THE
WORLDWIDE
GUIDE TO
MOVIE
LOCATIONS

TONY REEVES

Library of Congress Cataloging-in-Publication Data

Reeves, Tony.
    The worldwide guide to movie locations / Tony Reeves.— 1st ed.
        p.   cm.
    Includes index.
    ISBN 1-55652-432-3
    1. Motion picture locations.   2. Motion pictures—Catalogs.   I. Title.

PN1995.67 .A1 R44 2001
791.43′75′025—dc21   2001046143

Picture on page 91 Northeast Wyoming; Picture 8a on page 135 courtesy HRH group of hotels; Page 184 Greg Reis, Mono Lake Committee; Page 196 Oak Alley Plantation; Page 234 Red Fox Inn, Middleburg; Page 275 Drunken Duck Inn and The Langdale Chase Hotel; Page 280 Dan Hatzenbuhler Stock Studios/Dallas CVB; Page 281 Nik Klaassen/Flinders Ranges Research; Page 302 Dallas Convention and Visitors Bureau; Page 320 Reen Pilkington; Page 321 Mansfield Reformatory, Ohio; Page 380 Dunsmuir House and Gardens; Page 394 Trustees of Reservations, Great House at Castle Hill; Page 400 The Parkwood Estate, Oshawa.

Front cover, back cover and all other interior photographs © 2001 Tony Reeves.

ACKNOWLEDGMENTS

Thanks to the following people for their invaluable help: Arizona Film Commission; James Cary-Parkes; Chicago Film Office; Simon Cork; Stephen K. Crocker; Veronica Lynch, Dallas Convention and Visitors Bureau; Malcolm Davis; Terry Deal; Dallas Denton-Cox; Nigel Hatton; Hawaii Film Commission; Matthew Hodson; Sabina Bailey, HRH Group of Hotels; Steen Mangen; Lucy Chancellor Weale, Melbourne Film Office; Mono Lake Committee; City of Monrovia; Ontario Film Development Corporation; Julie Nixon, City of Oshawa; City of Palm Springs; Carolyn Partrick; Greater Philadelphia Film Office; Pittsburgh Film Office; Glen Platts; Vicky Powell; Colin Richardson; Ray Arthur, Ridgecrest Film Commission; Gillian Rodgerson; Norman Warwick; Wyoming Film Office.

PUBLISHER'S NOTE

Every effort has been made to ensure that the information given in this book was correct at the time of going to press. However, details such as travel information and phone numbers can change. The publishers cannot accept responsibility for any consequences arising from the use of this book.

We would be delighted to receive any corrections for incorporation into the next edition.

PRIVACY

Please note that many of the locations detailed in this book are private property, and are not open to the general public. Please respect the privacy of the owners, and be aware that access of any kind is often prohibited.

Did you enjoy this book? We love to hear from our readers. Please e-mail us at: **readerfeedback@titanemail.com** or write to Reader Feedback at the above London address.

791.4375
REE
2001

CONTENTS

IF YOU FILM IT, THEY WILL COME...

- In 1994, the Queen Elizabeth Suite of the Crown Hotel, Amersham in Buckinghamshire, suddenly became booked up for years ahead.
- Since 1977, the number of visitors to America's oldest national park, Devil's Tower in Wyoming, has increased by three quarters.
- And in 1989, the tiny town of Dyersville, Iowa (population 3,825) became a major tourist mecca.

There's a simple connection. All three places had recently appeared in successful films. The Crown was the hotel where Hugh Grant rattled the four-poster with Andie MacDowell in *Four Weddings and a Funeral*; Steven Spielberg picked the peculiar rock monolith of Devil's Tower as the alien rendezvous in *Close Encounters of the Third Kind*; and it was near Dyersville that Kevin Costner built his supernatural baseball pitch in *Field of Dreams*. By 1992, 60,000 visitors had motored out to see the field, and with each passing year the numbers have increased.

Movie locations have become today's historic sites. Romantics queued to spend their honeymoons in Amersham, awestruck stargazers looked up to Devil's Tower and dads swung a bat with their sons out in Dyersville. After the release of John Boorman's backwoods nightmare *Deliverance*, Rayburn County in Georgia saw a sudden boom in rafting holidays, which is just plain scary.

According to the Irish Minister for Arts, Culture and Heritage, more than one in six visitors to the Republic in 1993 cited a reference to film as their reason for visiting. After the release of *Gorillas in the Mist*, and before the present troubles, Rwanda's tourism increased by twenty per cent.

Travel guides map out the world for us in terms of high culture – history, architecture and literature – but there's an irresistible drive to seek out those places to which we have a more emotional link.

Unlike reading fiction or an historical account, film lets us into a story directly. We experience the sights and sounds first hand and, now that we all have video and DVD collections, we are more and more familiar with the backdrops to favourite scenes. The age-old thrill of standing on the site of significant events is vastly amplified once we've experienced those events directly, and can replay them constantly.

For me, a trip to the States turned out to be something of a life-changing event. A few years earlier, I'd moved down to London from a dull Midlands town, and found that I'd landed in the heart of Movie Gothic territory. Around the corner from my Earl's Court bedsit, John Landis was filming *An American Werewolf in London*. On the way to the local shops, I'd pass the gloomy apartment block where Catherine Deneuve went murderously batty in *Repulsion*. A few minutes walk in the opposite direction I found the house where sinisterly camp gentleman's gentleman Dirk Bogarde played mindgames with aristocrat James Fox in *The Servant*. And my journey to work took me past the extravagant blue-tiled mansion where Joseph Losey shot his bizarre psychodrama *Secret Ceremony* with Elizabeth Taylor and Mia Farrow, and the site of Carl Boehm's home in *Peeping Tom*.

Okay, I was a bit of a movie freak, but the fascination of living within the landscape of cinema would probably have remained on the back burner if I'd not had that chance to visit America. The magic name of Hollywood had me taking out a whopping bank loan and heading for West Coast USA. San Francisco was actually my first destination. It was a strange sensation to find that I already knew the hills Steve McQueen bounced down in *Bullitt*, the zigzag streets navigated by *The Love Bug*, the square where Gene Hackman eavesdropped on *The Conversation* and, of course, the prison island where Burt Lancaster served time as the *Birdman of Alcatraz*. But above all, the cool pastel colours and misty coastal light marked the city out as the backdrop to Hitchcock's *Vertigo*. This was unmistakably the dreamy world of Madeleine and Scottie, overlooked by Coit Tower, the landmark Kim Novak uses to trace James Stewart's flat.

Los Angeles, and its excitingly seedy suburb, Hollywood, turned out to offer more glimpses of movie heaven. The gleaming white Griffith Observatory is forever haunted by the image of a tearful James Dean holding out the handful of bullets at the climax of *Rebel Without a Cause* (they're savvy enough to have erected a bust of the actor in the grounds). The old carousel on the Santa Monica pier is instantly recognisable from *The Sting*, despite the studio's best efforts to relocate it to Chicago. And in the bustle of downtown, the sudden calm of the Bradbury Building's elaborate lobby instantly conjures up the dystopian landscape of *Blade Runner*.

Apart from these tantalisingly arbitrary guidebook tidbits, there was precious little detail on California's awesome film history. Even here, at the very heart of the movie industry, it seemed the boisterous, extrovert young member of the arts family was not yet mature enough to merit serious attention. In the UK, it wasn't until 1996, when the realisation dawned that this pushy little newcomer had actually reached the age of 100 and could be regarded as respectable, that the first coy plaques recording cinema history began to appear.

I wanted a guide to my favourite art form that, like cinema itself, would be worldwide and not restricted by geography. In the best tradition of 'let's put on the show right here...', I began to compile the guide myself, not for a second appreciating the scale of the task I was taking on.

So, here is the first worldwide guide to our cinematic heritage, a world tour from the Western prairies through the mean streets of New York and the stately homes of England to the extravagant palaces of Europe. I've tried to include a selection of the best-known foreign language films too, but the world's cinematic output is simply too vast for one book, so there's little of Hong Kong's output, and I couldn't even begin to start on Bollywood. But I hope that the most familiar and iconic images are here.

There are also eleven colour features, with maps, each covering a particular theme: 'Swinging London' picks out a selection of the cinematic landmarks in the UK capital; a 'Star Wars World Tour' highlights George Lucas' imaginative universe, from the first *Star Wars* film, *A New Hope*, to *The Phantom Menace*; 'Star Trek, USA' takes you to the otherworldly landscapes of the cult film series; 'The World of James Bond' is a handy guide to the best of 007's globe-trotting highlife; 'Salzburg's Sound of Music' takes you round the sites of the world's best-loved musical; some of the stately homes that have formed the backdrop to classic costume dramas are covered in 'English Heritage'; while in the States there are two views of Los Angeles, the scuzzy 'Tarantino's LA' and the stylish 'LA Neo-Noir' locales, plus two contrasting views of the Big Apple, the classy 'Woody Allen's Manhattan' and gritty 'New York's Mean Streets'; and finally, 'Vertigo's San Francisco', which immerses you in the dark world of one of cinema's great innovators.

If you're staying at home, *The Worldwide Guide to Movie Locations* is a fascinating look at the trickery and the expertise that go into movie-making. Practical problems or budgetary restrictions often prevent filmmakers from shooting on the locations they'd ideally like. There's an unsung genius in the way an inventive director (or location scout) can reorder the world's geography to suit a picture's needs. The Coen brothers, needing a New York restaurant for *Barton Fink*, which was made in Los Angeles, used the gleaming deco interior of the *Queen Mary*, the old liner permanently berthed at Long Beach. The spectacular Id Club in *Species* is the wildly elaborate foyer of a Hollywood cinema. And when Laurence Olivier returns to his Roman villa in *Spartacus*, the camera misses by inches the kitschily twenties marble statue at the monumental swimming pool of newspaper magnate William Randolph Hearst, where the scene was shot. The list goes on...

But the real joy of this book is as a travel guide, and I hope you get the chance to visit at least some of the sites. Do go and see. These places may not be here forever. Norma Desmond's *Sunset Blvd.* mansion was bulldozed in the sixties to make way for an office building; the London Hilton now stands on the site of Park Lane House, the Embassy in Hitchcock's glossy remake of *The Man Who Knew Too Much*; and even the *Reservoir Dogs'* warehouse was razed to the ground. Since taking photos for this book, the Hawthorne Grill, held up by Honey-Bunny and Pumpkin at the beginning of *Pulp Fiction*, has also been torn down. The Ambassador Hotel, a location for films from the 1937 *A Star Is Born* to Tony Scott's *True Romance*, and where Bobby Kennedy was assassinated in 1968, lives on borrowed time while the city of Los Angeles and property developers tussle over whether to turn the site into a school or a shopping mall.

But plenty of locations still remain. My own top pleasures fall into two categories. There's the buzz that comes with a box-office classic, the instantly recognisable cinematic icon. It's hard to beat the thrill of standing in Luke Skywalker's sunken homestead from the original *Star Wars*; lingering before the white wooden church, unchanged since Gary Cooper pleaded for help in *High Noon*; recognising the high street where Celia Johnson and Trevor Howard couldn't help bumping into each other in *Brief Encounter*; cycling over the bridge that Bruce the Shark swam under to get into the 'safe' inlet in *Jaws*; catching the sunlight streaming down through the tracks of the elevated railway above the car chase of *The French Connection*; or just walking the Burbank street where the T-Rex ran amok in *The Lost World: Jurassic Park*.

But no less exciting are the more personal favourites: the dank, narrow waterways of Venice, every bit as spooky as they appeared in *Don't Look Now*; the dizzying vista of *Zabriskie Point*; the surreally monstrous Sicilian mansion used as the customs house in *L'Avventura*; burger and fries in the still wonderfully eccentric *Bagdad Cafe*; tracking down the twin railway bridges that rattled the Bijou fleapit in *The Smallest Show on Earth*; and resisting the urge to macarena at the vegetable stall in the supermarket from *Go*. But for me, tops would have to be the tiny Californian coastal resort where Hitchcock filmed *The Birds*. Settling down in front of the TV to watch the Oscars, with a balcony view over Bodega Bay, was close to my idea of movie heaven.

Whatever your tastes, the adventure starts here. Going to the movies will never be quite the same again.

Tony Reeves
London, January 2001

HOW TO USE THE GUIDE

The *Worldwide Guide to Movie Locations* is listed alphabetically by film title – taking note of word spaces (*The Man Who Knew Too Much* comes before *Manhattan*), the only exception being numbered sequels, which are listed in numerical order. Foreign language films are generally listed in the original language (Visconti's *The Leopard* is listed as *Gattopardo, Il*), but there is an alternative titles index at the back of the book. For handy recognition, the year, director and main stars of each film are included at the beginning of the entry. After these details, but before the full entry, the main locations – city, county, US state or country – are listed. Since you might want to check out the movie sites in a particular area, these locations are cross-referenced with a gazetteer at the back of the book.

Apart from listing the key locations you can see and visit, I've also included a record of those which have gone and a note of those which never existed. Fans still turn up in Atlanta hoping to visit 'Tara', unaware that Scarlett's mansion was no more than a wood and plaster frontage on the Selznick backlot in Culver City. The places you can actually see are picked-out in **bold type**. Since opening hours and admission charges are constantly subject to change, I've not included the details but, wherever possible, I've listed a phone number (with area but not international code) or a website address. If you are planning to visit a particular location, it's always advisable to check ahead. Historic houses in the UK are often closed during winter months, and there's always the possibility that commercial establishments such as hotels, restaurants and bars may have ceased business.

Many of these locations advertise themselves and welcome visitors; however, just as many are private properties. Feel free to visit and take a discreet look, but please don't ever disturb residents or trespass on private property. Any disturbance of people's privacy can only hinder future listings.

A

A BOUT DE SOUFFLE (aka *Breathless*)
(1959, dir: Jean-Luc Godard)
Jean-Paul Belmondo, Jean Seberg, Daniel Boulanger.
● **PARIS; MARSEILLES**

Seberg's hotel: Les Rives de Notre Dame

Godard's début full-length feature was one of the first movies to escape the confines of the studio, and was shot (apart from the opening scene of Belmondo hotwiring a car in the **Vieux Port of Marseille**) on the streets of **Paris**.

Jean Seberg's Left Bank hotel, the riverfront Hotel de Suede – as it was in 1959 – lies in the shadow of Notre Dame, and was used as a make-do studio for most of the film's interiors. One of the film's sites that's been given a substantial revamp and, with an eye to its location, a change of name, **Les Rives de Notre Dame** can be seen at **15 quai St Michel** at the junction of rue Xavier Privas (*metro: St Michel*).

The café, where Belomondo orders a breakfast he can't afford, is now a drugstore. It was Le Royale St Germain, at the intersection of the boulevard St Germain and the rue de Rennes opposite the St Germain des Pres metro station. Wannabe-journalist Seberg is out selling the *New York Herald Tribune* on the **Champs Elysées**, where Belmondo catches up with her. The old office of the *Trib*, out of which Seberg works, has undergone a major facelift (it now houses a pensions company), but the brass plaque to the left of the doorway still records that from 1930 to 1978 this was the paper's home. In front of the office, Godard puts in a cameo appearance as the weasely snitch who tips off the law. You can see the new frontage just off the Arc de Triomphe end of the Champs, at **21 rue de Berri** (*metro: George V*).

Much of the subsequent action centres around the Champs. The entrances to the **George V metro** station itself are where Belmondo gives the slip to the detectives before striking poses in front of Humphrey Bogart stills in a movie house lobby. The much-modernised cinema is the **Cinema Normandie, 116 bis Champs Elysées**, next to the Lido de Paris. At the top of the Champs stood the Pergola, the spacious first floor café where Seberg meets journalist Van Doude, and southwest is the avenue Montaigne, home of Paris' swishest designer stores. Here, in front of the **Christian Dior store, 30 avenue Montaigne**, Seberg dreams of posh frocks while Belmondo shows off his savvy, knowing that this is the

The old *New York Herald Tribune* office: 21 rue de Berri

place to make phone calls for free.

Briefly leaving the city centre, Seberg interviews novelist M Parvulesco on the terrace of what was, in 1959, Paris' main airport, **Orly**, about 45 minutes south of the city.

Back on the Champs, it's Seberg's turn to be tailed, through crowds watching a (real) visit of General de Gaulle and President Eisenhower to the Tomb of the Unknown Soldier beneath the Arc de Triomphe. Like Belmondo, Seberg's evasive action also ends, unsurprisingly, in a movie house. She leaves the cops flummoxed, ducking through the **Cinema Mac-Mahon, 5 avenue Mac-Mahon** just off L'Étoile, which is still very much in business and pretty much unchanged.

Seberg dodges the cops: Cinema Mac-Mahon

The photographer's apartment: 11 rue Campagne Première, Montparnasse

The night scenes shift south of the Seine to the pseud's paradise that was the Left Bank. Belmondo and Seberg take off for St-Germain in a stolen car, taking time to admire the sparkling lights of **Place de**

Belmondo gets breathless: rue Campagne Première, Montparnasse

8

la Concorde *en route*. They end up further south in the midst of the clutch of famously arty hangouts on the **boulevard Montparnasse** at its junction with boulevard Raspail (*metro: Vavin*). The Kosmos (it's lost the quaint K to become **Le Cosmos**) at **101 boulevard Montparnasse**, and **Le Select** at **99**, the two bars used as backdrop to the scene, are still serving, as is **La Rotonde**, which the couple drive past on the way to the haven of 'Zumbach's girlfriend's place'.

This is the photographer's apartment where the pair spend their last night, only a couple of blocks south of boulevard Montparnasse, at **11 rue Campagne Première**. Running northeast from boulevard Raspail, the quiet sidestreet has long been a magnet for artists. Modigliani, Miro, Picasso, Ernst, Giacometti and Kandinsky have all, at some time, called it home. Belmondo makes his doomed attempt to outrun a police bullet down the centre of the red-brick road, ending up literally breathless at the southern T-junction with boulevard Raspail (*metro: Raspail*). See also *Breathless*, the LA-set remake.

A PROPOS DE NICE

(1930, dir: Jean Vigo)
● NICE

Haunt of the rich: Hotel Negresco, Promenade des Anglais

The first of Vigo's three surreal, experimental movies (he died four years later at the age of 29) is a wickedly satirical documentary contrasting the lives of the rich and the poor in France's Riviera city, a favourite resort of the well off since the 19th century. While Cannes and Monaco, flanking Nice on either side, have prospered,

Extravagant grave monuments: Protestant Cemetery

and thus suffered from crass redevelopment, Nice – although hardly downmarket – has an endearing, somewhat decaying, down-at-heel feel.

Vigo, though, turned his camera toward the monied grotesques of the thirties on the **Promenade des Anglais**, the grand seaside parade that was built in the 1820s and supposedly paid for by the local English community to provide work for the unemployed after the failure of the 1822 orange crop. Of the sumptuous hotels seen here, including the Hotel Ruhl and the Palais de la Mediterranée, only the mega-grandiose **Hotel Negresco, 37 Promenade des Anglais** still lords it over the seafront. This temple to opulence, which houses an enormous chandelier whose twin hangs inside the Kremlin, boasted the presence of twelve kings at its opening. Incidentally, it was outside the Negresco that dancer Isadora Duncan came to a terrible end when a trailing scarf snagged in the wheels of her Bugatti. The Ruhl has been demolished to make way for the bland Casino Ruhl, while the Mediterranée is merely a gutted shell.

Vigo constructs his film around Nice's carnival, still held over the twelve days of Lent until Shrove Tuesday, when King Carnival is ceremonially burned. It's a raucous but good-natured event, with parades and a Battle of the Flowers.

The impressionist jigsaw also takes in the naval fleet, filmed in the beautiful bay at **Villefranche**, just east of Nice, and the extravagantly tasteless grave monuments of the **Protestant Cemetery** on the hill overlooking the old town.

ABOMINABLE DR PHIBES, THE

(1971, dir: Robert Fuest)
Vincent Price, Joseph Cotten, Peter Jeffrey.
● HERTFORDSHIRE; LONDON

Style and wit triumph over a shoestring budget and speed of shooting in this horror outing, filmed mostly on campy thirties sets built at Elstree Studios. To see the exterior of Phibes'

Dr Phibes' mansion: Rosary Priory High School, Bushey

mansion, head for the Elstree Road between Bushey and Elstree in Hertfordshire. At the junction with the A409 you can't miss the looming tower of the **Rosary Priory High School** – a Victorian Gothic extravaganza that used to be the Caldecote Towers Hotel (also seen in Tom Selleck actioner *High Road to China*) (*rail: Elstree or Stanmore*). The cemetery where Phibes and his wife were supposedly laid to rest is the overgrown and creepy old section of **Highgate Cemetery**, on the west side of **Swain Road, London** N6 (*tube: Archway*). The newer section of Highgate is generally open (*admission charge*), but you can only see the much more impressive older section with a guided tour on Sundays.

ABOUT LAST NIGHT...

(1986, dir: Edward Zwick)
Rob Lowe, Demi Moore, James Belushi.
● CHICAGO

Hiding behind the coy title is David Mamet's play *Sexual Perversity in Chicago*, and Chicago does form the backdrop for this mostly spot-on look at the tug between friendships and relationships. If you want to check out the singles bar where Lowe and Belushi dispense their own brand of charm and sensitivity, it's **Mothers, 26 West Division Street** at North Dearborn Street, toward the south of Chicago's Gold Coast district. But if you prefer the look of the

The singles bar: Mother's, West Division Street

boisterous beer garden beneath the rumble of the Howard elevated trailway, where Lowe and Moore bump into each other after a couple of one-night stands, it's **Kelly's, 949 West Webster Avenue** at North Sheffield Avenue. Close to DePaul University, it's obviously a student bar.

ABSOLUTE BEGINNERS

(1986, dir: Julien Temple)
Eddie O'Connell, Patsy Kensit, James Fox.
● LONDON

Julien Temple's series of pop promos, vaguely inspired by Colin MacInnes' cultish novel of West London life in the fifties, was the great hope of Goldcrest Films, but in fact helped sink the company. The terrific sets (and it's almost totally set-bound), including a garishly stylised Soho and a meticulous recreation of Napoli, Notting Hill's gloriously seedy bedsit area, were built at Shepperton Studios. Out in the real world, Eddie O'Connell's 'Have You Ever Had it Blue' number was filmed on the **Albert Bridge, SW11**, between Chelsea Embankment and Battersea Park.

ABSOLUTE POWER

(1997, dir: Clint Eastwood)
Clint Eastwood, Gene Hackman, EG Marshall.
● MARYLAND; WASHINGTON DC; LOS ANGELES

Eastwood meets the FBI: Corcoran Gallery of Art, 17th Street, Washington DC

This movie adaptation of David Baldacci's novel was fatally tailored to fit director/star Eastwood's needs by veteran screenwriter William Goldman. Set in Washington DC, much of the movie was actually shot in Baltimore, Maryland. Elder statesman EG Marshall's mansion, where the veteran housebreaker Eastwood sees the special agents protect sleazy Pres Hackman by blowing away his mistress, is the **Maryvale School for Girls, 11300 Falls Road, Brooklandville**, north of Baltimore. The art gallery where Eastwood is confronted by good FBI man Ed Harris is real DC. It's the **Corcoran Gallery of Art, 17th Street** at New York Avenue NW, just south of the White House (*metro: Farragut West*). Another genuine DC location is the hotel where Eastwood delivers a stolen necklace to the devious Chief of Staff Judy Davis. Cheekily, this is the **Watergate Hotel, 2650 Virginia Avenue NW** (*metro: Foggy Bottom*). And yes, this is part of the same complex housing the burgled Democratic offices (at number 2600).

ABYSS, THE

(1989, dir: James Cameron)
Ed Harris, Michael Biehn, Mary Elizabeth Mastrantonio.
● SOUTH CAROLINA

Close encounters of the submarine kind when an oil rig crew aboard the *Deepcore* submersible drilling platform in the Caribbean investigate something very strange under the sea. The nightmarish production (which star Ed Harris refused to talk about) fared poorly on initial release, but was finally rewarded with a successful second life on video, which at last makes sense of the plot by restoring the vital tsunami – giant tidal wave – climax.

Cameron's locations reflect the hard, industrial feel of his movies – *Aliens* used a power station, *T2* disused steel mills – *The Abyss'* underwater scenes were filmed in an uncompleted nuclear power station. The Duke Power Company's Cherokee Power Station never went on line and was subsequently abandoned only to be snapped up by movie entrepreneur Earl Owensby – owner of the Owensby Studios in North Carolina. He rented the facility out to *The Abyss'* production company, who built the film's *Deepcore* sets inside the two gigantic concrete tanks. When filled, they became, at 7.5 million gallons and 2.6 million gallons, two of the largest freshwater containers in the world. You can see them just outside **Gaffney**, 45 miles east of Greenville on Route 29, South Carolina.

ACCATTONE

(1961, dir: Pier Paolo Pasolini)
Franco Citti, Franca Pasut, Silvana Corsini.
● ROME

Pasolini's first film, the relentlessly downbeat story of doomed thief and pimp Vittorio (*aka* Accattone – 'Scrounger'), starred the then-unknown non-actor Franco Citti, who went on to be a Pasolini regular and appeared as a Sicilian minder in the *Godfather* movies. Contributions to the script came from Citti's younger brother Sergio (who actually plays his brother in the movie) and director-to-be Bernardo Bertolucci. Filming in Rome, the movie studiously avoids the *Roman Holiday* sights and picturesque ruins in favour of the dismal slums and concrete tower blocks of the suburbs. The one touch of Ancient Romanesque is Stella's tearful meeting with her manipulative pimp among the statues of the **Via Appia Antica** after a disastrous first attempt at prostitution. Most of the movie was filmed in the middle of the **Pigneto district**, east of the city. The first shots were filmed in the slums of **Via Fanfulla da Lodi**, which runs between Via Prenestina and Via del Pigneto.

ACCIDENT

(1967, dir: Joseph Losey)
Dirk Bogarde, Stanley Baker, Michael York.
● OXFORDSHIRE; SURREY; LONDON

Cool observation rules in one of the major Pinter/Losey/ Bogarde collaborations of the sixties, as the car-crash death of aristocratic student Michael York triggers off a series of flashbacks charting the status games played on a university campus. It was filmed largely around Oxford University, though the site of the titular accident is miles to the south in Surrey.

The university locations include Oxford's **St John's College** on **St John's Street**, where mousy don Bogarde experiences a bout of mid-life angst. The quads here are open to the public, usually on weekday afternoons, but check in advance for opening times. The entrance to Bogarde's rooms can be seen at the southeast corner of the elaborately gargoyled inner **Canterbury Quad**. In the

Bogarde's rooms: Canterbury Quad, St John's College, Oxford

grounds of **Magdalen College** you can see the bridge where Michael York invites Bogarde for an ultimately humiliating punt along the Cherwell. The entrance is on the High Street toward Magdalen Bridge (*admission charge*). Being a Pinter adaptation, the boys have to play their little games, and here it's a bizarre 'football game', which must still give the film's insurers nightmares. The rough and tumble – roughly based on the Eton Wall Game – was shot in the classical grandeur of Robert Adams' Great Hall of **Syon House, Brentford**, where Bogarde keeps goal in front of the cast of a Dying Gladiator (even in 1773 this bronze copy cost a cool £300 when bought in Rome). Syon House, set in grounds landscaped by Capability Brown, is on the north bank of the Thames eight miles west of London, off the A4 between Brentford and Isleworth (*tube/rail: Gunnersbury Park*). The Great Hall is open to the public (© *020.8560.0881, admission charge*). You can see more of its elegant rooms and corridors in *The Madness of King George*. Bogarde's house, scene of the accident, is **Norwood Farm Hall**, on **Elveden Road** north of the Esher bypass, Cobham, Surrey (*rail: Oxshott*).

ACCION MUTANTE

(1993, dir: Alejandro de la Iglesia)
Antonio Resines, Enrique San Francisco.
● **SPAIN**

Wildly OTT exercise in bad taste from Almòdovar alumnus Iglesia, blending *Alien*, *Mad Max* and *The Patty Hearst Story*. An incompetent gang of deformed terrorists exact revenge on the smug 'beautiful people' and kidnap the daughter of a wealthy businessman, taking her to an alien planet. Shot largely in Madrid and Bilbao, the dry, yellowed surface of the planet Axturias is the wild deserted region of **Bardenas Reales** in Navarra, northeastern Spain. Take the N121 south from Pamplona toward Tudela and see the strange wind-blasted desert east of the road near Arguedas.

ACE IN THE HOLE (aka *The Big Carnival*)

(1951, dir: Billy Wilder)
Kirk Douglas, Jan Sterling, Porter Hall.
● **NEW MEXICO; LOS ANGELES**

Washed up in the Mid-West, wise-ass New York hack Kirk Douglas sees a chance to break back into the bigtime by milking the human interest story of a cave-in victim, even when it means holding off a rescue attempt. The hick town home of Douglas' paper, the *Sun-Bulletin*, is **Albuquerque**, central New Mexico, where director Wilder grabbed vérité-style shots using a concealed camera mounted on a truck.

Although the underground scenes were filmed on a mock-up back at the **Paramount Studios** on **Melrose Avenue** in Hollywood, the desert location really is New Mexico. You won't be able to follow the trail to the old Indian Cliff Dwellings at the Minosa Trading Post where Richard Benedict was entombed, though. The film used a gigantic set, claimed at the time to be the largest constructed for any movie other than a war film. Towering 237 feet into the air and covering an area 1,200 by 1,600 feet, it incorporated the cliff dwellings, the Indian settlement and the ensuing carnival. You can visit the breathtaking New Mexico desert where the mammoth set was built some twenty miles to the west of **Gallup**, I-40, on the Arizona border. I-40, incidentally, is part of the old Route 66.

ACE VENTURA, PET DETECTIVE

(1994, dir: Tom Shadyac)
Jim Carrey, Sean Young, Courteney Cox.
● **MIAMI, FLORIDA**

Ace Ventura's apartment: Campton Apartments, Washington Avenue

Jim Carrey shot to overnight megabucks stardom with his love-it-or-loathe-it manic shtick, as the animal-friendly 'tec tracking down the Miami Dolphins' kidnapped mascot Snowflake. It was filmed around Miami, Florida, where Carrey keeps a secret menagerie in his 'Surfside' apartment, the **Campton Apartments, Washington Avenue** – alongside the artsy rock venue Cameo Theatre at 1445 near Espanola West – in the newly-revitalised art deco district of South Beach.

The football stadium Snowflake disappears from is the real home of the Miami Dolphins, the **Joe Robbie Stadium, 2269 NW 199th Street**, a hi-tech 73,000 seater sports arena about sixteen miles northwest of downtown Miami. If you fancy catching a game, there's a Metro-Dade Transit Authority bus from town (© *305.638.6700*).

You can also visit the exclusive seafront villa of fish-collector Udo Kier, where Carrey skips the party to find a shark in the cellar. It's **Villa Vizcaya, 3251 South Miami Avenue** at 32nd Road in Coconut Grove on the coast of South Miami, built in 1916 as the winter home of magazine founder James Deering. A smaller-scale Xanadu, the Italian Renaissance mansion is packed with European artefacts – Roman sarcophagi, Catherine de Medici's fire-

Udo Kier's seafront estate: Villa Vizcaya, Coconur Grove

place, the contents of Italian villas. There are formal gardens and tours of the building (© *305. 579.2708, admission charge*). A frequently-used location, you can also see the villa in *Absence of Malice, Airport '77* and *Any Given Sunday*.

The African villages of the dismal sequel, *Ace Ventura: When Nature Calls*, were constructed on the **777 Ranch**, at **Hondo** near San Antonio, Texas (© *830. 426.3476*). A 15,000 acre wildlife reserve, the ranch is open to the public for safari tours and, yes, you can ride the same zebra-striped jeep seen in the movie. More scenes were shot in Texas, at **Camp Waldemar**, **Botany Bay Plantation** and **Cherokee Plantation** in South Carolina; and in Canada, at the **Panorama Resort**, British Columbia.

ACROSS 110th STREET
(1972, dir: Barry Shear)
Anthony Quinn, Anthony Franciosa, Yaphet Kotto.
● **NEW YORK CITY**

Quentin Tarantino pays homage to this classic seventies actioner by playing Bobby Womack and JJ Johnson's theme tune over the credits of *Jackie Brown*. Black and Italian gangs vie for control of Harlem, while black and Italian cops jockey for control of the precinct, in this gritty, documentary-style thriller. Taken from the novel *Across 110th* by Wally Ferris, the movie makes terrific use of real locations. The opening credits sequence sets the tone as the white mobsters' '68 Cadillac drives north through Manhattan to **110th Street**, the northern boundary of Central Park, dividing the Upper West Side from Harlem (the road sign which metamorphoses into the title credit is 'Lenox Avenue/110th Street'), then on to **125th Street**, past Harlem landmark the **Apollo Theater**, at **253**. The Italians' party was shot at Central Park's southern boundary, **Central Park South**.

Of the 60 or so locations used, the majority were in Harlem itself, where the production shot in real police stations, bars and private apartments. There's not much to search out as many of the buildings were already condemned, a boon to film-makers who wanted to pepper walls with bullet holes. Still under construction at the time of filming, though, was the half-built highrise from which Tony Franciosa and his henchmen dangle the hapless Ed Bernard. It's the **Federal Building, 125th Street** at Lenox Avenue, Harlem. The final, bloody shoot-out is on **Lenox Avenue** between 141st and 142nd Streets.

ADAM'S RIB
(1949, dir: George Cukor)
Katharine Hepburn, Spencer Tracy, Judy Holliday.
● **LOS ANGELES; NEW YORK CITY**

One of the great Tracy-Hepburn comedies, with lawyer Hepburn defending Judy Holliday against a charge of attempted murder, while husband Tracy acts for the prosecution. Set in New York, it was filmed mainly on MGM's stages in Culver City, LA, using a few location scenes to add authenticity. The office, outside which Holliday waits for erring husband Tom Ewell before following him down into the subway, is on **Bowling Green, Broadway** at Bat-

Hepburn and Tracy make up at the tax office: Bayard Street, New York

tery Place, Lower Manhattan. Tracy and Hepburn drive to court on **Franklin D Roosevelt Drive** alongside the East River – courtesy of a little back projection. The forbidding court exterior, with its ironic motto, 'Equal and exact justice to all men of whatever state or persuasion', can still be seen in Manhattan's Chinatown. It's the **Criminal Courts Building**, known as 'The Tombs', **100 Centre Street** between Leonard

Tracy and Hepburn clash in court: Criminal Courts Building, Centre Street

and White Streets. The accountant's office, where Tracy and Hepburn reunite while filing their tax returns, is on **Bayard Street**, in the shadow of The Tombs, beneath the Bridge of Sighs, which linked the Municipal Prison to the courthouse.

ADDAMS FAMILY, THE
(1991, dir: Barry Sonnenfeld)
Raul Julia, Anjelica Huston, Christopher Lloyd.
● **LOS ANGELES**

Coen brothers' cinematographer Sonnenfeld turned first-time director with the movie version of the sixties TV show of the fifties cartoons. It was shot at the **Hollywood Center Studios, 1040 Las Palmas Avenue**, mainly on Stage 3/8, which coincidentally happened to be the studio where the original TV series was filmed. This studio, built in 1919 as the Jasper Studio, survived under various names until, in 1980, it became the ill-fated Zoetrope Studios as part of Francis Ford Coppola's scheme to run a large independent production facility.

Sadly, there's no Addams Mansion to see. The frontage of the house was built for the film on a mountain overlooking the Burbank Hills at **Toluca Lake**. (The TV pilot did use a real house, on Adams Boulevard, just south of Hollywood. You can still see it during the show's opening credits, but a painting was substituted for the run of the series.) The film's locations include the charity auction, where the Addamses buy back their own finger trap, which was filmed in LA's 1924 **Wilshire Ebell Theater**. You can see the building's Renaissance-style façade at **4401 West 8th Street** near Lucerne Boulevard, midtown. The school theatre, where Wednesday and Pugsley stage a Peckinpahesque version of Shakespeare, is the **Brentwood Theatre** on the grounds of the **Sawtelle Veteran's Administration Medical Center, 11000 Wilshire Boulevard** in Westside. The Wampum Court Motel, to which the family are exiled, was in **Sylmar**, northern LA, off the Golden State Freeway in the San Fernando Valley.

ADDAMS FAMILY VALUES
(1993, dir: Barry Sonnenfeld)
Raul Julia, Anjelica Huston, Christopher Lloyd.
● CALIFORNIA

Homicidal serial bride Debbie sets her sights on Uncle Fester when she's hired to look after new arrival, baby Pubert. There's no single conjugal home for Fester and Debbie, as their wedded bliss was shot in a conflation of mansions in Pasadena and the Palos Verdes Peninsula, southwest of LA.

If you're entranced by the prospect of a holiday at Camp Chippewa – America's Foremost Facility for Privileged Young Adults – the delightfully WASP summer camp to which Wednesday and Pugsley are despatched, you can visit it at **Sequoia Lake** near the entrance to the **Sequoia National Forest**, fifty miles east of Fresno, central California, though I can't guarantee you'll get 'Kumbaya' around the campfire *every* night.

As the name suggests, the forest is home to giant sequoia trees, the largest living things on the planet. You'll find a Visitor Centre at Grant Grove (© *209. 335.2315*), where the 3,000-year-old giants, named for US war heroes, include the General Grant and the Robert E Lee. A few miles to the southeast on Route 180 – called the General's Highway – stands the biggest of the lot, General Sherman, 275 feet tall and weighing 1385 tons. Sequoia Lake is just off the General's Highway, a couple of miles from Grant Grove. The arrival of the campers was shot at **Camp Sequoia** itself, while the cheesy Thanksgiving musical pageant, gloriously subverted by Wednesday, was staged on the other side of the lake at **Camp Tulequoia**.

ADVENTURES OF BARON MUNCHAUSEN, THE
(1989, dir: Terry Gilliam)
John Neville, Eric Idle, Sarah Polley.
● SPAIN; ITALY

Heaven's Gate, Ishtar and *The Cotton Club* were elbowed out of the way as Gilliam's lavish fantasy hit the record books as the biggest lossmaker in movie history, reputedly clocking in at minus $48 million on what was originally budgeted as a $23.5 million movie. It might have cost the earth, but at least the money is right up there on the screen.

Shot largely at Rome's **Cinecittà Studios**, the movie, which utilised the services of longtime Fellini collaborators cinematographer Giuseppe Rotunno and art director Dante Ferretti, needed a staggering 67 sets.

The Turkish Camp was filmed at the standard Euro-desert location of **Almeria** on the coast of southern Spain. More interesting is the Mediterranean town besieged by the Turks. This ghost town, once home to 4,500 people and boasting an eclectic mix of Baroque and Gothic architecture, was mercilessly bombed during the Civil War in 1938. Left deserted and unrestored for fifty years, it was remembered by Ferretti as a location he had once scouted for Sidney Lumet's aborted project *No Pasaran*. The remains of **Belchite** can be found 25 miles southeast of Zaragoza in Aragon.

A big budget, full colour version had already been made in 1943 at Europe's largest film studio – the **UFA (Universum Film Aktien Gesellschaft) Studios** – at the behest of Josef Goebbels, to perk up German morale during WWII. The reputation of the studios, built in 1917, plummeted from the heights of classic German films of the twenties and thirties, including *Nosferatu, The Cabinet of Dr Caligari, Metropolis* and *The Blue Angel*, to Nazi propaganda vehicles like the infamous *Jud Süss*. Now the DEFA Studios, they are in serious trouble and may no longer even be in existence, at **Oberlandstrasse 26, Babelsberg** in Potsdam on the outskirts of Berlin.

ADVENTURES OF PRISCILLA, QUEEN OF THE DESERT, THE
(1994, dir: Stephan Elliott)
Terence Stamp, Hugo Weaving, Guy Pearce.
● NEW SOUTH WALES, AUSTRALIA; SOUTH AUSTRALIA; NORTHERN TERRITORY, AUSTRALIA

The Abba-inspired three-pack of drag queens in this feel-good Aussie road movie take a journey through the outback in a silver-painted bus, christened 'Priscilla', to a booking in Alice Springs. The trip starts out from **Sydney** – oohs and aahs for the **Opera House** and the **Harbour Bridge** – before striking out across the inhospitable desert of New South Wales. The first major stop-off is **Broken Hill**, an outback mining town about 750 miles west of Sydney, where Mitzi, Felicia and Bernadette raise eyebrows when they go shopping on **Argent Street**, the main drag (pun definitely intended).

The eccentric hotel the girls check into is **Mario's Palace, Sulphide Street** at Argent (yes, all the street names – Bromide, Chloride, Oxide, reading like a chemistry textbook – reflect the town's mining history) (© *80.88.1699*). Mario, who appears

"Tack-o-rama...": Mario's Palace, Broken Hill, New South Wales, inside...

... and outside

as himself in the movie, is likely to be presiding. If you're in the area, a few miles northwest of Broken Hill is the ghost town of Silverton, one of the most used Australian locations (see *Mad Max 2* for details), and a few miles further on from here you'll find the next stop, the **Mundi Mundi Plain Lookout**, where the dragsters find themselves stranded after Priscilla breaks down.

Help appears in the shape of good-hearted Bob and his strange wife, Cynthia, who give the three a lift to **Coober Pedy**, a further 500 miles west in central South Australia. Another mining town, Coober Pedy is tougher, rougher and even hotter than Broken Hill. The terrain is so inhospitable, in fact, that most dwellings are built underground (the name means 'white man in a hole'). The strange mining-scarred landscape is another favourite location, providing the post-apocalyptic wastelands of *Mad Max Beyond Thunderdome* and Wim Wenders' *Until the End of the World*. If you want to try out the subterranean accommodation, the stopover here is the **Underground Motel, Umoona Road** (© *80.72.5324*), to the north of town.

From here the journey heads north a few hundred miles into Northern Territory, finally arriving at the ostensible destination, **Alice Springs**, where it's best bib and tucker for the dressy nightspot they perform at – **Lasseter's Casino** on **Barrett Drive**.

King's Canyon is the site of Felicia's triumphant climb. The spectacular gorge, a cousin of the USA's Grand Canyon, is in the **Watarrka National Park** at the western end of **Ernest Giles Road**, a couple of hundred miles west of Alice Springs. The original script specified the much more iconic Ayers Rock – and what an image that would have been – but Ayers (Uluru) is a significant feature of Aboriginal culture, and the idea of three drag queens traipsing over it was a complete no-no.

Felicia fulfils her dream: King's Canyon, Watarrka National Park

ADVENTURES OF QUENTIN DURWARD, THE

(aka *Quentin Durward*)
(1955, dir: Richard Thorpe)
Robert Taylor, Kay Kendall, Robert Morley.
● **FRANCE; SUSSEX**

Brash, colourful period romp from a Walter Scott story, with a host of Brit character actors strutting their stuff. A somewhat wooden Robert Taylor is sent by camp old Ernest Thesiger to woo Kay Kendall. Robert Morley is the devious monarch and George Cole the devious gypsy spy. Credibility is not the film's strong point.

Ernest Thesiger's Scottish castle is **Bodiam Castle**, a

medieval fortress near Robertsbridge in East Sussex (© *01580.830436, admission charge*).

The French locations, however, actually are in France. The Duke of Burgundy's chateau at Peronne, where Taylor first meets Kendall, is the **Château de Chambord**, eleven miles east of Blois in the Loire Valley. The largest of the Loire châteaux, Chambord was built by François I between 1520 and 1535 (© *54.20.31.32, admission charge*). The court of Louis XI at Plessis les Tours is another Loire château, **Château de Chenonceau**, six miles southeast of Amboise. Built earlier than Chambord (1513-21) by tax collector Thomas Bohier, it was later owned by François I, Henri I – who gave it to his mistress Diane de Poitiers – and Catherine de Medici (Henri's widow, who snatched it back on the king's death). Its gallery is built out on arches over the river Cher (© *47.23.90.07, admission charge*). Filming also took place at **Château de Maintenon**, twelve miles north of Chartres, the home of Madame de Maintenon, mistress of Louis XIV (*admission charge*).

ADVENTURES OF ROBIN HOOD, THE

(1938, dir: William Keighley, Michael Curtiz)
Errol Flynn, Olivia de Havilland, Basil Rathbone.
● **CALIFORNIA**

This great Errol Flynn vehicle cost $1.9 million, yet surprisingly recouped only $1.5 million at the box office. It proved enormously expensive because, as well as the sets, they used the spanking new Technicolor system.

Sherwood Forest is **Bidwell Park, Chico**, with its authentic oaks and sycamores. And its less authentic wild vines. Not to mention the plaster trees and rocks imported by art director Carl Jules Weyl.

Chico, 30 miles east of I-5 and halfway between Sacramento and Redding, Northern California, is actually built around the ten mile-long park, which was donated by the widow of city founder William Bidwell. Here is the spot where Flynn's men stage the raid on Basil Rathbone's treasure caravan. At **Big Chico Creek**, running through **Chico Canyon** in the park, Robin challenges Little John to a longstaff fight and duels with Friar Tuck in the creek.

Robin Hood's camp, site of the huge banquet following the treasure raid, when Olivia de Havilland begins to thaw out, was about a mile from the park entrance, around Hooker, the world's largest oak tree – 92 feet tall, 149 feet across its branches and named after British naturalist Sir Joseph Hooker. Bidwell Park was also used for some exterior shots in *Gone With the Wind*. Chico is on the Seattle-Sacramento railway line, and also on the north-south Greyhound route (*Visitors Bureau* © *916. 342.4258*).

The archery tournament, where the too-cocky Robin gets arrested, was filmed in Busch Gardens, Pasadena. Don't bother to look for them. The gardens, seen also in *Citizen Kane*, have long since gone the way of many of LA's great landmarks. Extra shots for the attack on the treasure caravan were filmed in the **Sherwood Lake** and **Sherwood Forest** area. No, not on a location trip to England – this Sherwood Forest can be found about fifteen miles west of LA, south of Westlake Village on Potrero Road, just off Highway 101 near the Santa Monica Mountains. The name is no coincidence, as it comes from the area's use as a location in the 1922 Douglas Fairbanks Robin Hood movie.

The lower part of Nottingham Castle (its upper reaches are a matte painting) was built on the old Warners' Calabasas Ranch. This too has gone. The area is now a golf course and housing development south of Ventura Freeway on the road toward Westlake. The streets of Nottingham are 'Dijon Street' on the Warners' Burbank backlot, and the interiors were shot here too. In the Lighting Prop Shop on the **Warners' Studio Tour** you can still see the chandeliers from the production, along with other treasures, such as the lamps from Rick's Bar in *Casablanca*. This tour, unlike the Universal Studios theme park, is the real thing – a small-scale guided tour around the surprisingly unchanged and low-tech lot where Jack Warner kept his stars on a short leash and his movies on a tight budget. You need to book ahead (© *818. 954.1951*) and you'll find the tour entrance at **4000 Warner Boulevard** off the Ventura Freeway, Burbank.

ADVISE AND CONSENT

(1962, dir: Otto Preminger)
Don Murray, Charles Laughton, Henry Fonda.
● **WASHINGTON DC; LOS ANGELES**

A cracking cast, including Charles Laughton in his last role as a scheming Southern senator, have a ball in the White House when there's trouble as President Franchot Tone attempts to appoint liberal Henry Fonda as Secretary of State. The astonishing amount of co-operation Preminger managed to get from government departments for a film exposing chicanery, blackmail and closet homosexuality seems to indicate an unhealthy pride in their Machiavellian image.

The movie was filmed almost entirely on real DC locations; virtually the only purpose-built set is the thoroughly convincing full-size recreation of the Senate Chamber (a long-standing rule forbids photography here), at Columbia Studios on Gower Street in Hollywood. Alan Drury, author of the original book, sits behind one of the hundred desks.

The centre of all the game-playing and manipulating is, of course, the **Capitol**, home of the US Congress, where scenes were filmed in the **Great Rotunda** beneath the capitol's dome, and in the historic **Reception Room** just off the Senate Chamber. The building is open to the public (© *202.225.6827*) and there are free guided tours (though when the Senate or House are in session you'll need to

Political machinations: US Capitol Building, Washington DC

Charles Laughton investigates: Treasury Building, Washington DC

show ID and get a pass from the Appointment Desk for the Senate side or the Doorkeeper's office for the House side). The tour entrance is on East Capitol Street, Capitol Hill (*metro: Capitol South, Union Station*).

Charles Laughton arranges a clandestine meeting with the mysterious 'Mr Fletcher' on the Ellipse of the **Mall**, the two-mile stretch of lawn neatly separating DC into north and south, in front of the **Washington Monument**, the 555-foot obelisk on the Mall at 15th Street (there's a free elevator to the top if you're willing to queue) (*metro: Smithsonian*). He investigates the employment record of weaselly Burgess Meredith at the **Treasury Building, Pennsylvania Avenue NW** at 15th Street. If you book in advance (© *202.622.0896*) you can tour the magnificent interior of this imposing Greek Revival building (*metro: Farragut West, McPherson Square*). The canteen, where Don Murray receives one of the series of threatening phone calls, is also in the Treasury Building.

The hearing of the 'Sub-committee of the Senate Foreign Relations Committee' – which tries, unsuccessfully, to discredit Fonda – was filmed in the **Caucus Room**. The airport, used by Murray for his stealthy trip to New York, is **DCA**, Washington National, over the Potomac, three and a half miles south of downtown on the George Washington Memorial Parkway. Franchot Tone's address to the White House Press Corps was shot in the ballroom of the Sheraton-Park Hotel, now the **Sheraton Carlton, 923 16th Street NW** at K Street (*metro: Farragut West, McPherson Square*), in the Crystal Room, where DC journos do regularly interview politicians (© *202.638.2626 or 800. 325.3535*).

AFRICAN QUEEN, THE

(1951, dir: John Huston)
Humphrey Bogart, Katharine Hepburn, Robert Morley.
● **ZAIRE; UGANDA; LONDON; LOS ANGELES**

As WWI breaks out, Hepburn takes Bogart gunning for the beastly Hun, who've caused the death of her preacher-brother in German East Africa. There's a surprising amount of location filming in Africa for the period – seemingly as an excuse for macho director Huston to go hunting elephants (see Peter Viertel's thinly-disguised book of the shoot, *White Hunter, Black Heart*, or Clint Eastwood's film version). Katharine Hepburn has also penned her own wonderfully idiosyncratic version of events in *The Making of The African Queen, or How I Went to Africa with Bogart, Bacall and Huston and Almost Lost My Mind*.

Even so, much of the African jungle was recreated at Worton Hall Studios in Isleworth, southwest London. The interior of Robert Morley's First Methodist Church at Kungdu was built here, to match an exterior constructed in Africa. A none-too-convincing double stands in for Morley, who never left England – just look at the cross-cutting between Hepburn with Morley in London and Hepburn with the congregation in Africa. The doomed church and the village of Kungdu were built on the shore of Lake Albert at **Port Butiaba, Uganda**, up near the border with Zaire. Morley's funeral was filmed in Zaire itself (then the Congo), on a hillside about two and a half miles upriver from the village of **Biondo**, on the **Ruiki** – the river

Still in service: the *African Queen*, Key Largo, Florida

which stands in for the Ulanga in the early scenes of the *Queen* chugging down to confront the Germans.

The *Queen* going over the falls is a model made by monks from the local monastery at Ponthierville in Zaire (nuns made the tiny Bogart and Hepburn), filmed on the falls above the town, while the German fort at Shona was shot back at Worton Hall.

The reedy lake where a becalmed Hepburn and Bogart finally confront the *Louisa* is a small offshoot of Lake Albert at Murchison Falls, up the Nile among the crocs and the hippos, now **Kabalego Falls** in Uganda's National Park of the same name. They've changed since the movie filmed here. Once, the Nile was forced under pressure through a tiny gap in the rocks, but flooding in 1961 burst through the rocks and there are now two falls. Although the area suffered greatly during Uganda's recent troubled history, the park – Uganda's largest – is now open again. Paraa Safari Lodge and Chobe Safari Lodge, the two camps nearest the Falls are once again functioning after having been destroyed and looted. If you plan to visit, it's still a good idea to check ahead on local conditions.

The ending, with the scuppered little steamer finally blowing the gunboat to smithereens, filmed back in Isleworth again. The *African Queen* itself wasn't really blown up at all. It still exists and you can see it at Key Largo, first of the Florida Keys on Route 1 at Florida's southern tip. It's been berthed outside the **Holiday Inn, MM100, Key Largo, Oceanside** since the early eighties, though it does occasionally scuttle off to appear in parades around the US (*© 305.451.4655*).

AFTER HOURS

(1985, dir: Martin Scorsese)
Griffin Dunne, Rosanna Arquette, Verna Bloom.
● NEW YORK CITY

Manhattan's SoHo district is the setting for the best of eighties 'yuppie nightmare' genre movies. Word proces-

Rosanna Arquette conks out: Howard Street, SoHo

sor Griffin Dunne ventures down to this expensive, if rundown, artsy enclave to meet the goofy Rosanna Arquette. If you really want to follow him, take the subway down to

Spring Street, the station where the near-penniless Dunne fails to talk his way onto the platform when ticket prices are suddenly hiked up. **28 Howard Street** at Crosby Street is the spacious loft of dour sculptress Kiki Bridges where Arquette inconsiderately conks out.

A few blocks west you can sample burgers in the

Griffin Dunne finds shelter: Moondance Diner, Sixth Avenue

wonderfully stylish stainless-steel diner which Dunne scuttles back to through the course of an increasingly frantic night. It's the **Moondance Diner, 80 Sixth Avenue** at Grand Street in SoHo. A genuine diner, and good value.

Further west still is the Terminal Bar, where John Heard pours beer and Dunne keeps company with a brace of leather queens. If you want to try a beer here, it's an Irish tap room, the

Dunne's workplace: Metropolitan Life Building, Madison Avenue

The Terminal Bar: The Emerald Pub, Spring Street, SoHo

Emerald Pub, 308 Spring Street at Renwick Street, and over the road at **307** you can see the apartment of 'Miss Beehive 1965', disaffected barmaid Teri Garr. Heard's place, where Dunne's problems escalate after he's mistaken for a burglar, was further along the road on the corner of Greene Street at 128 Spring Street. The site has since been redeveloped. The elaborate iron gates of Dunne's workplace, outside which he's finally dumped, are those of the **Metropolitan Life Tower, Madison Avenue** between 23rd and 24th Streets by Madison Square Park.

AGAINST ALL ODDS

(1984, dir: Taylor Hackford)
Jeff Bridges, Rachel Ward, James Woods.
● LOS ANGELES; MEXICO

James Woods, the shifty owner of Hollywood nitespot Jake's Palace, hires washed up football player Bridges to find Rachel Ward in this convoluted remake of the 1947

Jake's Palace: Hollywood Palace Theater, North Vine Street, Hollywood

film noir *Out of the Past* (aka *Build My Gallows High*). The 'Palace' is the **Hollywood Palace Theater, 1735**

The Mayan football pitch: Chichen Itza, Mexico

The pyramid: El Castillo, Chichen Itza

Bridges disposes of the body: Sacred Cenote, Chichen Itza

North Vine Street opposite the Capitol Records Tower, by Hollywood Boulevard. Built as the Hollywood Playhouse in 1927, the theatre became El Capitan in 1942, venue for many TV shows including *This Is Your Life* in the fifties. It became the Palace in 1964 and is now a rock/jazz nightclub (*© 213.462.3000*).

Bridges' investigations take him down Mexico way – the exotic island resort on which he finds Ward is the tiny, and relatively unspoiled, island of **Cozumel**, off the east coast of Mexico's Yucatan Peninsula, a mere 30 minute flight from that wildly over-developed tourist mecca Cancun. 75 miles south of Cancun, Route 307, at **Tulum** on the mainland coast, you can see the Mayan ruins where Bridges and Ward finally get together. Although not the most spectacular ruins, the alabaster temples are unique, being the only Mayan site built directly on the coast (*© 988. 3.1505, admission charge*).

The much more spectacular ruins where Coach Sully catches up with the pair is the Toltec site of **Chichen Itza**. Amazingly, Ward's speech about Mayan football is generally true. A form of soccer was played in the 272-feet long pitch seen here, and the game did indeed end in ritual sacrifice with the beheading of the losing team (though some claim this fate was awarded to the winners as an honour). The square mile of ruins tends to be overrun by tourists – best to get there early in the day. Buses run from Cancun or Merida. Visit on the spring or autumn equinox to see the awesome optical illusion created when carefully engineered shadows become the body of giant plumed snake god Quetzlcoatl writhing down from the temple at the top of **El Castillo** (the giant pyramid you can see in the background of the movie) to the carved serpent head at the bottom.

After killing Coach Sully, Bridges disposes of the body in the **Sacred Cenote**, a 200-foot wide well half a mile into the jungle north of the site. He seems to be following tradition – precisely why the dank water is so well stocked with skeletons isn't known, but the most popular theories involve screaming sacrificial victims being hurled down the 70-foot drop.

AGATHA
(1979, Michael Apted)
Vanessa Redgrave, Dustin Hoffman, Helen Morse.
● **YORKSHIRE; AVON; LONDON**

The fictionalised story of Agatha Christie's 1926 disappearance originally centred on the relationship between Ms Christie and her husband's mistress. Enter Hoffman in a small role as an unlikely American interviewer. Out goes the central female relationship, and in comes the Redgrave-Hoffman romance.

Christie leaves London for Harrogate, where much of the movie filmed, though the more fittingly period **York Station** is used for her arrival. The hotel she stays in is the real thing; whatever her motives, Ms Christie did spend her mysterious retreat at the **Old Swan Hotel, Swan Street** in Harrogate. In 1926 it was called the Hydro Hotel, but the film opts to keep the present name. She plots a strange revenge at **Harrogate's Royal Baths, Parliament Street**, the town's famous hot springs, still open to the public. The photogenic town of Bath was also used as a stand-in for twenties Harrogate.

AGE D'OR, L'
(1930, dir: Luis Buñuel)
Gaston Modot, Lya Lys, Max Ernst.
● **PARIS; SPAIN**

Buñuel and his co-writer Salvador Dali set out to top the eye-slitting and sexual symbolism of their first collaboration, *Un Chien Andalou*, with a provocatively incendiary mix of sex, scatology and blasphemy (originally titled *La Bête Andalouse*). They succeeded in spades. During the film's first run, at Studio 28 in Paris, riots broke out, led by an unholy alliance of outraged rightwing Catholics, patriots and anti-Semites. The screen was showered with ink and the foyer exhibition of Surrealist art was destroyed. Nevertheless, more than 60 years on, **Le Studio 28** (named after the year it opened) is still showing movies, and you can visit it at **10 rue de Tholoze** in Montmartre (*metro: Blanche or Abesses*). *L'Age d'Or* itself was immediately banned, and it remained virtually unshown until the early seventies.

It's been claimed that the villa seen in the movie is the home of the Vicomte de Noailles, the wealthy aristo crat who funded many Surrealist projects, but although the movie was conceived and written here, it was largely filmed in Paris. Nevertheless, the Villa de Noailles was the centre of the hi-jinks and zany parties with which Dali,

The Dali-esque coastline: Cabo de Creus, Cataluña

Picasso and others tried desperately to shock the bourgeoisie. And Man Ray did shoot one of his surreal films here. You'll find the Villa de Noailles in Parc St-Bernard, Hyères, in the south of France, on the N96 between Toulon and St Tropez. Built for the Noailles in 1923, and recently restored, there are guided tours around the villa on Friday afternoons from mid-June to mid-September (book in advance from the Tourist Office, © 04.94.65.18.55).

A mixture of silent and sound footage, much of *L'Age d'Or* is studio-shot. The silent scenes were shot at the **Billancourt Studios, 50 Quai du Pont-du-Jour** on the Seine's north bank in southwest Paris (*metro: Billancourt or Marcel Sembat*), and the sound sequences at the Studios de la Tobis, Epinay-sur-Seine. Exteriors were also filmed at Montmorency, Seine-et-Oise, and in the 16th Arrondissement.

The striking, Dali-esque landscape of the opening scene is **Cabo de Creus**, on the Costa Brava, Cataluña. The rocky outcrop is the tail-end of the Pyrenees, trailing out to form Spain's most easterly point. The young Dali holidayed at nearby Cadaques, and in later life lived at Port Lligat.

AGE OF INNOCENCE, THE
(1993, dir: Martin Scorsese)
Daniel Day-Lewis, Michelle Pfeiffer, Winona Ryder.
● **NEW YORK STATE; PENNSYLVANIA; PARIS**

Scorsese's lush film of Edith Wharton's novel used a variety of period locations around New York State to conjure up the pre-high-rise Manhattan of the 1870s, including frat houses, yacht clubs, gravel pits, private homes and clubs, although the New York Academy of Music, where Daniel Day-Lewis first claps eyes on Michelle Pfeiffer during a performance of *Faust*, was actually filmed in Philadelphia. The impressive red and gilt opera house is the **Philadelphia Academy of Music, South Broad Street** and **Locust Street**, (© 215.893. 1930), home of the Philadelphia Orchestra. An ideal setting, the opulent interior of the building, which dates from 1857, is modelled after La Scala in Milan.

Back in New York, the Beauforts' house, to which everyone retires for the post-opera ball, can be found bang in the centre of Manhattan. It's the **National Arts Club, 15 Gramercy Park South** at Irving Place in the Gramercy district (*subway: 23rd Street or 14th Street and Union Square, Routes 4, 5 & 6*). Previously known as the Tilden House, the Victorian Gothic building was home to Samuel J Tilden, the city Governor who

The opera house: Philadelphia Academy of Music, South Broad Street

The Beauforts' house: National Arts Club, Gramercy Park South

Daniel Day-Lewis and Winona Ryder in the white aviary: Enid A Haupt Conservatory, Bronx Park

brought about the downfall of the notoriously corrupt 'Boss' Tweed, builder of the New York County Courthouse. In 1874 the house was remodelled by the co-designer of Central Park, Calvert Vaux, while the period redecoration added for the movie so pleased the members that they kept it. If you're lucky, you may get a peek inside as the club occasionally houses exhibitions (© 212.477.2389). You can see more of it, including the exterior, in Woody Allen's *Manhattan Murder Mystery*. Filming also took place at **Old Westbury Gardens** on Long Island (see *North by Northwest* for details).

The town of **Troy**, on the Hudson River's east bank across from Albany, upstate New York, stood in for 19th century New York. Once a thriving business centre to rival Manhattan, the town failed to achieve the same success and, fortunately for the film-makers, missed out on the high-rise redevelopment. 23rd Street exteriors were filmed here, while **River Street**, downtown Troy, stands in for turn-of-the-century Wall Street. Mrs Mingott's pooch-filled salon in 'a wilderness near Central Park' is the **Phi Kappa Phi Fraternity House, 49 Second Street**, of Troy's Rensselaer Polytechnic Institute (Troy is in Rensselaer County).

Daniel Day-Lewis' parents' house is the **Federal Gale House, First Street**, a Hall of Residence of another of Troy's three colleges, the Russell Sage College. The law office is the **Rice Building** at First and River Streets. **Washington Park** stands in for Manhattan's Gramercy Park. Troy has a Visitor Information Center which you'll find at 251 River Street (© 518.270.8667). The stretch of River Street south of the centre was period dressed for the movie and, although most of the stores are empty, the set decoration has been kept.

Over in the Bronx you can find the delicate white aviary in which Day-Lewis walks with Winona Ryder. The **Enid A Haupt Conservatory of Bronx's Botanical Gardens, 200th Street** at Bronx Boulevard in Bronx Park (© 718.220.8700, admission charge) might look familiar to Londoners, since its design is based on Kew Gardens' Great Palm House.

Other US locations in the New York area included the Boston park where Day-Lewis casually bumps into Pfeiffer (in Brooklyn) and the formal garden in Florida, where he tries to gee-up the marriage plans (actually Long Island). The European scenes, however, really were shot in Paris, including inside the **Louvre**.

AGONY AND THE ECSTASY, THE

(1965, dir: Carol Reed)

Charlton Heston, Rex Harrison, Diane Cilento.

● **ITALY**

It's all agony and little ecstasy in this dull 15th century sitcom, as slow and temperamental interior designer Charlton Heston tussles with tightwad Pope Rex Harrison. Heston is meant to be Michelangelo, commissioned to paint the ceiling of the Sistine Chapel. The real chapel was, not surprisingly, out of the question for filming, and was duplicated in Rome's Cinecittà Studios, where sections of the plaster set were gradually removed to reveal a huge photographic reproduction of Michelangelo's original. The 'wet plaster' which constantly drips into Heston's mouth is chocolate pudding, by the way.

Heston chooses the marble for his sculptures from the quarries actually used by Michelangelo at **Carrara**, southeast of La Spezia up in the Apuan Alps of Tuscany. You can take a trip up to see some of the 400 separate quarries in three valleys – Fantiscritti, Collonata and Torano – which have supplied the best quality marble since Roman times. St Peter's Square, circa 1508, was recreated in one of Italy's finest medieval squares, the **Piazza del Popolo** at **Todi**, 25 miles south of Perugia off the E45 in Umbria.

AGUIRRE, THE WRATH OF GOD

(1972, dir: Werner Herzog)

Klaus Kinski, Ray Guerra, Helena Rojo.

● **PERU**

Kinski is one of Pizarro's lieutenants taking a raft party down river to discover El Dorado but instead discovering megalomania. You'll need to be an adventurous traveller to follow in his footsteps. Herzog's wild epic was filmed, spectacularly, in the near-inaccessible **Andes of northwest Peru**, literally hundreds of miles from the nearest city, on the lands of the Aguaruna and the Lauramarca Indians.

AIR FORCE ONE

(1997, dir: Wolfgang Petersen)

Harrison Ford, Glenn Close, Gary Oldman.

● **RUSSIA; CALIFORNIA; OHIO; WASHINGTON DC**

A scenery-chewing Russian terrorist (the new Nationalist breed, not the old Commie type) hijacks America's First Plane with President Harrison Ford on board. For the early sequences, a second unit captured shots of **Red Square** in Moscow, but Harrison Ford stayed in LA to make his Russian speech. Similarly, Moscow Airport is actually **Los Angeles International Airport**. Ramstein Air Force Base, Germany is **Rickenbacker International Airport, Columbus** in Ohio. Permission to use airports determined the locations for much of the rest of the film. The Presidential Palace, Kazakhstan is **Case Western Reserve University, Cleveland**, while the vast Russian prison, where Jurgen Prochnow is incarcerated, is **Mansfield Reformatory, Mansfield** (also used for exteriors for *The Shawshank Redemption*). And although the lawn was recreated in a park in LA, it is the real **White House** in Washington DC in the long shots.

AIRPLANE!

(1980, dir: Jim Abrahams, David Zucker, Jerry Zucker)

Robert Hayes, Julie Haggerty, Peter Graves.

● **LOS ANGELES**

A wild hit'n'miss spoof, based not on *Airport* but on Arthur Hailey's play *Flight Into Danger* (filmed as *Zero Hour!* in 1957 with Dana Andrews as the shell-shocked pilot having to land a 'plane after the crew goes down with food poisoning). The featured airport is **Los Angeles International**, LAX, southwest of the city at the end of **Sepulveda Boulevard**, where the 747s really do press their noses alarmingly close to the Departure Lounge windows. The space shuttle in *Airplane II: The Sequel* still takes off from LAX.

AIRPORT

(1970, dir: George Seaton)

Burt Lancaster, Dean Martin, George Kennedy.

● **MINNESOTA; CALIFORNIA**

First of the major airliner-in-danger movies that spawned so many imitations throughout the seventies. Lincoln International Airport, where a frazzled Burt Lancaster has to cope with blizzards, a suicide bomber and Oscar-winning stowaway Helen Hayes, is **Minneapolis-St Paul International Airport** on **Cedar Avenue** just to the south of Minneapolis where, rather than resorting to models, a real Boeing 707, rented at a cost of $18,000 a day, was actually landed in a snowstorm at -43° as the film froze in the camera. The interiors were shot inside a grounded 707 installed at Universal Studios in Hollywood.

In the first sequel, *Airport '75*, stewardess Karen Black takes the controls of a stricken 747. The doomed flight takes off from **Dulles International Airport**, which serves Washington DC but is actually about twenty miles to the west on Dulles Access, Route 267, in Virginia. Charlton Heston and George Kennedy are flown in to **Salt Lake City Airport**, west of the city, to take charge. The mid-air helicopter-to-747 transfer stunt was filmed over the Heber Valley, east of the Wasatch Range in Utah. Other airports used in the production include **Los Angeles International**; the old **Van Nuys Airport** (also seen in *Casablanca*) **6590 Hayvenhurst Avenue**, Van Nuys, northwest LA; and **Edwards Airforce Base** north of LA in the Mojave desert.

To add variety to the midair crisis plot, the plane in *Airport '77* plummets to the bottom of the ocean. A cast of Hollywood stalwarts gamely bounce about on a jet set mounted on cantilevers in the Universal Studio, Hollywood. Millionaire James Stewart's museum-home is in Florida. It's **Villa Vizcaya, 3251 South Miami Avenue**. A familiar location, you can also see this Italianate mansion in *Any Given Sunday*, and its grounds in *Absence of Malice*. For further details, see *Ace Ventura, Pet Detective*. Filming also took place at **Burbank Airport**; **Los Angeles international**; and **Dulles International** in Virginia. The offshore filming was, as usual, around the San Diego area, while underwater scenes were filmed on the Universal backlot and at **Wakulla Springs** near Tallahassee, Florida (a regular subaqua location – see also *Creature From the Black Lagoon*).

For the third sequel, *Airport '80: The Concorde*, it's the supersonic luxury jet in trouble as arms dealer Robert Wagner tries to prevent passenger Susan Blakely publishing damning evidence against him. The Concorde touches down and takes off from **Dulles International Airport** near DC, in Virginia. It's heading for Charles de Gaulle Airport in Paris, but missile and F-15 fighter plane attacks mean an emergency landing with nets at **Le Bourget,** Paris' original airport, north of the city. Hotel scenes were shot back in LA at our old friend the **Biltmore Hotel, 506 South Grand Avenue,** downtown (see *The Fabulous Baker Boys* for details). The final forced landing in the Alps was filmed at **Alta** in Utah, southeast of Salt Lake City.

ALAMO, THE

(1960, dir: John Wayne)
John Wayne, Laurence Harvey, Richard Widmark.
● TEXAS

Wayne's lumbering epic, a long, long way from the historical truth, actually began filming in Mexico – there's not much of the real Alamo left – but this proved too expensive. Even so, at $7,500,000, *The Alamo* was the costliest movie made at the time. The production was closed down and restarted at **Brackettville** on Highway 90, about 100 miles west of San Antonio toward Del Rio, West Texas, where Wayne leased 400 acres of a 22,000 acre ranch belonging to one JT 'Happy' Shahan, and the Alamo was rebuilt. The full-sized facsimile, which took two years to complete, used the original plans, the traditional adobe techniques and, without any apparent irony, a largely Mexican workforce of 5,000. It was claimed at the time to be

The Alamo: the full-size facsimile was rebuilt in Brackettville, Texas...

...only part of the real complex still stands on Alamo Plaza in San Antonio

the biggest movie set outside Hollywood.

And it's still there, as a tourist attraction as well as a location for many subsequent movies. Extensions acquired over the years include a section of San Antonio which metamorphoses over its length to become Fort Worth of the 1880s. Alamo Village, open May to September, can be found just north of Brackettville itself, on Route 674 (© 512.563.2580).

Wayne's mentor, John Ford, proved unable to resist giving advice to his old pal until Wayne packed him off to film second unit shots. Ford's scenes include the wide shot of Santa Ana's initial approach on the Alamo and the Mexican soldiers crossing the river.

The real **Alamo**, in **San Antonio**, was founded as the Mission San Antonio de Valero in 1718, the first in a chain of missions built along the San Antonio River to extend the frontier of the Spanish empire and convert the Native Americans to Catholicism. It was closed down in 1793 and its lands given to the 39 mission Indians, then occupied on and off by the various forces in control of Texas until it achieved immortality in 1836 when 188 Texan volunteers were massacred, rather pointlessly, by Santa Ana's troops. Among those who perished in the massacre were American folk heroes Jim Bowie and Davy Crockett, hence Hollywood's fascination with this bit of US history. The only survivor of the massacre was a black servant found hiding in the chapel and played, memorably, by blonde Joan O'Brian in *The Alamo*.

Although the town of San Antonio is shaded by alamo (cottonwood) trees, the name actually comes from a Spanish Cavalry unit from the pueblo of El Alamo de Parras who occupied the old mission in 1801. The chapel, built in 1756, and the Long Barrack are virtually all that remain of the fortified complex, though the site now also contains the extensive Alamo Memorial Museum (© 210. 225.1391), which occupies a 4.2 acre site on Alamo Plaza. Entry is free, but watch your dress and behaviour here – the place has taken on the status of a holy shrine. Bare chests and loud shirts are out, hushed voices and solemn patriotism very much in.

ALEXANDER NEVSKY

(1938, dir: Sergei Eisenstein)
Nikolai Cherkassov, Nikolai Okhlopkov, Andrei Abrikosov.
● RUSSIA

13th century Prince Nevsky defeats Teutonic knights in a battle on the ice of Lake Peipus in Northern Russia, to music by Prokofiev. This state-funded film is set largely in the city of Novgorod, about 100 miles south of St Petersburg, but the city had changed too much to allow location filming. Although the 13th century cathedral is still there, it's surrounded by modern buildings and no longer as gleaming white as it once was. The city sets were built just outside Moscow, at enormous expense. Despite the film's wintry look, *Nevsky* was actually filmed during the summer, with snow simulated by white sand shipped in from the beaches of the Baltic Sea, cotton wool perched in the tree branches and the actors showered with salt. Lake Peipus was also mocked-up on the set, with the artificial ice floes supported by collapsible pontoons that gave way on cue.

As an homage, Ken Russell virtually recreates this sequence at the end of his 1967 thriller *Billion Dollar Brain* (the third film to feature Michael Caine as Harry Palmer), where it's the private army of batty General Midwinter disappearing beneath the ice.

ALFIE
(1966, dir: Lewis Gilbert)
Michael Caine, Shelley Winters, Millicent Martin.
● **LONDON**

Alfie recuperates in the sanatorium: York House, Twickenham

Caine shot to stardom as a callous cockney womaniser forced to face up to mortality, abortion and formidable American matrons. The various locations are, unsurprisingly, around London. The opening scene ('I suppose you think you're goin' to see the bleedin' titles now...'), despite establishing shots of Westminster, was actually filmed on **Camley Street**, NW1, behind King's Cross station, with the famous Victorian gasometers much in evidence in the background. The industrial buildings where Alfie's steamed-up car is parked have

The christening: St Mary's, Battersea

gone, and the site is currently Camley Street Natural Park, a wildlife preserve, but not for long. The site is up for redevelopment and even the gasometers are scheduled to be moved. Catch it while you can.

You'll find Alfie's seedy bedsit in Notting Hill Gate, at **22 St Stephen's Gardens** off Chepstow Road, W2 (*tube: Royal Oak*). It hasn't really changed at all, apart from a little pedestrianisation of the area, which means that Jane Asher would no longer be able to jump straight onto a convenient bus. Over the Thames from World's End, Chelsea, you can see the green spire of **St Mary's, Battersea Parish Church** on **Battersea Church Road**, SW11, where Julia Foster spends her lunchbreaks with nerdy but dependable bus conductor Graham Stark, and Alfie balefully watches her baby's Christening.

The sanatorium where Alfie recuperates after a shadow is found on his lung, and where he seduces fellow patient's wife Vivien Merchant, is **York House and Gardens, York Street** (the A305), Twickenham, conveniently close to the film studios (*rail: Twickenham*). The seventeenth century mansion, alongside the new Civic Centre, is now council offices, but the ornamental gardens are open to the public (entrance to the left of the house on Sion Road).

Alfie and his friend Murray Melvin take a walk along side the **Grand Union Canal** by the Lock-Keeper's cot-

tage at King's Cross, with the gasometers in the background. He photographs voracious Shelley Winters at the Tower of London, while the lobby of Winters' apartment (complete with Tretchikoff 'Green Lady' painting) is actually the **Dorchester Hotel, Park Lane**, W1 (a *huge* £15 a week).

ALICE
(1990, dir: Woody Allen)
Mia Farrow, Alec Baldwin, William Hurt.
● **NEW YORK CITY**

Another trip with Woody Allen around the classier joints of Manhattan, as the well-heeled but rather distracted Mia Farrow visits Chinatown herbalist Keye Luke and picks up some very peculiar concoctions to help sort out her tangled life. The swanky clothes store where she takes the first lot of magical 'erbs is

Swanky shopping: Valentino Boutique, on New York's East Side

Mia Farrow eavesdrops invisibly: Polo Ralph Lauren Store, Madison Avenue

the Euro-design showcase the **Valentino Boutique, 825 Madison Avenue** between 68th and 69th Streets on the East Side, after which Farrow soon finds herself eloquently talking jazz with Joe Mantegna. She gets cold feet and ducks out of her assignation, leaving him waiting at the recently renovated **penguin tank** in the **Central Park Zoo**, east Central Park at 64th Street.

The illicit romance with Mantegna takes off again when they both take their kids to the **Big Apple Circus**, which performs every winter, from October to January, at the **Lincoln Center, Columbus Avenue** between West 62nd and West 65th Streets on the West Side, (© 212.168.3030). The pair get invisible together at NY's oldest Italian restaurant, **Barbetta**, an elegant townhouse at **321 West 46th Street** near 8th Avenue (© 212. 246.9171). It's a favourite of Allen's, seen also in his *Celebrity*. Later, Farrow invisibly follows her gossipy friends into the deluxe **Polo Ralph Lauren Store**, with its pricey antiques, walnut fittings and oriental carpets, in the **Rhinelander Mansion, 867 Madison Avenue** at 72nd Street.

ALICE DOESN'T LIVE HERE ANY MORE
(1974, dir: Martin Scorsese)
Ellen Burstyn, Kris Kristofferson, Billy Green Bush.
● **LOS ANGELES; ARIZONA**

After being widowed, Ellen Burstyn determines to return to her roots in Monterey and resume her career as a singer. With her young son, she eventually fetches up in **Tucson**, Arizona, where she lowers her sights a little to work in a diner. Mel and Ruby's Bar-B-Q was filmed in a real Tucson diner, and all the other joints where Burstyn tries to get work as a lounge singer are genuine Tucson bars, too. The giant cow skull-fronted restaurant where Burstyn stops off *en route* from Phoenix to Tucson is actually the **Big Horn Restaurant** in **Amado** on I-9, a good 30 miles to the south of Tucson.

The Monterey Dining Room billboard seen at the end of the movie, when Burstyn decides to stay on and give her relationship with farmer Kristofferson another chance, is not a piece of heavy-handed 'happiness-in-your-own-backyard' symbolism, but an actual Tucson sign that strayed into the closing shot by luck.

ALICE IN DEN STADTEN (aka *Alice in the Cities*)
(1974, dir: Wim Wenders)
Rudiger Vogler, Yella Rotlander, Lisa Kreuzer.
● **WUPPERTAL, GERMANY; NEW YORK CITY; AMSTERDAM**

The cities being New York, Amsterdam and Wuppertal, as burnt out photographer Vogler journeys from America to Germany after being lumbered with a little girl. The Boardwalk where the movie opens is set in Queens, NY, at **Rockaway Beach** by Beach 67th Street. Also in Queens, Vogler sells his car within earshot of the organ at **Shea Stadium, 126th Street**, Flushing, and has to catch the subway at **Willet's Point/Shea Stadium** station on the Main Street-Flushing Line 7. He takes the young Alice to see the view from the outside Observation Deck of the **Empire State Building, 350 Fifth Avenue**, before they depart for Europe from **JFK Airport**. The European destination is Amsterdam's **Schiphol Airport**, and there's a brief jaunt around the canals of the city centre before the last leg of the journey takes them to Germany. If you fancy a ride on the creaky old suspension railway the pair take to find Alice's Grandma's house, you'll find it in **Wuppertal**, about thirty miles north of Cologne. The railway – amazingly, built in 1900 – rattles along for eight miles, 39 feet above the city's streets, linking eighteen stations between Vohwinkel and Oberbarmen, and has reputedly never had an accident in its history.

ALIEN
(1979, dir: Ridley Scott)
Sigourney Weaver, John Hurt, Tom Skerritt.
● **BERKSHIRE**

Not surprisingly, there's nothing to see of this movie, set as it is entirely aboard a space freighter, with weirdly effective alien planet sets – and the creature itself – based on designs by Swiss artist HR Giger. It was shot at Shepperton Studios, west of Shepperton Green off the B376 in Surrey, and at longtime home of Hammer Films, Bray Studios, Down Place in Berkshire

ALIENS
(1986, dir: James Cameron)
Sigourney Weaver, Michael Biehn, Carrie Henn.
● **LONDON**

Director Cameron's penchant for industrial locations (see *The Abyss* and the *Terminator* movies) takes him from Pinewood Studios to the cavernous disused **Acton Lane**

Power Station on Acton Lane, London W3.

ALIEN³
(1992, dir: David Fincher)
Sigourney Weaver, Charles Dance, Paul McGann.
● **NORTHUMBERLAND**

Filmed mostly at Pinewood Studios, the surface of the alien planet was **Blast Beach** alongside **Dawdon Colliery** on the Northumberland coast, blackened with years of pit detritus. The area was recently cleaned up in an extensive restoration programme. There was more filming at the nearby, and recently closed, **Blyth Power Station** in Bedlington.

ALL ABOUT EVE
(1950, dir: Joseph L Mankiewicz)
Bette Davis, George Sanders, Anne Baxter.
● **NEW YORK CITY; SAN FRANCISCO; NEW HAVEN, CONNECTICUT**

Clever use of location adds a little East Coast authenticity to this largely studio-bound story of ruthless ambition, set in Manhattan's theatreland, which got a record fourteen Oscar nominations, and bagged six of them, including biggies Best Picture, Direction and Screenplay.

Manipulative Eve Harrington, first seen as a sweet, unassuming little mite, hangs around the stage door of NY's **John Golden Theater, 252 West 45th Street** at 8th Avenue (© *212.239.6200*), for a glimpse of her idol, Margo Channing. Though the alley beside the Golden, where helpful Celeste Holm offers to take Eve backstage, is a studio set, the establishing longshot is real. Doubles stood in for the two stars, who remained back at the Fox studios in Hollywood, a standard technique of the period used throughout the film.

The cast did make it a little further up the West Coast, though, to San Francisco to film theatre interiors, where a pre-stardom Marilyn Monroe appears as George Sanders' protegé – Miss Caswell, 'a graduate of the Copacabana school of acting.' The Golden's interior is the **Curran Theater, 445 Geary Street**, downtown San Francisco (©

415.474.3800). Built in 1922, the theatre is still a popular venue for the latest big musicals.

Celeste Holm gets a stand-in for her entrance into New York's famous **21 Club, 21 West 52nd Street** near Fifth Avenue (© *212.582.7200*), where she bumps into Eve. The real 21, a pretty exclusive drinking club which started up

The New York theatre: John Golden Theater, West 45th Street

...and the West Coast interior: Curran Theater, Geary Street, San Francisco

during Prohibition as a speakeasy, was given a new lease of life in 1987 when, after years of decline, it was renovated. It features frequently as a symbol of worldly success in such films as Oliver Stone's *Wall Street* and Woody Allen's *Manhattan Murder Mystery* – where you can see the club's jockey-covered frontage.

Footsteps on the Ceiling, in which Eve finally gets the plum role, opens at the **Shubert Theater, 247 College Street, New Haven**, Connecticut, a traditional out-of-town try-out venue for Broadway-bound shows, and the hometown of Yale University. Once again, doubles are used for the long shots, while Anne Baxter and George Sanders stroll past rear projection of the Shubert and the nearby Taft Hotel.

The swanky apartment to which Eve finally retires, clutching her Sarah Siddons award, was shot on NY's **Fifth Avenue**, again with a stand-in.

ALL QUIET ON THE WESTERN FRONT

(1930, dir: Lewis Milestone)
Lew Ayres, Louis Wollheim, John Wray.
● **CALIFORNIA**

WWI seen through the eyes of young soldiers from the German side, this anti-war epic still packs a punch. The huge sets were constructed on Universal's backlot, and recycled over the years (you can catch them again in James Whale's classic *Frankenstein*). The trench scenes were filmed at the **Irvine Ranch** near Santa Ana, Route 405 in Orange County southeast of LA, while more scenes were shot at **Balboa**, on the southern California coast between Newport and Laguna Beaches. With only 150 extras, Milestone was forced to employ bravura techniques for the battle scenes. And in the classic final shot, it's the director's own hand reaching for the butterfly.

ALL THAT JAZZ

(1979, dir: Bob Fosse)
Roy Scheider, Jessica Lange, Ann Reinking.
● **NEW YORK CITY**

Fosse's story of a workaholic, sexually compulsive choreographer, which seems more than a little autobiographical, was filmed on location around New York. The opening 'cattle call' audition for aspiring hoofers was staged in Manhattan's **Palace Theater, Seventh Avenue** at 47th Street (*© 212.730.8200*) in the Theatre District.

ALL THE KING'S MEN

(1949, dir: Robert Rossen)
Broderick Crawford, Joanne Dru, John Ireland.
● **CALIFORNIA**

An initially decent man finds political fame, corruption and, ultimately, assassination in this *film à clef* based on the career of Louisiana Governor Huey Long. Set in the South, it was shot largely on location around northern California. The city of **Suisun**, off I-80 to the northeast of San Francisco, was used for the election scenes, and the locale given a more folksy, funky feel with 50 tons of topsoil dumped onto the paved streets. Nearby **Fairfield** and **Stockton**, Route 5, east of San Francisco, stood in for Southern towns.

ALL THE PRESIDENT'S MEN

(1976, dir: Alan J Pakula)
Robert Redford, Dustin Hoffman, Jason Robards.
● **WASHINGTON DC; LOS ANGELES**

The third of Pakula's excellent paranoia trilogy (following *Klute* and *The Parallax View*) which manages to make the potentially uncinematic uncovering of the Watergate story truly gripping, is brilliantly photographed around a spookily benighted DC by Gordon Willis.

Authenticity is all. The break-in was actually filmed in the **Watergate Complex** (not far from the Georgetown house used for *The Exorcist*), with Frank Wills – the very security guard who discovered the taped door – recreating the moment on the exact spot (the arresting officer, by the way, is future *Amadeus* Oscar-winning actor F Murray Abraham). The Democratic offices were on the sixth floor of the complex at **2600 Virginia Avenue NW**, west of downtown DC (*metro: Foggy Bottom*). If you feel like a souvenir, you can pick up a bottle of Watergate Whisky from the store in the complex.

Base 1, the lookout, is stationed – as he was – on the balcony directly opposite, which belongs to the **Howard Johnson Motor Lodge, 2601 Virginia Avenue NW** at New Hampshire Avenue, and yes, if you wish, you can book the room used by the burglars (*© 202.965.2700; 800.654.2000*).

Washington Post reporters Bob Woodward and Carl

Woodward and Bernstein's office: The Washington Post Building

Bernstein work out of the paper's building at **1150 15th Street NW** between L and M Streets, downtown DC (*metro: Farragut North*). On Mondays, between 10am and 3pm, there's a tour of the building, which takes in the actual newsroom (book ahead on *© 202.334.7969*). The movie's city room, in which the pair worry away at

The lookout: the Howard Johnson Motor Lodge

The burglary: The Watergate complex

the burglary story, is, however, an elaborate set built on soundstages at Warner Brothers' Burbank lot. The 32,000 square-foot set cost half a million dollars, and the obsessive detail went further than just reproducing all 250 of the reporters' and editors' desks in their correct positions and the graphics on the walls – it went as far as filling the wastepaper baskets with real waste from the actual *Post* offices, *correctly assigned to each department.*

Genuine DC locations include, of course, the **Capitol Building** – the entrance for tours is on East Capitol Street, Capitol Hill (© *202.225.6827*) (*metro: Capitol South, Union Station*).

The magnificent circular reading room, where the duo sort through the White House book-request slips, is the domed, marble Main Reading Room in the Jefferson Building of the **Library of Congress, First Street SE** between East Capitol Street and Independence Avenue (© *202.707.5000*) (*metro: Capitol South, Union Station*).

The concert building outside which Redford catches a cab for his first assignation with enigmatic insider Deep Throat is the **Kennedy Center for the Performing Arts, Rock Creek Parkway** at New Hampshire Avenue NW (*metro: Foggy Bottom*). The complex, which opened in 1971, houses two theatres, a concert hall and an opera house (© *202.416.8000*). The highrise wilderness where Redford keeps the rendezvous can be found over the Potomac River in **Arlington**, Virginia, though, if you want to see the car park itself, you'll need to visit LA. The sinister garage is under the **ABC Entertainment Center** on **Avenue of the Stars** at Constellation Boulevard, Century City.

Hoffman meets up with his phone company contact at the site of all those sixties anti-war demos, **Lafayette Park**, north of the White House, on Pennsylvania Avenue and H Street NW between Jackson and Madison Places (*metro: Farragut West*). The lead takes him to the County Justice Building of Miami where he tricks his way into meeting official Ned Beatty. The building is no more Miami than it is DC. It's **Los Angeles City Hall, 200 North Spring Street**, downtown, the home of *Dragnet* and *Superman.* Also in LA, you'll find the burger joint where Redford and Hoffman hatch the plot to get Sloane to confirm Haldeman's name (McDonald's in **Santa Monica**), and disgraced lawyer Donald Segretti's apartment, overlooking the Marina in **Marina del Rey.**

The FBI works out of the **J Edgar Hoover FBI Building, 10th Street and Pennsylvania Avenue NW**, downtown DC, though the interior of the building, where Woodward and Bernstein badger the agent, is, surprise, not the real FBI HQ at all, but once again City Hall, LA. The genuine FBI Building offers free tours, which include a firearms demo, from the entrance on East Street NW between 9th and 10th Streets (© *202.324.3000*) (*metro: Metro Center, Gallery Place, Federal Triangle*).

ALL THE PRETTY HORSES

(2000, dir: Billy Bob Thornton)
Matt Damon, Lucas Black, Rubén Blades.
● **TEXAS; NEW MEXICO**

Damon is a Texan drifter in the forties, who crosses the

border into Mexico to find only hardship. Texas filming took place in **San Antonio**, at the old **Cadillac Bar, 212 South Flores Street**, downtown. The film was also shot all over New Mexico, including the **State Penitentiary, Santa Fe**; the Rio Grande Gorge rim at **Taos**; Plaza Blanca and the Chama River at **Abiquiu**; **Las Vegas** and **San Jose** (New Mexico towns, not their more famous Nevada and California namesakes).

ALPHAVILLE

(1965, dir: Jean-Luc Godard)
Eddie Constantine, Anna Karina, Akim Tamiroff.
● **PARIS**

Sci-fi fantasy with special agent Lemmy Caution travelling across space (by car, naturally) to investigate the bleak futuristic city of Alphaville, represented by a quirkily photographed sixties Paris. The Electricity Board building is used as an ominous computer centre. Caution's hotel is the **Scribe Hotel, 1 rue Scribe**, by the Place de l'Opéra. This rather grand edifice, which was the Allied

Lemmy Caution's hotel: Scribe Hotel, Paris

Forces' press HQ during WWII, has another place in cinema history. An inscription round the corner, at the hotel's boulevard des Capucines entrance (no 14) records that here, in the Salon Indien of the Grand Café, the Lumière Brothers first demonstrated cinematic projection on 28 December, 1895.

Quentin Tarantino pays homage to the director by naming the diamond shop, site of the robbery, in *Reservoir Dogs* Karina's, after *Alphaville*'s co-star who was at the time married to Godard, and also by calling his production company, A Band Apart, after Godard's 1964 movie, *Bande à Part*.

ALTERED STATES

(1980, dir: Ken Russell)
William Hurt, Blair Brown, Bob Balaban.
● **NEW YORK CITY; MASSACHUSETTS; LOS ANGELES; MEXICO**

No love lost between scriptwriter Paddy Chayevsky (who took his name off the film) and director Ken Russell in this story of an obsessed scientist using a mix of drugs and sensory deprivation to investigate primal states of consciousness. The faculty where William Hurt conducts his first tentative experiments is New York's **Columbia University**, between Amsterdam Avenue and Broadway, West 114th and West 120th Streets up towards Morningside Heights. Popular with wacko paranormal investigators, it spawned the trio of *Ghostbusters* a few years later.

Hurt relocates to Boston, where he lives in the **Beacon Hill** district and continues his experiments at **Harvard Medical School**. The bizarre rock formations he flies out to are in Mexico (they're for real – the *Fantasy Island* set at Burbank which the studio wanted to use was too Disneyfied for Russell), and he returns via Boston's Logan

Airport. The evolutionarily regressed Hurt visits the animals in **Bronx Zoo**, the largest urban zoo in the States, **Bronx Park** on **Southern Boulevard**, NY. The scenes with Hurt regressing further to some kind of primal blob were filmed at the **Biltmore Hotel, 506 South Grand Avenue**, downtown LA.

AMADEUS
(1984, dir: Milos Forman)
F Murray Abraham, Tom Hulce, Simon Callow.
● **CZECHOSLOVAKIA**

Shaffer's fantasia on the rivalry between composers Salieri and Mozart was filmed almost entirely in real castles and palaces throughout Czechoslovakia. Only four sets were built for the movie – Schikanader's Volkstheater, where Simon Callow stages a surreal comedy; Salieri's hospital room; the interior of Mozart's apartment; and the staircase where he meets his father, at Prague's **Barrandov Studios**. The famous studios, in the suburb of Hlubocepy, were founded in 1933 by President Vaclav Havel's uncle Milos.

The relatively unchanged **Old Town (Staré Mesto)** of **Prague** stands in for 18th century Vienna. The opera performances, *Seraglio, Marriage of Figaro* and *Don Giovanni*, were filmed here in the unchanged **Tyl Theatre, Zelezna ulice 11** (Zelezna Street) at Havirska Street. Built in 1783 for Count Anton von Nostitz-Rieneck, as the Nostitz Theatre, it became the German Theatre in the mid-19th century until 1945, when it was renamed for Czech dramatist and actor Josef Kajetan Tyl. It's now Czechoslovakia's National Theatre. During his lifetime, Mozart was always more appreciated in Prague than in Vienna, and the composer actually chose to stage the première of *Don Giovanni* at the Tyl, on 29 October 1787.

To the west, reached by the Charles Bridge (Karluv

Most) over the Vltava River, you'll find the **Lesser Town (Malá Strana)**, a picturesque quarter of winding streets, taverns and old houses which provided more period backdrops. North of the Mala Strana is the residential district of Hradcany, where the aristocracy built their swish palaces. Here you can see the Emperor's Palace – actually the recently restored **Gryspek**

The opera performances: Tyl Theatre, Prague

The Emperor's palace: Gryspek Palace, Hradcany Square

Palace, the Prague residence of Cardinal Tomasek, in **Hradcany Square** (Hradcanské námestí) opposite St Vitus Cathedral. Originally a Renaissance mansion, it was bought by Ferdinand I from the Royal Private Secretary – Florian von Gryspek – and presented to the Catholic Archbishop of Prague. During the 16th century it was rebuilt and extended before being remodelled in the Baroque style between 1675 and 1688. In 1764 Johan Joseph Wirch reworked it into Rococo style and decorated the interior in sumptuous splendour. You can see the results, but it's not easy. The Palace is only open to the public one day a year, between 9am and 5pm on Maundy Thursday.

Salieri's first encounter with the brattish Mozart uses the equally lavish interior of the Baroque palace at **Kromeriz**, northern Moravia in the eastern part of the Czech Republic. The palace and its gardens are open for guided tours. More austere interiors for Salieri were found in the former **Palace of the Grand Prior of the Knights of Malta, Maltese Square** (Maltézské námestí), which for a while was Prague's Museum of Musical Instruments, but is now a private liberal arts college.

AMANTS, LES (aka *The Lovers*)
(1958, dir: Louis Malle)
Jeanne Moreau, Alain Cuny, Jean-Marc Bory.
● **FRANCE**

Jeanne Moreau is married to stuffy old Alain Cuny and carrying on an affair in Paris too, when she suffers a sudden Gallic attack of *amour fou* and takes off with a younger hunk, in Malle's early New Wave movie. Moreau and Cuny's villa is a composite of an actual villa in **Dijon** – as it's supposed to be – together with exteriors shot near Paris. The neighbouring roads were filmed around Burgundy, while the grounds were actually way to the south in Provence. The small village where Moreau and her beau-to-be stop off en route to Dijon is **Montbard**, 45 miles northwest of the city on the River Brenne and the Canal du Bourgogne.

AMANTS DU PONT NEUF, LES (aka *The Lovers on the Bridge*)
(1990, dir: Leos Carax)
Juliette Binoche, Denis Lavant, Klaus-Michael Gruber.
● **FRANCE**

A bizarre romance between middle-class artist Binoche, who's losing her sight, and nihilist fire-eating street-punk Lavant, set on the Pont Neuf in Paris during the 1989 Bicentennial celebrations. The Paris locations you can see include the street where Lavant is hit by a car at the beginning of the movie – **boulevard Sebastopol**, which runs north/south from Strasbourg St Denis Metro to Chatelet – and the **Nanterre Night Refuge** to which he's taken.

The metro station, inside which Lavant impresses Binoche with his acrobatics, is **Pont Neuf** itself; while the one with the illuminated pavement, where Binoche is chased, is **Montparnasse Bienvenue**. Beyond Pont Neuf, the iron-latticed bridge to which Binoche retires after drugging café patrons, is the wooden-planked **Pont des Arts** leading from the Institut de France to the Louvre. And it really is the **Louvre** Binoche steals into at night for a pri-

The real thing: Pont Neuf, Paris

vate viewing of the Rembrandt self-portrait. The shot of Binoche taking an uncomfortably close peek at the painting with a cigarette lighter was reputedly snatched while the ever-present Louvre guard had popped out to the toilet.

The Pont Neuf itself was closed for renovations from 1989 to 1991, and its turrets provide shelter for the movie's down-and-out characters. If the Paris background looks sparsely populated, though, that's because, for the most part, the film was made on a giant set which recreates the Seine river fronts in forced perspective. Which also explains why, until Claud Berri's mammoth adaptation of *Germinal* came along in 1993, *Pont Neuf* was the most expensive French movie ever made. The real bridge was scheduled to be used for filming, with a set taking over for the spectacular night-time scenes, but when Denis Lavant injured a tendon in his wrist the production moved full-time to the set, which had then to be extended to accommodate daytime shooting.

40 bulldozers set to shifting a quarter of a million cubic tons of earth to recreate the River Seine in a field near **Montpellier**, in **Lansargues**, southwest of Nimes down toward the south coast. But money ran out, and in December 1988 the production closed down. After an aborted five week shoot in 1989, a new producer and even rumours of Elia Kazan or Robert De Niro taking over as director, the production finally wrapped in January 1990, with a final cost rumoured at between 100 and 160 million francs.

The real **Pont Neuf** – the New Bridge, actually the oldest existing bridge across the Seine, completed in 1607 – crosses the river in a series of twelve arches by the western tip of the Ile de la Cité, dividing it neatly into two sections (*metro: Pont Neuf*).

AMARCORD

(1974, dir: Federico Fellini)
Puppella Maggio, Magali Noel, Armando Brancia.
● **ITALY**

Fellini's typically imaginative, anecdotal look at small-town Italian life in the thirties won the 1973 Best Foreign Picture Oscar. Like all of his later films, it was shot on the huge Stage 5 at Cinecittà outside Rome. The town of Borgo, built in the studio by Art Director Danilo Donati, is based on Rimini on Northern Italy's Adriatic coast. The Grand Hotel exterior, though, where Bisceine has a dubious adventure with the sheik's wives, was too large even for Cinecittà. It's a five-storey hotel which you can see in **Anzio**, on the coast 35 miles south of Rome.

AMATEUR

(1994, dir: Hal Hartley)
Martin Donovan, Isabelle Huppert, Elina Lowensohn.
● **NEW YORK CITY**

Fiercely indie director Hartley deserts his usual Long Island

locales for central Manhattan, and even ventures, quirkily, into thriller territory as amnesiac heavy Donovan gets involved with virgin nymphomaniac nun Huppert and a pair of oddball hitmen.

The café where Elina Lowensohn meets Damian Young and puts in a fateful phone call to Amsterdam was the **Angelika Film Center, 611 Broadway** at West Houston Street in Greenwich Village. The couple are sub-

The café: Angelika Film Center, Greenwich Village

sequently tracked down to the concourse of **Grand Central Station**. The public phone where a manic Young, suffering the after-effects of a little improvised electroconvulsive therapy, gets arrested, is at the corner of **Fifth Avenue and 19th Street**, just northwest of Union Square.

Donovan is finally gunned down when he accompanies Huppert back to her convent. This normally quiet haven is a blissfully useful escape from Manhattan. A cluster of medieval European buildings transported to and rebuilt in the US, **The Cloisters** overlook the Hudson River in Fort Tryon Park north of Washington Heights. If you need to chill out, The Cloisters are open every day except Mondays from 9.30am to 4.45pm, entrance on **West 193rd Street** at Fort Washington Avenue (© 212. 923.3700, *subway: 190th Street*).

AMAZING COLOSSAL MAN, THE

(1957, dir: Bert I Gordon)
Glenn Langan, Cathy Downs, William Hudson.
● **NEVADA**

The fallout from a nuclear explosion in the Nevada desert causes colonel Glenn Langan to grow ten feet a day in this sci-fi flick from cheapo FX merchant Bert Gordon. A combi-

The end of the Colossal Man: Hoover Dam, near Boulder City, Nevada

nation of real location work and model shots has Langan wreaking havoc on the endearingly modest **Las Vegas Strip**, as it appeared in 1957. Although some of the fifties Vegas landmarks are no more, including the crown he rips from the roof and the revolving Silver Slipper, 50 feet tall Las Vegas Vic, whom Langan apparently crumples up, still towers over the **Pioneer Club, 25 East Fremont Street**, even if he's not puffing away on a cigarette any more. The Colossal Man is eventually toppled from the edge of the **Hoover Dam**, east of Vegas near Boulder City. The spectacular dam, which blocks the Colorado River to form Lake Mead and power all that neon, was built between 1930 and 1935 and took some 96 lives in the process. It's 30 miles east of Vegas, and Route 93 – the Flagstaff road from where Mr Colossal plummets into the waters of the Colorado – runs along the top. The Visitor Centre, from which you can descend 44 storeys to the base on a guided tour, features in *Lost In America*, and there's a new one scheduled to open.

AMERICAN BEAUTY

(1999, dir: Sam Mendes)
Kevin Spacey, Annette Bening, Wes Bentley.
● CALIFORNIA

The aerial shots of the neat, bland chequer-board neighbourhood in Sam Mendes' Oscar-winning drama, are the suburbs of California state capital, **Sacramento**, as are the streets where Kevin Spacey jogs with his neighbours. Sadly though, you won't be able to visit Spacey's family house. The very specific sightlines needed as the characters constantly peer into each other's houses, meant that the movie had to be shot on the controlled environment of the studio backlot. One real location is the school, where Spacey lusts after his daughter's friend Mena Suvari, which is **South High School, Torrance**, in LA's South Bay area.

AMERICAN GIGOLO

(1980, dir: Paul Schrader)
Richard Gere, Lauren Hutton, Hector Elizondo.
● CALIFORNIA

Gere's neighbourhood: Westwood

Gere is a high-class rent boy who discovers the downside of Tinseltown when he's framed for murder. Schrader's movie, which borrows its striking visual style from Bertolucci's *Il Conformista*, was filmed round a cool, slick, pastel LA – particularly **Westwood Village**, a one-time exclusive enclave between Hollywood and Bel-Air, where Gere's stylish home, the Westwood Hotel Apartments, is supposedly sited. The building was actually the Sunset Plaza Apartments, which stood at 1220 Sunset Plaza Drive, Mount Olympus, to the north of Beverly Hills. It has been home to Mitzi Gaynor, Katharine Hepburn and James Dean, but lost the fight for preservation as part of Hollywood's history and was demolished in 1987. The diner where Gere is questioned by Detective Sunday really was in Westwood, and was the Me & Me, 10975 Weyburn Avenue, in the shadow of Mann's Village Theatre, the white Spanish-Moderne tower in the background at 961 Broxton Avenue. It's on the main drag, **Westwood Plaza**, that bored society wife Lauren Hutton trails Gere until 'accidentally' bumping into him in **Tower Records**. The white Spanish-domed structure seen here is a Westwood landmark dating from 1929 and currently housing **Eurochow**, one of Mr Chow's drop-dead stylish designer restaurants. Westwood is home to the University of California, and the quiet wooded glade where Hutton tells him she's going away for a while is the University's **Mathias Botanical Gardens**, an eight-acre tree-shaded canyon southeast of the campus, off Hilgard and Le Conte Avenues.

Gere drives a couple of miles east to Beverly Hills,

where he takes clients to legendary 'Pink Palace', the **Beverly Hills Hotel**, recently reopened after extensive renovation. The Mission Revival-style building, dating from 1912, which in its time has been home to Howard Hughes, Gable and Lombard, Chaplin and – reputedly – site of Monroe's liaisons with the Kennedy brothers, is tucked discreetly away behind thick shrubbery at **9641 Sunset Boulevard** near Rodeo Drive (℗ *310.276.2251, 800.283.8885*). The open air café where Gere gets an ominous warning was itself on **Rodeo Drive**, opposite the Polo Ralph Lauren store at 444, but establishments on this image-obsessed strip come and go as fashion dictates. Further east, in Hollywood, is the gay disco where Gere has to go to fix up an alibi, **Probe, 836 North Highland Avenue** near Melrose Avenue. The glitzy restaurant where our dishevelled hero gets short shrift when he pleads for help was **Perino's, 4101 Wilshire Boulevard** at Norton Avenue. This classic Hollywood restaurant is now closed (see *Mommie Dearest* for details). Gere takes Route 111 east out of LA for his assignment with the creepy voyeur and his wife, which was filmed in **Palm Springs**.

Gere gets an alibi: Probe, Highland Avenue

Gere appeals for help: Perino's, Wilshire Boulevard

AMERICAN GRAFFITI

(1973, dir: George Lucas)
Richard Dreyfuss, Ronny Howard, Paul LeMat.
● CALIFORNIA

Dismissed as 'a disgrace' and 'unreleasable' by the suits who know the business, *Graffiti* not only grossed millions and spawned a wave of pale imitations, but earned a pair of Oscar nominations for George Lucas as both writer and director. The film was inspired by Lucas' own adolescent years cruising the Strip in Modesto, on Highway 99

The teens cruise the main drag: Petaluma Boulevard, Petaluma

The movie theatre: Mystic Theater, Petaluma

Dreyfuss joins the Pharaohs: Kentucky Street, Petaluma

The cop car stunt: Petaluma Boulevard

between Stockton and Fresno in central California. And Modesto is the town to head for if you've got the wheels and want to show them off. The regular cruise has moved from its sixties location – Tenth Street between G and K Streets – to McHenry Avenue. There is actually a 'Graffiti night' on the first Saturday after graduation day (some time in the middle of June – call the visitors' bureau [© 209.577.5757] to check the date). Modesto now even boasts roller-skating waitresses at the A&W Root Beer Drive-In, close to the cruise strip, at 1404 G Street.

Despite all this razzmatazz, Modesto is not where the movie was shot. The two towns used, which had barely changed since the sixties, were **Petaluma** in Sonoma County and **San Rafael** in Marin County, on Highway 101 north of San Francisco. San Rafael, now all rather gentrified, was the first choice for filming but the disruption caused by initial shooting on **Fourth Street**, downtown, led to the production being moved to another location. You'll instantly recognise Petaluma as Graffiti-town. Proud of its varied and well-preserved architecture, Petaluma has provided the backdrop for a whole slew of movies including Francis Coppola's *Peggy Sue Got Married*, Joe Dante's *Explorers*, Paul Verhoeven's *Basic Instinct*, legendary turkey *Howard the Duck* and the controversial nineties remake of *Lolita*. You can take a walking tour of the town's many movie sites, with a guide from the tourist information office at 799 Baywood Street (© 707. 762.2785). The boys drive up and down **Petaluma Boulevard North**, on **D Street** and **Washington Street**, the main drag used in the movie.

Richard Dreyfuss is drafted into the Pharaohs gang in front of the **Old Opera House, 149 Kentucky Street**. And the used car lot, where Dreyfuss chains the axle of the police car, can still be recognised. It's a vacant lot alongside the **McNear Building, 15-23 Petaluma Boulevard North**. The State Movie Theater (showing *Dementia 13*, the horror movie a young Francis Ford Coppola directed for Roger Corman) is the **Mystic Theater** in the McNear at number 23. The high school is **Tamalpais High School, 700 Miller Avenue, Mill Valley**.

Sadly, the film's most famous location, Mel's Drive-In, with its rollerskating waitresses, no longer exists. It was real, and actually situated in the city of San Francisco itself, on the corner of South Van Ness and Mission Street. It closed down and was, amazingly, demolished. The good news is, it was one of a chain, and a surviving classic Mel's can be found at 3355 Geary Boulevard.

AMERICAN PIE

(1999, dir: Paul Weitz)
Jason Biggs, Chris Klein, Natasha Lyonne.
● **LOS ANGELES**

Dog Years, six blocks from downtown: Myrtle Avenue, Monrovia

Hormonally-fuelled teen comedy, with four high school boys vowing to lose their virginity before graduation. Set in the fictitious town of East Great Falls, the school is **Long Beach Polytechnic High School, 1600 Atlantic Avenue** at Pacific Coast Highway in Long Beach, southern LA. Neighbourhood scenes were filmed in Monrovia, LA's eastern suburb, where Dog Years, the coffee shop hangout, was created in an empty property at **402 South Myrtle**.

AMERICAN PSYCHO

(2000, dir: Mary Harron)
Christian Bale, Jared Leto, Reese Witherspoon.
● **ONTARIO; NEW YORK CITY**

Comparing cards in Harry's Bar: the Boston Club, Front Street, Toronto

New York style in Ontario: The Senator, Victoria Street, Toronto

Bret Easton Ellis' notorious eighties-set slasher satire gets a stylish but restrained treatment from director Harron. Set in the exclusive bars and restaurants of New York's yuppie circuit, the movie was actually shot largely in Toronto, Ontario, with the real new York featured only in a sprinkling of establishing shots.

Harry's Bar, where the guys compare cards and where Patrick Bateman finally confesses all to a disbelieving lawyer, was the upper crust Boston Club, **4 Front Street East**, which is now closed. The other supposedly-New York upper-crust hangouts are forties-style diner the **Senator, 249 Victoria Street**; kitschy Pacific Rim restaurant **Monsoon, 100 Simcoe Street**; old dance hall-turned-theatre space, the **Phoenix, 410 Sherbourne Street**; the wood-beamed Wild West roadhouse **Montana, 145 John Street**; and the aptly-named **Shark City, 117**

Another New York eaterie: Montana, John Street, Toronto

Eglinton Avenue East. Street scenes were filmed around Toronto's Cabbagetown district, while the spectacular shootout with the police was shot on **Pearl Street** between Simcoe and Duncan Streets, just around the corner from Monsoon.

AMERICAN WEREWOLF IN LONDON, AN

(1981, dir: John Landis)
David Naughton, Jenny Agutter, Griffin Dunne.
● **LONDON; SURREY; WALES**

The Slaughtered Lamb: The Black Swan, Martyr's Green

A pub full of character actors rhubarbing away on the Yorkshire Moors can only mean bad news for two American backpackers. The moors were filmed around the Black Mountains in Wales, and East Proctor is in reality the tiny village of **Crickadarn**, about six miles southeast of Builth Wells off the A479. If you want to join the locals here for a pint at The Slaughtered Lamb, you'll have quite a journey. Although the exterior is an empty cottage dressed up for the movie, the interior, where Lila Kaye tends bar and a frighteningly young Rik Mayall plays chess, is in Surrey. It's **The Black Swan, Old Lane** at the junction with Ockham Lane, **Martyr's Green**, about a mile northwest of Effingham Junction (rail: Effingham Junction) between Guildford and Leatherhead.

Jenny Agutter's flat: Coleherne Road, Earl's Court

The hospital where David Naughton recovers from a nasty wolf bite was the **Princess Beatrice Maternity Hospital on Finborough Road** at Lillie Road in Earl's Court, London SW5. The building is still there, and is now a hostel for the homeless. Around the corner at **64 Coleherne Road, SW10**, you can see nurse Jenny Agutter's flat, where Naughton does some shape-shifting to 'Bad Moon Rising' (tube: Earl's Court).

Unusually, the tube station, where the city gent gets chomped, was filmed, during the wee small hours, at **Tottenham Court Road** tube (London Transport's all-purpose location, the closed Aldwych Station in the Strand, is almost invariably used for filming). The undead victims pop up in a studio recreation of the old Eros News Cinema (now H Samuels, the jeweller) on the corner of Shaftesbury Avenue in Piccadilly Circus. And once again Landis demonstrates his talent for staging major set-pieces in impossible locations by setting the climactic mayhem smack in the middle of **Piccadilly Circus** itself.

The dull and belated sequel, *An American Werewolf in Paris*, was shot largely in Luxembourg.

AMERIKANISCHE FREUND, DER (aka *The American Friend*)

(1977, dir: Wim Wenders)
Dennis Hopper, Bruno Ganz, Gerard Blain.
● **GERMANY; FRANCE; NEW YORK CITY**

Wenders films Patricia Highsmith's *Ripley's Game* as a Hitchcockian thriller, with Dennis Hopper as shady wheeler-dealer Tom Ripley turning essentially decent picture framer Zimmerman (Bruno Ganz) into a contract killer. The book's French location, Fontainebleau, is shifted to the scuzzy harbour area of Hamburg.

A few miles west of downtown Hamburg on the grand Blankenese road you'll find Ripley's grand, if dilapidated, mansion, where shifty French crook Raoul Minot calls to hire a killer. It's **Saulenvilla, Elbchaussee 186**, overlooking the riverside suburb of Ovelgonne high, above the north bank of the Elbe.

Back in Hamburg itself, you can see Zimmerman's picture-framing shop – actually a hat shop, and still in existence – it's **Lange Strasse 22**, on the corner of Kleine Pinnes, just to the south of the S-bahn Reeperbahn Station near the sleazy St Pauli district. A little to the east, on the corner of **Davidstrasse** and the waterside road of St Pauli-Hafenstrasse, near to the old St Pauli Fishmarkt, is Zimmerman's waterfront apartment. And it's on Hamburg's **U-bahn railway** that Minot makes his proposition to Zimmerman, on the stretch from St Pauli at the eastern end of the Reeperbahn along the Elbe waterfront to Rodingsmarkt in the Altstadt.

Zimmerman's shop: Lange Strasse, Hamburg

Convinced he's suffering from a terminal blood disease, Zimmerman's increasingly panicky visits to his doctor take him down the endless escalators (there's a giant lift now) to the oppressive **Old St Pauli-Elbtunnel** (a new motorway tunnel a couple of miles to the west was completed in 1974). Built between 1907 and 1911 to relieve the pressure on the Elbe ferry to the docks of Steinwerder, the twin tunnels are not for claustrophobes. 490 yards long, the carriageways are a mere

The road tunnel: St Pauli-Elbtunnel, Hamburg

Ripley's mansion: Saulenvilla, Hamburg

six feet wide. They're closed at night and on Sundays, but the rest of the time there's free entry (on foot – vehicles pay a toll). The funfair Zimmerman takes his family to is the **Hamburger Dom**, held every year in November/December in the **Heiligengeistfeld**, also in the St Pauli district.

Zimmerman is taken to Paris for a second opinion on his illness. The hospital where he undergoes tests is the **American Hospital, 63 boulevard Victor-Hugo, Neuilly-sur-Seine**, northwest Paris (*metro: Anatole France*). Convinced he's on the way out, Zimmerman agrees to carry out a hit on the Paris Metro as his victim changes trains at Etoile. He actually manages to complete the task one station further west on the RER 'A' line, on an escalator at **La Defense Station**, west of the city centre.

His second assignment is to whack the mob boss (a cameo from movie director Samuel Fuller), on the no-longer operating Munich-Hamburg Express, where Ripley turns up to help out. The flight of steps down which Sam Fuller (or his stunt double, at least) finally takes a tumble are further away from Saulenvilla than they appear in the movie, toward the waterfront.

The opening scene, which was filmed in New York City, features another cameo appearance, from veteran movie-maker Nicholas Ray, who directed Hopper alongside James Dean in *Rebel Without a Cause*.

AMISTAD

(1997, dir: Steven Spielberg)
Anthony Hopkins, Djimon Hounsou, Morgan Freeman.
● **RHODE ISLAND; CONNECTICUT; MASSACHUSETTS; LOS ANGELES**

Amid accusations of plagiarism and Disneyfication, Spielberg followed the success of his grown-up movie, *Schindler's List*, with another worthy slice of history. The opening mutiny scenes are a mix of studio and location filming. Daytime exteriors filmed aboard two different schooners at two separate locations – on the east coast, the *Amistad* is played by Maryland's state ship, the *Pride of Baltimore*, while over on the west coast, a 'floating city' was constructed a mile off the coast of San Pedro, the harbour south of Los Angeles (Spielberg learned his lessons about seaborne shoots on *Jaws*). The boat here was the state ship, too, the *Californian*. The port is **Mystic Seaport**, Connecticut, home of America's leading maritime museum, where a reproduction of the schooner is to be built to help teach history. And, yes, it's the town featured in *Mystic Pizza*. More material was shot around **Groton Long Point**, Connecticut.

Most of the filming, however, took place in **Newport**, Rhode Island, where the prison exteriors were built. The major location is the city's historic **Washington Square**. Here, the **Colony House**, dating from 1739 and once the site of Rhode Island's colonial government, provided two locations for the major courtroom scenes. The arraignment of the Africans was shot in the Colony's ground floor, and the next courtroom scenes, in the Appellate Court, were filmed in the upstairs courtroom of Colony House. When permission to film the climactic scene in the real Supreme Court Building, Washington DC was refused, the courtroom was reproduced on a local soundstage. More scenes were filmed in Massachusetts, at the **Massachusetts State House, Boston**.

AMITYVILLE HORROR, THE

(1979, dir: Stuart Rosenberg)
James Brolin, Margot Kidder, Rod Steiger.
● **NEW JERSEY**

The true (!) story of a family hounded out of their Long Island home by apparently supernatural phenomena. The lesson for potential housebuyers is to make sure that a) the previous owner was not your double and responsible for slaughtering his entire family, and b) that your house isn't built over a festering pit of demonic slime. The home of the real George and Kathleen Lutz at 112 Ocean Avenue, Amityville, proved such popular attraction for tourists that the local mayor imposed a parking ban on the street. The movie, though, didn't use the actual location, but was filmed at a riverside house in the town of **Tom's River**, on the Garden State Parkway, Ocean County, about twenty miles south of Asbury Park on the New Jersey coast and at **Scotch Plains**, New Jersey. The prequel, *Amityville II: The Possession*, returned to the Tom's River house for the exteriors, but was largely shot at the **Churubuscu Studios** in **Mexico City**.

AMSTERDAMMED

(1988, dir: Dick Maas)
Huub Stapel, Monique van de Ven, Hidde Maas.
● **AMSTERDAM**

Enjoyable, low-budget indie-horror with an eco-message has something murderous lurking in the canals of central Amsterdam, and Maas makes excellent use of the narrow, threatening waterways.

The first victim meets a nasty end by the bridge at the junction of the two canals, **Keizersgracht and Reguliersgracht**. The two conservationists are clipped on the southern shore of main waterway **Het Ij**, north of **Havens Oost**, at the end of the 28 bus route. The Salvation Army collector turns up, with toes turned up, on the north shore of the Amstel at **Oude Turfmarkt** just to the south of Dam Square.

ANACONDA

(1997, dir: Luis Llosa)
Jennifer Lopez, Ice Cube, Jon Voight.
● **BRAZIL; LOS ANGELES**

A giant, and largely computer generated, snake picks off members of a jungle expedition in this tongue-in-cheek thriller. Although much of the movie was shot in the jungle around **Manaus** in Brazil, you don't have to travel quite so far to enjoy the *Anaconda* experience. Watch how the lush foliage gives way to, er, palm trees toward the film's climax. The later action sequences were filmed in California, in the **Los Angeles State and County Arboretum**, a 127-acre botanical garden which must be one of the most filmed locations in the world. Its tropical foliage has been seen in *Tarzan* movies, *Road* movies, *The African Queen*, TV's *Fantasy Island* (the kitschy little Queen Anne cottage is here) and literally hundreds of others. It's at **301**

North Baldwin Avenue, Arcadia, east of Pasadena (© *818.821.3222*).

ANALYZE THIS
(1999, dir: Harold Ramis)
Robert De Niro, Billy Crystal, Lisa Kudrow.
● NEW YORK STATE; NEW JERSEY; FLORIDA

De Niro is the mob boss who begins to get anxiety attacks, Crystal the hapless shrink hired to cure him. Filming took place around New York: at **Katonah**; **Todt Hill, Staten Island** (near to the *Godfather* mansion); and **Sing Sing Penitentiary, Ossining**. The hospital is at **Elmhurst**, Queens.

New Jersey locations include **Montclair** and **Jersey City** (site of the shootout), and **Fort Lauderdale**, Florida, was also used. Lisa Kudrow's (first) wedding takes place at the expensive **Sheraton Bal Harbour Hotel, 9701 Collins Avenue** at 96th Avenue, **Bal Harbour, Miami Beach**, Florida (© 305. 865.7511).

ANASTASIA
(1956, dir: Anatole Litvak)
Ingrid Bergman, Yul Brynner, Helen Hayes.
● PARIS; HERTFORDSHIRE; COPENHAGEN, DENMARK

Lavish filming of Marcelle Maurette's play, with Ingrid Bergman winning an Oscar as the woman who might or might not be the surviving daughter of the slaughtered Romanov family. Bergman is discovered in Paris' Russian neighbourhood between the Arc de Triomphe and Parc Monceau. The Russian Orthodox church, where Easter is being celebrated at the beginning of the film, is the **Cathedral of St Alexander Nevsky, 12 rue Daru** (*metro: Courcelles*). 'Anastasia' contemplates suicide at the foot of the steps below **Pont Alexandre III** over the Seine.

The final seal of approval needs to be given by crusty-but-lovable Dowager Empress Helen Hayes. In the real life incident on which the play was based, Anastasia's visit to the Empress was conveniently delayed so many times that the old woman died before the claim could be tested. In the movie, however, Bergman is taken to visit the Empress in Copenhagen. Second unit filming, including **Copenhagen Railway Station** and the nearby **Tivoli Gardens**, can't disguise the fact that the Empress' palace is none other than **Knebworth House**, near Stevenage, Hertfordshire (see Tim Burton's *Batman* for details).

ANATOMY OF A MURDER
(1959, dir: Otto Preminger)
James Stewart, Ben Gazzara, Lee Remick.
● MICHIGAN

As Hollywood moved toward more realistic, 'adult' subjects in the late fifties, the glossy artifice of the studios began to look increasingly inappropriate. While scouting exterior locations, Otto Preminger made the bold decision to dispense with studio filming and move the entire production up to the book's setting of Michigan's water-hemmed Upper Peninsula, filming on real locations when possible. Although Robert Traver's book was based on actual events – the trial of a soldier accused of shooting

the man he believes raped his wife – the blue-collar town of Iron City and the nearby lakeside resort of Thunder Bay are fictional. Their real life counterparts, where Preminger filmed, are **Ishpeming** and **Marquette**. Marquette is on the Lake Superior coast of Michigan's Upper Peninsula, I-41, and Ishpeming about fifteen miles west.

Behind the 'Traver' pseudonym was Michigan Supreme Court Justice John Voelker, and Voelker's house in Ishpeming became the home and law office of his alter ego Paul Biegler (James Stewart). Similarly, the 1905 red sandstone **Marquette County Courthouse** was used for the courtroom scenes. Transformed into a temporary studio, the entire second floor of the building was taken over by the film company, with defendant Ben Gazzara held in the cells there. Also in Marquette was the waterfront lunchstand where Stewart and old soak Arthur O'Connell debate whether to defend Gazzara, and the hospital, where O'Connell ends up after a road smash.

Barney Quill's bar, scene of the murder, is two different places – the interior is the Tripoli Bar in Ishpeming (supposedly where the actual shooting occurred and, legend has it, where the bullet holes were preserved by the proprietor). In the movie, it's the bar of the Thunder Bay Inn, which was actually Marquette's Big Bay Inn (though a contemporary photograph of the location clearly shows the sign 'Bay View Inn'). The motel didn't have a bar, so the one-storey Tavern Bar extension was built, and subsequently preserved as a tourist attraction.

Over in Ishpeming are the law library, where Stewart digs out legal precedent – not a law library at all but **Ishpeming Public Library** on **Main Street** – and **Ishpeming Railroad Depot**, the station where Arthur O'Connell meets the army psychiatrist. The Thunder Bay trailer park where Gazzara and Lee Remick live, and the scene of the rape, is a real trailer camp about 25 miles west of Ishpeming at **Michigamme** on I-41.

ANDERSON TAPES, THE
(1971, dir: Sidney Lumet)
Sean Connery, Dyan Cannon, Martin Balsam.
● NEW YORK CITY

Sean Connery is an ex-con unprepared for the modern world of surveillance as he heads a gang out to rob an entire luxury apartment block. Lumet's paranoid thriller

The lavish apartment block: 91st Street on the Upper East Side

was filmed on location around Manhattan. Connery is released from the notorious **Riker's Island** in Queens (see *Carlito's Way* for details), and he arrives in Manhattan at the **Port Authority Bus Terminal** on **Eighth Avenue**. The lavish Italianate palazzo they set their sights on is at **1 East 91st Street** on Fifth Avenue, overlooking Central Park. One of New York's largest private houses, the last on Millionaire's Row, it was built in 1918 for banker Otto Kahn and became the Convent of the Sacred Heart (if you're going to take a vow of poverty, you might as well do it in a millionaire's mansion on the Upper East Side), and is now a girls' school. Some interiors were shot at the **New York Production Center Studios**, 221 West 26th Street, but the mansion's oval staircase is the real thing.

ANDREI ROUBLEV
(1966, dir: Andrei Tarkovsky)
Anatoly Solonitsin, Ivan Lapikov, Nikolai Grinko.
● RUSSIA

Epic life of the 15th century artist, virtually the inventor of Russian icon painting who freed the art form from its foreign influences.

At the beginning of the film, Rublev works at the **Church of the Holy Trinity**, part of the **Monastery of the Trinity St Sergius** in **Zagorsk**, 50 miles northeast of Moscow. Zagorsk, now an industrial town, grew up around the Monastery, which houses the remains of the Saint and, in the Church of the Assumption, the remains of usurper tsar Boris Godunov. Rublev's *Icon of the Trinity* here is a copy – the original is in the Tretyakov Gallery, south of the Moskva in the Zamoskvarechye district of Moscow.

The painter spends most of his life at the **Andronnikov Monastery** in Moscow – which now houses the Andrei Rublev Museum. It's north of Ulianovskaya Street, east of the city centre by the Yaouza River (*Kursk Station*). He decorates the Cathedral of the Dormition in Vladimir, the city which is sacked, a hundred miles east of Moscow.

You can also see an early icon by Rublev in the Cathedral of the Annunciation in the Kremlin. It was painted in 1405 for a smaller church on the site, which was demolished to make way for the cathedral. These are the places where the events actually took place, and can be visited.

ANGEL (aka *Danny Boy*)
(1982, dir: Neil Jordan)
Stephen Rea, Veronica Quilligan, Ray McAnally.
● IRELAND

Neil Jordan's first film, a fable set against the Troubles in Northern Ireland, was filmed largely in the town of **Bray**, on the Irish coast, about ten miles south of Dublin.

The seafront of the unnamed town: Bray

ANGEL AT MY TABLE, AN
(1990, dir: Jane Campion)
Kerry Fox, Alexian Keogh, Karen Ferguson.
● NEW ZEALAND; SPAIN; PARIS; LONDON

Jane Campion's lovingly filmed version of Janet Frame's autobiography follows the New Zealand writer's progress from clumsy, withdrawn schoolgirl through eight years of misdiagnosed institutionalisation to her final literary success. The movie was largely shot in New Zealand, with exteriors around **Auckland**, and interiors filmed at **Morningside**. The older Frame travels to Europe, staying in

London and Paris, and finds a short-lived idyll in the tiny coastal town of **Puerto de la Selva** on the north of the Cabo de Creus peninsula. North of the Costa Brava, it's near to Salvador Dali's former home at Port Lligat.

ANGEL HEART
(1987, dir: Alan Parker)
Mickey Rourke, Robert De Niro, Lisa Bonet.
● NEW YORK CITY; NEW YORK STATE; NEW ORLEANS, LOUISIANA

De Niro hires PI Mickey Rourke to track down a debtor, but since their respective characters are called Lou Ciphre and Angel, it's clear we're not in for a straight crime film.

Despite the fifties setting, Parker makes great use of real locations in New York and Louisiana. The scuzzy New York of the time was recreated around the nineteenth century tenements of **Eldridge Street**, on Manhattan's Lower East Side, where the 1955 prices in the shop windows nearly led to riots. Although the same area is also used for some of the Harlem scenes, the Mission and the procession are the real **Harlem**, as is the Lincoln Presbyterian Hospice where Rourke visits bandleader Spider, which was shot at the **Harlem Hospice** on **138th Street**.

Down in the East Village, you can find the bar where Rourke gets hold of pictures of Johnny Favorite. It's **Vazak's Bar, 108 Avenue B** at the corner of Tomkins Square. Vazak's is a familiar 'lowlife atmosphere' bar seen in plenty of other movies, including *"Crocodile" Dundee* and *The Godfather Part II*.

The Poughkeepsie nursing home where Rourke impersonates a hospital inspector is **Rhinebeck**, in Albany, upstate New York toward the Catskills, which had been home to the former secretary, recently deceased, to Franklin D Roosevelt. The neighbourhood of sweaty junkie Dr Fowler, supposedly at 419 Kitteredge, was filmed over on **Staten Island**. In Brooklyn, the venerable **Coney Island, West 10th Street** at Surf Avenue on the South Shore, repainted glumly to suit the film's monochrome look, serves as the rundown, rat-infested amusement park where Rourke looks for Madame Zora.

And on to New Orleans, sort of. Rourke's arrival in Louisiana by train was shot at **Hoboken Railway Station**, just over the Hudson from Lower Manhattan. You can reach this impressive marble wonder on a Port Authority Trans-Hudson train from the PATH station on the lowest level of the World Trade Center.

The real Big Easy shooting was largely around the Victorian houses and shops in the old Irish section along **Magazine Street**, New Orleans. The streetcar was filmed on the main **St Charles Avenue track**. Charlotte Rampling's house was a boarded-up property behind Royal Street, while the slave quarters at the back doubled as Rourke's hotel. The touristy shots of New Orleans take in the arches by the market on **Decatur Street, St Peter Street** alongside St Louis Cathedral.

The church where Rourke indulges in a little profane language is **St Alphonsius, 2029 Constance Street**, parallel to Magazine Street. The racetrack, though, doesn't exist – it was specially built in an empty field. The gumbo shack where Rampling's father gets his face boiled is a disused New Orleans bus depot and the flashbacks to a post-war Times Square were also, confusingly, filmed in New Orleans. If you want to visit the plantation village where Rourke meets up with Lisa Bonet, it's the **Laurel Valley Village Museum**, a perfectly preserved sugar plantation dating from 1840, on Route 308, two miles south of Thibodoux. The plantation, still in use in the 20th century, once covered 5,000 acres and is pretty much as seen in the movie – only the cemetery is faked. Thibodoux is on Route 1, 50 miles west of New Orleans on the Bayou Lafouche. The Red Rooster, where Rourke meets up with Toots Sweet, is actually the popular **Maple Leaf Club, 8316 Oak Street,** New Orleans.

ANGELA'S ASHES
(2000, dir: Alan Parker)
Robert Carlyle, Emily Watson, Joe Breen.
● IRELAND

The ashes of controversy were fanned into flame when Alan Parker decided to film Frank McCourt's grim, poverty-ridden autobiography on the actual locations in **Limerick**, in the west of Ireland. In the end, much of the movie was shot in **Cork**, at **Cobh Harbour**, and on sets in Dublin.

ANNA AND THE KING
(1999, dir: Andy Tennant)
Jodie Foster, Chow Yun Fat, Mano Maniam.
● MALAYSIA

Retread of *Anna and the King of Siam* (which was shot almost entirely in the studio in Hollywood, like the musical version, *The King and I*). Plans to film on genuine Thai locations were scuppered by protests of historical inaccuracy from the Thai Film Board (both previous versions were banned in Thailand). The original Anna Leonowens, on whose memoir the story is based, is thought to have significantly exaggerated her importance in, and influence on, the Siamese court to the detriment of King Mongkut. After protracted negotiations, Twentieth Century Fox moved the production to Malaysia.

Most of the movie was filmed in **Ipoh**, Perak, Malaysia, and Anna's traditional village house is in **Parit**. King Mongkut's Grand Palace was recreated at a secret location, but part of the palace was filmed in **Rumah Besar Papan**, a Mandailing mansion in **Papan**, about ten miles from Ipoh. In the port of **Penang**, Penang Island, colonial buildings and a local Khoo kongsi temple became a 19th century Siamese port. Filming also took place at **Langkawi Island** and **Shah Alam, Selangor**.

ANNA AND THE KING OF SIAM
(1946, dir: John Cromwell)
Irene Dunne, Rex Harrison, Gale Sondergaard.
● LOS ANGELES

The much elaborated story of an English governness who supposedly brought Western values to the court of King Mongkut has long been a source of contention in Thailand – both this film and the musical remake, *The King and I*, remain banned there. Exotic scenes for the Irene Dunne version were filmed in the lush surroundings of the **Los Angeles State and County Arboretum, 301**

North Baldwin Avenue, Arcadia, east of Pasadena (*©* *818.821.3222*). See *The African Queen* for details.

ANNA KARENINA
(1935, dir: Clarence Brown)
Greta Garbo, Fredric March, Basil Rathbone.
● CALIFORNIA

A second stab at Tolstoy's novel (Garbo starred in a 1927 silent version called *Love*), filmed largely in a Hollywood studio, though the racetrack and steeplechase scenes were shot up the coast on the beautiful **Monterey Peninsula**.

ANNE OF THE THOUSAND DAYS
(1969, dir: Charles Jarrott)
Richard Burton, Genevieve Bujold, Anthony Quayle.
● KENT; LONDON

The Tudor garden: Penshurst Place, Kent

An uninspiring account of Henry VIII and Anne Boleyn's doomed marriage, filmed on sets at Shepperton Studios, where the major interiors were built (they were later reused for Hammer's *Countess Dracula*).

Real locations include Anne Boleyn's actual childhood home of **Hever Castle**, between Sevenoaks and East Grinstead, three miles south of Edenbridge in Kent (*rail: Hever*). The double-moated house, set in 40 acres of garden, is open mid-March to early November (*©* *01732. 865224*). The rare, authentic Tudor garden belongs to **Penshurst Place**, one of the finest 14th century manor houses in England, in Penshurst village a couple of miles east of Hever Castle (*rail: Penshurst*), and now home of the Viscount de l'Isle, former Governor General of Australia. The house is open from the beginning of April to the beginning of October (*©* *01892. 870307*). The hunting scenes were shot in London's **Richmond Park**.

ANNÉE DERNIÈRE À MARIENBAD, L' (aka *Last Year in Marienbad*)
(1961, dir: Alain Resnais)
Delphine Seyrig, Giorgio Albertazzi, Sacha Pitoeff.
● MUNICH, GERMANY

If, in the sixties, you saw a serious bunch of students hunched over a table mysteriously moving matchsticks around, chances are they were film society members playing out Sacha Pitoeff's fiendish game from this art house movie *par excellence*. Well, was it Marienbad? Or Frederiksbad? Or neither? Sorry to be so prosaic, but it was **Munich**. Three overwrought baroque castles were knitted together to make a single, vast, labyrinthine hotel. You could go crazy trying to untangle Resnais' sinuous jigsaw, one location flowing seamlessly into another, the layout of the garden endlessly changing and doors not always opening onto the same room. Not surprisingly, the major location, a gigantic rococo palace where elegantly attired guests play arcane games, was once home to the famously extravagant King Ludwig I. It's **Schloss**

Nymphenburg, 200 years in the building and half a mile from wingtip to wingtip, in a northwest suburb of the city. Ludwig, while struggling with his sexuality, managed to scandalise society by commissioning a series of portraits of women – including notorious courtesan Lola Montes – which now hang in the palace's Schönheitengalerie (The Gallery of Beauties). The largest of its kind in Germany, the palace is set in 500 acres of parkland, varying from the wild to the geometrically formal French-style gardens seen in the film. Nymphenburg can be reached by the number 12 streetcar or the 41 bus from downtown Munich. It's open Tuesdays to Sundays.

In the grounds is the hunting lodge, **Amalienburg**, second of the movie's locations. If 'hunting lodge' conjures up images of rustic simplicity, you're in for a surprise. The interior is even more florid than Nymphenburg; a white, green and gold rococo fantasy centered around the sumptuous Spiegelsaal, the Hall of Mirrors. Resnais has loads of fun here with the endless reflections, seen over the opening monologue and used as the setting for the concert on Seyrig and Albertazzi's final evening.

The plainer exterior, seen as Frederiksbad in Albertazzi's memories and in the framed pictures throughout the film, is the **Neues Schloss** of **Schloss Schleissheim**, housing the Bayerische Staatsgalerie collection of baroque art. Find it to the northwest of Munich, on the S-1 urban line and the 292 bus to Oberschleissheim. You won't be able to see the classical statue of Charles III and his wife, which appears to move constantly about the gardens, though. Based on characters in a painting by Poussin, it was built specially for the movie. You can pose in the formal gardens, but if you want to appear as stylish as the cast, the trick is to organise your own accessories. Unlike the trees, the humans cast impossibly long, dramatic shadows – these were actually painted onto the ground.

The real Marienbad, by the way, or more properly Marianske Lazne, which has no connection with the movie at all, is a spa town in the Czech Republic about 80 miles west of Prague, south of Karlovy Vary.

ANNIE HALL
(1977, dir: Woody Allen)
Woody Allen, Diane Keaton, Shelley Duvall.
● **NEW YORK CITY; LOS ANGELES**

Oscar-winner for Best Picture, and seen by many as his best film, Allen's innovative, episodic account of the on/off relationship between East Coast Jewish intellectual Alvy Singer and the WASPish Annie, who eventually takes root on the West Coast, was filmed mainly around New York. The young Alvy's childhood home is under the Cyclone Ride at **Coney Island**, entrance on **West 10th Street** at Surf Avenue on Brooklyn's South Shore, subway lines D, Q, N, B and F. The wooden house actually burned down

The West Coast health-food restaurant: Sunset Boulevard, West Hollywood

in May 1991, but the Cyclone is still there, and so is **Steve's Famous Clam Bar**, seen in the flashback, at **515 Atlantic Avenue** at Third Avenue.

As usual, Allen visits a clutch of NY cinemas. The picture house showing Bergman's *Face to Face*, where Alvy is recognised from TV as he waits for Annie, is the **Beekman Cinema, 1254 Second Avenue** at East 65th Street on the East Side. He conjures Marshall McLuhan out of the air to silence a loudmouth pseud in the queue at the **New York Theater**, while the final movie house, where Alvy bumps into Annie taking her new guy to see *The Sorrow and the Pity,* is – was – the Thalia Cinema, which stood at 250 West 95th Street on the Upper West Side until 1987. Annie's apartment is on **70th Street**, between Lexington and Park Avenues (the number remains a mystery as we don't see the exterior). The beach and the beach house, where Alvy and Annie have problems with lobsters, is **The Hamptons**, the exclusive South Shore enclave at the far eastern end of Long Island on Route 27, while the sporty club where Alvy and Annie first meet is the **Wall Street Tennis Club**. The inevitable visit to **Central Park** sees the couple mocking nerdy passers-by.

Over on the West Coast – anathema to Woody Allen – was the health food restaurant where Alvy tries the alfalfa sprouts with mashed yeast, before Annie turns down his proposal. Then, it was the Source Restaurant, but food fads change and it's now the **Cajun Bistro, 8301 Sunset Boulevard** in West Hollywood.

ANOTHER COUNTRY
(1984, dir: Marek Kanievska)
Rupert Everett, Colin Firth, Cary Elwes.
● **OXFORDSHIRE; NORTHAMPTONSHIRE**

Eton College unsurprisingly passed up the opportunity to house this film of Julian Mitchell's play about a gay public schoolboy who defects to Moscow, loosely based on the life of Guy Burgess. The setting was finally supplied by the quads of **Brasenose College** (the fountain was added for the movie) in the centre of Oxford, entrance at Radcliffe Square opposite the Radcliffe Camera. The quads are open to the public (*admission free*), usually on week day afternoons, but it's best to check times in advance. You can see the oval windows, where besotted Rupert Everett passes the note to Cary Elwes, along the eastern wall of the small central quad. The church parade, where the students sing while Everett makes cow eyes at young Elwes, was filmed in the **Old Schools Quadrangle** of the **Bodleian Library**, north of Radcliffe Square.

The college: Brasenose College, Oxford

Church parade: Old Schools Quadrangle, Oxford

Interiors were filmed at the family seat (since 1508) of the Spencers, **Althorp** in Northamptonshire – Earl Spencer himself appears as an extra in the film. The estate is now more famous as the burial site of Princess Diana. It's open to the public with prior bookings, six miles northwest of Northampton on the A428.

ANOTHER WOMAN

(1988, dir: Woody Allen)
Gena Rowlands, Mia Farrow, Ian Holm.
● **NEW YORK CITY**

Academic Gena Rowlands goes through an emotional crisis when she overhears Mia Farrow's therapy sessions in one of Allen's non-comedy films. The little theatre where Rowlands bumps into old pal Sandy Dennis and dreams an off-off-Broadway version of her life is the **Cherry Lane Theater, 38 Commerce Street** between Bedford and Barrow Streets in Greenwich Village (© *212.989 .2020*). Originally built as a brewery, it was converted in 1924 to house avant garde theatre productions. It also features in Spike Lee's jazz movie *Mo' Better Blues*, where its exterior is the Beneath the Underdog club; as the Provincetown Playhouse in Warren Beatty's epic *Reds* and as an escape route in Peter Yates' 1988 Cold War thriller *The House on Carroll Street*.

ANY GIVEN SUNDAY

(1999, dir: Oliver Stone)
Al Pacino, Jamie Foxx, Cameron Diaz.
● **FLORIDA; TEXAS**

Oliver Stone's power-playing drama of American football treads familiar territory and spends too much time on the football pitch. Set largely in Florida, the home of the fictitious Miami Sharks is the **Orange Bowl Stadium, 1400 NW 4th Street**, Miami. The mayor's party is held in that familiar old standby of Miami movies, **Villa Vizcaya, 3251 South Miami Avenue** at 32nd Road, an Italianate mansion south of Miami in Coconut Grove (for details, see *Ace Ventura, Pet Detective*). The nightspot where Jamie Foxx bumps into his ex is the **Cardozo Hotel, 1300 Ocean Drive**, South Beach (see *There's Something About Mary* for details). More scenes were shot in Miami's southern suburb of **Homestead**, and the home of the Dallas Knights, scene of the climactic game, is in the real Lone Star state – it's the **Texas Stadium, Irving**.

APACHE

(1954, dir: Robert Aldrich)
Burt Lancaster, Jean Peters, John McIntire.
● **CALIFORNIA; ARIZONA**

Burt Lancaster is the last warrior refusing to submit to 'relocation' in Florida after the subjugation of the Apache nation. The opening scene of Geronimo's surrender, with the Cavalry and Indians facing off among angular sandstone formations, was filmed at **Vasquez Rocks County Park, Escondido Road**, California. Named after 19th century outlaw Tiburcio Vasquez, who hid out here, the spectacular location – an outburst of the San Andreas fault where spurs of rock have been thrust out of the earth – has been used in hundreds of Westerns and sci-fi movies,

Geronimo's surrender: Vasquez Rocks, California

including *The Flintstones* and *Austin Powers*. The park is in the high desert north of LA, between Newhall and Acton, off Route 14 (*admission free*).

The forested landscapes are in **Tuolumne County**, east of San Francisco on the Nevada border in the Sierra Nevadas, while the stark red sandstone buttes where Lancaster hides out with Jean Peters can be found in Arizona at **Sedona**, south of Flagstaff, Route 89A. More scenes were filmed at the Warners' Calabasas Ranch which was in the San Fernando Valley north of LA. It's now a golf course.

APARAJITO (aka *The Unvanquished*)

(1956, dir; Satyajit Ray)
Kanu Banerjee, Karuna Banerjee, Pinaki Sen Gupta.
● **INDIA**

The second of Ray's acclaimed Apu trilogy, based on the novels by Bibhutibhusan Banerjee, follows the life of the young village boy determined to pursue his education in the city as first his father, and then his mother, die.

Aparajito opens in **Varanisi**, the post-independence name of Benares in the northern province of Uttar Pradesh (confusingly, Varanisi is also referred to by the old name of Kashi), to which Apu's family move at the end of *Pather Panchali*, the first film of the trilogy. Varanisi is the major Hindu holy city (home to over two thousand temples and shrines), built on the sacred Ganga River. The opening sequence gives a picture of bustling life on the ghats, the stepped landings on the river banks, where priests recite, a muscleman swings a club and bodies are burned. Young Apu passes the time on the ghats and it's here, negotiating the steps, that his father Harihar collapses. Apu returns to the landings to fetch a bowl of Ganga water for the dying Harihar. 81 ghats line this four mile stretch of the Ganga's western bank.

The incense-filled temple to which Apu accompanies his mother is Varanisi's chief shrine, the **Vishvanath Temple** (Vishvanath is an alternative name for Shiva, Lord of the Dance). Built in 1750, the gilded decoration from 1939 has earned it the name of the Golden Temple. It's set back from the Ganga between Dasashwarnedh and Manikarnika Ghats, and is not open to non-Hindus. You can get the best view from the roof of the house opposite, which makes a small charge for the privilege.

After Harihar's death, Apu and his mother leave the city for a remote village in Bengal (the name is given as Mansapota, and the nearby school Apu attends is in

35

Arboal), but Apu has ambitions beyond life as a village priest and takes the train to Calcutta where he studies at the University. He arrives at eastern India's main rail terminal, **Howrah Station** on the north bank of the Hoogly River, and sees the English street sign on Harrison Road.

APARTMENT, THE
(1960, dir: Billy Wilder)
Jack Lemmon, Shirley MacLaine, Fred MacMurray.
● **NEW YORK CITY**

Wilder's snappy satire scooped Best Picture, Writer and Director Oscars. Jack Lemmon features as an insurance clerk obliged to let out his apartment to philandering boss Fred MacMurray. The Consolidated Life of New York, where Lemmon works, was a brand new (in 1960) $13 million skyscraper in Manhattan's commercial district, which provided the exterior and lobby scenes. When Lemmon waits in vain for Shirley MacLaine (while she's being wined and dined by sleazeball MacMurray), it's outside the **Majestic Theater, 247 West 44th Street** between Broadway and 8th Avenue, where the hit musical of the day, *The Music Man*, was playing (© *212.246 .0730*). It's a real New York bar where a morose Lemmon builds up an impressive collection of cocktail olives, on the West Side at **205 Columbus Avenue**, between West 69th and West 70th Streets. The address of the titular brownstone house itself is given as 51 West 57th Street, on the West Side close to Central Park, though the apartment used was actually on **59th Street**.

APOCALYPSE NOW
(1979, dir: Francis Ford Coppola)
Martin Sheen, Marlon Brando, Robert Duvall.
● **PHILIPPINES**

Coppola films Joseph Conrad's *Heart of Darkness* as a total Vietnam experience, a series of overwhelming cinematic set-pieces. Filmed on the island of **Luzon** in the Philippines, the nightmare shoot was recorded in Eleanor Coppola's book *Notes* and her amazing documentary film, *Hearts of Darkness*.

The Wagnerian helicopter attack on the quiet village was filmed at **Baler** on the northeastern coast of Luzon (the northern island of the Philippines, home to the capital, Manila). The helicopters, provided by President Marcos, were being used to put down Filipino insurgents at night, and occasionally during the day too, when they would suddenly veer off mid-shot. The surfing beach, fresh with the smell of napalm, subsequently commandeered by Robert Duvall is **Baler Bay**, and is indeed just being discovered as *the* place to ride the waves in the Philippines. Baler is about 120 miles northeast of Manila, reachable by a seven-hour bus journey.

As the disaster toll mounted (star Harvey Keitel was replaced by Martin Sheen, who suffered a heart attack) the sets, originally located at **Iba**, on Luzon's west coast, northwest of Manila, were wrecked by Hurricane Olga. Many had to be recreated at **Pagsanjan**, about an hour and a half's drive southeast of Manila. The trippy Do Long bridge was built here, on the Magdapio River, as was Kurtz's compound. Pagsanjan is worth the visit – to reach

it, take the South Expressway from Manila as far as you can go, turn left to Calamba, then right, and it's signposted. Alternatively, there's a bumpy three hour bus ride. There's also a thrilling, and extremely wet, boat trip up the rapids to Pagsanjan Falls (also known as Magdapio Falls). Check with the local travel agencies, as some of the boatmen have been known to rip off tourists. The four mile paddle upriver to the falls passes the site of Brando's nightmare empire, and it's followed by a scary, whitewater ride back over fourteen sets of rapids.

The local Ifugaos were recruited to play extras and disembodied heads (their bodies concealed in boxes buried beneath the set) in Kurtz's kingdom, and the climactic hacking to death of a water buffalo – which Coppola managed to capture on film – is part of their ritual celebration, though whether an elaborate set and romantic backlighting are part of the tradition isn't made clear.

APOLLO 13
(1995, dir: Ron Howard)
Tom Hanks, Bill Paxton, Kevin Bacon.
● **LOS ANGELES; TEXAS; FLORIDA**

Very special FX in this surprisingly gripping account of the ill-fated 1970 moonflight. There's far less location filming than you might imagine, since the gigantic Saturn V rockets, which carried the moon missions from Cape Kennedy, have long since been replaced by recyclable shuttles. As a consequence, much of the movie was tricked up in Hollywood. The Saturn V launched in the movie is a one-twentieth scale model, while most of the sequence is computer generated. Mission Control, too, was filmed in the studios at Universal.

To achieve the authentic feeling of weightlessness, director Howard filmed the Apollo capsule scenes on a set built inside a KC-135 cargo plane used for NASA training flights. The jet followed a 30,000 feet parabolic trajectory before going into a roller-coaster dive, giving 23 seconds of weightlessness to get a shot in the can. The effect on stomach contents of ten days filming under these conditions earned the KC-135 the nickname the Vomit Comet. The plane flew from **Ellington Field, Texas**.

Rather like some enormous dinosaur, NASA's moving parts are a long, long way from its brain though, fortunately for space buffs who'll doubtless want to explore the real thing, both sites can be visited. The launch site, which provided backgrounds for the faked take-off, is of course the **Kennedy Space Center, Merritt Island, Flori-**

Saturn V rocket: Lyndon B Johnson Space Center, Houston

da (© *407.452.2121*). Merritt Island, most of which is a wildlife reserve, can be reached by I-405 from Titusville, on the coast 50 miles east of Orlando, or Route 3 north on Bennett Causeway from the town of Cocoa. Two bus tours, Red and Blue, cover the site – the Red Tour ($7) takes in the Space Center, where you can see the 52-storey Vehicle Assembly Building. This massive structure, where the Saturn rockets were built, is seen in the movie, but the open door is another piece of computer generated trickery. Even if NASA had been persuaded to open the 400-foot-high doors for filming, there wouldn't have been a Saturn inside. Sophisticated motion-control techniques were used to add the rocket to a genuine helicopter shot. You can see one of the old Saturn rockets on the Space Center tour, though.

The other place to see a Saturn V is in the Rocket Park at the Lyndon B Johnson Space Center in Houston, site of the real Mission Control. You can tour most of this facility, including Shuttle training vehicles, laboratories, samples of moon rock and, if it's not closed for a launch, the actual Mission Control Room itself. Open every day except Christmas, 9am to 4pm, entrance is free. It's about twenty miles south of Houston on I-45 (© *713.244.2100*).

You can also visit the Florida motel with an ocean view where Mrs Lovell spends the night before the launch, and where she ominously loses her wedding ring in the shower. It's actually in Los Angeles: the **Safari Inn Motel, 1911 Olive Avenue**, Burbank (© *818.845.8586*). This sixties themed motel with illuminated 'African' sign can also be seen as Clarence and Alabama's hideaway in Tony Scott's film of Quentin Tarantino's *True Romance*. Gary Sinise's and Kevin Bacon's apartments were in the **Ambassador Hotel, 3400 Wilshire Boulevard**, midtown LA. The hotel closed in 1989 and is now used only as a movie location. It's currently under threat of demolition.

APT PUPIL
(1998, dir: Bryan Singer)
Ian McKellen, Brad Renfro, Elias Koteas.
● CALIFORNIA

Queasily exploitative Stephen King adaptation, from the director of *The Usual Suspects*, about a schoolboy's growing fascination with an ageing ex-Nazi war criminal. The school is **Eliot Middle School, 2184 North Lake Avenue, Altadena**, east of Los Angeles. Filming also took place around the LA suburb of **Alhambra**.

ARABESQUE
(1966, dir: Stanley Donen)
Gregory Peck, Sophia Loren, Alan Badel.
● LONDON; BERKSHIRE; OXFORDSHIRE; SOUTH WALES

Veteran director Donen invests this lightweight sub-Hitchcock comedy thriller with lurid sixties visuals, as Professor Gregory Peck is marked for death after he deciphers some mysterious Egyptian hieroglyphics. The university where Peck lectures is, of course, Oxford, and you can see the rather grand quad where he's propositioned at **St John's College** on St Giles Street. It's the inner Canterbury Quad (which also appears in Joseph Losey's *Accident*).

Touristy locations include **Regents Park Zoo**; **Trafalgar Square** (unable to use a helicopter shot, Donen took his camera up Nelson's Column using block and

Gregory Peck's college: St John's, Oxford

tackle); the **British Museum**; the Royal Enclosure at **Ascot Racetrack** in Berkshire, and **Waterloo Station**.

The climactic chase, with helicopter-borne villains pursuing Peck and Loren under a railway viaduct, was filmed at **Abertillery**, twelve miles north of Newport, Gwent in South Wales. Road, rail, gas and electricity were cut off during the stunt filming, and 350 people from the nearby village had to be evacuated – though £2 'disturbance money' was handed out to each family. Ms Loren's wardrobe, by comparison, cost £53,500.

ARABIAN NIGHTS
(1974, dir: Pier Paolo Pasolini)
Ninetto Davoli, Franco Citti, Franco Merli.
● NORTH AFRICA; MIDDLE EAST; NEPAL; INDIA

Final part of Pasolini's Trilogy of Life, following *The Decameron* and *The Canterbury Tales*, beautifully filmed in North Africa and the Middle East. The African scenes were shot in the northeast of the continent in **Ethiopia** and **Eritrea**, and over the Red Sea in **Yemen**. Filming also took place in **Nepal** and **India**. The wedding scene was shot at **Esfahan** in central **Iran** in the courtyard of the spectacular pale-blue tiled **Mesjed-e Imam** (formerly the Mesjed-e Shah), completed in 1638 after 26 years of work. It's on the south side of the Meidun-e Imam, the huge square in the centre of Esfahan.

ARACHNOPHOBIA
(1990, dir: Frank Marshall)
Jeff Daniels, John Goodman, Julian Sands.
● CALIFORNIA; VENEZUELA

Jaws with spiders. The fictional Californian coastal town of Canaima, where the house and barn were built for the movie, is **Cambria**, which you'll find ten miles south of San Simeon toward San Luis Obispo on Highway 1. The jungle scenes were shot near Angel Falls in Venezuela, at a place actually called **Canaima**.

ARMAGEDDON
(1998, dir: Michael Bay)
Bruce Willis, Ben Affleck, Steve Buscemi.
● NEW YORK CITY; LOS ANGELES; TEXAS; SOUTH DAKOTA; WASHINGTON DC; FLORIDA; NEW MEXICO; FRANCE; TURKEY; INDIA; CHINA

An asteroid the size of Texas is hurtling towards Earth. The Space Shuttle launch is for real, filmed at the **Kennedy Space Center** in Florida (see *Apollo 13* for details). Filming also took place at NASA's six million-gallon neutral buoyancy tank at the **Johnson Space Center, Houston**, Texas. Establishing reaction shots were taken in New York,

Asteroid fragments rain down on New York... : Grand Central Station

... but land in LA: Main Street

Washington DC and at **Pilot Point**, **Aubrey** and **Denton**, Texas. The surface of the asteroid, where the shuttles *Independence* and *Freedom* crash-land, was in the **Badlands National Park,** South Dakota. Director Bay also used a historic Craftsman-style house in Los Angeles; **Edwards Air Force Base**, north of LA; the **Shrine Auditorium, 665 West Jefferson Boulevard** (see *A Star Is Born* for details); the **Very Large Array National Radio Astronomy Observatory** near Magdalena in New Mexico (see *Contact* for details) and the **Fletcher Oil Refinery, 24721 Main Street, Carson** between Sepulveda and Lomita Boulevard.

More global atmosphere shots were filmed in **San Michele**, France; the **Blue Mosque** and **Ortakoy**, Istanbul, Turkey; at the **Taj Mahal** and the **Red Fort**, India and in **Shanghai**, China. The opening meteor shower blitzing 53rd Street, New York was actually filmed in Los Angeles, around **Fourth Street** and **Main Street**, by the old **Barclay Hotel** (seen also in *As Good As It Gets*).

ARMY OF DARKNESS

(1993, dir: Sam Raimi)
Bruce Campbell, Embeth Davidtz, Marcus Gilbert.
● CALIFORNIA

The third *Evil Dead* movie goes back to the Middle Ages for this bloody romp, filmed mainly on the La Brea Stage in Hollywood. The 13th century English castle was constructed in the, no doubt, geographically accurate High Desert of California at **Acton**, just off Route 14 north of LA. Filming also took place at **Vasquez Rocks** (see *Apache* for details).

AROUND THE WORLD IN EIGHTY DAYS

(1956, dir: Michael Anderson)
David Niven, Cantinflas, Shirley MacLaine.
● LONDON; PARIS; SPAIN; INDIA; HONG KONG; JAPAN; CALIFORNIA; COLORADO; OKLAHOMA

Statistics first: 50 guest stars; 68,894 people on screen (count 'em); eight different countries filmed; four million air-passenger miles travelled; 112 exterior locations; 140 sets in six Hollywood studios, plus studios in England, Hong Kong and Japan; 34 species of animal; 33 assistant directors. The plan was to use a director from each country to direct each sequence, but Brit director Anderson, who kicked off with an efficient – if uninspired – job in London was handed the whole assignment by producer Mike Todd. Associate Producer William Cameron Menzies, the brilliant production designer who storyboarded

Cantinflas and the pennyfarthing: Upper Cheyne Row, Chelsea

Noël Coward's employment agency: Grosvenor Place, Victoria

Gone With the Wind, was responsible for the exterior locations in Europe, Colorado and Oklahoma.

The opening scenes were shot in London, beginning with **Rotten Row, Hyde Park**. The Scots Guards parade was filmed at **Wellington Barracks**, the unofficial shots taken by a camera hidden in a vegetable stall. Niven accepts the challenge to travel around the world at the **Reform Club**, a real London club still going strong, at **104 Pall Mall, SW1** (though, along with Baggott's Employment Office and Lloyd's of London, the interiors were recreated at Elstree). Cantinflas pedals his pennyfarthing along **Upper Cheyne Row** off Oakley Street just north of Albert Bridge, Chelsea, SW3, to **Victoria Square**, a quiet square tucked away to the northwest of Buckingham Palace Road, SW1 (where the Schlegel sisters, in Merchant-Ivory's film of *Howards End* live). The building used as Hesketh-Baggott's Employment Office, where John Gielgud complains to agency boss Noël Coward, is unchanged. It's **5, Lower Grosvenor Place** on the corner of Victoria Square, SW1 (*tube: Victoria*).

Niven and Cantinflas arrive in Paris at the **Gare du Nord**, rue du Faubourg Saint Martin. They travel by taxi to Thomas Cook's in the arcades of the **rue de Rivoli**, via **Place Vendôme** and rue de Castiglione. The film ran into a spot of trouble with the law here when around forty out-of-period cars were spirited away out of camera range without permission. Don't bother trying to look for the dinky French village from which Niven and Cantinflas make their balloon ascent – it's simply a studio set.

The Spanish seaport where the balloon lands is also a studio set, though some scenes were filmed on the road near **Toledo**, and the bullfight was staged in **Chinchon**, about 25 miles southeast of Madrid on the M311 Valencia road. The arcaded town square, Plaza Mayor, with its photogenic wooden loggias was dressed up for a fiesta and the 6,500 inhabitants were togged up in period gear. Plaza Mayor is actually used for bullfights in the late summer, but a more civilised way to see the square is to try the many little restaurants overlooking it.

The Suez docks were recreated on a soundstage at the RKO Studios in Hollywood, were we get the first sight of the HMS *Mongolia*, which takes Niven and co to Bombay. With a bit of ingenuity from the art department, the same boat reappears throughout the movie, as the SS *Rangoon* from Calcutta to Hong Kong, the SS *General Grant* to San Francisco, and finally the ill-fated *Henrietta* from New York to Liverpool.

The Indian train journey is real enough, but the Bombay street and the Pagoda of Pillaji, where a browned-up Shirley MacLaine escapes ritual suttee are pure Hollywood. The waterfront dive on the Calcutta to Hong Kong leg is back at RKO – the junk journey to Yokohama features real views of Mount Fuji, but RKO again provides the Japanese theatre where Cantinflas performs. The San Francisco election rally and Clancy's, the Barbary coast dive, where George Raft pairs up with Marlene Dietrich as Frank Sinatra tinkles the ivories, are all Hollywood.

The transcontinental railway journey, with Buster Keaton (talking!) as a guard, was filmed on the **Durango and Silverton Narrow Gauge Railway**, running 45 miles between Durango and Silverton alongside Route 550 through the spectacular 3,000 foot San Juan Mountains in southwest Colorado. You can ride on the train (travel to Silverton by bus and make the one-way journey back; or you can get further information from 479 Main Avenue, Durango, Colorado [© *303 247.2733*]), but the return journey will take up a whole day. The stampede of buffalo (2,448 of them – go ahead, doubters, count them) was shot in Oklahoma, as was the Indian pow-wow with Cantinflas being burned at the stake, at **Lawton**, about 70 miles southwest of Oklahoma City on I-44 in the southwest of the state.

The final sea journey from New York to Liverpool, with the *Henrietta* dismantled to feed its own furnace, was filmed offshore at **Newport Beach**, just south of LA.

ARTHUR

(1981, dir: Steve Gordon)
Dudley Moore, John Gielgud, Liza Minnelli.
● NEW YORK CITY; NEW YORK STATE

Any pretensions Steve Gordon may have had toward saying something about alcoholism are scuppered by Moore's (unbelievably Oscar-nominated) one-note, end-of-the-pier drunk, and the waspish Gielgud effortlessly walks off with the film.

If you're in the same tax bracket, why not enjoy a meal at the classy restaurant where Moore shocks fellow diners with hooker Gloria, the **Oak Room** at the **Plaza Hotel, Fifth Avenue** at 59th Street (© *212. 759.3000*). But please don't imitate Liza Minnelli by shoplifting at **Bergdorf-Goodman's** posh department store, **754 Fifth Avenue** between 57th and 58th Streets. On the Upper East Side, visit Moore's Grandma's house, the **Carnegie Mansion, 2 East 91st Street**, familiar from *Marathon*

Arthur and the hookers: Plaza Hotel, 59th Street

Liza Minnelli shoplifts: Bergdorf-Goodman, Fifth Avenue

Arthur's Grandma's: Carnegie Mansion, Upper East Side

Man, *Working Girl* and Sean Connery thriller *The Next Man*.

Over on Long Island, the swanky country homes of Arthur's fiancée Susan and her father can be

Opting out of the wedding: St Bartholomew's, Fifth Avenue

found in **Glen Cove** and **Manhasset**. Filming also took place at the **Knole Estate, Old Westbury** on Long Island, and the stables were at **Caumsett**, on the Marshall Field III estate, now a State Park. You can find the church, where Moore opts out of the arranged marriage, on Park Avenue, naturally. It's the Byzantine-styled, Episcopalian **St Bartholomew's, 109 Fifth Avenue**.

AS GOOD AS IT GETS

(1997, dir: James L Brooks)
Jack Nicholson, Helen Hunt, Greg Kinnear.
● NEW YORK CITY; LOS ANGELES

Oscars for Nicholson and Hunt in this enjoyable but soft-centred feelgood movie, as waitress Helen Hunt, gay neighbour Greg Kinnear and Verdell the dog soften up bigoted obsessive-compulsive writer Nicholson. Nicholson and Kinnear's apartment block is **31-33 12th Street** between Fifth and Sixth Avenues in the West Village, New York. Helen Hunt lives at **1 Windsor Place** in the rather nice Prospect Park district of Brooklyn. The Café 24 Heures, where Hunt works, is actually way over on the west coast. It was constructed on the ground floor of the rundown **Barclay Hotel**, on the corner of **Fourth Street** and **Main Street**, in a decrepit area of downtown (the junction appears as New York again in *Armageddon*). The seafront restaurant, supposedly in Chesapeake Bay, Baltimore, can be found down in Long Beach, south of LA. It's **Khoury's Restaurant, 110 North Marina Drive** on the Alamitos Bay Landing Center. The pier is **Seal Beach Pier, Main Street, Seal Beach**.

The Cafe 24 Heures: Barclay Hotel, Fourth Street, downtown LA

ASCENSEUR POUR L'ECHAFAUD (aka *Lift to the Scaffold/Frantic*)
(1957, dir: Louis Malle)
Maurice Ronet, Jeanne Moreau, Georges Poujouly.
● PARIS

Dumping the Merc: Pont de Bir-Hakeim

Louis Malle's first feature is a tightly-made thriller with a cool Miles Davis score. Ronet plots with Moreau to kill her husband – his boss – but their scheme goes awry

The suicide pact: Boulevard de Grenelle

when a local tearaway takes Ronet's car for a murderous joyride while Ronet is trapped in a lift overnight. The innovative camera-work shows a distracted Moreau walking down the **Champs Elysées** at night, illuminated only by the light from shop windows. The motel where the joyriders kill the German tourists was in Normandy, as there were none in Paris then.

They dump the car on the **Pont de Bir-Hakeim**, the double-decker road and rail bridge just west of the Eiffel Tower. Originally the Passy Viaduct, the bridge was renamed in 1949 to commemorate the Free French Army's battles against Rommel in the Libyan Desert in 1942 (*metro: Bir-Hakeim, Passy*). You'll probably be more familiar with it from Bertolucci's *Last Tango in Paris*. The subsequent botched suicide pact at the girlfriend's apartment is just south of the Pont de Bir-Hakeim, at **55 boulevard de Grenelle**. The art nouveau building is largely unchanged, but is slightly more upmarket, and probably not home to many teenage shop assistants these days.

ASPHALT JUNGLE, THE
(1950, dir: John Huston)
Sterling Hayden, Louis Calhern, Marilyn Monroe.
● LOS ANGELES; KENTUCKY

The inner-city setting of Huston's prototype caper movie was intended to be non-specific. Locations scouted included St Louis and Cincinnati, but in the end the crew simply filmed around **LA**, apart from the final sequence, shot at horse-racing capital **Lexington** in Kentucky.

ASSAM GARDEN, THE
(1985, dir: Mary McMurray)
Deborah Kerr, Madhur Jaffrey, Alec McCowen.
● GLOUCESTERSHIRE

Deborah Kerr (in her first film since 1969's *The Arrangement*) is a widow who, returning to England from Assam, tends an Eastern garden planted by her late husband.

Locations had been scouted from Kew Gardens in Richmond up to the west coast of Scotland (where semi-tropical plants flourish in the warm Gulf Stream) when the

film company found an ideal two-acre exotic wild garden, dating from 1910, which had been laid out, just as in the story, by a returnee from India. **Priors Mesne**, overlooking the Severn Estuary near **Aylburton**, four miles south of Lydney in the Forest of Dean, appeared as the subject of the 1899 book *A Gloucestershire Wild Garden* and so impressed writer Elizabeth Bond as a girl that it inspired her to write *The Assam Garden*. The garden is privately owned and not normally open to the public, though it may be possible to visit through the National Gardens Scheme Charitable Trust, where many private gardens are open to the public for one day a year.

ASSASSIN (aka *Point of No Return*)
(1993, dir: John Badham)
Bridget Fonda, Gabriel Byrne, Anne Bancroft.
● CALIFORNIA; LOUISIANA; WASHINGTON DC

Another US remake, virtually shot-for-shot, of a Euro-original, the French arthouse hit *Nikita*, with Bridget Fonda talking over as the criminal given a reprieve and a makeover if she takes on the job of government hitperson. The original's Paris and Venice are exchanged for California's **Venice Beach** and **New Orleans** at Mardi Gras. The initial robbery, Fonda's training and first assignment were filmed in **Washington DC**. On release, she takes an apartment on LA's Venice Beach (in this version, she takes up with a photographer in the supermarket queue, not the check-out boy – so much for the classless US). The assassin's next assignment, delivering a bomb, takes place at the **JW Marriott Hotel, 2152 Avenue of the Stars** (✆ *310.277.2777*) in Century City – once part of the old Fox backlot.

The idyllic Venice trip of the French movie is replaced by a jaunt to the New Orleans Mardi Gras, taking in the crowds along **Bourbon Street** in the French Quarter.

ASSAULT ON PRECINCT 13
(1976, dir: John Carpenter)
Austin Stoker, Darwin Joston, Laurie Zimmer.
● LOS ANGELES

Carpenter's reworking of Howard Hawks' *Rio Bravo* sees an unlikely mixed-race street gang besieging a near-deserted police station. The precinct is actually Precinct 9, in the fictitious Anderson, and the movie was originally called *The Anderson Alamo*. The title was changed to *The Siege*, before distributor Irwin Yablans came up with the final

Precinct 13: Police and Fire Station of Venice, Venice Boulevard

catchy, if inaccurate, moniker.

Shot on a shoestring, the movie uses a patchwork of locations around LA, and the interiors were filmed at the Producers Studio, now **Raleigh Studios**. The streets near the station are in Watts, LA's troubled South Central area; the view across the street from the precinct is North Hollywood, but Anderson Police Station, Division 14 itself is the old **Police and Fire Station of Venice**, on the northeast corner of **Venice Boulevard** and Pisani Drive, Venice.

ATALANTE, L'

(1934, dir: Jean Vigo)
Jean Dasté, Dita Parlo, Michel Simon.
● **FRANCE**

Vigo's dreamy, poetic movie, with Dita Parlo as barge captain Jean Dasté's wife, seduced away from romantic shipboard life by the lure of Paris. The dozen or so cats aboard the barge, so much a part of the movie's feel, were Vigo's idea, replacing the dog specified in the script.

The opening wedding scene was staged at the village of **Maurecourt** on the Oise, just north of the Seine, about twenty miles northwest of Paris. Canal scenes were filmed at nearby **Conflans-Sainte-Honorine**, a centre for river navigation on the Seine (there's a River Craft Museum here). The journey to Paris continues along the **Canal de Ourcq**, northeast of the city, into the marina at **Bassin la Villette** (also seen in Jean-Jacques Beineix's *Diva*) and on to the Canal St Martin, where the barge docks at the **Quai de la Loire**, northeast from Jaures metro station. The cabaret where Dita Parlo is tempted toward city life by a pedlar is the Charentonneau Dance Hall in **Maisons Alfort** to the southeast of Paris (though the interior is a set). The railway station where Parlo is robbed is the **Gare d'Austerlitz**, which had to be shot in the closed station after midnight, populated with friends of Vigo dragged from the bars of St-Germain-des-Pres.

ATLANTIC CITY

(1980, dir: Louis Malle)
Burt Lancaster, Susan Sarandon, Michel Piccoli.
● **ATLANTIC CITY, NEW JERSEY; CANADA**

Enjoyably quirky low-life comedy drama, scripted by playwright John Guare and filmed in the famed old East Coast resort as the grand old hotels were being demolished and the quaint seaside tradition metamorphosed into a flashtrash ersatz Vegas (casino gambling was legalised in 1977). The action, of course, centres on the famous **Boardwalk**. The elephant-shaped building seen at the beginning, as Susan Sarandon's disreputable relatives ride into town, is **Lucy the Margate Elephant**, a Victorian folly, originally built of wood and tin. She's six storeys high, has spiral stairs in her legs and houses a museum of Atlantic City memorabilia. You'll find Lucy at **9200 Atlantic Avenue** (© *609.823.6473, admission charge*). Sarandon trains to be a dealer at the Resorts International Casino, now **Merv Griffin's Resorts Casino Hotel, North Carolina Avenue** at the Boardwalk (© *609.344.6000*), Atlantic City's first casino. The seafood restaurant where she shares a celebration meal with Lancaster is the rather pricey **Knife and Fork Inn**, at **Albany** and **Atlantic Avenues** (© *609.344.1133*). The constantly moving car park where Sarandon's ne'er-do-well husband meets his end is the **Park Mobile**. The film was a Canadian 'tax shelter' movie, which is why most of the supporting cast are Canadian, and the interiors were filmed in **Montreal**.

ATTACK OF THE KILLER TOMATOES!

(1978, dir: John de Bello)
David Miller, George Wilson, Sharon Taylor.
● **SAN DIEGO, CALIFORNIA**

Sadly, this promisingly titled shocker turns out to be just a deliberate spoof. The town menaced by the fiendish fruits is **San Diego**, Southern California.

AU REVOIR LES ENFANTS

(1987, dir: Louis Malle)
Gaspard Manesse, Raphael Fejto, Francine Racette.
● **LOIRE**

The newcomer at a Catholic boarding school in Occupied France has to hide the fact that he's Jewish. Filming took place in the town of **Provins**, 50 miles southeast of Paris in the Loire district, at the **Institution Sainte-Croix**, where the church of Saint-Croix was enlarged in the 13th century to house a piece of the true cross (no, really), brought back from the Crusades.

AUSTIN POWERS: INTERNATIONAL MAN OF MYSTERY

(1997, dir: Jay Roach)
Mike Myers, Elizabeth Hurley, Michael York.
● **LOS ANGELES; LAS VEGAS, NEVADA**

Mike Myers' spoof of swingin' sixties spy movies covers such clichéd territory that it has no right to be as funny as it is. Apart from a couple of stock second-unit shots, there was no filming in England, though a neat process shot manages to place a Bob's Big Boy smack in the middle of Piccadilly Circus. The London scenes were filmed on the Paramount backlot in LA. The opening shot is of the **Valley of Fire State Park**, near Las Vegas, Nevada. The action swiftly moves to Las Vegas proper, where Myers and Elizabeth Hurley arrive at the **Stardust Resort and Casino, 3000 Las Vegas Boulevard South** (© *702. 732.6111*), though the casino interiors were filmed in the **Riviera Hotel and Casino, 2901 Las Vegas Boulevard South** (© *702. 732.5110*). Sixties musical legend Burt Bacharach, who used to score the kind of camp romp being parodied – think *Casino Royale* or *What's New, Pussycat?* – plays

Powers' stays in Vegas: Stardust Casino, Las Vegas

Lotte Fagina's place: The Imperial Palace, Las Vegas

piano on the upper deck of Myers' red double-decker on the glittering Vegas Strip. Alotta Fagina's penthouse is in the Oriental-themed **Imperial Palace, 3535 Las Vegas Boulevard South** (© *702.731.3311*). The Imperial's other gimmick is a vast collection of some 700 vintage cars, including motors owned by Elvis, Hitler and Al Capone. The interiors are a bit less glamorous – they were filmed at a sewage filtration plant at Van Nuys. The final escape from Dr Evil's underground complex was shot in **Vasquez Rocks County Park, Escondido Road**, northeast of Newhall, California. For details of the park, which has long been used for such films as *The Flintstones* and *Bill & Ted's Bogus Journey*, see *Apache*.

AVALON

(1990, dir: Barry Levinson)
Armin Mueller-Stahl, Aidan Quinn, Elizabeth Perkins.
● **BALTIMORE, MARYLAND**

Levinson, in glowingly nostalgic mode, charts the fortunes of an immigrant family over several generations. Filmed in his hometown of Baltimore, though the titular district of Avalon is fictional, with any amount of cross-references. The terraced house that Aidan Quinn and Elizabeth Perkins leave for 'the suburbs' is **3107 Cliftmont Avenue** off Erdman Avenue, west of Cliftmont Park – the same house Danny De Vito and Barbara Hershey move *into* in Levinson's *Tin Men*. The house they move to is Levinson's real-life childhood home in Forest Park, west of the city centre, also seen in *Tin Men*. And young Elijah Wood sees the diner from Levinson's film of the same name being lowered onto a vacant lot (the diner itself currently stands at 400 East Saratoga Street at Holliday Street, downtown). The forties street scenes were filmed on **Appleton Street**, running south from North Avenue, south of Druid Hill Park in southwest Baltimore. Kirk and Kaye's television store is actually a bookstore – the **19th Century Bookshop, 1047 Hollins Street** at Union Square. The discount warehouse the business moves to, which subsequently burns down, is at **Fells Point** on the north west branch of the Patapsco River. The family sleep out by Druid Lake in **Druid Hill Park** when the summer gets too stifling, and just south of the park, at the corner of **Mason Street and Linden Avenue** stands the house where the family circle meetings are held. The rundown cinema where Wood watches *King of the Rocket Men*, and where the streetcar ploughs into Perkins' car, is the **Senator, 5907 York Road**, way north of the city centre toward Anneslie at Belvedere Avenue.

AVANTI!

(1972, dir: Billy Wilder)
Jack Lemmon, Juliet Mills, Clive Revill.
● **ITALY**

Blackish comedy with Jack Lemmon in Italy collecting the body of his recently deceased father and falling for the daughter of his father's similarly deceased mistress. The aeroplane scene, with Lemmon swapping his golf pants for a suit and tie, was filmed aboard an Alitalia DC8 at Rome's **Leonardo da Vinci Airport (Fiumicino Airport)**, 22 miles southwest of the city. His problems with immigration were shot in the Main Terminal.

The sun-baked resort island where Lemmon and Juliet Mills overcome their grief is **Ischia**, largest of the Neapolitan islands, off Italy's Amalfi coast, south of Naples (although most of the interiors were shot in Rome's Palatino Studios). If you want to visit Ischia like Jack Lemmon, fast and expensively, take the hydrofoil from Naples. Better, though, to take a boat to the island, famous mostly for its spa waters and mud baths. You won't find Lemmon's elegant, old-world hotel on Ischia at all, but back on the Italian mainland, south of the Bay of Naples on the Sorrentine Peninsula. It's the pricey **Hotel Excelsior Vittoria, Piazza Tasso, Sorrento** (© *010.39.87.81.900*), where tenor Enrico Caruso once stayed, immortalising the town in the song 'Return to Sorrento'.

AVVENTURA, L'

(1960, dir: Michelangelo Antonioni)
Monica Vitti, Gabriele Ferzetti, Lea Massari.
● **ROME; SICILY, ITALY**

A group of middle and upper class Italians visit a deserted volcanic island. When one of them disappears, the ensuing search drifts into indolence, and the mystery is never solved.

The opening scene, outside Anna's father's villa, was filmed on the outskirts of **Rome** – that's the dome of St Peter's in the background. Her boyfriend Sandro's home is Lady Montague's

Before the journey: Ponte Fabricia, Rome

apartment, on **Isola Tiberina**, a tiny island in the Tiber between Palatino and the Trastevere district. It's reached by **Ponte Fabricio**, the oldest surviving bridge over the river. Sandro's apartment is just to the left of the bridge (which you can glimpse though the open window in the film). In front of it is the tiny square where Claudia waits.

From here, it's south to the Tyrrhenian Sea and a yacht cruise around the volcanic **Lipari**, or Aeolian, islands. There are fourteen islands, seven of them inhabited. Panarea, smallest of the inhabited islands, is where the cast and crew stayed during filming. Anna disappears from **Lisca Bianca**, a deserted, jagged volcanic rock about three miles east, where the futile search begins. A couple of miles north is the steeply conical island of **Basiluz-**

The decayed interior of the customs house: Villa Palagonia, Bagheria

The staircase of the customs house: Villa Palagonia, Bagheria

zo, the first the party encounters *en route* to Lisca Bianca.

Sandro and Claudia report Anna's disappearance to the authorities on the Sicilian mainland at Milazzo (the nearest Sicilian port to the Liparis, and where you'll depart from if you want to visit). The grand, if faded, Customs House is definitely worth a visit, but you won't find it in Milazzo. It's actually the **Villa Palagonia** in **Bagheria**, way to the west near Palermo. This bizarre confection, designed by Palatino, has a garden which was initially populated by 200 grotesque statues – giants, dwarves, hybrids – commissioned by the villa's owner, the clearly mad Ferdinand, Prince of Palagonia as caricatures of his wife's supposed lovers. The interior of the villa was equally crazy – chairs with legs of unequal length, cushions containing hidden spikes and mirrors hung at weird angles. The cushions and chairs have gone, and the number of lovers is down to 62, but the building is being restored and you can visit. It's on **Piazza Garibaldi**, along Corso Umberto, a short walk from Bagheria railway station. Alternatively, there's an AST bus from Palermo's Piazza Lolli to Bagheria every half hour. The villa is open daily between 9am and 1pm, then 4pm and 7pm.

Sandro and Claudia begin travelling around Sicily, following up possible sightings of Anna. First, they take the train from **Milazzo** along the northern coast. Sandro alights at **Castoreale**, although once he hits the platform, the location becomes the more atmospheric **Cefalu**, overshadowed by the great rocky headland, further west along the coast toward Palermo. He continues the search on the island's northeast tip, in **Messina**, where he encounters publicity-hungry 'writer' Gloria Perkins. Claudia, meanwhile, rests up at the Villa Montaldo (or Montalto in the published script), where Giulia is seduced by the Princess' grandson. It's actually the **Villa Niscemi** near Palermo, home to Princess Lampedusa, who plays Princess Montaldo in the movie. The villa, on **Piazza Niscemi**, Via di Fante near the entrance to the Parco Della Favorita north of Palermo towards Mondello, was the inspiration for the house of Tancredi in Giuseppe de Lampedusa's *The Leopard,* filmed in 1963 by Luchino Visconti – see *Gattopardo, Il*). It's since been acquired by the Comune. The villa's terrace looks out to the distant heights of San Ferracavallo and Monte Gallo to the west, and the Gulf of Palermo to the east. Sandro moves on to Troina to question the pharmacist who may have seen Anna, though the scene was shot on the **Catanian Plain**.

Here, Claudia catches up with him and together they travel south toward the town of **Noto**. The eerily deserted modern town they stop at is one of the newly-built Cassa del Mezzogiorno towns near **Caltanisetta**, in the centre of the island. The railway tunnel, where Sandro and Claudia finally get it together is **Santa Panagia**, just north of Siracusa (Syracuse) on the southeast coast.

Even further south and inland a little is their destination, the impressively Baroque town of **Noto**, where they stay at the fictitious Trinacria Hotel. Noto was built of honey-coloured limestone at the end of the 17th century, when the existing town was destroyed in an earthquake. It looks, as Sandro observes, like an elaborate stage set. From the tower of the **Chiesa del Collegio**, the Collegio church where Claudia rings the bells, there's a view of the stunning **Piazza Municipio** overlooked by the **Duomo** and its wide, stepped approach. Sandro tries to get into the **Museo Civico**, housed in the Convent of Santissimo Salvatore to the right of the Duomo. He doesn't have much luck, but you might fare better. In the Piazza Municipio he accidentally-on-purpose spills ink over the student's architectural drawing. The building used as the Trinacria is behind the Museo Civico, its balcony overlooking the imposing facade of the **Church of San Francesco** on **Piazza Immacolata**.

The movie ends in **Taormina**, amid the lavish surroundings of an impossibly grand hotel, where Sandro, having betrayed the missing Anna with Claudia, now cheats on Claudia with the dreadful Gloria Perkins. The **San Domenico Hotel, Piazza San Domenico 5**, Taormina (*℡ 0942.23701*) is one of the world's most famous luxury hotels, housed in a 15th century monastery. The final scene, a wordless, numb acceptance between Claudia and Sandro, takes place on one of the hotel's terraces before the ruined tower of the church of San Domenico, with the peak of Mount Etna on the horizon.

AWAKENING, THE

(1980, dir: Mike Newell)
Charlton Heston, Susannah York, Jill Townsend.
● **LONDON; EGYPT; CAMBRIDGESHIRE**

Some great locations, but sadly this adaptation of one of *Dracula* author Bram Stoker's lesser novels, *The Jewel of Seven Stars*, never rises from the tomb. It was the first film from director Mike Newell, who went on to make crowd pleaser *Four Weddings and a Funeral* and the superb *Donnie Brasco*.

Unlike many more lively mummy movies, which made do with the cramped sound-stages of Hollywood or Bray,

Mummy's resting place: Museum of Egyptian Antiquities, Cairo

this snoozer scores a first by actually making it to the **Valley of the Kings** in Egypt, intended to be the last resting place of the Pharaohs, until graverobbers and archaeologists gave premature notice of eviction. The valley is just a part of the **Theban Necropolis**, a vast complex of tombs and temples over the Nile from Luxor, some 600 miles south of Cairo, a favourite tourist stopoff. The river marks an age-old boundary between the City of the Dead, on the west bank, and Luxor, City of the Living, on the east. Beyond the Valley of the Kings lies the Valley of the Sorcerer and the twin sandstone peaks overlooking Queen Kara's tomb, which archaeologist Charlton Heston discovers and unwisely opens just at the moment his wife goes into labour. A ferry from the docks at Luxor will take you over to the Necropolis, but to enter the various monuments you need to purchase tickets in advance from the kiosk by the ferry landing-stage. The ruined temple Heston later visits with his grown-up daughter can also be found in the complex. This is the **Ramesseum**, mortuary temple of

The British Museum: University College, Gower Street, London

Rameses II, which the Pharaoh had built on the Nile's flood plain, unfortunately.

Cairo, the destination of long-dead Queen Kara and her treasures, provides an authentic backdrop as the restive mummy is housed in the city's justly renowned **Museum of Egyptian Antiquities**. One of the world's great collections – the museum boasts among its exhibits the contents of Tutankhamun's tomb – it can be found in downtown Cairo's main square, **Midan el-Tahrir** on the east bank of the Nile. Extracting maximum value from the location trip, the Egyptian capital features again as Heston returns to retrieve the apparently crumbling mummy. This time, it's Islamic Cairo, the historic district east of the city centre. Heston strides manfully through the souk, the famously bustling bazaar overlooked by the needle-thin minarets of the **Sultan Hasan Mosque-Madrasa** on **Sharia el-Qala**. You can visit the historic mosque (*admission free*), but remember the rules of modest dress and check prayer times in advance. The domed and peculiarly deserted mosque also seen is one of the most sacred, and is closed to non-Muslims, presumably why Heston isn't in the shot. It's **Sayyidna el-Husayn Mosque** on the **Midan el-Husayn**, said to house the head of Hussein, grandson of Mohammed.

In London, at the British Museum, you can see the head and shoulders missing from a giant statue of Rameses II at the Ramesseum in Luxor. Although Heston supposedly works and lectures in the British Museum, the colonnaded front is actually that of **University College** on **Gower Street**. The interior of the museum's Egyptian Room is bogus too, mocked up in the studio. The radio telescope installation, where Heston's suspicions about the movements of the Seven Stars – the Great Bear constellation – are confirmed, is real, though. Cambridge University's **Mullard Observatory**, where the first pulsar was discovered, can be found west of Cambridge at **Lords Bridge**.

AWAKENINGS

(1990, dir: Penny Marshall)
Robin Williams, Robert De Niro, Max von Sydow.
● **NEW YORK CITY**

An unusually subdued Robin Williams plays Dr Malcolm Sayer, a character based on Oliver Sacks, the introverted psychiatrist who woke near-comatose patients with the drug L-Dopa, only to see them react violently to the drug's side effects and lapse back into their vegetative state. Set almost entirely in Brooklyn, where the movie opens in the thirties with young Leonard (who grows up to be Robert De Niro) carving his name on a bench at the foot of **Manhattan Bridge**. Fast-forward to 1969, and Dr Sayer arrives at the (fictitious) Bainbridge Hospital, where Leonard and the other vegetative patients are resident. Bainbridge is the real **Kingsboro Psychiatric Center, 681**

Clarkson Avenue off Utica Avenue in Brooklyn, dressed as the late sixties by production designer, the late Anton Furst. Sayer's home is on **City Island** in the Bronx, only a few steps from Oliver Sacks' real home, while the house of Leonard's mother is a brownstone in Brooklyn's classy **Park Slope** district. Leonard's elementary school can also be found in Park Slope.

The botanical garden, where Dr Sayer relaxes, is the **Enid A Haupt Conservatory** in the **New York Botanical Garden, 200th Street** at Southern Boulevard in Bronx Park, the Bronx (see Martin Scorsese's *The Age of Innocence* for details). The dance hall, where the newly-awakened oldsters find out that Prohibition is over, is **Casa Galicia, 3922 30th Street, Long Island City** in Queens (*© 718.472.1002*).

AWFULLY BIG ADVENTURE, AN

(1995, dir: Mike Newell)
Georgina Cates, Hugh Grant, Alan Rickman.
● **DUBLIN**

The Liverpool Playhouse: Dame Theatre, Dublin

Full marks to Hugh Grant, risking his newly-acquired star status after the phenomenal success of *Four Weddings and a Funeral* by playing the seedily manipulative gay theatre director in Newell's film of Beryl Bainbridge's backstage tragedy.

Set in Liverpool during the forties, the movie was filmed, apart from a couple of establishing shots of the Mersey, in Dublin, as once again the Irish government scored with the tax breaks. The Playhouse is actually the beautiful 1,300 seat Victorian **Dame Theatre, 72 Dame Street** (*© 677.7744*) near the Temple Bar district.

Not far away is another Dublin institution, the tea-room where members of the company swap gossip. It's **Bewley's Oriental Café, 78-79 Grafton Street**. Dublin Docks stand in for Liverpool's Merseyside equivalent, where grand actor

Company gossip: Bewley's Oriental Cafe

Alan Rickman rides his motorbike.

The theatre's rehearsal space might look familiar – it's the same ornate, arched rehearsal room, above a snooker hall, used by the band in Alan Parker's *The Commitments*, which you can find south of the city centre on **Lower Camden Street**.

B

BABE
(1995, dir: Chris Noonan)
James Cromwell, Magda Szubanski, Christine Cavanaugh.
● NEW SOUTH WALES, AUSTRALIA

An irresistible animal fantasy written by George Miller, who made the *Mad Max* movies. Hoggett's Farm was built in the rolling green countryside of **Robertson**, 80 miles south of Sydney, on the Illawara Highway in the Southern Highlands of New South Wales.

BABE, PIG IN THE CITY
(1998, dir: George Miller)
Magda Szubanski, James Cromwell, Mickey Rooney.
● NEW SOUTH WALES, AUSTRALIA

It's a return to **Robertson** (see *Babe*) for the Hoggett's farm scenes in this commercially unsuccessful but dark and imaginative sequel directed by George Miller. The Flealands Hotel and its quirky neighbourhood were constructed at the new **Fox Studios** in **Sydney**. The art deco Metro Theatre is a copy of the real music venue at **624 George Street**, central Sydney, which also happens to house the film company's production offices.

BABETTE'S FEAST
(1987, dir: Gabriel Axel)
Stephane Audran, Birgitte Federspiel, Bodil Kjer.
● DENMARK

Exiled Parisian chef Audran manages to bring unwanted gastronomic pleasure into the lives of an austere Danish religious community by cooking the mother of all banquets. Filmed in **Vendsyssel**, the northernmost island of Jutland, Denmark. The military scenes were shot at the garrison town of **Naestved**, 50 miles southwest of Copenhagen, Sjaelland – the home of the Royal Guard Hussars.

BABY DOLL
(1956, dir: Elia Kazan)
Carol Baker, Karl Malden, Eli Wallach.
● MISSISSIPPI

'The dirtiest American picture ever legally exhibited' said *Time* magazine of this Tennessee Williams adaptation, which sparked a boom in shortie-nighties. Director Kazan likes to work on real locations, so the movie was shot in the South, at the small town of **Benoit, Mississippi**, on Route 1, about twenty miles north of Greenville close to the Arkansas border.

BACK TO THE FUTURE
(1985, dir: Robert Zemeckis)
Michael J Fox, Christopher Lloyd, Lea Thompson.
● LOS ANGELES

Fox is the teen who has to engineer his own parents' romance after being whisked back to the 1950s in this enjoyably slam-bang fantasy. The setting of Mill Valley is fictitious, and the movie was filmed around LA. The

Doc Emmett's house: Gamble House, Westmoreland Place.

town square is a huge set, built on the Universal lot, where it was badly damaged in the fire of the late eighties, but plenty of the other locations are real. Doc Emmett's

Marty McFly's mother's house: Bushnell Avenue, Pasadena

house, 1640 Riverside Drive, Mill Valley, is one of LA's great architectural joys, the 1908 **Gamble House, 4 Westmoreland Place** in Pasadena, just a little to the south of the Pasadena Historical Society. Built for the Gamble family (as in Proctor and...), this charming, Japanese-influenced wood shingle house is open to the public (© *818.793.3334*). The Doc's workshop, where the time-travelling DeLorean is stored, is actually the **Gamble House bookshop**, alongside the main house. The front door on which Fox knocks, though, and the house interior, is the 1907 **RR Blacker House**, a similar Japanese-inspired design by Charles and Henry Greene, at **1177 Hillcrest Avenue, Oak Knoll**, Pasadena.

The fifties neighbourhood of Fox's Mom-to-be is also Pasadena. Lea Thompson's house, where Fox gets hit by a car, is **1727 Bushnell Avenue** in South Pasadena. And big lummock Biff lives just down the road at **1809 Bushnell Avenue**. A few miles further south you'll find Mill Valley High School, down in Whittier, southeastern LA, hometown of Richard Milhaus Nixon. And indeed the school, **Whittier Union High School, 12417 Philadelphia Street** at Pierce Avenue, is where Tricky Dickie graduated in 1930. The 'Enchantment Under The Sea' dance, though, where Fox finally unites his parents and invents rock 'n' roll, was filmed in Hollywood, in the gymnasium of the **First United Methodist Church of Hollywood, 6817 Franklin Avenue**.

To the east of Whittier, in the anonymous sprawl of industrial estates aptly called City of Industry, is the Twin Pines Mall where Doc Emmett gets gunned down by irate Libyans. It's the **Puente Hills Mall** on the southeast corner of the Pomona Freeway exit, Highway 60, at **Azusa Avenue**.

BACK TO THE FUTURE PART II

(1989, dir: Robert Zemeckis)
Michael J Fox, Christopher Lloyd, Lea Thompson.
● CALIFORNIA

The confusing sequel (shot back-to-back with *Part III*), which flips from past to future, revisits many of the familiar locations. The school is, once again, **Whittier High** in Pasedena, and the 'Enchantment' dance was carefully recreated at the **First United Methodist Church of Hollywood**. The Mill Valley town square at Universal was dressed to represent alternative futures – one good, one nightmarish – while Biff's Vegas-style 'Pleasure Palace', in the nightmare future, is no more than a nine-foot model.

BACK TO THE FUTURE PART III

(1990, dir: Robert Zemeckis)
Michael J Fox, Christopher Lloyd, Mary Steenburgen.
● ARIZONA; CALIFORNIA

The final part of the trilogy sends Fox zooming back to the Wild West, and what location could be more iconic than **Monument Valley**, Arizona? See *Stagecoach* for details of this familiar, but still breathtaking, Western backdrop. The railroad scenes were shot on the **Sierra Railroad** between Jamestown and Sonora – a stretch of track also seen in films such as *Bad Day at Black Rock* and *High Noon*. It's on Route 108 east of Stockton, California. The 1885 version of the Mill Valley square was reconstructed up here. Once again, Doc Emmett's place is the **Gamble House** (see *Back to the Future*), though this time the interiors were on a Universal soundstage.

BACKBEAT

(1993, dir: Iain Softley)
Stephen Dorff, Sheryl Lee, Ian Hart.
● HAMBURG; LONDON; LIVERPOOL; WALES

The story of Stu Sutcliffe, a founder member of the Beatles, who left the group and died of a brain haemorrhage before they hit the bigtime.

The Liverpool pub: Cheney Street, Kings Cross, London

Set, unsurprisingly, in Liverpool and Hamburg, much of the film was actually shot in London. The opening scene, where Sutcliffe and Lennon get involved in a fight at the Anchor Pub, Liverpool filmed on the familiar cobbles of **Cheney Street**, London NW1, behind Kings Cross Station – a location seen in many films including *The Ladykillers*, *Chaplin* and *Richard III*, its days are numbered as the area is sadly due for extensive redevelopment.

The Hamburg trip takes the boys to the notorious **Reeperbahn**, where the band starts out playing

The Top Ten Club, Hamburg: The Dome, Tufnell Park

cruddy basement clubs. Interiors, though, are largely London again. The Kaiserkeller filmed in a side-street off Ladbroke Grove, W10; the Top Ten Club is **The Dome, Dartmouth Park Road, Tufnell Park**, N19, on Junction Road opposite Tufnell Park tube station; while the deco-ish Polydor Record Company where the band signs a record deal, is a private residential block in Highgate, **High Point, North Road**, N1. Success, after Sutcliffe's death, takes the boys to the Star Club for the *Twist and Shout* number, which filmed in the **National Club, 234 Kilburn High Road**, London NW6. The remote lighthouse they escape to for a little r&r can be seen at **Point of Air**, three miles east of Prestatyn off the A548, on the coast of North Wales.

Hamburg's Star Club: National Club, Kilburn

BACKDRAFT

(1991, dir: Ron Howard)
William Baldwin, Kurt Russell, Scott Glenn.
● CHICAGO

Ron Howard's firefighter epic has great conflagrations but sudsy plotlines. It filmed in the Chicago neighbourhoods of **Oak Park** (home to the Frank Lloyd Wright museum and many of his houses – the elevator shaft scenes filmed here) and **Hinsdale**. The fire stations are at **Archer and Sacramento Streets**; and the **Southside Firehouse**, West Cermak Road, in Chinatown a few yards west of the Cermak-Chinatown el station on the Lake/Dan Ryan line. The funeral scene was shot in the prestigious 1860 **Graceland Cemetery**, last resting place of Chicago's 19th century notables and such household names as architect Mies van der Rohe, storeowner Marshall Field and sleeping-car inventor George Pullman. It's on **North Clark Street** at Irving Park Road, Wrigleyville. The final huge parade of 2,000 firefighters was shot in central Chicago, on **Michigan Avenue**, at the foot of the famous Wrigley Building.

The firehouse: Southside Firehouse, West Cermak Road

The funeral parade: Michigan Avenue, Chicago

BAD BOYS

(1995, dir: Michael Bay)
Will Smith, Martin Lawrence, Tea Leoni.
● FLORIDA

Another slam-bang Simpson-Bruckheimer actioner, with mismatched cops Lawrence and Smith tracking down a

Trouble at the party: Biltmore Hotel, Anastasia Avenue, Coral Gables

Will Smith's apartment: Tyler Adams Hotel and Apartments

mega-stash of heroin lifted from the cop station. The druggy party, where Tea Leoni dives into the pool after witnessing a double murder, is at the **Biltmore Hotel, 1200 Anastasia Avenue** at De Soto Boulevard, Coral Gables, southwest Miami (*©305. 445.1926*). Built in 1926, and designed by the architects of the Waldorf-Astoria and Grand Central Station in New York, the hotel has had a chequered history, closing down and being resold several times. It's now a national historic landmark and offers one-hour walking tours. Will Smith's stylish apartment is in the **Tyler-Adams Hotel and Apartments** (previously the Collins Park Hotel), **2030 Park Avenue** in Miami's art deco district.

BAD DAY AT BLACK ROCK

(1955, dir: John Sturges)
Spencer Tracy, Robert Ryan, Anne Francis.
● **CALIFORNIA**

Tracy arrives in a small town with a big secret in this excellent, pared-down suspenser. 'Black Rock' has nothing to do with it – the script was called *Bad Day at Hondo* until John Wayne turned up in 1953 with a movie called *Hondo*. Writer Millard Kaufman stopped for gas in the tiny town of Black Rock, Arizona, and a new title was born. Most of the film was shot on the lot at MGM, though some exteriors were lensed on the edge of Death Valley, at **Lone Pine** on Route 395, California (also the location for 1989 horror comedy *Tremors* and Bogart's *High Sierra*, among many others).

BAD LIEUTENANT

(1992, dir: Abel Ferrara)
Harvey Keitel, Frankie Thorn, Zoe Lund.
● **NEW YORK CITY**

Keitel finds redemption: Port Authority Bus Terminal, Eighth Avenue

Although Keitel is frighteningly intense as a doomed Catholic cop who witnesses the rape of a nun, the movie plays like Andy Warhol filming a rejected Scorsese script on a grant from the Catholic Truth Society. It was filmed around New York's Little Italy area, in the Bronx and in Jersey City. The grocery store where Keitel sorts out the

Keitel deals with the robbery: Median Foods, Seventh Avenue

robbery is **Median Foods, 461 Seventh Avenue** near 35th Street, midtown Manhattan. He finally attains redemption, handing over the money which would have saved his life, to the two rapists, at the **Port Authority Bus Terminal** on **Eighth Avenue** between West 40th and West 42nd Streets.

BAD TASTE

(1988, dir: Peter Jackson)
Peter Jackson, Mike Minett, Peter O'Herne.
● **NEW ZEALAND**

Semi-pro exercise in gross-out schlock, made over four years on a budget of twopence. The house where aliens package up fat-free humans for intergalactic consumption is a protected colonial homestead, the **Gear House, Okowai Road, Papakowhai, Porirua** (*©04.237.8540*), in a picturesque harbour town about twenty minutes north of Wellington, New Zealand. Filmed also at **Titahi Bay**; **Pukerua Bay**; and **Makara Beach**, Wellington.

BAD TIMING

(1980, dir: Nicolas Roeg)
Art Garfunkel, Theresa Russell, Harvey Keitel.
● **VIENNA, AUSTRIA; LONDON; MOROCCO; NEW YORK CITY**

Garfunkel is a psychoanalyst whose obsessive infatuation with Russell leads to tragedy. Fittingly, the movie filmed mainly in the home of psychoanalysis, the cluttered, elegant Jugendstil city of Vienna where Freud himself probed tortured psyches.

Theresa Russell's florid apartment building is on **Schoenebroene Schlosstrasse**. The gallery she visits with Garfunkel to see the Klimt paintings is the **Neue Galerie**, on the second floor of the **Stallburg**, the stables of the famous Riding School in the Hofburg Palace complex. The entrance is at Reitschulgasse 2, on the northern corner of Josefsplatz between Stallburgasse and Braunerstrasse. The Klimts, Schieles and other paintings were moved in the late eighties though, and they're now on display in the Osterreichisches Galerie des 19. & 20. Jahrundert (the Austrian Gallery of 19th and 20th Century Art) in the Oberes Schloss Belvedere. The Belvedere Palace stands on a hill southeast of the Schwarzenberg Palace overlooking Vienna in acres of formal gardens.

The large, elegant coffee house, where Art Garfunkel meets Daniel Massey, is the landmark **Cafe Landtmann, Dr Karl Lueger Ring 4**, a historic hangout for politicians, next to Vienna's Burgtheater.

The flashback scenes to Morocco were filmed at **Ouarzazate**, a favourite North African location seen in films as diverse as *Jewel of the Nile*, *The Last Days of Sodom and Gomorrah* and Bertolucci's *The Sheltering Sky*, while the film's coda was shot in New York City.

BADLANDS

(1973, dir: Terrence Malick)
Martin Sheen, Sissy Spacek, Warren Oates.
● COLORADO

The first film from the enigmatic Malick who, after one more feature (*Days of Heaven* in 1978) didn't release a film for over twenty years until 1999's *The Thin Red Line*. *Badlands* is clearly an influence on *Natural Born Killers* and Malick's style was shamelessly ripped off for the Tarantino-scripted, Tony Scott-directed *True Romance*. The film was inspired by the case of Charles Starkweather and his fourteen-year-old girlfriend, Caril Fugate, who killed ten people in 1958, including Fugate's mother, stepfather and half-sister. The real events took place in Lincoln, Nebraska, but although Malick's version is transposed to the Badlands of South Dakota, it was shot in **La Junta**, I-50, Otero County, southeast Colorado; and **Las Animas**, about 25 miles to the east.

BAGDAD CAFE

(1988, dir: Percy Adlon)
Marianne Sagebrecht, CCH Pounder, Jack Palance.
● CALIFORNIA

German tourist Sagebrecht brings a touch of magic to a humble roadside stop-off in Adlon's whimsical fantasy. The cafe was the Sidewinder Cafe, now – unsurprisingly – renamed the **Bagdad Cafe**, on the famed old Route 66 between the east and west off-ramps of I-40 at **Newberry Springs**, east of Barstow on Highway 40, California. The strange light reflections come from the 100-acre field of mirrors of the Department of Energy's **Solar One Power Plant** at **Daggett**, east on the main highway I-40 out of Barstow.

The Bagdad cafe: Bagdad Cafe, Newberry Springs

BALLAD OF CABLE HOGUE, THE

(1970, dir: Sam Peckinpah)
Jason Robards, Stella Stevens, David Warner.
● NEVADA; ARIZONA

Peckinpah followed up *The Wild Bunch* with this slow, eccentric, likeable and gentle Western. The film's base was at Echo Bay, 53 miles northeast of Las Vegas near to Lake Mead, but the actual location is the **Valley of Fire**, a few miles to the north off I-15. Hogue's castle is a real hotel bought and transported, complete with furniture, from Bishop, just over the border in Central California. The interiors lensed at **Apache Junction**, a Western movie town east of Phoenix, Arizona.

BARABBAS

(1961, dir: Richard Fleischer)
Anthony Quinn, Silvana Mangano, Jack Palance.
● ITALY

In Dino de Laurentiis' huge US/Italian co-production, Quinn is the thief pardoned in place of Christ and sentenced to work in the silver mines, who converts to Christianity and winds up as a gladiator. The mines Barabbas sweats in are genuine sulphur mines on the volcanic slopes of **Mount Etna** in Sicily. The vast, gladiatorial amphitheatre, where 300 combatants slog it out in true epic style, is the **Arena di Verona** in the **Piazza Bra** in the centre of **Verona**. One of the largest and best preserved in the world, it dates from the first century AD.

The first scene, of the crucifixion, famously incorporates a genuine total eclipse of the sun for the moment of Christ's death. It was shot on 15 February 1961 at **Roccastrado**, 120 miles north of Rome.

BAREFOOT IN THE PARK

(1967, dir: Gene Saks)
Jane Fonda, Robert Redford, Mildred Natwick.
● NEW YORK CITY

Bob and Jane are struggling newlyweds in this film of an early Neil Simon play. The park, where Jane Fonda gets uptight lawyer Redford to get shoeless and loosen up is New York's **Washington Square**, Greenwich Village. Other NY locations include **West 10th Street**, a deli on Sixth Avenue and Lower Fifth Avenue. Fonda and Redford's apartment is **111 Waverly Place**, off Washington Square's northwest corner.

Bob and Jane's apartment: Waverly Place, Greenwich Village

BARRY LYNDON

(1975, dir: Stanley Kubrick)
Ryan O'Neal, Marisa Berenson, Patrick Magee.
● IRELAND; WILTSHIRE; SUSSEX; GLOUCESTERSHIRE; YORKSHIRE; GERMANY

To achieve the breathtaking look of his film of the Thackeray novel, Kubrick pushed the technology of the time, demanding specially ground lenses which enabled him to film on real locations using available light and even, amazingly, to film by candlelight. The production was initially based at Waterford in southeast Ireland. **Carrick-on-Suir**, fifteen miles to the northwest, is where Redmond Barry – as the hero starts out – joins the English militia. The stone walls and towers of **Kells**, nine miles south of Kilkenny, are the backdrop to the scenes of the English Redcoats, while the German encampment, where Barry meets Captain Potsdorf, is **Cahir Castle**, ten miles west of Clonmel in Tipperary. **Dublin Castle** is used for the elegant hotel and the casino, where he pursues his career as a card player.

After terrorist threats, the production decamped to England, where interiors were shot in two grand Wiltshire houses: **Wilton House**, two and a half miles west of Salisbury on the A30; and the Marquis of Bath's pile, **Longleat House** in Warminster.

Redmond Barry becomes Barry Lyndon when he marries a rich widow, the Countess of Lyndon, in the chapel of **Petworth House** in the centre of Petworth, five and a half miles east of Midhurst, West Sussex. The exterior of the vast estate he marries into is **Castle Howard** (the familiar setting for TV's *Brideshead Revisited*), fifteen miles northeast of York off the A64 in Yorkshire. The interior, where Barry scuppers his chance of being awarded a title after an ugly scuffle with his stepson, is one of the lavish state rooms of **Corsham Court**, four miles west of Chippenham off the A4, and also in Wiltshire.

For the Berlin exteriors, the film uses the complex of elegant palaces and parks at **Potsdam**. Although geographically southwest of Berlin, the town was, until 1990, part of East Berlin.

BARTON FINK
(1991, dir: Joel Coen)
John Turturro, John Goodman, Judy Davis.
● **LOS ANGELES**

The Coen Brothers' cryptic movie sends a Left-ish, Odetts-style Broadway playwright to a literal Hollywood hell. There's no real East Coast here though. New York's Belasco Theater (the real location for Woody Allen's *Bullets Over Broadway*), where Fink's drama of the common working man triumphs, is actually LA's beautifully preserved 1926 **Orpheum Theater, 842 South Broadway**, downtown LA (a popular location seen also in *Dead Again*, *Ed Wood*, *Last Action Hero* and *The Doors*). The stylish 'Sardi's'-type restaurant and bar, where Fink gets the call to the West Coast, was filmed in the deco bowels of the **Queen Mary** at her dry dock on **Pier J** at the end of Long Beach Freeway, Long Beach.

Moving to Hollywood, Fink checks into the dismally claustrophobic Hotel Earle. Although the hotel room and corridors are sets, the lobby is the entrance of the restored 1931 grand movie palace the **Wiltern Theater**, in the **Wiltern Center, 3790 Wilshire Boulevard** at Western Avenue, midtown LA.

The studio commissary of Capitol Pictures, where Fink meets the cynical director, filmed in the now closed and shuttered **Ambassador Hotel, 3400 Wilshire Boulevard** at Catalina Street, midtown. The famous hotel, scene of Bobby Kennedy's 1968 assassination, has frequently been used as a movie location. It was recently acquired by Donald Trump to be developed as a mall

The lobby of Fink's Hotel Earle: Wiltern Centre, Wilshire Boulevard

Fink celebrates at the USO dance: Ballroom, Park Plaza Hotel, South Park View Street

complex, though the city of LA wants to build a school on the site (keep up with events at *www.cocoanutgrove.org*). Catch it while – and if – you can. The 'adjoining' men's toilet where burned-out writer Mayhew loses his lunch, is about a mile to the east in the **Park Plaza Hotel, 607 South Park View Street** overlooking MacArthur Park. Its toilets obviously have a strange fascination, as they also feature as the scene of Tim Roth's dope cover story in *Reservoir Dogs*. The USO dance, where a celebratory Fink inadvertently starts a brawl, was also filmed at the Park Plaza, in the wood-panelled Ballroom (a familiar venue seen in *Chaplin, New York, New York, Hook* and many other films).

The exterior corridor leading up to Bill Mayhew's bungalow on the Capitol lot is on the **Columbia Pictures' lot** (previously the MGM Studio), **10202 West Washington Boulevard**, Culver City, though the interior of the bungalow is once again the Ambassador Hotel. The office of production executive Ben Geisler is a bungalow on the lot of the **Hollywood Center** (previously Francis Coppola's ill-fated Zoetrope Studios) at **1040 North Las Palmas Avenue** off Romaine Street in Hollywood.

The bizarre closing scene was shot near **Zuma Beach** on the west side of Point Dume, west of Malibu.

BASIC INSTINCT
(1992, dir: Paul Verhoeven)
Sharon Stone, Michael Douglas, George Dzundza.
● **SAN FRANCISCO**

By wrapping a potentially interesting idea (role-reversal serial killer movie) in a Hitchcock pastiche, Verhoeven's movie comes over as a confused piece of homophobic misogyny. The director chooses a *Vertigo*-esque San Francisco, with Sharon Stone sporting the inappropriate Hitchcock uniform of sexual repression, all tightly-clenched hair and severe grey suit. Michael Douglas' apartment (even the staircase here is modelled on that of the belltower in *Vertigo*) is **1158 Montgomery Street**. Following Stone's grilling in the film's most notorious scene, teetotal Michael Douglas decides to desert the Evian at **Tosca, 242 Columbus Avenue**, a pricey media persons' hangout (this is obviously a well

Michael Douglas' apartment: Montgomery Street, San Francisco

Douglas falls off the wagon after grilling Sharon Stone: Tosca, Columbus Avenue

paid police force). The Police HQ where Stone does for knickers what Clark Gable did for vests, filmed at Warners' studio in Hollywood, as did Johnny Boz's churchified rock club – a set based on NYC's Limelight Club.

The Stetson Bar, though, is real. It's **Raw Hide II, 280 Seventh Street**, south of Market, a lesbian C&W bar in San Fran. The exterior, and the diner next door, were false fronts constructed in a deserted alley beneath the **Transbay Terminal Deck**, Mission Street at First Street.

Filming also took place in **Rohnert Park** and **Petaluma** (the northern Californian town where *American Graffiti* filmed); and at the Dominican College in Marin County. The chase filmed up **Kearney Street**'s steep sidewalk steps on Telegraph Hill. Sharon Stone's swish Stinson pad was actually shot south of San Fran at a beachfront estate on a rocky bluff, on **Spindrift Road, Carmel Highlands** (which is why it seems to be reached via the **Bixby Bridge** on Highway 1, California's Big Sur coastline). The plush home, on the same road as Clint Eastwood's place in *Play Misty For Me*, is not visible from the street, but you can visit **Garrapatta State Beach**, Route 1 about eight miles to the south, where the beach scenes were shot.

The climax, with Jean Tripplehorn taking the bullet, was staged at **2201 Broadway, Oakland**, just over the Bay Bridge from San Francisco.

BASKET CASE

(1982, dir: Frank Henelotter)
Kevin van Hentenryck, Terri Susan Smith.
● **NEW YORK STATE**

Enjoyably grungy horror comedy with Duane and his evolutionarily challenged ex-Siamese twin Belial, out for revenge on the doctors who separated them. Shot in New York city, primarily around Times Square, on the kind of budget that barely runs to shoestrings, studio work was out of the question. The movie was filmed in friends' houses at **Glens Falls**, on the Hudson River north of Albany, I-87; in New York lofts; and at a mid-Manhattan welfare hotel which threatened to sue if its name was mentioned (which is a bit odd as it's credited in the movie). Now gone, it was the Hotel Broslin near Times Square.

BATMAN

(1989, dir: Tim Burton)
Michael Keaton, Jack Nicholson, Kim Basinger.
● **LONDON; HERTFORDSHIRE; BEDFORDSHIRE**

Burton's Gotham City, a nightmare fantasy of New York, was actually built in England. The late Anton Furst's set

Wayne Manor: Knebworth House, Hertfordshire

covered most of the 18 soundstages at Pinewood Studio. Wayne Manor, though, is real, and is a conflation of two buildings. The exterior is **Knebworth House**, a Gothicised Tudor manor house 28 miles north of London on the A1 (*℡01438.812661, admission charge, rail: Stevenage*). It also provided gloomy Gothic mansions for, among others, Ken Russell's *Lair of the White Worm*, Gene Wilder's *Haunted Honeymoon* and Ingrid Bergman's Oscar-winning *Anastasia*.

The interiors are **Hatfield House, Hatfield** a Jacobean pile (*℡01707.262823, admission charge, rail: Hatfield*). The gaming room, where Kim Basinger asks "Who's Bruce Wayne?", was filmed in the Long Gallery here. Wayne's arsenal, with its two-way mirror, was shot in the Marble Hall, while the library, where Alfred advises Bruce Wayne to get married, is the library.

The Axis Chemical Works, where Jack Nicholson plunges into the chemical sludge, was shot at a disused power station in **Acton Lane**, West London. The exploding exterior was **Little Barford Power Station**, a couple of miles south of St Neots in Bedfordshire.

The first sequel, 1992's *Batman Returns*, was shot in the US, and was completely studio-bound, taking up all seven of Warner's large LA soundstages, plus one at Universal, where the Penguin's lair was built.

BATMAN & ROBIN

(1997, dir: Joel Schumacher)
George Clooney, Chris O'Donnell, Alicia Silverstone.
● **LOS ANGELES**

Mainly studio-bound clunker, getting more and more like the old TV series. The grounds of Wayne Manor are **Greystone Park, 905 Loma Vista Drive**, Beverly Hills (see *The Loved One* for details).

BATMAN FOREVER

(1995, dir: Joel Schumacher)
Val Kilmer, Chris O'Donnell, Jim Carrey.
● **LOS ANGELES; NEW YORK STATE**

As the directorial reins were handed over to Joel Schumacher, the series came up with an eclectic mix of East and West Coast locations. Wayne Manor undergoes another transformation, to Long Island mansion. This time it's the **Webb Institute of Naval Architecture** (previously The Braes), **Welwyn Preserve** on **Crescent Beach**, Glen Cove on the north shore of Long Island.

Chase Meridian's office, exterior: Surrogate's Court, Chambers Street

Pan-Asia Town, scene of Two-Face's opening robbery, is over on the West Coast. It's a sec-

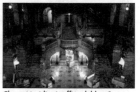

Chase Meridian's office, lobby: Surrogate's Court, Chambers Street

Gotham City: Exchange Place, New York

tion of **Figueroa Street**, downtown LA, dressed with a flurry of neon signs. The Gotham backstreets where O'Donnell takes the Batmobile for a spin and encounters the dayglo streetgang, filmed on the old Hennessy Street set, a section of New York's Greenwich Village built on the backlot at Warner Bros' Burbank Studios. But more Gotham Cityscapes were found in New York, on **Exchange Place**, the ultimate concrete canyon, running between Broadway and William Street, a block north of Wall Street in Lower Manhattan.

Edward Nygma's bash at the Ritz Gotham Hotel: Museum of the Native American, Broadway

Not far away is the grandiose entrance to the Ritz Gotham Hotel, where Jim Carrey holds his wild bash. It's the **Smithsonian Museum of the Native American** – previously the old US Customs House – **Broadway** at Bowling Green, Lower Manhattan. In a flash, it's back to the West Coast for the 'Ritz' interior, which is the foyer of the venerable **Pantages Theater, 6233 Hollywood Boulevard**, Hollywood (see *The Bodyguard* for details). Chase Meridian's office is New York. The exterior, where the Batmobile arrives, the imposing arched marble foyer with its double staircase, are those of the 1911 **Surrogate's Court, 31 Chambers Street** at Center Street, Lower Manhattan, also the site of the climax of *Romeo Is Bleeding*. The building is open to the public. Meridian's bizarre nouveau-ish apartment is a studio set, but you can see the room it's based on in Prague Castle. Similarly with the Gotham City Police headquarters rooftop, where the bat-signal is located. Although this is a set, you can see the two real art-deco buildings that inspired it: one in lower Manhattan, at **60 Wall Street**, the other over in downtown Los Angeles – the turquoise terra-cotta **Eastern Columbia Building, 849 South Broadway** (for details see *Predator 2*, which featured this architectural gem as a location). Still on the west coast Broadway is the dazzling **Los Angeles Theater, 615 South Broadway**, whose glittering lobby is used as Gotham's Excelsior Grand Casino (see *Chaplin* for details). The exterior of Two-Face's lair is the monumental façade of New York's **Manhattan Bridge**, while the Riddler's Claw Island lair is a, slightly enhanced, view of **Alcatraz Island** in the bay at San Francisco in longshot, and the old **ARCO Refinery, Carson**, California, for closer views.

BATTAGLIA DI ALGERI, LA (aka *Battle of Algiers*)
(1965, dir: Gillo Pontecorvo)
Brahim Haggiag, Jean Martin, Yacef Saadi.
● ALGERIA

The first feature film made in Algeria (and nominated for

an Academy Award as Best Foreign Film) covers the final days of the country's struggle against French rule in 1954. Despite the utterly convincing documentary style, no actual newsreel footage was used. Pontecorvo filmed entirely on location, and with a non-professional cast, largely in the **Casbah** of Algiers, where the events depicted had taken place. When houses needed to be blown up, full-size buildings were erected in the narrow streets, largely from expanded polystyrene. Ali's house, where he dies when it's destroyed the end of the movie, was reconstructed on the site of the real house.

BATTLE OF THE SEXES, THE
(1960, dir: Charles Crichton)
Peter Sellers, Constance Cummings, Robert Morley.
● EDINBURGH

Blackish comedy, based on a Thurber story, filmed by veteran director Crichton who later made *A Fish Called Wanda*. Efficiency expert Constance Cummings, American *and* female, is dispatched to shake up traditional Scottish tartan weavers, The House of MacPherson. She arrives at Edinburgh's **Waverley Station**, just off Princes Street. The House of MacPherson itself is on

The tobacconist: Lawnmarket, Edinburgh

George Street, Edinburgh, but the film plays with the city's geography, giving it a photogenic view across Princes Street to Waverley Bridge and the Balmoral Hotel. The tobacco shop, where Sellers buys cigarettes, is on **Lawnmarket** opposite St Giles Cathedral. The car shunt was filmed in **Grassmarket** at **King Stable's Road** beneath Edinburgh Castle. The remote Scottish Highlands, where the crofters work, were actually in **Holyrood Park** Edinburgh.

View from the House of MacPherson: Princes Street, Edinburgh

The car shunt: Grassmarket, Edinburgh

BATTLESHIP POTEMKIN (aka *Potemkin*)
(1925, dir: Sergei Eisenstein)
A Antonov, Grigori Alexandrov, Vladimir Barsky.
● UKRAINE

Eisenstein's silent classic is a fictionalised account of the 1905 revolutionary uprising in the Black Sea port of **Odessa**. The massacre on the steps (an episode invented by Eisenstein) is one of cinema's most innovatory sequences, and probably runs second only to *Psycho*'s shower murder as the most parodied of movie images – just watch those prams bouncing down steps in movies as diverse as Terry Gilliam's *Brazil* or Brian de Palma's *The Untouchables*. Odessa is a charming Ukranian resort on the northern shore of the Black Sea, though as the area gets more industrialised, the sea is becoming increasingly polluted.

The steps – originally the Richelieu Steps, named for Odessa's first governor, the Duke of Richelieu, whose statue stands at the top of them – were built between 1837 and 1841, and designed in perspective, reducing from 21 metres wide at the base to 13 at the top, to look more imposing from below. They run from the grand 19th century buildings of **Primorsky Bulvar** (Primorsky Boulevard) to the now-busy road of **ulitsa Suvorova** along the seafront. If you can't manage the steps, there's now an Odessa Escalator running alongside, though it's yet to feature in a movie. Odessa is about two hours by air from Moscow, or twenty-four hours by express train.

BEACH, THE
(1999, dir: Danny Boyle)
Leonardo DiCaprio, Tilda Swinton, Robert Carlyle.
● **THAILAND**

Notoriously filmed on **Phi Phi Leh Island**, near Phuket, Thailand, amid allegations of ecological vandalism when imported palms were planted to make the 'perfect' beach even more perfect. DiCaprio's naïve traveller sets out to find the fabled beach from the bustling backpack chaos of **Khao San Road**, downtown Bangkok. **Khao Yai National Park**, **Krabi** and **Phuket** were also used.

BEACH BLANKET BINGO
(1965, dir: William Asher)
Annette Funicello, Frankie Avalon.
● **LOS ANGELES**

This archetypal beach movie, and many others of the period, was shot at **Surfrider Beach** – the surfers' paradise, alongside Malibu Pier, and at **Zuma Beach**, Malibu, LA.

BEAST FROM TWENTY THOUSAND FATHOMS, THE
(1953, dir: Eugene Lourié)
Paul Christian, Paula Raymond, Cecil Kellaway.
● **NEW YORK CITY; LOS ANGELES**

Inspired by Ray Bradbury's short story 'The Foghorn' (about a surviving prehistoric lizard mistaking the sound of a foghorn for the mating call of another dinosaur), this monster-on-the-loose pic was animated by stop-motion genius Ray Harryhausen and directed by production designer Lourié, who designed *La Grande Illusion* and *La Regle du Jeu*, among many others, for Jean Renoir. Made quickly and cheaply, it's set in New York, but filmed mostly in the studio in Hollywood. The real New York locations include the **Fulton Fishmarket**, where the rhedasaurus comes ashore from the East River, and **Wall Street**, Lower Manhattan. The climax, with the monster being killed at Coney Island, filmed in the Amusement Park at **Long Beach**, LA.

The dinosaur skeleton dominating the museum set is the one Cary Grant painstakingly assembled in Howard Hawks' *Bringing Up Baby*, which was discovered in an old RKO warehouse.

BEAT THE DEVIL
(1954, dir: John Huston)
Humphrey Bogart, Jennifer Jones, Gina Lollobrigida.
● **ITALY**

Campy, culty spy spoof – or, as Bogart put it, "only the phonies liked it." It filmed in the small medieval town of **Ravello**, high on a mountainside about four miles above Amalfi, south of Naples, in Campania, Italy. The ill assorted bunch of shady characters sit around bars in the **Piazza Duomo**. Bogart's villa is the **Villa Cimbrone** here. The terrace decorated with marble busts, where Bogart takes Jennifer Jones, is the Terrace of Infinity, the villa's famous Belvedere overlooking the Amalfi coast – "the most beautiful view in the world" according to Gore Vidal, who took up residence in Ravello. The villa, dating from before the 11th century, has included DH Lawrence and Greta Garbo – who famously conducted an affair with conductor Leopold Stokowski here – among its guests. And for trivia buffs, the clapper-boy on the movie was composer and lyricist-to-be Stephen Sondheim.

BEETLEJUICE
(1988, dir: Tim Burton)
Michael Keaton, Alec Baldwin, Geena Davis.
● **VERMONT**

Keaton is full-tilt hyperactive as the exorcist-in-reverse, evicting unwanted living souls from the home of newly-deads Baldwin and Davis. The dinky little town nestling in the rolling green hills, where Baldwin and Davis set up home, just has to be New England. And it is. The location is **East Corinth**, Vermont, just off highway 25 near the New Hampshire border.

BEGUILED, THE
(1971, dir: Don Siegel)
Clint Eastwood, Geraldine Page, Elizabeth Hartman.
● **LOUISIANA**

Great fun, as the priceless Geraldine Page grimly saws off injured soldier Clint Eastwood's leg, in a Confederate Ladies' school. Actually, it's the **Ashland-Belle Helene House** (also used in the Clark Gable-Yvonne de Carlo melodrama *Band of Angels*), one of the many beautiful plantation houses on the Mississippi between New Orleans and Baton Rouge, Louisiana. It's at **7497 Ashland Road**, off the River Road, about five miles north of Darrow. Bought by the Shell Oil company, it's sadly no longer open to the public.

BEING THERE
(1979, dir: Hal Ashby)
Peter Sellers, Shirley MacLaine, Melvyn Douglas.
● **NORTH CAROLINA; LOS ANGELES; WASHINGTON DC**

Downbeat, deadpan Sellers, as Chance the naïve gardener, becomes a major celeb as his tiddly little gardening homilies are taken for deep wisdom in this overlong satire.

The grand mansion: Biltmore House, Asheville, North Carolina

The Washington Mansion: Fenyes Mansion, West Walnut Street, Pasadena

The interior of the dowdy Washington house, where Chance suddenly finds himself unemployed and homeless on the death of his employer, filmed in the **Fenyes Mansion, 470 West Walnut Street, Pasadena**, northeast of LA. You can visit the house – it's the headquarters of the Pasadena Historical Society.

After wandering the streets of Washington DC, the grandiose mansion he finds himself guest in after a minor accident is **Biltmore House** on the Biltmore Estate, **Asheville**, western North Carolina (*open to the public, website at www.biltmore.com*). The Biltmore House is a 255-room French Renaissance-style chateau built in the 1890s for the Vanderbilts. It was designed by Richard Hunt Morris, whose other claim to fame on the design front is the plinth for the Statue of Liberty. The grounds were landscaped by Edward Law Olmos, who also landscaped New York's Central Park. The house contains the Vanderbilt's collection of paintings and it's open to the public. It's on Route 25, three blocks north from Route 40. More interiors were shot in the **Craven Estate, 430 Madeline Avenue**, west of Orange Grove Boulevard, Pasadena (see *Enemy of the State* for details).

BELL, BOOK AND CANDLE
(1958, dir: Richard Quine)
James Stewart, Kim Novak, Jack Lemmon.
● NEW YORK CITY

Adaptation of John Van Druten's stage comedy with James Stewart as a NY publisher slowly coming to the conclusion that girlfriend Novak and her weird family are witches. Set largely in a studio-reconstruction of Greenwich Village. Stewart and Novak are magically transported to the roof of the **Flatiron Building, 175 Fifth Avenue**, the oddly-shaped skyscraper occupying the trian-

The big clinch: Flatiron Building, Fifth Avenue

gular block where Broadway crosses East 23rd Street. Built in 1902, it was, in its day, the tallest building in the world.

BELLBOY, THE
(1960, dir: Jerry Lewis)
Jerry Lewis, Alex Gerry, Bob Clayton.
● MIAMI, FLORIDA

Jerry Lewis, who wrote and directed, is, well, a bellboy who is, well, clumsy. Filmed at Miami's Fontainbleu Hotel (also seen in *Goldfinger* and *The Bodyguard*) – now the **Fontainbleau Hilton Resort and Spa, 4441 Collins Avenue**, Miami Beach.

BELLE DE JOUR
(1967, dir: Luis Buñuel)
Catherine Deneuve, Michel Piccoli, Genevieve Page.
● PARIS

Buñuel supposedly hated Joseph Kessel's novel about a bored, masochistic wife of a wealthy Parisian surgeon who spends her afternoons working in a brothel, but nevertheless turned it into a surreal masterpiece. The elegant café terrace, where Catherine Deneuve is picked up for the Duc's incestuously necrophilic fantasy, is the **Chalet de la Grande Cascade** by the Second Empire artificial waterfall near the Longchamp Crossroads in the **Bois de Boulogne**. It's a very glitzy restaurant, and if you don't have a car it's quite a schlep (*metro: Ranelagh*) along Route de l'Hippodrome. Behind Deneuve on the restaurant terrace you can see Buñuel talking business with Robert and Raymond Hakim – producers of the movie. And it's their office, with the movie stills outside, where Pierre Clementi robs a deliveryman in the lift. The building, since gutted and turned into an Italian restaurant, can be seen at **79 Champs Elysées**.

Madame Anais', the classy brothel where ice-cool Deneuve confronts a bizarre spectrum of sexualities, is at **1 square Albin-Cachot**, a tiny cul-de-sac south of rue Leon Maurice Nordmann between rue de la Sante and rue de la Glacière (*metro: Glacière*).

Deneuve meets the necrophile: Chalet de la Grande Cascade, Bois de Boulogne

BELLE ET LA BÊTE, LA (aka *Beauty and the Beast*)
(1946, dir: Jean Cocteau)
Jean Marais, Josette Day, Mila Parely.
● FRANCE

Cocteau's surreal and visually dazzling version of the old fairy tale. The merchant's house is **Rochecorbon**, a tiny manor built below the level of the road at Tours. Don't confuse this with Roche Courbon Chateau, between La Rochelle and saintes in the Poitou-Charentes area, which is famed – confusingly – as the 'Sleeping Beauty' castle. The Beast's castle is the 17th century **Chateau Raray** in Picardy, about six miles northeast of Senlis. It's not open to the public, but any interior could only be a disappointment after seeing Cocteau's imaginative anthropomorphic architecture, though you can view the exterior.

BELLY OF AN ARCHITECT, THE

(1987, dir: Peter Greenaway)
Brian Dennehy, Chloe Webb, Serge Fantoni.
● ROME

Greenaway's beautifully filmed puzzle links architecture, pregnancy and stomach ailments. Architect Dennehy is first seen at **Ventimiglia** station, the

The picnic: baths of the Villa Adriana, Tivoli

crossing point from France into Italy on the south coast, ten miles east of Monte Carlo, but from here on, Greenaway sets the action against the classical buildings of Rome. Dennehy's apartment overlooks the **Tomb of Augustus**, in the piazza Augusto, east of the via del Corso. He works in the **Victor Emanuel Building**

Vittorio Emanuele Building, Piazza Venetia

on the piazza Venezia; stops to write a postcard to deceased architect Boulée on Mussolini's **Foro Italico**; and writes another in the **piazza del Popolo** at the north end of via del Corso.

The picnic, with the vomit-eating doggie, is at the baths of the **Villa Adriana**, Hadrian's villa in Tivoli, fifteen miles east of Rome. He writes another postcard in **St Peter's Square**, Vatican City. The weirdo collecting the noses from statues is in the **Forum** overlooking the Foro Traiano on the eastern side of the piazza Venezia. Dennehy photographs the belly of a Bernini nude in the **piazza Navona** – site of Emperor Domitian's racecourse. Statues are being restored in Mussolini's **Foro Italico Stadium**. The dying Dennehy gets roaring drunk before the floodlit **Pantheon** in the piazza della Rotonda.

BEN HUR

(1926, dir: Fred Niblo)
Ramon Novarro, Francis X Bushman, Carmel Myers.
● ITALY

Much troubled epic filming of General Lew Wallace's religiose tome, which began filming in Egypt – though none of the Egyptian footage was eventually used – but decamped to Italy. The impressive sea battle filmed off **Livorno** on Italy's northeastern coast.

BEN HUR

(1959, dir: William Wyler, Andrew Marton)
Charlton Heston, Stephen Boyd, Jack Hawkins.
● ITALY

Elephantine remake of the 1926 epic, filmed at Rome's enormous Cinecittà Studios, where the stupendous chariot race was shot by second unit director Marton. The gigantic Circus, modelled on the circus at Antioch, was cut out of a huge rock quarry and filled with 40,000 tons of white sand, imported from Mediterranean beaches. Full-sized galleys were floated on a titanic man-made lake. So who says size isn't important? The film took a record eleven Oscars, and gave birth to a wonderfully entertaining feud between star Heston and writer Gore Vidal, who claims he added a homosexual subtext to the script, which Heston denies. Watch the movie.

The Nazareth scenes were shot in **Fiuggi**, famous as a spa town since the 11th century, 50 miles east of Rome. Hur's camel journey from the galleys back to Judea, was shot at **Nettuno**, famed for its Medieval town walls, on the coast 30 miles south of Rome. The oasis, where he meets up with Scot Finlay Currie and Welsh sheik Hugh Griffith, is **Folliano**. The valley of lepers, where Hur's mother and sister serve out their time, is a rock quarry in Rome.

BÊTE HUMAINE, LA (aka *Judas Was a Woman*)

(1938, dir: Jean Renoir)
Jean Gabin, Simone Simon, Fernand Ledoux.
● PARIS

Melodramatic filming of Emil Zola's novel, with Gabin as the doomed train driver plotting with *femme fatale* Simon to murder her station-master husband. Gabin's engine breaks

Jean Gabin plans murder: Gare St Lazare, rue St Lazare

down at **Le Havre Station**, where there was much location filming. A section of Simone's apartment was built on a raised platform in the railroad yard at Le Havre to allow views of the sidings from the window. Similarly, Gabin's Paris apartment overlooks the exit of the enormous **Gare St-Lazare**, the third largest railway station in the world, rue St Lazare. The rail journey filmed was from Evreux to Le Havre. The village where Gabin stops off to see his godmother, is **Breaute-Beuzeville** in Normandie

BEVERLY HILLS COP

(1984, dir: Martin Brest)
Eddie Murphy, Judge Reinhold, Steven Berkoff.
● DETROIT, MICHIGAN; LOS ANGELES

Eddie Murphy's first outing as Axel Foley helps out the Motortown economy by writing off any number of cars in the opening chase through picturesque Detroit. Once in Beverly Hills we get the establishing tourist shots of the **Beverly Hills Hotel** and **Rodeo Drive**, before Murphy bullshits his way into the fictional Beverly Palms Hotel,

The shootout at the restaurant: Acapulco, North La Cienega Boulevard

Upmarket cop shop: City Hall, Beverly Hills

The Beverly Palms Hotel: Biltmore Hotel, South Grand Avenue, LA

Robbery at the jewellers: North Highland Avenue, Hollywood

supposedly on Wilshire Boulevard, in actuality the 700-room **Biltmore Hotel, 506 South Grand Avenue**, a smart Spanish-Italian Renaissance landmark, not in Beverly Hills at all but downtown LA. Built in 1923, it's been a frequent movie location over the years, from *The Sting* to *Independence Day*. It hosted the Oscars, too, during the thirties. Murphy pulls off the banana-in-the-exhaust-pipe gag opposite the Biltmore, on **Pershing Square**. Being Beverly Hills, the cop station is no ordinary precinct, but the splendid 1932 Spanish-Baroque **Beverly Hills City Hall, North Crescent Drive** at Santa Monica Boulevard. The exclusive club, in which Murphy embarrasses Steven Berkoff, is the **Athenaeum**, the dining club of the California Institute of Technology, at **551 South Hill Avenue** in Pasadena.

BEVERLY HILLS COP II

(1987, dir: Tony Scott)
Eddie Murphy, Judge Reinhold, Ronny Cox.
● **LOS ANGELES**

Axel Foley hares back to LA when police chief Bogomil is gunned down. Police HQ, once again, is ostensibly **Beverly Hills City Hall**, and the establishing long shots certainly are. But look carefully. When Ronny Cox drives away, it's a different building altogether. All the scenes involving actors, and which therefore require expensive film permits, feature **Pasadena City Hall, 100 North Garfield Avenue**

The upmarket cop shop changes: City Hall, Pasadena

Eddie Murphy's classy squat: Walden Drive, Beverly Hills

at Holly Street, Pasadena. LA's eastern suburb is significantly cheaper to film in than swanky Beverly Hills. Its city hall is smaller, but even more extravagant, than the Beverly Hills counterpart. Unfortunately, it looks nothing like the Beverly Hills building.

The jewellery store robbed by Brigitte Nielsen was once the magnificently kitsch Max Factor Museum (see the incredible Beauty Calibrator!), now sadly closed. The pink granite deco building stands at **1666 North Highland Avenue** just off Hollywood Boulevard. You can see the 'nodding donkey' oil wells, where Bogomil is tailed, at **Baldwin Hills** on La Cienega Boulevard, southeast of Culver City. The house undergoing renovation, where 'Beverly Hills Building Investigator' Foley squats for the duration of the movie, is not 1603 Hillcrest Road, it's **614 Walden Drive**, which runs north from Santa Monica Boulevard to Lomitas Avenue, east of Los Angeles Country Club – and it is really in Beverly Hills. The shoot-out restaurant where Taggart passes himself off as Gerald Ford, however, is not. At the time it was French restaurant 385 North, but it's now Mexican restaurant **Acapulco, 385 North La Cienega Boulevard** in Hollywood. The Beverly Hills Gun Club is once again the **California Institute of Technology's Athenaeum Club** (see *Beverly Hills Cop*). The concrete mixer chase does end at a real enough location: the bunnyman's warren, Hugh Hefner's **Playboy Mansion, 10236 Charing Cross Road** off Mapleton Drive, running between the western reaches of Sunset Boulevard and Los Angeles Country Club.

BEVERLY HILLS COP III

(1994, dir: John Landis)
Eddie Murphy, Judge Reinhold, Theresa Randle.
● **CALIFORNIA**

John Landis takes the helm for the second sequel, disowned by virtually everyone involved as a big mistake. It has all the Landis trademarks: sprawling self-indulgence, great set pieces and oodles of cameos. Once again, the cop shop is **Beverly Hills City Hall.** The Wonderworld amusement park is Paramount's 100 acre theme park, the **Great America Amusement Park, Great America Parkway, Santa Clara**, in the South Bay area south of San Francisco. The Alien Attack ride, however, is the Earthquake attraction on the Universal Studio Tour, **Universal Studios, 100 Universal City Plaza** just off the Hollywood Freeway (*℡ 818.508.9600*). The 'Private Security Agents Convention', where camp gallery owner Bronson Pinchot, from the first film, turns up selling the Annihilator 2000, shot in a location which also featured in *Beverly Hills Cop*. It's the **Biltmore Hotel**, which featured as the Beverly Palms in the earlier film. The suspect truck, which turns out to be empty, is discovered by **Santa Monica Pier**. The snooty bar where Murphy is recognised as Uncle Dave's shooter, is on **Rodeo Drive**, with the Regent Beverly Wilshire Hotel in the background.

BIG

(1988, dir: Penny Marshall)
Tom Hanks, Elizabeth Perkins, Robert Loggia.
● **NEW YORK CITY; NEW YORK STATE; NEW JERSEY**

The toyshop: FAO Schwarz, Fifth Avenue

Best of the body-swap movies which surfaced at the same time, originally for Robert De Niro, though the boy-man Josh now seems the part Tom Hanks was born to play. Young Josh's home is over the Hudson River from Manhattan, in New Jersey at **Cliffside Park**. At the fair here, beneath the **George Washington Bridge**, he gets his wish to be big granted and promptly relocates to central Manhattan, fetching up in standard sleazy **Times Square**. Also in Manhattan is the toyshop, where the grown-up Josh gets to dance on the fab giant keyboard, **FAO Schwarz, 745 Fifth Avenue** at 58th Street. The deserted funfair, where he finally gets to reverse the growing-up process, is **Playland**, an amusement park at **Rye**, on the banks of Long Island Sound, New York State, west of Yonkers on Highway 95.

BIG BLUE, THE

(1988, dir: Luc Besson)
Rosanna Arquette, Jean-Marc Barr, Jean Reno.
● **FRANCE; ITALY; CORSICA; THE VIRGIN ISLANDS; NEW YORK CITY; GREECE; PERU**

Luc Besson's beautiful, but pretentious, underwater movie was filmed in several locations, including Corsica; Paris; New York City; the Virgin Islands; Peru; and in the Alps. Diving scenes were shot at **Taormina** on the east coast of Sicily. The aquarium is **Marineland** in **Antibes** on the French Riviera. The stranded boat is on **Amorgos**, one of the Greek Cyclades Islands, where there was filming at **Le Grand Bleu** bar, naturally, and also on **Manganari**, an out of the way Greek island, where Luc Besson spent some of his childhood, and which inspired the film.

BIG BUSINESS

(1929, dir: James W Horne)
Stan Laurel, Oliver Hardy, James Finlayson.
● **LOS ANGELES**

The Laurel and Hardy movie in which they try to flog a Christmas tree to grouchy foil Finlayson and end up dismantling his home. The house they used is still there at

10282 Dunleer Drive between Rancho Park and the Santa Monica Freeway, West LA.

BIG CHILL, THE

(1983, dir: Lawrence Kasdan)
Kevin Kline, William Hurt, Glenn Close.
● **SOUTH CAROLINA**

Kevin Costner, who's suicide brings together a bunch of erstwhile sixties students, ended up being cut from the movie. Kevin Kline's smart white mansion, where everyone gathers for the wake and to rake over old ashes, is **Tidalholm, 1 Laurens Street, Beaufort** on the coast of South Carolina. A private house, not open to the public, Tidalholm was built in 1853 for cotton merchant Edgar Fripp, and is one of many mansions in the area reflecting the wealth made by Sea Island cotton.

BIG EASY, THE

(1987, dir: Jim McBride)
Dennis Quaid, Ellen Barkin, Ned Beatty.
● **NEW ORLEANS, LOUISIANA**

Ellen Barkin hates Dennis Quaid so much that you just know they're going to end up together while investigating corruption in a touristy New Orleans.

A body is discovered in the fountain of the **Piazza d'Italia** on **Poydras Street**, near Tchoupitoulas Street, one of several 'European' – French, Spanish, British – themed piazzas in the area. Quaid takes Barkin to a recreation of the famous Tipitina's, a music joint and local institution. Visit the real thing at 501 Napoleon Avenue. Ellen Barkin, obviously doing pretty well for herself, later receives a phone call at **Antoine's**, a very expensive French-Creole restaurant – and the oldest eatery in the US under continuous family ownership – at **713 St Louis Street** in the French Quarter.

BIG LEBOWSKI, THE

(1998, dir: Joel Coen)
Jeff Bridges, John Goodman, Steve Buscemi.
● **LOS ANGELES**

The vaguely retro bowling alley, where John Goodman and Buscemi hang out in the Coens' goofball spin on *The Big Sleep*, is **Hollywood Star Lanes, 5227 Santa Monica Boulevard**, Hollywood.

If there's a Beverly Hills mansion featured in a Hollywood movie, chances are it will have been filmed in the eastern suburb of Pasadena, which is packed to bursting

The bowling alley: Hollywood Star Lanes, Santa Monica Boulevard, Hollywood

with lavish estates but charges only a fraction of the rate for film permits. Perversely, *The Big Lebowski*'s Pasadena mansion is a conflation of two Beverly Hills estates. The exteriors are a grand estate on Charing Cross Road, just northwest of Los Angeles Country Club. The interiors are the **Greystone Mansion, 905 Loma Vista Drive**. The mansion, and its expansive landscaped grounds, are a frequently used location. See *The Loved One* for details. Julianne Moore's artist's loft is above the Palace Theater, at **630 South Broadway**, downtown LA. Bridges and Goodman discuss the possible provenance of Bunny's toe at **Johnie's, 6101 Wilshire Boulevard** at Fairfax Avenue, opposite the huge golden cylinder of the old May & Co department store. The café, where the German nihilists drink with the toeless woman, is **Dinah's, 6521 South Sepulveda, Culver City**. The final scattering of ashes is on a bluff at **Palos Verdes**, south of LA.

BIG SLEEP, THE

(1946, dir: Howard Hawks)
Humphrey Bogart, Lauren Bacall, Elisha Cook Jr.
● **LOS ANGELES**

General Sternwood hires Philip Marlowe to protect his wild daughter in the classic noir treatment of Raymond Chandler's novel. Filmed entirely in the studio, but many locales are based on real locations. Marlowe's Cahuenga Building was the Guaranty Building, now the Bank of America, 6331 Hollywood Boulevard, down the road from Mann's Theater. Geiger's shifty bookshop is actually Book Treasury, 6707 Hollywood Boulevard, and the apartment at which Joe Brody is murdered is on the corner of Palmerston Place and Kenmore near Franklin Avenue.

BILL & TED'S EXCELLENT ADVENTURE

(1989, dir: Stephen Herek)
Keanu Reeves, Alex Winter, George Carlin.
● **ARIZONA**

Likeably dorky fun with the Valley Boys zizzing about in time for a school history project. And for once, it's somewhere else pretending to be California. San Dimas (east of LA) was in reality filmed in Arizona, at **Phoenix** and **Scottsdale**, plus **Cococino National Forest**, around Flagstaff. For the sequel, *Bill & Ted's Bogus Journey* (originally intended to be *Bill & Ted Go to Hell*), the locale becomes a real LA suburb, **Northridge** in the San Fernando Valley. The spectacular landscape where B&T come face to face with Death is **Vasquez Rocks County Park, Escondido Road**, northeast of Newhall (see *Apache* for details).

BILLION DOLLAR BRAIN

(1967, dir: Ken Russell)
Michael Caine, Oscar Homolka, Francoise Dorleac.
● **LONDON; FINLAND**

Third of the Harry Palmer films has the seedy agent delivering a flask full of eggs to a European destination and becoming involved with a Right-wing American loony's plan for world domination. Director Russell, in his second feature, can't resist turning the climax into a pastiche of the battle on the ice from Eisenstein's *Alexander Nevsky*.

Harry Palmer's dingy digs, over the surgical appliance shop, are at **297 Pentonville Road** at the junction with Gray's Inn Road opposite Kings Cross Station, N1 (*tube: Kings Cross*). He views the contents of the flask with the aid of a pedoscope (remember those foot X-ray machines that every upmarket shoe shop once had?) at **Whiteley's** in Queensway, W2, the Bayswater mega-department store recently given a new lease

Harry Palmer's squalid digs: Pentonville Road, Kings Cross

of life with a major overhaul (*tube: Bayswater*). His Finnish assignment takes him to the capital, **Helsinki**, and 85 miles west at the frozen Baltic port of **Turku**. The Texan scenes were shot in the studio in England.

BILLY LIAR

(1963, dir: John Schlesinger)
Tom Courtenay, Julie Christie, Wilfred Pickles.
● **YORKSHIRE; LONDON**

When the New Wave of the sixties shifted the focus of British cinema from the middle class Home Counties to the working class inner cities, it wasn't all grim up north. Schlesinger incorporated fantasy sequences and broad satire into this adaptation of Keith Waterhouse and Willis Hall's play about an undertaker's clerk who lives a rich fantasy life but ultimately blows his chance of real escape with swinging free spirit Julie Christie. Filmed mainly around Bradford, where Tom Courtenay clowns about on the city's war memorial on **Prince's Way** (shockingly disrespectful, less than twenty years after the end of WWII). The shop which served as the undertakers where Billy works can be found nearby, at the foot of the steps on **Southgate**, off Sunbridge Road. The pompous Victorian pretender he walks in, with one of his two fiancées, can be found northeast of the city centre. The grimy monuments of **Undercliffe Cemetery** overlook Bradford, on **Undercliffe Lane,**

The undertaker's: Southgate, central Bradford

Billy and his girlfriend: Undercliffe Cemetery, Bradford

Acting up in the city centre: War Memorial, Princes Way, Bradford

Billy's house: Hinchcliffe Avenue, Baildon

Billy chickens out at Bradford Central: Marylebone Station, London

off Otley Road. Although he appears to walk to the city centre in a couple of minutes, Billy's home is in one of the nicer suburbs, about four miles north of the city, at **37 Hinch-cliffe Avenue, Baildon**, north of Shipley (*rail: Baildon*).

The dance hall, where Billy's romantic entanglements catch up with him, was the old Locarno, now gone, which stood on Manningham Lane. Billy's review of the victorious troops in the fantasy realm of 'Ambrosia' filmed at **Leeds Town Hall**. Look out for director Schlesinger, in a characteristic Hitchcock-style cameo, as a Russian officer in one of the fantasy sequences. The final scene, set on Central Station, Bradford, with Christie leaving for the Big City, was shot in the capital itself, ironically, on London's **Marylebone Station**.

BILLY THE KID
(1941, dir: David Miller)
Robert Taylor, Brian Donlevy, Ian Hunter.
● ARIZONA

The ever-wooden Spangler Arlington Brugh (a wise name change to Robert Taylor, I think) takes over as Billy the Hero in this remake filmed in **Monument Valley** and at **Sedona**, Arizona. This was the first time the great red mesas and buttes of the spectacular valley were glimpsed in glorious Technicolor. See *Stagecoach* for further details of Monument Valley.

BIRDCAGE, THE
(1996, dir: Mike Nichols)
Robin Williams, Nathan Lane, Gene Hackman.
● FLORIDA

The Birdcage Club: Carlyle Hotel, Ocean Drive, Miami Beach

This Hollywood remake of the seventies French farce *La Cage Aux Folles* uses the plot as a blunt instrument to clobber the hypocritical mores of the sup-

posed Moral Majority. Robin Williams is incredibly restrained as the butch half of a gay partnership while Nathan Lane whoops and squeals as the undisguisable queen. Worth seeing for the sight of Gene Hackman in drag alone. The locale is moved from the South of France to the wonderful Art Deco district of South Miami Beach. The Birdcage Club is actually the splendid **Carlyle Hotel, 1250 Ocean Drive** at 13th Street (© *305.532.5315*).

BIRDMAN OF ALCATRAZ
(1962, dir: John Frankenheimer)
Burt Lancaster, Karl Malden, Thelma Ritter.
● CALIFORNIA

The Federal Bureau of Prisons was not best pleased with the idea of filming the story of Robert Stroud, and offered no cooperation, so Leavenworth (where Stroud was

Longtime home of the Birdman: Alcatraz Island

originally imprisoned) and Alcatraz were constructed on studio backlot. Strangely, the original director was the veteran of Ealing comedies, Charles Crichton, who made a belated comeback with *A Fish Called Wanda*, but he left after just three weeks of work.

The real **Alcatraz Island**, which once housed 'Machine Gun' Kelly and Al Capone, is seen in a long shot from San Francisco Bay. See *Escape From Alcatraz*, which did film at the real lcation, for details on visiting the national monument.

BIRDS, THE
(1963, dir: Alfred Hitchcock)
Tippi Hedren, Rod Taylor, Suzanne Pleshette.
● CALIFORNIA

Hitchcock's film of the Daphne du Maurier short story (originally set in Cornwall) uses lots of process shots, but as usual he plays fair with the geography. Tippi Hedren is first seen in San Francisco's **Union Square**, heading to the pet shop – where Hitch puts in his cameo with a pair of fluffy dogs. Notice the crafty edit here, covered by the news-stand flashing by the camera, from the real San Fran

The attack on the school: Bodega Lane, Bodega

Sheltering from the bird attacks: the Tides Hotel, Bodega Bay

cisco to the pet shop, which was a set at Universal studios in Hollywood.

Rod Taylor drives north up the California coast to **Bodega Bay**, centre of the bird attacks. Bodega Bay, once a small fishing village on the coast 50 miles north of San Francisco, really is a centre for bird migration, and the air can be disconcertingly thick with squawking and chattering. It's a great place for birdwatching, and even amateurs can check out the different species on a chart at the tourist office. The Tides Restaurant, in which the assorted locals shelter from the bird attacks, has expanded into an unrecognisable hotel complex. The big surprise is that there is no town. No post office, no gas station, little more than a cluster of holiday accommodation. The aerial view of Bodega Bay is largely a painting. In fact, many of the Bodega Bay scenes, including the post office itself, were shot on a set back at the Universal lot, where Hitchcock felt more in control of the elements.

A few miles inland is the quaint village of **Bodega**, where you can see Suzanne Pleshette's schoolhouse, at **17110 Bodega Lane**, which, in the movie, appears to be just up the hill from the bay. The house was originally a schoolhouse, a local community centre and for a while a guest house. It's now a private residence.

BIRDY

(1984, dir: Alan Parker)
Matthew Modine, Nicolas Cage, John Harkins.
● PHILADELPHIA, PENNSYLVANIA; CALIFORNIA; NEW JERSEY

Much friendlier birds here. Modine is a traumatised war vet who's retreated into silence, Cage his physically damaged friend. Set in Philadelphia, which certainly provides the city backdrops, much of the movie was filmed around northern California. The hospital in which Modine is incarcerated is **Agnew's State Hospital** at **Santa Clara**, just south of San Francisco (the sets were built here). The elevated railway, where Cage and Modine clamber among the girders to catch pigeons, is **46th Street Station** at the corner of Market Street and 46th Street to the west of the city. The pair take a renovated '53 Ford to the coast, but Atlantic City, where the scene is set, has been extensively redeveloped. The fairground scenes actually filmed 30 miles to the south of Philly at **Wildwood** on the Jersey coast. The Atlantic City jail, where they end up, is a wing of the women's prison at Philadelphia's House of Correction. The statue of William Penn can be seen atop the

rather overblown **Philadelphia City Hall, Penn Square** at Broad and Market Streets.

BIRTH OF A NATION, THE

(1915, dir: DW Griffith)
Henry B Walthall, Mae Marsh, Miriam Cooper.
● LOS ANGELES

Griffith's Civil War epic and hymn of praise to the Ku Klux Klan was filmed around LA long before Hollywood became the centre of the film industry. The 'Battle of Petersburg' was staged north of the city in LA's San Fernando Valley. Much of the location shooting took place around the area now occupied by Forest Lawn Hollywood Hills Cemetery, the last resting place of Charles Laughton, George Raft, Stan Laurel, Buster Keaton and Liberace, **6300 Forest Lawn Drive** in Burbank.

BLACK NARCISSUS

(1947, dir: Michael Powell, Emeric Pressburger)
Deborah Kerr, Kathleen Byron, David Farrar.
● SUSSEX

Director Powell turns this unlikely melodrama, about a group of nuns attempting to set up a convent in the Himalayas, into a bizarrely beautiful experience. Amazingly, the far eastern locations were created almost entirely in the studio at Pinewood, while the jungle scenes filmed in deepest Sussex. The lush forest was shot at **Leonardslee Gardens**, one of the largest woodland gardens in the UK, planted with exotic blooms. It's about four miles from Horsham in Sussex (*rail: Horsham Station*), and is open from the beginning of April to the end of October (*© 01403.891212, admission charge*).

BLACK RAIN

(1989, dir: Ridley Scott)
Michael Douglas, Andy Garcia, Ken Takakura.
● OSAKA, JAPAN; NEW YORK CITY; CALIFORNIA

The seething, industrial city of Osaka is a gift to the man who directed *Blade Runner*, as semi-sleazy NY cop Douglas tracks a Yakuza-style mobster to Japan. Scott gets much the same feeling of a polluted Oriental urban nightmare blasted by banks of neon. Osaka is home to several enormous underground shopping malls, and the extravagant mall with pretensions to being a cathedral where Andy Garcia unwisely responds to the taunting of a sinister biker, is the **Hankyu Umeda Mall**, near to Umeda and Osaka Stations.

The sinister underground mall: Hankyu Umeda Mall, Osaka

The house of the mob chief isn't a Japanese location at all, but at Los Feliz in the heart of LA. Previously featured as Harrison Ford's apartment block in *Blade Runner*, it is Frank Lloyd Wright's **Ennis-Brown House, 2607 Glendower Avenue**, a concrete Mayan temple-style home on the slopes below the Griffith Park Observatory. For details of this much-filmed landmark, see *The House on*

Haunted Hill. The climactic motorbike chase sequence also filmed back in California, when the money for Japanese filming ran out. It was shot in the **Napa Valley** region of Northern California.

BLACKMAIL

(1929, dir: Alfred Hitchcock)
Anny Ondra, Donald Calthrop, John Longden.
● **LONDON**

The climactic chase: drinking fountain at the British Museum

Hitchcock's first talkie (it started out as a silent), with Anny Ondra killing her assailant after fighting off an attempted rape. The climactic chase takes place in the **British Museum**, mocked up in the studio with huge photographs of the galleries, though the exterior is real enough.

BLADE

(1998, dir: Stephen Norrington)
Wesley Snipes, Stephen Dorff, N'Bushe Wright.
● **LOS ANGELES; BRITISH COLUMBIA**

N'Bushe Wright's apartment: Chester Williams Building, Fifth Street

The Pearl vampire club: South Broadway at 8th Street

The hospital: South Broadway, downtown LA

Blood-drenched cartoon strip, filmed with bags of style and energy on some spectacular sets and downtown LA locations. The interior of the hospital, where N'-Bushe Wright is attacked by the crispy fried vampire, and from which Snipes makes a flying escape, is a disused facility in Boyle Heights, but the exterior is the elaborate white terracotta building at **610 South Broadway**, coincidentally one of the buildings Harold Lloyd dangled from in *Safety Last*. Wright's apartment is the **Chester Williams Building, 215 Fifth Street**, directly opposite John Doe's apartment from *Se7en*. The Pearl vampire club is a dressed-up shop front on **South Broadway** at the northwest corner of 8th Street, just opposite the ornate Tower Theater at 802. Studio filming was in Vancouver

BLADE RUNNER

(1982, dir: Ridley Scott)
Harrison Ford, Rutger Hauer, Sean Young.
● **LOS ANGELES**

Somehow, Ridley Scott's film of Philip K Dick's novel *Do Androids Dream of Electric Sheep?* has mutated in critical opinion from so-so spectacle to a classic of modern cinema. More to do with 20/20 hindsight than the release of the, admittedly far superior, Director's Cut which restores the equivocal unicorn while removing Harrison Ford's deliberately dirgy voiceover (he hoped it would prove unusable) and the tacked-on happy ending (which consists of some second unit footage from Stan-

The tunnel to Deckard's home: Second Street Tunnel, Figueroa Street

The futuristic police station: Union Station, Alameda Street, downtown LA

Exterior of Sebastian's home: Bradbury Building, South Broadway

Deckard confronts Batty in toymaker Sebastian's waterlogged home: Bradbury Building, South Broadway, downtown LA

Deckard's apartment building: Ennis-Brown House, Glendower Avenue, Silverlake

ley Kubrick's *The Shining*). Harrison Ford is a Blade Runner (a title taken from William Burroughs, replacing Dick's box-office killer), a tracker-down and eliminator of very human looking replicants. Rutger Hauer is the replicant in love with life.

The polluted, rainswept, Orientalised LA futurescape, which has provided the pattern for countless dystopian fantasies, is the old Warners' backlot gangster street transformed with miles of neon and acres of glass. The excellent model shots incorporate existing LA landmarks including the cylindrical towers of the Bonaventure Hotel (itself a fave LA location) at 404 South Figueroa Street, downtown LA. The cop station of the future, to which Ford is hauled, is an office set built within the vast concourse of another favourite LA location, the 1939 Spanish Revival-style **Union Station, 800 North Alameda Street**, downtown, seen in many films, including *The Way We Were*, *The Driver* and *The Replacement Killers* (which shares many of *Blade Runner*'s locations).

The waterlogged home of toymaker Sebastian, where Ford is menaced by androids and has the final showdown with Rutger Hauer, is the **Bradbury Building, 304 South Broadway** at Third Street. Outside, it's an unremarkable red-brick block, but the central courtyard, illuminated by skylights (through which the illuminated blimp is seen in the movie), is a joyous fantasy of wrought-iron grillwork, marble and brickwork surrounding open-cage elevators. It was a bit decrepit when *Blade Runner* was filmed, but it's since been lovingly restored and now houses offices. The ground floor is open to the public. The exterior of the Bradbury Building filmed at the junction of **Broadway and Third Street**, but there's plenty of set dressing so don't look for the massive pillars. The interior of the scuzzy Yukon Hotel is the **Pan Am Building, South Broadway** at Third Street, opposite the Bradbury Building, downtown LA. You may recognise it as the apartment of the comatose 'Sloth' victim in *Se7en*.

The tunnel through which Harrison Ford approaches his apartment is the **Second Street Tunnel**, running between Figueroa Street and Hill Street, downtown LA. His home turns out to be Frank Lloyd Wright's terrific **Ennis Brown House, 2607 Glendower Avenue**, Silverlake, below Griffith Park. A few storeys were added optically, and casts taken from the building's trademark concrete blocks to be used for the interior studio shots. See William Castle's classic fifties schlocker *The House on Haunted Hill* for details of the house.

BLAIR WITCH PROJECT, THE
(1999, dir: Daniel Myrick, Eduardo Sánchez)
Heather Donahue, Michael C Williams, Joshua Leonard.
● MARYLAND

The surprise smash hit of 1999 was a made-for-peanuts fake documentary, supposedly edited down from amateur footage of three student filmmakers who disappeared in the 'Black Hills Forest' near Burkittsville, Maryland, while following up a local legend about the titular witch. Filmed in **Burkittsville**, Maryland. Don't expect a warm welcome, though, if you visit. Locals are not best pleased with the attention their town has received – even booing the filmmakers out of town when they returned to discuss filming a sequel. Joshua Leonard's house is in **Wheaton**, Maryland, just north of Washington D.C.. The Black Hills Forest is **Seneca Creek State Park**, about 25 miles west of Burkittsville. The 200-year-old house featured in the film has been saved from demolition by the film's distributors. It's the **Griggs House** in **Patapsco State Park**, western Baltimore County.

BLAZING SADDLES
(1974, dir: Mel Brooks)
Cleavon Little, Gene Wilder, Harvey Korman.
● LOS ANGELES

The last really sidesplitting Mel Brooks movie, graced with a smidgeon of anti-racist sentiment. The backlot at **Warner Bros, 4000 Warner Boulevard** in Burbank gets a starring role in the climactic fight scene, ending up at **Mann's** (originally Grauman's) **Chinese Theater, 6925 Hollywood Boulevard**. The theatre opened in 1929 with the première of DeMille's *King of Kings* and you'll hardly need reminding of the 180 or so hand-, foot-, nose- and whatever-prints of the famous gracing its forecourt, the tradition begun accidentally (oh yeah), by Norma Talmadge, Mary Pickford or Douglas Fairbanks Sr, according to which version of the legend you choose to believe.

BLITHE SPIRIT
(1945, dir: David Lean)
Rex Harrison, Kay Hammond, Constance Cummings.
● BUCKINGHAMSHIRE

Noël Coward considered his play "the best thing I ever wrote", but was far from pleased with David Lean's movie version. Harrison's marriage is threatened by the appearance of the ghost of his former wife (coated in dreadful green make-up). The opened-up countryside scenes filmed near the studios around the village of Denham, on the A40, Buckinghamshire. The house is **Fairway, Denham**.

BLOB, THE
(1958, dir: Irvin S Yeaworth Jr)
Steven McQueen, Aneta Corseau, Olin Howlin.
● PENNSYLVANIA

Low budget sci-fi with carnivorous jello from space feasting on bit part players in a small town until a young (well, 28) Steven McQueen pops it in the freezer. The terrorised town is **Valley Forge**, fifteen miles west of Philadelphia, Pennsylvania, on I-76. Most of the movie interiors and exteriors were filmed in the Valley Forge Studios. Real locations include **Jerry's Supermarket** (where the Blob is played by a weather balloon – for much of the rest of the time it's a chunk of silicone wobbling about on miniature sets); the exterior of the **Colonial Theater** – the town's terrorised cinema; the doctor's office and the **Downington Diner**, scene of the movie's climax and (in 1989 at least) still the town's main tourist attraction. The not-half-bad updated remake (*The Blob*, 1988, directed by *The Mask*'s Chuck Russell), with spectacularly gloopy FX and a fine cast of character players, was filmed in **Abbeville**, on Route 14, twenty miles south of Lafayette in Lafayette County, southern Louisiana.

BLOCKHEADS
(1938, dir: John G Blystone)
Stan Laurel, Oliver Hardy, Billy Gilbert.
● LOS ANGELES

Ollie finds Stan still guarding a WWI trench twenty years after the end of the war, at an 'old soldiers' home', the Veterans Administration complex in LA. The entrance

The final chase: West 8th Street at South Westlake Avenue, downtown LA

of the complex, used for filming, has been demolished but it stood at the junction of Sawtelle Boulevard and Ohio Avenue, west of the San Diego Freeway between Westwood Village and West LA (it's also the hospital where hundred-and-something Dustin Hoffman rasped out the story of *Little Big Man*). Shotgun-wielding Billy Gilbert chases the pair down an alleyway between two buildings in the final scene. The pretty-much unchanged alleyway can still be seen between the **St Arthur Apartments, 2014 West 8th Street** and the **Westmont, 807 South Westlake Avenue**, just south of MacArthur Park in Midtown LA.

BLOOD SIMPLE
(1984, dir: Joel Coen)
John Getz, Frances McDormand, Dan Hedaya.
● TEXAS

The Coen brothers' dazzling post-noir début film was shot in the area of state capital Austin and nearby Round Rock, Texas. The movie's $1.5 million budget was raised by hawking around a three-minute trailer while younger brother and producer Ethan Coen worked as a statistical typist at Macy's.

Dan Hedaya's Neon Boots bar no longer exists. It was

the Starliner on Little Cisco Road off Braker Lane at North Lamarr in the Walnut Forest area of northeast Austin (there's now a mall on the site). The over-

Dan Hedaya hires the hitman: Mount Bonnell Park, Austin

look, where Hedaya instructs M Emmet Walsh to kill John Getz, is **Mount Bonnell Park**, above Lake Austin – not a lake at all but a stretch of the Colorado River – on Mount Bonnell Road at the western end of 35th Street, Austin, behind Camp Mabry National Guard Installation. Walsh traces the illicit lovers to the **Heart Of Texas Motel, 5303 W Highway 290**, (*© 512.892.0644*) down in southwest Austin near Oak Hill on Route 71/290, the Fredericksburg Road.

Hutto is a little town, population 659, about twenty miles northeast of Austin on Route 79 and it's two miles south of Hutto on **Farm Road 1660** you can find the ploughed field where the victim of the botched murder is buried. The darkroom where Walsh burns the incriminating photos is the **Old Grove Drug Building** on **Sixth Street**, Austin. Also on Sixth Street, above a restaurant, is the apartment building McDormand moves into, which is the scene of the bloody climax.

BLOW OUT
(1981, dir: Brian De Palma)
John Travolta, Nancy Allen, John Lithgow.
● PHILADELPHIA, PENNSYLVANIA

This aural version of Antonioni's *Blowup*, with Travolta as a movie sound engineer who captures the suspicious death of a state governor on tape, was filmed around De Palma's home town, Philadelphia. The car 'accident' is on **Wissahickon Bridge** over **Wissahickon Creek** southwest of Philadelphia. Travolta meets Nancy Allen at **30th Street Station, 30th Street** just over the Schuylkill River (site of the murder in *Witness*), and it's here that John Lithgow garrots a prostitute and later stalks Allen. From the 30th Street Subway, Lithgow and Allen take the Franklin Bridge Express to **Penn's Landing** on the Delaware River. Following in his jeep, Travolta careers through the central plaza of **Philadelphia City Hall, Penn Square** at Broad Street, before crashing into the window display at **Wanamaker's Department Store, Market and 13th Streets** (the department store also used in *Mannequin*). Travolta finally catches up with Lithgow and Allen, too late, atop the **Port of History Building** at Penn's Landing.

BLOWUP
(1966, dir: Michelangelo Antonioni)
David Hemmings, Vanessa Redgrave, Sarah Miles.
● LONDON

And the real thing, Antonioni's landmark mystery, with photographer Hemmings (a role earmarked for Terence Stamp) accidentally capturing something suspicious on film. The eerie park where Hemmings may or may not have photographed something is **Maryon Park**, south of Woolwich Road, SE7 (*rail: Woolwich Dockyard*). Antonioni notoriously manipulated reality to achieve his visual effects, painting paths black and grass green. The bushes, where the 'body' was hidden,

Steps up to the mysterious site: Maryon Park

David Hemmings' studio, exterior: Pottery Lane, Holland Park

David Hemmings' studio, interior: Princedale Road, Holland Park

were added, and houses overlooking the park were false flats. The tennis court, where students mimed the surreal tennis match in the park, is still there, unchanged. The antique shop (it was a grocery store) was in Clevely Close, at the park's northeast corner. It's since been demolished and the corner redeveloped.

David Hemmings' studio scenes filmed in the studio of John Cowans, **49 Princes Places**, off Princedale Road, Notting Hill, although the exterior is nearby **77 Pottery Lane**, W11, next to the Earl of Zetland pub, north of Holland Park Avenue (*tube: Holland Park*)

BLUE HAWAII

(1961, dir: Norman Taurog)
Elvis Presley, Joan Blackman, Nancy Walters.
● **HAWAII**

The Elvis of the movie years rarely ventured beyond the soundstage, so there aren't too many Presley locations, but he could always be tempted out to Hawaii, where this story of a GI turned beachcomber was shot. Featured is the **Coco Palms Resort, 241 Kuhio Highway, Kapaa** (*tel: 808.822.4921*), which opened in 1953, on Coconut Coast, on the east of the island of Kauai between Lihue and Anahola, and the **Hanauma Bay Beach Park** on the southeastern point of Oahu.

BLUE LAGOON, THE

(1949, dir: Frank Launder)
Jean Simmons, Donald Houston, Noel Purcell.
● **FIJI**

H de Vere Stacpole's novel about two shipwrecked children growing up on a desert island and discovering (discreet) sex, was shot half in the studio at Pinewood and half on an island north of **Vitu Levu**, the main island of the Fiji archipelago. The 1980 Hollywood remake, replacing the Britishly chaste Simmons and Houston with Brooke Shields and Christopher Atkins, was photographed by veteran cinematographer Nestor Almendros, seemingly under the impression it was some contribution to the art of cinema, again in Fiji, on the deserted island of **Nanuya Levu**.

BLUE LAMP, THE

(1949, dir: Basil Dearden)
Jack Warner, Jimmy Hanley, Dirk Bogarde.
● **LONDON**

Hanley is the idealistic young police officer, and Warner

his older mentor, PC Dixon, gunned down by young hoodlum Bogarde, only to rise from the dead for a long-running TV series. *The Blue Lamp* was one of the first British movies to move out onto the streets for much of its filming, around Ladbroke Grove, Paddington Green and Edgware Road.

Dixon's beat: Westbourne Terrace Road Bridge, Little Venice

Site of Bogarde's hideout: Lord Hills Road, W9

Many of the West London locations have now gone, including the old Harrow Road Police Station out of which Dixon works, although the Blue Lamp of the title has been retained and you can see it still hanging outside the new station on Harrow Road, W9. The bridge, where Dixon passes the time with a little improvised verse, can still be seen in Little Venice, the **Westbourne Terrace Road Bridge** over the Grand Union Canal. Bogarde's hideout has been demolished but the site is still recognisable on **Lord Hills Road** at the Canal in W9.

The Metropolitan Theatre, where Bogarde establishes his alibi by ostensibly watching Tessie O'Shea's act, closed in 1962 and has been demolished. It stood at 267 Edgware Road. The Coliseum Cinema where Dixon gets shot has also been demolished – the site is now occupied by council buildings. The climactic car chase, around Notting Hill and North Kensington, climaxes at the White City dog stadium on White City Road, off Wood Lane W12, Shepherds Bush. The stadium was torn down in the 1980s and BBC offices now stand on the site.

BLUE VELVET

(1986, dir: David Lynch)
Kyle McLachlan, Laura Dern, Isabella Rossellini.
● **NORTH CAROLINA**

Disturbed, disturbing, visually glorious, nastily sadistic, but one of Lynch's most satisfying movies to date. The apparently sweet and easy Lumbertown – "at the sound of the falling tree" – is the movie city (it's home to several movie studios) of **Wilmington**, North Carolina, and many of the locations can easily be recognised.

The general vista of Lumbertown is the view of Wilmington across the Cape Fear River toward Water Street. Arlene's Restaurant, where MacLachlan and Dern hatch their plan to uncover Lumbertown's

Laura Dern's school: New Hanover High School, Market Street

Lumbertown – at the sound of the falling tree: Wilmington, across the Cape Fear River

Site of the Brothers' hotel: West Van Buren Street

Lumbertown Police Station: Wilmington Police HQ, Redcross Street

Arlene's Restaurant: New Hanover Human Resources, Fourth Street

secrets, isn't a restaurant at all, but the **New Hanover Human Resources Office** at **4th and Chestnut Streets**. Laura Dern's school is the **New Hanover High School, 1307 Market Street**. The police station, where Kyle McLachlan first glimpses the strange Man in Yellow, is the **Wilmington Police Headquarters, 115 Redcross Street**. Isabella Rossellini's gloomy Deep River apartment block, where McLachlan witnesses one of the creepiest sex scenes in film history, is the **Carolina Apartments, Market Street** at Fifth Avenue.

Isabella Rossellini's Deep River apartment: Carolina Apartments, Market Street, Wilmington

BLUES BROTHERS, THE

(1980, dir: John Landis)
John Belushi, Dan Aykroyd, Carrie Fisher.
● ILLINOIS; WISCONSIN

Enormously overblown and expensive slapstick chase movie went from box office disaster to cult status mainly because of the terrific soundtrack, the great array of soul stars on display and Belushi's charisma. It was filmed, of course, around Chicago, employing Landis' usual breath-taking knack of persuading the authorities to allow him to stage major set pieces in busy public places.

John Belushi is released from the **Joliet Correctional Center**, north of the suburb of Joliet on Highway 53, itself south of the city. The new Bluesmobile demonstrates its prowess by leaping across the **East 95th Street Bridge** over the Calumet River at Calumet Harbor, south Chicago, down near the Indiana border. The Brothers' digs, 'Hotel For Men Only. Transients Welcome', no longer exists. It wasn't blown up by Carrie Fisher (that was a large photograph of the building pasted on to flyaway polystyrene blocks), but it has since been demolished. It stood at **22 West Van Buren Street**, at the last check, still a vacant lot beneath the el-train.

The Soul Food Restaurant, where the waitress is Aretha Franklin and John lee Hooker plays outside, is on **Maxwell Street**, centre of the bustling Maxwell Street flea market at the junction with South Halstead Street, just southeast of the University of Illinois campus. Much of the area has since been demolished. The Nazis turn up at the brothers' official address, **1060 West Addison Street** – which just happens to be the home of the Chicago Cubs, **Wrigley Field**. The shopping mall the brothers drive their car through is the **Dixie Mall, Harvey**, a suburb of south Chicago over the Little Calumet River.

The Palace Hotel Ballroom, "up north on Lake Wazupumani," where the Blues Brothers get their first major gig, is actually down south. it's the **South Shore Country Club, South Shore Drive** at East 71st Street. The 1916 Mediterranean-style building, on the coast toward Calumet Harbor, was recently renovated.

The climactic chase through central Chicago, under the el, ends up at the prestigious **Richard J Daley Center** building (named for Mayor Daley, who died in office in 1976). The building stands on the block bounded by Randolph, Dearborn and Clark Streets and Washington Boulevard. On the open plaza south of the Center on Washington Boulevard is the 50-foot-tall **Chicago Picasso Sculpture**, the cubist head Jake and Elwood use for a landmark. Amazingly, Landis got permission for the Bluesmobile to crash through the Daley Center win-

The expensive climax: Richard J Daley Center

dows. The brothers' ultimate destination, **City Hall-County Building**, is west of the Daley Center over Clark Street. It's here they barricade themselves in while the National Guard abseil down the side of the building. The 'Cook County' clerk, who receives their payment, is that other expert in expensive, lumbering monsters, Steven Spielberg.

Other locations used by the movie include the northwestern suburb of **Park Ridge**; **Wauconda**, 25 miles northwest of Chicago on Route 12; **Waukegan**, 25 miles north on the coast near the Wisconsin border and **Milwaukee**, on the coast over the border in Wisconsin itself.

After the death of Belushi, a sequel was never a good idea. And choosing to film much of *Blues Brothers 2000* in Canada didn't help. Chicago sets the scene, but much of the filming was done in **Toronto** and **Kingston**, Ontario. The Kentucky fairground is **Markham Fairgrounds**, Toronto.

BODY DOUBLE

(1984, dir: Brian De Palma)
Craig Wasson, Melanie Griffith, Deborah Shelton.
● **LOS ANGELES**

Craig Wasson and Melanie Griffith eat out: Spago's, Horn Avenue

De Palma recycles more Hitchcock plots, this time a mix of *Vertigo* and *Rear Window*. The film opens at the **Tail 'o' the Pup, 329 San Vicente Boulevard**, midtown, the hotdog stand that looks like, well, a hotdog. The Cascade Theater, where Wasson auditions and meets Gregg Henry, is actually the **Callboard Theater, 8451 Melrose Place** near Orlando Avenue/La Cienega Boulevard in West Hollywood (the frontage does clearly read 'Callboard'). Wasson shops at LA landmark **Farmers' Market, 6333 West 3rd Street** at Fairfax Avenue, and drinks in **Barney's Beanery**, a venerable Hollywood hangout – Jean Harlow allegedly picked up men here, and it's where Jim Morrison pees against the bar in Oliver Stone's *The Doors* – at **8447 Santa Monica Boulevard**, West Hollywood. The bizarre home-on-a-stalk that Wasson occupies is architect John Lautner's **Chemosphere House, 3105 Torreyson Place**, off Mulholland Drive, in the Hollywood Hills. From here, Wasson spies on Deborah Shelton in her house in the hills on **Miller Drive**. Shelton buys expensive undies on Rodeo Drive – underneath all the swish dressing, Bellini's is the **Louis Vuitton** luggage store in the **Rodeo Collection**, the exclusive mall at **421 North Rodeo Drive**. Wasson takes Melanie Griffith to celeb hangout, **Spago's Restaurant, 1114 Horn Avenue**, overlooking West Hollywood.

BODY HEAT

(1981, dir: Lawrence Kasdan)
William Hurt, Kathleen Turner, Richard Crenna.
● **FLORIDA; HAWAII**

Steamy near-remake of *Double Indemnity*, with lawyer Hurt plotting with Turner to kill her husband. Originally set in Atlantic City, the locale was changed to Florida for the movie. It was shot around the **Lake Worth** area of Palm Beach, southern Florida. The bridge is at **Delray Beach**, the boardwalk is **Hollywood Beach**, south of Fort Lauderdale down toward Miami. Filming also took place on the glorious Garden Isle of **Kauai**, Hawaii.

BODYGUARD, THE

(1992, dir: Mick Jackson)
Kevin Costner, Whitney Houston, Gary Kemp.
● **LOS ANGELES; FLORIDA**

Houston performs after the death threat: Mayan Theater, South Hill Street

Costner is the bodyguard hired to protect performer Houston from a murderous nut.

The wild, pre-Columbian nightmare of a theatre, where Houston defies the threats to perform (and in the ensuing chaos provides the image for the movie poster) is the **Mayan Theater, 1038 South Hill Street**, downtown LA. It's followed the standard pattern of grand 'themed' movie theatre in the twenties (along with the Chinese and the Egyptian), a sixties slump into porno house and revival as a nightclub. You can see its incarnation as an XXX movie dive in the 1973 Jack Lemmon Oscar-winner *Save the Tiger*.

The working class bar where Costner and Houston stop off for a drink, is the venerable institution **Joe Jost's, 2803 East Anaheim Street** in Long Beach.

Houston nips off to perform at an Aids charity benefit (with not a red ribbon in sight?) at the **Fontainebleau Hilton Hotel, 4441 Collins Avenue**. Yes, that's where Bond stymied the crooked poolside card game in *Goldfinger*. The killer pursues Houston to a wintery retreat at **Fallen Leaf Lake, Fallen Leaf Road** running south from Route 89 at the southern tip of Lake Tahoe, on the California side of the Nevada border.

The climactic Academy Awards

The Oscar ceremony was filmed in the Pantages Theatre, Hollywood Boulevard

... but the arrival was shot downtown: Park Plaza Hotel

65

ceremony was filmed at two different locations. You won't find the imposing exterior with its enormous Egyptian statues in any guide book to Hollywood: it's the imposing frontage of the Park Plaza Hotel, overlooking MacArthur Park. The 37-foot tall statues were added by Production Designer Jeffrey Beecroft. And to confuse things further, the luscious black and gold zigzag *moderne* interior is a few miles away in Hollywood. It's the 1929 **Pantages Theater, 6233 Hollywood Boulevard**, which, in the fifties, actually was home to the Academy Awards ceremony. The Rotary Club dinner epilogue filmed in the familiar Crystal Ballroom of LA's **Biltmore Hotel** (seen in *The Fabulous Baker Boys* and *Splash!* among many other films), **506 South Grand Avenue**, on Pershing Square, downtown.

BOMBSHELL (aka *Blonde Bombshell*)
(1933, dir: Victor Fleming)
Jean Harlow, Lee Tracy, Franchot Tone.
● **LOS ANGELES**

Wisecracking Hollywood-set farce. The nightclub scene filmed in the famous, but sadly now closed, Cocoanut Grove of the **Ambassador Hotel, 3400 Wilshire Boulevard** at Catalina Street, midtown (see *Barton Fink* for details).

BONFIRE OF THE VANITIES, THE
(1990, dir: Brian De Palma)
Tom Hanks, Melanie Griffith, Bruce Willis.
● **NEW YORK CITY; LOS ANGELES**

Fatally miscast and drastically cut down, De Palma's film is little more than a trot through the plot of Tom Wolfe's satirical novel. The whole story of the making of the movie is chronicled with painful detail in Julie Salamon's fascinating *The Devil's Candy* (and what a movie that would make).

'Master of the Universe' Hanks lives at **800 Park Avenue** near 75th Street, naturally on Manhattan's prestigious East Side (*subway: 77th Street*), although his lobby filmed in number 77, way down south of Midtown. His workplace is the Bond Trading Room at **Merrill-Lynch** in **Two, World Financial Center**, the tallest of architect Cesar Pelli's assymetrical four-tower complex occupying the landfill site at Manhattan's southern tip. Merrill Lynch cooperated with this less-than-sympathetic portrayal of NYC life on condition that their name was not mentioned. Oops.

Home of the 'Master of the Universe': Park Avenue, the East Side

Lost in a controversial caricature of the Bronx in the High Bridge district on **167th Street**, between Sherman and River Avenues (*subway: 167th Street Station, Green Route to Woodlawn*), Hanks and Griffith get involved in the fateful hit-and-run accident under the **Third Avenue Bridge**, where Third Avenue crosses the East River north of East Harlem. Hanks finds himself taken to the aus-

tere deco fortress of the **Bronx County Courthouse Building, 851 Grand Concourse** at the southwest corner of East 161st Street. The local subway station is 161st Street/Yankee Stadium a couple of blocks west, but this is not the one Willis hustles Hanks into, which was a fake entrance built on the sidewalk to keep the action flowing smoothly.

Rev Bacon (a caricature of Al Sharpton) exploits the case with a demo for the media at a housing project on **171st Street** between Fulton and Third Avenues, just west of Crotona Park in the Bronx. Out on bail, Hanks attends a post-opera party, which was filmed way across on the West Coast, among the stuffed predators in the **Los Angeles County Museum of Natural History**, part of the Exposition Park complex of museums and galleries, downtown LA on Exposition Boulevard.

Back on the East coast, the courthouse used for Hanks' – much cut-down – trial scene is over in Queens. It's the **Queens County Courthouse** on Sutphin Boulevard in the Jamaica District. The lionisation of Willis, which opens and closes the movie, is held in the Grand Central-sized Plaza of the **Winter Garden** with its enormous arched window overlooking the Hudson River. Coincidentally, it's part of the same lavish Battery Park City complex housing the Merrill-Lynch offices.

BONNIE AND CLYDE
(1967, dir: Arthur Penn)
Warren Beatty, Faye Dunaway, Gene Hackman.
● **TEXAS**

This stylish and violent mythologising of two much uglier gangsters was filmed around Dallas, Texas, at many of the sites where the actual events happened. The three banks raided are the real banks, which had been left unchanged after closing down during the Depression in the thirties. They're at **Pilot Point**, 50 miles north of Dallas on Route 377; **Red Oak**, just south of Dallas; and **Venus**, Route 67 about twenty miles southwest of Dallas (a town also seen in *The Trip to Bountiful*). The other locations, Arcadia, Louisiana, Dexter, Iowa and Joplin, Montana, also filmed in Texas. Among the small, unmodernised towns used are **Midlothian** and trusty old **Waxahachie** (the location for *Places in the Heart* and *Tender Mercies*, both also just south of Dallas; **Rowlett**; **Maypearl** (south of Venus); **Garland** (Route 66, northeast Dallas); and **Ponder** (Route 156, 25 miles north of Fort Worth).

The real-life killing of Parker and Barrow took place in Dexter, about 80 miles northwest of Des Moines, just north of Route 30 in Carroll County, Iowa. The bloody 'Ring of Fire' shooting was filmed at **Lemmon Lake**, a privately-owned preserve on Trinity River a few minutes from downtown Dallas.

BOOGIE NIGHTS
(1997, dir: Paul Thomas Anderson)
Mark Wahlberg, Burt Reynolds, Julianne Moore.
● **LOS ANGELES**

Anderson's rose-tinted look at the fall of the porn film industry in the seventies bursts with style and energy. It was filmed largely in the San Fernando Valley north of

The Hot Traxx disco: Sherman Way, Reseda

LA. The Hot Traxx disco has cleaned up its act a little, and is in fact a church, Iglesia Cristiana Nuevo Empezar, **18419 Sherman Way** at Canby Avenue, **Reseda**.

The dazzling opening shot of Sherman Way, Reseda

Just west, on Sherman Way, you can see the, now-closed, Reseda picture house used for the opening credits. Jack Horner's house is in **West Covina**. Horner's porno warehouse is the real thing, **Gourmet Video** in Van Nuys.

BOOM!

(1968, dir: Joseph Losey)
Elizabeth Taylor, Richard Burton, Noël Coward.
● SARDINIA

A minor Tennessee Williams play, *The Milk Train Doesn't Stop Here Anymore*, customised to become a vastly expensive Burton-Taylor vehicle. The rich and decrepit Mrs Goforth (Taylor, 36) is visited by a young and beautiful Angel of Death (Burton, 43) in a sixties art gallery perched on a cliff, where Noël Coward (in a bitchy role written for a woman) pops in to dish dirt. The house was purpose-built at **Capo Caccia** on the coast of Sardinia. Perverse to the end, Tennessee Williams considered it the most perfect filming of one of his plays. What *was* he on when he saw it?

BOOMERANG

(1947, dir: Elia Kazan)
Dana Andrews, Jane Wyatt, Lee J Cobb.
● CONNECTICUT; NEW YORK STATE

Innovative semi-doc melodrama based on a true story of murder in small-town USA. An innocent man is saved but, unusually, the real killer is not unmasked. Also unusually for this period, it was shot entirely on location, a Kazan trademark. The street scenes were filmed in **Stamford**, Connecticut, the court scenes in the courthouse of **White Plains**, New York.

BORN FREE

(1966, dir: James Hill)
Virginia McKenna, Bill Travers, Geoffrey Keen.
● KENYA

The Adamsons raise lion cubs, and have to train Elsa the grown lioness to live in the wild. This was filmed on the actual location, at **Naro Moru** in Meru National Park, surprisingly the least spoiled, least visited of Kenya's parks. A replica of the Adamsons' house was built on a 750-acre equatorial farm here in the Kenya Highlands, with filming on the surrounding plains and along the **Naro Moro River**.

BORN ON THE FOURTH OF JULY

(1989, dir: Oliver Stone)
Tom Cruise, Raymond J Barry, Willem Dafoe.
● TEXAS; PHILIPPINES; MEXICO

Cruise makes a bid for the traditional disability Oscar, complete with lank hair and a beard, as real-life Viet-vet Ron Kovic, who led opposition to the Vietnam War after being paralysed from the waist down. The movie was made at Los Colinas Studios in Dallas, Texas, and both Kovic's neighbourhood of Massapequa, Long Island, and the Miami scenes were actually filmed around the Dallas area. The Vietnam scenes were shot in the Philippines.

The Kovics' Long Island home is on **Creekside Drive**, off Houghton Road, southwest Dallas near the Hawn Freeway. Young Ron's high school is **Henderson Elementary School, 2200 South Edgefield Avenue, Elmwood** in **Oak Cliff**, Dallas. After the killings at Kent State University, Abbie Hoffman leads protests at **Dallas Hall**, home of **Dedman College, Boaz Lane** off Daniel Avenue, on the campus of **Southern Methodist University**. The Chicago Convention Center is the **Dallas Convention Center, 650 South Griffin Street**.

BOUCHER, LE (aka *The Butcher*)

(1969, dir: Claude Chabrol)
Stephane Audran, Jean Yanne, Antonio Passalia.
● FRANCE

A typically Hitchcockian thriller from Chabrol, as a serial killer haunts a small French town. It's filmed around the Dordogne area of France. The town is **Tremolat**, a beautiful little village close to the Cingle de Tremolat, a great bend in the Dordogne River about 70 miles east of Bordeaux.

BOUDU SAUVÉ DES EAUX (aka *Boudu Saved From Drowning*)

(1932, dir: Jean Renoir)
Michel Simon, Charles Granval, Marcelle Hainiaa.
● PARIS

Simon is the tramp rescued from a suicide bid who makes life hell for the family who take him in. Sound familiar? It was remade by Hollywood in 1985 as *Down and Out in Beverly Hills*.

Boudu saved from drowning: Pont des Arts

The Renoir original was filmed at the Seine in Paris, and at Joinville, Marne. Studio filming was at the Eclair Studios, Epinay. Boudu makes his leap from the

Pont des Arts, the wooden-planked pedestrian link between the Louvre on the Right Bank and the Institut de France on the Left. The bookshop belonging to Granval, who saves him, is on the **Quai de Conti**, on the Left bank between the Pont des Arts and the Pont Neuf. The building used is still there.

BOUND

(1996, dir: Larry Wachowski, Andy Wachowski)
Jennifer Tilly, Gina Gershon, Joe Pantoliano.
● **LOS ANGELES**

Taut little off-centre noir from the Wachowski brothers, who went on to make the phenomenally successful *The Matrix*. Like the sci-fi blockbuster, the brothers set the action in their home town of Chicago while filming elsewhere. The deco apartment block where neighbours Tilly and Gershon enjoy what readers of one magazine

The apartment block: Talmadge Apartments, LA

voted the most popular kiss in screen history is actually the **Talmadge Apartments, 3278 Wilshire Boulevard** at Berendo Street, midtown LA.

BOUNTY, THE

(1984, dir: Roger Donaldson)
Anthony Hopkins, Mel Gibson, Laurence Olivier.
● **TAHITI; NEW ZEALAND; LONDON; MIDDLESEX; WILTSHIRE**

The old *Mutiny on the Bounty* warhorse, told in flashback from Bligh's court martial. Scripted by Robert Bolt and slated to be directed by David Lean, it was finally helmed by Donaldson, who has since hived off into empty bozo movies like *Species* and *Dante's Peak*. You can find the building used for Lieutenant Bligh's home in Twickenham.

It's one of the elegant terraced houses running along the western edge of Marble Hill Park. Built in 1721, it was once home to poet Alfred Lord Tennyson, and you can see it at **15 Montpelier Row**, south of Richmond Road to the southwest of Richmond Bridge (*tube: Richmond, rail: St Margaret's*).

The galleried club, where Bligh invites Fletcher Christian

Bligh's home: Montpelier Row, Twickenham

to sail with him, is the **Reform Club** in Pall Mall, St James, SW1. Bligh's court martial filmed at two separate locations. The exterior is the **Royal Naval College** at Green-

The court martial exterior: Royal Naval College, Greenwich

wich, SE10 (*rail: Greenwich*), but the grand interior, where Laurence Olivier presides, is the Double Cube Room of **Wilton House, Wilton**, two and a half miles west of Salisbury on the A30 in Wiltshire. It's open to the public (*admission charge*).

The South Seas location is the island of **Moorea**, close to Tahiti. Four sets, the landing site, the Polynesian village where Bligh meets the King, the Dutch port of Coupand, in Timor and the breadfruit gardens, were built here. The *Bounty* itself was built at **Whangarei** on the North Island of New Zealand and here, and further south at **Gisbourne**, most of the boat's scenes and the Pitcairn Island scenes were shot.

BOYFRIEND, THE

(1971, dir: Ken Russell)
Twiggy, Christopher Gable, Max Adrian.
● **HAMPSHIRE**

Pastiche upon pastiche upon pastiche as a thirties style Hollywood director watches a tatty British company stage a fifties send-up of a twenties musical. Messy, long and mostly fun, with a couple of leaden moments, this was filmed on location at Portsmouth's **Theatre Royal, Guildhall**. Walk past the Guildhall itself in the town centre. Ken

The theatre: Theatre Royal, Portsmouth

Russell vowed never to work at Elstree again after interior sets built there collapsed.

BOYS DON'T CRY

(1999, dir: Kimberley Peirce)
Hilary Swank, Chloe Sevigny, Peter Sarsgaard.
● **TEXAS**

Based on a true story, which happened in Falls City, Nebraska, when Brandon Teena, a popular, handsome new boy in town, was brutally murdered and found to be Teena Brandon, a lesbian living as a boy. Shot in and around **Austin**, Texas, the courthouse was in **Greeneville**, Texas.

BOYS' TOWN

(1938, dir: Norman Taurog)
Spencer Tracy, Mickey Rooney, Henry Hull.
● **NEBRASKA**

Tracy pulls all the stops out (he really wanted to be a priest) as Father "There's no such thing as a bad boy" Flanagan in this teary true-life biopic filmed on location in the real **Boys' Town** on the western edge of Omaha, Nebraska.

BOYZ'N'THE HOOD

(1991, dir: John Singleton)
Cuba Gooding Jr, Larry Fishburne, Ice Cube.
● **LOS ANGELES**

23-year-old Singleton's film, about the vicious circle of black-on-black violence, was filmed in the area he grew up in, LA's South Central district. The focus of the movie is Inglewood, an area just east of LA International Airport. The opening scene, where a pool of blood becomes a source of fascination to the schoolkids, took place at the junction of **Lawrence Street and Woodworth Avenue**, south of Hollywood park in southern Inglewood. Young Tre attends **Woodworth Elementary School**. A block east is the notorious north-south cruising strip of **Crenshawe Avenue**, where the piddling slight that escalates into tragedy is set.

BRADY BUNCH MOVIE, THE
(1995, dir: Betty Thomas)
Shelley Long, Gary Cole, Michael McKean.
● **LOS ANGELES**

Knowing send up of the cutesy seventies TV series. The original Brady Bunch house stood on Dilling Street in North Hollywood, but it had changed too much to be used for the movie. A similar house on **Firmament Avenue, Sherman Oaks**, was dressed for the part. West Dale High School is **Taft High School, 5461 Winnetka Avenue, Woodland Hills**.

BRAINDEAD (aka *Dead Alive*)
(1992, dir: Peter Jackson)
Timothy Balme, Diana Penalver, Elizabeth Moody.
● **NEW ZEALAND**

More wildly emetic schlock-horror from the director of *Bad Taste*, filmed in **Wellington**, New Zealand, and at the **Pinnacles**.

BRANNIGAN
(1975, dir: Douglas Hickox)
John Wayne, Judy Geeson, Richard Attenborough.
● **LONDON**

The free-for-all: Leadenhall Market

A US cop comes to London to apprehend an escaped villain, in John Wayne's only English picture. The criminal mastermind is quite obviously the English Tourist Board, as every event takes place in front of a famous London landmark. The muffed postal drop filmed in the middle of **Piccadilly Circus**, where the villains manage to escape through sewers. The most famous scene is the car leap across a half-opened **Tower Bridge**. Scotland Yard seems to jump the Thames too, since the view from the windows is obviously south of the river. These scenes were shot in **St Thomas' Hospital**.

The obligatory pub fight, where everyone ends up flailing at everyone else, filmed in **The Lamb** in the centre of the Victorian arcaded **Leadenhall Market** at the foot of the new Lloyds Building (*tube: Bank*).

BRASSED OFF
(1996, dir: Mark Herman)
Ewan McGregor, Pete Postlethwaite, Tara Fitzgerald.
● **YORKSHIRE; MIDLANDS; LONDON**

Set in the fictitious town of 'Grimley' and using the famous Grimethorpe Colliery Band, this was shot in Doncaster,

Birmingham and London. The brass band championship was filmed at **Halifax Piece Hall**, while the finals were staged at the **Royal Albert Hall**, Knightsbridge.

The brass band championship: Piece Hall, Halifax

BRAVEHEART
(1995, dir: Mel Gibson)
Mel Gibson, Patrick McGoohan, Sophie Marceau.
● **IRELAND; SCOTLAND**

Best Film and Best Director, according to the Academy Awards. Hmmm. There was much controversy when it was admitted that this story of Scottish independence was to be filmed largely in Ireland, but the Republic is on the ball with tax breaks and the use of its army. The village of Lanark, where William Wallace lives as a child and later falls in love with Murron, was one of the few locations actually in Scotland. The medieval Scottish village was constructed in the **Glen Nevis Valley** at the foot of Britain's highest peak, Ben Nevis. The village set was completely dismantled and the area returned to its former state, though the Braveheart Car Park, constructed to service the location, has been retained. The filming site is up the glen, past the car park, and below the road's highest point. The design of the village houses was based on those of St Kilda, a tiny island off the Scottish coast, inhabited until the late 18th century, but now a tourist attraction.

More Scottish landscapes were filmed at **Loch Leven** and **Glen Coe**. Wallace's trek up to the spectacular peak was shot on the **Mamores**. The interior of Mornay's castle is another Scots location, filmed in the **Edinburgh Council Chamber**.

Everything else in the movie was filmed in Ireland, within a 30 mile radius of Dublin. The fortified English town of York is **Trim Castle**, a massive ruin kitted out for the movie with wooden buttresses and a seven-ton gate. The London square was also created at Trim, on the other side of the castle wall. (Trim Castle can be seen in Sam Fuller's war movie, *The Big Red One*). The town of Trim is about 26 miles northwest of Dublin on the River Boyne, Co Meath. About five miles northeast of Trim is **Bective Abbey**, which was used as the courtyard of Longshanks' castle and the dungeons, where Wallace is imprisoned.

Edinburgh Castle is tall, square-towered **Dunsoghly Castle**, dating from 1450 and the only castle in Ireland to retain its original medieval trussed roof. It's about two miles northwest of Finglas, northern Dublin off the N2 between Kilshane Bridge and Pass If You Can. Another English stockade was constructed around an old hunting lodge at **Coronation Plantation**. Westminster Abbey is **St Nicholas Church, Dunsany Castle**. The escape from Mornay's castle, after bloodily crushing his skull, filmed at **Blessington Lakes**, where a 45-foot tower was specially constructed. Most interiors filmed in Dublin's Ardmore Studios. The battles of Stirling and Falkirk were staged at the **Curragh and Ballynmore Eustace**, a large, privately-owned stretch of land, and on the studio lot at Ardmore.

BRAZIL
(1985, dir: Terry Gilliam)
Jonathan Pryce, Michael Palin, Robert De Niro.
● **LONDON; KENT; CUMBRIA;**
BUCKINGHAMSHIRE; PARIS

The glum, fifties-style setting of Terry Gilliam's visually stunning fantasy is a mixture of elaborate sets built at Lee Studios, and cunning location work. The vast clerks pool in the Department of Records, where Jonathan Pryce works, and the deserted corridors of the Expediting Department, are the interior of the old deserted CWS Flour Mill at the Royal Victoria Dock. The mill also provided the grim passageways and stairwells, as well as the exterior, of Shangri La Towers, the unfortunate Buttle's tower block.

Mentmore Towers, in the village of **Mentmore**, Buckinghamshire, was built in the 1850s for the Rothschild family. Designed by Sir Joseph Paxton, the architect of Crystal Palace, it's modelled on the Elizabethan Wollaton Hall near Nottingham. In 1977 the house hit the headlines when the entire contents were sold by Sothebys. A hidden stash of silverware was discovered beneath a trapdoor. The house became headquarters of the Maharishi University of Natural Law, but was recently put up for sale. It is no longer open to the public. The house's grand Entrance Hall, with its white marble staircase leading up to the glass-roofed Grand Hall, is used as the pompous restaurant where Pryce meets his mother, oblivious to a pyrotechnic terrorist attack.

The flamboyant setting for Katharine Helmond's facial surgery is the famous Arab Hall of **Leighton House, 12 Holland Park Road**, London W14 (*tube: High Street Kensington*), albeit camped up with Michelangelo's David in its alcoves. This Victorian gem, decorated in gilt and blue Islamic tiles – the fantasy creation of Royal Acadamician Frederick Lord Leighton – is part of the Leighton House Museum, open free of charge every day except Sundays. It contains more restored Victorian interiors, along with paintings by Leighton himself and contemporaries Burne-Jones, Millais and Watts. Find it north of the western reaches of Kensington High Street.

Helmond's cluttered home is the Billiard Room of the old **National Liberal Club, 1 Whitehall Court** at Whitehall Place, seen in many other movies, including *The Elephant Man*. The dramatic spiral staircase is also here. The club has since been incorporated into the **Royal Horseguards Hotel**. The industrial complex is the **BP Oil Refinery** on the **Isle of Grain**, Kent.

Pryce's neighbourhood is **Marne-la-Vallée**, a modern satellite town about twenty miles east of Paris on the RER

Katharine Helmond's plastic surgery: Leighton House, Kensington

line. The main location is the **Palais d'Abraxis Apartments**. Also in Marne-la-Vallée is the delirious pathway to the funeral parlour in Pryce's climactic

fantasy. The pink deco interior of the Chapel of Our Lady of the Checkout Counter itself is the **Rainbow Room**, on the top floor of the old Biba store, High Street Kensington.

The brief country idyll filmed in the Lake District in Cumbria. The torture chamber is the interior of one of the giant cooling towers of Croydon Power Station. The complex has since been demolished, though the names of the new streets on the site – Ampere, Volta, Faraday, Galvani – record its history, and there's even a Brazil Close. The station also provided the exterior of the Ministry, and though most, including the imposing entrance, has gone, you can still see some of the monumental deco brickwork at the foot of the two huge chimneys now on the site of the IKEA Superstore on Ampere Way.

BREAKFAST AT TIFFANY'S
(1961, dir: Blake Edwards)
Audrey Hepburn, George Peppard, Mickey Rooney.
● **NEW YORK CITY**

A film of the book would have been nice, but this cleaned-up jaunt through the edited highlights is jolly enough to be going on with, and Audrey Hepburn is, as always, a treat. Holly Golightly is the

Coffee and Danish at the ready?: Tiffany's, Fifth Avenue

flighty social butterfly with a past, who enjoys nothing more than an alfresco breakfast gazing in the window of swish jewellery store, **Tiffany's, 727 Fifth Avenue** at 57th Street.

The green and white candy-striped awning of Golightly's apartment building, where Mickey Rooney donned rubber eyelids as an an unlikely Japanese landlord, may have gone, but you'll still recognise the townhouse at **169 East 71st Street**, on the East Side, New York.

Holly Golightly's apartment: East 71st Street,

BREAKFAST CLUB, THE
(1985, dir: John Hughes)
Emilio Estevez, Judd Nelson, Molly Ringwald.
● **CHICAGO**

Archetypal Hughes teen-movie with the five principals whiling away an afternoon's detention. This being John Hughes, the setting is inevitably Chicago, in this case Des Plaines, and featuring **Main North** and **Glenbrook North High Schools**.

BREAKING AWAY
(1979, dir: Peter Yates)
Dennis Christopher, Dennis Quaid, Daniel Stern.
● **INDIANA**

Enormously likeable little middle-America movie, a sort of *Rocky* for cyclists, but done with wit and style. Made by a Brit director, it got a surprise Oscar nomination for Best Picture, and actually picked up the Academy Award for Steve Tesich's quirky script. The movie was made entirely on location in **Bloomington**, Indiana, 40 miles southwest of Indianapolis, and on the campus of the screenwriter's alma mater, **Indiana University, 107 South Indiana Avenue**. The area's old limestone quarries, where Christopher and his buddies hang out, are a legacy of the town's past, hence Cutters, the students' term for locals.

BREAKING THE WAVES
(1996, dir: Lars Von Trier)
Emily Watson, Stellan Skarsgard, Katrin Cartlidge.
● **SCOTLAND; DENMARK**

Beautifully shot and affectingly acted, this story of a virginal bride sexually degrading herself to please her paralysed husband is horribly miscalculated. Danish scenes were filmed in **Hellerup** and **Lyngby**, while the Scottish scenes were shot at **Mallaig** and **Glendale** on the Isle of Skye, and at **Morar**.

BREATHLESS
(1983, dir: James McBride)
Richard Gere, Valerie Kaprinsky, Art Metrano.
● **LOS ANGELES**

Brilliantly good-looking (with great LA locations) and bravely unlikeable remake of Godard's trash-culture landmark A Bout de Souffle, gaining oodles of cool credentials courtesy of Tarantino, who lists it as one of his faves. The action is transferred from sixties mono Paris to eighties pastel California. Locations included the **University of California**, Los Angeles; **Westwood** and **Venice Beach**. The terrific murals, a feature of LA's Venice area, are the ones near **Windward Avenue** and **Speedway**. The nightmarishly futuristic hotel is the **Westin Bonaventure, 404 South Figueroa**, downtown LA.

BRIDE, THE
(1985, dir: Franc Roddam)
Sting, Jennifer Beals, Quentin Crisp.
● **FRANCE**

Oddball remake of The Bride of Frankenstein with Sting creating Jennifer Beals, assisted by Quentin Crisp (continuing the gay tradition – in the original, gay director James Whale cast his lover Colin Clive as Dr Frankenstein and the wonderfully fey Ernest Thesiger as Dr Pretorius). Set in Budapest in the 1840s, it filmed mainly in France. The main square of Budapest, where the Monster carries Rappaport into town, is **Sarlat-la-Caneda**, a beautifully preserved town of medieval, Renaissance and 17th century buildings. It's 90 miles north of Toulouse in the Perigord region.

The longshots of the town where the circus camps, are of **Carcassonne**, the walled city 50 miles southeast of Toulouse, and also seen as Nottingham Castle in Robin Hood, Prince of Thieves. More old town locations filmed in **Perouges**, twenty miles northeast of Lyon. Frankenstein's chateau is **Chateau de Cordes**, a 15th century chateau renovated in the 17th century, just north of Orcival, southwest of Clermont-Ferrand.

BRIDE OF CHUCKY
(1998, dir: Ronny Yu)
Jennifer Tilly, Brad Dourif, Alexis Arquette.
● **ONTARIO**

Fourth in the series, with tongue very firmly in cheek, filmed in Ontario, Canada, at **Brampton; Pickering** and Toronto itself. Jennifer Tilly kills the cop and first picks up the Chucky doll in the derelict, but landmark structure at **45 Parliament Street**. The pair hide out in Room 121 of the wonderfully fifties **Hillcrest Motel, 2143**

"Well, hello dolly" – Jennifer Tilly picks up Chucky: Parliament Street

The motel: Hillcrest Motel, Lakeshore Boulevard West, Toronto

Lakeshore Boulevard West on the shore of Lake Ontario (© 416.255.7711). The gorgeous wedding chapels can be found on the strip near sideshows and waxworks of the gloriously tacky **Clifton Hill** in Niagara Falls. Sets were constructed in warehouses at **373 Front Street East; 15 Fraser Avenue** and **153 Eastern Avenue**. Filming also took place at an old army camp in **Oshawa**.

BRIDE OF THE MONSTER
(1955, dir: Edward Wood Jr)
Bela Lugosi, Tor Johnson, Tony McCoy.
● **LOS ANGELES**

Another classic from the widely acknowledged Worst Director of All Time (it's the film with the fake octopus seen in Tim Burton's Ed Wood), shot, exotically, in **Griffith Park**, Los Angeles.

BRIDGE ON THE RIVER KWAI, THE
(1957, dir: David Lean)
Alec Guinness, William Holden, Sessue Hayakawa.
● **SRI LANKA**

The first of Lean's large-scale epics, Bridge was filmed on location in Sri Lanka, in the small community of **Kitulgala** on the Kelani River. The bridge itself, 425 feet long and rising 90 feet above the water, cost a quarter of a million dollars to build. The cast and crew stayed at the **Government Rest House** in Kitulgala, which overlooks the site of the bridge. A few stumps from the movie bridge still remain on either side of the river. The British HQ, from which Jack Hawkins leads a force to blow up the bridge, is the **Peradeniya Botanic Gardens** on the outskirts of **Candy**, Sri Lanka, where Mountbatten did indeed have his station command from 1943 to 1945. There was more filming in the Sri Lankan capital of Colombo, at the **Mount Lavinia Hotel, 104 Hotel Road** (©0094.1717. 450). The real River Kwai itself can be seen in the 'Vietnam' sequences of The Deer Hunter. The real Bridge on the River Kwai, still standing, looks nothing like Lean's romanticised version. It's a concrete and girder structure standing, not amongst Sri Lanka's lush jungle vegetation, but on a scrubby Thai plain. You can take a River Kwai excursion, plus train ride, from Bangkok.

BRIDGE TOO FAR, A

(1977, dir: Richard Attenborough, Sidney Hayers)
Dirk Bogarde, James Caan, Michael Caine.
● NETHERLANDS

Long, long account of the disastrous WWII Allied parachute drop into the Netherlands, filmed at **Deventer**, 40km north of Arnhem, and at **Nijmegen**, south of Arnhem. Filming also took place at **Brinkhorst**; **Bemmel**; **Lent** and **Grave**, all in the Netherlands.

BRIDGES OF MADISON COUNTY, THE

(1995, dir: Clint Eastwood)
Meryl Streep, Clint Eastwood, Annie Corley.
● IOWA

The nearest America has come to *Brief Encounter*, with tight-assed mid-West puritanism standing in for English repression. Madison County is a real district of Iowa (it's John Wayne's birthplace), and the bridges are for real too. You'll find them in the area of **Winterset**, the town Streep visits to buy her new frock, and where scarlet woman Lucy is ostracised by the locals. Winterset is about 30 miles southwest of Des Moines, Iowa, on I-169. The unique bridges were covered by order of the county, using cheap lumber to protect the expensive flooring timbers. Of the original 19, which were named for the closest resident, only six remain. The bridges seen in the movie are the **Roseman Bridge**, built in 1883, which Eastwood is trying to find when he calls on Streep's farmhouse and where the ashes are scattered, and the longest, the **Holliwell Bridge** over Middle River southeast of Winterset, where the pair meet up after the visit to Winterset. Meryl Streep's farmhouse was an abandoned ruin in the northeast of the county, renovated for the movie. It's been kept as a tourist attraction, open from May to October (*admission charge*).

The cafe is the **Northside Cafe**, Winterset. The general store is **M Young & Co** feed store building. A closed Conoco gas station became the 1965 Texaco station – it's now the **Memory Station** gift shop. The Blue Note Lounge filmed inside Winterset's **Corner Tavern** (though the exterior is another building). The stone bridge, where Eastwood and Streep enjoy a picnic getaway, can be found in Winterset's **City Park**, just south of the Cutler-Donahue covered bridge. The river crossing, where Streep's children discuss her diaries, is **Pammel State Park**, southwest of Winterset.

BRIEF ENCOUNTER

(1945, dir: David Lean)
Celia Johnson, Trevor Howard, Joyce Carey.
● LANCASHIRE; BUCKINGHAMSHIRE; LONDON

Milford Junction railway station, supposedly in Kent, where Howard and Johnson meet up for their chastely clandestine afternoons, is **Carnforth Station** in Lancashire, about five miles north of Lancaster. The station is still

standing and in use, though much of it is closed and boarded up. The tea room (the interior of which was recreated in the studio at Denham) is gone, but the platform tunnels and platform one, where Celia nearly takes a dive under the boat train, are still recognisable. Carnforth was chosen because of its distance from the German airfields and the subsequent relaxation of the blackout regulations so far north (this was early 1945). You can plainly see station signs with the names of northern towns in the film. The lugubrious voice of the station announcer, by the way, is writer Noël Coward himself.

Milford High Street: Station Parade, Beaconsfield

Celia Johnson bumps into Trevor Howard: Burke's Parade, Beaconsfield

The accident on the boating lake: the Long Bridge, Regent's Park

The rest of the film was shot in the Home Counties, with some of the busier railway shots filmed at Watford Junction. Milford High Street can be found in **Beaconsfield**, Buckinghamshire. The barrel organ on the corner by Harris's plays on **Station Parade**, alongside Beaconsfield Station, and Celia bumps into Trevor outside Boots, a few hundred yards south on **Burke's Parade**.

The cinema where they see the trailer for *Flames of Passion* was a picture house in Victoria, London, though the deco exterior was an entrance to the Denham Studios,

The railway station: Carnforth, Lancashire

The railway station: Carnforth, Lancashire

since demolished, on the North Orbital Road, Denham. The hospital where Howard works is a set built for Alexander Korda's 1945 Robert Donat-Deborah Kerr comedy, *Perfect Strangers*. The boating lake is slap in the middle of London's **Regent's Park**. You can see the **Long Bridge**, which Trevor Howard clings to, in the bird sanctuary in the centre of the park, northwest of the Inner Circle opposite the entrance to the Open Air Theatre.

BRIGHTON ROCK (aka *Young Scarface*)
(1947, dir: John Boulting)
Richard Attenborough, Hermione Baddeley, William Hartnell.
● SUSSEX

The Star and Garter pub: Dr Brighton's, Little East Street

Cuddly Attenborough is surprisingly menacing as babyfaced teenage hoodlum in Graham Greene's adaptation of his own book, which was filmed mostly on location in a seedy forties **Brighton**. Opening at **Brighton Station**. Pinkie and the mob catch up with Kolley Kibber at the Star and Garter pub, now **Dr Brighton's**

Kibber flees for his life: Queens Road

on the sea front at Little East Street. Kibber flees through **The Lanes**, up **Queens Road** and back to the station, where the gang is waiting for him. He catches a number six bus and gets off at the **Clock Tower**. Running down **Church Street** to **Brighton Pavilion**, he's finally killed on **Palace Pier**. The racecourse is, of course, **Brighton Racecourse**.

BRING ME THE HEAD OF ALFREDO GARCIA
(1974, dir: Sam Peckinpah)
Warren Oates, Gig Young, Isela Vega.
● MEXICO

Peckinpah continued his love affair with the dusty south in this strange, slow movie, which was shot entirely on atmospheric Mexican locations, many around Mexico City. 'El Jefe', who gives the command of the title, rules from the **Hacienda de San Juan**, a 200-year-old fortress north of Mexico City near to Teotihuacan (Place of the Gods), an amazing area of pyramids and temples covering seven square miles. Oates works in the **Tlaquepaque Bar** in Plaza Garibaldi, Mexico City. The bizarrely colourful graveyards are in Mexico City.

BRITANNIA HOSPITAL
(1982, dir: Lindsay Anderson)
Leonard Rossiter, Graham Crowden, Joan Plowright.
● LONDON

Last, and by far the least, of Lindsay Anderson's trilogy, which began so brilliantly with *If...*, wobbled a bit with the eccentric *O Lucky Man!* but finally crashed to earth with this cringingly banal, state-of-the-nation allegory, filmed at the huge, sprawling **Friern Hospital, Friern Barnet**

Britannia Hospital: Friern Barnet Hospital, New Southgate

Road, just west of New Southgate Station in London N11. True to the spirit of the movie and the times, it's now closed.

BROADWAY DANNY ROSE
(1984, dir: Woody Allen)
Woody Allen, Mia Farrow, Nick Apollo Forte.
● NEW YORK CITY; NEW JERSEY

The deli where the group of old comics recounts the tale of failed theatrical agent Danny Rose is the **Carnegie Delicatessen & Restaurant, 854 Seventh Avenue**, near West 54th Street, NY. The New York deli, it claims to serve the best pastrami and corned beef in the world, and they do serve a Broadway Danny Rose sandwich. Check out the mouthwatering website, complete with virtual tour and soundbites, at *www.nyctourist.com/ivrs/carndeli_1*. Danny signs up his woeful clients at the **Brill Building, 1619 Broadway** between West 49th and West 50th Streets.

BROKEN ARROW
(1996, dir: John Woo)
John Travolta, Christian Slater, Samantha Mathis.
● ARIZONA; MONTANA

FX-heavy adventure romp with baddy Travolta making off with the military's atomic weapons. Set in Utah, it was filmed in Arizona, around the spectacular red sandstone landscapes of **Glen Canyon**; **Lake Powell** and the town of **Page**. Railway scenes filmed on a 40-mile stretch of private railroad at **Livingston**, Montana.

BROWNING VERSION, THE
(1951, dir: Anthony Asquith)
Michael Redgrave, Jean Kent, Nigel Patrick.
● DORSET

A film version of Terence Rattigan's venerable play, about crusty teacher Crocker-Harris faceing up to personal crises on his premature retirement. Filmed at **Sherborne School, Sherborne** in Dorset. In 1994 Mike Figgis (*Leaving Las Vegas*) filmed a decent remake with Albert Finney taking over the schoolmaster's gown. The school interiors were again shot at **Sherborne**, though the exteriors are **Milton Abbey School, Milton Abbas**, also in Dorset.

BUCKET OF BLOOD, A
(1959, dir: Roger Corman)
Dick Miller, Barboura Morris, Antony Carbone.
● LOS ANGELES

Before he made the cult *Little Shop of Horrors*, Corman directed this little number from the same scriptwriter, Chuck Griffith. After accidentally killing his landlady's cat, nerdy sculptor Miller (now a permanent fixture of Joe Dante's movies) covers it in clay, calls it 'Dead Cat', becomes a proto-Damien Hirst and moves on to human sculptures. The film was shot in five days, mainly on studio sets, but with location filming around **Venice Beach**.

BUFFY THE VAMPIRE SLAYER
(1992, dir: Fran Kazui)
Kristy Swanson, Luke Perry, Paul Reubens.
● **LOS ANGELES**

Swanson is a California airhead destined to be the Ms Van Helsing of the West Coast in this witty spoof horror which didn't set the box office alight but nonetheless spawned a TV series. It was shot around LA. Buffy works out in the frequently filmed ballroom of the **Park Plaza Hotel, 607 South Park View Street**, mid-town LA. Her school is the familiar old **John Marshall High School, 3939 Tracy Street, Silverlake**, which numbered the young Leonardo DiCaprio among its students.

Buffy's school: John Marshall High School, LA

BUGSY
(1991, dir: Barry Levinson)
Warren Beatty, Annette Bening, Ben Kingsley.
● **CALIFORNIA**

Biopic of the man who, according to legend, built Las Vegas. The real Bugsy – sorry, Benny – Siegel was gunned down, shot through the eyes (see the tasteful picture in Kenneth Anger's *Hollywood Babylon*) at his home in Beverly Hills, **810 Linden Drive**.

The 1940s Beverly Hills of the film, though, is largely represented by the suburb of Pasadena, where the houses of Jack Dragna and Bugsy himself were filmed. Virginia Hill's home is in LA's Wilshire district in the Hancock Park area. Siegel is met on arrival in LA by George Raft at the wonderful Spanish-style **Union Station, 800 North Alameda Street**. There's impressive attention to detail – the famous sign in the hills, glimpsed only briefly in the background during the drive to Hollywood, actually reads 'HOLLYWOODLAND', as it did until 1949.

The Flamingo of the movie looks very different to the Vegas of today, and had to be rebuilt in its original form out in **Thermal**, south of I-10 between Palm Springs and Salton Sea in the Southern California desert. You can see shots of the Vegas strip in 1950, four years after the original Flamingo opened, in Charlton Heston's first Hollywood movie *Dark City*. The pink neon Flamingo as it's seen today appears at the end of *Bugsy*. Bugsy's rose garden (it was alleged, only half jokingly, that several of his enemies rested beneath it) was finally paved over in 1990, and in 1993 Siegel's on-site penthouse was demolished to make way for the new water park. The respectably renamed Flamingo Hilton is at 3555 Las Vegas Boulevard South.

The Hotel Nacional de Cuba, where the gang leaders gather to discuss Bugsy's future, is a conflation of two buildings. The grandiose lobby is the familiar **Park Plaza Hotel, 607 South Park View Street**, downtown LA. The exterior is the astonishing **Castle Green Apartments, 99 South Raymond Avenue** at East Green Street just south of Colorado Boulevard in central Pasadena. This Moorish fantasy, which you have to see to believe, was built at the turn of the century as an annexe to an older hotel across Raymond Avenue. The older hotel was demolished in the thirties, leaving the stump of the strange connecting bridge straddling the avenue.

The Hotel Nacional de Cuba: Castle Green Apartments, Pasadena

...while the lobby is the oft-used Park Plaza Hotel

BULL DURHAM
(1988, dir: Ron Shelton)
Kevin Costner, Susan Sarandon, Tim Robbins.
● **NORTH CAROLINA**

Sarandon is a baseball obsessive who makes a point of initiating new players, which sounds tacky but it all works. It was filmed around North Carolina with locations in **Raleigh**; **Greensboro**; **Asheville**; **Burlington** and **Wilson**. The ball games were shot at **Durham Athletic Park, 426 Morris Street, Durham**.

BULLETS OVER BROADWAY
(1994, dir: Woody Allen)
John Cusack, Chazz Palminteri, Dianne Wiest.
● **NEW YORK CITY**

Once again, Woody Allen manages to turn the mean streets of New York into a warmly glowing visual treat. The theatre where Woody stand-in John Cusack gets his play staged with dubious finances is the **Belasco Theater, 111 West 44th Street** between 6th and 7th Avenues. You might recognise the hotel lobby of Cusack's mob backer, Nick Valenti, as the place where Luca Brasi gets garrotted in *The Godfather*. It's been renovated since the seventies, but the **Edison Hotel, 228 West 47th Street** (© *212. 840.5000*) is still a deco delight.

On the Upper West Side you'll find the stable where gangster-cum-playwright Cheech is quizzed: the **Claremont Riding Academy, 175 West 89th Street** between Amsterdam and Columbus Avenues (where the hippies got their horses for the Central park ride in Milos Forman's film of *Hair*). Even further north is Helen Sinclair's penthouse apartment, on

The stables: Claremont Riding Academy, West 89th Street

110th Street at Riverside Drive, though the beautiful early 20th century roof, with its rare view of a skyscraper-free Manhattan skyline is an office building on **Nassau Street**, down in Lower Manhattan. The Three Deuces nightclub was filmed in central Manhattan, in the ballroom of the **New Yorker Hotel, 481 Eighth Avenue** (℗ *212.971.0101*). The ballroom also appeared, albeit differently decorated, in Woody Allen's *Radio Days*. The old movie theatre, under the elevated railway tracks, is over the East River in Williamsburg, Brooklyn.

BULLITT

(1968, dir: Peter Yates)
Steve McQueen, Robert Vaughn, Jacqueline Bisset.
● **SAN FRANCISCO**

Witness Johnny Ross is spotted: Mark Hopkins Hotel, Nob Hill

Bullitt meets up with an informant: Enrico's, Broadway

Brit director Yates set the industry standard for car chases in this SF based police actioner. Detective Frank Bullitt has to track down killers before the fact leaks out that a prize witness has been offed. The doomed witness, Johnny Ross, is first spotted by the baddies in the lobby of the deluxe **Mark Hopkins Hotel, 1 Nob Hill** at California

Frank Bullitt's apartment: Taylor Street

Street (℗ *415.392.3434; website: hotels.san-francisco.interconti.com*). As you might deduce from the address, this grand SF institution was built on the site of one of the city's most prestigious mansions. See it also in *The Betsy* and *Daddy's Gone a-Hunting*. But it's downhill for Ross from here: the rather less grand hotel where he is installed stood on Embarcadero, at the foot of the double-deck **Oakland Bay Bridge**, and has since been demolished

You can see Bullitt's apartment, unchanged, at **1153-1157 Taylor Street**, a

...and the shop where he stocks up: VJ Groceries, Taylor Street

stylish 1906 three-story frame building at the corner of Clay Street. Over the road you can still shop at **VJ Groceries**, where Bullitt stocks up on TV dinners. The church,

where Robert Vaughn serves a writ of habeas corpus on the police chief, is **Grace Cathedral, 1051 Taylor Street**, a couple of blocks south of Bullitt's home. The bar where Bullitt meets up with informant Eddie is also still in existence. It's **Enrico's, 504 Broadway** at the corner of Kearney Street. The car chase (the car is a Mustang Shelby) was filmed largely on **Fillmore Street**, between Broadway and Vallejo

Robert Vaughn serves a writ: Grace Cathedral

Street. The climactic shoot-out took place in **San Francisco International Airport**.

BUNNY LAKE IS MISSING

(1965, dir: Otto Preminger)
Carol Lynley, Keir Dullea, Laurence Olivier.
● **LONDON**

Preminger's weird black comedy, with a wonderful cast of eccentrics, filmed on location around London as policeman Olivier tries to track down the missing, but possibly imaginary, daughter of possibly batty Carol Lynley. Lynley's flat, where Noël Coward is the grossly lubricious landlord, was just off Trafalgar Square but has since been demolished. The Little People's Garden School, from which Bunny disappears, is still there, however. It's **South Hampstead High School, 5 Netherhall Gardens**, near Finchley Road, Hampstead, NW3 (*tube: Finchley Road*). Don't be fooled by the Frognal End, NW3 street signs – there's no such place. The glorious art nouveau pub where Olivier takes the distraught Lynley for a drink is the **Warrington Arms, 93 Warrington Crescent** – once a favourite haunt of Marie Lloyd – in Maida Vale, W9 (*tube: Maida Vale*). The grand Hampstead home of Keir Dullea, and scene of the climax, was once home to actor Gerald du Maurier. It's **Cannon Hall, 14 Cannon Place** at Squire's Mount tucked away off East Heath Road, NW3, just off Hampstead Heath (*tube: Hampstead*).

The Little People's Garden School: Netherhall Gardens, Hampstead

Laurence Olivier takes Carol Lynley for a drink: the Warrington Arms, W9

Frognall End, Keir Dullea's mansion: Cannon Hall, Hampstead

BUS STOP

(1956, dir: Joshua Logan)
Marilyn Monroe, Don Murray, Betty Field.
● ARIZONA; IDAHO

The film of William Inge's play, about a dim macho cowboy's attempt to woo a singer during a bus stop in a small Western town was shot on location in **Phoenix**, Arizona, and at **Sun Valley** and **Ketchum**, close together on Route 75, the scenic highway north from Twin Falls by the Sawtooth National Forest, Idaho. The **North Fork Store**, seen in the movie, is about ten miles north of Ketchum on Route 75 in the National Forest itself. During Arizona filming, MM stayed at the Sahara Motor Hotel, 401 North 1st Street, Phoenix.

BUSTER

(1988, dir: David Green)
Phil Collins, Julie Walters, Larry Lamb.
● LONDON; LEICESTERSHIRE; BERKSHIRE; MEXICO

Mother-in-law's place: Abady House, Westminster

A yucky attempt to turn thuggery into folksy fun, filmed mostly on location, though almost entirely north of the Thames. Buster's flat is in Hackney, E8, standing in for "Saarf Lonnon". Mother-in-law Sheila Hancock's flat is **Abady House, Page Street** near Regency Street, on the Grosvenor Estate, Westminster, SW1 (*tube: Pimlico*). The period-looking entrance is real, and still there unchanged. The altogether posher area he moves to after the robbery is **Wraysbury**, northwest of Staines in Berkshire (*rail: Wraysbury*).

The train robbery (which in real life was carried out on the Euston-Northampton line near Tring, Hertfordshire) was shot on the two-and-a-half mile stretch of Northampton's Central Steam Railway between Loughborough and Rothley, Leicestershire.

Buster's Mexico bash filmed in the restaurants, bars and beaches of **Acapulco**, Mexico.

BUSY BODIES

(1933, dir: Lloyd French)
Stan Laurel, Oliver Hardy, Tiny Sandford.
● LOS ANGELES

Laurel and Hardy change the record: Canon Drive, Beverly Hills

This short features Laurel and Hardy working in a saw-mill, and driving to work with the phonogram under the car bonnet. They motor along **Canon Drive** in Beverly Hills – stopping to change the record of course, outside **517 North Canon Drive**, which is still unchanged today.

BUTCH CASSIDY AND THE SUNDANCE KID

(1969, dir: George Roy Hill)
Paul Newman, Robert Redford, Katharine Ross.
● UTAH; COLORADO; MEXICO

A spiffing romantic Western, originally written for Jack Lemmon (Butch) and Paul Newman (Sundance). Butch's first (real life) bank hold-up was at **Telluride** in the spectacular Uncompahgre National Forest, Route 550, southwest Colorado, and the **New Sheridan Hotel, 231 West Colorado Avenue** boasts a bar used in the movie.

The railway robberies filmed on the **Durango-Silverton Narrow Gauge Railway** in southwest Colorado (see *Indiana Jones and the Last Crusade* for details). The breathtaking leap into the river was a less than breathtaking hop six feet onto a hidden platform (apparently Redford has a fear of heights). It was filmed at **Trimble Bridge** on the **Animas River**, near Durango, southwest Colorado.

The spectacular landscapes filmed in southwest Utah, at **St George**, on Route 15 in Washington County; **Snow Canyon** a few miles north on Route 18 (also, notoriously, locations for John Wayne's disastrous Genghis Khan pic *The Conqueror*); and in **Zion National Park**. Katharine Ross' house, site of the famous but rather twee musical interlude, was built for the movie and still stands in **Grafton**, a crumbling ghost town near Rockville, also Washington County.

The New York scenes were to have been shot on the *Hello Dolly* set at Twentieth Century-Fox in Hollywood, but since *Dolly* was yet to be released, studio head Richard Zanuck objected to revealing the expensive new showpiece, so the montage of period photos was used. The Bolivian scenes were shot in **Taxco** and **Curenavaca** to the south of Mexico City, Mexico.

BUTCHER BOY, THE

(1997, dir: Neil Jordan)
Eamonn Owens, Stephen Rea, Fiona Shaw.
● IRELAND

Jordan's imaginative film of Patrick McCabe's novel, about a psychotic young boy troubled by bizarre visions, was filmed in the author's home town of **Clones**, Co Monaghan, on the A34 about 35 miles west of Dundalk.

C

CABARET
(1972, dir: Bob Fosse)
Liza Minnelli, Joel Grey, Michael York.
● GERMANY

Toned down from the stage musical, this is still a stylish filming of Christopher Isherwood's stories of pre-war Berlin. The Kit Kat Club was built in Munich's Bavaria Studios. Michael York's arrival in Berlin Hauptbahnhof station was shot on the old railway station at **Lubeck**, northeast of Hamburg. The baron's castle is **Schloss Eutin**, about 20 miles from Lubeck in Schleswig-Holstein. The lake district exteriors and interiors were shot on the estate of the Duke of Oldenburg. Filming also at **Dohlem**, with street scenes shot around **Berlin**, and in the **Tiergarten**, as well as in **Munich**.

CABLE GUY, THE
(1996, dir: Ben Stiller)
Jim Carrey, Matthew Broderick, George Segal.
● CALIFORNIA

Socially challenged cable TV installer Carrey barges into Matthew Broderick's life. Carrey's private retreat, a 60-foot satellite dish, was built in California's **Angeles Forest**, north of LA, and rebuilt in the old Spruce Goose Hangar at Long Beach for studio filming. Believe it or not, the medieval theme restaurant, where Carrey and Broderick are roped into a serious jousting tournament, is for real. You can find **Medieval Times** in the Buena Park district south of LA near Knott's Berry Farm. It's at **7662 Beach Boulevard**. Call ahead for details of shows (℗ *714.521.474*).

CADDYSHACK
(1980, dir: Harold Ramis)
Chevy Chase, Rodney Dangerfield, Bill Murray.
● FLORIDA

Clumpy farce set around a golf course, filmed at the **Rolling Hills Golf and Tennis Club, 3501 West Rolling Hills Circle** at South West 36th Street, Davie, about ten miles from downtown Fort Lauderdale, Florida. The waterside hi-jinks filmed at the **Boca Raton Hotel and Country Club, 501 East Camino Real** in the wealthy coastal resort of **Boca Raton**, north of Fort Lauderdale.

CAGE AUX FOLLES, LA (aka *Birds of a Feather*)
(1978, dir: Edouard Molinaro)
Ugo Tognazzi, Michel Serrault, Michel Galabru.
● FRANCE

Molinaro's amiable farce, centering around a gay nightclub (remade by Hollywood as *The Birdcage*) was shot on the charming, and surprisingly unspoilt,

Tognazzi and Serrault argue: Place de l'Ormeau, St Tropez

waterfront of **St Tropez** on the French Riviera. There is no Cage Aux Folles club, of course, but you will recognise the **Place de l'Ormeau**, at the end of **rue de l'Ormeau**, as the spot behind the club where Tognazzi and Serrault argue after stomping out.

CAGED HEAT
(1974, dir: Jonathan Demme)
Juanita Brown, Erica Gavin, Barbara Steele.
● LOS ANGELES

Jonathan Demme's first feature was a women-in-prison melodrama, made for exploitation king Roger Corman, in the old **Lincoln Heights Jail, 421 North Avenue 19, Lincoln Heights**, LA.

CANDYMAN
(1992, dir: Bernard Rose)
Virginia Madsen, Tony Todd, Xander Berkeley.
● CHICAGO

Clive Barker's horror story is transposed from its UK setting of Liverpool to Chicago, where the vengeful spirit of an executed slave is traced to the troubled housing projects of **Cabrini Green**.

CANTERBURY TALE , A
(1944, dir: Michael Powell, Emeric Pressburger)
Eric Portman, Sheila Sim, Dennis Price.
● KENT

Wartime oddity from the Powell-Pressburger team with Price, Sim and John Sweet undertaking a latterday pilgrimage to Canterbury, while an unhinged magistrate pours glue onto women's hair during the wartime blackout.

The railway station, where the pilgrims meet up, is **Selling**, the stop before Canterbury East on the Kent Coast line from Victoria. The village of Chillingbourne is fictitious – a composite of several villages in the area around Canterbury. Eric Portman's house is **Wickhambreux Court** in the village of **Wickhambreux**, about five miles east of Canterbury, north of the A257. Just southeast of Wickhambreux on the A257 itself is the village of **Wingham**, where you'll find the **Red Lion Hotel, Canterbury Road**. The blacksmith's shop was at **Shottenden**, six miles west of Canterbury, off the A28. The hall, where Eric Portman delivers his lecture on the Pilgrim's way, is the town hall at **Fordwich**, a couple of miles northeast of Canterbury.

The exterior of **Canterbury Cathedral** is real enough, but the organ sound is that of St Alban's Cathedral (Canterbury's having been dismantled for wartime safety reasons), and the nave was rebuilt in the studio at Denham (the stained glass windows at Canterbury had been boarded up).

CANTERBURY TALES, THE
(1971, dir: Pier Paolo Pasolini)
Pier Paolo Pasolini, Hugh Griffith, Laura Betti.
● AVON; ESSEX; GLOUCESTERSHIRE; SUFFOLK; SUSSEX; WORCESTERSHIRE; SICILY, ITALY

All the exuberance of Chaucer with, happily, *all* of the

concomitant crudities of his period. The second part of Pasolini's folksy medieval 'Trilogy of Life' (coming between *The Decameron* and *The Arabian Nights*) explicitly concentrates on the bawdiness of the tales. Filmed on location around real English villages including: **Chipping Campden**, ten miles south of Stratford-upon-Avon on the B4035 in Gloucestershire; **Lavenham** (the site of witch burning in *Witchfinder General*), ten miles south of Bury St Edmunds on the A1141 in Suffolk; **St Osyth**, a couple of miles west of Clacton-on-Sea on the B1027 in Essex; **Bath** in Avon; **Battle**, five miles northwest of Hastings in Sussex; and **Rye**, eight miles northeast of Hastings, also in Sussex.

The 'Hell' scenes, with the giant Devil farting friars from his arse (I told you it contained the crudities of his period), were shot in the volcanic landscapes of Sicily.

CAPE FEAR

(1962, dir: J Lee-Thompson)
Robert Mitchum, Gregory Peck, Polly Bergen.
● **GEORGIA**

Psycho con Mitchum terrorises the family of lawyer Peck, whom he blames for a long prison stretch. Cape Fear River is actually in movie-heavy North Carolina (you can see it in *Blue Velvet* and *Track 29*) but this movie was shot in and around **Savannah**, Georgia.

CAPE FEAR

(1991, dir: Martin Scorsese)
Robert De Niro, Nick Nolte, Jessica Lange.
● **FLORIDA**

Scorsese's first studio genre picture is a big, violent, widescreen remake of the 1962 thriller with De Niro as the crazy con, Nolte protecting his family and cameos from the stars of the original. It was shot in Florida, around Fort Lauderdale and its southern suburb Dania, I-95 north of Miami, and in the subtropical wilderness of the Everglades, down on Florida's southern tip. If you want to visit, the main entrance to the Everglades National Park is on Route SR 9336 from Florida City, or off Route 41 at Shark Valley and Everglades City.

You'll find the college, where De Niro seduces Lewis into a bout of finger-sucking, in West Broward County, just east of *Caddyshack*'s Rolling Hills Golf Club. It's **Broward Community College, 3501 SW Davie Road**. De Niro clings to the underside of the family car at **Seminole Indian Truck Stop, North US Highway 27**.

The attack on De Niro, where he taunts Nolte, filmed on **Brickel Avenue**. New Essex is **Hollywood Boulevard** in West Broward, where the ice cream store is the **Rainbo Cafe, 1909 Hollywood Boulevard**.

CAPTAINS COURAGEOUS

(1937, dir: Victor Fleming)
Spencer Tracy, Freddie Bartholomew.
● **MAINE; CALIFORNIA**

Spoiled rich kid Bartholomew falls overboard and learns his lessons living among poor fisher folk. Based on a Rudyard Kipling story, and winning Tracy an Oscar, it was filmed in cutesy seaport **Camden** on the coast of Maine,

I-1, 40 miles southwest of Bangor, and at **Monterey Bay**, on the central California coast.

CAR WASH

(1976, dir: Michael Schultz)
Franklin Ajaye, Sully Boyar, Richard Pryor.
● **LOS ANGELES**

Hi jinks at a car wash in LA. Major traffic problems ensued when the Pointer Sisters did their big number. The De Luxe Car Wash, an existing facility kitted out with all modern

Site of the carwash: Rampart Boulevard at Sixth Street, downtown LA

gimmicks, stood on **Rampart Boulevard** at Sixth Street, near Lafayette Park, downtown LA. It's since been demolished.

CARLITO'S WAY

(1993, dir: Brian De Palma)
Al Pacino, Sean Penn, Penelope Ann Miller.
● **NEW YORK CITY**

Pacino is the ex-con trying, unsuccessfully, to go straight in De Palma's gutsy thriller. Scuzzy lawyer Sean Penn involves him in a crazy plot to spring a client from the notorious **Riker's Island Prison Barge**. The island, in the East River north of Astoria, Queens, is reached by the Riker's Island Bridge from Hazen Street in Steinway just west of La Guardia Airport. The nightclub where a coked-up Penn lets slip about the prison break was the **Copacabana, 10 East 60th Street** at Madison Avenue on the east Side (it's now closed, but see *Goodfellas* for details). Pacino,

Pacino watches Miller: Joffrey Ballet School, Sixth Avenue

released from prison, watches old flame Penelope Ann Miller from a rainswept roof. The dance class is at the **Joffrey Ballet School** on the corner of **Sixth Avenue** and 10th Street in the village. The turreted Gothic building past which Pacino follows Miller is the old **New York Public Library** on Sixth Avenue. The

Penelope Ann Miller's Greenwich Village apartment: Gay Street

Pacino and Miller mull over old times: Le Figaro Cafe, Bleecker Street

The elaborate shootout: Grand Central Station

coffee house where Pacino and Miller talk over old times is **Le Figaro Cafe, 168 Bleecker Street** at MacDougal Street. Miller's apartment is **17 Gay Street** in Greenwich Village. It's at the end of **Gay Street**, at the junction with **Waverly Place**, that Pacino is arrested.

Dodging the bad guys, Pacino jumps onto the South Ferry subway train at **125th Street Station** on Park Avenue in Harlem. The final confrontation takes place all over **Grand Central Station**, 42nd Street at Park Avenue, with a shootout on the Park Avenue elevator.

CARNAL KNOWLEDGE
(1971, dir: Mike Nichols)
Jack Nicholson, Ann-Margret, Art Garfunkel.
● **VANCOUVER; NEW YORK CITY; MASSACHUSETTS**

Nicholson and Garfunkel meet up: Wollman Skating Rink, Central Park

Top notch directing and acting of a brilliantly cynical Jules Feiffer sex comedy. Largely New York set, it was mainly shot in and around Vancouver, Canada. The skating rink, where a lone white-clad skater signals the passing of time and Nicholson and Garfunkel meet up to mull over their lives, is Central Park's **Wollman Memorial Skating Rink**, 59th Street at 6th Avenue. The rink was recently rebuilt, courtesy of Donald Trump.

Nicholson and Garfunkel's college years were filmed at **Smith College, Northampton**, Massachusetts (see *Who's Afraid of Virginia Woolf?* for details).

CARNIVAL OF SOULS
(1962, dir: Herk Harvey)
Candace Hilligoss, Frances Feist, Sidney Berger.
● **KANSAS; UTAH**

Weird, offbeat little indie horror movie – a one-off from the director Harvey – made, apart from the lead role, with a non-professional cast. It was shot around Harvey's hometown of **Lawrence**, Kansas, about 30 miles west of Kansas City on Highway 70. The opening car smash filmed in **Kaw Bridge, Lawrence**. The bizarre carnival itself was a rundown funfair, the **Saltair Pavilion**, I-80, west of Salt Lake City, Utah. The wooden pavilion seen in the film has since been replaced by a tacky Vegas-style complex, but you can see a scale-model of the original inside.

CAROUSEL
(1956, dir: Henry King)
Gordon Macrae, Shirley Jones, Cameron Mitchell.
● **MAINE**

Macrae returns from the dead to make amends for his wast-

ed life in a muted version of Rodgers and Hammerstein's superb musical, which unwisely changes key scenes for the cinema. Based on Ferenc Molnar's play *Liliom*, *Carousel* transposes the action from Hungary to the New England seaside. One of the few musicals of the period to pop its head out of the studio gates, it was shot mainly at the prettified Maine coastal port of **Boothbay Harbor**, off I-1, around 30 miles south of Augusta. Filming also took place at **Newcastle**, Maine.

CARRIE
(1976, dir: Brian De Palma)
Sissy Spacek, Piper Laurie, William Katt.
● **LOS ANGELES**

Arguably the best filming of a Stephen King story so far, with repressed teen Spacek wreaking revenge on her cruel classmates and her religious-nut Mom Laurie. Bates High School (what else would it be called in a De Palma movie?) is a conflation of **Hermosa Beach Community Center** (which used to be the Pier Avenue School), **Pier Avenue** at Pacific Coast Highway, Hermosa Beach between Manhattan Beach and Redondo Beach, Highway 1 south of LA International Airport; and **Pacific Palisades High School**. The interior of the gym was reconstructed at **Culver City Studios, 9336 Washington Boulevard**, Culver City, for the final conflagration – the same studio where they burned Atlanta for *Gone With the Wind*.

John Travolta and co get the bucket of blood that ends Carrie's night out from a pig farm in the industrial town of Vernon, southeast LA. The farm coyly hides behind images of porkers scampering in green meadows. It's the cutesy **Farmer John's Pig Mural**, one of the biggest murals in the world. Covering an entire city block, it was begun in 1957 by movie industry artist Les Grimes, who died in a fall from scaffolding while working on the project. You can see it at **3049 East Vernon Avenue, Vernon**, LA.

Bates High School: Hermosa Beach Community Center, Hermosa Beach

CARRY ON AGAIN DOCTOR
(1969, dir: Gerald Thomas)
Jim Dale, Kenneth Williams, Charles Hawtrey.
● **BERKSHIRE**

Ooh, Doctor Nookey! Bodily functions always gave the hospital Carry Ons a head start, and this is one of the best. Long Hampton Hospital is the Ceremonial Entrance to **Maidenhead Town Hall, St Ives Road, Maidenhead**, also used in *Carry On Doctor* and *Carry On Behind*. The

Dr Nookey's surgery: Park Street, Windsor

Long Hampton Hospital: Maidenhead Town Hall

Moore-Nookey Clinic (go on, say it out loud) is Heatherden Hall, the building at the heart of the Pinewood Studios complex, regularly drafted in for the low-low-budget series (it was the hospital in *Carry On Nurse*, for example). It's actually the studio administrative building. After returning from the tropical island with a lucrative slimming cure, Dr Nookey sets up his consulting rooms at **12 Park Street, Windsor**, just a few doors away from the familiar location seen in *Carry On Loving* and *Carry On Regardless*.

CARRY ON AT YOUR CONVENIENCE
(1971, dir: Gerald Thomas)
Sidney James, Kenneth Williams, Charles Hawtrey.
● **BUCKINGHAMSHIRE; SUSSEX**

Filming took place at **Black Park Country Park**, Buckinghamshire; and in **Brighton**.

CARRY ON BEHIND
(1975, dir: Gerald Thomas)
Kenneth Williams, Elke Sommer, Kenneth Connor.
● **BERKSHIRE; BUCKINGHAMSHIRE**

Featuring **Maidenhead Town Hall, St Ives Road, Maidenhead**, Berkshire. Windsor Davies' shop is on **Farnham Common**, between Slough and Maidenhead, Buckinghamshire.

CARRY ON CAMPING
(1969, dir: Gerald Thomas)
Sidney James, Barbara Windsor, Bernard Bresslaw.
● **BUCKINGHAMSHIRE**

The camping shop: High Street, Maidenhead

The shop, where Charles Hawtrey is shown how to stick the pole up (sigh), was Courts (now closed), **19 High Street, Maidenhead**, at the corner of St Ives Road. Sid James and Bernard Bresslaw look into the St Ives Road window and, yes, that's Maidenhead Town Hall – the 'hospital' from *Carry On Doctor* and *Carry On Again Doctor* – in the background. The holiday camp scenes were filmed at cold, wet **Burnham Beeches**. Chayste Place, the finishing school for young ladies, is, once again, Heatherden Hall, the Pinewood studios administration building.

CARRY ON COLUMBUS
(1992, dir: Gerald Thomas)
Jim Dale, Bernard Cribbins, Rik Mayall.
● **SURREY**

A sad, limp end to a long series, intended to be carried along on the supposed wave of Columbus-mania due to hit in 1992. This time around, Chris fetches up on the beach at **Frensham Ponds** on the A287, four miles south of Farnham, Surrey.

CARRY ON COWBOY
(1965, dir: Gerald Thomas)
Kenneth Williams, Sidney James, Jim Dale.
● **BUCKINGHAMSHIRE**

Filmed at **Black Park Country Park** and **Chobham Common**.

CARRY ON DICK
(1974, dir: Gerald Thomas)
Sidney James, Barbara Windsor, Kenneth Williams.
● **BERKSHIRE; BUCKINGHAMSHIRE**

The Reverend Flasher's church: St Mary's, Hitcham Lane, Burnham

The countryside is, naturally, the much-used **Black Park**, alongside Pinewood Studios, and **Maidenhead Thicket**. Sid James' church is **St Mary's, Hitcham Lane**, just west of **Burnham** in Buckinghamshire. Its prominently-featured WWI war memorial is never really explained. The stocks (the ever-patrician Kenneth Williams refused to do the movie if this scene remained) are at **Stoke Poges**, north of Slough.

CARRY ON – DON'T LOSE YOUR HEAD
(1967, dir: Gerald Thomas)
Kenneth Williams, Sidney James, Jim Dale.
● **BUCKINGHAMSHIRE; SURREY**

Set, of course, in the French Revolution. The French Chateau, which is about as near as you'll get to the real thing in the UK, is **Waddesdon Manor**, at the west end of Waddesdon village, on the A 41 six miles northwest of Aylesbury. This French Renaissance-style chateau was built for the Rothschild family. It's now owned by the National Trust and open to the public (℗ *01296.651142, admission charge*). It features also in *Isadora* and *Never Say Never Again*. More period scenes used **Cliveden** near Taplow, Buckinghamshire (see *Help!* for details) and **Clandon Park**, West Clandon east of Guildford, Surrey (*rail: Clandon*). (℗ *01483.222482, recorded info: 01483.223479, admission charge*).

CARRY ON GIRLS
(1973, dir: Gerald Thomas)
Sidney James, Bernard Bresslaw, Kenneth Connor.
● **BUCKINGHAMSHIRE; SUSSEX**

Tired old formula jokes as 'Women's Libbers' attempt to disrupt a seaside Beauty Contest. The town of Fircombe is, of course, Brighton and the hotel, significantly grander than it's supposed to be in the film, is Brighton's **Grand Hotel** on the seafront, now most famous as the site of the IRA's 1984 bomb attack on members of the Conservative party.

CARRY ON LOVING

(1970, dir: Gerald Thomas)
Sidney James, Hattie Jacques, Richard O'Callahan.
● BERKSHIRE

Kenneth Williams' house: Adelaide Square, Windsor

The Parkway Hotel: Ye Harte and Garter, Windsor

Once again, most of the filming is around **Windsor**, Berkshire (the castle walls are a pretty recognisable backdrop to many scenes). Much Snogging-on-the-Green railway station, where Charles Hawtrey gets arrested for following Sid James into the gents toilet, is the **Windsor and Eton Station**, which looks very different now. The Wedded Bliss Agency was on the fourth floor **15 Park Street** at Sheet Street – back in 1961, Sid James' Helping Hands employment agency operated out of the basement of the same building. The Parkway Hotel, where nerdy Richard O'Callahan meets the photographer's model, is the side entrance, Garter's Bar, to **Ye Harte and Garter Hotel, Jubilee Arch,** at the entrance to Windsor Station off Sheet Street. Kenneth Williams' rather posh home can be seen halfway along **Adelaide Square**.

CARRY ON REGARDLESS

(1961, dir: Gerald Thomas)
Sidney James, Kenneth Connor, Joan Sims.
● BERKSHIRE; LONDON; SCOTLAND

Number five in the series is a series of unconnected sketches linked by an Employment Agency gimmick: 'Helping Hands Ltd', which operates from the basement of **15 Park Street** at Sheet Street, just to the south of Windsor Castle, Windsor. The sinister man who wants a fourth at bridge is supposedly staying at the **Dorchester Hotel, Park Lane,** London. His garbled phone call sends Kenneth Connor to the **Forth Bridge** (courtesy of back-projection) in a parody of *The 39 Steps*. Kenneth Williams and monkey are barred from the bus in front of the railway arch on **Goswell Road**, Windsor. The 'zoological gardens' over the road, that Williams takes the chimp to, is **Alexandra Park**.

CARRY ON SERGEANT

(1959, dir: Gerald Thomas)
William Hartnell, Kenneth Williams, Bob Monkhouse.
● SURREY

Little post-war conscription comedy that unexpectedly

spawned the seemingly endless series of increasingly bawdy romps. Dour army officer Hartnell (the original *Doctor Who*) licks a shower of conscripts into shape. Filmed at the home of the Queen's Royal West Surrey Regiment (HM took her driving lessons here), the Victorian Stoughton Barracks, which in 1995 was converted into luxury housing and renamed **Cardwells Keep, Stoughton Road,** Stoughton north of Guildford, Surrey.

CARRY ON UP THE KHYBER

(1968, dir: Gerald Thomas)
Sidney James, Bernard Bresslaw, Kenneth Williams.
● WALES; SCOTLAND; BUCKINGHAMSHIRE

This *Carry On* seemed to have a slightly higher budget. The Himalayas were shot in Snowdonia, around the **Llanberis Pass**. The British colonial home is, of course, Heatherden Hall, the old Pinewood studio building.

CARS THAT ATE PARIS, THE

(1974, dir: Peter Weir)
Terry Camillieri, John Meillon, Melissa Jaffa.
● NEW SOUTH WALES, AUSTRALIA

The début movie of Peter Weir, who went on to make *The Truman Show*, is a black comedy about a small, out-of-the-way town where the inhabitants make a living from engineering road accidents and selling the spare parts. The little town of Paris is **Sofala**, an old gold-rush town in the Turon River Valley, about 30 miles from Bathurst in the Western Plains, west of Sydney, New South Wales.

CASABLANCA

(1942, dir: Michael Curtiz)
Humphrey Bogart, Ingrid Bergman, Paul Henreid.
● LOS ANGELES

A confused production, with script changes from day to day and no ending decided during filming, yet all the pieces fell perfectly into place for one of the great weepies of all time. It's based on the unproduced play *Everybody Comes To Rick's* by Murray Burnett and Joan Alison.

The film is almost entirely studio-bound, shot on Warners' Burbank lot, and, with Jack Warner's customary thrift, using sets from previous productions. Eastern sets were rehashed from *The Desert Song*, while the railway station was leftover from the Bette Davis weepie *Now Voyager*. If you want to see the original plane from the movie, and you're willing to suspend your disbelief, it's rumoured that it's included in the *Casablanca* tableau at the Disney-MGM Studios Theme Park in Orlando, Florida, where audio-animatronics recreate 'great scenes from the movies'. You can definitely see the large hanging lamps from Rick's Bar in the Lighting Prop Shop on the Warner Bros Studio Tour.

The farewell on the tarmac was filmed, not at an actual airport, but at Warners', on Stage 21 or Stage 1 – according to which version you believe.

There is one location to be visited, though. The arrival of Captain Strasser (the splendidly nasty Conrad Veidt) was filmed at the old Metropolitan Airport at Van Nuys near Burbank. The site has since been incorporated into

The runway of Casablanca Airport: Waterman Drive, Van Nuys

Van Nuys Airport, 6590 Hayvenhurst Avenue, occupying the area between Woodley Avenue to the east, Balboa Boulevard to the west, and Roscoe Boulevard and Vanowen Street. The art deco control tower has sadly been demolished, but you can still see one of the old hangars from the movie. When the airport was realigned, the two hangars no longer stood within the terminal boundaries. Used as engineering workshops, they stood on **Waterman Drive**, a tiny private street running west from Woodley Avenue between Blythe and Arminta streets, to the northeast of the airport lot. Sadly, one has already been demolished, but one remaining trace of *Casablanca* still survives.

CASINO
(1995, dir: Martin Scorsese)
Robert de Niro, Sharon Stone, Joe Pesci.
● **LAS VEGAS, NEVADA; CALIFORNIA**

Scorsese's crackling account of the takeover of Vegas by faceless corporations suffered by coming hard on the heels of the magnificent *Goodfellas*. It was filmed largely, of course, in Vegas itself. The fictitious Tangier casino is the **Riviera Hotel and Casino, 2901 Las Vegas Boulevard South** (℡ *702. 732.5110*). Joe Pesci's death scene was filmed in **Fresno**, California. Filming also took place at **Baker**, in the Mojave Desert, and **Hanford**, California. The kitschy motel, where Joe Pesci enjoys a brief fling with Sharon Stone, is **La Concha, 2955 Las Vegas Boulevard South** (℡ *702.735.1255*).

The fictitious Tangier casino: Riviera Hotel and Casino, Las Vegas Boulevard

Joe Pesci enjoys a fling with Sharon Stone: La Concha, Las Vegas Boulevard

CASTAWAY
(1986, dir: Nicolas Roeg)
Amanda Donohoe, Oliver Reed, Georgina Hale.
● **LONDON; SEYCHELLES**

Oliver Reed advertises for a 'beautiful woman' to retire with him to a South Seas island. Donohoe replies. She should have known better. This was filmed (unusually, in continuity) around London and in the Seychelles. Donohoe initially works in the tax office at **Charles House, High Street Kensington**. The less-than-idyllic paradise was shot on the islands of **Praslin**, **Cousin** and **La Digue**.

CAT BALLOU
(1965, dir: Eliot Silverstein)
Jane Fonda, Lee Marvin, Michael Callan..
● **COLORADO**

Jane Fonda hires drunken has-been gunslinger Marvin to kill a villain (Marvin again) in revenge for the death of her father. Spoof Western made at the **Buckskin Joe Studio** theme park west of Cañon City, Colorado.

CAT ON A HOT TIN ROOF
(1958, dir: Richard Brooks)
Elizabeth Taylor, Paul Newman, Burl Ives.
● **NEW YORK STATE**

Bowdlerised Tennessee Williams adaptation, buoyed up by a great cast on top form. The Deep South mansion is actually the **Coleman Estate, Muttontown**, near Glen Cove, one of Long Island's grand North Shore mansions.

CAT PEOPLE
(1982, dir: Paul Schrader)
Natassja Kinski, Malcolm McDowell, John Heard.
● **NEW ORLEANS, LOUISIANA**

Schrader makes explicit the themes hinted at in Val Lewton's understated 1942 classic. Natassja Kinski turns into a panther at the zoo in **Audobon Park**, New Orleans. Her house is on the corner of **Chartres** and **Esplanade**, opposite the Germaine Wells Mansion.

CATCH 22
(1970, dir: Mike Nichols)
Alan Arkin, Jon Voight, Richard Benjamin.
● **MEXICO**

For years, Orson Welles wanted to film Joseph Heller's surreal anti-war novel, but – as with *Moby Dick* – he had to settle for playing a cameo role in someone else's film. This was filmed at **Guaymos**, a seaport and fishing village on the west coast of northern Mexico, Route 15, about 300 miles south of the border at Nogales.

CATCH US IF YOU CAN (aka *Having a Wild Weekend*)
(1965, dir: John Boorman)
The Dave Clark Five, Barbara Ferris, Robin Bailey.
● **LONDON; DEVON**

For a short while in the mid-sixties, the Tottenham Sound of the Dave Clark Five was tipped to eclipse the Beatles, and the Five duly launched their imitation *Hard Day's Night*. While the Beatles had Richard Lester, the Five scored by choosing first-time director John Boorman. They play stuntmen (Dave Clark's pre-drumming occupation) who escape the boredom of London for a series of encounters with an array of the country's top-notch (and underrated) character actors in the West Country. The island they retreat to which turns out, symbolically, to be still connected to the mainland at low tide, is **Burgh Island**, connected by the strange sea-tractor – seen at the end of the movie – to Bigbury-on-Sea, Devon, twelve miles east of Plymouth on the B3392.

C'EST ARRIVÉ PRES DE CHEZ VOUS (aka *Man Bites Dog*)
(1992, dir: Remy Belvaux, Andre Bonzel, Benoit Poelvoorde)
Benoit Poelvoorde, Remy Belvaux, Andre Bonzel.
● BELGIUM; FRANCE

This very nasty black comedy takes no prisoners, as a documentary crew follows extrovert serial killer Poelvoorde around suburban Belgium. Shot around **Namur**, 35 miles southeast of Brussels, Belgium. Poelvoorde dumps his victims into the marble quarry at **Neuville**, five miles north of Lyon, France.

CET OBSCUR OBJET DE DESIR (aka *That Obscure Object of Desire*)
(1978, dir: Luis Buñuel)
Fernando Rey, Carole Bouquet, Angela Molina.
● FRANCE; SPAIN

On a journey from Seville to Madrid, Fernando Rey tells the story of his sexual obsession with the changeable (played alternately by Bouquet and Molina) Conchita. The opening scenes, where Rey pours a bucket of water over Conchita, were shot at **Seville Railway Station**. Rey is robbed, and meets up again with Conchita, at his hotel in Lausanne, Switzerland. Back in Seville, where Rey meets up – yet again – with Conchita, he goes of to see **Seville Cathedral** (the third largest in Europe, after St Peter's in Rome and St Paul's in London) and the adjoining **Giralda Tower**, originally a minaret. And it's in **Madrid** that Rey and Conchita go off to an explosive future.

CHAN IS MISSING
(1982, dir: Wayne Wang)
Wood Moy, Marc Hayashi, Laureen Chew.
● SAN FRANCISCO

Looking for Chan: Ross Alley, Chinatown

The first feature-length US movie to be produced entirely by a Chinese-American cast and crew was also Wang's first US movie (before *The Joy Luck Club* and *Smoke*). Two taxi drivers fruitlessly try to track down Chan, who's disappeared with $2,000. It was shot around San Francisco's Chinatown, the largest Chinese community in the US outside of New York, which grew up in the early 19th century around Portsmouth Square when Chinese immigrants fled war and famine in Canton. It covers the area between Broadway, Bush Street, Powell Street and Kearny Street to the east. Grant Avenue, running north-south through the area, is tourists' Chinatown. **Stockton Street**, running par-

allel and just to the west, is its real heart. Much of *Chan Is Missing* was filmed around **Ross Alley**, a small street between Grant and Stockton.

CHANT D'AMOUR, UN
(1950, dir: Jean Genet)
Lucien Senemaud, Java,
● PARIS

Not surprisingly, the French authorities denied permission for Saint Genet to use a real prison for his movie of brutal, romantic love. Exterior shots of La Sante prison at **Fresnes** (where Genet wrote *The Miracle of the Rose* while in residence) were filmed clandestinely from an apartment over the road. The prison interiors were staged on sets built above Nico Papatakis' La Rouge Rose basement nightclub, which stood on the rue de Rennes in Paris' Saint-Germaine-des-Pres district. The fantasy forest scenes filmed on Jean Cocteau's estate at **Milly la Foret** near Fontainebleau.

CHANT OF JIMMIE BLACKSMITH, THE
(1978, dir: Fred Schepisi)
Tommy Lewis, Freddy Reynolds, Angela Punch.
● NEW SOUTH WALES, AUSTRALIA

The casual racism of turn-of-the-century Australia explodes in shocking violence. Filmed in New South Wales, at **Armidale**, around the **Bundarra Dorrigo State Forest**; at **Dubbo**, **Gulgong**, **Mudgee**, **Rylstone**, and at **Kempsey**, **Port Macquarrie**.

CHAPLIN
1992, dir: Richard Attenborough)
Robert Downey Jr, Dan Aykroyd, Geraldine Chaplin.
● CALIFORNIA; LONDON; SUSSEX; SWITZERLAND

Attenborough's bio-pic is a disappointing skim through the life of the great sentimentalist, but it uses a slew of interesting locations.

Chaplin's early life in London's Lambeth filmed behind Kings Cross Station at the junction of the cobbled **Cheney Road** and **Battle Bridge Road, NW1**. The houses – including Charlie's home – are a vast set which took four months to build, though the gasometers are real enough (they probably look familiar, having been seen in *The Ladykillers*, *Alfie*, *Backbeat* and *Shirley Valentine* as well as many other films, ads and TV shows). The site is currently under threat of redevelopment for the Kings Cross channel tunnel terminal.

The scene of little tot Chaplin saving the day when his mother's

The Aldershot theatre: Wilton's Music Hall, E1

Chaplin's Lambeth home: Cheney Road, Kings Cross

stage act takes a nose dive, set in Aldershot, was filmed in the famous **Wilton's Music Hall, 1 Grace's Alley, Wellclose Square**, off Cable Street, E1. The hall, built in 1858, was the first and one of the most successful of London's music halls. It was taken over by scandalised Methodists in the 1880s, and run as a mission until 1956, when it became a rag warehouse. For many years it lay dilapidated, used only for film shoots (including *Isadora* and *The Krays*) and music videos (Frankie Goes To Hollywood's 'Relax' must have had the Methodists whizzing round in their graves). It's now home to the Broomhill Opera.

Chaplin's first comic success was filmed at the beautiful **Hackney Empire, 291 Mare Street, E8**. The stageside box, in which he makes his appearance as a belligerent tippler, was built especially for the movie. The Cane Hill Asylum, where Chaplin's disturbed mother is incarcerated, was shot inside the disused **St Pancras Hotel**, above **St Pancras Station, Euston Road, NW1**. Closed for years, it is occasionally open to the public (one day a year) to view the stunning Victorian interior.

The riverside audition for Fred Karno was filmed in the grounds of the former Astor estate at **Cliveden** (see *Help!* for details of Cliveden). After being snubbed at a snobbish restaurant, Chaplin takes his first love, Hetty Kelly, for a cup of tea at the old Covent Garden vegetable market, where it was possible to get a cuppa at any hour of the day or night – or even get a beer at seven in the morning, due to the special license arrangements for the Garden porters. In the seventies, the market moved to a modern site in Nine Elms, so the scene was actually shot at **Smithfield Meat Market** between Charterhouse Street and Long Lane, EC1. You can see the real Covent Garden market, as it was in its heyday, in Hitchcock's *Frenzy*.

Chaplin soon takes off for the fledgling movie industry of the States. Mack Sennett's Keystone Studio, where Chaplin got his first job, stood at 1712 Allessandro Street. Chaplin's own studio, where he made *The Immigrant*, *The Floorwalker* and *Easy Street* in 1916 and 1917, was located at 1025 Lillian Way, south of Santa Monica Boulevard between Eleanor and Romaine Streets. No trace of either remains. Hollywood in the twenties was still a town of citrus groves, so the studios were recreated north of LA at **Fillmore**, Route 126 between Ventura and Valencia. The 'Hollywoodland' sign, where Chaplin plays with Fairbanks, was recreated too.

Chaplin's first comic success: Hackney Empire

The mock-Tudor studio is a recreation of the one Chaplin used from 1918 onwards, though this, amazingly, has survived. It's now the home of A&M Records, at **1416 La Brea Avenue**,

Chaplin returns to the London pub: The Salisbury, Haringay

between Sunset Boulevard and Fountain Avenue. Chaplin's footprints are preserved in concrete on Stage 3. Charlie's home was on Summit Drive in Beverly Hills, but

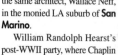

Baiting J Edgar Hoover: Ballroom of the Park Plaza Hotel, downtown LA

the film utilises a house built by the same architect, Wallace Neff, in the monied LA suburb of **San Marino**.

William Randolph Hearst's post-WWII party, where Chaplin upstages FBI boss J Edgar Hoover with his breadroll dance, is held in the much-used Ballroom of the **Park Plaza Hotel, 607 South Park View Street** overlooking Macarthur Park in downtown LA (see *New York,*

The premiere of *Limelight*: Los Angeles Theater, downtown LA

New York for details of this legendary movie location).

Returning to England, the train journey from Southampton to London was filmed on the dependable old **Bluebell Line** – a five mile stretch of track between Horstead Keynes and Sheffield Park, northeast of Haywards Heath in Sussex. The enthusiastic welcome to the capital, which actually took place at Waterloo Station, was filmed on **St Pancras Station**, one of the least changed of London's great termini. The Covent Garden pub, where Chaplin discovers he's no longer just one of the lads, is the grand, but rather faded, **Salisbury, Green Lanes** at the corner of St Ann's Road, Harringay, N15.

The shipbound scene, of Chaplin heading back to the States, was shot aboard the **Queen Mary** at her berth on Pier J in Long Beach, LA – the Manhattan skyline was added later. The première of *Limelight* was filmed in the dazzling foyer of the 1931 Second Empire-style **Los Angeles Theater, 615 South Broadway** in the vibrant – if a bit down at heel – Hispanic centre of downtown LA.

Anthony Hopkins' fictional biographer interviews the elderly Chaplin at the real Chaplin estate, courtesy of his widow Oona, who had given the film her blessing. It's in **Vevey**, twelve miles east of Lausanne on the north shore of Lake Leman in Switzerland. The closing scenes, of Chaplin's belated Lifetime Achievement Oscar award, though shot on a set at Shepperton Studios, were intercut with shots of the actual ceremony at the current home of the Academy Award ceremonies, the **Dorothy Chandler Pavilion**, part of the Music Center, **135 North Grand Avenue** between First and Temple Streets in LA's Bunker Hill district.

CHARADE

(1963, dir: Stanley Donen)
Audrey Hepburn, Cary Grant, Walter Matthau.
● **PARIS**

Lightweight, blackish comedy thriller of the kind they can't seem to make anymore, set in Paris. Hepburn and

Grant stay at the **Hotel Saint Jacques** (where Grant famously takes a shower in his suit), near the St Jacques metro on the Left Bank. Hepburn is lured to the Centre Gardens of the **Palais Royal**, while the movie climaxes in the **Comedie Français, 2 rue de Richelieu** (*metro: Palais-Royal*).

CHARGE OF THE LIGHT BRIGADE, THE
(1936, dir: Michael Curtiz)
Errol Flynn, Olivia De Havilland, David Niven.
● **CALIFORNIA**

Exciting adventurer, with little or nothing to do with the Crimea. A full-scale replica of the Chukoti Garrison, the Indian fortress, was built at Lasky Mesa, a desolate windswept spot, dry, covered in tumbleweed and crawling with tarantulas, according to de Havilland's autobiography. Lasky Mesa, a 7,000 acre tract of land north of LA, was bought up by the studio for filming, and many movies were shot here. The area, between Agoura and Woodland Hills, is now known as the **Ahmanson Ranch**, and is scheduled for redevelopment. See *Gone With the Wind*, part of which filmed here, for details.

CHARGE OF THE LIGHT BRIGADE, THE
(1968, dir: Tony Richardson)
Trevor Howard, John Gielgud, David Hemmings.
● **TURKEY; LONDON**

This vastly underrated, darkly iconoclastic sixties version, with a quirky script from Charles Wood and stunning animated sequences from Richard Williams, could hardly be more different from the Curtiz version. There were endless legal wrangles over the script, which was accused of borrowing heavily from Cecil Woodham-Smith's book *The Reason Why*. Laurence Harvey, who owned rights to the book, was given a role, but eventually cut from the movie.

John Gielgud's office, the Horseguards HQ, was filmed in the Governor's Office of the old **Royal Mint** (before its function was moved to South Wales), **Cartwright Street**, E1, northeast of the Tower of London (*tube: Tower Hill*). The arrival of the troops was shot in **Istanbul**, Turkey. The charge itself, the 'Valley of Death' was filmed near the villages of **Saraycik** and **Pacenek**, about 30 miles from Ankara in central Anatolia.

CHARIOTS OF FIRE
(1981, dir: Hugh Hudson)
Ben Cross, Ian Charleson, Nigel Havers.
● **SCOTLAND; MERSEYSIDE; BERKSHIRE; BUCKINGHAMSHIRE; YORKSHIRE**

This overrated flagwaver is purportedly based on truth but traditionally Hollywoodised, hence the Best Picture Oscar. Although set partly in France, it was shot entirely in the UK. The famous slo-mo run along the beach which opens the movie, supposedly at Broadstairs, Kent, is **West Sands** at St Andrews on the Fife coast, where the Carlton Hotel is actually the clubhouse of the Royal and Ancient Golf Club.

Sensitive to accusations of anti-Semitism, Harold Abrahams' old university, Caius College, Cambridge,

refused permission to film on its property, and **Eton College** in Windsor stands in. A familiar location, Eton is also seen in *Henry VIII and His Six Wives, Young Sherlock Holmes* and *The Madness of King George*. Abrahams' "College Dash" around the Great Court of Trinity College is around the School Quad.

The race around Trinity College, Cambridge: Eton College, Windsor

Abrahams' romantic dinner: Cafe Royal, Edinburgh

Meanwhile, the zealous Eric Liddell is awarding prizes at the Highland games, a scene shot at **Sma Glen**, on the A822 a few miles north of Crieff, Perthshire. **Inverleith**, in Edinburgh, is the rugby ground where Liddell preaches to the crowd after the Scotland-Ireland meet, while the Scotland-France International shot at **Goldenacre**, the grounds of Heriot's Rugby Club on **Bangholm Terrace in Edinburgh**.

Liddell runs to the religious meeting: Assembly Hall, Edinburgh

The London restaurant, to which Abrahams takes singer Sybil Gordon after seeing her in *The Mikado*, is the **Oyster Bar** of Edinburgh's **Café Royal, 17 West Register Street** at Rose Street. Liddell, his obsession with running vying with his faith, is late for the religious meeting at the **Assembly Hall** on the **Mound** in Edinburgh, and afterwards, with his sister Jennie, looks out over the city from **Holyrood Park**. The vast estate, where aristocratic Lord Lindsay comforts Sybil before leaping over hurdles topped with glasses of champagne, is **Hall Barn**, south of Beaconsfield in Buckinghamshire. A 17th century private house built for poet Edmund Waller, the estate can also be seen in the 1994 film of *Black Beauty*. The relatively unchanged **York Station** stands in for London's Kings Cross, while Dover Station, from which the athletes leave for the Olympic Games in France, is the port of **Birkenhead**, over the Mersey from Liverpool.

Much of Paris is actually Merseyside. The British Embassy ball, where the Prince of Wales tries to persuade Liddell to run on the Sabbath, is **Liverpool Library and Town Hall**, and the French café is the no-longer-used chapel of the **Royal Hospital**, Liverpool. The Church of Scotland in Paris, where Liddell preaches, really is in Scotland. It's the **Broughton McDonald Church, Broughton Place** in Edinburgh. The Paris Stade des Colombes, venue for the climactic Olympics, is the **Bebington Oval Sports Centre, Old Chester Road, Wirral** on Merseyside.

CHARLEY VARRICK

(1973, dir: Don Siegel)
Walter Matthau, Andy Robinson, Joe Don Baker.
● NEVADA

Matthau is a small time bank robber finding himself with a stash of mob money in this tight little thriller from the dependable Siegel. The

The Tres Cruces bank: Courthouse Museum, Genoa

town of Tres Cruces is **Genoa**, a few miles south of Carson City in Nevada, close to the California border. The Tres Cruces Western Fidelity Bank is Genoa's **Courthouse Museum, 191 First Street**.

CHARME DISCRET DE LA BOURGEOISIE, LE

(aka *The Discreet Charm of the Bourgeoisie*)
(1972, dir: Luis Buñuel)
Fernando Rey, Delphine Seyrig, Stephane Audran.
● PARIS

A group of ever-so-well-mannered bourgeois are constantly frustrated in their attempts to get together for a meal in Buñuel's surreal black comedy, filmed around Paris. The house of

Fernando Rey's house: rue de Franqueville, Passy-la-Muette

super-cynical Fernando Rey, smuggling cocaine in his diplomatic bag, is on **rue de Franqueville** at rue Verdi, near Ranelagh Gardens in the embassy-infested Passy-La Muette district, 16th arrondissement.

CHASE, THE

(1966, dir: Arthur Penn)
Marlon Brando, Robert Redford, Jane Fonda.
● CALIFORNIA

Smalltown festerings surround escaped, but sympathetic, con Redford. Good-looking, but a bit disappointing considering the names involved – Arthur Penn directing a Lilian Hellman script with a cast to die for. Texas-set, it was actually filmed in **Chico**, north of Sacramento, California.

CHASING AMY

(1997, dir: Kevin Smith)
Ben Affleck, Joey Lauren Adams, Jason Lee.
● NEW JERSEY; NEW YORK CITY

Kevin Smith's pan-sexual love story is set, like his earlier *Clerks* and *Mallrats*, on the western tip of the New Jersey coast, around Red Bank, Leonardo and Asbury Park, with just a glimpse of Manhattan. Ben Affleck and Jason Lee's apartment is **30 Broad Street, Red Bank**, above Jack's Music Shop. The Manhattan Comicon convention, where Affleck first meets Joey Lauren Adams, is held in

the **Berkely Cartaret Hotel and Convention Center, Ocean Avenue** at Deal Lake Drive on the **Asbury Park** shorefront. The park, where they open up to each other, is **Victory Park, River Road, Rumson** out on the western-most tip. Lee's motormouth pal reveals the story behind Adams' Fingercuffs nickname outside **Quick Stop, 58 Leonard Avenue** in **Leonardo** – the famous location for Smith's breakthrough movie, *Clerks*. Affleck grills Adams at the ice hockey match at **Ocean Ice Palace, 197 Chambersbridge Road, Brick**. And of course, Jay and Silent Bob put in their trademark appearance, at the **Marina Diner, Highway 36** at **East Road, Belford**.

CHEYENNE AUTUMN

(1964, dir: John Ford)
Richard Widmark, Carroll Baker, Karl Malden.
● UTAH; COLORADO; WYOMING

With this story of the forced resettlement of the Cheyenne nation in the 1860s, John Ford tries to make amends for years of whooping savages. The Cheyenne, played by Navajos and Dolores Del Rio, are dispossessed of their grassland home and relocated 1,500 miles away in the harsh north. The effect of this dislocation is somewhat dissipated by the fact that they hardly ever seem to leave **Monument Valley**. Ford also used the area around **Moab**, Utah, including **White's Ranch; Castle Valley; Professor Valley; Fisher Canyon; Arches National Park** and **Mexican Hat**. Filming also took place at **Gunnison Canyon** in Colorado and **Fort Laramie**, Wyoming.

At this point in his career, Ford was tending toward the slipshod in some of his movies, and the Kennedy assassination, which occurred during filming, added to Ford's mood of disaffection. Much of the Monument Valley location work was simply filmed in front of the crew's base at **Goulding's Lodge**.

CHIEN ANDALOU, UN

(1928, dir: Luis Buñuel)
Simone Mareuil, Pierre Batcheff, Jaime Miravilles.
● PARIS

Buñuel and Salvador Dali's classic surreal short filmed in Paris' Ursuline Studios, and at **Le Havre**.

CHILDREN OF THE DAMNED

(1964, dir: Anton M Leader)
Ian Hendry, Alan Badel, Barbara Ferris.
● LONDON

Message-heavy sequel to *Village of the Damned* with the eerie blond children, now a multi-racial bunch, claiming an anti-war purpose. The church in which they hole up for the explosive finale is **St Dunstan-in-the-East, St Dunstan's Hill**, north of Lower Thames Street, EC3. Severely damaged in the Blitz of 1941, only the shell and the steeple (which is by Christopher Wren) remain.

Church of the damned: St Dunstan-in-the-East

CHILD'S PLAY
(1988, dir: Tom Holland)
Catherine Hicks, Chris Sarandon, Brad Dourif.
● CHICAGO

A superior jokey shocker, directed by the writer of *Psycho II*, with dying psycho Brad Dourif possessing the 'Good Guy' doll, leading to a string of sequels. Catherine Hicks' quartzite stone-clad apartment block, in which the creepy Chucky doll goes on the rampage, is the **Brewster, 2800 North Pine Grove Avenue** at West Diversey Parkway in Chicago's Lake View district.

House of Chucky: North Pine Grove Avenue, Chicago

CHIMES AT MIDNIGHT
(1966, dir: Orson Welles)
Orson Welles, Keith Baxter, John Gielgud.
● SPAIN

Welles' adaptation of both parts of *Henry IV* (incorporating bits of *Henry V*) was made under impossible conditions in Spain, and contains the best battle scene in any movie, ever. Typical of his underfunded European movies, Welles cobbles together various locations. Backgrounds were filmed against the oldest and best preserved medieval walls in Spain, at **Avila**, 50 miles northwest of Madrid on the Salamanca road. The two miles of wall are defended by 88 towers. The battle and the Gadds Hill robbery used the **Casa de Campo** – once a royal hunting area, it's now a huge, popular park in Madrid, reached by metro or bus (route 33).

Henry IV's palace is mostly **Castillo de Montjuich**, situated in Parque de Montjuich on a hill overlooking Barcelona. Built as a castle in 1640, it now houses the Military Museum. Further scenes of Henry's court were filmed at the castle of **Cardona**, which was also used for Henry V's coronation. The rear of Cardona became Hotspur's castle. Cardona is about 50 miles northwest of Barcelona, and the castle is now a lavish parador (hotel). The remainder of the coronation scene was shot in a Madrid church. The snow scenes were staged to the north at **Soria** and in the Basque region. Soria's Romanesque 12th century (though largely rebuilt in the 16th century) **Cathedral of San Pedro** was also used.

Other villages used include **Calatanazor**, a medieval town about twelve miles west of Soria; **Colmenar Viejo**, north of Madrid; **Guipuzcoa**; and **Puerto de San Vicente**, 65 miles west of Toledo. Street scenes were filmed in **Pedraza**, an old town about 55 miles north of Madrid. The Plaza Mayor here is one of Castile's most beautiful squares, and there are many preserved old streets as well as the town's medieval walls.

CHINA SYNDROME, THE
(1979, dir: James Bridges)
Jack Lemmon, Jane Fonda, Michael Douglas.
● CALIFORNIA

Timely thriller with a message, which was about to be written off as anti-nuke eco-hysteria when Three Mile Island went into an 'impossible' meltdown. Not surprisingly, there was no location filming in a real nuclear plant, but three conventional power plants in the LA area stood in (despite a large amount of hostility, directed particularly at 'Hanoi Jane'). The main exterior is the **Scattergood Power Plant, 12700 Vista del Mar** – the coast road running by Los Angeles Airport – at Playa del Rey.

CHINATOWN
(1974, dir: Roman Polanski)
Jack Nicholson, Faye Dunaway, John Huston.
● LOS ANGELES

It was reportedly a fraught production, but Polanski added bags of atmosphere and a tragic ending to Robert Towne's brilliant script (based on the corruption involved in LA's water programme) and a classic neo-noir resulted. Although the film uses plenty of period LA locations, there are some stunning sets: the interior of the Hall of Records, the Department of Water and Power, Gittes' living room and the interior of the old house in Pasadena are all fake.

The Brown Derby: The Windsor, West Seventh Street

The sinister Mar Vista Rest Home: Eastern Star Home, Sunset Boulevard

"It's Chinatown": Ord Street, Chinatown

The lake at the centre of the intrigue is the real thing. **Lake Hollywood**, a reservoir built by Water Commissioner William Mulholland in 1925 as part of the water programme, can be reached by entrances on Lake Hollywood Drive (north) and Weidlake Drive (south). Jack Nicholson tails the water commissioner in a rowing boat across the palm-fringed fifteen-acre lake in **Echo Park**, at Glendale Boulevard and Park Avenue, Silver Lake. The dry river bed, where mysterious flows of water indicate that something fishy is going on, is the **Big Tujunga Wash** at Foothill Boulevard, Sunland. Nicholson gets his nose sliced open (by director Polanski) at **Point Fermin**, Point Fermin Park, Gaffey Street at Paseo del Mar, San Pedro, south LA. He goes to see John Huston, the power behind the plotting, on **Catalina Island**, just off the LA coast. That's the 1928 white Spanish-Moderne **Avalon Casino** by the landing stage at the northwest end of Crescent Bay (it contains a beautiful 1,000 seater cinema, a grand ballroom plus a small museum and art gallery), **1 Casino Way, Avalon**.

Dunaway's mansion is one of Pasadena's grand houses on **South Oakland Avenue**. She supposedly meets up with Nicholson at the old Brown Derby restaurant, but the scene was shot in the **Windsor**, an expensive French restaurant at **3198 West Seventh Street**, behind the Ambassador Hotel, midtown LA. The Mar Vista Rest Home, where the pair go to "find a place for dad" and discover a whole load of unwittingly rich inmates, is the **Eastern Star Home, 11725 Sunset Boulevard**, on the road's western reaches in Brentwood. The uncompromisingly downbeat climax was filmed in LA's real Chinatown, on **Ord Street**.

CHITTY CHITTY BANG BANG

(1968, dir: Ken Hughes)
Dick Van Dyke, Sally Anne Howes, Lionel Jeffries.
● **BUCKINGHAMSHIRE; AUSTRIA; FRANCE; GERMANY**

Straightforward musical film of Ian Fleming's children's story about the eccentric inventor who transforms a clapped-out racing car into a magical toy. In-joke spotters will

Dick Van Dyke's home: Smock Windmill, Cadmore End

have twigged that the original owner of of the dilapidated racer is James Bond's Q, Desmond Llewellyn.

Dick Van Dyke's windmill home is the **Smock Windmill**, a genuine restoration still at **Cadmore End** on the B482 about four miles west of High Wycombe in Buckinghamshire.

The kingdom of Vulgaria: Schloss Neuschwanstein

It seems the car has pretty miraculous powers already. When Van Dyke drives Sally Anne Howes and the kids down to the beach from Cadmore End, they end up by the sea at **St Tropez** in the South of France. Gert Frobe's airship hovers over the hillside near the village of **Turville**, just southwest of Cadmore End.

Followed by Chitty, the balloon flies to the mythical child-hating kingdom of Vulgaria. The town square, where Robert Helpmann's creepy Childcatcher and the cavalry (with horses from the famous stud farm near Munich) search for the kiddies, is **Rothenburg ob der Tauber**. Rothenburg was fortunate enough to be both economically devastated by the Thirty Years War and hidden away from major commercial routes, which meant that over the years it has never been modernised. Now, although a bit of a tourist trap, it's a perfectly preserved 17th century wonder, about 45 miles west of Nurnberg toward Stuttgart, in Bavaria.

Baron Bomburst's Vulgarian castle, subliminally familiar as the model for Disneyland's Sleeping Beauty castle, is Ludwig II's marvellously kitsch fantasy of **Schloss Neuschwanstein**, about 150 miles to the south of Rothenburg. Built between 1870 and Ludwig's mysteri-

ous death in 1886, not by an architect but by a theatrical set designer (one C Jank, who was responsible for designing the original production of Wagner's *Tannhauser*) high above the Schwansee and the Alpsee. There are guided tours (there's a bus service from Schwangau, about a mile away), but in summer it can get mighty packed.

CHUNGKING EXPRESS

(1994, dir: Wong Kar-wai)
Takeshi Kaneshiro, Brigitte Lin, Tony Leung Chiu-wai.
● **HONG KONG**

All the rough energy of *A Bout de Souffle* in Wong Kar-wai's brace of stories set in flashy, frenetic downtown Hong Kong, as two lovelorn cops (in separate stories) cope with being dumped. The teeming tourist hotel, which provides the movie's title, is the **Chungking House** (aka Chungking Mansions), **40 Nathan Road** in the **Tsim Sha Tsui** district of Kowloon. The house, a 75-room traditional stopover for backpackers, is an old apartment block, divided up into guest houses of varying quality. The public areas are a bit grubby and, some say, rife with petty crime (*©* 852.2366 .5362). The bar where Kaneshiro meets mysterious, blonde-wigged drug-dealer Lin, is **Bottoms Up**, in the **Mohan's Building**, also in Tsim Sha Tsui. The fast food place, where Kaneshiro hangs out and site of the second story, is **Midnight Express, 3 Lan Kwai Fong** in the Central District.

CINCINNATI KID, THE

(1965, dir: Norman Jewison)
Steve McQueen, Edward G Robinson, Karl Malden.
● **NEW ORLEANS, LOUISIANA**

McQueen is the Kid, an itinerant card player in this Depression era poker movie shot in **New Orleans** Louisiana. The film was begun by Sam Peckinpah who was fired by the studio when he insisted on filming (albeit fleetingly) nudity – a definite no-no for a major studio in 1965.

CINEMA PARADISO

(1988, dir: Giuseppe Tornatore)
Philippe Noiret, Jaques Perrin, Salvatore Cascio.
● **SICILY, ITALY**

Lushly-scored wallow in cinematic nostalgia, with Noiret as the old picture palace projectionist who bequeaths a love of movies, literally, to his young assistant. Much of the filming was around the town of **Bagheria**, birthplace of the director Tornatore, a short bus ride to the east of Palermo in northern Sicily (the Villa Palagonia here was featured in Antonioni's *L'Avventura*). The town square, where the old cinema frontage stood, is in the village of **Palazzo Adriano**, about 30 miles south of Palermo, and close to the towns of Prizzi and Corleone, both of which have passed their names on to Hollywood.

More Sicilian scenes were filmed at **Palermo** itself; **Cefalu**; **Castelbuono** and **Lascari**.

CITADEL, THE

(1938, dir: King Vidor)
Robert Donat, Rosalind Russell, Ralph Richardson.
● **SOUTH WALES**

Donat is an idealistic young doctor in a mining village,

tempted by the easy life of London in this film of AJ Cronin's novel. The village scenes filmed in **Abertillery**, north of Pontypool, Gwent, South Wales.

CITIZEN KANE

(1941, dir: Orson Welles)
Orson Welles, Joseph Cotten, Everett Sloane.
● **LOS ANGELES; NEW YORK STATE**

Another classic from the heyday of the studio film, *Kane* was shot almost entirely in the old **RKO Studio, 780 Gower Street** at Melrose Avenue, Hollywood. The studio, built in 1920 as the Rob-ertson-Cole Studios, was bought by Howard Hughes in 1948, and subsequently by Lucille Ball in 1957. It has since been incorporated into the Paramount Studios, but you can't miss the giant RKO globe built onto the corner of the sound-stage on the north-west corner of Gower Street and

The original Xanadu: Hearst Castle, San Simeon

The old RKO Studio, Gower Street at Melrose Avenue, Hollywood

Melrose Avenue.

As an economy measure, Welles incorporated what had supposedly been 'film tests' into the finished movie. Thus, the projection room, where the opening newsreel is shown, was the real RKO projection room (with Joseph Cotten and a then-unknown Alan Ladd among the reporters); Susan Alexander's nightclub was an old Western set; and her attempted suicide had no set at all, just a couple of flats.

For real interest, though, check out Hearst Castle, the original architectural hotchpotch on which Kane's 'Xanadu' was based, in idea if not visually. The building was never completed and now never will be. Away from the impressive façade, at the rear of the building, the elaborate decoration and the thin coating of stone runs out to reveal the concrete structure beneath. Just like a movie set, in fact. Hearst Castle is on Coastal Highway 1, on the central California coast near to San Simeon, just about halfway between Los Angeles and San Francisco. It's now owned by the state, is more properly known as the Hearst State Historical Monument, and is open to the public for four tours every day except Thanksgiving, Christmas Day and New Year's Day. For details, see the website at

www.sansimeonsbest.com/hearst_castle.

Views of Xanadu in the fake documentary at the beginning of the movie are shots of **Oheka Castle, 135 West Gate Drive, Huntington**, on Long Island, New York. This private house (*website: www.oheka-castle.com*) was built in 1919 for tycoon Otto Hermann Kahn (hence the name), who also commissioned the lavish Manhattan mansion used for *The Anderson Tapes*. There are plans to turn the castle into a luxury health spa.

The grounds of Xanadu were filmed in Busch Gardens, Pasadena, an estate built by the Busch brewing family. These vast, landscaped gardens have long since vanished, but portions of the old layout can be glimpsed in back gardens of some of the grand houses in the area. You can see the remnants of the landscaping in the gardens of properties around **Arroyo Boulevard** between Bellefontaine Street and Madeline Drive.

CITY SLICKERS

(1991, dir: Ron Underwood)
Billy Crystal, Daniel Stern, Jack Palance.
● **NEW YORK CITY; NEW MEXICO; COLORADO**

In New York, city boy commuter Crystal takes the **East River Tram, Second Avenue** between East 59th and East 60th Streets, to Roosevelt Island. The western scenes

Crystal travels to work: East River Tram, the East Side

were filmed in Northern New Mexico, and at **Steward's Ranch** on Lightner Creek near Durango on Route 160, southwest Colorado.

CLAMBAKE

(1967, dir: Arthur H Nadel)
Elvis Presley, Shelley Fabares, Bill Bixby.
● **LOS ANGELES; FLORIDA**

Another production line vehicle, as rich kid Presley swaps places with a Miami Beach ski instructor. Filmed mainly on the lot at Universal Studios, Hollywood, the movie did venture out to the wilds of Florida – the finale was staged at the Orange Bowl Regatta in **Miami Marine Stadium, 3601 Rickenbacker Causeway**, Virginia Key toward Key Biscayne. Filming also took place at **Cape Florida Lighthouse, 1200 South Crandon Boulevard** at the very tip of Key Biscayne. Built in 1825, it's 95 feet tall and the oldest structure in South Florida. Open for tours (*©305.361.5811, admission charge*).

CLASH BY NIGHT

(1952, dir: Fritz Lang)
Barbara Stanwyck, Paul Douglas, Robert Ryan.
● **CALIFORNIA**

Melodramatic complications occur when Barbara Stanwyck returns from the big city to the fishing town she was brought up in, takes up with an old flame and is soon a-cheatin' on him. Lang, who always preferred studio filming, for once took a film crew up the coast to **Monterey,** where he filmed location shots on **Cannery Row**.

CLERKS

(1994, dir: Kevin Smith)
Brian O'Halloran, Jeff Anderson, Marilyn Ghigliotti.
● **NEW JERSEY**

Kevin Smith's micro-budget indie production, famously financed by credit cards and filmed in the convenience store where the director was working, **Quick Stop Groceries, 58 Leonard Avenue, Leonardo,** on the western tip of New Jersey. The video store is **RST Video,** next door at number 60. The undertaker's is **Postens Funeral Home, 59 East Lincoln Avenue, Atlantic Highlands**.

CLIENT, THE

(1994, dir: Joel Schumacher)
Susan Sarandon, Tommy Lee Jones, Brad Renfro.
● **TENNESSEE; ARKANSAS; LOUISIANA**

Another legal thriller from the John Grisham production line, with Susan Sarandon acting for underage witness Brad Renfro. Inevitably, it was filmed in the South, in Memphis and New Orleans. The movie kicks off in Memphis. Sneaking a furtive smoke with his little brother, young Renfro is involved in the suicide of a mob lawyer who lets slip where the body of a senator is buried. The woods where the lawyer shoots himself are in the **John F Kennedy Park, 4575 Raleigh-LaGrange Road** in Memphis. Renfro and his traumatised brother are whisked off to the Elvis Presley Wing of the Saint Peter Charity Hospital, actually the **Memphis Regional Medical Center, 877 Jefferson Avenue,** known as 'the Med'.

In Hollywood, no matter how poor someone is, there'll always be a high flying lawyer willing to work for nothing, and sure enough, Renfro stumbles across Sarandon, who works out of the high-rise **Sterick Building, 9 North Third Street,** a location actually specified by Grisham in the book. The seedy café, where the bad guys hire a PI to keep an eye on the kid, is a familiar Memphis location seen in Jim Jarmusch's *Mystery Train* and in Jerry Lee Lewis biopic *Great Balls of Fire,* the **Arcade Restaurant, 540 South Main Street**. Ossie Davis' courthouse is the **Memphis County Courthouse, 140 Adams Avenue,** and the Women's Detention Hall, where Renfro gets banged up, is the **Criminal Justice Center, 201 Poplar Avenue**.

The bad guys operate out of New Orleans. LaPaglia and his uncle are bugged in the **Germanic Red Room** of **Antoine's Restaurant, 713 St Louis Street** (*©* *504.581.4422*), another Grisham favourite, also seen in *The Pelican Brief.* The movie's climax supposedly takes place in New Orleans, with Sarandon driving over the Huey P Long Bridge, but the boathouse, where the senator is buried, is a country inn on **Horseshoe Lake,** near **Hughes,** Arkansas, about 30 miles west of Memphis.

CLIFFHANGER

(1993, dir: Renny Harlin)
Sylvester Stallone, John Lithgow, Michael Rooker.
● **ITALY**

Vertiginous thriller with Sly dangling around, supposed-

ly in the Colorado Rockies. For decades the Rockies and Sierras have masqueraded as every mountain range in the world, from the Alps to the Himalayas, but for once it's Euro-mountains passing themselves off as their US cousins. The environmental lobby, fearful of potential damage to the Rockies' ecology, meant that most of *Cliffhanger* was filmed in the Italian Dolomites at **Cortina d'Ampezzo,** near the German border, on **Mount Falzarrago**. Studio work meant it was the last major production, at the time of writing, to be made at Rome's declining Cinecittà Studios. The plane hijack *did* film over the Rockies, at 14,000 feet, where a US Treasury DC9 was 'hijacked' by a Lockheed JetStar.

CLOCKERS

(1995, dir: Spike Lee)
Harvey Keitel, Mekhi Phifer, Delroy Lindo.
● **NEW YORK CITY**

Richard Price's novel of 24-hour drug dealers – the 'Clockers' of the title – was set in New Jersey, and was due to be filmed by Martin Scorsese. Scorsese subsequently stepped back to become producer with Spike Lee taking over direction and so, naturally, the location leapt across Manhattan to Brooklyn. It was filmed on the **Gowanus Housing Projects,** between Wyckoff and Baltic Streets, Hoyt and Bond Streets in the Boerum Hill section of Brooklyn. The little park where the Clockers hang out, and Delroy Lindo runs his business, is on the south side of **Wyckoff Street** between Hoyt and Bond Streets. Strike's apartment, Rodney's grocery store and the church where Victor turns himself in can all be found in the immediate area. Don't bother looking for Moby's restaurant, where the murder takes place, or the Kool Breeze bar opposite. Along with the police station, they were simply abandoned buildings dressed up for the movie

CLOCKWORK ORANGE, A

(1971, dir: Stanley Kubrick)
Malcolm McDowell, Patrick Magee, Adrienne Corri.
● **LONDON; HERTFORDSHIRE; BUCKINGHAMSHIRE; MIDDLESEX**

For many years, Kubrick's refusal to allow the film to be shown in the UK gave his blackly comic version of Anthony Burgess' novel about free will and control an undeserved reputation as a fearsome video nasty. Set vaguely in the north, judging by the accents, the film was made almost entirely on location around London and the Home Counties, with the notoriously travel-phobic Kubrick choosing locations from architectural guides. Virtually the only purpose-built set, the Korova Milk Bar, was constructed in a factory just off Borehamwood High Street near to the MGM Studios (where *2001* had been shot).

Alex's estate is part of the un-speakable concrete

The Ludovico Medical Facility: Lecture Centre, Brunel University, Uxbridge

The tramps' revenge: Albert Bridge, Chelsea Embankment

disaster that is **Thamesmead South**, a vast, grim, windswept collection of tower blocks connected by intimidating walkways. The benighted subways patrolled by the Droogs, though, are over in West London, in **Wandsworth**. The Flat Block Marina is Thamesmead's artificially created **Southmere Lake**. Alex reasserts his dominance over fellow Droogs here by dumping Dim in the water and slicing his outstretched hand at **Binsley Walk** on the Lake's western shore overlooked by the blocks of Yarnton Way. More futuristic cityscapes filmed in the sixties concrete shopping centre of **Friar's Square** in **Aylesbury**, Buckinghamshire. Another urban disaster, the centre was closed down in 1990 and drastically remodelled as a much more friendly redbrick indoor mall.

Alex's apartment in Municipal Flat Block 18A, Linear North is a flat in the village of Elstree. Kubrick was ever the perfectionist: the couple who lived here moved out while £5,000 was spent on redecoration. With filming over and the flat restored to its original state, they returned only to be moved out again so two close-ups could be shot. The cat woman's house is a real mansion in the Hertfordshire countryside. Also in Hertfordshire is 'Home', Patrick Magee's futuristic pad and site of the notorious 'Singin' in the Rain' rape of Adrienne Corri (when the two met in Hollywood, Gene Kelly allegedly snubbed Kubrick for the use of this number in the scene). The house is **Skybreak**, tucked invisbly away in the tiny village of **Warren Radlett**, Hertfordshire.

The chrome and glass record shop, where Alex picks up two girls for a spot of high speed 'in and out', was the old Chelsea Drugstore which stood on the Kings Road at the northwest corner of Royal Avenue (it closed in the 1970s and is now a McDonald's).

The Ludovico Medical Facility, where Alex undergoes the gross aversion therapy, is the campus of **Brunel University** in **Uxbridge**, Middlesex. The giant overhanging concrete monstrosity is the Lecture centre in the middle of campus, opposite which Alex is received into the Art Centre. The campus is on Kingston Lane off Hillingdon Hill about a mile south of Uxbridge (*tube: Uxbridge*).

The newly defenceless Alex meets an earlier victim on the **Chelsea Embankment** at Oakley Street, SW3, and it's under **Albert Bridge** that the tramps take their revenge.

CLOSE ENCOUNTERS OF THE THIRD KIND

(1977, dir: Steven Spielberg)
Richard Dreyfuss, Melinda Dillon, François Truffaut.
● **ALABAMA; WYOMING; CALIFORNIA; WASHINGTON DC; INDIA**

Spielberg resurrected the Cinema of Awe not seen since the days of the great religious epics (just count the references to *The Ten Commandments*) as earth is visited by friendly aliens. The opening sandstorm, and the ship strand-

The landing site: Devil's Tower, Black Hills National Forest

ed in the Sahara Desert seen in the Special Edition, were filmed in California's Mojave Desert. More desert scenes were shot at **Tequisquiapan** and **Bernal**, Querétaro, Mexico. Howard K Smith, the news anchorman, shot his scenes in **Washington DC**. The footage of Truffaut making recordings in India was filmed in **Bombay**. The air traffic control center is in **Palmdale**, California.

Most of the filming, however, was in Alabama, where dirigible hangars, larger than any Hollywood soundstage, were found to house the enormous sets. Consequently, the whole production moved to Alabama. The landing site was the biggest indoor set ever built, constructed at the former air force base, now an industrial complex in Mobile. The hangars are numbers 5 and 6, Building 17 of the **Brookley Field Industrial Complex, Old Bay Street, Mobile**. Other sets built in the hangars include the road bend where the cop cars attempt to follow the alien craft into space, and the interior of the Dreyfuss house. The mountainside scenes used artificial boulders, with only twelve basic shapes carefully placed at differing angles to prevent patterns becoming obvious. Dreyfuss' house is a real house in Mobile, while Jillian's mother's house is in **Baldwin County** to the east of Mobile. The big evacuation scene filmed at **Bay Minette** over the Mobile and Tensaw Rivers, 30 miles northeast of Alabama on Route 31.

Apart from the 'strip' itself, the landing site is real and has since become a major tourist attraction. The striking sawn-off peak of **Devil's Tower National Monument** can be found in the northeast corner of Wyoming in the **Black Hills National Forest**. According to native legend, the strange formation was made by giant bears clawing at a mountain to reach a princess on the summit. According to science, it's the plug of an extinct volcano. Devil's Tower was designated the US' first national monument, in 1906. It's open all year round, and there's a visitor centre open from April to October, about three miles from the entrance. It's 33 miles northeast of Moorcroft, I-90. Nearest airports are Gillette, Wyoming, and Rapid City, South Dakota. Details at *www.gorp.com/gorp/resource/us_nm/wy_devil.htm*.

CLOSELY OBSERVED TRAINS (aka *Closely Watched Trains*)

(1966, dir: Jiri Menzel)
Vaclav Neckar, Jitka Bendova, Vladimir Valenta.
● **CZECHOSLOVAKIA**

An apprentice railway guard at a small country station in

Czechoslovakia discovers sex and love during WWII, but when he becomes a saboteur this small, closely observed comedy takes a tragic turn. It was shot on the railway station at **Lodenice** in Czechoslovakia.

CLUELESS

(1995, dir: Amy Heckerling)
Alicia Silverstone, Stacey Dash, Brittany Murphy.
● **LOS ANGELES**

Spot-on updating of Jane Austen's *Emma* (and closer to the spirit of the original than the 1996 straightforward period version), set in Beverly Hills. Alicia Silverstone's school is **Occidental College, 1600 Campus Road** in Eagle Rock, which you may recognise as California University from TV's *Beverly Hills 90210*. She shops, of course, on Rodeo Drive – the steps and fountain are **Rodeo II**, opposite the Wilshire Beverly Hotel. The shopping mall is **West Side Pavilion, 10800 Pico Boulevard**, and the skateboarding scene uses the parking lot of **Shoreline Village, 407 Shoreline Village Drive**, Long Beach. The bizarre 'witch's cottage' Silverstone wanders past in Beverly Hills is the **Spadena House, 515 Walden Drive**, originally built as a movie set. For details, see Roger Corman's *The Undead*.

COAL MINER'S DAUGHTER

(1980, dir: Michael Apted)
Sissy Spacek, Tommy Lee Jones, Levon Helm.
● **KENTUCKY; VIRGINIA; TENNESSEE**

Brit director Apted's biopic of C&W singer Loretta Lynn won Spacek an Oscar for the title role. It was filmed in **Whitesburg** and **Jenkins**, Kentucky, and just over the border at **Wise** in western Virginia. Spacek also gets to perform at the Grand Ol' Opry in the **Ryman Auditorium, 116 Opry Place**, Fifth Avenue North between Broadway and Commerce Street, Nashville, Tennessee.

COCKTAIL

(1988, dir: Roger Donaldson)
Tom Cruise, Bryan Brown, Elisabeth Shue.
● **NEW YORK CITY; ONTARIO; JAMAICA**

Cruise and Brown juggle bottles: TGI Fridays, First Avenue

Cruise learns the value of true lurve, and how to juggle bottles, in this predictable, flashy fluff, filmed mainly around New York. The East Side bar where Cruise and Brown practise their synchronised juggling was TGI Friday's (it has since closed down) which stood at **1152 First Avenue** at 63rd Street (though the interi-

Once again, Toronto masquerades as New York: Beardmore Building

ors were filmed at a recreation of the bar in a Canadian studio). Cruise's success takes him to Jamaica, where the beach bar scenes were staged at **Port Antonio**.

Previously Soupy's Tavern, now Stoopy's, Dundas east, Toronto

Much of the filming took place in Toronto, at **Soupy's Tavern** (now **Stoopy's**), **376 Dundas East**; **Lee's Palace, 529 Bloor West**; the **Old Don Jail**; **Knox College** at the University of Toronto; **Casa Loma**; **Canada Life Building**; the **Beardmore Building** and **St John's Norway Cemetery**.

COCOON

(1985, dir: Ron Howard)
Don Ameche, Wilford Brimley, Hume Cronyn.
● **FLORIDA; BAHAMAS; CALIFORNIA**

Enjoyably hokey, feelgood fantasy as alien Brian Dennehy and pals unwittingly rejuvenate a bunch of oldsters. Filming took place in the retirement haven of St Petersburg on Florida's west coast. The old folks' home is the **Sunny Shores Rest Home, 125 56th Avenue South**, while the 'magical' pool is part of a large neo-Spanish estate on **Park Street**, St Petersburg, where the poolhouse was specially built. The scenes on the 'Manta III' boat were shot offshore at **Tierra Verde** in the **Boca Ciega Bay**, and at **Nassau** in the Bahamas. The ballroom, where the folks strut their stuff, is the old Mediterranean revival style **Coliseum Ballroom, 535 Fourth Avenue North**, downtown St Petersburg (℃ *813.892.5202*). Wilford Brimley is rejected when he applies for his driving licence at the **St Petersburg Municipal Building**.

The lame, quick cash-in sequel, *Cocoon: The Return*, moved from St Petersburg to Miami, with more filming in San Francisco – the old folks' bungalows are the Sunrise Court Apartments, Miami. Jack Gilford and Elaine Stritch have a date at the **Desiree Supper Club, 9674 Coral Way** (℃ *305.559.0969*) in Miami, and filming also took place at the **Miami Seaquarium, 4400 Rickenbacker Causeway**, Virginia Key (℃ *305.361.5705*).

COLLECTOR, THE

(1965, dir: William Wyler)
Terence Stamp, Samantha Eggar, Mona Washbourne.
● **LONDON; KENT; LOS ANGELES**

Stamp is far too attractive to be the repressed and unhinged butterfly collector who kidnaps art student Eggar to add to his 'collection' in this psychological thriller. Stamp stalks Eggar in Hampstead, kidnapping her in the tiny **Mount Vernon** lane, off Holly Hill just up the hill from

The kidnapping: Mount Vernon, Hampstead

Hampstead tube station. The house where Stamp holds Eggar prisoner is a 400-year-old farmhouse in Tudor style in a vast estate near **Edenbridge**, ten miles northwest of Tunbridge Wells on the B2026 in west Kent. The local village is **Westerham**, five miles to the north. The interiors, however, were reconstructed on soundstages in the US, at Columbia's Gower Street Studio in Hollywood.

COLOR OF MONEY, THE
(1986, dir: Martin Scorsese)
Paul Newman, Tom Cruise, Mary Elizabeth Mastrantonio.
● ILLINOIS; NEW JERSEY

Cruise first grabs Newman's attention: Fitzgerald's, Berwyn

Scorsese's kinetically thrilling follow up to Robert Rossen's 1961 *The Hustler* has Newman coming back to the role of pool hall king Fast Eddie Felson, ostensibly grooming talented tyro Cruise for pool stardom. Though the story takes off from Chicago and heads across the States to the Atlantic City tournament, it was filmed

Studying human moves: O'Brien's Steakhouse, North Wells Street

on real locations almost entirely in the city of Chicago.

The pool hall where Cruise first grabs Newman's attention by trashing John Turturro is **Fitzgerald's, 6615 West Roosevelt Road** in Berwyn, west of the city (*rail: Berwyn*). Established as a pool hall in 1915, you can see Fitzgerald's as the Suds Bucket, site of the raucous dance, in *A League of Their Own*. The Sir Loin Inn, where Newman takes Cruise and Mastrantonio for a meal and a lesson in human moves, is **O'Brien's Steakhouse, 1528 North Wells Street** near West North Avenue in the Old Town district (*©312.787.3131*).

Another Chicago bar turned into a pool hall for the movie was the **Gingerman Tavern, 3720 North Clark Street** at West Waveland Avenue northwest of Wrigley Field in Wrigleyville. Real pool halls include **St Paul's Billiards** (it was formerly

Bar-cum-pool hall: Gingerman Tavern, North Clark Street

'Crossing the US' – in Chicago: Zum Deutschen Eck, Southport Avenue

the Vaudeville Theatre), **1415 West Fullerton Avenue** in Lincoln Park-De Paul, where Cruise gets beaten up; **Chris's Billiards, 4637 North Milwaukee Avenue** between

The Nine-ball Classic in Atlantic City: Navy Pier, Chicago

Laurence and Montrose in northwest Chicago; the **Gaslight, 2858 North Halsted** at West Diversey and **North Center Bowl, 4017 North Lincoln Avenue**, where a disillusioned Newman finally ditches Cruise. More scenes were filmed at German oompah restaurant **Zum Deutschen Eck, 2924 North Southport Avenue** at Diversey in north Chicago.

The Nine-ball Classic Tournament is held at the oft-used **Resorts International Hotel** on the Boardwalk at Atlantic City, New Jersey, but even this turns out to be Chicago. Although there are establishing shots of the hotel, the giant arched hall of the climactic poolathon is the **Navy Pier**, east of the Streeterville district. This 3,000 foot pier was built in 1916 (it was intended to be one of a pair but its partner never materialised) when Lake Ontario was used for commercial shipping. Post-thirties it fell into decline, until major renovations in 1976. The pier entrance is on **Streeter Drive** at 600 East Grand Avenue near lake Shore Drive just north of the Chicago River.

Similarly, Tom Cruise's Atlantic City hotel is in Chicago. It's the **Blackstone Hotel, 636 South Michigan Avenue** at East Balbo Drive (*© 312.427.4300*), the same venue that hosted the bloody banquet in Brian De Palma's *The Untouchables*.

COLOR PURPLE, THE
(1985, dir: Steven Spielberg)
Whoopi Goldberg, Margaret Avery, Oprah Winfrey.
● NORTH CAROLINA; CALIFORNIA

Spielberg in worthy David Lean mode, aiming for Oscars but missing again, films a tidied-up version of Alice Walker's novel about an abused black woman who finally finds her own freedom. Set in Georgia, it was filmed in the area around **Wadesboro** in North Carolina, including the old **Wadesboro Courthouse**, and in the towns of **Marshville**; **Ansonville** and **Lilesville**, 20-30miles east of Charlotte (most of the African scenes were shot in North Carolina, too).

COMMITMENTS, THE
(1991, dir: Alan Parker)
Robert Arkins, Andrew Strong, Michael Aherne.
● IRELAND

Raucous filming of Roddy Doyle's novel about a Dublin soul band. Set in the fictitious Barrytown, based on Kilbarrack, a working class estate in Dublin's Northside, and shot on no fewer than 44 locations, mixing Dublin's bland Northside estates with the older, characterful city centre. The opening scene, with Jimmy trying to offload cassettes, filmed on **Sherriff Street**, Dublin. Jimmy's home is in

Getting rid of the keyboard player: Bray Head Hotel, Bray

The band splits up at Gallagher's: Sir John Rogerson's Quay

Darndale. Joey the Lips' mother's house is on **Pembroke Road** in Ballsbridge. The concert, where Jimmy decides to get rid of the keyboard player, is the **Bray Head Hotel** in **Bray**, on the coast south of Dublin. The church, where 'A Whiter Shade of Pale' is played on the organ, is **St Francis Xavier's, Gardiner Street**. The Commitments' rehearsal room is above a Snooker Hall on **Lower Camden Street**. The local hall where the band starts out is the **Guide Hall** in **Synge Street**. The music bar, Gallagher's, where the band finally falls apart during a gig while waiting for Wilson Pickett to turn up, is the **Waterside Rock Bar** on **Sir John Rogerson's Quay**. It's on the quay that Jimmy finally encounters Pickett's limo.

CON AIR

(1997, dir: Simon West)
Nicolas Cage, John Malkovich, John Cusack.
● **LAS VEGAS, NEVADA; UTAH; LOS ANGELES**

Another hi-octane thriller, and an A-list cast, from the Jerry Bruckheimer stable, with a whole psycho ward of super-convicts hijacking a plane. The initial boarding, suppos-edly at Oakland Airport, over the bay from San Francisco, is **Salt Lake City** in Utah. Likewise, the desert landing, where serial killer Steve Buscemi gets added to the mix, at Carson City, Nevada, uses the local airport at **Ogden**, Utah. The desert landing in Death Valley is at **Wendover**, on the formless salt flats of the Utah-Nevada border.

The plane is finally brought to earth on the Strip in Las Vegas and, as in *Mars Attacks!*, the cameras incorporate the last moments of a Vegas landmark into a fictitious sce-nario. This time it's the demolition of the venerable Sands Hotel, which is seemingly trashed when the plane careers through its lobby. To complete the illusion, 250 feet of the Vegas Strip were also mocked up, with the plane wing apparently clipping the neon guitar of the Hard Rock Café. The road tunnel is LA's **Second Street Tunnel**, between Hill Street and Figueroa Street, downtown. Filming also took place around **Moab**, Utah, at **Determination Towers** in **Mill Canyon**.

CONAN THE BARBARIAN

(1981, dir: John Milius)
Arnold Schwarzenegger, Sandahl Bergman, James Earl Jones.
● **SPAIN**

Self-styled 'Zen fascist' Milius' po-faced and pompous

film of the pulp character was shot in Spain, at freezing **Segovia** and the blazing desert of **Almeria**. The slightly more enjoyable sequel, *Conan the Destroyer*, was filmed in Mexico, at **Samalayuca**, 50 miles south of El Paso on Route 45, and at **Juarez**.

CONFORMISTA, IL

(1969, dir: Bernardo Bertolucci)
Jean-Louis Trintignant, Stefania Sandrelli, Pierre Clementi.
● **PARIS; ROME**

Trintignant's hotel: Gare d'Orsay, rue de Bellchasse

Strange psycho-political thriller from Bertolucci, with a deeply re-pressed Trin-tignant succumb-ing to fascism in thirties Italy. Trin-tignant's hotel, where he awaits orders from his fascist bosses to kill an anti-Nazi profes-sor, is part of Paris' old **Gare d'Orsay, 1 rue de Bellchasse**, (see Orson Welles' *The Trial*, which filmed within the station, now an art museum). The professor's address and phone number in the movie are actually those of Jean-Luc Godard, included as a joke after the two direc-tors had fallen out.

In Rome, Trintignant crosses the **Sant' Angelo Bridge** to the **Colosseum**. And it's inside the Colosseum that Trintignant comes face to face with the chauffeur he thought he had killed years before.

CONQUEROR, THE

(1955, dir: Dick Powell)
John Wayne, Susan Howard, Pedro Armendariz.
● **UTAH**

John Wayne as Genghis Khan? In a Howard Hughes clunk-er? What should have been simply a hoot turned into some-thing much more sinister due to Dirty Harry – that's the nickname given to a nuclear test explosion at Yucca Flats in Nevada which dumped fallout around the area, includ-ing St George in Utah. And it was in **Snow Canyon State Park**, ten miles to the northwest of St George, that *The Conqueror* was filmed the following year. To make mat-ters worse, lorryloads of the local red earth were shipped back to the RKO studio in Hollywood for studio scenes.

By 1979 many of the stars – including Wayne and Hayward – the director Powell and many of the crew had died of cancer. Wayne was 72, Hayward 57, Agnes Moorehead 68 and Powell 59. Coincidence? If you real-ly want to visit (this was 45 years ago, after all), St George is way down in the southwest corner of Utah near the Arizona border on I-15.

CONQUEST (aka *Marie Walewska*)

(1937, dir: Clarence Brown)
Greta Garbo, Charles Boyer, Reginald Owen.
● **CALIFORNIA**

Garbo plays Walewska, Napoleon's Polish mistress, in this

classy melodrama. The island of Elba, Napoleon's place of exile, is **Point Lobos** on the Monterey Peninsula south of San Francisco.

CONTACT

(1997, dir: Robert Zemeckis)
Jodie Foster, Matthew McConnaughey, Tom Skerritt.
● **ARIZONA; WASHINGTON DC; NEW MEXICO; PUERTO RICO; VIRGINIA; FIJI**

Rational scientist Foster is the recipient of apparent alien messages in this ultimately disappointing adaptation of Carl Sagan's novel.

There's so much tricksy effects work in the film, and it's not confined to the sci-fi elements, that location spotting is a dodgy business. Young Foster's home is in **Herndon**, Virginia, though the interiors were filmed on a soundstage in LA. The huge radio telescope is the **Arecibo Observatory** in Puerto Rico, the largest single-dish site in the world, and the same one seen during the opening of *Goldeneye*. It's not quite as pristine as it looks in the movie and had to be cleaned up with a little computer generated help. It's operated by Cornell University, and if you want to visit, there is a visitor centre, open Wednesday to Friday, 10am to 4pm and Saturday, Sunday and most holidays from 9am to 4pm. Visit the website at *www.naic.edu*. The collection of telescopes is the imaginatively-named **Very Large Array**, 27 dishes arranged along three thirteen-mile arms on the San Augustin Plains at **Socorro**, New Mexico. The visitor centre is on Route 52, and there's a walking tour of the site. Website at *www.aoc.nrao.edu/AOC*. Don't look for a nearby canyon rim to sit on and contemplate the universe, though. Despite appearances, the apparently neighbouring canyon is the spectacular **Canyon de Chelly**, a great gash running through Defiance Plateau, near Chinle in Arizona. See *MacKenna's Gold* for details, or check out the website at *www.nps.gov/cach*. The dishes in the background were added later.

Similarly, though more obviously, tricked up is the vast machine designed to send Jodie Foster through a wormhole in space. The CGI image was added to shots of the real Cape Canaveral coast in Florida (see *Apollo 13* for details of the US' premier rocket launching centre). The wild and wacky UFO encampment was also a good way away from the Array, this time at **Victorville**, a standard Hollywood desert location in the Mojave, California. Also in California is the airport where Foster boards John Hurt's private plane, which shot at **Van Nuys Airport, Burbank**, another favourite location dating back to *Casablanca* and before.

Washington DC locations include the **Hotel Washington, 15th Street** at Pennsylvania Avenue NW (*metro: Metro Center*) (© *202.638.5900*), site of the formal party – the hotel's **Sky Terrace** has spectacular views over the White House and the Mall; and the finale, which was filmed, not at the Capitol Building as it appears, but on the steps of the more easily available **Treasury Building, Pennsylvania Avenue NW at 15th Street**. And, yes, that's a computer generated image of the Capitol's dome reflected in the car window to complete the illusion.

CONVERSATION, THE

(1974, dir: Francis Ford Coppola)
Gene Hackman, John Cazale, Allen Garfield.
● **SAN FRANCISCO**

The Godfather and *Apocalypse Now* notwithstanding, this is arguably Coppola's masterpiece, an audio reworking of Antonioni's *Blowup* with surveillance expert Hackman apparently uncovering a plan to kill a pair of illicit lovers. Set in San Francisco, where the crucial conversation is recorded in **Union Square**. Hackman's bizarre con-

Recording the conversation: Union Square

Hackman's dream: Alta Plaza Park, Steiner Street

fessional dream was filmed in **Alta Plaza Park, Steiner Street**, site of the car-down-the-steps stunt in *What's Up, Doc?*. The forbidding, black, X-braced building, where Hackman frets after being dismissed by a young Harrison Ford, is the **Alcoa Building, 1 Maritime Plaza** on Battery Street between Clay and Washington Streets.

COOGAN'S BLUFF

(1968, dir: Don Siegel)
Clint Eastwood, Lee J Cobb, Don Stroud.
● **NEW YORK CITY; CALIFORNIA**

A western sherriff rides into the Big Apple and shows the city boys how things get done. It's the old loner against the system story again, which Siegel had already tried in *Madigan* with Richard Widmark, and returned to with Eastwood in *Dirty Harry*. Where possible, Siegel liked to avoid studios and film on location. The opening scene, set in Arizona, was shot in the Mojave Desert near Mojave itself, California.

From here on, it's New York City, with Clint arriving (and departing at the end of the movie) by helicopter on the helipad of the **Pan Am Building**, towering over Grand Central Station at **200 Park Avenue**. You won't be able to make a similar entrance, though. The noisy, unpopular pad was closed down in 1977 after a fatal accident, in which, incidentally, the director of the notorious (but faked) movie *Snuff*, Michael Findlay, was apparently decapitated.

The cop station is NY's **23rd Precinct**. The ghastly, homophobic Pigeon Toed Orange Peel Disco scene did film in the studio. It's Universal's old opera house set, built for the 1925 Lon Chaney *Phantom of the Opera*. Coogan's and Julie's love scene was filmed in **Fort Tryon Park**, north of Washington Heights overlooking the Hudson River. The final motorbike chase was shot around **The Cloisters**, a collection of architectural bits from various monasteries in southern France and Spain, in Fort Tryon Park, **West 193rd Street** at Fort Washington Avenue towards Inwood.

COOL HAND LUKE

(1967, dir: Stuart Rosenberg)
Paul Newman, George Kennedy Jo Van Fleet.
● CALIFORNIA

An Academy Award for George Kennedy, and a nomination for Newman in this Christ-ish allegory with Newman suffering on a chain gang. Shot in the **San Joaquin River delta** area near **Stockton**, California.

COP LAND

(1997, dir: James Mangold)
Sylvester Stallone, Robert De Niro, Ray Liotta.
● NEW JERSEY

Set in the fictional town of Garrison, New Jersey, just across the George Washington Bridge from Manhattan, the movie was filmed in **Edgewater**, New Jersey. The sheriff's department is actually Edgewater's public water and electric works building. The shooting takes place on the **George Washington Bridge**.

COTTON CLUB, THE

(1984, dir: Francis Coppola)
Richard Gere, Gregory Hines, Diane Lane.
● NEW YORK CITY

Diane Lane's luxury pad: Apthorp Apartments, Broadway

The potentially fascinating story of Harlem's legendary nightclub where, in the twenties, all-white audiences flocked to watch black performers, suffered from a horribly troubled production. Producer Robert Evans, who was to have directed, was replaced by script doctor Coppola. Al Pacino and Sylvester Stallone were considered for the role that eventually went to Richard Gere. Richard Pryor was replaced by Gregory Hines. Roy Radin, a vaudeville producer, offered to raise finance from contacts in Puerto Rico, but subsequently turned up shot dead in a canyon north of LA.

The Cotton Club was meticulously recreated by designer Richard Sylbert at the **Kaufmann-Astoria Studios, 34-12 36th Street** in Queens. Original menus were copied, authentic flowers of the period were used and the superb Art Direction got a well-deserved Oscar nomination.

Location shooting took place around Manhattan. The rather sinister party to which Gere is invited by Dutch Schultz, and where rival mobster Flynn is bloodily stabbed, filmed in the **Plaza Hotel, Fifth Avenue** at 59th Street. The grand block where Diane Lane is kept in luxury by Schultz is the **Apthorp Apartments, 2211 Broadway** between West 78th and West 79th Streets.

The Abyssinian church, where Gregory Hines proposes to Lonette McKee, is the ballroom of **Prospect Hall** in Brooklyn. Another section of the hall is used for the Hoofers' club, where the old troupers go through their paces, and also the scene in the black bar where Hines tells Laurence Fishburne that he wants Mike the bouncer killed.

The machine gun revenge attack by Cage's men on Julian Beck, which backfires horribly when children are mown down, was filmed on **West 131st Street** in Harlem.

The elaborately theatrical finale was staged in **Grand Central** terminal, 89 East 42nd Street.

COUNTY HOSPITAL

(1932, dir: James Parrott)
Stan Laurel, Oliver Hardy, Billy Gilbert.
● LOS ANGELES

Stan and Ollie's hospital: Culver City Hall, Culver City

The Laurel and hardy pic where Stan visits Ollie in hospital and nearly wrecks the place. The hospital is actually **City Hall, 9770 Culver Boulevard** at Duquesne Avenue, Culver City in LA. The city hall has been rebuilt, but the old frontage has been incorporated into the new design and is still recognisable.

CRASH

(1997, dir: David Cronenberg)
James Spader, Deborah Kara Unger, Holly Hunter.
● ONTARIO, CANADA

Cronenberg's controversial film of JG Ballard's perverse novel about people getting sexual excitement from car wrecks, filmed on stretches of highway in **North York**, northern Toronto.

CRAZIES, THE (aka *Code Name: Trixie*)

(1973, dir: George A Romero)
Lane Carroll, WG McMillan, Harold Wayne Jones.
● PENNSYLVANIA

Chemical weapons are accidentally spilled into a town's water supply. Guess what happens. This Romero shocker was filmed in **Evans City** (the location for the same director's *Night of the Living Dead*) north of Pittsburgh; and in nearby **Zelienople**, both just off Route 79.

CREATURE FROM THE BLACK LAGOON

(1954, dir: Jack Arnold)
Richard Carlson, Julie Adams, Ricou Browning.
● FLORIDA; LOS ANGELES

Way up the Amazon, a group of scientists discover a scaly creature, half-man, half-amphibian, in the Daddy of all fifties creature-features. Much of the Amazon lagoon is Park Lake on the Universal backlot in Hollywood, where the *Rita* explores the creepy backwaters. The opening 'Creation of the World' sequence filmed on the **Will Rogers State Beach** at Pacific Palisades, where Sunset Boulevard reaches the ocean. Dr Maia's camp, where the fossilised man and the mangled native bodies are found (and the creature makes a grab for Julie Adam's ankle) is **Sierra Canyon**, Chatsworth, northwest of LA.

Julie peers at fish in the **Hermosa Beach Aquarium, Route 1** south of LA toward Palos Verdes. The speedboat, supposedly in Brazil's Morajo Bay, was filmed at **Portuguese Bend**, an area of spectacular rock faults on **Palos Verdes Drive South** on the south coast of the Palos Verdes Peninsula.

The second unit location filming of the excellent underwater scenes (it's diver Ricou Browning in the rubber monster suit) was at **Wakulla Springs**, fourteen miles south of Tallahassee on Route 267 in northern Florida. Wakulla Springs has an unknown depth – no diver has yet reached the bottom – 'Wakulla' is a Native word which means 'Mysterious Waters'. It's been the setting for countless underwater film sequences, including the old *Tarzan* movies.

CREEPSHOW

(1982, dir: George A Romero)
Carrie Nye, Viveca Lindfors, Leslie Nielsen.
● PENNSYLVANIA; NEW JERSEY

Compendium of Stephen King (who also stars in one episode) stories in slam-bang comic book style, filmed, like almost all of Romero's work, near Pittsburgh. The main location was the **Penn Hall Academy**, set in wooded grounds near **Monroeville** (the Mall location for Romero's *Dawn of the Dead*). The interiors were shot in the academy's gymnasium.

Father's Day: John Amplas returns from the dead to wreak vengeance on his family. Filmed at a Gothic-style mansion in **Fox Chapel**, a swanky suburb of Pittsburgh a couple of miles to the north, just off I-28, with the grounds dressed as the overgrown cemetery.

Something to Tide You Over: Ted Danson and Gaylen Ross come back from the dead to wreak vengeance on Leslie Nielsen. It's away from Pittsburgh, which sadly doesn't have a coastline, for the beach scenes, which were filmed at **Island Beach State Park** on the New Jersey Coast.

The Crate: The creepy science lab and college campus are Penn Hall itself.

The Lonesome Death of Jordy Verrill: Stephen King mutates into a giant plant. A meteor crater and a house overrun by mutoid plants were constructed on a hillside near to Penn Hall.

They're Creeping Up on You: More Penn Hall interiors, overrun this time by 28,000 (go ahead, count 'em) giant five-inch cockroaches, bussed in from bat-guano caves in Trinidad.

Creepshow II followed, with three more Stephen King chillers. King, having his say this time around, insisted that one of the episodes, *The Hitchhiker*, was shot in his hometown, **Bangor**, Maine.

CRIES AND WHISPERS

(1972, dir: Ingmar Bergman)
Harriet Andersson, Ingrid Thulin, Liv Ullmann.
● STOCKHOLM, SWEDEN

Harriet Andersson dies slowly of cancer, tended by sisters Ingrid and Liv, and earthmother Kari Sylwan in Bergman's beautiful, elegaic movie. The mansion setting is the **Taxinge-Nasby estate**, a decayed old manor house which was in such a dilapidated state that the film crew

were allowed to do what they liked, which included painting the interior walls of the house blood-red (a favourite Bergman device). The mansion is outside Mariefried in the Malar district west of Stockholm.

CRIMES AND MISDEMEANORS

(1989, dir: Woody Allen)
Woody Allen, Martin Landau, Mia Farrow.
● NEW YORK CITY

Parallel stories, one satiric, one deadly serious, as media nerd Allen struggles to make documentaries and eye surgeon Landau rids himself of his mistress.

Site of the Bleecker Street Cinema: 144 Bleecker Street, Greenwich Village

Woody Allen retires to the Bleecker Street Cinema with his niece, to watch Hitchcock's only screwball comedy *Mr and Mrs Smith*, the 1937 Edward G Robinson movie *The Last Gangster*, Betty Hutton in 1943's *Happy Go Lucky* and Alan Ladd in *This Gun for Hire*. The movie house stood at **144 Bleecker Street** in Greenwich Village, but has since closed down – in 1996 it was a video store. It was, incidentally, also the cinema where Aidan Quinn worked as projectionist in *Desperately Seeking Susan*. Smug Alan Alda offers Woody Allen a directing job during a party at the swanky restaurant **Tavern On The Green, Central Park West** at 67th Street, in Central Park itself on the West Side (see *Ghostbusters* for details).

Allen and Joanna Gleason make up a foursome with Alan Alda and Mia Farrow at the One Fifth Restaurant, which was at **1 Fifth Avenue** at Eighth Street, just to the north of Washington Square in the Village, but has now gone. Take a look at the deco highrise that housed the restaurant. This was the original choice for Sigourney Weaver's possessed apartment block in *Ghostbusters*. The wedding party that ends the movie was filmed in the **Waldorf-Astoria Hotel, 301 Park Avenue** between East 49th and East 50th Streets, midtown.

CRIMES OF THE HEART

(1986, dir: Bruce Beresford)
Jessica Lange, Sissy Spacek, Diane Keaton.
● NORTH CAROLINA

Kooky whimsy alert! It's Beth Henley on the loose again, with Bruce Beresford's adaptation of her marshmallow-centred, would-be black comedy play, which did win a Pulitzer Prize. The Mississippi-set story was filmed at **Harper House, 211 Caswell Avenue, Southport**, south of Wilmington on North Carolina's south coast (Southport is also the location for *I Know What You Did Last Summer* and TV series *Dawson's Creek*). The Botrelle mansion, where Spacek shoots her husband, is the **Orton Plantation, 9149 Orton Road**, I-33 on the Cape Fear River between Southport and Wilmington. The house isn't open to the public but the gardens are (© *910.371.6851; www.ortongardens.com/*)

CRIMSON PIRATE, THE
(1952, dir: Robert Siodmak)
Burt Lancaster, Nick Cravat, Eva Bartok.
● NAPLES, ITALY

Burt flashes his many, many teeth and goes through his acrobatic routines in a pirate romp that somehow turned into a campy spoof. The West Indies was faked up at **Teddington Studios**, and on an island in the **Bay of Naples**.

"CROCODILE" DUNDEE
(1986, dir: Peter Faiman)
Paul Hogan, Linda Koslowski, John Meillon.
● QUEENSLAND, AUSTRALIA; NORTHERN TERRITORY, AUSTRALIA; NEW YORK CITY

Mick Dundee's hotel: Plaza Hotel

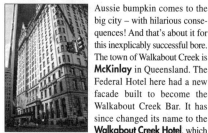

The fight scene: Cortlandt Alley

Aussie bumpkin comes to the big city – with hilarious consequences! And that's about it for this inexplicably successful bore. The town of Walkabout Creek is **McKinlay** in Queensland. The Federal Hotel here had a new facade built to become the Walkabout Creek Bar. It has since changed its name to the **Walkabout Creek Hotel**, which doubled the price of the property when it was subsequently sold. The outback scenes were filmed in **Kakadu National Park**, Northern Territory, including at the **UDP Falls**. All very wild and beautiful, until you realise that UDP stands for Uranium Development Project. Kakadu National Park begins 93 miles east of Darwin and stretches for 62 miles to the western border of Arnhem Land, an Area set aside solely for the use of Aboriginals, and from the northern coast 50 to 120 miles south. To get there, head south 22 miles from Darwin to Humty Doo then turn east onto the Arnhem Highway which leads through the park to Park Headquarters at Jabiru.

The New York hotel where Hogan stays is, of course, the ubiquitous **Plaza Hotel, Fifth Avenue** at 59th Street. The interior was recreated in the studio – Plaza bathrooms don't actually have bidets, but as it's such a hilarious joke, who cares? Hogan scares off muggers with his huge knife on the plaza in front of the **Municipal Building**, east side of Centre Street at Chambers Street. The alley where he gets into a fight is the oft-used **Cortlandt Alley**, running between Canal and Franklin Streets alongside Broadway in Lower Manhattan.

The bar, where Dundee – hilariously – gets fixed up with a man dressed as a woman, is **Vazac's**, called the Seven and B, **108 Avenue B** on the corner of Tomkins Square in the East Village (see it also in, amongst many other films, *Godfather II*, where the Rosato Brothers

attempt to garotte Pentangelli).

The happy-ending subway is **Columbus Circle**, at the SW corner of Central park – geographically nonsensical as the nearest subway to the Plaza, but it does allow cute views of Central Park for the climax.

The equally 'hilarious' sequel reversed the formula, starting out in NYC before heading Down Under.

CROSS OF IRON
(1977, dir: Sam Peckinpah)
James Coburn, James Mason, Maximillian Schell.
● FORMER YUGOSLAVIA

Peckinpah's only war movie, shot in what was northern Yugoslavia, in the area between Trieste and Zagreb. A deserted factory complex at **Obrov**, about twenty miles southeast of Trieste, was the setting for the scenes in the trenches.

CROW, THE
(1994, dir: Alex Proyas)
Brandon Lee, Ernie Hudson, Michael Wincott.
● NORTH CAROLINA

Dark, Gothic thriller, notorious for the on-set accident which killed Brandon Lee. The Detroit setting was recreated almost entirely on the backlot of the De Laurentiis Studio, **Wilmington**, North Carolina. A few interiors were found in Wilmington itself, the town familiar as Lumbertown in David Lynch's *Blue Velvet*.

CRUEL INTENTIONS
(1999, dir: Roger Kumble)
Sarah Michelle Gellar, Ryan Phillippe, Reese Witherspoon.
● NEW YORK STATE; LOS ANGELES

The Valmont house: Fifth Avenue at 79th Street

First-time director Roger Kumble's updating of *Les Liaisons Dangereuses* as a dark teen movie is set in New York high society, but much of it was actually filmed in LA. Mrs Rosemont's house, the country estate, is **Old Westbury Gardens** on Long Island (see *North By Northwest* for details).

The interior of the house filmed in two mansions and a hotel on the West Coast. The interiors are both in the exclusive Hancock Park district of LA – one the **Otis Chandler Mansion**, the other the home of screenwriter Shane Black; while the indoor swimming pool, where Phillippe gives innocent virgin Witherspoon an eyefull, is the **Biltmore Hotel, 506 South Grand Avenue**, downtown LA (see *Ghostbusters* for details of this familiar location). Also in Hancock Park is the old people's home, where Phillippe and Witherspoon do good works, which is is the **Ebell Club, 4400 Wilshire Boulevard**. The interior of Cecile's, where she takes cello lessons, is on **Blue Jay Way** in the Hollywood Hills, the shrink's office of the opening scene, is downtown LA, and Joshua Jackson's modern place is in **Brentwood**.

The Valmont house is the **Ukranian Cultural Center, Fifth Avenue** at 79th Street. The interior of Witherspoon's home is the **Marriott Essex House Hotel, 160 Central Park South**. The dress shop, where Gellar passes on a bit of gossip, is on **Robertson Boulevard**, LA, while Penn Station, where Phillippe enjoys a moist-eyed reconciliation with Witherspoon, is actually one of the stations on the new subway system in downtown LA.

CRUISING
(1980, dir: William Friedkin)
Al Pacino, Karen Allen, Paul Sorvino.
● **NEW YORK CITY**

Pacino goes into the closet as an undercover cop investigating a series of bloody murders connected to NY's gay S&M scene in this voyeuristic, homophobic exploitationer from the director of the gay self-loathefest, *Boys in the Band*. It was filmed on location around New York, despite much noisy disruption from gay activist groups who got wind of the project.

Friedkin did manage to film in real leather bars, many of which are still in existence, including the **Badlands, 388 West Street** at Christopher Street in Greenwich Village. The gay sex shop is next door, the **Underground Erotic Emporium, 390 West Street** at Dock Strip. Other locales include the **Eagle's Nest, 142 Eleventh Avenue** at West 21st Street in Chelsea; and around the famous gay areas of Christopher Street and West Street in the Village. Police scenes were filmed at **Police Plaza** in the **Municipal Building** on the east side of Centre Street at Chambers Street.

CRY-BABY
(1990, dir: John Waters)
Johnny Depp, Amy Locane, Ricki Lake.
● **BALTIMORE; MARYLAND**

Mainstream, post-Divine, Waters without the shock value of the earlier pictures but still with a great sense of camp and a cast including Joe Dallesandro, Patty Hearst, Willem Dafoe and former porn star Traci Lords. It's a pastiche of fifties teen flicks, centering on the running battle between the Straights and the Drapes, with Depp as the badboy crybaby leader of the Drapes. And, of course, it has to be Baltimore. Turkey Point, the redneck Riviera hangout of the Drapes, is the **Milford Mill Swim Club, 3900 Milford Mill Road**, Windsor Mill. Depp ends up incarcerated in the **Maryland House of Correction**.

CRY FREEDOM
(1987, dir: Richard Attenborough)
Kevin Kline, Penelope Wilton, Denzel Washington.
● **ZIMBABWE**

Attenborough follows *Gandhi* with another liberal epic, charting Donald Woods' escape from South Africa after the death in custody of his friend Steve Biko. It was not shot in South Africa.

According to Woods, an irate South African film producer announced he was filming his own version – *Biko:*

the True Story – thus demonstrating the country's freedom of expression. The producer's offices were raided by the Security Police and the film was never made.

Location filming for *Cry Freedom* was in neighbouring Zimbabwe, largely in and around the capital Harare. It was here, in the well-to-do suburb of **Avondale**, that the exterior of the Woods' house was built on a vacant lot on **Ridge Road** (interiors were filmed back at Shepperton Studios).

Woods' newspaper office is in central Harare; the flashback to Biko's cross-examination at the SASO trial was shot in the **High Court, Harare**; the Soweto demonstrations were staged in **Bulawayo**; Biko takes Woods to see how South African blacks live at **Mbare township**; he addresses football game spectators at **Gweru**; Biko's fatal incarceration was shot in real police cells in Harare.

The King Williams Town mortuary, where Woods views Biko's body, is a gymnasium in **Mutare**, and the funeral, involving 15,000 Shona extras, was shot in the **Chibuku Stadium**, a soccer ground in the Harare suburb of **Chitungwiza**.

Woods begins hitching to freedom from **Gweru**; the town of **Shurugwi** stands in for SA's Stutterheim – the **Grand Hotel** here, closed for more than a year, was partly renovated for the New year's Eve party; the border post at Telle Bridge was constructed by the **Macheke River**, near the border with Mozambique; Woods' arrival at Maseru was shot at Mutare.

Maseru Airport is the **Charles Prince Airport**, a small civil airfield for charter flights about eleven miles west of Harare; Johannesburg Airport is in fact **Sandown Racetrack** in England.

CRYING GAME, THE
(1992, dir: Neil Jordan)
Stephen Rea, Jaye Davidson, Miranda Richardson.
● **IRELAND; LONDON**

IRA man Rea becomes involved with the partner of the British soldier he was supposed to kill. The opening Irish scenes were filmed on location at **Laytown** in South Armagh. Rea moves to London and meets up with hairdresser Dil (Davidson's Oscar nomination was for Best Actor, giving away the big plot twist) at Millie's Hairdressing Salon, Spitalfields, in reality an empty clothing factory at **3 Fournier Street**. The Metro Bar, where Davidson sings the title song, was the London Apprentice pub, a famous gay bar at **333 Old Street**, now a straight pub simply called **333**. The exterior, however, is an empty

Exterior of the Metro Bar: Coronet Street, Hoxton

Jaye Davidson's apartment: Hoxton Square

The attack on the judge: Eaton Place, SW1

property behind the pub on the corner of the quaintly cobbled **Coronet Street** and Boot Street, Hoxton, N1. The 'Metro' logo is still visible. The wasteland behind, where Rea sorts out Davidson's problem, has since been built up. The gardens where he skulks to watch Davidson are in nearby **Hoxton Square**. Davidson's apartment, where the goldfish meet a sad end on the pavement, is **9 Hoxton Square**.

Irish terrorist Miranda Richardson spies on the couple at the **Clifton Restaurant, 126 Brick Lane**, E1. Davidson follows Rea to the **Lowndes Arms, 37 Chesham Street**, SW1, northeast of Sloane Square, which happens to be opposite the 'discreet knocking shop' where the IRA carry out their bloodily bungled attack on the judge, **100 Eaton Place**.

CUL-DE-SAC

(1966, dir: Roman Polanski)
Donald Pleasence, Lionel Stander, Jack MacGowran.
● **NORTHUMBERLAND**

Absurdist black comedy, with Stander and MacGowran as unlikely gangsters terrorising Donald Pleasence, sporting an even more unlikely frock, in his remote island castle. Shot in bleak monochrome on the island of **Lindisfarne**, off the coast of Northumberland.

CURSE OF FRANKENSTEIN, THE

(1957, dir: Terence Fisher)
Peter Cushing, Christopher Lee, Hazel Court.
● **BUCKINGHAMSHIRE**

The movie that put Hammer films on the map, when the studio decided to remake the 1931 Universal classic in colour, with splodges of gore and body parts. After a spate of legal wrangling with Universal, who jealously guarded their contribution to the story and copyrighted the make-up design (which is why Lee looks such a mess), Hammer began their production line of horrors. Baron Frankenstein's Swiss chateau, steeped in gloom to disguise its Englishness, is Oakley Court, now the **Oakley Court Hotel**, next door to Hammer's Bray Studios in Buckinghamshire, where the rest of the movie – and most of their subsequent output – was shot. (See *The Rocky Horror Picture Show*, which also filmed here, for details of Oakley Court). And, yes, that is Melvyn Hayes playing the young Frankenstein.

CURSE OF THE CRIMSON ALTAR

(1968, dir: Vernon Sewell)
Boris Karloff, Christopher Lee, Rupert Davies.
● **MIDDLESEX;**
HERTFORDSHIRE

Great cast, and a good photographer in John Coquillon – who did such an excellent job on the English countryside in *Witchfinder General* – are wasted in this occult thriller from the team who brought you giant moths in *The Blood Beast Terror*. And wouldn't you know it, it's the very same

location. The 1870 Norman Shaw house was once home to lyricist W S Gilbert (of Gilbert and Sullivan), who ultimately drowned in its lake. It's now the **Grim's Dyke Hotel, Old Redding** at Harrow Weald north of Harrow off the A409 (*www.grimsdyke.com*). Apart from horror movies, the house has been used for *The Prime of Miss Jean Brodie* and the semi-documentary *It Happened Here*.

The cursed house: Grim's Dyke Hotel

The local village in the movie is **Ridge Village**, three miles west of Potters Bar in Hertfordshire.

CYRANO DE BERGERAC

(1990, dir: Jean-Paul Rappeneau)
Gerard Depardieu, Anne Brochet, Vincent Perez.
● **FRANCE; HUNGARY**

Lavishly filmed version of Edmund Rostand's verse drama – the precursor of all Hollywood self-sacrificing 'women's weepies' – with Depardieu in excellent form as the poet-swordsman afraid to declare his love because of his spectacularly outsize nose. The movie was shot in various picturesque towns around France.

The town on the river, where Cyrano first reveals his feelings for Roxane, is **Moret-sur-Loing**, about 45 miles southeast of Paris, near Fontainebleau in the Ile-de-France region. Impressionist Alfred Sisley lived here until his death in 1899 and it features in many of his paintings. The streets where Cyrano acts mad and stalks de Guiche are in **Le Mans** (home of the 24-hour Grand Prix), 125 miles southwest of Paris on the River Sarthe in the Loire valley. The Gothic walls and flying buttresses in the background are the superb medieval **Cathedral of Saint-Julien**, last resting place of Richard the Lionheart's widow, Queen Berengaria.

Other period backgrounds include the town of **Dijon**, the capital of Burgundy in the Côte d'Or, and **Uzes**, fifteen miles north of Nimes in the Languedoc-Rousillon area.

The abbey where the dying Cyrano is finally reunited with Roxane is the **Abbey de Fontenaye**, three miles northeast of the little industrial town of Montbard, northwest of Dijon. Founded by St Bernard in 1118, the abbey was turned into a paper mill during the Revolution but restored in 1906.

The interiors and the balcony scene were filmed in **Budapest Studios**, Hungary, while the Battle of Arras was staged on the city's outskirts.

D

DAD'S ARMY
(1971, dir: Norman Cohen)
Arthur Lowe, John Le Mesurier, John Laurie.
● BUCKINGHAMSHIRE

Movie of the much-loved British TV series of the seventies about the Home Guard, constantly anticipating invasion by the Germans during WWII. The fictional village of Warminster on Sea is **Chalfont St Giles**, on the A413 between High Wycombe and Rickmansworth in Buckinghamshire.

DAM BUSTERS, THE
(1954, dir: Michael Anderson)
Michael Redgrave, Richard Todd, Ursula Jeans.
● LINCOLNSHIRE; LAKE DISTRICT; WALES

Michael Redgrave is Barnes Wallis, inventor of the bouncing bomb which effectively destroyed German dams during WWII. The airfield scenes were filmed on the actual location of **Scampton** (also used for the 1990 WWII airborne movie *Memphis Belle*), about five miles north of Lincoln in Lincolnshire, and at the village of **Hemswell**, a few miles further north. The testing of the bouncing bombs was staged at **Gibraltar Point**, on the Lincolnshire coast near Skegness, while a second unit crew filmed attacks on the 'dams' at **Lake Windemere** in the Lake District and at **Elan Valley** in Powys, Wales.

DAMNED, THE (aka *These Are the Damned*)
(1961, dir: Joseph Losey)
Macdonald Carey, Shirley Anne Field, Oliver Reed.
● DORSET

Strange, creepy sci-fi about a bunch of radioactive kids kept sealed underground. An English film from American director Losey, made for Hammer Films, and shot around the seaside resort of **Weymouth** in Dorset, where the children are imprisoned in caves within the cliffs to the north of the town.

DANCE WITH A STRANGER
(1985, dir: Mike Newell)
Miranda Richardson, Rupert Everett, Ian Holm.
● LONDON

Straightforward account of the case of Ruth Ellis, the last woman to be hanged for murder in Britain, after shooting her wastrel upper class boyfriend. Studio filming took place in a disused aircraft component factory in north London.

Set in the fifties, the street exteriors were mostly filmed in tight close-up to avoid the necessity of extensive period dressing. Scenes were shot at **Well Walk, Hampstead, NW3**, but not at the real site of the murder.

It was outside the Magdala Tavern, South Hill Park, NW3, opposite Hampstead Heath railway station that David Blakeley was gunned down. The pub still exists, and bullet holes can still be seen in its frontage, where a plaque commemorates the event.

DANCES WITH WOLVES
(1990, dir: Kevin Costner)
Kevin Costner, Mary McDonnell, Graham Greene.
● SOUTH DAKOTA; WYOMING; KANSAS

'Kevin's Gate' jeered the cynics during this first directorial effort, but a Best Picture Oscar got Costner the last laugh. The soft-centred but well-meaning tear-jerker was filmed on location in South Dakota, mainly near the **Triple U Standing Butte Ranch** outside **Pierre**, on Route 14 at the Missouri River, central South Dakota, where 3,500 buffalo constitute the world's largest privately-owned herd. The herd dictated the location, and the location in turn necessitated changing the subjects of the story from the Comanche of Oklahoma and Texas – as in Michael Blake's original novel – to the Sioux.

The Tennessee civil war battle was also filmed outside Pierre. The winter camp is **Spearfish Canyon** outside Rapid City, Route 90 in southwest South Dakota. Native Americans were recruited as extras from the Rosebud, Pine Ridge and Eagle Butte Reservations.

Costner sets out from Fort Hays, Kansas, about 100 miles west of Salina on I-70. A purpose-built set was constructed about four miles south of Rapid City, and the buildings have since been re-sited as a tourist attraction on Tomahawk Drive.

The wagon ride from Fort Hayes to Fort Sedgewick was filmed in the **Sage Creek Wilderness Area** of **Badlands National Park**, while a Second Unit shot the spectacular scenery of **Jackson**, Wyoming.

DANGEROUS LIAISONS
(1988, dir: Stephen Frears)
John Malkovich, Glenn Close, Michelle Pfeiffer.
● FRANCE

Lush adaptation of Christopher Hampton's play of Laclos' novel, *Les Liaisons Dangereuses*. The thuddingly literal title translation was a reaction to the assumption that foreign movies are box office poison in the US. It was filmed largely at the **Chateau de Champs-sur-Marne**, overlooking the Marne about twelve miles east of Paris. The 18th century chateau was rented by Madame de Pompadour, who spent a small fortune on improvements (the original owner, who had gone bankrupt, keeled over and died on its steps as he was about to be arrested).

Mme de Rosemonde's country house is **Chateau Maisons-Lafitte**, a superb 17th century French Renaissance chateau about twelve miles northwest of Paris, in which Louis XIV, XV and XVI stayed.

The theatre where the Gluck opera is performed is the **Theatre Montansier**, alongside the Palace of Versailles.

DANTE'S PEAK
(1997, dir: Roger Donaldson)
Pierce Brosnan, Linda Hamilton, Jeremy Foley.
● IDAHO; WASHINGTON STATE

One of the brace of volcano movies to hit the screen in

'97. Where *Volcano* blew up LA, Donaldson's movies dumps hot lava over the Pacific Northwest. The fictional town of Dante's Peak is **Wallace**, in the Bitteroot Mountains, part of the Western Rockies in Idaho. The interior of the crater is **Mount St Helens**, Washington State.

DANTON

(1982, dir: Andrzej Wajda)
Gerard Depardieu, Wojciech Pszoniak, Patrice Chereau.
● FRANCE

Des Moulins' printing shop: Cour de Commerce St Andre

Veteran Polish director Wajda filmed an adaptation of the play *The Danton Affair* by Stanlislawa Przybszewska, about the rift between revolutionary puritan Robespierre and the libertarian Danton, shot around Paris. The printing shop belonging to Camille Des Moulins (played by brilliant opera and theatre director Patrice Chereau), closed down by the revolutionary guards, is the Via Gallery on the **Cour de Commerce St Andre** opposite the rear entrance to the historic Le Procope café (one of the world's oldest cafés, its patrons have included Rousseau, Voltaire, Balzac and Benjamin Franklin as well as revolutionaries Marat, Napoleon and the real Robespierre and Danton. The entrance is at 13 rue l'Ancienne Comedie). A prototype guillotine was supposedly set up outside number 9 Cour de Commerce St Andre, St Germain-des-Pres (*metro: Odeon*).

DARK PASSAGE

(1947, dir: Delmer Daves)
Humphrey Bogart, Lauren Bacall, Agnes Moorehead.
● SAN FRANCISCO

A framed convict escapes, meets Lauren Bacall and is transformed by plastic surgery into Humphrey Bogart. To avoid showing the pre-Bogie face, the entire opening sequence of the movie uses a radical subjective point-of-view.

The prison Bogart escapes from, in a barrel, is **San Quentin**, Marin County, across the Bay from San Francisco (see *I Want to Live* for details of the notorious prison). The impressive spinning barrel shot is repeated in another San Fran-based movie, *Foul Play*. On the road south, Bacall is stopped and questioned by the law, in a scene adapted this time by Hitchcock for *Psycho*. Crossing the Golden Gate Bridge, she gets an attack of paranoia by the mar-

Lauren Bacall's stunning apartment: Montgomery Street

vellous art deco toll gates. The gates have, however, been updated since the forties. Amazingly unchanged is Bacall's impossibly stylish deco apartment, where Bogart hides out. It looks like an art direector's fantasy, but you can still see the silver, white and glass marvel at **1360 Montgomery Street** at Filbert Street. When the house was up for sale in 1996, a lifesize cutout of Bogart was cheekily exhibited in the window. It's at the top of the **Filbert Steps**, the endless stairs Bogart struggles up after his plastic surgery at the beginning of the movie.

DARLING

(1965, dir: John Schlesinger)
Julie Christie, Dirk Bogarde, Laurence Harvey.
● LONDON; BUCKINGHAMSHIRE; SURREY; FLORENCE, ITALY

An Oscar for Christie as the ambitious actress ending up as – would you believe? – 'Princess Diana', trapped in a loveless marriage, in this cynical satire from Schlesinger.

Bogarde's home: South End Road, Belsize Park

Christie flirts with TV producer Bogarde (in a part originally written as a US columnist and intended for Montgomery Clift) on the Thames foreshore by **Strand on the Green** at Chiswick, W4. Bogarde's family home is on **South End Road**, Belsize Park overlooking Hampstead Heath, NW3.

Christie retreats to the country at **Skindles** in Maidenhead. She meets Laurence Harvey at his pad at **40-41 Wimpole Street**, W1, goes shoplifting with Roland Curram at **Fortnum and Mason's** in Piccadilly and lives unhappily ever after in Rome, actually a palazzo in Florence.

DAWN OF THE DEAD (aka *Zombies*)

(1978, dir: George A Romero)
David Emge, Ken Foree, Scott Reiniger.
● PENNSYLVANIA

Second of Romero's zombie trilogy finds the crumbly flesh-eaters taking over a suburban shopping mall – cue satire on consumerism. The mall is the huge 143-shop **Oxford Developments Mall, Monroeville**, 30 miles southeast of Pittsburgh, Pennsylvania, on I-76. Surprisingly, 130 of the stores in the mall cooperated with shooting. One local bank even loaned $20,000 in notes for the scene where now-useless money flutters through the air (it was covered by a cheque to cover losses). The rooftop hideout (there isn't one in the mall) was an empty warehouse in downtown Pittsburgh.

DAY AT THE RACES, A

(1937, dir: Sam Wood)
The Marx Brothers, Margaret Dumont.
● LOS ANGELES

This mid period Marx-ism, with the brothers causing chaos at the races, was shot at the **Santa Anita Racetrack, 285**

The racetrack: Santa Anita Racetrack, Arcadia

West Huntington Boulevard, Arcadia, between LA and Pasadena. With its towering palms and distinctive green and yellow wrought ironwork, the Santa Anita has been a favourite with Hollywood punters since 1934 (it's where the James Mason fell off the wagon in the 1954 *A Star Is Born*).

DAY OF THE DEAD
(1985, dir: George A Romero)
G Howard Klar, Ralph Marrero, John Amplas.
● **PENNSYLVANIA; FLORIDA**

Third of Romero's zombie trilogy finds the zombies vastly outnumbering the living, who are holed up in an underground bunker and indulging in some nastiness of their own. Most of the filming took place in a limestone mine at **Wampum**, 35 miles northwest of Pittsburgh, toward New Castle, Pennsylvania. The giant elevator to the underground compound was the Nike missile base outside Pittsburgh, though the entrance (the elevator platform) was built in a field on **Sanibel Island**, off the west coast of Florida, near Fort Myers. Sanibel Island was also used for the beach from which the heroes manage to escape at the end of the movie. The city of the dead, rendered suitably decayed for the filming, is **Fort Myers** itself.

DAY OF THE JACKAL, THE
(1973, dir: Fred Zinnemann)
Edward Fox, Michel Lonsdale, Eric Porter.
● **FRANCE; AUSTRIA; ITALY; LONDON**

In 1963, the OAS hires a professional hitman to assassinate General de Gaulle. Zinneman's detailed, episodic filming of Frederick Forsyth's novel was filmed all over Europe.

Fox, the coldly professional gunman, initially meets up with the OAS leaders in Vienna's **Prater** park, home of the familiar Big Wheel, seen in *The Third Man*.

The UK locations are now largely defunct: Fox consults *Le Figaro* in the old circular **Reading Room** at the **British Museum Library**. He gets a false birth certificate at **Somerset House** in the **Strand**, where all UK births, marriages and deaths were recorded until the register moved to St Catherine's House. Somerset House has since found fame as a regular movie location, in *Goldeneye* (as St Petersburg), *Portrait of a Lady*, *Wilde* etc. The British police operate from the old **Scotland Yard** building on **Victoria Embankment** north of Westminster Bridge, SW1.

The town where Fox collects his customised pack-

away gun from Cyril Cusack and his fake ID from Ronald Pickup, is **Genova** on the coast of northern Italy. His fraught border crossing back into France is at **Ventimiglia** on the coast road a few miles east of Monaco. He meets up with Delphine Seyrig in a hotel, supposedly near Grasse, ten miles northwest of Cannes on the N85, but actually a dilapidated chateau near Paris, and he catches his train to Paris at **Tulle**, arriving at the **Gare d'Austerlitz**, Place Valhubert on the Quai d'Austerlitz.

The Jackal's assassination attempt on De Gaulle: rue de Rennes, Montparnasse

The Jackal makes his attempt on de Gaulle from a hotel window opposite the Montparnasse Bienvenue metro station. The hotel can be seen virtually unchanged at **150 rue de Rennes** on the place du 18 Juin 1940, at the boulevard du Montparnasse.

For the 1997 'remake' see *The Jackal*.

DAY OF THE LOCUST, THE
(1975, dir: John Schlesinger)
William Atherton, Karen Black, Burgess Meredith.
● **LOS ANGELES**

Atherton is the naïve art director whose experience of the madness of Hollywood in the thirties leads to apocalyptic visions of the burning of LA. Schlesinger's film of Nathanael West's bitingly satirical novel so perfectly captures the feel of thirties LA that, like *Chinatown*, it's surprising to find much of the movie was filmed on the Paramount lot.

Atherton's San Bernardino Arms apartment was built over the Paramount tank where Charlton Heston parted the Red Sea in *The Ten Commandments*. Its design was based on the home of author West, where he wrote *Day of the Locust*, the mock-Tudor Parva Sed Apartments, 1817 North Ivar Street, Hollywood (which are just down the road from the Alto Nido Apartments, at 1851, where scribe William Holden tapped the keys in *Sunset Boulevard*).

Karen Black's kitschy pink stucco cottage is also on the Paramount backlot, the blue sky behind it no more than a painted backdrop, which meant that filming had to be ended each day when shadows of telegraph poles began to creep across the 'sky'.

And as ever, the Hollywood sign is not real. It is, in reality, quite inaccessible. You certainly can't drive up to it. Two letters of the sign were erected in a more convenient area of the Hollywood Hills.

But there are real locations: the posh bordello, which supplies wannabe-actress Faye (Black) with a little part-time work, is a mansion on **Cerro Crest Drive** in Beverly Hills which was once owned by stripper Gypsy Rose Lee. The movie producer's house, with a horse in the swimming pool, is Frank Lloyd Wright's glorious Mayan pyramid-style **Ennis-Brown House, 2607 Glendower Avenue** below Griffith Park in Los Feliz (for details of this much-used location, see *The House on Haunted Hill*). Burgess

The movie producer's home: Ennis-Brown House, Glendower Avenue

Big Sister's Temple: the Hollywood Palladium, Sunset Boulevard

Meredith attempts to sell his patent medicine in the scarily exclusive neighbourhood of **Whitley Heights**, modelled on an Italianate village, and reputedly where Bette Davis lived in *Now, Voyager*. If it's not yet gated, as many exclusive streets now are, it can be reached by Milner Road off Highland Avenue, south of the Hollywood Bowl. When he succumbs to a heart attack, Meredith's funeral service is conducted at the 1930s deco Mausoleum of **Inglewood Memorial Park Cemetery**, northeast corner of **Manchester Avenue** at Prairie Avenue, Inglewood, south Central LA. Big Sister's Temple, where Geraldine Page works miracles, is the ballroom of the old **Hollywood Palladium**, big band mecca of the forties, at **6215 Sunset Boulevard**, and site of the fan convention in sci-fi spoof *Galaxy Quest*.

The movie studio at the centre of the action is, of course, **Paramount, 5451 Marathon Street**. See that other great exposé of Tinseltown, *Sunset Blvd* for further details of the Paramount lot. The apocalyptic riot scene is triggered by a hysterical première at Grauman's Chinese Theater, 6925 Hollywood Boulevard. The famous landmark still stands in all its kitsch cod-Oriental glory, as Mann's Chinese Theater, but it would have been impossible to stage a scene of this size and complexity on Hollywood's main thoroughfare. Instead, three blocks of Hollywood Boulevard were recreated on three adjoining soundstages at Paramount, which also allowed for the addition of a convenient, if non-existent, street to be situated directly opposite the movie palace.

DAY OF THE TRIFFIDS, THE

(1962, dir: Steve Sekely)
Howard Keel, Nicole Maurey, Kieron Moore.
● **LONDON; SPAIN**

Disastrous filming of John Wyndham's sci-fi novel about killer plants from space. A dazzling meteor shower blinds most of the world's population, apart from Howard Keel who is recovering from an eye operation in London's **Moorfield Eye Hospital, City Road**, EC1. The blinded train driver crashes into, and causes a panic at, **Marylebone Station**, NW1. Keel goes to find his ship via **Piccadilly Circus, Charing Cross** and **Westminster Bridge**. The climax of the movie takes place in **Alicante**, Spain.

A troubled production, it all but ended the career of Hungarian director Steve (Istvan) Sekely. Of the 300 mechanical triffids built, only seven full-sized monsters eventually made it onto the screen. Plus, when the assem-

bled film ran a mere 55 minutes, veteran Freddie Francis was brought in to shoot a totally unconnected subplot about Kieron Moore and Janette Scott trapped in a Cornish lighthouse.

DAY THE EARTH CAUGHT FIRE, THE

(1961, dir: Val Guest)
Edward Judd, Janet Munro, Leo McKern.
● **LONDON**

A surprisingly downbeat and detailed sci-fi, with global warming going to extremes after nuclear tests tilt the earth's axis, which also contains the priceless credit: 'Beatnik music by Monty Norman'. Much of the realism comes from the decision to film in the old black glass, deco office of the *Daily Express*, **121 Fleet Street**, EC4. The newspaper editor is actually played by Arthur Christiansen, the *Express*' editor for 25 years, who also acted as technical advisor.

The Met Centre, where reporter Judd tries to ferret out the truth, is actually the **Board of Trade Building** in Westminster. The CND rally filmed, of course, in **Trafalgar Square**, in the days when anti-bomb protesters regularly marched from Aldermaston, between Reading and Newbury. Judd takes his son to the old Battersea Funfair. The famous fair finally closed for good in the 1970s, but you can still visit the site in Battersea Park on the south bank of the Thames across from Chelsea.

DAY THE EARTH STOOD STILL, THE

(1951, dir: Robert Wise)
Michael Rennie, Patricia Neal, Hugh Marlowe.
● **WASHINGTON DC**

Michael Rennie, aided by his robot friend Gort, arrives on earth with a mission to stop all wars. Filmed in Washington DC, the flying saucer touches down on the **Ellipse**, the 52-acre green oval between the White House and the Mall.

"Klaatu barada nikto!": the Ellipse, Washington DC

DAYS OF HEAVEN

(1978, dir: Terrence Malick)
Richard Gere, Brooke Adams, Sam Shepard.
● **ALBERTA, CANADA**

Hardships of farmlife in the Texas panhandle during the early 1900s. Visually one of the most stunning movies ever, with the cinematography of the late Nestor Almendros picking up a well-deserved Oscar. Reclusive director Malick had made only one other movie, the superb *Badlands*, and didn't make another until *The Thin Red Line* in 1998.

Days of Heaven was filmed, not in Texas at all, but at **Banff** and **Lethbridge** in Alberta, Canada, among an Amish-like people called Hutterites whose way of life, set apart from modern society, pretty much approximated the period of the movie. Authentic grain silos and steam driven farm machines were loaned by private collectors.

Unbelievably, the original 70mm prints of this visual masterpiece were lost forever when a studio employee, ordered to trash unwanted reels of the Tom Cruise boy-racer flop *Days of Thunder*, destroyed the wrong title.

DAZED AND CONFUSED
(1993, dir: Richard Linklater)
Jason London, Joey Lauren Adams, Milla Jovovich.
● TEXAS

More Texan slackers from Linklater, and once again the location is the state capital, Austin, along with **Georgetown**, about twenty miles north on I-35. Robert E Lee High is **Bedichek Middle School, 6800 Bill Hughes Road** in Austin, and the local burger joint is the **Top Notch Restaurant, 7525 Burnet Road**. The alfresco party filmed in **West Enfield Park**, beneath the Moontower that the lads attempt to climb, the towering lighting system built for the local power plant.

DEAD, THE
(1987, dir: John Huston)
Angelica Huston, Donal McCann, Rachael Dowling.
● DUBLIN, IRELAND; CALIFORNIA

House of the dead:
Usher's Island, Dublin

Director John Huston was seriously ailing when he came to film this James Joyce story, and the interiors for what turned out to be his final film were shot in a warehouse north of LA in Valencia, on I-5. The exteriors, though, really are Dublin. The house is **15 Ushers Island**. Other genuine Irish locations include the **Halfpenny Bridge** over the Liffey; **Temple Bar; Anglesea Street** and **Henrietta Street**.

DEAD AGAIN
(1991, dir: Kenneth Branagh)
Kenneth Branagh, Emma Thompson, Derek Jacobi.
● LOS ANGELES, CALIFORNIA

Enjoyably flashy reincarnation thriller set in LA, with Emma Thompson as an amnesiac apparently haunted by memories of a past life in which she was brutally murdered.

The forties monochrome flashbacks see private dick Branagh as an orchestra conductor wooing Thompson. Branagh's grand mansion is **380 South San Rafael Avenue** in Pasadena. You can't see this oft-used mansion from the road, but you may recognise its entrance as the spot where

The entrance to Branagh's mansion:
San Rafael Avenue, Pasadena

Steve Martin grabs clandestine shots of Eddie Murphy leaving his estate in Hollywood satire *Bowfinger*. The concert hall, where Branagh conducts, is the beautifully preserved 1926

Orpheum Theatre, 842 South Broadway, downtown LA, still functioning as a movie house (and seen in plenty of films from *Ed Wood* to *Last Action Hero*), while the glamorous Syd's restauarant is **Perino's**, the legendary LA restaurant, **4101 Wilshire Boulevard** at Norton (see it also in *American Gigolo*).

The climax: High Tower, High Tower Drive

In the present day, the elaborate Gothicky bridge, where Branagh gets beaten up by faker Campbell Scott, is **Shakespeare Bridge**, on Franklin Avenue between Myra Avenue and St George Street, in the Los Feliz district. The jail is good old **Lincoln Heights Jail, 421 North Avenue 19, Lincoln Heights**. No longer used as a jail, the building is a frequent film location – seen in films as diverse as *A Star Is Born* and *A Nightmare on Elm Street*.

The climax of the movie was written for the location. Emma Thompson's striking, Italianate apartment complex is **High Tower, High Tower Drive**, off Camrose Drive west off Highland Avenue, North Hollywood, where the tower houses an outdoor elevator. The same complex was home to Philip Marlowe in Robert Altman's *The Long Goodbye*.

DEAD CALM
(1989, dir: Philip Noyce)
Nicole Kidman, Sam Neill, Billy Zane.
● QUEENSLAND, AUSTRALIA

Shipbound suspenser, with wacko Zane threatening Kidman and Neill aboard their yacht, filmed at **Hamilton Island**, Queensland, and at **Whitsunday Passage** on the Great Barrier Reef.

DEAD MAN
(1996, dir: Jim Jarmusch)
Johnny Depp, Gary Farmer, Lance Henriksen.
● ARIZONA; OREGON; WASHINGTON STATE

Strange black and white Western from Jarmusch, shot in **Cococina National Forest, Sedona**; **Camp Verde** and **Peoria**, Arizona; **Grants Pass**, Oregon; and **Neah Bay**, Washington State.

DEAD MEN DON'T WEAR PLAID
(1982, dir: Carl Reiner)
Steve Martin, Rachel Ward, Carl Reiner.
● LOS ANGELES

Since Reiner's homage to *films noir* ingeniously incorporates clips from Hollywood classics, most of the movie is filmed on sets which accurately match up to their forties counterparts, but there are a couple of real LA locations, notably **Union Station, 800 North Alameda Street**, downtown, where Martin is followed onto the train by Cary Grant (in a clip from Hitchcock's *Suspicion*). See *Blade Runner* for details of Union Station. Martin researches at **Los Angeles Central Library South Flower Street** at West Fifth Street, downtown LA (see *Ghostbusters* for details).

DEAD OF NIGHT

(1945, dir: Cavalcanti; Charles Crichton; Robert Hamer; Basil Dearden)
Mervyn Johns, Roland Culver, Frederick Valk.
● **BUCKINGHAMSHIRE**

The ghostly wedding: St Mary the Virgin, Turville

Brilliant compendium of ghost stories framed by a recurring nightmare. Light relief is provided by a golfing ghost story with Basil Radford and Naunton Wayne (the Charters and Caldicott team from Hitchcock's *The Lady Vanishes*). The golf course, supposedly the Royal & Ancient at St Andrews in Scotland, is **Stoke Poges Golf Course, Stoke Poges**, (for details, see *Goldfinger*, which uses the same location for Bond's game with Auric Goldfinger). The church where the deceased Wayne haunts Radford's wedding is **St Mary the Virgin** at **Turville**, Buckinghamshire – the village and church also used in the excellent wartime drama, *Went the Day Well*.

DEAD POETS SOCIETY

(1989, dir: Peter Weir)
Robin Williams, Robert Sean Leonard, Ethan Hawke.
● **DELAWARE**

Delaware's only claim to movie fame, so far, is this well-done, if mechanically predictable, tearjerker from the 'inspiring teacher who formed me' genre. Welton Academy is **St Andrew's School, Noxontown Pond Road, Middletown**, a private school situated in 2,000 acres of farmland about two miles from Noxontown Pond, between Wilmington and Dover, northern Delaware.

The theatre where Robert Sean Leonard plays Puck (elevated to "the lead role") in *A Midsummer Night's Dream*, is the historic **Everett Theatre** of St Andrew's, which was renovated specially for the film. The town is the old colonial town of **New Castle**, six miles south of Wilmington on Route 9, where Leonard's father's house is situated, in the affluent suburb of **Westover Hills**. The cave, where the society meets, is **Wolf Cave**, a registered historic landmark, although the interior was recreated in a New Castle warehouse.

DEAD RINGERS

(1988, dir: David Cronenberg)
Jeremy Irons, Genevieve Bujold, Heidi Von Palleske.
● **ONTARIO, CANADA**

Bujold makes a disturbing discovery: the elegant conservatory of Casa Loma

Weird drama about identical twin gynaecologists, which should have won Irons the Oscar he later picked up for *Reversal of Fortune*. The movie filmed in Toronto.

You won't be able to eat at either of the film's restaurants. Giannino's, the swanky Italian joint with the elaborate murals has now closed, while the elegant place where Genevieve

The ending, outside the twins' apartment: Trinity Square Park, Toronto

Bujold discovers she's been dating two men is simply the conservatory of **Casa Loma, 1 Austin Terrace**. See *X-Men*, where this faux-medieval folly became Professor Xavier's academy, for details. The Irons' apartment is **Bell Trinity Square, 483 Bay Street** behind the Eaton Place shopping complex, and it's just outside, in **Trinity Square Park**, that the movie ends.

DEATH IN VENICE

(1971, dir: Luchino Visconti)
Dirk Bogarde, Bjorn Andresen, Silvana Mangano.
● **ITALY**

Suggested by Thomas Mann's slim novella, Visconti's film works as a superb romantic tearjerker with immaculate production design. As in the book, Gustav von Aschenbach's sumptuous hotel is, of course, the **Grand Hotel des Bains, Lungomare Marconi 41**, on the east shore of Venice's Lido, though interiors were filmed at Cinecittà Studios in Rome. The Lido, a narrow sliver of land, nine miles long but barely a mile wide, is a ten minute boat ride from Piazza San Marco. To reach the hotel from the vaporetto stop on the Lido, take Gran Viale Santa Maria Elizabetta across the island to the sandy eastern shore. The Hotel des Bains is is on the corner of Santa Maria Elizabetta, over the main road from the private beach – surprisingly, it's not actually on the beach as it seems to be in the film (don't confuse it with the elaborate Moorish Hotel Excelsior, which *is* on the beach further to the south). The hotel is closed during winter months, from November to March (℃ 5260201).

The obsessed

Aschenbach stalks Tadzio: dietro la Fenice

Questioning the locals: Campiello dei Calegheri

The truth from the bank manager: Banca Commerciale Italiana, Piazza San Marco

Aschenbach's hotel: Hotel des Bains, Venice Lido

Von Aschenbach follows Tadzio through the maze of tiny canalside paths behind La Fenice opera house, **dietro la Fenice**. The tiny campo, where Aschenbach's questions elicit no more than stony silence, is the **Campiello dei Calegheri**, just west of the opera house. The bank, where the English manager is more forthcoming, is the **Banca Commerciale Italiana**, in the northeast corner of Piazza San Marco. The flashbacks to von Aschenbach's marriage were filmed in a plum orchard about 100 miles northwest of Venice at **Bolzano** in the Dolomites.

DEATH ON THE NILE

(1978, dir: John Guillermin)
Peter Ustinov, David Niven, Bette Davis.
● **EGYPT; WARWICKSHIRE**

Leaving on the Nile cruise: Hotel Pullman Cataract, Aswan

Forget the plot, enjoy the cast, in this second of the stylishly period, star-studded Agatha Christie adaptations which followed the success of *Murder on the Orient Express*. The country home of ghastly rich bitch, and victim-to-be, Lois Chiles, is **Compton Wynyates**, eight miles west of Banbury in Warwickshire. It's now a private home, and not open to the public.

Chiles and Simon MacCorkindale take off on honeymoon to Egypt, where jilted Mia Farrow follows them to the giant pyramids at **Giza**. You too can follow in their footsteps and climb the Great Pyramid, though be aware it's not officially allowed, and it is quite dangerous. People are regularly killed bouncing down the stone steps. Poirot is first seen here, by the **Sphinx**.

The grand Nile hotel, where everyone assembles and from which the 'Karnak' departs, is the **Hotel Pullman Cataract** (previously and better known as the Old Cataract Hotel), **Sharia Abtal el Tahrir, Aswan** (© *316000*). The stop-off, where the first attempt on Chiles life occurs when a chunk of rock plummets from an ancient temple, is **Luxor**. The huge temple complex is **Karnak**, where you can see the avenue of ram-headed sphinxes, and the **Temple of Amun** where Chiles is nearly killed. Farrow turns up again at **Abu Simbel**.

DEATH WISH

(1974, dir: Michael Winner)
Charles Bronson, Hope Lange, Vincent Gardenia.
● **NEW YORK CITY; ARIZONA**

A huge box-office success, but Bronson was horribly miscast as the drippy-liberal conscientious objector who becomes a vigilante anti-hero only after his wife and daughter have

Bronson's apartment: Riverside Walk, East Side

been viciously attacked. Set, and largely filmed, in New York. Bronson's apartment is **33 Riverside** at 75th Street on the East Side, and it's in nearby **Riverside Park**, overlooking the Hudson River, that he blasts his first kill. The architectural office, where he works, is **2 Park Avenue** at 32nd Street in the Murray Hill district.

Bronson was originally to have been inspired by *High Noon*, but the film company couldn't get the rights to a clip of the movie. Instead, Bronson gets a whiff of old frontier life during a business trip to Tucson, Arizona, when he watches an Old West shoot-out at the **Old Tucson Studios, 201 South Kinney Road**, a movie-lot turned tourist attraction near Tucson.

DEEP END

(1970, dir: Jerzy Skolimowski)
John Moulder-Brown, Jane Asher, Diana Dors.
● **LONDON; GERMANY**

Sexual awakenings among the young staff of a London swimming baths. The baths are the **Fulham Pools, North End Road** at Fulham Broadway, SW6, though the corridors were

The swimming baths: North End Road, Fulham

recreated in a studio in Munich. The actual pool is closed down, but the building is still clearly marked.

DEER HUNTER, THE

(1978, dir: Michael Cimino)
Robert De Niro, John Cazale, John Savage.
● **PENNSYLVANIA; WEST VIRGINIA; OHIO; WASHINGTON STATE; THAILAND**

The controversial Vietnam movie, accused of both racism and of inaudible dialogue (though it received an Oscar nomination for its sound, and an even more inexplicable nomination for its totally unbelievable script), is nominally set in the blue-collar steeltown of Clairton, about ten miles south of Pittsburgh, Pennsylvania. The town, however, is an amalgamation of eight different locales. Three are in Pennsylvania: the real **Clairton; McKeesport**, over the Monongahela River; and **Pittsburgh** itself. Two are towns to the west in the sliver of West Virginia between the Ohio River and Pennsylvania: **Weirton** and **Follansbee**. And three more are just over the Ohio River down in Ohio State: **Steubenville** and **Mingo Junction** on Route 7, and **Struthers**, which is about 25 miles north, near to Youngstown. Similarly, the steelworks, dominating the town, is a different plant from scene to scene. The opening steel factory scenes were shot in US Steel's **Central Blast Furnace, Cleveland**, though only after a nervous studio insured its stars to the tune of $5million – the plant is known locally as the Widowmaker.

The church where John Savage weds Rutanya Alda is Cleveland's **St Theodosius Russian Orthodox Cathedral, 733 Starkweather Avenue**, claimed to be an exact replica of the Czar's cathedral inside the Kremlin, Moscow. The raucous reception is held in the same city's **Lemko Hall, 2335 West 11th Street**. The Eagle Supermarket, where Meryl Streep works, is also on Starkweather Avenue.

Welsh's Bar, where De Niro and his macho pals play pool, was built behind an existing storefront on **Commercial Street** in **Mingo Junction**. Plenty of product placement here, with all the bottles of Rolling Rock neatly turned to face camera, and De Niro's ringing endorsement, "A good beer – it's the best around." To be fair, it is the local brew, from the Latrobe Brewery between Pittsburgh and Johnstown, Southern Pennsylvania. The bowling alley is the **Bowladrome Lanes, 56 State Street, Struthers**, Ohio.

The deer hunt itself, set in the Allegheny Mountains, was shot 10,000 feet above sea level in the **Heather Meadows** area of **Mount Baker**, Washington State, close to the British Columbian border.

The Vietnam scenes filmed in Thailand, with **Bangkok** standing in for Saigon, and in the **Katchanburi** district of north Thailand near to the Burmese border. The prison camp, where the VC obligingly allow the boys to play Russian roulette with three bullets (with one bound they're free...) was built on the **River Kwai** (as in *Bridge On...*). The 1973 evacuation of downtown Saigon was staged on **Throng Wad Road** in Bangkok, with 6,000 enthusiastic extras responding to a call for 800. The US Airfield is Bangkok's main international terminal, **Don Muang Airport**.

Back in the States, De Niro finds Savage an embittered patient in Cleveland's (real) **Veteran's Administration Hospital**. Walken is buried (after a pretty impressive run as a professional Russian Roulette player) in the **Pennsylvania Versailles Cemetery, McKeesport**.

The hugely successful theme music was originally written for the 1970 David Hemmings-Samantha Eggar tearjerker *The Walking Stick*, where it was heard by practically no one.

DEFIANT ONES, THE

(1958, dir: Stanley Kramer)
Sidney Poitier, Tony Curtis, Theodore Bikel.
● CALIFORNIA

Typically worthy Kramer melodrama, with white racist Curtis escaping from a chain gang only to find himself manacled to Sidney Poitier. The film is set, of course, in the Deep South, but the movie was filmed largely on the Newhall Land and Farming Company, a 40,000 acre movie lot on the northern border of LA. **Newhall** is still popular – the 'raptor attack in the long grass in *The Lost World: Jurassic Park* was shot there. It's a couple of miles to the west of I-5 on Route 126 up toward Valencia. The railroad scenes, with Poitier and Curtis clambering aboard the freight train, were filmed around fifteen miles to the northwest at **Piru** (where Judy Garland and James Mason flee to get married in *A Star Is Born*). The hazardous river crossing scene was shot even further north up in Kern County, on the Kern River (another popular location – it was the same river crossed in John Ford's *Stagecoach*).

DEJEUNER SUR L'HERBE (aka *Lunch on the Grass*)

(1959, dir: Jean Renoir)
Paul Meurise, Catherine Rouvel, Jacquline Moran.
● FRANCE

Renoir's whimsical romance sees a scientist specialising in artificial insemination taking off for a country idyll, and practising a spot of the real thing with the maid. Of course, he's humanised and finally marries her. It was filmed at **Les Collettes** forest in the Auvergne area, and in and around **Cagnes-sur-Mer** on the Côte d'Azur.

DELIVERANCE

(1972, dir: John Boorman)
Jon Voight, Burt Reynolds, Ned Beatty.
● GEORGIA

What's more disturbing, the backwater hell that the four city guys find themselves in, or the fact that the movie generated a whitewater rafting tourist boom in the area? *Deliverance* was filmed at **Rabun Gap** and in Rabun County, up in the northeastern corner of Georgia. The river Reynolds and co canoe down is the **Chattooga River**, defining the border of South Carolina. The waterfall is the **Tallulah Falls**.

DEMOLITION MAN

(1993, dir: Marco Brambilla)
Sylvester Stallone, Wesley Snipes, Sandra Bullock.
● CALIFORNIA

In this underrated satire, Stallone is a rogue cop brought out of deep freeze to combat psycho-criminal Snipes in the crime-free, politically-correct 21st century West Coast sprawl of San Angeles. Nigel Hawthorne is chief villain, establishing his Hollywood cred for the film role of *The Madness of King George*, which he originated on the London stage.

Sandra Bullock's futuristic apartment: Pacific Design Center, Melrose Avenue

San Angeles of the future: Museum of Contemporary Art, Grand Avenue

San Angeles, the Santa Barbara-Los Angeles-San Diego Metroplex, is a conflation of all three cities. The giant spiral prison set is based on Frank Lloyd Wright's Guggenheim Museum in New York – producer Joel Silver is a devotee of the architect and lives in a landmark Wright house in LA. The poster on Bullock's office wall is for *Lethal Weapon III*, another Silver production. Sandra Bullock's futuristic apartment block can be found in the inner court of the **Pacific Design Center, 8687 Melrose Avenue** in West Hollywood. The San Angeles Police Department HQ, out of which Bullock works, is the **Prudential Building, Thousand Oaks Boulevard**, north of Highway 101, Westlake Village in the San Fernando Valley.

More futuristic locations were found at the **New LA Convention Center, 1202 South Figueroa Street** between Pico Boulevard and 11th Street, downtown LA; the **Museum of Contemporary Art, 250 South Grand Avenue**, downtown LA; **Sawpit Dam, Monrovia Mountain Park, North Canyon Boulevard**, north of Monrovia, east of LA; and the **San Diego Convention Center**.

DERNIER METRO, LE (aka *The Last Metro*)
(1980, dir: François Truffaut)
Catherine Deneuve, Gerard Depardieu, Jean Poiret.
● **PARIS**

Truffaut's claustrophobic drama has Depardieu hiding out from the Nazis during the occupation. It was shot in Paris on a very tight budget, largely on sets built in a disused chocolate factory in **Clichy**.

DESERTO ROSSO, IL (aka *The Red Desert*)
(1964, dir: Michelangelo Antonioni)
Monica Vitti, Richard Harris, Rita Renoir.
● **ITALY**

Beautiful to look at, with fascinating use of colour, and filmed in the industrial landscape of **Ravenna** in northern Italy.

DESIREE
(1954, dir: Henry Koster)
Marlon Brando, Jean Simmons, Merle Oberon.
● **CALIFORNIA**

Miscast life of Napoleon. As in the similarly-themed *Conquest*, the isle of Elba was shot at **Lone Cypress, Pebble Beach** on the Monterey coastline, central California.

DESPERADO
(1995, dir: Robert Rodriguez)
Antonio Banderas, Salma Hayek, Joaquim de Almeida.
● **MEXICO**

Rodriguez turns in a virtual revamp of his low-budget calling card *El Mariachi*. Long on visual pyrotechnics and short on narrative, it was shot at **Ciudad Acuna**, Coahuila, Mexico.

DESPERATELY SEEKING SUSAN
(1985, dir: Susan Seidleman)
Rosanna Arquette, Madonna, Aidan Quinn.
● **NEW YORK CITY; NEW JERSEY**

Screwball romantic comedy with bored Arquette chasing up Madonna's cryptic personal ads. New Jersey coastal resort Atlantic City is the site of the hotel where La Ciccone takes polaroids of herself. Arriving in New York, she deposits her luggage at the world's largest and busiest bus terminal, the **Port Authority Bus Terminal, 8th Avenue** between 40th and 42nd Streets. Arquette lives over the

Spying on Madonna: Gangway 1, Battery Park

The shopping street: St Mark's Place, Greenwich Village

Hudson River in New Jersey, where her pricy-looking apartment overlooks the George Washington Bridge. She reads Madonna's ad while at the hairdressers, **Nubest & Co Salon, 1482 Northern Boulevard**, Manhasset, spies on Madonna's tryst at **Gangway 1, Battery Park** on Manhattan's southernmost tip, and subsequently follows her to the East Village. The lively hippy-punk shopping street where Arquette upsets the street stall is **St Mark's Place**, the stretch of 8th Street between Third Avenue and Tomkins Park Square, and buys Madonna's jacket at funky second-hand store **Love Saves The Day, 119 Second Avenue** at East 7th Street.

Aidan Quinn worked as a projectionist at the old Bleecker Street Cinema, which stood at **144 Bleecker Street** between Thompson Street and La Guardia Place, Greenwich Village, seen also in Woody Allen's *Crimes And Misdemeanors*. It's now a video store. Also gone is the dance club where Arquette's husband gets to meet up with Madonna, which was Danceteria, at 30 West 21st Street in the heart of Chelsea.

New Jersey locations include **Tenafly** and **Edgewater**, northern New Jersey, north of New York, west of the Hudson; and **Lakehurst**, between New York and Atlantic City. Shooting also took place at **Roslyn Heights**, Nassau County, Long Island.

DEVIL IN A BLUE DRESS
(1995, dir: Carl Franklin)
Denzel Washington, Jennifer Beals, Don Cheadle.
● **CALIFORNIA**

A stylish private eye movie from Walter Mosley's novel, set in 1948 Los Angeles, and filmed entirely on location around LA, in **Malibu, Pasadena** and in **Piru**, 40 miles to the north. The forties black centre of Central Avenue was recreated in a frequently used, and run-down, area of downtown Los Angeles, along four blocks of **Main Street**, around the **Regent Theater, 448 South Main Street**. As few photographs of Central Avenue survive, the store names, Lovejoy's Breakfast Club, Bluebird Market, Waters and Sons Record Shop, were taken from

Central Avenue of the forties: South Main Street, downtown LA

a period directory of black businesses. The mansion is **Mayfield Senior School, 500 Bellefontaine Street**, Pasadena, the interior of which became Richard Attenborough's house in *The Lost World: Jurassic Park*.

DEVIL RIDES OUT, THE

(1968, dir: Terence Fisher)
Christopher Lee, Charles Gray, Patrick Mower.
● **HERTFORDSHIRE; BUCKINGHAMSHIRE**

Disappointingly ordinary filming of a potentially scary story, with Lee as an aristocrat, on the side of the angels for once, rescuing his friends from a devil-worshipping cult. The conjuring of Satan was filmed in **Black Park Country Park**, Buckinghamshire. Villain Mocata's house is **High Canons, Buckettsland Lane, Well End**, a couple of miles to the north of Borehamwood in Herfordshire (a much used location seen in *Half Moon Street*, *Rentadick*, *Murder on the Orient Express* and lots of TV shows). Close to Elstree-Borehamwood Studios, it's a private house and not visible from the road.

DEVILS, THE

(1970, dir: Ken Russell)
Oliver Reed, Vanessa Redgrave, Gemma Jones.
● **NORTHUMBERLAND**

Brilliantly cinematic, pitch black comedy account of John Whiting's play, based in turn on Aldous Huxley's book *The Devils of Loudun*. One of Russell's, and Britain's, greatest movies. The walled city of Loudun was built, from terrific designs by Derek Jarman, at **Pinewood**. The exterior, seen behind the rotting corpses of the opening scenes, is the 12th century Norman keep of **Bamburgh Castle**, sixteen miles north of Alnwick in Northumberland. It's open Easter to October (*© 01669.620314, admission charge*).

DEVIL'S ADVOCATE, THE

(1997, dir: Taylor Hackford)
Keanu Reeves, Al Pacino, Charlize Theron.
● **NEW YORK CITY; FLORIDA**

Ambitious young countryboy lawyer Reeves finds himself working for Pacino's high-flying New York corporation. The small town he originally hails from is **Gainesville** on I-75 in northern Florida, but he's soon off to the Big Apple.

The New York locations are divided between the courts and corporate offices of Lower Manhattan and the swish penthouses of the East Side. The city's grand courthouses are on **Foley Square** in the Civic Center district, and Reeves is seen leaving the **Surrogate's Court, 31 Chambers Street** (Nicole Kidman's office in *Batman Forever* and site of the bloody climax of *Romeo is Bleeding*). Sinister Pacino, who could clearly afford to travel the city in a stretch limo, chooses to descend into

the **Chambers Street Subway Station**. Penta Plaza, his company office, is **Continental Plaza, Wall Street**, with its spectacular view of three bridges crossing the East River, but the rooftop scene, where he tempts Reeves, filmed 50 floors up on top of the **Continental Tower**. In reality, there's no water garden up there, and this cool feature was added digitally. Pacino's apartment is naturally one of NY's most prestigious addresses, **Fifth Avenue at 94th Street, Carnegie Hill**.

The property developer's apartment: Trump Tower, Fifth Avenue

Reeves' wife, Charlize Theron, is taken power shopping by the ghastly rich-bitch wives in SoHo, at **Yohji Yamamoto's, 103 Grand Street**.

The deliriously kitsch, nouveau stinking-rich living room of property developer Alex Cullen could belong to only one person. It's the real apartment of Donald Trump, occupying the top four floors of **Trump Tower, 725 Fifth Avenue**.

Pacino boils the holy water: Central presbyterian Church, Park Avenue

'St Andrew's Catholic Church', where Pacino gets the font water to boil at his satanic touch, is **Central Presbyterian Church, 593 Park Avenue** near 64th Street.

DIAMONDS ARE FOREVER

(1971, dir: Guy Hamilton)
Sean Connery, Jill St John, Charles Gray.
● **LAS VEGAS, NEVADA; CALIFORNIA; AMSTERDAM; GERMANY**

Connery returned as Bond, for his last appearance in the mainstream series, in one of the better films, unfortunately hampered by production problems and soured by a streak of gratuitous homophobia.

The diamond smuggling plot naturally takes Bond to Europe's gem capital, Amsterdam, where shocked sightseers see the body of the old lady being hauled from the **Amstel Canal** at the **Skinny Bridge**. Bond girl Tiffany Case's apartment is on the third floor of **Reguliersgracht 36**.

But, of course, Bond is soon off to glossier locations, in this case Las Vegas. Apart from the car chase through the parking lot of the Mint, which was filmed on the Universal lot, the Vegas exteriors were shot in the casino city itself. The Slumber Mortuary, where Bond nearly gets cremated, is the **Las Vegas Visitors Bureau** building on Highway 10. Although there was no shortage of over-the-top decor in Vegas, the designers decided to built the fantasy interior at Pinewood. Full advantage was taken of the 'theme' casinos though, with Bond and Tiffany Case meeting up in **Circus Circus, 2880 Las Vegas Boulevard South**, where trapeze artists dangle over the heads of the punters.

Willard Whyte's Whyte House is the **Las Vegas Hilton** (then the Las Vegas International Hotel). At the **Riviera Hotel and Casino, 2901 Las Vegas Boulevard South** (*©* *702.732.5110*) (the major location for Martin Scorsese's *Casino*), Bond wins $50,000 and Plenty O'Toole, though Sammy Davis Jr's cameo ended up on the cutting room floor. Bond stays, naturally, at the home of the bare-breasted Folies Bergère revue, **The Tropicana, 3801 Las Vegas Boulevard South**. The car chase, filmed on **Fremont Street**, meant that Vegas' main drag had to be cordoned off for three nights.

The Techtronics Missile Laboratories are the **Johns Manville Gypsum plant** on the outskirts of Vegas. Whyte's winter home, the **Elrod Residence, 2175 Southridge Drive, Palm Springs**, designed by Frank Lloyd Wright acolyte John Lautner. Blofeld launches his satellite from the **Vandenberg Air Force Base**, on the coast between San Luis Obispo and Santa Barbara, I-1, southern California. The anti-aircraft guns were mounted on a temporary oil rig which was installed off the coast of Southern California near Oceanside, Route 5, between Los Angeles and San Diego.

It was a confused and troubled production, leading to some eccentric continuity as the disparate shots were matched up. The most famous blooper is the stunt car careering down a narrow alley on its two left-hand wheels and emerging from the alley on its right side.

DIE HARD

(1988, dir: John McTiernan)
Bruce Willis, Alan Rickman, Bonnie Bedelia.
● LOS ANGELES

Willis, armed with only a sweaty singlet, saves an office block from a bunch of terrorists, but the whole movie gets hijacked by histrionic villain Alan Rickman anyway. The block is on Fox's ex-backlot again; the Nakatomi tower is the 34-story **Fox Plaza, 2121 Avenue of the Stars**, part of the Century City complex, where thousands of dollars worth of Italian marble were imported to replace any glitzy Fox marble that got chipped during the slam-bang climax.

The Nakatomi Building: Fox Plaza, Avenue of the Stars

DIE HARD II: DIE HARDER

(1990, dir: Renny Harlin)
Bruce Willis, Bonnie Bedelia, William Atherton.
● WASHINGTON DC; COLORADO; MICHIGAN; CALIFORNIA

"How can this be happening again?" wonders Willis, as he tackles terrorists once more, this time at **Washington Dulles International Airport**, some 26 miles west of downtown DC along Route 66 at Herndon (which is actually in East Virginia). Much of the movie was shot at Colorado's **Stapleton International Airport**, at the eastern end of East 32nd Avenue in Denver, and in **Brecken-**

ridge, Route 9, south of I-70 west of Denver in the Rocky Mountains. The plane crash, which called for stiff winds, was staged at **Tehachapi Pass** in the Mojave Desert, and the search for survivors at **Alpena**, on the shore of Lake Huron, northern Michigan, Route 23.

The little church taken over to become the baddies' HQ is **Highland Lake Church**, in **Mead**, on I-35 about 30 miles north of Denver, Colorado (the steeple and front of the church destroyed in the explosion were fakes added for the movie).

DIE HARD WITH A VENGEANCE

(1995, dir: John McTiernan)
Bruce Willis, Samuel L Jackson, Jeremy Irons.
● NEW YORK CITY; SOUTH CAROLINA; MARYLAND

Alan Rickman turns out to have a brother who's almost, but not quite, as theatrical, and bent on revenge. Part three is set in New York, where Irons sets up a disaster to divert attention while he robs the **Federal**

"As I was going to St Ives...": Broadway at 72nd Street

Reserve Bank, 33 Liberty Street in Manhattan's Financial District. Willis and Jackson play Simon Says, following instructions at **Tomkins Square Park**, East Village, solving the "As I was going to St Ives..." riddle on **Broadway** at **72nd Street**, and careering through Central Park in a commandeered taxi. Filming also took place at **Yankee Stadium** in the Bronx and in **Charleston**, South Carolina. The

Jeremy Irons robs the bank: Federal Reserve Bank, Liberty Street

ending was filmed at the **Truckers Inn, I-95 and Route 175, Jessup**, Maryland.

DIE, MONSTER, DIE (aka *Monster of Terror; The Color Out of Space*)

(1965, dir: Daniel Haller)
Boris Karloff, Nick Adams, Susan Farmer.
● BERKSHIRE

When Roger Corman came over to England in the sixties to make *The Masque of the Red Death* and *The Tomb of Ligeia* , his talented Art Director, responsible for the look of the stylish Poe movies, came over too, and directed this sci-fi horror. Adams is the young American looking up his English fiancée only to find that her father is Boris Karloff, while her mother is not only bed-ridden but heavily veiled. This is not good news. Karloff's house is Oakley Court, now the **Oakley Court Hotel**, a Victorian Gothic fantasy on the A308 between Maidenhead and Windsor, next to Hammer's old studios at Bray (for details of Oakley Court, see *The Rocky Horror Picture Show*).

DIM SUM
(1984, dir: Wayne Wang)
Laurene Chew, Kim Chew, Victor Wong.
● **SAN FRANCISCO**

Wayne Wang follows up his Hollywood début, *Chan Is Missing*, with a generation gap comedy also set among the Chinese-American community and again filmed in San Francisco's **Chinatown**, but also in the **Richmond** district – San Fran's New Chinatown around Clement Street to the north of Golden Gate Park.

DINER
(1982, dir: Barry Levinson)
Steve Guttenberg, Daniel Stern, Mickey Rourke.
● **BALTIMORE, MARYLAND**

Levinson's ensemble piece sees a group of college students gather to talk through problems at their local diner in 1959. The eaterie was shipped in from a diner graveyard in Oakland, New Jersey, after the owner of an existing establishment upped his asking price. It was installed on a vacant lot at Boston Street and Montford Avenue, overlooking the North West Harbor south of Patterson Park. The art department thought it would look great facing the rippling water, but director Levinson favoured logic over appearance and had it turned to face the street. The area has since been redeveloped, but you can still see the diner, which was relocated to **400 East Saratoga Street** at Holliday Street.

Guttenberg celebrates his wedding at the **Engineer's Society, 11 West Mount Vernon Place**. The diner can also be seen in two other Levinson films, *Tin Men* and *Avalon* – where it's shown being lowered into place. It also featured as the Capitol Diner in *Sleepless in Seattle*.

DINOSAURUS
(1960, dir: Irvin S Yeaworth)
Ward Ramsay, Paul Lukather, Greg Martell.
● **VIRGIN ISLANDS**

A bunch of dinosaurs and a caveman are brought back to life on a tropical island, filmed at **St Croix**, in the Virgin Islands.

DIRTY DANCING
(1987, dir: Emile Ardolino)
Jennifer Grey, Patrick Swayze, Jerry Orbach.
● **VIRGINIA; NORTH CAROLINA**

This teen coming-of-age movie queasily drags in serious issues as flippant plot devices. Set in the Catskills in the sixties, the mountains are actually the Appalachians, the main location being the **Mountain Lake Hotel, Mountain Lake**, off I-460 west of Roanoke, Virginia. There was more filming at **Lake Lure**, southeast of Asheville, North Carolina, a picturesque area which had been a major location during the silent movie era.

DIRTY DOZEN, THE
(1967, dir: Robert Aldrich)
Lee Marvin, Ernest Borgnine, Robert Ryan.
● **HERTFORDSHIRE**

Twelve convicted GIs in WWII Britain are given a chance to avoid the death sentence or a life stretch by undertaking a suicide mission behind enemy lines.

The fictitious Marston-Tyne Military Prison, where Lee Marvin chooses his recruits, is **Ashridge Management College**, once a Tudor manor house (and home to the young Elizabeth I), but greatly added to over the years and now a huge Victorian Gothic complex.

Manoevres in the Devon village: Aldbury, Hertfordshire

Marston-Tyne Military Prison: Ashridge College, Little Gaddesden

It's down a toll road from the village of **Little Gaddesden**, about six miles northeast of Hemel Hempstead in Hertfordshire (*rail: Tring*).

The military airbase, where 'Major' Donald Sutherland seriously pisses off Robert Ryan while inspecting troops, is **Hendon Aerodrome**, fifteen miles north of London. The Devon village, Red Force Division 1 HQ, where the Dozen disrupt military manoevres and capture the commanding officers, is the historic village of **Aldbury**, with its duckpond and stocks on the village green, a couple of miles to the west of Little Gaddesden in Herfordshire. This popular location can also be seen in Gainsborough's period melodrama *Jassy* and in the Swinging Sixties comedy thriller *Crossplot*.

You won't, however, be able to visit the French chateau, target of the mission. Solid and imposing as it looks, the entire building was no more than a giant set built on the backlot at MGM Studios in Borehamwood. It was 2400 feet across, 50 feet high and set in a turfed area the size of two football pitches.

DIRTY HARRY
(1971, dir: Don Siegel)
Clint Eastwood, Andy Robinson, Harry Guardino.
● **SAN FRANCISCO**

Some dubious right-wing tub-thumping mars this brilliantly made thriller, gratuitously linking CND peace symbols to the psycho-villain, Scorpio.

The movie was shot almost entirely around San Francisco, where Scorpio starts off taking potshots at SF citizens from the rooftop of the **Bank of America World HQ, 555 California Street** at Kearney Street (the building, incidentally, used for the entrance to *The Towering Inferno*). The rooftop pool, where the first victim splashes about, is on top of the **Holiday Inn at**

The threat to kill a priest: Saints Peter and Paul, Filbert Street

The search for Scorpio: Broadway

Scorpio is spotted on the rooftop: Stockton Street

Chinatown, 750 Kearny Street between Washington and Merchant Streets.

Detective Harry Callahan is soon summoned to the mayor's office – and it is the real Mayor's Office in San Francisco's City Hall, conveniently empty over a Memorial Day weekend. The imposing dome can be seen on Polk Street between McAllister and Grove.

The shootout around the café, when Harry spots a robbery in progress and gets to use his "How lucky do you feel?" spiel for the first time, is the only studio section. It was filmed at Warner Bros Burbank lot in LA, where car crashes are easier to set up, which is why San Francisco suddenly looks so *flat*.

The Police Department Harry works out of was the old Pacific Gas and Electric Building, 245 Market Street in the Financial District. The 'copter discovers Scorpio on the rooftop of 1606 Stockton Street, overlooking Washington Square, where he's choosing another victim. The twin-spired Italianate church over the way is Saints Peter and Paul, 666 Filbert Street, to which he returns to carry out his threat of blowing away a Catholic priest.

The night-time search for the killer takes Harry and his college kid partner down Broadway, past such local colour as Big Al's and the Roaring Twenties clip joints. The railway station is Forest Hill MUNI Station, between Twin Peaks and Mount Davidson.

Harry is lead around town to meet with Scorpio at the 100-foot tall concrete cross which tops Mount Davidson, San Francisco's highest peak, at 398 feet. The path up to the peak begins at the corner of Myra Way and Sherwood Court. He eventually tracks the killer down to Kezar Stadium, Kezar Drive in Golden Gate Park. And when the suspect is released, Harry tails him to a strip joint – the Roaring Twenties again, on Broadway.

The final showdown takes the hijacked school bus over the Golden Gate Bridge onto Sir Francis Drake Boulevard and through the Waldo Tunnel on Highway 101. The climax, where Scorpio is finally wasted, was at the old rock quarries of Larkspur, about ten miles north of the Golden Gate Bridge. The area has since been completely redeveloped as Larkspur Landing.

DIRTY ROTTEN SCOUNDRELS

(1988, dir: Frank Oz)
Michael Caine, Steve Martin, Glenne Headly.
● FRANCE

A remake of 1964's *Bedtime Story*, with Caine and Martin taking over from David Niven and Marlon Brando as two conmen vying for the hand of Glenne Headly on the French Riviera. Set in the fictitious Beaumont-sur-Mer, it was mainly filmed at Beaulieu-sur-Mer, an elegant Edwardian resort east of Nice, where the Grand Hotel de Cap-Ferrat stands in for Beaumont's Grand. More Riviera locations were found at Nice itself; the fishing port of Villefranche-sur-Mer to the east and at Antibes, between Nice and Cannes. Beaumont's airport is the Aerodrome International Cannes-Mandelieu, while its casino is the glass-enclosed Rotonde in Beaulieu-sur-Mer. The harbour is the yacht harbour at Juan les Pins, the art gallery, the Fondation Ephrussie de Rothschild, Villa Ile-de-Frances, Cap Ferrat. Villa Hier, a private home on the coast of Cap d'Antibes, was used for Caine's luxury pad, and tons of sand were brought in to bury the naturally stony beach.

DISORDERLY ORDERLY, THE

(1964, dir: Frank Tashlin)
Jerry Lewis, Glenda Farrell, Everett Sloane.
● LOS ANGELES

Whitestone Sanitarium and Hospital, where orderly Jerry Lewis wreaks havoc is the Greystone Mansion, 905 Loma Vista Drive in Beverly Hills. The mansion itself isn't open to the public but the extensive parkland grounds are (see *The Loved One* for details).

Whitestone Sanitarium: Greystone Mansion, Loma Vista Drive

DIVA

(1981, dir: Jean-Jacques Beineix)
Frederic Andrei, Wilhelmina Wiggins Fernandez.
● PARIS

The pirated concert: Theatre des Bouffes du Nord, boulevard de la Chappelle

The remains of Bohringer's warehouse: quai de la Seine

Parisian postman Andrei secretly tapes a concert by his heroine, opera diva Fernandez, and finds the bootleg cassette becoming the MacGuffin in a drugs'n'prostitution racket... but forget the plot, this is Paris and style is all.

Fernandez's bootlegged concert filmed at the Theatre des Bouffes du Nord, 37 bis, boulevard de la Chappelle in the 18th arrondissement. Long abandoned and used as a warehouse, it was taken over by the legendary Peter Brook as the base for his international rep company. Though the theatre was renovated, it was not redecorated, hence the quaintly distressed

Quaid's college: Austin State Capital

The woman who plants the compromising cassette in Andrei's postbag gets a stiletto in the back at the **Gare St Lazare** (the world's third largest railway station), on **rue St-Lazare**, while another witness gets the stiletto treatment on **boulevard Barbes**, alongside the boulevard de la Chappelle.

The chase: Etoile-Foch enertainment complex

Andrei meets Deruaz shoplifting at the **Lido Musique** record store on the **Champs Elysées**, and returns a stolen frock to Ms Fernandez at her suite in the impossibly luxurious **Hotel Royal Monceaux, 35-39 avenue Hoche**, just off the place Charles de Gaulle. He escapes assassins by riding his bike into the Paris Metro. The moving pavement is at the **Opera Station**.

The opera singer's hotel: Hotel Royal Monceaux, avenue Hoche

Richard Bohringer's warehouse apartment has since been demolished – it stood on **quai de la Seine** at rue de Crimée in the Bassin de la Villette. Andrei's meeting with a prostitute was filmed by one of Hector Guimard's few remaining glass art nouveau 'butterfly roof' metro stations on the **avenue Foch**. He is chased into the nearby **Étoile-Foch** entertainment complex with its arcades and bowling alley.

DJANGO

(1966, dir: Sergio Corbucci)
Franco Nero, José Bódalo, Eduardo Fajardo.
● SPAIN

Paella Western, filmed at **Colmenar Viejo**; **La Pedriza** and **Torremocha de Jarama**, Madrid.

D.O.A.

(1950, dir: Rudolph Maté)
Edmond O'Brien, Pamela Britton, Neville Brand.
● SAN FRANCISCO; LOS ANGELES

O'Brien is slipped a fatal dose of slow poison and sets out to track down his own killer before the inevitable end in this noir thriller made on location in San Francisco and Los Angeles. O'Brien finally meets up with his murderer at the **Bradbury Building, 304 South Broadway**, downtown LA (see *Blade Runner* for details of this landmark building).

D.O.A.

(1988, dir: Rocky Morton, Annabel Jankel)
Dennis Quaid, Meg Ryan, Charlotte Rampling,.
● TEXAS

Enjoyably stylish remake, with Quaid as a poisoned Professor of English. I'll just run that by you again: Dennis Quaid as a Professor of English. This time around, the story is filmed in state capital **Austin**, Texas. The college where Quaid teaches is the **State Capitol Building, Congress Avenue** between 11th and 14th Streets. When a student takes a swan dive out of the window, Quaid drowns his sorrows at the **Continental Club, 1315 South Congress Avenue**, one of Austin's many popular and packed music bars.

DO THE RIGHT THING

(1989, dir: Spike Lee)
Danny Aiello, Spike Lee, Ossie Davis.
● NEW YORK CITY

Racial tensions erupt during a blistering heatwave in New York. Lee's controversial polemic was shot in the Bedford-Stuyvesant area of Brooklyn. Sal's Famous Pizzeria stood on **Stuyvesant Street** between Quincy and Lexington. A metal plaque was set into the sidewalk to mark the location, but it's since been stolen.

DOCTOR DOLITTLE

(1967, dir: Richard Fleischer)
Rex Harrison, Samantha Eggar, Anthony Newley.
● WILTSHIRE; WEST INDIES; CALIFORNIA

Puddleby-on-the-Marsh: Castle Combe, Wiltshire

This dreadful, big budget, musicalised version of Hugh Lofting's story was astonishingly nominated for an Oscar as Best Film. To portray the little coastal town of Puddleby-on-the-Mars, the filmmakers chose the 'prettiest village in England', **Castle Combe** in Wiltshire. The troubled production ran into problems from the start. Since Castle Combe is miles from the sea in the middle of the English countryside, the tiny river which flows through the village was transformed into a seafront, and the unspoiled loveliness of the location, which

The doctor's house: Castle Combe

had attracted 20th Century-Fox in the first place, was transformed. The subsequent disruption, along with the constant high-decibel playback of the music tracks, resulted in plummeting relations with the locals. One villager was apparently intercepted carrying sticks of dynamite, with the intention of removing the set once and for all. Nevertheless, in the main street you can still recognise the sea front, the jail, and the Doctor's house. The British summer, though, trundled glumly on, and the poor weather deteriorated further, until production was halted and cast and crew headed for LA where the village was recreated on Hollywood soundstages. The beach scenes with the giant snail were filmed at **Marigot Bay, Santa Lucia** in the West Indies. Almost inevitably, the film crew arrived just in time for the rainy season.

DR. DOLITTLE
(1998, dir: Betty Thomas)
Eddie Murphy, Ossie Davis, Oliver Platt.
● **CALIFORNIA**

Out with the music, in with elaborate special effects for this update set in San Francisco, where the doctor's apartment is on **Webster Street**. The carnival is at **Aquatic Park** near Fisherman's Wharf, and the scene with the tiger was filmed at **Coit Tower** (see *Vertigo* for details). Filming also took place in **Pacific Heights**; and out of San Fran at **Big Bear**; Pasadena and **Lake Sherwood**, California.

DOCTOR IN THE HOUSE
(1954, dir: Ralph Thomas)
Dirk Bogarde, Kenneth More, Donald Sinden.
● **LONDON**

St Swithin's' Hospital: University College, Gower Street

First of many film and TV adaptations of Richard Gordon's *Doctor* books, with Bogarde, More, Sinden and Donald Houston as suspiciously elderly medical students (33, 40, 31 and 31 years old respectively) romping through every bedpan and thermometer joke known to mankind. St Swithin's Hospital is played by **University College, Gower Street**, south of Euston Road by Euston Square tube station. The fairground is the old Battersea Funfair which, until the 1970s, was in Battersea Park over Albert or Chelsea Bridges from Chelsea Embankment.

DR NO
(1962, dir: Terence Young)
Sean Connery, Joseph Wiseman, Ursula Andress.
● **WEST INDIES; LONDON**

Ian Fleming's sadistic, humourless snob disappeared for all time when Sean Connery adopted the name James Bond. First of a series of campy villains is veteran stage actor Wiseman hiding behind rubber eyelids, operating out of the fictional Crab Key in the West Indies.

The opening scenes are in **Kingston, Jamaica**, where the 'three blind mice' amble through **Harbour Street**, downtown. John Strangway is gunned down by the 'mice' and spirited away after a bridge game at the Queens Club, now the **Liguanea Club**, a fitness club in **New Kingston** (© *926.8144*). Strangway's cottage, where his secretary is offed and Bond later picks up a clue, stood on **Kinsale Street**, north of Kingston in the foothills of the Blue Mountains. It's now gone.

Time to bring in 007. Bond's first big-screen appearance is at the chemin-de-fer table of Le Cercle, at **Les Ambassadeurs, Hamilton Place**, behind the Hilton Hotel, off Park Lane, London (recreated in the studio, though a couple of years later the Beatles would be bopping the night away in *A Hard Day's Night* in the real thing). If you fancy your luck, the club is still going.

After a little banter with Miss Moneypenny, Bond begins a long tradition by swanning off to the West Indies. He is met by the impostor 'Mr Jones' at **Norman Manley International Airport**, halfway along the Palisadoes, the ten-mile spit which protects the harbour at **Kingston**, Jamaica. The meeting with the Colonial Secretary, at Government House filmed at the Governor General's mansion, **King's House**, in central Kingston. The waterfront where Bond searches out Quarrel is **Morgan's Harbour**, near Port Royal at the western tip of the Palisadoes.

Miss Taro's bungalow on the fictitious Magenta Drive is a villa at the pricy **SuperClub Grand Lido Sans Souci Hotel**, in Ocho Rios – a convenient location, since the crew were staying there – in the foothills of the Blue Mountains. 96 suites, eight deluxe rooms and seven penthouses. Even in low season it will knock you back $250 a night, and no kids – it's couples and over-16s only (© *876.974.2353*).

The waterfalls outside **Ocho Rios** provide Crab Key's shore, where Bond and Quarrel arrive. The beach where bikini-clad Andress famously rises from the the waves to grace countless schoolboys' bedroom walls, is **Laughing Waters**, then a private section of Roaring River which was the hideaway estate of recluse, and Bond fan, Mrs Minnie Simpson. You'll find the cascades a mile west of Dunn's River, three miles west of Ocho Rios, near to the hydroelectric power station.

Dr No's bauxite mine on Crab Key is a real bauxite mine, the **Kaiser Terminal** on the A3 coast road near Ocho Rios on the north shore, and the mangrove swamp where the dragon tank captures Bond and Honey is **Falmouth**, about 40 miles to the west.

DR STRANGELOVE OR: HOW I LEARNED TO STOP WORRYING AND LOVE THE BOMB
(1963, dir: Stanley Kubrick)
Peter Sellers, George C Scott, Sterling Hayden.
● **SURREY**

Kubrick's black farce filmed almost entirely in the studio at **Shepperton**. The airborne shots were taken from a B-17 bomber over the Arctic, Greenland, Iceland, Canada's Northwestern Territories and the Rockies. Location filming took place at London Airport. The computer scenes were filmed in the computer room at IBM, where the IBM 7090 – one of only three in the world – was insured by the film company for four million dollars. NY shutterbug WeeGee (played by Joe Pesci in biopic *The Public Eye*) acted as advisor to the stills photographer on the movie.

DOCTOR ZHIVAGO
(1965, dir: David Lean)
Omar Sharif, Julie Christie, Alec Guinness
● **SPAIN; FINLAND; CANADA**

Lean's lumbering, sugarcoated romance, loosely based on

bits of Boris Pasternak's novel, always seems to teeter on the verge of being a musical. Despite the endless snowscapes, most of the film was shot in Spain, with the major sets constructed in **Canillas**, a little suburb of Madrid. The Christmas card cottage, with its dinky icicles and plaster snow, was built in the mountainous region 100 miles northeast of Madrid at **Soria**. Other Spanish locations included **Granada**; **Guadalajara**; **Aljalvir** and **Aranjuez**.

The train sequence was filmed in Finland, on the railway laid during the 1940 Russian invasion, at the town of **Joensuu**, some 400 miles north of Helsinki. The refugees' trek filmed at **Lake Phyhaselka** in Finland, 100 miles from the real Russian border. There was even a little second unit filming in the Canadian Rockies, providing more mountain views for the train sequence. The giant hydroelectric dam, which bookends the story, is **Aldeadavila Dam** on the Douro River, 55 miles west of Salamanca.

DODGE CITY

(1939, dir: Michael Curtiz)
Errol Flynn, Olivia de Havilland, Anne Sheridan.
● **CALIFORNIA**

For this early colour movie, Dodge City was rebuilt partly in the studio at Warner Bros, and part on location at **Modesto**, 80 miles south of Sacramento, where the dusty plains stood in for Kansas. Longhorn cattle were rounded up for the shoot, existing fences pulled down and a period railroad train mocked up.

DOG DAY AFTERNOON

(1975, dir: Sidney Lumet)
Al Pacino, John Cazale, Chris Sarandon.
● **NEW YORK CITY**

Writer Frank Pierson picked up an Oscar for his screenplay, while Pacino, Sarandon and Lumet got nominations, for this based-on-real-life story of incompetent bank robbers, one of whom was trying to get money to finance his boyfriend's sex change. The Brooklyn bank where the couple are holed up was actually a garage on **10th Street** in Flatbush, Brooklyn.

DOGMA

(1999, dir: Kevin Smith)
Ben Affleck, Linda Fiorentino, Matt Damon.
● **PENNSYLVANIA; NEW JERSEY**

The Catholic Church got pretty upset over Kevin Smith's rambling but imaginative satire, which sees Affleck and Damon as a pair of dispossessed angels attempting to re-enter Heaven via a loophole in Catholic doctrine.

There are only glimpses of Smith's usual stomping ground of **Red Bank** and **Asbury Park** (where the old man is battered at the opening of the movie), for, although the movie is set in New Jersey and Illinois, most of it was in fact shot around Pittsburgh. For instance, General Mitchell Airport, Milwaukee, where Affleck and Damon tempt a nun to go AWOL, is **Pittsburgh International Airport**, and the Mexican restaurant, in which Linda Fiorentino's supernatural mission is explained by angel Alan Rickman is the **Franklin Inn, 2313 Rochester Road, Franklin Park** (© *412.366.4140*), northwest Pittsburgh.

On Pittsburgh's North Side, muse Salma Hayek wows 'em as a stripper in silver bra and specs at the **Park View Cafe, 2 East North Avenue** at Federal Street. Down southwest of the city in **Dormont** you'll find the **Dormont Cafe, 2887 West Liberty Avenue**, where demonic Jason Lee is dispatched by a holy golf club. Also in Dormont was Mooby's Fast Food joint, an old Burger King restaurant, site of Chris Rock's revelations about the real Christ, now a Rite Aid drugstore at **3210 Banksville Road**, Highway 19, opposite Dormont Park.

In Pittsburgh itself you can't miss the Mooby Corp Building, **USX Tower, 600 Grant Street** – Pittsburgh's tallest skyscraper – and the Software Engineering Institute of **Carnegie Mellon University, 4500 Fifth Avenue** between Dithridge and Craig Streets, which was used for the Mooby boardroom, where Matt Damon guns down the directors. The posh restaurant where Rickman makes the astonishing revelation that God has gone missing, is the **Grand Concourse Restaurant** (© *412.261.1717*), the restored waiting room of Pittsburgh's old P & LE railway station in **Station Square**. St Michael's Church, supposedly in Red Bank, NJ, where Cardinal Glick's Catholicism WOW! movement replaces the depressing crucifix with the upbeat Buddy Christ – and site of the apocalyptic climax – is the **Everlasting Covenant Cathedral, 130 Larimer Avenue** in **East Liberty** (watch out though, this isn't a particularly comfortable section of town).

DOGS OF WAR, THE

(1980, dir: John Irvin)
Christopher Walken, Tom Berenger, Colin Blakeley.
● **BELIZE**

Mercenaries in West Africa, from a Frederick Forsyth novel. The major location is **Chateau Caribbean, 6 Marine Parade** (© *02.30800*) on the east coast. It's now a luxurious colonial-style hotel.

The West African location, now a hotel: Chateau Caribbean, Belize

DOLCE VITA, LA (aka *The Sweet Life*)

(1960, dir: Federico Fellini)
Marcello Mastroianni, Anita Ekberg, Anouk Aimée.
● **ROME**

Fellini's first non-narrative visual delirium introduced the word *paparazzi* to the world, and the hacks and the sybarites of Rome. It was mostly filmed on sets at Cinecittà Studios outside Rome, but Anita Ekberg's much-publicised frolic in the fountain was filmed on location. Like Marilyn Monroe's subway grating scene in *The Seven Year Itch*, the shoot was given plenty of advance

Ekberg's frolic: Trevi Fountain, Rome

publicity and was shot at the **Trevi Fountain** in a freezing January in front of 5,000 onlookers, some of whom had paid to rent rooms overlooking the site.

DONNIE BRASCO
(1997, dir: Mike Newell)
Al Pacino, Johnny Depp, Anne Heche.
● NEW YORK CITY

The director of the enjoyable, if over-rated, *Four Weddings and a Funeral* changed genres radically to come up with one of the best New York gangster movies, based on the true story of agent Joe Pistone (Depp), who, in the seventies, infiltrated the mob under the name Donnie Brasco.

Pacino and Depp first meet: Mare Chiaro: Mulberry Street, Little Italy

Filming *Donnie Brasco* on Mott Street

Pacino is brilliant as the doomed middle-ranker who unwittingly signs his own death warrant by vouching for the fraudulent Brasco.

It's set mostly in New York, and was all shot there – even the short Miami episode. The Little Italy bar where Pacino and Depp first meet is **Mare Chiaro, 176 Mulberry Street** between Broome and Grand Streets. The bar, also known as **Tony's**, has been seen in many movies including *Nine 1/2 Weeks*, *State of Grace* and *The Godfather, Part III* – a list of its film credits hangs on the wall. Although photos of the owner with the likes of Frank Sinatra decorate the bar, the relentless encroachment of Chinatown on the area of the old Little Italy means that this once-Italian bar is now Chinese run.

Depp meets up with his contacts in **Katz's Delicatessen, 205 East Houston Street** between Ludlow and Orchard Streets in the East Village, most famous as the restaurant where Meg Ryan faked it for Billy Crystal in *When Harry Met Sally....* Depp and Pacino meet up with the mob boss on **Mott Street** in Little Italy, where the Genco olive oil company had its offices in *The Godfather*.

DONOVAN'S REEF
(1963, dir: John Ford)
John Wayne, Elizabeth Allen, Lee Marvin.
● HAWAII

John Ford's clumpingly macho comic knockabout is set on a South Seas island, but was filmed on the island of **Kauai**, Hawaii (see *Jurassic Park* for details). "I believe in God, as we all do, but I respect the beliefs and customs of my people," says the native woman, hedging her bets, as she prays to the god of the canyon.

You can find the stunning **Waimea Canyon**, 'the Grand Canyon of the Pacific', in the wilderness on the west side of the island. Take Kaumualii Highway (Highway 50),

running along the south coast, to Waimea, then head north on Waimea Canyon Road. Two lookouts on the road, Waimea Canyon Lookout and Puu Hinahina, both give breath-taking views across the mile-wide valley.

DON'T LOOK NOW
(1973, dir: Nicolas Roeg)
Donald Sutherland, Julie Christie, Hilary Mason.
● VENICE, ITALY

Dank, crumbling, off-season Venice provides the setting for Roeg's reinvention of a Daphne du Maurier short story as a dazzling cinematic mosaic. Donald Sutherland is the disbelieving architect, doomed by a refusal to accept his own extrasensory powers. The Europa Hotel, where Sutherland and Christie stay, is a conflation of two classy – and pricy – Venetian establishments. The lobby and the exteriors are the **Hotel Gabrielli Sandwirth, Castello 4110, Riva degli Schiavoni**, (*℡ 5231580*), a converted Gothic palace overlooking the San Marco Canal just east of the Piazza San Marco. The hotel interior – location for one of cinema's most convincing sex scenes – is over to the west of Piazza San Marco, the expensive **Bauer Grunwald, San Marco 1459, Campo San Moise** (*℡ 5207022*).

The church Sutherland is restoring is way down in the southwest of the city. It's **San Nicolo dei Mendicoli,** one of the oldest in

Sutherland and Christie's hotel – exterior: Hotel Gabrielli Sandwirth, Riva degli Schiavoni

...and the interior: Hotel Bauer Grunwald, Campo San Moise

The church Sutherland restores: San Nicolo dei Mendicoli, Campo San Nicolo

The church interior: San Nicolo dei Mendicoli

The detective trails Sutherland around the city: San Polo

Christie faints at the restaurant: Ristorante Roma, Canal Grande at Ponte Scalzi

The sisters' hotel: La Fenice et des Artistes, Campiello Fenice

Sutherland follows the mysterious little figure: Calle di Mezzo

Venice and restored – in real life – during the seventies (though you won't see the mosaic worked on in the movie, which was nothing more than a prop). The church, which is open to the public from 10 till noon in the mornings and 4.30 to 7.30 in the afternoon, is on **Campo San Nicolo**, a small square surrounded on three sides by the Rio di San Nicolo and the Rio delle Terese. To get to it, you need to follow the Canale della Giudecca waterfront, the Fondamenta delle Zattere, west past the Stazione Marittima toward the rather glum, industrial San Marta area.

The suspicious detective follows Sutherland through the **San Polo** district in the centre of the northern curve of the Grand Canal's reverse 'S', to the southwest of Venice's second largest square, the Campo San Polo: the **Calle di Castel Forte** and the **Ponte Vinanti**.

The restaurant in which Sutherland and Christie meet the two strange sisters is the **Ristorante Roma**, near to the Ponte Scalzi over the Grand Canal by the railway station, Stazione Ferrovia Santa Lucia.

After Julie Christie collapses, she's taken to hospital from the landing stage on the north side of the Grand Canal here. The sisters stay at **La Fenice et des Artistes, San Marco 1936, Campiello Fenice** alongside, and serving, the Fenice Opera House which burned to the ground in such mysterious circumstances, west of Piazza San Marco.

The narrow canal, to which Sutherland finally follows the tiny red-coated figure, is the **Calle di Mezzo**, northeast of Piazza San Marco, to the gates of the **Palazzo Grimani** (at the junction of Rio di Santa Maria Formosa and Rio di San Severo – don't confuse it with the *other* Palazzo Grimani on the Canal Grande), where he finds out that – oops! – it's not his daughter after all. The Palazzo has been deserted for years, but in 1998 was in the process of being ren-

The funeral: Church of San Stae, Campo San Stae

Sutherland finally meets the mysterious figure: Palazzo Grimani, Calle di Mezzo

ovated. The gated entrance to the Palazzo, through which Sutherland enters, can be seen on Calle di Mezzo.

The funeral, which ends the film, is at the 17th century **Church of San Stae** (a contraction of San Eustachio) at **Campo San Stae** on the northern curve of Canal Grande.

DOORS, THE

(1991, dir: Oliver Stone)
Val Kilmer, Meg Ryan, Frank Whaley.
● CALIFORNIA; NEW YORK CITY; PARIS

Stone's wackily mystical biopic of Doors singer/songwriter/poet Jim Morrison was shot at getting on for 80 locations, mainly around California. The band first comes together at LA's Bohemian hangout, **Venice Beach**. Getting out of LA for a couple of scenes, they visit **San Francisco**, in its full sixties incarnation, and outrage Ed Sullivan in **New York** (though Morrison didn't actually sing "Girl we couldn't get much *higher*" on live TV after being ordered to change the line).

In LA, quite a few of the city's venerable institutions are seen. The Doors perform at the **Whisky-a-Gogo, 8901 Sunset Boulevard** in West Hollywood. The bar, where bad boy Morrison takes a pee against the counter, is **Barney's Beanery, 8447 Santa Monica Boulevard**, a longstanding West Hollywood drinking hole – it's alleged that Jean Harlow used to pick up men here. After his breakdown,

Morrison on auto-destruct: Chateau Marmont, Sunset Boulevard

Morrison pees against the bar: Barney's Beanery, Santa Monica Boulevard

Morrison's grave: Père Lachaise Cemetery, Paris

Morrison enjoys a drink on the window ledge above the traffic at the **Chateau Marmont, 8221 Sunset Boulevard**, built in 1929 and long a residential hotel for the likes of Boris Karloff, Greta Garbo, Errol Flynn and Harlow again. But most famously, it was here in 1982 that another personality programmed to auto-destruct, John Belushi, OD'd on coke and heroin. The New Haven concert, brought to a halt when Morrison is arrested for abusing the cops, filmed in the beautiful **Orpheum Theater, 630 South Broadway**, downtown LA. More footage was filmed at the disused **Ambassador Hotel, 3400 Wilshire Boulevard**, midtown LA.

The desert scenes were shot in **Providence Mountains State Park**, a 5,900 acre recreation area on a mountain slope overlooking a vast expanse of desert. Way out in the middle of nowhere, take I-40 about 100 miles east of Barstow, then turn northwest on the Essex Road. There was trouble for the movie company when the fake Native American pictographs painted for the movie proved more difficult to remove than had been promised.

The final scene was filmed at Morrison's grave in Paris' largest cemetery, the **Père Lachaise, 65 boulevard de Menilmontant** in the 20th arrondissement. The much-graffitied grave is in the 16th section. From the main entrance, take the Avenue Principale to the Avenue de Puits, turn right and follow the Avenue Casimir-Perier. Other celeb graves seen in the movie include Oscar Wilde (Jacob Epstein's sphynx), Bizet, Marcel Proust, Sarah Bernhardt, Balzac and Rossini. You can also find the tomb of Abelard and Heloise, and the graves of Simone Signoret, Edith Piaf, Gericault, Chopin, Colette, Isadora Duncan, director Max Ophuls, Marie Walewska (Bonaparte's mistress, played on screen by Garbo in *Conquest*) and cinema pioneer Georges Mélies.

DOUBLE INDEMNITY

(1944, dir: Billy Wilder)
Barbara Stanwyck, Fred MacMurray, Edward G Robinson.
● **LOS ANGELES**

Fred MacMurray is the insurance salesman ensnared by femme fatale Stanwyck to bump off her – well-insured – hubby. Stanwyck's house, supposedly in Los Feliz, can be found in the maze of tiny winding lanes in the Hollywood Hills, at **6301 Quebec Drive**, off Beachwood, north from Franklin Avenue. In the movie it stood alone, overlooking Hollywood, but now, although unchanged, it is packed into a densely built up area of pricy properties. Pasadena Station was filmed at the **Glendale Amtrak**

Barbara Stanwyck's house: Quebec Drive, Hollywood Hills

Station on Cerritos Avenue off Vassar Avenue by Forest Lawn Memorial Park.

DOUBLE LIFE OF VERONIQUE, THE

(1991, dir: Krzysztof Kieslowski)
Irène Jacob, Wladyslaw Kowalski, Philippe Volter, .
● **POLAND; FRANCE**

Irène Jacob picked up the Best Actress award at Cannes for her dual role in this story of two identical women, one Polish, one French, whose lives mysteriously cross. It was filmed in **Krakow**, Poland, and in **Clermont-Ferrand**, France.

DOWN AND OUT IN BEVERLY HILLS

(1986, dir: Paul Mazursky)
Bette Midler, Nick Nolte, Richard Dreyfuss.
● **LOS ANGELES**

A remake of Jean Renoir's 1932 *Boudu Sauvé Des Eaux*, with Nolte as the bum who tries to drown himself in Midler and Dreyfuss' swanky pool, but ends up staying on

Midler and Dreyfuss' swanky home: North Bedford Drive, Beverly Hills

with the family. Nolte searches for his lost dog in the **Rodeo Collection**, a swishy shopping mall on Rodeo Drive. Midler and Dreyfuss' house is in the real Beverly Hills for once (it's so expensive to film here, Pasadena usually stands in) at **802 North Bedford Drive** off Sunset Boulevard.

DRACULA

(1931, dir: Tod Browning)
Bela Lugosi, Helen Chandler, Edward Van Sloan.
● **LOS ANGELES**

The first Hollywood version of Bram Stoker's vampire story, though it had been filmed, unofficially, in Germany in 1921 by FW Murnau, as *Nosferatu. Dracula*, kicking off Universal's cycle of stylish, atmospheric horror movies of the thirties and forties, is basically a filming of the British stage adaptation by Hamilton Deane, which had opened in London in 1927 with 23 year-old Raymond Huntley (the pompous civil servant of the *St Trinian's* and dozens of other British movies) as the Count. The role was created on Broadway by the Hungarian classical actor Lugosi, who went on to land the film role after Lon Chaney Sr, who was terminally ill, and Conrad Veidt, who returned to his native Germany, passed over the project.

The Transylvania and Yorkshire sets were all built, and subsequently much recycled, at Carl Laemmle's **Universal Studios**, north of Hollywood (see *Frankenstein* for details of the studio).

The exteriors of Castle Dracula are cunningly revamped from the 'medieval' style sets of old Universal silents by assistant designer Herman Rosse. The sets for the Transylvanian inn and its yard were built at Universal on what is now the site of the Studio Tour tram stops. Arriving in England, Dracula contrives an invitation to Lucy and Mina at the Albert Hall – actually the old *Phantom of the Opera* set (which was still in use in 1973 – see it as the burlesque house in *The Sting*). One real location, the opening shots of Renfield's coach careeriing through the eerie Mittel-European landscape, was filmed at **Vasquez Rocks**, the area of tortured sandstone formations near to LA seen in so many Westerns and, later, in sci-fi movies (see *Apache* for details of Vasquez Rocks).

DRACULA (aka *Horror of Dracula*)

(1958, dir: Terence Fisher)
Christopher Lee, Peter Cushing, Melissa Stribling.
● BERKSHIRE; BUCKINGHAMSHIRE

Hammer Films repeated the Universal pattern and, after their successful remake of *Frankenstein*, set out to refilm all the thirties classics with colour and gore. *Dracula* filmed almost entirely on the lot at Hammer's **Bray Studios, Down Place**, between Maidenhead and Windsor. The Transylvanian countryside filmed alongside Pinewood Studios in **Black Park Country Park**.

DRACULA

(1979, dir: John Badham)
Frank Langella, Laurence Olivier, Kate Nelligan.
● CORNWALL

Dracula's castle: St Michael's Mount

Seward's asylum: King Arthur's castle Hotel, Tintagel

Frank Langella put in the fangs (after playing the role in a Broadway version) with Olivier wielding the garlic and stake in this lush, romantic melodrama.

Though made in England, film doesn't use the book's setting of Whitby in Yorkshire, but filmed in Cornwall. Count Dracula's castle is **St Michael's Mount**, half a mile offshore – it's connected by a causeway – from **Marazion**, three miles east of Penzance in Cornwall. Home of Lord St Levan, the 17th century castle is a National Trust property and open to the public, Monday to Friday, April to October (© *01736.710507*).

Seward's asylum, run by Donald Pleasence, is the mock-Gothic **King Arthur's Castle Hotel, Tintagel**. The village, where Dracula tries to board ship, is **Mevagissey**, a fishing village way to the west, five miles south of St Austell.

DRACULA AD 1972

(1972, dir: Alan Gibson)
Christopher Lee, Peter Cushing, Christopher Neame.
● LONDON; HERTFORDSHIRE

Ghastly attempt to update the fag end of the Hammer series

to the Swinging Seventies, set around the Kings Road, Chelsea, years after Chelsea's sixties heyday. The church is obviously a set, but the groovy coffee bar where the

The groovy seventies coffee bar: King's Road, Chelsea

trendy young things gather is now Italian restaurant **La Bersagliera, 372 Kings Road** up towards World's End. The country scenes filmed at **Tykes Water Lake** at **Aldenham** Country Park, west of Elstree between Bushey and Borehamwood, Hertfordshire.

DRAGNET

(1954, dir: Jack Webb)
Jack Webb, Richard Boone, Ben Alexander.
● LOS ANGELES

The movie of the fifties TV series remade, spoofily, in the eighties and pastiched as *Badge of Honor* in *LA Confidential* ("Just the facts, ma'am..."). The most famous image, seen on the LAPD badge, is of the 1928 **Los Angles City Hall, 200 North Spring Street**, downtown LA. There's an observation deck on the 27th floor. Also featured is the much more modern **Parker Center** (the former Police Administration Building) to the southwest of City Hall at **150 North Los Angeles Street**.

The police department: Parker Center, North Los Angeles Street

DRAGONHEART

(1996, dir: Rob Cohen)
Dennis Quaid, voice of Sean Connery, David Thewlis.
● SLOVAKIA

A period fantasy adventure filmed in Slovakia. The opening scene was shot at the ruin of **Cachtice Hrad**, once home to the notorious Erzsebet Bathory, the legendary Blood Countess, alleged to have bathed in the blood of virgins and whose story was wildly mytholgised in Hammer's *Countess Dracula*. The ruined tower can be found above the town of Cachtice. The movie uses the beautiful landscapes of the Slovakian National Park near the medieval town of **Levoca**, while Einon's castle is **Spis Castle** in eastern Slovakia, one of the largest castles in Europe, set against the backdrop of the Tatra Mountains, overlooking the protected ancient towns of Spisska Kapitula and Spisska Podhradie.

DRAUGHTSMAN'S CONTRACT, THE

(1982, dir: Peter Greenaway)
Anthony Higgins, Janet Suzman, Anne Louise Lambert.
● KENT

The first of Greenaway's elegant, game-playing features,

with Higgins as the draughtsman, commissioned by Janet Suzman to produce a series of drawings, but subsequently drawn into an enigmatic murder plot. The country house is **Groombridge Place**, a 1655 moated house set in landscaped grounds, four miles southwest of Royal Tunbridge Wells on the Kent/Sussex border. The grounds (but not the house itself) are open to the public daily from Easter to the end of October (*© 01892. 863999, admission charge*).

DRESSED TO KILL
(1980, dir: Brian De Palma)
Michael Caine, Angie Dickinson, Keith Gordon.
● **NEW YORK CITY; PHILADELPHIA**

The New York art gallery: Philadelphia Museum of Art, 26th Street

De Palma continues to work through his Hitchcock obsession with a stylish and nasty revamping of *Psycho*, set in New York. Shrink Michael Caine's office is the basement at **162 East 70th Street** near Lexington Avenue on the East Side. He's supposed to do some work at the Bellevue Hospital

Michael Caine's office: East 70th Street, East Side

on First Avenue, where Ray Milland suffered DTs in *The Lost Weekend*, but the institution we actually see is the interior of the **Tweed Courthouse, 52 Chambers Street** in the Civic Center.

And the art gallery where Angie Dickinson picks up a bit of rough trade before the film's most contentious sequence, isn't all it seems. Supposedly New York's Metropolitan Museum of Art on Fifth Avenue at 82nd Street, the gallery interior is actually the **Philadelphia Museum of Art, 26th Street** at Benjamin Franklin Parkway. Philadelphia is the city De Palma grew up in and features regularly in his movies.

DRIVER, THE
(1978, dir: Walter Hill)
Ryan O'Neal, Bruce Dern, Isabelle Adjani.
● **LOS ANGELES**

Dern is 'The Cop' (it's an existential thriller, so the characters have no names) determined to lock up 'The Driver', a speedy getaway expert. Walter Hill's fast-paced, pared-

Site of the famous Torchy's: West Fifth Street, downtown LA

down thriller was filmed on the streets of LA.

The bar Dern operates out of was Torchy's, **218 1/2 West Fifth Street**, downtown LA. Obviously a

fave Hill location, you can see Torchy's as the San Francisco redneck bar of *48 Hours*. Torchy's has since closed and the premises is currently an electrical goods store. O'Neal meets up with Adjani on the illuminated walkways of LA's futuristic **Westin Bonaventure Hotel, 404 South Figueroa Street** (see *In the Line of Fire* for details of the Bonaventure). The luggage deposit boxes, where bags are stored and switched and Dern sets up O'Neal for the climax, are at **Union Station, 800 North Alameda Street.**

DRIVING MISS DAISY
(1989, dir: Bruce Beresford)
Jessica Tandy, Morgan Freeman, Dan Aykroyd.
● **GEORGIA**

Worthy middlebrow sentimentality, centering on the growing friendship between wealthy Miss Tandy and chauffeur Freeman, filmed around the stately homes of Atlanta, Georgia. Miss Daisy's gracious mansion is **822 Lullwater Road** in the **Druid Hills** area of the city.

DRUGSTORE COWBOY
(1989, dir: Gus Van Sant)
Matt Dillon, Kelly Lynch, James Remar.
● **OREGON**

Set in 1971, this small scale study of the lives of a group of drug addicts was filmed in Portland, Oregon. Dillon and Lynch's apartment is the **Irving Apartments, 2127 Northwest Irving Street** in the centre of town. The pharmacy they rob is **Nob Hill Pharmacy, 2100 Northwest Glison Street** at Northwest 21st Avenue, a couple of blocks south.

DRUM, THE (aka *Drums*)
(1938, dir: Zoltan Korda)
Sabu, Roger Livesey, Raymond Massey.
● **WALES**

Action melodrama, set in the Indian Raj. The Northwest Frontier of India actually filmed around **Harlech** in North Wales.

DUCK SOUP
(1933, dir: Leo McCarey)
The Marx Brothers, Margaret Dumont, Louis Calhern.
● **LOS ANGELES**

Groucho is Rufus T Firefly, who becomes President of Freedonia in one of the best of the Marx film outings. Although deco-ish Freedonia is firmly set in **Paramount Studios**, the garden party of rival Sylvania, where Groucho (surprise!) insults Margaret Dumont ("All I can offer you is a Rufus over your head.") filmed at the **Arden Villa, 1145 Arden Road**. You might recognise the villa as the Carrington mansion from TV's *Dynasty* and as George Cukor's estate in *Gods and Monsters*. It's a

Freedonia: entrance to the Arden Villa, Arden Road, Pasadena

private home in Pasadena, east of LA, not visible from the street.

DUCK, YOU SUCKER (aka *A Fistful of Dynamite*)
(1971, dir: Sergio Leone)
Rod Steiger, James Coburn, Romolo Valli.
● SPAIN

Mexican bandit Coburn and IRA man Steiger join forces in 1913 to rob a bank. Like many Spaghetti Westerns, it was filmed in the dry desert area of **Almeria**, Southern Spain.

DUEL
(1971, dir: Steven Spielberg)
Dennis Weaver, Jacqueline Scott, Eddie Firestone.
● CALIFORNIA

Spielberg's first theatrical feature (though it was originally made for American TV) remains one of the great cinematic débuts, despite being made in a mere two weeks. The simple plot has nerdy driver Weaver threatened by a monster truck and its unseen driver. The movie opens in downtown LA where Weaver drives down **South Broadway**, and heads north on Highway 5, the Golden State Freeway toward Bakersfield. Most of the filming is on **Route 14** and in the **Angeles National Forest** just north of LA. The gas station where he gets the warning about the radiator hose, and phones his wife from the launderette, is **Acton**, just south from Route 14. He finally trashes the monster at **Soledad Canyon**, off Route 14 toward Ravenna.

DUEL IN THE SUN
(1946, dir: King Vidor; Josef Von Sternberg; William Dieterle, B Reeves Eason and David O Selznick)
Jennifer Jones, Joseph Cotten, Gregory Peck.
● CALIFORNIA; ARIZONA

Massive, lurid vanity project from Selznick, intended to outwind *Gone With the Wind* and to showcase his protegée Jennifer Jones. Jones is the 'half-breed' Indian girl who falls in love with the son of the ranch family she lives with and sparks off family feuds. It was filmed out in the blazing desert of Arizona, on the Texas Ranch, now the **Triangle T Ranch** near **Dragoon**, and at **Lasky Mesa**, west of the San Fernando Valley in California (see *The Charge of the Light Brigade* for details). Original director Vidor walked off the movie, fed up, like many another director, with Selznick's relentless 'hands on' approach to producing. Dieterle took over, with contributions from veterans von Sternberg and Reeves Eason, along with – naturally – Selznick himself.

DUELLISTS, THE
(1977, dir: Ridley Scott)
Keith Carradine, Harvey Keitel, Edward Fox.
● FRANCE; SCOTLAND; LONDON

Scott's first feature, complete with trademark atmospheric mists and lush visuals, is Joseph Conrad's story about a series of obsessive duels fought between two officers, during the Napoleonic Wars. It was filmed around the beautiful medieval village of **Sarlat La Caneda**, 35 miles southeast of Perigueux in the Dordogne. There was also some filming at **Aviemore**, on the A9 southeast of Inverness, Scotland. Period interiors were shot in classy restaurant **Simpsons** on the **Strand**, London.

DUMB AND DUMBER
(1994, dir: Peter Farrelly)
Jim Carrey, Jeff Daniels, Lauren Holly.
● COLORADO; UTAH; RHODE ISLAND

Carrey and Daniels travel from Providence to Aspen, to return Lauren Holly's money-packed briefcase, in the film that launched the Farrelly brothers' brand of hi-jinx, lo-taste filmmaking.

Most of the film was shot in Colorado and Utah. There is a little scene-setting in Providence, Rhode Island, but Mary Swanson's New England mansion is actually in Utah. It's **La Caille**, a 20-acre estate built in 1975, at **Quail Run**, **Little Cottonwood Canyon** in the city of **Sandy**. Most of the transcontinental journey, the highways, fast-food joints and truckstops, were filmed around **Fort Morgan** (boyhood home of bandleader Glenn Miller) on the eastern plains of Colorado.

The arrival of Carrey and Daniels in Aspen actually filmed on **Main Street, Breckenridge**, which is at a higher altitude than the swanky ski resort, and more likely to be snow-covered in late spring. It's not unlikely that Breckenridge was a damn sight cheaper too. The mini-bike ride through Aspen was shot on **Main Street, Park City** in Utah. The lavish Danbury Hotel, where Carrey and Daniels dip into the case of money to buy a Lamborghini and stay in the Presidential Suite, is the **Stanley Hotel, 333 West Wonder View Avenue, Estes Park** (*© 001.970.586.3371*) in Colorado. The grandly imposing hotel became the inspiration for the Overlook in *The Shining* after Stephen King stayed there in 1973. The Kubrick movie didn't film here, but the TV remake, sanctioned by King (who hated the big screen version) did. The Avalanche Bar & Grill, where Carrey waits in vain for Lauren Holly, is the Stanley's bar. Daniels is meanwhile meeting up with her at **Copper Mountain Resort** in Breckenridge, which is where he licks the frost on the ski lift.

The Snowy Owl Benefit was filmed in the **Union Pacific Railroad Department**, a former train station, built in 1909, and now a historic landmark building in **Salt Lake City**, Utah. The Aspen chalet and the home of baddie Nicholas Andre both filmed in **Dee Valley**, adjoining Park City, Utah. Most interiors were filmed, by the way, in **Intermountain Studios**, Orem in Utah, the studio built by the Osmonds for *The Donnie and Marie Osmond Show*...

DUNE
(1984, dir: David Lynch)
Kyle MacLachlan, Francesca Annis, Brad Dourif.
● MEXICO

Lynch's third movie is a huge, confused sci-fi epic condensing a series of cult books. It's never less than visually amazing, though, and the extended TV cut is more comprehensible. It was filmed in Mexico, at the **Churubuscu Studios**.

E

Elliot's house: Dos Rios Drive, Tujunga

E.T. THE EXTRA-TERRESTRIAL
(1982, dir: Steven Spielberg)
Henry Thomas, Drew Barrymore, Peter Coyote.
● LOS ANGELES

In its day, the biggest-grossing movie ever, Spielberg's tearjerking fantasy was filmed largely on the soundstages at **Culver Studios** (previously Pathe, Pathe-de Mille

The flying bikes: White Oak Boulevard, San Fernando Valley

and RKO-Pathe Studios), **9336 Washington Boulevard** in Culver City, where many other movie greats, including *King Kong* and *Gone With the Wind*, were shot. All the interiors, apart from the high school, were filmed here, along with some of the exteriors too, including the rear of the house and the backyard where Elliot leaves a trail of M&Ms to tempt the alien.

The redwood forest scenes are in the **Redwood National Park** at **Crescent City**, Route 101 in far northern California near the Oregon border.

You'll find Elliot's frog-infested school in LA; it's **Culver City High School, Elenda Street** at Franklin Avenue. The principal was played by Harrison Ford, whose role ended up on the cutting room floor, though I suppose true fans might be able to recognise the back of his head and shoulder, which are supposedly still in the finished film.

The neighbourhood chosen for the movie was Northridge – the epicentre of 1994's disastrous quake – northwest LA in the San Fernando Valley. The Halloween and chase scenes filmed in the **Porter Ranch** district and the flying bicycle chase on **White Oak Boulevard** between Tribune and San Fernando Mission Roads, but Elliot's house is about fifteen miles to the east.

Spielberg wanted a more dramatic backdrop and headed off to the foothills of the San Gabriel Mountains. The actual house is **7121 Dos Rios Drive, Tujunga**, a suburb north of Burbank.

EAGLE HAS LANDED, THE
(1976, dir: John Sturges)
Michael Caine, Donald Sutherland, Robert Duvall.
● BERKSHIRE; CORNWALL; FINLAND

WWII thriller, with Germans infiltrating an English village as part of a plot to kill Churchill. The snowy railway marshalling yard on the Russian-Polish border, where Caine unsuccessfully attempts to save a Jewish prisoner, was filmed in the goods yard of Lapland's capital, **Rovaniemi** – the biggest town on the Arctic circle – in Finland.

Cornwall stood in for the Channel Islands and Berkshire for East Anglia. Occupied Alderney – a Channel Islands town – was recreated at the harbour of **Charlestown** in Cornwall, on the coast eighteen miles southeast of Newquay. The German communications post was built at the edge of the harbour, while the George and Dragon, the pub Donald Sutherland gets ejected from, is the town's **Pier House Hotel**. Also in Cornwall was Landsvoort Airfield, where the captured DC3 is held, which was the RAF station at **St Mawgans**, five miles from Newquay.

The East Anglia village of Studley Constable, Norfolk is actually **Mapledurham**, on the A329 just northwest of Reading, Berkshire. Real locations include the church, where the villagers are held hostage, which was the **Church of St Margaret** (which now houses a small exhibition of photographs taken during the production) and the watermill, where the fake Polish soldier blows the Nazis' cover. a fake waterwheel was added to the 15th century structure, it's fully restored and working, producing flour you can buy in the gift shop. You won't be able to sink a pint at the Spyglass and Kettle though, or shop at the local store, both of which were built on still recognisable sites in the village. The Manor House, to which Churchill is taken, is the 16th century Elizabethan **Mapledurham House**. It's open to the public on summer weekends (© *01189. 723350*). Mapledurham is four miles northwest of Reading on the north bank of the Thames.

The villagers held hostage: Church of St Margaret, Mapledurham

The Nazis' cover blown: the watermill

George and Dragon pub: Pier House Hotel, Charlestown

EARTHQUAKE
(1974, dir: Mark Robson)
Charlton Heston, Ava Gardner, Genevieve Bujold.
● LOS ANGELES

Sunset-Vine Tower,
Sunset Boulevard

The San Andreas Fault finally writes off LA in this rather downbeat addition to the seventies disaster movie genre, shot in the short-lived gimmick of Sensurround. The movie was filmed in and around LA, apart from the opening scene of the San Andreas fault which shot at **Carrizo Plains**, about 100 miles to the north. The first ominous traces of impending disaster are dis-

Survivors congregate at Wilson Plaza:
Ahmanson Center, Wilshire Boulevard

covered at the **Mulholland Dam** on Lake Hollywood up in the Hollywood Hills (see *Chinatown* for details). The city of LA itself was conjured up from a mixture of models,

sets and real locations. Among the landmark buildings reproduced in miniature were the Taft Building at the corner of Hollywood and Vine (which for many years was HQ of the hated puritanical Hays Office) and the Capitol Records Tower, 1750 Vine Street, an architectural stack of 45s with a stylus jutting from its roof.

The street scenes are largely in Hollywood, around the famous Hollywood and Vine intersection (though much of the action was filmed on the 'New York' street on the Universal backlot), and just south is Charlton Heston's office block, the **Sunset-Vine Tower, 6290 Sunset Boulevard** at Vine. At 20 storeys, it's Hollywood's tallest structure, built in 1964, after the abolition of height restrictions. Wilson Plaza, the disaster centre, is the **Ahmanson Center Building, 3701 Wilshire Boulevard** at Oxford Avenue, though the shopping mall was the **Broadway Plaza, 700 West Seventh Street** at Broadway, downtown. The cantilevered houses, where Genevieve Bujold is caught in the quake, can be seen on **Coldwater Canyon** north of Hollywood. The devastated roadway was a stretch of unfinished freeway near Glendale.

EAST OF EDEN
(1955, dir: Elia Kazan)
James Dean, Raymond Massey, Julie Harris.
● CALIFORNIA

This adaptation of John Steinbeck's epic novel was largely made in the book's setting of northern California, around **Salinas** and the coastal town of **Mendocino** (standing in for much-changed Monterey). The family mansion is no more, however. The Denslow-Morgan-Preston Mansion burned down a year after filming, and the site at 45200 Little Lake Street now houses the Mendocino Art Center and Gallery. It's close to Angela Lansbury's house from

TV's *Murder, She Wrote*, at the corner of Little Lake and Ford Streets. **Salinas Valley** hosted most of the location shooting (the beanfields and the ice-house of the Trask farm filmed here), and there was more filming in the city of Salinas itself at the **Spreckels Sugar Factory**. The funfair, though, was built back on the Warners' lot in Burbank.

EASY RIDER
(1969, dir: Dennis Hopper)
Peter Fonda, Dennis Hopper, Jack Nicholson.
● LOS ANGELES; ARIZONA; NEW MEXICO; NEW ORLEANS, LOUISIANA

This surprise low-budget sixties smash, revolutionising the studios and launching dozens of variable quality imitations, was shot in sequence, apart from the New Orleans Mardi Gras scene, which was actually first in the can. Always know where you're heading.

The cross-country journey, which follows much of the famed old Route 66, begins in LA. The opening druggy deal (a cameo from legendary record producer Phil Spector) was shot at **Los Angeles International Airport**, but from there on the movie was filmed on the hoof across the American southwest. The key scene of Fonda tossing his Rolex to the ground was staged in the ghost town of **Ballarat**, east of Route 178, between Trona and Stovepipe Wells on the western edge of Death Valley. But it's way south again, heading east on I-40, that Fonda and Hopper cross the Colorado River into Arizona at **Topock**. From here, the journey takes Route 95 alongside the Colorado River before turning south along I-60 to Routes 71 and 89, the scenic route into **Flagstaff** going through the towns of Prescott and Cottonwood.

From Flagstaff, it's north on 89, where you can find the **Magic Mountain gas station** (no longer operational) and the geological wonders of the **Painted Desert** and **Monument Valley**. The town parade was filmed in **Las Vegas** – not the glitzy casino city of Nevada but the tiny frontier town in New Mexico. Thrown into jail for "parading without a licence", the pair meet up with star-to-be Jack Nicholson. Although the exterior of the old jail can be seen in Las Vegas, at **157 Bridge Street**, the interiors filmed in **Taos**, once home to DH Lawrence, and the writer's last resting place. The town jail is now an art gallery, **Bryans Gallery, Camino de la Placitas** in the town square.

Next stop is the scary redneck café, also long gone, which stood in the small town of **Morganza**, Louisiana,

Fonda dumps the Rolex: Ballarat ghost town

by the Mississippi, about 30 miles northwest of state capital Baton Rouge. From here, it's just a short hop, past the clutch of plantation houses familiar from so many other movies, to New Orleans and Mardi Gras.

ECLISSE, L' (aka *The Eclipse*)
(1962, dir: Michelangelo Antonioni)
Alain Delon, Monica Vitti, Francesco Rabal.
● ROME

Another of Antonioni's cool, classic sixties studies of bourgeois alienation, along with *L'Avventura* and *La Notte*, set in the soulless suburbs of Rome. After leaving her husband, Monica Vitti dives into an affair with heartless young stockbroker Alain Delon, whom she meets in the bustle of the **Rome Stock Exchange**.

ED WOOD
(1994, dir: Tim Burton)
Johnny Depp, Martin Landau, Sarah Jessica Parker.
● LOS ANGELES

Burton's surprisingly moving tribute to the legendary 'Worst Director of All Time' filmed at 68 real locations around LA. Amazingly, Burton managed to find period locations, including the suburbs of **Torrance**; **Sierra Madre**; **Long Beach**; **Norwalk**; **Gardena** and **Eagle Rock**, and even managed to find unchanged corners among the tacky, redeveloped streets of Hollywood.

Wood's appalling stage venture filmed at **Theatre/Theater, 1713 Cahuenga Boulevard** at Hollywood Boulevard. The fledgling director finds encouragement in the reviews with the rest of the cast at **Boardner's Bar, 1652 North Cherokee Avenue**, a traditional old Hollywood hangout since the 1940s, just off Hollywood Boulevard. To the left of Boardner's you can see the vacant shop premises dressed as the Hollywood Funeral Home, where Wood first sees Bela Lugosi testing coffins. Wood begins to assemble his extended family of oddballs when

The funeral home: North Cherokee Avenue

he encounters wrestler Tor Johnson at the **Olympic Auditorium, Grand Avenue** at Olympic Boulevard, downtown LA – it's the venue where the boxing scenes from the *Rocky* movies and *Raging Bull* were filmed. The Brown Derby restaurant, where Wood hosts a fundraiser, is long gone. It was recreated in the grounds of the Ambassador Hotel on Wilshire Boulevard, opposite which you can actually see the shell of the famed hat-shaped landmark. You can also see the church attended by the cast of *Plan 9* when Wood gets some unorthodox funding. It's the

Ed Wood reads the reviews: Boardner's Bar, North Cherokee Avenue, Hollywood

Wood meets Welles: Musso and Frank's Grill, Hollywood Boulevard

Toluca Lake First United Methodist Church, 4301 Cahuenga Boulevard in Burbank.

There were a couple of authentic locations: the *Bride of the Monster* sequence, with Lugosi battling a rubber octopus, was filmed where the real Ed Wood actually shot his classic in **Griffith Park**, and Wood's home in the movie is the director's last apartment in Hollywood. His inspirational meeting with

Wood gets funding for his masterpiece: Toluca First United Methodist Church, Burbank

idol Orson Welles was shot in another classic Hollywood landmark, the oldest restaurant in the city, **Musso and Frank's Grill, 6667 Hollywood Boulevard** (not far from Boardner's and the funeral home). Pretty unbelievably, Wood's film premières at the wonderful **Pantages Theater, 6233 Hollywood Boulevard** at El Centro, though the cinema interior is actually the slightly less grandiose **Orpheum Theater, 842 South Broadway**, downtown Los Angeles, seen in *Dead Again* and *Last Action Hero*.

EDIPO RE (aka *Oedipus Rex*)
(1967, dir: Pier Paolo Pasolini)
Franco Citti, Silvana Mangano, Alida Valli.
● ITALY; MOROCCO

Pasolini's heavily Freudian filming of the Greek myth is bookended by the birth of a child in the 1930s and his maturity in the 1960s. For the ancient Greek towns of Corinth and Thebes, Pasolini used the beautiful fortified kasbahs and the spectacular deserts of southern Morocco.

The updated prologue and epilogue filmed in Pasolini's hometown of Bologna, Italy. The present-day Oedipus becomes a blind beggar playing his flute on the steps of **San Petronio**, one of the world's largest churches, on the **Piazza Maggiore**, while his boy, Angelo, chases pigeons in front of the **Palazzo Communale**.

EDUCATING RITA
(1983, dir: Lewis Gilbert)
Michael Caine, Julie Walters, Michael Williams.
● DUBLIN, IRELAND

Academy nominations for the two leads in Willy Russell's adaptation of his own Liverpool-set play. Though still ostensibly set in Liverpool, the movie was shot entirely around Dublin, where the university campus is **Trinity College**, and Caine's rooms are in the **Graduates Memorial Building**. The pub, where Rita begins to feel alienated from her family at a dismal singalong, is a conflation of two Dublin institutions. The interior is the hangout of Trinity

Caine's rooms at college: Graduates Memorial Building

The grim family singalong, exterior: The Dame Tavern, Dame Court

But the interiors filmed over the street: The Stag's Head, Dame Court

students, the **Stag's Head, 1 Dame Court**, while the exterior is just over the road, the **Dame Tavern, 18 Dame Court**. Twenties, the restaurant where Rita waits tables alongside ditsy Maureen Lipman, is **Dobbins Wine Bistro, 15 Stephens Lane**. A very drunk Caine looks for Rita at the old Flamingo disco, now gone, which was sited in the revamped **Stillorgan Park Hotel, Stillorgan Road** in Blackrock. Rita leaves for summer school from Dublin's **Pearse Street Station**, while the wedding of Rita's pregnant younger sister was filmed at the **Church of the Holy Family, Aughrim Street**, in an area often used as a location – scenes for *Michael Collins*, *My Left Foot* and *The Boxer* were shot in the church's parish district.

EDWARD SCISSORHANDS
(1990, dir: Tim Burton)
Johnny Depp, Winona Ryder, Dianne Wiest.
● FLORIDA

The twee little pastel neighbourhood where Scissorhands sculpts bushes is **Tinsmith Circle, Carpenter's Run** in Lutz, about five miles north of Tampa on Route 41, Florida. 44 houses here were made over for the movie. Sadly, they're not always candy-coloured, nor do they sport quirky topiary. The dinosaur, elephant, Elvis and penguin shaped bushes were metal and chickenwire frames covered with greenery. The beauty salon, where Kathy Baker tries to seduce Edward, is in the **Southgate Shopping Center, 2500 South Florida Avenue**, Lakeland, east of Tampa.

84 CHARING CROSS ROAD
(1987, dir: David Jones)
Anthony Hopkins, Anne Bancroft, Judi Dench.
● LONDON; NEW YORK CITY

This transatlantic romance, conducted entirely by letter, between American bibliophile Bancroft and English bookseller Hopkins, was based on true events. The bookshop at number 84, on the northeast corner of Cambridge Circus, has been modernised and is now a restaurant – for the film it was mocked up at **Shepperton Studios**. Hopkins's north London Muswell Hill home and neighbourhood was actually filmed in the southwest of the city in **Richmond**. The

mock-Tudor pavilion alongside which Hopkins sits can be seen in **Soho Square**. Period accuracy demanded that **Madison Avenue**, in the New York scenes, be returned to its original two-way traffic system.

EL (aka *This Strange Passion*)
(1953, dir: Luis Buñuel)
Arturo De Cordova, Delia Garces, Luis Beristain.
● MEXICO

De Cordova is the bourgeois gentleman who whisks Delia Garces off her feet (and it is her feet he first falls for – this being a Buñuel movie), only to descend into dangerous paranoia. The movie, hailing from the Spanish director's period of Mexican exile, was shot in **Mexico City**. The less-than-happy couple spend their fraught honeymoon in **Guanajuato**, an elegant, muy-European city about 200 miles northwest of Mexico City.

EL CID
(1961, dir: Anthony Mann)
Charlton Heston, Sophia Loren, Herbert Lom.
● SPAIN

From the golden age of epics, this ranks as one of the best, unusually deserting toga country for the story of legendary Spanish hero Don Rodrigo de Bivar.

The movie was shot at three studios around Madrid, **Chamartin, Sevilla** and **Cea**, as well as on real Spanish locations. Burgos Cathedral, site of the coronation scene, has seen quite a few changes since the 11th century and a full-sized mock-up was built at the Sevilla Studios.

The tournament, where an embittered Sophia Loren gives her favour to Heston's opponent, filmed at a real location, before the 15th century gothic castle of **Belmonte**, built for writer and warrior Don Juan Manuel. One of the best preserved of its kind in Spain, and now declared a national monument, the castle is perched on a hilltop overlooking the province of La Mancha about 75 miles southeast of Madrid on the road between Alcazar de San Juan and Olivares.

The Cid's exile filmed in the **Guadarrama Mountains**, north of Madrid, and more period scenes were shot around **Valladolid** – known as 'castle country' – in Old Castille, 100 miles northwest of Madrid.

For the final battle scenes Valencia was played by the walled city of **Peñiscola**, an old fortress town built on a promontory surrounded by the sea on three sides. It's on Spain's east coast 60 miles north of Valencia itself. The fortress walls, dating from the time of Phillip II, are emblazoned with his coat of arms and the castle once served as the papal court of Pope Benedict XIII, whose chapel and rooms can be visited. The giant Moorish gates installed for the movie were left behind as a gift to the city.

EL DORADO
(1967, dir: Howard Hawks)
John Wayne, Robert Mitchum, James Caan.
● ARIZONA

Hawks' solid Western filmed at the **Old Tucson Studios, 201 South Kinney Road**, Tucson. Built for the 1940

Western *Arizona*, the studio is still in use – *Tombstone* was filmed here in 1993 – and also functions as a Western theme park, open daily (℡ *602.883.6457*).

ELECTION
(1999, dir: Alexander Payne)
Matthew Broderick, Reese Witherspoon, Chris Klein.
● **NEBRASKA; NEW YORK**

Snappy high school satire, filmed around **Omaha**, Nebraska. Director Payne used his own childhood neighbourhood of **Dundee**. The high school is **Papillion-La Vista Senior High, 504 South Washington Street, Papillion**.

ELECTRA GLIDE IN BLUE
(1973, dir: James William Guercio)
Robert Blake, Billy Green Bush, Jeannine Riley.
● **UTAH; ARIZONA**

Cult biker/cop movie, following in the wake of *Easy Rider*, the only movie from Guercio, the manager of the rock band Chicago – he wrote the music for the film too. Filmed at **Phoenix** and **Carefree** in Arizona, it features a great mythic final shot of **Monument Valley**.

ELEPHANT MAN, THE
(1980, dir: David Lynch)
John Hurt, Anthony Hopkins, John Gielgud.
● **LONDON**

One of Lynch's more mainstream films, this eerie Romantic fantasy is overlaid with an obsessive attention to the detail of industrial Victoriana. There's little left to see of the film's London locations; Lynch seems to have been one step ahead of the developers all the way.

The smoke-wreathed opening London street scenes filmed on the South Bank by London Bridge along **Shad Thames**, a familiar location – seen also in *The French Lieutenant's Woman* – now lost to inevitable gentrification as the warehouses are converted into wine bars and restaurants; and in the tiny knot of cobbled streets off **Clink Street** and **St Mary Overies Dock** behind Southwark Cathedral and Borough Market, SE1. Here, too, the atmosphere is long gone. The warehouses have actually been demolished, though the old street plan and cobbled roads have been retained. The area is worth a visit, having the remains of the Bishop of Winchester's 14th century Palace banqueting hall and the old Clink prison (which became the generic name for all subsequent lock-ups), now open as a museum.

Dr Carr-Gomm's office: Liberal Club, Whitehall Place

Gone, too, is the old Eastern Hospital on Hom-

'I am a man!': Liverpool Street Station

erton Row, Lower Clapton, E9, replaced by the spanking new Homerton Hospital. The Eastern stood in for the London Hospital on Whitechapel Road, E1, where the real John Merrick actually stayed. This hospital still exists, opposite Whitechapel Tube Station, but its modern annexes rendered it unsuitable for filming. The corridors of the hospital and Dr Carr-Gomm's office were filmed inside the **Liberal Club, 1 Whitehall Court** at Whitehall Place, SW1, now incorporated into the Royal Horseguards Hotel.

The wonderfully decrepit Victorian railway station where Merrick arrives back in London after his escape from the freak show is the old **Liverpool Street Station, Bishopsgate**, EC2. Since filming the station has been thoroughly gutted. The wooden walkways, photogenic grime and white-tiled toilets have gone, but if you look up at the sparkly clean brick walls above the entrance to Platform 1 you'll recognise the shell of the building seen in the movie. The walkway, where Merrick was pursued by the mob, followed roughly the same path as its replacement above the platform entrances. The bright new Liverpool Street station can be seen in Brian De Palma's *Mission: Impossible*.

ELIZABETH
(1997, dir: Shekhar Kapur)
Cate Blanchett, Joseph Fiennes, Kathy Burke.
● **DERBYSHIRE; NORTHUMBERLAND; COUNTY DURHAM; YORKSHIRE; BERKSHIRE; MIDDLESEX**

Power politicking in the Tudor court, using real locations all over England. **Haddon Hall**, south of Bakewell, Derbyshire (℡ *01629.812855*), is substituted for Hatfield House, Elizabeth's childhood home, and itself a frequent location, though much altered during the Jacobean period.

Several locations were found in Northumberland. The burning of the martyrs at Bishopsgate, London is **Alnwick Castle** (℡ *01665.510777*), as is Leith Castle, where Mary Queen of Scots rides after the battle. Not far away you'll find the hunting lodge, where Elizabeth and Dudley meet, and also the Leith Castle apartment of Mary of Guise, which are both **Chillingham Castle** (℡ *01668.215359*). Seven miles south of Alnwick is **Warkworth Castle** (℡ *01665.711423*), seat of the Percy family, in which the cells of the Tower of London were filmed, while the torture chamber and the apartment of Walsingham were **Aydon Castle**, near Corbridge (℡ *01434.632450*)

County Durham provided the Whitehall Palace river pageant, which is **Raby Castle**, Staindrop, about twelve miles west of Darlington (℡ *01833.660202*); and **Durham Cathedral**, the **Chapter House** of which became the Whitehall Palace State Room, and its nave, the queen's royal court.

North Yorkshire stands in for the Tower of London courtyard, the French bordello and the armoury, which are **Bolton Castle** (where the real Mary, Queen of Scots was imprisoned for siz months), six miles from Leyburn (℡ *01969.623981*), while Elizabeth's coronation takes place in **York Minster**. Lord Arundel's home is **Dorney Court**, a Tudor manor house near Maidenhead, Berkshire (℡ *01628.604638*). The final scene, and the coronation party, are **St Alban's Church, Teddington**, Middlesex, now a community arts centre.

ELVIRA MADIGAN
(1967, dir: Bo Widerberg)
Pia Degermark, Thommy Berggren, Lennart Malmer.
● SWEDEN

Lovingly photographed tragedy that seemed like the ultimate doomed romance back in the sixties. Army officer Berggren runs off with tightrope-walker Degermark, but their idyll is short lived, and, rather than be parted, the pair opt for a suicide pact. Filmed in **Skane**; **Nordsjallend** and **Karlbergs slott och Solliden** in Stockholm.

EMERALD FOREST, THE
(1985, dir: John Boorman)
Powers Boothe, Meg Foster, Charley Boorman.
● BRAZIL; LINCOLNSHIRE

After searching for eleven years in the Brazilian jungle, dam engineer Boothe meets up with the young son taken by Indians. This wonderful-looking drama filmed on location in Brazil. Boothe's Amazco office is a government building on the waterfront of **Belem**, on the south of the Amazon delta. The dam being constructed is over the Araguaia River at **Tucurui**, about 200 miles to the south. For the dam burst sequence, a scaled down model was built across a stream in the rather less exotic location of **Spilsby**, Lincolnshire. Jungle locations are **Paraty** and **Carajas**, while the waterfall, where Boothe finally meets his son, is at **Itatiata**.

EMMA
(1996, dir: Douglas McGrath)
Gwyneth Paltrow, Toni Collette, Jeremy Northam.
● DORSET; BUCKINGHAMSHIRE; HAMPSHIRE; MIDDLESEX

Straightforward filming of the Jane Austen novel, upstaged by the more spirited nineties update, *Clueless*. The fictional village of Highbury is **Evershot**, eight miles south of Yeovil in Dorset, where scenes filmed on **Fore Street** and at the **Old Manor**, standing in for the schoolhouse. Mrs Weston's house, Randalls, is **Mapperton**, five miles northeast of Bridport, Dorset, and seen also in *Restoration*. The gardens here are open to public in summer (℡ *01308.862645*). Other period locations include include **Stratfield Saye**, home of the Duke of Wellington, between Reading and Basingstoke (℡ *01256.882882*); **Claydon House**, Middle Claydon, thirteen miles northwest of Aylesbury in Buckinghamshire – an 18th century house with rococo decoration (℡ *01296.730349*); **Stafford House** at West Stafford, east of Dorchester and **Breakspear House, Bury Street, Ruislip**, a disused old people's home in Middlesex.

EMMANUELLE
(1974, dir: Just Jaeckin)
Sylvia Kristel, Marika Green, Alain Cuny.
● SEYCHELLES

The wife of a French Embassy official explores the possibilities of soft-focus sex in Siam in this classic of seventies softcore kitsch, which actually filmed in an old Plantation House on the island of **La Digue** in the Seychelles. The house stands on the road between the main, and only, town of La Reunion and the main beach at Grand Anse.

EMPIRE OF THE SUN
(1987, dir: Steven Spielberg)
Christian Bale, John Malkovich, Miranda Richardson.
● SHANGHAI, CHINA; SPAIN; BERKSHIRE; LONDON; CALIFORNIA

Spielberg's Leanian epic, based on JG Ballard's autobiographical novel, has Bale as a boy surviving on his wits after being separated from his parents during the WWII Japanese invasion of Shanghai. It was filmed largely on location in Shanghai, and in Spain.

Bale's colonial home in Shanghai did film in that city's English settlement. The style was so similar to stockbroker belt England that it proved possible to shoot interiors in a bungalow at Sunningdale, on the A30 between Egham and Camberley, on the exotic Berkshire/Surrey border, southwest of London.

The downtown Shanghai scenes were filmed in the old colonial financial district overlooking the Huangpu River waterfront, a virtually unchanged area of the city, where Spielberg coordinated the enormous crowd scenes of mass panic around the **Bund** (now called the Zhongshan Dongyilu).

The hotel, from which Bale signals to the Japanese warship, is the **Peace Hotel**, called the Cathay in the forties. This grand deco building, dating from the twenties, with its distinctive pyramid roof, is at **20 Nanjiang Dong Lu** (Nanjing Street). One of the famous stopovers for the English abroad, it was here that Noël Coward wrote *Private Lives* (℡ *8621.63216888; www.shanghaipeacehotel.com*). The bridge, clogged with panicking crowds below the hotel, is the **Waibaidu Bridge** over Suzhou Creek, flowing into the Huangpu by Huangpu Park, the small green area once notoriously barred to the native Chinese.

The Japanese detention centre filmed inside part of the huge, abandoned gasworks complex at **Becton** on the Thames in East London, where Kubrick famously filmed the Vietnam scenes for *Full Metal Jacket*. The prison camp set was built near **Jerez**, 80 miles northwest of Seville in southwest Spain.

EMPIRE STRIKES BACK, THE
(1980, dir: Irvin Kershner)
Mark Hamill, Carrie Fisher, Harrison Ford.
● NORWAY

The script for part V of the *Star Wars* saga was the last work of Leigh Brackett, veteran screenwriter of *The Big Sleep* and *Rio Bravo*.

The Millennium Falcon was built on a huge soundstage at Elstree, where most of the filming took place – 64 sets and 250 scenes over a four month shoot. The ice planet Hoth was the **Hardanger Jøkulen Glacier**, at **Finse**, the highest railway station in Norway.

ENEMY OF THE STATE
(1998, dir: Tony Scott)
Will Smith, Gene Hackman, Lisa Bonet.
● WASHINGTON DC; MARYLAND; LOS ANGELES

Flashy, visceral surveillance thriller from the hyperactive Scott, with Will Smith under threat after witnessing the murder of a politician. Set in Washington DC, filming took

SWINGING LONDON

WEST LONDON: On the Thames at **Strand-on-the-Green**, Chiswick W4, stands the historic **City Barge** pub, where the Beatles discovered a tiger in the cellar in *Help!* (**1a**). East of the railway bridge, Julie Christie dallied with Dirk Bogarde on the muddy waterfront in John Schlesinger's *Darling* (**1b**). In nearby Hammersmith, stands the 'White Pad' at **1 Melrose Terrace**, W6 (**2**), centre of all the frenetically surreal happenings in *The Knack*, while the normally bustling **Shepherd's Bush Market** on **Goldhawk Road** (**3**) was the dark passageway where unfortunate rocker Ray Winstone took a bloody beating from the mod gang in *Quadrophenia*. Notting Hill has more than its share of classic locations. Michael Caine's *très* sixties pad, jammed with thrift shop bric-a-brac in *The Italian Job* was **18 Denbigh Close** (**4a**), off Portobello Road. At **25 Powis Square** (**4b**) stands the now-gentrified home of burned-out rock star Mick Jagger in *Performance*, and on **Lancaster Road** at St Mark's Grove (**4c**) stands the pub which became Camden's legendary, but fictitious, Mother Black Cap in *Withnail and I*. Further east is the home of compulsive womaniser *Alfie*, at **22 St Stephen's Gardens**, W2 (**4d**). David Naughton did some shape-shifting in Earl's Court to become *An American Werewolf in London* in the flat of nurse Jenny Agutter at **64 Coleherne Road**, SW10 (**5**).

CENTRAL LONDON: Although the old vegetable market has moved south of the river, you can still down a pint at **The Globe, Bow Street**, WC2 (**6**), where Jon Finch worked in Hitchcock's *Frenzy*. And while the old Scala Theatre, used for the concert scenes in *A Hard Day's Night*, has gone, the alleyway opposite the site on **Charlotte Street**, (**7**), from which the Fab Four emerge in time for their TV appearance, still remains.

THE CITY AND EAST LONDON: Near to Smithfield Market is **Vic Naylor, 40 St John Street**, EC1 (**8**), which became JD's Bar in Guy Ritchie's *Lock, Stock and Two Smoking Barrels*. The eerie park, where David Hemmings might or might not have witnessed a murder in Antonioni's *Blowup* is **Maryon Park** (**9**), south of Woolwich Road, SE7. Finally, at **Binsley Walk** in **Thamesmead South**, you'll find the Flat Block Marina, home to Alex and the Droogs in *A Clockwork Orange* (**10**).

129

STAR WARS WORLD TOUR

TUNISIA: George Lucas took the architecture of Tunisia as the basis for the look of the desert planet Tatooine in the original *Star Wars* movie – *Episode IV: A New Hope*. Perhaps the most famous location is in the desert town of **Matmata**, where the dwellings are carved from the soft sandstone to escape the blistering desert heat. The interior of Luke Skywalker's homestead is the circular inner courtyard of the **Sidi Driss Hotel** (**1a,1b** & **1c**), where you can see the breakfast nook (**1d**) with murals and tiling added for the film. The Mos Eisley cantina was shot in the sponge-fishing town of **Ajim** on the Ile de Jerba off the central coast. The exterior of Luke's home and the featureless desert wastes are the vast, white salt lake of **Chott El Jerid** (**1e**), to the west, occupying the centre of the country all the way to the Algerian border. On the western edge of the Chott is the oasis town of Nefta. You'll need a four-wheel-drive vehicle, and probably a guide, to visit the dunes of **Chott el Gharsa**, north of Nefta, where the Mos Espa sets (**1f** & **1g**) for *Episode I: The Phantom Menace* still stand. The remains of two sets can be seen here, along with

the strange, angular rock formations from the desert fight with Darth Maul. Young Anakin's slave quarter home can be found behind the main square of **Medenine** (**1h**), a town about 35 miles southeast of Matmata. The rear of the slave-quarters, where he works on the pod racer with Jar Jar, and where his mother drops portentous hints about a virgin birth, is the deserted **Hotel Ksar Hadada, Ksar Hadada** (**1i** & **1j**) near Ghomrassen, south of Medenine toward Tataouine.

CALIFORNIA: Since the bantha of *A New Hope* was in reality a disguised elephant hired from Marine World, its scenes were shot in California's **Death Valley** (**2**). The desert of the second sequel, *Return of the Jedi*, is also California, the endless sand dunes of **Buttercup Valley** (**3**), near Yuma, in the southeast corner of the state. At the opposite end of the state you'll find the monster trees from the Moon of Endor on the temperate Pacific coast, almost at the Oregon border. They are the giant Redwood groves of the **Jedediah Smith Redwood State Park, 4241 Kings Valley Road, Crescent City** (**4**).

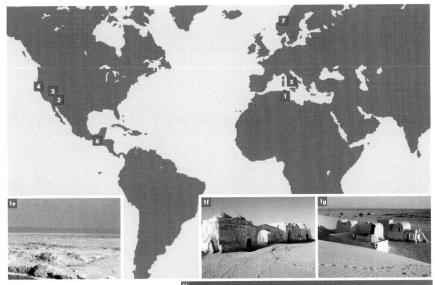

ITALY: The staterooms and staircases of Queen Amidala's palace for *The Phantom Menace* are the overwhelming marble interiors of **Palazzo Reale**, the Royal Palace, on **Piazza Carlo III, Caserta** (**5a** & **5b**) directly opposite the railway station, about 15 miles north of Naples.

GUATEMALA: The rebel base of *A New Hope*, on the fourth moon of Yavin, is the giant Mayan temple complex at **Tikal** (**6**), in the 222-square-mile rainforest of the **Parque Nacional Tikal**, northern Guatemala.

NORWAY: The ice planet Hoth, in *The Empire Strikes Back*, is the **Hardanger Jøkulen Glacier**, at **Finse** (**7**).

STAR TREK, USA

As you'd expect from a series set in space, the first three *Star Trek* movies were almost entirely studio-bound, but there's been an increasing use of real locations, almost always in California.

SAN FRANCISCO: The original TV series ended in 1969, but it wasn't until 1979 that *Star Trek* made it to the big screen. That film was nearly all shot in a studio, but it did site the Starfleet Academy alongside the Golden Gate Bridge in San Francisco. The Golden Gate academy was seen again in *Star Trek VI: The Undiscovered Country*. In *Star Trek IV: The Voyage Home* the *Enterprise* crew zoom back to 1986 San Francisco. They split up at the junction of **Columbus, Kearney** and **Pacific Avenues** (**1**).

NOVATO: The lakeside campus of Camp Khitomer, site of the climactic peace conference of *Star Trek VI: The Undiscovered Country*, is the **Fireman's Fund Building, 777 San Marin Drive** (**2**) in the town of Novato in Marin County, north of San Francisco.

MONTEREY: On the coast 115 miles south of San Francisco is the **Monterey Bay Aquarium, 886 Cannery Row** (**3**), which became the Sausalito Cetacean Institute where Kirk and the crew find the humpback whales in *Star Trek IV: The Voyage Home*.

BISHOP: In central California, toward the Nevada border, the foothills of the spectacular Sierra Nevada range become distinctly Alpine in character. Nineteen miles west of Bishop, up in the Inyo National Forest, is the peaceful reservoir of **Lake Sabrina** (**4a** & **4b**). A near-inaccessible peak overlooking the lake was used as the mountaintop refuge of the Ba'ku people in *Star Trek: Insurrection*.

OWENS LAKE: South of Lone Pine on I-395, central California, this vast, dry lake bed (**5**) became the Planet of Galactic Peace in *Star Trek V: The Final Frontier*.

TRONA: South toward Ridgecrest in the Mojave Desert are the **Trona Pinnacles** (**6**), an area of bizarre tufa spires formed when the area was beneath a long-vanished sea, which became the surface of the planet Shakari, where Captain Kirk has a close encounter with 'God' in *Star Trek V: The Final Frontier*.

LOS ANGELES: The superbly art deco **Union Station, 800 North Alameda Street** (**7**) in downtown LA was transformed into the thirties nightclub for the holodeck scene in *Star Trek: First Contact*. The snowy wastes of the Knik Glacier in Alaska were used as the surface of Rura Penthe, the penal asteroid Kirk is banished to in *Star Trek VI: The Undiscovered Country*, but the penal colony was built in **Bronson Canyon** in LA's Griffith Park.

VALLEY OF FIRE: Over the border in Nevada, about 50 miles east of Las Vegas, is the dazzling red **Valley of Fire State Park** (**8**), which became Viridian 3, where James T Kirk finally passed into history in *Star Trek Generations*.

SAN FRANCISCO

LAS VEGAS

LOS ANGELES

MONTEREY BAY AQUARIUM

PORTOLA SARDINES

THE WORLD OF JAMES BOND

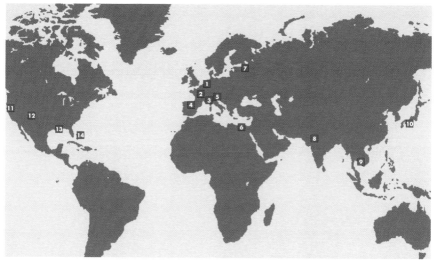

AMSTERDAM: The gem capital of Europe naturally featured in *Diamonds Are Forever*. A canal trip may take you past the **Skinny Bridge**, where the old lady's body is dragged from the water. Bond girl Tiffany Case lives in one of the city's elegant, narrow canal houses at **Reguliersgracht 36 (1)**.

PARIS: In *A View to a Kill*, villainess May Day parachutes from the **Eiffel Tower**, but its Jules Verne Restaurant was recreated in the studio. Risk a Seine boat trip under the elaborate **Pont Alexandre III (2)**, from which Bond leaps into the pleasure cruiser.

COTE D'AZUR: A natural Bondian haunt. There's usually a casino scene, and in *GoldenEye*, Bond plays at the most famous of all, the **Casino de Monte Carlo Casino (3a)** in Monaco. It's from the **Bay of Monte Carlo (3b)** that Xenia Onatopp steals the super-dooper helicopter. Visit at night when the lights twinkle and gleam. Monte Carlo by day is a grimly ugly example of unbridled development. Take the coast road west to the beautiful little fishing village of **Villefranche-sur-Mer**, a popular filming location used for the motorbike chase in the non-mainstream Bond, *Never Say Never Again*, a remake of *Thunderball*. Largo's Palmyra fortress is **Fort Carré d'Antibes** at Antibes, a little further west along the coast.

SPAIN: The stylish new **Guggenheim Museum, Bilbao** (**4**) is used as a backdrop to the opening teaser of *The World Is Not Enough*.

VENICE: Featured in two Bond movies, though blink and you'll miss its appearance at the end of *From Russia With Love*, when Bond's gondola passes under the **Bridge of Sighs** and out to the Canal Grande. He spends more time in the city in *Moonraker*. The entrance to Drax's glassworks is **Venini, 314 Piazzetta dei Leoni** (**5**), northeast of San Marco. The boat chase ends with Bond hovering across **Piazza San Marco**, where you can see the **Torre dell'Orologio**, the clock tower in which Bond slugs it out with the baddies.

CAIRO: Stop off to witness the touristy *son et lumière* at the **Pyramid of Cheops** (**6**) as seen in *The Spy Who Loved Me*.

ST PETERSBURG: True, most of *GoldenEye's* spectacular tank chase was shot on a set in Hertfordshire, but the imposing square is the real **Palace Square** (**7**).

UDAIPUR: The Maharani converted two of his spectacular palaces into luxury hotels, both of which are seen in *Octopussy*. Bond stays at the **Shiv Niwas Hotel** (**8a**) on the lake shore, but a short boat ride will take you out to the fabulous **Lake Palace Hotel** (**8b**), Octopussy's floating palace, in the middle of

Lake Pichola. You may not have a barge rowed by handmaidens, but even the movie cheated by using a hidden motor.

THAILAND: Bond makes a spectacular descent down the side of the **Westin Banyan Tree Hotel**, Bangkok in *Tomorrow Never Dies*, while south at Phuket you can see **Khow-Ping-Kan** (**9**), the island lair of Scaramanga from *The Man With the Golden Gun*, in **Phang Nga Bay**, Phuket on the Malay Peninsula.

JAPAN: The Ninja Training School of *You Only Live Twice* is **Himeji Castle** (**10**), Himeji, 33 miles west of Kobe.

SAN FRANCISCO: The State Office Building in *A View to a Kill* is **San** Francisco City Hall (**11a**); the opening of the **Lefty O'Doul Bridge, Third Street** (**11b**) provides an ending for the firetruck chase.

LAS VEGAS: The Whyte House of *Diamonds Are Forever* is the **Las Vegas Hilton** (**12a**). Spend a few bucks in **Circus Circus** (**12b**), the themed casino with acrobats performing overhead.

NEW ORLEANS: The **French Quarter** (**13**) of New Orleans is used for the Jazz funeral of *Live and Let Die*.

BAHAMAS: Finally, to the Bahamas for the original *Thunderball*, and Largo's other Palmyra estate, on **New Providence Island** (**14**).

SALZBURG'S SOUND OF MUSIC

MIRABELL GARDENS: (**1**) Behind the Mirabell Palace. At the northern end of the gardens are the 'Do Re Mi' steps and the Pegasus Fountain, to the south the 'leaping' entrance statues (**2**).

RESIDENZPLATZ: (**3**) Where Maria splashes in the Residenzbrunnen (Residence Fountain) on her way to the Von Trapp house, and, later, Nazi troops march after the Anschluss.

ROCK RIDING SCHOOL: (**4**) The family performs 'Edelweiss' at the song festival before escaping over the border.

WINKLER TERRACE: (**5**) Take the lift to this restaurant terrace overlooking the city. The kids begin 'Do Re Mi' here, and it is also used as the convent terrace (the abbey actually looks south over the nondescript suburbs). Follow the path southeast along the Monchsburg Cliffs.

NONNBERG ABBEY: (**6**) You can peek into the courtyard (seen in the film) and the chapel (which isn't). Go west to Leopoldskroner Teich. From the west shore of the lake look across to the palace of Leopoldskron.

LEOPOLDSKRON: (**7**) A private establishment, which supplied the Von Trapp mansion's lakeside terrace.

SCHLOSS FROHNBURG: (**8**) To see the front entrance of the Von Trapp mansion, head south on the small cycle track of Hellbrunner Allee. Soon you'll recognise the yellow-painted wall where Maria alights from the bus ('I Have Confidence in Me') and pauses before the forbidding gates.

SCHLOSS HELLBRUNN: (**9**, off the map). To avoid constant trespassing, the '16 Going on 17' pavilion was moved from the grounds of Leopoldskron to Schloss Hellbrunn.

MONDSEE: (**10**, about 15 miles east of Salzburg) the cathedral of Mondsee was used for the wedding of Maria and captain Von Trapp.

Will Smith's law firm: 430 Madeline Avenue, Pasadena

A Hollywood institution: Canter's, North Fairfax Avenue

place at **Dupont Circle**, the Georgetown district and the steps of the **Treasury Building**. Brill's hideout was the old Dr Pepper plant in the industrial section of Baltimore, which was demolished for the movie. Also Baltimore is the chase through the **Consolidated Coal** yards on **Newgate Avenue**, down toward the Patapsco River. More locations were faked in LA, including Will Smith's law office, which is the **Craven Estate, 430 Madeline Drive, Pasadena** (used also in *Being There*). Two famed LA restaurants were roped in for filming: **Canter's, 419 North Fairfax Avenue**, Hollywood, and **Chasen's, 246 North Canon Drive**, in Beverly Hills.

ENFANTS DU PARADIS, LES (aka *Children of Paradise*)

(1945, dir: Marcel Carné)
Jean-Louis Barrault, Arletty, Pierre Brasseur.
● FRANCE

Carné's great classic of theatre life in 1840s Paris was filmed during the German occupation, amid accusations of collaboration. It's set on Paris' Boulevard du Temple, near the working-class districts of Sainte-Antoine and Saint-Denis in the 3rd and 10th arrondissements, named after the Order of the Knights Templar who were once associated with the area. The Boulevard was a strolling area, with pedlars and showmen's booths and, though it was suppressed after the 1789 Revolution, it boomed again after the restoration, becoming the 'Boulevard du Crime', after the number of theatres presenting melodramas, or the shifty mountebanks operating outside. Only one of the original theatres remains, the Theatre Dejazet.

The Boulevard was recreated, at a cost of five million francs, by designer Alexander Trauner on the studio lot at the **Studios la Victorine** in **Nice**, where close on 50 building and theatre façades were erected. The site of this vast outdoor set is now the studio parking lot. Most of the interiors filmed at Victorine too, though some scenes were shot at the **Joinville and Francoeur Studios** in **Paris**. The Studios la Victorine are still there (they feature in Truffaut's *Day for Night*), at **16 avenue Edouard Grinda**, Nice.

ENGLISH PATIENT, THE

(1996, dir: Anthony Minghella)
Ralph Fiennes, Juliette Binoche, Kristin Scott Thomas.
● ITALY; TUNISIA

Minghella's visually lush adaptation of Michael Ondaatje's WWII romance is set in Italy and Egypt, though the daz-

Ralph Fiennes Egyptian desert camp: Camel's Neck, near Nefta, Tunisia

zling desertscapes are in fact Tunisia. 1940s Cairo is **Tunis**, the Egyptian original being a much more developed city these days, while the the city's Medina filmed in **Sfax**, on the Tunisian coast. The invasion of Tobruk shot in the port of **El Mahdia**, between Sfax and Sousse. Ralph Fiennes' desert camp is in the western Tunisian desert near to **Nefta**, not too far from the set of *Star Wars Episode I: The Phantom Menace*, beneath the strange rock formation called, for obvious reasons, the **Camel's Neck**. A guided desert safari with four-wheel drive vehicle is the only practical way to see the location. The huge shimmering salt lake is **Chott el Jerid**, the dry lake you'll need to cross to reach Nefta, and the cave where Kristin Scott Thomas dies, which is near the old Bedu caravan post of **Tozeur**. Locations can be easily reached on expeditions or tours available to those based at the beach resorts of Hammamet, Sousse or Monastir (Tunisian Tourist Office: ✆ 020.7224.5561).

The old Shepheard's Hotel, Cairo – the wartime watering hole for explorers, diplomats and spies which was destroyed in the fifties – is not Egypt either. Nor Tunisia. It's the **Grand Hotel des Bains** in Venice, the setting for Visconti's *Death in Venice*. The actual Italian locations include the village, which is **Pienza** in Tuscany, and the chapel where Binoche studies the frescoes. This is the 13th century **Bacci Chapel** in the church of **San Francesco** at **Arezzo**, also in Tuscany. The frescoes, painted between 1453 and 1466 by Piero Della Francesca, have recently been restored. Reservations are required to view them, and, no, you can't light flares or dangle from the ceiling.

ENTER THE DRAGON

(1973, dir: Robert Clouse)
Bruce Lee, John Saxon, Jim Kelly.
● HONG KONG

British Intelligence enlists the aid of martial arts master Lee in Hollywood's first flirtation with the martial arts genre, made, on a minuscule budget, at Kowloon's **Golden Harvest Studios** – a former textile mill. The museum and dungeon sets were built here, with Hong Kong's drunks and vagrants drafted in as extras. And since no respectable Hong Kong woman would play a hooker, real prostitutes were brought in from the city's Maze Nightclub.

The location filming took place around Hong Kong itself, and Kowloon. The opening credits record the bustle of Hong Kong's **Barker Street**. Jim Kelly wanders through the narrow streets of the city's giant produce markets. The trip through the junks and sampans to the island fortress of villain Han was shot in **Aberdeen Harbour**, behind a small strip of land on the ocean side of Hong Kong. Han's Castle still overlooks Aberdeen Harbour, and though it's now surrounded by highrises, the steps up from the harbour can still be seen. The tournament fields were actually the tennis courts of Hong Kong attorney MW Lo. Surrounded by eight-foot walls, they're built into the hillside above **Tai Tam Bay**, prime site of the Japanese invasion of 1941.

ENTERTAINER, THE

(1960, dir: Tony Richardson)
Laurence Olivier, Joan Plowright, Roger Livesey.
● **LANCASHIRE; YORKSHIRE**

The old music hall: Alhambra Theatre, Bradford

Olivier recreates his Royal Court stage role, as failed seaside comedian Archie Rice, in John Osborne's bilious state-of-the-nation play. It's set and was mainly filmed on the blowsy seafront of faded resort **Blackpool**, the two-week-holiday escape for workers of the industrial north, but the theatre scenes were shot over the Pennines in the **Alhambra Theatre, Bradford**, Yorkshire.

ENTERTAINING MR SLOANE

(1969, dir: Douglas Hickox)
Beryl Reid, Harry Andrews, Peter McEnery.
● **LONDON**

Beryl Reid's cemetery home: Camberwell Old Cemetery, Honor Oak

Joe Orton it's not, but an enjoyable black comedy anyway with priceless performances. The Midlands semi, sited by a rubbish tip, becomes a Gothic folly in a London cemetery. The movie filmed in **Camberwell Old Cemetery** at **Honor Oak** in South London. The lodge where Beryl Reid entertains Peter McEnery is at the cemetery entrance on **Forest Hill Road**, opposite Marmora Road, SE22. A Grade II listed building, the 1856 house was in a sad state of disrepair when it was put on the market by owners Southwark Council for £100,000 in 1993: the conservatory gone, the stained glass windows replaced by breeze-blocks.

ERASERHEAD

(1978, dir: David Lynch)
Jack Nance, Charlotte Stewart, Jeane Bates.
● **PHILADELPHIA, PENNSYLVANIA; LOS ANGELES**

Lynch's first full-length movie is a claustrophobically oppressive nightmare of sexual guilt, filmed in a grim,

industrial cityscape around Philadelphia. The interiors were shot in the stables of the American Film Institute, then at the **Greystone Mansion, 501 North Doheny Road**, Beverly Hills. The mansion itself, and the extensive grounds, are familiar locations seen in *The Loved One*, *The Disorderly Orderly* and *Death Becomes Her*. This grand estate was built for oil magnate EL Doheny. In 1929, Doheny's son and his male secretary were discovered shot here, in an assumed murder/suicide.

ESCAPE FROM ALCATRAZ

(1979, dir: Don Siegel)
Clint Eastwood, Patrick McGoohan, Roberts Blossom.
● **SAN FRANCISCO**

Dark, downbeat account of the only documented escape from the notorious Rock, though the escapers' implied survival remains a moot point. Some interiors had to be recreated at Paramount in Hollywood, but much of the movie was actually shot at the disused prison of **Alcatraz Island** in San Francisco Bay. Extensive renovations were made to the crumbling structure, which have

The real interior of Alcatraz Prison

helped to preserve it as a tourist attraction. The paint used to restore the site to its earlier appearance needed to be easily removable so as not to obscure graffiti left from the 1969-71 occupation of the island by Native Americans, which is now regarded as a legitimate part of the island's history.

The island functioned as a Federal prison, in effect little more than a dumping ground for problematic convicts, from 1934. Despite the prison's fame, most inmates were not household names, though celeb inmates included "Machine Gun" Kelly, Robert Stroud, The Birdman (see *Birdman of Alcatraz*), and of course, Al Capone. Capone, who was moved to the Rock after continuing to run his empire from behind bars in Atlanta, still sought to buy influence by offering to pay for an extension to the exercise yard. His kind offer wasn't taken up and the King of Crime was relegated to working in the prison laundry.

By 1963, when the concept of confinement without hope of reformation had become outdated and the cost of maintaining the island prohibitive, the prison was closed. Alcatraz is now a national park and can be visited by boat from Fisherman's Wharf in San Francisco. Visit the website at *www.nps.gov/alcatraz*.

ESCAPE FROM NEW YORK

(1981, dir: John Carpenter)
Kurt Russell, Lee Van Cleef, Donald Pleasence.
● **ST LOUIS, MISSOURI; NEW YORK CITY**

Kurt Russell is sent in to rescue President Donald Pleasence, after his plane is downed in the island of Manhattan, now (in the distant future of 1997) a maximum security prison. Most of the the futuristic NY of John Carpenter's cult thriller is not the Big Apple at all, but St Louis, Missouri. The fight scene, ostensibly in the Big Apple's Madison Square Garden, is the **Grand Hall** of **Union**

Station, 1 St Louis Union Station, a then-vacant railway terminus, now been renovated as a vast mall/hotel complex. 59th Street Bridge is St Louis' **Chain of Rocks Bridge**. Russell finds cabby Ernest Borgnine happily singing along to the shabby remnants of a Broadway show at the **Fox Theater, Grand Avenue** at Washington. Brain's hideout is the **Civil Courts Building, 12th** at Market. The plane crash site is the corner of **Broadway and St Charles Street**, downtown St Louis, an area which had recently been devastated by a huge fire.

ESCAPE FROM THE PLANET OF THE APES
(1971, dir: Don Taylor)
Roddy McDowall, Kim Hunter, Bradford Dillman.
● **CALIFORNIA**

Three of the futuristic apes travel back to 20th century LA in this second sequel to *Planet of the Apes*. Filming took place at the **Natural History Museum of Los Angeles County**, LA and south of **San Clemente**, California.

ET DIEU... CREA LA FEMME (aka *And God... Created Woman*)
(1957, dir: Roger Vadim)
Brigitte Bardot, Curt Jurgens, Jean-Louis Trintignant.
● **FRANCE**

Director Roger Vadim not only put Bardot on the map, as the original 'Sex Kitten', but also **St Tropez**, in this widescreen sex melodrama. Considering its reputation, the tiny fishing port is, visually at least, astonishingly unchanged since the fifties and you'll recognise most of the film's locations. Bardot's home is in the **La Ponche** district, north of the Old Town, but most of the film was shot on the picturesque waterfront. It's still a jumble of tiny pastel-coloured cafés, and you can see Curt Jurgens' office on **Quai Jean Jaurès**. The sea wall and steps, where La Bardot pouted and wiggled, are on **Môle Jean Réveille**, across the port from Belvedere de la Marine. Nearby is the gentle slope of **Quai Frédéric Mistral**, which was the site of the Bar des Amis, outside which Jean-Louis Trintignant gets involved in a fistfight and in the basement of which

Site of Curt Jurgens' office: quai Jean Jaurès, St Tropez

Site of the bar: Quai Frédéric Mistral, San Tropez

The newsagent where Bardot worked: San Tropez

the movie climaxes. The bar is now a souvenir shop, Bleu Continu. Tucked away behind the cafés here is the newsagent where Bardot worked, now a vacant building, **2 rue du Cepoun Louis Sanmartin**, at the junction with Montée Honnorat Coste.

EVERY WHICH WAY BUT LOOSE
(1978, dir: James Fargo)
Clint Eastwood, Sondra Locke, Ruth Gordon.
● **CALIFORNIA; NEW MEXICO; COLORADO**

This bozo knockabout comedy, featuring a lovable orangutan alongside Clint, was a surprise box office smash, spawning an equally dumb sequel, *Any Which Way You Can*. It was shot around the southwest, from LA's **San Fernando Valley** through **Santa Fe** and **Taos**, New Mexico, to **Denver**, Colorado.

EVERYONE SAYS I LOVE YOU
(1996, dir: Woody Allen)
Woody Allen, Goldie Hawn, Edward Norton.
● **NEW YORK CITY; PARIS; VENICE, ITALY**

Allen's musical for non-singers and non-dancers, filmed in New York, of course. The jewellery store is the city's première diamond salon, **Harry Winston Inc, 718 Fifth Avenue** at West 56th Street.

Allen's Venetian stay: Gritti Palace Hotel, Canal Grande

The dancing corpses perform at **Campbell's Funeral Parlor** on Madison Avenue. Allen's European jaunt takes in **Paris**, where he dances with Goldie Hawn on the banks of the Seine, and **Venice**, where he stays at the luxurious **Gritti Palace Hotel, San Marco 2467, Campo Santa Maria del Giglio** (℃ *794611*).

EVIL DEAD, THE
(1982, dir: Sam Raimi)
Bruce Campbell, Ellen Sandweiss, Betsy Baker.
● **TENNESSEE; MICHIGAN**

Raimi's influential, gory, energetic shocker was financed by Detroit dentists and filmed in 16mm, with five benighted teensters stuck in a wooden cabin in a possessed forest. The location is near a campground area at **Morristown**, north of I-81, about 40 miles northeast of Knoxville in East Tennessee. The animation sequences were filmed in a basement in Raimi's hometown, **Detroit**, Michigan.

EVIL DEAD II
(1987, dir: Sam Raimi)
Bruce Campbell, Sarah Berry, Dan Hicks.
● **NORTH CAROLINA; MICHIGAN**

More fun in the woods. The little cabin is now at **Wadesboro**, 40 miles east of Charlotte on Highway 74, North Carolina. Studio filming was at the **De Laurentiis Studios** in **Wilmington**, North Carolina, with additional work in **Detroit**, Michigan once again.

EVITA
(1996, dir: Alan Parker)
Madonna, Jonathan Pryce, Antonio Banderas.
● ARGENTINA; HUNGARY

Alan Parker brings visual grandeur to the ropey old Lloyd Webber-Rice cart-horse. The production managed to film in **Buenos Aires** (in the face of much artificially induced anti-Madonna hysteria), but it's often **Budapest** standing in for the Argentinian capital. The great coup, of course, was filming 'Don't Cry For Me Argentina' on the balcony of the **Casa Rosada, Government House**, on the **Plaza de Mayo**. The railway station is in Argentina too; the **British Victorian Retiro Station**.

The possessed house: Prospect Avenue, Georgetown

The modernisation of Buenos Aires sent the production company to Europe, however. The tank invasion was filmed in **Liberty Square**, Budapest. Evita's grandiose funeral was shot, not on Buenos Aires' Avenida de Mayo, but on Budapest's **Constitution Avenue** near the Parliament building. But even Budapest presented problems. Evita's lying in state wasn't staged in the Basilica of St Stephen as had been planned, but in the city's **Museum of Ethnography**.

The *boliche* (bar/restaurant) where Magaldi performs, and the various nightclubs and hotels where Evita works her way to the top, are sets at Shepperton. The real Evita, by the way, appeared at the Colon Opera House in Buenos Aires, and is buried in the Recoleta Cemetery.

EXCALIBUR
(1981, dir: John Boorman)
Nigel Terry, Helen Mirren, Nicol Williamson.
● IRELAND

Boorman's Arthurian fantasy eschews real castles as too naturalistic, and films in the wild landscapes of southern Ireland in Wicklow, Kerry and Tipperary. The forests are the 400-year-old natural oak woods at **Lough Dan** in the Wicklow Mountains, twenty miles south of Dublin, and **Childer's Wood**, near Roundwood for jousting scenes and for Arthur and Guinevere's wedding. Battle scenes feature the primaeval settings of **Wicklow Head**, on the east coast at Wicklow, and **Lamb's Head**, County Kerry.

Cahir Castle, seen in Stanley Kubrick's *Barry Lyndon* is used for the early 'dark ages' scenes.

EXORCIST, THE
(1973, dir: William Friedkin)
Linda Blair, Ellen Burstyn, Max Von Sydow.
● WASHINGTON DC; NEW YORK CITY; IRAQ

Massively hyped on release, picketted by fundamentalist Christians – the kind of publicity you just can't buy – *The Exorcist* set new standards for gross-out horror movies. Author William Peter Blatty's stated intention was a movie about Catholic faith. Director Friedkin wisely dumped Blatty's flakily religiose 'Thousand Points of Light' ending, with souls twinkling in Heaven.

The opening scene of Father Merrin confronting the demon Pazuzu shot in pre-Saddam Hussein Iraq. The location was a genuine archaeological dig near **Al Mawsil**, and the town where Father Merrin suffers is **Hatra**.

Movie actress Chris MacNeil (a character supposedly based on Shirley MacLaine) is shooting a movie about

student protest on the campus of **Georgetown University**, Washington DC – author Blatty's alma mater. It's on campus that the **Dahlgren Chapel** is obscenely desecrated. Father Karras visits his sick mother in New York's **Goldwater Memorial Hospital** on Roosevelt Island in the East River (for a long time the site of madhouses and prisons – it was here Mae West served her eight day sentence in the 1930s for appearing in her play *Sex*). The hospital appeared again in the very different *Exorcist II: The Heretic*.

Burstyn's student protest movie: Georgetown University

The desecrated church: Dahlgren Chapel, Georgetown

The possessed house itself stands at **3600 Prospect Avenue** at 36th Street NW, close to the Potomac River in Georgetown, southwest DC, but it's not quite as seen in the movie. You won't be able to spot the window of Regan's room, from which the ominous shaft of light floods in the poster image. This wing of the house was no more than a false front built for the movie.

The flight of steps: M Street

You can, though, find the flight of steps down which Father Karras hurtles, alongside the house, leading down from Prospect Avenue to **M Street**.

The complex interior set, with moving walls and refrigeration, was built at the Ceco Studios (now called Cameramart), **450 West 54th Street** between 9th and 10th Avenues in New York.

EXORCIST II: THE HERETIC
(1977, dir: John Boorman)
Richard Burton, Linda Blair, Louise Fletcher.
● NEW YORK; ARIZONA; LOS ANGELES

Not remotely similar in style or content to *The Exorcist*. The Georgetown house was mocked up on a soundstage at Warner Bros' Burbank Studio when permission was refused to film there again. Louise Fletcher's clinic, where she investigates Linda Blair's nightmares, was the disused **Goldwater Hospital, Roosevelt Island** in the East River, New York. The hospital, reached by the Aerial Tramway seen in *City Slickers*, also featured as the institution Father Karras' mother was confined to in *The Exorcist*. Linda Blair's New York apartment is the black, accordion-pleated **CBS Building, Sixth Avenue** between 52nd and 53rd Streets, although the rooftop terrace, where Blair teeters 35 stories up, is the **Warner Communications Building, between Fifth and Sixth Avenues** overlooking 51st Street and St Patrick's Cathedral.

The African Mission Center is at **Lone Rock**, on the shore of the artificially-created Lake Powell, near Page in northern Arizona. Also near Page is the village at the base of the Ethiopian Rock Church, at **Crazy Canyon**. Both *The Greatest Story Ever Told* and *Planet of the Apes* used the same spectacular rockscapes. The mud city of Jepti was a set built at the Burbank studios, based on the real African villages of Mopti and Djenne in Mali.

EXORCIST III

(1990, dir: William Peter Blatty)
George C Scott, Brad Dourif, Jason Miller.
● **WASHINGTON DC; NORTH CAROLINA**

This confusing, and quite batty, religious shocker follows on from the original *Exorcist* rather than *Exorcist II: The Heretic* and is, incidentally, quite horrific. Directed by the writer of the original story, it was filmed once again in the Georgetown area of Washington DC, making more use of the locale than the other movies. Once again, the campus of **Georgetown University**, and the steps alongside **M Street** and the Prospect Avenue house are featured. The heavenly dream-sequence, set in what looks like a combination of Grand Central Station and a hospital, was filmed in the disused Ideal Cement Factory building at **Wilmington**, North Carolina (also the site of Dinohattan in *Super Mario Bros*). And if Nicol Williamson's exorcism scene seems a tad irrelevant, that's because it was tacked on (at a cost of $4 million) after main filming had finished, presumably to justify the title.

EXPLORERS

(1985, dir: Joe Dante)
Ethan Hawke, River Phoenix, Jason Presson.
● **CALIFORNIA**

Dante's enjoyable, satirical sci-fi has Hawke, Phoenix (in his first movie) and Presson as three schoolkids who visit, in their homemade spacecraft, aliens whose knowledge of

Ethan Hawke spies on his dream girl: D Street, Petaluma

Earth derives entirely from stray TV signals. The small US town the kids take off from is **Petaluma**, in Sonoma County, Route 101, 30 miles north of San Francisco, and

also the location for George Lucas' *American Graffiti*. The movie opens on Petaluma's D Street, and the house where Ethan Hawke spies on his dream girl is **920 D Street**. The drive-in, where the spacecraft crashes into the snack bar, is the **Pickwick Drive-In Theater** in the **Pickwick Recreation Center, 1001 West Riverside Drive**, Burbank.

EYES WIDE SHUT

(1999, dir: Stanley Kubrick)
Tom Cruise, Nicole Kidman, Sydney Pollack.
● **LONDON; BEDFORDSHIRE**

After all the hype and the secrecy, Kubrick's final movie was greeted with a strangely muted reception, but there's no denying how gorgeous it all looks.

Greenwich Village, New York: Hatton Garden

Although it's set in New York, there are only the most fleeting glimpses of the real city, courtesy of a Second Unit. The Long Island mansions were found in the Home

The masked orgy, exterior: Mentmore Towers

Counties, the Greenwich Village streets constructed at Pinewood or faked in corners of central London.

The big party scene, where Cruise attends to host Sydney Pollack's hooker after she ODs on a speedball, filmed at **Luton Hoo** (see *Four Weddings and a Funeral* for details). Most of the Greenwich Village street scenes were shot on huge and elaborately detailed sets at Pinewood (the proliferation of T-junctions is a dead giveaway), but for a few shots, London streets were dressed as New York. After enquiring too closely about the fate of his musician friend, Cruise is stalked by a sinister man along **Worship Street**, EC2, just off City Road near Old Street in the City, and into **Hatton Garden**. **Berner Street** and **Eastcastle Street** also became Greenwich Village. The interior of Club Sonata, the New York jazz club is **Madame Jo-Jo's, Brewer Street**, in Soho. Filming also took place in the Royal Suite of the **Lanesborough Hotel, 1 Lanesborough Place**, SW1. Knebworth House (Wayne Manor in Tim Burton's *Batman*) was screentested, and rejected, for the masked 'orgy' scene. In the end, two separate locations were used. The exterior is **Mentmore Towers**, in the village of **Mentmore**, Buckinghamshire (see *Brazil* for details). It is no longer open to the public. The exotic interior, with its Indian-style carvings, is **Elveden Hall**, a private house on the A11 about four miles west of Thetford in Suffolk. The final Christmas shopping reconciliation scene was filmed on the ground floor of the famous toyshop **Hamley's, Regent Street**, London W1.

F

FABULOUS BAKER BOYS, THE
(1989, dir: Steve Kloves)
Jeff Bridges, Beau Bridges, Michelle Pfeiffer.
● SEATTLE, WASHINGTON; LOS ANGELES

The resort hotel: Greystone Mansion, Loma Vista Drive, Beverly Hills

Though this story of two cheesy lounge pianists, who find success but fall apart when they hook up with singer Michelle Pfeiffer, is set in **Seattle**, Washington State, it was made far from the rains and the mist, largely in sunny Los Angeles. The real Pacific Northwest is used to set the scene: Jeff Bridges is first seen leaving a one-night-stand on **First Avenue** at Vine Street in Seattle's Bohemian Belltown district. His apartment is a third-floor warehouse overlooking the city's famous Pioneer Square, above **Masin's Furniture Co, 220 Second Avenue South** at South Main Street. After the split-up, he thinks he sees Pfeiffer outside the **WestCoast Roosevelt Hotel, 1531 Seventh Avenue** at Pine Street (seen also in the biopic of France Farmer, *Frances*).

The piano showroom, where the auditions are conducted, is down south in Los Angeles' eastern suburb of **Pasadena**, and the deli in LA's **Fairfax** district. The brothers' gigs take in such familiar LA venues as the **Ambassador Hotel, 3400 Wilshire Boulevard**, which doubled as a number of sites (see the 1954 *A Star Is Born* for details); the **Variety Arts Theatre, 940 South Figueroa Street**, downtown and the **Hollywood Roosevelt Hotel, 7000 Hollywood Boulevard**, Hollywood. The upscale resort hotel is a combination job. The exterior is the **Greystone Mansion, 905 Loma Vista Drive**, Beverly Hills (see *The Loved One* for details), while you'll no doubt recognise the imposing lobby and the **Crystal Ballroom**, where Pfeiffer stops the show with her piano-lolling 'Makin' Whoopee', as the **Biltmore Hotel, 506 South Grand Avenue**, downtown (see *Beverly Hills Cop*).

FACE, THE (aka *The Magician*)
(1958, dir: Ingmar Bergman)
Max Von Sydow, Gunnar Bjornstrand, Ingrid Thulin.
● SWEDEN

Dry old stick Bjornstrand subjects charlatan Von Sydow's theatrical show to official scrutiny and lives to regret it. In keeping with the film's theme of theatricality, it's mostly studio-shot, but you can find Gunnar Bjornstrand's house and the cobbled street in the **Skansen Open Air Museum, Djurgardsslaten 49-51, Stockholm**. The museum, a collection of around 150 period buildings (and a zoo) has been a Stockholm attraction since 1891. It's open every day except Christmas (℃ *08.442.8000*)

FACE/OFF
(1997, dir: John Woo)
John Travolta, Nicolas Cage, Joan Allen.
● LOS ANGELES

Bogus priest Cage plants the bomb: New LA Convention Center, downtown

Woo's first real American success since relocation from Hong Kong, with Travolta and Cage having huge fun impersonating each other's mannerisms in this brazenly ludicrous face-swap thriller. The vast atrium, where bogus priest Nicolas Cage plants a bomb, is the **New Los Angeles Convention Center, Figueroa Street** between 11th Street and Venice Boulevard, downtown LA. See it also as the spaceport in *Starship Troopers*. The futuristic lab, where the face-swap takes place, is a private house in Agoura Hills, designed in 1993 by Ed Niles which, coincidentally, was also used for *Starship Troopers* (as Casper Van Dien's home). The speedboat climax filmed in **San Pedro Harbor**, south of the city.

FACULTY, THE
(1998, dir: Robert Rodriguez)
Josh Hartnett, Shawn Hatosy, Elijah Wood.
● TEXAS

More hip post-modern schlock irony from a script by *Scream*'s Kevin Williamson, directed by indie-meister Rodriguez, which was filmed at **Lockhart** ('The Barbeque Capital of Texas'), and also at state capital **Austin** and **San Marcos**. Herrington High is the **Texas School for the Deaf, 1102 South Congress Avenue**, Austin.

FAHRENHEIT 451
(1966, dir: François Truffaut)
Oskar Werner, Julie Christie, Cyril Cusack.
● FRANCE

Ray Bradbury's sci-fi novel filmed by Truffaut, with music by Bernard Herrmann and photography by Nicolas Roeg, was shot at Pinewood studios in England. The futuristic monorail, however, can be found in France, at **Chateauneuf-sur-Loire**, about fifteen miles from Orleans.

FALL OF THE ROMAN EMPIRE, THE
(1964, dir: Anthony Mann)
Stephen Boyd, Alec Guinness, Christopher Plummer.
● SPAIN

Last great of the great sixties epics, looking terrific because of the decision to build expensive three-dimensional sets. A vast reconstruction of the Roman Forum was built at the site of another Samuel Bronston production, *55 Days at Peking*, on the ranch of the Marques de Villabragima at **Las Matas**, sixteen miles from Madrid.

The opening scenes, of Marcus Aurelius' campaign against the barbarians, are in the **Sierra de Guadarrama** mountains above Segovia, north of Madrid. The battle against the Persians was shot 100 miles to the south of Madrid on a plain near **Manzanares El Real**. **Sagunto**, on the east coast, twenty miles north of Valencia, stood in for the Roman city of Ravenna. Coincidentally, Sagunto is one of the towns taken from the Moors by the subject of another Bronston epic, El Cid. Lakeside scenes were shot on the shore of **Lake Santillana**.

FALLEN IDOL, THE (aka *The Lost Illusion*)

(1948, dir: Carol Reed)
Bobby Henrey, Ralph Richardson, Michele Morgan.
● **LONDON**

The Embassy: Belgrave Square

The Embassy, where butler Ralph Richardson comes close to being falsely arrested for murder in this adaptation of a Graham Greene short story, is the headquarters of the St John's Ambulance organisation at the northeast corner of **Belgrave Square**, on Wilton and Grosvenor Crescents (*tube: Hyde Park Corner*). The maze of narrow mews streets where Richardson clandestinely meets with Michele Morgan, and where young Bobby Henrey gets lost, have moved seriously upmarket from the pub'n'café atmosphere of the movie. They are **Belgrave Mews** and **Kinnerton Street**, just to the north of Belgrave Square. The day out was filmed at **Regents Park Zoo**, at the old refreshment stand in front of the **Mappin Terraces**.

FALLING DOWN

(1993, dir: Joel Schumacher)
Michael Douglas, Robert Duvall, Frederick Forrest.
● **LOS ANGELES**

'You mean I'm the bad guy?': Venice Pier, Venice Beach

Michael Douglas, aka D-FENS, is having one of those days. Caught in a gridlock at **Lincoln Heights**, east of downtown LA, he makes the ultimate gesture of defiance. He gets out of his car and heads home to **Venice** *on foot*. How radical is that? Douglas' trek takes him down Wilshire Boulevard, past **The Dark Room, 5370 Wilshire Boulevard**, a camera shop built in gleaming black vitrolite as the front of a Leica camera. The Golden State Savings and Loan, where the disaffected customer stages his lone demonstration, is at **5350 Wilshire Boulevard**. At the corner of **Sunset Boulevard** and **Laurel Avenue**, way up in West Hollywood, he shoots up a phone booth. Home is Venice Beach, and it's on the seafront pier that D-FENS finally gets to realise that he's not the good guy. **Venice Pier** is on Ocean Front Walk at the end of Washington Street.

FAME

(1980, dir: Alan Parker)
Irene Cara, Lee Curreri, Gene Anthony Ray.
● **NEW YORK CITY**

The High School of Performing Arts: West 46th Street

The trials and tribulations of a bunch of aspiring hopefuls at New York's **High School of Performing Arts**. The school used to be at **120 West 46th Street**, until 1984, when the facility transferred to the Lincoln Center. The building, gutted by fire in 1988, but restored as the Jacqueline Kennedy Onassis High School, was used only for exteriors. Most of the actual filming took place in the disused Haaren High School, 10th Avenue at 59th Street, which closed down in 1976. It was also used for 1967's *Up the Down Staircase*. The Haaren has since been demolished.

FAMILY PLOT

(1976, dir: Alfred Hitchcock)
Karen Black, Bruce Dern, Barbara Harris.
● **CALIFORNIA**

The department store: Southwestern Law School, Wilshire Boulevard, LA

Hitchcock's last film, a lightweight comedy thriller, is set in San Francisco, but it's no *Vertigo*. Among the real San Fran landmarks is the **Fairmont Hotel, 950 Mason Street** (*© 415. 772.5000*), seen also in *Petulia* and *The Rock*, where Barbara Harris leaves a message for cabby Bruce Dern at the hotel's *porte cochere*. The cathedral, where Hitch stages the bravura sequence in which a bishop is kidnapped in full view of his congregation, is also for real. It's **Grace Cathedral, 1051 Taylor Street**, also used in *Bullitt*.

Kidnapping the bishop: Grace Cathedral, Taylor Street

But many of the locations are down the coast in LA. The department store, where Dern quizzes the chauffeur's daughter, was Bullock's, the 1928 art deco gem in midtown Los Angeles. Although the store has closed, the building lives on as the **Southwestern Law School,**

Barbara Harris leaves a message: Fairmont Hotel, Mason Street

Barlow Creek Cemetery: Pioneer Cemetery, Sierra Madre

3050 Wilshire Boulevard (for details see *Topper*). Barlow Creek Cemetery, where Katherine Helmond is tailed, is **Pioneer Cemetery** in **Sierra Vista Park, Sierra Madre Boulevard**, Sierra Madre, just northeast of Pasadena. The tiny cemetery was booked for filming months in advance and allowed to become wild and overgrown. Cathleen Nesbitt's Rainbird Mansion, supposedly in Pacifica, is a grand house in South Pasadena, while the out-of-control car chase was shot on **Angeles Crest**, LA.

FANNY AND ALEXANDER
(1982, dir: Ingmar Bergman)
Gunn Walgren, Ewa Froeling, Erland Josephson.
● SWEDEN

Surprisingly benign Dickensian drama from Bergman, with stern pastors, kindly old relatives and a happy ending. The major location is **Uppsala**, 40 miles north of Stockholm.

FANTASTIC VOYAGE, THE
(1966, dir: Richard Fleischer)
Stephen Boyd, Raquel Welch, Donald Pleasence.
● LOS ANGELES

Dotty sci-fi romp with a team of surgeons reduced to germ-size and injected into the body of a top scientist to perform delicate brain surgery. The HQ exteriors and the huge circular corridor are the **Los Angeles Sports Arena, 3939 South Figueroa Street**, home of the LA Clippers, in the Exposition Park area.

FAR AND AWAY
(1992, dir: Ron Howard)
Tom Cruise, Nicole Kidman, Thomas Gibson.
● IRELAND; MONTANA

More misty-eyed nostalgia over old Oireland as Cruise and Kidman emigrate to the New World. The Irish coastal scenes used the **Dingle Peninsula**, where, as for *Ryan's Daughter*, a village was built specially for the movie. The country estate, where poor country lad Cruise falls for the daughter of the landowner, is **Kilruddery**, near Bray just south of Dublin. Seat of the Earl of Meath, the house is still there (its fiery destruction was computer generated). Cruise and Kidman flee to the US, but filming continues in Ireland. Their arrival in turn-of-the-century Boston filmed on **Market Street**, behind the Guinness Brewery in **Dublin**. The bustling street scenes, with the brothel where

Cruise and Kidman arrive in Boston: Market Street, Dublin

Cruise stays, is **Temple Lane**, near the Ha'penny Bridge. Molly Kay's brothel, Cruise's lodging, was built on a vacant lot between a pub and a pizza parlour.

The Oklahoma Land Rush really is in the US, though. The spectacular land-grab was shot just outside **Billings**, Montana.

FAR FROM THE MADDING CROWD
(1967, dir: John Schlesinger)
Julie Christie, Alan Bates, Terence Stamp.
● DORSET; WILTSHIRE

Schlesinger brought all the naturalistic innovations of sixties new wave cinema, along with the atmospheric photography of Nicolas Roeg, to Thomas Hardy's tragic novel. Set in fictional Weatherbury (based on Puddletown, five miles northeast of Dorchester on the A35), the movie was shot in Dorset and Wiltshire.

Gabriel Oak's caravan, where the tragedy is set in motion when a rogue sheepdog drives his flock over a cliff, stood on the cliffs at **Scratchy Bottom**, between Worbarrow Bay and Osmington close to the spectacular sea-arch of **Durdle Door**, on the Dorset Coast Path. Bathsheba's humble farm was a disused farm building beneath the Hardy Monument (that's Captain Hardy, of "kiss me" fame, not the novelist) at **Portesham**, west of Dorchester. As Oak's fortunes are plummeting, Bathsheba's rise when she inherits Weatherbury Farm (based, in the book, on Waterston Manor in Puddletown), which in the movie is represented by **Bloxworth House**, a 17th century brick house near **Bere Regis** (it's occasionally open to the public).

Oak arrives in Weatherbury to look for work. The steep cobbled street is **Gold Hill**, familiar to a generation of British TV viewers from the 'Hovis' ad. It's behind the Town Hall of **Shaftesbury**, Wiltshire, on the A30 about twenty miles west of Salisbury. The hiring fair itself, though, is **Market Place, Devizes**, almost 30 miles to the north. On the square you can see the **Bear Hotel** (✆ 01380.722444), where the farm-owners relax, and the **Corn Exchange**, where Bathsheba proves she's more than a match for the local traders. Also in Devizes is **St John's Church**, used as All Saints, where Fanny fatally misses her wedding to Captain Troy.

The interior of Squire Boldwood's home is in Wiltshire, too; **Thornhill House** at the village of Sturminster Newton, between Shaftesbury and Sherborne, but its exterior is back in Dorset at **Friar Waddon House**, near Weymouth.

Gabriel Oak arrives in Weatherbury: Gold Hill, Shaftesbury

Captain Troy shows off his swordsmanship: Maiden Castle, Dorchester

Other locations near to Dorchester include Fanny's grave, in the graveyard of **St Nicholas** at **Sydling St Nicholas**, seven miles northwest of Dorchester (*rail: Maiden Newton*); the all-night party which is the **Tithe Barn, Abbotsbury**, near the coast, eight miles southwest of Dorchester and the grassy, stepped hillocks, where Captain Troy demonstrates his swordsmanship. This is **Maiden Castle**, a ten-acre neolithic camp a mile or two southwest of Dorchester on the road to Martinstown. The camp, which became a hill fort, was the site of a bloody battle during the Roman invasion. It subsequently became a Roman encampment.

The cockfight was shot in the six-storey 18th century folly **Horton Tower**, just outside **Horton**, about ten miles north of Bournemouth.

FAREWELL MY LOVELY (aka *Murder My Sweet*)
(1944, dir: Edward Dmytryk)
Dick Powell, Claire Trevor, Mike Mazurki.
● **LOS ANGELES**

The alternative title was meant to warn audiences expecting a musical, when crooner Dick Powell changed gear to become Philip Marlowe in one of the first films noir, an adaptation of Raymond Chandler's novel. Jules Amthor's apartment is **Sunset Towers, 8358 Sunset Boulevard** in West Hollywood (see *The Player* for details), where Marlowe is kept drugged up.

Marlowe is drugged up at Jules Amthor's: Sunset Towers, Hollywood

FAREWELL MY LOVELY
(1975, dir: Dick Richards)
Robert Mitchum, Charlotte Rampling, Sylvia Miles.
● **LOS ANGELES**

Atmospheric, and more explicit, remake with Mitchum a bit of a softie. Jules Amthor has become butch dyke Francis Amthor, "LA's famous madam" (with a young Sylvester Stallone as henchman). Her brothel is now the **Milbank and McFie Residence, 3340 Country Club Drive** at Arlington Avenue, between Pico and Olympic Boulevards, midtown (not open to the public). The swishy gilt White Orchid nightclub where Marlowe meets corrupt official Burnett, is the old Myron's Ballroom, now renamed **Grand Avenue, 1024 South Grand Avenue**, downtown LA (which you can also see in *New York, New York*).

FARGO
(1996, dir: Ethan Coen)
Francis McDormand, William H Macy, Steve Buscemi.
● **MINNESOTA; NORTH DAKOTA**

The Coens' inventive thriller (based on a 'true story'), was shot mainly around **Brainerd**, Minnesota, but, as luck would have it, a particularly mild winter meant that filming had to move north for snow scenes, as far as **Fargo** itself, and **Grand Forks**, North Dakota. Also featured is **Embers Restaurant, 7525 Wayzata Boulevard** at

Pennsylvania Avenue South in the St Louis Park area of Minneapolis. Although there is a giant Paul Bunyan statue in Brainerd (it's in the Paul Bunyan Amusement Center on the west edge of town, billed as 'The World's Largest Talking Animated Man', and he's seated), the statue seen in the movie was erected on **Pembina County Highway 1**, four miles west of **Bathgate**, North Dakota, up towards the Canadian border.

FAST TIMES AT RIDGEMONT HIGH
(1982, dir: Amy Heckerling)
Sean Penn, Jennifer Jason Leigh, Judge Reinhold.
● **LOS ANGELES**

This high school drama has a superior script from *Jerry Maguire* director Cameron Crowe. The high school is a combination of two valley schools: **Canoga Park High School, 6850 Topanga Canyon Boulevard** at Vanowen Street, and **Van Nuys High School, 6535 Cedros Avenue**, which has included Robert Redford and Jane Russell among its pupils, and, for a short while, Marilyn Monroe. The shopping mall is the old **Sherman Oaks Galleria, 15303 Ventura Boulevard**.

FATAL ATTRACTION
(1987, dir: Adrian Lyne)
Michael Douglas, Glenn Close, Anne Archer.
● **NEW YORK CITY; NEW YORK STATE**

Flashy re-run of vengeful-ex thriller *Play Misty for Me*, set in new York. The restaurant where Michael Douglas first claps eyes on Glenn Close is **Mr Chow of New York, 324 East 57th Street**, midtown, a branch of the

Michael Douglas' fatal mistake: Mr Chow of New York, East 57th Street

snobby Beverly Hills restaurant. Close's warehouse apartment can be seen at **675 Hudson Street** between 13th & 14th Streets, but the lift they make out in is actually around the corner, at **400 East 14th Street**. The funfair Close takes the kiddie to is **Rye Playland, Playland Parkway, Rye**, New York State.

Douglas' out-of-town house is a conflation of two properties: the exterior is in **Bedford**, just east of I-684 in Westchester County, New York State, where the new ending for the movie was shot (it's the old Irene Selznick estate), while interiors were filmed at a house in **Mt Kisco**. The medical centre is the **Westchester Medical Center, Valhalla**, New York State.

FATHER OF THE BRIDE
(1991, dir: Charles Shyer)
Steve Martin, Diane Keaton, Martin Short.
● **LOS ANGELES**

This syrupy remake of the 1950 Vincente Minnelli movie with Spencer Tracy trots out every known cliché about fathers, daughters and weddings. Steve Martin and Diane Keaton's home is **843 South El Molino Avenue** in

Martin and Keaton's house: 843 South El Molino Avenue, Pasadena

Pasadena. Wildly OTT Martin Short has a boutique in **Melrose Place** in West Hollywood. The wedding finally takes place at **Trinity Baptist Church, 2040 West Jefferson Boulevard**, Santa Monica.

FEAR EATS THE SOUL (aka *Angst Essen Seele Auf*)
(1973, dir: Rainer Werner Fassbinder)
Brigitti Mira, El Hedi Ben Salem, Barbara Valentin.
● **MUNICH, GERMANY**

Loosely based on Douglas Sirk's 1955 melodrama *All That Heaven Allows*, Fassbinder's film deals with the prejudice surrounding the relationship between Mira's older charwoman and Ben Salem's younger Moroccan immigrant. It was shot in Munich.

FEET FIRST
(1930, dir: Clyde Bruckman)
Harold Lloyd, Barbara Kent, Robert McWade.
● **LOS ANGELES; HAWAII**

Harold Lloyd dangles again: 848 South Broadway, downtown LA

Revisiting his famous silent *Safety Last*, Harold Lloyd plays a shoe salesman getting mixed up with crooks and – surprise! – ending up dangling from a tall building. This skyscraper can still be seen at **848 South Broadway**, on the corner of 9th Street, by the Orpheum Theater, downtown LA, and is still there unchanged. Filming also took place in the **Aloha Tower** area of **Oahu**, Hawaii.

FELLINI SATYRICON
(1970, dir: Federico Fellini)
Martin Potter, Hiram Keller, Max Born.
● **ITALY**

Fellini, as usual, conjures up most of his surreal, satiric images at **Cinecittà** studios in Rome. However, the shipboard scenes, with the giant fish and a one-eyed Alain Cuny marrying the hero, filmed at **Fregene** on the coast west of Rome, and on the **Isle of Ponza**, 35 miles out in the Tyrrhenian Sea from Gaeta – between Rome and Naples. Some scenes with Potter and Keller in the subterranean grotto, which couldn't be recreated at Cinecittà, were shot in the caverns beneath Rome's **Coliseum**.

FELLINI'S ROMA
(1972, dir: Federico Fellini)
Peter Gonzales, Stefano Majore, Anna Magnani.
● **ROME**

Brilliantly inventive kaleidoscopic collage of memories and images of Rome, filmed almost entirely on the soundstages at **Cinecittà**. The hallucinatory motorway ride into

Rome is for real – apart from the terminal traffic jam at a very deliberately artificial Coliseum – as is the closing motorbike tour of the city.

FEMALE TROUBLE
(1974, dir: John Waters)
Divine, Edith Massey, David Lochary.
● **BALTIMORE, MARYLAND**

The tragic life of Dawn Davenport, shot, naturally, around the less salubrious areas of Waters' native Baltimore. Dawn enjoys a traditional Christmas carol singing with Mom and Dad at her home in the **Orchard Hills** district. She strolls with resolutely heterosexual hairdresser and husband-to-be Gator around romantic **Fell's Point**, at the south end of Broadway overlooking North West Harbor. At Fell's Point and Broadway is the bridal shop where she purchases her ravishing see-through wedding gown, and she performs as 'The Most Beautiful Woman in the World' at the **Theater Club Theater**.

FEMME EST UNE FEMME, UNE (aka *A Woman Is a Woman*)
(1961, dir: Jean-Luc Godard)
Jean Paul Belmondo, Jean-Claude Biraly, Anna Karina.
● **PARIS**

Tribute to the Hollywood musical: Porte St Denis, rue du Faubourg St Denis

Always unpredictable, Godard followed up his groundbreaking *A Bout De Souffle* with this oddball tribute to the Hollywood musical. Filmed on the streets of Paris, at **Porte St Denis, rue du Faubourg St Denis**.

FERRIS BUELLER'S DAY OFF
(1986, dir: John Hughes)
Matthew Broderick, Alan Ruck, Mia Sara.
● **CHICAGO**

Matthew Broderick became a cult role model to the slacker generation when he bunked off school to spend a day bumming around Chicago. Broderick's school is **Glenbrook North High School, Dee Road**, Des Plaines (now Central Management Services for the State of Illinois, and previously used by Hughes in *The Breakfast Club*). Windy City landmarks visited include the Skydeck Observatory on the 103rd floor of the (then) tallest building in the world, the **Sears Tower**, between West Adams Street, West Jackson Boulevard, South Franklin Street and South Wacker Drive in the Loop (② 312. 875. 9696); **Wrigley Field**, home of the Chicago Cubs, **1060 West Addi-**

Playing hookey: The Art Institute of Chicago, South Michigan Avenue

Ferris Bueller's Chicago home: Country Club Drive, Long Beach, LA

The parade: Dearborn Street

son Street at North Clark Street in Wrigleyville and the Art Institute of Chicago, South Michigan Avenue at East Adams Street in the Loop (© 312.

443.3600). The parade Broderick joins with a rendition of 'Twist And Shout' is a real annual German-American parade filmed on **Dearborn Street**, intercut with a restaging for the movie on the following Saturday, when 10,000 locals turned up in response to ads on the radio and in newspapers. But even in a John Hughes movie, it's not all Chicago: Matthew Broderick's house is in LA. It's **4160 Country Club Drive**, just south of Virginia Country Club in Long Beach.

FEW GOOD MEN, A

(1992, dir: Rob Reiner)
Tom Cruise, Demi Moore, Jack Nicholson.
● **CALIFORNIA; WASHINGTON DC**

The US Naval Academy: St Elizabeth's Hospital, Washington D.C.

There was precious little co-operation from the US Marines, who objected strongly to the near-psychotic Jack Nicholson character in Aaron Sorkin's adaptation of his own stage drama. As a result, much of the movie was filmed on Warners' Burbank backlot. The US naval base at Guantanamo Bay, Cuba consists of several locations: the 'fenceline' is at **Crystal Cove State Park**, between Newport and Laguna Beaches south of LA; other parts of the base filmed at **Fort McArthur** and the **Point Magu Naval Air Station**. The meeting on the verandah of Nicholson's home was filmed at the home of the Coast Guard Commander in **San Pedro**, overlooking the harbour.

The real Washington DC does put in an appearance, though. Landmark sights include the **Memorial Bridge** over the Potomac, between the Lincoln memorial and Arlington Cemetery. Cruise's apartment is on a quiet street just to the northwest in Georgetown, but you'll look in vain for the newsstand on **18th Street**, where he picks up a paper. It was created purely for the movie. The US Naval Academy is actually **St Elizabeth's Hospital, 2700 Martin Luther King Jr Avenue SE**.

FIDDLER ON THE ROOF

(1971, dir: Norman Jewison)
Topol, Norma Crane, Leonard Frey.
● **FORMER YUGOSLAVIA**

The Broadway musical, based on the stories of Sholom Aleichem, survives the transition to the screen with the help of some pretty authentic European locations. The fictitious village of "Anatevka, just south of somewhere" is a skilful conflation of two former-Yugoslavian villages, **Lakenik** and **Mala Gorica**, in Croatia about 30 miles from Zagreb. Some buildings were constructed from scratch, and others built up with false fronts, but the film used many of the houses unchanged.

FIELD OF DREAMS

(1989, dir: Phil Alden Robinson)
Kevin Costner, James Earl Jones, Amy Madigan.
● **IOWA; MASSACHUSETTS**

"If you build it, they will come," promised the supernatural voices, and come they did. Kevin Costner's supernatural baseball feelgood weepie has provided Iowa with a major tourist attraction. The baseball field, now well signposted, is about four miles northeast of **Dyersville**, just off Highway 20, west of Dubuque. The diamond straddled two properties and after filming, half of it was ploughed up and returned to farming. But as tourists came, the farmer relented, and the field was restored. The baseball ground, where Costner and James Earl Jones receive subliminal messages on the scoreboard, is home of the Boston Red Sox, **Fenway Park, Boston**, in Massachusetts. The smallest major league ground in the States (and the site of Babe Ruth's first professional appearance in 1914), it's on **Yawkey Way** – the ticket office is at no. 4.

54

(1998, dir: Mark Christopher)
Ryan Phillippe, Salma Hayek, Neve Campbell.
● **NEW YORK CITY; ONTARIO, CANADA**

Recreation of the legendary NY druggery of the seventies, also featuring Mike Myers as ringmaster Steve Rubell. The exterior and the lobby are the real **Studio 54, 254 West 54th Street** between Broadway and Eighth Avenue, Manhattan. The interior was recreated (only slightly smaller than the original) in Toronto. After the owners of Studio 54 were jailed for tax evasion and drug offences, celebs drifted away from the club, and the emergence of Aids finally killed off the hedonistic, anything-goes scene. In 1986 the club closed. It came close to demolition, but has

The real thing: 254 West 54th Street, New York

New York, once again in Toronto: Drake Hotel, Queen Street West

survived as a performance space. Fittingly, it became home to Sam Mendes' production of *Cabaret*. Most of the film was shot up in Toronto, where locations include fake-Medieval folly **Casa Loma, 1 Austin Terrace** at Spadina Road; **Marine Terminal 28**; the **Tulip Restaurant, 1606 Queen Street East**; **Hillsdale Avenue East**; **Music Hall, 147 Danforth Avenue**; and the **Drake Hotel, 1150 Queen Street West**.

FIGHT CLUB
(1999, dir: David Fincher)
Ed Norton, Brad Pitt, Helena Bonham-Carter.
● LOS ANGELES

The scuzzy hotel: Bristol Hotel, West Eighth Street

As in *Se7en*, Fincher turns the normally sunny environs of LA into a dank, grim nightmare for this blacker-than-pitch adaptation of Chuck Palahniuk's satirical novel. Brad Pitt's glum squat on the fictitious Paper Street was a façade constructed down in LA's **San Pedro** harbour area. The exploding TV shop is on the corner of the 500 block of **Sixth Street**. Helena Bonham-Carter's digs is the **Bristol Hotel, 423 West Eighth Street**. The restaurant where she meets a confused Ed Norton is **Clifton's Restaurant, 648 South Broadway** between Seventh and Eighth Streets.

FINAL ANALYSIS
(1992, dir: Phil Joanou)
Richard Gere, Kim Basinger, Uma Thurman.
● CALIFORNIA

Gere takes Basinger: Bix Restaurant, Gold Street

A hokey-but-fun psycho-thriller, set in San Francisco but predictably sneaking in a few LA locations. In San Fran, Richard Gere takes Kim Basinger to **Bix Restaurant, 56 Gold Street**, a classy art deco eaterie between Sansome and Montgomery in the Jackson Square historic area. The tearoom is actually the chandeliered lobby of the Sir Francis Drake Hotel (now the Westin St Francis), **335 Powell Street** at Sutter Street, north of Union Square. The two hospitals in the movie are both wings of the abandoned **Presidio Hospital**, built in 1950 but damaged in the 1989 earthquake. Other SF locations include the rococo rotunda of the **San Francisco Courthouse** and the **Presidio Yacht Club** over the Golden gate Bridge in Marin County.

Much of the movie, though, is actually LA. The court-

room is the wood-panelled Ballroom of the **Park Plaza Hotel, 607 South Park View Street**, overlooking MacArthur Park, midtown LA. The fabulously stylish restaurant, where Basinger throws an alcohol-induced wobbly due to "pathological intoxication", is the art deco **Rex II Ristorante** in the **Oviatt Building, 617 South Olive Street**, downtown LA (seen also in *Indecent Proposal* and *Pretty Woman*). Other LA locations include the 1919 **Royce Hall**, one of the buildings of the original quadrangle of UCLA (University of California at Los Angeles), entrance at **405 Hilgard Avenue**, Westside.

Despite what the filmmakers would have us believe, you won't find a lighthouse alongside the Golden Gate Bridge. The climax combines a set built in LA with the real light at **Pigeon Point**, on the coast 50 miles south of San Francisco where, of course, the graveyard was added just for the movie.

FIRM, THE
(1993, dir: Sydney Pollack)
Tom Cruise, Gene Hackman, Jeanne Tripplehorn.
● MEMPHIS, TENNESSEE; CAYMAN ISLANDS; MASSACHUSETTS; WASHINGTON DC; ARKANSAS

There's trouble ahead when ambitious young Harvard grad Tom Cruise lands a job with a powerful but dubious law firm in Memphis. The opening Harvard scenes were actually filmed at **Harvard University, East Cambridge** and **Harvard Square**, Massachusetts. The impossibly luxurious hotel suite used for Bendini, Lambert and Locke's interview is in Boston's **Copley Plaza Wyndham Hotel, 138 St James Avenue** in Copley Square.

In Memphis, the rooftop party is atop the **Peabody Hotel, 149 Union Avenue** (home of the marching ducks who troop down from their penthouse to splash about in the lobby fountain every morning), and it's also in the Peabody that Cruise confronts the mob brothers at the end of the movie. Other Memphis locations include **Elmwood Cemetery**, scene of the funeral of the Firm's ex-employees; and Gary Busey's detective agency, which is in the **Cotton Exchange Building, 65 Union Avenue**. The greyhound track, where FBI agent Ed Harris is set up, is the **Southland Greyhound Park, 1550 North Ingram Boulevard** just over the Mississippi on I-40 or I-55 in West Memphis, Arkansas.

The firm's luxury getaway is on **Grand Cayman**, largest of the three Cayman Islands (*The Firm* was the first movie to be shot in these islands). The 'tax avoidance' meeting takes place at the grand 240-room **Hyatt Regency Grand Cayman Resort and Villas** at **Seven Mile Beach** on West Bay Road, north of Georgetown. And though Abanks Diving Lodge was a set, built on the island's North Sound, it was intended to be kept as a tourist attraction. The company's condo itself is the **Great House** on **Seven Mile Beach**. The night-time party, which leads to Cruise's little indiscretion on the beach, is at **Rumheads**, the beachside bar of the Holiday Inn.

On to Washington, where Cruise attends a seminar at the **Hotel Washington, 15th Street** at Pennsylvania Avenue NW (*℗ 202.638.5900*, used also in *Contact*); and a furtive meeting with the FBI takes place by the **Reflecting Pool** in front of the Lincoln Memorial, at the foot of the Mall. **Mud Island** in Memphis is the setting for the climactic chase. The 52-acre park contains the **Mississippi River Museum**, where Cruise tries to hide himself, as well as River Walk, a five-block long scale model of the Mississippi itself. The **Monorail**, and footbridge above, which lead to the island, both feature in the climax, and begin at **125 Front Street** at Adams Avenue, downtown.

FIRST KNIGHT
(1995, dir: Jerry Zucker)
Sean Connery, Richard Gere, Julia Ormond.
● **WALES; BUCKINGHAMSHIRE; HAMPSHIRE; HERTFORDSHIRE**

A long, long way from the *Airplane!* films, Jerry Zucker makes heavy, glum weather of this version of the familiar Knights of the Round Table legend. Camelot – well, a bit of it – was built alongside the lake at **Trawsfynydd**, on the A487, six miles south of Blaenau Ffestiniog in North Wales, but much of the city was computer generated. *First Knight* uses a bunch of other familiar locations: the thatched village was constructed on the National Trust's **Ashridge Estate**, near Tring in Hertfordshire (for details, see *The Dirty Dozen* which filmed at Ashridge College); the wedding was filmed in **St Albans Cathedral**; forest scenes were shot at **Burnham Beeches** – site of Robin Hood's camp in *Robin Hood, Prince of Thieves*; and in **Black Park Country Park**, the convenient woodland area adjoining Pinewood Studios familiar from literally hundreds of movies from James Bond to Hammer films. The battle scene filmed at the Roman road (known as The Devil's Highway) which runs to the north of **Stratfield Saye**, in Hampshire, about six miles south of Reading.

The wedding: St Alban's Cathedral

FISH CALLED WANDA, A
(1988, dir: Charles Crichton)
John Cleese, Jamie Lee Curtis, Kevin Kline.
● **LONDON; OXFORD; SURREY**

Superbly crafted black comedy, directed by Ealing veteran (*The Lavender Hill Mob*) Crichton. Kipling Mansions, Michael Palin's pad, and home to Wanda the fish, is **Aubrey House, 7 Maida Avenue, W2**, on the Grand Union Canal (if you're in the area, a few doors up you can see the flat shared by Lynn Redgrave and Charlotte Rampling in *Georgy Girl*).

The jewel robbery is staged in the centre of London's diamond trading district, **Hatton Garden**, EC1, north of Holborn, where Jamie Lee Curtis checks out **Diamond House, 37-38 Hatton Garden**. Hatton Garden,

Kipling Mansions: Maida Avenue, Maida Vale

incidentally, became Greenwich Village in Stanley Kubrick's *Eyes Wide Shut*. The getaway filmed quite a distance away, in Clerkenwell. Moustachioed Jamie Lee waits with the car in **Clerkenwell Green**, EC1, where Patricia Hayes is walking her dogs. The flight of steps where the robbers swap cars can be seen between **Roberts Place and Clerkenwell Close**, just to the north of Clerkenwell Green. The gateway where Michael Palin disposes of the evidence is **St John's Gate** on Clerkenwell Road at St John's Square. Patricia Hayes' house, where Palin makes a disastrous attempt on her life, is **69 Onslow Gardens**, South Kensington. The pet cemetery, where the little doggies get buried, is a real one: **Silvermere** at **Cobham** in Surrey.

Swapping cars after the robbery: Roberts Place

Jamie Lee Curtis comes on to barrister John Cleese: Osney Lane, Oxford

The Old Bailey interiors: Oxford Town Hall, St Aldgate's

Pat Hayes' house: Onslow Gardens, South Kensington

The legal scenes were filmed around the **Old Bailey**, EC4, and the **Inns of Court, Inner Temple Garden**, north of the Victoria Embankment, also EC4, a quiet, olde worlde square which can also be seen as 19th century London in Tony Richardson's *Tom Jones*. The interior of the Old Bailey, however, is actually **Oxford Town Hall**, St Aldgate's at Carfax in the centre of town. The prison, too, is in Oxford. The rusticated entrance to **HM Prison Oxford**, where Kline and Curtis first catch sight of barrister Cleese, is on New Road, alongside Castle Mound. The side street, where Curtis makes her move on Cleese, you can find a couple of blocks west behind Morrell's Brewery. It's **Osney Lane** between Woodbine Place and The Hamel.

St Trevor's Wharf, where Cleese borrows the luxurious pad for a doomed tryst with Curtis, is the **New Concordia Wharf, Bermondsey Wall West**, one of those renovated Thames-side warehouses, with a terrific view of Tower Bridge. The window-hanging stunt was filmed a couple of blocks down, in then undeveloped **Reed's Wharf**.

FISHER KING, THE

(1991, dir: Terry Gilliam)
Jeff Bridges, Robin Williams, Mercedes Ruehl.
● NEW YORK CITY; LOS ANGELES

Ex-DJ Bridges, plagued with guilt that he may have inadvertently caused a mass killing, finds redemption through Williams' winsomely mad tramp in Gilliam's twee Arthurian fantasy set in Manhattan.

The red castle: Hunter High School, Madison Avenue

A drunken Bridges talks to himself at the base of the gilt equestrian statue of General William Tecumseh Sherman, on the west side of **Fifth Avenue** by the Plaza Hotel. Robin Williams and his army of vagrants save Bridges from vigilantes at the foot of Manhattan Bridge. Williams watches the object of his affections, Amanda Plummer, at her place of work, the **Metropolitan Life Building, Madison Avenue** between 23rd and 24th Streets. Commuters break into a romantic waltz for Gilliam's big conceit in the Concourse of **Grand Central Station**. The Red Knight chasing Williams down Fifth Avenue was actually filmed on **Amsterdam Avenue** (where the traffic flows in the opposite direction). The 'red castle', where the Grail is kept, is the Squadron A and Eighth Regiment Armory, now **Hunter High School, Madison Avenue** at 94th Street on the Upper East Side.

All the interiors, apart from the Chinese restaurant which was a set in New York, were filmed in Los Angeles. Robin Williams' basement hideout is the boiler Room of the **Park Plaza Hotel, 607 South Park View Street**, downtown LA.

FISTFUL OF DOLLARS, A

(1964, dir: Sergio Leone)
Clint Eastwood, Gian Maria Volonté, Marianne Koch.
● SPAIN; ROME

First of the Spaghetti Westerns, which is a bit of a misnomer, since – apart from interiors at **Cinecittà** studios in **Rome** – the locations were filmed in Spain. The opening scene, of Eastwood stopping at the well as he rides into the grim town of San Miguel, is **Cortijo El Sotillo**, near the resort of San Jose in the Cabo de Gata, the coastal strip of southeastern Spain east of Almeria. The western landscapes are the familiar arid deserts of the area, used in countless movies since *Lawrence of Arabia* was shot here in 1962. The main street of San Miguel is **Hoyo de Manzanares**, near Colmenar, about 20 miles north of Madrid, a Western town built as a movie location whose sad state of disrepair exactly conveyed the death-haunted look Leone needed. The estate of the villainous Rojo brothers is part of the the museum of traditional life in Madrid's **Casa de Campo** park.

FITZCARRALDO

(1982, dir: Werner Herzog)
Klaus Kinski, Claudia Cardinale, Jose Lewgoy.
● PERU; BRAZIL

Kinski is the obsessed turn-of-the-century Irishman Fitzgerald, determined to build an opera house in the Amazonian jungle, even if that means physically dragging his ship over a mountain. The making of the movie is chronicled in Les Blank's documentary *Burden of Dreams*.

Kinski and Cardinale arrive at **Manaus**, at the junction of the Negro and Amazon Rivers in Northern Brazil, to hear a concert by Caruso. Their skiff docks at the Manaus waterfront landing, below the **Mercado** municipal market.

The opera house is the **Teatro Amazonas**, built at the height of the rubber boom between 1896 and 1910, when local Indians and poor whites were used as slave labour to make vast fortunes for the rubber barons. This dazzling palace, whose fountains flowed with French champagne on first nights, once hosted the likes of Jenny Lind, the Ballet Russes and Sarah Bernhardt – who, bizarrely, would mime to great arias as a stand-in soprano warbled away in the orchestra pit. It's on Manaus' **Placa Sao Sebastio**, and has recently been restored to all its glory.

Fitcarraldo returns to his house, which is about 900 miles up the Amazon in **Iquitos**, Peru. The house used to stand on the **Plaza de Armas**, the town centre of Iquitos, capital of the Department of Loreto. The square also contains the metal house of M. Eiffel, of Tower fame, and the boats from *Fitzcarraldo* are moored in the nearby port.

Two boats, with reinforced hulls, were used in filming: one to navigate the rapids (yes, they did it for real) and one to be dragged over the mountain. Herzog in fact went one better than the real Fitzcarraldo, who sensibly dismantled his boat and had it taken over the mountain in pieces. The *Molly Aida* was dragged by 500 Indian extras for over a mile, to a height of 600 feet. The launch, with the ship careering down into the river, was a one-take shot.

The river scenes were filmed in an inaccessible region of the River Urubamba near **Rio Comisea**, in the territory of the Machiguenges and the neighbouring Campas, several hundred miles to the south of Iquitos, with supplies brought in from the nearest town of Pucallpa, hundreds of miles downriver. The site of the actual boat-towing, 'Istmo de Fitzcarrald', is about 300 miles further south.

Peru can be a risky country to travel in, but most of the cities are safe enough (though robbery remains a constant danger). All the roads from Iquitos peter out a short way into the jungle; it's accessible only by air or water. If you really want to follow in Kinski's footsteps, there are jungle cruises up the Amazon from Iquitos.

FIVE EASY PIECES

(1970, dir: Bob Rafelson)
Jack Nicholson, Karen Black, Susan Anspach.
● OREGON; CALIFORNIA

Easygoing drama with disaffected Nicholson giving up middle class life to drift across US. Nicholson works at the oilfields near **Taft**, Kern County, California. Filming also took place at **Eugene; Portland** and **Florence**, Oregon.

FLASHDANCE
(1983, dir: Adrian Lyne)
Jennifer Beals, Michael Nouri, Lilia Skala.
● PENNSYLVANIA

Beals is a welder with ambitions to be a dancer in this movie, co-written by Joe Eszterhas and filmed in **Pittsburgh**, Pennsylvania. Beals runs into problems at Pittsburgh's famous **Carnegie Institute, 4400 Forbes Avenue, Oakland** (© *412.622.3131*), home of the Museum of Art and the Carnegie Museum of Natural History.

FLATLINERS
(1990, dir: Joel Schumacher)
Kiefer Sutherland, Kevin Bacon, Julia Roberts.
● CHICAGO

A bunch of med students use the college facilities after hours to explore the afterlife with death-and-resuscitation experiments. Filmed in Chicago, the university campus is that of tiny **Loyola University, 6225 North Sheridan Road** at West Devon Avenue on the Lake Michigan shore. The exterior of the Taft Building is the **Chicago Museum of Science and Industry, South Lake Shore Drive** at East 57th Street.

FLESH EATERS, THE
(1964, dir: Jack Curtis)
Martin Kosleck, Rita Morley, Byron Sanders.
● NEW YORK STATE

Gungy little indie low-budget shocker, with Kosleck breeding carnivorous plankton who chomp their way through the extras with a grossness rare for the time. It was filmed, with that sleazily effective air of cheapness, around the famous beaches of **Montauk**, last village of the Hamptons, way out at the far eastern tip of Long Island, Route 27.

FLINTSTONES, THE
(1994, dir: Brian Levant)
John Goodman, Elizabeth Perkins, Rick Moranis.
● CALIFORNIA

Bedrock: Vasquez Rocks County Park

Inspired casting is the best thing about this live-action version of the TV cartoon series. Downtown Bedrock, in case you don't recognise it, was constructed at the familiar location of **Vasquez Rocks County Park**, a spectacular outcropping of the San Andreas Fault, rearing up in a splurge of fantastic sandstone formations, **10700 Escondido Canyon Road**, off Highway 14 between Newhall and Palmdale, north of LA (for details see *Apache*). The rock quarry, where Fred works, is the **Cal Mat Quarry, Sun Valley**, Southern California.

FLY, THE
(1986, dir: David Croneneberg)
Jeff Goldblum, Geena Davis, John Getz.
● ONTARIO, CANADA

Goldblum mutates into a giant insect in Cronenberg's vis-

ceral remake of the 1958 culty sci-fi. Filmed in Toronto, mainly at the **Kleinburg Studios** to the north of the city. The opening conference, where Goldblum and Davis meet, was staged in **Walker Court**, at the **Art Gallery of Ontario, 317 Dundas Street W** at McCaul Street, downtown Toronto. The clinic, where Davis tries to get an emergency abortion after the horrendous maggot dream, is the **Chinese Consulate, 240 St George Street**, Yorkville, north of downtown. Goldblum's lab is a turn-of-the-century brick warehouse in a derelict section of Toronto that's since been gentrified.

Geena Davis meets nerdy Goldblum: Walker Court, Art Gallery of Toronto

Goldblum abducts Davis from the clinic: Chinese Consulate, St George Street

FOG, THE
(1979, dir: John Carpenter)
Adrienne Barbeau, Jamie Lee Curtis, Hal Holbrook.
● CALIFORNIA

Enjoyable early Carpenter spookster, with the long-drowned crew of a wrecked ship returning to wreak what the undead tend to wreak best. Filmed in the towns of **Port Reyes Station** and **Inverness** in Marin County, on the coast north of San Francisco, Highway 1. The lighthouse is the **Point Reyes Lighthouse**. Filming also took place at **Bodega Bay,** location of Hitchcock's *The Birds*.

The fogbound light: Point Reyes Lighthouse

FOLLOW THAT CAMEL (aka *Carry On – Follow That Camel*)
(1967, dir: Gerald Thomas)
Phil Silvers, Jim Dale, Charles Hawtrey.
● KENT

Basically 'Carry On Legionnaire', with Silvers as guest star. The desert location is **Camber Sands**, west of Dungeness on the south Kent coast.

FOOLISH WIVES
(1921, dir: Erich Von Stroheim)
Erich Von Stroheim, Mae Busch, Maud George.
● CALIFORNIA

Legendarily extravagant melodrama, directed by, and starring, one of cinema's great maverick talents in the days before the studios clamped down. Set in Monte Carlo, but filmed on the Monterey Peninsula in northern California. The gigantic Monte Carlo set was constructed at **Sea Lion Point** in the **Point Lobos State Reserve**. Filming also took place along **Seventeen Mile Drive** on the peninsula.

FOOTLOOSE
(1984, dir: Herbert Ross)
Kevin Bacon, Lori Singer, John Lithgow.
● UTAH

Bacon is the young newcomer who scandalises the small US town of Bomont, and upsets hellfire blatherer Lithgow with the godless concept of dancing. Fittingly, the town of **Payson**, which stood in for the fictitious Bomont, lies just south of Provo, the seat of Utah County on the shore of Lake Utah – more white, conservative and Mormon than the state capital itself. You can find Payson fifteen miles to the south on I-15. Filming also took place in **Provo** itself; in **American Fork** and at the **Lehi Roller Mills, Lehi** for the dance sequences.

FOR A FEW DOLLARS MORE
(1965, dir: Sergio Leone)
Clint Eastwood, Lee Van Cleef, Klaus Kinski.
● SPAIN

A fairly appropriate title for this sequel to the low budget *A Fistful of Dollars*, shot once again in Spain. The opening railway scene uses the stretch of line down in the southeast corner of the country between **Almeria** and **Guadix**. The main Western set was built outside **Tabernas**, about eight miles from Almeria, southern Spain, where it can still be seen as part of the **Mini Hollywood** tourist attraction (not to be confused with Little Hollywood and Western Leone, more attractions which have sprung up to capitalise on the area's fame). The town of Agua Caliente is **Los Albaricoques**, a tiny village in the Cabo de Gata Natural Park, north of San Jose, to the east of Almeria, while the church, where Indio and his gang hole up, is **Santa Maria** at **Turrillas**, about twelve miles to the northwest. Scenes were also shot at the Western sets of **Colmenar Viejo** and **Hoyo de Manzanares**, in Madrid; and at **La Calahorra**, Granada.

FOR WHOM THE BELL TOLLS
(1943, dir: Sam Wood)
Gary Cooper, Ingrid Bergman, Akim Tamiroff.
● CALIFORNIA

The near-inaccessible location for this epic Hemingway adaptation was in the **Sierra Nevada Mountains** north of Yosemite National Park, 50 or 60 miles west of Sacramento, and two hours north of Sonora, the nearest town.

FOR YOUR EYES ONLY
(1981, dir: John Glen)
Roger Moore, Carole Bouquet, Topol.
● GREECE; ITALY; SPAIN; BAHAMAS; LONDON

One of the better of the later Moore Bonds, after a ghastly opening teaser, with a 'wacky' Blofeld character being dumped into an industrial chimney – using the North Thames gasworks site at **Becton** in London, which was

alsoVietnam in Kubrick's *Full Metal Jacket*.

The mining of a spy ship in the Ionian Sea upsets the British Ministry of Defence. Those are the MoD's reassuringly solid doors on **Whitehall Court**, SW1. Melina's parents are gunned down on their yacht in **Corfu Harbour**.

At north Italian winter sports resort **Cortina d'Ampezza** (location for the original *Pink Panther*), in the Dolomites, Bond stays at the **Hotel Miramonte Majestic, localita Pezzie 103**. He meets arch-baddie Kristatos at the **Olympic Ice Rink**, built, like many of Cortina's facilities, for the 1956 Winter Olympics. As was the now unused **Olympic Ski Jump** and the **Bobsleigh Run** which feature in the ensuing chases.

After a brief sojourn in Corfu, Bond and Melina set off in search of St Cyril's. First stop is a wedding party staged at **Bouas-Danilia Village**, an authentic-looking, but fake, tourist attraction 9 km north of Corfu, off the Paleokastrita Road (it's very well advertised, and not as Disneyfied as it might sound). But the location used for St Cyril's is far less accessible. The dazzling mountaintop monastery is **Meteora**, 2 km north of Kalambaka in central Greece. There are actually five of the original 24 monasteries remaining perched on vertiginous pinnacles. They were built in such inaccessible places during the Serbian-Byzantine wars of the 14th century, when the only access was by removable wooden ladders. They can now be visited (by those with a good head for heights and suitably restrained clothing – which can be hired, if your bermuda shorts are a bit too *risqué*) via steps and ramps. The monastery featured in the film is **Aghia Triatha** (Holy Trinity), reached by a circular staircase of 139 steps. The inhabitants of the other monasteries, none too keen on the intrusion of a film crew, reportedly hung out their washing to disrupt shooting.

FOREIGN CORRESPONDENT
(1940, dir: Alfred Hitchcock)
Joel McCrea, Laraine Day, Herbert Marshall.
● LOS ANGELES

Hitchcock's wartime drama was, by necessity, almost totally studio-bound, filming at the independently-owned studios of Samuel Goldwyn. Almost 100 sets were built, ranging from a square in Amsterdam (needing a diversion of the Colorado River and a sewer system to provide the rainstorm); an 80-feet, three-tiered windmill; the cabin of a crashing plane (which alone cost $160,000 and was suspended on wires to plunge into the studio tank) to a gigantic mock up of London's Waterloo Station.

FOREVER YOUNG
(1992, dir: Steve Miner)
Mel Gibson, Jamie Lee Curtis, Elijah Wood.
● CALIFORNIA

Romantic fantasy with Gibson as a WW1 pilot put into deep freeze in 1939 and thawed out by young Elijah Wood 50 years later. The fictitious Alexander Field, where Mel crashes in 1939, was constructed on an old airstrip in **Moorpark**, on Route 118, northwest of LA on the road to Ventura. The 1992 version of the tower is at **Van Nuys Airport, 6590 Hayvenhurst Avenue** between Roscoe

Boulevard and Vanowen Street, Van Nuys (also used in *Casablanca* and in Laurel and Hardy's *The Flying Deuces*). The 1939 diner was built on a street corner in **Claremont**, north of Pomona to the east of LA, then aged, updated and moved five miles to **Northridge**, northern LA, for the 1992 scenes. The 'Wings of Freedom' airshow filmed at **Los Alamitos Army Airfield**, I-405 east of Long Beach.

The shingle cottage, built for the movie alongside an existing lighthouse but since dismantled, was on a rocky bluff at **Point Arena**, about 120 miles north of San Francisco, Route 1. The lighthouse is open for tours.

FORREST GUMP
(1994, dir: Robert Zemeckis)
Tom Hanks, Robin Wright, Gary Sinise.
● **SOUTH CAROLINA; GEORGIA; WASHINGTON DC; LOS ANGELES; UTAH; MAINE**

Moving affirmation of simple values or a reactionary celebration of bone-headed sentimentality? The Academy decided on the former and doled out a second Best Actor award to Hanks. The bench, on which Gump collars anyone who'll listen, was erected in **Chippewa Square, Savannah**, Georgia, and removed afterwards. If you really do want to ponder exactly how much like a box of chocolates life is, there's a similar seat nearby.

Many of the film's locations were found in a small area of South Carolina around **Beaufort**. The Vietnam scenes used **Fripp Island** and **Hunting Island State Park**, off the Beaufort coast. The fictitious town of Greenbow, Alabama, where the young Gump grows up, is **Varnville**, on Route 68 about 35 miles northwest of Beaufort. Many of the main street shops dressed for the movie have elected to retain the Gump look. The Gump boarding house, Jenny's house and the bus stop were constructed on the **Bluff Plantation, Twickenham Road**, just southeast of Yemassee, on the Combahee River between Varnville and Beaufort. The Four Square Baptist Church, where Gump prays for shrimp with the choir, is **Stoney Creek Chapel, McPhersonville**, Hampton County. In Beaufort itself, the **University of South Carolina** stood in for the University of Alabama, where Gump unwittingly gets involved with Governor George Wallace's attempt to prolong segregation, while its **Beaufort Performing Arts Center** became the Bayou le Batre Hospital. Bubba's Louisiana home was not in the fictitious Bayou La Batre, but at **Lucy Creek**, just southeast of Beaufort on **Ladys Island**.

Gump's marathon run takes him first to **Santa Monica Yacht Harbor** on the west coast, then to the **Marshall Point Lighthouse**, near **Point Clyde**, Maine, on the east. Three years, two months, fourteen days and sixteen hours later, he decides to go home at **Monument Valley** in Utah.

In Washington DC to meet Richard Nixon, Gump stays at the **Watergate Hotel, 2650 Virginia Avenue NW**, and reports mysterious men with torches in the building opposite (see *All the President's Men* for details of this location). He addresses the crowd at the **Lincoln Memorial** in DC, before meeting Jenny in the **Reflecting Pool**. After the anti-war demo, Gump hands over his Congressional Medal of Honor to Jenny on **Maine Avenue SW**, in front of the **Jefferson Memorial** in East Potomac Park.

FORT APACHE
(1948, dir: John Ford)
John Wayne, Henry Fonda, Shirley Temple.
● **UTAH**

Typical Fordian cavalry pic, with Fonda as a stiff-backed officer leading his men to defeat against those damn Injuns. Filmed at **Monument Valley** in Utah; also at nearby **Mexican Hat** and **Gooseneck**, on the San Juan River.

48 HOURS
(1982, dir: Walter Hill)
Eddie Murphy, Nick Nolte, Annette O'Toole.
● **CALIFORNIA**

Con Murphy is let out of jail to team up with cop Nolte in Hill's frantic comedy thriller, set in San Francisco, though mostly filmed around LA. The redneck C&W bar, where Murphy embodies its patrons' worst nightmares – "a nigger with a badge" – was **Torchy's, 218 1/2, West Fifth Street**, downtown LA. A favourite location with Hill (among others), it was Bruce Dern's hangout in *The Driver*. It's since closed down, and the property is currently an electrical goods store. Nolte and Murphy slug it out at the corner of **Fifth Street** and **Spring Street**, downtown LA.

The 1990 sequel, *Another 48 Hours*, was once again set, but this time also filmed, in San Francisco. The racetrack where Nolte shoots – and burns – a suspect is at **Hunter's Point**, a few miles south of downtown San Fran on Highway 101 – it's where you'll find Candlestick Park, the major league baseball stadium shaken up during a game in the 1989 quake. Much of the action centres around the sleazy **Tenderloin district**, between Union Square and the Civic Center. The final confrontation with the biker hitmen and the Ice Man filmed in the **Bird Cage Club**, one of the many strip joints on the Bay City's answer to Soho and 42nd Street, **Broadway**.

FOUL PLAY
(1978, dir: Colin Higgins)
Goldie Hawn, Chevy Chase, Dudley Moore.
● **CALIFORNIA**

Sub-Hitchcock, but enjoyable, comedy thriller, with Hawn and Chase thwarting an assassination attempt on a strangely vacuous Pope. Filmed in the movie-makers' dream city of San Francisco, with the inevitable, but pretty good, bouncy car chase, heading for a climax at the **San Francisco War Memorial Opera House** during a performance of *The Mikado*. The grand opera house building, and the lavish entrance hall are at **401 Van Ness Avenue**, at Grove Street, though the interior seen in the movie is that of the **Shrine Auditorium, 665 West Jefferson Boulevard**, downtown Los Angeles (see *King Kong*, 1933, for details). Goldie Hawn's apartment is **430 Vallejo Street**.

The assassination attempt: San Francisco War Memorial Opera House, Van Ness Avenue

FOUR FEATHERS
(1939, dir: Zoltan Korda)
Ralph Richardson, John Clements, C Aubrey Smith.
● **SUDAN**

AEW Mason's story of the man who becomes a hero after being sent the white feathers of cowardice, was filmed, in colour, partly in the Sudan. The lavish battle scenes have been recycled over the years, even reappearing in the 1955 Cinemascope remake *Storm Over the Nile*.

FOUR WEDDINGS AND A FUNERAL
(1994, dir: Mike Newell)
Hugh Grant, Andie MacDowell, Simon Callow.
● **LONDON; HERTFORDSHIRE; ESSEX; BEDFORD-SHIRE; SURREY; BUCKINGHAMSHIRE; HAMPSHIRE**

The lightweight romantic comedy which turned out to be the most successful British film of all time (until the Sheffield unemployed started dropping their trousers) was filmed entirely in London and the Home Counties.

You can find Hugh Grant's London flat at **22 Highbury Terrace**, on the northwest corner of Highbury Fields at the junction of Highbury Terrace Mews, N5.

Wedding No. 1 (Angus and Laura, at St John's Church, Stoke Clandon, Somerset) is held at **St Michael's Church** in the village of **Betchworth**, a couple of miles to the west of Reigate, Surrey (*rail: Betchworth, closed Sundays*). The reception, with the sheep, is **Goldington's**, a private home set in 52 acres of rolling Hertfordshire countryside. You can see the Georgian mansion just off **New Road**, **Church End** between Chorleywood and the village of Sarratt, north from the A404, Hertfordshire (*rail: Chorleywood*).

The black and white Tudor exterior of the Lucky Boatman, where Grant and MacDowell first get it together after the reception, is the half-timbered **Kings Arms, Amersham** (the northernmost terminus of the Metropolitan line) in Buckinghamshire, though you won't be able to book a room here, as it's just a bar. The interior is the **Crown Hotel**, a few doors along, at number 16, where you'll find the very four-poster in the hotel's Queen Elizabeth I honeymoon suite (though it's always been

Wedding No 1: St Michael's Church, Betchworth

Reception No 1: Goldington's, Church End

booked well in advance since the release of the film).

Wedding No. 2 (Bernard and Lydia at the Catholic St Mary of the Fields, Cripplegate, EC2) was filmed in the (Anglican) **Royal Naval College Chapel, King William Walk, Greenwich**, SE10. Although the future of the college is in doubt, the chapel is open to the public, and likely to stay that way (*rail: Greenwich*). The second reception (The Holbein Place) was staged at **Luton Hoo** stately home, a couple of miles south of Luton, 30 miles north of London off the M1, Bedfordshire. The 1767 Robert Adam house was, until recently, open to the public, and housed a fascinating collection of Romanov memorabilia. A frequent movie location, it's been seen in *A Shot in the Dark*, *Eyes Wide Shut*, *Never Say Never Again* and *Wilde*, and was recently put up for sale.

The restaurant, where MacDowell catalogues her sexual track record, was the Dome in **Wellington Street**, Covent Garden (now the **Café Rouge**). Grant hares off to meet his brother at the entrance to the **National Film Theatre** on the South Bank, and it's on the terrace of the South Bank that Grant explains to MacDowell about David Cassidy and the Partridge Family. MacDowell tries on wedding dresses at **Albrissi**, an interior design service at **1 Sloane Square** – actually at the start of Cliveden Place by Sloane Square.

Wedding No. 3, where MacDowell marries the stiff in the skirt at the chapel of Glenthrist Castle, Perthshire, was actually filmed in Surrey at **Albury Park**, just southeast of Guildford, which is open May to September (*admission charge*). The kilt-swirling interior of the castle is the Victorian Gothic house, home of Sir James Scott, Lord Lieutenant of Hampshire, **Rotherfield Park, East Tisted** on the A32 south of Alton, Hampshire (and, yes, it is available for wedding receptions). It's occasionally open to the public on Sundays and Bank Holidays during the summer (© *0142. 058.204*).

Simon Callow's funeral is held at **St Clement, West Thurrock**, Essex. This 'redundant' church – stranded in the wastes of an industrial estate – was restored by soap

The Lucky Boatman exterior...: Kings Arms, Amersham

...and the interior: The Crown Hotel, Amersham

Wedding No 2: Royal Naval Chapel, Greenwich

Reception No 2 at the Holbein Place: Luton Hoo, Luton

The funeral: St Clement, West Thurrock

Non-wedding No 4: St Bartholomew The Great, Smithfield

Hugh Grant's flat: Highbury Terrace, Highbury Fields

giants Procter and Gamble (whose giant formless grey cube overshadows it) in 1987 as part of the company's 150th anniversary. It's a nature reserve and pretty fiddly to get to. From West Thurrock (a couple of miles west of Grays railway station), take the Stoneness Road south from London Road, turn east into Headley Avenue and south again into St Clement's Road where the tiny church is tucked away between the titanic industrial monsters. The spectacular bridge in the background is the **Queen Elizabeth II Bridge** over the Thames alongside the Dartford Tunnel.

Non-wedding No. 4, at St Julian's, the church where Grant has second thoughts, is **St Bartholomew the Great, Smithfield**, hidden away behind its gatehouse *(tube: Farringdon or Barbican)*. The interior can also be seen in *Robin Hood, Prince of Thieves*, where it stands in for Nottingham Cathedral.

1492: CONQUEST OF PARADISE
(1992, dir: Ridley Scott)
Gerard Depardieu, Sigourney Weaver, Fernando Rey.
● COSTA RICA; SPAIN

Columbus' landfall, in this version of the story, takes place on a beach near to **Jaco**, Costa Rica. Ten major sets were constructed here, including the city of Isabel. Back in Spain, the production used several of the genuine historical locations in the cities of **Caceres**; **Trujillo**; **Seville**; and **Salamanca**. In Salamanca, scenes were filmed in the **Old Cathedral** (the city has twin cathedrals fused together as part of the same complex in the centre of town); in the **Convento of San Esteban**, a Dominican monastery built at the end of the 16th century, and also on the **Plaza Mayor**. In Seville, filming took place in the **Alcazar** – the royal palace – and in the **Casa de Pilatos** on **Plaza de Pilatos**, a lavish palace, supposedly a copy of Pontius Pilate's residence.

FRANKENSTEIN
(1931, dir: James Whale)
Boris Karloff, Colin Clive, Mae Clarke.
● LOS ANGELES

Mary Shelley's Gothic novel was turned into a classic movie by gay director Whale, starring his lover Colin Clive as the original doctor, and shot almost entirely on the Universal lot and stages. The European village was left over from Lewis Milestone's *All Quiet on the Western Front*.

The beautifully designed, and much copied, laboratory set survived for *Flash Gordon* serials, which also nicked the music from *Bride of Frankenstein*. The lakeside scene, where the Creature hurls the little girl into the water to see if she floats, was shot at **Sherwood Lake**, in Sherwood Forest northwest of LA.

FRANKENSTEIN MUST BE DESTROYED
(1969, dir: Terence Fisher)
Peter Cushing, Freddie Jones, Simon Ward.
● MIDDLESEX

Baron Frankenstein hides out: Stanmore Hall, Middlesex

No monster this time, but a spot of brain-swapping leaves poor old Freddie Jones with a stitched head. The house where Peter Cushing hides out is **Stanmore Hall, Wood Lane**, north of Stanmore off the A4140, Middlesex. The hall, with some modern additions, is now home to the Anglo-Swedish Consulting Service and though it can be glimpsed through the gates on Wood Lane just off Stanmore Hill. It's not open to the public.

FRANTIC
(1988, dir: Roman Polanski)
Harrison Ford, Emmanuelle Seigner, Betty Buckley.
● PARIS

Harrison Ford's Paris hotel: Grand Hotel, rue Scribe

Harrison Ford is an American in Paris whose wife is kidnapped. The posh hotel the couple stay in is the **Grand Hotel, 2 rue Scribe** (© 40.07.32.32; *metro: Opéra*), designed in 1860 by Charles Garnier, the man responsible for the ludicrously over the top Opera House nearby. It's been radically renovated since and now looks blandly modern in spite of being one of Europe's oldest luxury hotels.

Ford arranges an assignation with the kidnappers on the Yellow Level of the underground car park of the **Centre George-Pompidou, rue Saint Martin**, 4th arrondissement.

FRENCH CONNECTION, THE

(1971, dir: William Friedkin)
Gene Hackman, Roy Scheider, Fernando Rey.
● NEW YORK CITY; WASHINGTON DC; FRANCE

The doomed detective (though you need to read the script to find out that's what he is – the movie offers no clue) follows Fernando Rey and Marcel Bozzuffi through the streets

Devereaux's hotel: Doral Park Avenue Hotel, Park Avenue

of **Marseilles** at the beginning of the film. From here on in, though, it's New York. The lowlife bar where Hackman gets plastered is on **South Street** at Market Street at the foot of Manhattan Bridge on the Lower East Side. The toll bridge, where Tony Lo Bianco is tailed, is the **Triborough Bridge** to Randall's Island at the east end of 125th Street. At seven in the morning, Hackman and Scheider stake out **Ratner's Restaurant, 138 Delancey Street** on the Lower East Side at the entrance to the Williamsburg Bridge.

Scheider first bumps into Rey, 'Frog One', at the entrance to the **Roosevelt Hotel, East 45th Street** at Madison Avenue. Frog One's hotel is the **Westbury, 15 East 69th Street** at Madison Avenue on the East Side. He gives Hackman the slip by ducking into the fancy

flower shop, **Ronaldo Maia Flowers**, a couple of blocks away at **27 East 67th Street** at Madison, and slips away with the on-off routine on the subway at **Grand Central**. Lo Bianco and Rey meet up in Washington DC, in front of the **Capitol Building**.

Hackman's home is the **Marlboro Housing Project**, on

The stake-out: Ratner's, Delancey Street

Avenues V, W and X off Stillwell Avenue in Brooklyn, where Frog Two takes pot shots at him. He requisitions a passing car and begins the movie's famous chase sequence at **Bay 50th Street Station**.

Frog One's hotel: The Westbury, East 69th Street

The car chase filmed (over five weeks) beneath the **Bensonhurst Elevated Railway** – 26 blocks (count 'em) of Brooklyn's Stillwell Line from Bay 50th Street Station

Start of the chase: Bay 50th Street Station, Brooklyn

along **Stillwell Avenue**, into **86th Street** and finally right into **New Utrecht Avenue**, ending at **62nd Street Station**, where Frog Two gets shot. The chase was filmed, unusually and not entirely legally, at full speed, with real pedestrians and traffic, though there are five staged stunts too.

French TV celeb 'Devereaux' stays at the **Doral Park Avenue Hotel, 70 Park Avenue** at 38th Street in the Murray Hill district. Lo Bianco picks up the drug-stuffed car from the hotel's underground car-park just around the corner on **37th Street**. It's back to the Triborough Bridge for the final drug deal and shoot-out on **Wards Island**, where Lo Bianco's brother works.

FRENCH CONNECTION II

(1975, dir: John Frankenheimer)
Gene Hackman, Fernando Rey, Bernard Fresson.
● FRANCE

Superior sequel, filmed on location around **Marseille**.

FRENCH LIEUTENANT'S WOMAN, THE

(1981, dir: Karel Reisz)
Meryl Streep, Jeremy Irons, Leo McKern.
● DORSET; DEVON; BERKSHIRE; LONDON

A box office smash but a not too successful filming of John Fowles' novel, replacing the literary commentary with a present day parallel relationship. But the abiding image is of

Meryl's stunt double: The Cobb, Lyme Regis, Dorset

Meryl Streep (or rather, a stunt double) in a big cloak standing on the **Cobb** in **Lyme Regis**, Dorset. The Cobb is a curving 13th century breakwater built by Edward I to improve the harbour. Filming on location around Lyme Regis included the abandoned railway station, which actually closed in 1965; the **Undercliff**, the coastal area between Lyme Regis and Axmouth; and **Broad Street**, including the **Royal Lion Hotel**, and **Mr Chapman's Bookshop**, which has been left as it was dressed for the movie.

The Exeter scenes were actually filmed at **Kingswear**, over the River Dart from Dartmouth, in Devon. The bar and the bedroom scenes of the Endicott's Family Hotel were shot at the **Steam Packet Inn, Fore Street** here, while the **Royal Dart** was repainted in brown and cream to suit the 1867 setting. Exeter St David's Station was **Windsor Central Station**, Berkshire, which has since been radically modernised. Period street scenes were filmed in the narrow all-purpose byways between the warehouses of **Bermondsey** in London. The dock office is an elaborate set built on the Thames front at **Shad Thames**. Virtually all that is seen of the real location are the warehouses opposite.

FRENZY

(1972, dir: Alfred Hitchcock)
Jon Finch, Barry Foster, Barbara Leigh-Hunt.
● LONDON

A disappointing collision between Anthony Shaffer's black-

Barry Foster's flat: Henrietta Street, Covent Garden

Discussing the murders: Nell of Old Drury, Drury Lane

ly humorous script and the director's virulent misogyny, with Hitchcock, returning to film in London for the first time in many years, seemingly stuck in a thirties time warp.

A body is found in the Thames alongside **County Hall**, while a politician blathers on about pollution to an audience including a prurient, bowler-hatted Hitch, but most of the action centres around the old Covent Garden in the days when it was still a thriving fruit and veg market. In the mid-seventies, the market moved to Nine Elms near Vauxhall, and Covent Garden became a prettified tourist trap.

Many of the locations are still recognisable, however. **The Globe, Bow Street**, the public house from which Jon Finch is sacked from his job as a barman, can still be seen, though it's been completely renovated. The pub where he overhears the city gents drooling over the wave of sex killings remains unchanged. It's the **Nell of Old Drury, 29 Catherine Street**, WC2 opposite the Drury Lane Theatre. Villain Barry Foster's flat, where Hitch pulls off the eerie silent tracking shot up and down the stairs, is **3 Henrietta Street**. There's a barely perceptible cut as someone passes the camera – the interior is a studio set. Finch takes Anna Massey to the **Coburg Hotel, 129 Bayswater Road**, opposite Hyde Park. Barbara Leigh-Hunt's marriage bureau, where she is raped and strangled, has now gone. The narrow alleyway where it stood, which ran south from Oxford Street is now incorporated into the World of Football shop.

FRESHMAN, THE

(1990, dir: Andrew Bergman)
Matthew Broderick, Marlon Brando, Frank Whaley.
● **NEW YORK CITY; ONTARIO, CANADA**

Naïve film student Broderick manages to become entangled with the mob and a revoltingly decadent gourmet club when he arrives in New York. His college is the **Tisch School of the Arts**, part of New York University, southeast corner of Washington Square Park at **La Guardia Place**, Greenwich Village.

Predating *Scream*'s knowing post-modernism, Marlon Brando is cast as Sabatini, the man on whom *The Godfather* was supposedly based, while *The Godfather Part II* is the movie Broderick studies. Broderick reaches Brando's Italian-American social club via **Mulberry Street** (another little in-joke: Mulberry Street was a main Little Italy location for *The Godfather* movies). The club itself is **175 Hester Street**, an area now absorbed into Chinatown.

Broderick's first job for Brando is to deliver a Komodo dragon lizard from the JFK Cargo Terminal to New Jersey. Although it's set in New York, much of *The*

Brando's Italian-American club: Hester Street, Chinatown

Freshman was actually filmed in Canada. The shopping mall where the lizard escapes and gets to ride the glass elevator is the **Woodbine Centre**, Toronto, near to the Woodbine Racetrack. Broderick evades FBI agents by driving into the goods lift on **East 12th Street**, opposite Cinema Village in the East Village.

Other Toronto locations include **Front Street East**; **Wellington Street East**; **Dunvegan Road**; **St Joseph Street**; and **Seaton Street**.

FRIDAY THE 13TH

(1980, dir: Sean S Cunningham)
Betsy Palmer, Adrienne King, Harry Crosby.
● **NEW JERSEY**

Archetypal cheapo slasher, starting a series that seems to have run and run, and featuring an early appearance from Kevin Bacon. Camp Crystal Lake is **Camp No Be Bo Sco, 11 Sand Pond Road**, a boy scout camp founded in 1927, on **Lake Cedar**, just south of Blairstown on Route 818, northwest New Jersey.

FRIED GREEN TOMATOES AT THE WHISTLE STOP CAFÉ

(1991, dir: Jon Avnet)
Mary-Louise Parker, Mary Stuart Masterson, Kathy Bates.
● **GEORGIA**

Set in Birmingham, Alabama, this story of women's self-reliance and self-discovery, though toned down from the novel (in which the central friendship is explicitly lesbian), was filmed in **Juliette**, 60 miles southeast of Atlanta, Georgia east off I-75 toward Macon. The café was the general store on **McCrackin Road**. And guess what? Yes, it's since been renamed the Whistle Stop Café. The rail depot, however, was a dilapidated structure found in the middle of nearby woods, which was excavated, repaired and transported to sit alongside an existing track.

The Rose Hills Nursing Home, where Bates visits her mother and strikes up a life-changing friendship with Jessica Tandy, is the **Starcrest Nursing Home**, formerly a blacks-only hospital, in **Newman**, 30 miles southwest of Atlanta off I-85.

FRIENDLY PERSUASION

(1956, dir: William Wyler)
Gary Cooper, Dorothy McGuire, Anthony Perkins.
● **CALIFORNIA**

Cooper is the patriarch of a pacifist Quaker family caught up in the US Civil War. This was filmed in **Bidwell Park**, central California (see *The Adventures of Robin Hood*, for details) and on the **M and T Ranch**, Butte County.

FROM DUSK TILL DAWN
(1996, dir: Robert Rodriguez)
George Clooney, Quentin Tarantino, Harvey Keitel.
● CALIFORNIA

Mexico? No. But although the Tarantino-scripted, all-stops-out Western vampire splatterfest was made in the more accessible California, you won't be able to visit the Titty Twister bar. The elaborate trucker hangout was constructed from scratch, telegraph poles and all, on the featureless salt flats of **Calico Dry Lake Bed**, beneath the touristy Calico Ghost Town, on I-15 about a mile east of Barstow in the Mojave Desert.

Site of the Titty Twister bar: Calico Dry Lake Bed, Mojave Desert

FROM HERE TO ETERNITY
(1953, dir: Fred Zinneman)
Burt Lancaster, Deborah Kerr, Frank Sinatra.
● HAWAII; CALIFORNIA

Honolulu soaper centering around Pearl Harbor. That the army comes out significantly better than in the book is not entirely unconnected with the need to film in Hawaii's **Schofield Barracks, Wilkina Drive**, about ten miles north of Honolulu. But the film's most enduring image has to be Burt and Deborah rolling in the surf on **Kuhio Beach**, now helpfully called the '*From Here to Eternity* Beach', at **Halona Cove** by the Halona Blow Hole, east of Diamond Head, Waikiki, on Kalanianaole Highway.

FROM RUSSIA WITH LOVE
(1963, dir: Terence Young)
Sean Connery, Robert Shaw, Lotte Lenya.
● SCOTLAND; TURKEY; VENICE, ITALY

Much of the second Bond movie, which was still on a shoestring budget, was filmed in the grounds of Pinewood Studios, with the studio's main administration building standing in for SPECTRE headquarters in the opening scene.

Bond travels to Istanbul to collect potential defector Tatiana Romanova, whom he meets clandestinely on the picturesque **Bosphorus Ferry**. The mosque, where Donald Grant kills the agent, is the **Mosque of Saint Sophia**. Also in Istanbul is agent Krilencu's apartment, in the industrial section of the city. In Ian Fleming's book, the apartment has a huge billboard advertising *Niagara* outside, with a trapdoor in Marilyn's mouth. In the movie, the advert is for the Broccoli/Saltzman production *Call Me Bwana*, the mouth belonging to Anita Ekberg. Enough said.

The Orient Express leaves from Istanbul's **Sirkeci Station**, which also stands in for Belgrade and Zagreb stations. The motorboat chase was begun off the coast of Turkey, at a small village called **Pendik** near the Greek border, but delays and hassles led to it being abandoned and completed at **Crinan**, on the west coast of Scotland. The helicopter chase was filmed at **Lochgilphead** in Scotland. The final shot, of Bond sailing under the Bridge of Sighs in Venice, was captured by a second unit.

FUGITIVE, THE
(1993, dir: Andrew Davis)
Harrison Ford, Tommy Lee Jones, Sela Ward.
● ILLINOIS; NORTH CAROLINA

Big screen version of the long-running TV series, set in, and largely filmed around, Chicago. Harrison Ford, before being accused of his wife's murder, attends a charity fundraiser at the city's deluxe **Four Seasons Hotel, 120 East Delaware Place** at North Michigan Avenue on the Magnificent Mile. The hospital he works at is the **University of Chicago Hospital**, on the campus of the University of Chicago between East 57th and East 59th Streets and South University and South Ellis Avenues in the Hyde Park-South Kenwood district.

The breathtakingly staged train crash, which sets Ford free, was filmed on the Great Smoky Mountains Railway at **Dillsboro**, about 40 miles west of Asheville in the far western tip of North Carolina. A further 30 miles west at the Tennessee border is the **Fontana Dam** on the Little Tennessee River at **Lake Cheoah**, where Ford makes his spectacular dive into the white water (the drainage pipe was constructed for the movie).

The charity ball: Four Seasons Hotel, East Delaware Place

Ford checks out prosthetic limbs at **Cook County Hospital, Harrison Street** at South Wood Street, and makes a narrow escape from Chicago's **City Hall-County Building** after visiting a prisoner in the lock-up. The building, which also figures in the climax of *The Blues Brothers*, is on the block bounded by North Clark, North La-Salle, West Randolph and West Washington Streets. Ford escapes across the plaza outside, past the Picasso sculpture, to lose himself in a (real) St Patrick's Day Parade on **Dearborn Street**.

Ford confronts the villain: Chicago Hilton, South Michigan Avenue

Ford makes a narrow escape: City Hall-County Building, Chicago

The climax of the movie, with Ford finally confronting the real villain, occurs in the plush Grand ballroom of the **Chicago Hilton and Towers, 720 South Michigan Avenue** at East Balbo Drive in the South Loop.

FUGITIVE KIND, THE
(1959, dir: Sidney Lumet)
Marlon Brando, Anna Magnani, Joanne Woodward.
● NEW YORK STATE

The Deep South, festering with lushes, repression and terminal illness, is just waiting for Brando to drift into town. Yes, it's Tennessee Williams' play, *Orpheus Descending*. Director Lumet, like Woody Allen, doesn't like to stray too far from New York if he can help it, so this Mississippi town is actually in upstate NY. It's **Milton**, a small Hudson Valley town on Highway 9W near Poughkeepsie.

FULL METAL JACKET
(1987, dir: Stanley Kubrick)
Matthew Modine, Adam Baldwin, Vincent d'Onofrio.
● LONDON; CAMBRIDGESHIRE; NORFOLK

Kubrick's strange Vietnam movie, actually two films in one, looks like no other. No lush foliage or rolling green hills, but the bombed out ruins of a far eastern city. The first half, the training sequence on Paris Island filmed at PEA **Bassingbourn Barracks, Bassingbourn**, north of Royston on the A505 between Cambridge and Letchworth in Cambridgeshire. The Vietnam scenes famously filmed in the vast abandoned gasworks at **Becton**, on the north bank of the Thames, dressed by designer Anton Furst (who designed the brilliant Gotham City for Tim Burton's *Batman*) and planted with (wilting) palm trees. The delta helicopter scenes were filmed, not on the Mekong River, but over the **Norfolk Broads**.

FULL MONTY, THE
(1997, dir: Peter Cattaneo)
Robert Carlyle, Tom Wilkinson, Mark Addy.
● YORKSHIRE

Owing more to the spirit of Ealing than to radical politics, this amiable story of redundant steelworkers exploiting their natural assets was made around **Sheffield**, Yorkshire. The closed steelworks is **Sanderson Special Steels, Newhall Road**, in Newhall to the northwest of the city centre. A little to the south is the Sheffield and Tinsley Canal, where Gaz and Dave get stranded atop a sinking car alongside the **Bacon Lane Bridge** in Attercliffe. West a

Gaz stranded on the sinking car: Sheffield and Tinsley Canal, Attercliffe

Gaz's son's school: 73 Burton Street

The 'Full Monty': Idsworth Road

couple of miles, in Hillfoot, is the school where Gaz drops off his son, now the Sheffield Boxing Centre, **73 Burton Street** off Langsett Road. The **Langsett Music Centre** became the Job Centre where the lads' practice routine livens up the dole queue. The area is overlooked by Sheffield's Ski Village, and it's on **Pickering Road**, opposite this swanky new amenity, that Lomper's suicide attempt is thwarted. You can find the tiny park, where the lads make amends to Gerald after disrupting his job interview, southwest, over the A61 Penistone Road in front of the **Blake Pub, 53 Blake Street**, while **Crookes Cemetery**, where Lomper's mum is laid

Lomper's suicide attempt: Pickering Road

Making amends to Gerald: Blake Street

Site of the real Monty: Shiregreen Working Men's Club, Shiregreen Road

Gerald's gnome-infested house: Whirlow Park Road

to rest, is west of the city at Crookes, north of the A57 Manchester Road. Down to the southwest, in Whirlow, is Gerald's gnome-infested house, at **34 Whirlow Park Road**.

Millthorpe Working Men's Club, where the lads finally perform, is a combination of **Shiregreen Working Men's Club, 136 Shiregreen Lane**, in Shiregreen to the north of the city, where the routine was actually performed, and **Regency House, Idsworth Road**, off Firth Park Road, a furniture warehouse which supplied the club's exterior.

G

GALLIPOLI
(1981, dir: Peter Weir)
Mark Lee, Mel Gibson, Bill Kerr.
● SOUTH AUSTRALIA; EGYPT

Peter Weir's account of the tragic WW1 campaign (when the Australian and New Zealand Army Corps suffered shocking casualties after a badly organised attempt to secure the tactically important Dardanelles Strait in Turkey) was made mainly in Australia. Mark Lee's west Australia home is **Beltana**, in the Flinders Mountain Range, south Australia. The western Australian desert he crosses with Mel Gibson is the salt flat of **Lake Torrens**, to the west of the Flinders range. Anzac Cove, site of the disastrous battle, is **Port Lincoln**, down on the southern tip of the Eyre Peninsula on Spencer Gulf. The Egyptian bazaar scenes, though, really are **Cairo**.

GAME, THE
(1997, dir: David Fincher)
Michael Douglas, Sean Penn, Carroll Baker.
● CALIFORNIA; MEXICO

Michael Douglas' San Francisco mansion: Filoli, Woodside

A sinister survival game spirals out of control to turn the life of rich businessman Douglas upside down in Fincher's disappointingly contrived follow up to the magnificent *Se7en*. It's set in San Francisco, but Douglas' mansion is about 25 miles south of the city. It's the **Filoli Mansion, Canada Road, Woodside** – familiar from the opening credits of *Dynasty* (see *Heaven Can Wait* for details). San Francisco locations include the **Presidio**, the military base alongside the Golden Gate Bridge; **Embarcadero; Chinatown** and the **Sheraton Palace Hotel, 639 Market Street** in San Francisco's Financial District. It's the oldest grand luxury hotel in the city and, of course, extremely pricey. More scenes were shot at **Palo Alto**, south of the city.

Douglas finds himself dumped by the gamesters in Mexico, in **Mexicali**, Baja California.

GANDHI
(1982, dir: Richard Attenborough)
Ben Kingsley, Candice Bergen, Edward Fox.
● INDIA; LONDON

Ben Kingsley's performance and the big set pieces enliven this worthy, coffee-table epic biopic, which was made almost entirely in India, including the South African scenes. General Smuts' office is **Hyderabad House** in Delhi. The enormous funeral procession, as with so many other scenes, was filmed on the actual location of the real event, from **Rashtrapati Bhavan** – the Viceroy's Palace in Delhi – down **Rajpath** to **India Gate**. Scenes were also shot at

Porbandar, Gandhi's birthplace. The protest at the salt works and the Calcutta riots were shot in Bombay, with the shipboard scenes shot on board the *MS Dwarka* in the city's port. More filming took place at the **Aga Khan Palace** in **Pune**, southeast of Bombay. Also in Pune were the South African mosque scene and the protest in the Imperial Theatre. **Patna** in the northeast was the setting for the Champaran indifo farmers' riots, and the train scenes were staged in **Udaipur**. The assassination was filmed on the spot where Gandhi was actually shot, in the gardens of **Birla House, New Delhi**.

English locations included **Kingley Hall, Powis Road**, Bow E3, in the East End; **Buckingham Palace** and **10 Downing Street**. The Indian courtroom, where Trevor Howard presides over the great trial, was in **Staines Old Town Hall**.

GAS-S-S-S (aka *Gas! Or it Became Necessary to Destroy the World in Order to Save it*)
(1970 dir: Roger Corman)
Bud Cort, Cindy Williams, Robert Corff.
● DALLAS, TEXAS; NEW MEXICO

Corman's wildly anarchic, hit-and-miss satire, with a chemical leak wiping out everyone over the age of 25, was much butchered by the studio. The movie was shot around Dallas, where a huge pile-up was staged on the then newly completed, but not yet open, **LBJ Freeway** and in New Mexico, on the **Acoma Indian Reservation**, Route 40 west of Albuquerque.

GATTACA
(1997, dir: Andrew Niccol)
Ethan Hawke, Uma Thurman, Jude Law.
● CALIFORNIA

The sinister Gattaca Corporation of this dystopian sci-fi is Frank Lloyd Wright's **Marin County Civic Center, Civic Center Drive, San Rafael**, over the Golden

The Gattaca Corporation: Marin County Civic Center, San Rafael

Gate Bridge about 15 miles north of San Francisco. The low, blue-domed, futuristic centre, Lloyd Wright's last building, wasn't dedicated until after the architect's death in 1959. See it also in George Lucas' first movie, *THX1138*.

GATTOPARDO, IL (aka *The Leopard*)
(1963, dir: Luchino Visconti)
Burt Lancaster, Claudia Cardinale, Alain Delon.
● SICILY, ITALY

The location for Visconti's lavish version of Giuseppe di Lampedusa's epic novel could only be Sicily.

Visconti initially wanted to use the medieval village of Palma di Montechiaro to represent Donnafugata, the family home of the princes of Salina, but this would have meant

Site of the lavish ball: Palazzo Valguarnero Gangi, Palermo

building a road, and that's where the men in dark glasses stepped in (allegedly) to ask for their piece of the action. Visconti wisely moved the production to the decaying village of **Ciminna**, 30 miles south of Palermo. The Piazza of Donnafugata is Ciminna's square, where the façade of Salina's palace was constructed.

More of the movie was filmed in the gorgeous palazzo of **Villa Boscogrande, Via T Natale 91, Mondello**, a seaside resort north of Palermo. The villa is now a swish hotspot. The grand ball was staged in the **Palazzo Valguarnera Gangi, Piazza Croce dei Vespri in Palermo** itself. The ballroom is not open to the public, but the palazzo now houses a restaurant. And though the red-shirted Garibaldini filmed on the real streets of Palermo, a section of the town was rebuilt for the film.

GENERAL, THE

(1926, dir: Buster Keaton, Clyde Bruckman)
Buster Keaton, Marion Mack, Glen Cavender.
● OREGON

Keaton's classic is based on real events during the Civil War (also filmed – straight – by Disney in 1956 as *The Great Locomotive Chase*), when Union soldiers stole a train from Atlanta, Georgia, and attempted to drive it to Chattanooga, Tennessee. Striving for authenticity, Keaton wanted to use the real train, which was then still housed at the station in Chattanooga (Chattanooga Choo-Choo and Terminal Station, 1400 Market Street, now commemorates the first major public passenger service between the north and south), but Tennesseans didn't take kindly to their history being the subject of a comedy and refused permission. The railroad finally used for filming was at **Cottage Grove**, about twenty miles south of Eugene, off I-5, western Oregon.

GENEVIEVE

(1953, dir: Henry Cornelius)
Dinah Sheridan, Kay Kendall, John Gregson.
● BUCKINGHAMSHIRE; BERKSHIRE; LONDON

Two couples enter their vintage cars in the London to Brighton car race in this classic, irresistible comedy. In fact, most of the movie was shot on the roads around Pinewood Studios. The newsreel crew films the race in front of the gates of **Moor Park Golf Course, Anson Walk**, on the A404, between Rickmansworth and Northwood in Buckinghamshire. The **Jolly Woodman** pub can be found in

A newsreel crew films the race: Moor Park Golf Course, Anson Walk

Burnham, Berkshire, while the **One Pin Pub**, where the couples stop for a hair of the dog, can be found on **Parish Lane** at One Pin Lane in **Hedger-**

ley, Buckinghamshire. **Collinswood Road**, also in Hedgerley, and **Common Road, Fulmer**, provided more stretches of country road. By the time of shoot-

Stopping for a drink: The One Pin Pub, Hedgerley

ing, the old tramlines that used to run across Westminster Bridge had long gone, which meant that the close-ups of jammed car wheels had to be shot on lines in **Lewisham**.

GENOU DE CLAIRE, LE (aka *Claire's Knee*)

(1971, dir: Eric Rohmer)
Jean-Claude Brialy, Aurora Cornu, Béatrice Romand.
● HAUTE-SAVOIE, FRANCE

Another of Rohmer's navel-gazing moral tales among the young, middle-classes, filmed in the Haute-Savoie region of France, by **Lake Annecy**, some 60 miles east of Lyon at the foot of the Alps.

GEORGY GIRL

(1966, dir: Silvio Narizzano)
Lynn Redgrave, Alan Bates, Charlotte Rampling.
● LONDON

The clanking metal staircase leading up to the top-floor flat shared by Lynn Redgrave and Charlotte Rampling, in this Swinging Sixties comedy, can be seen in

James Mason's house: Harley Road, Primrose Hill

the alley off **Maida Avenue** alongside the Grand Union Canal at the corner of Edgware Road, and is actually the rear of **449 Edgware Road**. Further down Maida Avenue, between numbers 15 and 22, is **St Mary's Church**, where James Mason finally proposes to Redgrave. Maida Avenue is also the site of Michael Palin's flat in *A Fish Called Wanda*.

Mason's grand home, where

The stairs to Georgy's flat: Maida Avenue

Redgrave entertains nursery classes, is the former home of opera singer Dame Clara Butt, near Primrose Hill, at **7 Harley Road**, NW3. The registry office where Rampling finally marries Alan Bates is now the Council Tax Division of **Camden Council's Finance Department, Rosslyn Hill** at the corner of Belsize Avenue, Belsize Park.

GERMINAL

(1993, dir: Claude Berri)
Gérard Depardieu, Renaud, Miou-Miou.
● FRANCE

Berri's epic filming of Zola's novel, set in the Wallers-

Arenberg mine, was made in the region of the **Lewarde Mining Museum**, east of Douai, south of Lille in the Nord-Pas-de-Calais region near the Belgian border.

GET CARTER
(1971, dir: Mike Hodges)
Michael Caine, Ian Hendry, Britt Ekland.
● **TYNESIDE**

Jack Carter takes the train north to sort out the murder of his brother in this tough crime drama. Caine arrives at **Newcastle Railway Station**. The nearby pub where Caine sinks a pint, reputed to have had the longest bar in Europe, is no more. The shoot-up between Carter and the boys sent from London to bring him back, is around the ferry between North and South Shields. Newcastle's famed bridges are of course featured: Carter meets Margaret on the **Tyne Bridge** and he buys heroin to kill her on the **Swing Bridge**. The betting shop where Carter knifes Albert is in **South Shields**; the high-rise carpark, from which Brumby gets thrown, is in Gateshead. Already condemned, it is due to be demolished. Jack's brother's house was on **Frank Street, Benwell**; and the house where Jack himself stays on **Coburg Street, Gateshead**. The home of the villain played by John Osborne was the real-life house of a local fruit machine king, who was involved in a slot-machine scam linked to a local murder. It's **Dryderdale Hall, Hamsterley** in County Durham. The bleak ending is at **Blackhall Colliery** on the coast between Seaham and Hartlepool – near the location used for *Alien³*.

A 1972 black remake, *Hit Man*, with Bernie Casey and Pam Grier, was made around LA, featuring the astonishing **Watts Towers, 1765 107th Street, Watts**, and the **Milbank and McFie Residence, 3340 Country Club Drive** (see the 1975 *Farewell My Lovely* for details); while the latest remake, with Sylvester Stallone, was shot around Seattle, Vancouver and Las Vegas.

GET SHORTY
(1995, dir: Barry Sonnenfeld)
John Travolta, Rene Russo, Gene Hackman.
● **LOS ANGELES**

Loan enforcer John Travolta finds his vocation in movie production when he relocates from Miami to Hollywood, in Elmore Leonard's satirical thriller. The movie was actually made entirely in LA, including the Miami scenes, which were shot in the **Westside** neighbourhood and at an Italian eaterie in **Santa Monica**.

Travolta arrives at **LAX** airport, where much of the plot centres around the left-luggage boxes in the Southern Terminal, and stays at **Sunset Towers, 8358 Sunset Boulevard**, West Hollywood (see *The Player* for details). The **UTB Building, 6605 Hollywood Boulevard**, opposite celebrated underwear palace Frederick's of Hollywood, be-

Gene Hackman's office: UTB Building, Hollywood Boulevard

came the office of schlock movie producer Gene Hackman. When Travolta and Hackman drive along the western reaches of Sunset Boulevard, they spot egomaniac movie star Danny DeVito dining at **Café Med, 8615 West Sunset Boulevard**. Rene Russo's house is on **Carbon Canyon, Malibu**.

Travolta and Hackman spot de Vito: Café Med, West Sunset Boulevard

GETAWAY, THE
(1972, dir: Sam Peckinpah)
Steve McQueen, Ali MacGraw, Ben Johnson.
● **TEXAS**

A crooked deal gets Steve McQueen released from **Huntsville State Penitentiary**, Highway 190, about 60 miles north of Houston, to pull a bank job. He goes on the run with partner Ali MacGraw to **San Marcos**, northeast of San Antonio; **San Antonio** itself, on **River Walk**; and finally to **El Paso**, with a climactic shootout at the old Laughlin Hotel, before the couple ride off to Mexico. Shortly after filming, the Laughlin was demolished to make room for the Sheraton.

McQueen and MacGraw on the lam: River Walk, San Antonio

The 1994 remake, with Alec Baldwin and Kim Basinger, relocated the action to **Phoenix** and **Prescott, Arizona**.

GHOST
(1990, dir: Jerry Zucker)
Patrick Swayze, Demi Moore, Whoopi Goldberg.
● **NEW YORK CITY**

This New York-set supernatural comedy-thriller, from the director of *Airplane*, turned out to be a surprise smash. Demi Moore's pad is one of Tribeca's impressive and trendy cast iron apartment buildings, at **104 Prince Street** between Greene and Mercer, New York. Patrick Swayze is murdered on **Crosby Street** between Prince and Spring Streets, only to return and follow his murderer onto the subway at **Franklin Street**. The Italian restaurant where medium Whoopi Goldberg first meets Moore is **Mezzogiorno, 195 Spring Street** at Sullivan Street (℗ *212.334.2112*). And at the end of the movie, Goldberg donates the money to nuns at the base of the statue of George Washington in front of **Federal Hall, 28 Wall Street**.

Demi Moore's New York pad: Prince Street, Soho

GHOST AND MRS MUIR, THE

(1947, dir: Joseph L Mankiewicz)
Rex Harrison, Gene Tierney, George Sanders.
● CALIFORNIA

Gene Tierney falls for ghostly sea captain Harrison in this romantic fantasy, filmed at **Stillwater Cove** in **Pebble Beach** on the Monterey Peninsula, northern California.

GHOSTBUSTERS

(1984, dir: Ivan Reitman)
Bill Murray, Dan Aykroyd, Harold Ramis.
● NEW YORK CITY; LOS ANGELES

The haunted library, outside: New York Public Library, Fifth Avenue

The haunted library, inside: Los Angeles Central Library, Fifth Street

The firestation: North Moore Street, Tribeca

The phenomenally successful horror comedy is set in New York, but its locations are divided between the east and west coasts. The first of many supernatural appearances occurs in the **New York Public Library**, where the marble lions in the opening shots flank the wide flight of steps along **Fifth Avenue** between 40th and 42nd Streets. The haunted stacks, though, were filmed across the continent in the **Los Angeles Central Library, Fifth and Hope Streets**.

After getting the boot from New York's **Columbia University** (which doesn't have a Department of Parapsychology, or a Weaver Hall), Murray, Aykroyd and Ramis conceive their ghostbusting plan on the steps of the university's **Low Memorial Library**, on the **Upper Quadrangle** of the campus, north of College Walk, between Amsterdam Avenue and Broadway, West 114th and West 120th Streets. The fictitious Manhattan City Bank that hands out the loan is the **Irving Trust Building, 1 Wall Street**.

The dinky little firestation (yes, it is a real one) that serves as HQ can be seen at **14 North Moore Street**, off West Broadway in the Tribeca area, but the interior is a disused firestation on the west coast, in downtown LA.

Also in LA is the fictitious Sedgewick Hotel, where the Ghostbusters capture their first apparition in the ballroom. It's that old favourite, the **Biltmore Hotel, 506 South Grand Avenue**, downtown LA.

Back in New York, 'Spook Central', Sigourney Weaver's troubled apartment block, is **55 Central Park West** at 65th Street, with a few upper storeys added in by the studio art

department. The chosen location was originally to have been 1 Fifth Avenue in Greenwich Village, an art-deco apartment tower block with Gothic trimmings and stylised gargoyles, but local residents finally nixed the idea. The building housed the One Fifth restaurant, a location for Woody Allen's *Crimes and Misdemeanors*. Just across from Weaver's apartment, in Central Park, you can see the restaurant where Rick Moranis pounds on the window to escape a ravening hellhound. It's another much-used location, the **Tavern on the Green, Central Park West** at 67th

The university campus: Columbia University

The possessed apartment block: Central Park West

Street. The Ghostbusters vehicles can be seen on the Warners' Burbank lot if you take the Studio Tour of **Warner Bros, 4200 Warner Boulevard** (*© 818.972.8687*).

GHOSTBUSTERS II

(1989, dir: Ivan Reitman)
Bill Murray, Dan Aykroyd, Sigourney Weaver
● NEW YORK CITY

In the rather tired sequel, the museum is the old United States Customs House in New York, now the **Museum of the Native American, Broadway** at Bowling Green,

The museum: Museum of the Native American, Broadway

more recently seen as the site of the Riddler's flash party in *Batman Forever*.

GIANT

(1956, dir: George Stevens)
James Dean, Elizabeth Taylor, Rock Hudson.
● TEXAS

Edna Ferber's Texas family saga lives up to its name with a massive George Stevens production. The studio filming, on what turned out to be James Dean's last movie, was at Warners' Burbank studio, but the Texas landscapes were filmed at **Marfa**, a tiny town out on Route 90 in the West Texas desert between El Paso and Del Rio. Here the Reata ranch house set stood, until most of it finally crumbled away in the eighties. The ruins stand on the **Ryan Ranch**, west of Marfa. The land is private property, but the scaffold skeleton can be seen on the left from I-90, on the road toward Valentine. Little Reata can also be seen a few miles west of Marfa, on the right of I-90 – look for the windmill.

Memorabilia display in the lobby: Paisana Hotel, Marfa

Robert Altman's film *Come Back to the 5 & Dime Jimmy Dean, Jimmy Dean* featured a group of Deanophiles in the (fictitious) nearby town of McCarthy who collect bits of the old set, and in *Fandango* Kevin Costner and chums visit its crumbling remains.

The Paisana Hotel in Marfa contains a lobby display of signed photos and memorabilia from the movie. Although only lesser crew members stayed at the now rather forlorn and empty Paisana, the leads did hang out here in the evenings. And if you're visiting the town, you'll doubtless want to investigate Marfa's other claim to fame – the Marfa Mystery Lights.

GIARDINO DEI FINZI-CONTINI, IL (aka *The Garden of the Finzi-Continis*)
(1970, dir: Vittorio De Sica)
Dominique Sanda, Lino Capolicchio, Helmut Berger.
● ITALY

The Oscar for Best Foreign Language Film went to De Sica's study of an aristocratic family Jewish family in pre-WW2 Italy hiding their heads in the sand as Fascism threatens, which was shot in **Ferrara**.

GIGI
(1958, dir: Vincente Minnelli)
Leslie Caron, Maurice Chevalier, Louis Jourdan.
● PARIS; LOS ANGELES

Real location filming around the French capital adds bags of atmosphere to the musical version of Colette's novel about a young girl in *fin-de-siècle* Paris. The opening and closing scenes were filmed in the **Bois de Boulogne**, the vast tract of forested parkland to the west of the city. The scenes in **Maxim's, 3 rue Royale,** were actually filmed in the famed restaurant, while the ice skating scene uses the **Palais de Glace, 37 rue du Faubourg du Temple**. Louis Jourdan's elegant house is the **Musée Jacquemart-Andre, 158 boulevard Haussmann** in the 8th arrondissement. A luxurious 19th century classical mansion, with paintings and a furniture collection, it was bequeathed to the Institut de Franc and is open to the public. Bad weath-

The ice skating scene: Palais de Glace, rue du Faubourg du Temple

Louis Jourdan's house: Musée Jacquemart Andre, boulevard Haussmann

er meant that the beach scenes, scheduled to be filmed at Trouville, were shot later in Los Angeles, at **Venice Beach**.

GLADIATOR
(2000, dir: Ridley Scott)
Russell Crowe, Joaquin Phoenix, Oliver Reed.
● SURREY; MOROCCO; MALTA

The savage opening battle, set in Germania, was staged at **The Bourne** near **Farnham**, Surrey, and caused ructions among environmentalists after swathes of forest were cleared for filming – although this was an area scheduled for clearing by the Forestry Commission. The African town, where Russell Crowe is sold into slavery, is **Aït Ben Haddou**, near Ouarzazate in Morocco. The provincial arena was added to the existing village, which had already hosted films such as *Lawrence of Arabia*, *The Last Days of Sodom and Gomorrah* and *Jewel of the Nile*.

The vast Roman sets (with CGI additions) were constructed on the massive remains of **Fort Ricasoli** on **Malta**.

The African arena: Aït Ben Haddou

GLENN MILLER STORY, THE
(1954, dir: Anthony Mann)
James Stewart, June Allyson, Harry Morgan.
● CALIFORNIA

Biopic of the bandleader, and his search for 'the sound', featuring the ballroom of the **Santa Monica Pier**, at the foot of Colorado Avenue. The pawn shop stood on Clay Street, alongside **Angel's Flight**, downtown LA's tiny funicular railway, a much-loved landmark, which ran from Hill Street up to Clay Alley, demolished in 1969. The structure was kept in storage and has finally been restored. The surrounds are unrecognisable – the railway now runs up a grassy green slope – but you can ride it again.

Glenn Miller goes to the pawn shop: Angel's Flight, downtown LA

GLORY
(1989, dir: Edward Zwick)
Matthew Broderick, Denzel Washington, Morgan Freeman.
● GEORGIA; MASSACHUSETTS

Matthew Broderick in a story of the first black regiment in the US army. The Boston scenes filmed in **Savannah,**

Georgia. Once a great cotton port, Savannah slid into deep decline until the 1950s, when a giant restoration project was begun. The beautiful downtown area is now the USA's largest Urban Historic Landmark district.

The location for the parade, when the 54th finally gets its blue coats, is **River Street**, running along the south bank of the Savannah River, Savannah. Broderick's mansion is the **Hugh W Mercer House, Bull Street**, which runs south from River Street through Chippewa Square (the site of Tom Hanks' bench in *Forrest Gump*), a private home not open to the public. Readville Camp, Massachusetts was filmed in **Battlefield Park**.

The assault on Fort Wagner was shot 60 miles south on **Jekyll Island**, once the private playground of the stinking rich – we're talking Vanderbilts, Rockefellers and Astors – it was bought by the state of Georgia in 1947 (for $650,000 if you must know). The Battle of Antietam was staged near **McDonough**.

GO

(1999, dir: Doug Liman)
Sarah Polley, Desmond Askew, Scott Wolf.
● **LOS ANGELES; NEVADA**

Jons supermarket: South Central Avenue, LA

The Vegas hotel: Frontier Hotel and Casino, Las Vegas Boulevard South

LA checkout clerks get involved with drug busts, guns and stolen cars in Liman's dazzling, blackly funny follow-up to *Swingers*, made almost entirely on location around Los Angeles and Las Vegas. The store is **Jons, South Central Avenue** at East Adams Boulevard in LA, which was chosen for its unmodernised appearance. The filmmakers were horrified to find out that the owner had used the location fee to – you guessed it – smarten up his store before filming started. The inspiration for the store came from Ralph's Grocery in LA, known as 'rock'n'roll Ralph's', as it's sited in the middle of the stretch of guitar shops and academies on Sunset Boulevard in Hollywood. The Vegas locations are the **Riviera Hotel and Casino, 2901 Las Vegas Boulevard South** at Riviera Boulevard (*©* *702.734.5110*); and at the **Frontier Hotel and Casino, 3120 Las Vegas Boulevard South** (*©* *702.794.8200*).

GO-BETWEEN, THE

(1970, dir: Joseph Losey)
Dominic Guard, Julie Christie, Alan Bates.
● **NORFOLK**

Set in a golden Edwardian summer, Losey's film of the LP Hartley story (adapted by Harold Pinter) was made on location in Norfolk. Michael Redgrave, in one of the movie's ominous flash-forwards to a dull, grey present, arrives at **Norwich Station, Thorpe Road**. In happier times, his younger self is taken on a shopping expedition to Norwich by Julie Christie. While young Dominic Guard is sent to amuse himself in **Norwich Cathedral**, Christie clandestinely meets up with hunky farmer Alan Bates at the horsefair on **Tombland**. Off Tombland is **Tombland Alley**, along which Christie and Guard walk. The ghoulish name comes from the fact that bodies of plague victims are buried behind its walls.

The local village is **Heydon**, just west of the B1149, about eight miles west of Aylsham (*BR: Aylsham*). Here you'll find the **Church of St Peter and St Paul**, where the locals gather and where the older Redgrave walks in the graveyard. On the green opposite stands Julie Christie's cottage, where Redgrave is asked to carry one last message. The cricket match, though, is not in Heydon. You can see the green, now rough, overgrown and planted with a couple of decrepit goalposts, just south of the village of **Thornage**. The three skeletal trees overlooking the green are still recognisable, as are the farm outbuildings. The B1110 runs right through the green.

Southwest of Thornage is Melton Constable on the B1354, and a couple of miles south on the road to

The shopping expedition: Tombland Alley, Norwich

Leo is sent to amuse himself: Norwich Cathedral

Julie Christie's cottage: Heydon

The cricket match: Thornage

The country house: Melton Constable Hall, Melton Constable

Hindolveston is a large unmarked gate which is the entrance to **Melton Constable Hall**, now a private residence.

GO WEST
(1940, dir: Edward Buzzell)
The Marx Brothers.
● CALIFORNIA

The old railroad: Jamestown

The railway commandeered by Groucho & co in this Wild West caper is the old Sierra Railroad in northern California, seen in dozens of movies including *High Noon*, *My Little Chickadee* and *Unforgiven*. It still operates, as **Railtown 1897 State Park**, part of the California State Railroad Museum at **Fifth** and **Reservoir Street, Jamestown**, on Route 49 about 50 miles east of Stockton. At weekends from April through October, you can take a 40-minute round trip (© *916.445.6645; www.csrmf.org/railtown.html*)

GODFATHER, THE
(1972, dir: Francis Ford Coppola)
Marlon Brando, Al Pacino, Diane Keaton.
● NEW YORK CITY; LONG ISLAND; LOS ANGELES; LAS VEGAS, NEVADA; SICILY, ITALY

With mafia movies out of fashion and a relatively unknown director at the helm, Paramount was keen to cut costs by updating the movie to the present day and filming on its Hollywood lot. But as paperback sales hit 12 million copies, the studio reluctantly conceded to Coppola's demands, and much of the film was shot on real locations in New York.

Even the studio filming was done on the east coast, at New York's Filmways Studios, **246 East 127th Street, East Harlem** at Second Avenue. The studio has since closed down, and is now a huge supermarket called Foodways.

Luca Brasi is garrotted: Sofia's Restaurant, Edison Hotel, 47th Street

The wedding scene, at the Corleone compound on Long Island, did film on an island over the water from New York – not on Long Island, but

The Corleone mansion: Longfellow Road, Staten Island

Staten Island. The outdoor festivities were staged in the garden of **120 Longfellow Road**, in the affluent neighbourhood of Emerson Hill. The Corleone Mansion itself is next door at **110 Longfellow Road**. The Staten Island Rapid Transit Railway will take you from St George Station, four stops to Grasmere. From here, it's about a half hour's walk north to Longfellow Road, a leafy cul-de-sac running east from Ocean Terrace. Numbers 110 and 120 are the last houses at the end of the road.

The Genco Olive Oil office: Mietz Building, Mott Street

Michael Corleone learns that the Don has been shot: Radio City Music Hall

When Don Corleone sends his consigliore, Tom Hagen, to Hollywood, to make the studio head the infamous 'offer he can't refuse', there's a great newsreel shot of the old Hollywood, with **Hollywood United Methodist Church** on Highland Avenue (see *What Price Hollywood?* for details) and **Grauman's Chinese Theater** (as it then was) on Hollywood Boulevard still recognisable from the days before the area became swamped by tacky tourist shops.

Michael and Kay's hotel: The St Regis-Sheraton, East 55th Street

The Paramount lot, **5451 Marathon Street** at Bronson Avenue behind Melrose Avenue in Hollywood stands in for Woltz International Pictures'(see *Sunset Blvd* for details of the studio). After Woltz eventually agrees to meet up with Hagen, it's a rare case of an East Coast residence standing in for Hollywood. The bedroom of Woltz's villa, where the studio boss finds the head of his unfortunate horse, is the living room of **Falaise**, on **Sands Point Preserve**, the Guggenheim estate way out at **95 Middleneck Road** on Long Island. You can visit the Preserve, which also houses mansions seen in the 1998 update of *Great Expectations* and *Scent of a*

Barzini is gunned down: New York County Courthouse steps, Center Street

Michael becomes the Godfather: St Patrick's Cathedral, Mulberry Street

Woman in the summer months. It's about four miles north of Point Washington (there's a cab firm near the station), on the Long Island Railroad from New York's Pennsylvania Station, Seventh Avenue. The exterior of Woltz's mansion, seen also as Whitney Houston's estate in *The Bodyguard*, really is LA. It's supposedly the enormous Beverly Hills estate of silent star Harold Lloyd, **Greenacres, 1740 Green Acres Drive.** See *Westworld* for details.

Michael and Kay are staying at the grand St Regis Hotel, now the **St Regis-Sheraton, 2 East 55th Street** (*©* *212.767.0525*) on the corner of Fifth Avenue. Nearby stood Best & Co, the New York department store where they do their Christmas shopping, on Fifth Avenue between 51st and 52nd Streets in the fashionable stretch of 'Ladies' Mile'. Although already closed, the store briefly blazed back to life for filming before being demolished. Sadly, the model-train heaven, Polk's Hobby Shop, which stood at 314 Fifth Avenue near 31st Street, is also gone. This is where Tom Hagen stocks up on presents when Sollozzo's men invite him for a car ride. It has now been replaced by a pizza joint.

The bar, where Sollozzo meets up with Luca Brasi, is the **Edison Hotel, 228 West 47th Street.** You'll recognise the slightly redecorated corridor with its circular mirrors in Woody Allen's *Bullets Over Broadway*. It's inside what is now **Sophia's Restaurant**, the Edison's coffee shop, that Brasi is pinned down to the counter and garrotted.

The Genco Olive Oil premises, supposedly on Mulberry Street, outside which the Don is gunned down, was the **Mietz Building, 128 Mott Street**, a then-unchanged area between Little Italy and Chinatown. The relentless encroachment of Chinatown into Little Italy means that the building has since been gutted and has become a Chinese market, though the 'Mietz' name is still visible on the frontage. The art deco entrance was created especially for the movie. With astonishing speed, the news hits the papers while Michael and Kay watch *The Bells of St Mary's* at **Radio City Music Hall, 1260 Sixth Avenue** at 50th Street. The exterior of hospital where Michael visits his wounded father is the **Lincoln Medical Center, 234 East 149th Street** in the Bronx, though the deserted interior is the **New York Eye and Ear Infirmary, 310 East 14th Street** in the East Village.

Michael is subsequently picked up outside Jack Dempsey's Broadway Bar (another long-gone venue mocked up in NY for the movie), and taken towards New Jersey, which ought to mean taking the George Washington Bridge over the Hudson. The bridge used for the U-turn scene, however, is the **Queensboro Bridge** over the East River. Louis' Restaurant, where Sollozzo and McCluskey are gunned down over the veal, was the old Luna restaurant under the elevated White Plains Road IRT in **Belmont**, NY's largest Italian community.

Fleeing to Sicily, Michael goes to ground in the hills around Taormina. The village is **Forza d'Agro**, a small medieval community dominated by the ruins of a 16th century castle. To find it, head north a couple of miles from Taormina to the coastal town of Mazzaro, then turn left into the hills for another two and a half miles. Michael's wedding is celebrated at the small, wood-panelled **Bar Vitelli** in the village of **Savoca**, a few miles north of Forza d'Agro.

Back in NY, Sonny beats up bullying brother-in-law Carlo at **118th Street and Pleasant Avenue**, east of First Avenue in East Harlem, but soon gets his payback, blown away in a spectacular hail of bullets at tollbooths supposedly on the Jones Beach Causeway, Long Island, but actually built on the disused airfield **Floyd Bennett Field**, southeast of Brooklyn at the end of Flatbush Avenue. Bonasera's funeral parlour is the morgue at **Bellevue Hospital, First Avenue** at East 29th Street by the East River in the Gramercy district.

The Christening: Mount Loretto, Staten Island

The summit meeting of the Five Families takes place in the boardroom of the Penn Central Railroad above **Grand Central Station**, 42nd Street and Park Avenue, while Michael's foray into Las Vegas was filmed at the **Tropicana, 3801 Las Vegas Boulevard South** at Tropicana Avenue, on the Strip. After Don Corleone's lavish funeral, at the **Calvary Cemetery, Greenpoint Avenue** in Queens, overlooked by the Queens Expressway bridge crossing Newton Creek, Michael becomes Godfather in a ritual brilliantly intercut with the bloody murders of the family heads. Clemenza blasts Stracci and Cuneo in the lift of the **St Regis-Sheraton** (where Michael and Kay spent their night in NY); Moe Greene is shot through the eye in the steamroom of the **McBurney YMCA, 215 West 23rd Street** (*©* *212.741.9226*) and arch-enemy Barzini is gunned down by fake cop Al Neri on the steps of the **New York County Courthouse, 60 Centre Street** at Pearl Street, Lower Manhattan (see *Twelve Angry Men* for details of this popular location).

The christening itself took place inside NY's **Old St Patrick's Cathedral, 264 Mulberry Street** between East Prince and Houston Streets in Little Italy, though the exterior is the **Mission of the Immaculate Virgin, Hylan Boulevard, Mount Loretto**, down in the southwest corner of Staten Island (*rail: Pleasant Plains*).

GODFATHER PART II, THE

(1974, dir: Francis Ford Coppola)
Robert De Niro, Al Pacino, Lee Strasberg.

● **NEW YORK CITY; CALIFORNIA; NEVADA; CONNECTICUT; FLORIDA; SICILY, ITALY; ITALY; DOMINICAN REPUBLIC**

Arguably superior to part one, *The Godfather Part II* was the first sequel ever to win Best Picture at the Oscars.

The village of Vito Andolini's youth is supposedly Corleone, a real town about twenty miles south of Palermo in western Sicily, though the locale seen in the movie is around Taormina in the northeast. New York's Ellis Island, point of arrival for all the European immigrants during the first half of the century, where Vito Andolini becomes Vito Corleone, still exists but has long since fallen into disrepair. The film uses the **Old Fish Market** at Trieste, on the Adriatic, northern Italy.

The Corleone lakeside estate is **Fleur du Lac**, the Henry Kaiser estate on the western California shore of **Lake**

The attack on Pentangeli: PH Vazac's, Avenue B, East Village

Caffe Reggio, MacDougal Street, Greenwich Village

Tahoe. The lakeside area has been developed and the Corleone compound is now the boathouse of a private, gated, community.

De Niro's Little Italy, 1917 scenes were shot on **Sixth Street** in the East Village between Avenues A and B, tricked out in period dressing. A block north is the bar where the Rosato brothers try to garotte Pentangeli, **PH Vazac's, 108 Avenue B** at Seventh Street (known as 'Seven and B'), at the southeast corner of Tompkins Square Park in the East Village. A popular 'lowlife' bar, Vazac's can also be seen in *"Crocodile" Dundee* and *Angel Heart*, among many others. The ensuing shoot-out was filmed outside on **East 7th Street**.

When Michael Corleone visits Hyman Roth in Miami it's the real thing, but Cuba was obviously out of the question. The pre-revolutionary scenes were shot in the Dominican Republic, the eastern part of the island of Hispaniola (Gulf & Western, Paramount's parent company conveniently owns property in there). **Santo Domingo**, the island's capital on the southern coast, stood in for Havana, where Roth's hotel is **El Embajador Hotel, Avenue Sarasota** (© *809.2212131*), and Batista's palace, where the New Year's Party is cut short by revolution, is Santo Domingo's **Presidential Palace**.

The army post, where the FBI protect Pentangeli, is the **California Institute for Men, Central Avenue**, three miles south of **Chino**, Highway 60 to the east of LA.

Two other places claiming to have been used as locations, but not instantly recognisable, are the **Doheny Mansion, Chester Place**, on the campus of Mount St Mary's College, off West Adams Boulevard in Los Angeles and venerable coffee house **Caffe Reggio, 19 MacDougal Street** at West 3rd Street in Greenwich Village.

GODFATHER PART III, THE

(1990, dir: Francis Ford Coppola)
Al Pacino, Andy Garcia, Diane Keaton.
● NEW YORK CITY; ROME; NEW JERSEY; SICILY, ITALY

The overambitious end to the trilogy opens with Michael being awarded the Order of St Sebastian the Martyr at **Old St Patrick's Cathedral, 264 Mulberry Street**, Little Italy (site of the christening in *The Godfather*). The Italian-American street festival, during which Zasa is gunned down, is on **Elizabeth Street**, which runs parallel to Mott Street, the Little Italy location where Don Corleone was shot in the first film, and in fact, more filming took place at the **Mietz Building, 128 Mott Street**, which served as the Genco Olive Oil company in *The Godfather*. Other New

The operatic climax: Teatro Massimo, Palermo

York locations include the huge disco, **The Red Zone, 440 West 45th Street** and the **Waldorf Astoria Hotel, 301 Park Avenue**. Diane Keaton's home is the **Trevor Manse, Mill Neck**, a private home on Long Island. The helicopter attack on the Atlantic City mob convention was shot at **Cinecittà** studios in Rome, though the exterior was filmed at **Trump Castle, Atlantic City**.

The long-disused **Palermo Town Hall** was opened up and refurbished for Michael's return to Sicily. Sicilian locations from the previous *Godfather* movies were revisited, including the village of **Forza d'Agro** north of Taormina. Other Sicilian locations include the **Villa Platania**, near **Fiumefreddo**, about six miles south of Taormina and the **Marina de Cottone**. The toast to Anthony's début as an opera singer was filmed at the foot of the steps leading to **Villa Malfitano**. The archbishop's office is in the pentagonal **Villa Farnese**, at **Caprarola**, a small village about 30 miles north of Rome. Michael is absolved by the future Pope at the **Church of Santa Maria della Quercia** in **Viterbo**. The grandly operatic climax was shot at the **Teatro Massimo** in **Palermo**, and though renovation work meant that the interior opera scenes had to be filmed at Cinecittà, the tragic conclusion to the saga was staged on the opera house steps.

GODS AND MONSTERS

(1998, dir: Bill Condon)
Ian McKellen, Brendan Fraser, Lynn Redgrave.
● LOS ANGELES

Fictionalised account of the last days of the classic Hollywood director James Whale, and a putative relationship with hunky gardener Brendan Fraser. James Whale's actual house stands on Amalfi Drive in Pacific Palisades, but a similar house in **Altadena**, an eastern suburb of LA, was used for the movie exteriors. George Cukor's estate, site of the garden party where a ditsy Princess Margaret mistakes Whale for Cecil Beaton, is the **Arden Estate, 1145 Arden Road**, Pasadena – a frequently used location seen also in the Marx Brothers' *Duck Soup* and in TV's *Dynasty*. The villa is a private home, not visible from the street.

GODZILLA

(1998, dir: Roland Emmerich)
Matthew Broderick, Jean Reno, Hank Azaria.
● HAWAII; NEW YORK CITY

Nuclear fallout gives birth to a gigantic monster the size of a skyscraper which somehow manages to go to ground

Godzilla on the loose in New York: Fifth Avenue at 42nd Street

Godzilla's nest: Madison Square Gardens

in New York City. The tropical island where the giant footprint is originally discovered is **Kauai**, one of the Hawaiian islands (see *Jurassic Park* for details). In New York, the monster stomps around **Fifth Avenue** at 42nd Street before making its nest inside **Madison Square Gardens**, Seventh Avenue between West 31st and West 33rd Streets.

GODZILLA, KING OF THE MONSTERS
(1954, dir: Terry Morse, Inoshiro Honda)
Raymond Burr, Takashi Shimura, Momoko Kochi.
● **JAPAN**

The daddy of all creature features, with the radioactive lizard first appearing on the fictitious Odo Island, supposedly off the Izu Peninsula. The Odo scenes were filmed around **Toba City**, entrance to the Ise-Shima National Park on the Shima peninsula. The monster naturally heads for Japan's capital, and trashes **Tokyo**. Godzilla comes ashore at eastern Tokyo Bay, destroying a train at **Shinagawa Railway Station**, the large station serving the south and Yokohama. He stomps through Minato-Ku and Shimbashi on his way to the central shopping district, Ginza. He torches **Matsuzakaya Department Store, 6-10-1 Ginza, Chuo-ku** (*Subway: Ginza*), tears down the clock on the **Wako Department Store, 4-5-11 Ginza, Chuo-ku** at the main Ginza crossing, Yonchome, and heads northeast across **Sukiya Bridge**. He destroys the **Tokyo Marion Building** (previously the Nichigeki Theatre), **2-5-1 Yurakucho, Chiyoda-ku**, and crosses into the Akasaka district, home to the major government and media buildings, where he smashes the national assembly hall, the **Diet Building, Nagatacho 1-chome** (*Subway: Kokkaigijido*). Don't worry, the 1936 building still stands, and you can take a peek inside to watch a debate in progress (*admission free*). He then destroys **Kachidoki Bridge** at the mouth of the Sumida River, before returning to the ocean.

GOING MY WAY
(1944, dir: Leo McCarey)
Bing Crosby, Barry Fitzgerald, Rise Stevens.
● **LOS ANGELES**

The Best Picture of 1944, apparently,

St Dominic's: Santa Monica Catholic Church, California Avenue

was this sentimental story of young priest Bing Crosby taking over a tough New York parish. St Dominic's is actually **Santa Monica Catholic Church, 715 California Avenue**, Santa Monica.

GOLD RUSH, THE
(1925, dir: Charles Chaplin)
Charles Chaplin, Georgia Hale, Mack Swain.
● **CALIFORNIA**

Chaplin is a Yukon prospector who finally gets rich. The film includes the classic bread roll dance and shoe-eating scene. The snowy locations are at **Truckee**, in the Sierra Nevadas of California, Route 80, northwest of Lake Tahoe.

GOLDENEYE
(1995, dir: Martin Campbell)
Pierce Brosnan, Sean Bean, Izabella Scorupco.
● **LONDON; HERTFORDSHIRE; SURREY; ST PETERSBURG, RUSSIA; PUERTO RICO; FRANCE; SWITZERLAND; MONACO**

The increasingly moribund series was on the verge of retirement when it got a new lease of life with Pierce Brosnan. The opening teaser, Bond's spectacular bungee jump, at the 'Arkangel Chemical Weapons Facility – USSR', is actually the **Tusker Dam, Lake Verzasca**, at **Hittnau** in Switzerland. Bond's race with Xenia Onatopp, supposedly in the hills above Monte Carlo, uses the mountain roads around **Thorenc**, about 20 miles north of Grasse, way to the northwest. Nevertheless, Bond arrives at the **Casino de Monte Carlo**, Monaco, and it's from the bay at **Monte Carlo** that Onatopp steals the Stealth helicopter.

St Petersburg: Somerset House, The Strand

The Russian cathedral: St Sofia's Greek Cathedral, Bayswater

M's office is, finally, MI6's real HQ, in the spanking new building on the Thames by **Vauxhall Bridge**. Although there is some real filming in **St Petersburg** in Russia, much of the tank chase was filmed on a massive set, built at the old Rolls Royce aircraft plant in **Leavesden**, Hertfordshire.

Many of the other Russian locations were shot around the southeast of England: St Petersburg Airport, where Bond is met by Joe Don Baker, is actually the **Queen's Stand, Epsom Racecourse, Epsom**, Surrey, while the St Petersburg exterior where Baker fixes the motor is the courtyard of the recently restored **Somerset House** on the **Strand**. The Russian church is **St Sofia's Greek Cathedral, Moscow Road**, Bayswater, W2; and the St Petersburg interiors used the grandiose architecture of **Draper's Hall, Throgmorton Street, EC2** in the City. The massive radio telescope dish is **Arecibo**, in Puerto Rico (see *Contact* for details).

GOLDFINGER

(1964, dir: Guy Hamilton)
Sean Connery, Gert Frobe, Honor Blackman.
● MIAMI, FLORIDA; KENTUCKY; SWITZERLAND;
BUCKINGHAMSHIRE

The budget was still relatively modest for the third Bond, and, apart from a week's filming in Switzerland, all Sean Connery's scenes were shot in England. When Goldfinger cheats at cards at the Fountainebleau Hotel, now the **Fountainebleau Hilton Resort and Spa, 4441 Collins Avenue, Miami**, Florida, Connery was filming his scenes on a mock-up of the hotel at Pinewood. In fact, a lot of the filming was done not far from Pinewood in Buckinghamshire. The 'South American holdings' of the pre-credits sequence, are a storage tank complex at **Stanwell**, west of London between Staines and Hounslow; the cliff over which the Merc plummets is **Harefield Quarry**; while the Blue Grass Airfield, Kentucky is **Northolt Aerodrome**. Likewise, the golf match between Bond and Goldfinger, supposedly at Royal St George's, Sandwich in Kent, uses **Stoke Poges Golf Club**, on the A332 a couple of miles north of Slough. The clubhouse, in front of which Oddjob decapitates a statue with his lethal hat, is **Stoke Park House, Stoke Poges Lane**.

Though the exterior of the real **Fort Knox**, Kentucky, south of Louisville near the Indiana border, is briefly seen, the fort was recreated at **Black Park Woodland** behind the studio at Pinewood. A wholly fantastic interior (the problems of storing gold bullion make vaults boringly unphotogenic) was created on a soundstage. Bond trails Goldfinger's Rolls along Alpine roads and encounters Tilly Masterson at **Andermatt**, a small Swiss village, 50 miles south of Zurich in the shelter of the Leopontine Alps near the Simplon Tunnel. And although the long shots of Auric Enterprises are the **Pilatus Aircraft Factory** outside **Lucerne**, Switzerland, the scenes set in Goldfinger's complex use the familiar Pinewood studio buildings.

Bond plays Goldfinger at golf: Stoke Poges Golf Club, Slough

Goldfinger cheats at cards: Fontainebleau Hilton, Miami

GONE TO EARTH (aka *The Wild Heart*)

(1950, dir: Michael Powell, Emeric Pressburger)
Jennifer Jones, David Farrar, Cyril Cusack.
● SHROPSHIRE

Powell and Pressburger's wildly overblown period romance uses the Shropshire villages of **Much Wenlock**, twelve miles southeast of Shrewsbury on the A458; **Church Stretton**, twelve miles south of Shrewsbury on the A49 and **Craven Arms**, a further seven miles south on the A49.

GONE WITH THE WIND

(1939, dir: Victor Fleming; George Cukor, Sam Wood)
Vivien Leigh, Clark Gable, Olivia de Havilland.
● CALIFORNIA

Although people still arrive in Atlanta expecting to visit Scarlett's estate, not a frame was shot in Georgia. Virtually all the movie was filmed at what was then the Selznick International Studios. This studio, built by DW Griffith's contemporary and early innovator Tom Ince in 1916, passed into various hands over the years. In 1924 it was Pathe Studios, in 1925 the DeMille Studios (*King of Kings* was made here in 1927), in 1931 RKO-Pathe. Later, in 1957, it became Desilu-Culver and later still just **Culver Studios**. You can see the original studio building, unchanged, at **9336 Washington Boulevard** between Ince and Van Buren, Culver City. The Washington Boulevard frontage of the studio was used for the entrance to Twelve Oaks.

One of the earliest shots in the can was the burning of Atlanta, so early, in fact, that Scarlett O'Hara hadn't yet been cast. Legend has it that Vivien Leigh arrived during filming and instantly secured the part. What went up in flames was the old Selznick backlot, in a massive space-clearing operation. You can plainly see the giant gates of King Kong's Skull Island – bizarrely out of place in Atlanta – during the conflagration.

The few locations include the barbecue at Twelve Oaks, which used the long-gone Busch Gardens in Pasadena, an estate built by the Busch brewing family. Remnants of the landscaping can still be seen in gardens of the houses around Arroyo Boulevard between Bellefontaine Street and Madeline Drive (see *Citizen Kane* for details).

When Scarlett vows never to go hungry again, it's an early morning sunrise at **Lasky Mesa, Calabasas**, northwest of LA in the Simi Valley. Loads of movies were shot here, including the 1936 *The Charge of the Light Brigade*. The area, between Agoura and Woodland Hills, is now known as the **Ahmanson Ranch**, and is currently scheduled to be redeveloped. Gerald O'Hara's last ride was also filmed at Calabasas. The attack in Shantytown is at **Big Bear Lake** at San Bernardino, east of LA. Gerald's walk with Scarlett was shot on the **Reuss Ranch, Malibu Lake**.

The cotton fields of Tara and O'Hara's first horse ride

The entrance to Twelve Oaks: Culver Studios, Washington Boulevard, Culver City

are around **Chico**, way up in northern California, some 80 miles north of Sacramento. Filming took place around **Bidwell Park, Pentz Road**, and **Paradise Apple Orchard**. Various estates lay claim to be the inspiration for Tara. The staircase was supposedly based on an original at Cretien Point Plantation, about four miles from Sunset, between Lake Charles and Baton Rouge, Louisiana, while the avenue of oaks is based on one at Boone Hall Plantation, seven miles north of Charleston, near US17, South Carolina.

GOOD MORNING, VIETNAM
(1987, dir: Barry Levinson)
Robin Williams, Forest Whitaker, Tung Thanh Tran.
● THAILAND

Thalang, in Phuket Province, stood in for Saigon in Levinson's black comedy.

GOOD, THE BAD, AND THE UGLY, THE (aka *Il Buono, Il Bruto, Il Cattivo*)
(1966, dir: Sergio Leone)
Clint Eastwood, Eli Wallach, Lee Van Cleef.
● SPAIN

The last of the *Dollars* trilogy uses locations in both southern and northern Spain. The friary of Eli Wallach's good brother is **Cortijo de los Frailes**, which you can still see, between Los Albaricoques and the coastal resort of San Jose in the Cabo de Gata Natural Park east of Almeria. The sandy waste Wallach forces Eastwood to cross is the surrounding desert. Less arid landscapes were found to the north. At **Covarrubias**, about 20 miles southeast of Burgos, the spectacular Civil War scenes were shot along the banks of the River Arlanza, and you'll find the ruins of the **Monastery of San Pedro de Arlanza**, which became the military hospital. A few miles further southeast, at **Carazo**, the cemetery-cum-arena was built for the final confrontation.

GOOD WILL HUNTING
(1997, dir: Gus Van Sant)
Matt Damon, Robin Williams, Ben Affleck.
● BOSTON, MASSACHUSETTS; TORONTO, ONTARIO

Damon explains his gift: Au Bon Pain, Harvard Square

The toy store: Ontario Specialty Co, Church Street, Toronto

Co-stars Matt Damon and Ben Affleck picked up an Oscar for their screenplay, set around South Boston and Harvard Square. Although the publicity made great play of the Boston locales, much of the movie was actually made in Toronto. Real Boston locations include the college, where underachiever Damon works as janitor,

The South Boston Bar: Woody's L Street Tavern, Eighth Street

which is **Mass-achusetts Institute of Technology, Cambridge** – the exterior is MIT's **McLaurin Building**. Robin Williams' college is the **Bunker Hill Community Col-lege, Rutherford Avenue, Charlestown**, while Minnie

The Boston college bar: Upfront Bar & Grill, Front Street, Toronto

Driver's college room is over the Charles River, **Dunster House, Harvard University**, Cambridge. Harvard Square is the site of **Au Bon Pain, 27 Brattle Street**, where Damon tries to explain his gift to Driver, and also the now closed Tasty Café, where the two share a very messy pickle. Off Massachusetts Avenue was Harvard student hangout the Bow and Arrow Pub, now gone. The working class bar where Damon hangs out with Affleck and his buddies is **Woody's L Street Tavern, 658 East Eighth Street A**. Williams takes Damon for a heart-to-heart in the **Boston Public Garden**, southwest of downtown.

The University of Toronto supplied many of the film's interiors: **Knox College; Whitney Hall; St Michael's College** and **McLennan Hall**; while the **Central Technical High School** was also used. Dorm interiors were filmed at **Wycliffe College, Hoskin Avenue**. In downtown Toronto are the **Ontario Specialty Co, 133 Church Street** at Queen Street, the toy store where Damon demonstrates his magic trick, and the **Crown Life Building, 120 Bloor Street East**, the glossy corporate environment Damon rejects. The interior of the college bar, where Damon humiliates the history student, is the **Upfront Bar and Grill, 106 Front Street East**, downtown Toronto.

GOODBYE MR CHIPS
(1939, dir: Sam Wood)
Robert Donat, Greer Garson, Paul von Hernreid.
● DERBYSHIRE

Classic tearjerker from James Hilton's novel, following the life of a shy schoolmaster from 1870 to WWI. Made by MGM with an American director, Sam Wood, it was filmed in England. Brookfield School is **Repton School**, Repton, between Derby and Burton-upon-Trent, though the school was recreated in the studio for most scenes.

The 1969 musical remake used **Sherborne**, in Dorset. Sian Phillips' waterfront house is **59 Strand-on-the-Green**, on the north bank of the Thames just east of Kew Bridge,

London W4. The Alpine holiday is replaced by an Italian jaunt, taking in the ruins of **Pompeii** at the foot of Vesuvius; **Positano**, about fifteen miles to the south; and, further south, **Paestum**.

GOODFELLAS

(1990, dir: Martin Scorsese)
Ray Liotta, Joe Pesci, Robert De Niro.
● **NEW YORK CITY; NEW JERSEY; LONG ISLAND**

Scorsese's classic tracking shot: the old Copacabana, East 60th Street

Scorsese's great gangster movie, shot entirely on location around New York City, the borough of Queens and New Jersey. The Brooklyn home of anti-hero Ray Liotta is actually in **Astoria**, Queens, beneath the N line. Liotta shows off at the old Copacabana Nightclub (now closed), **10 East 60th Street** at Fifth Avenue in Manhattan. You can still see the entrance used for the electrifying tracking shot. The kitschy Bamboo Lounge, where Pesci does his scary "funny guy" turn was the Hawaii Kai Restaurant, **49th Street** at Broadway.

The Bamboo Lounge: 49th Street at Broadway

It's now a stylish Japanese restaurant and the glorious South Seas decor is only a memory. The airport scenes were shot at the cargo buildings of **Kennedy Airport**. The Airline Diner is the **Jackson Hole Wyoming Diner**, which stood at 6935 Astoria Boulevard in Queens. It has since been moved. The posh beach club, where Liotta goes with Lorraine Bracco after his first big airport job, is the **Catalina Beach Club at Atlantic Beach** on Long Island's southwest coast. The edgy meeting with a paranoid De Niro was filmed on **Smith Street** at 9th Street, alongside the Gowanus Canal, under the elevated railway F Line in Brooklyn's dodgy Red Hook district.

Filming also took place on the **Palisades Parkway**, which runs along the west bank of the Hudson River in New Jersey; at **Fort Lee**, just over the George Washington Bridge in New Jersey; at **New Rochelle** on Route 95 north of New York City; on **Coney Island Avenue** in Brooklyn; in Brooklyn's **Prospect Park** and at **Valley Stream**, Long Island. Liotta's trial, where he turns on boss Paul Sorvino, was filmed in **New York County Courthouse, 60 Centre Street**.

GORILLAS IN THE MIST

(1988, dir: Michael Apted)
Sigourney Weaver, Bryan Brown, John Omirah Miluwi.
● **RWANDA**

Powerful and moving biopic of anthropologist Dian Fossey, her battle to save Africa's mountain gorillas and her murder in 1985. The movie's location was determined by the habitat of the remaining 650 gorillas, which can be found in just two colonies, on the borders of Rwanda, Congo and Uganda. Fossey's **Karisoke Research Centre** struggles on in the **Virunga Conservation Area**, about ten miles west of Ruhengeri, Rwanda. Sigourney Weaver was so affected during the making of the movie (it was made less than three years after Fossey's murder) that she became Honorary Chairperson of the Dian Fossey Gorilla Fund International. While the conservation area remains so unstable, it might be better to just visit the DFGFI website at *www.gorillafund.org*.

GOSPEL ACCORDING TO ST. MATTHEW, THE

(aka *Il Vangelo Secondo Matteo*)
(1964, dir: Pier Paolo Pasolini)
Enrique Irazoqui, Margherita Caruso, Susanna Pasolini.
● **ITALY**

Non-professional actors, world music and stark monochrome cinematography – Pasolini's Marxist-Humanist version of the gospel story is a long, long way from Cecil B DeMille. Filmed around **Calabria** and **Puglia** in Southern Italy.

GÖTTERDAMMERUNG (aka *The Damned*)

(1969, dir: Luchino Visconti)
Dirk Bogarde, Ingrid Thulin, Helmut Berger.
● **GERMANY; AUSTRIA; ITALY**

The fall of a decadent Krupp-like family in Nazi Germany, filmed by Visconti as a wildly operatic melodrama.

The German locations include the Rhineland cities of **Dusseldorf** and **Essen**, both just north of Cologne. The steel mill scenes were filmed in Italy at the industrial city of **Terni** in Umbria, 50 miles north of Rome. The lakeside hotel setting for the 'Night of the Long Knives' orgy and massacre, set in Wiessee, were actually filmed on the southwestern tip of the **Atter See**, twenty miles southeast of Salzburg in Unterach.

GRADUATE, THE

(1967, dir: Mike Nichols)
Dustin Hoffman, Anne Bancroft, Katharine Ross.
● **CALIFORNIA**

The Taft Hotel, where graduate Benjamin conducts an illicit affair with neighbour Mrs Robinson, is actually the **Ambassador Hotel, 3400 Wilshire Boulevard**, midtown LA. The hotel has been closed since 1989 and is currently under threat of demolition (see the 1954 *A Star Is Born* for details).

Waiting at the Berkeley fountain: USC Campus, Los Angeles

The university, attended by Benjamin's real love, who happens to be Mrs Robinson's daughter Elaine, is supposedly Berkeley, over the Bay

The Taft Hotel: Ambassador Hotel, Wilshire Boulevard

The disrupted wedding: United Methodist Church, La Verne

from San Francisco. For the most part, though, it's the spacious Romanesque campus of the **University of Southern California (USC), Jefferson Boulevard**, bounded by Vermont Avenue, Exposition Boulevard and Figueroa Street, downtown LA. The fountain, where Benjamin mopes about waiting for Elaine, is in front of the **Edward L Doheny Jr Memorial Library**, between Hoover Boulevard and Childs Way. Elaine's dorm is the **Von Kleinsmid Center of International and Public Affairs** at USC.

The real Berkeley makes a showing, though. Benjamin drives south over the double-decker **Oakland Bay Bridge**, which is actually *away* from Oakland. If he had driven *toward* Oakland he would have been invisible on the bridge's lower deck. Elaine walks through **Sproul Plaza**, and the frat house is **Theta Delta Chi Fraternity House, 2647 Durant Avenue** between Rowditch and College. Benjamin follows Elaine to her meeting by the Monkey House in **San Francisco Zoo**, south of the Sunset district.

The gas station, where Benjamin tries to find out where Elaine is getting married by posing as a priest, is at **Winchester Canyon**, north of Santa Barbara. The church, where the wedding is finally disrupted, is not in Santa Barbara at all. It's the **United Methodist Church of La Verne, 3205 D Street, La Verne**, east of Los Angeles.

GRANDE ILLUSION, LA (aka *Grand Illusion*)
(1937, dir: Jean Renoir)
Jean Gabin, Pierre Fresnay, Erich von Stroheim.
● FRANCE

The Hallbach POW camp for officers, where Jean Gabin is initially incarcerated, is the army barracks at **Colmar**, in Alsace toward the German border. Winterborn, the fortress prison commanded by Erich von Stroheim that he's transferred to, is **Haut-Koenigsbourg Castle**, overlooking the village of St Hippolyte, about 60 miles to the southwest.

GRAPES OF WRATH, THE
(1940, dir: John Ford)
Henry Fonda, John Carradine, Jane Darwell.
● CALIFORNIA; OKLAHOMA

John Ford's moving, but politically softened, filming of Steinbeck's story of migrating farmers in the thirties was shot mainly on the Fox backlot on **Pico Boulevard, LA**, where the Hooverville settlement was built. Real Californian locations included the San Fernando Valley, and the river scene, which was shot at **Needles** on I-40 at the the Arizona border, but that's as far as the cast got. A second unit did

the location work, filming doubles leaving the farm in **McAlester**, Oklahoma, Highway 69, 100 miles south of Tulsa.

GREASE
(1978, dir: Randal Kleiser)
John Travolta, Olivia Newton-John, Stockard Channing.
● LOS ANGELES

Rydell High is a conflation of three schools. The art-deco façade is **Venice High School, 13000 Venice Boulevard**. The finale used the sports fields of **John Marshall High School, 3939 Tracy Street** in Silverlake, LA, seen also in the genuine 1957 juvenile delinquent movie *The Young Stranger* and the original *Buffy the Vampire Slayer* movie. The cars are raced along the concrete spillways of the Los Angeles River between the **First and Seventh Street Bridges**, east of downtown.

Grease II, the disappointing sequel with Maxwell Caulfield replacing Travolta and pre-stardom Michelle Pfeiffer stepping into Olivia Newton-John's stilettoes, used the **Excelsior High School** at **Norwalk**, southeast LA on Route 5.

Rydell High: Venice High School, Venice Boulevard, Venice

GREAT DICTATOR, THE
(1940, dir: Charles Chaplin)
Charles Chaplin, Jack Oakie, Paulette Goddard.
● CALIFORNIA

Chaplin contributed to the WWII war effort with a debunking of Hitler and Mussolini, by playing a Jewish barber mistaken for fascist dictator Adenoid Hynkel. Oakie is fellow fascist Napaloni. Mostly studio-bound in Hollywood of course, but Hynkel's oratory was shot up north in the **San Fernando Valley** and the war scenes and duck hunt were filmed around **Malibu Lake**, south of Mulholland Highway near Cornell in the Santa Monica Mountains. The exterior of Hynkel's palace, seen when Jack Oakie arrives, is **Pasadena City Hall, 100 North Garfield Avenue**, Pasadena (see *Beverly Hills Cop II* for details of this popular location).

GREAT ESCAPE, THE
(1963, dir: John Sturges)
Steve McQueen, James Garner, Richard Attenborough.
● GERMANY

After scouting locations around California, Stalag Luft III was eventually recreated in a pine forest behind the

Geiselgasteig studios near Munich. The railroad scenes were filmed on a stretch of line running between Munich and Hamburg. Steve McQueen's motorbike scenes were shot at **Fussen** on the Austrian border.

GREAT EXPECTATIONS
(1946, dir: David Lean)
John Mills, Bernard Miles, Valerie Hobson.
● KENT; LONDON

Perhaps the greatest Dickens adaptation, filmed mostly in the studio at Denham. The opening scenes used **St Mary's Marshes** on the south side of the Thames Estuary a few miles northeast of Rochester. It's here too, at high tide, that Pip and Herbert Pocket arrive and depart in a rowboat, and about a mile inland that Joe Gargery's forge was built. The Rotterdam Paddle Boat plied the **River Medway**. Pip's arrival in London was filmed in front of the real **St Paul's Cathedral**, the shots carefully angled to exclude modern buildings and bomb damage.

GREAT EXPECTATIONS
(1998, dir: Alfonso Cuarón)
Ethan Hawke, Gwyneth Paltrow, Anne Bancroft.
● NEW YORK STATE; FLORIDA

Surprisingly successful updating of Dickens, relocated to New York and Florida. The mansion of Anne Bancroft, the Miss Havisham character, is **Hempstead House**, one of three mansions open to the public on the Guggenheim Estate, **Sands Point Preserve** on the north shore of Long Island, seen also in *Malcolm X* and *Scent of a Woman*. See *The Godfather* (the horse's head scene was filmed on the estate) for details.

Miss Havisham's mansion: Hempstead House, Long Island

GREAT GATSBY, THE
(1974, dir: Jack Clayton)
Robert Redford, Mia Farrow, Bruce Dern.
● RHODE ISLAND; NEW YORK CITY

Scott Fitzgerald's novel is set on Long Island, centering on the uncrossable class divide between East Egg and West Egg, old and new money, separated by Long Island Sound. The encroaching urbanisation of new money forced Paramount to look elsewhere for locations, finally settling for Rhode Island.

Daisy's childhood home, where she meets Gatsby, is a white-pillared, Southern-style mansion on **Hope Street, Bristol**, about ten miles north of Newport off Route 114. The Gatsby Mansion is in **Newport**, Rhode Island. It's **Rosecliffe, Bellevue Avenue**, an imitation of the Petit Trianon at Versailles, built in 1909. The interior of Bellevue featured as the Swiss chateau gatecrashed by Arnold Schwarzenegger at the opening of *True Lies*.

The area is pretty damn exclusive – the stars of the movie rented cottages on the Hammersmith Farm Estate, owned by Jackie Onassis' parents, the Auchincloss family. The Kennedy wedding reception was held here, and it became the presidential hideaway during the early sixties. Ironically, **Hammersmith Farm, Ocean Drive**, ended up slumming it in the movie as Gatsby's West Egg Mansion. Both Rosecliffe and Hammersmith Farm are open to the public.

Other locations included **Marble House** in Rhode Island; and two grand New York hotels, the **Waldorf-Astoria Hotel, 301 Park Avenue** between East 49th and East 50th Streets and the **Plaza Hotel, Fifth Avenue** at 59th Street. Interiors were shot at **Pinewood Studios** in England, where the Conservatory, built as an extension to Pinewood's original building, Hertherden Hall, still stands.

GREAT RACE, THE
(1965, dir: Blake Edwards)
Jack Lemmon, Tony Curtis, Peter Falk.
● AUSTRIA; CALIFORNIA; OREGON

Elaborate, big-budget farce centering on the 1908 New York to Paris car race. Potsdorf is **Salzburg** in Austria. The railway scenes utilised the Sierra Railroad, which you can visit in **Jamestown**, northern California. Other US locations included the **Alabama Hills, Lone Pine**, central California and **Gearhart**, Oregon.

GREATEST SHOW ON EARTH, THE
(1952, dir: Cecil B DeMille)
Charlton Heston, Betty Hutton, James Stewart.
● FLORIDA; PENNSYLVANIA; WASHINGTON DC

DeMille's irresistible circus hokum, filmed in part at **Sarasota**, south of Tampa, on Florida's west coast, headquarters of the Ringling Brothers Barnum and Bailey Circus. The recently renovated Ringling Museum, based on John Ringling's mansion, based on the Doge's Palace in Venice, is half a mile south of the Sarasota-Bradenton Airport on US41 (☏ *813.355.5101*).

GREATEST STORY EVER TOLD, THE
(1965, dir: George Stevens)
Max von Sydow, Charlton Heston, Carroll Baker.
● UTAH; NEVADA; CALIFORNIA

The vast budget of this underrated epic demanded stars, stars, stars, but since the main roles went to relative unknowns, a series of absurdly distracting cameos disrupts the film.

Stevens wanted to film in Israel, but practical considerations, and the sway of unions, resulted in a decision to film entirely on US soil. So, lo and behold, it was discovered that 'Utah looks more like the Holy Land than the Holy Land'. In truth the locations are stunning, if geographically inaccurate, and the visuals fall apart only with the horribly studio-bound crucifixion, filmed at **Culver City Studios** after bad weather closed down location shooting.

The southwest US forms the backdrop for most of the movie, with the Colorado River standing in for the River Jordan and Navajo taking time off from playing Sioux, Cheyenne and Apaches to become the Roman army.

Kane County, on Utah's southern border, stood in for the Holy Land. The town of Bethlehem was reconstructed near **Moab**, between the spectacular Arches and

Canyonlands National Parks. The Sea of Galilee, though, is some way off in western Nevada. It's **Pyramid Lake**, within Pyramid Lake Indian Reservation, 30 miles north of Reno. Capernaum was built on the lake's shore. The cast and crew stayed in the town of Page, Arizona, near the Glen Canyon Dam. The opening of the dam had been held up for the shoot, and after filming, the area was flooded. Many of the film's locations now lie under the waters of Lake Powell.

GREED
(1924, dir: Erich von Stroheim)
Gibson Gowland, Zasu Pitts, Jean Hersholt.
● **CALIFORNIA**

Having rebuilt Monte Carlo on the Universal lot for *Foolish Wives*, extravagant genius Erich von Stroheim took an entirely different approach to his epic adaptation of Frank Norris' novel *McTeague* and made the movie on real locations, largely around San Francisco. Virtually taking over an entire city block, he not only used exteriors but filmed inside houses too, with his cast living and sleeping on the sets. The resulting 96 hours of film were edited down to a nine hour picture, then to five. Eventually the studio stepped in and slashed the movie down to little more than two hours.

McTeague's Polk Street dentist office can still be recognised at **611 Laguna Street** on the corner of Hayes Street. The church attended by McTeague and his new bride is St Paulus Lutheran Church, which stood at the corner of Eddy and Gough Streets (that's the church you can see in *Vertigo* opposite Mckittrick's Hotel) until it was destroyed by fire a few years ago. The famously shocking desert climax, with the treacherous McTeague handcuffed to the dead body of his one-time friend, was shot out in the blistering wilderness of **Death Valley**.

McTeague's dentist office: Laguna Street, San Francisco

GREEN MILE, THE
(1999, dir: Frank Darabont)
Tom Hanks, David Morse, Bonnie Hunt.
● **TENNESSEE; NORTH CAROLINA**

Another Stephen King prison drama from the director of *The Shawshank Redemption*, set in Cold Mountain Penitentiary, South Georgia, but made largely in Tennessee. The prison exterior is the old **Tennessee State Penitentiary, Nashville**, seen also in Sharon Stone's *Last Dance*. More scenes were shot at **Lewisburg**; **College Grove**; **Columbia**; **Nolensville**; and **Shelbyville**.

Georgia Pines nursing home is **Flat Top Manor** (*admission free*), the turn-of-the-century home of businessman Moses Cone, in the **Moses Cone National Park** on the Blue Ridge Parkway at **Blowing Rock**, between Asheville and Winston-Salem, North Carolina.

GREGORY'S GIRL
(1981, dir: Bill Forsyth)
Gordon John Sinclair, Dee Hepburn, Clare Grogan.
● **SCOTLAND**

The Scots town is **Cumbernauld**, a new town just north of Glasgow, where Gregory's school is **Abronhill High School**, in the Abronhill district. Gregory waits by the huge clock in the **New Town Plaza**. Filming also took place at **Partick Thistle FC** and at the **Cumbernauld Theatre**.

GREMLINS 2: THE NEW BATCH
(1990, dir: Joe Dante)
Zach Galligan, Phoebe Cates, Christopher Lee.
● **NEW YORK CITY; LOS ANGELES**

Wickedly funny and wildly self-indulgent sequel to the studio-bound *Gremlins*, cramming more in-jokes into its anarchic plot than you could possibly take in at one viewing. This time the little creatures get to New York, though the Chinatown shop where the gremlin is discovered is the New York Street set on the Warner Bros backlot in **Burbank**. In New York, Clamp Tower is **101 Park Avenue**, just to the south of Grand Central Station. The Cathedral of St Eva-Marie (think about it) is **St Patrick's Cathedral, Fifth Avenue** between 50th and 51st Streets.

Clamp Tower: Park Avenue, New York

GREYSTOKE: THE LEGEND OF TARZAN, LORD OF THE APES
(1984, dir: Hugh Hudson)
Christopher Lambert, Ralph Richardson, Ian Holm.
● **SCOTLAND; HERTFORDSHIRE; OXFORDSHIRE; LONDON; CAMEROONS**

Good-looking but clumsy retelling of the old warhorse. The screenplay credit goes to PH Vazak – the script was originally written by Robert Towne who, on seeing the movie, insisted on giving the writing credit to his dog. The dog in turn is named after PH Vazak's bar in Greenwich Village, itself a famous movie location (*The Godfather Part II*). The African scenes filmed in the **Cameroons**.

The Greystoke Mansion is **Floors Castle**, north of **Kelso** in Scotland, about 25 miles southwest of Berwick-upon-Tweed. It's open to the public (© *01573.23333, admission charge*). Floors provides the exterior and the ballroom, but the other interior scenes were filmed at **Hatfield House, Hatfield** in Hertfordshire, and at **Blenheim Palace, Woodstock** in Oxfordshire. The grand entrance hall, where Ralph welcomes Tarzan on his arrival and where James Fox proposes to Andie MacDowell in front of a blazing fire, is Hatfield's magnificent Marble Hall (see *Batman* for details). The elaborate staircase, down which Ralph Richardson famously slides on a tea tray, is also at Hatfield. It's the Grand Staircase, one of a few surviving Jacobean wooden staircases and a marvel of carving.

Tarzan is unwisely invited to the opening of the Greystoke Wing of the **Natural History Museum, Cromwell Road**, in the Dinosaur Hall. He liberates the captive ape, which has the good taste to head directly for Gilbert Scott's marvellously kitschy, and recently restored, **Albert Memorial**, down the road in **Kensington Gardens** opposite the Royal Albert Hall.

GRIFTERS, THE
(1990, dir: Stephen Frears)
Anjelica Huston, John Cusack, Annette Bening.
● **CALIFORNIA; PHOENIX, ARIZONA**

Neo noir from British director Frears, with Huston, Cusack and Bening as three con-artists involved in a queasily incestuous relationship. The hotel in LA where Cusack hangs out is the **Bryson, 2701 Wilshire Boulevard**, downtown (it also served as the rather seedier hotel that Mickey Rourke and Faye Dunaway dive into to avoid the cops in *Barfly* and was seen in the opening sequence of Paul Thomas Anderson's *Magnolia*). Filming also took place in **San Diego**. The race track is the **Turf Paradise Race Horse Track, 19th Avenue** at Bell Road, Phoenix, Arizona, and the airport is the **Sky Harbor Airport**, at Phoenix.

GROSSE POINTE BLANK
(1997, dir: George Armitage)
John Cusack, Minnie Driver, Alan Arkin.
● **MICHIGAN; CALIFORNIA**

The coffee shop: South Myrtle Avenue, Monrovia

There's a little scene-setting in **Detroit** and its classy suburb of **Grosse Pointe** itself, for this black comedy, but most of the movie was shot in LA's eastern suburbs of Pasadena, Duarte and Monrovia. The Grosse Pointe neighbourhood, where Cusack rekindles romance with old flame Minnie Driver, is the 400 block of **South Myrtle Avenue**, Monrovia. The café, where he meets up with rival hitman Dan Aykroyd, is **Natick's Hobby Shop, 405 South Myrtle Avenue**. Pointes High is **John Marshall High School, 3939 Tracy Street, Silverlake**, a familiar filming location seen in *Buffy the Vampire Slayer*, body-swap comedy *Like Father, Like Son* and fifties teen-flick *The Young Stranger*

GROUNDHOG DAY
(1993, dir: Harold Ramis)
Bill Murray, Andie MacDowell, Chris Elliott.
● **ILLINOIS**

Murray's stylus gets stuck in the groove of time, living the same day over and over again in smalltown USA. Punxsutawney, Pa. is actually **Woodstock**, 45 miles northwest of Chicago on Route 14, Illinois. The movie makes use of the old pre-Civil War courthouse and jail, the restored turn-of-the-century opera house and town square with its bandstand and gazebo.

GUNFIGHT AT THE O.K. CORRAL
(1957, dir: John Sturges)
Kirk Douglas, Burt Lancaster, Jo Van Fleet.
● **ARIZONA**

Another version of the legendary showdown between Wyatt Earp, Doc Holliday and the Clantons. The OK Corral was reconstructed at the Western facsimile town of **Old Tucson, 201 South Kinney Road**, (© *602.883.6457; www.oldtucson.com*), Arizona, now a major tourist attraction. The set was built for the 1940 Western *Arizona*, and has been seen in films such as *Rio Bravo*, *El Dorado* and *The Quick and the Dead*. The crew also ventured south to the town of **Elgin**, another favourite location, just down the road from the real Tombstone.

GUNGA DIN
(1939, dir: George Stevens)
Cary Grant, Victor McLaglen, Douglas Fairbanks Jr.
● **CALIFORNIA**

Site of the temple: Temple Pocket, Horseshoe Meadow Road

Spectacular epic set on India's North West frontier, with the ubiquitous **Alabama Hills**, at Lone Pine, on I-395, central California, standing in for the Himalayas. The location was put to similar use in, amongst other films, *The Charge of the Light Brigade* (1936) and *The Lives of a Bengal Lancer*. The Hills, striking rock formations, are west of the town of Lone Pine off Whitney Portal Road. The huge English fort was built on **Indian Springs Road**, south of Whitney Portal, against the backdrop of the Sierra Nevadas. The Temple of Kali was constructed in a hollow now known as **Temple Pocket** on **Horseshoe Meadow Road** – where a stone marker commemorates the shoot.

Site of the English fort: Indian Springs Road, Alabama Hills

GUNS OF NAVARONE, THE
(1961, dir: J Lee Thompson)
Gregory Peck, David Niven, Stanley Baker.
● **RHODES, GREECE**

Jolly adventure stuff, but being a Carl Foreman scripted movie, there's plenty of moral philosophising before we get to the bangs and crashes. Set on the island of Rhodes, the interiors were filmed at **Shepperton Studios**, the exteriors at – believe it or not – **Navarone**, on the island of Rhodes.

H

HACKERS
(1995, dir: Iain Softley)
Jonny Lee Miller, Angelina Jolie, Matthew Lillard.
● **NEW YORK CITY**

Engaging computer-age thriller, set in New York, at Grand Central Station and in the East Village. The high school is **Stuyvesant High School, 345 Chambers Street, Battery Park City**, New York.

HAINE, LA (aka *Hate*)
(1995, dir: Mathieu Kassovitz)
Vincent Cassel, Hubert Kounde, Saïd Taghmaoui.
● **PARIS**

Kassovitz' tough film about racism looks at a side of Paris rarely seen on screen, made on the streets of the **Chanteloupe-les-Vignes** estate.

HAIRSPRAY
(1988, dir: John Waters)
Divine, Ricki Lake, Colleen Fitzpatrick.
● **BALTIMORE, MARYLAND**

Divine's last movie is a blow for Chubby Lib and racial integration, set in a fictitious day-glo sixties, and filmed, of course, in Baltimore. Ricki Lake is Tracy Turnblad, a hefty teenager desperate to bop in the audience of the grossly white *Corny Collins Show*, Divine, her even heftier Mom. Tracy's high school is **Merganthaler Vocational Technical School, 3500 Hillen Road**.

HALLOWEEN
(1978, dir: John Carpenter)
Jamie Lee Curtis, Donald Pleasence, Nancy Loomis.
● **LOS ANGELES**

The original, and best, stalk'n'slash, with more scary stalking than gratuitous slashing. Set in the fictitious Illinois suburb of Haddonfield (producer Debra Hill grew up in Haddonfield, New Jersey), the movie blends locales in Hollywood and South Pasadena. Jamie Lee Curtis' house is in South Pasadena, on **Oxley Street** at the corner of Fairview Avenue, South Pasadena. Haddonfield High is **South Pasadena High School, Lyndon Street** at Fremont Avenue. Nichol's Hardware Store, robbed by Michael Myers ("just some rope, a knife and a Hal-

The high school: South Pasadena High School, Lyndon Street

The hardware store: Mission Street, South Pasadena

Site of the murders: Orange Grove Avenue, Hollywood

loween mask... must be kids") is **The Frame Shop, 964 Mission Street** at Meridian Avenue in South Pasadena. And on the opposite corner of Meridian is **Century House, 1000 Mission Street**, the now-bright-and-nicely-renovated Myers house. If the angle of the house looks a little odd, that's because the entire building was actu-

Jamie Lee Curtis babysits: Orange Grove Avenue, Hollywood

The old Myers house: Mission Street, South Pasadena

ally moved from its former position around the corner at 707 Meridian Avenue.

The Doyle and Wallace houses can be found in Hollywood, on the 1500 block of Orange Grove Avenue between Sunset Boulevard and Selma Avenue. The house where Jamie Lee Curtis babysits is **1530 Orange Grove Avenue**, and the scene of the murders is across the street at **1537 Orange Grove Avenue**.

HALLOWEEN II
(1981, dir: Rick Rosenthal)
Jamie Lee Curtis, Donald Pleasence, Jeffrey Kramer.
● **CALIFORNIA**

Michael Myers escapes again in a retread of the first movie. The town square is **Kersting Court, Sierra Madre Boulevard** at Baldwin Avenue, **Sierra Madre**, to the east of

The town square: Kersting Court, Sierra Madre

Pasadena. You might recognise the locale as Santa Mira from Don Siegel's original *Invasion of the Body Snatchers*.

The hospital, where much of the action takes place, is mainly **Morningside Hospital, 8711 South Harvard, Inglewood,** plus a little **Pasadena Community Hospital, 1845 North Fair Oaks Avenue,** Pasadena.

HALLOWEEN III: SEASON OF THE WITCH
(1983, dir: Tommy Lee Wallace)
Dan O'Herlihy, Tom Atkins, Stacey Nelkin.
● CALIFORNIA

Nothing at all to do with the *Halloween* series, apart from the name and the presence of John Carpenter as producer and composer. The original script was by Nigel Kneale (creator of *Quatermass*), who demanded his name be taken off the credits. Toymaker Dan O'Herlihy tries to enslave kids with a range of possessed Halloween masks. Set, confusingly, in Santa Mira (the fictional town where the original *Invasion of the Body Snatchers* is set: see *Halloween II*), but filmed in **Loleta**, on California's far northern coast, about ten miles south of Eureka.

HALLOWEEN 4: THE RETURN OF MICHAEL MYERS
(1988, dir: Dwight H Little)
Donald Pleasence, Ellie Cornell, Danielle Harris.
● UTAH

Following the non-Myers aberration *Halloween III*, *The Return...* was shot in **Ogden**, near Salt Lake City, Utah.

HALLOWEEN H20: 20 YEARS LATER
(1998, dir: Steve Miner)
Jamie Lee Curtis, Adam Arkin, Josh Hartnett.
● LOS ANGELES

Myers haunts the private school: Micheltorena Street, Silverlake

Twenty years after the events of the original *Halloween*, Michael Myers tracks down his sister, now the disturbed alcoholic head of a private school. The fictitious town of Summer Glen is **La Puente**, LA. The school is a mansion complex built for film star Antonio Moreno in the twenties. For many years it was a Franciscan convent, and it's now abandoned. Only the wrought iron gates and the gatehouse are visible. The **Canfield-Moreno Residence and Complex** is at **1923 Micheltorena Street, Silverlake,** LA (used also in *Scream 3*).

HAMLET
(1990, dir: Franco Zeffirelli)
Mel Gibson, Glenn Close, Alan Bates.
● SCOTLAND; KENT

Solid, traditional Shakespeare utilising real castle exteriors. Elsinore is a conflation of two British castles. The main one is **Dunnottar Castle**, set on a striking sandstone outcrop on Scotland's east coast, almost cut off from the mainland. It was one of the most impregnable of Scottish fortresses. To find it, head south from Aberdeen, through

Stonehaven on the A92. The battlements where the ghost appears and Ophelia's funeral were filmed here. The "To be or not to be..." soliloquy uses **Dover Castle**, overlooking Dover in Kent. it's open to the public from March to the end of October (*© 01304.211067, admission charge*). Another location was **Blackness Castle**, on the B903 east of Falkirk in West Lothian.

HAMLET
(1996, dir: Kenneth Branagh)
Kenneth Branagh, Julie Christie, Derek Jacobi.
● OXFORDSHIRE

Big, big widescreen production (the first British movie in years to be filmed in 70mm) shot largely in the studio. The exteriors of Elsinore are **Blenheim Palace**, in **Woodstock** village, eight miles north of Oxford. Home to the Duke of Marlborough, the house is open mid-March to the end of October (*© 0993.811325, admission charge*).

HANNAH AND HER SISTERS
(1986, dir: Woody Allen)
Mia Farrow, Dianne Wiest, Michael Caine.
● NEW YORK CITY; ITALY

The Mock-Tudor village: Pomander Walk

Another tour of Manhattan from Allen, revolving around the various relationships of sisters Mia Farrow, Barbara Hershey and Dianne Wiest, between three Thanksgiving dinners. Farrow's apartment is at the **Langham, 135 Central Park West**. Architect Sam Waterston takes Wiest and Carrie Fisher for a tour of his (and so, we presume, Allen's) favourite NY buildings, including the **Dakota Apartments, 172nd Street** at Central Park West (see *Rosemary's Baby*); the old bulging windows on West 44th Street; the glistening, deco **Chrysler Building, 405 Lexington Avenue** at East 42nd Street (see *Q – The Winged Serpent*); Abigail Adams' old stone house, **421 East 61st Street** at York and First Avenues on the East Side (it's now a museum and open to the public) and the **Waldorf-Astoria Hotel, 301 Park Avenue** between East 49th and East 50th Streets. He also takes them through the charming little mock-Tudor village of **Pomander Walk, 260-266 West 95th Street** to 94th Street. You'll be lucky to take such a romantic stroll through it, though – the street is generally locked to the public.

When Michael Caine 'accidentally' bumps into Barbara Hershey in the East Village, she takes him to the Pageant Print and Book Store – now the **Pageant Bar and Grill, 109 East Ninth Street**. They conduct their affair at the **St Regis-Sheraton Hotel, 2 East 55th Street** on the southeast corner of Fifth Avenue.

Allen takes a deeply unimpressed Wiest, who prefers coke'n'punk, to hear Bobby Short, regular jazz entertainer in the **Cafe Carlyle** in the **Carlyle Hotel, 35 East 76th Street** at Madison Avenue on the East Side. After her terrible singing audition, Wiest meets Carrie Fisher outside the **Booth Theatre, 222 West 45th Street** between Broadway and Eighth Avenue. The production briefly leaves New York when Waterston takes Wiest to the opera. The performance of *Manon Lescaut* was filmed at the **Regio Theatre, Turin**, Italy.

When hypochondriac Allen is found not to have a brain tumour, he dances out of the **Mount Sinai Hospital, East 98th to East 101st Streets** between Fifth and Madison Avenues on the Upper East Side. His brush with death takes him on a search for religion to the **Church of the Transfiguration, 1 East 29th Street** near Madison Square, but eventually he finds solace watching the Marx Brothers' *Duck Soup* at the **Metro Cinema, 2626 Broadway** at 99th Street on the Upper West Side.

HARD DAY'S NIGHT, A

(1964, dir: Richard Lester)
The Beatles, Wilfrid Brambell, Victor Spinetti.

● LONDON; WEST COUNTRY

Ringo goes walkabout: The Turk's Head, Twickenham

The groovy nightclub: Les Ambassadeurs, Hamilton Place

Lester, who started out making films with the Goons, set the style for pop movies for decades to come with his freewheeling, machine-gun edited, surreal day-in-the-life musical. The opening scenes of teen hysteria, presumably meant to be in Liverpool, were filmed at London's **Marylebone Station**. The journey shunts between Paddington Station, Minehead, Taunton and Newton Abbot in the West Country. The scene where the boys run alongside the train to annoy a grumpy commuter, is **Crowcombe**, north Somerset. And the final destination of the journey? Why, it's Marylebone Station, London.

The Beatles are driven to the Scala Theatre, which used to stand on **Charlotte Street**, just off Tottenham Court Road. A block of flats now occupies the site, but opposite you can still see the alleyway from which the Beatles emerge in time for the final concert. Wilfred Brambell, as Paul's grandad, excuses himself to go gambling at **Les Ambassadeurs** nightclub, **Hamilton Place**, behind the Hilton Hotel (see *Dr No* for details). The club's **Garrison Room** served as the nightclub where the group demonstrate those great sixties dances.

The TV studio, where the band rehearse and perform the climactic concert, is the Scala again, but when the four escape down the fire escape for a moment of pixilated fun, it's the iron staircase behind the Hammersmith Odeon (now **Labatt's Apollo**) they hurry down, only to land on the helicopter pad at **Gatwick Airport**. The scamperings about here are matched up with extra footage filmed on the **Thornbury Road Playing Fields**, south of the Great West Road, A4 (*tube: Osterley*).

Ringo takes off for a spot of meandering along the **Putney Towpath**, the south bank of the Thames just west of Kew Bridge. He samples pub sandwiches in the **Turk's Head, Winchester Road** at the corner of St Margaret's Grove, St Margaret's, Twickenham, conveniently close to the film studios. The chase sequence is around Notting Hill Gate, with the since-demolished St John's Secondary School, 83 Clarendon Road, used as the police station.

HARD TARGET

(1993, dir: John Woo)
Jean-Claude Van Damme, Lance Henriksen, Arnold Vosloo.

● NEW ORLEANS, LOUISIANA

Hong Kong action director Woo made his US début with this Van Damme flick, which was subsequently much altered by the studio, shot on location in New Orleans, in the **French Quarter**, and in one of the huge Mardi Gras float warehouses.

HARRY AND THE HENDERSONS (aka *Bigfoot and the Hendersons*)

(1987, dir: William Dear)
John Lithgow, Melinda Dillon, David Suchet.

● WASHINGTON STATE

Disney-ish Bigfoot fantasy which spawned the TV series. Set in the Pacific Northwest, where the family house, 437 Manning Drive, is in **Wallingford**. Lithgow searches for the missing Bigfoot in **Seattle**, where the inevitable **Space Needle** makes its trademark appearance. Forest scenes used the area around **North Bend**, east of Seattle on I-90, the location for David Lynch's *Twin Peaks*. The Hendersons' campsite is further east on I-90, near **Kachess Lake**, about 50 miles east of Seattle in the Wenatchee National Forest. Don Ameche's museum is at **Index**, on I-2 to the north.

HATARI!

(1962, dir: Howard Hawks)
John Wayne, Hardy Kruger, Elsa Martinelli.

● TANZANIA

Comedy-actioner with Wayne on the loose in Africa, rounding up animals for incarceration in zoos, filmed in the **Serengeti National Park**, Tanzania, around the foothills of Kilimanjaro's little twin, **Mount Meru**.

HAUNTING, THE

(1963, dir: Robert Wise)
Julie Harris, Claire Bloom, Richard Johnson.

● WARWICKSHIRE

A genuinely scary, low-key haunted house suspenser. Set in the United States, Hill House was supposedly 'built in the most remote part of New England he could find'. The great Gothic house is actually about five miles southeast of Stratford-upon-Avon in Warwickshire. Supposedly the most haunted house in Britain, the 60-room mansion has been converted into a hotel. The **Ettington Park Hotel**, is on the A34 in **Alderminster** (✆ *01789.450123*).

HAUNTING, THE
(1999, dir: Jan De Bont)
Liam Neeson, Catherine Zeta-Jones, Owen Wilson.
● FLORIDA; LINCOLNSHIRE

Audiences justifiably hooted at this ludicrous, FX-heavy remake. Hill House for the nineties is the gorgeously over-the-top **Harlaxton Manor**, an astonishing neo-Elizabethan folly which was home to mad Lord Peter O'Toole in *The Ruling Class*. Three miles from Grantham on the A607 in Lincolnshire, it's now Harlaxton College, the British Campus of the University of Evansville, Indiana. The carport entrance was added for the movie and the bizarre interiors – nothing like the real Harlaxton – were created on soundstages in the US. The Billiard Room, however, is Harlaxton's Great Hall. The kitchen scenes used **Belvoir Castle**, home of the Duke of Rutland, about seven miles from **Grantham** (see *Young Sherlock Holmes* for details).

HEAR MY SONG
(1991, dir: Peter Chelsom)
Adrian Dunbar, Ned Beatty, Shirley Anne Field.
● IRELAND; LANCASHIRE

The Liverpool club: Davenport Hotel, Merrion Square, Dublin

The Liverpool club is Dublin's Merrion Hall, now the **Davenport Hotel, Merrion Square**. The cliff which Dunbar is dangled over is at **Howth**, north of Dublin. Filming also took place at the **Cliffs of Moher** in County Clare. The tower, where Dunbar goes drinking with Ned Beatty (as singer Josef Locke), is **O'Brien's Tower** near the Cliffs of Moher.

HEAT
(1995, dir: Michael Mann)
Robert De Niro, Al Pacino, Val Kilmer.
● LOS ANGELES

Stylemeister Michael Mann remakes his own *LA Takedown* seven years on as a conscious love-letter to the architecture of LA. The opening robbery is on **Venice Boulevard** between Figueroa and Flower Streets beneath the Santa Monica freeway, south of downtown. The bank raided by De Niro and crew is **444 South Flower Street** at Fifth Street, downtown LA and the subsequent mother of all shoot-outs spills out onto the stretch of **South Figueroa Street** between Fifth and Fourth Streets.

The restaurant, where Amy Brenneman comes on to De Niro while he's studying a book on metallurgy, is the **Broadway Deli, 1457 Third Street** at

De Niro studies metallurgy: Broadway Deli, Third Street, Santa Monica

Broadway at the pedestrianised Third Street Promenade in Santa Monica (don't confuse it with the Broadway Bar and

The shootout: South Figueroa Street

Grill on the opposite corner). Not far away, on the Santa Monica sea front, is the Japanese restaurant Pacino stakes out, **Zen Zero, 1535 Ocean Avenue**.

Robbing the bank: Flower Street, downtown LA

De Niro and Pacino confront each other is one of the few remaining original **Bob's Big Boy, 4211 Riverside Drive** in Burbank. A brass plaque by the table commemorates the

The stakeout: Zen Zero, Ocean Avenue, Santa Monica

legendary spot. The hospital is **St Mary Medical Center, 1050 Linden Avenue** in Long Beach.

HEAT AND DUST
(1983, dir: James Ivory)
Julie Christie, Christopher Cazenove, Shashi Kapoor.
● INDIA; LONDON

More Forsterish Anglo-Indian culture clashing from the Merchant-Ivory-Jhabvala team, shot, of course, on location. The palace is **Hyderabad**; the house featured in the modern story is in the centre of the old city of Hyderabad, near the **Char Minar**. The club is in **Secunderabad** and the little bungalow is in **Gulmarg** in Kashmir. The views of England seen during the Indian duststorm are of **Richmond Park**.

HEATHERS
(1989, dir: Michael Lehmann)
Christian Slater, Winona Ryder, Shannen Doherty.
● LOS ANGELES

Teenage fantasies of revenge on the revolting, snobby 'Heathers' and the macho jocks are cranked up to murderous heights when mean 'n' moody crackpot Slater moves into Ryder's high school. This superb black comedy would have been even blacker had the original ending been kept. Set in Sherwood, Ohio, Westerburg High is a conflation of several schools, but the main location was the old Corvalis High School, now **Osaka Sangyo University of Los**

Westerburg High: Osaka Sangyo University of Los Angeles, Laurel Canyon Boulevard, Studio City

Angeles, 2921 Laurel Canyon Boulevard at Maxwellton Road about half a mile from Ventura Boulevard, Studio City in the San Fernando Valley. The school closed in 1987. The gym is **Verdugo Hills High School, Tujunga**, seen in many other movies, including *The Craft, one eight seven* and *River's Edge*. The **John Adams Middle School, 2425 16th Street, Santa Monica** was also used. The name Westerburg is a nod to Paul Westerberg, lead singer of Ryder's fave band of the time, The Replacements.

The jocks' 'cow pushing' takes place in a quiet corner of **Griffith Park**, LA.

HEAVEN CAN WAIT

(1978, dir: Warren Beatty, Buck Henry)
Warren Beatty, Dyan Cannon, Julie Christie.
● **CALIFORNIA**

The mansion: Filoli, Woodside

A remake, not of Ernst Lubitsch's 1943 *Heaven Can Wait*, but of the 1941 *Here Comes Mr Jordan*. The sumptuous mansion where Beatty finds himself ensconced is the **Filoli Mansion, Canada Road, Woodside**, off Highway 280 between San Francisco and San Jose. The mansion, whose name derives from the family motto: 'Fight, Love, Life', was seen in the opening credits of TV soap *Dynasty*, featured in Wayne Wang's *The Joy Luck Club* and was more recently seen as Michael Douglas' home in David Fincher's *The Game*. The house and gardens are open to visitors from February to October (© *650.364.8300, admission charge*). Visit the website at *www.filoli.org* for details and a virtual tour.

HEAVEN'S GATE

(1980, dir: Michael Cimino)
Kris Kristofferson, Christopher Walken, John Hurt.
● **MONTANA; IDAHO; OXFORDSHIRE**

As a film, *Heaven's Gate* is not the disaster that legend would have it, but it lost serious money and all but finished United Artists. The whole story is recounted in Stephen Bach's fascinating book *Final Cut*.

March to the graduation ceremony: New College Lane, Oxford

The prologue is set in Harvard University, but after the college refused permission for filming, Cimino amazingly decided on Oxford University as a stand-in, and the production decamped to England. The opening shot is **Tom Tower, Christ Church**. The band marches to the graduation ceremony under the **Bridge of Sighs** on **New College Lane**, to the **Sheldonian Theatre**, where Joseph Cotten gives the address. The alfresco dance uses the spacious quad of **Mansfield College, Mansfield Road**.

The Harvard graduation: Sheldonian Theatre, Oxford

The alfresco dance: Mansfield College Quad, Mansfield Road

The major location for the movie, though, is **Kalispell**, Montana, in Flathead County, where the roller rink was built. Kalispell is the gateway to Glacier National Park, Blackfoot Indian Territory. The town of Sweetwater was built over a parking lot in Glacier National Park on the edge of **Two Medicine Lake**. The mountain opposite is **Painted Teepee**. The Main Street of Casper, Wyoming is **Wallace**, Idaho, on I-90, a nondescript mining town, whose other claim to fame is as the home of Sweater Girl Lana Turner.

HELL IN THE PACIFIC

(1968, dir: John Boorman)
Toshiro Mifune, Lee Marvin.
● **SOUTH PACIFIC**

Boorman's allegorical two-hander has a US pilot and a Japanese officer marooned together on a tropical island. The location is **Palau Islands**, in the southwestern corner of Micronesia. The film used the wartime Japanese communication centre at **Airai** on the largest island of **Babelthuap**, alongside Palau's airport.

HELLO, DOLLY!

(1969, dir: Gene Kelly)
Barbra Streisand, Walter Matthau, Michael Crawford.
● **NEW YORK STATE; LOS ANGELES**

Two million dollars were spent by Twentieth Century-Fox on the famous turn-of-the-century New York Street, which still earns its keep on the Fox lot (you can see it in the sepia photo-montage of *Butch Cassidy and the Sundance Kid*). For location filming, the town of **Garrison**, on the Hudson River, upstate New York, was 'beautified' to the tune of half a million dollars. Garrison is on Highway 9d, about 30 miles north of New York City, just over the Hudson from West Point Military Academy. Some of the movie's dressing remains, including the gazebo in **Waterfront Park** (though this was replaced in the seventies when the original temporary wooden structure rotted), and the fake barbershop façade. Horace Vandergelder's Grocery Store is Garrison's bed and breakfast, **Golden Eagle Inn** (© *914.424.3067*), which retains the embossed 'V's on the hotel's doors.

Yonkers Railway Station is Garrison's own station.

HELLRAISER
(1987, dir: Clive Barker)
Andrew Robinson, Clare Higgins, Sean Chapman.
● **LONDON**

666 Lodovico Street: Dollis Hill Lane, NW2

The movie that launched the Cenobites, perverse pleasure-seekers from Hell, especially Pinhead. In the film, the house where Clare Higgins disposes of casual pick-ups to revive Sean Chapman with fresh blood, is known as '66 Lodovico Street'. The real house is actually much grander, and less dilapidated, than it appears in the movie, and it's the rear of the house that's seen. It's actually **187 Dollis Hill Lane**, NW2, high on the hill, the rear overlooking Cricklewood, where the interiors filmed at the **Production Village Studio, 100 Cricklewood Lane**.

HELP!
(1965, dir: Richard Lester)
The Beatles, Eleanor Bron, Leo McKern.
● **LONDON; WILTSHIRE; BUCKINGHAMSHIRE; AUSTRIA; BAHAMAS**

The Beatles second cinematic outing, this time in colour, is a more surreal, freewheeling affair. The four terraced houses, behind which the Fab Four inhabit a single luxury suite, are numbers **5,7,9 and 11 Ailsa Avenue**, west of St Margaret's Road just over Twickenham Bridge in St Margaret's, near Twickenham Studios. Ringo attempts, unsuccessfully, to have a sacrificial ring removed at classy jewellers **Asprey's, 165 New Bond Street**, W1. The 'Rajahama' Indian restaurant was the Dolphin Restaurant, now the **California Pizza Company, 8 Blandford Street**, W1, by Marylebone High Street.

The Beatles perform in the middle of a circle of Chieftain tanks, while being protected by the army, at **Knighton Down** on the B3086 about ten miles north of Salisbury at Larkhill on Salisbury Plain. When they hide out at Buckingham Palace, it's really **Cliveden** (site of the actual events recounted in *Scandal*), three miles northeast of Maidenhead on the B476 Hedsor road (*rail: Taplow*). Cliveden, a National Trust property once home to the Astor family, is open to the public (*© 01628.605069, admission charge*).

The riverside pub, with the Beethoven-loving tiger in the basement, is the historic **City Barge, 27 Strand-on-the-Green, Gunnersbury**, W4, east of Kew Bridge by Post Office Alley. The 15th century pub is named for the Lord Mayor's barge, which was moored nearby. For a really surreal experience, visit during high tide when the riverside terrace disappears and the front bar is awash with Thames water.

The ski scenes were filmed on the slopes at **Obertrauen** in Austria, while the sun-drenched beaches are at **Nassau** and on the surroundings of **New Providence Island** in the Bahamas. The airport is Nassau's itself. 'Another Girl' is performed on **Paradise Island** – a more appealing name to tourists than the original Hog Island. A major loca-

The 'terraced' luxury pad: Ailsa Avenue, St Margaret's

tion for *Thunderball*, the island is off New Providence's northeastern coast and is now linked by a concrete bridge. The upmarket eaterie is Paradise Island's famous **Cafe Martinique** (also seen in *Thunderball*), once the guest-house of Dr Axel Wenner-Gren, the man who bought an estate on, and developed Hog Island. It's on the shore of the man-made Paradise Lake (*© 809.326.3000*). The featured beaches are **Cabbage Beach**, the white sand beach behind Paradise Towers and Grand Hotel, and **Victoria Beach**, scene of the climactic chaos, down **Casuarina Drive** on the island's northwest shore.

HENRY: PORTRAIT OF A SERIAL KILLER
(1990, dir: John McNaughton)
Michael Rooker, Tom Towles, Tracy Arnold.
● **CHICAGO**

Controversial, low-key documentary-style film about a motiveless mass murderer, shot around Chicago, where Henry's pal, Otis, stalks victims on **Lower Wacker Drive**.

HENRY VIII AND HIS SIX WIVES
(1972, dir: Waris Hussein)
Keith Michell, Donald Pleasence, Charlotte Rampling.
● **HERTFORDSHIRE; KENT**

This historical drama was made in the wake of the successful BBC TV series and used the same star. Young Henry's jousting tournament was filmed at the unmistakably Jacobean **Hatfield House, Hatfield**, Hertfordshire (*rail: Hatfield*) (*© 01707.262823*). Catherine Howard is arrested at **Eton College**, meant to be Hampton Court, and executed in the School Quad here (see *The Madness of King George* for details of Eton). Filming also took place at **Woburn Abbey**, home of the Duke of Bedford, eight and a half miles northwest of Dunstable on the A4012 (*rail: Leighton Buzzard or Bletchley*) and **Allington Castle**, a couple of miles north of Maidstone in Kent (*rail: Maidstone*).

HENRY V
(1944, dir: Laurence Olivier)
Laurence Olivier, Leslie Banks, Robert Newton.
● **IRELAND**

Olivier's heroic wartime version of Shakespeare, filmed largely on stylised sets at the Rank Studios in Denham in England. Starting out in Shakespeare's Globe, the action becomes increasingly more naturalistic up to the thrilling set-piece Battle of Agincourt. Half a mile of track was laid on the estate of Lord Powerscourt in **Enniskerry**, near Dublin, for the famous shot following the charge of the French knights.

HENRY V
(1989, dir: Kenneth Branagh)
Kenneth Branagh, Derek Jacobi, Brian Blessed.
● **SUSSEX**

A more sober version for the eighties, shot on more naturalistic sets, but still largely in the studio at **Shepperton**. The prologue was filmed on the cliffs at **Crowlink**.

HERE WE GO ROUND THE MULBERRY BUSH
(1968, dir: Clive Donner)
Barry Evans, Judy Geeson, Angela Scoular.
● **HERTFORDSHIRE**

Gimmicky, very sixties coming-of-age sex comedy, co-scripted by American Larry Kramer – now a leading gay rights/Aids awareness activist in the US. It was filmed in swanky new town **Stevenage**, on the A602, north of London in Hertfordshire.

HESTER STREET
(1975, dir: Joan Micklin Silver)
Steven Keats, Carol Kane, Mel Howard.
● **NEW YORK CITY**

Hester Street: Morton Street, Greenwich Village

Quiet study of the life of Jewish immigrants on New York's East Side in the 1890s. The Lower East Side was recreated on the small block of **Morton Street**, between Seventh Avenue and Bleeker Street in the heart of Greenwich Village. The picnic was shot in **the Rambles** in Central Park. The Great Hall of Ellis Island, where the immigrants arrive in the US, is actually the **Tweed Courthouse, 52 Chambers Street**, another favourite NY location (see *Kramer vs Kramer* for details).

HIDDEN FORTRESS, THE (aka *Kakushi Toride No San Akunin*)
(1958, dir: Akira Kurosawa)
Minoru Chiaki, Kamatari Fujiwara, Toshiro Mifune.
● **JAPAN**

Widescreen historical drama, with much of the action seen from the point of view of two comic minor rogues, one short, one tall. Remind you of anything?. This is the movie that apparently inspired the structure of *Star Wars*. The landscape is the black volcanic slopes of **Mount Fuji**.

HIGH ANXIETY
(1977, dir: Mel Brooks)
Mel Brooks, Madeline Kahn, Harvey Korman.
● **CALIFORNIA**

This hit-and-miss Hitchcock parody signalled the start of Brooks' slide into mediocrity. Set in the quintessentially Hitch city of San Francisco, where the hotel lobby with glass lifts that triggers off Brooks' acrophobia, is the twenty-storey atrium of the **Hyatt Regency, 5 Embarcadero**

Center in San Francisco's Financial District – also seen as the lobby of *The Towering Inferno*. Filming also took place at **Fort Point**, beneath the foot of the Golden Gate

The Institute for the Very, Very Nervous: Mount St Mary's College, Bel-Air

Bridge, in homage to *Vertigo*. The Institute for the Very, Very Nervous, though, is in Los Angeles. It's the campus of **Mount St Mary's College, 12001 Chalon Road, Bel-Air**, which is just north of Bellagio Road where Hitchcock himself lived, at number 10957. The park used for the *Birds* parody, where Mel was actually splattered with mustard, is **Brookside Park**, north of

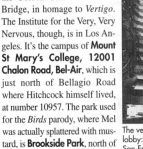

The vertigo-inducing lobby: Hyatt Regency, San Francisco

the Ventura Freeway toward the Rose Bowl at the western edge of Pasadena.

HIGH HOPES
(1988, dir: Mike Leigh)
Philip Davis, Ruth Sheen, Edna Dore.
● **LONDON; ESSEX**

Glum comedy of manners from Mike Leigh. Philip Davis and Ruth Sheen's flat is on **Stanley Passage**, behind Kings Cross Station, N1. It runs between Pancras Road and the famous stretch of Cheney Road by the gasometers, seen in *The Ladykillers* and *Chaplin* among many others. Davis and Sheen visit Karl Marx's tomb in **Highgate Cemetery**. Richard Rodgers' loved-or-loathed **Lloyd's Building** also puts in an appearance.

Davis and Sheen's flat: Stanley Passage, Kings Cross

HIGH NOON
(1952, dir: Fred Zinnemann)
Gary Cooper, Thomas Mitchell, Grace Kelly.
● **CALIFORNIA**

Sheriff Will Kane stands alone against the baddies, but fortunately wife Amy does not forsake him. The opening scenes, under the credits, were shot at the **Iverson Ranch** near Chatsworth, north of LA, but the fictitious Hadleyville, New Mexico was to have been played by the

The original choice for Hadleyville: Columbia State Park

Will Kane appeals for help: St Joseph's, Tuolumne City

Cowardly Sam Fuller's home: Columbia State Park

Main Street of Columbia State Park, a preserved goldrush town in northern California. By the time the crew arrived, however, spring had arrived and the bleak, bare main street of Columbia had burst into green leafiness. In the end, they used the Western Street at, by coincidence, Columbia Pictures in **Burbank**. Some of the real mining town remains in the picture, though. You can't miss the white picket fence of Sam Fuller, the cowardly friend who sends his wife to claim he's not at home. This is the **Wilson House** on Main Street, a few doors away from the Visitor Center, and the last privately-owned home in the town. **Columbia State Historic Park** is east of the town of Columbia, 45 miles northeast of Modesto in Tuolumne County (*open daily; © 209.532.4301*).

A few miles southeast of Columbia you'll find the church where Kane pleads for special deputies to face Frank Miller. It's **St Joseph's Catholic Church, Gardner Avenue** at Tuolumne Road in **Tuolumne City**, not a city at all but a tiny town just off Route 108. The railroad station was built alongside a watertower at **Warnerville**, a little to the southwest, about 14 miles east of Oakdale on the narrow gauge Sierra Railroad (see *Go West* for details of the railroad).

HIGH PLAINS DRIFTER
(1972, dir: Clint Eastwood)
Clint Eastwood, Verna Bloom, Marianna Hill.
● CALIFORNIA; NEVADA

Surreal revenge Western. The fictitious town of Lago was built, complete with interiors, at the strange lunar-like land-

Site of Lago: Mono Lake, central California

scape of **Mono Lake**, east of Yosemite National Park at the foot of the Sierra Nevadas. It's on Highway 395, central California. The opening and closing scenes of barren emptiness were filmed at **Winnemuca Dry Lake** near Fallon, east of Carson City, Nevada.

HIGH SIERRA
(1941, dir: Raoul Walsh)
Humphrey Bogart, Ida Lupino, Arthur Kennedy.
● CALIFORNIA

Bogart is 'Mad Dog' Earle, on the lam in this classic chase movie, which sees Bogie holed up in the mountains above **Lone Pine** , Route 395 in central California. **Cedar Lake** in the San Bernardino Mountains was also used. The final car chase takes off from Lone Pine, west along the winding **Whitney Portal Road** up toward the snowcapped High Sierras and Mount Whitney itself, which in 1941 (before Alaska joined) was the highest point in the US.

The climactic chase: Whitney Portal Road, Lone Pine, California

HIGH SOCIETY
(1956, dir: Charles Walters)
Bing Crosby, Grace Kelly, Frank Sinatra.
● RHODE ISLAND

The Philadelphia Story, laced with Cole Porter songs, is relocated to Rhode Island. The mansion, where Sinatra and Crosby vie for Grace Kelly is **Clarendon Court, Bellevue Avenue, Newport**. It's a private house, not open to the public, and was home to Claus von Bulow, the millionaire businessman cleared of the attempted murder of his wife, Sunny. The von Bulow story is told in *Reversal of Fortune* which, not surprisingly, wasn't filmed at Clarendon Court.

HIGHLANDER
(1986, dir: Russell Mulcahy)
Christopher Lambert, Sean Connery, Clancy Brown.
● SCOTLAND; NEW YORK CITY

A gobsmacking jumble of accents: Scot Connery plays Spanish nobleman Ramirez and Frenchman Lambert is immortal Scot Macleod, in this flashy nonsense made by a director of TV ads (and does it show). Macleod's home is the 13th century **Eilean Donan Castle** on an islet in **Dornie**, eight miles east of Kyle of Lochalsh on the A87, Wester Ross (© *01599.555202, admission charge*). The battle between the tribes was staged at **Glencoe**, on the A82 in Argyllshire. The beach, where Mcleod experiences the Quickening, is **Refuge Bay, Curtaig** near Morar, while

The confrontation with Kurgan: Silvercup Studios, Queens

the spectacular jagged peak where Ramirez teaches swordplay is **Cioch** in the **Cuillin Hills** on the Isle of Skye. In present day New York, Mcleod decapitates a rival swordsman in the carpark of **Madison Square Garden**. The scuzzy backstreet is the all-purpose fighting alley, **Cortlandt Alley**, between Canal and Franklin Streets alongside Broadway in Lower Manhattan (it's where Crocodile Dundee fights off muggers). The final confrontation with Kurgan is, conveniently, atop the **Silvercup Studios, 42-25 21st Street** in Queens, where the film's interiors were shot.

The first sequel, *Highlander II: The Quickening*, was made in Buenos Aires, Argentina, while *Highlander III: The Sorcerer* (aka *Highlander – The Final Dimension*) returned to Scotland, filming at Glencoe, **Glen Nevis** and **Ardnamurchan**.

HITCHER, THE
(1986, dir: Robert Harmon)
Rutger Hauer, C Thomas Howell, Jennifer Jason Leigh.
● **CALIFORNIA**

Not good news for student travellers. You will never, *ever* give anyone a lift after seeing this creepy chiller with hapless motorist Howell picking up psycho Rutger Hauer. The featureless desertscapes are around **Amboy, Barstow** and in **Death Valley**, California.

HOBSON'S CHOICE
(1953, dir: David Lean)
Charles Laughton, Brenda de Banzie, John Mills.
● **MANCHESTER**

Yorkshireman Laughton's great hammy turn as a tyrannical Lancashire patriarch, with some wonderfully grimy location filming around **Salford**, near Manchester, on the banks of the River Irwell.

HOLE IN THE HEAD, A
(1959, dir: Frank Capra)
Frank Sinatra, Edward G Robinson, Eleanor Parker.
● **MIAMI, FLORIDA**

Capra was well past his glory days when he filmed Sinatra as a hotel owner trying every trick in the book to stay in business. The hotel is the **Cardozo Hotel, 1300 Ocean Drive** at 14th Street, South Beach, Miami, an art deco gem restored in the eighties (*© 305.534.2135*), also seen in *There's Something About Mary*. Sinatra drives down Hotel Row on **Collins Avenue**.

HOLIDAY CAMP
(1947, dir: Ken Annakin)
Jack Warner, Kathleen Harrison, Flora Robson.
● **YORKSHIRE; LINCOLNSHIRE**

Comedy thriller, with the Huggett family (from BBC radio) and a murderer loose in that great British institution, the seaside camp. The fun spot was the old **Filey Holiday Camp**, a couple of miles south of the town of Filey on the Yorkshire coast between Scarborough and Bridlington. The railway station, where the happy campers arrive, is **Skegness Station** down on the Lincolnshire coast.

HOME ALONE
(1990, dir: Chris Columbus)
Macaulay Culkin, Joe Pesci, Daniel Stern.
● **CHICAGO**

Macaulay Culkin's house is to the north of Chicago, at **671 Lincoln Avenue, Winnetka** (*rail: Winnetka, Metra Commuter line from Northwestern Station*). Nearby is the green where Culkin visits Santa Claus, in front of **Winnetka Village Hall, Green Bay Road**. The green with the bandstand, where Culkin shops for a toothbrush, is one stop north of Winnetka, **Hubbard Woods**, while the church is way over in the western suburb of **Oak Park**. The airport from which the family leave is, of course, **Chicago O'Hare**. And the Paris airport at which they land? That's O'Hare too.

The MacAllister home: Lincoln Avenue, Winnetka

HOME ALONE 2: LOST IN NEW YORK
(1992, dir: Chris Columbus)
Macaulay Culkin, Joe Pesci, Daniel Stern.
● **NEW YORK CITY; CHICAGO**

Once again Culkin gets separated from his family, as they head for Florida and he catches a plane for New York. **671 Lincoln Avenue** and **Chicago O' Hare** reprise their roles from the first movie. Culkin stays at the **Plaza Hotel, Fifth Avenue** at 59th Street, New York, but this is a John Hughes-produced movie, and if it can be shot in Chicago, it will be. The luxury suite, in which the family is reunited at the end of the movie, supposedly overlooking Central Park, is the Conrad Hilton Suite of the **Chicago Hilton and Towers, 720 South Michigan Avenue**. Likewise, Eddie Bracken's toyshop is the unmistakable rusticated arch of the **Rookery Building, 209 South La Salle Street** at West Adams Street in the Loop (see *The Untouchables* for details).

HOME FROM THE HILL
(1960, dir: Vincente Minnelli)
Robert Mitchum, George Hamilton, George Peppard.
● **MISSISSIPPI; TEXAS**

Southern family saga filmed in lush colour around William Faulkner's home town of **Oxford**, on Route 6, west of Tupelo in northern Mississippi. The racing scene was filmed in an area of yellow sands near **Paris**, Texas, Route 82, north-east of Dallas (famous for *not* appearing in *Paris, Texas*).

HONDO

(1953, dir: John Farrow)
John Wayne, Geraldine Page, Ward Bond.
● MEXICO

Wayne defends Geraldine Page and her kid from Indians in New Mexico. Actually, it's old Mexico, at **Camargo** just over the Rio Grande, south of Laredo. When *Hondo* was released, a movie slated to be called *Bad Day at Hondo* needed a rethink, and so became *Bad Day at Black Rock*.

HONEYMOON IN VEGAS

(1992, dir: Andrew Bergman)
Nicolas Cage, James Caan, Sarah Jessica Parker.
● LAS VEGAS, NEVADA; NEW YORK CITY; HAWAII

Wacky comedy with Caan and Cage competing for Parker in a Vegas seething with Elvis impersonators. Filming took place at **Bally's Casino Resort, 3645 Las Vegas Boulevard South** (℗ *702.739.4111*). Apart from Las Vegas itself, where Cage gets to fly over the crazily spired and turreted 4,000-room (the largest in the world – at the time) **Excalibur Hotel**, on the corner of Tropicana Avenue and the Strip, there's location filming in New York. And Caan's Hawaiian estate was shot on the island of **Kauai**. The restaurant is the **Inn on the Cliffs, 3610 Rice Street**. Cage and Caan fight outside the **Kauai Marriott Resort and Beach Club**.

HOOK

(1991, dir: Steven Spielberg)
Robin Williams, Dustin Hoffman, Maggie Smith.
● LOS ANGELES; HAWAII

A misguided, sentimental gloss on the Peter Pan story, filmed almost entirely in the studio on the same sound-stages at the old MGM lot as *The Wizard of Oz*, **9336 Washington Boulevard, Culver City**. The few exterior shots of Neverland are the Hawaiian garden isla of **Kauai**, with the addition of much matte painting. Spielberg returned to Kauai to much greater effect for *Jurassic Park*. The Great Ormond Street banquet, held to honour Wendy, was filmed in the Ballroom of the **Park Plaza Hotel, 607 South Park View Street**, downtown LA.

HORROR HOSPITAL

(1973, dir: Antony Balch)
Michael Gough, Robin Askwith, Dennis Price.
● HERTFORDSHIRE

Trash horror at its trashiest, as Dr Michael Gough rules a bizarre health hotel – 'Hairy Holidays – fun and sun for the under thirties', which seems to be constantly awash with blood. Brittlehurst Manor turns out to be none other than **Knebworth House**, Hertfordshire (see Tim Burton's *Batman* for details).

HORSE SOLDIERS, THE

(1959, dir: John Ford)
John Wayne, William Holden, Constance Towers.
● LOUISIANA; MISSISSIPPI

Ford lost heart in this Civil War Western after the accidental death of a veteran stuntman. It was shot in the mangrove swamps of southern Louisiana; at **Natchez**, Mississippi, where the cadet school scenes were staged in the **Jefferson Military College**; and on the Homochitto River, Mississippi, some twenty miles south of Natchez, where the fatal accident occurred.

HOSPITAL, THE

(1971, dir: Arthur Hiller)
George C Scott, Diana Rigg, Barnard Hughes.
● NEW YORK CITY

Paddy Chayev-sky's scathingly black satire on the state of the US medical system survives Hiller's characterless direction. The hospital, where the mortality rate among the

The hospital: Metropolitan Hospital Center, First Avenue, Upper East Side

staff outstrips that of patients, is the **Metropolitan Hospital Center, 1902 First Avenue** on the Upper East Side.

HOT SHOTS!

(1991, dir: Jim Abrahams)
Charlie Sheen, Valeria Golino, Cary Elwes.
● CALIFORNIA

Top Gun spoof, not in the *Airplane!* league. The funeral takes place at the **Hollywood Memorial Cemetery, 6000 Santa Monica Boulevard**, between Gower and Van Ness, Hollywood (where the screenwriter was buried in Robert Altman's *The Player*). The flying sequences were shot above the Ridgecrest area of central California.

HOTEL DU NORD

(1938, dir: Marcel Carné)
Jean-Pierre Aumont,
Annabella, Louis Jouvet.
● PARIS

The real hotel: Hotel du Nord, quai de Jemappes, Paris

Marcel Carné's beautifully atmospheric, romantic tragedy, set in a canalside Parisian hotel, was made largely in the studio, but you can see the real hotel, which still exists: **Hôtel du Nord, 102 quai de Jemappes**, on the Canal St-Martin.

HOTEL NEW HAMPSHIRE, THE

(1984, dir: Tony Richardson)
Beau Bridges, Rob Lowe, Jodie Foster.
● QUEBEC, CANADA

John Irving's novel may not make a successful movie, but individual episodes are fun. The province of Quebec, Canada, stands in for New Hampshire. The hotel is the 140-room **Hotel Tadoussac, 165 rue Bord de l'Eau** (℗ *418.235.4421*). Tadoussac is on Route 138 on the north shore of the St Lawrence (there's a free ferry), about 170 miles east of Quebec.

HOUR OF THE WOLF (aka *Vargtimmen*)
(1967, dir: Ingmar Bergman)
Max von Sydow, Liv Ullmann, Ingrid Thulin.
● **SWEDEN**

Bleak, powerful Bergman, from his peak period. Artist alter-ego von Sydow suffers nightmares straight out of thirties Universal horror movies on a bleached out Frisian island. The island is a composite of the rocky headland at **Hovs Hallar** in southwest Sweden (where von Sydow memorably met Death in *The Seventh Seal*) and the island of **Faro**, off the island of Gotland in the Baltic Faro. The setting of many later Bergman films, it is a very private island, off limits to foreigners.

HOUSE
(1986, dir: Steve Miner)
William Katt, Kay Lenz, George Wendt.
● **CALIFORNIA**

The possessed house: Melrose Avenue, Monrovia

William Katt inherits the spooky house where an old lady died and gets hounded by his dead buddy from Vietnam. The outrageously gingerbread Victorian house can be found at **329 Melrose Avenue, Monrovia**, east of Pasadena, California.

The sequel, *House II: The Second Story*, uses another folly, the Romanesque **Stimson House, 2421 South Figueroa Street, Exposition Park**, south of downtown LA, now owned by the nuns of Mount St Mary's College.

HOUSE OF USHER, THE (aka *The Fall of the House of Usher*)
(1960, dir: Roger Corman)
Vincent Price, Myrna Fahey, Mark Damon.
● **LOS ANGELES**

The first of Corman's stylish, low-budget Poe adaptations, this was all studio shot of course, using matte paintings for the house exteriors. Canny as ever, though, Corman took advantage of a fire that swept through the Hollywood Hills to get the shots of Damon's journey through 'blighted' countryside with ashes and charred trees. For the final conflagration, Corman got permission to burn down a huge barn, on the verge of demolition, in Orange County, south LA. The spectacular footage of blazing rafters collapsing was to become a familiar favourite over the years as it cropped up with alarming regularity at the climax of Corman movies.

HOUSE ON HAUNTED HILL, THE
(1958, dir: William Castle)
Vincent Price, Richard Long, Carol Ohmart.
● **LOS ANGELES**

Price is the millionaire holding an all-night party in the supposedly haunted house cared for by jittery Elisha Cook Jr, in William Castle's classic gimmicky schlocker. The gimmick this time, Emergo, had a plastic skeleton trundled

The house on 'Haunted Hill': Ennis-Brown House, Los Feliz

out from behind the screen over the heads of the audience. Pretty scary. Castle eschews standard Gothic, and uses Frank Lloyd Wright's superb **Ennis-Brown House**, a Mayan-temple influenced structure built of pre-cast concrete blocks. The house, built in 1924, suffered years of neglect. After the release of the movie, it was nightly besieged by bozos, hurling bottles. It was slightly damaged in the 1994 quake, too. A frequent location for movies, ads and music videos, you can see the house as a movie producer's home in *Grand Canyon* and *Day of the Locust*; as a villain's hideout in *Black Rain* and *The Karate Kid III*, but perhaps most famously as Harrison Ford's futuristic home in *Blade Runner*. It's a private home now, and struggling to be preserved. There are occasional tours. The house is on a slope below Griffith Park, at **2607 Glendower Avenue**, Los Feliz, LA (℗ *213.660.00607*).

For the campy 1999 remake, the amusement park was largely a model, based on a real park in Orlando, Florida. The house itself consisted of miniatures and matte paintings. Only the entrance is real. It's the art deco frontage of the **Griffith Observatory, 2800 East Observatory Road** in Griffith Park, LA (see *Rebel Without a Cause* for details).

HOUSE ON 92nd ST., THE
(1945, dir: Henry Hathaway)
William Eythe, Lloyd Nolan, Signe Hasso.
● **NEW YORK CITY**

Highly influential documentary-style drama, with the FBI rooting out Nazi spies in New York, this was one of the first Hollywood movies to get right out of the studio. The house, supposedly on the north side of 92nd Street near Madison Avenue, where Elsa Gowns fronted for the spy ring, was actually 53 East 93rd Street. It's now demolished, but its twin, 55, is still standing. Other NY locations include the **Brill Building, 1141 Broadway**.

HOW GREEN WAS MY VALLEY
(1941, dir: John Ford)
Walter Pidgeon, Maureen O'Hara, Donald Crisp.
● **LOS ANGELES**

John Ford's romanticised dream of life in a Welsh mining village was to have been directed by William Wyler, who prepared the movie and worked on the script. Its heart is sort of in the right place, but sentimentality wins out. The village was a huge set built at the Fox Ranch, **Malibu Creek State Park, Las Virgenes Road**, off Mulholland Highway, Calabasas.

HOW THE WEST WAS WON

(1962, dir: Henry Hathaway, John Ford, George Marshall)
Carroll Baker, Henry Fonda, Gregory Peck.

● **SOUTH DAKOTA; COLORADO; WEST KENTUCKY; UTAH**

Long, sprawling history of the West, filmed as a Cinerama spectacular. The giant format caused all sorts of headaches, including the problem of where to place the microphones in such a wide-open, spacious frame.

The Henry Fonda section – the railroad and the buffalo stampede directed by George Marshall – was shot at **Custer State Park**, near Rapid City, South Dakota. Fonda's cabin, though, was in California, just off **Whitney Portal Road**, above **Lone Pine**, Route 395, against the breathtaking backdrop of Mount Whitney and the High Sierras. The site is now the Lone Pine Campground, a couple of miles west of the town. The Indian attack used the **Alabama Hills**, the striking red rock formations above Lone Pine (see *Gunga Din* for details). The Civil War section, directed by John Ford, naturally uses **Monument Valley**, Utah.

Other locations included **Paducah** on Route 24 in West Kentucky; and **Duck Creek Village**, 30 miles east of Cedar City, Utah (also the location for TV series *My Friend Flicka* among many others). There is a bit of padding, too, from other movies to bulk out the epic. You can see Santa Ana's army from John Wayne's *The Alamo* and battle scenes from Edward Dmytryk's 1958 *Raintree County*; while the modern day epilogue, with Spencer Tracy's voiceover lauding the wonders of the freeway system, is taken from the travelogue demo *This Is Cinerama*.

Site of Fonda's homestead: Lone Pine Campground

HOW TO MARRY A MILLIONAIRE

(1953, dir: Jean Negulesco)
Lauren Bacall, Marilyn Monroe, Betty Grable.

● **NEW YORK CITY**

Betty, Betty and Norma Jean share an apartment at **36 Sutton Place South**, by the East River in New York. Fred Clark is less than thrilled to be greeted as driver of the fifty millionth

Where to marry a millionaire: Sutton Place South, East Side

vehicle across NY's **George Washington Bridge**, West 178th Street crossing the Hudson River to Fort Lee, New Jersey. Also featured is the **Rockefeller Center**, West 48th to West 51st Streets between Fifth and Sixth Avenues, then only partially completed. It was Marilyn who, in 1957, ceremonially detonated the first dynamite charge to begin the excavation of the Time-Life Building.

HOWARDS END

(1992, dir: James Ivory)
Emma Thompson, Vanessa Redgrave, Anthony Hopkins.

● **LONDON; OXFORDSHIRE; SURREY; SHROPSHIRE; DEVON; WORCESTER**

The third of the impeccably produced Merchant-Ivory Forster adaptations uses a slew of real locations. Starting off in London: the cream-painted home of Emma Thompson and Helena Bonham-Carter – the fictitious 6 Wickham Place – is in **Victoria Square**, a quiet square hidden away just north of Victoria Station, SW1, whose photogenic charm was also used in *Around the World in Eighty Days*. Not far away, the courtyard of a converted Edwardian apartment block, the **St James Court Hotel, Buckingham Gate**, SW1 (℃ *020.7834.6655*) was used for the exterior of Anthony Hopkins' grandiose London residence. You can glimpse the landscaped courtyard, with its Shakespearian figures and central fountain, through the hotel's imposing gateway. The interior staircase, where Hopkins proposes to Vanessa Redgrave, is the office of movie producer Albert Broccoli, **South Audley Street** in Mayfair.

At the other end of the social scale, Sam West's modest home is on **Park Street** behind Borough Market, Borough SE1; another popular (though threatened) location you'll probably recognise from *Lock, Stock and Two Smoking Barrels* and *Keep the Aspidistra Flying*. The rainswept exterior of the Ethical Hall is near the Bank of England in the City of London, but the interior, where West picks up the wrong umbrella, is **Oxford Town Hall, St Aldgate's** at Carfax in the centre of town (another favourite, it featured as the interior of the Old Bailey in *A Fish Called Wanda*).

Emma Thompson's home, Wickham Place: Victoria Square, SW1

Sam West's modest home: Park Street, Southwark

Emma Thompson meets her brother: Magdalen College, Oxford

Buying the railway tickets: St Pancras Station ticket hall

Chelsea Embankment, where Anthony Hopkins gives West some bad, as it turns out, career advice, is actually **Chiswick Mall**, W4. The Porphyrion Insurance Company where Sam West initially works is the abandoned **Pearl Assurance Building, High Holborn**, WC1 (which was also used for the offices of Hopkins' Rubber Company), and the bank where he subsequently applies for a job is **Baltic Exchange, St Mary Axe** off Leadenhall Street, EC3, severely damaged by the IRA bomb attack on the City.

More venerable landmarks abound: Thompson and Redgrave are driven from the Mall through London's **Admiralty Arch** at the southwest corner of Trafalgar Square in a gasp-inducing money-shot, which seems to include every horse-drawn period carriage in the British Isles. The station where they buy tickets to Hilton is **St Pancras Station**, Euston Road, NW1, and Thompson takes lunch with Hopkins at **Simpsons-in-the-Strand**.

Out of London, Emma Thompson's brother studies at **Magdalen College, Oxford** where she meets him on the bridge over the Cherwell (you can explore the grounds – for details see Joseph Losey's *Accident*). The country cottage to which she retreats is at **Blackpool Sands**, where it overlooks the English Channel near Dartmouth, Devon.

In Surrey, south of **Englefield Green** on the A30 west of Egham, you can't miss the chimneyed and turretted outline of the **Royal Holloway and Bedford New College**, which was used for the nursing home in which Vanessa Redgrave expires. Built in 1887 as a women's college for pill manufacturer Thomas Holloway, and now part of the University of London, its elaborate design was inspired by France's Chateau de Chambord. Howards End itself, in the fictional village of Hilton, is **Peppard Cottage** on Peppard Common just off the B481, in the village of **Rotherfield Peppard** just to the west of Henley-on-Thames, Oxfordshire. Not nearly as remote as it appears in the movie – it's only a couple of doors from the village pub – the cottage was once owned by Lady Ottoline Morrell, who entertained members of the Bloomsbury group here around the turn of the century. Hilton was filmed in Worcestershire: the 'George Tavern' can be found in the village of **Upper Arley**, west off the A442 about six miles northwest of Kidderminster, and Hilton Station is **Bewdley**, a couple of miles to the south, on the Severn Valley Railway.

Hopkins' country mansion, where all the chickens come home to roost at the nightmarish wedding reception, is **Brampton Bryan**, on the A4113 about twelve miles west of Ludlow, Shropshire.

HUD
(1963, dir: Martin Ritt)
Paul Newman, Patricia Neal, Melvyn Douglas.
● **TEXAS**

Melodrama on a Texas ranch, with reckless son Newman

and stern father Douglas, from a novel by Larry McMurtry, author of *The Last Picture Show*. It was filmed in **Claude**, Route 287, about twenty miles east of Amarillo in the north Texas panhandle.

HUDSON HAWK
(1991, dir: Michael Lehmann)
Bruce Willis, Danny Aiello, James Coburn.
● **NEW YORK CITY; HUNGARY; ITALY; LONDON**

Big-budget misfire from the director of the wonderful *Heathers*. Set partly in New York, it features a 'wacky' chase over the **Brooklyn Bridge**. The prison is the notorious **Sing Sing Prison**, on the Hudson River, north of NYC. Filming also took place in **Budapest; Rome**; London and at **Castello di San Leo**, the gigantic medieval fortress, where Cagliostro was imprisoned and died, about fifteen miles southwest of Rimini, Italy.

HUDSUCKER PROXY, THE
(1994, dir: Joel Coen)
Tim Robbins, Jennifer Jason Leigh, Paul Newman.
● **CHICAGO**

Set in 1950s New York, *Hudsucker* relies mainly on huge stylised sets, but for authentic deco locations the movie decamped to Chicago. The Hudsucker Building is Chicago's **Merchandise Mart**, on the north bank of the Chicago River between Wells and Orleans Streets. Built by Marshall Field in 1931, the Mart boasted the largest floor area of any building in the world until the construction of the Pentagon in Washington DC. The charity ball was filmed in the ballroom of the **Blackstone Hotel, 636 South Michigan Avenue** (see *The Untouchables* for details).

The Hudsucker Building: Merchandise Mart, Chicago

HUNCHBACK OF NOTRE DAME, THE
(1939, dir: William Dieterle)
Charles Laughton, Cedric Hardwicke, Maureen O'Hara.
● **LOS ANGELES**

One of Laughton's really great performances, in a totally irresistible film. This RKO movie uses the set built at Universal in Hollywood for the 1923 Lon Chaney silent version. The bell tower interior is supposedly the Tuscan-style campanile of the **Mudd Hall of Philosophy, University Avenue** at Exposition Boulevard, on the campus of the **University of Southern California**, south of downtown LA (see *The Graduate* for details). The University claims it was used for the Lon Chaney version, but Mudd Hall wasn't built until 1928, so it's not likely.

HUNGER, THE
(1983, dir: Tony Scott)
Catherine Deneuve, Susan Sarandon, David Bowie.
● **LONDON; NEW YORK CITY**

Deneuve and Bowie are fashion-plate vampires staving off

The New York clinic: Senate House, Malet Street

the years with lashings of the red stuff in this designled horror. Set in New York, much of the movie was made in the UK. The disco is **Heaven**, the vast gay dance-spot under the Arches at Charing Cross in London. The art deco NY clinic is the foyer of **Senate House, the University of London, Malet Street**, seen also as the king's neo-fascist bunker in Ian McKellen's thirties-set *Richard III*.

Shakespeare's King Leo: 68th Street Playhouse, Third Avenue

and Greene Streets in SoHo. The cafe is run by Dean & DeLuca, the nearby gourmet food store. Woody Allen teaches creative writing to Juliette Lewis at **Barnard College**, part of the familiar **Columbia University**, over Broadway, west of the main campus, **West 116th Street and 120th Streets** between Claremont Avenue and Broadway in Morningside Heights. Sydney Pollack and his ditsy new girlfriend see Kurosawa's version of Shakespeare's '*King Leo*' at the **68th Street Playhouse, Third Avenue** at 68th Street.

HUNT FOR RED OCTOBER, THE
(1990, dir: John McTiernan)
Sean Connery, Alec Baldwin, Scott Glenn.
● CALIFORNIA; WASHINGTON STATE; NORTH CAROLINA; LIVERPOOL

Soviet admiral Connery hijacks his own 'invisible' submarine and attempts to defect, in this Cold War thriller made around **San Diego**, California, and at **Port Angeles** on Route 101, north of Seattle, on the Strait of Juan de Fuca, Washington State. The Russian Embassy, where shifty Joss Ackland bluffs and sweats, is actually **Sessions House**, a courtroom in Liverpool. Studio filming was at **Wilmington Studios**, North Carolina, and scenes were also shot in the Function Room of the **Park Plaza Hotel, 607 South Park View Street**, midtown LA.

HURRICANE, THE
(1999, dir: Norman Jewison)
Denzel Washington, Vicellous Reon Shannon.
● NEW JERSEY; TORONTO, ONTARIO

Dubious biopic of the wrongly-jailed boxer Rubin 'Hurricane' Carter, filmed in New Jersey, on many of the real locations, and in Toronto, Ontario. Jail scenes were shot at **Rahway State Penitentiary, Woodbridge Road, Rahway** (seen also in *Malcolm X*) on Route 1 on the River Rahway, and at **Trenton State Prison**, New Jersey. The robbery scene used the real **Lafayette Bar and Grill, Patterson**, New Jersey, which had to be restored for filming.

Much of the movie, though, was shot north of the border in Toronto, at: **Dupont Street** at Dundas Street; the **Harbourfront**; **Kingswood Road**; **15** and **53 Fraser Avenue**; **Riverside Drive**; **St Joseph's Health Centre, 30 The Queensway**; **Booksworth, 347 Bay Street**; the **Old City Hall**; the **Winchester Hotel, 537 Parliament** at Gerrard; **11 King Street West** and **Branksome Hall School, 10 Elm Avenue**.

HUSBANDS AND WIVES
(1992, dir: Woody Allen)
Woody Allen, Mia Farrow, Judy Davis.
● NEW YORK CITY

Multi-focused drama of marital, post-marital and extramarital relationships, recorded semi-documentary style. Mia Farrow has lunch with newly-single Judy Davis at the **Dean & DeLuca Cafe, 121 Prince Street** between Wooster

HUSH... HUSH, SWEET CHARLOTTE
(1964, dir: Robert Aldrich)
Bette Davis, Olivia de Havilland, Joseph Cotten.
● LOUISIANA

This troubled follow-up to the hugely successful *What Ever Happened to Baby Jane?* was all but completed with the re-teaming of Bette Davis and Joan Crawford, when Crawford's persistent illnesses brought production to a halt (read Shaun Considine's wickedly gossipy book, *Bette and Joan: The Divine Feud* for the fascinating details). The company aimed high for a replacement: not surprisingly, grandes dames Vivien Leigh and Katharine Hepburn both turned down the role in this Southern Gothic melodrama, which eventually went to Olivia de Havilland.

The Greek Revival mansion with its three-storey spiral staircase (mind those bouncing heads) is the **Houmas House**, just west of **Burnside** on Route 44 between New Orleans and Baton Rouge. It's open for tours, conducted by knowledgeable guides in Antebellum costume.

The Southern mansion: Houmas House, Burnside, Louisiana

HUSTLER, THE
(1961, dir: Robert Rossen)
Paul Newman, Jackie Gleason, George C Scott.
● NEW YORK CITY; LOS ANGELES

Rossen's downbeat, lowlife pool-hall movie, with Newman as Fast Eddie Felson – the character he returned to 25 years later in *The Color of Money*. Filming took place at LA's **Union Station, 800 North Alameda Street**, with studio work at the **Edison Studio, Decatur Avenue and Oliver Place** in the Bronx, NY.

I

I CONFESS
(1953, dir: Alfred Hitchcock)
Montgomery Clift, Anne Baxter, Karl Malden.
● QUEBEC

When Hitchcock needed a deeply Catholic environment to make this story of a priest riddled with sexual guilt and bound by the rules of the confessional, he headed north to Canada, filming in French Québec, around the narrow streets of the old quarter. Anne Baxter's politician husband speechifies at Québec's **Parliament Building, Grande Allée est** at avenue Dufferin (*guided tours; admission free*). She meets up with Clift on the **Lévis Ferry**, crossing the St Lawrence River from Lower Town (why do characters in films always meet furtively aboard ferries?). After Clift's inconclusive trial in the **Halls of Justice**, the real murderer hides out in the city's magnificent landmark **Chateau Frontenac Hotel, 1 rue des Carrieres** (© *418.692.3861*). Clift's church, Sainte Marie, is **Eglise Saint-Zéphirin de Stadacona** (Stadacona was the name of the native village which stood on the site Québec City now occupies).

I KNOW WHAT YOU DID LAST SUMMER
(1997, dir: Jim Gillespie)
Jennifer Love Hewitt, Sarah Michelle Gellar, Ryan Phillippe.
● NORTH CAROLINA; CALIFORNIA

This Kevin Williamson-penned slasher used mostly real locations – the fishing village is just what it says, **Southport**, North Carolina, also the location for *Crimes of the Heart* and *The Birds II: Lands End* (the disappeared-without-out-trace TV movie sequel to the Hitchcock classic), as well as Williamson's TV series, *Dawson's Creek*. The 'Shivers' store is a real department store on the town square.

The car accident was filmed on a scary stretch of the Pacific Coast Highway, **Meyers Grade** and **Timber Cove Roads**, north of **Jenner**, northern California. Other northern California locations include **Campbell Cove** at **Bodega Bay** (the famous setting for Hitchcock's *The Birds*); **Kolmer Cove**, north of Fort Ross and **Schoolhouse Beach** near Carmel. The college is **Duke University, Durham**, North Carolina.

The inevitable sequel, *I Still Know What You Did Last Summer*, moved down to Mexico, to be shot at **El Tecuan Marina Resort** and at **El Tamarindo, Jalisco**, on Mexico's Gold Coast. Filming also took place at the **University of Southern California**, in the Exposition park area of downtown LA.

I KNOW WHERE I'M GOING!
(1945, dir: Michael Powell, Emeric Pressburger)
Wendy Hiller, Roger Livesey, Pamela Brown.
● SCOTLAND

Wendy Hiller travels out to the Hebrides to marry a rich old man, but finds love on the way. Filmed in the Western Isles and Mull, the house, Erraig, where Wendy Hiller first stops, is the house of **Carsaig**, on the south coast of Mull.

Livesey shows Hiller **Moy Castle** at **Lochbuie**, a few miles east. Hiller moves out of Erraig to stay at Sorne, actually a Victorian castle set in Italianate grounds, called **Torosay**. The isle of Kiloran is the small isle of **Colonsay**, to the south of Mull. The whirlpool is **Corrievrechan**, between Scarba and Jura.

I LOVE YOU TO DEATH
(1990, dir: Lawrence Kasdan)
Kevin Kline, Tracey Ullman, Joan Plowright.
● WASHINGTON STATE

Underrated little black comedy with a sparkling cast, shot in **Tacoma**, Washington State. Kevin Kline's pizzeria (specially created for the movie) is the **Bostwick Building, 764 Broadway**, on the city's Antique's Row. The fabulous coffee-pot shaped café where Ullman hires doped-out William Hurt and River Phoenix to knock off her husband is, amazingly, for real – it's **Bob's Java Jive, 2102 South Tacoma Way**. The police station, where the attempted murderers are questioned, is the **Elks Club Building, 565 Broadway**. Also seen are **Stadium Bowl High School, 111 North E Street** and the **Holy Rosary Church, 512 South 30th Street**.

Tracy Ullman hires the flaky hitmen: Bob's Java Jive, Tacoma

I SEE A DARK STRANGER (aka *The Adventuress*)
(1945, dir: Frank Launder)
Deborah Kerr, Trevor Howard, Raymond Huntley.
● IRELAND; DEVON; ISLE OF MAN

If you can believe Deborah Kerr as an IRA activist who spies for the Germans, you'll swallow the plot of this thriller. A rare movie to have been shot on the **Isle of Man**. The Irish scenes were shot near Dundalk and in Dublin, with more filming in Devon.

I WANT TO LIVE!
(1958, dir: Robert Wise)
Susan Hayward, Simon Oakland, Virginia Vincent.
● CALIFORNIA

An Oscar for Susan Hayward as Barbara Graham, sent to the gas chamber on dubious evidence, in Robert Wise's downbeat, semi-documentary style anti-capital punishment drama, with filming at the real **San Quentin State Prison**, at **San Rafael** on I-580 just over the Toll Bridge

The prison: San Quentin, San Rafael

from Richmond, California. If you want to visit this notorious facility, there's a Visitor Center and Museum. You'll need to call ahead to book (℗ *415.454.8808*), and remember to take along photographic ID.

ICE COLD IN ALEX (aka *Desert Attack*)
(1958, dir: J Lee Thompson)
John Mills, Sylvia Syms, Anthony Quayle.
● LIBYA

Desert suspenser shot on location just outside the Libyan capital, Tripoli, in pre-Gaddhafi days, though the famous bar scene – later ripped off for a beer ad – was filmed in the studio at Elstree. And, yes, it *was* real lager, six pints of which were downed by John Mills before the shot was in the can.

ICE STORM, THE
(1997, dir: Ang Lee)
Kevin Kline, Joan Allen, Sigourney Weaver.
● CONNECTICUT; NEW YORK CITY

The soulless neighbourhood of Ang Lee's seventies-set family drama is **New Canaan**, on the northeast fringe of Stamford, Connecticut, home to seventies architects like Philip Johnson, who designed the original 'glass house'. Both the stunning seventies-built glass-walled home of Sigourney Weaver and the fifties-style house of Kevin Kline and Joan Allen can be found here. Filming also took place in **Greenwich**, Connecticut. Katie Holmes' New York apartment is on Park Avenue.

IF....
(1968, dir: Lindsay Anderson)
Malcolm McDowell, David Wood, Richard Warwick.
● GLOUCESTERSHIRE

Dazzling first part of the trilogy that slid spectacularly downhill from the patchy but enjoyable *O Lucky Man!* to the dire *Britannia Hospital*. The public school where Malcolm McDowell leads a revolt, set against a surreal background of the British class system, is **Cheltenham College** in Gloucestershire.

IMITATION OF LIFE
(1959, dir: Douglas Sirk)
Lana Turner, Juanita Moore, Susan Kohner.
● LOS ANGELES

Lush, glossy melodrama with Lana Turner as a Hollywood actress and Juanita Moore her black maid whose daughter, Susan Kohner, passes for white. Kohner gets to perform at Hollywood's old Moulin Rouge nightspot. It opened in 1938 as the Earl Carroll Theatre, with the first double revolving stage – 90 feet in diameter. It became the Moulin Rouge in 1953, and later the **Aquarius Theatre**. See it at **6230 Sunset Boulevard** between Argyle and El Centro, Hollywood.

IN A LONELY PLACE
(1950, dir: Nicholas Ray)
Humphrey Bogart, Gloria Grahame, Frank Lovejoy.
● LOS ANGELES

Bogart is an embittered Hollywood scriptwriter suspected of murder. **Beverly Hills City Hall, North Crescent Drive** at Santa Monica Boulevard (see *Beverly Hills Cop* for details) is featured, and filming also took place at the secluded European-style **Villa Primavera, 1300-1308 North Harper Avenue**, West Hollywood.

Bogart's place: Villa Primavera, North Harper Avenue, Hollywood

IN AND OUT
(1996, dir: Frank Oz)
Kevin Kline, Joan Cusack, Tom Selleck.
● NEW JERSEY; NEW YORK STATE

Kline is an English teacher outed during ex-student Dillon's Oscar acceptance speech (based on Tom Hanks' naming of his drama teacher when picking up the award for *Philadelphia* – though Hanks claims he checked with the teacher beforehand). Set in the fictitious town of Greenleaf, the movie was filmed around New York State and New Jersey, mainly at **Northport**, NY. Greenleaf High is **Pompton Lakes High School, Pompton Lakes**, New Jersey. The bar scenes were filmed in **Riverdale**, New Jersey. The Oscar exteriors were shot outside the **Lincoln Center for the Performing Arts**, New York. More scenes were staged in the Concert Hall at the Performing Arts Center of **Purchase College, 735 Anderson Hill Road, Purchase**, upstate New York.

IN COLD BLOOD
(1967, dir: Richard Brooks)
Robert Blake, Scott Wilson, John Forsythe.
● KANSAS; MISSOURI; NEVADA; COLORADO; TEXAS; MEXICO

Filming of the true story, as written by Truman Capote, of the murder of a family by two young punks. The semi-documentary style used the real-life locations, following the killers' flight from the scene of the murder, at **River Valley Farm**,

The real courthouse, used in the film: Finney County Courthouse, Garden City

River Road, Holcomb, Kansas, across Missouri, Nevada, Colorado, Texas and Mexico. The trial takes place in the actual courthouse used, **Finney County Courthouse, Garden City,** Kansas.

IN THE BLEAK MIDWINTER (aka *A Midwinter's Tale*)
(1995, dir: Kenneth Branagh)
Michael Maloney, Richard Briers, Joan Collins.
● **SURREY**

The church where the thesps rehearse *Hamlet* is **St Peter's Convent, Old Woking,** Surrey.

IN THE HEAT OF THE NIGHT
(1967, dir: Norman Jewison)
Sidney Poitier, Rod Steiger, Warren Oates.
● **ILLINOIS**

Detective Poitier ends up earning the respect of redneck bigot Rod Steiger in this worthy odd-couple cop movie, which won the Oscar for Best Picture (in the year of *The Graduate* and *Bonnie and Clyde*). Sparta, Mississippi really is **Sparta,** but in Illinois, about 40 miles southeast of St Louis. More scenes were filmed in the towns of **Belleville** and **Freeburg** on Route 15, the road to St Louis.

IN THE LINE OF FIRE
(1993, dir: Wolfgang Petersen)
Clint Eastwood, John Malkovich, Rene Russo.
● **WASHINGTON DC; LOS ANGELES**

Clint's DC hangout: Old Ebbitt Grill, Fifteenth Street

It's the old psycho-developing-an-affinity-with-unorthodox cop story again, with Malkovich taunting and seducing Presidential guard Eastwood. Set, not surprisingly, in Washington DC, where Eastwood drinks at traditional hack hangout the **Old Ebbitt Grill, 675 Fifteenth Street NW.** He chills out

Clint chills out: The Lincoln Memorial

with an ice cream on the steps of that inevitable DC location the **Lincoln Memorial,** in front of the Reflecting Pool.

The Denver hotel where Eastwood stays with Rene Russo is the familiar old **Biltmore Hotel, 506 South Grand Street,** on Pershing Square, downtown LA (see *Beverly Hills Cop* for details). He follows the Pres to LA, where the assassination attempt, and final shoot-out, take place at the futuristic high-rise glass-towered **Westin Bonaventure Hotel, 404 South Figueroa Street,** downtown LA (℡ *213.624.1000*). Another old favourite location, here showing off its **California Ballroom** – the largest in LA – the Bonaventure has been seen in plenty of movies including real-time thriller *Nick of Time,* Barry Levinson's

Rain Man, futuristic fantasy *Strange Days,* classic mockumentary *This Is Spinal Tap* and James Cameron's *True Lies.*

IN THE MOUTH OF MADNESS
(1995, dir: John Carpenter)
Sam Neill, Julie Carmen, Jürgen Prochnow.
● **ONTARIO, CANADA**

Set in New York, but made around Ontario, at **Scarborough,** east Toronto; and **King City,** north of Toronto. The New England village of Hobbs End is **Unionville,** about

The library: Saulter Street Library, Toronto

twenty miles from Toronto. Carpenter once more sneaks in an homage to Nigel Kneale – who wrote the script for *Halloween III* – by naming the village after the fictitious London tube station in *Quatermass and the Pit.* The library is the **Saulter Street Library,** Toronto.

IN THE NAME OF THE FATHER
(1993, dir: Jim Sheridan)
Daniel Day-Lewis, Pete Postlethwaite.
● **LIVERPOOL; MANCHESTER; DUBLIN**

Slightly dramatised but basically true story of Gerry Conlon and his father Guiseppe, two of the 'Guildford Four', wrongly imprisoned for the 1974 pub bombing. The Guildford pub is actually the **Brunswick Vaults, Tithebarn Street,** Liverpool – with a specially built addition blown up. The Old Bailey court is a conflation of **Liverpool Museum,** (at the front) and **Manchester Town Hall** (at the rear), while the interior is **St George's Hall,** Liverpool. The gaol, with the familiar metal stair, is **Kilmainham Gaol, Dublin** (see it also as Noël Coward's place of incarceration in *The Italian Job*). Exterior shots used **St Patrick's Institution** courtyard, and **Mountjoy Prison.**

IN WHICH WE SERVE
(1942, dir: David Lean, Noël Coward)
Noël Coward, Bernard Miles, John Mills.
● **HERTFORDSHIRE**

Lightly-disguised story of Lord Mountbatten, in the best stiff-upper-lip tradition. Mostly studio-bound, but the flashback picnic is on **Dunstable Downs,** Hertfordshire.

INDECENT PROPOSAL
(1993, dir: Adrian Lyne)
Demi Moore, Woody Harrelson, Robert Redford.
● **LOS ANGELES; LAS VEGAS, NEVADA**

Redford offers a million dollars for a night with Demi Moore. The Vegas casino, where Harrelson and Moore try to recoup their money and get the modest proposal, is the **Las Vegas Hilton, 3000 Paradise Road.** The 1,500 room hotel adjoins the Las Vegas Convention Center, about three quarters of a mile east of the Strip (it was the Whyte House in *Diamonds Are Forever*). The restaurant with the bizarre

Redford's estate: Huntington Library, San Marino

Harrelson loses his cool: The Oviatt Building, South Olive Street

Kiss and make up: Paradise Cove Pier, Malibu

singing statues, similar to Disneyland's kitschy Enchanted Tiki Room, is the Hilton's **Benihana Village**, a (very) stylised Japanese village setting. The images of Moore haunt a distraught Harrelson on the 46 television screens of the casino's **Race and Sports Room**. The waterfalls and volcanic flames can be seen a couple of miles south of the Hilton, outside the **Mirage Hotel, 3400 Las Vegas Boulevard South**.

Redford's Mediterranean-style estate to the north is the **Huntington Library, 1151 Oxford Road, San Marino**. Moore's real estate office is in the glorious deco **Crossroads of the World, 6671 Sunset Boulevard** at Cherokee, Hollywood. Designed to look like a stately liner docking among a fantasy of Spanish, French, Moorish and English villages, it was built in 1936 as an outdoor shopping mall. See it also as one of the great period backdrops for *L.A. Confidential*. The property she shows Redford around is the **Greystone Park and Mansion, 905 Loma Vista Drive, Beverly Hills** (see *The Loved One* for details).

The art deco restaurant, outside which Harrelson confronts Moore and Redford, was Rex-II Ristorante in the **Oviatt Building, 617 South Olive Street** at Sixth Street just off Pershing Square, downtown LA. More liner-inspired design – the interior of the restaurant was based on thirties floating luxury palace, the *Rex*. See the drop-dead stylish interior in Phil Joanou's ditzy thriller *Final Analysis*. It's since closed, and reopened as Cicada, a northern-Italian style place that's a favourite of Nic Cage (✆ 213.488.9488).

The kiss'n'make up ending was shot on the pier at **Paradise Cove**, a private beach west of Malibu, entrance on the 28100 block of the Pacific Coast Highway.

INDEPENDENCE DAY

(1996, dir: Roland Emmerich)
Will Smith, Jeff Goldblum, Bill Pullman.
● **CALIFORNIA; NEVADA; WASHINGTON DC**

A youthful fighter pilot president, a rainbow coalition of heroes and flying saucers fifteen miles wide in this surprise smash. The First Lady's hotel is the **Biltmore Hotel, 506 South Grand Street**, downtown LA, from which she escapes in the chopper (see *Beverly Hills Cop* for details). The desert airforce base is **Wendover Airport** in Nevada, where Will Smith drags the captured alien across **White Sands**. The skyscraper on which the new-agers gather to welcome the aliens, and which is the first target to get zapped, is the roof of the **First Interstate World Center**, north side of 5th Street west of Grand Avenue, downtown LA. The tunnel traffic jam was filmed in LA's **Second Street Tunnel** between Hill Street and Figueroa Street, downtown.

The aliens' target: First Interstate World Center, downtown LA

INDIANA JONES AND THE LAST CRUSADE

(1989, dir: Steven Spielberg)
Harrison Ford, Sean Connery, River Phoenix.
● **UTAH; COLORADO; VENICE, ITALY; JORDAN; SPAIN**

The third Indiana Jones film begins in **Moab**, in Utah. It's **Sevenmile Canyon**, in the spectacular **Arches National Park**, where River Phoenix, as the young Indy, spends the movie's prologue. But why are the fantastic rock formations suddenly replaced by featureless grassland the moment the train appears? Well, that's because the railway scenes were filmed on the **Cumbras and Toltec Railroad** in Southern Colorado. And it's a railroad you can travel, too. The return journey, taking a whole day, runs from Antonito, Route 285, south of Alamosa in Southern Colorado, 30 miles southwest through the San Juan Mountains to Chama in northern New Mexico.

The school where Indy teaches is **Rickmansworth Masonic School, Chorleywood Road** (A404) just a couple of minutes north of Rickmansworth Station. Also in the UK is the classically grand setting for the Berlin rally,

Indiana Jones takes class: Rickmansworth Masonic School, Hertfordshire

The Venetian church: Church of San Barnaba, Campo San Barnaba, Venice

Home of the Grail, Canyon of the Crescent Moon: Petra, Jordan

Berlin Airport: New Horticultural Hall, Westminster

The Himalayas: Mammoth Lakes, California

Thirties Shanghai: Macau

where Indy manages to get the Führer's autograph, which is **Stowe School** in Buckinghamshire. This former home of the Duke of Buckinghamshire, set in grounds landscaped by Capability Brown, is four miles north of Buckingham town and usually open to the public for the first two weeks in April and from July through to the beginning of September (© *0280.813650*). The stern interior of Berlin Airport is the **New Royal Horticultural Hall**, on the corner of **Greycoat** and **Elverton Street** in Westminster, SW1. It's occasionally open for exhibitions. See it as Berlin again in *The Saint* and looking similarly fascist for Ian McKellen's rally in *Richard III*.

The search for the Grail takes Indy to Venice, where he finds a clue in the **Church of San Barnaba, Campo San Barnaba**, south of Rio di San Barnaba off the Canal Grande southeast of the campo Santa Margherita in the Dorsoduro district. If you want to see the real interior, the 1749 church is open daily from 7.30am to noon and 4.30pm to 7pm. And although the Venice waterfront starts out as real, we're soon back in England, chasing around **Tilbury Docks** in Essex.

The fictitious Iskenderun (it was, apparently, a small sultanate south of Turkey and north of Syria) is **Granada** in Spain. The railway station, where Denholm Elliott is besieged by beggars, is **Guadix Station**, about thirty miles east of Granada on the N342.

The Grail, it turns out, resides in the Canyon of the Crescent Moon, in actuality, **Al Khazneh**, the Treasury of the rock city of **Petra** in the Edom Mountains of southwest Jordan. Petra is a three-hour drive from the Jordanian capital of Amman (though you can reach it more easily from Aqaba or from Eilat in Israel), at the end of a three-quarter-mile trek (on foot, camel or horse) through the Siq, a narrow rock fissure in the cliffs.

INDIANA JONES AND THE TEMPLE OF DOOM
(1984, dir: Steven Spielberg)
Harrison Ford, Kate Capshaw, Ke Huy Quan.
● **SRI LANKA; CALIFORNIA; MACAU**

The 'Shanghai, 1935' opening of the second Indiana Jones adventure, is the **Rua de Felicidade**, near to the Floating Casino in the rather sleazy Inner Harbour district of Macau, over the Pearl River Estuary from Hong Kong (see *The Man With the Golden Gun* for details). The Pink City of Jaipur was chosen as the Maharajah's abode, but the Indian authorities demanded script changes, so the palace was finally built at **Elstree Studios**. There was some filming, though, in Sri Lanka, where the Indian village was built amid the tea bushes on the **Hantane Tea Estate** high above the town of **Kandy**. The rope-bridge sequence was also filmed in Sri Lanka, on a 300 foot-deep gorge near a dam construction site (which meant a convenient supply of engineers and equipment to string the bridge).

Shanghai Airport is actually the **Hamilton Air Force Base**, at **Novato**, north of San Francisco, California. Also in California, just south of Yosemite National Park, **Mammoth Mountain**, a ski area, stands in for the Himalayas. Other locations include the **Tuolumne River**, which runs through Yosemite in its own 'Grand Canyon', and the **American River**, running from Lake Folsom to Sacramento.

INN OF THE SIXTH HAPPINESS, THE
(1958, dir: Mark Robson)
Ingrid Bergman, Curt Jurgens, Robert Donat.
● **WALES; HAMPSHIRE**

Missionary Ingrid Bergman cheerfully leads a bunch of orphans over the Himalayas. The original intention was to film in Taiwan, China, but derogatory references to the practice of foot-binding upset the Chinese authorities. Snowdonia stands in for the Himalayas, around the villages of **Beddgelert** and **Capel Curig**. The walled city was built at **Nantmor**, at the foot of the Cwm Bychan Valley near Beddgelert.

INNERSPACE
(1987, dir: Joe Dante)
Martin Short, Dennis Quaid, Meg Ryan.
● **CALIFORNIA**

Comedy take on *Fantastic Voyage*, set in San Francisco. The angular glass church, used for Quaid and Ryan's wedding at the end of the movie, is Frank Lloyd Wright's **Wayfarer's Chapel, 5755 Palos Verdes Drive South,**

Portuguese Bend at Abalone Cove, **Rancho Palos Verdes**. It was designed in 1949 to blend in with a grove of redwood trees, which have now gone. Filming also took place in **Northridge**, in the San Fernando Valley, north of LA.

INNOCENTS, THE
(1961, dir: Jack Clayton)
Deborah Kerr, Megs Jenkins, Michael Redgrave.
● SUSSEX

Creepily atmospheric adaptation of Henry James' *The Turn of the Screw*. Are the kiddies possessed, or is it the festering imagination of prissy governess Deborah Kerr? The house and grounds are **Sheffield Park**, 40 acres of gardens and lakes designed by Capability Brown, at **Dane Mill**, five miles northwest of Uckfield, on the east side of the A275 between east Grinstead and Lewes in Sussex. The gardens are open to the public on certain days of the week (*©* *01825.790231, admission charge*). A bizarre prequel, *The Nightcomers* starring Marlon Brando, was filmed by Michael Winner.

INTERNAL AFFAIRS
(1990, dir: Mike Figgis)
Richard Gere, Andy Garcia, Laurie Metcalf.
● LOS ANGELES

Mike Figgis' dark and uncomfortable police corruption thriller is a riff on *Othello*, with Gere cast against type as a nasty Iago character. Set around LA, where the LAPD HQ is naturally **City Hall, 200 North Spring Street**. Andy Garcia spies on his wife's furtive lunch with Gere at the restaurant of the venerable **Hollywood Roosevelt Hotel, 7000 Hollywood Boulevard**, Hollywood.

Garcia spies on Gere: Hollywood Roosevelt Hotel

INTERVIEW WITH THE VAMPIRE: THE VAMPIRE CHRONICLES
(1994, dir: Neil Jordan)
Tom Cruise, Brad Pitt, Kirsten Dunst.
● SAN FRANCISCO; LOUISIANA; PARIS

You can see the disused building used as St Martin's Hotel, where Christian Slater gets Brad Pitt's story, at the corner of **Market Street** with **Golden Gate Avenue** and **Taylor Street** in San Francisco. Pitt's estate is **Oak Alley**

PHOTOGRAPH COURTESY OAK ALLEY PLANTATION

Pitt's estate: Oak Alley Plantation, Vacherie

Plantation, 3645 Los Angeles Highway 18, Vacherie in Louisiana. One of the restored mansions between New Orleans and Baton Rouge (it was also used for the remake of *The Long, Hot Summer*), Oak Alley, built in 1839, takes its name from the avenue of 28 oaks leading up to it. The house is open to the public most days, from 9am to 5pm (*©* *504.523.4351, admission charge*). The Parisian hotel is actually the **Paris Opera House**.

The St Martin Hotel: Market Street

INTOLERANCE
(1916, dir: DW Griffith)
Mae Marsh, Lillian Gish, Constance Talmadge.
● LOS ANGELES

Griffith's vast historical drama, linking four stories of intolerance through the ages, was a landmark in cinema. The vast 'Babylon' set, with its rearing elephants, has always been a symbol of overblown Hollywood epics. It's long since vanished of course. It stood at 4500 Sunset Boulevard at the junction with Hollywood Boulevard in Silverlake.

INTRUDER, THE (aka *The Stranger*)
(1961, dir: Roger Corman)
William Shatner, Frank Maxwell, Beverly Lunsford.
● MISSOURI

Roger Corman's message pic about racism in the Deep South was filmed in southeast Missouri at **Sikeston**, on Highways 55 and 57. Initially co-operative locals were given watered down and edited versions of the script, but once the full story began to leak out, enthusiasm declined somewhat. The film company managed to grab a bit more location shooting at nearby **East Prairie High School**, before hotfooting it out of town.

INVASION OF THE BODY SNATCHERS
(1956, dir: Don Siegel)
Kevin McCarthy, Dana Wynter, King Donovan.
● LOS ANGELES

Despite the tacked-on 'safe' ending, Don Siegel's sci-fi noir remains a classic. The fictional town of Santa Mira was based on Mill Valley, on Highway 1 over the Golden Gate Bridge from San Francisco, which is where the director wanted to film. But wouldn't you know it, Allied Artists discovered that the area around their East Hollywood studio in Silverlake looked just like Mill Valley. The studio, now KCET TV Studios, still stands at **4401 Sunset Boulevard**. Much of the movie was shot in the studio, in a mere 23 days. The studio entrance itself features as Santa Mira's hospital. Location shooting was at nearby **Glendale;**

Escaping the pod people: Westshire Drive, Hollywood Hills

Santa Mira town square: Sierra Madre

Chatsworth in northwest LA; and the neighbourhood of **Los Feliz**. Santa Mira town square is the square of **Sierra Madre**, a sweet little community to the east of Pasadena. Much revamped, you can still recognise the square at the junction of **Sierra Madre Boulevard** and **Baldwin Avenue**.
More of Santa Mira was shot at **Beachwood Canyon** and **Belden Drive** in the maze of roads east of the Hollywood freeway south of Hollywood Reservoir. The flight of steps, up which McCarthy and Wynter escape from the pod people, can be seen at **2744 Westshire Drive**, at the corner of **Beachwood Drive** and **Woodshire Drive**. At the top of the steps, they hide out in the **Bronson Canyon Caves**, to the north in Griffith Park.

INVASION OF THE BODY SNATCHERS
(1978, dir: Philip Kaufman)
Donald Sutherland, Brooke Adams, Leonard Nimoy.
● **SAN FRANCISCO**

The updated remake, set in, and filmed in, San Francisco. Don Siegel, director of the original, puts in an appearance, and Kevin McCarthy repeats his role in a tiny cameo, before being run down by a car at the corner of **Leavenworth** and **Turk**. Donald Sutherland lives on **Union Street** near Castle, and works at the **Department of Public Health, 101 Grove Street**. Brooke Adams lives at **720 Steiner Street**, one of the bunch of cutesy Victorian houses overlooking Alamo Square, and backed by the San Fran skyline, that are used is countless bay City movies. The humans escape down Montgomery Street to the **Filbert Steps**. A third version, called *Body Snatchers*, was made by Abel Ferrara at an abandoned army base, Craig Field, in **Selma**, Alabama.

IPCRESS FILE, THE
(1965, dir: Sidney J Furie)
Michael Caine, Guy Doleman, Nigel Green.
● **LONDON**

First of three 1960s Harry Palmer spy movies from Len Deighton's books (a series revived in straight-to-video productions years later), shot on location around London. The station from which the scientist disappears is **Marylebone Station**, NW1.

IRON HORSE, THE
(1924, dir: John Ford)
George O'Brien, Madge Bellamy, Cyril Chadwick.
● **NEVADA**

In 1923, Paramount had a great hit with its epic Western

The Covered Wagon, and Fox determined to repeat the success with a grand-scale picture of its own. At $450,000, the story of the building of the first transcontinental railroad turned out to be Fox's most expensive movie at the time. It was made on location at **Wadsworth**, 30 miles east of Reno on Route 80, Nevada. Three shack towns, which became instant ghost towns once shooting was over, were built to house the crew, the cooks and the 5,000 extras.

IRON MASK, THE
(1929, dir: Allan Dwan)
Douglas Fairbanks, Nigel de Brulier, Belle Bennett.
● **CALIFORNIA**

Dumas' follow up to *The Three Musketeers*, a big silent adventure, used **Point Lobos** on the Monterey Peninsula, south of San Francisco, for its exteriors.

ISADORA (aka *The Loves of Isadora*)
(1968, dir: Karel Reisz)
Vanessa Redgrave, Jason Robards, James Fox.
● **LONDON; DEVON; BUCKINGHAMSHIRE; FRANCE; ITALY; YUGOSLAVIA**

Reisz's episodic biopic of the eccentric American dancer (inspired by Ken Russell's delirious TV movie, *Isadora, the Biggest Dancer in the World*, which starred the sublime Vivian Pickles) takes in locations around the world.
The US theatre, where 'Peppy Dora' earns $300 with high kicks to take her family to Europe, is **Wilton's Music Hall, 1 Grace's Alley, Wellclose Square**, off Cable Street, E1. Long disused but recently rediscovered, see *Chaplin* for details. Bellevue, the French school 'ten miles from Paris', bought for Isadora by sewing machine heir Paris Singer, can be found in Buckinghamshire. It's the extraordinary **Waddesdon Manor**, a Victorian mansion built atop a Home Counties hill in the style of a Loire Valley chateau for Ferdinand de Rothschild. You can see it at the west end of Waddesdon village, six miles northwest of Aylesbury on the A41. Owned by the National Trust, the house and grounds are open to the public from March to December (*rail: Aylesbury*) (© *01296.822850, admission charge*). You can also see the chateau in *Never Say Never Again* and in *Carry On – Don't Lose Your Head*. Paris Singer's dazzling English home is the real thing – **Oldway Mansion, Paignton** in Devon. It's now Paignton's Civic Centre, though the grounds and tennis courts are open to the public. Theatre scenes were shot at the **Theatre Royal, Drury Lane**, WC2. More London filming took place in the **British Museum, Great Russell Street**, WC1, where Isadora is enthralled by the Parthenon's Elgin Marble.
The Berlin Theatre is the National Theatre at **Rijeka** in the former Yugoslavia. The Nice scenes, set during the twenties at the end of Isadora's career, were shot at **Opatija** on the Croatian coast. Henri's Bar, the beach bar where Isadora finally meets Mr Bugatti, was built at **Mostenica Beach**, Yugoslavia. It was so popular, and sturdy, that locals asked to keep it. Filming also took place at **Ptuj** and **Zagreb** in the former Yugoslavia.
The grotesque car accident – far more spectacular and unbelievable than the movie version – actually occurred outside the Hotel Negresco on the seafront at Nice, itself

a movie location seen in Jean Vigo's *A Propos De Nice* and *The Day of the Jackal*.

ISLAND OF LOST SOULS
(1933, dir: Erle C Kenton)
Charles Laughton, Bela Lugosi, Richard Arlen.
● CALIFORNIA

Remade twice as *The Island of Dr Moreau*, the chilling first adaptation of HG Wells' novel uses **Catalina Island**, off the coast of LA, as Moreau's kingdom.

IT ALWAYS RAINS ON SUNDAY
(1947, dir: Robert Hamer)
Googie Withers, John McCallum, Jack Warner.
● LONDON

Downbeat crime melodrama set in the slummy, post-war East End of London. Most of the film was shot around the **Petticoat Lane** area, but some was filmed around Chalk Farm, at **Hartland Road**, NW1, with Holy Trinity Church in the background. The final chase was shot in the **Temple Mills Railway Yard, Stratford**, E15.

IT HAPPENED AT THE WORLD'S FAIR
(1963, dir: Norman Taurog)
Elvis Presley, Gary Lockwood, Joan O'Brien.
● SEATTLE, WASHINGTON STATE

Presley and Lockwood are a couple of pilots letting loose in Seattle, at the World Fair. Featuring now famous Seattle landmarks like the **Space Needle** (see *The Parallax View* for details) and the city's **Hallweg Monorail**, which were built specially for the fair.

IT SHOULDN'T HAPPEN TO A VET
(1976, dir: Eric Till)
John Alderton, Colin Blakely, Lisa Harrow.
● YORKSHIRE

More stories of Yorkshire vet James Herriot during the thirties, a sequel to *All Creatures Great and Small*. This time around, the vets' practice, Skeldale House, is on the corner of the village green in **Reeth**, on the B6270, some twenty miles southwest of Darlington.

ITALIAN JOB, THE
(1969, dir: Peter Collinson)
Michael Caine, Noël Coward, Benny Hill.
● TURIN, ITALY; LONDON; IRELAND

The interior of Wormwood Scrubs where Mr Bridger (Noël Coward) masterminds the job, is actually **Kilmainham Gaol, Dublin** (seen also in *In the Name of the Father*). Michael Caine's coming out do is at the **Royal Lancaster Hotel**. His oh-so-sixties bric-a-brac cluttered flat is **18 Denbigh Close**, off the north end of Portobello Road, W11, next to Alice's junk shop.

The robbery takes place in Turin during a massive traffic jam. The jam starts by the **Palazza Madama** on **Piazza Castello**. Unlike BMC, manufacturers of the Mini, who offered minimal co-operation, Fiat offered limitless help. The rooftop leap, in fact, was filmed on the roof of the Fiat factory, dressed to look like a Turin street. The chase through the sewer was staged in England. Although the entrance and exit were filmed in Turin, the length of sewer used was a new pipe system being installed in Coventry.

The famous ending, dreamed up by a Paramount executive in Hollywood, hated by director Collinson and star Caine, and assigned to a second unit, was shot above a reservoir at **Ceresole Reale**, about 40 miles northwest of Turin.

IT'S A MAD MAD MAD MAD WORLD
(1963, dir: Stanley Kramer)
Spencer Tracy, Jimmy Durante, Milton Berle.
● CALIFORNIA

Zillions of stars fill out three hours-plus of widescreen slapstick, concerning a stash of buried loot. The movie was shot all over southern California, in millionaires' desert playground **Palm Springs**, and south of LA in **Long Beach**. The 'W' everybody is looking for, which turns out to be four palm trees, was in the park at **Portuguese Point**, on the southwest tip of the Palos Verdes Peninsula.

IT'S A WONDERFUL LIFE
(1946, dir: Frank Capra)
James Stewart, Henry Travers, Donna Reed.
● LOS ANGELES

Hard to believe that this classic was a box office failure on its first release. The town of Bedford Falls, where elderly angel Henry Travers convinces suicidal Stewart that life hasn't been in vain, was totally recreated with a huge 3-block-long set on RKO's **Encino Ranch** in the San Fernando Valley. The gym floor which opens up to reveal a swimming pool is still in action at **Beverly Hills High School, 255 South Lasky Drive**, at Moreno Drive in Beverly Hills, where the 'Swim-Gym' is still signposted.

The dance-hall-swimming pool: Swim-gym, Beverly Hills High School

IVANHOE
(1952, dir: Richard Thorpe)
Robert Taylor, Joan Fontaine, Elizabeth Taylor.
● NORTHUMBERLAND

Colourful historical fluff, including filming at **Bamburgh Castle**, east of Belford in Northumberland. The castle is open daily from April to October (*© 01669.620314, admission charge*).

J

JFK
(1991, dir: Oliver Stone)
Kevin Costner, Joe Pesci, Gary Oldman.

● **DALLAS, TEXAS; NEW ORLEANS, LOUISIANA; WASHINGTON DC**

Somehow, Oliver Stone got permission to use many actual sites for his contentious film about the Kennedy assassination, including **Dealey Plaza** itself, in Dallas, where the President was murdered by persons unknown. The sixth floor of the Texas Book Depository, now the **Dallas County Administration Building, 411 Elm Street**, is a fascinating museum telling the various stories of the assassination. Vast amounts of background detail are available on self-operated videos and recorded commentaries. The museum is open seven days a week (© *214.747.6660, www.jfk.org/home.htm*). The movie actually filmed on the seventh floor, which not only interfered less with the museum, but compensated for the growth of the tree outside, over which Lee Harvey Oswald is supposed to have shot.

Other genuine locations include the boarding house Oswald occupied in 1962, to which he returned after the shooting (and where police officer Tippit was killed), at **1026 North Beckley Avenue**; the **Texas Theater, 231 West Jefferson Street**, where Oswald was arrested and the old **Dallas City Jail, Main Street** at Harwood, where he was shot by Jack Ruby.

Not every location is so real, however. Parkland Hospital, where JFK's body is taken immediately after the shooting, is actually **St Joseph's Hospital, 5909 Harry Hines Boulevard, Fort Worth**, Texas. Jack Ruby's seedy nightclub, The Carousel, is, ironically, represented by the elegant Venetian Room of the **Fairmount Hotel, 1717 North Akard Street** at Ross Avenue, downtown Dallas. The New Orleans bar in which DA Costner watches the TV news reports of the shooting is the arty, laidback **Napoleon House, 500 Chartres Street** at the corner of St Louis Street in the French Quarter. Sleazeball Ed Asner's office is at **531 Lafayette Street**, with the other entrance around the corner at **544 Camp Street**, just west of the French Quarter.

Costner's office is in the **Louisiana Supreme Court Building, 400 Royal Street**, New Orleans. His confrontation with lawyer John Candy takes place over a meal at **Antoine's Restaurant, 713 St Louis Street**, New Orleans. The climactic court scene was filmed in the actual location of the Clay Shaw trial, the **Criminal Courts Building, Tulane and Broad Streets**.

Washington DC filming includes JFK's last resting place, **Arlington National Cemetery** at Arlington Memorial Bridge (*metro: Arlington Cemetery*); and Costner's clandestine meeting with Donald Sutherland at the **Lincoln Memorial**, 23rd Street NW (*metro: Foggy Bottom*).

JABBERWOCKY
(1977, dir: Terry Gilliam)
Michael Palin, John Le Mesurier, Warren Mitchell.

● **WALES**

Gilliam's imaginative, blood and mud-soaked Dark Ages fantasy will appeal to fans of *Monty Python and the Holy Grail*. The medieval locales are **Chepstow Castle**, Chepstow, Gwent, near the M4 Severn Bridge on the England-Wales border; and **Pembroke Castle**, Pembrokeshire, down towards Wales' southwest tip; as well as **Bosherston Quarry**, about seven miles south.

JACKIE BROWN
(1997, dir: Quentin Tarantino)
Pam Grier, Samuel L Jackson, Robert Forster.

● **LOS ANGELES**

Apart from the occasional directorial flourish, you'd hardly recognise this Elmore Leonard adaptation as the work of the man who made *Pulp Fiction*. The bar 'near the airport', where Jackson and Robert De Niro hang out, is the **Cockatoo Inn, 4334 West Imperial Highway** at Hawthorne Boulevard, which is indeed not far from Los Angeles International. The vast shopping mall, further south in the South Bay area, is the **Del Amo Fashion Center, Hawthorne Boulevard**. Robert Forster's Cherry Bail Bonds office is at **724 East Carson Street, Carson**.

The shopping mall: Del Amo Fashion Center, Hawthorne Boulevard

The lone gunman?: Texas Book Depository, Dealey Plaza

The airport bar: The Cockatoo Inn, West Imperial Highway, Hawthorne

JAMÓN, JAMÓN

(1992, dir: José Juan Bigas Luna)
Javier Bardem, Jordi Mollà, Penélope Cruz.
● SPAIN

Bigas Luna's sexual satire was made in the **Monegros** region of Spain.

JANE EYRE

(1996, dir: Franco Zeffirelli)
Charlotte Gainsbourg, William Hurt, Anna Paquin.
● DERBYSHIRE; YORKSHIRE

Unlike the studio-bound forties Hollywood version, starring Joan Fontaine and Orson Welles, florid Italian director Zeffirelli went on location for Thornfield Hall, using **Haddon Hall**, just south of Bakewell in Derbyshire. Open to the public from March to September (*© 01629.812855, admission charge*). Haddon Hall is also seen as Edward VI's estate in *Lady Jane*. Jane Eyre meets Rochester at **Brimham Rocks**, near Pateley Bridge, north Yorkshire.

JASON AND THE ARGONAUTS

(1963, dir: Don Chaffey)
Todd Armstrong, Honor Blackman, Niall MacGinnis.
● ITALY

Jason goes in search of the Golden Fleece in this showcase for the animation of Ray Harryhausen. Music score by the magnificent Bernard Herrmann. Location filming took place at **Palinuro**, Italy.

JASSY

(1947, dir: Bernard Knowles)
Margaret Lockwood, Dennis Price, Patricia Roc.
● HERTFORDSHIRE

The village: Aldbury

The mansion: Moor Park Golf Club, Batchworth Heath

Colourful Gainsborough melodrama with gypsy servant Lockwood falling for her master and the priceless Esma Cannon swooning in the witness box. The local village is **Aldbury**, off the A41, six miles northwest of Hemel Hempstead (see *The Dirty Dozen* for details). The grand house is **Moor Park Golf Club, Anson Walk** in Batchworth Heath on the A404 north of Northwood.

JAWS

(1975, dir: Steven Spielberg)
Roy Scheider, Richard Dreyfuss, Robert Shaw.
● MASSACHUSETTS

Dazzlingly directed thriller that launched the Spielberg phenomenon and spawned a shoal of sloppy sequels and

Amity Island: Edgartown, Martha's Vineyard

copies. The fictitious Amity island is swanky holiday retreat **Martha's Vineyard**, off the coast of Massachusetts. The prestigious resort remains relatively unspoiled since its heyday as a whaling centre in the 19th century, and the movie's locations remain unchanged. The town centre, where Chief Brody gets materials for the 'Beach closed' signs, is the junction of **Water Street** and **Main Street**, **Edgartown**, the one-time whaling town on the east coast. At the end of Daggett Street, at the northern end of town, you'll find the **Chappaquiddick Island Ferry**, where the Mayor has a quiet word about boating accidents. The ferry takes pedestrians, bikes and up to three cars at a time.

The Mayor has a word: Chappaquiddick Island ferry, Edgartown

West of the coast road north from Edgartown toward the popular resort of Oak Bluffs is **Joseph A Sylvia State Beach**, where the swimmers are panicked by the attack on the Kintner boy. Alongside is the **American Legion Memorial Bridge**, under which the shark

The site of Quint's workshop: Menemsha Harbor

The *Orca* sets out: Menemsha Harbor

The 'safe' inlet: Sengekontacket Pond

swims to the 'safe' inlet, **Sengekontacket Pond**, where Brody's son is traumatised by the attack.

Across the island, toward the southwest tip, is the tiny fishing port of **Menemsha**. It was here, at the end of the harbour inlet between the General Store and the Galley Restaurant, that Quint's workshed was built. A permanent structure would have had to meet the island's strict building regulations, so the area was restored to its original state after shooting, back to an empty lot. The *Orca*'s scenes were filmed over 155 days at sea between Oak Bluffs and East Chop, under well-documented nightmare conditions.

The great shock moment, when Dreyfuss discovers the old fisherman's nibbled head in the wrecked boat, was added as an afterthought. The 'head' shot was staged in the swimming pool of the movie's editor, Verna Field.

JAWS 2
(1978, dir: Jeannot Szwarc)
Roy Scheider, Lorraine Gary, Murray Hamilton.
● **MASSACHUSETTS; FLORIDA**

Without Spielberg's genius for staging set pieces, this is a boring plod from one chomping to the next. It's back to **Martha's Vineyard** again, but this time just about encompassing the whole island – **Edgartown**; **Chappaquiddick**; **Oak Bluffs**; **Menemsha**; **Gay Head**; **East Chop**; **Squibnocket**; **Vineyard Haven**; **Sengekontacket**; **Harthaven**; **Katama**; **Mattekeeset**; **Takemmy Trail**; **Chilmark**; **Pohognut** and **Mayhew Lane**. As if that weren't enough, production delays meant that some of the beach scenes had to be shot at **Navarre Beach**, off Route 98 between Pensacola and Fort Walton beach, northern Florida.

JAWS 3-D
(1983, dir: Joe Alves)
Dennis Quaid, Bess Armstrong, Louis Gossett Jr.
● **FLORIDA**

From bad to worse as Bruce the Shark heads south to Florida only to pop up, in glorious 3-D, in the unlikely setting of Orlando's **Sea World Aquatic Park**, between Orlando and Disneyworld on Interstate 4, Florida.

JAWS THE REVENGE
(1987, dir: Joseph Sargent)
Lorraine Gary, Mario Van Peebles, Michael Caine.
● **MASSACHUSETTS; BAHAMAS**

All that's left is *Abbott and Costello Meet Jaws*. **Martha's Vineyard** is Amity again, but Chief Brody's widow hops off to the Bahamas. And guess what's waiting?

JAZZ SINGER, THE
(1927, dir: Alan Crosland)
Al Jolson, May McAvoy, Warner Oland.
● **LOS ANGELES**

The legendary 'first sound film', with Jolson blacked up as the cantor's son bent on a singing career, was shot in Warner Bros' old Hollywood facility before the company moved to its Burbank lot in 1929. The building still stands, and is now home to independent TV channel KTLA, at **5858 Sunset Boulevard** between Bronson and Van Ness Avenue.

JEAN DE FLORETTE
(1986, dir: Claude Berri)
Gérard Depardieu, Yves Montand, Daniel Auteuil.
● **PROVENCE, FRANCE**

Depardieu is the hunchbacked city boy, blindly determined to make a success of his inherited patch of Provençal farmland. What he doesn't know is that greedy neighbour Montand has blocked up the spring that would feed his plot, and has thus set tragedy in motion. The film was made back to back with *Manon Des Sources*, less a sequel than a second half, which reaches the tragic conclusion.

Both movies were made on location around Provence in the south of France, mainly in the village of **Cuges les Pins**, and at nearby **Sommieres**. Other locations included **Mirabeau**, **Vaugines** and **Ansouis**.

JEREMIAH JOHNSON
(1972, dir: Sydney Pollack)
Robert Redford, Will Geer, Stefan Gierasch.
● **UTAH**

Originally titled *Liver Eatin' Johnson*, from a story by Edward Anhalt and John Milius, the movie was shot around **Alpine Loop** and in **Provo Canyon**, Utah. The area is now part of Redford's Sundance Resort.

JERK, THE
(1979, dir: Carl Reiner)
Steve Martin, Bernadette Peters, Catlin Adams.
● **LOS ANGELES**

Martin's first starring role, as the dorkish white son of black sharecroppers who makes, and then loses, a fortune. The millionaire mansion he buys stood at 9561 Sunset Boulevard, Beverly Hills. It shot to fame in 1978 when the then-owner, Sheikh Al-Fassi, stopped the traffic by having its classical nude statues painted in anatomically correct colours. The mansion was badly damaged by fire in 1979 and has since been demolished.

JERRY MAGUIRE
(1996, dir: Cameron Crowe)
Tom Cruise, Cuba Gooding Jr, Renee Zellweger.
● **LOS ANGELES; ARIZONA; NEW YORK CITY**

Crowe's Oscar-winning tale of a sports agent uses 70 locations around Los Angeles, plus scenes shot in **Tempe** and **Phoenix**, Arizona. The SMI headquarters is a huge set built at Sony Studios in **Culver City**, an homage to the vast, impersonal office of Billy Wilder's *The Apartment*. Cuba Gooding Jr's climactic football game was shot in the **Sun Devil Stadium**, on the campus of **Arizona State University**, Tempe. The film also used **John Wayne Airport**, **Santa Ana** in LA, **Manhattan Beach**, south of LA, and **Times Square**, New York.

JESUS CHRIST SUPERSTAR
(1973, dir: Norman Jewison)
Ted Neeley, Carl Anderson, Yvonne Elliman.
● **ISRAEL**

A bunch of flared seventies tourists act out Lloyd-Webber's dire, dated musical in the middle of the desert. Jesus is a wimp and the villains are camp. Judas gets the best role and rises from the dead. To cap it all, Tim Rice wrote the lyrics. Filmed in Israel, at the ruins of **Pratzim**.

JÉSUS DE MONTRÉAL (aka *Jesus of Montréal*)
(1989, dir: Denys Arcand)
Lothaire Bluteau, Catherine Wilkening, Remy Girard.
● **MONTRÉAL, CANADA**

A powerhouse performance from Bluteau as an actor playing Christ in a radical passion play, performed on the **Way of the Cross, St Joseph's Oratory, 3800 chemin Queen Mary**, Mont-Royal, overlooking the city, it's the highest point of Montréal.

JEWEL OF THE NILE, THE
(1985, dir: Lewis Teague)
Michael Douglas, Kathleen Turner, Danny DeVito.
● **FRANCE; MOROCCO; UTAH**

Sequel to *Romancing the Stone* with novelist Turner accepting an invitation from a Middle Eastern potentate and getting involved in a Holy War. The opening scenes were shot at **Nice** on the French Riviera. The Middle Eastern scenes filmed in Morocco. The village is **Aït Ben Haddou**, near Ouarzazate, a location familiar from *Gladiator, The Last Days of Sodom and Gomorrah* and seen in *Lawrence of Arabia*.

The gateway Douglas crashes the jet plane through was built for the movie and can still be seen – complete with jet plane-shaped hole. The climax, at the royal city of Khadir, used the **Royal Square** of **Meknes** in northern Morocco. It was a trouble-ridden production: sets built in the desert were washed away by freak floods; posters and flags for the rally scene had to be remade when it was discovered that the words on them were blasphemous; while the original production designer and location manager were killed in a plane crash. More desert shots used **Zion National Park** in Utah.

The plane runs amok: Aït Ben Haddou, Morocco

JOHNNY BELINDA
(1948, dir: Jean Negulesco)
Jane Wyman, Lew Ayres, Charles Bickford.
● **CALIFORNIA**

Gushy melodrama, with deaf and dumb Wyman on trial for the murder of her rapist. Set on the island of Cape Breton, the movie was shot around **Mendocino** on the northern California coast, and at the **Pebble Beach-Pacific Grove** waterfront of central California.

JOHNNY GUITAR
(1954, dir: Nicholas Ray)
Joan Crawford, Mercedes McCambridge, Sterling Hayden.
● **ARIZONA**

Bizarre Freudian Western, in lurid colour, with a glorious face-off between Crawford and McCambridge. Filmed at Republic's standing Western set in **Sedona**, Route 89A, south of Flagstaff, Arizona, and at **Oak Creek Canyon** between Flagstaff and Sedona.

JOHNNY MNEMONIC
(1995, dir: Robert Longo)
Keanu Reeves, Dolph Lundgren, Ice-T.
● **ONTARIO, CANADA**

Keanu's pre-*Matrix* sci-fi extravaganza, which fell flat on its virtual face, is set in the New Jersey and Beijing of 2021, but was filmed in Toronto and Montréal. The Beijing hotel is in Toronto's south-western suburb of **Mississauga**. In Toronto itself, Udo Kier's New Jersey nightclub is the

Udo Kier's nightclub: Opera House, Queen Street East, Toronto

The hospital: Union Station, Toronto

Opera House, 735 Queen Street East, priest Dolph Lundgren's church is **Riverdale Presbyterian Church, 662 Pape Street**; and doctor Henry Rollins' makeshift hospital is **Union Station**. Reeves' recovered childhood memories are of **Casa Loma, 1 Austin Terrace** (see *X-Men* for details) and the staircase of nearby **Spadina House, 285 Spadina Road**.

JOHNNY SUEDE
(1991, dir: Tom DiCillo)
Brad Pitt, Calvin Levels, Alison Moir.
● **NEW YORK CITY**

Retro-style, silly hair, surreal humour: a cult film-by-numbers, filmed around 44 separate locations in **Williamsburg**, a tough section of north Brooklyn by the East River. DiCillo went on to make *Living in Oblivion*, about the making of a cheapo cult movie with a pretentious, preening, temperamental Hollywood star.

JOUR DE FÊTE
(1948, dir: Jacques Tati)
Jacques Tati, Guy Decomble, Paul Frankeur.
● **FRANCE**

Tati's début feature-length film, about a village postman embarking on an American-style efficiency drive. The cute little village is **Sainte-Severe-sur-Indre**, about 40 miles south of Bourges in the Loire. The village is just south of the D943 Tours-Montlucon road (*rail: Le Châtre*).

JOURNAL D'UNE FEMME DE CHAMBRE, LE
(aka *The Diary of a Chambermaid*)
(1964, dir: Luis Buñuel)
Jeanne Moreau, Michel Piccoli, Georges Geret.
● FRANCE

Moreau is the maid working for a family of bourgeois sexual misfits with a fascist manservant, in this adaptation of Octave Mirbeau's novel (previously filmed, in a softer version, in the studio, by Jean Renoir in 1946). The little town is **Milly-la-Foret**, twelve miles west of Fontainebleau. Film director Jean Cocteau lived here, and decorated its Chapelle Saint-Blaise-des-Simples, where his tomb now lies.

JOURNEY TO THE CENTER OF THE EARTH
(1959, dir: Henry Levin)
James Mason, Pat Boone, Arlene Dahl.
● SCOTLAND; NEW MEXICO

The military parade: Mound Place, Edinburgh

The centre of the earth: Carlsbad Caverns, New Mexico

Professor Lindenbrook sets off from (and returns to) **E d i n b u r g h University**, South Bridge. The scenes were shot in the university's **Old Quad**. He absent-mindedly gets mixed up in a military parade at **Mound Place**. Some of the more spectacular underground scenes of this Jules Verne adaptation were filmed in the **Carlsbad Caverns, Carlsbad**, in the southeast corner of New Mexico (see *The Spider* for details).

JUBILEE
(1978, dir: Derek Jarman)
Jenny Runacre, Little Nell, Toyah Wilcox.
● LONDON

Jarman's contribution to the Queen's Silver Jubilee year, this bilious view of seventies punk, seen through the eyes of a time-travelling Queen Elizabeth, filmed at **Rotherhithe**. Queen Bess and her astrologer, John Dee, wander along the cliffs at **Winspit**. The nightclub, which is **Westminster Cathedral** on the outside, is the now-defunct Catacomb, a once-notorious gay club on Finborough Road at the junction of Old Brompton Road in Earls Court, SW10. Jordan performs 'Rule Britannia' on stage at the **Theatre Royal, Drury Lane**, in front of the mirrored set for *A Chorus Line*.

JULES ET JIM
(1961, dir: François Truffaut)
Oskar Werner, Jeanne Moreau, Henri Serre.
● FRANCE

Truffaut's classic triangular affair between Jean Moreau,

Frenchman Henri Serre and German Oskar Werner before and after WWII, filmed in Paris and the South of France. Paris scenes were shot in the hidden gardens of **Villa Castel** behind passage Plantin, up a narrow flight of steps at 83 rue Couronnes in Belleville (*metro: Couronnes*). On rue du Transvaal, at the top of passage Plantin, is a wrought iron gate through which you can catch a glimpse of these very private gardens.

The 'hidden' garden: Villa Castel, Paris

Filming also took place near to the German border in Alsace and on the Côte d'Azur in the picturesque town of **St Paul-de-Vence**, about 12 miles north of Cannes. The final cremation and funeral was staged in Paris' **Père Lachaise** cemetery (see *The Doors* for details).

JULIA
(1977, dir: Fred Zinnemann)
Jane Fonda, Vanessa Redgrave, Jason Robards.
● NORFOLK; CUMBRIA; OXFORDSHIRE; FRANCE

Fonda plays Lillian Hellman in a dubious account of her friendship with anti-Nazi activist Julia during the 1930s. The American scenes were shot in the UK; with **Winterton-**

The Vienna hospital: Hôpital Villemin, Paris

on-Sea, nine miles north of Great Yarmouth in Norfolk, standing in for Nantucket. Hellman and Dashiell Hammett's beach house was built on the sand dunes here. The Adirondack Mountains were actually around **Keswick** in the Lake District, Cumbria. The boating scenes take place on **Lake Derwentwater**. The Oxford University scenes used **St John's College, New College** and the **University Library, Oxford**.

In Paris, Julia stays at the swanky **Hotel Meurice, 228 rue de Rivoli**, home over the years to King Alphonse XIII of Spain, and to Salvador Dali (who stayed for 30 years). During WWII, it actually served as Nazi HQ (*metro: Tuileries; Concorde*). Over the rue de Rivoli, in the **Jardin de Tuileries**, alongside the Place de la Concorde, Maximilian Schell asks Fonda to smuggle $50,000. The 1934 Paris riots were filmed in the preserved city of **Versailles**, the town built alongside the more famous chateau (an early example of town planning, with a grid-like layout). Fonda walks in the small hours in the six-acre **Jardin du Palais Royal**, between the rue de Montpensier and rue de Valois (*metro: Palais Royal*). The railway station she departs from is the **Gare du Nord**, dressed to be circa 1937.

The Vienna Hospital is played by the **Hôpital Villemin**, a now-disused military hospital still standing alongside Paris' Gare de l'Est on the **rue du Faubourg Saint Denis**, built to take wounded WWI soldiers direct from the railway station. Austria and Berlin scenes were both filmed in **Strasbourg**, with **Strasbourg Station** standing in for Berlin's railway terminal and **Strasbourg University** passing itself off as the University of Vienna. The streets of Strasbourg were also used for the Florisdorf riots. The German frontier checkpoint is **Shirmack Station**, 40 miles west of Strasbourg.

JUMANJI
(1995, dir: Joe Johnston)
Robin Williams, Bonnie Hunt, Jonathan Hyde.
● **NEW HAMPSHIRE; MAINE; BRITISH COLUMBIA, CANADA**

Williams plays yet another man-boy, this time spewed from a sinister board game after growing up in limbo. Set in Brantford, New Hampshire, the movie was shot around **Keene** and **Swanzey**, southern New Hampshire; and **North Berwick** and **Kennebunk**, south of Portland, Maine. **Tsawwassen**, on Route 17 in Delta, the peninsula south of Vancouver, British Columbia was also used.

JUNGLE FEVER
(1991, dir: Spike Lee)
Wesley Snipes, Annabella Sciorra, Spike Lee.
● **NEW YORK CITY**

Snipes is a NY architect who has an affair with Italian-American secretary Sciorra in Lee's excellent film about the difficulties caused by an inter-racial relationship. Snipes'

Harlem institution: Sylvia's Restaurant, Lenox Avenue

neighbourhood is one of Harlem's middle class enclaves, **Strivers' Row**, around West 138th and West 139th Streets. Built as houses for upper-middle class white families in the Harlem real estate boom of 1919, they became the focus for well-to-do African Americans, the 'Strivers', who have included the likes of WC Handy, Noble Sissle and Eubie Blake. Sciorra's area is **Bensonhurst**, South Central Brooklyn. Traditionally an Italian-Jewish community, it was here that Yusuf Hawkins, a young black man, was beaten to death in August 1989. Lee determined to film in Bensonhurst despite intense local animosity, including bomb threats and disruption, during which cinematographer Ernest Dickerson was hit by a rock.

Featured is **Sylvia's Restaurant, 326 Lenox Avenue** at 125th Street, Harlem's legendary soulfood restaurant. Get there early on Wednesdays, for free tickets to amateur night at the Apollo Theater.

JUNIOR BONNER
(1972, dir: Sam Peckinpah)
Steve McQueen, Ida Lupino, Robert Preston.
● **ARIZONA**

Low-key family drama, with ageing rodeo star McQueen returning to his hometown. The movie was filmed in **Prescott**, Arizona, the setting of screenwriter Jeb Rose-

brook's story, with the real Prescott Rodeo as background.

The bar to which everyone retires between sessions, and the setting for the brawl, is the **Palace Bar**. The railway station is, naturally, **Prescott Railroad Station**. Robert Preston and Ida Lupino's reconciliation was shot on the back stairs of the **Palace Hotel**.

JURASSIC PARK
(1993, dir: Steven Spielberg)
Sam Neill, Laura Dern, Jeff Goldblum.
● **HAWAII; CALIFORNIA**

Spielberg's blockbuster was filmed mainly on **Kauai**, smallest and most beautiful of the major Hawaiian islands, despite the best efforts of Hurricane Iniki, which flattened the sets.

The Badlands dig: Red Rock Canyon, near Ridgecrest, California

The Badlands archaeological dig filmed on mainland USA, in a section of **Red Rock Canyon** near **Ridgecrest**, only accessible to four-wheel drive vehicles in California's **Mojave Desert**, but the Isla Nublar locations are all in Hawaii. The waterfall, where John Ham-

Isla Nublar: Kauai, Hawaii

mond's helicopter touches down (the helipad was a temporary structure for the movie), is inaccessible by land, but most of the Kauai helicopter tours will point out the **Manawaiopuna Falls** in **Hanapepe Valley**. The site of the giant 'Jurassic Park' gates is almost as hard to get to. They stood alongside **Blue Hole**, a water-filled canyon near the centre of Kauai, which you can reach via a five-hour hike from Wailua, on the eastern coast. The electrified fence was erected in Kauai's **Olokele Valley**, while more scenes were shot at **Lawai**. The Gallimus stampede, where the leaping herd of dinosaurs move like a flock of birds, used the most populous and developed of the islands, Oahu – specifically at the **Kualoa Ranch, Kamehameha Highway, Ka'a'awa Valley**. The ranch is open to visitors, and the fallen tree, under which Sam Neill and the kids sheltered, is still there as a great photo opportunity. Take Kamehameha Highway north from Honolulu, about twenty miles. The entrance is on the left, opposite the Kualoa Regional Park (© *800.231.7321 or, Kualoa Ranch and Activity Club, PO Box 650, Kamehameha Highway, Ka'a'awa, Hawaii 96730*).

K

KAGEMUSHA (aka *Shadow Warrior*)
(1980, dir: Akira Kurosawa)
Tatsuya Nakadai, Tsutomo Yamazaki, Kenichi Hagiwara.
● JAPAN

The shadow warrior is a lookalike hired to impersonate a clan chief in this stirring period epic. Kurosawa filmed at several castles around Japan, using low-angle shots to avoid intrusive modern surroundings. The spectacular battle scenes were shot on the north island of Hokkaido. The tiered white castle is **Himeji Castle**, the 'White Heron' castle, situated on a bluff overlooking the town of Himeji, 33 miles west of Kobe. It's about ten minutes walk from Himeji Station, from where you can see it clearly. It is seen also in *Ran*, Kurosawa's version of *King Lear*, and in the Bond movie *You Only Live Twice*.

KALIFORNIA
(1993, dir: Dominic Sena)
Brad Pitt, Juliette Lewis, David Duchovny.
● GEORGIA; CALIFORNIA

Sena's flashy thriller uses scuzzy landscapes around Atlanta, Georgia, and the **Alabama Hills**, above Lone Pine, central California. The desert café is the closed and boarded-up **Ludlow Café, Ludlow** on I-40, about 30 miles east of Newberry Springs (site of the *Bagdad Cafe*), in the southern California desert. More desert scenes were filmed further west on I-40 at **Amboy**. The old Bradbury Textile Warehouse, the Pittsburgh murder site, is actually **Murrays Mill, 1200 Foster Street, Atlanta**, Georgia, previously the E Van Winkle Gin and Machine Works, and now a listed historical site.

KANAL (aka *They Loved Life*)
(1956, dir: Andrzej Wajda)
Teresa Izewska, Tadeusz Janczar, Emil Kariewicz.
● WARSAW, POLAND

A fact-based story of Polish patriots hiding in the sewers from the Nazis during the 1944 Warsaw uprising. The manhole cover is at the corner of **Dluga** and **Miodowa** streets, down from the Krasinski Palace, Warsaw. A nearby wall plaque commemorates the events depicted.

KARATE KID, THE
(1984, dir: John G Avildsen)
Ralph Macchio, Noriyuki 'Pat' Morita, Elisabeth Shue.
● ARIZONA

Rocky remade as a teen movie, and by the same director, too, filmed at **Sedona**, Arizona. In *The Karate Kid Part II*, Pat Morita flies back to Japan to see his ailing father, and finds there are old scores to settle. The island of **Oahu, Hawaii**, stands in for Japan. Old rivalries are warmed over again in the second sequel, *The Karate Kid III*. Villain Thomas Ian Griffith's stylish home is the Frank Lloyd Wright-designed **Ennis-Brown House, 2607 Glendower Avenue, Los Feliz, LA**. For full details of this concrete

Mayan temple, see *The House on Haunted Hill*.

KENTUCKY FRIED MOVIE, THE
(1977, dir: John Landis)
Marilyn Joi, Saul Kahan, Marcy Goldman.
● LOS ANGELES

Hit-and-miss sketches, in this early appearance of John Landis and the *Airplane* team of Zucker-Zucker-Abraham, who produced. The feel-a-round cinema is the **Rialto Theater, 1023 South Fair Oaks** Avenue at Oxley Street, South Pasadena (see Robert Altman's *The Player*, which also filmed here). The 'Deathseekers' sketch was shot at the **Pasadena Department of Water and Power**.

KES
(1969, dir: Ken Loach)
David Bradley, Colin Welland, Lynne Perrie.
● YORKSHIRE

No-hope life in the industrial north, shot in Loach's effective semi-documentary, semi-improvisational style around the tiny village of **Tankersley**, at Junction 36 of the M1 between Sheffield and Barnsley, and **Barnsley** itself, Yorkshire. The countryside where David Bradley learns to train the kestrel is **Hoyland Common, Hoyland Road, Hoyland**, just northeast of Tankersley. He goes to school at **St Helen's County Secondary School, St Helen's Way, St Helen's**, northeast Barnsley.

KEY LARGO
(1948, dir: John Huston)
Humphrey Bogart, Lauren Bacall, Claire Trevor.
● LOS ANGELES; FLORIDA

A disparate bunch of people are holed up in a Key Largo hotel while a devastating hurricane threatens. Largo is one of the Florida Keys, the curving chain of islands linked by a coral reef, running from Miami to Key West. It's claimed that the movie was filmed at the recently rebuilt Caribbean Club bar, but this might be a bit of wishful thinking by the owners. Director Huston maintained that the whole film was shot at **Warners, Burbank**, including the sea sequences in the studio tank. The only kosher locations are some establishing shots, near the beginning of the movie, of Florida's **Overseas Highway**, which runs between the islands.

KID FOR TWO FARTHINGS, A
(1955, dir: Carol Reed)
David Kossoff, Celia Johnson, Diana Dors.
● LONDON

A young boy believes that his one-horned goat is a unicorn in this sentimental whimsy set in a 'corblimey' version of London's East End. Fashion Street is **Petticoat Lane**, E1. Also featured is **Aldgate**, with St Paul's Cathedral looming strangely large and seemingly just at the end of the road.

KID MILLIONS
(1934, dir: Roy Del Ruth)
Eddie Cantor, Ethel Merman, Ann Sothern.
● **CALIFORNIA**

Eddie Cantor is the East Side kid who inherits a fortune in this musical fantasy, which used locations at **Calabasas**, north of LA, and the sandy desert of **Yuma** down toward the Arizona border.

KIDNAPPED
(1960, dir: Robert Stevenson)
Peter Finch, James MacArthur, Peter O'Toole.
● **SCOTLAND**

This vesion of the Robert Louis Stevenson adventure, also filmed in 1938 and 1948 in Hollywood, was shot by Disney at Pinewood studios and on location in Scotland. The Scots locations are **Ardgour**; in the remote wilderness near Fort William; **Ballachulish**, near Glencoe in Argyll and **Glen Nevis**. A further remake, in 1971 with Michael Caine and Trevor Howard, used **Seil Island**, about ten miles southwest of Oban; and **Stirling Castle, Stirling** (*admission charge*).

KILL ME AGAIN
(1989, dir: John Dahl)
Val Kilmer, Joanne Whalley-Kilmer, Michael Madsen.
● **NEVADA**

Reno: the Biggest Little City in the World

The climax: Valley of Fire, Nevada

John Dahl's multiple-cross film noir, with debt-ridden PI Kilmer helping femme fatale Joanne Whalley-Kilmer fake her own death. Where else could it be set but the gambling state of Nevada?

The opening robbery is at **Winnemucca**, on I-80 in the north of the state. It's in **Reno** (with the familiar 'Biggest Little City in the World' sign across its main street) that Val Kilmer has his office. Whalley-Kilmer fetches up at the ever-popular **Las Vegas Hilton, 3000 Paradise Road** (this is also where Robert Redford made that *Indecent Proposal* and featured as Willard Whyte's Whyte House in the Bond movie *Diamonds Are Forever*). The Kilmers set off for **Lake Mead**, where a second death is faked. Mead is the huge artificial lake created when the Colorado River was blocked up by the Hoover Dam. You'll find the getaway Echo Bay Motel at **Echo Bay** on Lake Mead's northwest shore. You can see the wild red sandstone landscapes forming the backdrop to the last part of the movie in nearby **Valley of Fire State Park**, about 50 miles northwest of Las Vegas, off Route 169 (see *Star Trek Generations* for details).

KILLER ELITE, THE
(1975, dir: Sam Peckinpah)
James Caan, Robert Duvall, Mako.
● **SAN FRANCISCO**

The English novel *Monkey in the Middle* by Robert Rostand, transposed to San Francisco because Caan wouldn't make the picture outside the US. But it looks good, and uses plenty of SF locations including, inevitably, **Chinatown; the Bethlehem Steel Pier** and **San Francisco International Airport**, where, to placate the airlines worried about an apparent breach of security, Peckinpah convinced them that a character falling down dead had suffered a heart attack. Of course, he added the gunshot later. The climactic fight takes place at **Suisun Bay**, where the Navy's 'mothball fleet' is stationed.

KILLER KLOWNS FROM OUTER SPACE
(1988, dir: Stephen Chiodo)
Grant Cramer, Suzanne Snyder, John Allen Nelson.
● **CALIFORNIA**

Killer klowns on the loose: Santa Cruz Boardwalk

Aliens, looking astonishingly like circus clowns, begin to take over a small town, but who's going to believe the kids who've seen them? This enjoyably trashy horror was shot on the **Santa Cruz Beach Boardwalk, Santa Cruz**, on the California coast south of San Francisco (see *The Lost Boys* for details of the boardwalk).

KILLERS, THE
(1964, dir: Don Siegel)
John Cassavetes, Lee Marvin, Angie Dickinson.
● **LOS ANGELES**

Remake of the 1946 movie of the Hemingway story, and Ronald Reagan's last movie. Set around LA, where Angie Dickinson's house is at **Toluca Lake**.

KILLING FIELDS, THE
(1984, dir: Roland Joffe)
Sam Waterston, Haing S Ngor, John Malkovich.
● **THAILAND; CALIFORNIA**

New York Times reporter Sidney Schanberg escapes the fall of Phnom Penh in 1975, but his photographer, Dith Pran, left behind and presumed killed, survives the Pol Pot regime. Tragically, Dr Haing S Ngor, who won the Best Supporting Actor Oscar as Pran, was gunned down in a robbery outside his LA home in 1996. It's another film with Thailand standing in for Vietnam (as well as Cambodia), with much of the film being shot around **Phuket**. The French Embassy is the **Colonial Town Hall, Narisarn Road** at Toh Sae Road in Phuket Town, southeast of the island. The Phnom Phen Penh Hotel is the **Railway Hotel, Hua Hin**, which you can reach by narrow gauge train from Hua Lampong station, Bangkok.

There was also filming in San Francisco.

KILLING OF SISTER GEORGE, THE
(1968, dir: Robert Aldrich)
Beryl Reid, Susannah York, Coral Browne.
● LONDON

George drinks at the Marquis of Granby: The Hollybush, Hampstead

This crass commercialisation of Frank Marcus' black comedy, about a TV soap star on the verge of losing her job and her young female lover, is saved by terrific performances, especially from Beryl Reid, who originated the role on stage. The film has the distinction of having been banned in Norwich. The club Reid invites snooty BBC lady Coral Browne to, with its mix of genuine butch dykes and femme movie extras, was the Gateways, the legendary but now long-gone lesbian club which stood in Bramerton Gardens, just off the Kings Road, Chelsea, SW10. The pub, The Marquis of Granby, which Reid drinks in at the opening of the movie, is actually the wonderful old **Hollybush, 22 Holly Mount NW3**, tucked away behind Heath Street in Hampstead (*tube: Hampstead*). It's still there, and virtually unchanged. Over the opening credits, Reid stomps through the narrow stepped passages between **Heath Street** and **Hampstead Grove**, before popping out on the other side of London at the **Embankment**, near Chelsea.

KILLING ZOE
(1994, dir: Roger Avary)
Eric Stoltz, Jean-Hugues Anglade, Julie Delpy.
● PARIS; LOS ANGELES

The Paris hotel: Mondrian Hotel, West Hollywood

This heist movie is set in Paris, but the French capital is seen only in establishing shots. The rest of the movie is faked up in Los Angeles, around **Long Beach** (where the gang HQ used a penthouse suite) and in the downtown area (where the bank hold-up was staged). The coolly chic Parisian hotel where Eric Stoltz meets Julie Delpy is West Hollywood's exclusive **Mondrian Hotel, 8440 Sunset Boulevard** (*✆ 213.650.9999*).

KIM
(1950, dir: Victor Saville)
Errol Flynn, Dean Stockwell, Paul Lukas.
● INDIA; CALIFORNIA

Colourful adventure from the Rudyard Kipling novel, with plenty of actual filming in India, at **Jaipur** and **Bundi**, as well as use of the spectacular **Alabama Hills**, overlooking Lone Pine in central California. The Hills, striking rock formations set against the dramatic backdrop of the snowcapped Sierra Nevada range, have featured in countless movies, often, as here, doubling for India and the Him-

alayas (see *Gunga Din, King of the Khyber Rifles* and *The Lives of a Bengal Lancer*) as well as Western landscapes for *How the West Was Won* and *Joe Kidd*. An annual Lone

'Indian' landscapes: Alabama Hills, California

Pine Film Festival celebrates the area's cinematic legacy, and even the place names reflect the importance of the movie industry. The track leading up to the most frequently used area is called Movie Road. For detailed maps of film locations in the area, check out Dave Holland's invaluable guide *On Location in Lone Pine*, available locally.

KIND HEARTS AND CORONETS
(1949, dir: Robert Hamer)
Dennis Price, Alec Guinness, Valerie Hobson.
● KENT

Best, and blackest, of the Ealing comedies has embittered heir Price killing off the eight members of the D'Ascoyne family standing between him and his right-

Chalfont, family seat of the D'Ascoynes: Leeds Castle, Kent

ful inheritance. Chalfont, the family seat, is **Leeds Castle**, four miles east of Maidstone on the B2163 (*rail: Bearsted*). The Norman castle was turned into a royal palace by Henry VIII, and stands in the middle of a lake surrounded by 500 acres of parkland. It's open to the public daily, except Christmas Day (*✆ 01622.765400, admission charge*).

KIND OF LOVING, A
(1962, dir: John Schlesinger)
Alan Bates, June Ritchie, Thora Hird.
● LANCASHIRE; MANCHESTER

Stan Barstow's novel of northern working class life is set in the fictitious Cressley, Yorkshire, but was filmed in Lancashire. The house newly-weds Alan Bates and June Ritchie share with disapproving mother-in-law Thora Hird is on **Radcliffe New Road, Radcliffe**. The wedding takes place at **St John's Church**, Radcliffe, Manchester. Also in Radcliffe is Beacon's Park, where Bates and Ritchie spend their evenings, which is actually the town's **Coronation Park**. The arcade where the couple go on a date with an unwanted third party is the **Miller Arcade** in **Preston** (which now sports one of the plaques erected in 1996 to mark the centenary of cinema).

KINDERGARTEN COP
(1990, dir: Ivan Reitman)
Arnold Schwarzenegger, Pamela Reed, Linda Hunt.
● LOS ANGELES; OREGON

Odd mix of cutesy kidsy comedy with violent bookends.

The mall in the opening scene is **Main Place, 2800 North Main Street, Santa Ana**, in LA. Flying from LA to Portland, Oregon, Arnie drives along the scenic Route 26, **Sunset Highway**, through **Tillamook** and **Clatsop State Forests**, to Astoria, the 'San Francisco of the Northwest', a Victorian gingerbread town at the mouth of the Columbia River (already familiar from *Short Circuit* and *The Goonies*). Astoria Elementary School, where he takes a teaching post under headmistress Linda Hunt, is **Astor Elementary School, 3550 Franklin Avenue**, with its glorious views over the Columbia River and the spectacular toll bridge to Washington State.

KING CREOLE
(1958, dir: Michael Curtiz)
Elvis Presley, Carolyn Jones, Walter Matthau.
● **NEW ORLEANS, LOUISIANA**

Presley is a nightclub singer getting involved with gangsters in this film of Harold Robbins' *A Stone for Danny Fisher*. The book was set in New York City, but the movie plumps for the more picturesque New Orleans.

KING KONG
(1933, dir: Merian C Cooper, Ernest B Schoedsack)
Fay Wray, Robert Armstrong, Bruce Cabot.
● **LOS ANGELES; NEW YORK CITY**

The New York theatre: Shrine Auditorium, LA

The landing on Skull Island was filmed at **San Pedro**, home of LA harbour, south LA near Long Beach – the mountains were painted on glass.

Several leftover sets were used by penny-pinching RKO, including the native village (from King Vidor's 1932 *Bird of Paradise*, and the giant wall from DeMille's 1927 *King of Kings*) on the lot at the **Culver Studios, 9336 Washington Boulevard** in Culver City. In turn, the giant Skull Island gates were reused for *Gone With the Wind*, where – bizarrely – they can clearly be seen during the burning of Atlanta. Skull Island itself was shot in Hollywood's own wilderness, the caves at **Bronson Canyon**, about a quarter of a mile from the end of Canyon Drive in Griffith Park.

The interior of the New York theatre, where Kong is exhibited is LA's **Shrine Auditorium, 649 West Jefferson Boulevard**, south of downtown LA. And, of course, it's atop the **Empire State Building, Fifth Avenue** at 34th Street, New York, where Kong finally meets his end.

KING KONG
(1976, dir: John Guillermin)
Jeff Bridges, Charles Grodin, Jessica Lange.
● **NEW YORK CITY; HAWAII**

A knowing, campy remake which misses by miles the juddery charm of the original. Skull Island is the inaccessible **Na Pali Coast** on the northern shore of Kauai, Hawaii, where camp is set up on **Honopu Beach**. In New York,

Kong climbs one of the twin towers of the **World Trade Center**, finally plummeting into the **World Trade Center Plaza**.

Skull Island: Na Pali Coast, Kauai

KING OF COMEDY, THE
(1983, dir: Martin Scorsese)
Robert De Niro, Jerry Lewis, Sandra Bernhard.
● **NEW YORK STATE**

Vastly underrated character piece, with De Niro excruciating as a small-time comic who kidnaps a surprisingly low-key Jerry Lewis to get a spot on TV. It's New York-set, where Jerry Lewis' office is **Paramount Plaza, 51st Street** at Broadway and the bar is **Club 478, 9th Avenue** between 36th and 37th Streets in the Theater-Garment district. The restaurant scene is, naturally, at showbiz hangout **Sardi's, 234 West 44th Street** at Broadway. Lewis' country retreat is in Nassau County, Long Island.

Jerry Lewis' office: Paramount Plaza, 51st Street

KING OF KINGS
(1927, dir: Cecil B DeMille)
HB Warner, Jacqueline Logan, Ernest Torrence.
● **LOS ANGELES**

DeMille's life of Christ is heavy on Magdalen's debauchery, but maybe a tad lacking in Christian humility. The Sea of Galilee was filmed at **Catalina Island**, off the coast of LA. The Garden of Gethsemane was, modestly, built in the backyard of CB's East Hollywood home, at **2000 DeMille Drive**, off Los Feliz, which has remained completely unchanged since the old showman's death there in 1959.

KING OF KINGS, THE
(1961, dir: Nicholas Ray)
Jeffrey Hunter, Robert Ryan, Frank Thring.
● **SPAIN**

With director Ray, of *Rebel Without a Cause*, and heart-throb star Hunter, it was inevitable that the movie would be dubbed *I Was a Teenage Christ* (although, personally, I prefer *Suddenly Last Supper*). This life of Christ is actually not bad. It was filmed in Spain, mainly on huge sets erected near Madrid. Nazareth is **Manzanares el Real**, about twenty miles north of Madrid. Christ delivers the Sermon on the Mount at **Chinchón**, 20 miles southeast of Madrid. The River Jordan is **Aldea del Fresno**; the Sea of Galilee is **Lago Alberche** and Golgotha is **Navacerrada**, Madrid.

KING OF MARVIN GARDENS, THE
(1972, dir: Bob Rafelson)
Jack Nicholson, Bruce Dern, Ellen Burstyn.
● NEW JERSEY; PENNSYLVANIA

Nicholson is a radio talk show host, Dern his flaky, ambitious brother, in this downbeat character study filmed mainly around the sadder parts of the East Coast's flash gambling capital, **Atlantic City**, New Jersey. Filming also took place in **Philadelphia**, Pennsylvania.

KING OF NEW YORK
(1990, dir: Abel Ferrara)
Christopher Walken, David Caruso, Larry Fishburne.
● NEW YORK CITY

In Ferrara's cult thriller, drug lord Walken operates out of New York's **Plaza Hotel, 59th Street** at Fifth Avenue. The climactic shoot out is staged in **Times Square**.

KING OF THE KHYBER RIFLES
(1953, dir: Henry King)
Tyrone Power, Michael Rennie, Terry Moore.
● CALIFORNIA

Tyrone Power is the conflicted half-Indian officer with the Khyber Rifles pitched against his step-brother in this standard Cinemascope adventure, which once again uses the rocky landscape of the **Alabama Hills**, west of Lone Pine on Route 395, central California to represent India's Khyber Pass, and the snow-topped Sierra Nevadas as the Himalayas (see *Kim* for more details).

KING SOLOMON'S MINES
(1950, dir: Compton Bennett, Andrew Marton)
Stewart Granger, Deborah Kerr, Richard Carlson.
● KENYA; TANGANYIKA; BELGIAN CONGO; UGANDA; NEW MEXICO; CALIFORNIA

Classic adventure, shot on location in Africa, in Kenya; Tanganyika; the Belgian Congo and Uganda. Also partly filmed in **Death Valley**, California. The underground mines are the breathtaking **Carlsbad Caverns, Carlsbad**, on I-285, southeast New Mexico (see *The Spider*).

KINGS GO FORTH
(1958, dir: Delmer Daves)
Frank Sinatra, Tony Curtis, Natalie Wood.
● CALIFORNIA

WWII melodrama with GIs Sinatra and Curtis vying for supposedly mixed-race Natalie Wood. Set in the South of France, filming took place at **Yankee Point**, Monterey County, northern California, and in **Lower Carmel Valley**.

KINGS OF THE ROAD (aka *Im Lauf der Zeit*)
(1975, dir: Wim Wenders)
Rudiger Vogler, Hanns Zischler, Lisa Kreuzer.
● GERMANY

Wenders' long, rambling road movie, with Vogler and Zischler travelling from town to town fixing movie projectors. The 80 cinemas in the original script were eventually whittled down to twelve as the journey from **Luneburg** to **Passau** passes through **Lower Saxony, Hessen** and **Bavaria**. The VW factory is in **Wolfsburg**.

KISS BEFORE DYING, A
(1991, dir: James Dearden)
Matt Dillon, Sean Young, Max von Sydow.
● LONDON; HERTFORDSHIRE; PENNSYLVANIA; VIRGINIA; NEW YORK CITY; MIDDLESEX

Remake of the 1956 movie of Ira Levin's novel. Set in the US, the movie was made on both sides of the Atlantic. US locations included **Charlottesville**, central Virginia, and **Philadelphia**, Pennsylvania. Matt Dillon tosses the suitcase into the East River from **Manhattan Bridge**, in the real Manhattan, but the New York country estate, where he goes fishing with industrialist Max von Sydow, is **Brockett Hall, Marford Road, Lamsford** in Hertfordshire (see *Night of the Demon* for details). And Philadelphia Central Police HQ is the **First National Bank of Chicago, First Chicago House, 90 Long Acre**, in London.

Max Von Sydow's New York estate: Brockett Hall, Hertfordshire

The Philadelphia police station: Long Acre, London

KISS ME DEADLY
(1955, dir: Robert Aldrich)
Ralph Meeker, Albert Dekker, Cloris Leachman.
● CALIFORNIA

Bizarrely arty filming of the Mike Hammer thriller, with location filming at **Malibu**, north of LA, and in the decrepit area which was Bunker Hill, now massively rebuilt. Forget Internet theories about the strange glow from the suitcase in *Pulp Fiction* – it's an homage to the final scene of *Kiss Me Deadly*, when the radioactive briefcase is finally opened.

KISS ME, STUPID
(1964, dir: Billy Wilder)
Dean Martin, Kim Novak, Ray Walston.
● CALIFORNIA; NEVADA

Sour satire from Wilder. Set in the fictitious Climax, Nevada, it was shot around **Twentynine Palms** in Nevada and in the **Aquarius Theatre, 6230 Sunset Boulevard** between Argyle and El Centro, Hollywood, in the days when it was the Moulin Rouge (see *Imitation of Life* for details).

KISS OF DEATH
(1947, dir: Henry Hathaway)
Victor Mature, Brian Donlevy, Coleen Gray.
● NEW YORK STATE; NEW JERSEY

Crime drama given a semi-documentary treatment, with Richard Widmark stealing the show as the grinning killer. Convicted of robbery, Mature is packed off to **Sing Sing Penitentiary, Ossining**, New York State. Filming in New

York included the **Chrysler Building** and **Hotel Marguery**. The courts are the **Criminal Courts Building**, known as 'The Tombs', **100 Centre Street** between Leonard and White Streets (see *Adam's Rib* for details). Filming also took place at the **Academy of the Holy Angels, Fort Lee**, New Jersey. A 1995 remake, designed to kickstart the movie career of *NYPD Blue*'s David Caruso (it didn't), was filmed around New York and **Elmhurst**.

KLUTE
(1971, dir: Alan J Pakula)
Donald Sutherland, Jane Fonda, Charles Cioffi.
● **NEW YORK CITY**

Excellent, moody thriller, with Sutherland investigating the disappearance of a scientist and getting involved with neurotic hooker Fonda. It was shot on the streets of New York, and at the now defunct Filmways Studios, 246 East 127th Street at 2nd Avenue in East Harlem. It's since become a giant Foodways supermarket.

KNACK... AND HOW TO GET IT, THE
(1965, dir: Richard Lester)
Rita Tushingham, Michael Crawford, Ray Brooks.
● **LONDON**

Flashy, surreal filming of Ann Jellicoe's stylised stage play, set in a very swinging sixties London. Naïve Rita Tushingham arrives in the city at **Victoria Coach Station, SW1**. The street scenes are around Shepherd's Bush and Notting Hill Gate; the swimming pool is **Ruislip Lido, Ruislip**, west London, and Ray Brooks' wildly sexist fantasy takes place at the **Royal Albert Hall, Kensington**. The famous 'white pad', where much of the movie is set, is **1 Melrose Terrace, W6**.

KNIGHTS OF THE ROUND TABLE
(1953, dir: Richard Thorpe)
Robert Taylor, Ava Gardner, Mel Ferrer.
● **CORNWALL; DEVON**

Hollywoodised Arthurian legend, with filming at **Tintagel** on the northern coast of Cornwall. The castle was built atop **Haytor Vale** on Dartmoor, Devon.

KRAMER VS KRAMER
(1979, dir: Robert Benton)
Dustin Hoffman, Meryl Streep, Jane Alexander.
● **NEW YORK CITY**

Tug-of-love tearjerker, mostly set around the swanky Upper East Side of New York. Hoffman and Streep's son attends **PS6 (Public School 6), Madison Avenue** at 82nd Street, near to the Metropolitan Museum of Art. The Copper Kettle, opposite, from which Streep watches, is now gone.

Hoffman runs four blocks with his son to the **Lenox Hill Hospital, 100 East 77th Street** at Park Avenue. Also featuring the marvellous silver art deco **Chrysler**

The school: PS6, Madison Avenue

Building, **405 Lexington Avenue** at East 42nd Street and the **Tweed Courthouse, 52 Chambers Street** in the Civic Center district. The courtroom (unusually, both inside and out) where Streep and Hoffman slug it out for custody of the close-ups, is **Federal Hall, 26 Wall Street** at Nassau Street in the Financial District.

KRAYS, THE
(1990, dir: Peter Medak)
Gary Kemp, Martin Kemp, Billie Whitelaw.
● **LONDON**

Quirky, non-naturalistic film about London's notorious gangster twins. 'Fortress Vallance', the Krays' actual home, stood at 178 Vallance Road, Bethnal Green, E2, but the area has

Fort Vallance: Caradoc Street, Greenwich

since been redeveloped. The search for a suitably unchanged terraced street for the Kray's house led to a Greenwich sidestreet off Trafalgar Road, **Caradoc Street, SE10**.

The imposing exterior of the Krays' nightclub is **Richmond Theatre, The Green, Richmond** (*℘ 020.8940.0088*), where the operettas were staged in Mike Leigh's *Topsy-Turvy*. The inte-

The Krays' club: Richmond Theatre

rior, though, is **Wilton's Music Hall, 1 Grace's Alley, Wellclose Square**, off Cable Street, **E1**, seen also in *Chaplin* and *Isadora*.

The pub that gets smashed up is the **Royal Oak, Columbia Road**, by the famous flower market (also seen in *Lock, Stock and Two Smoking Barrels*, and used as the time-warped local in TV's *Goodnight Sweetheart*).

Shooting up the pub: Royal Oak, Hackney

KUNDUN
(1997, dir: Martin Scorsese)
Tenzin Thuthob Tsarong, Gyurme Tethong, Tulku Jamyang Kunga Tenzin.
● **MOROCCO**

Scorsese's film about the early life of the Dalai Lama was never going to be an easy prospect, and put the director on the list of people banned from Tibet. With the actual locations out of the question, Scorsese returned to the country where he filmed his previous controversial film, *The Last Temptation of Christ*, Morocco. The village where the Dalai Lama is born is **Timlougite**, between Ouarzazate and Marrakech. Dungkhar Monastery is actually **La Kasbah de Toubkal**, a field study centre at **Imlil**.

The movie premiere drug bust: Gramercy Place, Hollywood

L.A. CONFIDENTIAL
(1997, dir: Curtis Hanson)
Russell Crowe, Guy Pearce, Kevin Spacey.
● **LOS ANGELES**

Although it's set in the fifties, Hanson's stylish cop corruption actioner was filmed almost entirely on real locations around LA. Only the decrepit Victory Motel, site of the final shoot-out, is a purpose-built set, constructed among the 'nodding donkey' wells of the **Baldwin Hills** oilfields near Culver City. The *Badge of Honor* TV show, for which Kevin Spacey acts as advisor, is obviously based on *Dragnet*, and similarly uses **LA City Hall** on the LAPD badge as its logo. It's out of City Hall that the cops operate. The familiar pyramid-topped highrise can be seen at **200 North Spring Street**, downtown. Sleazy journo Danny DeVito's office is beneath the illuminated spire and revolving globe of the **Crossroads of the World, 6671 Sunset Boulevard** in Hollywood, a glorious thirties shopping mall designed as an ocean liner, complete with portholes (see *Indecent Proposal* for details). DeVito sets up the 'movie première pot bust' in a bungalow at **1714 Gramercy Place**, west of Western Avenue just off Hollywood Boulevard in Hollywood. The impressive-looking El Cortez theater, where *When Worlds Collide* is premièring, is fictitious. An illuminated marquee was built onto the front of the imposing, but abandoned, bank building at **5620 Hollywood Boulevard**.

Just a little to the west is Nick's Liquor Store, where Russell Crowe first sees Veronica Lake look-alike Basinger, which was recreated on **Larchmont Boulevard**, just south of the Paramount Studios on Melrose Avenue. The Nite Owl Cafe, site of the massacre, is in downtown LA: the **J&J Sandwich Shop, 119 East 6th Street**, opposite the **Pacific Electric Building, 610 South Main Street**, where Russell Crowe dangles the terrified DA from a window.

The terraced home of Basinger's high-class pimp is Richard Neutra's 1929 **Lovell House**. Neutra's masterpiece was built for vegetarian health freak Lovell (it's known as the Lovell Health House). It's a private residence, **4616 Dundee Drive, Los Feliz**, below the Griffith Observatory, which you can see on the skyline in the movie. The house where the prostitute is being held, supposedly Avalon Street, in South Central, was on **Avenue 28** in the

Lincoln Heights district.

Before deciding to check on the actor-cum-hustler, Spacey downs a drink at the **Frolic Room, 6245 Hollywood Boulevard**, a surviving forties neon-lit bar alongside the **Pantages Theater**. He subsequently finds the body of the murdered actor in room 203 of the

Patchett's house: Lovell House, Dundee Drive

The Nite Owl Cafe: J&J Sandwich Shop, Sixth Street

Hollywood Center Motel, 6720 Sunset Boulevard, an original twenties motel, enlarged in the 1950s. The other Hollywood bar, festooned with celebrity photos, where Crowe and Pearce hassle Johnny Stompanato and the 'real' Lana Turner, is another famous landmark, the **Formosa Cafe, 7156 Santa Monica Boulevard** near La Brea Avenue. This Chinese restaurant was a regular hangout for Bogart, Monroe and Gable, among others. And it's still going strong, just over the road from the old Goldwyn Studios. Stompanato, by the way, was the underworld hood stabbed to death in the bedroom of Turner's Beverly Hills mansion in 1958 – allegedly by her daughter Cheryl Crane.

Mrs Leffert's house, where a body is found in the crawl space, is in **Elysian Park**, while Basinger's 1927 house is on **Wilcox Avenue**, next to the Wilshire Country Club in the Rossmore district of Hollywood. Navarette's hide-out, supposedly on the now-redeveloped Bunker Hill, filmed on **San Marino Street** near the intersection of Olympic Boulevard and Hoover Street west of Macarthur Park. Bidwell's house, 'south of Jefferson', was in **Angelino Heights** near Echo Park.

L.A. STORY
(1991, dir: Mick Jackson)
Steve Martin, Victoria Tennant, Sarah Jessica Parker.
● **LOS ANGELES**

Amiable romantic satire, set in a determinedly cosy, white-bread Los Angeles. KYOY, where Steve Martin works as a wacky weatherman, is **KCET, 4401 Sunset Boulevard**. Although now a TV station, it used to be Allied Artists film studio, and before that, Monogram Pictures. You can see the building in Don Siegel's original

The TV studio: KCET, Sunset Boulevard

The hotdog stand: Tail o'the Pup, San Vicente Boulevard

'Full service': Gilmore Service Station, Highland Avenue

Invasion of the Body Snatchers. L'Idiot restaurant is the **Ambassador Hotel, 3400 Wilshire Boulevard** (see the 1954 *A Star is Born* for details). The bank is an old Bank of America building at **650 South Spring Street**, a frequently used location seen in another Steve Martin vehicle, *All of Me* and *Se7en*, among others. The art gallery Martin rollerskates through is the **Los Angeles County Museum of Art, 5905 Wilshire Boulevard**, midtown (© *213.857.6000, admission charge*), while the gallery where he critiques abstract art is the Museum of Contemporary Art, 250 South Grand Avenue (© *213.626.6222*). Richard E Grant grabs a bite to eat at the **Tail o'the Pup, 329 San Vicente Boulevard** at Beverly Boulevard, midtown – the fast-food stand in the shape of a giant hot-dog. The 'full service' garage is the **Gilmore Service Station, Auto Repair & Snack Shop, 859 Highland Avenue** at Willoughby.

L-SHAPED ROOM, THE
(1962, dir: Bryan Forbes)
Leslie Caron, Brock Peters, Tom Bell.
● LONDON

The boarding house in Brockash Road: St Luke's Road, Notting Hill

Compendium of sixties issues, with unmarried mother-to-be Caron arriving in London (an international star was cast to get the movie off the ground) and sharing a bug-ridden house with an interesting cross-section of bedsit residents. Filmed around London's Notting Hill area, the boarding house on the fictitious Brockash Road can be seen at **4 St Luke's Road** at Westbourne Park Road, W11.

LACOMBE, LUCIEN
(1974, dir: Louis Malle)
Pierre Blaise, Aurore Clement, Holger Lowenadler.
● FRANCE

Lacombe is a young peasant who, on being turned down by the Resistance, drifts into collaboration with the Nazis and pays the price. The town is **Figeac**, on the Cele River. Standing at the junction of the N140, N122, D122 and D653 roads in the north of the Midi-Pyrenees region, 45 miles northwest of Rodez, the town has an 11th century

church and a mint dating from the 13th century.

LADRI DI BICICLETTE (aka *Bicycle Thieves*)
(1948, dir: Vittorio De Sica)
Lamberto Maggiorani, Enzo Staiola, Lianella Carell.
● ROME

Long-term unemployed worker Maggiorani finally manages to get a bill-posting job, only to find his much-needed bike has been stolen. De Sica's neo-realist classic, a staple of earnest film societies for decades, was shot on the streets of Rome. Maggiorani's home is in the dismal government housing project of **Citta Valmelaina** on the Via Salaria in Rome's northern outskirts. Maggiorani drops off his son at **Porta Pingiana**, and picks him up at night at the piazza at **Porta Pia** in the Montesacro district. Together, they look for the stolen bicycle in the market at **Piazza Vittoria**, before glimpsing the thief at the market of **Porta Portese** to the south of the Trastevere district.

LADY FROM SHANGHAI, THE
(1948, dir: Orson Welles)
Orson Welles, Rita Hayworth, Everett Sloane.
● MEXICO; CALIFORNIA

Welles' weird film noir used locations in Mexico and northern California. The yacht scenes were shot on board Errol Flynn's boat, the *Zaca*, at **Acapulco Bay**, in Mexico.

The aquarium: Steinhart Aquarium, Golden Gate Park

Rita Hayworth dives into the ocean from the landmark **Morro Rock**, Morro Bay, northwest of San Luis Obispo on the southern California coast.

The restaurant was Sally Stanford's Valhalla, since taken over by the Chart House chain. It's still in existence as the **Chart House, 201 Bridgway**, Sausalito (© *415.332.0804*), over the Golden Gate Bridge from San Francisco. The aquarium is the **Steinhart Aquarium, Music Concourse**, part of the California Academy of Sciences in Golden Gate Park (© *415.750.7145, www.calacademy.org/aquarium*). The most famous sequence, the dazzling Hall of Mirrors shoot out, was of course filmed in the studio, where a near-full-size funhouse was built at Columbia Studios. The exteriors, though, were Playland, now gone, which used to stand at the western end of Golden Gate Park.

LADY VANISHES, THE
(1938, dir: Alfred Hitchcock)
Margaret Lockwood, Michael Redgrave, Paul Lukas.
● LONDON; HAMPSHIRE

Hitchcock's Switzerland-set comedy thriller was made almost entirely in the old Gaumont-British Studios, which stood until recently in Lime Grove, W12, alongside the Goldhawk Road-Shepherds Bush tube line. The railway scenes used the British Southern Railway boat train and the now long-gone Longmoor Military Railway in Hampshire, a frequent movie location. A 1979 remake, with Cybill Shepherd and Elliott Gould, was made on location in Austria, at **Feistritz im Rosental**, on the line between Klagenfurt and Rosenbach.

LADYKILLERS, THE
(1955, dir: Alexander Mackendrick)
Alec Guinness, Katie Johnson, Herbert Lom.
● **LONDON**

The robbery: Battle Bridge Road, King's Cross

Site of Mrs Wilberforce's house: Frederica Street today

Dumping the bodies: Copenhagen Tunnel, King's Cross

Classic Ealing black comedy, with little old lady Katie Johnson unwittingly giving houseroom to Alec Guinness (in a role intended for Alistair Sim) and his gang of robbers, posing as a string quintet. The locale is London's King's Cross, in the days before the area became synonymous with drugs and prostitution. The robbery begins by the Victorian gasometers in **Goods Way**, behind King's Cross Station, and actually takes place in **Battle Bridge Road**. The stretch of cobbled road, backed by the picturesque ironwork of the gasometers, is a familiar location seen in films as diverse as *The Missionary*, *L'accompagnatrice*, *Alfie*, *Backbeat* and *Chaplin*. The area is sadly threatened by redevelopment.

Johnson's house is at the end of a cul-de-sac facing St Pancras Station in Euston Road, NW1. From the view of the station, the house is clearly meant to be in Argylle Street, running south from Euston Road. Yet Argylle Street is not a cul-de-sac, and the railway lines run north. Although the view *from* the house is Argylle Street, the house itself was in Frederica Street, about a mile to the north, running west from Caledonian Road facing Pentonville Prison. The house is actually a full-size set built at the end of this small cul-de-sac. In keeping with the off-kilter storyline, the set was built without any true right-angles. Regrettably, the whole street has since been redeveloped as a housing estate and no trace remains of the old houses seen in the movie.

The tunnel entrance where the bodies are dropped into goods trailers was indeed behind Frederica Street. It's the entrance to the **Copenhagen Tunnel**. There are three separate tunnels, and the one used for the movie conveniently serves the line to the King's Cross goods yards. It can't

be seen any longer from Frederica Street, but Vale Royal, a cul-de-sac running east from York Way, N7, leads to a car park from which you can see the weed covered plot of land where Alec Guinness and Herbert Lom had their final shoot out, and the decayed grandeur of the tunnel entrances. The lethal old-fashioned signals have gone.

LAIR OF THE WHITE WORM, THE
(1988, dir: Ken Russell)
Amanda Donohoe, Hugh Grant, Catherine Oxenberg.
● **HERTFORDSHIRE**

Rural worm-worship, from a Bram Stoker story, with Donohoe as a reptilian high priestess, which is by turns hilarious and surreal. Hugh Grant's ancestral pile, D'Ampton Hall, is **Knebworth House**, 28 miles north of London on the A1, Hertfordshire (see Tim Burton's *Batman* for full details).

LAND THAT TIME FORGOT, THE
(1974, dir: Kevin Connor)
Doug McClure, John McEnery, Susan Penhaligon.
● **CANARY ISLANDS**

A shipwrecked crew find themselves on an island of prehistoric monsters, in this adventure taken from an Edgar Rice Burroughs story. The prehistoric landscape can be found at **La Palma**, Santa Cruz de Tenerife, Canary Islands.

LASSIE COME HOME
(1943, dir: Fred M Wilcox)
Roddy McDowall, Donald Crisp, Elizabeth Taylor.
● **CALIFORNIA; WASHINGTON STATE**

First of the Lassie movies, although, as everyone now knows, Lassie was a laddie. Filming took place at the glorious **Point Lobos State Reserve**, a stretch of rocky coastline four miles south of Carmel on Highway 1, central California, and also at **Lake Chelan**, Washington State.

LAST ACTION HERO
(1993, dir: John McTiernan)
Arnold Schwarzenegger, Art Carney, Charles Dance.
● **NEW YORK CITY; LOS ANGELES**

Mega-hype, mega-budget, mega-star, even ads on NASA rockets, but this surprisingly witty in-joke of a movie still bombed in the summer of dino-mania. The interior of the Pandora Theater, where Austin O'Brien uses his magic ticket to enter the movie world, is the **Orpheum Theater, 842 South Broadway**, downtown

Interior of the Pandora Theater: Orpheum Theater, South Broadway, LA

Jack Slater IV première: RKO Twin Theatre, Times Square, NY

Leo the Fart's funeral: Hyatt Regency, Long Beach, LA

LA. This gem of a cinema, recently restored, can also be seen in *Dead Again* and *Ed Wood*. Schwarzenegger's fictitious blockbuster, *Jack Slater IV*, premières on the other coast, at the **RKO Twin Theater, Times Square** in New York, where a giant inflatable Arnie sways about on the sidewalk.

The house where Schwarzenegger almost gets blown up is on the **1100 block of Angelina Street**, downtown LA. In a re-run of *Terminator 2*'s road-into-flood channel leap, a car flies into the LA River channel at the **First Street Bridge**. Leo the Fart's lavish mob funeral filmed atop the roof of the 502-room **Hyatt Regency Hotel, 200 South Pine Avenue** at Shoreline Drive in Long Beach, south LA. The La Brea Tar Pits, in reality on Wilshire Boulevard, midtown, were recreated alongside the Hyatt. O'Brien's school, Lincoln Elementary is a standing set built on the Culver City lot during the twenties, while Elsinore in the *Hamlet* fantasy scene is the castle built for Francis Coppola's *Bram Stoker's Dracula*.

LAST DAYS OF SODOM AND GOMORRAH, THE (aka *Sodom and Gomorrah*)
(1962, dir: Robert Aldrich, Sergio Leone)
Stewart Granger, Pier Angeli, Stanley Baker.
● MOROCCO

'Twin cities of sin': Aït Ben Haddou, Morocco

God destroys two cities, notorious for their gross decadence (though this doesn't seem to go much beyond leering), while tight-ass Stewart Granger and his snotty-nosed cronies escape. This turgid epic was directed by Robert Aldrich (*What Ever Happened to Baby Jane?*) and a pre-*Dollars* Sergio Leone. Touted as a real shocker in its day, the film now ambles along on Saturday afternoon TV, but at least has the benefit of spectacular location filming. The battle scenes and the flood were staged near Marrakech in Morocco. The twin cities of sin are portrayed by **Aït Ben Haddou**, the spectacular desert town about twenty miles northwest of Ouarzazate on the Marrakech road.

LAST DETAIL, THE
(1973, dir: Hal Ashby)
Jack Nicholson, Otis Young, Randy Quaid.
● VIRGINIA; NEW HAMPSHIRE; MASSACHUSETTS; WASHINGTON DC; NEW YORK CITY

Nicholson and Young are naval officers escorting Quaid to jail, and giving him one last night of freedom on the way. Quaid is taken from the US naval base at **Norfolk**,

Virginia, to **Portsmouth**, New Hampshire. The first stop on the journey is Washington DC, where Quaid is taken to visit his mother's house. Next stop is New York City, then Quaid loses his virginity in a brothel in Boston, Massachusetts, with filming at **South End** and **Boston Common**.

LAST EMPEROR, THE
(1987, dir: Bernardo Bertolucci)
John Lone, Joan Chen, Peter O'Toole.
● CHINA

Bertolucci's visually luscious epic, charting the life of the last imperial ruler of China, scored a first in being able to use the **Forbidden City** of Beijing.

The emperor's childhood: The Forbidden City, Beijing

LAST HOUSE ON THE LEFT, THE
(1972, dir: Wes Craven)
Sandra Cassel, Lucy Grantham, David Hess.
● CONNECTICUT; NEW YORK CITY

Wes Craven's first movie, a cult shocker loosely based on Ingmar Bergman's *The Virgin Spring*. It was made on a shoestring, guerilla-style, in **Westport**, I-95, on the southwest coast of Connecticut, where the woods belong to a public reservoir just outside town. More scenes were shot in **Manhattan.**

LAST OF THE MOHICANS, THE
(1992, dir: Michael Mann)
Daniel Day-Lewis, Russell Means, Madeleine Stowe.
● NORTH CAROLINA

Fenimore Cooper's story of the French-Indian wars, made on location in the Blue Mountains of North Carolina, at **Massacre Valley** in Burke County, and further west on Highway 40, at in the grounds of the **Biltmore Estate, Asheville**. Much of the filming took place in **Chimney Rock Park**, US 74 and 64, 25 miles southeast of Asheville, where you'll find **Inspiration Point**, site of the love scene between Day-Lewis and Stowe,

The climactic fight: Hickory Nut Falls, Chimney Rock Park

and **Hickory Nut Falls**, where the climactic fight takes place. The park's map lists the movie sites.

A 1936 Hollywood version, with Randolph Scott, didn't stray much further than standard Hollywood locales the **Iverson Ranch, Iverson Lane, Chatsworth,** about 30 miles north of LA; **Kern River** and **Sherwood Lake.**

LAST PICTURE SHOW, THE

(1971, dir: Peter Bogdanovich)
Jeff Bridges, Timothy Bottoms, Cloris Leachman.
● TEXAS

Bogdanovich never came close to equalling this achingly atmospheric evocation of smalltown life in the fifties, from Larry McMurtry's novel. The one-street town of Anarene, Texas is actually **Archer City,** Texas – "one street

The picture house, Anarene: Archer City, Texas

and a traffic light" as a local described it. The burned-out shell of the Royal picture house is still crumbling away, at **115 East Main Street.**

LAST TANGO IN PARIS

(1972, dir: Bernardo Bertolucci)
Marlon Brando, Maria Schneider, Jean-Pierre Léaud.
● PARIS

Bertolucci's tragic romance was lusciously photographed on location around Paris by Vittorio Storaro. Tormented widower Brando meets Maria Schneider on the **Pont de Bir-Hakeim,** in the 15th and 16th arrondissements. Originally the Passy Viaduct, the bridge was renamed in 1949 to commemorate battles against Rommel in the Libyan desert.

The apartment: rue de l'Alboni, Passy

The apartment in which they energetically consummate the perversely anonymous romance, 1 rue Jules Verne, is actually **1 rue de l'Alboni** at the end of the bridge in Passy. The wrought iron doorway can be seen at the top of the steps at the northern end of the bridge. At the foot of the steps you'll recognise, somewhat revamped, the bar from which Schneider makes a phone call. It's the **Kennedy Eiffel Bar, avenue du President Kennedy.**

The last tango: Salle Wagram, avenue de Wagram

More drastically changed is the salon where Brando and Schneider disrupt the tango competition at the movie's climax. The old, neo-Classical **Salle Wagram** has been remodelled as a disco. You can find it just down the road from the Arc de Triomphe at **39 avenue de Wagram.**

LAST TEMPTATION OF CHRIST, THE

(1988, dir: Martin Scorsese)
Willem Dafoe, Harvey Keitel, Barbara Hershey.
● MOROCCO

Scorsese's absurdly controversial, but actually quite reverential, version of Nikos Kazantzakis' fantasia on the life of Christ took years to get off the ground, and was obliged to use Morocco as a stand-in for the Holy Land. Nazareth and Magdala were both filmed in the village of **Oumnast** (Umnast), about 15 miles south of Marrakech.

Jerusalem was going to be a set until the filmmakers discovered **Mekenes** (Meknes), which provided the **Moulay Ismael Stables** for the interior of the Temple, the Passover baths and the palace of Pontius Pilate. Sultan Moulay Ismael ruled Mekenes for 55 years, from 1672 to 1727, during which time he embarked on a massive building programme and turned the city into a spectacular walled capital with over 50 palaces. The stables are part of his Villa Imperiale, a huge complex of palaces, gardens, barracks and the stables below Mekenes' Medina. From the Ville Nouvelle, cross the River Oued Boufekrane, which divides the city, and take the Rue Rouamzine and Rue Dar Smen to the gateway, Bab Mansour. Moulay Ismael's Mausoleum is here, but past that, a corridor leads to the Heri as-Souani (or the Dar el-Mar). Called the 'stables', these high-vaulted rooms were, in all probability, store rooms and granaries.

The final 35-minute 'temptation' sequence was filmed in the Atlas Mountains and around the Roman ruins of **Volubilis,** about twenty miles north of Mekenes.

LAVENDER HILL MOB, THE

(1951, dir: Charles Crichton)
Alec Guinness, Stanley Holloway, Sidney James.
● LONDON; MIDDLESEX; PARIS

Mild-mannered Alec Guinness masterminds a daring bullion robbery in this Ealing classic, and as the plot involves smuggling gold disguised as Eiffel Tower souvenirs,

The police chase ends in chaos: Bramley Arms, Notting Hill

there's filming in Paris, but most of the movie was shot around post-war London. The airport scene was originally scripted as Victoria Station, but it cost ten times as much to close down a major London terminus than to close a small Home Counties airfield, and the scene was shot at **Northolt Airport,** Middlesex. The London chase ends at the **Bramley Arms** in Notting Hill, London.

LAWN DOGS

(1998, dir: John Duigan)
Kathleen Quinlan, Sam Rockwell, Mischa Barton.
● KENTUCKY

Lawn man Rockwell's friendship with a ten year-old girl is misunderstood in Duigan's smalltown drama, made in **Prospect,** on the Cincinnati Highway, Route 42, about five miles north of Louisville, Kentucky.

The Arabian desert: Wadi Rumm, Jordan

LAWRENCE OF ARABIA

(1962, dir: David Lean)
Peter O'Toole, Omar Sharif, Alec Guinness.
● JORDAN; SPAIN; MOROCCO; LONDON;
SURREY; CALIFORNIA

The Cairo hotel: Palaçio Español, Seville

Lean's last really great movie, before his taste for the overblown ballooned. The opening scene, of Lawrence's fatal motorbike ride (supposedly in Wales), is **Chobham**, Surrey. Lawrence's memorial service did actually use the steps in front of **St Paul's Cathedral** in London, but the interior was recreated in a Spanish studio. In fact, all the interiors, and much of the rest of the film, was shot in Spain. The town of Aqaba was built at a beach called **Playa del Algorocibo** near Carboneros, close to Almeria in southern Spain. The attack on the train filmed at **Genovese Beach, San Jose** on **Cabo del Gato** (Cape of the Cat) nearby.

For many of the Middle Eastern settings, Lean used the heavily Moorish city of Seville. The Cairo hotel, where Lawrence's companion is refused a drink after the desert crossing, is the **Palaçio Español**, a semi-circular arcaded building in the **Plaza de España, Seville**, built for the 1929 Spanish-American exhibition. The courtyard of the Officers' Club, Cairo, is Seville's luxurious **Alfonso XIII Hotel, 2 San Fernando 41004** (*© 5422.2850*). Lawrence and Allenby meet in another Seville landmark, the **Casa de Pilatos, Plaza de Pilatos**, built in 1519, and supposedly a copy of Pontius Pilate's surprisingly 16th century Jerusalem house. Jerusalem's civic buildings are Seville's **Plaza of the Americas**, and the British headquarters a trade exhibition centre (still decorated with Spanish tapestries which were too expensive to move), while Damascus town hall, the Arab council chamber, is a local casino.

But of course, the real visual splendour of *Lawrence* lies in its breathtaking Jordanian desertscapes. Lawrence's first introduction to the desert is the black basalt landscape of **Jebel Tubayq**, near the Saudi Arabian border, as is much of the trekking and the caravan across the Nefud. Feisal's camp, and the well where Lawrence first gets his Arab drag, are the spectacular red cliffs of **Wadi Rumm**, twenty miles north of the Gulf of Aqaba.

Omar Sharif's spectacular camel ride entrance (of course, Sharif wasn't actually in this, his most famous scene) used the mudflats at **Jafr** in Jordan, as did the rescue of the lost Arab boy, Gasim. More scenes were filmed in Morocco, at the spectacular desert town of **Ait Ben-haddou**, about fifteen miles northwest of Ouarzazate. Just outside Ouarzazate, the giant Glaoui Kasbah was converted into a hotel, now the Kasbah Tifoultoutte, specially to house the cast. It's about three miles from Ourzazate on the P31 (*© 04.88.46.36*).

Extra desert shots were filmed in the States, on the **Imperial Sand Dunes**, Highway 78, east of El Centro, southern California close to the Mexican border.

LE MANS

(1971, dir: Lee H Katzin)
Steve McQueen, Siegfried Rauch, Elga Andersen.
● FRANCE

The racetrack through Le Mans was taken over for twelve weeks for McQueen's car race movie. The old historic town of **Le Mans** lies 125 miles southwest of Paris on the River Sarthe. An excellent motor museum is attached to the racing circuit. You can see another side of this historic town in *Cyrano De Bergerac*.

LEAGUE OF THEIR OWN, A

(1992, dir: Penny Marshall)
Geena Davis, Tom Hanks, Madonna.
● ILLINOIS; INDIANA; KENTUCKY; NEW YORK
STATE

Davis leads a women's baseball team in this comedy, made largely in **Chicago** and its northern suburb, **Evanston**. Harvey Field is **Wrigley Field, 10060 West Addison**

The dance: Fitzgerald's, West Roosevelt Road, Berwyn

Street at North Clark Street, home of the Chicago Cubs in the Wrigleyville district of northern Chicago. Racine Field is **Bosse Field, Garvin Park** between North Main Street and Heidelbach Street, Evanston. The bar, where the team lets rip at the dance, is **Fitzgerald's, 6615 West Roosevelt Road, Berwyn**, a western suburb of Chicago. This popular bar can also be seen in *The Color of Money* and *Adventures in Babysitting*. To find it, take the Des Plains A Branch 'el' to Harlem Avenue, Berwyn.

Garry Marshall's estate is the **Cantigny Mansion, One South 151 Winfield Road, Wheaton**, two miles north of I-88, west of Chicago. Formerly home to the publisher of the *Chicago Tribune*, the mansion is open to the public (*www.rrmtf.org/cantigny*). The various small towns were found around Indiana, while the boarding house is on the corner of **Fifth Street and Main Street, Henderson**, Kentucky. The movie ends tearily at the **National Baseball Hall of Fame and Museum, 25 Main Street, Cooperstown**, New York State (*© 607.547.7200, www.baseballhalloffame.org/index.htm*).

LEATHER BOYS, THE
(1963, dir: Sidney J Furie)
Colin Campbell, Dudley Sutton, Rita Tushingham.
● LONDON; SUSSEX

The biker hangout: The Ace Café, North Circular Road, London

Campbell's marriage to Tushingham is rocky enough, when gay biker Sutton comes along to confuse the poor lad. Slice of working class sixties life, filmed entirely on location by Canadian Furie. The holiday camp is the old Butlin's Camp at **Bognor Regis** on the south coast of Sussex. The biker café was the Ace Café on London's **North Circular Road**. Built as a lorry stop in 1938, and rebuilt in 1949, its 24-hour service led to it becoming a legendary biker hangout. It closed its doors as a café in 1969, to reopen as a tyre warehouse, but recently, the old Ace has been bought and now opens up again at weekends. It's on the A406 North Circular Road at **Beresford Avenue**, near Stonebridge Park tube station (*www.acecafe-london.com*).

LEAVING LAS VEGAS
(1995, dir: Mike Figgis)
Nicolas Cage, Elisabeth Shue, Julian Sands.
● NEVADA; CALIFORNIA

Cage bumps into Shue: The Flamingo, Las Vegas Boulevard

Shue and Cage talk beneath the Circus Circus clown

Nicolas Cage gives it all up to drink himself to death in Las Vegas. The LA bar of the opening scenes is the **Cock and Bull Pub, 2947 Lincoln Boulevard, Santa Monica**. And although the Vegas exteriors are real enough, the casino interiors were shot 90 miles south in **Laughlin**, on the Arizona border. Founded in 1966 by Don Laughlin, the town has grown to become a mini-Vegas with small-scale counterparts of its big sister's casinos. The movie was shot in the Gold River Casino and Resort. Since bought up by entrepreneur Alan Paulson, it's now the **River Palms Resort Casino, 2700 South Casino Drive** (© *702.298.2242*).
Leaving LA, Cage takes one of the world's great drives, the six-hour trip on I-15 through the Mojave Desert to Vegas. The movie makes up for its Laughlin interiors by setting key scenes in front of a slew of Strip landmark casinos. Cage first bumps into hooker Elisabeth Shue at a

stop light on Las Vegas Boulevard outside the **Flamingo Hilton and Tower, 3555 Las Vegas Boulevard South**, the starting point of the new Las Vegas, opened in 1946 by 'Bugsy' Siegel (see *Bugsy* for the history). Shue, in turn, finds Cage in front of **Bally's, 3645 South Las Vegas Boulevard**. They talk in front of the giant illuminated clown of **Circus Circus, 2880 Las Vegas Boulevard South**. Shue is picked up by the college jocks on the aerial walkway in front of the toytown turrets of **Excalibur, 3850 Las Vegas Boulevard South**. The waterfall, where she hails a cab after the rape, is at **Mirage, 3400 Las Vegas Boulevard South**.

LEGENDS OF THE FALL
(1994, dir: Edward Zwick)
Anthony Hopkins, Brad Pitt, Aidan Quinn.
● ALBERTA, CANADA; BRITISH COLUMBIA, CANADA; JAMAICA

Set in Montana, Hopkins' homestead retreat was a ranch in the **Ghost River** area, 40 miles west of Calgary, Alberta. The WW1 trenches were also filmed here. Brad Pitt's African travels are actually **Ocho Rios** in Jamaica, and the town of Helena, where Aidan Quinn sets up his business, is Vancouver's Gastown area, east of downtown. **Powell Street** and **Maple Leaf Square** were period dressed. The **Hotel Europe**, on Helena's main street, is at **43 Powell Street**.

Helena: Powell Street, Vancouver

LÉON (aka *The Professional*)
(1994, dir: Luc Besson)
Jean Reno, Gary Oldman, Natalie Portman.
● NEW YORK CITY; NEW JERSEY; PARIS

Luc Besson's stylish thriller with hitman Reno versus rampantly OTT crooked cop Oldman is set in New York, but most of the studio shooting took place in Paris. Real NY sites include Spanish Harlem, Chinatown and Wall Street; plus **Hoboken** and **West New York**, New Jersey. Tony's,

Natalie Portman's hotel: 97th Street

...and inside: The Chelsea Hotel

Danny Aiello's restaurant, supposedly in Little Italy, is **Guido's, 511 9th Avenue** at West 38th Street (© *212.564.8074*) south of the Port Authority Bus Terminal. The exterior of Natalie Portman's hotel is **71 97th Street** at Park Avenue on the Upper East Side, but the stairwell and corridors are those of the **Hotel Chelsea, 222 West 23rd Street**, between Seventh and Eighth Avenues (© *212.243.3700*) (see *Sid and Nancy* for details).

LETHAL WEAPON
(1987, dir: Richard Donner)
Mel Gibson, Danny Glover, Gary Busey.
● **LOS ANGELES**

The shootout: Hollywood Boulevard

First in the hugely successful series of actioners pairing suicidally on-the-edge Gibson with staid, middle-aged Glover. The movie was shot all over LA – on the southwest peninsula of **Palos Verdes**; the beachside community of **Santa Monica**; **Studio City** in the San Fernando Valley and **Inglewood** in South Central – as well as at **El Mirage**, the dry lake bed about 20 miles west of Victorville in the Mojave Desert.

The opening leap: International Tower, Ocean Boulevard, Long Beach

The circular apartment block, where a drugged-out woman plummets to her death in the opening scene, is the **International Tower, 700 Ocean Boulevard East**, a block of condominiums in Long Beach. The rooftop from which Gibson survives a leap with the unwilling suicide, is the **Emser Building, 8431 Santa Monica Boulevard** in West Hollywood. The villains' nightclub, where Gibson is tortured, is the – now closed – **Ritz Theater** on Hollywood Boulevard (next door to 6652). The shoot-out is on Hollywood Boulevard outside the Vogue Cinema.

The successful leap: Emser Building, West Hollywood

LETHAL WEAPON 2
(1989, dir: Richard Donner)
Mel Gibson, Danny Glover, Joe Pesci.
● **LOS ANGELES**

Glover and Gibson protect Pesci from nasty South Africans, while causing maximum mayhem around LA. Villain Joss Ackland's stilt house, demolished by Gibson, still survives (a mock-up was erected above Valencia, north of LA, for the destruction scene). The real house, designed by John Lautner, can be seen at **7436 Mulholland Drive** in the Hollywood Hills. And Mulholland Drive was convenient for the thrilling car chases. The tunnel chase is through the much-used **Second Street Tunnel**, downtown LA. The hotel, from which Gibson makes a leap into the pool, is the **Park Hyatt Los Angeles** (previously the JW Marriott

Hotel), **2152 Avenue of the Stars**, Century City. Danny Glover's house stands on the **Warner Bros Ranch, 3701 West Oak Street** (not generally open to the public). Filming also took place at the **Westin Bonaventure Hotel, 404 South Figueroa Street**, downtown LA.

LETHAL WEAPON 3
(1992, dir: Richard Donner)
Mel Gibson, Danny Glover, Joe Pesci.
● **LOS ANGELES; FLORIDA**

More of the same, largely set in LA, though the International Control Systems Building, blown up at the opening of the movie, was in Florida. It was the Soreno Building,

Gibson and Glover demoted: Olvera Street, downtown LA

Orlando's City Hall, South Orange Avenue, downtown, which was being demolished. The movie is one of the first to use the spanking new, and long-awaited, LA Subway, about five miles of which had been completed by the time of filming. Gibson and Glover are demoted to uniform patrol in the Plaza at **Olvera Street**, the heart of LA's historic centre.

LETHAL WEAPON 4
(1998, dir: Richard Donner)
Mel Gibson, Danny Glover, Joe Pesci.
● **LOS ANGELES; NEVADA**

For the opening flamethrower sequence, a fake gas station was constructed on the corner of **First Street** at Elm Street, downtown LA. Much of the subsequent action takes place around LA's **Chinatown**. And, for no apparent reason, the highway chase used **I-215** between **Pecos Road** and **Windmill Lane**, Las Vegas, Nevada, much to the anger of inconvenienced locals.

LIAR LIAR
(1997, dir: Tom Shadyac)
Jim Carrey, Maura Tierney, Cary Elwes.
● **LOS ANGELES**

One joke sitcom storyline, with Carrey as the LA lawyer condemned to tell the truth for 24 hours by his son's birthday wish. Filming took place at LA's City Jail, and the Supe-

The Superior Court Building: Los Angeles City Hall

rior Court Building, where Carrey fights his cases, is **Los Angeles City Hall, 200 North Spring Street**, downtown LA. The court steps are City Hall's West Entrance. The restaurant where Cary Elwes proposes to Carrey's ex-wife is **Bistro Garden, 12950 Ventura Boulevard**, Studio City, an indoor version of the Beverly Hills favourite. The airport climax is at **Los Angeles International Airport**, LAX, and some scenes were shot in **South Pasadena**.

LICENCE TO KILL
(1989, dir: John Glen)
Timothy Dalton, Carey Lowell, Robert Davi.
● **MEXICO; FLORIDA**

Perhaps the most 'serious' of the Bonds. Bond's old buddy Felix Leiter marries Della Churchill at **St Mary's Star of the Sea Catholic Church, 1010 Windsor Lane, Key West** in Florida. Also in Key West, though supposedly in Bimini in the Bahamas, is the fictitious Barrelhead Bar. It's the **Harbor Lights Bar, 711 Eisenhower Drive**. You can see the real Bimini at the end of *Silence of the Lambs*. After Bond decides to go it alone when Leiter loses a leg to villain Sanchez's sharks, he gets his licence to kill revoked during a confrontation with M at the **Ernest Hemingway Museum, 907 Whitehead Street** at Truman Avenue, Key West. The 1851 Spanish-Colonial house was home to the writer from 1931 until his death in 1961. It's open daily, 9am to 5pm (© *305.296.5811, admission charge*). Other Florida locations include **Garrison Bight Marina** on **Garrison Bight Causeway; Overseas Highway**, where the police escort plunges into the sea; and **Key West International Airport, South Roosevelt Boulevard**, where Bond learns of Sanchez's escape.

Most of the movie was made in Mexico (at Churubuscu Studios). Villain Sanchez's house is the **di Portanova Estate**, on the beach near **Las Brisas** in Acapulco. Isthmus City is fictitious, most of it being filmed around **Mexico City**. Banco De Isthmus is the main Post Office of Mexico City. Bond's El Presidente hotel is, on the inside, the splendid art nouveau **Gran Hotel de la Ciudad de Mexico, Calle 16 de Septiembre** (© *5510.4040*) at the Zocale, the city's gigantic square. It was built in 1899 to accommodate the Centro Mercantil, Mexico City's first shopping centre. The exterior is the **Biblioteca de la Banca de Mexico** (Library of the Bank of Mexico), while the exterior of Sanchez's office is **El Teatro de la Ciudad, 36 Donceles**.

The Isthmus Casino, where Taliso Soto helps Bond out, is the **Casino Espagnol**, Mexico City. Televangelist Wayne Newton's home, the Olimpatec Meditation Institute, is the **Otomi Ceremonial Center**, a bizarre structure built for the native Otomi people in 1980 at **Toluca**, 35 miles west of Mexico City on Route 15. Bond and Leiter find Sanchez at **Isla de Mujeres**, near Cancun, where all the underwater sequences were shot. The climactic chase, at Paso El Diablo, the drug runners' rendezvous, is **Rumorosa Pass**, a winding stretch of road about 50 miles west of Mexicali, just over the border from California.

LIFE AND DEATH OF COLONEL BLIMP, THE
(1943, dir: Michael Powell, Emeric Pressburger)
Roger Livesey, Deborah Kerr, Anton Walbrook.
● **LONDON**

Powell and Pressburger's masterpiece proved enormously controversial at the time, not least for Walbrook's sympathetic German character. The film is almost totally set-

bound. For the opening raid on Blimp's Royal Bathers' Club, the army trucks ('borrowed' for the movie) thunder down Western Avenue, round Marble Arch and into Berkeley Square. Blimp's London house, despite being demolished by a bomb in the movie, still stands unchanged, at **15 Ovington Square, SW3**, off the Brompton Road, Knightsbridge (*tube: South Kensington*). The tiny tree-filled square opposite is Ovington Square.

Blimp's London home: Ovington Square, South Kensington

LIFE AND TIMES OF JUDGE ROY BEAN, THE
(1972, dir: John Huston)
Paul Newman, Anthony Perkins, Ava Gardner.
● **ARIZONA**

Mythmaking script by ultra-rightist poseur John Milius, saved by John Huston's quirky treatment. The real town of Langtry, where eccentric judge Bean embodied the 'law

The real courthouse/opera house: Langtry, Texas

west of the Pecos', is named in honour of Bean's obsession, singer Lillie Langtry. The combined saloon, courthouse and opera house have been preserved as the Judge Roy Bean Visitor Center. Langtry is on US 90, southwest Texas near the Mexican border. For the movie, though, the town was reconstructed in the Arizona desert near **Tucson**.

LIFE LESS ORDINARY, A
(1997, dir: Danny Boyle)
Ewan McGregor, Cameron Diaz, Holly Hunter.
● **UTAH; CALIFORNIA**

The *Shallow Grave* and *Trainspotting* team's third feature was shot in **Salt Lake City**, Utah and **Los Angeles**.

LIGHT SLEEPER
(1992, dir: Paul Schrader)
Willem Dafoe, Susan Sarandon, Dana Delany.
● **NEW YORK CITY**

The third part of Schrader's loose trilogy, which began with *Taxi Driver* and *American Gigolo*. Willem Dafoe is the insomniac drug dealer in New York, where piles of rubbish, deliberately positioned by the design department to indicate moral decay, were constantly removed by the city's too-diligent sanitation department. Filming took place at the **Hotel Pennsylvania, West 32nd Street** by Penn Station; expensive restaurant **Palio, 151 West 51st Street** in the Equitable Center; the **Paramount Hotel, 235 West 46th Street**, between Broadway and 8th Street and La Côte Basque, the French restaurant to which Sarandon takes Dafoe, which has now gone. It stood at 5 East 55th Street.

LION IN WINTER, THE
(1968, dir: Anthony Harvey)
Peter O'Toole, Katharine Hepburn, Anthony Hopkins.
● WALES; FRANCE; IRELAND

James Goldman's play, about the stormy relationship between Henry II and Eleanor of Aquitaine, may not make for the most cinematic experience, but a crackling script bursting with everybody's favourite quotes and some blistering performances make for high-octane entertainment. The interiors were filmed at Bray Studios near Dublin.

The beach scenes are **Marloes Sands**, west of Milford Haven, Pembrokeshire. Various castles around Wales and in the south of France provided the exteriors. The main location is the **Abbey of Montmajour**, near Fontvieille in the south of France. Eleanor's landing was staged on the River Rhone. The ending was shot at **Tarascon**, France.

LITTLE BIG MAN
(1970, dir: Arthur Penn)
Dustin Hoffman, Chief Dan George, Faye Dunaway.
● MONTANA; ALBERTA, CANADA; CALIFORNIA

Arthur Penn's picaresque tale of the hundred-and-something survivor of Little Big Horn. The Battle of Little Big Horn itself was shot on the actual site, now the **Custer Battlefield National Monument**, on the Little Big Horn River, Route 94, about 60 miles east of Billings, Montana, and the neighbouring Crow Reservation on Route 90. The winter scenes were filmed in Canada, at **Morley** near Calgary, Alberta. The present-day hospital bookend scenes, with a wheezy centenarian Hoffman, were filmed in the now-demolished Sawtelle Veterans Hospital, west Los Angeles.

LITTLE SHOP OF HORRORS, THE
(1960, dir: Roger Corman)
Dick Miller, Jonathan Haze, Jack Nicholson.
● LOS ANGELES

The original, low-budget spoof horror that inspired the campy musical was shot almost entirely on a tiny studio set in two days, between Christmas and New Year, 1959. The second unit filmed exteriors on skid row and at the **Santa Fe rail yards** in downtown LA, with the real inhabitants acting up for the cameras.

LITTLE VOICE
(1998, dir: Mark Herman)
Jane Horrocks, Brenda Blethyn, Michael Caine.
● YORKSHIRE

Slim vehicle (from the play originally directed by *American Beauty*'s Sam Mendes) for Jane Horrocks as a seriously introverted northern girl with an uncanny flair for vocal impersonation. Set, and filmed, in **Scarborough**, on the Yorkshire coast, where Horrocks and Blethyn's house is on the corner of **Barwick Terrace** and **Barwick Street**. Boo's Nightclub, where

Boo's Nightclub: Clayton Bay, Yorkshire

Horrocks is cajoled into performing, is the disused **Haven Holidays** site at **Clayton Bay**, on the A165 a few miles to the south of Scarborough.

LITTLE WOMEN
(1933, dir: George Cukor)
Katharine Hepburn, Joan Bennett, Paul Lukas.
● NEW HAMPSHIRE

Louisa May Alcott's book about four sisters growing up, filmed by 'women's director' Cukor, with location filming in **Concord**, New Hampshire.

LITTLE WOMEN
(1994, dir: Gillian Armstrong)
Susan Sarandon, Winona Ryder, Gabriel Byrne.
● BRITISH COLUMBIA, CANADA; MASSACHUSETTS

Remake, filmed in **Cobble Hill**, British Columbia, Canada, and Vancouver and Victoria, BC. More period settings were found at **Historic Deerfield, Deerfield**, the museum of New England history housed in a 330 year-old village in Massachusetts, off I-91 about ten miles south of Greenfield (© *413.774.5581*, *www.historic-deerfield.org*).

LIVE AND LET DIE
(1973, dir: Guy Hamilton)
Roger Moore, Yaphet Kotto, Jane Seymour.
● LOUISIANA; JAMAICA; NEW YORK CITY

One of the better Moore Bonds, playing like an homage to *North by Northwest*, opening with a murder at the United Nations, the hero hiding from an aerial attack in an overgrown field and a final scene on a train. The **United Nations Building** is on **46th Street** at First Avenue, New York, and Bond is duly dispatched to the Big Apple.

The NY consulate of the fictitious San Monique is on **69th Street**, midtown Manhattan. Bond tails a lead from the Oh Cult Voodoo Store, **33 East 65th Street** on the East Side, up Fifth Avenue to the Fillet of Soul on 'Lenox Avenue and 124th Street' in Harlem. The Fillet actually filmed on the Upper East Side on **Second Avenue at 94th Street**. The ensuing fight scene was shot on **118th Street**, edging towards the real Harlem, with more Harlem scenes using **117th Street**.

The trail leads to the island of San Monique which is, inevitably for a Bond movie, in the West Indies. Bond's hotel, where Baron Samedi performs his tourist-voodoo nightclub act, is the **Sans Souci Hotel, 2171 Magenta Drive** in **Ocho Rios**, Jamaica (which featured as Miss Taro's home in the first Bond movie, *Dr No*). The cemetery was a set built on a hill three miles north of the Montego Bay-Falmouth road. The bus chase (it's a London double-decker under the San Monique logo), used the **Montego Bay-Lucea Highway**.

The derelict wharf, where Bond and Rosie try to board Quarrel's yacht, is at **Montego Bay**. Rosie's breakfast veranda is a bungalow at **Half Moon Bay**.

To New Orleans International Airport (**Moisant Field** in **Kenner**, fifteen miles east of the Big Easy itself), where Bond is spirited away to the Bleeker Flying School – in actuality the **Lakefront Airport** – where several planes get thoroughly trashed. The crocodile farm (the 'Trespassers will be eaten' sign is actually for real) is Ross Kananga's farm, home to 300 crocs and 'gators, not in Louisiana at all but back in Jamaica, some 20 miles from Montego Bay. Kananga himself, whose name was confusingly nicked for the film's villain, performs the running-over-the-crocs stunt.

Bond escapes by boat, ready for the big set piece chase through the Louisiana bayous. The boat jumps over Highway 11 at the **Crawdad Bridge**, just outside Phoenix on the Mississippi, south of New Orleans. The interrupted wedding was filmed at the **Treadway Estate**, a former Indian reservation in Louisiana's Bayou country, 30 miles from New Orleans. The boats scoot over the lawn at the **Baldwin Estate**, Lousiana. The police riverblock is at **Miller's Bridge**. Adam dies among the rusting wrecks of the boatyard at **Slidell**. The Southern Yacht Club marina is on the shores of **Lake Pontchartrain**.

LIVES OF A BENGAL LANCER, THE
(1935, dir: Henry Hathaway)
Gary Cooper, Franchot Tone, Richard Cromwell.
● **CALIFORNIA**

Heroics on India's Northwest Frontier, a project originated some years earlier by *King Kong* co-creator Ernest Schoedsack and intended to be made on location, but little of the Indian footage remains. The film was shot on the fantastic rocky outcrops of the **Alabama Hills** above **Lone Pine**, I-395, central California (see *Kim* for details).

LIVING DAYLIGHTS, THE
(1987, dir: John Glen)
Timothy Dalton, Maryam d'Abo, Jeroen Krabbe.
● **MOROCCO; AUSTRIA; GIBRALTAR; LONDON**

First of the po-faced Bonds, reacting against the increasingly flip Moore movies. The opening war games teaser filmed on **Gibraltar**. Bond's HQ, Universal Exports, is on the south side of London's **Trafalgar Square**. Bond meets Saunders at the **Prater Café** in Vienna's Prater Park, alongside the fairground with *The Third Man*'s Big Wheel, which of course has to be incorporated into the action. The Vienna hotel is the **Hotel Im Palais Schwarzenberg, Schwarzenbergplatz 9**. Situated in 15 acres of park in the heart of Vienna, it was built 300 years ago as a palace, and gutted by the Nazis. Part of the building is now the hotel. The theatre is the **Sofiensale Theater**, and filming also took place in the grounds and palace of **Schonbrunn**. The Afghan airport is **Ouarzazate Airfield** in Morocco (an often-used location – for details of Ouarzazate see *Lawrence of Arabia*). The militaristic villa of villain Joe Don Baker is the **Forbes Museum, Palace El Mendoub, Tangier** (though the interior was recreated in the studio) which was founded by and belonged to millionaire Malcolm Forbes.

LOCAL HERO
(1983, dir: Bill Forsyth)
Denis Lawson, Peter Riegert, Burt Lancaster.
● **SCOTLAND; TEXAS**

Canny locals of a small Scottish village exploit a Texan oil company in a movie that harks back to the great days of the Ealing comedy. The fictitious Scots village of Fer-

ness is a conflation of two separate locations. The beach is **Morar Beach**, at **Camusdarrach**, 37 miles from Fort William. The village is **Pennan**, over on the other side of Scotland, on the north Grampian coast, 36 miles north of Abberdeen on the B9032. It's at Pennan that you'll find the phone box, which is now the subject of a preservation order. The church is simply a cottage with added set dressing, though the interior is **Our Lady of the Braes Roman Catholic Church** at **Polnish**. The hotel, likewise, was filmed at a private house. The interior is the **Lochailort Inn**, **Lochailort** on the A861, Invernesshire. The village shop is at **Pole of Itlaw**, south of Banff on the B9121 in Banffshire and the village hall is in **Hilton** on the A948, about 15 miles north of Aberdeen. Skywatching Burt Lancaster heads Knox Oil at its HQ in **Houston**, Texas.

LOCH NESS
(1995, dir: John Henderson)
Ted Danson, Joely Richardson, Ian Holm.
● **SCOTLAND; LONDON**

Most of the filming is actually on the real **Loch Ness** itself, though it's prettied up with a few extra locations. The ruined castle is **Urquhart Castle**, which *is* on Loch Ness (and can be seen in Billy Wilder's excellent *The Private Life of Sherlock Holmes*), although it's intercut with shots of the more striking **Eilean Donan Castle** (seen also in *Highlander*). The pier and the bay are at **Lower Diabag** on **Loch Torridon**, along with Joely Richardson's hotel. Filming also took place at the villages of **Dores**; **Foyers**; and **Fort Augustus** on Loch Ness, and at the **Natural History Museum** in South Kensington, London.

LOCK, STOCK AND TWO SMOKING BARRELS
(1998, dir: Guy Ritchie)
Jason Flemyng, Dexter Fletcher, Nick Moran.
● **LONDON**

A great black comedy, drawing on *Performance*, *The Long Good Friday*, *Pulp Fiction* and *The Italian Job* among scores of other movies. The gang's hang-

The hideout: Park Street, Borough

out, also used in that other slice of seedy London low life, *Howards End*, is **15 Park Street, SE1**, a wonderfully undeveloped street opposite Borough Market. Dog's place, next door, is **13 Park Street**. Filming also took place in **Brick Lane, E1**; the card game was staged in **Repton Boxing Gym** – an old haunt of the Kray twins. The office of the seedy Soho sex club is actually **Bethnal Green Town Hall**. JD's bar is **Vic Naylor, 40 St John Street**, Smithfield, EC1.

LOCK UP YOUR DAUGHTERS!
(1969, dir: Peter Coe)
Christopher Plummer, Susannah York, Tom Bell.
● **IRELAND**

A brace of Restoration comedies, combined into a musical for London's Mermaid Theatre and then filmed, without the songs. **Kilkenny**, 60 miles southwest of Dublin, stands in for 18th century London.

LOLITA
(1962, dir: Stanley Kubrick)
James Mason, Sue Lyon, Peter Sellers.
● **BUCKINGHAMSHIRE**

Lolita's New Hampshire home: Packhorse Road, Gerrards Cross

Kubrick couldn't have filmed Nabokov's controversial novel in the US, so he moved to the UK. And stayed. Although the story is set in urban America, it was made almost entirely at Elstree Studios. A second-unit in the States provided the briefest of establishing shots and the back-projection sequences, but all the rest is England. Shelley Winters' lodgings in West Ramsdale, New Hampshire, where James Mason develops an obsession with nymphet Sue Lyon, is **Highburgh House, Packhorse Road, Gerrards Cross** (*rail: Gerrards Cross*), about half a mile north of the railway station, in Buckinghamshire. And it's on Packhorse Road that Shelley Winters gets hit by a car.

LOLITA
(1997, dir: Adrian Lyne)
Jeremy Irons, Melanie Griffith, Dominique Swain.
● **CALIFORNIA; LOUISIANA; NEW MEXICO; NORTH CAROLINA; TEXAS**.

Lolita's real America: Petaluma Boulevard, Petaluma

Controversial remake, with 14-year-old Swain in the lead, which had problems being released, particularly in the US. Filming took place all over the States: **Petaluma** (the town in *American Grafitti*) at the **Mystic Theater** and **D Street and Petaluma Boulevard**; **New Orleans**, Louisiana; **Las Cruces**, New Mexico; the **Chinqua Penn Plantation**, North Carolina; **Wilmington** (home of *Blue Velvet*), North Carolina; and **El Paso, Lake Buchanan, Luckenbach, Richmond, San Antonio** and **Wharton** in Texas.

LONELINESS OF THE LONG DISTANCE RUNNER, THE
(1962, dir: Tony Richardson)
Tom Courtenay, Michael Redgrave, James Fox.
● **SURREY**

Courtenay is the borstal boy with stamina in this dour character study filmed on location around London. The borstal is **Ruxley Towers**, which until recently could be seen disused and crumbling away at the end of **Ruxley Ridge**, off Common Road, **Claygate**, just southeast of Esher in Surrey (*rail: Claygate Station*). The facility had been used by

the army as a NAAFI facility, but recently it has been substantially renovated and is enjoying a new lease of life as a private, and very luxurious home.

The borstal: Ruxley Towers, Claygate

LONELY ARE THE BRAVE
(1962, dir: David Miller)
Kirk Douglas, Walter Matthau, Gena Rowlands.
● **NEW MEXICO**

A sombre passing-of-the-Old-West movie, adapted by Dalton Trumbo from Edward Abbey's novel *Brave Cowboy*. Shot in the **Manzano Mountains** south of Albuquerque, New Mexico.

LONELY PASSION OF JUDITH HEARNE, THE
(1987, dir: Jack Clayton)
Maggie Smith, Bob Hoskins, Wendy Hiller.
● **DUBLIN**

Sad little downbeat character study with heartbreaking performances, set and filmed in Dublin. American widower Bob Hoskins takes Maggie Smith to the **Shelbourne Hotel, St Stephen's Green**. Smith's house is **47 Blessington Street**.

LONG DAY'S JOURNEY INTO NIGHT
(1962, dir: Sidney Lumet)
Ralph Richardson, Katharine Hepburn, Jason Robards.
● **NEW YORK STATE**

Judith Hearne's home: Blessington Street, Dublin

Filming of Eugene O'Neill's autobiographical play, set in 1912 Connecticut, with Richardson as the actor father, and Hepburn as the druggie mother. The Connecticut house was found at **21 Tier Street** on **City Island**, a new England-style community on a 230-acre island in Long Island Sound, connected to Pelham Bay Park on the Bronx's eastern coastline by a causeway.

LONG GOOD FRIDAY, THE
(1980, dir: John Mackenzie)
Bob Hoskins, Helen Mirren, Derek Thompson.
● **LONDON; SCOTLAND**

One of the few British thrillers that can stand up against the best from the US, as gangland boss Hoskins is unwittingly caught up in shady deals with the IRA. Filmed around London, with Scotland standing in for Belfast. Much of the action centres around London's **St Katherine's Dock**, just downstream from Tower Bridge. The street where Paul Barber gets grilled, while a gang of kids guard Hoskins' car, is **Villa Road, Brixton, SW9**. The Boulevard Restaurant, now gone, where the distraught widow of Hoskins' chauffeur spits in the face of his henchman, was on **Wigmore Street, W1**. The Mafia contacts stay at the **Savoy Hotel**, in the **Strand**, where Hoskins is abducted during the cracking ending (that's a young Pierce Brosnan wielding the gun).

LONG GOODBYE, THE
(1973, dir: Robert Altman)
Elliott Gould, Nina Van Pallandt, Sterling Hayden.
● **LOS ANGELES; MEXICO**

Updating of Chandler's novel by veteran screenwriter Leigh Brackett, who also worked on the screenplay for the 1946 *The Big Sleep*. Reviled on release, it's now regarded as a classic. Made almost entirely on location around LA, at **Malibu** Sheriff's office; a rest home in **Pasadena**; the new skyscraper at **9000 Sunset Boulevard**; offices in **Westwood** and **Hollywood**; and **Lincoln Heights Jail**. Nina van Pallandt's home is Robert Altman's own **Malibu Colony** beachfront house. Elliot Gould's apartment is the beautiful Italianate **High Tower, High Tower Drive** off Camrose Avenue, Hollywood (see *Dead Again* for details). Filming also took place in Mexico.

LONG, HOT SUMMER, THE
(1958, dir: Martin Ritt)
Paul Newman, Joanne Woodward, Orson Welles.
● **LOUISIANA**

An overheated, in every sense, Deep South melodrama from stories by William Faulkner. The town of Frenchman's Bend, where drifter Newman settles, is **Clinton**, 30 miles north of Baton Rouge. Joanne Woodward's mansion is **Asphodel, East Felicia Parish** one of the many plantation houses along the Mississippi between New Orleans and state capital Baton Rouge (*www.asphodelplantation.com*). The church, where Newman wins a picnic with Woodward at the fundraiser, is **St Andrew's Episcopal Church**.

LONG KISS GOODNIGHT, THE
(1996, dir: Renny Harlin)
Geena Davis, Samuel L Jackson, Brian Cox.
● **ONTARIO, CANADA; NEW JERSEY**

Slam-bang action-er, with happily married Davis waking from an eight-year bout of amnesia to discover that she was previously a lethal CIA assassin. Set in New Jersey, the

Samuel L Jackson's home: Heward Avenue, Toronto

film was shot mainly in Canada, although when Davis and incompetent PI Jackson hide out in **Atlantic City**, New Jersey, they stay in the **Taj Mahal**. Canadian locations included **Collingwood**, on Nottawasaga Bay, northwest of Toronto; **Hamilton**, south Toronto; **Historic Unionville**, in **Markham**, north Toronto; **Milton**, west Toronto; **Concord**; **Dundas**; **Halton Hills**; **Milford Bay**; **Scarborough**; **Uxbridge**; **Wasaga Beach**; **Windmere** and **York Region**. Samuel Jackson's home is **134 Heward Avenue**, off Queen Street East, eastern Toronto. Geena Davis dumps

him from the car in front of the **Canary Restaurant, 409 Front Street East** at Cherry Street (a regular location, seen in Jean-Claude Van Damme's *Maximum Risk* and Bette Midler weepie *Stella*) down toward the Port of Toronto. Chesterman Station, site of the massive shoot-out and the leap into the frozen canal, is **Old Hamilton Train Station**, which you might recognise as the station where Magneto demonstrates his powers in *X-Men*. The climax was filmed at **Niagara Falls**, though the bridge is actually unharmed.

Geena Davis dumps Samuel Jackson: Cherry Street

LONG RIDERS, THE
(1980, dir: Walter Hill)
The brothers Carradine, Keach, Quaid and Guest.
● **GEORGIA; TEXAS; CALIFORNIA**

Hill's excellent Western casts four sets of Hollywood brothers as the James gang. It utilises excellent locations around **Parrott**, Georgia; as well as Texas and northern California.

LONGEST DAY, THE
(1962, dir: Andrew Marton, Ken Annakin, Bernhard Wicki)
John Wayne, Rod Steiger, Robert Ryan.
● **FRANCE**

Countless stars line up in this account of the 1944 D-Day landings, which was filmed on the **Normandy** beaches – codenamed Gold, Juno, Sword, Utah and Omaha – where the action actually took place.

LOOK BACK IN ANGER
(1959, dir: Tony Richardson)
Richard Burton, Mary Ure, Claire Bloom.
● **LONDON**

John Osborne's bilious attack on, well, everything, the original kitchen sink drama, transferred from the Royal Court stage to film. London location filming was at **Deptford Market**; **Dalston Junction** and **Stratford East**.

LOOK WHO'S TALKING
(1989, dir: Amy Heckerling)
John Travolta, Kirstie Alley, Olympia Dukakis.
● **BRITISH COLUMBIA, CANADA**

Bruce Willis voices Mikey the Talking Baby in this one-joke movie, and Travolta's career gets a false restart. Set in New York, where Travolta is a Yellow Cab driver, but the Big Apple has never looked so clean, bland and anonymous. No art deco, and no quirky skyscrapers. That's because it was filmed in Canada, on the

Kirstie Alley's New York apartment: Thurlow Street, Vancouver

streets of downtown **Vancouver**, British Columbia, with barely an establishing shot of NYC. As Travolta's cab rushes Kirstie Alley to hospital, he races along **Hornby Street**, past Vancouver Art Gallery, and along **Burrard Street**, downtown Vancouver. When Travolta drives Alley to Grandpa's they pass the **Hotel Georgia, 801 West Georgia Street**, and a couple of minutes later pass it again in the opposite direction. Some cab driver.

Kirstie Alley's apartment building is **784 Thurlow Street at Robson Street**. Mikey braves the traffic to bring Travolta and Alley together by an English theme-pub, the **Jolly Taxpayer, 828 West Hastings Street** at Howes Street.

Look Who's Talking Too was also made in Vancouver, though there's a little more New York on view in that movie.

LOOT

(1970, dir: Silvio Narizzano)
Hywel Bennett, Lee Remick, Richard Attenborough.
● **SUSSEX**

The entrance to McLeavy's Hotel: Bear Road

Joe Orton's stage farce is transmuted into a gaudy, frenetic black comedy, now set in a **Brighton** boarding house. The cemetery, where Mrs McLeavy doesn't get buried, is **Lewes Road Cemetery**, east of the town centre. The out-of-control funeral careers down **Bear Road**. The entrance to McLeavy's Hotel can be seen at the top of Bear Road, at Warren Road opposite Brighton Racecourse.

LORD OF THE FLIES

(1963, dir: Peter Brook)
James Aubrey, Tom Chapin, Hugh Edwards.
● **PUERTO RICO**

Brook's attempt to film William Golding's novel, about a party of English schoolboys reverting to savagery after a plane crash leaves them stranded on a deserted island, filmed at **Frenchman's Cove**, east of Port Antonio, Puerto Rico.

The 1990 American remake, changing the English schoolboys for US military cadets, was shot on the Garden Isle of **Kauai**, Hawaii.

LOST BOYS, THE

(1987, dir: Joel Schumacher)
Jason Patric, Corey Haim, Dianne Wiest.
● **CALIFORNIA**

A teenage vampire gang in smalltown California. Good ideas – the vampire lair is a Victorian hotel lobby which slipped into a fault in the 1906 earthquake – and a good cast are squandered. "I sensed that with this picture I could have fun without the result becoming camp" said director Schumacher. Well, there you go.

Santa Carla is **Santa Cruz**, an eccentric coastal town between San Mateo and Monterey on the California coast south of San Francisco. The main attraction is the town's lively **Santa Cruz Beach Boardwalk, 400 Beach Street**, California's only surviving traditional seafront funfair.

The rollercoaster: Santa Cruz Beach Boardwalk, California

Here you'll find the wonderful 1911 carousel the boys are barred from at the opening of the movie, and the old wooden rollercoaster.

LOST HIGHWAY

(1996, dir: David Lynch)
Bill Pullman, Patricia Arquette, Balthazar Getty.
● **CALIFORNIA**

Lynch's foray into fluid identities is his most disturbing and successful effort since *Blue Velvet*. Bill Pullman's home is Lynch's own – he designed it himself – hidden away in the **Hollywood Hills**. The desert locale is **Silurian Dry Lake**, east of Route 127, between Baker and Shoshone in the Mojave Desert. The Lost Highway

The Lost Highway Hotel exterior: Death Valley Building, Death Valley Junction

The Lost Highway Hotel interiors: Amargoso Hotel, Death Valley Junction

Hotel is a conflation of two buildings. The corridors are the **Amargoso Hotel, Death Valley Junction**, a tiny, one-street town on Route 127, north of Shoshone near the Nevada border. The exterior is the more photogenic **Death Valley Building**, directly opposite.

LOST HORIZON

(1937, dir: Frank Capra)
Ronald Colman, Jane Wyatt, John Howard.
● **CALIFORNIA**

The opening airlift of Capra's classic fantasy was filmed at the old Los Angeles Metropolitan Airport, now incorporated into **Van Nuys Airport, 6590 Hayvenhurst Avenue, Van Nuys**, with the San Bernardino Mountains standing in for the mountains of Baskul. The Metropolitan Airport also featured as Casablanca Airport in *Casablanca*. The plane refuels at **Lucerne Dry Lake**, east of Victorville in the Mojave Desert. The aerial shots of the Himalayas are actually the High Sierras northwest of **Lone Pine**, central California. The Lamasery of Shangri-La was built on the Columbia Ranch at 4000 Warner Boulevard, Burbank, and the Valley of the Blue Moon, with its Tibetan village, is in **Sherwood Forest** beyond the San Fernando Valley.

The waterfall scene used **Tahquitz Canyon** (it's closed to the public, and you need a special permit to visit it). Tahquitz Canyon is part of Palm Canyon, stretching for some 15 miles in the Low Desert close to Palm Springs, 107 miles east of LA. You can find the spot from which Ronald Colman looked down onto the valley of Shangri-La northwest of Los Angeles, near Ventura. About ten miles north of Ventura is Ojai. From Ojai, follow Route 150, **East End Drive**, for about three miles to the spot, a promontory with a stone bench, inscribed 'The Ojai Valley'.

The clunky musical remake in 1973 used old sets from *Camelot* at Warners Burbank Studio, perked up with a bit of Oriental tat, and LA gardens with white sheeting laid down for snow. The snowbound opening scenes are at **Mount Hood, Oregon**, home of the Overlook Hotel in Stanley Kubrick's *The Shining*.

LOST PATROL, THE
(1934, dir: John Ford)
Victor McLaglen, Boris Karloff, Wallace Ford.
● **ARIZONA**

British army patrol in the Mesopotamian desert during WWI are picked off by Arabs. The desert scenes were filmed around **Yuma**, southwest Arizona.

LOST WEEKEND, THE
(1945, dir: Billy Wilder)
Ray Milland, Jane Wyman, Philip Terry.
● **NEW YORK CITY**

Grim, realistic study of alcoholism, made on location in New York. The bar is **PJ Clarke's Saloon, 915 Third Avenue** at East 55th Street. This wonderful institution is, amazingly, still open for business, a tiny oasis among the highrise real estate of the East Side. The rumble of the old 'Third Avenue el' – the elevated railway which ran past the bar – meant that many of the scenes had to be re-shot in the studio. Milland dries out at **Bellevue Hospital, First Avenue** at East 29th Street. Milland's painful trek along **Third Avenue**, north from 55th Street to 110th Street in search of a pawnbroker, was shot by a hidden camera inside a bakery truck one quiet Sunday.

LOST WORLD: JURASSIC PARK, THE
(1997, dir: Steven Spielberg)
Jeff Goldblum, Julianne Moore, Pete Postlethwaite.
● **CALIFORNIA; HAWAII**

Richard Attenborough's house, where Jeff Goldblum has his arm twisted to travel out to the previously unmentioned Isla Sorna, is actually a Catholic girls' school in Pasadena, **Mayfield Senior School, 500 Bellefontaine Street** (seen also in *Devil in a Blue Dress*). And while Site B again used *Jurassic Park*'s main location on the island of **Kauai**, Hawaii, for scene setting, much of the action was

John Hammond's house: Mayfield Senior School, Pasadena

filmed on mainland USA, in northern California near to Eureka, at **Patrick's Point**.

T Rex on the loose in San Diego: Golden Mall, Burbank

The T-rex wreaks havoc on landing at **San Diego**, supposedly in the city's Gaslamp district. But once again, there's a bit of sleight of hand. San Diego only features in a bit of Second Unit footage to establish the locale. Most of the filming was much closer to the studio in **Burbank**, at **Golden Mall** on **San Fernando Boulevard** between **Palm Grove** and **Orange Grove**, which were renamed with San Diego street signs. The Starbucks coffee shop is at **300 San Fernando Boulevard**. The bookshop where the screenwriter David Koepp, in a cameo as 'Unlucky Bastard' gets chomped by the T-rex, is **Crown Books, 301 San Fernando Boulevard**. The InGen dock where the T-rex boat crashes ashore is actually **San Pedro** harbour in LA. The house where T-rex takes a drink from the swimming pool and snacks on a dog is in **Granada Hills**, a Valley suburb of LA, and here too is the gas station, where the trademark '76' ball rolls down the street. It's the **Chevron Filling Station, Balboa Boulevard** at the corner of **Rinaldi**.

T Rex trashes the gas station: Balboa Boulevard, Granada Hills

LOVE AFFAIR
(1939, dir: Leo McCarey)
Irene Dunne, Charles Boyer, Maria Ouspenskaya.
● **NEW YORK CITY**

First of three versions of the classic tearjerker, with Dunne and Boyer meeting aboard ship, and pledging to reunite at the **Empire State Building, 350 Fifth Avenue**. Dunne misses the appointment when she's hit, and crippled by, a cab.

LOVE AFFAIR
(1994, dir: Glenn Gordon Caron)
Warren Beatty, Annette Bening, Katharine Hepburn.
● **NEW YORK CITY; FRENCH POLYNESIA**

Third version of the timeless story (the second was *An Affair to Remember*). Beatty and Bening meet up when their flight to Sydney is forced to land at **Moorea**, French Polynesia, but the rendezvous is still the **Empire State Building**. Filming also took place at **Essex House, 160 Central Park South**, in midtown Manhattan.

LOVE AND DEATH
(1975, dir: Woody Allen)
Woody Allen, Diane Keaton, Harold Gould.
● **PARIS; HUNGARY**

Back in the days when Woody Allen strayed, occasionally, outside Manhattan, he went to Europe to make this funny Bergmanesque version of *War and Peace*, filmed on real locations in **Budapest** and Paris.

LOVE AT FIRST BITE
(1979, dir: Stan Dragoti)
George Hamilton, Susan St James, Richard Benjamin.
● **NEW YORK CITY**

Spoofy Dracula story, with Hamilton's count fleeing Transylvania to take up residence in New York. He stays in luxury at the **Plaza Hotel, Fifth Avenue** at 59th Street. Shrink Richard Benjamin, unable to convince Manhattanites that Dracula walks among them, is committed to **Bellevue Hospital, First Avenue** at East 29th Street. Susan St James' apartment is the **Langham, 135 Central Park West**, seen also in *Hannah and Her Sisters*.

LOVE BUG, THE
(1969, dir: Robert Stevenson)
Dean Jones, Michele Lee, David Tomlinson.
● **CALIFORNIA**

The 'Crookedest Street in the World': Lombard Street, San Francisco

Disney fun, with the anthropomorphic VW's first outing, set in San Francisco. And, of course, any comedy car chase set in the Bay City has to take in the self-proclaimed 'Crookedest Street in the World', the **1000 block of Lombard Street**, between Hyde and Leavenworth. The eight switchbacks were introduced in 1922, not by a movie company, but as a practical way of rendering the street accessible to cars. If you want to see it, go on foot or take the Hyde-Powell cable car which runs along the top of the street, as it can get seriously clogged with sightseers. Filming also took place on the **Monterey Peninsula**, on the coast south of the city.

LOVE STORY
(1970, dir: Arthur Hiller)
Ryan O'Neal, Ali MacGraw, Ray Milland.
● **MASSACHUSETTS; NEW YORK CITY**

Rich kid O'Neal gives up the family fortune to marry working class student McGraw, but it's a bad deal as she's dying from one of those mysterious Hollywood diseases devoid

Love means...: Oxford Street, Cambridge

of visible symptoms. O'Neal and McGraw meet at **Harvard**. Along with the sequel, *Oliver's Story*, legal drama *The Paper Chase* and misfiring comedy *Soul Man*, it's one of the few features actually filmed on the hallowed campus. Filming took place at **Harvard Yard** and **Tercentury Theatre**. The intimidatingly grand mansion belonging to Ray Milland, O'Neal's unbending father, is .

The college campus: Harvard Yard

the **Phipps Estate House, Old Westbury Gardens, 71 Old Westbury Road** on Long Island (see *North by Northwest* for details), though the gate leading to it is that of **Planting Fields**, on Long Island.

After their DIY marriage, O'Neal and McGraw set up home in a modest woodframe house at **119 Oxford Street, Cambridge**. It's on the doorstep here that McGraw gets to utter the immortal 'Love means never having to say you're sorry'. After graduation, the couple move to New York City. The skating scene is at the **Wollman Skating Rink** in Central Park. When McGraw is taken ill, they catch a cab by Central Park opposite the **Hotel Pierre**.

LOVED ONE, THE
(1965, dir: Tony Richardson)
Robert Morse, John Gielgud, Rod Steiger.
● **LOS ANGELES**

Tony Richardson's satire on the movie business and the American funeral industry, based on the Evelyn Waugh novel, is a bit hit and miss, but the hits are priceless, including Liberace

Whispering Glades: Greystone Park, Loma Vista Drive, Beverly Hills

as an oleaginous coffin salesman. Robert Morse arrives at **Los Angeles International Airport, LAX**. Megalopolitan Studios, where he goes to work, is the MGM lot. Behind the Megalopolitan logo is the Metro-Goldwyn-Mayer sign of the Irving Thalberg Building. Whispering Glades is the 16-acre **Greystone Park**, the grounds of **Greystone Mansion, 905 Loma Vista Drive, Beverly Hills**. The park, open daily to the public, disguises a massive underground reservoir. By the way, it's often said in guidebooks that John Gielgud's home in the movie is the Spadena House, Beverly Hills' quirky Witch's House – seen in Roger Corman's 1957 *The Undead* – but it ain't.

LUST FOR LIFE
(1956, dir: Vincente Minnelli)
Kirk Douglas, Anthony Quinn, James Donald.
● **HOLLAND; FRANCE; BELGIUM**

Minnelli's biopic of Van Gogh was shot in Europe on many of the real locations. Including **Vught** and **Bois-la-Duc** in Holland, **Paris**, and **St Remy** and **Arles** in Provence. The Petit Wasmes mine disaster was staged at **Le Borinage** in south Belgium, using 200 unemployed miners as extras. The final wheatfield scenes, of Van Gogh's suicide, are at **Auvers-sur-Oises**.

M

MA NUIT CHEZ MAUD (aka *My Night at Maud's*)
(1969, dir: Eric Rohmer)
Jean-Louis Trintignant, Marie-Christine Barrault.
● **FRANCE**

Trintignant is obliged to crash down with his mate's girl-friend during a snowstorm. Naturally, they flirt, discuss Jansenism, consider marriage and don't have sex. Trintignant, however, eventually realises he really loves a blonde he's seen on a bicycle. The town is **Clermont-Ferrand**, though the interior of Maud's apartment was recreated in a small studio on the rue Mouffetard in Paris. The epilogue is on the island of **Belle Ile** off St Nazaire, and in **Paris**.

MACBETH
(1971, dir: Roman Polanski)
Jon Finch, Francesca Annis, Martin Shaw.
● **NORTHUMBERLAND; WALES**

Misguided attempt to film Shakespeare's dark nightmare as a too-naturalistic historical bloodbath. Some nice visuals though. Dunsinane is **Bamburgh Castle** in Northumberland (see *The Devils* for details). Inverness is **Lindisfarne Castle** on Holy Island (see Polanski's earlier film, *Cul-De-Sac*, for details). The movie also uses locations in Wales – the opening beach scenes are **Morfa Bychan**, near Portmadoc.

McCABE AND MRS MILLER
(1971, dir: Robert Altman)
Warren Beatty, Julie Christie, René Auberjonois.
● **BRITISH COLUMBIA, CANADA**

Altman's bleakly atmospheric Western, trashed on release, has since gained classic status. The frontier town was built in its entirety – cabins, saloons, barbershop, whorehouse, church, general store and sawmill – in **West Vancouver**, British Columbia, and gorgeously photographed by Vilmos Zsigmond.

MACKENNA'S GOLD
(1969, dir: J Lee Thompson)
Gregory Peck, Omar Sharif, Telly Savalas.
● **ARIZONA; UTAH**

Bizarre, epic Western, with loads of guest stars attempting to track down the legendary Valley of Gold. The striking desert landscapes are **Glen Canyon**, Utah; and the magnificent **Canyon de Chelly**, Arizona. The sheer, red cliffs of Canyon de Chelly are peppered with caves and the ruins of Indian villages (*www.nps.gov/cach*). The visitor centre is at Chinle, about three miles from Route 191.

MAD MAX
(1979, dir: George Miller)
Mel Gibson, Joanne Samuel, Hugh Keays-Byrne.
● **VICTORIA, AUSTRALIA**

Mel Gibson shot to fame as futuristic, leather-clad cop Max Rockatansky, unhinged by the murder of his wife and child, in George Miller's low budget actioner, which spawned increasingly spectacular sequels. Filmed on the roads around Melbourne. The Halls of Justice cop station/garage, where Max is seduced by the souped-up motor, is the **Southern Car Park** of **Melbourne University**.

MAD MAX 2 (aka *The Road Warrior*)
(1981, dir: George Miller)
Mel Gibson, Bruce Spence, Vernon Wells.
● **NEW SOUTH WALES, AUSTRALIA**

Sequel takes on an epic sweep, and the visual style launched a slew of rip-offs. It was made at the deserted (except for film crews, that is) ghost town of **Silverton**, about fourteen miles northwest of Broken Hill. Once a booming silver town – producing one third of the world's silver – Silverton is now a frequent location, seen in films such as *Razorback* and the TV remake of *A Town Like Alice*. Memorabilia from the various movies shot here is on display. The stretch of road used for the climactic smash-up can be seen just outside town.

The final smash-up: Silverton, New South Wales

MAD MAX BEYOND THUNDERDOME
(1985, dir: George Miller)
Mel Gibson, Tina Turner, Frank Thring.
● **SOUTH AUSTRALIA; NEW SOUTH WALES, AUSTRALIA**

The main location for the third part of the trilogy is the strange, moonlike landscape, scarred by opal mining, around **Coober Pedy** in South Australia. The name means 'White Man's Burrow' – most of the homes here, even the church and the rooms of two of the five motels, are dug out of the ground. You can visit the underground dwelling seen at the end of the movie. It's **Harry's Crocodile Nest**, three miles outside Coober Pedy itself (*admission charge*).

Also featured is **The Castle**, part of the Breakaways, the end of a mountain chain around 20 miles from town. You can fly out to Coober Pedy, or take a daily bus from Adelaide or Alice Springs (expect a lengthy journey, 530 miles from Adelaide, 455 from Alice). To drive there, take National Route 1 from Adelaide to Port Augusta, then continue on Route 87, Stuart Highway. The town is seen also in *The Adventures of Priscilla, Queen of the Desert*. There was more filming at a vast, empty brick pit in the **Blue Mountains**, 50 miles west of Sydney.

MADIGAN

(1968, dir: Donald Siegel)
Richard Widmark, Henry Fonda, Harry Guardino.
● **NEW YORK CITY; LOS ANGELES**

Cop-with-a-grudge movie, which Siegel later recycled as *Dirty Harry*. This time round it's Richard Widmark, with plenty of sleazy Brooklyn locations. Henry Fonda's apartment is on **57th Street**, Manhattan. The final shoot-out in Harlem was actually shot in downtown LA, with a bit of clever effects work taking out the LA Civic Center and replacing it with a NY skyscraper.

MADNESS OF KING GEORGE, THE

(1994, dir: Nicholas Hytner)
Nigel Hawthorne, Helen Mirren, Rupert Everett.
● **OXFORDSHIRE; LONDON; SUSSEX; BERKSHIRE; WILTSHIRE; MIDDLESEX**

Stage director Nicholas Hytner's film adaptation of Alan Bennett's play, *The Madness of George III*, uses a slew of real locations. The opening concert is the sumptuous 17th century Double Cube Room of **Wilton House**, in the town of **Wilton**, two and a half miles west of Salisbury on the A30, Wiltshire. The house and grounds are open in summer (*admission charge, © 01722. 746720*). Another popular location, Wilton House can be seen in *Barry Lyndon*, *The Bounty* and *Mrs Brown* among many others. See *The Music Lovers* for details.

The Palace of Westminster, exterior: School Yard, Eton College

Windsor Castle has been extensively remodelled since George III's reign, so the film uses the exterior of **Arundel Castle, Arundel**, in West Sussex (*rail: Arundel*), the 12th century home of the Duke of Norfolk. The castle is open Sunday to Friday in summer (*admission charge; © 01903. 883136*). The entrance is on Lower Lodge Mill Road, Arundel, just north of the A27 between Worthing and Chichester.

The Palace of Westminster interior: Convocation, Oxford

The Palace of Westminster, too, has changed beyond recognition. The exterior is the **School Yard** of **Eton College**, north of Windsor, Berkshire. The steps lead up to the north porch of **College Chapel**. Between the buttresses at the foot of the steps, the game of Eton Fives originated. You can see the same yard in stacks of other films, including *Chariots of Fire*, *Young Sherlock Holmes*, *The Fourth Protocol* and *Henry VIII and His Six Wives*. The public entrance to the school (it's generally open from April to mid-October) is on Slough Road (*admission charge*). The House of Commons interior, with Bennett himself as an MP, used **Convocation** in Oxford, with the adjoining **Divinity School** standing in for the lobby. Both are part of the Bodleian Library complex, **Catte Street**, and are open to the public. About ten miles east of Oxford is the location used for Kew Gardens, where the King is sent to be cured by strict doctor Ian Holm. It's **Thame Park, Thame Park Road**, just southeast of the village of Thame. A private house, it was bought with the intention of conversion into a hotel, but the plans fell through and the house currently stands empty.

The music recital: Naval College, Greenwich

Windsor Castle: Arundel Castle, Sussex

The House of Commons' lobby: Divinity School, Oxford

The Queen's royal apartments are **Broughton Castle**, a moated 14th century Medieval castle which was much enlarged in 1550. The home of Lord and Lady Saye and Sele, it's two miles southwest of Banbury, Oxfordshire, on the B40355 Shipston-on-Stour road. It's open to the public Wednesdays and Sundays in summer (*admission charge; © 01295.262624*). You can also see the castle in *Shakespeare in Love* and *Three Men and a Little Lady*.

The Prince of Wales' lodgings also used Wilton House, as well as at the **Royal Naval College, Greenwich**, London SE10 (*rail: Greenwich*). It's in the lavish **Painted Hall** of the Royal Naval College that the royal family suffers through the handbell concert. In Wren's building, until recently used as the dining room of the naval hospital, painter James Thornhill collaborated with architect Nicholas Hawksmoor for nineteen years on this *trompe l'oeil* extravaganza. It was here that the body of Lord Nelson lay in state, and the Painted Hall is open to the public. The Long Gallery, in which the King sees Pitt, is at **Syon House** (*rail: Brentford or Syon Lane*), on the north bank of the Thames between Brentford and Isleworth. The Prince of Wales' breakfast room is also Syon House (*admission charge; © 020.8560.0881*). See *Accident* for details.

MAGIC FLUTE, THE

(1974, dir: Ingmar Bergman)
Josef Kostlinger, Irma Urrila, Hakan Hagegard.
● **SWEDEN**

Mozart's opera filmed (*à la* Busby Berkeley) as a stage performance which opens up cinematically. The theatre is the **Drottingholm Palace** in the royal park outside Stockholm, though filming inside proved impractical and the interior was recreated at the Swedish Film Institute at Rasunda.

MAGNIFICENT AMBERSONS, THE

(1942, dir: Orson Welles)
Joseph Cotten, Dolores Costello, Tim Holt.

● LOS ANGELES

Welles' second feature was butchered by the studio after a disastrous preview in Pomona, while the director was in South America filming *It's All True*. The historical context was hacked out, and a ghastly happy ending tacked on, by Welles' then-editor Robert Wise. It was made almost entirely in the studio, at the RKO Studios, 780 Gower Street in Hollywood. Just about the only scenes not filmed at RKO are the snow sequences which were shot, for authenticity, in an ice house in East Los Angeles.

MAGNIFICENT OBSESSION

(1954, dir: Douglas Sirk)
Jane Wyman, Rock Hudson, Agnes Moorehead.

● CALIFORNIA

Remake of a 1935 movie, with Sirk's customary Technicolor gloss. Rock Hudson is responsible for the death of Jane Wyman's husband, and for blinding her. To atone he becomes a surgeon. Filming took place at **Lake Arrowhead**, an upscale resort in the San Bernardino Mountains, off I-15 east of LA.

MAGNIFICENT SEVEN, THE

(1960, dir: John Sturges)
Yul Brynner, Steve McQueen, James Coburn.

● MEXICO

Seven hired guns fight off bandits in this remake of Kurosawa's *The Seven Samurai*, made on sets constructed in the desert at **Cuernavaca** near Mexico City.

MAGNOLIA

(2000, dir: Paul Thomas Anderson)
William H Macy, Julianne Moore, Tom Cruise.

● CALIFORNIA; NEVADA

Anderson's daring, Altmanesque, multi-centred drama is, like his earlier *Boogie Nights*, set in the director's own neighbourhood, the San Fernando Valley, of Bur-

The suicide leap: Bryson Hotel, Wilshire Boulevard

bank, North Hollywood and Van Nuys, north of LA, and the film is named for one of the main east-west thoroughfares, Magnolia Boulevard. The nine-storey building where the unsuccessful suicide becomes a successful homicide, is the **Bryson, 2701 Wilshire Boulevard**, downtown LA, seen also in *The Grifters*.

MAHLER

(1974, dir: Ken Russell)
Robert Powell, Georgina Hale, David Collings.

● CUMBRIA; HERTFORDSHIRE

Russell fantasia on the music of Mahler, limited by the budget, was shot mainly in the Lake District, where the

composer's waterside cabin was constructed on **Lake Derwentwater**. Other locations include **Borrowdale** and **Keswick**, with the woodland scenes shot close to Pinewood Studios at **Black Park Country Park**.

MAJOR DUNDEE

(1965, dir: Sam Peckinpah)
Charlton Heston, Richard Harris, James Coburn.

● MEXICO

Violent Western set, and filmed, in Mexico, mainly at that old standby Western town **Durango**, with interiors shot at Churubuscu Studios in Mexico City. For the opening massacre, the Rostes ranch was built at **La Marquesa**, 25 miles southwest of Mexico City. Other exteriors are various Mexican towns, including **Cuautla**; **Tequesquitengo**; **Tehuixtla** and **Vistahermosa** – all south of Mexico City on the route to Acapulco, as is the setting for the final battle sequence on the Rio Balsas near **Chilpancingo**.

MALCOLM X

(1992, dir: Spike Lee)
Denzel Washington, Angela Bassett, Theresa Randle.

● NEW YORK CITY; NEW YORK STATE; CAIRO, EGYPT; MECCA, SAUDI ARABIA; SOUTH AFRICA

Welcoming Joe Louis: The Apollo, 125th Street, Harlem

Spike Lee's epic biopic of the black leader and activist was filmed (and not without a struggle: see *By Any Means Necessary* – Lee's book on the making of the film) largely around New York.

The grand opening shot is supposed to be Dudley Street Station, Roxbury, a black area of Boston, but is actually Brooklyn, with NYC transit trains painted as Boston trains of the forties. Malcolm X's childhood home, in Omaha, Nebraska, was filmed in **Peekskill**, on Route 9, New York State. The bravura dance sequence in Boston's Roseland is the ballroom of the since-demolished Diplomat Hotel, 108 West 43rd Street. The New England shoreline is at **Hempstead House, Sands Point Preserve, Port Washington**. When Malcolm X returns to Boston after falling foul of a Harlem numbers boss, the burglary at Beacon Hill was shot at a classy apartment on Manhattan's **Park Avenue**.

In New York, X gravitates to Harlem. The Paradise Bar, where he hangs out and begins running numbers, is the **Lenox Lounge, 288 Lenox Avenue**, Harlem's recently-restored thirties gem, also seen in John Singleton's update of *Shaft*. Charleston State Prison, where X converts to Islam, is **Rahway State Penitentiary, Rahway**, on Route 1, New Jersey, on the River Rahway. The reborn Malcolm X lectures at **Columbia University, 114th-120th Streets**, between Broadway and Amsterdam Avenue, and tentatively enjoys a first date with Betty Shabazz at the **American Museum of Natural History, Central Park West** at West 79th Street. The ecstatic welcome for Joe Louis, and the march from the police station to the hospital after the release of brother Johnson, were filmed on 125th Street by the famous **Apollo Theater, 253 West 125th Street.**

The **Audobon Ballroom, 3940 Broadway** at West 166th Street in Washington Heights, scene of Malcolm X's assassination, was actually used for exterior shots. The Audobon was acquired by the city in the mid-seventies, and Columbia University currently has plans to develop the site as a research complex. The Audobon interiors used the Diplomat Ballroom again.

The real Mecca scenes were filmed by a second unit, as only a totally Islamic crew was allowed into the country. The Mecca scenes filmed in Cairo feature the **Mohammed Ali Mosque.** The epilogue was shot at **Phakamani Combined School, Soweto** in South Africa, where Nelson Mandela speaks the film's closing lines, and in the **Alexander** township.

MALLRATS
(1995, dir: Kevin Smith)
Shannen Doherty, Jeremy London, Jason Lee.
MINNEAPOLIS; NEW JERSEY

Follow-up to *Clerks*, with a bunch of bickering teens hanging out in the local shopping mall, the **Eden Prairie Center Mall, Prairie Center Drive** off I-212 in Minneapolis. Filming also took place in New Jersey.

MALTESE FALCON, THE
(1941, dir: John Huston)
Humphrey Bogart, Mary Astor, Sydney Greenstreet.
● **CALIFORNIA**

Huston's directorial début, the classic 'tec story, set in San Francisco but filmed almost entirely at Warner Bros studios in Burbank. The only shots of the real San Fran are a glimpse of the **Golden Gate Bridge**; a few atmospheric night shots; and the murder of Spade's partner, Archer, on **Bush Street.** Not featured in the film, but in the book, is John's Grill, 63 Ellis Street. Sam Spade eats here, and the still-extant joint features a collection of memorabilia.

MAN BETWEEN, THE
(1953, dir: Carol Reed)
James Mason, Hildegard Neff, Claire Bloom.
● **BERLIN**

Rerun of *The Third Man*, from the same director, filmed in Berlin, though permission to use East Berlin was refused after the previous film. Location filming had to be fast, as the photogenic postwar ruins were being repaired. Locations include the ruined **Moritzplatz**; the famous **Resi Restaurant**, where tables were linked by telephone; and the **Funk Tower Sports Arena**, used as a camp for refugees form the East.

MAN CALLED HORSE, A
(1970, dir: Elliot Silverstein)
Richard Harris, Judith Anderson, Jean Gascon.
● **MEXICO**

English aristocrat Harris is captured by Indians, and endures all kinds of hardships, including the stomach-churning Sun Vow Ceremony, to become a Sioux. Set in 1820's Dakota, it was shot in the standard Western location of **Durango**, Mexico.

MAN FOR ALL SEASONS, A
(1966, dir: Fred Zinnemann)
Paul Scofield, Wendy Hiller, Robert Shaw.
● **OXFORDSHIRE; HAMPSHIRE**

Worthy, well-acted version of Robert Bolt's play about Thomas More's crisis of conscience over Henry VIII's divorce. Despite what guide books say, there was no filming at Hampton Court Palace. Wolsey's palace is no more than a movie set. Thomas More's house on the Thames at Chelsea, however, is real. It's **Studley Priory**, a one-time Benedictine monastery, now a hotel, at **Horton-cum-Studley**, about seven miles northeast of Oxford. The Thames is the **River Beaulieu**, flowing through the estate of **Beaulieu Abbey**, on the B3504, south of Southampton in Hampshire. The river wall built alongside was reproduced at Studley Priory, allowing characters to leap across counties in one bound!

MAN FROM LARAMIE, THE
(1955, dir: Anthony Mann)
James Stewart, Arthur Kennedy, Donald Crisp.
● **NEW MEXICO**

Another terrific Mann-Stewart collaboration, with Stewart tracking down the bad guys who caused his younger brother's death. It was shot around **Santa Fe** and **Taos**, New Mexico.

MAN IN THE IRON MASK, THE
(1939, dir: James Whale)
Louis Hayward, Warren William, Alan Hale.
● **LOS ANGELES**

Costume fun, with Dumas' tale of Louis XIV's imprisoned twin brother and the Three Musketeers. The forest scenes are in the **Los Angeles State and County Arboretum, 301 North Baldwin Avenue, Arcadia**, east of LA.

MAN IN THE IRON MASK, THE
(1998, dir: Randall Wallace)
Leonardo DiCaprio, Gérard Depardieu, Jeremy Irons.
● **FRANCE**

Riding high on the success of *Titanic*, DiCaprio plays the dual role of Louis XIV and his twin brother in Alexander Dumas' romance. This period romp used real French locations, including **Fontainbleau Castle; Pierrefonds Castle**, a reconstructed Medieval fortress about 60 miles northeast of Paris; **Vaux-le-Vicomte**; the village of **La Ferté-Alais**, about 25 miles south of Paris and the town of **Le Mans**, France.

MAN IN THE WILDERNESS
(1971, dir: Richard C Sarafian)
Richard Harris, John Huston, John Bindon.
● **SPAIN**

After undergoing all kinds of tribulations in *A Man Called Horse*, Richard Harris becomes a fur trapper surviving hardships in northwest Canada during the 1820s. It's actually the desert of **Almeria**, southern Spain.

MAN ON THE MOON
(1999, dir: Milos Forman)
Jim Carrey, Paul Giamatti, Courtney Love.
● CALIFORNIA; NEW YORK STATE

The eaterie where Kaufman works: Jerry's Deli, Ventura Boulevard

Milos Forman's fantasia on the life of the legendary media guerilla Andy Kaufman, fated to be best remembered as a loveable sitcom character. Its many locations are found around LA and in New York.

Scenes of Kaufman's childhood home were filmed in his actual neighbourhood of **Great Neck**, northeastern Long Island, New York, though not at the real house. The Carnegie Hall show, transposed to the end of Kaufman's life, uses the real **Carnegie Hall, 154 West 57th Street** for exteriors (see *Carnegie Hall* for details), but the interior, with the Mormon Tabernacle Choir, the Rockettes and Santa Claus, is across the States, in the **Los Angeles Theatre, 615 South Broadway**, downtown LA (you can see the same lavish theatre in *Batman Forever*, *New York, New York* and *Chaplin*).

Also in LA are the Memphis wrestling scenes, which use the **Olympic Grand Auditorium**, downtown LA. The eaterie, where Kaufman works, is the real thing, still very much in operation: **Jerry's Deli, 12655 Ventura Boulevard, Studio City**. Street scenes are on **Main Street, La Puente**, which also featured as the town in *Halloween H20*.

MAN WHO FELL TO EARTH, THE
(1976, dir: Nicolas Roeg)
David Bowie, Candy Clark, Rip Torn.
● NEW MEXICO; NEW YORK CITY

For once, Bowie is perfectly cast in Roeg's anti-naturalistic mosaic – although, bizarrely, *Jurassic Park* author Michael Crichton was the director's first choice for the role. The dry, desert locale is New Mexico. The small desert town, where innocent alien Bowie takes up with Candy Clark, is **Artesia**, down in the southeast corner of the state, 30 miles north of Carlsbad on I-285. The church, where Bowie proves he can't sing, is the **Presbyterian Church of Artesia**. The rocket scenes used the **White Sands Missile Range, Alamogordo**, off I-70 in southern New Mexico. Trapped on Earth, Bowie finally ends up in New York.

MAN WHO KNEW TOO MUCH, THE
(1934, dir: Alfred Hitchcock)
Leslie Banks, Edna Best, Peter Lorre.
● LONDON

Leslie Banks and Edna Best track down their kidnapped child in this early Hitchcock thriller. The opening scenes are set in a very stagey *faux* St Moritz, with a few stock shots of Alpine skiers, but the action soon moves to London. The atmospheric Wapping scenes were filmed on a huge set, though there's a shot of the real **Tower Bridge**, when it was still surrounded by working docks and cranes. The attempt to assassinate the European diplomat was filmed, like the more famous remake, in the **Royal Albert Hall, South Kensington**.

MAN WHO KNEW TOO MUCH, THE
(1956, dir: Alfred Hitchcock)
James Stewart, Doris Day, Bernard Miles.
● MOROCCO; LONDON

Stewart and Day are drawn into the plot: Main Square, Marrakech

Hitch's big-budget, colour remake of his own modest 1934 spy thriller utilised lots of real locations. Stewart and Day are dragged into the plot to assassinate an ambassador after their son is kidnapped in Morocco. The opening scenes were filmed in the souks and the main square of **Marrakech**, and the couple stay in the famous **La Mamounia Hotel, Avenue Bab Jdid** (© 448981), set in seven acres of garden within the old city walls.

The Marrakech Hotel today: La Mamounia, Avenue Bab Jdid

Back in london, Stewart follows a red herring to 'Ambrose Chapel', which turns out to be a taxidermist's. Hitchcock meant to film the scene on a set in Hollywood, but eventually plumped for the real premises of Gerrard Family Taxidermists, who specialised in supplying stuffed animals to Hollywood studios, were used for both the exterior and interior shots. The company has gone, and the street has been redeveloped, but you can still see **Plender Street** and **Royal College Street, NW1**, where Stewart arrives by taxi, in **Camden Town**. The real Ambrose Chapel, where Doris Day is imprisoned, was St Saviour's church hall in **Brixton**. St Saviour's church is still there, but the church hall has gone. The Embassy, too, has gone. It was Park Lane House, demolished to make way for the Hilton Hotel on Park Lane. The climax was shot in the **Royal Albert Hall, South Kensington**.

Stewart looks for Ambrose Chapel: Plender Street, Camden Town

MAN WHO SHOT LIBERTY VALANCE, THE
(1962, dir: John Ford)
James Stewart, John Wayne, Vera Miles.
● ARIZONA

Dishwasher Stewart becomes a hero when everyone thinks

231

he shot baddie Marvin, but actually it was John Wayne. Late period Ford, which is either a dark masterpiece or a shoddy failure, according to taste. No Monument Valley this time, in fact, no wide open spaces at all. It was made almost entirely in the studio at **Old Tucson, 201 South Kinney Road**, the movie set cum tourist attraction near Tucson, Arizona.

MAN WHO WOULD BE KING, THE
(1975, dir: John Huston)
Sean Connery, Michael Caine, Christopher Plummer.
● MOROCCO

Huston's film of Rudyard Kipling's Northwest Frontier fable is set in India, Afghanistan and Kafiristan, but was shot entirely on location in the Atlas Mountains near **Ouarzazate**, Morocco.

MAN WITH THE GOLDEN GUN, THE
(1974, dir: Guy Hamilton)
Roger Moore, Christopher Lee, Britt Ekland.
● HONG KONG; MACAU; THAILAND

Bond traces Scaramanga's golden bullet to gun expert Lazar in Macau, the former Portuguese enclave west of Hong Kong, where he inevitably gravitates toward the casino, the **Floating Macau Palace, Inner Harbour, Rua das Lorchas**. As its name suggests, the casino is a converted vessel moored on the peninsula's western shore. He takes the ferry across the bay to **Kowloon**, the mainland suburb of Hong Kong, where he follows Maud Adams to the **Peninsula Hotel, Salisbury Road** at Nathan Road (© 852.2920. 2888; www.peninsula.com) which does indeed run a fleet of green Rolls Royces, and was also seen in the 1955 anti-Commie adventure *Soldier of Fortune*, with Clark Gable and Susan Hayward.

Also in Kowloon are the fictitious Bottoms Up club, which was situated amid the neon dazzle of the **Tsim Sha Tsui** shopping district, and Hai Fat's estate, the **Dragon Garden** on **Castle Peak Road, Castle Peak**. MI6 field  HQ is deep inside the tilted, rusting hulk of the Queen Elizabeth, which was grounded in Hong Kong harbour.

The trail of Scaramanga leads to Bangkok, and a boat chase through the klongs, the network of canals criss-crossing the city. The karate school is the **Ancient City**, the world's largest outdoor museum, with its scaled-down versions of the famous buildings and temples of Bangkok. It's about 20 miles east of town on **Sukhumvit Highway** in Changwat Samut Prakan (*admission charge;* © 226.1936). The

Bond arrives in Kowloon: Peninsula Hotel

Following the bullet: Floating Macau Palace, Macau

kickboxing match, at which Bond first meets Scaramanga, was filmed in Bangkok's **Ratchadamnoen Stadium, Ratchadamnoen Nok Road** (© 281.4205).

But, most famously, Scaramanga's island hideout is **Khow-Ping-Kan**, one of a chain of tiny jungle-covered limestone pillars in **Phang Nga Bay** at Phuket, on the tip of the Malay peninsula. At the time of filming it was a remote and undiscovered paradise. Now, it's overrun by tourists, taking the 54 mile bus journey north from Phuket Town, and the boat trip out to see 'James Bond Island'.

MAN WITH TWO BRAINS, THE
(1983, dir: Carl Reiner)
Steve Martin, Kathleen Turner, David Warner.
● LOS ANGELES

Wildly silly comedy, played to the hilt by a game cast, with Sissy Spacek voicing the disembodied brain Steve Martin falls in love with. The Austrian hotel, where Martin honeymoons, is the **Castle Green Apartments, 99 South Raymond Avenue, Pasadena**. For details, see *The Sting* which also used this fabulously bizarre Moorish fantasy.

MAN WITHOUT A FACE, THE
(1993, dir: Mel Gibson)
Mel Gibson, Nick Stahl, Margaret Whitton.
● MAINE

Gibson's first directorial outing, and he also plays the lead, a disfigured man who forms a bond with fatherless Nick Stahl. Gibson's house is a private home on **Deer Isle**. He shops in **Lincolnville General Store, Rockport**, Maine. Holyfield Academy is **Bowdoin College, Brunswick**, about 100 miles south of Rockport.

MANCHURIAN CANDIDATE, THE
(1962, dir: John Frankenheimer)
Frank Sinatra, Laurence Harvey, Angela Lansbury.
● NEW YORK CITY; WASHINGTON DC

Strangely baroque thriller, with a brainwashed Laurence Harvey programmed to carry out a political assassination. The locations are split between Washington DC and New York. Laurence Harvey's apartment is **67 Riverside Drive** at 79th Street, on the West Side. The bar, where the barman inadvertently sends Harvey to go jump in the lake, was Jilly's, on 52nd Street at Eighth Avenue.

Laurence Harvey's apartment: Riverside Drive

It was a real NY hangout of the Rat Pack, owned by Sinatra's pal and bodyguard Jilly Rizzo, who plays the barman in the movie. Harvey obediently plops into the Lake in Central Park, between the **Ramble** and **Cherry Hill**.

MANHATTAN
(1979, dir: Woody Allen)
Woody Allen, Diane Keaton, Mariel Hemingway.
● NEW YORK CITY; NEW JERSEY

The prologue to Woody Allen's stylish monochrome hymn

to New York is a montage of the city's iconic images including the thirties-style, stainless steel **Empire Diner, 210 Tenth Avenue** between West 22nd and West 23rd Streets; the **Staten Island ferry**; the **Lincoln Center**; and the **Temple of Dendur**, an Egyptian complex rebuilt in the **Metropolitan Museum of Art** on Fifth Avenue, illuminated within its purpose-built, glass-walled gallery.

The film is burdened with the line destined to haunt Allen forever ("I'm dating a girl who does homework") during the opening foursome at **Elaine's, 1703 Second Avenue** between 88th and 89th Streets on the East Side – a restaurant to be seen in rather than eat in (© *212.534. 8103*). He has an inauspicious meeting with neurotic poseur Diane Keaton at an exhibition in Frank Lloyd Wright's white spiral **Guggenheim Museum, 1071 Fifth Avenue** at 89th Street, but begins a guarded flirtation after a second meeting in the Sculpture Gallery of **MOMA, the Museum of Modern Art, 11 West 53rd Street**. It's afterwards that the pair famously watch dawn breaking from a bench on **Riverview Terrace** on **Sutton Square**, beneath the **Queensboro Bridge**. The stunning image inspires the movie's famous poster, but there's no bench here and the view is now disfigured by a series of bollards.

The speciality food store, where Allen and Mariel Hemingway diss Keaton, is **Dean and DeLuca Inc, 560 Broadway** between Prince and Spring Streets in SoHo. Allen kvetches to Michael Murphy in **Rizzoli's Bookstore, 31 West 57th Street** between Fifth and Sixth Avenues (where De Niro and Streep meet in *Falling in Love*), after throwing in his TV job. Keaton and Murphy meet furtively at the perfume counter of **Bloomingdale's, 59th Street** between Lexington Avenue and Third Avenue, while Allen collects his kid from ex-wife Meryl Streep for a meal and some guy stuff, at the (since closed, but now newly-renovated) **Russian Tea Room, 150 West 57th Street** between Sixth and Seventh Avenues, the showbiz hangout seen also in *Tootsie*.

An electrical storm in Central Park causes an increasingly friendly Allen and Keaton to duck into the **Hayden Planetarium**, part of the **American Museum of Natural History** at **Central Park West** on 81st Street. Mariel Hemingway's school is the progressive **Dalton School, 61 East 91st Street** on the Upper East Side. The pizza place, where she tells Allen she's off to London, is **John's Pizza, 278 Bleecker Street** at Morton Street and Seventh Avenue in Greenwich Village. It's small and usually packed, unsurprising since it was recommended by the director as the best pizza in New York.

Allen plays squash with Murphy at the **Uptown Racquet Club, Park Avenue** between 52nd and 53rd Streets, visits the **Whitney Museum of American Art, 945 Madison Avenue** at 75th Street, with Keaton, and watches art movies with her at the now gone Cinema Studio, 1966 Broadway. Still there, though, is **Zabar's, 2245 Broadway** at 80th Street, where Allen and Keaton gaze at the gourmet delights on display.

It's on an outing to the **Palisades** at **Englewood Cliffs**, across the Hudson River in New Jersey, where Allen gets to see Meryl Streep's published account of their marital break-up.

MANHATTAN MURDER MYSTERY

(1993, dir: Woody Allen)
Woody Allen, Diane Keaton, Alan Alda.
● **NEW YORK CITY**

Minor Allen comedy, grown out of ideas rejected from *Annie Hall*, which began life as a murder mystery. Allen and Keaton are an East Side married couple who begin to suspect their kindly old neighbour may have bumped off his wife. The couple stake out their cultural parameters by watching a NY Rangers hockey game at **Madison Square Garden, Seventh Avenue** between West 31st and West 33rd Streets, Chelsea, and taking in Wagner at the **Lincoln Center** on the West Side.

Keaton voices her first suspicions over a meal at fave Allen hangout, **Elaine's, 1703 Second Avenue** between East 88th and East 89th Streets on the Upper East Side (see *Manhattan* for details). Allen and Keaton take their son to the **21 Club, 21 West 52nd Street** between Fifth and Sixth Avenues, midtown, where you can see its cheery frontage of tiny jockeys. The grand, olde worlde establishment, where Keaton attends a wine tasting and sees the supposedly-dead neighbour on a bus, is the **National Arts Club, 15 Gramercy Park South** at Irving Place (see Martin Scorsese's *The Age of Innocence* for details). Anjelica Huston gives Allen a poker lesson at the **Cafe des Artistes, 1 West 67th Street** at Central Park West and Columbus Avenue on the West Side (see *My Dinner With Andre* which – supposedly – filmed here). The fictitious Hotel Waldron, where a body is discovered, is **Hotel 17, 225 East 17th Street** in the East Village, though the interior is the venerable **Chelsea Hotel, 222 West 23rd Street**, between Seventh and Eighth Avenues, Chelsea.

MANHUNTER

(1986, dir: Michael Mann)
William L Petersen, Brian Cox, Tom Noonan.
● **GEORGIA; NORTH CAROLINA; WASHINGTON DC; MISSOURI**

From the novel preceding *Silence of the Lambs*, and filmed by visual stylist Michael Mann four years before that film. This time, Hannibal Lecter is incarcerated, not in an underground dungeon from a Universal horror movie, but in a glossy, white, hi-tech facility. It's **Atlanta High Museum of Art, 1280 Peachtree Street** (© *404.892.3600*, *admission charge*), in the Ansley Park Area of Atlanta, Georgia. In Atlanta, investigator Will Graham stays at the luxury, 50-storey **Atlanta Marriot Marquis, 265 Peachtree Center Avenue** (© *404.521.0000*). The FBI works out of the **District Building, 1350 Pennsylvania Avenue NW** at 14th Street, Washington DC. And it's in front of here, on **Freedom Plaza** by the National Theater, that the innocent jogger gets busted. The airport where the Lear jet touches down is **Lambert International Airport, St Louis**, Missouri.

Wilmington in North Carolina, the self-styled 'East Coast Hollywood', with its slew of studio facilities, hosted more of the filming. The hospital was Wilmington's New Hanover Memorial Hospital, now expanded to become part of the **New Hanover Regional Medical**

Center, 2131 South 17th Street, and Will Graham's Florida beach house (supposedly at DeSoto Avenue, Captiva) is on nearby **Mansonboro Island**, North Carolina.

MANON DES SOURCES (aka *Manon of the Spring*)
(1986, dir: Claude Berri)
Yves Montand, Daniel Auteuil, Emmanuelle Béart.
● **FRANCE**

The concluding part of *Jean de Florette* sees the departed Depardieu's daughter grown up and revenging herself on the greedy neighbours who caused her father's death. The village is **Cuges Les Pins** in Province, with additional filming in **Sommieres**.

MARATHON MAN
(1976, dir: John Schlesinger)
Dustin Hoffman, Laurence Olivier, Roy Scheider.
● **NEW YORK CITY; PARIS**

Olivier in the diamond district: 47th Street

Hoffman jogs: Jogging path, Central Park

Final confrontation: Reservoir, Central Park

Schlesinger's stylish thriller is set in Paris and New York. Dustin Hoffman runs on the 1.6 mile jogging path surrounding the **Reservoir**, between 86th and 96th Streets in Central Park. His brother, Roy Scheider, gets knifed at the **Lincoln Center**, west of Broadway between 62nd and 66th Streets on the West Side. The Russian Embassy is a favourite NYC location, the **Carnegie Mansion, 22 East 91st Street** at Fifth Avenue on the Upper East Side, seen in *Arthur* and *Working Girl* among others.

The street where old Nazi Laurence Olivier gets an understandable panic attack is in the overwhelmingly Jewish Diamond District, **47th Street** between Fifth and Sixth Avenues. The trade here grew up in the thirties when dealers fleeing Nazi persecution in European diamond centres, such as Amsterdam and Antwerp, took advantage of an area that provided both low rent and proximity to the monied customers of Fifth Avenue.

The final confrontation between Hoffman and Olivier is staged at the **North Gate House** of the **Reservoir** in Central Park's, though the ironwork grid interior is a studio set, built by designer Richard MacDonald to resemble the layout of an Elizabethan stage.

MARNIE
(1964, dir: Alfred Hitchcock)
Tippi Hedren, Sean Connery, Diane Baker.
● **PENNSYLVANIA; NEW JERSEY**

Strange psycho-drama with Connery titillated by the sexually frigid kleptomaniac Tippi Hedren. Obviously very studio-bound, leaving acres of room for film students to debate whether Hitchcock was deliberately concocting a disquietingly unreal atmosphere, or had simply lost interest after an embarrassing incident when star Hedren allegedly rebuffed his advances. Marnie arrives in Philadelphia at **30th Street Station**. She's spotted by a man from her shady past at the **Atlantic City Racetrack**, New Jersey.

Marnie's Virginia hotel: The Red Fox Inn, Middleburg

Marnie arrives in Philadelphia: 30th Street Station

The horse-riding scenes use the 'Horse and Hunt Capital' of the US, **Middleburg**, a small town in the shadow of the Blue Ridge Mountains, northwestern Virginia, about 35 miles west of Washington DC. Marnie's hotel is the historic **Red Fox Inn, 2 East Washington Street** (*© 540.687.6301*). Dating from 1728, the Red Fox is one of the oldest inns in the US and still in business.

MARS ATTACKS!
(1996, dir: Tim Burton)
Jack Nicholson, Glenn Close, Pierce Brosnan.
● **LAS VEGAS, NEVADA; ARIZONA; WASHINGTON DC**

Burton's homage to fifties sci-fi is based on a series of notorious sixties bubble gum cards. The fictitious Perkinsville, Texas is **Burns**, Kansas, 40 miles northeast of Wichita – this is where the donut shop inspired by LA's wacky original was built. The opening scene of burning cattle, taken directly from the gum cards, is in **Lawrence**, Kansas.

The Martian landing site, Pahrump, Nevada, is **Red Lake**, a dust bowl 20 miles from Kingman, Arizona. But it's not long before the little green folk have set their sights on the nation's capital and, naturally, the glitz of Las Vegas. Washington exteriors include the **Washington Monument** and the **Mall**. Pam Grier's neighbourhood is a row of houses in the NW region of DC. The burned out house stood at the corner of **4th and Massachusetts**.

In Vegas, Tom Jones performs at the **Luxor Hotel, 3900 Las Vegas Boulevard South** (*© 702.262.4000*) the giant (30 storey, 2,520 rooms) and, of course, absolutely authentic Egyptian pyramid on the southern reaches of the Strip (the aerial tramway connects it with the Excalibur to the north and Mandalay Bay to the south). Jack Nicholson's Galaxy Hotel is – was – Howard Hughes' Landmark Hotel, a 356-foot tower opened in 1969 near the Hilton, which was actually demolished during the making of the movie (not *for* the making of the movie, of course). At 31 storeys, it was once the tallest building in Nevada but was constantly plagued by financial problems and finally closed in 1990. The neon graveyard is the old sign yard of **Yesco**, the Young Electric Sign Company, which has been making glitter city's twinkling signs for years.

MARY, QUEEN OF SCOTS
(1971, dir: Charles Jarrott)
Vanessa Redgrave, Glenda Jackson, Patrick McGoohan.
● TYNESIDE; NORTHUMBERLAND; SUSSEX
SCOTLAND

Gistorical pageant, climaxing with a totally invented meeting between the two main characters. Featured locations are **Alnwick Castle**, off the A1, 30 miles north of Newcastle-upon-Tyne; and **Bamburgh Castle**, on the coast a further 16 miles to the north (see *The Devils* for details). Vanessa Redgrave steps ashore at **Seahouses**, a few miles from Bamburgh. Filming also took place at **Hermitage Castle**, on the B6399, ten miles south of Hawick, in the Scottish Borders. Hermitage is open from April to September (*admission charge; © 013873.762225*). The meeting between Elizabeth and Mary was filmed at **Parham House, Pulborough**, on the A283 about 10 miles northwest of Worthing, Sussex (*rail: Pulborough*). Parham is open to the public on certain days from Easter to the end of October (*admission charge; © 01903.744888*).

M*A*S*H
(1970, dir: Robert Altman)
Donald Sutherland, Elliott Gould, Tom Skerritt.
● CALIFORNIA

Black comedy set in the Korean war marred, like so many of Altman's movies, by misogyny and homophobia, but given bite by the blood – sorely missing from the sanitised TV series. The South Korean tent encampment was built on the Twentieth Century Fox lot in **Malibu Creek State Park, Las Virgenes Road** and Mulholland Drive, at Calabasas in the Santa Monica Mountains, northwest of LA. The climactic football game was shot in a playground in LA's **Griffith Park**.

MASK, THE
(1994, dir: Charles Russell)
Jim Carrey, Cameron Diaz, Peter Riegert.
● LOS ANGELES

Carrey is ideal casting, if you can stand him, in this live action cartoon. Edge City is, of course, LA. The Edge City Bank, where nerdy Stanley Ipkiss works, is the old Bank of

Entrance to the Coco Bongo Club: Ambassador Hotel

America building, **650 South Spring Street**, downtown LA. The Coco Bongo Nightclub is a combination of two LA hotels: the exterior is the entrance to the **Cocoanut Grove**

The Coco Bongo Club: Terrace Room, Park Plaza Hotel

of the **Ambassador Hotel, 3400 Wilshire Boulevard**, midtown (see the 1954 *A Star Is Born* for details). The interior, though, beneath the dressing of palm trees, deco light fittings and the violet waterfall, is the **Terrace Room** of the **Park Plaza Hotel, 607 South Park View Street**, downtown LA. The mask is finally returned to the river from the **Sixth Street Viaduct**, downtown.

MATINEE
(1993, dir: Joe Dante)
John Goodman, Simon Fenton, Omri Katz.
● FLORIDA

Goodman is a fifties exploitation producer, not a million miles away from William Castle, previewing his sci-fi schlocker *Mant* ('Half man, half ant!') in a Florida cinema during the real horror of the Bay of Pigs crisis. Set down at the tip of the Florida Keys in Key West, the town is actually **Cocoa**, I-95, on the Florida coast east of Orlando. The Key West Strand Theater is the **Cocoa Village Playhouse, 3000 Brevard Avenue**, Cocoa (*© 321.636.5050*). Built in 1924 as the Aladdin Theater, a movie palace, it's been taken over by Brevard Community College and now presents live theatre. The real pink, deco Key West Strand Theater can be seen at 527 Duval Street between Petronia and Olivia Streets. The one-time movie palace, built by Cuban craftsmen in 1918, now lives on as a rock and reggae music venue.

MATRIX, THE
(1999, dir: Andy Wachowski, Larry Wachowski)
Keanu Reeves, Laurence Fishburne, Hugo Weaving.
● NEW SOUTH WALES, AUSTRALIA

This hi-hi-hi-tech thriller is set, like their previous movie *Bound*, in the Wachowski brothers' hometown of Chicago. Hence the references to 'the Loop', the Windy City's downtown district. But, also like *Bound*, it wasn't filmed there. The futuristic metropolis is **Sydney**. The helicopter takes off from the roof of the **Aon Tower, 201 Kent Street**. Morpheus is held in the **Colonial State Bank Centre, Martin Place**. The helicopter crashes into the **BT Tower** on the corner of **Market Street**. Neo lands on the roof of the **Allianz Building** (formerly the MMI Centre) on the other side of Market Street. The train station, where Neo battles Agent Smith, was shot on a section of track behind the silos at **White Bay** on the Balmain side of the Anzac Bridge. Neo's band ends up in the old post office in **Railway Square**, with extra stories added digitally. The phone box crushed by a truck was at an overpass on **Hickson Road**. Interiors were shot in the Fox Studio at **Moore Park**.

MATTER OF LIFE AND DEATH, A (aka *Stairway to Heaven*)

(1946, dir: Michael Powell, Emeric Pressburger)
David Niven, Kim Hunter, Marius Goring.
● DEVON

Powell and Pressburger's elaborate fantasy stars Niven as a WWII fighter pilot trapped in a surreal limbo after his plane crashes. The giant moving staircase to Heaven is an escalator, specially built by the London Transport Passenger Board and Rowson, Drew and Clydesdale. The two-gear, twelve-horsepower engine could run at speeds of 30 and 60 feet per minute. The film's mostly studio-bound, but The Burrows, the deserted beach Niven mistakes for heaven, where he encounters the strange goatherd, is **Saunton Sands**, on the B3231, on the north Devon coast south of Ilfracombe and west of Barnstaple.

MAURICE

(1987, dir: James Ivory)
James Wilby, Rupert Graves, Hugh Grant.
● LONDON; CAMBRIDGESHIRE; WILTSHIRE; GLOUCESTERSHIRE; SICILY, ITALY

Picking up the guardsman: The Black Friar

After their success with *A Room With a View*, the Merchant-Ivory team turned EM Forster's posthumously published gay novel *Maurice* into a lush Mills and Boon romancer. The Cambridge scenes were actually filmed at Forster's old University. Exterior shots are of **Trinity College, Cambridge**, at the **Quad** and under the **Wren Library**. The Gothic William IV Porter's Lodge is **King's College**, and the Latin grace was also shot there, in the Dining Hall. The punt trip is on the River Cam at **Clare Bridge**, and the romantic scene between Wilby and Grant in the field is near **Ely** in Cambridgeshire.

In London, Maurice bumps into his old schoolmaster by the Assyrian statues in the **British Museum, Bloomsbury**, while the marvellous art-nouveau pub where his pal with a taste for the military runs into problems is the **Black Friar, 174 Queen Victoria Street**, EC4, over the road from Blackfriars railway station. The subsequent trial for indecency was staged in **Salisbury Town Hall**, Salisbury, Wiltshire, which also served as Wilby's London office. Wilby and Grant take their minds off the proceedings by attending a concert at the **Wigmore Hall**.

Hugh Grant's country house, where Wilby is noticed by groundsman Rupert Graves, is **Wilbury Park, Newton Toney**, a private house owned by actress Maria St Juste, on the A338 halfway between Andover and Salisbury, Wiltshire. The boathouse in the grounds where they meet up is, however, in the grounds of **Crichel** in Dorset. Hugh Grant's London home is the **Linley-Sambourne house, 18 Stafford Terrace**, just off High Street Kensington, W8 (see *A Room With a View* for details).

The family meal, before Hugh Grant sets off for the Continent, is in the **Café Royal, Regent Street**, W1. His European travels take him to a Grecian amphitheatre, actually at **Segesta**, near Castellammare in northwest Sicily. The docks, where Wilby just manages to reach Graves before he emigrates, are **Gloucester Docks** on the Severn.

MAXIMUM RISK

(1996, dir: Ringo Lam)
Jean-Claude Van Damme, Natasha Henstridge, Jean-Hugues Anglade.
● FRANCE; NEW YORK CITY; ONTARIO, CANADA; PENNSYLVANIA

Ringo Lam made *City on Fire*, the heist-gone-wrong movie which provided the template for *Reservoir Dogs*, but dented his reputation with this Hollywood début. There is a great use of locations, though. Van Damme plays identical twins, one of whom is killed during a chase through the picturesquely narrow streets of

The chase in the South of France: Villefranche-sur-Mer

The Russian Baths: The Stables, Casa Loma, Toronto

Villefranche-sur-mer, east of Nice. He confronts his mother at the **Hermitage du Col d'Eze, Avenue des Diables Bleus, Eze** between Villefranche and Monaco. Chantal's cottage is **La Seguinière Restaurant, La Gaude**, north of Cagnes. Filming in Nice included streets near the **Promenade des Anglais**; the **Palais Hispania** office building near Nice train station; the church **l'Eglise du Port** and the **Flower Market, Cours Saleya**.

The chase in New York: Yonge Street, Toronto

The lawyer's office, which gets burned out is supposedly on Place Pigalle in Paris, but all the scenes here are still squarely in the South of France. The office can be found on **Zamenhof Square**, Nice. Van Damme hot-foots it to New York where he picks up the archetypal novel-writing cabbie by the **Brooklyn Bridge**. The action centres around **Little Odessa**, with a chase to **Brighton Beach Station**, though the station here is actually in northern Philadelphia, and the chase scene was filmed in Canada on **Yonge Street**, Toronto's main north-south thoroughfare – and the longest street in the world, and along Bloor Street, taking in **Sam the Record Man**'s store at **2252 Bloor Street West**. The Bohemia Club is the **Left Bank Restaurant, 567 Queen Street West**, downtown Toronto; the holding cell is in Toronto's **Old City Hall, Queen Street West** at Bay Street; and the seedy New York hotel is the **Waverley Hotel, 484 Spadina Avenue**, also in Toronto. More Toronto locations include the **Canary Restaurant, 409 Front Street East** and the **Zanzibar Strip Club, 359 Yonge Street**. The Russian-style bath-house is the stables of **Casa Loma, 1 Austin Terrace** at Spadina Road, a European castle built for Sir Henry Pellatt in1913. This grandiose folly is a frequently used movie location (*Cocktail*, *54* and *X-Men* among many others), and open to the public (© *416.923.1171, admission charge*). The final shoot-out is back in Nice, supposedly at the Banque Nationale de Provence, which is actually the **Palais de Justice, Place du Palais Square**. The interior of the banque, though, is the **Canada Permanent Trust Building, 320 Bay Street**, in the financial district of Toronto. The final car chase is through the streets of Nice's **Vieille Port**.

MEAN STREETS
(1973, dir: Martin Scorsese)
Harvey Keitel, Robert De Niro, David Proval.
● **LOS ANGELES; NEW YORK CITY**

The Volpe bar: Via Tutto, Cleveland Place

Scorsese's archetypal picture of Italian-Americans in Little Italy, NY, had only eight days filming in the Big Apple (and that stretched from a planned four). And it filmed in Belmont, too, the Italian community in the Bronx, standing in for the much-changed Manhattan locale. But all the interi-

De Niro and Keitel's heart to heart: Mulberry Street, Little Italy

ors, and plenty of the exteriors too, are in LA, including the final shooting and car crash. Tony's Bar is a soundstage set in Hollywood. Charlie's apartment is an office building on Hollywood Boulevard. The churchyard where Keitel and De Niro have a heart to heart is real New York though, the **Old St Patrick's Cathedral, 264 Mulberry Street** between East Houston and Prince Streets in Little Italy (seen also in *The Godfather*). The bar was **23 Cleveland Plaza**, now Via Tutto (© *212.841.0286*), a small Tuscan restaurant just north of Broome Street and the Police Building.

MEDITERRANEO
(1991, dir: Gabriele Salvatores)
Diego Abatantuono, Claudio Bigagli, Giuseppe Cederna.
● **DODECANESE, GREECE**

The Oscar winner for Best Foreign Language Film 1993. The island setting is **Kastellorizo**, a tiny island with one hotel and no restaurant, in the Aegean off the coast of Turkey.

MEET JOE BLACK
(1998, dir: Martin Brest)
Brad Pitt, Anthony Hopkins, Claire Forlani.
● **NEW YORK CITY; RHODE ISLAND; NEW JERSEY**

Pitt plays Death in this overlong romantic fantasy, based on the stage play *Death Takes a Holiday*, previously filmed in 1934 with Fredric March. Anthony Hopkins' mansion is the **Aldrich Mansion, Warwick**, Rhode Island. Filming also took place in **Teaneck**, New Jersey and New York.

MEN IN BLACK
(1997, dir: Barry Sonnenfeld)
Tommy Lee Jones, Will Smith, Rip Torn.
● **NEW YORK CITY; NEW JERSEY; LOS ANGELES**

The jewellery store: MacDougal Street, Greenwich Village

The forbidding MIB HQ is actually the **Holland Tunnel Ventilator Shaft** on **Battery Place**, north of Battery Park. The alien landing site is the home of the 1964-65 New York Worlds Fair in **Flushing Meadow**, Union Turnpike-44th Avenue, Queens. Here you'll find the two towers and the **Unisphere**, the giant hollow globe trashed by the flying saucer (reconstructed in the studio in Hollywood). Will Smith encounters his first alien by **Grand Central Station**. A short chase later and they're climbing up the **Guggenheim Museum, Fifth Avenue** at East 89th Street. The Rosenberg Jewellery store, which gets blown up, is at **54 MacDougal Street**, Greenwich Village, while the 'squid birth' is at **Liberty Park, Jersey City**, the tip of New Jersey opposite the Statue of Liberty.

Men in Black HQ: Ventilator shaft, Battery Place

The alien site: Flushing Meadow, Queens

MEPRIS, LE (aka *Contempt*)
(1963, dir: Jean-Luc Godard)
Brigitte Bardot, Michel Piccoli, Jack Palance.
● **ROME; CAPRI, ITALY**

Piccoli is a screenwriter on a film of *The Odyssey*, whose

marriage to Bardot is falling apart. Palance is the producer, veteran Fritz Lang (as himself) is the director. The extraordinary modernistic building is the **Casa Malaporte**, on the south of Capri, designed in 1942 by Curxio Malaporte and Adalberto Libera, with its funnelled staircase and curving white wall on the roof.

MICHAEL COLLINS
(1996, dir: Neil Jordan)
Liam Neeson, Julia Roberts, Alan Rickman.
● IRELAND

Historical biopic with Neeson in the title role. The 1922 Dail was filmed in a reading room of **Trinity College**, Dublin. The GPO Building, which still bears the bul-

The barge: Ha'penny Bridge, Dublin

let holes of the uprising, was recreated as the biggest set ever built in Ireland, at a cost of £1.5 million, at **Broadstone**, Dublin. The Bloody Sunday massacre of the crowd and players at a Gaelic football match by the Black and Tans at Croke Park was shot at the **Carlisle Grounds, Bray**. The pier Neeson, Aidan Quinn and Roberts stroll on is **South Pier, Dun Laoghaire**. The barge was moored at the **Ha'penny Bridge**, Dublin. Filming also took place at **Dame Street**; **Grafton Street**; **Four Courts**; **City Hall**; **Dublin Castle** and the **Iveagh Buildings** – all in Dublin.

MIDNIGHT COWBOY
(1969, dir: John Schlesinger)
Jon Voight, Dustin Hoffman, Sylvia Miles.
● NEW YORK CITY; TEXAS; FLORIDA

Jon Voight turns himself into a cowboy stud to escape his dreary life washing dishes at **Miller's Restaurant, Big Spring**, Hwy-80 between Midland and Abilene, west Texas. Moving to New York, he stays at the now-gone Claridge Hotel, which stood on Times Square. Still there is the apartment of gorgeous chick Sylvia Miles, **114 East 72nd Street** on the East Side, where it all ends in tears when he asks her for money. The fictitious Berkeley Hotel for Women, where Hoffman fantasises that Voight's studly prowess is the key to luxury, was the Gotham Hotel. Gutted and refurbished in the eighties, but still recognisable, it's now the **Peninsula Hotel, 700 Fifth Avenue**. The final bus journey was shot on the **Miracle Mile** stretch of **Coral Gables**, Florida.

Berkeley Hotel for Women: The Peninsula Hotel, Fifth Avenue

Sylvia Miles' apartment: East 72nd Street

MIDNIGHT EXPRESS
(1978, dir: Alan Parker)
Brad Davis, Randy Quaid, John Hurt.
● MALTA; TURKEY

Billy Hayes, the young, gay American student imprisoned for smuggling dope, is heterosexualised in this version of his ordeal in the Turkish prison system. The real location of the story, Sagamilcar Prison, Istanbul, was obviously out of the question. The prison set was constructed in **Fort St Elmo**, an old British army barracks in Malta. Built in 1850 on the site of the legendary great Siege of Malta in 1565, it's at the top of the Valetta Peninsula. The exterior balconies and courtyards are real. Filming also took place in the historic **Knight's Hall**, dating from 1574; and at the **Dominican Church, Rabat**.

MIDNIGHT RUN
(1988, dir: Martin Brest)
Robert De Niro, Charles Grodin, Yaphet Kotto.
● NEW YORK CITY; LOS ANGELES; CHICAGO; ARIZONA; NEVADA; MICHIGAN; NEW ZEALAND

Cross-continental chase movie that calls in just about everywhere, starting from LA, where De Niro gets his mission (to retrieve mob accountant Grodin from New York) at the bail bonds office in the scruffy downtown area. Catching up with Grodin, that old standby plot device, fear of flying, kicks in and the pair leave for LA from New York's **Grand Central Station**.

The little local station where FBI agent Yaphet Kotto boards the train only to find that De Niro and Grodin have already slipped off to take the bus, is **Niles Station, 598 Dey Street, Niles**, on I-33 down in the southwest corner of Michigan toward the Indiana border (seen also in *Only the Lonely*). The bus ride ends in Chicago, where marksmen are waiting at **Chicago Bus Terminal**, on **North State Street** at Lake Street.

The smalltown diner, where De Niro and Grodin can't even afford breakfast, is in **Globe**, Arizona. The helicopter attack is at **Salt River Canyon Bridge**, on I-60 about 35 miles north of Globe, where the pair end up in the Salt River, although the rapids were filmed in warmer water in New Zealand. Grodin attempts to steal a plane at the **Cameron Indian Reservation**. Other Arizona locations include **Flagstaff Train Station**; **Williams**; **Cottonwood**; and **Sedona**. Bad guy Dennis Farina operates out of **Las Vegas**, and it's at **McCarran International Airport** that De Niro exchanges Grodin for that Macguffin of the eighties, computer discs.

MIDSUMMER NIGHT'S DREAM, A
(1999, dir: Michael Hoffman)
Kevin Kline, Rupert Everett, Michelle Pfeiffer.
● ITALY

A lush adaptation, shot in Italy. The bustling town square and the theatre are in **Montepulciano**, Tuscany. Theseus' palace consists of two separate locations. The interior was filmed at **Villa d'Este**. The exterior, and the wedding feast, were at **Palazzo Farnese** in **Caprarola**. The magic forest is a studio set, constructed at Cinecittà in Rome. Filming also took place at **Sutri**, near to Caprarola.

MIDSUMMER NIGHT'S SEX COMEDY, A
(1982, dir: Woody Allen)
Woody Allen, Mia Farrow, Jose Ferrer.
● **NEW YORK STATE**

Woody Allen's spin on Bergman's *Smiles of a Summer Night*, was shot at **Pocantico Hills**, on Route 448, north-east of Tarrytown, upstate New York. Ferrer's mansion house was specially built for the movie. After alterations were made to bring the property into line with building regulations, it was sold as a habitable house.

MIGHTY APHRODITE
(1995, dir: Woody Allen)
Woody Allen, Mira Sorvino, F Murray Abraham.
● **NEW YORK STATE; ITALY**

The amphitheatre: Teatro Greco, Taormina

Woody Allen's Manhattanites are graced with a classical Greek chorus commenting on the action. Their amphitheatre is the **Teatro Greco, Taormina** on Sicily. The racetrack is **Belmont Racetrack**, Nassau County, Long Island, and there was more filming at **North Tarrytown** and the village of **Quogue**, New York.

MILAGRO BEANFIELD WAR, THE
(1988, dir: Robert Redford)
Chick Vennera, Carlos Riquelme, Sonia Braga.
● **NEW MEXICO**

The adobe church, Truchas

Redford's second outing as director, an eco-sound peasants-versus-authorities whimsy, was to have been filmed in Chimayo, north of Santa Fe, New Mexico. As the locals haggled and upped their price, the company moved ten miles east along Hwy-76 to **Truchas**, where the sets were built and the movie eventually made.

MILDRED PIERCE
(1945, dir: Michael Curtiz)
Joan Crawford, Ann Blyth, Zachary Scott.
● **LOS ANGELES**

Darkly glittering deco *noir*, with Joan Crawford clawing her way up in the restaurant business, only to be snubbed by her ungrateful daughter, creepily prefiguring *Mommie Dearest*.

Crawford is seduced by smooth-talking Zachary Scott in the stylish Malibu beach house of *Snake Pit* director Anatole Litvak. After the shooting of Scott, Joan is hauled off to **Los Angeles City Hall, 200 North Spring Street**, downtown LA.

MILLER'S CROSSING
(1990, dir: Joel Coen)
Gabriel Byrne, Albert Finney, John Turturro.
● **LOUISIANA**

More wonderful weirdness from the Coens, this time set in the twenties. The anonymous, Prohibition-era city is an unrecognisable, non-touristy New Orleans. Leo's club is the old worlde-style downstairs dining room of New Orleans' staid **International House**. The gigantic panelled room, where Tom confronts Johnny Caspar, is **Gallier Hall, 545 St Charles Avenue**, formerly City Hall. The Greek revival-style building, designed in 1845 by James Gallier Sr, stands opposite Lafayette Square. Another of its large rooms was used as the Mayor's office. The exterior and the foyer of Caspar's house were filmed at the exclusive **Louis S McGehee School, 2343 Prytania Street**. Leo's home is actually four separate locations: **Northline**; a street in the **Old Metairie** section of town (where the car is blown up); and two purpose-built sets. The sets were built in the huge garage belonging to the estate agents Toye Brothers on **Annunciation Street**.

Unchanged period exteriors were shot on **Magazine Street**, downtown, and on **Picayune Street** (the nighttime scene between Tom and Verna). The shoot-out between the police and members of Leo's social club, the Sons of Erin, was staged on **Church Street**.

Miller's Crossing itself, the wood where Tom has to carry out the killings, is a forest plantation about 30 miles east of Baton Rouge, near Hammond, on Route 190.

MILLION DOLLAR HOTEL
(2000, dir: Wim Wenders)
Jeremy Davies, Milla Jovovich, Mel Gibson.
● **LOS ANGELES**

This must be the first movie inspired by a rooftop. If you saw U2's video for 'Where the Streets Have No Name', you'll have seen the huge rooftop sign for the Million Dollar Hotel. Well, actually, it was a recreation built on top of a liquor store. This is the real thing, atop what is now the **Frontier Hotel, 111 West Fifth Street** at Main Street, in one of the scuzzier sections of downtown LA.

MILLION POUND NOTE, THE (aka *Man With a Million*)
(1954, dir: Ronald Neame)
Gregory Peck, Jane Griffiths, Ronald Squire.
● **LONDON**

Gregory Peck is a penniless American in London given, for a bet, the unchangeable note of the title by upper crust Wilfrid Hyde White and Ronald Squire in this forerunner of Eddie Murphy's *Trading Places*. Hyde White's grand Belgravia mansion is **47 Belgrave Square**, SW1. Peck chases the windborne note down Belgrave Square and around the corner to **Montrose Place**.

The Belgravia mansion: Belgrave Square

MIRACLE ON 34th STREET (aka *The Big Heart*)
(1947, dir: George Seaton)
Edmund Gwenn, Maureen O'Hara, Natalie Wood.
● NEW YORK CITY

Edmund Gwenn pretends to be a real Santa at **Macy's Department Store**, the biggest in the world, **Herald Square, Broadway** at 34th Street. He's sent for observation to **Bellevue Hospital Center, First Avenue** between 25th and 30th Streets on the Lower East Side. Santa stands trial at **New York County Courthouse, 60 Centre Street** in the Civic Centre district.

MIRACLE ON 34th STREET
(1994, dir: Les Mayfield)
Richard Attenborough, Elizabeth Perkins, Mara Wilson.
● NEW YORK CITY; CHICAGO

Mawkish remake of a story long past its sell-by date. This time around, Macy's wanted nothing to do with the production, so the department store becomes the fictitious CF Cole's. It's still set in New York, but that's not where you'll find most of the film's locations. There were only five days filming in the Big Apple. Apart from a couple of establishing shots, New York is restricted to the opening Thanksgiving Day Parade on **Central Park West** between 72nd and 78th Streets – and Perkins and Dylan McDermott's night out at the **Wollman Skating Rink** in Central Park. The clue to the film's real location comes in the opening credits. Like most John Hughes productions, *Miracle* was filmed in Chicago. The exterior of CF Cole's is the **Art Institute of Chicago, South Michigan Avenue** at East Adams Street in the Loop. Central Park Zoo, where Santa gets propositioned by the rival superstore, is actually **Lincoln Park Zoo, 2200 North Cannon Drive** at West Webster Avenue in Lincoln Park, north of the city centre. St Francis' church, where Perkins and McDermott finally submit to an arranged marriage, is **Holy Name Cathedral, 735 North State Street** at East Chicago Avenue.

MISERY
(1990, dir: Rob Reiner)
Kathy Bates, James Caan, Richard Farnsworth.
● NEVADA

The country store: Main Street, Genoa

Bates picked up an Oscar as the demented fan, nurse and jailer of injured writer Caan in a Stephen King story of a beleaguered scribbler. Set in the fictitious Silver Creek, Colorado, it was shot near Reno, Nevada. The Silver Creek Lodge is an innaccessible Forest Service lodge. The country store and post office are **2299 Main Street**, in **Genoa**, a beautiful little town just west of I-395, south of Reno, also seen in Don Siegel's *Charley Varrick*. The road where Caan crashes his car is the **Old Donner Pass**, on I-80, west of Reno on the Nevada-California border, where the Donner party, heading west, survived the disastrous winter of 1846 by resorting to cannibalism.

MISFITS, THE
(1961, dir: John Huston)
Marilyn Monroe, Clark Gable, Montgomery Clift.
● NEVADA

Monroe's divorce: Washoe County Courthouse, Reno

Monroe loses her wedding band: Truckee River Bridge, Reno

Sad, atmospheric movie which can't escape the shadow of the untimely deaths of the three principals. Gable's heart gave out a few weeks after the arduous shoot was over, while Monty Clift's system finally caved in after years of pills and booze in 1966, and what actually happened to Marilyn in 1962 is anybody's guess. Centering around the roping of wild mustangs in the desert, the film starts around **Reno**, Nevada, where Monroe is getting a divorce at the **Washoe County Courthouse, 5 Virginia Street** between Mill and Court Streets, before following tradition by tossing her wedding band into the Truckee River. The casino where Gable and Monroe gamble was the now-gone Mapes Casino, in the Mapes Hotel, 30 North Virginia Street, Reno. Most of the company stayed in the hotel. Marilyn and Arthur Miller occupied room 614, while Monty was discovered naked in the lift after one of his notorious barbiturate and alcohol cocktails.

The rodeo town is **Dayton**. Don't expect this tiny, one-street town to be bustling, but you can still eat at **Mia's Restaurant**, the bustling bar in the movie, in the Odeon Hall building, **Pike Street**. The roping of the stallions was filmed on the white salt flats of **Pyramid Lake**, about 30 miles north of Reno. Eli Wallach's ranch is **Quail Canyon Ranch**, off Pyramid Highway.

The bar in the rodeo town: Mia's, Odeon Hall, Dayton

MISSION, THE
(1986, dir: Roland Joffé)
Robert De Niro, Jeremy Irons, Ray McAnally.
● COLOMBIA; ARGENTINA

Big themes, big vistas, big music. Irons and De Niro bring

Jesus to the natives in their different ways. This was the worthy project that the profit from Hugh Hudson's ghastly *Revolution* was supposed to finance.

Location filming took place in Colombia and Argentina. The falls over which the crucified priest plunges are the **Iguazu Falls**, at the junction of the Parana and Iguazu Rivers on the borders of Brazil, Paraguay and Argentina. 350 of the Wuanana Tribe played the dooomed Guaranis.

Father Gabriel's San Carlos Mission was built in the jungle around **Santa Marta**, Colombia, on land owned by the brewery producing the country's most popular beer. Being Colombia, it also happened to be on an extremely popular drug route, which necessitated the posting of armed guards on the set, night and day.

The city of Ascension is the walled 16th century **Old Town** area of **Cartagena**, on the northeast coast of Colombia. Another mission was constructed here. Although only a temporary structure, built of plaster, the owner of the land asked for it to be left as a tourist attraction.

MISSION: IMPOSSIBLE
(1996, dir: Brian De Palma)
Tom Cruise, Jon Voight, Vanessa Redgrave.
● **LONDON; CZECH REPUBLIC; SCOTLAND; VIRGINIA**

The American embassy: Natural History Museum, Prague

The embassy, where the doomed mission begins, is the rather rundown **Natural History Museum, Václavské nám 68** in Prague. As the mission falls apart, Jon Voight falls into the Vltava River from the famous **Charles Bridge**. Other Prague locations include **Wenceslas Square** at the centre of the old town and the **Lichtenstein Palace, Malostranské nám 13** on Kampa Island. Vanessa Redgrave's art deco HQ is the **Europa Hotel, Václavské nám 25**, also on Wenceslas Square (*©42.2.2365274*)

Max's HQ: Europa Hotel, Prague

The exterior of the CIA Building in **Langley**, Virginia is the real thing, but the interior is London's old **County Hall**, on the south bank. The London safe house is aboove Liverpool Street underground station, **Liverpool Street** at **Broad Street**, EC2, and Cruise meets up with Voight on **Liverpool Street Station**, mightily revamped since its dilapidated appearance in *The Elephant Man*. The sup-

Jon Voight is shot: Charles Bridge

posedly cross-channel railway scenes were filmed in Scotland, on stretches of line between **Annan** and **Dumfries**, and **Dumfries** and **New Cumnock**.

Relaxing: Anchor Tavern, Bankside

The terrace pub, where Cruise finally unwinds, is the **Anchor Tavern, Bankside** by Southwark Bridge.

MISSION: IMPOSSIBLE 2
(1999, dir: John Woo)
Tom Cruise, Thandie Newton, Anthony Hopkins.
● **NEW SOUTH WALES, AUSTRALIA; UTAH**

John Woo's stylish but empty sequel was made almost entirely in Australia, around Sydney, New South Wales, except for the dizzying rock climbing scene (it really is Tom Cruise in all but one shot, though supporting cables were removed digitally), which was shot at **Dead Horse Point State Park**, about fifteen miles southwest of Moab, near the location of the final scene of *Thelma and Louise*, in southeast Utah.

Villain Dougray Scott's island hideout is **Bare Island Fort**, at the entrance to Botany Bay, south of Sydney. His other waterside retreat was built at **Ashton Park**, on the **Mosman** waterfront. The racecourse, where Thandie Newton steals the images from the digital camera, is **Royal Randwick Racecourse** in Sydney's suburb of Randwick. The motorbike chase was filmed at **Boora Point** near Malabar. More action scenes took in the area around **Governor Macquarie Tower** and **Governor Phillip Tower**, modern twin buildings near **Circular Quay**, Sydney

The Seville scenes were also shot in Australia, at **Argyle Place** in **The Rocks**, Sydney's revived historic core on the western shore of Sydney Cove, and at Sydney's most expensive mansion, **Boomerang**, on the waterfront at **Elizabeth Bay**.

MISSISSIPPI BURNING
(1988, dir: Alan Parker)
Gene Hackman, Willem Dafoe, Frances McDormand.
● **MISSISSIPPI; ALABAMA**

Fictionalised account of the investigation into the deaths of three Civil Rights workers in the sixties, causing much controversy by placing white – and fictitious – FBI agents at the centre of the story. Based on the murder of Andrew Goodman, Michael Schwerner and James Chaney in Philadelphia, East Mississippi, in 1964, the film was shot in Mississippi and Alabama. Chaney's funeral was filmed in **Cedar Hill Cemetery, Vicksburg**, Mississippi. Also in Mississippi is the Jessup County sherriff's office, which is **Vaiden Courthouse**. The town square of Philadelphia, 1964 is **Lafayette**, Alabama. The movie theatre was given a $25,000 makeover – it's been closed since the sixties and is now actually an auto supply store. Much of the film was shot in small towns around Jackson, Mississippi. Filming also took place at the **Ross Barnett Reservoir**, to the northeast of Jackson, Mississippi; and at **Bovina**, Mississippi.

MRS BROWN (aka *Her Majesty, Mrs Brown*)
(1997, dir: John Madden)
Judi Dench, Billy Connolly, Antony Sher.
● ISLE OF WIGHT; SCOTLAND; WILTSHIRE

An Oscar nomination for Judi Dench as Queen Victoria in this account of her friendship with Scots ghillie John Brown. Windsor Castle is played by **Wilton House, Wilton** near Salisbury (see *The Music Lovers* for details). The Scottish scenes are at **Duns Castle**, about 16 miles from Berwick. The 1320 private home is not generally open to the public, except by prior arrangement (*© 01361.883211*). And it is, famously, the real **Osborne House**, on the Isle of Wight, to which the Queen retreats. The house, just outside East Cowes on the isle's north shore, is open to the public from March to October (*© 01983.200022, admission charge*).

MRS DOUBTFIRE
(1993, dir: Chris Columbus)
Robin Williams, Sally Field, Pierce Brosnan.
● CALIFORNIA

This coarse, sentimental comedy, which really took off at the box office, is set around San Francisco. The TV studio, where Robin Williams gets a job boxing and shipping cans, is **KTVU 2** over on the East Bay. In East Bay, too, you'll find the restaurant where Williams performs his quick-change routine during two fraught meals. It's **Bridges Restaurant, 44 Church Street, Danville**, east of Oakland. Also in the area is the **Claremont Resort Hotel, Claremont Avenue** at Ashby Avenue in the Tilden Regional Park area north of Berkeley. Built in 1915, the Victorian-style resort is where Mrs Doubtfire sabotages Sally Field's flirtation with charmer Pierce Brosnan. Mrs Doubtfire takes the kids to cycle and play soccer at **Crissy Field**, the green area on the Bay just east of the Golden Gate Bridge. She fends off a mugger on **Columbus Avenue** (the elegant, pale green Flatiron Building in the background is the HQ of Francis Coppola's movie empire). Williams and Field live at **2640 Steiner Street** at Broadway in Pacific Heights.

The Doubtfire house: Steiner Street

MR BLANDINGS BUILDS HIS DREAM HOUSE
(1948, dir: H C Potter)
Cary Grant, Myrna Loy, Melvyn Douglas.
● LOS ANGELES

Grant and Loy are New Yorkers doing up their ideal Con-

necticut country home (an idea rejigged in 1986 as *The Money Pit*, with Tom Hanks). The dream house was built on the Fox Ranch, now the 4,000-acre **Malibu Creek State Park**. The land was owned by film producer George Hunter, who subsequently converted the house into a ranch home. And it's still there, housing the offices of the Santa Monica Mountains Conservancy Foundation, at **3800 Solstice Canyon Road**, Malibu Canyon Road between Mulholland Highway and Cold Canyon Road, in the Santa Monica Mountains above Malibu.

MISTER ROBERTS
(1955, dir: John Ford, Mervyn LeRoy)
Henry Fonda, James Cagney, Jack Lemmon.
● MIDWAY; HAWAII

Ford and Fonda, in their eighth film together, fell out over the filming of Thomas Heggen and Joshua Logan's comic-sentimental tale about WWII shipboard life. Fonda, who played the role on stage, objected to the Fordian knock-about coarsening. Ford was eventually hospitalised, to be replaced by veteran Warner Bros director LeRoy. The film was made at **Midway Island** in the Pacific and at the **Kanoehoe Marine Corps Air Station** in Hawaii.

MR SMITH GOES TO WASHINGTON
(1939, dir: Frank Capra)
James Stewart, Claude Rains, Jean Arthur.
● LOS ANGELES; WASHINGTON DC

Archetypal Capra little-man-against-bureaucracy fable. Mr Smith does indeed go to Washington, but only just. Most of the movie was made in LA, with some background filming in the nation's capital. James Stewart disembarks at DC's (recently restored) **Union Station, Massachusetts Avenue NE**, where the first building he sees is the reassuring dome of the **US Capitol**.

MO' BETTER BLUES
(1990, dir: Spike Lee)
Denzel Washington, Joie Lee, Wesley Snipes.
● NEW YORK CITY

Lee's New York-set film about the confused life of a jazz trumpeter, played by Denzel Washington, looks stunning. The opening shot of 'Brooklyn, 1969' was filmed on the west side of **Prospect Park** in the classy **Park Slope** area of the borough. Bleek's loft was shot on **Brooklyn Heights** near the waterfront, in the shadow of the Brooklyn Bridge, while Clarke's apartment is in a landmark building in the **Fort Greene** neighbourhood.

The Beneath the Underdog club is a composite. The interior is a studio set, but the exterior is Greenwich Village's **Cherry Lane Theater, 38 Commerce Street**, between Bedford and Barrow Streets, dressed as West 52nd Street in the fifties. You can also see the Cherry Lane in Woody Allen's *Another Woman*, Warren Beatty's *Reds* and *The House on Carroll Street*.

Clarke works as a cashier in the jazz section of **Tower Records, 692 Broadway** at East Fourth Street in the Village. The birth of Bleek's son is at **Harlem Hospital, 135th Street** at Lenox Avenue. The brownstone stoop, where Indigo waits for Bleek, is on **141st Street** between Convent Avenue and Hamilton Place, Harlem.

The Dizzy Club is the 350-seat **America Restaurant, 9 East 18th Street** between Broadway and Fifth Avenue, northwest of Union Square – once the ultimate trendy restaurant. The alleyway where Giant and Bleek are bloodily beaten up, is **Shinbone Alley**, off Bond Street between Broadway and Lafayette Street in the East Village.

MOBY DICK
(1956, dir: John Huston)
Gregory Peck, Richard Basehart, Friedrich Ledebur.
● **IRELAND; CANARY ISLANDS**

Orson Welles staged Herman Melville's tale on stage in London's West End and desperately wanted to direct the movie, but ultimately the job went to Huston, and Welles was compensated with the small role of Father Mapple. The New Bedford harbour the *Pequod* sails from is **Youghal**, about 25 miles east of Cork, in County Cork on the southern coast of the Republic of Ireland. Scenes at sea were filmed in St George's Channel off the coast of Fishguard, South Wales.

Filming dragged on, partly due to visa difficulties with Huston and Peck, who could only work 90 days in England, which meant they had to hotfoot it out of Britain every Friday, spend the weekend in Paris, and commute back for work on Monday. When the waters became too cold for filming, the crew upped and moved to Las Palmas in the Canaries, where the ending, with Richard Basehart floating on the coffin, was shot. The scene in which Peck, lashed to a rotating, 20-foot section of rubber whale, is finally dragged under, was saved until last. Just in case...

MODESTY BLAISE
(1966, dir: Joseph Losey)
Monica Vitti, Terence Stamp, Dirk Bogarde.
● **NETHERLANDS; ITALY; LONDON; HAMPSHIRE**

Losey's too self-consciously camp spy spoof uses locations in London, Amsterdam, the Bay of Naples and the slopes of Vesuvius. Modesty is lured out of retirement at the crush bar of the **Opera House, Covent Garden**, though the lobby of the Ritz Hotel is a set at Shepperton. Her private plane takes off from the security airfield at **Farnborough** in Hampshire. Filming in Amsterdam includes the notorious **Walletjes**, the Red Light District between Centraal Station, the Dam and the Nieuwmarkt, and the **Old Square**, with its House of Dolls, which is also the setting for the rally of barrel organs. Fluttery villain Bogarde's hideout is the castle and chapel of **St Alessio**, near Messina on the northeast coast of Sicily. The cliffs below are at **Tindari**, on Sicily's northwest coast, which also supplied the stretch of desert sand and volcanic rock, as well as the beach finale. The freighter is in the **Bay of Naples**, and the car chase along the top of **Mount Vesuvius**.

MOGAMBO
(1953, dir: John Ford)
Clark Gable, Ava Gardner, Grace Kelly.
● **TANGANYIKA; UGANDA**

Remake of Victor Fleming's 1932 movie *Red Dust*, transposed from an Indo-China rubber plantation to Africa, but with Gable reprising his role as the man torn between brassy showgirl Gardner and prim-but-married Kelly, during a gorilla hunt. Notching up 67 location days, it was the biggest film to have been made in Africa at the time, and one of the biggest headaches, being hampered by temperamental stars, outbreaks of amoebic dysentry and the chorus of animal noises, not to mention the Mau Mau rebellion. The locations were Tanganyika's **Serengeti Plain** and Uganda's **Kagera River**, with its spectacular rapids and falls.

MOMMIE DEAREST
(1981, dir: Frank Perry)
Faye Dunaway, Diana Scarwid, Steve Forrest.
● **LOS ANGELES**

Hilariously kitsch classic biopic of Joan Crawford, based on daughter Christina's 'revenge' autobiography, filmed as an old-fashioned Crawford melodrama. The real Crawford house, not available for filming, can still be seen

Crawford dines out: Perino's, Wilshire Boulevard

at 426 North Bristol Avenue, north from Sunset Boulevard in Brentwood. When Crawford married Douglas Fairbanks Jr, the house was named 'El Jodo' (*à la* 'Pickfair'). The movie house was a mansion just off the western reach of Sunset Boulevard. MGM Studios, where La Crawford makes her movies, is at **10202 West Washington Boulevard** in Culver City. The wonderful art deco frontage seen in the movie, however, can no longer be seen from the street: it's the eastern entrance at the end of Grant Avenue off Madison or Clarington Avenues, now part of the MGM lot. Crawford dines at **Perino's, 4101 Wilshire Boulevard** at Norton Avenue. The classic restaurant is now closed and up for sale, but you can still see its deco pink exterior. Originally called the Hi-Hat, Perino's in its heyday stood at 3929 Wilshire Boulevard, near Western Avenue. See it in *Sunset Blvd.*, opposite the shop where William Holden gets kitted out by Gloria Swanson. Young Christina is bundled off to **Chadwick School, 26800 South Academy Drive** on the Palos Verdes Peninsula, south of LA.

MON ONCLE (aka *My Uncle*)
(1956, dir: Jacques Tati)
Jacques Tati, Jean-Pierre Zola.
● **FRANCE**

Tati's comedy, pitting the eccentric uncle, M. Hulot, against a soulless modern world, took the Oscar for Best Foreign Language Film. Hulot's old neighbourhood is **Saint-Maur-des-Fossés**, Paris.

MONA LISA
(1986, dir: Neil Jordan)
Bob Hoskins, Cathy Tyson, Michael Caine.
● **LONDON; SUSSEX**

Cabdriver Bob Hoskins is hired to ferry high-class hook-

Tyson's haunt: St Ermin's, Caxton Sreet

er Tyson between assignations in a sleazy-looking London. Tyson's regular haunts include the **Ritz** in Piccadilly, and the florid pink **Hilton St Ermin's Hotel, Caxton Street, SW1**, where Hoskins turns up in his splendid new gear. Tyson is dumped by Hoskins in the traffic at **Hyde Park Corner**, but he relents and gets kitted out in style at **Tommy Nutter's**. The search for Tyson's friend takes in the **King's Cross** area, and the strip- and peep-joints of **Soho**. Michael Caine issues his orders from the **Raymond Revuebar, Walker's Court**. There's trouble from the heavies on **Brighton Pier**, and a bloody shoot-out in the **Royal Albion Hotel**, Brighton.

MONEY PIT, THE

(1986, dir: Richard Benjamin)
Tom Hanks, Shelley Long, Alexander Godunov.
● **NEW YORK CITY; NEW YORK STATE; FLORIDA**

Updating of *Mr Blandings Builds His Dream House*, with Hanks and Long going through all kinds of hell fixing up their bargain mansion. The house is **Northway, Feeks Lane, Lattingtown**, northeast of Glen Cove on the north coast of Long Island, off Route 107. The New York scenes feature the romantic **Cafe des Artistes** restaurant, in the **Hotel des Artistes, 1 West 67th Street** at Central Park West, and the **Apthorp Apartments, 2211 Broadway** between West 78th and West 79th Streets on the West Side. The house featured at the end is **Villa Vizcaya, 3251 South Miami Avenue** at 32nd Road in Coconut Grove on the coast south of Miami, Florida (see *Ace Ventura – Pet Detective* for details).

MONSIEUR HULOT'S HOLIDAY (aka *Les Vacances de Monsieur Hulot*)

(1953, dir: Jacques Tati)
Jacques Tati, Nathalie Pascaud, Michèle Rolla.
● **FRANCE**

The hotel, where M Hulot causes unintentional havoc, can still be seen, though now revamped since the movie was made in the fifties. It's the **Hotel de la Plage, 37 rue Commandant Charcot, St Marc-sur-Mer** (℗ *02.40.91.9901, www.hotel-de-la-plage-44.com/htgb/ home.htm*) on the mouth of the Loire, between swanky resort La Baule and naval base St Lazaire, about 45 miles west of Nantes, Loire Valley West.

MONTE CARLO OR BUST (aka *Those Daring Young Men in Their Jaunty Jalopies*)

(1969, dir: Ken Annakin)
Tony Curtis, Gert Frobe, Peter Cook.
● **FRANCE; SWEDEN; MONACO**

Big budget (ie unfunny) slapstick, shot in **Paris** and Sweden, with the inevitable climax at **Monte Carlo**, in the days before the once-elegant resort was swallowed up in a sea of concrete blocks.

MONTY PYTHON AND THE HOLY GRAIL

(1975, dir: Terry Gilliam, Terry Jones)
Graham Chapman, John Cleese, Michael Palin.
● **SCOTLAND**

King Arthur and his men, accompanied by their trusty coconut shells, approach **Doune Castle**, a 14th century fortification on the A84 a few miles northwest of Stirling (℗ *01786.841742, admission charge*). The Bridge of Death is at the **Meeting of the Three Waters**, where the mountain waterfalls become the River Cae in Glen Coe. The island castle where the Grail resides turns out to be **Castle Stalker**, 20 miles north of Oban. The 15th century stronghold is a quarter of a mile from the shore of Loch Linhe and occasionally open to the public subject to tides and weather (*admission charge; ℗ 01883.622768*).

MONTY PYTHON'S LIFE OF BRIAN

(1979, dir: Terry Jones)
Graham Chapman, John Cleese, Eric Idle.
● **TUNISIA**

Graham Chapman gets mistaken for the Messiah and makes a pretty good job of the position in this brilliant satire. The Holy Land is Tunisia, where most of the film was shot in the **Ribat**, the fortified monastery at **Monastir**, previously the setting for Zeffirelli's terminally pious

TV production, *Jesus of Nazareth*. Monastir, with its airport, is the centre of the Gulf of Hammamet's tourist coast. Though the town itself is small and away from the hotel complexes. The Ribat, with its maze of walls and passages, is open to the public (*admission charge*). The **Kasbah** of **Sousse**, the major city about 25 miles west of Monastir. The Kasbah is now a museum, containing a collection of Roman mosaics. The final crucifixion scene uses the landscape around **Tataouine**, the town that gave its name to Luke

Brian falls from the tower: Ribat, Monastir

The city walls: the Kasbah, Sousse

"Welease Woger": Ribat, Monastir

Skywalker's home planet in the Tunisia-shot *Star Wars*, toward the south of the country.

MONTY PYTHON'S THE MEANING OF LIFE

(1983, dir: Terry Jones)
Graham Chapman, John Cleese, Eric Idle.

● LONDON; BUCKINGHAMSHIRE

Mr Creosote: Porchester Hall, Queensway

More sketches, varying in quality. The 'Find the Fish' interlude was filmed at **Chicheley Hall, Newport Pagnell** in Buckinghamshire (*a d m i s s i o n charge; © 01234. 391252*). The restaurant, where the disgustingly obese Mr Creosote explodes, is **Porchester Hall, Porchester Centre, Queensway**, London W2. The 'Every Sperm Is Sacred' production number was filmed on the backstreet between **Bankfield Street** and Hargreaves Street in **Colne**, Lancashire. Terry Jones' house was **17 Bankfield Street**.

Every sperm is sacred...: Bankfield Street, Colne

MOONRAKER, THE

(1958, dir: David MacDonald)
George Baker, Sylvia Syms, Marius Goring.

● WILTSHIRE; KENT

Civil War swashbuckling suspenser. The opening scene, with Cavalier George Baker meeting his fellow conspirators, is at **Stonehenge** on Salisbury Plain, Wiltshire. Oliver Cromwell's HQ is **Leeds Castle**, near Maidstone in Kent (see *Kind Hearts and Coronets* for details). The Royalist house raided by Cromwell's troops is **Lacock Abbey**, a Gothicised 13th century abbey in Lacock, three miles south of Chippenham in Wiltshire. The house, home of the Talbot family, including the Medieval cloisters seen in the movie, is open daily (except Tuesday) from the beginning of April to the end of October (*admission charge; © 01249.730227*).

MOONRAKER

(1979, dir: Lewis Gilbert)
Roger Moore, Lois Chiles, Michael Lonsdale.

● RIO DE JANEIRO, BRAZIL; VENICE, ITALY; NEVADA; CALIFORNIA; FLORIDA; FRANCE; GUATEMALA

After the terrifically vertiginous opening sequence, *Moonraker* turns out to be just about the klutziest of the Bond

movies. Bond arrives at **LA International Airport**, to investigate the disappearance of a space shuttle, and takes a helicopter ride over the city to visit the estate of sauve villain Drax. Drax's lavish mansion was "brought stone by stone from France". Not quite. It is a French chateau, but it stayed firmly on the other side of the Atlantic. It's the 17th century chateau **Vaux-le-Vicomte**, twenty miles southeast of Paris. Built for Fouquet, Louis XIV's finance minister, its grandeur provoked a fit of envy in the King. With the hubris of a Bond villain, Louis had Fouquet thrown into prison and began planning the even more sumptuous Versailles.

Bond follows a lead to Venice, where Drax has his glassworks and museum off St Mark's Square. The glassworks' entrance is **Venini, 314 Piazzetta dei Leoni**, northeast of St Mark's. The cheesy boat chase (a motorised gondola which turns into a hovercraft for no discernible reason) ends with Bond hovering across **St Mark's Square**, to some of the most ridiculous reaction shots in movie history. The clock, behind which Bond slugs it out with the baddies, is the face of the **Torre dell'Orologio**, the clock tower at the north of St Mark's Square. Of course, the villain crashes through a fake. The clock's workings, if you want to check out what they really look like, can be visited. The training camp is **San Nicolo al Lido, Riviera San Nicolo**, a monastery on the northwest coast Venice's Lido.

It's on to Rio de Janeiro for a fight with Jaws on the cable car lift to **Sugarloaf Mountain** (only in longshot – the fight itself filmed on a Pinewood mock-up) and to Guatemala for yet another motorboat chase, leading to Drax's jungle hideout. A US shuttle is sent up to battle Drax's forces from the **Vandenberg Airforce Base**, between San Luis Obispo and Santa Barbara on Coastal Highway 1, southern California (also where Blofeld launched his satellite in *Diamonds Are Forever*).

MOONSTRUCK

(1987, dir: Norman Jewison)
Cher, Nicolas Cage, Danny Aiello.

● NEW YORK CITY; TORONTO, ONTARIO

Cher has to choose between safe, homely Aiello and his dangerous brother Cage in this enjoyable tale of mix 'n' match relationships among Italian-Americans in Brooklyn Heights. Set in New York, of course, but filming took place in Toronto too.

The Cammareri Brothers' bakery: Henry Street, Brooklyn

New York interiors: Keg Mansion Restaurant, Jarvis Street, Toronto

Cher's house: Cranberry Street, Brooklyn Heights

Cher lives in the up-market brownstone Italian neighbourhood just over the Brooklyn Bridge from Manhattan's southern tip, at **19 Cranberry Street** on the corner of Willow Street, overlooking the East River. Nicolas Cage lost his hand and his fiancée, but still works, at **Cammareri Bros Bakery, 502 Henry Street**, a few blocks south. The restaurant where Danny Aiello proposes to Cher is supposedly Greenwich Village's Grand Ticino Restaurant, 228 Thompson Street between Bleecker and West Third Streets, but it's actually one of the scenes shot in Ontario. He takes Cher to the **Metropolitan Opera House** in the **Lincoln Centre, Broadway** at 64th Street. Other Toronto locations include **Colborne Street** and **Victoria Street; Dufferin Street** and **St Claire Avenue** and the **Keg Mansion Restaurant, 515 Jarvis Street**.

MOSQUITO COAST, THE
(1986, dir: Peter Weir)
Harrison Ford, Helen Mirren, River Phoenix.
● **BELIZE**

The Belize hotel: Hotel Mona Lisa, Haulover Creek

Harrison Ford sheds his solidly dependable image to become loopily Messianic after leaving the rat race and taking his family off to live a simple self-sufficient life in the jungle. The movie was shot in Belize City and its water-logged surrounds, in Belize. The hotel is the **Hotel Mona Lisa** on the south side of **Haulover Creek** just past the new 3-storey market. The bridge, made in Liverpool and opened in 1923, is the only manually-operated swing bridge left in the Americas. The creek is named for the fact that cattle were once winched over the waterway, which divides the city.

MOST DANGEROUS GAME, THE (aka *The Hounds of Zaroff*)
(1932, dir: Ernest B Schoedsack, Irving Pichel)
Leslie Banks, Joel McCrea, Fay Wray.
● **CALIFORNIA**

Excellent, much-imitated horror thriller with Banks as the villainous hunter of human prey. Joel McCrea – or, rather, stuntman Wes Hopper who filmed the scene – swims

ashore on the rocky beach near **San Pedro**, south LA. The clifftop scenes were filmed at **Redondo**, while the views of the cove from Banks' studio-bound chateau are the cliffs at **Marineland**, the southwestern tip of the Palos Verdes Peninsula.

MOULIN ROUGE
(1952, dir: John Huston)
Jose Ferrer, Zsa Zsa Gabor, Suzanne Flon.
● **PARIS**

The real Moulin Rouge, Clichy

Lautrec in Paris: Pont Alexandre III, Paris

John Huston's biopic of painter Toulouse Lautrec was made almost entirely on location in Paris, with a complex system of gels and filters to produce a wonderful cinematic equivalent of the painter's style. Real locations include **Maxim's, 3 rue Royale** and the wildly elaborate **Pont Alexandre III**, seen also in *A View to a Kill*. The real Moulin Rouge can still be visited, in **Clichy**.

MOVE OVER, DARLING
(1963, dir: Michael Gordon)
Doris Day, James Garner, Thelma Ritter.
● **LOS ANGELES**

James Garner sees his macho rival, Chuck Connors, showing off on the trampoline by the pool at the **Beverly Hills Hotel, 9641 Sunset Boulevard**. Doris Day's home is on the corner of **Wyton Drive** in Beverly Hills.

MUCH ADO ABOUT NOTHING
(1993, dir: Kenneth Branagh)
Kenneth Branagh, Emma Thompson, Keanu Reeves.
● **ITALY**

Branagh's sunny Shakespearian romp, shot in the 15th century **Villa Vignamaggio**, home of the Gheradini family, reputedly the family of the model for the Mona Lisa. Built after the Florentines destroyed their place in Montagliari, the villa is near **Greve**, in Chianti, on a side road off the SS222 to Lamole. If you want a souvenir, the vineyard in the surrounding park has its own label.

MUMMY, THE
(1999, dir: Stephen Sommers)
Brendan Fraser, Rachel Weisz, Arnold Vosloo.
● **MOROCCO; BUCKINGHAMSHIRE; KENT; SURREY**

Splurgy horror comedy, knee-deep in CGI effects. Set in Egypt, of course, but filmed mainly in Morocco. The lost city of Hamunaptra was a set built at an old fort inside a dormant volcano near **Erfoud**. It's not all quite so exotic, though.

The port of Giza, where the party boards the Nile ship, is actually **Chatham Docks** in Kent, and after the ship goes down in flames, they come ashore at **Frensham Ponds**, on the A287about five miles south of Farnham in Surrey. The interior of the Museum of Antiquities in Cairo is **Mentmore Towers** at Mentmore, Buckinghamshire (see *Brazil* for details).

MURDER AHOY

(1964, dir: George Pollock)
Margaret Rutherford, Lionel Jeffries, Charles Tingwell.
● **BUCKINGHAMSHIRE**

Miss Marples' cottage: Denham

Fourth, and last, of the sixties Agatha Christie series, with Miss Marple investigating a murder shipboard. Miss Marples' Milchester cottage can be seen on **Village Road** at the Misbourne Bridge in the village of **Denham**, Buckinghamshire.

MURDER AT 1600

(1997, dir: Dwight H Little)
Wesley Snipes, Diane Lane, Daniel Benzali.
● **ONTARIO, CANADA**

Searching the archives: Metro Archive, Toronto

The DC dinner: Manulife Building, Bloor Street, Toronto

Snipes investigates a murder inside the White House, but although the film is naturally set in Washington DC, it was filmed largely in Canada, around Toronto: at **Etobicoke**, west Toronto, and **Mississauga**, southwest Toronto; **North York**, north Toronto and **Scarborough**, east Toronto. The archives Diane Lane searches are Toronto's **Metro Archives, Spadina Road**. The black tie function is held at the **Manulife Building, 200 Bloor Street East**, and Snipes follows the President's son to the **Venus Nightclub, 184 Pearl Street** between Soho Street and Spadina Avenue.

The motel is the **Hillcrest Motel, 2143 Lakeshore Boulevard West** (see *Bride of Chucky* for details). Other Toronto locations include the grand **Royal York Hotel, 100 Front Street West**, opposite Union Station; the **Paddock Tavern, 178 Bathurst Street** and the **County Court, 361 University Avenue**.

MURDER AT THE GALLOP

(1963, dir: George Pollock)
Margaret Rutherford, Flora Robson, Robert Morley.
● **BUCKINGHAMSHIRE; HERTFORDSHIRE**

Second of the Margaret Rutherford-Miss Marple movies is an adaptation of Agatha Christie's *After the Funeral*, with Marple investigating the demise of a man scared to death by a pussycat. Suspicious, huh? Shot around the village of **Denham**, on the A4020, northwest of Uxbridge; at **Aldenham**, to the northeast of Watford; and at **Hilfield Castle, Hilfield Lane**, just off the A41 north of Bushey in Hertfordshire.

Miss Marple investigates: Aldenham

MURDER BY DEATH

(1976, dir: Robert Moore)
Alec Guinness, Peter Sellers, Maggie Smith.
● **BERKSHIRE**

Enjoyably broad detective spoof, written, amazingly, by Neil Simon. The Gothic home of prissy writer Truman Capote, where the world's top detectives are gathered, is Oakley Court, now the **Oakley Court Hotel, Windsor Road** between Maidenhead and Windsor (see *The Rocky Horror Picture Show* for details of this much-used location).

MURDER IN THE FIRST

(1995, dir: Marc Rocco)
Christian Slater, Kevin Bacon, Gary Oldman.
● **CALIFORNIA**

Buddy-weepie with idealistic, young, Armani dressed lawyer Christian Slater representing no-hoper Kevin Bacon and exposing the brutal regime of Alcatraz in the thirties, while the soundtrack shamelessly rips off Vaughan Williams. The real **Alcatraz Island** is used for much of the movie, though the dungeon where Bacon is kept in three years of solitary darkness was meticulously recreated in the studio. The courthouse building is **San Francisco City Hall**, though once again the courtroom itself is a studio set. Slater catches the cable car on **Hyde Street**, where there's a truly great view of the Bay with Alcatraz Island smack in the centre. The elegant law office building Slater works out of, though, is in downtown Los Angeles. It's the **Bradbury Building** (see *Blade Runner* for details of this extraordinary Victorian office block).

MURDER ON THE ORIENT EXPRESS

(1974, dir: Sidney Lumet)
Albert Finney, Ingrid Bergman, Lauren Bacall.
● **PARIS; TURKEY; FORMER YUGOSLAVIA; LONDON; HERTFORDSHIRE**

First, and best, of the star-studded, immaculately period Agatha Christie adaptations that have blossomed into a genre of their own. Finney's enjoyably hammy Poirot solves a murder on the snowbound Orient Express. The movie was made mainly at Elstree Studios, with a wonderfully old-fashioned revolving drum passing painted scenery past the windows. The Express departs with style from the shabby **Landy Train Repair Depot** in St Denis, Paris, expertly dressed by veteran set designer Tony Walton. And look out for the fluffy foam posing as snow, wafting about in the breeze as the train is finally dug out by the snowplough.

The snowbound scenes were shot in the **Jura Mountains** of the former Yugoslavia. The arrival of the passengers by ferry was shot in Turkey on the Bosphorus. The Istanbul restaurant of the opening is the Moorish foyer of the old **Finsbury Park Astoria**, now a church, on **Seven Sisters Road**, north London. The Armstrong home on Long Island, New York, scene of the flashback kidnapping, is **High Canons, Buckettsland Lane** in Hertfordshire (see *The Devil Rides Out* for details).

MURDER, SHE SAID

(1961, dir: George Pollock)
Margaret Rutherford, Charles Tingwell, Muriel Pavlow.
● **LONDON; BUCKINGHAMSHIRE**

First of the cosy sixties Miss Marple mysteries with the priceless, though miscast, Margaret Rutherford (Christie herself loathed the casting). Adapted from *4.50 From Paddington*, the opening did indeed film on **Paddington Station**. The railway embankment is at **Gerrards Cross**, southeast of Beaconsfield, Buckinghamshire, convenient for Rutherford's home on nearby Elm Close.

MURIEL'S WEDDING

(1994, dir: P J Hogan)
Toni Collette, Bill Hunter, Rachel Griffiths.
● **AUSTRALIA**

Dumpy Muriel marries a hunk in this broad Aussie satire, set in the gorgeous, but sadly fictitious, beachside community of Porpoise Spit. It was filmed in **Coolangatta**, Queensland and in Sydney, New South Wales. Sydney locations include **Sea World Nara Resort; Surfers Paradise; House of Jean Fox** and **Park Avenue Bridal, Parramatta; Oxford Street, Darlinghurst; St Mark's Anglican Church** at **Darling Point;** and **Ryde Hospital**.

MUSIC BOX, THE

(1932, dir: James Parrott)
Stan Laurel, Oliver Hardy, Billy Gilbert.
● **LOS ANGELES**

Laurel and Hardy, on peak form, won an Oscar for Best Short Feature as two delivery men attempting to heave a piano up an endless flight of steps. The steps are still there, though the wide open lawns either side are now built up, and you'll have a job spotting the tiny opening. A plaque marks the location. It's between the buildings at **923-927 Vendome Street**, south of Sunset

The Music Box steps: Vendome Street

Boulevard in Silverlake, north of downtown LA.

MUSIC LOVERS, THE

(1970, dir: Ken Russell)
Richard Chamberlain, Glenda Jackson, Christopher Gable.
● **LONDON; BERKSHIRE; HAMPSHIRE; WILTSHIRE; BUCKINGHAMSHIRE; AVON**

Much of Russell's overheated, overpowering black comedy fantasia on the life of florid composer Tchaikovsky was shot at Bray Studios, near Windsor, where a huge section of 19th century Moscow, including the opening fairground and the glittering domes of the Kremlin, was built on the backlot.

The deliberately kitsch country idylls around the Davidov house, the Moscow Public Gardens and the fields and forests for the First Piano Concerto sequence, were filmed in **Milford-on-Sea**, just east of Christchurch on the Hampshire coast, in **Salisbury** and Russell's native **Southampton**. The lavish interior of Brailov, Madame von Meck's house, is **Wilton House**, in the village of Wilton, two and a half miles west of Salisbury on the A30, Wiltshire. A veteran of many

The firework party at Brailov: West Wycombe House

movies, including *Barry Lyndon, The Bounty, The Madness of King George* and *The Return of a Man Called Horse*, it was originally a Tudor manor house, remodelled in the 17th century by Inigo Jones. The lavish interior includes the famous Single Cube and Double Cube rooms. Wilton is open in summer (*admission charge*; © 01722.746.729).

The suicide attempt: Grand Union Canal, Camden

The exterior of the estate, however, is **West Wycombe House**. Madame von Meck sits writing in one of the gardens' faux-classical temples. The entrance, where Tchaikovsky delivers his scores, and the scene of the disastrous fireworks party at which he is outed by the vengeful Count

Tchaikovsky's wedding: St Sofia's Cathedral, Bayswater

Madame von Meck at Brailov: the lake at West Wycombe

Chiluvsky, is the house's two-storey colonnaded south front. The alfresco performance of *Swan Lake* is performed on the lawns before the north front, with the great lake as backdrop. West Wycombe Park is south of the Oxford Road (A40), two and a half miles west of High Wycombe, Buckinghamshire. The park is open April to August, the house from June (*admission charge; © 01494.524411*). You can see the house in many other films, including *Agatha Christie's Dead Man's Folly* and Clint Eastwood's *White Hunter, Black Heart.*

Tchaikovsky and Nina are married in **St Sofia's Cathedral**, a Greek orthodox church, appropriately enough in **Moscow Road, Bayswater** (it's also the Russia church seen in *Goldeneye*). The composer's tragi-comic suicide attempt was staged on the **Grand Union Canal**, where the composer jumps into the murky water beneath the Euston railway line alongside **Gloucester Avenue Bridge** between Camden Lock and Regent's Park, NW1. The asylum, where Nina is ultimately confined, is the disused **Royal Artillery Barracks, Artillery Place, Woolwich**, SE18.

MUTINY ON THE BOUNTY

(1935, dir: Frank Lloyd)
Charles Laughton, Clark Gable, Franchot Tone.
● **CALIFORNIA; TAHITI**

Macho man Gable leads the revolt against sadistic Laughton in this classic version of the familiar story, filmed at all-purpose nautical location, **Catalina Island**, 22 miles off the coast of LA, and on location in Tahiti. It's claimed that the *Balclutha*, now berthed at San Francisco's Maritime Museum on Hyde Street Pier, can be seen in the movie, but the real star, the *Bounty* itself, was played by the *Ellen*. The ship also starred in *Hawaii* before being sold by Columbia Studios. She's now safely berthed in an earthquake-proof concrete cradle, also in San Francisco, where she's been transformed into a restaurant. The **Sailing Ship Restaurant** is at **Pier 42, the Embarcadero** by the South beach Yacht Harbor, South of Market. Further scenes were shot in **Monterey Harbour**, south of San Francisco.

MUTINY ON THE BOUNTY

(1962, dir: Lewis Milestone, Carol Reed, George Seaton)
Trevor Howard, Marlon Brando, Richard Harris.
● **TAHITI; BORA BORA; HAWAII**

The number of directors attests to the nightmare of the production, as Brando plays Fletcher Christian as a prissy British fop with, for reasons best known to himself, his ears plugged. The *Bounty* was built specially for the movie in Nova Scotia, and sailed through the Panama Canal to Tahiti at a cost of $750,000. It was diesel powered, and actually a third larger than the original – which didn't need to accommodate movie cameras.

Carol Reed was replaced as director by veteran Lewis Milestone, after the stone fishing scene and Howard's awkward dance filmed in **Bora Bora**. Location filming continued in Tahiti (apart from some early scenes shot in **Honolulu**, Hawaii). Then it was back to Culver City for studio filming, and back again to Tahiti for retakes as George Seaton finally took over from Lewis Milestone.

MY BEAUTIFUL LAUNDRETTE

(1985, dir: Stephen Frears)
Daniel Day-Lewis, Gordon Warnecke, Saeed Jaffrey.
● **LONDON**

Young Asian entrepreneur Gordon Warnecke employs one-time racist Day-Lewis to make sock-washing a feelgood experience in this little gem of a movie. The news-

The launderette: Wilcox Road, Wandsworth

agent's shop is **News Point, 169-171 Wandsworth Road** at Albion Avenue, Stockwell, SW8. The railway bridge, under which Warnecke gets attacked, is over **Stewarts Road**, near Ascalon Street, Wandsworth, SW8. The launderette itself is now a secondhand shop, **Low Gear, 11 Wilcox Road, SW8**, off Wandsworth Road, two doors away from... a launderette.

MY BEST FRIEND'S WEDDING

(1997, dir: P J Hogan)
Julia Roberts, Rupert Everett, Dermot Mulroney.
● **CHICAGO**

Julia Roberts arrives at America's busiest air terminal, the vast **O'Hare Airport**, seventeen miles northwest of the city, to move in on Chicago's high society. The prospective bride's father owns the Chicago White Sox baseball team, who play at **Comiskey Park, 333 West 35th Street** at Shields Street. Other upscale Chicago locales include the exclusive **Union League Club, 65 West Jackson Boulevard**; the Conrad Hilton Suite is at the **Hilton Hotel and Towers, 730 South Michigan Avenue** (© 312.922.4400); the Gold Coast Room of the **Drake Hotel, 140 East Walton Place** at Michigan Avenue (© 312.787.2200); **Union Station** and the office tower at **77 West Wacker Drive**. The swanky restaurant is the expensive and exclusive (for weekends you'll need to book a month ahead) **Charlie Trotter's, 816 West Armitage Avenue** at North Halsted Street, south of DePaul University (© 773.362.6228, *www.charlietrotters.com*). The bride's parents' intimidating estate is the **Cuneo Museum and Gardens, 1350 North Milwaukee Avenue, Vernon Hills**, on Route 60 about 35 miles northwest of Chicago itself, (© 847.362.3042, *www.lakeonline.com/cuneo/*). A mansion built in 1914 for Thomas Edison's partner, Samuel Insull, it was bought by Chicago businessman John Cuneo in 1937 and remained the family home until 1990. It's now open to the public. The wedding is scheduled to take place on Chicago's Magnificent Mile, at the **Fourth Presbyterian Church, 125 East Chestnut Street** at Michigan Avenue.

MY BRILLIANT CAREER

(1979, dir: Gillian Armstrong)
Judy Davis, Sam Neill, Wendy Hughes.
● **NEW SOUTH WALES, AUSTRALIA**

Davis is the 19th century proto-feminist heroine who resists a life of wifely duties to become an independent writer.

Filming took place at **Hay**; Macarthur homestead at **Camden Park** and **Captain's Flat, Micalago**.

MY DARLING CLEMENTINE
(1946, dir: John Ford)
Henry Fonda, Linda Darnell, Victor Mature.
● **ARIZONA**

The ending: Monument Valley

Fonda and Mature are Wyatt Earp and Doc Holliday in this classic Ford Western, set in Tombstone, Arizona (way down south on Hwy 80, near the Mexican border), but filmed in the much more spectacular **Monument Valley** in northern Arizona, on the Utah border. The conical peak where Fonda and Darnell have their final clinch can be seen on Hwy 163 just north of Kayenta. Notice how the kiss is a cutaway, shot in the studio? It wasn't originally in the movie, but was added as an afterthought when it was decided a bit of physical contact was needed. The film was further 'improved' by producer Zanuck chopping out 30 minutes of footage.

The real Doc Holliday, by the way, is buried at Glenwood Springs, 150 miles west of Denver on I-70, Colorado, under a headstone reading 'He died in bed'.

MY DINNER WITH ANDRE
(1981, dir: Louis Malle)
Wallace Shawn, André Gregory.
● **NEW YORK CITY; VIRGINIA**

Extended mealtime conversation, from a two-hander play, which, against all the odds, somehow manages to be fascinating. If you want to relive the experience (expensively) with a friend, the restaurant is the romantic but pricy **Cafe des Artistes** in the **Hotel des Artistes, 1 West 67th Street** at Central Park West, Manhattan (✆ *212.877.3500, jacket and tie required*). The hotel was once home to the likes of Isadora Duncan, Alexander Woollcott, Noël Coward and Norman Rockwell. Not quite as simple as it seems, though. Due to budgetary restrictions, a non-union crew was used, which meant relocating from New York. The restaurant's interior was recreated in the Grand Ballroom of the, then closed-down **Jefferson Hotel, Franklin Street** at Adams Street in Richmond, Virginia. The grandiose Beaux Arts building, dating from 1895, had been damaged by fire, but reopened in its full splendour again as the Jefferson Sheraton in 1986 (✆ *804.788.8000*).

MY GIRL
(1991, dir: Howard Zieff)
Dan Aykroyd, Jamie Lee Curtis, Anna Chlumsky.
● **FLORIDA**

An undertaker's daughter grows up during the seventies. Worth the price of admission to see Macaulay Culkin stung to death by bees. Filmed in Florida, Madison, Pennsylvania was actually **Sanford**, twenty miles north of Orlando. The Sultenfuss Funeral Parlor is **555 Sanford Street, Bar-**

tow, Route 60, 40 miles east of Tampa. Filming also took place at **Ocoee Christian Church, Ocoee** near Lake Apopka on the western outskirts of Orlando; the old **Plant City High School, Plant City**, I-4 between Tampa and Lakeland, and **Mirror Lake**, near Clermont, west of Orlando. The café, where Chlumsky and Aykroyd see Culkin's mother, is **Cafe Jake's, 112 East First Street, Sanford**.

MY LEFT FOOT
(1989, dir: Jim Sheridan)
Daniel Day-Lewis, Brenda Fricker, Ray McAnally.
● **IRELAND**

Oscars for both Day-Lewis, as Christy Brown, and Fricker, as his mother, in the story of the writer's achievements using only the toes of his left foot. It was filmed on location around Dublin and Wicklow and at MTM Ardmore Studios. The opening charity gala was staged in **Kilruddery House** (the manor house that 'burned down' in *Far and Away*), just south of Bray, near Dublin. Christy Brown's house is on **St Kevin's Square, Bray**. The art exhibition used film producer Noel Pearson's home in **Old Conna**, near Bray. Christy Brown learns that Dr Cole is to marry at **Locks Restaurant, 1 Windsor Terrace, Portobello** (✆ *4538352*) on the bank of the Grand Canal in Dublin. The ending was shot at the stone monument atop **Victoria Hill, Killiney**, on the coast near Dublin.

MY OWN PRIVATE IDAHO
(1991, dir: Gus Van Sant)
River Phoenix, Keanu Reeves, William Richert.
● **OREGON; WASHINGTON STATE; ITALY**

Phoenix and Reeves are hustlers, film director Richert (who made the underrated River Phoenix movie *Jimmy Reardon*) a Falstaff figure in Van Sant's quirky update of Shakespeare's *Henry IV*, or, more accurately, of Welles' *Chimes at Midnight*. Shot in **Portland** and **Maupin**, Oregon; in **Seattle**, Washington State and in Italy.

MYSTERY TRAIN
(1989, dir: Jim Jarmusch)
Youki Kudoh, Masatoshi Nagase, Joe Strummer.
● **MEMPHIS, TENNESSEE**

More oddball minimalism from Jarmusch: three tales centering on a sleazy hotel, filmed around a very decrepit-looking Memphis, particulary the **Chaucer Street**

Memphis landmark, home of the Blues: Beale Street

area. The hotel itself, the Arcade Hotel, has since been demolished, though the featured **Arcade Café, 540 South Main Street**, can still be seen. Among the sites featured are the legendary **Sun Studios, 706 Union Avenue**, and **Schwab's Dry Goods Store, 163 Beale Street**. Beale Street, once the throbbing heart of Memphis' blues scene, has had a major makeover and is now clean and safe, but bland and featureless as a movie set.

N

NAKED

(1993, dir: Mike Leigh)
David Thewlis, Katrin Cartlidge, Lesley Sharp.
● LONDON

Mike Leigh's bit-
ter comedy took
Best Director and
Best Actor (for
Thewlis) at Cannes
in 1993. You can
see the house
where Mancunian
David Thewlis
holes up at **33 St**

The Scots drifter: Lina Stores, Brewer
Street

Mark's Rise, off Downs Park
Road, E8 (*rail: Dalston Kings-
land*). The Soho shop doorway
where Thewlis meets manic
Scots drifter Ewen Bremner is
**Lina Stores Ltd, 18 Brewer
Street** at Greens Court, W1.

NAKED CITY, THE

(1948, dir: Jules Dassin)
Barry Fitzgerald, Don Taylor,
Howard Duff
● NEW YORK CITY

Thewlis' London home: St
Mark's Rise, Dalston

The first of the eight million stories, this police procedure
thriller was shot, influentially, on the streets of New York
– a real change from the studio-bound productions out of
Hollywood. The cop station, used both for interiors and
exteriors, is the **10th Precinct, 230 West 20th Street** in
Chelsea. Why this precinct is investigating a murder committed at **52 West 83rd Street**, way up on the Upper West
Side, is a mystery left unexplained. Other NY locations
include **Wall Street** in the Financial District; and the foyer
of the old Roxy Theater, which stood on the northeast corner of 50th Street and Seventh Avenue, demolished in
1960. The final cop vs killer confrontation was shot at the
Williamsburg Bridge, where the villain takes a nosedive
into the East River. The entrance to the bridge, which leads
to Washington Plaza, Brooklyn, is at Delancey and Clinton Streets in Chinatown.

The title, bought up by Universal, came from a book
of photographs by famed shutterbug Weegee (portrayed
by Joe Pesci in *The Public Eye*), who advised on the picture and helped find locations.

NAKED GUN: FROM THE FILES OF POLICE SQUAD!, THE

(1988, dir: David Zucker)
Leslie Nielsen, Priscilla Presley, Ricardo Montalban.
● LOS ANGELES

The big screen spin-off from *Police Squad*, the inexplicably short-lived TV series by the makers of *Airplane!*, was
filmed around LA. The press conference, to announce the
arrival of Queen Elizabeth II, is held at LA's **City Hall, 200 North Spring Street**, downtown, and Her Majesty's reception is at the **Ambassador Hotel, 3400 Wil-**

The royal reception: Ambassador Hotel, Wilshire Boulevard

shire Boulevard (see the 1954 *A Star Is Born* for details).
Villain Ricardo Montalban's office is the **Park Plaza Hotel,
607 South Park View Street**, overlooking MacArthur
Park. Just across the park is the **Vagabond Cinema, 2509
Wilshire Boulevard**, where Leslie Nielsen and Priscilla
Presley have a good laugh over Oliver Stone's *Platoon*.
Harbour scenes are **Los Angeles Harbor, San Pedro**,
south of the city, and the car chase is on **Santa Fe Avenue**
and the **Fourth Street Viaduct**, downtown. The baseball
ground climax uses two different grounds: the exterior and
the longshots are the **Anaheim Stadium, 2000 Gene
Autrey Way**, Anaheim in Orange County, home to the
California Angels and the LA Rams; while the interiors
are the **Dodger Stadium, 1000 Elysian Park Avenue**,
north central LA.

For the first sequel, *Naked Gun 2 1/2; The Smell of
Fear*, Nielsen struggles with his wetsuit on the pier in **San
Pedro Harbor**, south LA.

NAKED GUN 33 1/3: THE FINAL INSULT, THE

(1994, dir: Peter Segal)
Leslie Nielsen, Priscilla Presley, George Kennedy.
● LOS ANGELES

It's a return to the villain's hideout from the first *Naked
Gun* movie for Nielsen's dream, a parody of *The Untouch-
ables'* shootout, which turns the cavernous lobby of the
Park Plaza Hotel, 607 South Park View Street into a
railway station. The station bookstore is the hotel's recep-
tion desk. The courtroom is the **LA County Municipal Courts
Building, 110 North Grand Avenue**, and the Academy
Awards are presented at the **Shrine Auditorium, 649 West
Jefferson Boulevard**, south of downtown LA.

NAKED LUNCH, THE

(1991, dir: David Cronenberg)
Peter Weller, Judy Davis, Ian Holm.
● ONTARIO, CANADA

William Bur-
roughs' unfilmable
book is hetero-
sexualised and hy-
bridised with a
Burroughs-bio by
squelchmeister
Cronenberg.
Largely studio-

A remaining location: Backstage
Cinema, Balmuto Street, Toronto

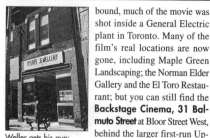

Weller gets his gun: Youri's Jewellery, Queen Street, Toronto

bound, much of the movie was shot inside a General Electric plant in Toronto. Many of the film's real locations are now gone, including Maple Green Landscaping; the Norman Elder Gallery and the El Toro Restaurant; but you can still find the **Backstage Cinema, 31 Balmuto Street** at Bloor Street West, behind the larger first-run Uptown Cinema; and the **Dunlan Restaurant, 1745 Dundas Street West**. The pawn shop, where Burroughs stand-in Weller gets the gun for the fatal William Tell game, is **Youri's Jewellery, 702 Queen Street West**.

Burroughs wrote the book in Room 9, Hotel el Muniria, 1 rue Magellan in Tangier, Morocco.

NAME OF THE ROSE, THE
(1986, dir: Jean-Jacques Annaud)
Sean Connery, Christian Slater, F Murray Abraham.
● GERMANY

Medieval whodunnit, which potters through Umberto Eco's plot while jettisoning the novel's philosophical *raison d'être*. Reversing the usual procedure, the 'Italian' monastery, where monk Connery and sidekick Slater investigate, is an enormous set on the outside, but real inside.

The interior is **Koster Eberbach**, a 12th and 14th century Cistercian monastery surviving in the Taunus Mountains in the heart of the Rheingau district which, after secularisation in 1803, became a prison and then a lunatic asylum. During WWI it was a military rehabilitation centre, and is now maintained by the state wine authorities of the Rheingau. Situated 20 miles southwest of Frankfurt, you can visit the monastery and, if arranged in advance, take a guided tour at weekends.

NANNY, THE
(1965, dir: Seth Holt)
Bette Davis, Jill Bennett, Wendy Craig.
● LONDON; HERTFORDSHIRE

Bette Davis looks after the kids: Chester Terrace, NW1

Bette Davis, in her post-*Baby Jane* phase, is the murderous nanny in this Hammer psycho-shocker. The posh London house, where she acts as a scary Mary Poppins to the kids, is on **Chester Terrace** alongside Regent's Park, London NW1. You can see the clinic, where one of her little charges is sent for psychiatric assessment, up in Hertfordshire. It is in fact **Wall Hall College**, the University of Hertfordshire, north of Aldenham, between Watford and Radlett, which was also used as the children's hospital in the 1957 Anna Neagle tearjerker *No Time For Tears*.

NASHVILLE
(1975, dir: Robert Altman)
Geraldine Chaplin, Keith Carradine, Ronee Blakley.
● TENNESSEE

Altman's brilliant multi-focused satire on the US via the Nashville country music industry filmed, of course, in **Nashville**, Tennessee. The climactic Replacement Party

The climactic political rally: The Parthenon, Centennial Park, Nashville

political rally was filmed at the city's replica of Athens' **Parthenon**, complete with Elgin marbles, in **Centennial Park**. Find it west of the city (© *615.259.6358, admission fee*).

NATIONAL LAMPOON'S ANIMAL HOUSE
(1978, dir: John Landis)
John Belushi, Tim Matheson, Donald Sutherland.
● OREGON

Start of the bozo campus comedy genre, shot at the **University of Oregon, Eugene**, on Hwys 99 and 126 (the university that turned down filming of *The Graduate*). Oregon weather being what it is, the snow had to be swept away before shooting, and the lawns painted green. The homecoming parade was filmed on the Main Street of **Cottage Grove**, twenty miles south of Eugene. Delta House stood at 751 East 11th Street, Eugene, but has since been demolished.

NATIONAL VELVET
(1944, dir: Clarence Brown)
Elizabeth Taylor, Mickey Rooney, Anne Revere.
● CALIFORNIA

Rooney and Taylor train a horse which goes on to win the Grand National. The old Warner Bros Ranch, where much of the movie was shot, is now the **Calabasas Golf Club, 4515 Park Entrada**, Calabasas, off Hwy-101 northwest of LA in the Santa Monica Mountains. On the edge of the golf course you can still see some of the old barn buildings from the movie. More scenes were filmed at the **Polo Field, Pebble Beach**, south of Monterey, on the central California coast.

NATURAL, THE
(1984, dir: Barry Levinson)
Robert Redford, Robert Duvall, Glenn Close.
● NEW YORK STATE

Hollywood bought up Bernard Malamud's odd Arthurian-baseball novel and totally reversed the ending to make an entirely different point. Set in the twenties and thirties, the movie was shot entirely within the environs of **Buffalo**, upstate New York, which was fairly unmodernised, and happened to have a period baseball stadium, the 40,000-seater **War Memorial Stadium, Jefferson and Best Streets**, home of the Buffalo Bisons. Much of the stadium has since been dismantled to form a sports complex. Filming also took place at the **Buffalo Psychiatric Center, 400 Forest Avenue**. The farmhouse is in **South Dayton**, about 40 miles southwest of Buffalo, where the the railway station is **South Dayton Station**. Chicago's Wrigley Field is actually the playing field of **Bennett High School, 2895 Main Street**, close to the ice cream parlor where Redford meets Glenn Close, **Parkside Candy Store, 3208 Main Street**.

NATURAL BORN KILLERS

(1994, dir: Oliver Stone)
Woody Harrelson, Juliette Lewis, Robert Downey Jr.
● NEW MEXICO; ARIZONA; ILLINOIS; INDIANA

Stone's adaptation of Tarantino's script was filmed all over the US, in New Mexico at **Albuquerque**; **Taos**; **Gallup**; **Redrock**; **San Jose**; **Farmington** and **Shiprock**. The bridge,

The media scrum at Mickey's trial: Chicago Cultural Center, Washington Street, Chicago

where Mickey and Mallory marry, is the **Taos Gorge Bridge** over the Rio Grande, seven miles north of Taos itself. M&M's trail of mayhem passes through Arizona, at **Winslow** and **Holbrook**.

The media scrum outside the courthouse, following the arrest of Mickey and Mallory, is at the **Chicago Cultural Center, 78 East Washington Street** at Randolph Street, Chicago, though the trial was shot in **Hammond City Court, 5925 Calumet Avenue, Hammond**, south of the city, just over the state border in Indiana. The prison is **Stateville Correctional Facility** at **Joliet**, Hwy-53, south of Chicago (where John Belushi was incarcerated at the beginning of *The Blues Brothers*).

NAZARIN

(1958, dir: Luis Buñuel)
Francisco Rabal, Marga Lopez, Rita Macedo.
● MEXICO

Mexican priest Rabal's literal attempts to follow Christianity result in futility. Though he does, at least, end up with a pineapple. Buñuel, not surprisingly, subverts Benito Perez Galdos' evangelical novel. What is surprising, though, is that the film was subsequently awarded a prize by the Office Catholique International du Cinema at Cannes. It was made in **Mexico City** and villages in the region of **Cuautla**. With typical perversity, whenever cinematographer Gabriel Figueroa had set up a beautifully composed shot, with Popocatepetl majestically looming in the background, Buñuel would avoid the picturesque by reversing the angle of the shot to film the banal view in the opposite direction.

NEGOTIATOR, THE

(1998, dir: F Gary Gray)
Samuel L Jackson, Kevin Spacey, JT Walsh.
● CHICAGO; LOS ANGELES

The Police Department Internal Affairs Division, where negotiator Spacey spars with pissed-off cop Jackson, is

77 West Wacker Dive, on the Chicago River, Chicago. The rooftop landing site for the SWAT team is the Quaker Oats Building across the river. Subsidiary locations were found around Los Angeles, including the Chicago park, which is actually the duck pond in **El Dorado Park**, Long Beach.

NET, THE

(1995, dir: Irwin Winkler)
Sandra Bullock, Jeremy Northam, Dennis Miller.
● CALIFORNIA; MEXICO; WASHINGTON DC

Bullock is a computer whiz who finds herself in receipt of hot info, in this Hitchcockian thriller for the keyboard age. The opening scene, of the homophobic politician offing himself, is in Washington DC, at **Haines Point**, the southernmost tip of West Potomac Park on the Tidal Basin. The bizarre sculpture rising out of the ground is Seward Johnson's 'The Awakening'. Bullock's home is in **Venice** on the coast of LA. After a holiday in Cozumel, Mexico, – actually **Miguelterra, Ciudad Real** – Bullock finds herself stripped of her i.d. and her identity at **LAX, Los Angeles International Airport**. She tries to meet up with fellow computer nerd Cyberbob on **Santa Monica Pier**; at the famous carousel seen in *The Sting*. The succeeding rainswept car chase is along **Templin Highway**, north of Los Angeles.

Bullock finally tracks down the net conspiracy to San Francisco, where the HQ of the 'Cathedral' corporation can be seen at **1 Post Street** at Market Street. The climactic Pan-Pacific Computer Convention used a real Apple convention at the **Moscone Center, Howard Street** between Third and Fourth Streets in San Francisco.

NETWORK

(1976, dir: Sidney Lumet)
Peter Finch, Faye Dunaway, William Holden.
● NEW YORK CITY; ONTARIO, CANADA

Paddy Chayevsky's blackly satirical satire on US TV gets a great Lumet treatment, and a posthumous Oscar for Peter Finch as the Mad Prophet of the Airwaves. Set in New York, much of the movie was made in **Toronto**, but there are some real NY locations. Holden's office is the **MGM Building, 1350 Avenue of the Americas** at 55th Street. He shares a lovenest with ambitious TV exec Faye Dunaway at the **Apthorp Apartments, 2211**

Holden's office: the MGM Building, Avenue of the Americas

Broadway between West 78th and West 79th Streets on the West Side. The pair meet up at showbizzy hangout **Elaine's Restaurant, 1703 Second Avenue** between East 88th and East 89th Streets on the East Side (see Woody Allen's *Manhattan* for details). The boardroom, where Finch gets a lecture from wacko business man Ned Beatty after putting the station's financial security in jeopardy, is the **New York Public Library, Fifth Avenue** between 40th and 42nd Streets.

NEVER ON SUNDAY
(1960, dir: Jules Dassin)
Melina Mercouri, Jules Dassin, Georges Foundas.
● GREECE

An American in Greece falls for prostitute Mercouri and tries to reform her. Filmed at **Piraeus**, about 30 miles west of Athens, where the leads take in a performance of *Medea* in the amphitheatre.

NEVER SAY NEVER AGAIN
(1983, dir: Irvin Kershner)
Sean Connery, Klaus Maria Brandauer, Kim Basinger.
● BAHAMAS; FRANCE; SPAIN; BEDFORDSHIRE; BUCKINGHAMSHIRE

Shrublands: Luton Hoo, Hertfordshire

Bond plays wargames with Largo: Waddesdon Manor

The end of the motorbike chase: Villefranche-sur-Mer

Largo's Palmyra estate: Fort Carré d'Antibes

Remake of *Thunderball*, by a different production company, but with Connery and an excellent supporting cast. Shrublands, the health club where Bond is sent by M to eliminate 'free radicals', is **Luton Hoo**, Luton, open to the public until recently. You can see the house in loads of films, including *Eyes Wide Shut*, *A Shot in the Dark* and *Wilde*. See *Four Weddings and a Funeral* for details.

Largo's yacht *Flying Saucer* is the 300-foot *Nabila*, which belonged to Adnan Khashoggi but is now the property of Donald Trump – renamed the *Trump Princess*. The motorbike chase was shot in the narrow streets of **Villefranche-sur-Mer**, a picturesque old fishing port east of Nice on the Côte d'Azur.

The 3-D Domination game between Bond and villain Largo was filmed in the French Rococo room of **Waddesdon Manor**, English home of the Rothschild family, seen also in *Carry On – Don't Lose Your Head* and *Isadora*. It's at the west end of Waddesdon village (*rail: Aylesbury*), six miles northwest of Aylesbury on the A41, and open to the public (*admission charge;* © *01296.653226;*

www.waddesdon.org.uk).

A 110-foot freighter was scuppered for the movie on New Providence Island in the Bahamas, at **Clifton Wall** on the south side. The hotel where Fatima Blush attempts to blow up Bond is the expensive, and revamped, **Best Western British Colonial Beach Resort, 1 Bay Street** at Marlborough Street west of Nassau Harbour (© *242.322.3301*), a 1923 Spanish-American style affair built on the site of the 17th century Fort Nassau. Bond walks through the **Straw Market** in Nassau, and the outdoor bar is on Nassau dock.

Largo's Palmyra fortress (in *Thunderball*, it was on New Providence Island in the Bahamas) is the disused **Fort Carre d'Antibes, Route du Bord du Mer**, north of the harbour at Antibes on the Côte d'Azur.

NEVERENDING STORY, THE
(1984, dir: Wolfgang Petersen)
Barret Oliver, Gerald McRaney, Noah Hathaway.
● BRITISH COLUMBIA, CANADA

Munich is actually the old **Gastown** district, just east of downtown, Vancouver, British Columbia.

NEW JACK CITY
(1991, dir: Mario Van Peebles)
Wesley Snipes, Ice T, Chris Rock.
● NEW YORK CITY; NEW YORK STATE

Cops versus drug dealers, filmed on the streets of New York City, and in Nassau County, Long Island. The mansion is **Hempstead House**, on **Sands Point Preserve, 95 Middleneck Road, Port Washington**, Long Island, seen also in *Scent of a Woman* and the 1998 *Great Expectations*. See *The Godfather*, which shot scenes at another mansion on the Preserve, for details.

NEW YORK NEW YORK
(1977, dir: Martin Scorsese)
Liza Minnelli, Robert De Niro, Lionel Stander.
● LOS ANGELES

De Niro plays the Sullivan House: the Ballroom, Park Plaza Hotel, LA

The nightclub: Grand Avenue, South Grand Avenue, downtown LA

Scorsese's brave attempt to put real characters into an old-style glossy musical wasn't made in New York at all, but in LA, largely on soundstages at MGM. Creepily, Liza Minnelli was assigned her mum's old dressing room. De Niro had Garbo's. Real locations can all be found in downtown LA, including the **Biltmore Hotel, 506 South Grand Avenue** on Pershing Square. The Sullivan House, where De Niro stands in when bandleader Frankie Harte has to bail out Fowler, is the Ballroom of the **Park Plaza Hotel, 607 South Park View Street** overlooking MacArthur Park. One of the most-used locations in LA , if not the world, you can see its wood-panelled Ballroom in *Barton Fink, The Big Picture, Chaplin, Hocus Pocus, Hook, Mr Saturday Night, Mobsters, Primal Fear, Stargate* and *What's Love Got to Do With It?* among many others, as well as in countless TV series and music videos. Its Terrace Room was featured in *The Mask*; its lobby in *Naked Gun 33¹/₃* and *Wild at Heart*; its exterior in *The Naked Gun, Tango and Cash* and *The Phantom*; its bathrooms in *Reservoir Dogs* and even its boiler room in *The Fisher King*. The towering structure, with its spectacular vaulted lobby, was built in the twenties as the Elks Building and long served as a hotel, but as the area around it, particularly Macarthur Park, became associated with drug related violence, it became increasingly deserted and finally closed its doors in 1998. It's now exclusively used for movie shoots and private functions. Other period-style nightspots include the old Myron's Ballroom, now renamed **Grand Avenue, 1024 South Grand Avenue**, and the lobby of the splendid **Los Angeles Theater, 615 South Broadway**.

commercialisation of the area, and the cute cabins where the couple stay have gone to make way for the main road overlooking the falls. Some of the locations remain unchanged.

Monroe and her lover: the walkways alongside the American Falls

you can still visit **Table Rock House** alongside the Horseshoe Falls, and see the ricketty-looking wooden walkways alongside the **American Falls** from the Maid of the Mist boat tour, which will take you to the foot of the falls. You can't request your favourite tune to be played on the bells, though. The bell tower, through which Monroe communicates to her lover, is the Falls Museum.

The bell tower: the Museum

NEW YORK STORIES
(1989, dir: Martin Scorsese, Francis Coppola, Woody Allen)
Nick Nolte, Rosanna Arquette, Woody Allen.
● **NEW YORK CITY**

Life Lessons: Nick Nolte is a painter in Martin Scorsese's section, filmed in a loft in **SoHo/Tribeca**.
Life Without Zoe: Coppola's mawkish story, written by his daughter, is the weakest of the three. Zoe lives in the deluxe, showbizzy **Sherry-Netherlands Hotel, 781 Fifth Avenue** at East 59th Street. The party scene was shot, imaginatively, in the arched underpass at **Bethesda Fountain** in Central Park, where the usual bums were moved out, and the space decorated to look like a mansion interior.
Oedipus Wrecks: Woody Allen's section is by far the best, with domineering mother Mae Questel (the voice of cartoon character Betty Boop) disappearing, only to materialise in the sky above Manhattan to discuss her son's shortcomings. The restaurant is the **Tavern on the Green**, in Central Park at Central Park West and 67th Street.

NIAGARA
(1953, dir: Henry Hathaway)
Marilyn Monroe, Joseph Cotten, Jean Peters.
● **ONTARIO, CANADA**

Monroe is the femme fatale planning to bump off hubby Joseph Cotten (in a role meant for James Mason) at the eponymous falls. The movie was shot on location on the Canadian side of the **Horseshoe Falls** before the massive

Double crossing at the Falls: Table Rock House

NIGHT OF THE DEMON (aka *Curse of the Demon*)
(1958, dir: Jacques Tourneur)
Dana Andrews, Niall MacGinnis, Peggy Cummins.
● **HERTFORDSHIRE; LONDON; WILTSHIRE**

Brilliant and genuinely scary filming of MR James' classic horror story 'Casting the Runes', slightly let down by the studio's insistence on giving the ambiguous demon thump-

Lufford Hall: Brocket Hall, Welwyn Garden City

ing great close-ups at the beginning of the movie. The opening scenes are at **Stonehenge** on Salisbury Plain, Wiltshire. Demon raiser MacGinnis follows Dana Andrews to the huge circular **Reading Room of the British Museum**, where the fatal runes are handed over. MacGinnis' mansion, Lufford Hall, Warwickshire, is **Brocket Hall** just west of Welwyn Garden City in Herfordshire. The mansion, also seen in TV movie *Murder With Mirrors* and the 1991 remake of *A Kiss Before Dying*, was home to the disgraced Lord Brocket, jailed for an insurance fraud. The house has since been sold and is now a private residence. You can see it from the public footpath running east from Marford Road, almost opposite the Crooked Chimney public house. The demon finally materialises on the railway line at **Bricket Wood**, between St Albans and Watford.

NIGHT OF THE IGUANA, THE
(1964, dir: John Huston)
Richard Burton, Ava Gardner, Deborah Kerr.
● **MEXICO**

Burton is the ex-priest turned tour guide having problems

with Gardner, Kerr and nymphet Sue Lyon in this comparatively lightweight Tennessee Williams play, filmed on location on the west coast of Mexico at **Puerto Vallarta**. Although tourists have been visiting the town since the thirties, it was Huston's film that put Puerta Vallarta on the map. There's actually a statue of the director in the park on Isla Río Cuale, the quiet island in the middle of Río Cuale, the river flowing through town. Much of the publicity centred around the Burton-Taylor romance, then at its height, and Burton, Taylor and Huston all stayed at La Jolla de Mismaloya Resort and Spa (*© 322.3.0660*), **Mismaloya Beach**, six miles south of town, where the movie was shot. The movie is shown nightly at Iggy's, the hotel's nightclub. You can still visit the stone buildings constructed for the movie, on the southern point above the beach.

Burton and Taylor actually bought houses in Puerto Vallarta on 'Gringo Gulch', the hilly neighbourhood of American expats on the north bank of Rio Cuale. Joined by a bridge, the two properties are now a guest house, Casa Kimberley, Zaragoza 445 (*© 322.2.1336*).

NIGHT OF THE LIVING DEAD
(1968, dir: George A Romero)
Judith O'Dea, Duane Jones, Karl Hardman.
● PITTSBURGH, PENNSYLVANIA

First of the US zombie movies to move into hitherto unexplored areas of grossness, with the low-budget, black and white look adding to the grungy atmosphere. Made, like most of Romero's output, around his native Pittsburgh, this one features **Evans City**, to the north of Pittsburgh itself, where the cemetery at the opening of the movie is situated. The farmhouse, which has since been demolished, stood on the banks of the Monongahela River. The farmhouse cellar was the basement of production company Latent Image, Carson Street, on Pittsburgh's South Side, and the TV studio was Karl Hardman's Studio in Pittsburgh.

For the 1990 colour remake, directed by Romero's make-up wiz Tom Savini, Pittsburgh was once again the setting. The farmhouse is in **East Buffalo**, Pennsylvania.

NIGHT PORTER, THE
(1974, dir: Liliana Cavani)
Dirk Bogarde, Charlotte Rampling, Philippe Leroy.
● ROME; VIENNA, AUSTRIA

When concentration camp survivor Rampling recognises the night porter of her hotel as a sadistic SS commandant, she embarks on a bizarre sado-masochistic relationship with him, in Cavani's queasily exploitative melodrama. The concentration camp scenes used a condemned TB sanatorium on the via Tuscolona in Rome. The present-day setting is Vienna, where Rampling attends performances by her conductor husband at the home of light opera, the **Volksoper, Währingerstrasse** at Währinger Gürtel.

NIGHTBREED
(1990, dir: Clive Barker)
Craig Sheffer, Anne Bobby, David Cronenberg.
● BUCKINGHAMSHIRE; ONTARIO, CANADA

Barker's fascination with the 'beauty' of horror, first seen

in *Hellraiser*, continues with this story of a young man and a psychiatrist obsessed with an ancient race of monsters. Set in the fictitious Shere Neck in Canada (there was actually a week of location shooting around **Calgary**, Ontario), the movie was made largely at **Pinewood Studios** in Buckinghamshire, utilising the actual studio buildings. Sheriff Eigerman's office is the Producer's Office at Pinewood; both the interior and exterior of Shere Neck Police Station are the Production Office complex; and the Necropolis was built on Pinewood's muddy backlot.

NIGHTCOMERS, THE
(1971, dir: Michael Winner)
Marlon Brando, Stephanie Beacham, Thora Hird.
● CAMBRIDGESHIRE

A gift to pub trivia quizzes – 'Which film featured both Marlon Brando and Thora Hird?' – this tacky prequel to the excellent *The Innocents* explains how gardener Quint's SM relationship with governess Miss Jessel gives the children Miles and Flora ideas beyond their years. Bly House (which was Sheffield Park, Sussex, in the 1961 movie) is **Sawston Hall**, a stone-built Tudor manor house five miles south of Cambridge on the A130. It's now a private school, the Cambridge Centre for Languages.

NIGHTMARE ON ELM STREET, A
(1984, dir: Wes Craven)
John Saxon, Ronee Blakely, Heather Langenkamp.
● LOS ANGELES

Wild, surreal, reality-shifting movie, elmstreets ahead of the stalk 'n' slashers it's usually bracketted with. Many of the interiors were shot inside the old **Lincoln Heights Jail, 421 North Avenue 19, Lincoln Heights**, near downtown LA, a frequent movie location. Heather Langenkamp's house, where Freddy Krueger

Freddie terrorises the teens: North Genessee Avenue, Hollywood

Johnny Depp's house: North Genessee Avenue, Hollywood

stalks her, is **1428 North Genessee Avenue**, between Fountain Avenue and Sunset Boulevard, West Hollywood. And just over the road at **1419 North Genessee Avenue**, is the house where boyfriend Johnny Depp (in his movie début) gets liquidised.

NINE 1/2 WEEKS
(1986, dir: Adrian Lyne)
Mickey Rourke, Kim Basinger, Margaret Whitton.
● NEW YORK CITY

Flash-trash ads director Lyne films a softcore promo for SM lite in New York. Shooting took place at literary hangout the **Algonquin Hotel, 59 West 44th Street** between Fifth and Sixth Avenues, midtown; funky Italian bar **Mare Chiaro, 176 Mulberry Street**, Little Italy (seen in *Donnie Brasco* among many other films); and at the **Hotel Chelsea, 222 West 23rd Street** (see *Sid and Nancy* for details).

NINETEEN EIGHTY-FOUR
(1984, dir: Michael Radford)
John Hurt, Richard Burton, Cyril Cusack.
● **LONDON; WILTSHIRE**

Victory Square: Alexandra Palace, north London

Designed like a forties dystopian nightmare, and made during the period in which the original story was set (April-May 1984) at Twickenham Studios and on location around London, including the disused **Battersea Power Station**, off Battersea Park Road, and the old railway station which used to serve it (used also in Ian McKellen's *Richard III*). Victory Square is the shell of **Alexandra Palace**, Muswell Hill, N22, after it had been gutted by fire. It has since been completely renovated. The Golden Country is the Wiltshire countryside.

NIXON
(1995, dir: Oliver Stone)
Anthony Hopkins, Joan Allen, James Woods.
● **WASHINGTON DC; CALIFORNIA**

Nixon meets Mao: Plaza Room, Park Plaza Hotel, South Park View Street

Long, impressionistic and surprisingly sympathetic biopic of Tricky Dicky. Nixon meets the anti-war protesters (an unlikely scene, but actually based on fact) in the **Lincoln Memorial** in Washington DC. The wheeling and dealing is conducted at the **Santa Anita Racetrack, 285 West Huntington Boulevard, Pasadena** east of LA (for details see the 1954 *A Star Is Born* which also filmed at this landmark track). Nixon's initial meeting with Chairman Mao in China is actually the Plaza Room of the **Park Plaza Hotel, 607 South Park View Street**, midtown LA (see *New York, New York* for details of the Park Plaza). The White House is the Sony Studios set built for *The American President*, while the White House gate is **El Dorado Park** near Studebaker Road and East Los Arcos Street in Long Beach. More scenes were shot at the **Greystone Mansion, 905 Loma Vista Drive**, Beverly Hills.

NO WAY OUT
(1987, dir: Roger Donaldson)
Kevin Costner, Gene Hackman, Sean Young.
● **WASHINGTON DC; VIRGINIA**

This engaging Costner vehicle, complete with trick ending, was filmed around Washington DC, actually in the foyer and corridors of the **Pentagon**, though of course, most of this secure facility was reconstructed in the studio. The party, where Costner first meets soon-to-be-murdered Sean Young, is at the **Omni Shoreham Hotel, 2500 Calvert Street NW** (*© 202.234.0700*) in Rock Creek Park, to the northwest of the city. The foot chase takes Costner to the 'Georgetown Subway'. Georgetown, however, isn't on a subway line. The station complex is actually the **Georgetown Park Mall** (also scene of a major shoot-out in *True Lies*), **M Street** at Wisconsin Avenue. The fancy green and gold design seems clearly based on LA's stunning Bradbury Building (Sebastian's home in *Blade Runner*). Gene Hackman's house, where Costner witnesses the murder, stood on **South Arlington Ridge Road** near Pentagon City, but has now gone.

NORTH BY NORTHWEST
(1959, dir: Alfred Hitchcock)
Cary Grant, Eva Marie Saint, James Mason.
● **NEW YORK CITY; NEW YORK STATE; ILLINOIS; SOUTH DAKOTA; CALIFORNIA**

Hitchcock in peak lightweight form with the greatest of all comedy thrillers. Grant is an advertising exec working in the now demolished CIT Building, which stood at 650 Madison Avenue (Hitch makes his cameo appearance under the credits here, just missing the bus). Grant is mistakenly abducted, in place of the mysterious Mr Kaplan, from the **Plaza Hotel, West 59th Street** at Fifth Avenue.

James Mason's house, supposedly 169 Baywood, Glen Cove, where Grant is force-fed bourbon by creepy Martin Landau, is the redbrick mansion at **Old Westbury Gardens, 71 Old Westbury Road**, the Phipps Estate, a few miles south of the real Glen Cove, Long Island. The estate, north of Westbury on the Long Island Railroad from New York's Pennsylvania Station, is open to the public between May and December (*admission charge; © 516.333.0048*).

Cary Grant gets abducted: Plaza Hotel, 59th Street

Grant follows a lead to the **United Nations Headquarters, First Avenue** between 42nd and 48th Streets, where he's framed for murder. You can tour the General Assembly Building, quite safely, from the entrance at 46th Street (*© 212.963.*

The murder frame-up: United Nations Building, First Avenue

Grant is held in Glen Cove: Old Westbury Gardens, Long Island

Grant meets up with Eva Marie Saint: Omni Ambassador East, Chicago

7113). Grant escapes on the Twentieth Century from **Grand Central Station, East 42nd Street** at Park Avenue, and meets the compliant Eva Marie Saint, who helps him evade redcaps when they arrive at Chicago's **LaSalle Street Station, 414 South LaSalle Street** between West Van Buren Street and West Harrison Street.

In one of cinema's most famous scenes, Grant goes to meet the strange Mr Kaplan by taking the Greyhound bus to Indianapolis and getting off at the Prairie Stop on Route 41, where he's attacked by the crop-dusting plane. Far from Indiana, the crop fields are actually at **Wasco**, near Bakersfield on Route 99, in the desert 80 miles north of LA. A favourite road of Hitchcock's – it links Hollywood to the vineyards of Northern California – it's the same stretch of road on which James Dean met his fate.

Grant, though, survives and continues his dogged pursuit of Kaplan to the **Omni Ambassador East Hotel, 1301 North State Parkway** at East Goethe Street, Chicago (© *312.787.7200*). Built in 1926, to mirror the 1919 Ambassador West over North State Street at 1300, the Ambassador East, and its luxurious Pump Room restaurant, was another favourite of Hitchcock's.

The futuristic home of villain James Mason is a studio mock-up of a Frank Lloyd Wright house. The climax on Mount Rushmore was shot mainly in the studio – the authorities weren't going to allow any disrespect to the dead presidents (at one point, Hitchcock wanted Grant to be given away by a sneeze while hidden inside a huge presidential nostril). The real **Mount Rushmore** can be visited in the Black Hills National Forest, Route 385 southeast of Rapid City, South Dakota.

NORTHWEST PASSAGE
(1940, dir: King Vidor)
Spencer Tracy, Robert Young, Walter Brennan.
● OREGON

Tracy hunts for the eponymous passage. Filmed in the **Cascade Mountains** of Oregon.

NOSFERATU
(1922, dir: F W Murnau)
Max Schreck, Alexander Granach, Gustav von Wangenheim.
● GERMANY

Imaginative horror, actually Bram Stoker's *Dracula* under a pseudonym to avoid copyright, with location filming in **Westphalia** and on the **Baltic Coast**.

NOSFERATU, PHANTOM DER NACHT (aka *Nosferatu the Vampyre*)
(1979, dir: Werner Herzog)
Klaus Kinski, Isabelle Adjani, Bruno Ganz.
● GERMANY; NETHERLANDS; CZECHOSLOVAKIA

Remake of the 1921 silent classic, with Kinski copying

Max Schreck's original appearance. The Carpathian Mountains are actually the **High Tatra** mountainous region on Czechoslovakia's border with Poland. Period locations include the towns of **Pernstein** and **Telc** in Czechoslovakia; and **Lubeck**, West Germany. The plague of rats is at **Delft** in the Netherlands, and features the 17th century town square. To the alarm of the authorities, not to mention local residents, 11,000 laboratory rats were released, without permission. Well, this is a Herzog movie.

NOTHING SACRED
(1937, dir: William Wellman)
Carole Lombard, Fredric March, Walter Connolly.
● NEW YORK CITY; CALIFORNIA

The press builds Lombard into a national celeb when it's believed she's dying from a rare disease. March is the cynical hack who brings her to New York. Filming took place at the **Rockefeller Center**, which was then only just beginning to be built. It now occupies 22 acres from West 48th Street to West 51st Street between Fifth and Sixth Avenues. March and Lombard sail the East River, beneath the **Brooklyn Bridge**. Scenes were also shot at **Agoura Hills**, north of Los Angeles, and **San Pedro**, the harbour to the south.

NOTTING HILL
(1999, dir: Roger Michell)
Hugh Grant, Julia Roberts, Rhys Ifans.
● LONDON

The team behind *Four Weddings and a Funeral* follows up with another Transatlantic romance as mega-movie star Roberts falls for mild-mannered English bookseller Grant. The title is the setting, though the famously cosmopolitan locale – site of race riots in the fifties – seems to have been ethnically cleansed:

The bookshop: Nicholls Antique Arcade, Portobello Road

this is the whitest

Hugh Grant's flat: Westbourne Park Road, Notting Hill

Notting Hill you'll ever see. First off, there is no Travel Book Company, the down-at-heel shop owned by Grant. The store is **Nicholls Antique Arcade, 142 Portobello Road**. The real Travel Bookshop, on which Grant's establishment was based, can be seen around the corner in Blenheim Crescent. Grant's flat, with its heavily-featured shabby blue door, was, in fact, the home of screenwriter Richard Curtis, put on the market for a cool £1.3 million just before the film's release. As you can imagine, it's a tad more impressive inside than the film version, which was recreated in the studio. The real flat, a converted chapel, has a courtyard garden, a 1,000 square foot reception room and a galleried mezzanine. The famous scuffed

The failed restaurant: Golborne Road, W10

blue door was sold off and can no longer be seen at **280 Westbourne Park Road**, just off Portobello Road.

The disused shop where Grant first bumps into Roberts is now **Coffee Republic**. Roberts and Grant see a movie at Notting Hill's **Coronet Cinema**, and afterwards enjoy a meal at **Nobu**, the dizzyingly expensive Japanese restaurant of the **Metropolitan Hotel, Park Lane** (© 020.7447.4747). At the other end of the scale, the failed restaurant of Grant's friend is **Portfolio**, an art store on the corner of **Golborne Road and Bevington Road, W10** at the northern reach of Portobello Road market. Previously an art gallery, it also became an eaterie – Brad Dourif's diner – in a film which took a totally different look at the area, Hanif Kureishi's *London Kills Me*. The private communal gardens Grant and Roberts break into at night is **Rosmead Gardens, Rosmead Road, W11**.

And outside Notting Hill, there's no shortage of London landmarks to seduce the US tourist dollar. Roberts stays at the **Ritz, Piccadilly**, which rarely permits filming inside, but on this occasion gave unprecedented cooperation to the film company. The site of Julia Roberts' Henry James movie is **Kenwood, Hampstead Lane, NW3**, on Hampstead Heath. The Adam mansion, once home to Lord Mansfield, holds the Iveagh Bequest of old master paintings, and, amazingly, entry is free. Roberts' press conference, at which Grant proposes, is held in the **Lancaster Room** of the **Savoy Hotel, the Strand**, while the wedding reception uses the Zen Garden of designer Anouska Hempel's minimalist **Hempel Hotel, Craven Hill, W2** (*www.the-hempel.co.uk*) and the movie première, the **Empire, Leicester Square**.

NOVECENTO (aka *Nineteenhundred*)
(1976, dir: Bernardo Bertolucci)
Robert De Niro, Gerard Depardieu, Burt Lancaster.
● **ITALY**

Bertolucci's examination of Italian fascism, in a family saga spanning 45 years, was beset by problems. Maria Schneider left the production, and Orson Welles was replaced by Burt Lancaster. Like the director's earlier *Before the Revolution*, the movie was shot around **Parma** in the province of Emilia, Northern Italy.

NOW, VOYAGER
(1942, dir: Irving Rapper)
Bette Davis, Paul Henreid, Claude Rains.
● **LOS ANGELES**

Davis is the mother-dominated spinster given a new lease of life by psychiatrist Rains, only to fall for married Henreid in this classic tearjerker. Filming allegedly took place at **Whitley Terrace** in the Italianate-style hilltop village of Whitley Heights, reached by Milner Road, east of Highland Avenue and north of Hollywood Boulevard. The terrace is actually seen in *Day of the Locust*, where Burgess Meredith peddles his quack medicine.

NUIT AMERICAINE, LA (aka *Day For Night*)
(1973, dir: François Truffaut)
Jacqueline Bisset, Jean-Pierre Aumont, Valentina Cortese.
● **NICE, FRANCE**

Truffaut puts his love affair with the cinema centre-screen with this backstage movie about the making of a romantic melodrama (dedicated to Dorothy and Lilian Gish). The film-within-the-film, *Je Vous Presente Pamela*, is being made at the famed **Studios la Victorine, 16 avenue Edoard Grinda**, in Nice, where, almost 30 years earlier, Marcel Carné filmed the classic *Les Enfants du Paradis*.

Jacqueline Bisset arrives, and holds a press conference, at **Nice-Côte d'Azur Airport**. The Atlantic Hotel, where the cast act out more dramas than before the camera, is Nice's **Hotel Windsor, 11 rue Dalpozzo**. The man from the British insurance company, who deals with a claim on the death of the leading man, might look familiar. It's writer Graham Greene, in an uncredited cameo.

The film studio: Studios la Victorine, Nice

NUTTY PROFESSOR, THE
(1963, dir: Jerry Lewis)
Jerry Lewis, Stella Stevens, Del Moore.
● **ARIZONA**

One for French cineastes, as nerdy chemistry prof Lewis metamorphoses into lounge lizard Buddy Love. The campus is **Arizona State University, Tempe**.

NUTTY PROFESSOR, THE
(1996, dir: Tom Shadyac)
Eddie Murphy, Jada Pinkett, James Coburn.
● **LOS ANGELES**

Successful remake with top-notch FX. The university campus is a conflation of LA's two higher learning establishments, the **University of California**, in Westside; and **UCLA**, Los Angeles. Filming also took place at the inevitable **Biltmore Hotel, 506 South Grand Avenue**, downtown LA, and in Beverly Hills. Dean Richmond's office is **Mayfield Senior School, 500 Bellefontaine Street**, Pasadena (see *The Lost World: Jurassic Park* for details).

O

OCTOPUSSY
(1983, dir: John Glen)
Roger Moore, Maud Adams, Louis Jourdan.
● INDIA; UTAH; MIDDLESEX

Beautifully photographed, but one of the least of the series. The South American Air force Base of the opening scene is **Northolt Aerodrome** in Middlesex, but the spectacular landscapes flown over are **Moab**, southwest Utah. The exterior of **Sotheby's, 35 Bond Street**, W1, where the Fabergé egg is put up for auction, is real, though the interior was recreated in the studio at Pinewood.

Bond in Berlin: Kurfürstendamm

Bond travels to **Udaipur** in India (via the Taj Mahal, naturally, despite its being several hundred miles out of the way in Agra). He stays at the luxurious **Shiv Niwas Hotel**, part of the City Palace, one of three palaces owned by the Mewar royalty. A second, also converted into a hotel, became the floating Palace, Octopussy's island home, the **Lake Palace Hotel** in **Lake Pichola**, both now part of the HRH Group of Hotels. The third, Summer Palace, overlooking the area, is used for Louis Jourdan's retreat, where Bond is held captive.

In Berlin, Bond is driven down the main shopping drag, **Kurfürstendamm**, to the one-time crossing point into East Germany, Checkpoint Charlie. Bond's escape from Karl Marx-Stadt was staged in the **Nene Valley Railroad** yard and station. Feldstadt, the US Air Force Base in Germany, is the RAF base at **Upper Heyford**.

ODETTE
(1950, dir: Herbert Wilcox)
Anna Neagle, Trevor Howard, Peter Ustinov.
● FRANCE

True-life story of the woman who spied for the French resistance during WWII, filmed in **Annecy**; **Cannes**; **Cassis** and **Marseilles**, France.

OF MICE AND MEN
(1939, dir: Lewis Milestone)
Burgess Meredith, Lon Chaney Jr, Betty Field.
● CALIFORNIA

Milestone wanted to film Steinbeck's story at the actual ranch in the Salinas Valley, Northern California, that the author had used as a model, but it turned out to be a ruin. Eventually, the film company rented out William Randolph Hearst's ranch at **Agoura**, off Route 101 in the Santa Monica Mountains, northwest of LA, and built the ranch house there. There was more filming on the **Monterey Peninsula** in northern California. The 1992 remake, with Gary Sinise and John Malkovich, was shot around Santa Barbara.

OFFICER AND A GENTLEMAN, AN
(1982, dir: Taylor Hackford)
Richard Gere, Debra Winger, Louis Gossett Jr.
● WASHINGTON STATE

Richard Gere suffers hell in a pristine white uniform at **Fort Worden State Park, Port Townsend**, a restored former coastal artillery army base on the Olympic Peninsula. The papermill where Debra Winger works was the old Champion International Corporation, bought up in 1985 and now the **Simpson Tacoma Kraft Company, 801 Portland Avenue, Tacoma**, on Commencement Bay. The inn is the **Tides Inn, 1807 Water Street, Port Townsend** (© 360.385.0595, www.tides-inn.com).

OH MR PORTER
(1937, dir: Marcel Varnel)
Will Hay, Moore Marriott, Graham Moffatt.
● HAMPSHIRE

Classic comedy with Will Hay and sidekicks Marriott and Moffatt foiling gun-runners and posing as ghosts at a little Irish railway station. Buggleskelly Station was in fact the already-near-derelict **Cliddesden Halt**, dressed up by designer Alex Vetchinsky. It's closed now of course, but if you can pick your way through the weeds, you can see the remains just south of Basingstoke on the Basingstoke-Alton line in Hampshire. The old Victorian engine, also near derelict, was the Gladstone. Sadly, the engine was sold for scrap in 1941.

OH! WHAT A LOVELY WAR
(1969, dir: Richard Attenborough)
John Mills, Ralph Richardson, John Gielgud.
● SUSSEX

Joan Littlewood's stage production put the words and songs from WWI into the mouths of a pierrot troupe. Attenborough's opened-up film was never going to

Stylized backdrop to WWI: West Pier, Brighton

capture the poignancy of the stage images, but instead utilises the faded grandeur of Brighton's now-closed and decrepit **West Pier**, the surrounding seafront area and **Brighton Railway Station**. The church parade filmed in the picturesque ruins of the 13th century **Bayham Abbey**, a mile and three quarters west of Lamberhurst, near Tunbridge Wells, east Sussex.

OKLAHOMA!
(1955, dir: Fred Zinnemann)
Gordon MacRae, Shirley Jones, Rod Steiger.
● ARIZONA

Not the obvious choice to direct a big musical and, true to form, Zinnemann takes the whole shebang out on loca-

Oklahoma?: San Rafael Valley, Arizona

tion. Oklahoma itself was out – the corn may well be as high as an elephant's eye, but the oil rigs are even higher. A suitable landscape was eventually found in Arizona, at **San Rafael Valley**, near to Nogales on the Mexican border. The corn was brought to the required height with the aid of the University of Arizona's Agriculture Department. The railway station, scene of the big musical number, is **Elgin**, twenty miles west of Tombstone.

OLVIDADOS, LOS (aka *The Young and the Damned*)

(1950, dir: Luis Buñuel)
Alfonso Mejia, Roberto Cobo, Estela Inda.
● MEXICO

Buñuel's breakthrough movie – it won the prize for Best Direction at Cannes in 1951 – is a semi-documentary, semi-surreal, determinedly unsentimental look at poverty and crime among the young gangs of a city's rundown suburbs. It was shot in Mexico City in an incredible 21 days.

OMEN, THE

(1976, dir: Richard Donner)
Gregory Peck, Lee Remick, David Warner.
● LONDON; SURREY; ROME; ISRAEL

The seminal horror film that spawned a whole genre of Antichrist movies. Before things start to get nasty, young spawn-of-Satan Damien and his family enjoy a day out on **Parliament Hill**, north London. US Ambassador Gregory Peck works, naturally, at the **American Embassy** in **Red Lion Square**, where he is confronted by crazy priest

The crazy priest gets spiked: All Saints Church, Putney

Patrick Troughton (TV's second *Doctor Who*), who spouts passages from Revelations alongside the Thames at Putney. His nearby church, where he gets spiked by the lightning conductor, is **All Saints Church, Fulham**, which is actually on the north side of Putney Bridge. Meanwhile, Damien is beginning to betray his diabolical leanings by throwing a major wobbly arriving at **Guildford Cathedral** and upsetting the monkeys at **Windsor Safari Park**.

The palatial home of the US Ambassador, supposedly on Seven Hills Road, is **Pyrford Court,**

The entrance to the home of the US Ambassador: Pyrford Court, Surrey

Pyrford, a couple of miles east of Woking in Surrey. A private home, it's well hidden behind a thick screen of trees and not visible from the road. You can, though, see the elaborate gatehouse, **The Bothy**, out of which Gregory Peck makes his final desperate drive, on the south side of **Pyrwood Common Road** near Upshot Lane. The funeral of the Ambassador is at **Brookwood Cemetery, Brookwood**, Surrey – once the country's largest cemetery.

ON A CLEAR DAY YOU CAN SEE FOREVER

(1970, dir: Vincente Minnelli)
Barbra Streisand, Yves Montand, Jack Nicholson.
● NEW YORK CITY; SUSSEX

Barbra Streisand regresses: Brighton Pavilion, Sussex

In this strange reincarnation musical, hypnotist Yves Montand sings 'Come Back to Me' from the roof of the **Pan-Am Building** in Central Manhattan, sending out his thought waves to Streisand at the corner of **Lexington Avenue**; in **Central Park** and at the **Lincoln Center**. The regression scenes used the **Brighton Pavilion**, Brighton, Sussex in England.

ON GOLDEN POND

(1981, dir: Mark Rydell)
Henry Fonda, Katharine Hepburn, Jane Fonda.
● NEW HAMPSHIRE

Henry Fonda's final film, and the only one with his daughter Jane, is a predictably sugary affair. The titular pond is **Squam Lake**, just off Hwy-93 between Plymouth and Meredith, southeastern New Hampshire. Boat trips from Holderness will take you past the house used in the movie, which is a private home. The *Thayer IV* can be seen at the Holiday Inn Docks, Key Largo, on Florida's southern tip.

ON HER MAJESTY'S SECRET SERVICE

(1969, dir: Peter Hunt)
George Lazenby, Diana Rigg, Telly Savalas.
● SWITZERLAND; PORTUGAL; BUCKINGHAMSHIRE

A bit more story this time around, but a bit less Bond, with the chiselled woodenness of TV adman George Lazenby. The opening sequence, of Bond rescuing Tracy from the sea, was shot on **Guincho Beach** near Cascais, west of Lisbon, Portugal. Draco's home, scene of the birthday party, is the **Da Vinho Estate** at **Zambuljal**. Bond stays at the **Palacio Hotel, Rua Do Parque, Estoril**, near Lisbon (*© 35121.4648000*).

The office of solicitor Gumpold, where Bond demonstrates that exciting new invention the photocopier, is the **Schweizerhof Hotel, Bahnhofplatz 11, Berne**, Switzerland (*© 31.326.8080*).

M's house is **Thames Lawn**, a riverfront mansion at

261

Marlow, near the Pinewood Studios in Buckinghamshire. Bond researches heraldry at the **Royal College of Arms, Queen Victoria Street**, EC4, near Blackfriars (*www.college-of-arms.gov.uk*), where he discovers that the Bond family motto is 'Orbis non sufficit' – The world is not enough. Good title for a film.

The stock-car rally was staged at **Lauterbrunnen**, two miles from Murren in Switzerland, and the skating rink is nearby **Grindelwald**.

Blofeld's mountaintop allergy clinic is **Piz Gloria**, a revolving restaurant at the 10,000-foot peak of **Schilthorn Mountain**, above Murren. The five-storey complex, with its own cable-car lift, was still under construction when the movie's locations were being scouted. Permission to film was granted on condition that the film company furnish the interior and build a helipad. They forked out to the tune of £60,000. The restaurant is still in business.

ON THE BEACH

(1959, dir: Stanley Kramer)
Gregory Peck, Ava Gardner, Fred Astaire.
● **AUSTRALIA; CALIFORNIA**

Depressing post-nuclear warning, starting from the grim premise that Australia is the only landmass to have survived – for the time being – atomic devastation. Made mostly on location in **Melbourne**, Australia, but including a nightmarish submarine trip to a disturbingly deserted **San Diego**.

ON THE TOWN

(1949, dir: Gene Kelly)
Gene Kelly, Frank Sinatra, Jules Munshin.
● **NEW YORK CITY; LOS ANGELES**

Three sailors enjoy 24 hours of shore leave in New York. Kelly wanted to film entirely on location, but the studio wanted it all shot in Hollywood. The compromise, despite the way it looks in the completed movie, was a mere week's location filming. Nevertheless, NY landmarks include **Liberty Island**; the **Empire State Building** at Fifth Avenue and 34th Street; **Central Park**; **Federal Hall, 26 Wall Street**; **Coney Island**; **Rockefeller Plaza**, between Fifth and Sixth Avenues and 49th and 50th Streets; and the roof of the 70-storey **RCA Building** (now the GE Building), Sixth Avenue. The opening shot of the singing longshoreman, and the closing shots, were filmed in the **Brooklyn Naval Yard**, just across the East River over the Manhattan Bridge, at Flushing Avenue.

ON THE WATERFRONT

(1954, dir: Elia Kazan)
Marlon Brando, Eva Marie Saint, Karl Malden.
● **NEW JERSEY**

Kazan's drama of mob rule among the longshoremen's unions was made on location on the waterfronts of **Hoboken**, New Jersey (the birthplace of Frank Sinatra). There's a PATH commuter train from the lower level of the World Trade Center. The piers and warehouses are long gone, and Hoboken is now a squeaky clean middle class suburb, but some of the movie's locations remain. The church scene was filmed at **Our Lady of Grace Church, 400**

Karl Malden's church: Our Lady of Grace Church, Hoboken

Willow Avenue, though the park in front of the church is **Stevens Park**, four blocks away, in front of **St Peter and St Paul Church, 400 Hudson Street**, which is also the church used for the interior shots.

Brando and Eva Marie Saint walk in the park: Stevens Park, Hoboken

ONCE UPON A TIME IN AMERICA

(1984, dir: Sergio Leone)
Robert De Niro, James Woods, Elizabeth McGovern.
● **ITALY; FRANCE; CANADA; NEW YORK CITY; NEW JERSEY; FLORIDA**

Leone's vast epic, tracing the lives of a group of NY gangsters from 1922 to 1968, used an astonishing range of locations, including **Rome; Venice; Paris; Toronto** and New York – where an entire city block was reconstructed. The Brooklyn neighbourhood is on **8th Street South** near Bedford Avenue, beneath the **Williamsburg Bridge**. **Hoboken Railway Station** in New Jersey and the **Don CeSar Palace, 3400 Gulf Boulevard, St Petersburg Beach** in Florida (© *813.360.1881*) were also used.

The Long Island restaurant: Hotel Excelsior, Lido, Venice

The Brooklyn neighbourhood: South 8th Street, Brooklyn

New York's Grand Central Station, in the thirties flashbacks, is the **Gare du Nord** in Paris.

The lavish Long Island restaurant, where De Niro takes his dream date, is actually the **Hotel Excelsior, Lungomare Marconi 41** on the Lido in Venice. Built in the 1900s, the Excelsior was the world's top resort hotel and is a favourite of the film festival crowd.

ONCE UPON A TIME IN THE WEST
(1969, dir: Sergio Leone)
Henry Fonda, Claudia Cardinale, Charles Bronson.
● SPAIN; ROME; ARIZONA

After limbering up with his *Dollars* trilogy, Leone went for the epic with this long, slow, operatic revenge Western. Filming began in Arizona, but after trouble with US crews and the problem of too many damn telegraph poles, it was back to **Almeria**, southern Spain, and the Cinecittà Studios in Rome. The real Arizona scenes include **Monument Valley**. A clue to which shots filmed in the States is the use of genuine US locomotives.

ONE-EYED JACKS
(1961, dir: Marlon Brando)
Marlon Brando, Karl Malden, Pina Pellicer.
● CALIFORNIA

Sam Peckinpah's original script was discarded and Calder Willingham brought in, and Stanley Kubrick was replaced as director by Brando himself for this long, slow Western. The $1.8 million budget ballooned to $6 million, and the film to five hours. Cut down to two hours and twenty minutes, and with a new ending, the film nevertheless managed to recoup $12 million at the box office, which almost redeemed it. Just pray there's not a director's cut lying about.

It was filmed on the west coast of California, north of **Cypress Point, Pebble Beach** and at **Pfeiffer Beach** in **Big Sur**.

ONE FLEW OVER THE CUCKOO'S NEST
(1975, dir: Milos Forman)
Jack Nicholson, Louise Fletcher, Brad Dourif.
● OREGON

This manipulative and contrived allegory was shot in a wing of the **Oregon State Mental Hospital, Center Street** between 24th and 25th Streets, **Salem**, on Hwy-5 about 50 miles south of Portland, Oregon. A condition of filming at the hospital was that the period not be updated from the original 1963. After all, we don't treat people like that any more.

ONE FROM THE HEART
(1982, dir: Francis Coppola)
Frederic Forrest, Teri Garr, Raul Julia.
● LOS ANGELES

A simple two-hander set in Vegas became a bloated monster when the director decided to rebuild the city elsewhere. That Francis Coppola wanted to explore the possibilities of the medium is admirable, but the extravagant visuals totally overwhelm the modest little story. All the Las Vegas scenes were recreated on soundstages at the **Hollywood Center** (then Zoetrope Studios), **1040 North Las Palmas Avenue**, off Romaine Street in Hollywood.

OPPOSITE OF SEX, THE
(1998, dir: Don Roos)
Christina Ricci, Martin Donovan, Lisa Kudrow.
● CALIFORNIA

Cracking comedy drama with a mission to offend, following the emotional fallout after narrator Ricci runs off with her gay step-brother's boyfriend. Set mainly in Indiana, the movie was made in California. The art deco seafront hotel in which Donovan and Kudrow stay when they follow Ricci to Santa Monica is the **Georgian Hotel, 1415 Ocean Avenue**, near the Santa Monica Pier (*℗ 310.395.9945, www.georgianhotel.com*). The motel where Ricci's monotesticular boyfriend gets shot is the classic sixties-style **Royal Sun Inn, 1700 South Palm Canyon Drive, Palm Springs** (*℗ 760.327.1564, www.royalsuninn.com*). The peaceful lakeside cabin over the Canadian border is actually on **Big Bear Lake**, San Bernardino, east of LA.

ORDINARY PEOPLE
(1980, dir: Robert Redford)
Timothy Hutton, Donald Sutherland, Mary Tyler Moore.
● ILLINOIS

Ordinary, very rich people actually. Redford's classy soap is set in the *très* upper middle class suburb of **Lake Forest**, on the Lake Michigan shore north of Chicago. Opening scenes filmed outside **Marshall Fields'** department store in Market Square, Chicago. Many of the interiors were filmed in the abandoned laundry room of Fort Sheridan Military Compound, converted into a temporary studio.

ORLANDO
(1993, dir: Sally Potter)
Tilda Swinton, Quentin Crisp, Billy Zane.
● RUSSIA; HERTFORDSHIRE

Tilda Swinton is the Elizabethan nobleman who, at the behest of Queen Elizabeth I (Quentin Crisp – who else?), remains ageless but changes sex in Potter's imagina-

The great house: Hatfield House, Hertfordshire

tive film of the Virginia Woolf story. Olde London was recreated in St Petersburg. The arid deserts and Muslim townscapes are **Khiva** in Uzbekistan (to travel to this beautifully preserved museum-city, check out the Central Asia Experience at *www.trans-siberian.co.uk*). The Great House, which forms a recurring backdrop, is **Hatfield House**, Hertfordshire (see *Batman* for details). Queen Elizabeth's lavish banquet, with ten thousand roses and four thousand tulips, was filmed in the house's Great Hall. The young Gloriana did, in fact, spend much of her youth on this estate, though not in the house itself, which is Jacobean.

ORPHÉE (aka *Orpheus*)
(1949, dir: Jean Cocteau)
Jean Marais, François Périer, Maria Casarès.
● FRANCE

Classic of poetic cinema, with Maria Casarès as Death, and Orpheus entering alternative worlds through liquid mirrors. Eschewing camera tricks, Cocteau used vats of mercury for the dazzling effects. Location filming was at the medieval ruins of **Les Baux-de-Provence** near Arles in southern France.

OTELLO
(1986, dir: Franco Zeffirelli)
Placido Domingo, Katia Ricciarelli, Justino Diaz.
● ITALY; CRETE, GREECE

Typically lush Zeffirellian filming of Verdi's opera, financed by Cannon's usually downmarket Golan-Globus team as their contribution to Art.

The main garrison setting is the 13th century **Hohen-staufen Castle** at **Barletta**, on the northern coast of Puglia, Route 16, 40 miles northwest of Bari (it's been undergoing a slow process of restoration since the seventies and is not at present open to the public).

The harbour exteriors are the port of **Heraklion** in Crete, where virtually an entire keep and monumental entrance were added to the existing Venetian buildings.

Otello's galleon, built at a cost of $80,000, was filmed, not on the coast of Crete, but on the Italian coast north of Rome after the rest of filming had been completed. The ship is still in existence, and could recently be seen moored at Marseilles.

OTHELLO
(1951, dir: Orson Welles)
Orson Welles, Suzanne Cloutier, Michael MacLiammoir.
● ITALY; MOROCCO

After filming *Macbeth* in three weeks on a cardboard set in Hollywood, Welles took a drastically different approach, and made this classic Shakespearian adaptation on location around Europe over a period of years. Michael MacLiammoir (who played Iago) tells the whole story, hilariously, in his memoir, *Put Money in Thy Purse*.

The use of locations is dizzying, as Welles cuts from country to country in mid-scene. Many of the Venice scenes are the real thing. Othello and Desdemona's secret wedding was filmed at **Santa Maria dei Miracoli** (seen also in *Don't Look Now*) alongside the Rialto in Venice. Brabantio's house is the **Palazzo Contarini-Fasan** on the Canal Grande at **Rio delle Ostreghe** near Piazza

Othello's house: Ca' d'Oro on the Canal Grande

San Marco. And indeed, it is known as Desdemona's House. The circular tower, supposedly at the rear, down which Brabantio's servants rush, is the **Palazzo Contarini dal Bovolo**, tucked away in a tiny courtyard at **Calle della Vida 4299**, at the corner of Rio dei Fuseri and Rio di San Luca. The unique spiral stair is seen also in the Brit-farce *Blame It on the Bellboy*. The midnight council assembles at the pink and white marble **Palazzo Ducale**, the Doge's Palace. The imposing staircase is the **Scala dei Giganti**, the Giant's Staircase, in the palace courtyard. Othello's house is the elaborate Gothic palace of the **Ca' d'Oro**, on the Canal Grande.

Brabantio's house: Palazzo Contarini-Fasan

The rear of Brabantio's house: Palazzo Contarini dal Bovolo

Most of the Cyprus scenes were filmed in **Essaouria**, on the coast of Morocco, about 40 miles west of Marrakech. The 18th century town, previously known as Mogador, is surrounded by Gothic battlements, which are used for the opening funeral procession, the torture of Iago and the jealousy scenes.

The senate: Scala dei Giganti, Palazzo Ducale

The famous steam bath scene was filmed in a local hammam (yes, steam bath) at Essaouria. A spot of improvisation was needed here. The costumes hadn't arrived in time for filming so the setting was dictated by the need for the characters to be wearing only towels. **Safi**, about 30 miles to the north, supplies the steps where Cassio regrets his drunken brawl. Though the town itself is pretty industrialised nowadays, it does still retain its old walled and turretted Medina. The brawl itself was staged in the 15th century **Portuguese Cistern** at **El Jadida**, on the coast a further 30 miles to the north. It's a vaulted underground chamber which dazzlingly mirrors the pillars and roof in the water which covers the floor. Find it in the city's Medina, known as the Cite Portugaise, at the north end of Boulevard de Suez. It's open to the public (*admission charge*). The fight is brought to a halt by the entrance of Othello – in the **Palazzo Papale** in **Viterbo**, Italy.

Brabantio's scenes were shot at **Torcello**, a peaceful green island six miles northeast of Venice, in the church cloisters, along with the scenes of Othello's rage. Othello strikes Desdemona in the 8th century **San Pietro Church**, a former cathedral externally remodelled in the 12th century, at **Tuscania**, ten miles from Viterbo. The senate scenes used the Umbrian town of **Perugia**, between

ENGLISH HERITAGE

BLICKLING HALL: (**1**) A Jacobean mansion northwest of Aylsham in Norfolk, it became Maryiot Cells, home of high-waywoman Lady Skelton, *The Wicked Lady*, in 1945.

DYRHAM PARK: (**2**) Six miles north of Bath, this 17th century house was used as the exterior of Darlington Hall in the Merchant-Ivory filming of *The Remains of the Day*.

THAME PARK: (**3**) A private house on Thame Park Road southeast of the village of Thame, near Oxford. It had been sold and stood deserted, after plans to convert it into a hotel fell through, when it was used to portray Kew Gardens, where George III is sent to be cured in *The Madness of King George*.

BROUGHTON CASTLE: (**4**) Two miles southwest of Banbury in Oxfordshire, the home of Lord and Lady Saye and Sele was Viola's house in *Shakespeare in Love*.

STUDLEY PRIORY: (**5**) Now a hotel, as the name suggests Studley Priory was once a Benedictine monastery. Standing in the village of Horton-cum-Studley, about seven miles northeast of Oxford, the priory was Thomas More's Chelsea home in *A Man for All Seasons*.

PEPPARD COTTAGE: (**6**) A private home on Peppard Common, in the village of Rotherfield Peppard west of Henley-on-Thames, it made an ideal *Howards End* in the Merchant-Ivory film.

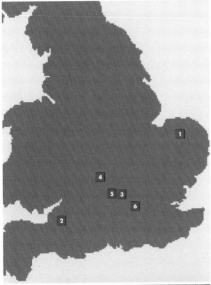

265

TARANTINO'S LA

Tarantino's movies favour the fringes of the city, away from the palm-fringed tourist sites. *Reservoir Dogs* centres on the northeastern suburb of Highland Park, while *Jackie Brown* uses the South Bay area.

RAYMOND THEATRE (1), 129 North Raymond Avenue, in the neighbouring eastern city of Pasadena, is the venue for Bruce Willis' 'Battle of the Giants' boxing match in *Pulp Fiction*. It was also used for the concert scenes of *This Is Spinal Tap*.

HIGHLAND PARK (2): Heading west into LA proper is Highland Park, the neighbourhood of the robbery and the ensuing shoot-out of *Reservoir Dogs*, around 55th and 56th Avenues. Mr Orange gets the bloody gunshot outside **5518 Marmion Way (2a)** near Avenue 56. There's no trace of the Dogs' warehouse, but you'll still want to pay homage at the site on the corner of **Figueroa Street and 59th Avenue (2b)**.

PAT AND LORRAINE'S (3), 4720 Eagle Rock Boulevard at North Avenue 46, is the diner where the Dogs discuss Madonna lyrics at the opening of the movie.

SAFARI INN (4), 1911 Olive Boulevard, Buena Vista. Wonderfully kitschy themed motel where Clarence and Alabama hide out in Tony Scott's film of Tarantino's *True Romance*. The Safari was also the Florida motel where the astronauts' wives waited in *Apollo 13*.

JOHNIE'S COFFEE SHOP (5), 6101 Wilshire Boulevard at Fairfax Avenue in midtown LA, is the fifties style diner where Mr Orange meets up with his contact in *Reservoir Dogs*.

RAE'S (6), 2901 Pico Boulevard at 29th Street, Santa Monica, is the Detroit diner where Clarence and Alabama eat pie after the Sonny Chiba triple bill in *True Romance*. The Detroit movie house was also in LA.

COCKATOO INN (7), 4334 West Imperial Highway at Hawthorne Boulevard. Currently closed, the Cockatoo is the bar near the airport where Jackson and De Niro hang out in *Jackie Brown*.

HAWTHORNE GRILL (8), 13763 Hawthorne Boulevard at 137th Street. A little further south is the site of the Hawthorne Grill, held up by Honey-Bunny and Pumpkin at the beginning of *Pulp Fiction*. For a couple of years it stood empty, but has finally been demolished.

DEL AMO FASHION CENTER (9), Hawthorne Boulevard at Sepulveda Boulevard. Way down in the South Bay area is the vast, sprawling shopping mall of *Jackie Brown*, where the scam is played out.

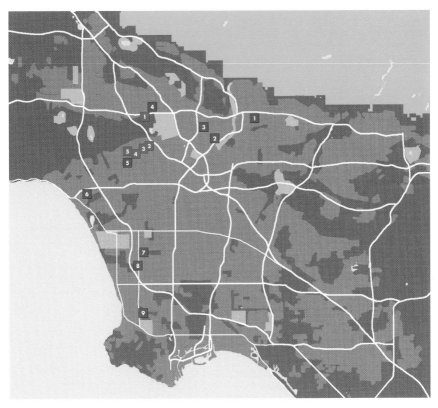

LA NEO-NOIR

Still fairly rundown, but capable of dripping style on screen, is the Hollywood of the thirties and forties. The noir city gleamed in the forties but blazed into colour with the neo-noirs of the nineties, particularly Curtis Hanson's fifties-set *LA Confidential*.

BOB'S BIG BOY (**1**), **4211 Riverside Drive**, Burbank. Kicking off in the Valley: although Michael Mann's *Heat* is a love letter to LA architecture, it never reveals the wonderful forties exterior of the cafe where De Niro and Pacino fence with each other.

THE FROLIC ROOM (**2**), **6245 Hollywood Boulevard**. Into Hollywood proper for *LA Confidential*, and the neon bar alongside Pantages Theater where Kevin Spacey drowns his sorrows.

CROSSROADS OF THE WORLD (**3**), **6671 Sunset Boulevard**. Danny DeVito's magazine office is sited in this nautical whimsy, built to resemble an ocean liner.

HOLLYWOOD CENTER MOTEL (**4**), **6720 Sunset Boulevard**. A twen-

ties motel, remodelled in the fifties and retaining its period look, where Spacey discovers the body of the murdered actor.

FORMOSA CAFE (**5**), **7156 Santa Monica Boulevard** near La Brea Avenue. A legendary hangout (more for the booze than the Chinese food) for Hollywood royalty such as Bogart, Monroe and Gable, where Guy Pearce insults the 'real' Lana Turner.

WOODY ALLEN'S MANHATTAN

Woody Allen's Manhattan is a stylish deco dream of a city, subtly spiced with danger and decay. It's a city of supper clubs, lounge entertainers and to-be-seen-in restaurants where white, middle-class media folk indulge midlife crises.

EAST SIDE: Allen gave us one of the most striking images of the city in *Manhattan*, the view of the Queensboro Bridge from **Riverview Terrace**, at **Sutton Square (1)**, actually just above the tiny park, at the end of 59th Street. There's no bench here though, so bring your own.

Elaine's, 1703 Second Avenue (2): A pricey showbiz eaterie on the East Side between 88th and 89th Streets, where Allen makes up a foursome in *Manhattan*, and Diane Keaton voices suspicions in *Manhattan Murder Mystery*.

70th Street (3), between Lexington and Park Avenues, was the site of Keaton's apartment in *Annie Hall*.

MIDTOWN: **Barbetta, 321 West 46th Street (4)**: The elegant Italian restaurant where Mia Farrow gets invisible in *Alice*; seen also in Allen's *Celebrity*.

Carnegie Deli, 854 Seventh Avenue (5) is where the old comics reminisce in *Broadway Danny Rose*. You can get a Broadway Danny Rose Sandwich.

Russian Tea Room, 150 West 57th Street (6): Allen takes his son to this recently-renovated, wildly extravagant NY institution to ogle women in *Manhattan*. The restaurant is also featured in *Tootsie*.

Cafe des Artistes, 1 West 67th Street (7): Lushly romantic, mural-filled restaurant of the Hotel Des Artistes, in which Anjelica Huston gives Woody a poker lesson in *Manhattan Murder Mystery*. This was also the setting (though not the actual location) for *My Dinner With Andre*.

The Langham, 135 Central Park West (8): Mia Farrow's real-life apartment, used in *Hannah and Her Sisters*.

Edison Hotel, 228 West 47th Street (9) just off Times Square. The deco 46th Street entrance is the lobby of the mobster's lavish apartment in *Bullets Over Broadway*. Also the site of a gruesome killing in *The Godfather*.

Belasco Theater, 111 West 44th Street (10), where John Cusack's play is rehearsed in *Bullets Over Broadway*.

UNION SQUARE: **National Arts Club, 15 Gramercy Park South (11)**: Keaton attends a wine tasting in *Manhattan Murder Mystery*. The magnificent interior is seen also in *The Age of Innocence*.

Hotel 17, 225 East 17th Street (12): Searching for clues at the fictitious Hotel Waldron in *Manhattan Murder Mystery*.

CHELSEA: **Empire Diner, 210 Tenth Avenue (13)**: Great old fashioned stainless steel diner, a NY icon seen in the opening montage of *Manhattan*.

GREENWICH VILLAGE: **John's Pizza, 278 Bleecker Street (14)**. Recommended as the best pizza in New York, seen in *Manhattan*.

Chumley's, 86 Bedford Street (15): a one-time speakeasy, one of the jazz clubs in *Sweet and Lowdown*.

Cherry Lane Theater, 38 Commerce Street (16): Gena Rowlands' off-off-Broadway dream in *Another Woman*.

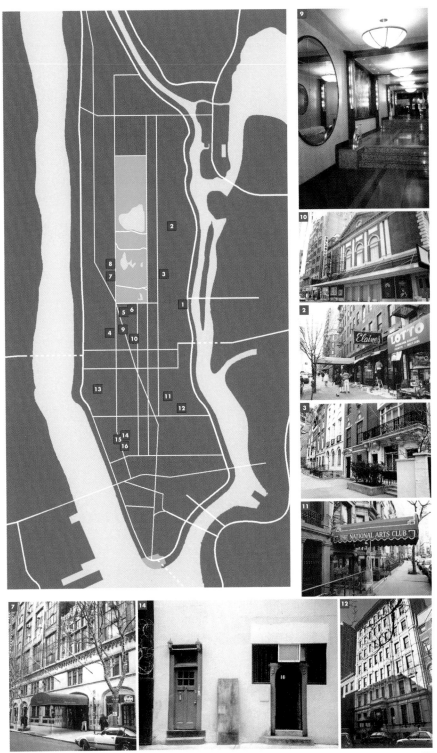

NEW YORK'S MEAN STREETS

The other side of New York is drugs, guns and tough talk, the backdrop to urban crime thrillers since movies moved from the studios to the street in the late forties.

10th Precinct, 230 West 20th Street (**1**): Where it all started, the cop station in one of the first street-level NY location thrillers: *The Naked City*.

Cleveland Plaza, Little Italy (**2**): The, now gentrified, neighbourhood of Martin Scorsese's seminal *Mean Streets*, on the western fringe of Little Italy. The Volpe bar stood at no. 23.

Mare Chiaro, 176 Mulberry Street (**3**): Now engulfed by Chinatown, an original Italian bar oozing atmosphere, where Johnny Depp and Al Pacino meet up in the sublime *Donnie Brasco*.

226 13th Street, East Village (**4**): Site of the final bloody shoot up at the end of Scorsese's masterpiece *Taxi Driver*.

621 Hudson Street, Greenwich Village (**5**): Now an upscale restaurant, this was the 'No Name Bar' in the original *Shaft*.

5-7 Minetta Street, Greenwich Village (**6**): Al Pacino's Village apartment in Sidney Lumet's police corruption thriller *Serpico*.

Guido's Restaurant, 511 Ninth Avenue (**7**): Tony's restaurant, supposedly in Little Italy, is down in the Garment District, in Luc Besson's stylish *Leon*. Great location, great food.

P J Clarke's, 915 Third Avenue (8): A great survivor among the highrises, this richly atmospheric bar is where Ray Milland destroys his liver in Billy Wilder's *The Lost Weekend*.

Lenox Lounge, 288 Lenox Avenue, Harlem (9): Recently restored to its deco glory, a Harlem legend seen in the remake of *Shaft* and in Spike Lee's *Malcolm X*.

New Utrecht Avenue, Borough Park, Brooklyn, (10): Arguably the greatest car chase in cinema, under the Bensonhurst Elevated Railway, in *The French Connection*.

8th Street South, Williamsburg, Brooklyn (11): The twenties neighbourhood of Sergio Leone's magnificently sprawling epic *Once Upon a Time in America*.

VERTIGO'S SAN FRANCISCO

FORT POINT (**1**), **Marine Drive** off Long Avenue. Make the journey down beneath the vast superstructure of the Golden Gate Bridge, to the spot where Scottie thwarts Madeleine's suicide attempt. Careful though, there is *no* flight of steps.

900 LOMBARD STREET (**2**) at Jones Street, at the foot of the famous 'crookedest street in the world', was Scottie's apartment, to which Madeleine finds her way by looking for Coit Tower.

ESSEX SUPPER CLUB (**3**), **537 Montgomery Street** in the Jackson Square Historic District was, in 1958, Ernie's Restaurant, once of Hitchcock's own favourites, where Scottie first gets a glimpse of Madeleine on the arm of Gavin Elster. For the movie, Ernie's was meticulously recreated in the studio.

BROCKLEBANK APARTMENT (**4**), **1000 Mason Street** at Sacramento Street. Atop Nob Hill, across from the Mark Hopkins Hotel, is Elster's luxury apartment block outside which Scottie begins tailing Madeleine.

YORK HOTEL (**5**), **940 Sutter Street** between Hyde and Leavenworth Streets. Plusher (it houses the Plush Room cabaret spot) than it was in the fifties, the York was Judy's lodging, the Hotel Empire, in which she is finally transformed into Madeleine.

MISSION DOLORES (**6**), **320 Dolores Street** at 16th Street. Behind the old adobe Misión San Francisco De Asis (for which the city is named) you can visit the tiny atmospheric cemetery, where Madeleine seeks out the grave of 'Carlotta Valdes'.

MISSION SAN JUAN BAUTISTA (**7**). The site of the climax, outside the city in the quiet little town of San Juan Bautista, about 90 miles to the south.

Rome and Florence. Desdemona's bedchamber is the 13th century round church of **Santa Maria della Salute** in Viterbo.

OTHELLO
(1995, dir: Oliver Parker)
Laurence Fishburne, Kenneth Branagh, Irène Jacob.
● **ITALY**

This time, the medieval battlements are the **Castello Orsini** at **Bracciano**, on Lake Bracciano, about 25 miles northwest of Rome.

OUR DANCING DAUGHTERS
(1928, dir: Harry Beaumont)
Joan Crawford, Anita Page, Johnny Mack Brown.
● **CALIFORNIA**

Flapper-era melodrama which catapulted Crawford to fame, with location filming at **The Lodge, Pebble Beach**, northern California.

OUT OF AFRICA
(1985, dir: Sydney Pollack)
Meryl Streep, Robert Redford, Klaus Maria Brandauer.
● **KENYA; TANZANIA**

Karen Blixen's book describes her experiences in Africa, attempting to grow coffee in the Ngong Hills outside Nairobi. The film charts a doomed affair with Denys Finch Hatton. Finch Hatton was a bald, six-foot four Old Etonian with a penchant for Latin and Greek poets. Robert Redford plays him. That's Hollywood. The settings are more authentic though. The small town that was Nairobi in 1914 was built from scratch on farmland at **Langata**, about 30 miles from the modern city. The Osgood and Norfolk Hotels, bazaar, church, and even the railway station were reproduced. Karen Blixen's house is now used as a government building, and the surrounding area developed. An existing farmhouse at the **Ngong Dairy** in **Karen** (yes, named for Blixen), not far from Langata and from the real house, was renovated to replicate the original. The Kikuyu village and the façade of the Muthiaga Club – where Karen marries Bror Blixen – were also constructed on the dairy's grounds. The real Muthiaga Club now stands in one of Nairobi's wealthier suburbs.

African landscapes were supplied by the **Masai Mara**, Kenya's part of the Serengeti Plain and the **Rift Valley**, west of Nairobi. The wildebeest migration was captured by a second unit at the **Ngorongoro Crater** and **Lake Manyara** in Tanzania.

OUT OF SIGHT
(1998, dir: Steven Soderbergh)
George Clooney, Jennifer Lopez, Ving Rhames.
● **FLORIDA; MICHIGAN; LOUISIANA; CALIFORNIA**

Elmore Leonard adaptation, shot largely around sunny Florida and in gloomy Detroit, Michigan. Belle Glade Correctional Institution is **Angola State Prison** in Louisiana, with real convicts playing extras. Lompoc Federal Penitentiary is a holding centre for immigration violations in **Palmdale**, California. The prison library is in the familiar old **Lincoln Heights Jail, 421 North Avenue 19**, Lin-

coln **Heights**, near downtown LA.

The Florida hotel, where Clooney and Rhames stay, is an old folks favourite, the **Tyler Adams Hotel and Apartments, 2030 Park Avenue, Miami Beach**.

Clooney and Rhames' hotel: Tyler Adams Hotel, Park Avenue, Miami

In Detroit, the gym where Clooney and Rhames confront Snopop and White Boy Bob is a venerable institution, **Kronk's Recreation Center, 5555 McGraw Street**, and the boxing scenes were staged in the **State Theater, 2115 Woodward Avenue**. Ripley's mansion is in the **Bloomfield Hills** section of the Motor City.

OUTBREAK
(1995, dir: Wolfgang Petersen)
Dustin Hoffman, Morgan Freeman, Rene Russo.
● **CALIFORNIA; HAWAII**

Hoffman works to contain a lethal African virus imported to West Coast USA. The Zaire scenes are the island of **Kauai**, Hawaii (see *Jurassic Park* for details of this beautiful island). The infected town of Cedar Creek is **Ferndale**, where the façade of the hospital lab was built onto a bank on Main Street.

OUTLAW – JOSEY WALES, THE
(1976, dir: Clint Eastwood)
Clint Eastwood, Chief Dan George, Sondra Locke.
● **UTAH; ARIZONA; CALIFORNIA**

Violent revenge Western, shot in **Kanab**, Utah; **Glen Canyon** and the artificial **Lake Powell** in Arizona and **Oroville**, Butte County, California.

OUTSIDERS, THE
(1983, dir: Francis Ford Coppola)
Ralph Macchio, C Thomas Howell, Matt Dillon.
● **OKLAHOMA**

SE Hinton's novel, directed by Coppola using a cracking cast of then-unknowns, was made back-to-back with the more arty *Rumble Fish* in **Tulsa**, Oklahoma.

OX-BOW INCIDENT, THE
(1943, dir: William A Wellman)
Henry Fonda, Harry Morgan, Dana Andrews.
● **CALIFORNIA**

The ever-upright Fonda stands up against a Nevada lynchmob in this powerful Western, which makes use of the barren rock formations of the **Alabama Hills**, at **Lone Pine**, I-395 in central California (see *Kim* for details of this popular location).

P

PACIFIC HEIGHTS

(1990, dir: John Schlesinger)
Melanie Griffith, Matthew Modine, Michael Keaton.
● CALIFORNIA

San Fran yuppies Griffith and Modine let a room in their Pacific Heights home to the sinister, cockroach-breeding tenant from Hell, Michael Keaton. Although the

The Pacific Heights house: 19th Street, Potrero Hill

address is given as 275 Pacific Street in the top-notch area of northern San Francisco up toward Marina, the house seen in the movie isn't on Pacific Heights at all, but tucked out of the way south of the city in the downmarket Potrero Hill District, **1243 19th Street** at Texas Street. When Keaton flees to LA, Griffith catches up with him at the **Park Hyatt Los Angeles** (then the JW Marriott Hotel), **2151 Avenue of the Stars** in Century City, (© *310.277.2777*), the site of the old Fox lot (and yes, it's a Twentieth Century Fox movie). It's here that Schlesinger puts in a Hitchcock-like cameo.

PAINT YOUR WAGON

(1969, dir: Joshua Logan)
Clint Eastwood, Lee Marvin, Jean Seberg.
● OREGON

A new plot is grafted onto the songs of the old stage musical, as a dearth of womenfolk pushes Clint and Lee to polyandry, sharing wife Jean Seberg. In an unusual turnabout, it was the director, stagey old Joshua Logan, who wanted to shoot the movie on the Paramount lot, and the studio who insisted on location shooting. As it turns out, the location is the movie's only real asset. No Name City, the goldrush shanty town, was built at **East Eagle Creek**, up in northeast Oregon, near to Baker City, within the Wallowa-Whitman National Forest.

PAL JOEY

(1957, dir: George Sidney)
Frank Sinatra, Rita Hayworth, Kim Novak.
● SAN FRANCISCO

Rodgers and Hart's musical about shifty nightclub entertainer Joey is set in San Francisco. Rita Hayworth's mansion is actually the **Coit Memorial Tower, Telegraph Hill Park** on Telegraph Hill Boulevard. This SF landmark was built for Lillie Hitchcock Coit to

Chez Joey: The Spreckels Mansion, Washington Street, San Francisco

'beautify the city'. Did it? See *Vertigo* for details. The Chez Joey nightclub is the grand **Spreckels Mansion, 2080 Washington Street**, overlooking Lafayette Park in Pacific Heights, seen also in the 1969 thriller *Eye of the Cat*. It's a private home, bought by writer Danielle Steele in 1990.

PALE RIDER

(1985, dir: Clint Eastwood)
Clint Eastwood, Michael Moriarty, Carrie Snodgress.
● IDAHO

Clint helps out prospecting families harassed by the big guys in a spectacular Western which was made around **Sun Valley**, in central Idaho, and the nearby **Sawtooth National Recreation Area**, on I-75.

PANDORA AND THE FLYING DUTCHMAN

(1951, dir: Albert Lewin)
Ava Gardner, James Mason, Nigel Patrick.
● SPAIN

Ava Gardner is the heartless tease who falls for the ghostly sea captain in this dour fable from eccentric director Albert Lewin. The little coastal town is **Tossa De Mar**, near Gerona, on Spain's Costa Brava, about 65 miles northeast of Barcelona.

PANTHER

(1995, dir: Mario Van Peebles)
Kadeem Hardison, Bokeem Woodbine, Joe Don Baker.
● CALIFORNIA

The story of sixties revolutionaries the Black Panthers, and the underhand tactics used by the FBI to undermine the movement, is set largely in Oakland, over the bay from San Francisco. It's on the double-decked **Oakland Bay Bridge**, linking Oakland with San Francisco, that the cops intimidate one of the Panthers. The Oakland Army Induction Center, where the Panthers' rally is staged, is the familiar **Park Plaza Hotel, 607 South Park View Street**, overlooking Macarthur Park, downtown LA (see *New York, New York* for details). Filming also took place at **Alameda County Courthouse, 1225 Fallon Street**, Oakland, and the **California State Capitol Building, Ninth Street** between L and N Streets, Sacramento.

PAPER MOON

(1973, dir: Peter Bogdanovich)
Ryan O'Neal, Tatum O'Neal, Madeline Kahn.
● KANSAS; MISSOURI; LOS ANGELES

The O'Neals, real life father and daughter, are Bible-selling con artists in the US midwest of the thirties. The period-looking towns are **Hays**, I-70,

Kendall Alley, Pasadena

central Kansas, which served as the film's base; **Lacrosse**, 30 miles to the south on I-283; and **St George** on I-55 just southwest of St Louis, Missouri. Filming also took place in the historic **Kendall Alley** in LA's eastern suburb, Pasadena (also seen in *Pulp Fiction*).

PAPILLON
(1973, dir: Franklin J Schaffner)
Steve McQueen, Dustin Hoffman, Victor Jory.
● JAMAICA

McQueen and Hoffman suffer the privations of the notorious French Guyana prison colony, in this epic filmed mainly in Jamaica, where the huge Devil's Island prison set was built at **Falmouth** and interiors lensed at **Montego Bay**. The Indian village is at **Ocho Rios** (a major location for the first Bond movie, *Dr No*) and the arrival of the prison ship filmed at **Kingston**. The work camp is **Paradise Jungle Park** at **Savannah-la-Mar**, the western end of Bluefields Bay, a 1,000-acre private estate about 30 miles south of Montego Bay (*admission charge, © 809.999.5771*).

PARADINE CASE, THE
(1947, dir: Alfred Hitchcock)
Gregory Peck, Alida Valli, Charles Laughton.
● LONDON; LAKE DISTRICT

Although Hitchcock's courtroom melodrama, his last picture for David O Selznick, was made at the RKO Studio in Hollywood, it's set in the UK, where a second unit captured location shots. In London, the exterior of the **Central Criminal Court, the Old Bailey**, EC4, where Alida Valli was tried for murder, is real, still showing the extensive bomb damage sustained during the Blitz, but the courtroom was meticulously recreated in the studio. Similarly, Bow Street Police Station and the old Holloway women's prison were recreated from photographs. Defence lawyer Gregory Peck's house is **60 Portland Place** at Weymouth Street, W1. When he investigates Valli's past in Cumberland, the Station Hotel, where he stays, is the **Drunken Duck Inn, Barngate**, off the B5286 just southwest of Langdale Chase. Hindley Hall, the Paradine estate, is a mock-Eliza-

Gregory Peck's house: Portland Place, W1

Gregory Peck stays at the Station Hotel: Drunken Duck Inn, Barngate

The Paradine estate: Langdale Chase Hotel, Cumbria

bethan manor house built in 1891, now the **Langdale Chase Hotel**, on the A591 between Brockhole and Ambleside on the north shore of Lake Windermere, Cumbria (© *015394.32201*).

PARALLAX VIEW, THE
(1974, dir: Alan J Pakula)
Warren Beatty, Paula Prentiss, Hume Cronyn.
● LOS ANGELES; WASHINGTON STATE

Brilliant conspiracy thriller with echoes of the Kennedy assassination, the centre of Pakula's great paranoia trilogy between *Klute* and *All the President's Men*. The opening political assassination takes place atop Seattle's **Space Needle, 203 Sixth Avenue North**, the familiar landmark erected for the 1962 World's Fair and featured, not surprisingly in Elvis Presley's 1962 *It Happened at the World's Fair*. It's open to the public and, for a fee, you can zoom up to the 518-foot high Observation Deck. The children's train, where Beatty meets up with Kenneth Mars, is **Woodland Park Zoo, 5500 Phinney Avenue North**, Seattle. The dam at fictitious Salmontail, where Beatty comes close to being drowned, is the **Lake Chelan Dam, Chelan**, on Route 97 in central Washington State. The final assassination filmed at the **Los Angeles Convention Center**, Figueroa Street, downtown LA – a building that's since been much enlarged and revamped.

The assassination: Space Needle, Seattle

PARENT TRAP, THE
(1961, dir: David Swift)
Hayley Mills, Maureen O'Hara, Brian Keith.
● CALIFORNIA

Twins (both Hayley Mills) try to reconcile their separated parents. Filming took place at **Monterey Peninsula Airport**; the Lodge of **Pebble Beach Golf Course** and **Cypress Point**, Pebble Beach. The 1998 remake, set in London and San Francisco, features the villa of the Staglin Family Vineyard, a private estate in the Napa Valley, northern California.

PARIS, TEXAS
(1984, dir: Wim Wenders)
Harry Dean Stanton, Dean Stockwell, Nastassja Kinski.
● TEXAS

Paris, Texas, a real enough town, is the Godot of film locations. Lots of waiting, but it doesn't actually turn up. Harry Dean Stanton is found at the opening of Wenders' soft-centred road movie in **Marathon**, a tiny town north of the

The Texas motel: Marathon Motel, Highway 90, Marathon, West Texas

spectacular Big Bend National Park. The motel he stays in is the **Marathon Motel and RV Park**, West Highway 90, a stunningly picturesque jumble of log cabins on the desert highway, alongside the railway, with breathtaking views over the West Texas desert to the Chisos Mountains (*© 915.386.4241*). The cross-state journey takes Stanton and Stockwell to **Port Arthur** and **Houston**.

Paris itself, on I-82, 90 miles northwest of Dallas, is a cutesy little town, totally destroyed by fire and rebuilt in the twenties, since when it's largely been unchanged. Paris capitalises on its exotic European name, though with only the most tenuous grasp of the idiom. A local fashion shop is wonderfully named *Le Anne's*.

PASSAGE TO INDIA, A
(1984, dir: David Lean)
Judy Davis, Victor Bannerjee, Peggy Ashcroft.
● INDIA

After the critical trouncing of *Ryan's Daughter*, Lean retired, hurt, from the fray until this acclaimed comeback. It has to be said, though, that it's another overblown epic. Set in the fictitious Chandrapore, most of the movie was shot around **Bangalore**, southern India, where sets, including the British quarter, the bazaar and Dr Aziz's house, were built on the grounds of **Bangalore Palace** in the centre of the city. Filming also took place at the **Bangalore Club, FM Cariappa Road**. The pivotal Marabar Caves location, where Judy Davis crucially succumbs to the exotic atmosphere, is the rock formation at **Ramanagaram**, about 30 miles from Bangalore. The ending of the movie is **Srinagar** in Kashmir, northern India, where, forbidden to buy property, the English lived in houseboats on the sytem of canals.

PASSENGER, THE (aka *Profession: Reporter*)
(1975, dir: Michelangelo Antonioni)
Jack Nicholson, Maria Schneider, Jenny Runacre.
● SPAIN; LONDON; NORTH AFRICA; GERMANY

Jack Nicholson steals the passport and assumes the identity of a dead man. Filming at the, then, brand new **Brunswick Centre** in Bloomsbury, opposite Russell Square tube station. Also in Chad; Algeciras; in Munich; and in Barcelona, where Nicholson rides the cable car above the city and wanders the bird markets of Rambla promenades. Ending at the **Hotel de la Gloria, Osuna**, Spain.

PASSION FISH
(1992, dir: John Sayles)
Mary McDonnell, Alfre Woodard, David Strathairn.
● LOUISIANA

Sayles' film about the relationship between paralysed soap star McDonnell and her attendant nurse Woodard was made at **Jennings** and **Lake Arthur**, Louisiana.

PASSPORT TO PIMLICO
(1949, dir: Henry Cornelius)
Stanley Holloway, Margaret Rutherford, Betty Warren.
● LONDON

When bomb damage uncovers documents revealing that Pimlico belongs to the Duchy of Burgundy, the neigh-

bourhood declares independence from the post-war Britain of rationing and licensing laws in this archetypal Ealing comedy. It was made, not in Pimlico, but about a mile east, over the Thames where a huge set was built on a cleared bomb site on the **Lambeth Road, SE1**. Although the bomb-flattened area has been totally redeveloped, if you stand on the Lambeth Road between Hercules Road and Kennington Road and look north toward Lambeth Bridge, you can clearly recognise the railway arches that dominated the set.

Pimlico declares independence: Lambeth Road, SE1

PAT GARRETT AND BILLY THE KID
(1973, dir: Sam Peckinpah)
James Coburn, Kris Kristofferson, Bob Dylan.
● MEXICO

Another slow, bloody Peckinpah hymn to dusty, sweaty machismo, which exists in various versions. After all his past treks around Mexico with *Major Dundee* and *The Wild Bunch*, Peckinpah this time stayed firmly in the time-honoured Western location of **Durango**, about 500 miles northwest of Mexico City, an area seen in many, many movies including *Cahill, US Marshal, Chisum, The Undefeated, The Unforgiven* (1960) and *The War Wagon*.

PATHER PANCHALI
(1955, dir: Satyajit Ray)
Subir Banerji, Kanu Banerji, Karuna Banerji.
● INDIA

Family life in a poverty-stricken Indian village, the first of Ray's Apu trilogy. The village of Gopalnagar is the novel's setting but proved to be unsuitable for filming. Ray settled on **Boral**, six miles from Calcutta's city centre, where the ruined house and the pond stand.

PATHS OF GLORY
(1957, dir: Stanley Kubrick)
Kirk Douglas, Adolphe Menjou, Ralph Meeker.
● MUNICH, GERMANY

Kubrick's WWI drama, set in the French trenches, was made in Munich. The grand palace is the **Neues Schloss** of **Schloss Schleissheim**, to the northwest of the city. For full details, see *L'Année Dernière à Marienbad*, for which the Schloss provided exteriors.

PATRIOT GAMES
(1992, dir: Phillip Noyce)
Harrison Ford, Sean Bean, Anne Archer.
● LONDON; MARYLAND; VIRGINIA; CALIFORNIA

Messy, exploitative thriller pitting the CIA against the Hollywood wing of the IRA, clearly aimed at US audiences who won't notice the bizarre London geography. US agent Harrison Ford, leaving a lecture at the 'Royal Naval Academy' in Greenwich, south of the Thames in southeast London, manages to turn a corner and witness terrorist attack on the 'Queen Mother's cousin' outside an extraordinary version of 'Buckingham Palace'. This 'palace' actually is in Greenwich. It's **Greenwich Naval College** (the film-makers wanted ex-GLC HQ County Hall, but couldn't get permission). See *Four Weddings and a Funeral* for details. The IRA uses an improbable dusty old secondhand book-shop in the swingingly posh **Burlington Arcade, Piccadilly** to transmit its messages. When rumbled, the villain legs it out of the arcade and down to the nearest tube station. Green Park, maybe, which is conveniently next door? Nope. It's **Aldwych Station**, over a mile away – the station London Transport makes available for filming.

Back in the US of A, Ford visits the **CIA HQ in Lang-ley**, East Virginia, just over the Potomac from Washington DC. And, unlike Buckingham Palace, it's the real thing – the entrance and the lobby, at least. So you can bet that this isn't going to be a CIA dirty tricks movie. *Mission: Impossible* also filmed in the lobby of CIA HQ, but for the corridors managed to use – County Hall in London. The *Patriot Games* interior is a set of course. Just who are those helpful signs, like 'Terrorism Assessments', meant for? Casual visitors?

Ford attends the **US Naval Academy at Annapolis**, I-301 on Chesapeake Bay, Maryland. The car chase is along Highway 301/50, over the Severn River Bridge. The climactic motor boat chase, supposedly in Chesapeake Bay, was shot in the two-million-gallon tank on the lot at Paramount in Hollywood. The North African terrorist camp was at **Brawley**, Route 86, south of Salton Sea in Southern California down near the Mexican border.

PATTON (aka *Patton – Lust For Glory*)
(1970, dir: Franklin Schaffner)
George C Scott, Karl Malden, Michael Bates.
● **SPAIN; GREECE; SICILY; ITALY; MOROCCO; CHESHIRE**

Epic biopic of the WWII general, with an Oscar-winning script co-written by Francis Coppola and a famously declined Best Actor Oscar for Scott, and made mostly on location.

The Battle of the Bulge, which took place in the Ardennes in Belgium, was recreated in the Segovia highlands, 80 miles northwest of Madrid. Patton's advance across France used the Pamplona region of Basque Spain. Spain also supplied the various terrains of North Africa, Sicily, Italy, France and Germany. The scene of amphibious landings is Sicily; while the Roman ruins and the reviewing of Moroccan troops actually filmed in Morocco. More filming took place in Greece.

The Battle of El Guettar is the familiar desert outside **Almeria** in southern Spain. After the battle, Patton meets his new aide de camp in the **Governor's Palace**, Almeria. The long hallway, down which Patton exits from Eisenhower's office after a rebuke, is the **Tapestry Room** at **La Granja** (which you might recognise as the scene of the climactic ball in Richard Lester's *The Three Musketeers*). Patton has his portrait painted at the castle of **Riofrio**, outside Segovia (another *Musketeers* location).

Patton's wartime HQ, where he dedicates the service club and offends the Russians, was filmed in the real location, **Peover Hall, Over Peover**, an Elizabethan manor house near **Knutsford**, Cheshire in the north of England. The house and gardens are open to the public from April to October (℃ *01743.708100*).

PAWNBROKER, THE
(1965, dir: Sidney Lumet)
Rod Steiger, Jaime Sanchez, Geraldine Fitzgerald.
● **NEW YORK CITY**

Steiger's pawn-broker shop no longer exists, but it stood at **1642 Park Avenue**, currently still a vacant lot, just north of 116th Street in East Harlem. You can still recognise

Site of Steiger's pawnbroker shop: Park Avenue, East Harlem

the neighbouring buildings though, which are largely unchanged. The Radiant Bar at 116th Street is now Ochun Botanica, a florist.

PEE-WEE'S BIG ADVENTURE
(1985, dir: Tim Burton)
Pee-Wee Herman, Jan Hooks, Elizabeth Daily.
● **LOS ANGELES; TEXAS**

Fun first feature-film outing for Tim Burton. The shopping mall, where Pee-Wee shops for magic stuff and gets his bike stolen, is the **Santa Monica Place Shopping Mall, Fourth Street** at Broadway, Santa Monica, LA. He searches for his bike at the **Alamo, Alamo Plaza, San Antonio**, Texas. The Pee-Wee Herman version of the Alamo tour is loads more fun than the dull solemnity of the real thing, basement or no basement (for full details see *The Alamo*). The film studio is, of course, **Warner Bros, 4000 Warner Boulevard, Burbank**. You can tour the studio, too. Unlike the Universal Studios theme park approach, WB has a small tour (up to twelve people), which needs to be booked ahead (℃ *818.954.1744*).

PEEPING TOM
(1960, dir: Michael Powell)
Carl Boehm, Anna Massey, Moira Shearer.
● **LONDON**

Reviled on release, but now lauded as one of the great British movies. Boehm, the disturbed son of a sadistic film-maker, has a fear fixation and a lethal movie camera. Boehm's house stood at 5 Melbury Road, off High Street Kensington near Holland Park. Although number 7 still stands, its neighbour was demolished to make way for a block of flats. Director Powell not only plays the obsessed father, but lived over the road at 8 Melbury Road, which *is*

Karl Boehm's first murder: Newman Arms, Newman's Court

The newsagent: Percy Street, W1

still there. An impressive Norman Shaw Victorian artist's property with enormous windows, the house's garden was used for home movie footage.

Boehm's first victim, Brenda Bruce, is picked up in **Newman's Court**, just off Oxford Street, and takes the killer up to her room above the **Newman Arms** alongside. The newsagent's, where furtive businessmen buy their adult magazines, is on the corner of **Percy Street** at Rathbone Place, just behind Tottenham Court Road.

PEGGY SUE GOT MARRIED
(1986, dir: Francis Coppola)
Kathleen Turner, Nicolas Cage, Barry Miller.
● **CALIFORNIA**

The Donut Hole Cafe:
Millie's Chili Bar,
Petaluma

An Oscar-nominated star turn from Kathleen Turner, regressing to her seventeen year-old self at a school reunion and rekindling romance with her cheesy husband. Look out for an early appearance by Jim Carrey, as a member of Nic Cage's vocal group. The movie was filmed in the towns of **Petaluma** and **Santa Rosa** in northern California. Petaluma, a small, unchanged town, is a frequent ly used period backdrop, most famously for *American Graffiti*. Peggy Sue's sixties home is **226 Liberty Street**, between Prospect and Washington Streets, Petaluma.

Peggy Sue's house: Liberty Street

Boyfriend Charlie's house: D Street

Cage, her boyfriend Charlie, lives at **1006 D Street**. The Donut Hole Cafe, where the young Peggy Sue enjoys a flirtation with mean 'n' moody poet Kevin J O'Connor is **Millie's Chili Bar, 600 Petaluma Boulevard** at H Street. Filming also took place on **H Street** at the Petaluma River.

Peggy Sue's high school: Santa Rosa
High School

The high school is **Santa Rosa High School, 1235 Mendocino Avenue** at Pacific. Santa Rosa was also the high school in *Inventing the Abbotts*, and was to have been Woodsboro High in Wes Craven's *Scream*, but the school authorities refused permission when they read the script, hence the bitchy 'No thanks at all to...' credit at the end of that movie.

PELICAN BRIEF, THE
(1993, dir: Alan J Pakula)
Julia Roberts, Denzel Washington, Sam Shepard.
● **LOUISIANA; NEW YORK CITY; WASHINGTON DC**

Riggs National Bank, Pennsylvania
Avenue, Washington DC

Another John Grisham thriller, in the capable hands of paranoia specialist Pakula. The opening scene was filmed in front of the **Supreme Court** in Washington DC. Denzel Washington meets his editor John Lithgow at **Mount Vernon**, the home of George Washington. The offices of White and Blazevich are the law offices of Howrey and Simon in the **Warner Building, 1299 Pennsylvania Avenue**. DC filming also took place in the courtyard of the FBI's **Hoover Building, 10th Street** at Pennsylvania Avenue; the **Washington Monument**; **Pershing Park**; **National Cathedral**; **Riggs National Bank, 1503 Pennsylvania Avenue** at 15th Street; **Dulles Airport** and the library, conference rooms and offices of the **Georgetown University Law Center, 600 New Jersey Avenue NW**. The Oval Office reuses the set built for Kevin Kline-Sigourney Weaver movie *Dave*.

In New Orleans, law scenes were shot at **Tulane University, New Orleans**. French Quarter locations include **Bourbon Street** and **Spanish Plaza, Riverwalk**, on the banks of the Mississippi, where Roberts meets the fake FBI agent. Roberts and Shepard dine at **Antoine's Restaurant, 713 St Louis Street** in the French Quarter (though the restaurant's frontage was mocked up in the city's warehouse district for the explosion which kills Shepard).

In NYC, Pakula used the enormous, 50-storey **Marriott Marquis Hotel, 1535 Broadway** at 45th Street (*℗ 212.398.1900*) overlooking Times Square. The 1,877 room hotel boasts the world's tallest atrium, New York's largest ballroom, and also incorporates the Broadway Theater.

Julia Roberts meets the fake FBI agent:
Riverwalk, New Orleans

Marriott Marquis Hotel,
Broadway, New York

PEOPLE VS LARRY FLYNT, THE

(1996, dir: Milos Forman)
Woody Harrelson, Courtney Love, Edward Norton.
● **MEMPHIS, TENNESSEE; LOS ANGELES; WASHINGTON DC**

The final victory for free speech: Supreme Court Building, DC

Biopic of the publisher of *Hustler*, reinvented in the person of cute fighter for free speech Woody Harrelson. The real Flynt has a wicked cameo as a judge. Most of the filming was around Memphis, Tennessee. The scenes of Flynt's childhood home in Kentucky were shot over the Mississippi River from Memphis itself, and his first nightclub (opened in Columbus, Ohio, in the seventies), was filmed in the city's downtown area. Most of the court scenes are Memphis too, where a train terminal served as the US Supreme Court. Flynt's Ohio estate, where he throws his lavish 1976 Bicentennial party, is the same Memphis estate Tom Cruise stayed at during filming of *The Firm*. Other Memphis locations include the famous **Peabody Hotel, 149 Union Avenue**; **Memphis State University**; the **Shelby County Arena** and a couple of correctional facilities.

The first courtroom clash with televangelist Jerry Falwell is at the courthouse of **Oxford**, Mississippi. In LA, real locations used include the **Flynt Publications Building** in Beverly Hills and Flynt's former home, **364 St Cloud Road**, Bel Air, where Harrelson is arrested. The outcome of the final Falwell hearing filmed on the steps of the **Supreme Court Building, First Street NE**, Washington DC.

PERFECT WORLD, A

(1993, dir: Clint Eastwood)
Clint Eastwood, Kevin Costner, Laura Dern.
● **TEXAS**

Eastwood and Costner team up for a chase movie made entirely on location in **Huntsville** and around Austin, Texas. Escaped convict Costner goes on the run with a young boy, kidnapping him on **Columbus Street**, off Bouldin Avenue, Austin. The fictitious town of Noodle is **Martindale**, where the shop held up by Costner is on **Main Street**. Filming also took place at the **State Capitol Building** in Austin. The various small Texan towns are **Taylor**; **Wimberley**; **Niederwald**; **Manor**; **Cedar Creek**; **Bastrop**; **Utley**; **Volante** and **Canyon Lake**.

PERFORMANCE

(1970, dir: Nicolas Roeg, Donald Cammell)
James Fox, Mick Jagger, Anita Pallenberg.
● **LONDON**

That old art movie chestnut, the personality swap, is made over by the dream teaming of Roeg and Cammell with such style and innovation that, alongside *Peeping Tom*, this has to be one of the best British movies ever. The run-

down Notting Hill house where gangster Fox hides out with burned-out rock star Jagger, is not 81 Powis Square (the address given in the movie), but **25 Powis Square**, W11, at Talbot Road, a couple of blocks east of Portobello Road. The picturesque squalor of the movie is long gone, and the house is now smartly renovated. The interiors were shot in a house in the much posher **Lowndes Square**, SW1, in Knightsbridge.

Jagger's druggy flat: Powis Square, Notting Hill

PERSONA

(1966, dir: Ingmar Bergman)
Liv Ullmann, Bibi Andersson, Gunnar Bjornstrand.
● **SWEDEN**

Yet another personality swap movie, but in Bergman's hands, an overwhelmingly cinematic experience, complete with Brechtian film break. It was made on the island of **Faro**.

PETER'S FRIENDS

(1992, dir: Kenneth Branagh)
Kenneth Branagh, Emma Thompson, Stephen Fry.
● **HERTFORDSHIRE**

The Brit Chill, as old college chums gather to rake over their lives. Stephen Fry's house is **Wrotham Park, Hill Road** at **Bentley Heath**, off the A1000 north of Barnet, Hertfordshire. Not visible from the road, and not open to the public, the house is occasionally hired out as a conference facility or a movie location (see it in Ken Russell's *Gothic* and in *Princess Caraboo*).

PETE'S DRAGON

(1977, dir: Don Chaffey)
Sean Marshall, Mickey Rooney, Helen Reddy.
● **CALIFORNIA**

Disney's long, part-animated fantasy, with Sean Marshall as the young boy with a pet dragon, is set in turn-of-the-century Maine. It was shot on the coast of California, where Mickey Rooney's lighthouse was built at **Morro Bay**, about 30 miles south of San Simeon on Highway 1.

PEYTON PLACE

(1957, dir: Mark Robson)
Lana Turner, Diane Varsi, Hope Lange.
● **MAINE**

Archetypal sex-in-a-small-town melodrama, which spawned the mother of all TV soaps. The little town is **Camden**, on the coast of Maine. Lana Turner's house is on **Chestnut Street** and her shop is on **Main Street**.

PHANTASM

(1979, dir: Don Coscarelli)
Michael Baldwin, Bill Thornbury, Reggie Bannister.
● **CALIFORNIA**

The spooky mausoleum of this bizarre horror-comedy is

Dunsmuir House and Gardens, 2960 Peralta Oaks Court, Oakland, over the bay from San Francisco, a location familiar from movies such as Mike Myers' *So I Married an Axe Murderer* and *A View to a Kill*. It is open to the public. Filming also took place at **Julian**, a southern California mining town about 40 miles northeast of San Diego.

PHANTOM OF THE PARADISE
(1974, dir: Brian De Palma)
William Finley, Jessica Harper, Paul Williams.
● LOS ANGELES; NEW YORK CITY; TEXAS

De Palma's wild rock spin on *The Phantom of the Opera* and *Faust* was shot on sets in LA, while its exteriors are mainly New York, but the Paradise rock palace, haunted by the disfigured composer, is in Dallas, Texas. It's the **Majestic Theater, 1925 Elm Street**, a baroque movie palace built in 1921 as the HQ of the Interstate theater chain. It was donated to the city of Dallas and subsequently restored.

The Paradise: Majestic Theater, Elm Street, Dallas

PHILADELPHIA
(1993, dir: Jonathan Demme)
Tom Hanks, Denzel Washington, Antonio Banderas.
● PHILADELPHIA, PENNSYLVANIA

Demme's determinedly mainstream movie about Aids prejudice is calculatedly set in the city of liberty, independence and brotherly love, kicking off with a montage of such Philadelphian images as the **Benjamin Franklin Bridge** over the Delaware River, the glitzy modernistic skyscrapers of **Liberty Place** and the Liberty Bell itself. Like most of Demme's movies, it was made almost entirely on real locations. The Action Aids office, where Hanks gets a check-up at the opening of the movie, is **1216 Arch Street** just east of City Hall,

Denzel Washington's law office: Chestnut Street

The Wheeler Building: Mellon Bank, Market Street

Washington gets freaked by the gay student: Pickwick Pharmacy, Market Street

opposite the Pennsylvania Convention Center. The office of the prestigious law firm, Wyant, Wheeler, Hellerman, Tetlow and Brown, where Hanks is initially a rising star, is that of Philly firm Mesirov, Gelman, Jaffe, Cramer and Jamieson (who donated their location fee to Aids charities), in the **Mellon Bank Building, 1735 Market Street**, west of City Hall. A little to the south is Denzel Washington's law office, **1901 Chestnut Street** on the corner of 19th Street. The pharmacy, where Washington's homophobia is provoked by a gay law student, is the **Pickwick Pharmacy, 1700 Market Street**, directly opposite the Mellon Bank Building. Washington delivers a summons to Jason Robards during a ballgame at the **Spectrum Sports Arena, Broad Street** at Pattison Avenue, home of the Philadelphia Kixx soccer team.

Tom Hanks gets a check-up at the Action Aids office: Arch Street

The trial scenes: Philadelphia City Hall

Hanks and Banderas' loft apartment is on **10th Street** at Bainbridge Street, and also on Bainbridge Street is the **Famous Fourth Street Delicatessen**, where Washington shops after the birth of his daughter. Hanks studies case law west of the city in the **University of Pennsylvania Fine Arts Library, Walnut Street**. The sauna, where Tom Hanks' coming out is thwarted by the partners' laddish banter, is in the **Raquet Club, 215 South 16th Street**. The trial scenes were filmed in Courtroom 243 of **Philadelphia City Hall, Penn Square**, at Broad and Market Streets. Hanks ultimately dies at **Mount Sinai Hospital, Fourth Street** at Reed.

PIANO, THE
(1993, dir: Jane Campion)
Holly Hunter, Harvey Keitel, Anna Paquin.
● NEW ZEALAND

Oscar-winning period drama, featuring some stunning locations, with Campion editing together several different locales. The exteriors of the Stewart and Baines houses are in **Walkworth**, just outside Auckland, North Island. The underwater sequence was staged at the **Bay of Islands**, and there was more filming at **Awakino Beach**. The spectacular beach of the shipwreck is **Karekare Beach, Karekare Road**, off Piha Road, near Glen Eden to the west of Auckland.

PICNIC
(1955, dir: Joshua Logan)
Kim Novak, William Holden, Rosalind Russell.
● KANSAS

Hunky stranger William Holden arrives in town and causes mayhem among the womenfolk in the Oscar-nominated filming of William Inge's play, which was shot in

Hutchinson, on I-50 about 40 miles northwest of Wichita, Kansas, and **Halstead**, 25 miles to the east. The waterfall scene was filmed in **Salina**, I-135, about 80 miles north of Wichita.

PICNIC AT HANGING ROCK
(1975, dir: Peter Weir)
Rachel Roberts, Helen Morse, Dominic Guard.
● VICTORIA, AUSTRALIA; SOUTH AUSTRALIA

Turn-of-the-century Aussie spin on Antonioni's *L'Avventura*, where schoolgirls on a picnic inexplicably disappear. **Hanging Rock** is real, and is where the picture was

Appleyard Girls' School: Martindale Hall, Mintaro, South Australia

shot. The weird jumble of stone columns can be found near **Woodend** in Victoria, about 35 miles northwest of Melbourne on the Calder Highway. The nearby extinct 3,320-foot volcano, Mount Macedon, gives excellent views of the rocks. Appleyard Girls' School is **Martindale Hall**, a period mansion in the Clare Valley near **Mintaro**, South Australia. You can visit the mansion (✆ *08.8843.9088*) and maybe pick up a bottle of Martindale Hall Chardonnay, which is produced on the estate.

PHOTOGRAPH COURTESY NIC KLAASSEN/FLINDERS RANGES RESEARCH

PINK FLAMINGOS
(1972, dir: John Waters)
Divine, Mink Stole, David Lochary.
● MARYLAND

The legendary masterpiece of John Waters' underground period, topped with its unrepeatable coda as Divine, to the tune of 'How Much Is That Doggy in the Window', eats freshly exuded doggy-do. Those who've only seen the video version (where the offending sequence is reduced to a series of stills) probably believe it was faked. If you've seen the original, you know it wasn't. Filmed, like all Waters' early movies, around **Baltimore**. The Marbles' house is **3900 Greenmount Avenue**. But what you really want to know is the where Divine ate that turd, which was outside **894 Tyson Street** at Reed.

PINK FLOYD – THE WALL
(1982, dir: Alan Parker)
Bob Geldof, Christine Hargreaves, James Laurenson.
● DEVON; LONDON; SURREY; YORKSHIRE

Pompous visualisation of Pink Floyd's concept album, a loose autobiography of Roger Waters, with hero Pink going through all the standard motions of rock star alienation. The wartime Anzio beach scenes, where young Pink's father is killed, were shot on **Saunton Sands**, south of Ilfracombe on the north Devon coast. Pink's childhood home is in **East Molesey**, Surrey, the playground is in **Bermondsey**, London and the recurring childhood dream was shot on **Epsom Downs**. The other kids' fathers return from war at **Keighley Station**, on the Keighley-Worth Valley Railway near Bradford in Yorkshire.

The US rock concert which gets out of hand, based on a Floyd concert at the Sports Arena in LA, was shot at **Wembley Arena** (apart from a brief second unit glimpse of LA, all the American scenes were filmed in the UK, on sets at Pinewood).When Pink metamorphoses, for no apparent reason, into a neo-fascist demagogue, he presides over a rally in the **Royal Horticultural Hall, Westminster** (see *Indiana Jones and the Last Crusade* for details). The snippet of football violence is in **Muswell Hill**, near Alexandra Palace. The school riot is at **Beckton Gasworks**, where Stanley Kubrick filmed the Vietnam scenes for *Full Metal Jacket*.

PINK PANTHER, THE
(1963, dir: Blake Edwards)
David Niven, Peter Sellers, Capucine.
● ITALY

The film that launched Inspector Clouseau is set mostly in the jet-set ski resort of **Cortina d'Ampezzo** in the Ampezzo Valley of the Italian Dolomites (see *For Your Eyes Only* for details). Filming also took place at the ancient village of **Rocca di Papa**, about fifteen miles west of Rome. The opening scene, of Capucine making a getaway, is in **Venice**. The dizzying, mile-high roads of Amalfi; the streets of Rome near the Coliseum and Florence were also used.

PLACE IN THE SUN, A
(1951, dir: George Stevens)
Montgomery Clift, Elizabeth Taylor, Shelley Winters.
● NEVADA; CALIFORNIA

Theodore Dreiser's *An American Tragedy* given the worthy Hollywood treatment by Stevens. Taylor is rich, Clift is poor, but Winters is pregnant. The location filming was at **Lake Tahoe** in Nevada; and nearby **Cascade Lake**, on Emerald Bay Road, over the border in California at Tahoe's southern tip. The story was based on the Gillette murder trial, which took place in New York State, at the Herkimer County Courthouse in Little Falls, off I-90, twenty miles east of Utica.

PLAGUE OF THE ZOMBIES, THE
(1966, dir: John Gilling)
Andre Morell, Diane Clare, John Carson.
● BUCKINGHAMSHIRE

Excellent little horror from Hammer's golden age, with a terrific dream sequence. The Cornish village, where wicked squire John Carson raises the dead to work in his tin mine, is a set at Bray Studios near Maidenhead. His house is the Victorian gothic extravagance alongside the studio, now the **Oakley Court Hotel** (see *The Rocky Horror Picture Show*, one of the dozens of movies filmed here, for details).

PLAN 9 FROM OUTER SPACE
(dir: Edward D Wood Jr, 1958)
Bela Lugosi, Tor Johnson, Vampira.
● CALIFORNIA

The legendary 'Worst Film of All Time', lovingly recreated in Tim Burton's *Ed Wood*, was made around **San Fernando**, north of LA.

PLANES, TRAINS & AUTOMOBILES
(1987, dir: John Hughes)
Steve Martin, John Candy, William Windom.
● LOS ANGELES; NEW YORK STATE; MISSOURI

Martin is an exec trying to make it home to Chicago (well, this is a John Hughes movie) for Thanksgiving, who gets lumbered with Candy, the world's worst travelling companion. Filmed in LA; **St Louis Lambert International Airport, St Louis**, Missouri and the **South Dayton Train Station, Buffalo**, New York.

PLANET OF THE APES
(1968, dir: Franklin Schaffner)
Charlton Heston, Roddy McDowall, Kim Hunter.
● CALIFORNIA; ARIZONA

The desert planet, run by apes, is the desert around **Page, Glen Canyon** and **Lake Powell**, northern Arizona. The ape village sets were built on the Fox Ranch in **Malibu Creek State Park, Las Virgenes Road** off Mulholland Highway, south from Route 101, northwest of LA. The final scene, when Heston realises he's been on Earth all along, was shot at a secluded cove on the far eastern end of **Westward Beach**, between Zuma Beach and Point Dume, Malibu.

Heston is back to Earth: Westward Beach, Malibu

PLATOON
(1986, dir: Oliver Stone)
Charlie Sheen, Willem Dafoe, Tom Berenger.
● PHILIPPINES

The first of Stone's Vietnam trilogy won the Best Picture Oscar. Powerful stuff, with a little help from Samuel Barber's 'Adagio'. Filmed, like so many other 'Nam movies, in the Philippines, in the jungle about 60 miles from Manila.

PLAY MISTY FOR ME
(1971, dir: Clint Eastwood)
Clint Eastwood, Jessica Walter, Donna Mills.
● CALIFORNIA

Clint's first movie as director is the original template for *Fatal Attraction*, with Jessica Walter obsessively stalking radio DJ Eastwood. It was made on the director's home territory of Monterey and Carmel on the Pacific coast south of San Francisco. The radio station is Carmel's own KRML. The pier restaurant, where Walter sabotages Eastwood's job interview, is in Monterey. Eastwood's house is on **Spindrift Road, Carmel Highlands** (the same road

as Sharon Stone's Stinson Beach home in *Basic Instinct*). The restaurant, where *Dirty Harry* director Don Siegel tends bar, is still there unchanged:

The bar: Sardine Factory, Monterey

it's the **Sardine Factory, 701 Wave Street** at Prescott, Fisherman's Wharf, Monterey.

PLAYER, THE
(1992, dir: Robert Altman)
Tim Robbins, Greta Scacchi, Whoopi Goldberg.
● CALIFORNIA

Altman bounced back into the limelight with this joyfully scabrous satire on the movie biz after several years of treading water with small-scale theatrical adaptations. The cinema, where paranoid studio exec Tim Robbins meets – and subsequently kills – the writer he thinks is sending death threats, is the **Rialto Theater, 1023 South Fair Oaks Avenue, Pasadena**. It's the same movie house premièring *Stab* in *Scream 2*. Robbins gets a message to meet 'Joe Gilles' (the name of William Holden's

Robbins meets the writer: Rialto Theater, Pasadena

The clifftop restaurant: Geoffrey's, Malibu

Burying the writer: Hollywood Memorial Cemetery, Santa Monica Boulevard

screenwriter character in *Sunset Boulevard*) in the patio of the St James' Club, formerly and now once again, the **Sunset Tower Apartments, 8358 Sunset Boulevard**, West Hollywood. Built in 1931, this luxury block once housed Errol Flynn, Clark Gable, Howard Hughes and the Gabor sisters. Legend has it, John Wayne kept a cow on the balcony. Whatever, it's a stunning zigzag moderne tower, recently restored, and seen in movies as diverse as Jean-Claude Van Damme's *A.W.O.L.*, *Farewell My Lovely* and *Get Shorty*.

Look out for the funeral scene, when the murdered writer is laid to rest. The tomb seen over the shoulder of sinister cop Lyle Lovett bears the family name Douras, the real handle of Marion Davies – born Marion Douras, longtime partner of William Randolph Hearst, the original model for Charles Foster Kane. Also glimpsed is the **Cathedral Mausoleum**, where Rudolph Valentino, Peter Finch and the ashes of Peter Lorre lie. And under the lawn behind the Douras monument lies actress Virginia Rappé, who died at Fatty Arbuckle's notorious sex and booze party at the St Francis Hotel in San Francisco, 1921 (chronicled in detail in the book *Hollywood Babylon*). The cemetery also contains the mortal remains of Tyrone Power, Douglas Fairbanks Sr, Cecil B DeMille, John Huston, Paul Muni and gangster Bugsy Siegel among others. Once a prime spot, adjoining the Paramount lot, the neighbourhood has declined and you'll now find the cemetery tucked away behind a mini-mall. It's the **Hollywood Memorial Cemetery, 6000 Santa Monica Boulevard**, between Gower and Van Ness, Hollywood.

The police station was the old Pasadena Police Station, which stood at Holly and Arroyo Parkway, Pasadena. It has since been demolished, but still extant are the clutch of Tinseltown landmarks Altman uses as backdrops. The star-studded charity ball is held in the **LA County Museum Of Art, 5905 Wilshire Boulevard** (see *LA Story* for details). The clifftop terrace restaurant, site of Burt Reynolds' cameo, is swanky **Geoffrey's, 27400 Pacific Coast Highway** in Malibu (© *310.457.1519*). And even more exclusive is the luxurious spa Robbins retreats to with Greta Scacchi: **Two Bunch Palms, 67-425 Two Bunch Palms Trail, Desert Hot Springs**, north of Palm Springs.

PLEASANTVILLE
(1998, dir: Gary Ross)
Tobey Maguire, Reese Witherspoon, Joan Allen.
● **LOS ANGELES**

Nineties teens find themselves trapped in the perfectly anodyne world of fifties monochrome soapland in Ross's technically brilliant satire. Sadly, there is no Pleasantville. The picture perfect town was built from scratch in Malibu Creek State Park.

PLEIN SOLEIL (aka *Purple Noon/Blazing Sun*)
(1960, dir: René Clément)
Alain Delon, Maurice Ronet, Marie Laforêt.
● **ITALY**

First filming of Patricia Highsmith's *The Talented Mr Ripley*, with Alain Delon as the amoral impostor. Mongebello this time was **Sant' Angelo**, on the southern tip of the island of **Ischia** in the Bay of Naples.

POINT BLANK
(1967, dir: John Boorman)
Lee Marvin, Angie Dickinson, Keenan Wynn.
● **CALIFORNIA**

The opening scene is on **Alcatraz Island** (see *Escape From Alcatraz* for details) in San Francisco Bay. Lee Marvin manages the hitherto impossible feat of swimming the treacherous waters to the city. From here on, the action of the movie is transposed from San Fran to Los Angeles, for its tougher visual appeal. The penthouse is at Santa Monica, and the ultra-modern ranch house is atop the **Curson Avenue Mall**.

POINT BREAK
(1991, dir: Kathryn Bigelow)
Patrick Swayze, Keanu Reeves, Gary Busey.
● **HAWAII; OREGON**

FBI agent Reeves goes undercover as a surfer to catch The Ex-Presidents, a bunch of bank robbers in rubber masks. Set in LA, the Southern California beach

The California beach: Sunset Beach, Oahu

scenes are actually in Hawaii, at the surfers' paradise locations of **Pipeline Beach, Sunset Beach** and **Waimea Bay**, on Oahu's north shore, Route 83. Lori Petty teaches new boy Reeves to surf at Oahu's Sunset Beach. The stormy finale, set at Bell's Beach, Australia, was filmed on the coast of Oregon at **Wheeler**, Ecola State Park, on coastal highway I-101, about twenty miles south of Cannon Beach and 60 miles west of Portland, though the titanic waves, where Swayze (or his stunt double) finally disappears, were filmed back on Oahu at Waimea.

POLLYANNA
(1960, dir: David Swift)
Hayley Mills, Jane Wyman, Karl Malden.
● **CALIFORNIA**

Gruesomely cheery orphan Hayley Mills brings a ray of sunshine into the lives of grumpy old townsfolk in this long, long version of the kiddie classic. The small

Pollyanna's house: Mableton Mansion, Santa Rosa

town is Santa Rosa, northern California, where Pollyanna's house is the **Mableton Mansion, 1015 McDonald Avenue** at 15th Street.

POLTERGEIST
(1982, dir: Tobe Hooper)
JoBeth Williams, Craig T Nelson, Heather O'Rourke.
● **LOS ANGELES**

Producer Spielberg is obviously the driving force, as malign forces enter a suburban household through the television set. The 'Freeling' house is on the small estate of **Forest Hills** in the Simi Valley north of LA.

Poltergeist II was set in Chicago, and featured the **John Hancock Center, North Michigan Avenue** between Chestnut and Delaware Streets.

POPIOL Y DIAMENT (aka *Ashes and Diamonds*)
(1958, dir: Andrzej Wajda)
Zbigniew Cybulski, Ewa Krzyzanowska, Adam Pawlikowski.
● **POLAND**

Cybulski is a James Dean-like partisan caught up in the

confusion of post-War Poland in Wajda's classic, which was filmed in **Lodz** and **Wroclaw**.

PORTRAIT OF JENNIE

(1948, dir: William Dieterle)
Joseph Cotten, Jennifer Jones, Ethel Barrymore.
● **MASSACHUSETTS; NEW YORK CITY**

Strange supernatural romance, with artist Joseph Cotten falling for ethereal muse Jennifer Jones. Set in New York, with filming in **Central Park**, and at the **Tavern on the Green**, Central Park West at 67th Street – a chance to see this much-used location before its 1974 revamp. The lighthouse of the stormy climax is **Graves End Light**, off Boston Harbor.

POSEIDON ADVENTURE, THE

(1972, dir: Ronald Neame)
Gene Hackman, Shelley Winters, Ernest Borgnine.
● **CALIFORNIA**

First of the seventies cycle of disaster movies, featuring the spectacular capsizing of a luxury liner. The pre-capsize *Poseidon* is the **Queen Mary**, permanently berthed at **Pier J, Long Beach** at the south end of Long Beach Freeway, south of LA. The art-deco treat has a restaurant, shops and accommodation in its tiny but glorious staterooms. See more of its plush interior in Ridley Scott's *Someone to Watch Over Me*, where it's used as the New York disco. A myth seems to have grown up that the upside-down ballroom is the Crystal Ballroom of the Biltmore Hotel, downtown LA. In fact, it was a full-size replica of the *Queen Mary*'s ballroom which was built on Stage 6 at the 20th Century Fox studio.

You can see the model liner used for filming among the many model ships in the Los Angeles Maritime Museum, Berth 84 at Los Angeles Harbor in San Pedro, just west of Long Beach.

POSTMAN ALWAYS RINGS TWICE, THE

(1981, dir: Bob Rafelson)
Jack Nicholson, Jessica Lange, John Colicos.
● **CALIFORNIA**

Remake of the 1946 film of James M Cain's novel, set in the fictional Sunland, supposedly near Glendale, which was too urbanised for filming. A patch of land was found on a ridge overlooking the old stagecoach trail near Lake Cachuma, east of Route 154 just north of Santa Barbara, southern California, where the set was built. Here, local barns were painted green, land bought up and allowed to grow wild. The mission-style Shell station was constructed, and the California bungalow erected alongside a gnarled oak. A second oak was planted to justify the name of Cain's roadside café, Twin Oaks.

PREDATOR

(1987, dir: John McTiernan)
Arnold Schwarzenegger, Carl Weathers, Jesse Ventura.
● **MEXICO**

Arnie meets up with a semi-invisible, near-invincible monster in the jungle. After the exciting build-up and demonstrations of truly scary prowess, the creature inex-

plicably resorts to fisticuffs. No contest. The movie was filmed in **Puerto Vallarta**, on the west coast of Mexico, 400 miles from Mexico City (see *The Night of the Iguana*, which put Puerto Vallarta on the map, for details). The set has since been turned into a restaurant, **El Edén**, off Hwy 200, between the Camino Real and La Jolla Mismaloya. It's a difficult place to get to, three miles along a dirt track. And there's no phone. Good luck! The jungle scenes used the lush greenery in the south of the country around **Palenque**.

PREDATOR 2

(1990, dir: Stephen Hopkins)
Danny Glover, Maria Conchita Alonso, Gary Busey.
● **CALIFORNIA**

The police building: Pacific Coast Stock Exchange, Spring Street

The dreadlocked, semi-invisible alien now turns up in futuristic downtown LA. The City of LA Police Administration building is actually the **Pacific Coast Stock Exchange, 618 South Spring Street**, downtown LA. The Lloyd Wright-style Mayan penthouse is a set, but the glorious peacock blue art-deco building, where the creature materialises, is real. It's the **Eastern Columbia Building, 849 South Broadway**, which you can also see in Antonioni's *Zabriskie Point*. The squeaky clean LA subway – there was no such thing in 1990 – is BART, the Bay Area Rapid Transport system beneath Oakland, across the bay from San Francisco.

The creature materialises: Eastern Columbia Building, Broadway

PRETTY BABY

(1978, dir: Louis Malle)
Keith Carradine, Susan Sarandon, Brooke Shields.
● **NEW ORLEANS, LOUISIANA**

Dubious but beautiful (photographed by Bergman collaborator Sven Nykvist) story of Shields' childhood in a turn-of-the-century New Orleans brothel. Bellocq's house is a Gothic mansion at **1221 Orange Street**, New Orleans, though the interiors were shot at the **Columns Hotel, 3811 St Charles Street**.

PRETTY IN PINK

(1986, dir: Howard Deutch)
Molly Ringwald, Andrew McCarthy, Jon Cryer.
● **LOS ANGELES**

Amiable enough teen comedy, written by John Hughes. The prom scene uses the often-seen Crystal Ballroom of the **Biltmore Hotel, 506 South Grand Avenue** overlooking Pershing Square, downtown LA.

PRETTY WOMAN
(1990, dir: Garry Marshall)
Richard Gere, Julia Roberts, Hector Elizondo.
● LOS ANGELES

The snotty clothes shop: Boulemiche Boutique, Santa Monica Boulevard

The Beverly Hills hotel: Regent Beverly Wilshire, Wilshire Boulevard

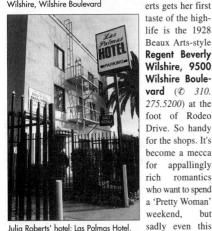
Julia Roberts' hotel: Las Palmas Hotel, Las Palmas Avenue, Hollywood

Fairy tale romance for the eighties, complete with designer labels to die for, as a poverty-row hooker who looks like a movie star crosses the path of a millionaire who also looks like a movie star. Only true love can possibly follow. As all the guide books point out, the intimidatingly luxurious hotel where Roberts gets her first taste of the high-life is the 1928 Beaux Arts-style **Regent Beverly Wilshire, 9500 Wilshire Boulevard** (℃ *310. 275.5200*) at the foot of Rodeo Drive. So handy for the shops. It's become a mecca for appallingly rich romantics who want to spend a 'Pretty Woman' weekend, but sadly even this amount of money can't buy a night in the suite used by Richard and Julia. Although the exterior and the lobby are the real Beverly Wilshire, the rooms were a set built at the Disney Studio in Burbank, and bear little resemblance to the real thing. The scene where the hotel manager teaches Julia Roberts about place settings was filmed in the ballroom of the now-closed **Ambassador Hotel, 3400 Wilshire Boulevard**, midtown (see the 1954 *A Star Is Born* for details).

Down to earth, Julia Roberts plies her trade alongside the tacky souvenir shops of **Hollywood Boulevard**. The Rodeo Drive boutique where she's snubbed by the staff, but gets her revenge bigtime – "Big mistake... huge" – and which goes to great pains to hide its name (come on, we know it's only a movie) is **Boulemiche Boutique**, which is actually on Santa Monica Boulevard, albeit on the corner of Rodeo Drive. But romantics, of course, would much rather check out the fire escape Richard Gere climbs to the strains of *La Traviata* than the overblown grandios-

ity of the Beverly Wilshire. It's attached to the **Las Palmas Hotel, 1738 Las Palmas Avenue**, just off Hollywood Boulevard.

PRICK UP YOUR EARS
(1987, dir: Stephen Frears)
Gary Oldman, Alfred Molina, Vanessa Redgrave.
● LONDON; MOROCCO

Neat Alan Bennett adaptation of John Lahr's biography of playwright Joe Orton, shot on various locations around London. For Orton and Kenneth Halliwell's flat, which was in Noel Road, Islington, N1, a house south of London in **Croydon** was substituted. Orton's boyhood in Leicester used nearby **Thornton Heath**, just north of Croydon. The exotic holiday is Morocco.

PRIMA DELLA RIVOLUZIONE (aka *Before the Revolution*)
(1964, dir: Bernardo Bertolucci)
Francesco Barilli, Adriana Asti, Morando Morandini.
● PARMA, ITALY

Bertolucci's second film is a loose adaptation of Stendhal's *Charterhouse of Parma*, with Francesco Barilli as a young bourgeois who carries on a passionate affair with his Milanese aunt, Asti, while tussling with the complexities of Euro-Communism. The movie was made in **Parma** itself (but don't go searching – there is no Charterhouse. It features only at the very end of the novel, when the hero retires to it, "in the woods by the Po, a couple of leagues from Sacca"), where Barilli and Asti hang around the main square, **Piazza Garibaldi**. The medieval church, where Cristina Pariset is found at the beginning is the 12th century **Baptistery** of Parma's **Cathedral of St Maria Assunta**, Piazza di Duomo. Barilli mooches around the aftermath of the Communist Summer Rally in the **Park Ducal**, the grounds of a Farnese palace over the Ponte Verdi from the town centre, while Asti and Barelli attend a performance of Verdi's *Macbeth*, at the **Teatro Regio** on the **via Garibaldi**.

PRIME OF MISS JEAN BRODIE, THE
(1969, dir: Ronald Neame)
Maggie Smith, Robert Stephens, Celia Johnson.
● EDINBURGH; MIDDLESEX

Maggie Smith takes over from Vanessa Redgrave, who originally played Brodie on stage to great acclaim, in the film of Muriel Spark's thirties-set novel. Rod McKuen growls what must be the least appropriate title song ever. A backdrop of real Edinburgh locations (minus TV aerials) includes the old **Grassmarket**; the **Vennel**; **Greyfriars Kirkyard**; the **Scottish National Museum** and **Edinburgh Castle** itself. Miss Brodie's home is the Victorian house at **5 Admiral Terrace**, opposite Lothian Regional Council Office, southwest of the city centre. Teddy Lloyd's studio is the Mary Tudor house at **1**

Miss Brodie's house: Admiral Terrace, Edinburgh

Marcia Blaine: Edinburgh Academy, Henderson Row

Candlemaker Row, on the corner of Merchant Street opposite Greyfriars Kirkyard. Although interiors were built in the studio, Marcia Blaine School was the Donaldson School for Deaf and Dumb Children, now part of **Edinburgh Academy, Henderson Row**. Cramond, the estate to which Miss Brodie retreats at weekends, is **Barnbougle Castle**, just outside Edinburgh by the Firth of Forth. Part of the Dalmeny Estate, it's home to the Earl and Countess of Roseberry. The library of Marcia Blaine was in Grim's Dyke House – now the **Grim's Dyke House Hotel** – former home of WS Gilbert (who drowned in the lake here) at **Old Redding** in Middlesex (see *The Curse of the Crimson Altar* for details).

PRINCE AND THE SHOWGIRL, THE
(1957, dir: Laurence Olivier)
Marilyn Monroe, Laurence Olivier, Sybil Thorndike.
● LONDON

The legendary mismatch of Olivier and Monroe in an adaptation of Terence Rattigan's *The Sleeping Prince* was shot almost entirely in the studio at Pinewood, apart from the scenes of the Foreign Office, filmed in **St James**, SW1. The fictitious theatre, where Monroe appears, is optically superimposed onto a shot of Trafalgar Square.

PRINCE OF FOXES
(1949, dir: Henry King)
Tyrone Power, Orson Welles, Everett Sloane.
● ITALY

The Borgias reinvented as a Warners gangster movie, filmed on a swathe of real Italian locations: in **Rome**; **Florence**; **Venice**; **San Gimignano**; **Terracina**; **San Marino** and the **Chapel of Palazzo Publico, Siena**.

PRISONER OF SECOND AVENUE, THE
(1975, dir: Melvin Frank)
Jack Lemmon, Anne Bancroft, Gene Saks.
● NEW YORK CITY

Blacker than usual Neil Simon, with married couple Lemmon and Bancroft driven to the verge of madness by urban life. Look out for Broadway director Gene Saks as Lemmon's brother and future Oscar-winners Sylvester Stallone (as a Central Park non-mugger) and F Murray Abraham (as a cab driver). Lemmon works, until unemployment strikes, on **Madison Avenue** at 47th Street. The apartment is on the Upper East Side, on the 14th floor of **385 East 88th Street** at Second Avenue, Yorkville.

PRIVATE FUNCTION, A
(1984, dir: Malcolm Mowbray)
Michael Palin, Maggie Smith, Richard Griffiths.
● YORKSHIRE

Alan Bennett's wartime comedy, with Maggie Smith turning into a suburban Lady Macbeth, urging her chiropodist

husband to evade the rigours of rationing by killing an illegal pig, was made in the village of **Barnoldswick**, about ten miles west of Skipton, Yorkshire, in **Bradford**, and to the east of Skipton on **Ilkley Moor**.

Barnoldswick

The cinema, where Maggie Smith plays the old fashioned organ, is further south. It's the **Regal Cinema, 2 Boroma Way, Henley-on-Thames**, Oxfordshire.

The Parade: Albert Road, Barnoldswick

PRIVATE LIFE OF SHERLOCK HOLMES, THE
(1970, dir: Billy Wilder)
Robert Stephens, Colin Blakely, Genevieve Page.
● LONDON; SCOTLAND; YORKSHIRE

Hugely underrated, affectionately romantic send-up of the Holmes myth, during which Holmes manages to chase the Loch Ness monster. The mysterious castle really is on Loch Ness. One of Scotland's largest, it's **Castle Urquhart**, a mile and a half southeast of Drumnadrochit on the Loch's west shore, about thirteen miles southwest of Inverness. It's open to the public.

The convincing-looking Baker Street is a vast and expensive set, 150 yards long, and built in perspective at Pinewood by veteran designer Alexander Trauner. It was subsequently much re-used. The railway scenes were filmed on the **Keighley and Worth Valley Railway** in Yorkshire.

PRIZZI'S HONOR
(1985, dir: John Huston)
Jack Nicholson, Kathleen Turner, Anjelica Huston.
● NEW YORK CITY; LOS ANGELES; LAS VEGAS, NEVADA

Nicholson and Turner are mob hitpersons, falling in love but hired to rub each other out in Huston's wonderful black comedy. The NYC neighbourhood is Brooklyn Heights, the well-to-do Italian-American area also seen in *Moonstruck*.

The opening wedding scene, where Nicholson first lays eyes on Turner, is at the

Nicholson's place: the Breukelen Apartments

Don Corrado's: Pierrepoint Place, Brooklyn

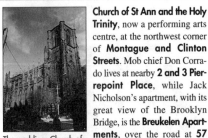

The wedding: Church of St Ann and the Holy Trinity

Church of St Ann and the Holy Trinity, now a performing arts centre, at the northwest corner of **Montague and Clinton Streets**. Mob chief Don Corrado lives at nearby **2 and 3 Pierrepoint Place**, while Jack Nicholson's apartment, with its great view of the Brooklyn Bridge, is the **Breukelen Apartments**, over the road at **57 Montague Street**. He contemplates marriage or murder on the nearby **Brooklyn Heights Promenade**.

PROBLEM CHILD

(1990, dir: Dennis Dugan)
John Ritter, Amy Yasbeck, Jack Warden.
● **TEXAS**

Sub-John Hughes kid-from-hell movie pitched somewhere between *Home Alone* and *The Omen*, made in and around Dallas, Texas. Directed by nerdy comedy actor Dennis Dugan (*The Spaceman and King Arthur*), who plays one of the dads, and with a theme song by the Beach Boys. St Brutus, the orphanage Ritter and Yasbeck collect their bundle of joy from was the Lady of Victory Catholic Boarding School, since closed, **3300 Hemphill Street, Fort Worth**. Junior's penpal is serving time in the **Old City Jail, Main Street** at Harwood, where Lee Harvey Oswald was held after the shooting of JFK.

PRODUCERS, THE

(1967, dir: Mel Brooks)
Zero Mostel, Gene Wilder, Kenneth Mars.
● **NEW YORK CITY**

Brooks' best comedy, set and made in New York at the **Production Center Studios, 221 West 26th Street**. The great moment, when Wilder's mousy accountant finally submits to Mostel's seduction and the fountain bursts into life, was shot in the central court of the **Lincoln Center**, Broadway between 62nd and 66th Streets.

PSYCHO

(1960, dir: Alfred Hitchcock)
Anthony Perkins, Janet Leigh, Martin Balsam.
● **LOS ANGELES; PHOENIX, ARIZONA**

Filmed at the Revue Studios, the television branch of Universal Studios rented for Hitchcock by Paramount. Filming began on Stage 18-A (which is where the shower murder – arguably the most famous scene in movies – was filmed). Marion Crane's car journey was, of course, done with rear projection. The road shots used were filmed on I-99 between Fresno and Bakersfield, California. A Second Unit filmed the opening shot

The Bates Motel house: Universal Studio, Hollywood

The garage: Century West BMW, Lankershim Boulevard

of Phoenix, Arizona, where Marion supposedly lives. Notice the Christmas decorations? The shot was filmed at the beginning of December, but Christmas doesn't get mentioned and the weather seems surprisingly hot. To cover this glitch, the time and date are added over the shot ('Friday, December the Eleventh...'), but the season is never referred to again.

The film was shot on a tiny budget, using a TV crew, mostly on the studio lot. The swamp, where Norman disposes of Marion's car, was intended to be filmed on location at Grizzly Island near Fairfield, north of San Francisco, but budget constraints meant that Hitch finally used 'Falls Lake' on the Universal-Revue backlot. The lake is named for the artificial falls built in the studio's early days. The fictitious town of Fairvale was simply the Universal lot's 'Main Street', and Fairvale Presbyterian Church can be seen on Circle Drive here. Fairvale Courthouse was the studio's main executive office, which has since been demolished. And, of course, the Bates house is now a main attraction on the Universal Studio Tour. The entrance is at **100 Universal City Plaza**, Universal City off the Ventura Freeway north of Hollywood (✆ *818.508.9600*).

A couple of real locations were used, however: Marion is stopped by the cop on I-5, the Golden State Freeway at **Gorman**, north of LA. And the used car lot where Marion changes her vehicle is still in operation. It's now **Century West BMW, 4270 Lankershim Boulevard** at Whipple Street and Valley Spring, just north of the studio. In 1960 it was Harry Maher's Used Car Lot, well stocked with Edsels, Fairlanes and Mercury's – one of the sponsors of Hitch's TV show was Ford.

PSYCHO

(1998, dir: Gus Van Sant)
Vince Vaughn, Anne Heche, Julianne Moore.
● **LOS ANGELES; PHOENIX, ARIZONA**

Oddball shot-for-shot remake in dazzling colour. The motel is the original, on the Universal lot in Hollywood, with a new house built in front of the familiar old Gothic mansion. The scene with the traffic cop was filmed at exactly the same spot at **Gorman**, north of LA, as the original.

PSYCHO II

(1983, dir: Richard Franklin)
Anthony Perkins, Vera Miles, Meg Tilly.
● **LOS ANGELES**

Having served 22 years in a mental institution, Norman

Bates returns to Fairvale. Marion Crane's sister is less than thrilled, as bodies start turning up again, in this jokey but unscary sequel.

The Bates house was moved when the Universal backlot was redesigned to accommodate the lucrative studio tour, and the motel set was torn down. When *Psycho II* went into production, the house had to be moved again, to a location which would match the original. Only a 40-foot section of the motel was rebuilt below, and the rest – neon sign included – is faked in with FX. Many of the original props and set dressing were hunted down in the studio to furnish the Bates Motel in its original style.

PSYCHO III
(1986, dir: Anthony Perkins)
Anthony Perkins, Diana Scarwid, Jeff Fahey.
● LOS ANGELES

Norman Bates at the tea dance: Park Plaza Hotel, South Park View Street

Perkins himself takes over direction, with Scarwid as a suicidal nun holed up in, of all places, the Bates Motel. The tea dance, where Norman takes his date, is the restaurant of the **Park Plaza Hotel, 607 South Park View Street**, downtown LA – later used as the hotel's breakfast room (see *New York, New York* for details of the Park Plaza).

PULP FICTION
(1994, dir: Quentin Tarantino)
John Travolta, Samuel L Jackson, Bruce Willis.
● LOS ANGELES

Tarantino's follow up to *Reservoir Dogs*, filmed around LA. The diner where Tim Roth and Amanda Plummer stage the hold-up was the Hawthorne Grill, 13763 Hawthorne Boulevard at 137th Street, Hawthorne, south of Los Angeles Airport. The grill stood empty for a while, and has now been demolished. Also vanished without trace is the motel where Bruce Willis hides out after winning the fight. It was the River Glen Motel, which stood at 2934 Riverside Drive off Los Feliz Boulevard, just to the west of the Golden State Freeway southeast of Griffith Park. The apartment block where Vince and Jules sample Big Kahuna burgers before wiping out the guys who crossed Marsellus, is on **Van Ness Avenue** just north of Hollywood Boulevard, Hollywood. Jack Rabbit Slim's is a huge set built in the film company's warehouse in Culver City. The raised dancefloor in the center of the diner is shaped,

Battle of the Giants: the Raymond Theatre, Pasadena

in case you hadn't noticed, as a tachometer, as an homage to Howard Hawks' *Red Line 7000* and Elvis Presley's *Speedway*. The dining areas are

Honey-Bunny and Pumpkin: Hawthorne Grill, Hawthorne

six vintage convertibles. The exterior is a disused bowling alley. The idea, though it's a long, long way away, was supposedly based on either architect John Lautner's diners or Ed Debevic's fifties-themed diner, 134 North La Cienega Boulevard near Beverly Hills. Marsellus' place is in **Beverly Hills**, the home of druggies Eric Stoltz and Rosanna Arquette is in **Echo Park**. The venue for the Battle of the Giants, where Bruce Willis makes a hasty exit after the fight, is the **Raymond Theatre, 129 North Raymond Avenue**, Pasadena.

PUMP UP THE VOLUME
(1990, dir: Alan Moyle)
Christian Slater, Scott Paulin, Ellen Greene.
● CALIFORNIA

Slater is the nerdy schoolkid moonlighting as subversive DJ Happy Harry Hard-on, stirring up insurrection in the fictitious dullsville town of Paradise Hills, Arizona. The town is actually **Saugus**, north of LA off I-5 east of Valencia. Behind all the 'HHH' logos of Hubert H Humphrey High School is **Saugus High School**.

PURPLE ROSE OF CAIRO, THE
(1985, dir: Woody Allen)
Mia Farrow, Jeff Daniels, Danny Aiello.
● NEW JERSEY; NEW YORK STATE

One of Allen's best movies, packing a wealth of ideas into its 82 minutes. Farrow is Aiello's bullied wife, who escapes into the fantasy world of movies at every opportunity, until her screen idol pops out of the silver screen into real life. The small town Allen chose for the thirties setting is **Piermont**, off I-9W, on the west bank of the Hudson River, New York State. The Jewel theater exterior is no more than a façade, masking a parking lot on Piermont's Main Street, but you can find the interior of the Jewel in south Brooklyn, in Woody Allen's home district of Midwood, toward Coney Island. It was the Kent Movie Theater, now the **Kent Triplex, 1168 Coney Island Avenue**. The deserted amusement park, where Daniels takes Farrow, is **Bertrand's Island, Mount Arlington**, north of Route 80 near Lake Hopatcong, northern New Jersey. The carousel is at **Prospect Park Zoo** in Brooklyn. The whorehouse, where Daniels begins to discover the joy of sex, is a shelter for the homeless on **West 71st Street**, belonging to Grace and St Paul's Lutheran Church, used also in *Radio Days*.

Q - THE WINGED SERPENT

(1982, dir: Larry Cohen)
Michael Moriarty, David Carradine, Candy Clark.

● **NEW YORK CITY**

A neat, satirical little monster movie written and directed by low-budget expert Larry Cohen. Michael Moriarty is splendidly sleazy as the smalltime crook who discovers the secret of a creature flying about chomping the heads off New Yorkers. The serpent of the title (which turns out to be an Aztec god, no less) has great taste in Art Deco architecture, choosing as its lair a cosy loft just beneath the gleaming spire of the **Chrysler Building, 405 Lexington Avenue** at 42nd Street.

The serpent's den: Chrysler Building

QUADROPHENIA

(1979, dir: Franc Roddam)
Phil Daniels, Leslie Ash, Sting.

● **LONDON; SUSSEX**

The Who's album is used as a framework for teen angst and a recreation of the early sixties running battles between the supersharp Mods and the leatherclad Rockers. The Who hailed originally from Shepherds Bush in west London, and this is where the London scenes are set. Jimmy rides

The Mods' hangout: Alfredo's, Islington

his scooter along **Goldhawk Road**, and it's from Goldhawk Road tube station that his greaser pal is chased into **Shepherd's Bush Market** and beaten up. The Rockers attack Spider after his scooter breaks down outside the **Bramley Arms**, Notting Hill. Opposite the Bramley is the scrapyard where Pete works. The Mods' London hangout is **Alfredo's, 4-6 Essex Road, Islington**, just north of the Angel tube station. This art deco institution, dating from the twenties, can

The riot: East Street, Brighton

Bellboy: Grand Hotel, Brighton

also be seen in *Mojo*.

Down in Brighton, the rival gangs congregate by the **Palace Pier**, in front of the now-closed Heart and Hand – then one of Brighton's most famous gay bars. The marquee of the cinema next door is advertising *Heaven Can Wait* – the Warren Beatty movie released in (whoops) 1978. East along the seafront, the Mods meet for breakfast at the **Waterfront Cafe** at the **Peter Pan Play Area, Madeira Drive**. Opposite the pier entrance you can see the exterior of the ballroom, where Jimmy upstages Ace by leaping from the balcony, which is now the **Brighton Sealife Centre**. Just across Old Steine is **East Street**, where the rioters get hemmed in by the law and

The alleyway: East Street, Brighton

The dance hall: Brighton Sea Life Centre

The café: Kings Road at Ship Street

Jimmy finally manages a quickie with Steph in the narrow alley by number 11, leading to Little East Street. The wrecked café is a little to the west, on the seafront at the corner of **Kings Road** and **Ship Street**.

The hotel, where Jimmy is ultimately disillusioned by the sight of Ace working as a bellboy is, of course, the **Grand Hotel, Kings Road** (℃ *01273.224300, www.grandbrighton.co.uk*). The spectacular white cliffs, off which Jimmy ultimately takes a dive on Ace's jazzed-up scooter, are almost twenty miles east of Brighton, at **Beachy Head**, southwest of Eastbourne.

QUATERMASS XPERIMENT, THE (aka *The Creeping Unknown*)

(1955, dir: Val Guest)
Brian Donlevy, Jack Warner, Richard Wordsworth.

● **BERKSHIRE; LONDON**

Film of Nigel Kneale's excellent and scary fifties TV series, with astronaut Richard Wordsworth succumbing to an alien fungus. His rocket falls to earth in a field

The ambulance races to the crash: Bray High Street

The mutating astronaut steals drugs: Queen Charlotte Street, Windsor

alongside Bray Studios near **Bray**, southeast of Maidenhead in Berkshire. The ambulances race through **Bray High Street** to the A308, past Bray Garage, which is still there, unchanged from its appearance in the film.

The chemist shop, where a slowly mutating Wordsworth steals drugs, is **Woods of Windsor, Queen Charlotte Street** (at 51 feet, ten inches, a plaque officially records this as the shortest street in Britain), a perfumery still going strong, just off Windsor High Street. The Frankenstein-like riverside scene with the little girl was filmed at **Deptford Creek**, south London.

But it's back to Windsor for the discovery of the slime trail glooping 30 feet up a sheer wall, which was filmed in the narrow alleyway of **Goswell Hill**, off Peascod Street. There's not a frame of the real Westminster Abbey in the climax of the movie, with the monster holed up in the abbey's scaffolding. After permission to film at the real location was, not surprisingly, refused, sections of the interior and exterior were recreated in the studio.

QUATERMASS II (aka *Enemy From Space*)
(1957, dir: Val Guest)
Brian Donlevy, John Longden, William Franklyn.
● **ESSEX; HERTFORDSHIRE.**

The second adaptation of a Nigel Kneale TV series is a genuinely frightening low-budget sci-fi. A hush-hush military research station, supposedly manufacturing artificial food, houses giant blobs from space.

The about-to-be-developed landscape is is the under-construction **Hemel Hempstead** new town in Hertfordshire. The military installation itself is Shell's giant Haven Refinery at **Canvey Island**, near to Southend-on-Sea in Essex.

QUATRE CENTS COUPS, LES (aka *The Four Hundred Blows*)
(1959, dir: François Truffaut)
Jean-Pierre Léaud, Patrick Auffay, Claire Maurier.
● **PARIS**

Truffaut's first feature film, introducing the character of Antoine Doinel as an adolescent, is one of the key movies of the French Nouvelle Vague movement, which moved film-making out of the studio and onto the streets of Paris. Doinel's house is **82 rue Marcadet**, running from Guy Moquet metro to Marcadet Poissonniers metro in the 16th Arrondissement. The kids insult a priest on the steps of **Sacre Coeur** in Montmartre.

Insulting the priest: Sacre Coeur, Montmartre

QUIET MAN, THE
(1952, dir: John Ford)
John Wayne, Maureen O'Hara, Barry Fitzgerald.
● **IRELAND**

Ex-boxer Wayne returns to the family roots to claim a wife in this colourful Irish romp, unlikely to appeal to feminists. Hard-man Ford, proud of his Irish ancestry, actually made the movie on location in Ireland around the village of **Cong**, between Lough Mask and Lough Corrib, Connemara; in the **Maam Valley** and in the grounds of **Ashford Castle**. The railway scene is **Ballyglunin**, on the line between Sligo and Limerick.

The Quiet Man Hostel on Abbey Street, in Cong, shows the movie every night, and also has a *Quiet Man* locations tour.

QUIZ SHOW
(1994, dir: Robert Redford)
Ralph Fiennes, John Turturro, Paul Scofield.
● **NEW YORK CITY; NEW YORK STATE**

The TV studio: NBC Building, Rockefeller Plaza

Redford's recreation of the famous fifties scandal, when TV execs ensured that handsome WASP Charles Van Doren triumphed on top-rating quiz show *Twenty-One* over Jewish Herbie Stempel. *Twenty-One* was recorded at the art deco **NBC Building, Rockefeller Plaza**, though the interiors of the NBC Studios of 1958 were recreated inside the **Red Zone, 440 West 45th Street**, a huge Manhattan disco (previously used for scenes for *The Godfather Part III*).

Herbie Stempel's blue-collar neighbourhood is Astoria, Queens, while the Van Doren patrician family home in Cornwall, Connecticut is actually in Ossining, New York State. Columbia University, itself a familiar film location for such movies as *Ghostbusters*, is here played by **Fordham University**, an 85-acre campus on **Webster Avenue** in the Bronx. As the scandal emerges, the Congressional hearings are held in the **New York Historical Society, 170 Central Park West** at 77th Street. The NBC Executive Offices are **Murdoch Hall**, a thirties art deco building over the Hudson River in Jersey City. Other locations include the lobby of the **Roosevelt Hotel, East 45th Street** at Madison Avenue midtown NY (© *212.661.9600*).

R

RABID

(1976, dir: David Cronenberg)
Marilyn Chambers, Frank Moore, Joe Silver.
● QUEBEC, CANADA

Cronenberg's early visceral horror has porn star Marilyn Chambers developing a bloodsucking growth in her armpit after experimental surgery. The hospital is **Notre Dame Hospital, 1560 Sherbrooke Street East**; the shopping mall is the **Cavendish Mall, 5800 Boulevard Cavendish** at Côte St Luc, and the hotel is the expensive **Hotel Meridian, 4 Complexe Desjardins** (℗ *514.285.1450*), downtown.

RADIO DAYS

(1987, dir: Woody Allen)
Woody Allen, Mia Farrow, Seth Green.
● NEW YORK CITY; NEW JERSEY

Allen usually borrows from Ingmar Bergman, but occasionally he takes Fellini as model. If *Stardust Memories* is his *8 1/2*, then *Radio Days*, in its fragmentary, evocative nostalgia, is a New York *Amarcord*. With his usual uncanny eye for period locations, Woody Allen conjures up both the working class neighbourhood of Queens and the stylish Manhattan of the forties. The neighbourhood of Little Joe (the young Allen) is Rockaway, the spit of land on the Atlantic coast of south Queens. His house is **180 Beach 115th Street** between Ocean Promenade – the Boardwalk – and **Rockaway Beach Boulevard**, the neighbourhood shopping centre, from the roof of which the schoolkids watch their teacher's naked dance. The radio repair shop, on the way back from which Little Joe meets his father working as a cab driver, is a few blocks east on **Beach 97th Street**. Rockaway's Playland, the amusement park Joe passes on the way to school while

Little Joe's neighbourhood: Beach 115th Street, Rockaway Park

coveting the Masked Avenger Secret Compartment Ring, stood at 185 Beach 97th Street, until it was torn down in 1987, shortly after *Radio Days* was filmed.

Little Joe's childhood home, and the house of his 'Communist' neighbours: Beach 115th Street, Rockaway Park

Built as Thompson's Amusement Park in 1938, its huge Atom Smasher rollercoaster, seen in the movie, was the one used in the 1952 spectacular, *This Is Cinerama*.

Watching the naked teacher: Rockaway Beach Boulevard at Beach 115th Street

Joe and his friends hang out at **Breezy Point**, on the north shore at the far west end of the Rockaway peninsula, and at **Coney Island Fishing Pier**, on the Boardwalk at 21st Street. Joe's school, where the anatomically explicit snowman is built, is **PS70, 30-45 42nd Street** in Manhattan, and the Hebrew class, where Joe steals the money meant for the Jewish National Fund, is the **Synagogue Congregation Mogen Abraham** on the Lower East Side.

Kids on the rooftop: Rockaway Beach Boulevard at Beach 115th Street

Little Joe gets a chemistry set: Macy's art deco entrance, West 34th Street

Listening to the radio: Nam Wah Tea Parlor, Doyers Street, Chinatown

Aunt Bea and her beau take young Joe to the movies at **Radio City Music Hall, 1260 Sixth Avenue**, where he's understandably overwhelmed by the spectacular gold-leaf foyer (also seen in *Annie*). The fast food establishment they visit was Horn and Hardart, then one of the few remaining automats in the city, which stood at 200 East 42nd Street. The site has since been redeveloped. Still going strong, though, is **Macy's, 34th Street** between Seventh Avenue and Broadway, where Joe gets a chemistry set with Aunt Bea's winnings from the radio quiz. The family bumps into the snotty radio whizz-kid at **Prospect Park Zoo, Flatbush Avenue** in Prospect Park, Brooklyn (℗ *718.399.7399*).

On the other side of the tracks, the nightclub, frequented by Manhattan sophisticates Roger and Irene, where Sally works as a cigarette girl, is the King Cole Dining Room of the **St Regis-Sheraton Hotel, Fifth Avenue** at East 55th Street (℗ *212.753.4500*). In fact, women weren't allowed into the King Cole Room until 1950 – and then only after 4pm. Roger and Irene's chic chrome-and-glass townhouse was one of the city's most famous gay discos, the Paradise Garage, which stood at **84 King Street**. Pumping out garage music from the late seventies through the eighties, its doors finally closed in 1987, though the building still remains. The broadcast network office, from where the 'Court of Human Emotions' is broadcast, is **Metropolitan Life's North Building, Madison Avenue** between 24th and 25th Streets. Sally gets sacked after recording a laxative ad at the **RCA Building, 50th Street** between Fifth and Sixth Avenues.

Among the bars where people gather to follow the tragedy of the little girl trapped down a well is the **Nam Wah Tea Parlor, 13 Doyers Street** at Pell Street, NY's oldest dim sum parlor, situated on an oddly angled street in Chinatown. The Great Tonino's is on **West 71st Street** (a location used in *The Purple Rose of Cairo*). The 'Malt shop counter', where the girls swoon to the radio crooner, is **Brummer's Confectionary** (sic), **Grand Street**, in Jersey City, New Jersey.

Among other New York landmarks used are the **Brill Building, 1619 Broadway** (see *The Sweet Smell of Success* for details of the Brill); and the **New Yorker Hotel, 481 Eighth Avenue** (*℗ 212.971.0101*). The ballroom also appeared, albeit differently decorated, in *Bullets Over Broadway*. Studio sets were built at the Kaufman-Astoria Studios, 34-12 36th Street in Queens.

RAGING BULL
(1980, dir: Martin Scorsese)
Robert De Niro, Cathy Moriarty, Joe Pesci.
● **NEW YORK CITY; NEW YORK STATE; LOS ANGELES**

Another masterpiece from the Scorsese-De Niro teaming, probably the best boxing picture ever, regularly cropping up in Ten Best lists, and made four years after *Rocky* scooped the Oscar for Best Picture.

The open-air pool where De Niro meets Cathy Moriarty is the **Carmine Street Public Pools, Seventh Avenue South** at Clarkson street in Greenwich Village. The long-shot ring and crowd scenes were filmed in LA at the **Olympic Auditorium, Grand Avenue** at Olympic Boulevard. Built for the 1932 Olympics, it was the site of the climactic fights in – yes – *Rocky I, II* and *III*. The dazzling fight sequences were shot in the controlled environment of the studio. The nursing home was the Lido Beach Hotel, now a private condo, on **Maple Boulevard, Lido Beach**

The outdoor pool: Carmine Street Public Pools, Greenwich Village

at Broadway on Long Island's southern shore. The Florida scenes were shot at **San Pedro**, Los Angeles Harbor west of Long Beach, kitted out with a couple of palm trees.

RAIDERS OF THE LOST ARK
(1981, dir: Steven Spielberg)
Harrison Ford, Karen Allen, Paul Freeman.
● **HAWAII; TUNISIA; FRANCE; CALIFORNIA**

The opening South American scenes of Spielberg's glorified Saturday morning feature were actually filmed on the garden isle of **Kauai** in Hawaii, to which the director would return for *Jurassic Park*. The location is the **Huleia River**, leading to Fern Grotto on the east coast, north of Lihue.

The classroom, where Ford teaches archaeology, is the **Conservatory of Music of the University of the Pacific, Stockton**, northern California. Studio sets, including the Raven Bar, the Peruvian temple, and the Well of Souls were built at Elstree in Hertfordshire. The German sub (it's the submarine from *Das Boot*) was shot at a genuine ex-German man base at **La Rochelle**, France.

The Egyptian scenes used the deserts of Tunisia – the vast dry salt lake of **Chott El Jerid** and, east toward the Algerian border, the oasis towns of **Nefta** and **Tozeur**. The film shares locations with *Star Wars*, including **Sidi Bouhel**, now known as Star Wars Canyon, east of Tozeur on the edge of the Chott. The ending was shot on the steps of one of the government buildings in downtown San Francisco.

RAILWAY CHILDREN, THE
(1970, dir: Lionel Jeffries)
Jenny Agutter, Bernard Cribbins, Dinah Sheridan.
● **YORKSHIRE**

Fine filming of E Nesbit's famous book about three Edwardian children and their mother, who have to move to Yorkshire when daddy is wrongly imprisoned. Bradford Recreation Division helpfully produces a guide to *The Railway Children* walk, which covers the main locations (info from the Countryside Warden Service, Third Floor, Provincial House, Bradford BD11 1NP (*℗ 01274. 752666 or 01535. 423329*).

The railway line used for film-

The railway station: Oakworth, Keighley and Worth Valley Railway

Perks' house: Oakworth

Three chimneys: Bent's Farm, Oxenhope

The doctor's house: Haworth Parsonage, Haworth

The Post Office: Tweed Room, Haworth

The paperchase: Mytholmes Tunnel

"You... you're the Rain Man": Big 8 Motel, El Reno

The gas station: Cogar

ing is the **Keighley and Worth Valley Railway**, mainly on the stretch between Keighley and Oxenhope, about five miles to the south. The station itself is **Oakworth**, about halfway between the two towns. Station-master Perks' house is just over the level crossing from the station. The children's home, Three Chimneys, can be found a couple of miles to the south of Oakworth in the village of **Oxenhope**. It's **Bent's Farm**, a little to the north of Oxenhope Station.

The village seen in the film is **Haworth**, halfway between Oakworth and Oxenhope, famous as home to the Brontës. You can see the shops, where the children collect presents for Perks' birthday, on **Main Street**, **Lodge Street** (the ironmonger's where the children get a shovel) and **Church Lane** (where the **Tweed Room** shop, with its little flight of stone steps, stood in for the Post Office and General Store). The Doctor's house is in fact the **Bronte Parsonage** itself, south of the village. You'll find the tunnel, where schoolboy Jim injures his leg during the paperchase, north of Haworth toward Oakworth. It's the **Mytholmes Tunnel, Mytholmes Lane**, while a few yards south on the line is the **Metal Bridge** seen in the 'goodbye' shot.

RAIN MAN

(1988, dir: Barry Levinson)
Dustin Hoffman, Tom Cruise, Valeria Golino.
● OHIO; KENTUCKY; INDIANA; OKLAHOMA; NEVADA; CALIFORNIA

Hard-hearted Cruise travels from LA, where his business operates out of the docks of **San Pedro**, to Cincinnati, after hearing of his father's death. The Oscar-grabbing movie travelled all over the US, but was based in Cincinnati for four weeks, using Indiana and Kentucky locations.

Skill with cards: Caesar's Palace, Las Vegas

The Cincinnati Trust, where Cruise learns the whereabouts of the $3 million trust fund, is the lobby of the **Dixie Terminal, 120 East Fourth Street** at Walnut Street, downtown Cincinnati. If Wallbrook, the home where he finds brother Raymond, looks a bit religiose, with statues of the virgin in the walls, that's because it's **St Anne's Convent, 1000 Saint Anne Drive, Melbourne**, just to the southeast of Cincinnati over the Ohio River on Route 8, Kentucky. Built 1919 by architect Howard McClorey, it now houses a Montessori school.

It's on to **Newport**, Kentucky, for the first night away from Wallbrook, spent at the **Vernon Manor Hotel, 400 Oak Street** (© 513.281.3300, www.vernon-manor.com), a 1924 landmark in the historic uptown district, loosely modelled on much-used movie location Hatfield House, Hertfordshire, in the UK. The bridge Cruise and Hoffman cross leaving town is the **John A Roebling Suspension Bridge**, a prototype for the designer's later Brooklyn Bridge in New York.

Also in Newport is the café where Hoffman reveals his amazing skills, by remembering the waitress's phone number and counting scattered toothpicks. It's **Pompilio's Bar and Restaurant, 600 Washington Avenue** (© 606.581.3065). A southern Italian restaurant, built in 1933, Pompilio's was granted one of the US's first post-Prohibition liquor licences.

To Ohio again, to **Greater Cincinnati International Airport**, where Hoffman quotes a few useful statistics, decides that road travel is preferable and the two take the highway, I-275, which happens to be the ring road around Cincinnati. Cruise and Hoffman's childhood home is a Tudor-style mansion on **Beechcrest Lane**, in Cincinnati's East Walnut Hills district, on the Ohio River's northern shore, northeast of downtown. Their father is buried in **Evergreen Cemetery**, Newport.

The film's crew based themselves in Oklahoma City for the cross-States journey. The motel in Amarillo, Texas, where Cruise realises that Hoffman is his imaginary friend, 'the Rain Man', is the **Big 8$ Motel, 1705 East 66th Highway**, El Reno, on I-40 about fifteen miles west of Oklahoma City. The sign, 'Amarillo's Finest', was added for the movie, and, much to the confusion of passing motorists, it's been retained as a feature of the motel. Cruise and Hoffman's room was 117. The gas station, where they stop to make a phone call, is a disused, and now once again dilapidated, stop at **Cogar**, about ten miles south of El Reno over the South Canadian River. Twenty miles west of El Reno, south of I-40, is **Hinton**, where Hoffman gets to watch Judge Wapner on the farmhouse TV. Way up about twenty miles north of Oklahoma City, on I-35, is the town of **Guthrie**, where Cruise takes Hoffman to see the doctor at the Guthrie Clinic, on the corner of **Oklahoma Street** and **Division Street**.

More road filming took place in South Nevada, *en route* to Las Vegas. The casino, where Hoffman demonstrates his skill with cards and Cruise teaches him to dance in the hotel suite, is the recently-enlarged **Caesar's Palace, 3570 Las Vegas Boulevard South** (© *702.731.7110*).

The LA mansion, where Cruise battles it out with the medical profession for custody of Hoffman, is the **Wattles Mansion, 1824 North Curson Avenue** on the south end of Runyon Canyon Park in Hollywood, a 1905 house and gardens built as the winter residence of an Omaha businessman. Cruise turns down $250,000 poolside in the **Westin Bonaventure Hotel, 404 South Figueroa Street**, downtown LA (see *In the Line of Fire* for details). The railway station, where Cruise tearfully sees Hoffman off, is **Santa Ana Train Station, 2800 North Main Street, Santa Ana**, southeast of LA.

RAINING STONES

(1993, dir: Ken Loach)
Bruce Jones, Julie Brown, Ricky Tomlinson.
● **MANCHESTER**

Loach's brand of hyper-realism brought to Jim Allen's story of an unemployed van driver trying to raise the loot for his daughter's confirmation dress. Filmed in **Middleton** near Manchester, on the **Langley Estate**, which writer Allen had helped to build. Jones attempts to sell bits of rustled sheep in the **Falcon** pub on the estate.

RAINMAKER, THE

(1997, dir: Francis Ford Coppola)
Matt Damon, Danny DeVito, Jon Voight.
● **TENNESSEE; CALIFORNIA**

Another Grisham legal thriller, with greenhorn Damon fighting the system to get a dying worker compensation from a big, bad company. The movie was shot in **Memphis**, Tennessee; and in **San Francisco**.

RAINTREE COUNTY

(1957, dir: Edward Dmytryk)
Elizabeth Taylor, Montgomery Clift, Lee Marvin.
● **MISSISSIPPI; KENTUCKY; TENNESSEE**

This attempt to out-wind *Gone With the Wind* was hampered by all kinds of problems, not the least of which was the traumatic car smash that ripped up Clift's face. Most of the studio interiors were filmed before the crash, the exteriors afterwards.

Locations were found in **Natchez**, on Hwy-61, Mississippi; in **Danville**, Hwy-127, 30 miles south of Lexington, central Kentucky; and **Paducah**, on I-24, McCracken County in far west Kentucky on the Illinois border. The ruined mansion is **Windsor**, near **Port Gibson**, Mississippi. Only 23 columns remain of this vast antebellum mansion, which was destroyed by fire in 1890.

The climax is at **Reelfoot Lake**, Tennessee, a weirdly beautiful place, scattered with cypress trees. The 13,000-acre lake was formed when an earthquake caused the Mississippi to overflow and flood a sunken forest. It's just west of Union City on the Missouri-Kentucky borders. Reelfoot Lake State Resort Park is a sanctuary for the rare American Bald Eagle, and there are eagle spotting tours.

RAISE THE RED LANTERN (aka *Dahong Denglong Gaogao Gua*)

(1991, dir: Zhang Yimou)
Li Gong, Jingwu Ma, Caifei He.
● **SHANXI PROVINCE, CHINA**

Yimou's ravishingly beautiful movie was shot in the old preserved **Qiao family villa** in **Qiaojiabao** near **Taiyuan**, the capital of Shanxi province, China. It's open as a museum. You can find details of a tour to the mansion from Shanghai at *www.shanghaitonight.com*.

RAISING ARIZONA

(1987, dir: Joel Coen)
Nicolas Cage, Holly Hunter, John Goodman.
● **ARIZONA**

The funniest, most inventive film of the year, made in, yes, Arizona, in Phoenix and its suburb Scottsdale. The supermarket, where Cage attempts to steal a pack of diapers and sets in motion the great car (and dog) chase, is in **Tempe**, in a long flat stretch of shopping centres outside Phoenix. Filming also took place at one of the **Denny's** restaurants in Scottsdale. The bank robbed by Goodman and William Forsythe is actually a restaurant, the **Reata Pass Steakhouse, 27500 North Alma School Parkway**, south from East Dynamite Boulevard, Scottsdale (© *480.585.7277*). The prison is the **Squaw Peak Water Treatment Plant, 20th Street**, Phoenix. 'Unpainted Arizona' is the **Home Depot, 12434 North Cave Creek Road, Cave Creek**, a northern suburb of Phoenix. The film's interiors used the historic 1925 **Jokake Inn**, now incorporated into the lavish **Phoenician Resort, 6000 East Camelback Road**, at the foot of Camelback Mountain, and Phoenix's **Old City Hall, 17th Street** at Second Avenue.

RAISING CAIN

(1992, dir: Brian De Palma)
John Lithgow, Lolita Davidovitch, Steven Bauer.
● **CALIFORNIA**

De Palma rehashes elements of *Psycho* once again, with a sadistic father plot borrowed from Michael Powell's *Peeping Tom*. The resulting film stretches credulity rather too far to be involving, but John Lithgow is always good value for money, and a villain with multiple personalities pro-

The police station: Mountain View City Hall, northern California

Climax at the sixties motel: Best Western Riviera Motel, Menlo Park

vides plenty of fun. Set in the fictitious California town of Bay View, the movie was shot in the area just south of San Francisco: **Los Altos; Mountain View; Menlo Park; Palo Alto** and **Woodside**, as well as in San Francisco itself. The kids' playground in Camino Park where the movie opens and ends, is **Shoup Park**, off University Avenue south of Burke Road, just to the west of G5, the Foothill Expressway, in Los Altos. The clock shop, where Davidovitch meets up with old flame Steven Bauer, is in the vast sprawl of the **Stanford Shopping Center** in Palo Alto. Also in Palo Alto is the hospital, where Bauer's wife expires on seeing him in a clinch with Davidovitch. It's the **Old Stanford's Children's Hospital, 520 Sand Hill Road**, which is near to the Woodside home of Shirley Temple, that exhibits the ex-moppet's Doll Collection in its lobby (*admission free*). Davidovitch's guilt-ridden dream, where she is impaled on the sword of an equestrian statue, uses the **Palace of the Legion of Honor** in San Francisco. The art museum, based on the Palace of the Legion d'Honneur in Paris, can be found on **Legion of Honor Drive** in **Lincoln Park** (see *Vertigo* for details). The vast, post-modern Bay View police station, where doctor Frances Sternhagen gives a *Psycho*-esque explanation, and from which Lithgow escapes in drag, is the postmodern three-storey **Mountain View City Hall, 500 Castro** between Church and Mercy Streets. The quintessentially sixties motel, where Lithgow-*père* hides out with the stolen kiddies, and where the movie climaxes, is the **Best Western Riviera Motel, 15 El Camino Real, Menlo Park** (*© 415.321.8772*).

RAMBO: FIRST BLOOD PART II
(1985, dir: George Pan Cosmatos)
Sylvester Stallone, Richard Crenna, Steven Berkoff.
● **MEXICO**

Rambo returns with bigger guns in this first sequel, shot around Acapulco, Mexico, where the compound, which had to serve as living accommodation for the crew, was built in the nearby jungle. CIA HQ is the **Acapulco Convention Centre, Costera Miguel Alemán**. Rambo kits himself out with knife and bow in the terrible privations of a room in the **Acapulco Plaza Hotel, Costera Miguel Alemán 123** (*© 001.5.9050*).

RAN
(1985, dir: Akira Kurosawa)
Tatsuya Nakadai, Satoshi Terao, Jinpachi Nezu.
● **JAPAN**

Kurosawa's epic version of Shakespeare's *King Lear* was made at various historic locations around Japan, including **Aso National Mountain Park** on the most westerly of Japan's four main islands, Kyushu, and **Kumamoto Castle**, Kumamoto, to the southwest of Aso National Park. The huge castle was entirely rebuilt, with a reinforced con-

crete frame, in 1960. **Nagoya Castle**, one of Japan's finest, destroyed by bombing in 1945 and also rebuilt with a reinforced concrete framework, was used too. It's one and a half miles northeast of Nagoya, on the south coast of Honshu, about 213 miles west of Tokyo. Also seen: **Gotemba**, again on Honshu, at the foot of Mount Fuji; and **Himeji Castle**, Himeji, west of Osaka (see *You Only Live Twice* for details). **Kokonoe** and **Shonai** are also featured.

RANSOM
(1996, dir: Ron Howard)
Mel Gibson, Delroy Lindo, Rene Russo.
● **NEW YORK CITY; NEW JERSEY**

Stinking rich airline exec Gibson risks all when the FBI fail to rescue his kidnapped son, snatched from a Junior Science Fair at **Bethesda Terrace** in Central Park, **Terrace Drive** at 72nd Street, just opposite

The Vanderbilt Bank: Madison Avenue at 90th Street

the famous Dakota Building. Gibson's luxury pad is on the Upper East Side, **Fifth Avenue** between 87th and 88th Streets, just

The shootout: Madison Avenue at 90th Street

south of the Guggenheim Museum, overlooking the Reservoir in Central Park. The wild goose chase with $2 million ransom money takes Gibson from **125th Street** in Harlem through the **Holland Tunnel**, which runs from Canal Street, SoHo, to 12th Street, Jersey City. He's soon deep into New Jersey, at **Paramus** on Route 4, going west to Route 208, and north on Saddle River Road to the rock quarry where small-fry gofer Donnie Wahlberg gets shot.

When the kidnap's mastermind is finally unmasked, he gets Gibson to wire money from the Vanderbilt Bank, actually a grand private house, **1261 Madison Avenue** at 90th Street, near the Gibson home. The final shootout takes place outside the Bright Lights shop, in reality **Roberta, 1252 Madison Avenue**.

REALITY BITES
(1994, dir: Ben Stiller)
Winona Ryder, Ethan Hawke, Ben Stiller.
● **TEXAS; LOS ANGELES**

Winona Ryder has to choose between yuppie Ben Stiller and slacker Ethan Hawke in Stiller's directorial début, set in Houston, Texas. After being fired from her job

Ethan Hawke comforts Winona Ryder: Tranquillity Park, Houston

at the TV studio, Ryder is comforted by Hawke by the cylindrical water features of **Tranquillity Park**, Houston. The coffee shop, where Ryder and Janeane Garofalo have a heart to heart, is actually in LA: it's **Johnie's Broiler, 7447 Firestone Boulevard, Downey**, seen also in Tina Turner biopic *What's Love Got to Do With It?*.

REAR WINDOW
(1954, dir: Alfred Hitchcock)
James Stewart, Grace Kelly, Raymond Burr.
● **LOS ANGELES**

Hitch's classic may be set in Greenwich Village, New York, but the movie was actually shot entirely on a gigantic set built at Paramount Studios in Hollywood. 31 apartments, twelve of which were fully furnished, can be seen from Stewart's window.

REBECCA
(1940, dir: Alfred Hitchcock)
Laurence Olivier, Joan Fontaine, Judith Anderson.
● **CALIFORNIA**

The Cornish coast: Point Lobos State Reserve, California

Hitchcock's first US film, adapted from Daphne du Maurier's novel and set in Monte Carlo and Cornwall, but made entirely in California. Manderley, of course, never existed. The house it was supposedly based on is Menabilly, on the east side of St Austell Bay, close to Fowey, Cornwall. The set for Hitchcock's Gothic mansion was built at the old Selznick Studios, on the site of the *Gone With the Wind* sets. The studio still stands, unchanged, but now called **Laird International Studios**, at **9336 West Washington Boulevard**, Culver City. The estate grounds were in the **Del Monte** area of California, while beach exteriors used **Catalina Island**, off the coast of LA. The rugged cliffs, where Joan Fontaine first meets Olivier, were filmed, using stand-ins, by a second unit at **Point Lobos State Reserve**, three miles south of Carmel. The delicate ecology of the area was endangered when the crew entered padlocked areas, bringing imported vines and ivy into contact with the native cypress trees. With poetic justice, most ended up hospitalised with poison ivy. You can visit the wildly beautiful state park, but the ground cover is still a mat of the very nasty weed. To remove it would upset the environmental balance, so warning notices are posted throughout.

REBEL WITHOUT A CAUSE
(1955, dir: Nicholas Ray)
James Dean, Natalie Wood, Sal Mineo.
● **LOS ANGELES**

James Dean's new school, Dawson High, at University and 10th is actually **Santa Monica High School, 601 Pico Boulevard** at 4th Street, Santa Monica, though some interiors were shot at **John Marshall High School, 3939 Tracy Street**, Los Feliz. Marshall High, apart from being

"I've got the bullets...": Griffith Observatory, Griffith Park

Leonardo DiCaprio's old school, has featured in lots of movies, including *Buffy the Vampire Slayer*, *Like Father Like Son* and fifties teen drama *The Young Stranger*.

Dawson High: Santa Monica High School, Pico Boulevard

The mansion, in which Dean, Sal Mineo and Natalie Wood play house, was also featured in *Sunset Blvd.*, and it stood at 641 Irving Boulevard at Wilshire Boulevard. Two years after *Rebel* was filmed, it was demolished. The planetarium visited by the schoolkids, and the site of the final shootout, is the **Griffith Observatory, 2800 East Observatory Road**, in Griffith Park. The film put the observatory firmly on the map, and there's now a bust of Dean in the grounds. Coincidentally, James Dean's first professional acting job was a Coca Cola commercial filmed in Griffith Park.

RED BADGE OF COURAGE, THE
(1951, dir: John Huston)
Audie Murphy, Bill Mauldin, Douglas Dick.
● **CALIFORNIA**

War hero Audie Murphy in a much-cut John Huston movie, now clocking in at under 70 minutes. Huston wanted to film this Civil War pic in Virginia, but finally had to settle for his own estate at **Calabasas**, northwest of LA in the Santa Monica Mountains off I-101, with further scenes shot at **Chico**, central California.

RED RIVER
(1948, dir: Howard Hawks)
John Wayne, Montgomery Clift, Walter Brennan.
● **ARIZONA**

Wayne and Clift follow Texas's Chisholm Trail, though this classic Western was filmed in southern Arizona at **Rain Valley**, 60 miles east of Tucson. Filming also took place in the **Coronado National Forest**, south of Benson. The river is the **San Pedro**.

RED SHOES, THE
(1948, dir: Michael Powell, Emeric Pressburger)
Moira Shearer, Anton Walbrook, Marius Goring.
● **LONDON; FRANCE; MONACO**

Powell and Pressburger's extravagantly romantic dance

drama opens at the **Royal Opera House, Covent Garden**, London, but soon star ballerina Moira Shearer is touring France, ending up in Monte Carlo. But be warned, the Monte Carlo of today is not the Monte Carlo of 1948. The classy elegance has been wiped away by crass development and the city is now a dump. The flower bedecked railway station, with its wrought iron decoration, has been replaced by a dismal concrete bunker. Shearer stays at the **Hotel de Paris, Place du Casino**, thankfully still standing and recognisable, tucked away behind the Casino. Also here is the **Monte Carlo Opera House**. The party spends an evening at **Villefranche-sur-Mer**, the beautiful little town on the coast just east of Nice, also seen in *Maximum Risk* and *Never Say Never Again*. The deserted mansion, with its atmospheric staircase, where Shearer visits Walbrook, is **Villa Leopolda, Avenue Leopold II**, east of Centre Ville, overlooking Villefranche.

The curving art nouveau terrace, from which Shearer ultimately flings herself, was demolished to make way for an ugly concrete walkway, and was way over the other side of the principality from the railway line onto which she falls.

RÈGLE DU JEU, LA (aka *Rules of the Game*)
(1939, dir: Jean Renoir)
Marcel Dalio, Nora Gregor, Jean Renoir.
● **FRANCE**

Renoir's classic satirical comedy concerning relationships among aristocrats and their servants during a shooting weekend at a French château was believed destroyed in a bombing raid during WWII. Although there was some damage to the film, the full version was eventually restored in 1959. The house used for locations is the 17th century **Château la Ferté-Saint-Aubin**, in the Sologne. The chateau, set in a vast park, is open for tours (*rail: Orleans, 11 miles, © 02.38.76.52.72, admission charge*).

REMAINS OF THE DAY, THE
(1993, dir: James Ivory)
Anthony Hopkins, Emma Thompson, James Fox.
● **DEVON; AVON; WILTSHIRE; SOMERSET**

The Merchant-Ivory team's thirteenth outing is a film of Kazuo Ishiguro's prizewinning novel, with Hopkins as the ultimate gentleman's gentleman, putting duty to the pro-Nazi Lord Darlington (Fox) before his buttoned-up feelings for housekeeper Thompson.

Darlington Hall is an ingenious conflation of several houses. The exterior is **Dyrham Park**, about six miles north of Bath, Avon, on the A46. It was built between 1692 and 1704 by William III's Secretary of State, William Blathwayt, on the site of a Tudor manor house. It's a National Trust property, open to the public from April through October, except Thursdays and Fridays (© *0127.582.2501*). Most of the interior is **Badminton House**, about 10 miles north of Bath off the B4040, which provided the entrance hall, Thompson's and Hopkins' parlours, and the conservatory where Hopkins' father collapses. **Powderham Castle**, a medieval pile dating from 1390 set in a deer park, supplied more interiors. It was damaged during the Civil War, then restored and much

altered in the 18th and 19th centuries. It's now the home of Lord and Lady Courtenay, and open to the public from May to October. The house is eight miles south of Exeter off the A379, Devon (© *01626.890 243/252*). Here you can see the Blue Staircase to the right of the entrance hall, the Library, Music Room, and the domed ceiling of the final scene with the trapped pigeon. **Corsham Court**, an Elizabethan and Georgian house, is the site of the conference in the 'Cabinet Room'. Four miles west of Chippenham off the A4 in Wiltshire, it's open from the beginning of January to the end of November (© *01249.712214*).

Tim Pigott-Smith proposes at the historic **George Inn, High Street, Norton St Philip**, six miles southeast of Bath, while Hopkins spends the night at the **Hop Pole Inn, Woods Hill, Lower Limpley Stoke** – a village used for another British classic. Limpley Stoke, a couple of miles south of Bath, appeared as the village of Titfield in the Ealing comedy *The Titfield Thunderbolt*. Hopkins eventually travels to meet Emma Thompson in **Weston-Super-Mare** on the Somerset coast about twenty miles west of Bristol. The hotel where he pulls up is the **Royal Pier Hotel, Birnbeck Road** (© *01934.626644*), and Thompson's boarding house is the **Highbury Hotel, Atlantic Road** (© *01934.621585*). They go for tea in the **Pavilion** and sit morosely together on the town's **Grand Pier**.

REPLACEMENT KILLERS, THE
(1998, dir: Antoine Fuqua)
Chow Yun-Fat, Mira Sorvino, Michael Rooker.
● **CALIFORNIA**

Visually lush, violent gunfest filmed around LA. The pre-Columbian fantasy disco of the first of the many shootouts is the **Mayan Theater, 1038 South Hill Street**, down-

The cartoon festival: Tower Theater, South Broadway

town LA, a cousin of Mann's Chinese Theater (see *The Bodyguard* for details). The cinema, where Chow Yun-Fat and Mira Sorvino thwart an attempt on the cop's son at a cartoon festival, is the **Tower Theatre, 802 South Broadway**, also downtown.

The film makes use of a clutch of locations previously seen in *Blade Runner*. Mr Wei's stylish home is, almost inevitably, Frank Lloyd Wright's **Ennis Brown House, 2607 Glendower Avenue**, Los Feliz, below Griffith Park. It was Harrison Ford's apartment block in the Ridley Scott film, but has also been used as the villain's lair in *Black Rain* and *The Karate Kid III*. See *The House on Haunted Hill* for details. Sorvino's dismal office was the Hotel Yukon in *Blade Runner*, as well as home to the emaciated Sloth victim in *Se7en*. It's the **Pan Am Building** on **South Broadway** at Third Street, opposite the Bradbury Building. The airport, where the replacement killers arrive and from which Yun-Fat finally departs, is actually the ever-adaptable **Union Station, 800 North Alameda Street**, also downtown LA. In *Blade Runner*, it became the police station.

REPULSION

(1965, dir: Roman Polanski)
Catherine Deneuve, John Fraser, Ian Hendry.
● LONDON

Madame Denise's beauty salon: Thurloe Place, South Kensington

Fish and chips for Deneuve: Dino's, South Kensington

Catherine Deneuve goes mad: Kensington Mansions, Trebovir Road

Brilliant, cold and terrifying case history, with sexually repressed and mystifyingly psychotic Deneuve killing off predatory males.

Madame Denise's beauty parlour, where Deneuve works, is still a beauty salon, at **31 Thurloe Place, South Kensington**, SW1. A couple of doors away is the **Hoop and Toy**, the pub where wannabe-boyfriend John Fraser drinks with his appalling cronies. He takes Deneuve for fish and chips at **Dino's**, also still doing good business, alongside South Kensington tube station. It's just opposite the tube station entrance where Deneuve is hassled by workman Mike Pratt. Deneuve's gloomy apartment block (though the incredible expanding interior was reproduced in the studio at Twickenham) is **Kensington Mansions, Trebovir Road**, off Warwick Road behind Earls Court tube station, SW5.

RESERVOIR DOGS

(1992, dir: Quentin Tarantino)
Harvey Keitel, Michael Madsen, Tim Roth.
● LOS ANGELES

Forget the ego and the irritating cameos, Tarantino's first movie really delivers. The diner, where the Dogs discuss Madonna lyrics and the ethics of tipping, is **Pat and Lorraine's, 4720 Eagle Rock Boulevard, Eagle Rock**, between Glendale and Pasadena, south of Ventura Freeway to the east of LA. The robbery of Karina's (named after Jean-Luc Godard's one-time wife Anna Karina) filmed a little to the east in the **Highland Park** district. More movie references abound – Mr Blue is "Dead as Dillinger" and Laurence Tierney (gangleader Joe Cabot) played Dillinger in 1945 for Monogram Pictures, the company to whom Jean-Luc Godard dedicated *A Bout de Souffle*. Mr Brown (Tarantino himself) gets shot, while Mr White kills the cops, in the alleyway between **55th and 56th Avenues** here. Mr Orange receives his bloody gunshot wound by **5518 Marmion Way**, near Avenue 56. Mr Pink shoots his way out and heads down **Figueroa Street** (play

Spot-the-camera crew in the shop windows in this scene), south of, and parallel to, Marmion Way. He gets hit by a car at the corner of **York Boulevard and 57th Avenue**, commandeers the motor and makes off on 57th.

The café, where Mr Orange meets up with his superior, is **Johnie's Coffee Shop, 6101 Wilshire Boulevard** at Fairfax Avenue (a familiar location – it's where Lily Tomlin works in *Short Cuts* and where Anthony Edwards receives news of the impending apocalypse in the underrated thriller *Miracle Mile*). His druggy cover story was filmed in the toilets of the **Park Plaza Hotel, 607 South Park View Street**, midtown LA. "The hotel has been featured many times in films," claimed Tarantino, "but I'm the only director that has used only its bathroom.". Maybe, but it's a close thing. The Park Plaza also supplied the men's room at Capitol Pictures for the Coens' *Barton Fink*, but it was used for the USO dance scene as well.

The graffiti-covered walls, where Orange rehearses his story, can be seen at the junction of **Beverly Boulevard** and **Second Street** and **Toluca Street,** just northwest of downtown (take care around here if you're visiting!).

The Dogs' warehouse has sadly been demolished, but you're sure to recognise the (currently empty) site at **Figueroa Street and 59th Avenue** in Highland Park. Fittingly, it was a former mortuary, and was also used for Mr Orange's scuzzy hotel room.

RETURN OF THE JEDI

(1983, dir: Richard Marquand)
Mark Hamill, Carrie Fisher, Harrison Ford.
● ARIZONA; CALIFORNIA

Studio filming for this, the third in the original trilogy, was again in England, but exteriors were further afield. Tatooine, which was found in Tunisia for *Star Wars*, is now **Buttercup Valley**, near Yuma in the Arizona desert (*Raiders of the Lost Ark* had run into problems filming in Tunisia, though Lucas returned to the country for *The Phantom Menace*). Jabba the Hutt's huge (80 feet high, 212 feet long) hover barge was built in Yuma. More otherworldly landscapes were found in **Death Valley** and at **Smith River**, California. The monster trees on the Moon of Endor, up to 300 feet tall and twenty feet in diameter, are the giant Redwood groves of the **Jedediah Smith Redwood State Park, 4241 Kings Valley Road, Crescent City**, northern California. *Jedi* was shot in strict secrecy, masquerading on location under the title *Blue Harvest – Horror Beyond Imagination*.

RETURN OF THE MUSKETEERS, THE

(1989, dir: Richard Lester)
Michael York, Oliver Reed, Frank Finlay.
● SPAIN

Over fifteen years after *The Three Musketeers*, Lester assembles most of the cast again to film Dumas' sequel, *Twenty Years After*, though the movie is probably now only remembered for Roy Kinnear's fatal riding accident during shooting. It revisits some of Spain's great landmarks, including the cities of **Toledo** and **Aranjuez**, south of Madrid; **Manzanares el Real**; **Riofrio**; **La Granja**; **Rascafria** and **Talamanca**, to the north of Madrid.

REVERSAL OF FORTUNE

(1990, dir: Barbet Schroeder)
Jeremy Irons, Glenn Close, Ron Silver.
● NEW YORK CITY; NEW JERSEY; NEW YORK STATE

The true story becomes a jet-black comedy, tiptoeing carefully through a legal minefield, as liberal lawyer Alan Dershowitz defends Claus von Bulow (an Oscar-winning Irons) against a charge of murder, after von Bulow's wife, Sunny, is found in a drug-induced coma. The von Bulow's house at the time was Clarendon Court, near Newport, Long Island. Not surprisingly, this is not used in the film, although you can see Clarendon Court on screen as the mansion in *High Society*. Schroeder used the **Knole Mansion, Post Road** in Old Westbury, just south of the Long Island Expressway on Long Island's North Shore (it's a private house, not open to the public). Interiors, though, were filmed at **Lyndhurst**, just south of **Tarrytown**, New York State. The crenellated castle of robber baron Jay Gould was donated to the National Trust for Historic Preservation by Gould's daughter in 1961.

Filming also took place in **Montclair**, New Jersey and in Manhattan. The hospital, where Sunny von Bulow lies comatose, is **St John's Hospital, Yonkers**, north of the Bronx. Dershowitz's law classes were filmed on the 34-acre campus of **City College**, between West 130th and West 140th Streets, and St Nicholas Terrace and Amsterdam Avenue in Hamilton Heights. Other locations include the area of **Flatbush**, Brooklyn; the **Carlyle Hotel, 35 East 76th Street** at Madison Avenue on the East Side; **Larchmont Yacht Club, New Rochelle** on Long Island Sound; the **Small Claims Court** and Jewish dairy restaurant **Ratner's, 138 Delancey Street** between Norfolk and Suffolk Streets on the Lower East Side, Manhattan.

REVOLUTION

(1985, dir: Hugh Hudson)
Al Pacino, Nastassja Kinski, Donald Sutherland.
● NORFOLK; DEVON; CAMBRIDGESHIRE; NORWAY

If a local whizz-kid, with a couple of flashy car commercials under his belt, came home to film the village pageant, the result might resemble *Revolution*. Legendary turkeys, like *Heaven's Gate*, are rarely as bad as their reputations. But this is the real thing, an appallingly made mess, loosely following a father and son through an endless American Revolution.

The sole good idea is the inventive use of locations, with **King's Lynn** in Norfolk standing in for 18th century Manhattan (Wall Street is still no more than an alleyway). The dockside warehouses are **South Quay** grain silos. New York Harbor, where Pacino and son sail into the middle of anti-English riots, is the area around King's Lynn's **Custom House**. Filming also took place in **King's Staithe Square**.

The American camp at Valley Forge is **Thetford**, in Norfolk, while the Brits camped in the **Burrator** area of southwest **Dartmoor**, Devon. More battle scenes used **Kingston** on the south coast. The Second Battle of Upper Manhattan shot at **Deancombe Valley**, above Burrator

reservoir. The Battle of Yorktown filmed at **Scobbiscombe Farm**, Kingston, and there was filming also at **Bigbury Bay**. A camera worth half a million pounds was lost at the Devon location when it tumbled over a cliff during the night. Philadelphia's state buildings are **Melton Constable Hall** in Norfolk (see *The Go-between* for details), and other Philadelphia scenes were filmed in **Ely**, Cambridgeshire.

RICHARD III

(1995, dir: Richard Loncraine)
Ian McKellen, Nigel Hawthorne, Maggie Smith.
● LONDON; SUSSEX; MIDDLESEX; LANCASHIRE

Filming of the Shakespeare history, based on Richard Eyre's National Theatre production, and making imaginative use of London and Home Counties locations to conjure up an alternative England with the Victorian Gothic style of King Edward's old order overtaken by the austere thirties look of Richard's neo-fascist dictatorship.

"Live with me and be my love...": St Cuthbert's Church, Earl's Court

The old order: Strawberry Hill House, Twickenham

The royal family's London palace is **St Pancras Chambers, Euston Road**, cheekily relocated to the banks of the Thames, though the interior is a crafty combination of **St Cuthbert's Church, Philbeach Gardens, Earl's Court, SW5** (the opening musical number), and the **Holbein Room** of **Strawberry Hill**

The seaside palace: Brighton Pavilion

The new order, Richard's HQ: Senate House, Malet Street

House, Waldegrave Road, Twickenham (*visits by appointment, ☎ 020.8892.0051*), the elaborately Gothic home of 18th century writer Horace Walpole. The royal breakfast is served in what is actually a vaulted pedestrian walkway beneath the chapel of **Lincoln's Inn Fields, WC2**, and the royal family's seaside retreat is a conflation of two Sussex landmarks, **Brighton Pavilion**, and the seafront terrace is the **De La Warr Pavilion**, Bexhill-on-Sea.

The Tower of London: Bankside Power station, now Tate Modern

The fascist rally, where Richard is offered the crown, is held in the **New Horticultural Hall**, on the corner of **Greycoat** and **Elverton Street** in Westminster, SW1 (seen in *Indiana Jones and the Last Crusade* and *The Saint*), while the backstage preparations are beneath **Earl's Court Exhibition Centre, Warwick Road, SW5**. The giant clockface, where Richard refuses to give Buckingham his promised title, is way up on the **Shell Building**, on the Embankment.

Richard's cold but stylish bunker is **Senate House, University of London, Malet Street** (which you might have seen as the New York clinic in Tony Scott's *The Hunger*), and his military HQ is **Steam Town**, a rail museum at **Carnforth** in Lancashire. Two of London's famous ex-power stations are also featured: Bankside Power Station, now the **Tate Modern**, is used as the Tower of London, and the deserted bulk of the old **Battersea Power Station** is the site of the climactic Battle of Bosworth.

RIDE THE HIGH COUNTRY (aka *Guns in the Afternoon*)
(1962, dir: Sam Peckinpah)
Joel McCrea, Randolph Scott, Mariette Hartley.
● **CALIFORNIA**

Randolph Scott came out of, and then went back into, retirement for this excellent early Peckinpah. The setting is the fictional Coarsegold, in Crane Valley, but the chosen location was over the mountains in the **Mammoth Lakes** region of the High Sierras, near Bishop, California. Peckinpah wanted to capture the change in terrain and vegetation as the party climbs and descends, but unseasonal bad weather cut short filming and the crew were forced to head back to LA, to the inevitable all-purpose **Bronson Canyon** in the heart of Griffith Park, where soapsuds were substituted for snow, and the tents were cut from the sails of the *Bounty* built for the 1962 version of *Mutiny on the Bounty*!

Other locations in the area include **Frenchman's Flat**; the **Conejo Valley**; the Fox Ranch in Malibu Canyon and even the MGM backlot.

The High Country: Bishop, central California

RING OF BRIGHT WATER
(1969, dir: Jack Couffer)
Bill Travers, Virginia McKenna, Roddy McMillan.
● **LONDON; SCOTLAND**

Following *Born Free*, Travers and McKenna are reunited in another animal pic, with Travers relocating to a Scottish village from London when he acquires a pet otter. The Scots location is **Easdale, Sell Island**.

RIO BRAVO
(1959, dir: Howard Hawks)
John Wayne, Dean Martin, Ricky Nelson.
● **ARIZONA**

Wayne and Martin hold out against a band of outlaws in this movie, which was reworked by Hawks as *El Dorado* in 1966, by Hawks again as *Rio Lobo* in 1970, and by John Carpenter in 1976 as *Assault on Precinct 13*. It was shot at **Old Tucson Studios, 201 South Kinney Road** near Tucson, built for the 1940 movie *Arizona*. The studio-cum-tourist attraction, claiming the largest Western street in the movie business, was restored at a cost of $1 million, including the set of *The High Chaparral*, which filmed here.

RIO GRANDE
(1950, dir: John Ford)
John Wayne, Ben Johnson, Maureen O'Hara.
● **UTAH**

More Ford-Wayne Injun-bashing, shot around **Moab**, in southeast Utah, at **White's Ranch**; **Professor Valley**; and **Onion Creek Narrows**.

RISKY BUSINESS
(1983, dir: Paul Brickman)
Tom Cruise, Rebecca De Mornay, Joe Pantoliano.
● **ILLINOIS**

It's the go-getting eighties, greed is good, and home-alone teen Cruise sets up a lucrative prostitution business while his parents are away. The movie was made around Chicago, where Cruise meets up with De Mornay in the Palm Court of the **Drake Hotel, 140 East Walton Place** (*© 312.787.2200*), also where faker Andy Garcia lives

Cruise meets De Mornay: Drake Hotel, East Walton Place, Chicago

Dunking the Porsche: Belmont Harbor, Lake Michigan

it up in *Accidental Hero* (aka *Hero*). Cruise's father's Porsche slips into the water at the marina of **Belmont Harbor** on Lake Michigan. Cruise's school is **Highland Park High School**, and the house, where he shot to fame dancing in his underwear, can be found on **Linden Street, Highland Park**.

RIVER OF NO RETURN
(1954, dir: Otto Preminger)
Robert Mitchum, Marilyn Monroe, Rory Calhoun.
● ALBERTA, CANADA

Scenic drama, made at **Banff**, in the Rockies of Alberta, Canada, where the raft scenes were filmed on the **Bow River**. Monroe stayed at the Banff Springs Hotel (where Betty Grable shot *Springtime in the Rockies*). The hotel is now used as the backdrop to a Japanese soap opera and, as a consequence, is full of Asian location hunters.

RIVER RUNS THROUGH IT, A
(1991, dir: Robert Redford)
Brad Pitt, Tom Skerritt, Craig Sheffer.
● MONTANA; WYOMING

Reverend Skerritt teaches his sons the art of fly fishing in Redford's family drama. Missoula is actually **Front Street, Livingston**, on I-91 in southern Montana. The extensive fishing scenes are south of town in **Paradise Valley** on the **Yellowstone River**; south of Bozeman on the **Gallatin River** and south of Big Timber on the **Boulder River**. There was also second unit filming at **Jackson**, Wyoming. And no fish were harmed during the filming of this movie.

RIVER WILD, THE
(1994, dir: Curtis Hanson)
Meryl Streep, Kevin Bacon, David Strathairn.
● MONTANA; OREGON; MASSACHUSETTS

Streep reinvents herself as an action woman in this white water action drama. At the film's opening, she trains on the **Charles River, Cambridge**, Massachusetts, but she's soon fiercely protecting her family in the wilderness. The **Kootenai River** in Montana is featured – where for the first time filming was permitted on ground sacred to the Kootenai Indians, but only on condition that the actual location, near Libby in the far northwest of the state, would not be revealed. About 80 miles to the east, the **Middle Fork** section of the **Flathead River** was also used, alongside Route 2, between West Glacier and Essex in the **Waterton Glacier International Peace Park**. Other scenes used the **Rogue River**, between Hog Creek and Argo Riffle, north of Medford in southwest Oregon.

RIVER'S EDGE
(1986, dir: Tim Hunter)
Crispin Glover, Keanu Reeves, Ione Skye.
● CALIFORNIA

A group of teenagers try to deal with one of their number becoming a murderer, based on a true story. The school is **Verdugo Hills High School, 10625 Plainview Avenue, Tujunga**, north of LA, also used in *one eight seven*, *The Craft* and *Heathers*.

ROAD TO MOROCCO
(1942, dir: David Butler)
Bob Hope, Bing Crosby, Dorothy Lamour.
● CALIFORNIA

The desert of Morocco is actually the sand dunes of **Imperial County**, way down in southern California toward the Arizona border.

ROB ROY
(1995, dir: Michael Caton-Jones)
Liam Neeson, Jessica Lange, Tim Roth.
● SCOTLAND

Dour version of the historical legend enlivened by Tim Roth's Oscar-nominated villain. The opening shot is of **Kinlochleven**. Rob Roy's cottage was built specially for the movie at **Bracorina**, on Loch Morar, but it was dismantled after filming. The home of the Marquis of Montrose, with its elegant 17th century gardens, is **Drummond Castle Gardens**, west of the Muthill Road about two miles south of Crieff. The castle is not open to the public, but you can visit the gardens (℗ *01764.681257, admission charge*). The village square is the courtyard of **Megginch Castle Gardens**, on the A90, eight miles east of Perth. Once again, you can visit the gardens, but not the castle (℗ *01821.642222, admission charge*). The gambling den, where Rob Roy faces Cunningham, is **Crichton Castle**, two miles south of Pathhead in Midlothian (℗ *01875.320017, admission charge*). Filming also took place at **Loch Earn**; **Glencoe** and at **Caig Falls Bridge, Loch Arkaig**.

ROBIN HOOD
(1991, dir: John Irvin)
Patrick Bergin, Uma Thurman, Jurgen Prochnow.
● CHESHIRE; WALES

Totally overshadowed by the flashy, attention-grabbing Kevin Costner movie made the same year, this version of the story is actually superior. It was largely shot around **Peckforton Castle**, on the A49 just south of the A51, between Chester and Nantwich, Cheshire, and also at the caves of nearby **Beeston Castle**. Also seen are **Tatton Park**, Cheshire, and the countryside around **Betwys-y-Coed** in North Wales.

ROBIN HOOD: PRINCE OF THIEVES
(1991, dir: Kevin Reynolds)
Kevin Costner, Alan Rickman, Morgan Freeman.
● SUSSEX; WILTSHIRE; YORKSHIRE; BUCKINGHAMSHIRE; NORTHUMBERLAND; LONDON; FRANCE

Costner's hyperactive, one-note extravaganza, famously using locations all over the UK, kicks off with Robin arriving home from the Crusades on a beach overlooked

Nottingham Cathedral: St Bartholomew the Great, Smithfield

by gleaming white cliffs. And where better than the **Seven Sisters**, on the Sussex coast west of Eastbourne toward Cuckmore Haven. You can access the clifftop path from car parks at Exceat Barn and Birling Gap, or view the Sisters from Seaford Head.

From the coast, Robin's trek north to Nottingham overshoots a little, to Northumberland in fact. In no time at all, he's giving directions to Morgan Freeman at **Sycamore**

The walled castle of Nottingham: Carcassonne, southern France

Gap, on **Hadrian's Wall** near to Housesteads Roman Fort. Housesteads is on the B6318 about 25 miles west of Newcastle-on-Tyne (*rail: Bardon Mill, 3 miles*). But it's soon back south, to Wiltshire, for the ruin of Locksley Castle, Robin's family home, which turns out to be **Wardour Castle**, between Salisbury and Shaftesbury, off the A30. Wardour has the great advantage for the movie of appearing either whole or totally wrecked according to which angle it's seen from. Then north again, to Yorkshire. The river, where Robin fights with Little John, is **Aysgarth Falls**, a series of broad limestone steps on the River Ure at Aysgarth, on the A684 about 25 miles west of Northallerton in the Pennines.

Robin Hood's Sherwood Forest camp was built near to the film studio at Shepperton, about 50 yards from a public footpath in **Burnham Beeches**, off the A335, north of Slough, Buckinghamshire. Maid Marion keeps her distance, though, at **Hulne Priory**, in Hulne Park, northwest of Alnwick on the A1 in Northumberland. Piggily villainous Harold Innocent plops out of the window to land in the courtyard of 12th century **Alnwick Castle** itself. Nottingham Castle square sat on the backlot at Shepperton, though the castle itself – in longshot – is the fortified city of **Carcassonne** down in the south of France close to the Spanish border (seen also in *The Bride*). The interior of Nottingham Cathedral is the **Church of St Bartholomew the Great**, a tiny church – repository of the bones of St Rahere – tucked away behind Smithfield, London, and seen also in *Four Weddings and a Funeral*.

ROBOCOP

(1987, dir: Paul Verhoeven)
Peter Weller, Nancy Allen, Ronny Cox.
● **DALLAS, TEXAS; NEW YORK STATE; PENNSYLVANIA**

Terrific black comedy actioner, with sleazoid techno-freaks incorporating dead cop Weller into a damn near indestructible law'n'order machine. Set in a futuristic New Detroit, the vaguely familiar skyline is eighties Dallas. The sinister OCP HQ is **Dallas City Hall, 1500 Marilla Street**, stretched to 95 storeys with some optical effects, though the dizzying Atrium is that of the **Plaza of the Americas Hotel, 650 North Pearl Street**. The rundown Detroit Police Precinct, Metro West is the old **Sons of Hermann Hall, 3414 Elm Street** at Exposition, built in 1911 by the Order of the Sons of Hermann, a German emigré's organisation. Other Dallas locations include the **Renaissance**

OCP HQ: Dallas City Hall, Marilla Street

Tower, 1201 Elm Street and music venue the **Bomb Factory, 2713 Canton Street**. The Detroit factory, in which Weller is shot to bits, was a disused car assembly plant at Long Island. The climax takes place at the **Duquesne Steel Works**, off Route 837, **Duquesne**, Pennsylvania.

ROBOCOP 2

(1990, dir: Irvin Kershner)
Peter Weller, Nancy Allen, Daniel O'Herlihy.
● **TEXAS**

Civic Centrum, exterior: Wortham Theater Center, Texas Avenue

Robocop takes on the newer, bigger version, Robocop 2, in this sequel, which found its futuristic cityscapes in **Houston**, Texas. Civic Centrum is a combination of the **Wortham Theater Center, 500 Texas Avenue** (outside) and the **George R Brown Convention Center, 1001 Avenue of the Americas** (inside). The OCP office this time around is the **Cullen Center, 1600 Smith Street**.

Civic Centrum, interior: George R Brown Convention Center

ROBOCOP 3

(1993, dir: Fred Dekker)
Robert John Burke, Nancy Allen, John Castle.
● **GEORGIA**

For the second sequel, Robocop takes up arms on behalf of Detroit's street people against the, once again, corrupt establishment. The Motor City is now played by **Atlanta**, Georgia, with filming on **Auburn Avenue**.

OCP HQ: Cullen Center, Smith Street

ROBOT MONSTER

(1953, dir: Phil Tucker)
George Nader, Claudia Barrett, Selena Royle.
● **LOS ANGELES**

Legendary movie dreck with the last six people on Earth pitted against a fabulously inventive monster – a guy in a gorilla suit wearing a diving helmet. Filmed in the thrilling glory of Tru-Stereo 3D, too. It was shot in the wilds of **Bronson Caverns**, Griffith Park, LA.

ROCK, THE

(1996, dir: Michael Bay)
Sean Connery, Nicolas Cage, Ed Harris.
● **CALIFORNIA**

High-octane actioner, with embittered major Harris and his crack troops taking over Alcatraz Island and pointing

Connery's luxury suite: Fairmont Hotel, Mason Street, San Francisco

Connery meets up with his daughter: Palace of Fine Arts, Lyon Street

Cage's Washington DC apartment: Hotel Rosslyn, West 5th Street, LA

some very nasty chemical warheads at the City by the Bay. Only ex-inmate and political prisoner Connery can sort the problem out, along with nervous scientist Cage. And it is the real **Alcatraz Prison** on Alcatraz Island in San Francisco Bay. It wasn't possible to close down the national monument, so filming had to accommodate tour parties milling around. See *Escape From Alcatraz* for visiting details, if you still want to risk a potential hostage situation. Nicolas Cage's apartment is supposedly in Washington DC, but the view from the window clearly shows the World Interstate Centre in downtown LA, while the sign on the roof, where he cavorts with his girlfriend, identifies it as the **Hotel Rosslyn, 112 West 5th Street** (℗ *213.624.3311*), downtown LA (also in Sam Raimi's *Darkman*).

The FBI agents set up mobile command HQ on **Pier 39** on San Francisco Bay. Cage is summoned to FBI offices in San Fran's **City Hall, Van Ness Avenue** at McAllister Street in the Civic Center. Connery demands, and gets, a penthouse suite at the **Fairmont Hotel, 950 Mason Street** on Nob Hill (℗ *415. 772.5000*), seen also in Hitchcock's final film, *Family Plot*. It's from here that Connery escapes after leaving the FBI boss dangling from the roof. But look again. The hotel that Cage chases Connery from is the **Biltmore**, on Pershing Square in downtown LA (see *Beverly Hills Cop* for details of this frequent movie location).

The San Fran ritual of a bouncy car chase down the city's hills is pepped up with a spectacular cable car crash, filmed in **Russian Hill**. Connery is apprehended when he meets up with his estranged daughter at the **Palace of Fine Arts, 3601 Lyon Street** between Jefferson and Bay Streets in the Marina district, a backdrop for both *Vertigo* and *Time After Time*. Built in 1915 for the Panama-Pacific Exhibition, the grandiose Romanesque buildings were retained and restored, and now house a kids' museum, the Exploratorium.

ROCKY

(1976, dir: John G Avildsen)
Sylvester Stallone, Burgess Meredith, Talia Shire.
● PHILADELPHIA, PENNSYLVANIA; LOS ANGELES

In the year of *Taxi Driver*, *All the President's Men* and

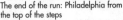

The Rocky steps: Philadelphia Museum of Modern Art, Benjamin Franklin Avenue

Network, this old fashioned fairytale of the underdog coming out on top took Oscars for Best Film and Best Director. The main location you'll want to see is, of course, the flight of 68 steps up to the **Philadelphia Museum of Modern Art, 26th Avenue** at Benjamin Franklin Avenues. But although *Rocky* is set in Philadelphia, the film's locations are split between the City of Brotherly Love and Los Angeles. Rocky's neighbourhood is South Philly. During training for his big break he runs past **Philadelphia City Hall** and through the **Italian Market, Ninth Street** between Federal and Christian Streets. The opening boxing match, though, with the religious

The end of the run: Philadelphia from the top of the steps

Rocky trains: the Italian Market, Ninth Street

The climactic fight: Olympic Auditorium, South Grand Avenue, LA

Rocky trains: Park Hyatt Philadelphia at the Bellevue, Broad Street

mural overlooking the ring, is in LA. It's the **Oscar de la Hoya Boxing Youth Center, 1114 South Lorena Street** in East LA. The press conference is held in the **Ambassador Hotel, 3400 Wilshire Boulevard**. The future of this LA landmark, bought up by Donald Trump, is currently in the balance. Catch it while it's still there, locked up and empty, and now used almost exclusively as a movie set (see the 1954 *A Star Is Born* for details). Rocky works out by pounding sides of beef at **Shamrock Meats Inc,**

3461 East Vernon Avenue at Alcoa Avenue, just south of the Los Angeles River in Vernon, southeast of downtown. The climactic fight itself, against Apollo Creed, is in Los Angeles, at the **Olympic Auditorium, 1801 South Grand Avenue** at Olympic Boulevard, downtown LA. It was built for the 1932 Olympics. The fight scenes for *Raging Bull*, and wrestling matches in *Ed Wood* and *Man on the Moon* also shot here.

ROCKY II

(1979, dir: Sylvester Stallone)
Sylvester Stallone, Talia Shire, Carl Weathers.
● PHILADELPHIA, PENNSYLVANIA; LOS ANGELES

Rocky hits the skids, but bounces back to win another fight, in this sequel with a budget eight times that of the original *Rocky*. Once again, Rocky trains in Philadelphia, runs in the **Italian Market**, trots up the steps of the **Museum of Modern Art** and triumphs over adversity in LA's **Olympic Auditorium** (see *Rocky* for details).

ROCKY III

(1982, dir: Sylvester Stallone)
Sylvester Stallone, Talia Shire, Carl Weathers.
● PHILADELPHIA, PENNSYLVANIA; LOS ANGELES

Rocky gets beaten early on, but don't worry – he wins out in the end, in LA's **Olympic Auditorium** again. The fight arena is the Crystal Ballroom of the **Biltmore Hotel, 506 South Grand Avenue**, downtown LA. Meanwhile, in Philadelphia, Rocky now has a statue atop the steps of the **Museum of Modern Art**. After filming, Stallone generously donated the statue to the museum. Errrm, thanks, but no thanks, they said, and the statue languished in Stallone's own backyard, until local petitions resulted in its being installed at the Spectrum Stadium, home of the Flyers hockey team and the 76ers basketball team (a location for the movie *Philadelphia*). Rocky trains at the ultra-luxurious **Park Hyatt Philadelphia at the Bellevue, Broad Street** at Walnut Street (© *215.893.1776*), just south of City Hall.

ROCKY IV

(1985, dir: Sylvester Stallone)
Sylvester Stallone, Dolph Lundgren, Carl Weathers.
● WYOMING; BRITISH COLUMBIA, CANADA

Rocky takes on Blond Bombshell Lundgren in laboured East-West allegory. Filmed in **Jackson**, Wyoming, passing itself off as Siberia. Replacing the Philadelphia steps is **Rendezvous Peak** at Jackson. Filming also in Vancouver, with local extras sweating through a summer heatwave under fur coast and winter wrappings. The fight, supposedly at Caesar's Palace, Las Vegas, was shot in the vast **Pacific National Exhibition Agrodome**, Vancouver (© *604.253.2311*), British Columbia.

ROCKY V

(1990, dir: John G Avildsen)
Sylvester Stallone, Talia Shire, Burt Young.
● LOS ANGELES

Brain-damaged Rocky takes on a protégé – who turns against him. Stallone's mansion is **160 San Rafael Avenue**, south of Colorado Avenue, Pasadena (seen also in *Mobsters*).

ROCKY HORROR PICTURE SHOW, THE

(1975, dir: Jim Sharman)
Tim Curry, Susan Sarandon, Richard O'Brien.
● BERKSHIRE

The cult movie to end all cult movies, despite being a bit *too* calculatingly camp and being constricted by its microbudget. Inte-

Frankenfurter's: Oakley Court Hotel, Windsor Road, Berkshire

riors filmed, fittingly, at Hammer Films' old Bray Studio. Frankenfurter's mansion is, conveniently, alongside the studio, and has naturally figured in a whole slew of horror movies. It was Oakley Court, a Victorian Gothic folly that lay for many years in a state of disrepair. It's been seen in dozens of movies, particularly Hammer films such as *The Curse of Frankenstein* and *The Plague of the Zombies*. It has since been renovated and is now the rather swanky **Oakley Court Hotel, Windsor Road, Water Oakley** (© *01753.609988*), on the A308 between Maidenhead and Windsor.

ROLLERBALL

(1975, dir: Norman Jewison)
James Caan, John Houseman, Maud Adams.
● GERMANY

Jewison's futuristic sci-fi was made in Europe, at Pinewood and in Munich. The Rollerball stadium is the vast, circular **Olympic Basketball Hall** in Munich.

ROMAN HOLIDAY

(1953, dir: William Wyler)
Audrey Hepburn, Gregory Peck, Eddie Albert.
● ROME

American newspaperman Peck romances Euro-princess Hepburn around the touristy sights of Rome, including the **Spanish Steps**. The **Mouth of Truth (Bocca della Verita)**, the carved stone face which supposedly bites the hands off liars, can be found in the church of **Santa Maria in Cosmedin, Piazza Bocca della Verita**. Filming also took place in the 19th century

The Mouth of Truth: Santa Maria in Cosmedin

Palazzo Brancaccio, Viale del Monte Oppio 7, now a conference centre, between the Colosseum and the Basilica of Santa Maria Maggiore; and one of Rome's largest palaces, **Palazzo Colonna, Piazza Santa Apostoli**. Open only on Saturdays, the entrance is on Via della Pilotta 17.

ROMANCING THE STONE

(1984, dir: Robert Zemeckis)
Kathleen Turner, Michael Douglas, Danny DeVito.
● NEW YORK CITY; MEXICO; UTAH; NEVADA

Kathleen Turner is a New York novelist dreaming of a

handsome hero who gets into trouble tracing her missing sister in Colombia and finding – guess what? Turner's apartment is **495 West End Avenue**, on the Upper West Side of Manhattan. The Colombian scenes were filmed, during a spectacularly wet rainy season, in Mexico – the cliffs at **Xica**; the fortress at **San Juan de Ulua**; the narrow roads of **Barraca Grande**; **Xalapa** and the jungles of **El Arsenal**. The desert scenes are **Washington County**, southwest Utah; and the **Mojave Desert** near Las Vegas, Nevada.

Turner's apartment: West End Avenue

ROMEO AND JULIET
(1968, dir: Franco Zeffirelli)
Leonard Whiting, Olivia Hussey, Milo O'Shea.
● **ITALY**

Beautiful to look at but slightly schmaltzy version of the Shakespeare play. After filming his *Taming of the Shrew* entirely in the studio, Zeffirelli takes the tearjerker out on location around Italy. Sites include the Tuscan hill town of **Pienza** – whose main square was recreated in the studio at Cinecittà. The fight scenes use the streets of the small medieval town of **Gubbia**, on the slopes of Mount Ingino in Umbria. More medieval backdrops were provided by the towns of **Tuscania**, on the River Marta, 50 miles northwest of Rome; and **Serravalle**, a walled village below the Meschio gorge, part of Vittorio Veneto, about 45 miles to the north of Venice. For Baz Luhrmann's nineties update, see *William Shakespeare's Romeo and Juliet*.

ROMPER STOMPER
(1992, dir: Geoffrey Wright)
Russell Crowe, Daniel Pollock, Jacqueline McKenzie.
● **MELBOURNE, AUSTRALIA**

Dorkish skinheads terrorise immigrants in Melbourne, in a controversial movie shot around the **Footscray** and **Point Addis** districts of Melbourne. The Vietnamese teens are attacked at **Footscray Station**.

ROOM AT THE TOP
(1958, dir: Jack Clayton)
Laurence Harvey, Simone Signoret, Donald Wolfit.
● **YORKSHIRE**

The screech of a train whistle and Mario Nascimbene's jazzy score heralded the arrival of the New Wave in Britain. And while Home Counties actors struggle embarrassingly with northern accents, this adaptation of John

Joe Lampton arrives at Warnley Town: Halifax Station

Braine's novel, about Joe Lampton, a working class lad with a whole plate of chips on his shoulder, still packs a punch. Many of the locations are surprisingly unchanged. The opening scene of Harvey arriving at the fictitious setting of Warnley Town station uses **Halifax Station**. Warnley itself is Bradford, where Harvey works in **Bradford City Hall**. The dance was filmed inside Bradford's art gallery, **Cartwright Memorial Hall** in Lister Park, **Keighley Road** a couple of miles northwest of the city centre. The posh home of Heather Sears, to which Harvey aspires, has been extended to become the **Jarvis Bankfield Hotel, Bradford Road, Bingley** (*℗ 01274.567123*). And you can still sink a pint in the pub where Harvey and Signoret meet up: the **Boy and Barrel, James Gate**.

Joe Lampton works for the council: Bradford City Hall

The dance: Cartwright Memorial Hall, Lister Park

Heather Sears' house: Jarvis Bankfield Hotel, Bingley

Joe Lampton meets Alice: Boy and Barrel pub, James Gate, Bradford

ROOM WITH A VIEW, A
(1986, dir: James Ivory)
Maggie Smith, Helena Bonham Carter, Julian Sands.
● **FLORENCE, ITALY; KENT; LONDON**

Perfect Merchant-Ivory drama from EM Forster's novel, blessed with a wonderful camp sensibility – just look at the interspersed captions – and a clutch of priceless cameos.

The Pensione Bertolini in Florence, where English-rosebud-abroad Bonham Carter finds herself in a room *without* a view, actually is in Florence. It's the **Quisisana e Ponte Vecchio Hotel, Lungarno Arnobusieri 4** alongside the Arno. Flouncy novelist Judi Dench whisks mag-

The Florence hotel: Pensione Quisisana e Ponte Vecchio

The fight in the piazza: Piazza della Signorina, Florence

Windy Corner: Foxwold, Brasted Chart

The village: Chiddingstone, Kent

gie Smith off to see the *real* Florence, starting at the statue of Grand Duke Ferdinand in the **Piazza Santissima Annunziata**, while Bonham Carter sets off to explore the sights alone. She's hassled by locals at the monument to Dante in the **Church of Santa Croce, Piazza Santa Croce 16** (unlike Michelangelo, Galileo, Machiavelli and Rossini who are buried in Santa Croce, Dante Alighieri has only a monument – he was exiled to, and died in, Ravenna). The bloody knife fight was filmed in the **Piazza della Signorina** – the site of the original 'Bonfire of the Vanities' when in 1497 followers of religious fanatic Savonarola burned all their worldly possessions. The idea really took off, and a year later they burned Savonarola too. There's a pretty fine selection of Florentine statuary seen here, including Cellini's 'Perseus holding the head of Medusa' and a copy of Michelangelo's 'David'. The huge fountain where the crowd try to revive the knife victim is Bartolommeo Ammannati's 1565 **Neptune Fountain**. Judged to be somewhat less successful than its neighbours, it's now known as Il Biancone – roughly, the Big White Lump. The drive out to the picnic was filmed on the road from Florence to Fiesde, and the picnic itself took place at **Villa di Maiano**, on a hillside near **Maiano**.

Back in England, Windy Corner, the home of the Honeychurch family in Summerstreet, is a private home (that of film critic John Pym), **Foxwold, Pipers Lane, Brasted Chart** south of Brasted west of Sevenoaks in west Kent – not visible from the road. The lake where Julian Sands, Rupert Graves and Simon Callow go skinny-dipping was created in the grounds here. Lucy's engagement party was filmed in the grounds of **Emmett's Garden**, a National Trust property just north of Ide Hill off New Road a couple of miles from Brasted. The five-acre garden, once densely wooded and, in spring, carpeted with bluebells, suffered heavily in the 1987 hurricane and is only slowly being restored to its former state. It's open to the public April to October. The railway station is **Horsted Keynes Station**, the northern terminus of the famous Bluebell Line, a few miles north of Haywards Heath in Sussex.

Daniel Day-Lewis' 'well appointed home' is the **Linley-Sambourne House, 18 Stafford Terrace**, London

W8. Built for *Punch* cartoonist Edward Linley-Sambourne in the 1870s, this unique perfectly preserved late Victorian house is managed by the Victorian Society and open to the public on Wednesdays and Sundays, March to October. You can find it just north of High Street Kensington (*© 020.8994.1019; tube: High Street Kensington*), and see it again, as Hugh Grant's London pad, in *Maurice*. Day-Lewis invites the Emersons to Summerstreet in the **National Gallery**.

The village of Summerstreet is **Chiddingstone**, a street of Tudor houses off the Edenbridge-Tonbridge road, B2027, at Bough Beech about 10 miles from Sevenoaks, Tonbridge or Tunbridge Wells in Kent, and about five from Emmett's. Here you can see the Reverend Beebe's church, **St Mary's**, opposite the row of houses. The sitting room, where Mr Emerson persuades Lucy to tell the truth, is a room in St Mary's rectory. The Emersons' house is **Chiddingstone Village Hall**. The London home of the two Miss Alans is **167 Queensgate**, South Kensington, SW7. At the time of filming this was the home of the Soviet representative for Estonia, but it's now a private residence.

ROPE
(1948, dir: Alfred Hitchcock)
John Dall, Farley Granger, James Stewart.
● **LOS ANGELES**

Hitchcock's first production away from control freak David O Selznick was an experiment with a single-take movie. Although there are no actual cuts, the twenty-minute maximum load of film stock required crafty blackouts to cover the changeover. The single penthouse set, with its view over 35 miles of New York skyline, needed 8,000 lightbulbs, 200 neon signs and even miniature smoking chimneys, and had to meet the technical challenge of the onscreen change from day to night. The film was shot entirely at The Warner Brothers studio in Burbank.

ROSEMARY'S BABY
(1968, dir: Roman Polanski)
Mia Farrow, John Cassavetes, Ruth Gordon.
● **NEW YORK CITY**

The Branford, the brooding Gothic building where newlyweds Farrow and Cassavetes set up home is, of course, the **Dakota Apartments, 1 West 72nd Street** at Central Park West, home to many celebs over the years, including Judy Garland, Lauren Bacall, Boris Karloff and

The gloomy Branford apartment building: Dakota Building, 72nd Street, West Side

Leonard Bernstein. It is most famously the last home of John Lennon, who was shot outside it in 1980. Over the road, in Central Park, is Lennon's memorial, Strawberry Fields. Ira Levin's original story was reputedly inspired by the Alwyn Court Apartments, a Renaissance-style block, decorated with terracotta dragons, at 180 West 58th Street.

ROUNDERS
(1998, dir: John Dahl)
Matt Damon, Edward Norton, John Turturro.
● **NEW YORK CITY; NEW JERSEY**

Damon is a gambling addict getting into hot water in John Dahl's poker drama, set in New York and Atlantic City. The City Law School, where Damon studies, is **Rutger's Law School, 123 Washington Street, University Heights, Newark**, New Jersey.

ROXANNE
(1987, dir: Fred Schepisi)
Steve Martin, Daryl Hannah, Rick Rossovich.
● **BRITISH COLUMBIA, CANADA**

Beautifully filmed updating of Rostand's *Cyrano de Bergerac*, which could have been a classic tearjerker without the cop-out ending. Shot on location in British Columbia, the photogenically precipitous streets and pine-clad hills are **Nelson**, in the southeast corner of the state, north of the US border.

RULING CLASS, THE
(1971, dir: Peter Medak)
Peter O'Toole, Harry Andrews, Arthur Lowe.
● **LINCOLNSHIRE; SURREY; BUCKINGHAMSHIRE; HAMPSHIRE; LONDON**

Peter Barnes' wild, black satire on the British upper class, with O'Toole as the gentle Jesus freak throwing his venal family into confusion when he inherits the earldom of Gurney. Harry Andrews' tutu-clad auto-erotic asphyxiation was filmed in the banqueting hall of the **Worshipful Company of Stationers and Newspaper Makers, Stationers' Hall, Ave Maria Lane**, EC4. The fantastical exterior of Gurney Manor is **Harlaxton Manor**, an extravagant neo-Elizabethan extravaganza a couple of miles west of **Grantham**, Lincolnshire. Owned by the University of Evansville, the house is open in May and June (*©* *01476.564541*). It's now probably more famous from the trashy remake of *The Haunting*. Interiors were filmed in **Cliveden** near Maidenhead, scene of the sixties sexual frolics portrayed in *Scandal*, and seen in The Beatles' movie *Help!*. The Gurney estate village is **Shere**, on the A25 between Guildford and Dorking in Surrey. The mental hospital is **Elvetham Hall**, now a conference centre, at **Hartley Wintney** near Fleet in Hampshire.

RUMBLE FISH
(1983, dir: Francis Ford Coppola)
Matt Dillon, Mickey Rourke, Diane Lane.
● **OKLAHOMA**

Filmed back-to-back with *The Outsiders*, and from another SE Hinton book, *Rumble Fish* couldn't be more different, with strange, dreamlike, bleached out monochrome photography, time-lapse landscapes and surreal set pieces. It was made on location in **Tulsa**, Oklahoma, (where the fish are released into the Arkansas River at the **21st Street Bridge**) and a few miles southwest down I-44 in the town of **Sapulpa**.

RUSH HOUR
(1998, dir: Brett Ratner)
Jackie Chan, Chris Tucker, Tom Wilkinson.
● **LOS ANGELES; HONG KONG**

The opening scene is **Hong Kong Harbour**, but Tom Wilkinson's home, despite the view of the city from the windows, is in LA. It's Frank Lloyd Wright's **Ennis Brown House**,

Hollywood sightseeing: Mann's Chinese Theater, Hollywood Boulevard

2607 Glendower Avenue, Silverlake, below Griffith Park (see *The House on Haunted Hill* for details). Chris Tucker takes Jackie Chan to see John Wayne's footprints at **Mann's Chinese Theater, 6925 Hollywood Boulevard** in Hollywood. The China Exposition is at the **New Los Angeles Convention Center, Figueroa Street** between 11th Street and Venice Boulevard, downtown LA. See it also in *Face/Off* and as the spaceport in *Starship Troopers*.

RYAN'S DAUGHTER
(1970, dir: David Lean)
Sarah Miles, Robert Mitchum, Christopher Jones.
● **IRELAND; SOUTH AFRICA**

The critical mauling of this vastly overblown epic caused David Lean to retire from the screen for fourteen years. Despite the visual splendour and some stunning sequences (the real storm is breathtaking), the small love story is uninvolving. The entire village of Kirrary was a set, now vanished, built near Carhoo on the **Dingle Peninsula**, down at the southwesternmost tip of Ireland. Most of the beach scenes were shot at **Inch Strand**, about twelve miles east of Dingle itself, and at **Coumeenoole Strand** near Dunquin. The beach where Rosie loses her parasol is at the **Cliffs of Moher**, County Clare, while other scenes used **Barrow Strand**, north of Tralee.

The highlight of the movie, the breathtaking storm sequence, uses the rocky coast at **Bridges of Ross**, 30 miles to the south. As the troubled shoot rolled on, and winter arrived, a new location had to be found. The suicide of Major Dorian was, bizarrely, filmed on a beach in South Africa, where the local white rock had to be painted black to match the Irish location.

S

SABOTAGE (aka *A Woman Alone*)
(1936, dir: Alfred Hitchcock)
Sylvia Sidney, Oscar Homolka, John Loder.
● LONDON

Foreign agent Oscar Homolka's Bijou cinema, the High Street Station and neighbouring street are a studio set, but Hitchcock's early suspenser contains more real London locations than any other feature film seen at the time. The opening scene sees sabotage at **Battersea Power Station** on the South Bank of the Thames, plunging into darkness central London landmarks like the Palace of Westminster, Trafalgar Square and Piccadilly Circus. It's in **Trafalgar Square** that Sylvia Sidney later meets up with undercover cop John Loder, before going for a meal at Simpson's in the Strand. The restaurant, one of Hitchcock's favourites and where he entertained the press to publicise the movie, was mocked up in the studio, but you can see the real thing in *Howards End*. The Lord Mayor's Show, where Sidney's young brother waits unknowingly with the bomb, was also faked. Supposedly in the Strand, the parade was shot in front of a giant photograph of the Law Courts.

SABOTEUR
(1942, dir: Alfred Hitchcock)
Robert Cummings, Priscilla Lane, Norman Lloyd.
● CALIFORNIA; NEW YORK CITY; NEVADA

Cummings is the innocent man suspected of being a wartime saboteur. Though made largely at Universal Studios in Hollywood, there are the usual Hitchcockian landmark locations, largely supplied by a second unit. Cummings thumbs across the desert near **Lone Pine**, on Route 395, central California, before arriving at the ghost town which overlooks the saboteurs' next target, **Boulder Dam**, over the Colorado River just outside of Las Vegas, Nevada. Arriving in New York, Priscilla Lane is held captive in the Rockefeller Center, and there's a shoot-out at a film screening in **Radio City Music Hall, 1260 Sixth Avenue** (though the deco interior was largely recreated in the studio).

A new ending was added, incorporating shots of the SS *Normandie*, supposedly in the Brooklyn Navy Yard. The ship had been renamed USS *Lafayette*, and burned in a suspicious fire at a Manhattan pier in February 1942. Listing under the weight of water used to extinguish the blaze, the ailing ship was inserted into the movie, a supposed victim of the saboteur. The Navy was not best pleased, but the shot remains. The famous climax atop the Statue of Liberty was filmed, of course, mainly in the studio.

SABRINA (aka *Sabrina Fair*)
(1954, dir: Billy Wilder)
Humphrey Bogart, Audrey Hepburn, William Holden.
● NEW YORK STATE

Wealthy brothers Holden and Bogart vie for the affections of chauffeur's daughter Hepburn in Wilder's romantic comedy, which was filmed at the **Welland House, Glen Cove**, on Route 107 northeast coast of Long Island, New York.

SABRINA
(1995, dir: Sydney Pollack)
Harrison Ford, Julia Ormond, Greg Kinnear.
● NEW YORK STATE; MASSACHUSETTS; FRANCE

The mansion of brothers Ford and Kinnear in this enjoyable, but unnecessary, remake is a stone's throw away from the house used in the original. A private home built in 1929 for financier Junius Spencer Morgan, and not open to the public, **Salutation House, Glen Cove**, became available for filming when it was put up for sale. The house was extensively renovated, and a whole false wing added onto the garage to serve as the chauffeur's quarters.

Ford whisks Julia Ormond away to the family's summer home on exclusive island resort **Martha's Vineyard**, off the coast of Massachusetts (see *Jaws* for details). The cottage itself (belonging to singer Billy Joel) overlooks the fishing port of **Chilmark** on the island's southwestern coast. The town they cycle to is **Vineyard Haven**, over on the island's northeastern coast. Ormond's stay in Paris takes in the usual touristy locations of the elaborate **Pont Alexandre III**; the **Place du Trocadero** at the foot of the Eiffel Tower; the **Louvre**'s stunning glass pyramid; and **Montmartre** and the **Sacre Coeur**. The final clinch is on the narrow, wooden **Pont des Arts**, just south of the Louvre.

SAFETY LAST
(1923, dir: Sam Taylor, Fred Newmeyer)
Harold Lloyd, Mildred Davis, Noah Young.
● LOS ANGELES

The De Vore Department Store: South Broadway

Silent comedian Harold Lloyd's stock-in-trade was a series of dizzying stunts involving dangling from the outside of tall buildings. In *Safety Last* he's a smalltown boy trying to impress his girlfriend by entering a skyscraper-climbing contest. The De Vore Department Store in the Bolton Building is a combination of two downtown LA structures, only one of which still survives. **801 South Broadway** can still be seen, but 908 South Broadway, where he famously hung from a clock face, has been demolished. It's not quite as dangerous as it looked. The clock face was built over a platform, and for the longshots, Lloyd hired 'human fly' Bill Struthers to climb the building. That's the LA Stock Exchange you can see in the background. Lloyd worked over the same ideas later in *Feet First*.

SAINT, THE
(1997, dir: Phillip Noyce)
Val Kilmer, Elisabeth Shue, Alun Armstrong.
● LONDON; OXFORDSHIRE; MIDDLESEX; KENT; RUSSIA

Val Kilmer is the master criminal who has amassed almost

The Saint's London base: Halcyon Hotel, Holland park

The Oxford pub: Trout Inn, Lower Wolvercote

The miraculous climax: Red Square, Moscow

$50 million by use of false moustaches and a string of instantly traceable names; Elisabeth Shue, the Oxford professor who, having solved the world's fuel problems, carries the formula in her underwear. While Hitchcock might have floated this material along effortlessly, this misfired thriller is sunk by the soggy ballast of cod psychology. The Saint's London base is the starry **Halcyon Hotel, 81 Holland Park, W11** (℃ *020.7 727.7288*), home to Hollywood royalty and visiting rock stars. Shue works out of **Queen's College, High Street, Oxford.** To seduce Shue, Kilmer poses opposite the white marble **Shelley Memorial** in **University College, High Street.** The statue, designed by Edward Onslow Ford, was intended for Shelley's grave in the English Cemetery, Rome, but proved too large and was presented to the college by Shelley's widow in 1894. See it in the domed chamber reached by a passageway in the northwest corner of the quad. The Oxford pub where Shue gets all soppy with 'St Thomas More' is the **Trout Inn**, a beautiful riverside pub (which has also been featured in TV's *Inspector Morse*) at **195 Godstow Road, Lower Wolvercote**, about three miles northwest of the city (℃ *01865.554485*).

Berlin Templehof airport is actually Westminster's **New Royal Horticultural Hall**, on the corner of **Greycoat and Elverton Streets** in Westminster, SW1 (it served much the same purpose in *Indiana Jones and the Last Crusade*). The real exotic location filming, though, is in Moscow's **Red Square**, where Kilmer escapes from the first chase, and looking stunning illuminated at night for the would-be miraculous climax. The Moscow hotel is the 1956 'Stalin Gothic'-style **Peking Hotel, 1/5 Bolshaya Sadovaya Street** (℃ *095.209.2215*). Filming in Moscow also took place at the **Foreign Affairs Ministry** building; at the **Aerostar Hotel** and at **Leningrad Station**. The finale, with Shue giving her secret to the world, is supposedly in Oxford's **Sheldonian Theatre**. The exterior is real enough, with Kilmer chased out past the Clarendon Building into **Catte Street**.

The inescapable feeling of déjà-vu, after seeing *Mission: Impossible* – sixties TV series made big with Hollywood star, London and Eastern Europe locations, impen-etrable plot – lurches into the realms of conspiracy theory with the reappearance of the improbably mugging Eurostar driver of the former film (David Schneider) in the rat-racing restaurant.

Scenes were also shot at **Harrow School**, Middlesex; the **Pearl Assurance Building, Holborn**, London and **Fort Amhurst, Chatham**, Kent.

SALO (aka *Salò O Le 120 Giornate Di Sodoma*)
(1975, dir: Pier Paolo Pasolini)
Paolo Bonacelli, Giorgio Cataldi, Caterina Boratto.
● ITALY

Pasolini's ice-cold and disturbing final film, still banned in the UK, transposes de Sade's *120 Days of Sodom* to the last days of fascist rule in northern Italy during WWII. Four upstanding pillars of the community spirit away a group of local youngsters for a terminally sadistic orgy. The estate is the decayed pre-Umbertine **Villa Mirra**, with overgrown gazebos and rose bushes choked by wisteria, at **Cavriana**, a few miles from Mantua, northern Italy. It's now the **Archaeological Museum of Alto Mantovano** (℃ *0376.806330*). Another Emilian villa not far from Bologna, and now a public park, was used for the scene in which the choicest local teens are chosen. For the final scenes of torture and death, the courtyard of Villa Mirra was recreated in the studio at Cinecittà, Rome.

And, for those foodies who enjoy recreating meals from the movies, the recipe for the coprophagic banquet scene is: Swiss chocolate mixed with broken biscuits, condensed milk and marmalade, extruded through plastic tubing. Enjoy.

SAMOURAI, LE (aka *The Samurai/The Godson*)
(1967, dir: Jean-Pierre Melville)
Alain Delon, François Périer, Nathalie Delon.
● PARIS

Director Melville had a cameo in Jean-Luc Godard's groundbreaking *A Bout de Souffle* and his cool, minimalist gangster movie was also made on the streets of Paris. Delon, like Jean-Paul Belmondo before him, dodges the law on the Champs Elysées by ducking through an entrance at **1 rue Lord Byron** (behind the Champs) to pop out at **116 bis**, by the Lido, and duck into the **George V metro station**. He takes the Vincennes line to **Porte d'Ivry** where he's shot and wounded on meeting his contact. There's a convoluted metro chase as the law follows Delon from the **Telegraphe metro** (near his apartment) to **Place des Fêtes**. He gets off at **Jourdain**. The law despatches cars to Place des Fêtes; **Botzaris** and **Pre Saint Gervais**. Delon finally gives them the slip at the world's largest subway interchange, **Chatelet Les Halles** (the setting for much of *Subway*), where he leaps off the travelator.

SAND PEBBLES, THE
(1966, dir: Robert Wise)
Steve McQueen, Richard Attenborough, Richard Crenna.
● TAIWAN; HONG KONG; LOS ANGELES

Vietnam parallels abound as the US gunboat, *San Pablo*, tangles with Chinese warlords on the Yangtse River in 1926. Wise's movie was made at **Taipei**, on the island of Taiwan, on the **Keelung** and **Tam Sui Rivers**. In the Tam

Sui district, 900 of the 5,000 locals were recruited as extras to storm across the **Changsha Bund** and hurl lighted torches at the *San Pablo*. The boat itself, at $250,000 the most costly action prop built at the time, was modelled on the *Villa Lobos*, which had been captured from Spain after the Spanish-American War. The climactic fight, with 30 Chinese junks, supposedly on the Chien River, was shot on the **Sai Kung** backwater inlet at Hong Kong.

The interiors were filmed back at Twentieth Century Fox in LA (you can see some of the sets recycled in Roger Corman's *The St Valentine's Day Massacre*).

SANDPIPER, THE
(1965, dir: Vincente Minnelli)
Elizabeth Taylor, Richard Burton, Eva Marie Saint.
● CALIFORNIA

Ponderous, soapy romance between California artist Elizabeth Taylor and Richard Burton, the minister/headmaster of her son's school. Taylor's shack was on the beach at **Monterey**, with more filming a little way down the coast at **Big Sur**.

SARABAND FOR DEAD LOVERS (aka *Saraband*)
(1948, dir: Basil Dearden, Michael Relph)
Stewart Granger, Joan Greenwood, Flora Robson.
● OXFORDSHIRE

Tragic historical romance, shot at **Blenheim Palace**, Sir John Vanbrugh's classic house, built for the Duke of Marlborough, and the birthplace of Sir Winston Churchill. It's open to the public from mid-March to the end of October (*admission charge; © 0993.811325*). You can find Blenheim southwest of Woodstock village, on the A44, eight miles north of Oxford.

SATANIC RITES OF DRACULA, THE (aka *Count Dracula and His Vampire Bride*)
(1973, dir: Alan Gibson)
Christopher Lee, Peter Cushing, Freddie Jones.
● LONDON; HERTFORDSHIRE

Another update, following the kitschy *Dracula AD 1972*, with the Count as a vampiric property developer in central London. Pelham House in Croxted Heath – headquarters of the Psychical Examination and Research Group, the front for a vampiric cult – is really **High Canons, Buckettsland Lane, Well End**, just to the north of Borehamwood in Hertfordshire. No stranger to such goings on, the house can be seen in plenty of other movies, including *The Devil Rides Out*.

SATURDAY NIGHT AND SUNDAY MORNING
(1960, dir: Karel Reisz)
Albert Finney, Shirley Anne Field, Rachel Roberts.
● NOTTINGHAMSHIRE; LONDON

A resentful factory worker has a fling with a married woman, but ultimately settles for dull conformity. One of the key British New Wave movies, which launched Albert Finney to instant stardom, it was made on location around Nottingham in the Midlands. Finney works at the **Raleigh Bicycle Factory** in **Radford**, where the story's author, Alan Sillitoe, had actually worked. The factory still survives,

though the surrounding streets have been demolished to provide car parking space. The pub, where Finney gets totally smashed, still exists; it's the **White Horse Inn, 313 Ilkeston Road** in Radford. The funfair scenes are at **Wimbledon** in London, and some interiors were shot in the studio at Twickenham.

SATURDAY NIGHT FEVER
(1977, dir: John Badham)
John Travolta, Karen Lynn Gorney, Barry Miller.
● NEW YORK CITY

Nik Cohn's account of social rituals is transformed into the disco hit of the seventies, with Travolta as the blue-collar kid from Brooklyn whose dancing opens up a new world over the East River. Travolta's neighbourhood is Bay Ridge. The opening scene is at **86th Street**, Brooklyn. The kids display macho bravado on the **Verrazzano Narrows Bridge**, where I-278 crosses New York Bay, south of Bay Ridge.

Travolta's home: 79th Street, Bay Ridge

Travolta's home is **221 79th Street, Bay Ridge**, in a smart middle class area of the borough. Not far away is the disco where white-suited Travolta provided the iconic image of seventies dance culture. In '78 it was 2001 Odyssey. It's now **Spectrum**, a gay men's dance club, **802 64th Street** at Eighth Avenue (*© 718.238.8213*).

The 2001 disco: Spectrum, 64th Street, Bay Ridge

SAVING PRIVATE RYAN
(1998, dir: Steven Spielberg)
Tom Hanks, Tom Sizemore, Matt Damon.
● HERTFORDSHIRE; IRELAND

The French village was built at the former British Aerospace factory in Hatfield, Hertfordshire. The harrowing Omaha Beach scenes were shot on **Curracloe Beach, Ballinesker**, just north of Wexford, about 70 miles south of Dublin, on the southeast coast of the Republic of Ireland (*rail: Wexford*).

SAYONARA
(1957, dir: Joshua Logan)
Marlon Brando, Miyoshi Umeki, Red Buttons.
● LOS ANGELES

Parallel romances in post-war Japan. The American Offi-

The American Officers' Club: Yamashiro, Sycamore Avenue, Hollywood

cers Club is **Yamashiro, 1999 North Sycamore Avenue**. A Japanese restaurant, built by hundreds of Oriental craftsmen in 1913-14, the cedar and teak replica of a Japanese palace comes complete with teahouse, gardens and an imported 600-year-old pagoda. It stands in the Hollywood Hills on a single track road, north of the suburb, with spectacular views over Hollywood.

SCANDAL

(1989, dir: Michael Caton-Jones)
John Hurt, Ian McKellen, Joanne Whalley-Kilmer.
● **LONDON; WILTSHIRE; MERSEYSIDE; NOTTINGHAMSHIRE**

Stephen Ward's flat: Bathurst Mews, Bayswater

Straightforward account of the Christine Keeler-John Profumo scandal that rocked British politics in the sixties, somewhat upstaged by McKellen's bizarre Samurai topknot, the misjudged result of shaving his hairline for the role rather than resorting to a wig.

Stephen Ward, the fall guy in the scandal who committed suicide, lived at 17 Wimpole Mews in Marylebone. Too redeveloped for filming, Ward's flat in the movie is **42 Bathurst Mews**, a cobbled mews in Bayswater.

The country house, where a monied elite indulged in poolside frolics, was, notoriously, Cliveden, home of the Astor family, two miles north of Taplow on the Hedsor Road near Maidenhead, Buckinghamshire. Although the house is open to the public during summer (though it's now being converted into a hotel), its connection with the Keeler-Profumo affair was not one the owners wanted to emphasise and permission to film was refused (although Cliveden has been seen in plenty of other movies, including *Help!*, where it stood in for Buckingham Palace). The country estate in the film is the much-used **Wilton House, Wilton**, three miles from Salisbury, Wiltshire and **Longleat House, Warminster**, also in Wiltshire.

There was additional filming in Liverpool, and the Old Bailey is a conflation of **County Hall**, London (see *Mission: Impossible* for details), and **Shire Hall, High Pavement**, Nottingham.

SCANNERS

(1980, dir: David Cronenberg)
Jennifer O'Neill, Patrick McGoohan, Stephen Lack.
● **QUEBEC, CANADA**

Telepaths with powerful mind-control abilities in Cro-

nenberg's influential sci-fi horror, made largely around **Montreal**. The railway station, though, is **Yorkdale Station** on the Downsview Line in **Toronto**, north of the city centre.

The railway station: Yorkdale, Toronto

SCARFACE

(1983, dir: Brian De Palma)
Al Pacino, Steven Bauer, Michelle Pfeiffer.
● **CALIFORNIA; FLORIDA; NEW YORK CITY**

When Fidel Castro opened up the harbour at Mariel in May 1980 to allow 125,000 Cubans to join relatives in the US, he took the opportunity to export some of the country's toughest criminals. Smalltime thug Tony Montana grabs the opportunity to make it as a big-time drug lord in Oliver Stone's loose reworking of the thirties gangster classic.

Set in Miami and Bolivia, the movie's locations are mostly divided between Florida and California. The Florida internment camp, where Pacino wins his freedom by killing a Castro agent, was constructed under the knot of freeway interchanges at the intersection of I-10, the Santa Monica freeway, and I-110, the Harbor Freeway, downtown LA behind the New LA Convention Center. Miami's 'Little Havana' district, where Montana starts out working at the El Paraiso lunch stand, was recreated at **Little Tokyo** in downtown LA. Montana's arrival in the art deco district of Miami Beach is impossible to fake, though, and was shot on **Ocean Drive** at 13th Street. The Sun Ray Apartments, where Montana's brother is dismembered by chainsaw, has been revamped to become **Johnny Rocket's, 728 Ocean Drive** between the Beacon and Colony hotels near 7th Street.

The movie's two estates, one supposedly in Bolivia, one in Florida, are both in the town of **Montecito**, on the California coast a few miles east of Santa

Tony Montana arrives in Miami Beach: Ocean Drive at 13th Street

Chainsaw at the Sun-Ray Apartment: Johnny Rocket's, Ocean Drive, Miami Beach

The bomb attempt in New York: Tudor City Place

Barbara. Sosa's South American estate, where Omar is ousted, is a rococo Spanish hacienda designed by architect Addison Mizener. Montana's own Coral Gables estate is **El Fureidis** ('Little Paradise'), a mediterranean villa built for Waldron Gillespie, a wealthy upstate New Yorker, by Bertram Goodhue. Neither estate is open to the public. The luxury hotel grounds, where Pacino and pal Steven Bauer ogle women, are of the **Fontainebleau Hilton Resort and Spa, 4441 Collins Avenue**, Miami (© *305.538.2000*; see *Goldfinger* for details).

In New York, the Gothic apartment block of the intended bomb victim is **5 Tudor City Place** at East 41st Street.

SCENES FROM A MALL
(1991, dir: Paul Mazursky)
Bette Midler, Woody Allen, Bill Irwin.
● **LOS ANGELES; CONNECTICUT; NEW YORK CITY**

The mall: Beverly Center, Beverly Hills

The mall, where Allen and Midler's marriage falls apart during a shopping trip, is, ostensibly, the **Beverly Center, Beverly Boulevard** at La Cienega Boulevard, midtown LA, which is, indeed, used for exteriors. But Woody Allen doesn't like to stray too far from New York, and certainly not to the abhorred West Coast. The interior of the mall, with its tiresome mimes, carol singers and sushi bars, is **Stamford Town Center, Atlantic Street, Stamford**, Connecticut, while most of the studio interiors were filmed in the Kaufman-Astoria Studios, Queens, New York.

SCENT OF A WOMAN
(1992, dir: Martin Brest)
Al Pacino, Chris O'Donnell, Gabrielle Anwar.
● **NEW YORK CITY; NEW YORK STATE**

College kid O'Donnell accompanies blind, suicidal ex-soldier Pacino on one last fling in New York. And it's nothing but the best. They stay at the **Waldorf-Astoria Hotel, 301 Park Avenue** (© *212.355.3000*) between East 49th and East 50th Streets, midtown Manhattan. They dine out

Pacino and O'Donnell in New York: Waldorf-Astoria Hotel, Park Avenue

in style in the **Oak Room** of the **Plaza Hotel, West 59th** Street at Fifth Avenue. Pacino dances a mean tango in the ballroom of the grand old European-style

Pierre Hotel, 2 East 61st Street at Fifth Avenue on the East Side. Pacino drives the car along the East River front, beneath the Williamsburg Bridge. O'Donnell's school is a conflation of two properties: **Hempstead House**, one of the four mansions (another was used

The tango: Hotel Pierre, East 61st Street

O'Donnell's School: Hempstead House, Long Island

as the estate where the movie producer gets a horse's head in his bed in *The Godfather*) on **Sands Point Preserve, 95 Middleneck Road, Port Washington** on Long Island, and the **Emma Willard School, 285 Pawlings Avenue, Troy** (the NY State town used as turn-of-the-century Manhattan in *The Age of Innocence*).

SCHINDLER'S LIST
(1993, dir: Steven Spielberg)
Liam Neeson, Ben Kingsley, Ralph Fiennes.
● **POLAND; ISRAEL**

Spielberg finally achieved respectability and got his long-delayed Oscar for this story of Oskar Schindler, the wheeler-dealing Gentile businessman who saved over a thousand Jews from the gas chambers. Initial controversy with the custodians of the Auschwitz Memorial, worried by the prospect of Hollywood schmaltz, was resolved by filming only outside the gatehouse of the Birkenau camp, in the Polish town of **Oswiecim**. Actually, several other Hollywood movies, including *Triumph of the Spirit*, had already filmed inside the camp.

The movie was made in **Krakow**, one of the few Polish cities to escape devastation during WWII, and listed by UNESCO as one of the world's great historic cities. Nothing, though, remains of Plaszów labour camp, which stood on the slope of Krzemionki Hill, to the east of the old town. The only set built for the movie, a replica of Plaszów, consisting of 34 barracks, seven watchtowers and even the road into the camp – paved with Jewish tombstones – was built, from the original plans, in a disused quarry at the foot of Krakus mound

Clearing the ghetto: Jozefa Street

The bridge over the Vistula: Krakowska Street

Oskar Schindler's factory: Lipowa Street, Krakow

close to the actual site. Amon Goeth's villa was reproduced above the camp, less than a mile from the original building, which still stands on Jerozolimska Street. Many of the real locations were used, including Schindler's own elegant apartment, at **7 Straszewskiego Street**, north of Kazimierz district and Wawel Hill.

For the wartime ghetto of Zgoda Square, which has been extensively redeveloped, the film uses **Szeroka Street** in the former Jewish district of Kazimierz. Nearby is **Ciemna Street**, where Poldek Pfefferberg narrowly escapes death after bumping into Amon Goeth by claiming that he had orders to clear the street. The expulsion of the Jews from the ghetto used the picturesque courtyard at **12 Jozefa Street**, linking to Meiselsa Street. The bridge over the Vistula, over which they are herded, is at the end of **Krakowska Street** (for the film, the crossing of the bridge had to be reversed). Schindler's factory is the real thing, virtually unchanged, at **4 Lipowa Street**. It now produces electrical components. The interiors, though, used the enamel factory in **Olkusz**, in the Malopolska province.

The church, where the Jews meet clandestinely, is Krakow's most important church, the 14th century **Church of St Mary's**. The railway station is **Krakow Glowny**. The Brinnlitz scenes used the quaint old town of **Niepolomice**, about 25 miles east of Krakow.

SCHOOL FOR SCOUNDRELS

(1960, dir: Robert Hamer)
Ian Carmichael, Alastair Sim, Terry-Thomas.
● **HERTFORDSHIRE**

Ian Carmichael is one of life's failures, taking lessons in one-upmanship from the cynical Sim in this film adaptation of Stephen Potter's books, from the director of *Kind Hearts and Coronets*. The railway station, at Yeovil, Somerset, is actually **Hertford East**, Hertfordshire. There was also filming at the **Edgwarebury Hotel, Edgwarebury Lane, Elstree**, Hertfordshire.

SCOTT OF THE ANTARCTIC

(1948, dir: Charles Frend)
John Mills, Derek Bond, James Robertson Justice.
● **NORWAY; ANTARCTICA; CORNWALL**

The story of Captain Scott's doomed expedition to the South Pole in 1912, with a score by Vaughan Williams. The location snowscapes are a glacier near **Finse** in Norway (an area which became Hoth in *The Empire Strikes Back*), with second unit shots from **Grahamland** in the

real Antarctic. The departure of the *Discovery* was filmed at the eastern breakwater of **Falmouth Docks**, down in southwest Cornwall.

SCREAM

(1996, dir: Wes Craven)
Neve Campbell, Courteney Cox, Skeet Ulrich.
● **CALIFORNIA**

First of that whole new genre, the post-modern, ironic slasher movie, from the pen of Kevin Williamson. It was made around northern California. Drew Barrymore's isolated house is on **Sonoma Mountain Road, Glen Ellen**, Route 12 southeast of Santa Rosa. Neve Campbell's home is on **Calistoga Road**,

Woodsboro town square: Healdsburg

Woodsboro Police Station: Healdsburg Police Station

north of Santa Rosa toward Calistoga. Woodsboro High was to have been Santa Rosa High School, but the school board pulled out when they read the script – hence the 'No thanks at all to...' credit at the end of the movie. In the end, the school was played by **Sonoma Community Center, 276 East Napa Street, Sonoma**, a few miles south of Glen Ellen. The town square of the fictitious Woodsboro, where the teens gather by the fountain to discuss the grisly details, is the **Town Square, Healdsburg**, and the cop station is **Healdsburg Police Station**. The video store, where film buff Jamie Kennedy works, is **Bradley Video, 3080 Marlow Road, Santa Rosa**. The mansion where the climactic bloodbath takes place is a private house, overlooking **Tomales**, just east of town, south from the **Petaluma Road**.

The bloodbath mansion: Tomales

SCREAM 2

(1997, dir: Wes Craven)
Neve Campbell, Liev Schreiber, David Arquette.
● **GEORGIA; CALIFORNIA**

Two years after the Woodsboro murders, Neve Campbell attends college, when the fictional version of the killings,

313

The premiere of *Stab*: Vista Theater, Hollywood

Stab, is released. Windsor College is **Agnes Scott College, Decatur** outside Atlanta, Georgia. The movie première of *Stab* was filmed at the little **Vista Theater, 4473 Sunset Drive, Hollywood** (seen as the Detroit movie house at the opening of *True Romance*), though the exterior is the **Rialto Theater, 1023 South Fair Oaks Avenue, Pasadena** (see *The Player* for details). *Stab* itself was shot in **Malibu**.

SCREAM 3

(2000, dir: Wes Craven)
Neve Campbell, David Arquette, Courteney Cox Arquette.
● **CALIFORNIA**

Stab 3 is in production and... well, figure out the convolutions for yourself. Set around Hollywood, the movie producer's office overlooks MacArthur Park, downtown. The mansion is the **Canfield-Moreno Residence and Complex, 1923 Micheltorena Street, Silverlake**, also seen as the private school in the *Halloween* sequel *H20*.

SEA OF LOVE

(1989, dir: Harold Becker)
Al Pacino, Ellen Barkin, John Goodman.
● **NEW YORK CITY; ONTARIO, CANADA**

Engrossing did-she-didn't-she thriller with Ellen Barkin suspected of bumping off lonely hearts. Set in New York, there are plenty of real locations, although much of the movie was made north of the border at the Kleinburg Studios in Toronto. The opening police scam, where Pacino

The singles set-up: O'Neal's Baloon, West 63rd Street

manages to execute a whole roomful of warrants, used the old Savoy Manor Ballroom on **East 149th Street**. It's now part of the Hostos Community College in Hamilton Heights. The first murder takes place at **365 West End Avenue**, near 78th Street on Manhattan's West Side. Pacino lives just to the north on 85th Street, Barkin even further north at **45 88th Street**. The second murder is on **Yellowstone Boulevard**, running north-south between the Long Island Expressway and Queens Boulevard, Queens.

The restaurant, where Pacino and Goodman set up an elaborate scam

The first murder: West End Avenue on the West Side

to check out the suspect singles, is **O'Neal's Baloon, 48 West 63rd Street** at Columbus Avenue near the Lincoln Center. Ellen Barkin sells swanky slingbacks at **Maud Frizon, 19 East 60th Street** on the East Side. There was more filming on **Broadway**; **Amsterdam Avenue**; **East 57th Street**; **Eighth Avenue** and the **Taft Houses** on Madison Avenue between 112th and 115th Streets in East Harlem.

Toronto locations passing themselves off as New York include **Jerry's Diner, 132 Dundas Street** (seen also in the New York-set *Cocktail* and the Bette Midler weepie *Stella*); **Metro Hall, St John Street**; **Sutton Place Hotel, 955 Bay Street** (featured in *The January Man* and *Suspect*); the **Horseshoe Tavern, 368 Queen Street West** and **St Nicholas Ukranian Catholic Church, 4 Bellwoods Avenue**.

Jerry's Diner, Dundas Street, Toronto

The New York bar: Horseshoe Tavern, Queen Street, Toronto

SEARCHERS, THE

(1956, dir: John Ford)
John Wayne, Jeffrey Hunter, Natalie Wood.
● **ARIZONA; COLORADO; UTAH; CALIFORNIA**

Arguably Wayne's best role, as Ethan Edwards, obsessively tracking down the niece abducted by Indians. The opening title, 'Texas 1868', is blatantly belied by a view of Ford's beloved **Monument Valley**, Arizona, where much of the film was shot, along with Utah, on the San Juan River at **Mexican Hat**, several miles to the north. Second unit filming, capturing snow scenes and buffalo herds, took

Ethan Edwards sets out: Monument Valley

Finding Scar: Twelve Dancers, Monument Valley

place all over the West, including **Aspen** and southwestern Colorado. The dusty climax, where Wayne finally meets up with, and accepts, Wood, is actually **Griffith Park**, Los Angeles.

SECONDS

(1966, dir: John Frankenheimer)
Rock Hudson, Richard Anderson, Salome Jens.
● **NEW YORK CITY; CONNECTICUT; CALIFORNIA**

Hudson is the middle-aged businessman offered a new lease of life by a sinister rejuvenation company in John Frankenheimer's classic scarer. Kirk Douglas (then starring in *One Flew Over the Cuckoo's Nest* on Broadway) bought the rights and was to have played the lead, but contractual obligations sent him elsewhere. The opening scene is New York's **Grand Central Station**. Train scenes use the commuter services of New York, **New Haven** and **Hartford**, Connecticut. Hudson's pre-op suburban home is in **Scarsdale**, a suburb of Westchester County. After rejuvenation, Hudson moves to the West Coast. The party scene, with Hudson drunkenly blurting out his secret (and Hudson really was drunk for the scene) was shot in John Frankenheimer's own beachfront house in **Malibu**.

SECRET CEREMONY

(1968, dir: Joseph Losey)
Elizabeth Taylor, Mia Farrow, Robert Mitchum.
● **LONDON; NETHERLANDS**

Elizabeth Taylor's Gothic mansion: Addison Road, Holland Park

Weird psycho-drama from the gloriously self-indulgent tail end of the sixties, with raven-wigged waif Farrow adopting blowsy Taylor as a substitute mom. The movie followed on from the location. Director Losey had long been fascinated by a bizarre house in West Kensington and chose to film this oddball melodrama here (though some interiors had to be recreated in the studio). The strange, brooding mansion, with tall chimneys and startling turquoise tiles is **8 Addison Road**, between Holland Park Avenue and High Street Kensington. The area has to be the centre of London Gothic – just around the corner in Melbury Road stood the house where Michael Powell filmed *Peeping Tom*. The bus ride is the 31 through Kentish Town. The holiday scenes were shot in **Noordmeyer** on the Dutch coast.

SECRETS & LIES

(1996, dir: Mike Leigh)
Brenda Blethyn, Marianne Jean-Baptiste, Timothy Spall.
● **LONDON**

Cannes award winner for Mike Leigh, and Brenda Blethyn as Best Actress, is light years away from the bleak pessimism of *Naked*, with Marianne Jean-Baptiste the black daughter tracing her white natural mother. Blethyn's ter-

raced house is **76 Quilter Road, Bethnal Green**, SE17. Jean-Baptiste gets a copy of her birth certificate from **St Catherine's House**, and meets up with her

Brenda Blethyn's terraced house: Quilter Road, Bethnal Green

mother at **Holborn Underground Station**. Timothy Spall's shop is a real photographer's studio, **Studio on the Green, 34 The Green, Winchmore Hill**; and his house is nearby at

Timothy Spall's studio: Studio on the Green, Winchmore Hill

87 Whitehouse Way at Hampden Way, **Southgate**.

SENSE AND SENSIBILITY

(1995, dir: Ang Lee)
Emma Thompson, Kate Winslet, Alan Rickman.
● **DEVON; WILTSHIRE; SOMERSET; LONDON**

Ang Lee brings a fresh sensibility to the English Heritage genre with his adaptation of the Jane Austen novel. Norland Park, home of the Dashwood family, is **Saltram House** , a George II house set in a landscaped park. It's open to the public from April through October (℃ *01752.336546*). Find it three and a half miles east of Plymouth between the A38 and the A379, in Devon. The Dashwoods' London home is **Chandos House, 2 Queen Anne Street**, near to Broadcasting House. This Grade I listed building, a Robert Adam mansion built in 1769, was recently compulsorily purchased from an investment company after years of neglect and is currently being restored.

The front room of Mrs Jennings' London house is the owner's home of the **Flete Estate**, eleven miles east of Plymouth, open Wednesdays and Thursdays, May to September. The rest of the house used **Mompesson House, Cathedral Close** on the north side of Choristers' Green in Salisbury. This furnished Queen Anne townhouse is also open May through October (℃ *01722. 335659*). Cleveland, home to the Palmers (Imelda Staunton and Hugh Laurie), is the striking Elizabethan **Montacute House**, Montacute village, four miles west of Yeovil in

Mrs Jennings' London house: Mompesson House, Cathedral Close, Salisbury

The London street: Queen's House, Greenwich

Somerset, which you might also have seen in Derek Jarman's *The Angelic Conversation*. You can visit April through October (℃ *01935.823289*). The ballroom scene, where Greg Wise encounters Kate Winslet, uses another familiar old location, **Wilton House, Wilton**, two and a half miles west of Salisbury on the A30 (℃ *01722.743115*), seen also in Ken Russell's *The Music Lovers* and in *The Bounty* amongst many other films.

The bustling London street scenes are the covered walkway at the carefully restored **Queen's House, Greenwich** (℃ *020.8858.4422*), a one-time royal palace, occupied by the dowager Queen Henrietta Maria, wife of Charles I. The final wedding was filmed at the church in the village of **Berry Pomeroy**, between Torbay and Totnes, Devon.

SENSO (aka *The Wanton Countess*)
(1953, dir: Luchino Visconti)
Alida Valli, Farley Granger, Massimo Girotti.
● **VENICE, ITALY**

Sumptuous melodrama from Visconti, with Valli as the Venetian noblewoman falling for an officer of the hated invading Austrian army. The opening scene, with loyal Venetians disrupting an opera performance, is **Teatro La Fenice**, Venice's ill-fated opera house. Burned down in 1836, and rebuilt – hence the name 'The Phoenix' – it was gutted by fire once again in 1996 and is currently still under wraps. Originally built in 1792, the lush red and gilt interior saw the premières of many famous works, including *Rigoletto* and *La Traviata*. It was the rallying point for Venetian patriots after the Austrian invasion of 1866. It stands on **Campo San Fantin**, west of the Piazza San Marco.

Alida Valli looks for Farley Granger: The Arsenale, Campo dell'Arsenale

Granger's barracks: Campo di Ghetto Nuovo

Meeting up at the well: Campo di Ghetto Nuovo

Valli and Granger walk at dawn: Fondamenta di Cannareggio

Granger's barracks are on the **Campo di Ghetto Nuovo**, a tiny island in the Cannareggio district linked by three bridges which was the original Jewish ghetto. The word 'ghetto' was a Venetian term for the iron foundry which once stood on this site. The Jews lived under a curfew – at night, the gates to the island would be padlocked. The uncharacteristic high-rise apartments are a result of this overcrowding. The well where Valli and Granger meet up is one of three in the centre of the campo.

As dawn rises, Valli and Granger walk along the nearby **Fondamenta di Cannareggio** on the Canale di Cannareggio. Valli looks for Granger at the **Arsenale, Campo dell'Arsenale**.

SERIAL MOM
(1994, dir: John Waters)
Kathleen Turner, Sam Waterston, Ricki Lake.
● **MARYLAND**

Standing alone in a genre all its own, the serial killer-feel-good movie, John Waters' best film since his underground trash days was shot, inevitably, around Baltimore, Maryland. The church where Turner eludes the cops is **Church of the Good Shepherd, 1401 Carrolltown Avenue**. The video store, where her son works and where you neglect to rewind at your peril, is **Video America, Cold Springs Lane**. Turner is finally arrested at a Camel Lips gig at the **Inner Harbor Concert Hall** (then Hammerjacks), **1101 South Howard Street**. Her subsequent trial was filmed in **Baltimore County Courthouse, 400 Washington Avenue, Towson**.

SERPICO
(1973, dir: Sidney Lumet)
Al Pacino, John Randolph, Jack Kehoe.
● **NEW YORK CITY**

Lumet's harrowing exposé of police corruption was based on real events and made on real locations around New York. Pacino crosses the **Williamsburg Bridge** from Brooklyn to start a new life in Greenwich Village. The apartment he moves into is **5-7 Minetta Street**.

He studies Spanish at **New York University** in Greenwich Village, on the east side of Washington Square Park. Though his classmate says she works in Caffe Reggio, 19 MacDougal Street at West 3rd Street, we don't – as is claimed in lots of NY guidebooks – actually get to see the famed Village hangout. You can, though, see the café, NY's oldest, in dull Sean Connery thriller *The Next Man*. Serpico takes in a ballet at the **New York State Theater**, on the south side of **Lincoln Center Plaza, 150 West 65th Street** at Broadway, on the West Side.

Serpico's Greenwich Village apartment: 7 Minetta Street

The subway station, where Serpico gives chase after seeing a burglary in progress, only to get shot at by the cops for his troubles, is **Ditmars Boulevard**, Astoria, in north Queens, at the end of the Broadway Local line. And, on the same line, he encounters a cop, stoned out of his mind after a drug lesson, at **57th Street Station**.

SERVANT, THE
(1963, dir: Joseph Losey)
Dirk Bogarde, James Fox, Sarah Miles.
● **LONDON**

Aristocrat James Fox's house: Royal Avenue, Chelsea

Bogarde is the sinister servant indulging in class-war power games with dissipated aristocrat Fox, in this classic sixties film of Robin Maugham's novel, by the Losey-Harold Pinter-Bogarde team. Fox's house is situated at **30 Royal Avenue**, Chelsea SW3, opposite the one-time home of Somerset Maugham, some of whose pictures were borrowed to give James' home a suitably 'homocentric' atmosphere. The wonderfully named 'Thomas Crapper, Sanitary Engineer', seen in the opening shot, was for a long while the Laura Ashley shop, in the King's Road opposite Royal Avenue, now The Vestry. Filming also took place at **St Pancras Station**.

SE7EN
(1995, dir: David Fincher)
Morgan Freeman, Brad Pitt, Kevin Spacey.
● **LOS ANGELES**

'Sloth': the Pan-Am Building, Third Street, downtown LA

The dismal, rain-swept city where Freeman and Pitt track down a serial killer, left deliberately vague in the movie, is neither New York nor Philadelphia, as has been claimed. It's downtown Los Angeles, with locations screened from the California sun, and rain machines in overdrive. The library where Morgan Freeman bones up on the Seven Deadly Sins is the old disused Bank of America building at **650 South Spring Street**. John Doe's place, where the killer narrowly escapes, is only a few blocks away, the **Alexandria Hotel, 218 West Fifth Street** at the southwest corner of South Spring Street. Once one of LA's most prestigious hotels, a favourite of movie stars in the twenties and

Paltrow confides in Freeman: Quality Coffee Shop, West Seventh Street

The library: South Spring Street, downtown LA

John Doe's apartment: Alexandria Hotel, West Fifth Street

thirties, it has suffered from the general decay of the surrounding area. The subsequent chase was filmed on **West Fifth Street**. Gwyneth Paltrow reveals she's pregnant to Morgan Freeman in the **Quality Coffee Shop, 1238 West Seventh Street**. The apartment of the comatose 'Sloth' victim is in the **Pan-Am Building, Third Street** at South Broadway, seen also in *Blade Runner* and just across from that movie's most famous location, the Bradbury Building.

SEVEN YEAR ITCH, THE
(1955, dir: Billy Wilder)
Tom Ewell, Marilyn Monroe, Evelyn Keyes.
● **NEW YORK CITY; LOS ANGELES**

Bimpy Tom Ewell gets hot and bothered by neighbour Monroe. Set in New York, though the movie was shot largely in Hollywood. The apartment, out of which Marilyn dangles Ewell's shoes, actually is in New York. See it on the East Side, unchanged, at **164 East 61st Street**. It was owned by Julian Bach, who received $200 worth of whiskey for the use of it.

At the time of filming, in September 1954, Monroe's marriage to Joe DiMaggio was falling apart. They were staying at Suites 1105 and 1106 in the St Regis-Sheraton Hotel, 2 55th Street at Fifth Avenue. The notorious subway grating scene was largely staged as a publicity stunt. The studio made sure that the press knew exactly when and where the scene was to be shot, and that Marilyn would be wearing an outfit that would 'stop the traffic' Around 2,000 people

Marilyn's New York apartment: East 61st Street, East Side

The subway grating: Lexington Avenue at 52nd Street

turned up to witness the filming, including an enraged DiMaggio. The crowd roared as Monroe's skirt billowed up, and one of the most enduring Hollywood images was born. The next day, Monroe was sporting bruises and within a few days she and DiMaggio had split. The close-ups of her legs were re-shot in Hollywood.

The subway grating was outside the Trans-Lux Theater, where Ewell and Monroe had just watched *The Creature From the Black Lagoon*. The Trans-Lux has since moved to 1221 Avenue of the Americas, but the subway grating can still be seen at the northwest corner of **Lexington Avenue** and **52nd Street**.

SEVENTH SEAL, THE

(1957, dir: Ingmar Bergman)
Max von Sydow, Gunnar Bjornstrand, Bibi Andersson.
● **SWEDEN**

One of the most enduring icons of Euro art cinema is that of Max von Sydow playing chess with Death, in Bergman's bleak period fable questioning religious faith, mostly filmed in the studios at **Rasunda**, Sweden. The opening scenes, of medieval knight von Sydow arriving at the rocky beach and confronting death, are **Hovs Hallar** in Skane Province, southwest Sweden. The site was used for the wider landscapes, too, including the stunning Dance of Death ending.

SEX, LIES, & VIDEOTAPE

(1989, dir: Steven Soderbergh)
James Spader, Andie MacDowell, Laura San Giacomo.
● **LOUISIANA**

Relationship problems down south, when Spader brings his video camera to town. Spot-on character piece shot on location in Lousiana state capital, Baton Rouge. The bar, where Steven Brill peddles his surreal chat-up lines and Laura San Giacomo serves drinks, is the **Bayou, 124 West Chimes Street** between Infirmary Drive and Highland Road, Baton Rouge. Not far way, east toward I-10, is the fern restaurant, **Zee Zee Gardens, 2904 Perkins Road** (*℃ 225.346.1291*).

SHADOW, THE

(1994, dir: Russell Mulcahy)
Alec Baldwin, John Lone, Penelope Ann Miller.
● **CALIFORNIA**

Mulcahy's visually stylish but empty period comic strip is set in NY, but uses a clutch of classic locations around LA, and **Alabama Hills** at Lone Pine, on Route 395, central California. The mansion is **Mayfield Senior School, 500 Bellefontaine Street**, Pasadena – Richard Attenborough's house in *The Lost World: Jurassic Park*. The rundown area in front of the Barclay Hotel at **Fourth and Main Street**s, downtown was also used.

SHADOW OF A DOUBT

(1943, dir: Alfred Hitchcock)
Joseph Cotten, Teresa Wright, Macdonald Carey.
● **CALIFORNIA**

Teresa Wright's favourite Uncle Charlie is actually the Merry Widow serial killer in Hitchcock's quietly understated thriller, co-scripted by playwright Thornton Wilder. Hitchcock's intention to film the whole movie on location, paying scrupulous attention to the details of small-town Americana, was ultimately compromised, but there's still plenty of filming in northern California, around **Santa Rosa**, on Route 101 about 50 miles north of San Francis-

co. Most of the city centre has been redeveloped, but you can still see the old railway station, where Uncle Charlie arrives. The railway itself is unused, but the station is now the tourist office, the **Old Railroad Depot, 9 Fourth Street**. You can buy the video of *Shadow of a Doubt* here. Amazingly, the

Uncle Charlie arrives in Santa Rosa: Old Railroad Depot, Fourth Street

Teresa Wright's home: McDonald Avenue, Santa Rosa

unchanged family home can still be seen just out of town at **904 McDonald Avenue** at 15th Street.

SHADOWLANDS

(1993, dir: Richard Attenborough)
Anthony Hopkins, Debra Winger, Joseph Mazzello.
● **OXFORDSHIRE; LONDON; HEREFORDSHIRE; LEICESTERSHIRE**

Dry old stick CS Lewis discovers emotional commitment with Joy Gresham just as she discovers she has terminal cancer, in this filming of William Nicholson's play. Lewis, author of *The Lion, the Witch and the Wardrobe*, is an Oxford don. The college, where he teaches and suffers the cynicism of his fellows, is **Magdalen College**, with its 15th century chapel and carved oak dining hall. Other Oxford locations include **Christ Church Meadow**; **Duke Humphrey's Library**, part of the Bodleian complex; the circular reading room of the **Radcliffe Camera**, where Lewis lectures, and the **Sheldonian Theatre**. The tea room, where he first meets Gresham, is the **Fellows Lounge** of the **Randolph Hotel, Beaumont Street** (*℃ 01865. 247481*). Both

Lewis' college: Magdalen College, Oxford

CS Lewis meets Joyce Gresham: Randolph Hotel, Beaumont Street

The wedding: BT Office, Hastings Street, Kings Cross

The choir at dawn: Magdalen College, Oxford

Hopkins and Winger, and director Attenborough, stayed at the Randolph during the Oxford shoot. What higher recommendation could you ask for? Oxford Station has been completely rebuilt, so the railway scenes used Britain's only perfectly preserved mainline steam facility, the **Great Central Railway, Loughborough Station**, Leicestershire (also used for railway scenes in *Buster*). The hotel Lewis and Gresham stay in, on their way to the Golden Valley, is **Pengethley Manor Hotel, Pengethley Park** (© *01989.730211*) off the A49 near Ross-on-Wye. The Golden Valley honeymoon is set in the rolling hills of Herefordshire at the Welsh border, but the real thing turned out to be just not photogenic enough. The stand-in is **Symond's Yat Rock** near Goodrich, about 30 miles away. The wedding is not Camden Town Hall as sometimes claimed, but just around the corner at, bizarrely, the back door of the **BT Office** in **Hastings Street** opposite Thanet Street. The windows opposite are Salvationist Publishing, and the period buses trundle up Judd Street.

SHAFT
(1971, dir: Gordon Parks)
Richard Roundtree, Moses Gunn, Charles Cioffi.
● **NEW YORK CITY**

The No-Name bar: Hudson Street, Greenwich Village

Roundtree is a black PI in New York in the movie which spawned not only two sequels and a television series, but the whole blaxploitation genre. Shaft's apartment is **55 Jane Street** in west Greenwich Village. Just across Hudson Street stood the No Name Bar, is now a restaurant, **Piccolo Angelo, 621 Hudson Street**. Another location is **Caffe Reggio, 119 MacDougal Street** at West Third Street (see *The Godfather Part II* for details). Much of the action centres on**125th Street** in Harlem.

Shaft's apartment: Jane Street, Greenwich Village

SHAFT
(2000, dir: John Singleton)
Samuel L Jackson, Christian Bale, Busta Rhymes.
● **NEW YORK CITY; NEW JERSEY**

Samuel L Jackson takes the mantle for this revisiting of the cult seventies hit. Shaft's favourite hangout is now the recently restored Harlem landmark bar the **Lenox Lounge, 288 Lenox Avenue**

between 124th and 125th Streets (© *212.427.0253*). The cop station exterior is in the Bronx, though the interior is a deserted Beaux Arts building in **Jersey City**, New Jersey. Other locales include the Brooklyn neighbourhoods of **Vinegar Hill; Red Hook; Bedford-Stuyvesant**; and **Crown Heights**. Villain Peoples Hernandez rules over the Dominican enclave in **Washington Heights**, way to the north of Manhattan. Featured also is the **River Diner, 452 11th Avenue** at 37th Street (© *212.868.1364*).

The diner: River Diner, 11th Avenue

SHAKESPEARE IN LOVE
(1998, dir: John Madden)
Joseph Fiennes, Gwyneth Paltrow, Judi Dench.
● **LONDON; BERKSHIRE; OXFORDSHIRE; HERTFORDSHIRE; NORFOLK**

Multi-Oscar winner, including Best Picture, as a hunky, young Shakespeare struggles to write *Romeo and Ethel, The Pirate's Daughter* and aristocrat Paltrow defies convention by wanting to act. The Rose Theatre is a set built for the movie. After filming, it was presented to Dame Judi with an eye to restoring it as a working theatre. The real Rose was actually uncovered during building work in Southwark in the late eighties, and a massive campaign was launched to preserve it. The property developers eventually agreed to preserve the theatre in the basement of the new building, but it sadly remains inaccessible.

Fireworks at Greenwich: Hatfield House, Hatfield

Shakespeare meets Viola at the dance: The Great Hall, Broughton Castle

Wessex informs Viola she is to be married: The Oak Room, Broughton Castle

Viola's home, the de Lesseps

Shakespeare woos Viola from the garden: Broughton Castle

Illyria: Holkham Beach

Site of Viola's balcony: Broughton Castle

house is **Broughton Castle**, home of Lord and Lady Saye and Sele, two miles southwest of **Banbury**, Oxfordshire. The dance, where Will first meets Viola, is the house's Great Hall, while it's in the Oak Room that Wessex informs Viola she is to be married. Viola's bedroom is a studio set, but for the exterior, a false wooden balcony was built onto Broughton Castle, overlookiing the formal gardens. The castle was also seen in *Joseph Andrews*, Tony Richardson's follow-up to *Tom Jones*, Trevor Nunn's *Lady Jane*, *The Madness of King George* and *Three Men and a Little Lady*. It's open to the public on various days between May and September (*admission charge; © 01295.262624*). The command performance of *Two Gentlemen of Verona* for Queen Elizabeth, in the Banqueting Hall at the Palace of White Hall, is in the **Great Hall** of **Middle Temple** in London. The Greenwich fireworks scene, where Viola meets the Queen, and Shakespeare accepts a bet in drag, used the rear of **Hatfield House** (see Tim Burton's *Batman* for details). The riverside scenes were shot on the Thames at **Barnes**. The interior of the church, where Shakespeare begs forgiveness after hearing about the murder of Kit Marlowe, is **Church of St Bartholomew the Great**, a tiny church – repository of the bones of St Rahere – tucked away behind Smithfield, and seen also in *Robin Hood, Prince of Thieves* and *Four Weddings and a Funeral*. The church exterior, after Viola's wedding to Wessex, is the courtyard of **Eton School**, Berkshire – which also served as the exterior of the Houses of Parliament in *The Madness of King George*. More filming took place at **Marble Hill House**, Twickenham.

The spectacular beach of 'Illyria' at the end is **Holkham Beach**, part of the Holkham Hall estate, three miles west of Wells-next-the-Sea on the A149 on the north coast of Norfolk.

SHAKESPEARE WALLAH
(1965, dir: James Ivory)
Shashi Kapoor, Geoffrey Kendal, Felicity Kendal.
● INDIA

Story of a British theatrical troupe crumbling during a tour

of India, filmed by the Merchant-Ivory-Jhabvala team on location. The opening is at **La Martiniere College, Dilkusha Road, Lucknow**, an enormous European-style palace. The company performs at the **Gaiety Theatre, Mall Road, Simla**, the spectacular hill station where the British made camp in 1819. The theatre, opened in 1887, still houses performances, though the bar is supposedly a greater attraction than the plays. Other locations include the hill station of **Kasauli; the Punjab; Alwar; Rajasthan** and **Bombay**.

SHALLOW GRAVE
(1994, dir: Danny Boyle)
Ewan McGregor, Kerry Fox, Christopher Eccleston.
● SCOTLAND

The flat: North East Circus Place, Edinburgh

Pitch black comedy thriller, set in Edinburgh but shot for the most part in Glasgow. The real Edinburgh New Town is used to set the scene in the opening car ride, racing down **St Vincent Street**, glimpsing St Stephen's Church before swinging left into North East Circus Place. The flat shared by McGregor, Fox and Eccleston is **6 North East Circus Place** on the corner of Royal Circus. The flat interior, though, was constructed in a warehouse in the Anniesland district of Glasgow.

The shallow grave: Rouken Glen Park, Thornliebank, Glasgow

McGregor's office is the newsroom of Glasgow's *Evening Times*, while Fox's hospital is the **Royal Alexandra Hospital** off Crow Road, Castlehead west of Glasgow city centre. This also houses the mortuary where Christopher Eccleston finally ends up.

The flooded quarry where the car is disposed of is **Mugdock Loch**, in **Mugdock Country Park, Mugdock Road** north of Milngavie (*rail: Milngavie*). The charity do, where Eccleston gets to assert his manhood, is in the **Townhouse Hotel, 54 West George Street**, Glasgow (*© 0141.332.3320*).

The grave itself, where Keith Allen is planted, is a wooded section of **Rouken Glen Park, Rouken Glen Road, Thornliebank** (*rail: Thornliebank*). The production team returned to Rouken Glen Park for the 'Sean Connery' scene in *Trainspotting*.

SHAMPOO
(1975, dir; Hal Ashby)
Warren Beatty, Julie Christie, Lee Grant.
● LOS ANGELES

Hot stuff in its day, a political satire with Beatty the priapic hairdresser seducing his glamorous female clients on

Christie's offer: site of Bistro, North Canon Drive, Beverly Hills

the eve of election night 1968, set, and filmed, in Beverly Hills. Jack Warden's mansion – which was in real life Warren Beatty's former home – is **1120 Wallace Ridge**, off Loma Vista Drive north of Sunset Boulevard. Sloshed Julie Christie offers Beatty a blow-job in the now-gone Beverly Hills eaterie, Bistro, 240 North Canon Drive, between Sunset and Santa Monica Boulevards. Also featured is the exclusive **Beverly Hills Hotel, 9641 Sunset Boulevard**.

SHANE

(1953, dir: George Stevens)
Alan Ladd, Jean Arthur, Brandon de Wilde.
● WYOMING

A mysterious stranger turns up to help a family of homesteaders in this epic Western. The luscious, Oscar-winning photography, by Loyal Griggs, makes full use of the location filming around **Jackson Hole**, Wyoming, at the southern end of the Grand Teton National Park. This has to be another of the great, all-time movie locations, regularly seen since silent movie days. Jackson Hole is a 50-mile-long, mile-high mountain valley overlooked by the Grand Tetons – the Big Breasts – a name bestowed by French trappers. To the original people of the land they were Teewinot – Many Pinnacles. Route 191 runs through the valley, alongside the Snake River, from Jackson north to Yellowstone National Park. The cabin itself, dilapidated but still standing, can be seen on **Gros Ventre Road**, just west of Kelly.

SHAWSHANK REDEMPTION, THE

(1994, dir: Frank Darabont)
Tim Robbins, Morgan Freeman, Bob Gunton.
● OHIO

Tim Robbins finds redemption during twenty years imprisonment. Shawshank State Prison, Maine is the **Ohio State Reformatory, Mansfield**, on I-30, 65 miles southwest of Akron, Ohio. The facility had lain dormant for four years and was scheduled for demolition.

PHOTOGRAPH COURTESY MANSFIELD REFORMATORY, OHIO

Shawshank State Prison: Mansfield Reformatory

SHE WORE A YELLOW RIBBON

(1949, dir: John Ford)
John Wayne, Joanne Dru, John Agar.
● ARIZONA; UTAH

Wayne as a cavalry officer on the verge of retirement in Ford's goodlooking, elegaic Western made – where else – in **Monument Valley**, Arizona and at **Mexican Hat** on the San Juan River, Utah. John Wayne's fort stands in the shadow of two of Monument Valley's most striking formations, **The Mittens**.

Site of the fort: The Mittens, Monument Valley

SHELTERING SKY, THE

(1990, dir: Bernardo Bertolucci)
Debra Winger, John Malkovich, Campbell Scott.
● MOROCCO; ALGERIA; NIGER

Long and meandering, but beautiful to look at, adaptation of Paul Bowles' novel, shot on location in Africa. Oran, the port of arrival, is **Tangier** in Morocco, where filming was held up for the arrival of King Hussein II's yacht. The movie begins and ends here, among the old colonial boulevards and the labyrinth of the Medina. The hotel is the **Hotel Palace, 2 Rue des Postes** (℡ 09.93.61.28), in the Medina. There was also filming at the **Hotel Continental, Rue Dar el Baroud**, also in the Medina.

The southern oasis area of Morocco, southeast of Ouarzazate toward the High Atlas mountains, hosted most of the shoot. The Hotel Majestic, Ain Krofa, is actually near Efroud, south of Er Rachidia, in the small town of **Rissani** close to the Algerian border. The arrival at the gates of El Gala used the market of **Gla Gla**. Debra Winger and the guide are followed by the ubiquitous Steadicam through the dry mud passageways of **Maadid**. The bicycle ride ends in the little town of **Zagora**, to the west, at the end of the spectacular Draa Valley. The love scene was filmed at the top of the strange, rather unreal, mountain overlooking the town and the surrounding desert.

The narrow streets of the historic core of Ouarzazate (in an area used for *Gladiator*, *Lawrence of Arabia* and *The Man Who Would Be King*, among others) leads to the movie's Hotel Transatlantique in Bou Noura, though the terrace of the hotel in Boussif is actually a replica in the hamlet of **Ait Saoun** and the exteriors of Bou Noura were filmed in the mud brick village of **Tamnougalt**, halfway between Ouarzazate and Zagora. The brothel is the **Kasbah** (the fortified palace) of Ouarzazate.

Algerian locations include the oasis **Beni Abbes**, where the fort of Sba, sheltered by the great dune, was built. Here

The brothel: Kasbah, Ouarzazate

also is the white room in which John Malkovich expires; and the Grand Erg Occidental mineral landscape. *The Sheltering Sky* was the first movie to film in Niger, one of the world's poorest countries, where the scene of Winger and Eric Vu-An in the mud room was shot in **Agadez**.

SHE'S ALL THAT

(1999, dir:Robert Iscove)
Freddie Prinze Jr, Rachael Leigh Cook, Matthew Lillard.

● LOS ANGELES

Nineties teen spin on *Pygmalion*, with Freddie Prinze Jr turning Rachel Leigh Cook into a Prom Queen. The high school is **Torrance High School, El Prado Avenue** at **Carson Street, Torrance**.

SHE'S GOTTA HAVE IT

(1986, dir: Spike Lee)
Tracy Camilla Johns, Tommy Redmond Hicks, John Canada Terrell.

● NEW YORK CITY

Spike Lee's first feature, a low-budget b&w comedy about Tracy Camila Johns' multiple entanglements, made in a mere twelve days in July 1985 on location in New York. Johns' loft is **1 Front Street**, Brooklyn, over what used to be the Ferry Bank Restaurant, now the Hot Spot – Brooklyn's only gay bar. The park is Brooklyn's **Fort Greene Park**, with its views across to Manhattan. It's southeast of Brooklyn Heights, bounded by De Kalb and Myrtle Avenues, St Edwards Street and Washington Park. A crypt below the park (not open to the public) holds the remains of some of the 12,000 American soldiers who died on British prison ships in Wallabout Bay between 1780 and 1783.

SHINE

(1996, dir: Scott Hicks)
Geoffrey Rush, Armin Mueller-Stahl, Lynn Redgrave.

● SOUTH AUSTRALIA; LONDON

Scott Hicks' Oscar-winning biopic of troubled pianist David Helfgott was made in South Australia, on 40 separate locations around Adelaide, including

Helfgott studies in London: Royal College of Music, Prince Consort Road

Carrick Hill and the **Adelaide Botanic Garden, North Terrace**. Helfgott performs at **Adelaide Town Hall, 126 King William Street**. The psychiatric hospital is **Glenside Hospital, 226 Fullarton Road, Eastwood**. In London, young Helfgott studies at the **Royal College of Music, Prince Consort Road, South Kensington**, SW7, opposite the Royal Albert Hall.

SHINING, THE

(1980, dir: Stanley Kubrick)
Jack Nicholson, Shelley Duvall, Danny Lloyd.

● OREGON

Nicholson is the blocked writer going barmy in a creepy snowbound hotel in Kubrick's very free adaptation of the Stephen King novel. The movie was shot almost entirely in the studio at Elstree in England, where the hotel interior was constructed. The exterior of the Overlook Hotel is the **Timberline Lodge, Mount Hood** in the Hood River area of Northern Oregon. Built during the Depression, it's 45 miles east of Portland, just east of Zig Zag on Route 26 (© *503.272.3311*). The interior sets were partly based on the Ahwanne Hotel, Yosemite, California.

The hotel which inspired the original story is the Stanley Hotel in Colorado, where King had stayed in 1973. The writer hated the Kubrick adaptation, which junked most of his plot in favour of atmosphere, and sanctioned a TV movie remake, which did indeed use the Stanley. For details of the hotel see *Dumb and Dumber*, which also filmed there.

SHIRLEY VALENTINE

(1989, dir: Lewis Gilbert)
Pauline Collins, Tom Conti, Joanna Lumley.

● LONDON; MERSEYSIDE; GREECE

Opening-up of Willy Russell's one-woman play about a Merseyside housewife who takes off for the Greek islands. Although it's set in Russell's native Merseyside, there's nothing more than a few establishing shots of Liverpool. Shirley Valentine's house is in Twickenham, not far from the film studios. Shirley's school is **Waldegrave School for Girls, Fifth Cross Road** in Twickenham. She buys exotic undies in **Littlewoods, Oxford Circus**, and gets her passport picture taken on **Marylebone Station**. The hotel, where she meets old school friend Joanna Lumley, is the luxurious **Marlborough Hotel, Bloomsbury Street**, WC1 (© *020.7636.5601*). The Greek island holiday des-

Shirley's school: Waldegrave School for Girls, Twickenham

Shirley meets her schoolfriend: Marlborough Hotel, Bloomsbury

tination where she finds liberation is the beach of **Aghios Ioannis**, southwest Mykonos, a couple of miles from Mykonos town, where she stays at the **Manoulas Beach Hotel**.

SHIVERS (aka *They Came From Within*)
(1975, dir: David Cronenberg)
Paul Hampton, Joe Silver, Barbara Steele.
● **QUEBEC, CANADA**

Early Cronenberg shocker, with gross sexually-transmitted parasites turning apartment dwellers into raving sex maniacs. The Starliner Towers high-rise block is a de luxe condo on **Nun's Island**, over the Pont Champlain in the St Lawrence river, southwest Montreal.

SHOOTING FISH
(1997, dir: Stefan Schwartz)
Stuart Townsend, Dan Futterman, Kate Beckinsale.
● **LONDON**

Entrance to the gasometer home: Lee Road, Mill Hill East

Townsend and Futterman are two orphans getting by as scam artists in this excellent caper comedy, which falls into sentimentality only toward the end. The gasometer, in which the boys live, can be seen at Mill Hill East, towering over the station at the terminus of the Northern Line. The entrance to their home is between **12** and **13 Lee Road, NW7**. They rummage in a rubbish skip in front of **Alexandra Palace**. The country home, which Kate Beckinsale saves, is **Poleseden Lacey**, a Regency villa near **Dorking**, Surrey (*admission charge ☎ 01372.452023*).

SHOOTIST, THE
(1976, dir: Don Siegel)
John Wayne, Lauren Bacall, James Stewart.
● **NEVADA**

Lauren Bacall's boarding house: Mountain Street, Carson City

Wayne's elegiac last turn as a gunfighter dying of prostate cancer (Wayne refused to succumb to the bladder cancer of the source novel). Although it's a Paramount movie, the street scenes were filmed on the Western Street of Warner Bros' Burbank lot. The sparkling location filming is **Carson City**, east of Lake Tahoe on I-395, Nevada. The buggy ride was filmed in **Washoe Lake State Park**. Lauren Bacall's boarding house, where Wayne sees out his final days, is the 1914 **Krebs-Paterson House, 500 Mountain Street**, Carson City. The house is one of the historic sites on the Kit Carson Trail, a two-and-a-half mile path through Carson City's historic district. Sound effects and recorded messages can be found on a special AM frequency at 24 of the houses – the Krebs-Paterson, of course, features the voice of John Wayne. Details from Carson City Chamber of Commerce, 1900 South Carson Street (☎ 775.882.1565).

SHORT CIRCUIT
(1986, dir: John Badham)
Steve Guttenberg, Ally Sheedy, Fisher Stevens.
● **OREGON**

Cutesy sub-*E.T.* fluff with a 'lovable' robot coming to life, marred by Fisher Stevens blacked up as a crass 'Goodness gracious me' Asian. It was made in **Astoria**, northeast Oregon. Ally Sheedy's house is **197 Hume Street**, Astoria. Filming also took place at **Bonneville Dam** on the Columbia River, Route 84, 30 miles east of Astoria and at **Cascade Locks**, a further ten miles east.

For the limp sequel, *Short Circuit 2*, Sheedy and Guttenberg are gone, and Stevens' ridiculous racial stereotype takes centre stage. The would-be cute robot makes it to the big city, but if NY looks a tad squeaky clean and airy, that's because it's actually Toronto.

SHORT CUTS
(1993, dir: Robert Altman)
Anne Archer, Lily Tomlin, Tim Robbins.
● **CALIFORNIA**

Lily Tomlin's coffee shop: Johnie's, Wilshire Boulevard

Altman weaves together a collection of Raymond Carver short stories, transplanting the locale from the Pacific Northwest to LA. The hospital is **Panorama Community Hospital, Panorama City** in the San Fernando valley, north of LA. The coffee shop, where Lily Tomlin works as a waitress, is **Johnie's Coffee Shop, Wilshire Boulevard** at Fairfax Avenue, midtown LA, seen also in *Reservoir Dogs* and *Miracle Mile*. The fishing trip is on the Kern River, and the final tragic outing, cut short by the earthquake, is **Bronson Canyon** in Griffith Park.

SHOT IN THE DARK, A
(1964, dir: Blake Edwards)
Peter Sellers, Herbert Lom, Elke Sommer.
● **HERTFORDSHIRE**

The French chateau: Luton Hoo, Luton

The French mansion of this follow-up to *The Pink Panther* is solidly Home Counties. It's **Luton Hoo**, Luton, in Hertfordshire. Until recently open to the public, it has since been put up for sale. See *Four Weddings and a Funeral* for details.

SHOWGIRLS

(1995, dir: Paul Verhoeven)
Elizabeth Berkley, Kyle MacLachlan, Gina Gershon.
● NEVADA

Paul Verhoeven's wildly trashy wallow in Vegas sleaze is set in Nevada's glitzy city of slot machines, but the musical numbers were staged at the **Horizon Casino Resort** (℡ *775.588.6211*) on I-50, Stateline, Lake Tahoe at the California border.

SID AND NANCY

(1986, dir: Alex Cox)
Gary Oldman, Chloe Webb, Drew Schofield.
● NEW YORK CITY; LONDON

Oldman and Webb are Sex Pistols 'bassist' Sid Vicious and girlfriend Nancy Spungen in this bleak fantasia on their doomed rela-

Sid and Nancy check out: The Hotel Chelsea, West 23rd Street

tionship (Sid OD'd while awaiting trial for Nancy's murder). Filming took place in London, and NYC, where the couple stay at, and Nancy dies in, the **Hotel Chelsea, 222 West 23rd Street**, between Seventh and Eighth Avenues (℡ *212.243.3700*). The landmark hotel, where you pay for the ambience more than for amenities, has been home to countless arty celebs over the years (as witnessed by the clutter of plaques around the entrance) including O Henry, Thomas Wolfe, Arthur Miller, Brendan Behan, Mary McCarthy, Vladimir Nabokov, Sarah Bernhardt and Dylan Thomas. The lobby and stairwells are decorated with works of art, of varying quality, donated by past residents. See the hotel's stairwell and corridors also in *Leon*.

SILENCE OF THE LAMBS, THE

(1991, dir: Jonathan Demme)
Jodie Foster, Anthony Hopkins, Scott Glenn.
● PITTSBURGH, PENNSYLVANIA; VIRGINIA; BAHAMAS

Although set in such wide-ranging locales as Ohio, West Virginia and Tennessee, Demme's superior thriller was made largely around Pittsburgh, western Pennsylvania.

Clarice Starling meets the entomologist at the **Carnegie Museum of Natural History** in the **Carnegie Institute, 4400 Forbes Avenue, Oakland** (it's where Jennifer Beals gets snubbed in *Flashdance*). The exterior of Lecter's place of internment, the Baltimore Hospital, was the Western Center, an old mental hospital in Canonsburg, on I-79 about fifteen miles south of Pittsburgh. It's since been demolished. Memphis Town Hall, where Lecter escapes from the holding cell and borrows the face of his guard, is the **Allegheny County Soldiers and Sailors Memorial Hall, 4141 Fifth Avenue**, a Civil War museum, part of the University of Pittsburgh. Many of the film's interiors were shot in the abandoned Westinghouse turbine factory (now known as **Keystone Commons**). The Grieg Funeral Home,

where Clarice views the body of the murder victim and has a flashback to her own father's funeral, was an empty house, formerly a real funeral parlor, on **Main Street, Rural Valley**, about 40 miles east of Pittsburgh. Filming also took place at **Allegheny County Jail, 950 Second Avenue**, Pittsburgh, and at the **Greater Pittsburgh National Airport**, to the west of the city.

Clarice Starling works out of the real **FBI training HQ, Quantico**, Virginia, on the US Marine Corps Base about 40 miles southwest of Washington DC.

Dr Lecter's tropical retirement home at the end of the movie is **Alice Town**, on the island of **North Bimini** in the Bahamas. The Bimini Islands, 50 miles off the coast of Florida, are the closest of the Bahamas to the USA. Famed for big game fishing and celebrated by Ernest Hemingway, who also took up residence here and wrote of the islands in *Islands in the Stream* (filmed by Franklin Schaffner with George C Scott, in 1977). The Biminis, like many islands in the Atlantic, were believed to have been the site of Atlantis, and are claimed to be home to the 'Fountain of Youth', the Healing Hole, which you can find on South Bimini.

SILVER STREAK

(1976, dir: Arthur Hiller)
Gene Wilder, Jill Clayburgh, Richard Pryor.
● ONTARIO, CANADA; ALBERTA, CANADA; CHICAGO; LOS ANGELES

Comedy thriller set on a transcontinental express train, climaxing at Chicago's **Union Station, 210 South Canal Street** (though the spectacular climactic crash is a mock-up built inside a Boeing aircraft hangar). Much of Union Station, Chicago is actually **Union Station, Toronto**. The real line is the Southern Pacific, from Boulder Dam to Chicago, though much of the movie was made in the

The crash at Union Station, Chicago: Union Station, Toronto

more controllable environment of the railroad yards in LA, and on the CPR Railway at **Calgary**, Alberta.

SIMPLE PLAN, A

(1998, dir: Sam Raimi)
Bill Paxton, Billy Bob Thornton, Bridget Fonda.
● MINNESOTA; WISCONSIN

In a winterbound small town, two brothers stumble upon a huge amount of money, which brings inevitable complications. The little town location is **Delano**, on I-12, about 25 miles west of Minneapolis, Minnesota. As unseasonably warm weather caused the snow to melt, the unit had to move north to Wisconsin to film snowscapes.

SINBAD AND THE EYE OF THE TIGER

(1977, dir: Sam Wanamaker)
Patrick Wayne, Taryn Power, Jane Seymour.
● JORDAN; SPAIN; MALTA

John Wayne's young lad stars in this dull sequel to *The Golden Voyage of Sinbad*, with the usual assortment of magicians, villains and Ray Harryhausen stop-motion monsters. It features the rose-red city of **Petra** in Jordan (see *Indiana Jones and the Last Crusade* for details). Filming also took place in Spain and Malta.

SINGLE WHITE FEMALE
(1992, dir: Barbet Schroeder)
Bridget Fonda, Jennifer Jason Leigh, Steven Weber.
● NEW YORK CITY

Bridget Fonda's apartment: The Ansonia, Broadway

Bridget Fonda invites mousy little Jennifer Jason Leigh to share her NY apartment, only to find she's living with a Bitch From Hell. Leigh works in **Rizzoli's Bookstore, 31 West 57th Street** between Fifth and Sixth Avenues, midtown. Fonda's Victoria apartment is supposedly 768 West 74th Street. Close, but not quite. It is, in fact, the gloriously embellished turn-of-the-century **Ansonia Hotel, 2109 Broadway**, between West 73rd and West 74th Streets. Not actually a hotel, the Ansonia is, as in the movie, a private apartment block. Its heavily soundproofed walls have made it an ideal home for musicians, and artists such as Caruso, Toscanini, Pinza and Stravinsky have stayed here. See it also as George Burns' home in Neil Simon's *The Sunshine Boys* and as Robert Redford's office in *Three Days of the Condor*.

SINGLES
(1992, dir: Cameron Crowe)
Campbell Scott, Kyra Sedgwick, Matt Dillon.
● SEATTLE, WASHINGTON STATE

The grunge club: Off-ramp, Eastlake Street, Seattle

Seattle's grunge scene is the backdrop for Cameron Crowe's quirky look at relationships. Rock venues featured include the **Off-Ramp, 109 Eastlake Street** at Denny Way and Stewart Street, and the **Re-Bar, 1114 East Howell Street** off Boren Avenue – a mixed straight-gay club. Kyra Sedgwick says 'yes' to Campbell Scott in the romantically-named **Gasworks Park, North Northlake** at Meridian North. Matt Dillon plays guitar on the grave of Jimi Hendrix in **Evergreen Memorial Cemetery** in **Renton**, east of Seattle.

Scott and Sedgwick meet up at **Virginia Inn, 1937 First Avenue** at Virginia Street. Opposite, at **1936 First Avenue**, is 'Expect The Best' dating agency, where *Batman* director Tim Burton cameos as a video director.

SISTER ACT
(1992, dir: Emile Ardolino)
Whoopi Goldberg, Maggie Smith, Kathy Najimy.
● CALIFORNIA; NEVADA

Nightclub singer Whoopi Goldberg, obliged to pose as a

nun after witnessing a murder, leads the convent to success in a choir competition. Harvey Keitel's casino, where Goldberg performs old Motown numbers, is the **Nevada Club, Commercial Street, Reno** on the outside, but the interior is over the road. It's **Fitzgerald's Casino, 255 North Virginia Street**, next to the famous 'Biggest Little City in the World' illuminated sign. Also in Reno, you can find the police station, which is actually **Reno Post Office, 50 South Virginia Street**, and the school that the young Goldberg attends: **St Thomas Aquinas Church, 310 West Second Street**. St Katherine's, the convent, where Goldberg hides out, is actually **St Paul's Church, 221 Valley Street** at Church, in San Francisco's quaint Victorian Noe Valley neighbourhood, just below the eastern slopes of Twin Peaks. Some interiors were shot in the **First United Methodist Church, 6817 Franklin Avenue**, Hollywood.

Goldberg performs in Reno: Fitzgerald's Casino, North Virginia Street

Young Goldberg's school: ST Thomas Aquinas Church, West Second Street

The police station: Reno Post Office, South Virginia Street

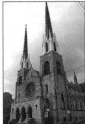

Goldberg hides out: St Paul's Church, Valley Street, Noe Valley

SIX DEGREES OF SEPARATION
(1993, dir: Fred Schepisi)
Will Smith, Donald Sutherland, Stockard Channing.
● NEW YORK CITY

Will Smith as a con man in NYC high society, adapted from John Guare's hit play. Donald Sutherland's apartment is **860 Fifth Avenue** (exterior), though the interior is **1049 Fifth Avenue**. Filming also took place at the **Metropolitan Museum of Art, 1000 Fifth Avenue** at 82nd Street.

Sutherland's apartment: Fifth Avenue

Cole's house: St Alban's Place

SIXTH SENSE, THE

(1999, dir: M Night Shyamalan)
Bruce Willis, Haley Joel Osment, Toni Collette.
● PHILADELPHIA, PENNSYLVANIA

Willis keeps the appointment: The Striped Bass Restaurant, Walnut Street

M Night Shyamalan's tricksy supernatural thriller, which turned out to be one of the year's unexpected smash hits, was shot around Philadelphia. You can find the garden street where young Osment and his mother live southwest of the city at **2302 St Alban's Place**, St Alban's Street at 23rd Street. Bruce Willis' more upmarket Locust Street home is really on **Delancy Street** in the, solidly respectable, Society Hill district.

The church to which haunted Osment retreats is **St Augustine's Roman Catholic Church, 4th Street** at New Street, near the entrance to the Benjamin Franklin Bridge. The restaurant, where Willis keeps an appointment with his wife, is the classy **Striped Bass, 1500 Walnut Street** (℗ 215.732. 4444), occupying the marble grandeur of a former brokerage house in the centre of town.

The church: St Augustine's Church, Fourth Street

SLACKER

(1991, dir: Richard Linklater)
Richard Linklater, Rudy Basquez, Jean Caffeine.
● TEXAS

Indie production, featuring a series of character encounters shot around **Austin**, Texas. The café featured is **Quackenbush's, 2121 Guadalupe Street** (℗ 512.472.4477).

SLEEPER

(1973, dir: Woody Allen)
Woody Allen, Diane Keaton, John Beck.
● COLORADO; CALIFORNIA

This untypical futuristic satire, with Allen as a Greenwich Village health food store owner waking up after 200 years

of cryogenic storage, uses an impressive array of sixties and seventies modernistic architecture. The 'clamshell' house of Dr Melik in the Central Parallel of the American Federation, where the newly-defrosted Allen is hidden from government agents, is architect Charles Deaton's **Sculpture House**, overlooking I-70 at **Genessee**, west of Denver, Colorado. The ovoid pod, perched on a stalk, was begun in 1963 by the architect, for himself, but never finished. It lay derelict for many years but has recently been purchased and renovated as a private home. More futurescapes were provided by the **Conservatory Building** of **Denver Botanical Garden, 1005 York Street** (℗ 303.331.4000), Denver. The countryside hideout is **Rancho San Carlos** in the **Carmel Valley** of northern California.

The sinister government complex, where Allen and Diane Keaton foil Project Aries, the plan to clone the quasi-fascist leader, is IM Pei's chunky, concrete **Mesa Lab** at the **National Center for Atmospheric Research, 1850 Table Mesa Drive, Boulder**, Colorado. Allen's living accommodation here, though, is actually in LA. It's the curvilinear **Robert Lee Frost Auditorium** of **Culver City High School, Elenda Street** at Franklin Avenue, Culver City in LA.

SLEEPERS

(1996, dir: Barry Levinson)
Brad Pitt, Kevin Bacon, Robert De Niro.
● NEW YORK CITY; NEW YORK STATE; CONNECTICUT

Glib revenge melodrama, supposedly based on a true story, though no one can find any substantiation of the events, filmed mainly around New York. For the sixties Hell's Kitchen neighbourhood, which has been radically redeveloped, the film uses **Greenpoint**, Brooklyn, where the church is **Holy Trinity Church**, and the courthouse the **County Courthouse, Yonkers**, New York State. The Wilkinson Home for Boys is **Fairfield Hills Hospital**, a facility for the mentally disabled near **Newtown**, Connecticut.

SLEEPLESS IN SEATTLE

(1993, dir: Nora Ephron)
Tom Hanks, Meg Ryan, Bill Pullman.
● SEATTLE, WASHINGTON STATE; CHICAGO; MARYLAND; NEW YORK CITY

Nora Ephron's cutesy romance, sparklingly photographed by longtime Bergman collaborator Sven Nykvist, was the sleeper of '93, and, although Vancouver was considered as a location, the real Seattle finally won out. Most of the Chicago, Baltimore and New York interiors are Seattle, too, plus some of the Baltimore exteriors. Tom Hanks leaves Chicago, and his unhappy memories, from the city's vast and modern **O'Hare International Airport**.

Moving to Seattle, he sets up home with his young son in a houseboat on **Westlake Avenue North**, on the west shore of Lake Union in the Queen Anne Hill district. The upscale neighbourhood also supplied characters' classy homes. Hanks' pal, director Rob Reiner, gives him some man-to-man advice about tiramisu – among other mysteries – in the **Athenian Inn, 1517 Pike Place** (℗ 206.624.7166), a breakfast and lunch eatery in the Main Arcade of Seattle's landmark Pike Place Market. It's in

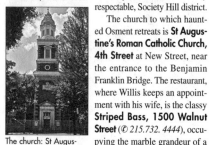

the market that Hanks shops with his prospective date, Victoria. He takes her for a meal at the **Dahlia Lounge**, one of Seattle's top restaurants, where Meg Ryan's detective surreptitiously photographs the couple. The restaurant, which stood at 1904 Fourth Avenuue, has recently moved premises, though not too far, to **2001 Fourth Avenue** at Virginia Street (© *206.682.4142*).

Ryan spies on Hanks playing with his son at **Alki Beach Park, Alki Avenue SW**, on the northwest shore of West Seattle. Supposedly in Baltimore, the New Year party, where Meg Ryan and Bill Pullman make plans for the future, is the **Dome Room** of the **Arctic Building, 700 Third Avenue** at Cherry Street, in Seattle's Business District. The 9-storey building was built in 1916 as a private club by men returning rich from the Klondike gold rush in the Yukon, hence the terracotta walrus heads decorating the façade. Supposedly in Washington DC, but actually in Baltimore, is the Capitol Diner, apparently in the shadow of the Capitol Building. It's the **Hollywood Diner, 400 East Saratoga Street** (© *410.962.5379*) – the original setting of Barry Levinson's *Diner*. Also in Baltimore are Ryan's apartment, at **904 South Broadway**, east of downtown and the **Sun Newspaper Building**, where she works.

In New York, Ryan and Pullman tentatively settle for unadventurous domesticity at **Tiffany and Co, 727 Fifth Avenue** at 57th Street, but in no time are splitting up in the **Rainbow Room, 30 Rockefeller Plaza** (© *212.632.5115*), the Rockefeller Center's pricy, highrise restaurant with its fabulous views over Manhattan.

The **Empire State Building, 350 Fifth Avenue** at West 34th Street, is only partly the real thing. The exterior and lobby are genuine enough, but for ease of filming, a slightly larger replica of the Observation Deck was built in a hangar at Sands Point Naval Base on Puget Sound.

SLEEPY HOLLOW

(1999, dir: Tim Burton)
Johnny Depp, Christina Ricci, Christopher Walken.
● **HERTFORDSHIRE; BUCKINGHAMSHIRE; LONDON**

Burton's filming of the Washington Irving story filmed largely on sets built at the Leavesden studios in Hertfordshire. The Western Woods were created on the soundstage. The village of Sleepy Hollow was built from scratch on the **Hambledon Estate**, near Marlow in Buckinghamshire. Turn-of-the-century New York is the central courtyard of **Somerset House, the Strand** in London. Christopher Walken rides the mechanical horse built for Elizabeth Taylor in *National Velvet*. The real US setting of Sleepy Hollow is now part of Tarrytown, New York State.

SLEUTH

(1972, dir: Joseph L Mankiewicz)
Laurence Olivier, Michael Caine, Alec Cawthorne.
● **DORSET**

Laurence Olivier's stately home, in this rather stagey adaptation of Anthony Shaffer's tricksy play, is **Athelhampton** (although the interior was recreated at Pinewood). One of England's finest medieval houses, Athelhampton was built in 1485 on the site of King Athelstan's palace, and

encircled by the River Piddle. It's about a mile east of Puddletown on the A35 Dorchester-Bournemouth road, and is open to the general public from Easter to the end

Laurence Olivier's country seat: Athelhampton, Dorset

of October (© *01305.848135, admission charge*).

SLIDING DOORS

(1998, dir: Peter Howitt)
Gwyneth Paltrow, John Hannah, John Lynch.
● **LONDON**

Gwyneth Paltrow's life takes off in two separate directions, depending whether or not she catches or misses a tube, in Peter Howitt's imaginative romance. The use of London locations is equally tricksy. Although the station Paltrow appears to exit and enter is **Embankment**, the spot where she actually misses/ catches the train is the Waterloo and City platform of **Waterloo Underground Station**. The attempted mugging, after Paltrow misses the train, takes place, strangely, outside the **Landmark**

Paltrow's flat: Princes Square, Notting Hill

Paltrow works or drinks: Bertorelli's, Charlotte Street

Rowing on the Thames: Lower Mall, Hammersmith

Hotel, Melcombe Place, opposite Marylebone Station. Paltrow lives with John Lynch at **62 Princes Square, Notting Hill**, W8. The restaurant where she either drinks with Hannah or works to support Lynch, is **Bertorelli's, 19 Charlotte Street**, behind Tottenham Court Road, W1. Paltrow and Hannah hang out and eventually reconcile, at **Albert Bridge**, Chelsea, SW3. They enjoy a post-rowing 'sponsored epileptic fit' at **The Blue Anchor, 13 Lower Mall, Hammersmith**, W6, alongside the Auriol Kensington Rowing Club.

Bitch From Hell Jeanne Tripplehorn works at **66 Chiltern Street**, though the entrance is actually on **Paddington Street**, W1. Her apartment is G4, **Pattern House, St John Street**, Clerkenwell, EC1, which is where Paltrow falls downstairs in the rather contrived ending. There was also filming at **Mas Cafe, All Saints Road**, Notting Hill.

SLIVER
(1993, dir: Phillip Noyce)
Sharon Stone, William Baldwin, Tom Berenger.
● NEW YORK CITY

The 'sliver' building (a spindly skyscraper making best use of a tiny sliver of real estate) of this weak sexploitation whodunnit, where voyeur Baldwin peeks in on his tenants, is NY's prestigious 32-storey **Morgan Court** in the Murray Hill area. One of Manhattan's last 'sliver' projects, it occupies a plot of land only 33 by 100 feet. An apartment here, though, sold for a cool million

The 'sliver' building: Madison Avenue

dollars just after the film's release. The building, supposedly 113 East 38th Street is at **211 Madison Avenue**, but it's the rear entrance around the corner on **East 36th Street**, fitted with a false glass arcade, that's used in the movie. A volcano sequence, shot in Hawaii and nearly resulting in tragedy when a helicopter carrying the cameraman crashed into a live crater, was cut from the final film.

SMALLEST SHOW ON EARTH, THE (aka *Big Time Operators*)
(1957, dir: Basil Dearden)
Bill Travers, Virginia McKenna, Margaret Rutherford.
● LONDON

Travers and McKenna inherit a fleapit cinema. Sadly, there is no 'Bijou', and never was, but you can still see the site where the frontage was erected. The

Site of the 'Bijou': Kilburn

old picture house was squeezed into the tiny gap between two railway bridges and rattled as trains thundered overhead. The two bridges can be seen just to the left of the entrance to **Kilburn Underground Station**, London NW6.

SMILES OF A SUMMER NIGHT
(1955, dir: Ingmar Bergman)
Gunnar Bjornstrand, Eva Dahlbeck, Harriet Andersson.
● SWEDEN

Ageing lawyer meets up with old flame ageing actress at an elegant country house, in this turn-of-the-century comedy of sexual manners, which provided the basis for the Stephen Sondheim musical *A Little Night Music*. The country house is **Jordeberga Castle**, three miles south of Malmo, Sweden. The theatre, at which Desiree appears, is based on a rococo gem in the town of Ystad.

SMOKEY AND THE BANDIT
(1977, dir: Hal Needham)
Burt Reynolds, Sally Field, Jackie Gleason.
● GEORGIA

Reynolds is a bootlegger who picks up disgruntled bride-not-to-be Field, sparking off a long and noisy chase by prospective father-in-law and sherriff Gleason. Filmed, like many of Reynolds' movies, in his home state of Georgia. You can see the motel and gas station sets on the **Burt Reynolds Ranch, 16133 Jupiter Farms Road, Jupiter**.

SNAKE EYES
(1998, dir: Brian De Palma)
Nicolas Cage, Gary Sinise, John Heard.
● NEW JERSEY; QUEBEC, CANADA

Thriller, set in the fictitious Atlantic City Boxing Arena, Atlantic City, New Jersey. The exteriors were filmed in the real East Coast gambling city, on its famous **Atlantic City Boardwalk**, at Donald Trump's **Taj Mahal Casino** and in **Bryant Park**. A section of the Boardwalk was also recreated in the carpark of **Egg Harbor High School, Egg Harbor Township**, a few miles out of town. Most of the film, though, was shot inside the **Montréal Forum, 2313 Ste-Catharine Ouest**, between Closse and Atwater in Montréal, Quebec. This venerable hockey venue, once home to the Montréal Canadiens, was temporarily closed down as it awaited redevelopment into an entertainment complex.

SOCIETY
(1989, dir: Brian Yuzna)
Billy Warlock, Devin DeVasquez, Evan Richards.
● LOS ANGELES

Imaginative script by Woody Keith and Rick Fry, about upper class slimesters literally feeding off the lower orders, is near scuppered by the ham-fisted direction of former producer Yuzna, though Screaming Mad George's FX are, erm, eye-popping. It was made around LA at mansions in **Pasadena** and **Malibu**; and in **Griffith Park**. The hospital is the **Veteran's Administration Medical Center** between Lassen and Plummer Streets in Northridge, northern LA. The school is **Birmingham High School**, which included Sally Field among its past students. No, don't even think about it...

SOME CAME RUNNING
(1959, dir: Vincente Minnelli)
Frank Sinatra, Shirley MacLaine, Dean Martin.
● INDIANA

Minnelli's colourfully soapy melodrama, from James Jones' novel of smalltown life after WWII, is set in Parkman, Illinois, but was made in **Madison**, on I-421, southwest Indiana by the Kentucky border. Arthur Kennedy's Hirsh Jewelry Store is actually Stanton's Shoe Store, **110 East Main Street**. Smitty's Bar was a vacant store nearby. Other genuine locations used include the local hotel, bank, and **Hanover College**.

SOME LIKE IT HOT
(1959, dir: Billy Wilder)
Marilyn Monroe, Jack Lemmon, Tony Curtis.
● SAN DIEGO, CALIFORNIA

The exteriors for this classic comedy were filmed in a mere seven days at **Coronado Beach** near San Diego, standing in for 1920s Miami. The hotel, where Lemmon and Cur-

The Miami hotel: Hotel del Coronado, San Diego

tis hide out in drag with Monroe, is the **Hotel del Coronado, 1500 Orange Avenue** (© *619.435.4131*). This 700-room Victorian fantasy, built in 1888, has long been frequented by the rich and famous, including no less than eight US presidents, Sarah Bernhardt, Charlie Chaplin, and – according to legend – it's where Edward met Wallis Simpson.

Its other connection with movie history is that this is where Frank L Baum wrote much of *The Wizard of Oz*, and its fussy Gingerbread appearance is said to have inspired the description of Oz. So, fittingly, Buddy Ebsen spent a month recuperating here from the effect of breathing in aluminium dust – and considering whether to sue MGM – after starting work as the original Tin Man.

The Coronado is also the setting for Richard Rush's brilliant, Oscar-nominated 1980 one-off, *The Stunt Man* with Steve Railsback and Peter O'Toole.

SOMEONE TO WATCH OVER ME
(1987, dir: Ridley Scott)
Tom Berenger, Mimi Rogers, Lorraine Bracco.
● **NEW YORK CITY; LOS ANGELES**

Working class cop Berenger is assigned to look after stinkingly rich witness Rogers in Ridley Scott's typically stylish thriller, set in New York, where much of the movie was shot. NY-scapes include the art deco tower of the **Chrysler Building, 405 Lexington Avenue** at East 42nd Street and the **Guggenheim Museum, Fifth Avenue** at East 89th Street.

Berenger's home is in **Long Island City** and there's swanky shopping at ultra-luxurious **Bergdorf Goodman, 754 Fifth Avenue** between West 57th and West 58th Streets. But with Scott, there's always an imaginative use of locations. The sumptuous art deco nightclub is actually the walnut and chrome interior of the luxury liner **Queen Mary**, berthed at **Pier J, Long Beach**, south of LA.

SOMMERSBY
(1993, dir: Jon Amiel)
Richard Gere, Jodie Foster, Bill Pullman.
● **VIRGINIA**

US remake of France's *The Return of Martin Guerre*, set in Tennessee during the Civil War. The brick mansion is now a hotel, the **Hidden Valley Bed and Breakfast, Hidden Valley Road, Warm Springs** in the George Washington National Forest, west Virginia. Originally Warwickton Mansion, it was built by slaves for Judge John Woods Warwick between 1848 and 1851. The town is **Lexington**, with filming on **Main Street** and **Washington Street**. The courtroom scenes were shot in **Charlotte**.

SONS AND LOVERS
(1960, dir: Jack Cardiff)
Dean Stockwell, Trevor Howard, Wendy Hiller.
● **NOTTINGHAMSHIRE**

DH Lawrence's semi-autobiographical novel, filmed by former cinematographer Jack Cardiff, and winning an Oscar for its cinematography by veteran Freddie Francis. Shot largely on location in Lawrence country around Nottinghamshire. The house is Lawrence's real childhood home in **Eastwood**, and the mine is **Brinsley Colliery** where Lawrence's father actually worked.

SOPHIE'S CHOICE
(1982, dir: Alan J Pakula)
Meryl Streep, Kevin Kline, Peter MacNicol.
● **NEW YORK CITY; YUGOSLAVIA**

Streep is a Polish concentration camp survivor plagued by guilt. The Pink Palace (which is in reality dull grey) is **101 Rugby Road, Flatbush** in Brooklyn. Meryl quaffs champagne on the **Brooklyn Bridge** and frolics with Kevin Kline at **Coney Island Amusement Park**. The Polish scenes were filmed in **Zagreb**, Yugoslavia, at the Jadvan Studios.

SOUND OF MUSIC, THE
(1965, dir: Robert Wise)
Julie Andrews, Christopher Plummer, Peggy Wood.
● **AUSTRIA; LOS ANGELES**

This phenomenally successful musical, based on a true story, was shot on lots of real locations around **Salzburg**, Austria, though plenty more were recreated in the 20th Century-Fox studios in Hollywood. The opening aerial shots are Salzburg's glorious Lake District, the **Salzkammergut**. The castles are **Fuchsl**, twelve miles east of Salzburg on the **Fuchslee**, clearest of the Salzkammergut lakes, and **Schloss Anif**, off E55 a few miles south of Salzburg. Maria's mountain, is **Mellweg**, near the Bavarian village of Schellenberg, about six miles from Salzburg. The birch trees were added for the movie and the babbling brook specially dug.

Convent interiors were recreated in the studio, but the exterior really is Maria's abbey. It's **Nonnberg Abbey, Nonnberg Gasse**, where you can visit the courtyard and peek into the chapel. The film cheats a little. The abbey looks out not to the picturesque old town of Salzburg, but to the nondescript southern suburbs. The reverse shot, of Maria leaving the abbey, was filmed across the city on the **Winkler Terrace** (where the 'Do Re Mi' number later begins). As Maria leaves to take up her post with the Von Trapps, 'I Have Confidence in Me' was filmed in Salzburg's Old Town, in the **Residenzplatz**, where

Arriving at the Von Trapp mansion: Hellbrunner Allee

Maria leaving: The entrance to Nonnberg Abbey...

...and the view from Winkler Terrace, across the city

Maria's wedding: Mondsee Cathedral

Maria's wedding: Mondsee Cathedral

you'll see the **Domplatz** arches, through which Maria enters, and the **Residenz Fountain**.

The Villa Von Trapp is a combination of two Salzburg locations. The tree-shaded lane, where Maria alights from the bus, is **Hellbrunner Allee**, running south from the old town. Here you'll recognise **Schloss Frohnburg**, a 17th century country house, now the Mozarteum Music Academy, which was used for the intimidating gates and front entrance of the villa. The lakeside terrace was filmed at **Schloss Leopoldskron**, a rococo castle on **Leopoldskroner Teich**, a small artificial lake on the southwest of the town. Now a private college, you can see Leopoldskron across the lake from **König Ludwig Strasse**. The real Villa Trapp, by the way, is in Aigen, 30 miles northwest of Linz in the very north of Austria near the German and Czech borders. The 'Do-Re-Mi' number begins atop the **Monchsberg Cliffs**, on Winkler Terrace which you can reach from the Monchsberg elevator in Anton Neumayrplatz, at the end of the Gstattengasse shopping street. The picnic is at the village of **Werfen**, 25 miles south of Salzburg in the Salzach River valley (the location for wartime action movie *Where Eagles Dare*). The number continues at **Mirabell Gardens**, on **Schwarzstrasse**, over the Salzach River behind Schloss Mirabell, where you'll find the fountains, statues and, famously, the flight of steps the children hop on. The little footbridge is **Mozart Steg**, north of Mozart Platz.

The Von Trapp gazebo, used for 'Sixteen Going on Seventeen', once stood in the grounds of Leopoldskron, but constant trespassing resulted in it being moved and reconstructed in the ornamental gardens of **Schloss Hellbrunn**, **Morzger Strasse**, south of the city.

Maria's wedding, which took place in Nonnberg Abbey, was shot in the baroque, twin-towered church of **Mondsee**, about fifteen miles east of Salzburg on the E55/E60.

The Anschluss scene, showing Austria's enforced unity with Nazi Germany, was staged back in the centre of town in **Residenzplatz**. The music festival, where the family perform their disappearing act, is at the **Felsenreitschule** ('Rock Riding School') on **Toscaninihof**, a massive rock arena built by the Romans for tournaments and part of the Festspielhaus. The cemetery, where the Von Trapps hide from the Nazis, is loosely based on St Peter's Graveyard just off Kapitelplatz, but was built in Hollywood. The mountain over which the family finally escapes to freedom is **Mount Obersalzburg** (once proposed as the site for Hitler's Eagle's Nest hideaway), near the village of Rossfeld, on the 319, twelve miles south of Salzburg.

Several companies offer *Sound of Music* tours which visit the locations: try Bob's Special Tours (℗ *0662. 872484*) or Panorama Tours, Mirabell Square (℗ *0662.871618; www.panoramatours.at*)

SOUTH PACIFIC
(1958, dir: Joshua Logan)
Mitzi Gaynor, Rossano Brazzi, Juanita Hall.
● **HAWAII; SPAIN**

There are some great Hawaiian locations for this musical, which suffers from Logan's over-enthusiastic use of lurid colour filters. Mitzi Gaynor washes her hair on

Mitzi washes her hair: Lumahai Beach, Kauai

Lumahai Beach, on Kauai. And just to the north, on the island's spectacular Na Pali Coast, is **Makahoa Point**, which stood in for the magic island of Bali Hai.

SOUTHERN COMFORT
(1981, dir: Walter Hill)
Keith Carradine, Powers Boothe, Fred Ward.
● **LOUISIANA; TEXAS**

Hill's tough Vietnam allegory, with National Guardsmen on an exercise in the Louisiana swamps caught in a cat-and-mouse game of death with local inhabitants, was shot on location in the swamps of Louisiana and at **Caddo Lake**, Texas.

SOUTHERNER, THE
(1945, dir: Jean Renoir)
Zachary Scott, Betty Field, Beulah Bondi.
● **CALIFORNIA**

Scott battles to save his cotton farm in Renoir's beautiful-looking film about the hardships of tenant farmers in Texas. The ramshackle farmhouse was built on the bank of the San Joaquin River near **Madera** on Route 99, north of Fresno.

SPACEMAN AND KING ARTHUR, THE (aka *Unidentified Flying Oddball*)
(1979, dir: Russ Mayberry)
Dennis Dugan, Jim Dale, Ron Moody.
● **NORTHUMBERLAND; DURHAM**

Disney adaptation of Mark Twain's *A Connecticut Yan-*

kee in King Arthur's Court with Dennis Dugan as a NASA engineer zapped back to Arthurian England. King Arthur's Camelot in Cornwall is really **Alnwick Castle**, Alnwick in Northumberland (*rail: Lesbury*). The 14th century fortress, the second largest inhabited castle in England – it's home to the Percys, Dukes of Northumberland – is open to the public (*© 01665.510777, admission charge*) and houses an impressive art collection. There was more filming at **Raby Castle**, Staindrop, near Darlington. Further scenes scheduled to be shot at Raby Castle, Staindrop, near Darlington, County Durham, never materialised (*© 01833.660202*).

SPANKING THE MONKEY
(1994, dir: David O Russell)
Jeremy Davies, Alberta Watson, Carla Gallo.
● **NEW YORK STATE**

Russell's taboo-breaking family melodrama, in low key style, was made on a shoestring and trailed awards from the Sundance Institute. At one point it attracted Faye Dunaway, who eventually dropped out. It was shot entirely in **Pawling**, a town of around 2,000 on Route 22, about 70 miles north of New York City near to the Connecticut border.

SPARTACUS
(1960, dir: Stanley Kubrick)
Kirk Douglas, Jean Simmons, Tony Curtis.
● **CALIFORNIA; SPAIN**

Crassus' villa: Hearst Castle, San Simeon

One of the best, if not the best, of the great epics, begun by Anthony Mann. Mann is responsible for the opening sequence, of a wickedly scene-stealing Peter Ustinov picking Spartacus from the Sicilian mines (actually the parched landscape of **Death Valley**, California) for his gladiator school. After two weeks of work, Mann was fired and the frantic search for a new director eventually turned up trumps with Stanley Kubrick.

Most of the film was shot on the Universal lot in Hollywood, although the spectacular battle sequences were filmed in Spain, with the Spanish army brilliantly executing the complex manoeuvres of the ancient Romans. The sound was something else. The roar of battle was the sound of 76,000 football fans attending a game between Michigan State and Notre Dame.

The exterior of Crassus' villa is the white marble swimming pool of newspaper magnate William Randolph Hearst at **Hearst Castle, San Simeon**, on California's Pacific coast halfway between Los Angeles and San Francisco. The model for Charles Foster Kane's Xanadu in *Citizen Kane*, the monument is now open to the public.

SPAWN
(1997, dir: Mark A Z Dippé)
Martin Sheen, Michael Jai White, John Leguizamo.
● **CALIFORNIA**

FX-heavy version of the dark comic strip. The Swiss Embassy is the **Fine Arts Building, 811 West 7th Street**, downtown LA (on the outside), while the interior is the **Los Angeles County Museum of Natural History, 900 Exposition Boulevard**, south of downtown. The Korean chemical plant is an oil refinery in **Carson**, California.

The Swiss Embassy: Fine Arts Building, West 7th Street, downtown LA

SPECIES
(1995, dir: Roger Donaldson)
Natasha Henstridge, Ben Kingsley, Michael Madsen.
● **CALIFORNIA; UTAH; PUERTO RICO**

Scientist Kingsley combines alien and human DNA to produce a speed-growing supermodel who, in the space of a few days, learns language, reading, dress sense and how to follow the instructions on a bottle of hair dye. Alien messages are first received at the **Arecibo Radio Telescope** in Puerto Rico, a familiar movie star seen in *Goldeneye* and *Contact*. The escape of young alien Sil filmed at the **Tooele Army Depot** in Northern Utah.

Sil's hideout: The Saharan Motor Hotel, Sunset Boulevard

The Victorian railway station is **Brigham City**, also Utah. She arrives, grown up and with an urge to mate, conveniently in LA, at **Union Station, 800 North Alameda Street**, downtown. The wedding dress shop where Henstridge picks up a little something to wear is at the intersection of Fifth Street and Broadway, downtown LA. The motel she checks into is the **Saharan Motor Hotel, 7212 Sunset Boulevard** at Alta Vista Boulevard in Hollywood (where the body of the murdered prostitute is discovered in Michael Mann's *LA Takedown*, his dry-run for *Heat*). You won't be able to pick up at the Id Club, to which Henstridge is directed in search of a man, as it's a fictional venue. You can see the elaborately decorated location though, which is the foyer of the **Pantages Theater, 6233 Hollywood Boulevard**, a movie palace now turned musical showcase (*© 310.410.1062*). The entrance to the Id uses the building's rear entrance on **Yucca Street** – that's the striking blue-and-white frontage of the Hollywood Palace Theater and the base of the Capitol Records Tower in the background. The team of oddball specialists on Henstridge's tail, almost literally, are based in the **Biltmore Hotel, 506 South Grand Avenue**, downtown LA – a frequent location, see *Beverly Hills Cop* for details. The car park where Henstridge is knocked down, and picked up by her next victim, is on **Appia Avenue** at Seaview Terrace, in Santa Monica alongside the Santa Monica Pier. The lavish house he takes her to is just to the north in Pacific Palisades. The car and helicopter chase was shot in the hills near Elysian Park just above the Dodger Stadium and alongside railroad yards at Union Station.

SPEED

(1994, dir: Jan De Bont)

Keanu Reeves, Sandra Bullock, Dennis Hopper.

● CALIFORNIA

Foiling the bomber: Gas Company Tower, West Fifth Street

Reeves chats to the bus driver: Firehouse Restaurant, Venice

The bus blows up: Main Street, Venice

The money drop: Pershing Square

Simple plot turned into mega-block-buster by cine-matographer-turned-director De Bont's high-octane direction. The office block where Hopper is foiled in his attempt to bomb the elevator is the 52-storey **Gas Company Towers, 555 West Fifth Street** at the northwest corner of Olive Street, downtown LA. Reeves celebrates his award at **The Derby, 4500 Los Feliz Boulevard** (*© 323.663. 8979*). The old Brown Derby Restaurant, it was renovated and reinvented as a swing venue in 1993. See *Swingers* for details.

Reeves chats to the bus driver at the **Firehouse Restaurant, 213 Rose Avenue** at Main Street, Venice, opposite the Koo Koo Roo Californian Kitchen with its landmark clown-ballet dancer sculpture hanging on the corner. The bus blows up on **Main Street**, just south of Rose Avenue, and this is where Reeves receives the phone call from Hopper. Sandra Bullock boards the bus at **Ocean Park Boulevard and Main Street**. Much of the bus ride was filmed on the I-105 in South Central LA around Watts. The spectacular bus jump on the unfinished freeway used the recently completed Glenn Anderson Freeway (Century Freeway). The yawning gap was added later with computer-generated imagery. The bus is finally diverted to the airstrips of **Los Angeles International Airport**. Kind of. The airport actually used for the filming is **Mojave Airport**, at Mojave in Kern County.

The money drop is at Fifth and Hill Streets, by the steps at the northeast corner of recently renovated **Pershing Square**, downtown Los Angeles. Here too is the station of the recently completed first section of the long-awaited LA subway, Metrorail Red Line at Pershing Square

Station. Most of the underground sequences were filmed on studio mock-ups, but it's on the real Hollywood Boulevard, at the near-completed **Hollywood Metrorail Station** just outside Mann's Chinese Theater between Highland and La Brea Avenues, that the train finally explodes into daylight.

SPIDER, THE (aka *Earth versus the Spider*)

(1958, dir: Bert I Gordon)

Ed Kemmer, June Kenny, Geene Persson.

● NEW MEXICO

Spider's lair: entrance to Carlsbad Cavern

A high school rock band revives an apparently dead giant spider, found in the spectacular **Carlsbad Caverns, Whites City**, on Route 180/62, south of Carlsbad, in the southeastern corner of New Mexico. The caverns, 83 separate caves forming one of the world's largest underground chambers, can be visited on tours of varying strenuousness (*© 505.7852232; www.carlsbad.caverns.national-park.com; admission charge*).

SPIDER'S STRATAGEM, THE (aka *Strategia del Ragno*)

(1970, dir: Bernardo Bertolucci)

Giulio Brogi, Alida Valli, Tino Scotti.

● ITALY

Brogi revisits the town where his father was murdered by fascists in the thirties, only to find that the truth is not so simple. Story by Jorge Luis Borges, photography by Vittorio Storaro, with Bertolucci directing. The strange setting is the town of **Sabbionetta**, a way outside Mantua. Built by a member of a wealthy Mantua family as the 'Ideal City', it never took off and now lies crumbling, dusty, and looking fabulous as a movie backdrop.

SPLASH

(1984, dir: Ron Howard)

Tom Hanks, Daryl Hannah, John Candy.

● NEW YORK CITY; LOS ANGELES

Mermaid Daryl Hannah follows Tom Hanks to New York, and turns up on **Liberty Island**, at the foot of the Statue of Liberty. Hanks works at **Fulton Fish Market, South Street** at Fulton Street. He lives at **25 Tudor City Place**, part of the kitschily Gothick Tudor City development, East 40th to East 43rd Streets between First and Second Avenues. Hannah learns English in an afternoon at the electrical department of **Bloomingdale's, 1000 Third Avenue** at

Daryl Hannah learns to speak: Bloomingdale's, Third Avenue

The little park: Sutton Place Park

Hannah incarcerated: American Museum of Natural History

Tom Hanks' apartment: Tudor City

East 59th Street. The fishy fountain she admires (don't go looking – it was just put there for the movie) is in the tiny park at **Sutton Place**, at the end of 57th Street, beneath the Queensboro Bridge (it's near to the same stunning view used for the poster of Woody Allen's *Manhattan*). Hannah and Hanks fall out at the **Wollman Memorial Rink**, 59th Street at Sixth Avenue in Central Park. It's not all kosher NY, though. The Presidential dinner, where Eugene Levy is mistaken for an assassin, filmed in the Crystal Ballroom of LA's **Biltmore Hotel**, a familiar location seen in *The Bodyguard* and *The Fabulous Baker Boys* among many others. And it's by the hotel's entrance, **506 South Grand Avenue** on Pershing Square, that Hannah gets drenched and comes out as a mermaid. Then it's back to New York, where she's incarcerated in the **American Museum of Natural History, Central Park West** at 79th Street.

SPLENDOR IN THE GRASS
(1961, dir: Elia Kazan)
Natalie Wood, Warren Beatty, Pat Hingle.
● NEW YORK STATE

Racy sounding title actually comes from a Wordsworth poem, though I bet he didn't spell it like that. And the following line, 'Glory in the flower', doesn't sound half so raunchy. Supposedly set in smalltown Kansas during the twenties, the film was actually made in New York, on **Staten Island**; and in upstate New York, at **High Falls**, northwest of Poughkeepsie. Natalie Wood's house, with the addition of a little dressing, is the corner house at **4144 Victory Boulevard, Travis**, west Staten Island.

SPY WHO LOVED ME, THE
(1977, dir: Lewis Gilbert)
Roger Moore, Barbara Bach, Curt Jurgens.
● CANADA; SCOTLAND; SARDINIA; EGYPT; BAHAMAS

The tenth Bond saga retains no more than the title from Ian Fleming (the author had refused permission to use the story, which he wasn't pleased with), in a lavish megaproduction, with Jurgens planning to rule an undersea kingdom after destroying terrestrial civilisation. The spectacular opening ski jump, supposedly at Berngarten, Austria, was filmed on the 3,000-feet **Asgard Peak**, 50 miles from the town of Pangnirtung, Auquittuq National park on the east coast of Baffin Island, Canada.

The naval establishment, where Bond is briefed about submarines, is **Faslane Submarine Base** on the Clyde near Glasgow. The Egyptian black-marketeer, Fekkesh, is killed during the spectacular lightshow shot at the **Pyramid of Cheops, Gaza**, near Cairo, Egypt. Before heading off to Jurgens' underwater hideout, Bond and KGB Major Amasova (Bach) stay at the huge **Hotel Cala de Volpe, Costa Smeralda**, perched, like a faux-Mediterranean village, atop the cliffs on the north coast of Sardinia (*© 39.0789.976.111*).

It was to film the interior of Jurgens' *Liparus* super-super-tanker, large enough to swallow up nuclear subs, that the vast 007 Soundstage was constructed at Pinewood. At 374 feet by 160 feet, and 53 feet high, it was the biggest in the world. It was badly damaged in a fire during the filming of Ridley Scott's *Legend* in 1985. The aerial shots of the supertanker swallowing a sub were achieved with models, filmed at **Coral Harbor, Nassau**, in the Bahamas.

STAGE FRIGHT
(1950, dir: Alfred Hitchcock)
Richard Todd, Marlene Dietrich, Jane Wyman.
● LONDON

Minor Hitchcock, with Jane Wyman (refusing to look too plain alongside the ineffably glam Marlene Dietrich) taking a maid's job to investigate the murder Richard Todd is accused of. Hitchcock returned to London to film this backstage murder mystery, which infuriated critics no end by breaking the rules and cheating in a flash-

Jane Wyman's class: RADA, Gower Street

Wyman meets the detective: Shepherd's Tavern, Shepherd Street, Mayfair

back sequence, and opens with a safety curtain rising on a view of St Paul's Cathedral towering above the post-war rubble. Todd eludes the police by crashing Jane Wyman's acting class at RADA, the **Royal Academy of Dramatic Art, 62-64 Gower Street**, WC1.

The house of Charlotte Inwood (Dietrich), scene of the murder, has sadly now been demolished. Although you may be able to recognise Hertford Street near the corner of Stanhope Row, W1, the block containing number 78 has gone to make way for the Hilton Hotel on Park Lane. A surviving location is the **Shepherd's Tavern, 50 Shepherd Street** at the corner of Hertford Street, where Wyman meets detective Michael Wilding over a brandy after her first visit to the Inwood house.

Iconic image: Monument Valley

STAGECOACH
(1939, dir: John Ford)
John Wayne, Claire Trevor, Thomas Mitchell.
● CALIFORNIA; UTAH

John Ford's Western classic is based on a short story, *Stage to Lordsburg*, by Ernest Haycox, published in *Collier's Magazine* in 1937, which was in turn based on Guy de Maupassant's *Boule de Suif*, set during the 1870 Franco-Prussian War. Wisely, John Wayne's character name was changed from Malpais Bill to the Ringo Kid.

The film established **Monument Valley**, on the Arizona-Utah border, as an icon of the American West, although, of the passengers, only John Wayne actually trekked out to Utah. None of the principals made it past California's San Fernando Valley.

Monument Valley, an area of striking, flat-topped mesas and buttes, was a tough location in 1938, at the end of a 200-mile dirt road from Flagstaff. The Navajo, already troubled by disease and unemployment, were employed to play Apaches – one of the many nations they were to play over the years. The Valley is not a National Park, as you might expect, but a Tribal Park still belonging to, and managed by, the Navajo nation. It can be reached on Route 163, 24 miles north from the town of Kayenta, Route 160. There's a visitor centre (*admission charge; © 435.727. 3353*). A 14-mile loop snakes through the valley, but not all roads are open to the public. You can see more of the park on a guided tour, from the parking lot at the visitor center.

But the Valley is only a part of *Stagecoach*. The river crossing is the Kern River, near to **Kernville**, 40 miles east of Bakersfield, California. The old wagon cut at **Newhall**, on I-5 – also called **Fremont Pass** – is the entrance to the dry lake. Nearby **Chatsworth** and **Calabasas** also provided locations. The chase by Indians was staged at the **Muroc Dry Lake** salt flats near Victorville, California, recreated by stunt artist Yakima Canutt from the 1937 Monogram movie *Riders of the Dawn*, which was filmed at the same location. To soften the ground for filming, 20 acres of ground had to be dug up by tractor. The real journey of the movie, though, is from the Western Street at Republic Studios (the town of Tonto) to the Goldwyn Studios (Lordsburg), where the interiors were shot.

STAND BY ME
(1986, dir: Rob Reiner)
River Phoenix, Wil Wheaton, Corey Feldman.
● OREGON; CALIFORNIA

Stephen King's untypical coming-of-age story, *The Body*,

was shot at **Eugene**, on Highway 5, eastern Oregon, about 100 miles south of Portland. The fictional New England town of Castle Rock, after which King named his production company, is **Brownsville**, a couple of miles west of I-5 to the north of Eugene. The railway viaduct is over the McCloud River in the **Mount Shasta** area of northern California.

STAR IS BORN, A
(1937, dir: William Wellman)
Fredric March, Janet Gaynor, Adolphe Menjou.
● LOS ANGELES

Second version (*What Price Hollywood?* was the first) of the classic Hollywood seesaw story, filmed in luscious Technicolor. Scenes were filmed at the **Hollywood Bowl,**

Classic Hollywood: The Hollywood Bowl, North Highland Avenue

2301 North Highland Avenue, LA. The Oscar ceremony was staged at the actual location used in the 1930s, the ballroom and nightclub of the **Ambassador Hotel, 3400 Wilshire Boulevard** (see the 1954 version for details). More scenes were shot at the pool patio of the plush **Beverly Hills Hotel, 9641 Sunset Boulevard**, Beverly Hills and the long-gone Trocadero Nightclub, which stood at 8610 Sunset Boulevard. The racetrack scenes are at the **Santa Anita Racetrack, 285 West Huntington Boulevard, Arcadia**, between LA and Pasadena (also used for the 1954 remake and for the Marx Brothers' *A Day at the Races*). The tear-jerky ending is in front of Grauman's (now **Mann's) Chinese Theater, 6925 Hollywood Boulevard**.

STAR IS BORN, A
(1954, dir: George Cukor)
Judy Garland, James Mason, Charles Bickford.
● CALIFORNIA

Expanded, musicalised, widescreen remake of the 1937 movie, charting the rise of singer Esther Blodgett and the fall of matinee idol Norman Maine. One of the most expensive movies of its time (pipped by *Duel in the Sun*), and Warners' costliest, it spanned a massive ten-month shoot, but was subsequently butchered by the studio. Shockingly, every copy, including the original negative, was cut – the ever-penny pinching Jack Warner wanting to retrieve every grain of silver. The three-hour-plus running time was hacked down to to two-and-a-half, and though a major restoration in 1983 unveiled the full stereo soundtrack, some scenes are permanently lost (the restored version bridges the gaps with still shots). George Cukor, who died before the restoration was complete, refused to watch the butchered version.

Production began during the hysterical flap caused by the arrival of television, with film companies desperately experimenting with every gimmick available. *Star* was thus filmed in Technicolor and Cinemascope. It was beaten by Twentieth Century Fox's *The Robe*, the first film

The Academy Awards: Ambassador Hotel, Wilshire Boulevard

Norman Maine's memorial: Church of the Good Shepherd, Beverly Hills

released in the new widescreen format, but Warner's cheekily managed to incorporate into the opening scene shots of the Fox epic's old-style searchlight première, at Grauman's (now **Mann's**) **Chinese Theater, 6925 Hollywood Boulevard**. The event is supposedly the 'Night of the Stars' benefit at LA's **Shrine Auditorium, 655 West Jefferson Boulevard**, south of downtown in the Exposition Park district. The bright, clear shots were specially filmed, in 'Scope, at the Shrine, and the grainier, newsreel footage is the Grauman's première. The Shrine, a massive 6,700-seat Moorish fantasy built in 1926, occasionally hosts the Oscars (the usual Dorothy Chandler pavilion isn't large enough to accommodate all the Academy members) – it was here that James Cameron became King of the World in 1998. Another king, *King Kong*, was exhibited here in 1933 (it was supposed to be New York), while one more lumbering colossus of the cinema, Arnold Schwarzenegger, was similarly exhibited 50 years later, clad in red, white and blue, when he and 2,000 other worthies became citizens of the USA.

The real Shrine stage and backstage areas were used for Blodgett's first encounter with wobbling star Norman Maine. The boorishly drunken Maine lurches on to the Cocoanut Grove at the **Ambassador Hotel, 3400 Wilshire Boulevard**, midtown. The exterior is real, though the Grove's campy, palmy interior was recreated in the studio at Warners'. The Ambassador – site of Oscar ceremonies in the thirties and of Bobby Kennedy's assassination in 1968 – has stood empty for many years, used only as a movie location. The threat of demolition currently hangs over the building.

The Oleander Arms, where Blodgett stays, was an apartment complex at the corner of Crescent Heights Boulevard and Fountain Avenue, West Hollywood. In 1983, when still photographs were taken for the film's restoration, the building was unchanged, but by 1984 it had been dismantled and carted away. Also gone is Robert's Drive-in Restaurant, where Blodgett works as a car-hop. It stood at Sunset Boulevard and Cahuenga. Similarly, the Bomba Club, where the desperate Esther tries out, unsuccessfully, for a singing job, which was downtown at 626 Spring Street.

The Oliver Niles Studio is, obviously, the Warners' lot itself, at **4000 Warner Boulevard, Burbank**. Cukor, though, reassigns buildings for visual effect: Norman Maine's lavish dressing room, where he gets rid of the blond wig and false nose foisted onto Esther, is one of WB's Executive Offices; the Publicity Department is actually the Wardrobe Building; the screening room, where studio head Niles watches a deafening Western, is the Sound Building. At the payroll window, a warehouse opposite the studio's Commissary, Blodgett finds out her new name is Vicki Lester, and a star is born.

Cut next is the scene, shot in the **Baldwin Hills**, of the nervous newcomer being sick on the way to the out-of-town preview of her first movie, *It's a New World*. The movie, which contains the classic 'Born in a Trunk' number, is showing at the fictitious Marcopia Theater, the exterior of which is on the Warners' New York Street, the interior, a balcony of the Shrine. The main feature advertised on the Marcopia's marquee is *Another Dawn*, the standard title always seen playing at cinemas in WB movies. The title was finally assigned to a 1937 Errol Flynn romance.

Maine and Lester sneak off to San Verdo for a quiet wedding. The tiny town used for the wedding scene is **Piru**, a main street and a railway line off I-126, north of LA.

At the studio, Vicki goes from bright and fresh-faced to exhausted and drained in one cut. A whole musical number, 'Lose That Long Face', was cut (but since restored). The New Orleans backdrop is the old Elysian Fields set from Elia Kazan's *A Streetcar Named Desire*, prettied up with a lick of white paint.

Cleaned-up and dried-out, Norman Maine turns up at the **Santa Anita Racetrack, 285 West Huntington Boulevard, Arcadia**, between LA and Pasadena. With its towering palms and distinctive green and yellow wrought ironwork, the Santa Anita has long been a favourite with Hollywood punters since 1934 (it's where the Marx Brothers spent *A Day at the Races* in 1937) and is still going strong. Fredric March ran into trouble here in the 1937 movie, and James Mason follows suit, falling off the wagon in spectacular fashion. Before you can say 'large scotch', Vicki Lester is racing along Sunset Boulevard (yes, that's the legendary but long-gone Schwab's Drugstore zooming by) to bail Norman Maine out of the drunk tank at frequent movie location **Lincoln Heights Jail, 421 North Avenue 19, Lincoln Heights**, near downtown LA.

At their Malibu beach house, Norman makes the ultimate Hollywood gesture of self-sacrifice for Vicki's career. It's not Malibu, though, but **Laguna Beach**, on I-1 south of LA, where he walks into the sea.

His memorial service is held at the **Church of the Good Shepherd, 505 North Bedford Drive, Beverly Hills** (affectionately known as Our Lady of the Cadillacs). Forbidden to use lighting within the church, Cukor silhouettes the emerging figures in sepulchral gloom against the stained glass windows before letting rip with a barrage of flashbulbs outside the church, where screeching fans rip off grieving Vicki's veil.

And the final shot is, once more, the Shrine Auditorium: "Hello everybody, this is Mrs Norman Maine..."

STAR IS BORN, A

(1976, dir: Frank Pierson)
Barbra Streisand, Kris Kristofferson, Gary Busey.
● ARIZONA; LOS ANGELES

Another star, another birth, but no Oscars this time, and no Ambassador. It's the **Arizona State University, Tempe,** Arizona. Filming also took place at that much-used location, LA's **Biltmore Hotel, 506 South Grand Avenue** on Pershing Square, downtown.

STAR TREK – THE MOTION PICTURE

(1979, dir: Robert Wise)
William Shatner, Leonard Nimoy, DeForest Kelley.
● CALIFORNIA

Studio-bound, determinedly epic, big-screen spin-off from the TV series. The glimpse of Earth locates the Starfleet Academy north of San Francisco, in the Presidio area alongside the **Golden Gate Bridge**. The TV series, when it wasn't in the studio, occasionally made use of the spectacular sandstone formations of Vasquez Rocks County Park, 10700 Escondido Canyon Road, northeast of Newhall, off Route 14 (see *Apache* for details).

STAR TREK IV: THE VOYAGE HOME

(1986, dir: Leonard Nimoy)
William Shatner, Leonard Nimoy, DeForest Kelley.
● CALIFORNIA

After a couple of totally studio-bound sequels, the series begins to use real locations with this eco-conscious adventure, as the crew of the *Enterprise* zoom back to 1986 San Francisco in time to save the whale. They split up at the junction of **Columbus, Kearny** and **Pacific Avenues**. The crew's purloined Klingon ship flies under the **Golden Gate Bridge**. Golden Gate Park, where the crew parks the 'Bird of Prey', is actually **Will Rogers State Park, 14253 Sunset Boulevard**, Pacific Palisades in LA. More filming took place at Vasquez Rocks State Park (see *Apache* for details).

The Sausalito Cetacean Institute, where the *Enterprise* crew find the two humpback whales, was supposedly over the Bay, just north of San Francisco. You can actually find it on the coast south of the city. It's the **Monterey Bay Aquarium, 886 Cannery Row, Monterey**. The aquarium, by the way, does not contain any whales, but does have loads of other fascinating stuff. Visit the aquarium's excellent website at *www.mbayaq.org*.

STAR TREK V: THE FINAL FRONTIER

(1989, dir: William Shatner)
William Shatner, Leonard Nimoy, DeForest Kelley.
● CALIFORNIA; WYOMING

Captain Kirk spends his shore leave climbing on **El Capitan** and **Inspiration Point, Yosemite National Park,** Wyoming (and ends up on the Paramount lot in Hollywood). 'Nimbus III in the Neutral Zone, the Planet of Galactic Peace' is **Owens Dry Lake** in the Mojave Desert, south of Lone Pine, central California, between Routes 395 and 136. The planet Shakari, where Kirk gets a wee bit suspicious at the appearance of 'God', is the **Trona Pinnacles**, an area of tufa spires rising up from Searles Dry

Lake Bed, Trona, near Ridgecrest, Kern County, central California. The strange columns, up to 140 feet tall and covering fifteen square miles, were formed by algae 10,000 years ago when the area lay underwater. The area is reached by a bumpy, seven-mile dirt road (it is accessible to 2-wheel-drive vehicles) off Route 78, about eight miles south of the town of Trona.

STAR TREK VI: THE UNDISCOVERED COUNTRY

(1991, dir: Nicholas Meyer)
William Shatner, Leonard Nimoy, DeForest Kelley.
● ALASKA; CALIFORNIA

'Definitely the very last', they said. The penal asteroid of Rura Penthe, where Kirk and McCoy are condemned to work in the dilithium mines for the assassination of the Klingon chancellor, is the **Knik Glacier, Chugach State Park**, north of Anchorage, Alaska, though the penal colony set was built back in LA, in **Bronson Canyon**, Griffith Park. Camp Khitomer, site of the peace conference, is a conflation of the **Firemen's Fund Building, 777 San Marin Drive**, off I-101 in Novato, Marin County, northern California (the live-action foreground and lake) and the **Brandeis-Bardin Institute, 1101 Peppertree Lane, Brandeis**, in the Simi Valley north of LA (the cylindrical building beyond the lake).

STAR TREK GENERATIONS

(1994, dir: David Carson)
Patrick Stewart, William Shatner, Malcolm McDowell.
● NEVADA; CALIFORNIA

A shot in the arm for the series as the *Enterprise*'s original captain hands over the baton to the Next Generation. Viridian 3, where Malcolm McDowell tries to return to the total joy of the Nexus, and where Kirk finally drops off the intergalactic perch, is **Silica Dome** in the **Valley of Fire State Park**, northwest of Las Vegas, Nevada. To reach the Valley, take I-15 north from Vegas for 33 miles. A signposted turnoff, Route 169, winds for another 18 miles to the park entrance, and on to the Visitor Center (© *702.397.2088; www.desertusa.com/nvval; admission charge*). Silica Dome, a dazzling white rounded peak among the fiery red sandstone outcrop, is off Fire Creek Road. Captains Kirk and Picard meet up near **Hart Flat**, Kern County, central California. The scenes of Captain Kirk riding his uncle's horse were filmed, with Shatner's own horse, on his own farm.

STAR TREK: FIRST CONTACT

(1996, dir: Jonathan Frakes)
Patrick Stewart, Jonathan Frakes, Brent Spiner.
● CALIFORNIA; ARIZONA

The crew battle the Borg in this action-packed entry in the series. The 'film noir' holodeck sequence was filmed in LA's stunning **Union Station, 800 North Alameda Street**, downtown (seen in lots of films, it was used as the police station in *Blade Runner*). Filming also took place in the **Angeles National Forest**, north of LA, and at the **Titan Missile Museum, 1580 West Duval Mine Road, Sahuarita, Green Valley**, Arizona (©

520.625.7736; www.pimaair.org/titan_01.html; admission charge). Home of the Titan II intercontinental ballistic missile, it's the only one of the 54 bases still in existence, now turned into a museum, after the programme was phased out in the eighties.

STAR TREK: INSURRECTION

(1998, dir: Jonathan Frakes)
Patrick Stewart, Jonathan Frakes, Brent Spiner.
● CALIFORNIA

Will Captain Picard actually defy the Federation to prevent the lo-tech, hippy Ba'ku being forcibly ejected from their paradise by the nasty Son'a? The idyllic Ba'ku colony was built at **Lake Sherwood, Thousand Oaks**, north of LA. The lake scenes used the **San Gabriel River** at the **San Gabriel Dam**, seven miles north of Azusa, Los Angeles. The Ba'ku mountain refuge filmed on an inaccessible (unless, like the cast and crew, you have access to a helicopter) mountaintop above the beautiful Alpine reservoir, **Lake Sabrina**, nineteen miles west of Bishop, Route 395, in the Inyo National Forest.

STAR WARS

(1977, dir: George Lucas)
Mark Hamill, Carrie Fisher, Harrison Ford.
● CALIFORNIA; TUNISIA; GUATEMALA

It may have been set in 'a galaxy far, far away', but you can visit some of it. For Luke Skywalker's home, the desert planet of Tatooine, George Lucas used the landscapes and native architecture of Tunisia (Tataouine is a real Tunisian town, some miles south of the movie location).

Luke's sunken home was in the troglodyte town of **Matmata**, where homes are burrowed into the soft local sandstone from the sides of circular pits. The interior is one of the inner courtyards of the **Sidi Driss Hotel** (*©* *216.230.066*), where you can still see the murals and some of the set dressing from the movie. Disturbed by the tourist influx, or just tired of living in the traditional pit homes, many of the residents have moved to the recent development of Nouvelle Matmata a few miles to the north. The exterior of the homestead, where Luke contemplates the two suns, is part of the vast **Chott el Jerid**, the dry, white salt flat stretching across central Tunisia to the oases of Tozeur and Nefta. The site of Luke's home, now a couple of filled-in circular pits, can be found a few miles south from Highway 3 on a turnoff just west of Nefta. The same turnoff, followed six miles north, leads to **La Grande Dune**, used for the Dune Sea, where C3P0 and R2D2 wander aimlessly. Take care on Highway 3, which leads into Algeria – if you inadvertently cross the border, you can end up in all kinds of trouble. The gully, where R2D2 is captured by the Jawas, now known locally as 'Star Wars Canyon' (you can see it again in *Raiders of the Lost Ark*), is **Sidi Bouhel**, east of Tozeur on the edge of the Chott el Jerid.

Mos Eisley, the sleazy spaceport where Luke and Obi-Wan meet Han Solo, is **Ajim**, a sponge fishing town near the Ile de Jerba. You can see the exterior of the Cantina here. A little to the north, overlooking the Gulf of Gabes, is Obi-Wan's remote home, and a mosque used as the entrance to Mos Eisley. Extra desert scenes, featuring

R2D2, Luke's landspeeder and the banthas, were shot in **Death Valley**, California, and cut in to match existing Tunisian footage. Underneath the bantha costume is an elephant hired from Marine World.

The rebel base, 'the Massassi Outpost on the fourth moon of Yavin', seen toward the end of the movie, is the giant Mayan temple complex at **Tikal**, Guatemala. The spectacular ruins, 2,500 years old and set in the 222-square-mile rainforest of the **Parque Nacional Tikal**, are in northern Guatemala, about 40 miles from Flores (there's a two-lane road, or you can travel by air from nearby Santa Elena Airport) and can be visited from the Tikal Visitor Centre.

STAR WARS EPISODE I: THE PHANTOM MENACE

(1999, dir: George Lucas)
Ewan McGregor, Liam Neeson, Natalie Portman.
● ITALY; TUNISIA

It's back to Tunisia for the Tatooine scenes, this time at **Tozeur** – also a location for *The English Patient.* Young Anakin's slave-quarter home is a ksar (originally a grain store) in **Medenine**, about 35 miles southeast of Matmata in southern Tunisia. The last remaining square of this once-vast complex has been turned into a bustling bazaar at avenue 7 Novembre in the centre of the town. The narrow street, where Anakin says goodbye to his mother, runs behind the square.

The fight with Darth Maul: Chott el Gharsa

Mos Espa: Watto's workshop, Chott el Gharsa

The exterior of Palazzo Reale, Caserta

The rear of the slave-quarters, where Anakin works on the pod racer, and where his mother reveals portentous hints about a virgin birth to Qui-Gon Jinn, is the **Hotel Ksar Hadada, Ksar Hadada** near Ghomrassen, south of Medenine toward Tataouine. No longer used as a hotel, this complex maze of crazily-angled ksar still bears traces of the plastic tiled set-dressing.

You'll need a four-wheel-drive vehicle, and probably a guide, to visit the sets of Mos Espa crumbling away among the dunes of **Chott el Gharsa**. The Chott is north of Nefta, an oasis town across the dry salt lake of Chott el Jerid in western Tunisia, near the Algerian border. The remains of two sets can be seen here, along with the strange, windblown, angular rock formations seen in the desert fight with Darth Maul. The site is near to the location of the desert camp in *The English Patient*.

The staterooms and staircases of Queen Amidala's Theed Palace on Naboo are the overwhelming marble interior of **Palazzo Reale**, the Royal Palace, **Piazza Carlo III, Caserta**, about 15 miles north of Naples in Italy. The baroque palace, built in 1752, for King Charles III of Naples to rival France's Versailles, is open to visitors. A regular rail service runs from Naples, and the palace is directly opposite the station at Caserta.

STARDUST MEMORIES
(1980, dir: Woody Allen)
Woody Allen, Charlotte Rampling, Jessica Harper.
● NEW JERSEY

Woody Allen's sour retread of Fellini's *8 1/2* was shot around New Jersey. Locations include the **Boardwalk** at **Asbury Park**, a rather faded resort on the North Jersey shore; **Ocean Avenue** in adjoining **Ocean Grove** to the south; and at **Planting Fields Arboretum, Planting Fields Road, Oyster Bay** on Long Island (© *516.922.9206*), 400 acres of gardens and woodland.

STARGATE
(1994, dir: Roland Emmerich)
James Spader, Kurt Russell, Jaye Davidson.
● CALIFORNIA; ARIZONA

School-of-Spielberg sci-fi spectacle, from the director who went on to make blockbuster *Independence Day*. The desertscapes are at **Yuma**, Arizona. Viveca Lindfors arrives at the cavernous lobby of the **Park Plaza Hotel, 607 South Park View Street**, downtown LA, where James Spader lectures in the Ballroom (see *New York, New York* for details of the Park Plaza).

STARMAN
(1984, dir: John Carpenter)
Jeff Bridges, Karen Allen, Charles Martin Smith.
● TENNESSEE; NEVADA; ARIZONA; IOWA; COLORADO; NORTH CAROLINA

Sci-fi fantasy road movie, with alien Bridges taking the form of widow Allen's recently deceased husband. This was filmed all over the US, in Tennessee; Iowa; Colorado; **Las Vegas**, Nevada; and at the **University of North Carolina**. You can visit the meteor crater, at which Bridges has his final rendezvous with his ship, about fifteen miles west of **Winslow**, Arizona, just to the south of I-40 (*admission charge: website: www.meteorcrater.com*)

STARS LOOK DOWN, THE
(1939, dir: Carol Reed)
Michael Redgrave, Margaret Lockwood, Edward Rigby.
● CUMBERLAND

After the success of the 1938 adaptation of *The Citadel*, a version of AJ Cronin's coalmining novel was next. Carol Reed wanted to make as much of the movie as possible on location, but sound recording problems necessitated some studio work, with one of the biggest sets ever built

at Twickenham constructed to match up with the real location of miners' cottages at **Great Clifton**, outside Workington. The colliery was the St Helen's Siddick Colliery at **Workington**, and the football match was shot at the Borough Park ground of **Workington FC**.

STARSHIP TROOPERS
(1997, dir: Paul Verhoeven)
Casper Van Dien, Dina Meyer, Neil Patrick Harris.
● WYOMING; SOUTH DAKOTA; LOS ANGELES

Compulsive controversialist Verhoeven follows up the disappointment of his would-be sexploitation shocker *Showgirls* with a violent and FX-laden monster movie set in a neo-

The spaceport: New Los Angeles Convention Center

fascist future. The bizarre rock formations of Tango Urilla, the alien world of sci-fi writer Robert Henlein's novel (most of which is dumped to leave more room for man-eating bugs) can be found in **Hell's Half Acre**, a county park west of Casper, Wyoming. A vast set was built here for the humans' command centre. More landscapes were shot at **Kadoka**, on Hwy-90, about 100 miles east of Rapid City in the Badlands of South Dakota. Van Dien's parents' home is a 1993 house designed by architect Ed Niles in the **Agoura Hills**, north of Malibu. It also features as the lab in John Woo's *Face/Off* and in *Mr Wrong*.

More futuristic locations around LA include the **California Institute of Technology (Caltech), 1201 East California Boulevard**, between Hill and Wilson Avenues, Pasadena (seen also in *Beverly Hills Cop*, *Real Genius* and *The Witches of Eastwick* among many others) and **The Pyramid, 1250 Bellflower Boulevard** at **California State University, Long Beach**. The spaceport is the concourse of the **New Los Angeles Convention Center, 1202 South Figueroa Street**, between Pico Boulevard and 11th Street, downtown LA – seen also in *Demolition Man* and *Face/Off*.

STAZIONE TERMINI (aka *Terminal Station/ Indiscretion of an American Wife*)
(1953, dir: Vittorio De Sica)
Montgomery Clift, Jennifer Jones, Gino Cervi.
● ROME

All kinds of problems lie behind the array of titles. Originally *Terminal Station*, the title was changed in the US to *Indiscretion of an American Wife* by hands-on producer David O Selznick, who was using the vehicle to showcase his then-wife Jennifer Jones, much to the annoyance of star Clift and writer Truman Capote. The final movie checks in at a savagely hacked 75

The railway station: Stazione Termini, Rome

minutes. It was made almost entirely on location on Rome's central train station, **Stazione Termini, Piazza dei Cinquecento**.

STEEL MAGNOLIAS
(1989, dir: Herbert Ross)
Shirley MacLaine, Sally Field, Dolly Parton.
● LOUISIANA

Robert Harling's terminally sentimental stageplay was filmed in **Natchitoches**, on I-1 between Shreveport and Alexandria, Louisiana. Dolly Parton's beauty parlor (based on that of Liz Landrum, who was allegedly appalled at the movie version, at 316 Sirod Street, Natchitoches) was a private house on **Henry Street**, with the addition of a fake bay window. The 'Easter Egg Hunt' takes place on a levee behind Natchitoches Chamber of Commerce, tricked out with 200 silk crocuses, tulips, irises and daisies. More stats – the production used thirteen three-tiered wedding cakes, 9,000 dyed Easter eggs and 600 roses. And if the crapping 'blackbirds' look a mite hefty, well, that's because they're actually pigeons, dyed with shoe polish.

STEPFORD WIVES, THE
(1975, dir: Bryan Forbes)
Katharine Ross, Paula Prentiss, Nanette Newman.
● CONNECTICUT

Ira Levin's wickedly dark allegory just about survives a monumental piece of miscasting which throws the whole concept out of whack (see screenwriter William Goldman's book *Adventures in the Screen Trade* for the full story). A leafy US suburb is a perfect heaven for the men, a town where beautiful, compliant women are just *thrilled* to do housework. Ross and the wonderful Prentiss get the creeps. Stepford is **Westport**, Route 95 on the south coast of Connecticut.

STING, THE
(1973, dir: George Roy Hill)
Paul Newman, Robert Redford, Robert Shaw.
● CHICAGO; LOS ANGELES

This phenomenally successful con movie is set in thirties Chicago, but many of the period locations were found around LA. In fact, much of the film was shot at Universal in Hollywood, on the backlot's all-purpose 'Main Street'. Paul Newman's carousel can be seen, still in action, on the **Santa Monica Pier**, at the end of Colorado Avenue, Santa Monica. Some tricky artwork turns the pier itself into Chi-

The Chicago carousel: Santa Monica Pier, Santa Monica

cago's 'el', the elevated railway. The Chicago 'el' seen in the movie is on the Universal backlot, where it was built for Norman Jewison's period comedy *Gaily Gaily*. Several real bars served as sets: the plush New York gambling casino is a lounge of the **Castle Green Apartments, 99 South Raymond Avenue, Pasadena**. A venerable old LA hotel, the Castle Green was drafted into service when the set-building budget began to run low. It was also used for corridors of the Chicago hotel. You can see the apartments' bizarre Moorish exterior in *Bugsy*. The bank is the Italian marble lobby of the 1912, seven-storey **Commercial and Savings Bank, Pasadena**. Nearby is the Chicago alleyway. The FBI hideout is the old **Koppel Plant**, a storage building for grain shipments in the San Pedro harbor district. The burlesque theatre is the old *The Phantom of the Opera* set at Universal Studios, in Hollywood.

The railway terminals of Joliet, Chicago and New York are all Chicago, though. Two of the railway terminals were no longer in use and had been converted into office space, which meant that renovations had to be stripped away and old ticket offices restored. The termini are **Union Station** (still in use); **La Salle Street Station** (still in use, but the period exterior seen in the movie has since gone); **Penn Central Freight Yards** and **Illinois Central Station**.

The limp 1983 sequel, imaginatively titled *The Sting II*, used the **Santa Cruz Boardwalk, 400 Beach Street, Santa Cruz**, on the coast south of San Francisco (see *The Lost Boys* for details).

STIR CRAZY
(1980, dir: Sidney Poitier)
Richard Pryor, Gene Wilder, Georg Stanford Brown.
● NEW YORK CITY; ARIZONA; NEVADA

Over-mugged farce with Pryor and Wilder wrongly banged up for a bank robbery after they move west from New York. The penitentiary is **Arizona State Prison, 1305 East Butte Avenue, Florence**, Arizona. More filming took place in the **Valley of Fire State Park**, Nevada.

STOLEN LIFE, A
(1946, dir: Curtis Bernhardt)
Bette Davis, Glenn Ford, Dane Clark.
● CALIFORNIA

Two Bette Davises, in a remake of a 1939 British movie which starred Elisabeth Bergner and Michael Redgrave. This movie, the first production from BD Inc (guess who's production company that was) was set in New England, but shot in California, at the snottily exclusive coastal resort of **Pebble Beach**, between Monterey and Carmel. The East Coast lighthouse was built at **Laguna Beach**, Orange County, south of LA, not far from Davis' home. It was claimed that Bette almost drowned filming the storm in the enormous seventeen foot deep tank on the Warners' lot.

STRADA, LA
(1954, dir: Federico Fellini)
Giulietta Masina, Anthony Quinn, Richard Basehart.
● ITALY

Masina is the maltreated, waif-like sidekick of macho travelling showman Quinn in Fellini's hauntingly magical fable, made on location around central and southern Italy, largely in **Viterbo**; **Ovindoli** and **Bagnoregio**.

STRAIGHT STORY, THE

(1999, dir: David Lynch)
Richard Farnsworth, Sissy Spacek, Harry Dean Stanton.
● **WISCONSIN; IOWA**

Exactly what it says. The Wizard of Weird produces a perfectly straightforward, low-key but affecting account of Alvin Straight's cross-country journey on his lawnmower to find his estranged brother. The film, shot chronologically, follows the real Alvin's route from **Laurens**, northwest Iowa, east across almost the entire width of the state, to **Mount Zion**, Wisconsin. He calls in at **New Hampton**; **West Bend**; **West Union** and **Clermont** in Iowa; then crosses the Mississippi into Wisconsin at **Prairie du Chien**, finally reaching Mount Zion.

STRANGE DAYS

(1995, dir: Kathryn Bigelow)
Ralph Fiennes, Angela Bassett, Juliette Lewis.
● **LOS ANGELES**

A techno-thriller from back when Millennium Eve was way in the future, set and shot in LA. The vast Millennium party is in front of the **Bonaventure Hotel, South Figuroa Street**, downtown (see *In the Line of Fire* for details).

STRANGERS ON A TRAIN

(1951, dir: Alfred Hitchcock)
Robert Walker, Farley Granger, Ruth Roman.
● **NEW YORK CITY; NEW YORK STATE; LOS ANGELES; WASHINGTON DC; CONNECTICUT**

Hitchcock sneakily managed to acquire the rights to Patricia Highsmith's novel for peanuts. Creepily camp Walker offers to swap murders with manly, strapping tennis player Granger, and before you can say 'criss cross', he's carried out his half of the bargain. Set largely in Washington DC, and the fictitious town of Metcalf. The opening scene, of Granger and Walker boarding the train, is DC's **Union Station, Massachusetts Avenue NE**, between First and Second Streets. After years of neglect, the grandiose Beaux Arts building was beautifully restored in 1988. Granger's hometown of Metcalf, where he rows with his wife, is the **Danbury** railroad stop, Connecticut, on I-84, 50 miles or so north of New York City on the New York state border. This is where Hitch makes his trademark cameo appearance, humping a double bass onto the train as Granger alights.

The amusement park, where Walker commits Granger's murder, and the site of the climactic carousel crash, is a conflation of a set constructed on the ranch of movie director Roland V Lee (*Son of Frankenstein*) in the LA suburb of Chatsworth, and the real **Canoga Park Fairground**, which supplied the Tunnel of Love, into which Walker follows his victim. Walker haunts Granger by hanging about on the steps of the **Jefferson Memorial, East Potomac Park**, 14th Street at East Basin Drive SW, Washington. After the suspenseful tennis match, suspicious cops tail Granger to New York's **Pennsylvania Station**, 31st-33rd

Streets between Seventh and Eighth Avenues.

Long shots for the climactic tennis game were taken at the Davis Cup match between America and Australia at the famous **West Side Tennis Club, 1 Tennis Place, Forest Hills** (*©* *718.268.2300*), while more tennis scenes used the **South Gate Tennis Courts**, southeast LA.

STRAW DOGS

(1971, dir: Sam Peckinpah)
Dustin Hoffman, Susan George, David Warner.
● **CORNWALL**

Down in deepest Cornwall, pacifist Hoffman turns to ultra-violence when local heavies lay siege to his farmhouse. The violence is all very jolly, but the rape scene is seriously leery. What might have worked in dusty Mexico seems wildly contrived in the West Country. The village is **St Buryan**, on the B3283 a few miles west of Penzance, toward Lands End.

STREETCAR NAMED DESIRE, A

(1951, dir: Elia Kazan)
Vivien Leigh, Marlon Brando, Kim Hunter.
● **LOS ANGELES; NEW ORLEANS, LOUISIANA**

The rather stagey adaptation of Tennessee Williams' play is set in steamy New Orleans, but was shot almost entirely at Warner Bros' Burbank Studio. Stanley Kowalski's bowling alley is one of the real locations, though not in the Deep South: it stood on Pico Boulevard in LA. There was some location

The real Desire Streetcar: Esplanade Avenue, New Orleans.

The real Elysian Fields, New Orleans.

work in the Big Easy, though. The railway station is the **L&N Train Station** at the foot of Canal Street, the wide north-south roadway bordering the French Quarter. By 1951, the streetcars had been replaced by buses, but an old Desire streetcar was trundled out of retirement for the shot. Sadly, almost all of the location filming was eventually cut from the movie. You can see a streetcar from the Desire line on display behind the Mint at 400 Esplanade Avenue, New Orleans. Elysian Fields, far from being a poetic invention of the playwright, is a real thoroughfare, a street of wooden shacks in a fairly poor neighbourhood.

STRICTLY BALLROOM

(1992, dir: Baz Luhrmann)
Paul Mercurio, Tara Morice, Gia Carides.
● **NEW SOUTH WALES, AUSTRALIA; VICTORIA, AUSTRALIA**

Winning, primary-coloured fantasy with drop-dead gorgeous Mercurio and plain-Jane Morice defying the carved-in-stone rules of ballroom dancing and, wouldn't you know, triumphing in style. Filming took place at the **Signal Room** near Pier 13, **Pyrmont**. The rooftop where Mercurio and Morice dance is estate agent **LJ Hooker's 322 Victoria Road** at Marrickville Road, **Marrickville**, Sydney. The joyous climax is at the **Melbourne Sports and Entertainment Centre, Swan Street**, Melbourne, Victoria.

STRIPTEASE
(1996, dir: Andrew Bergman)
Demi Moore, Burt Reynolds, Armand Assante.
● **FLORIDA**

Based on Carl Hiaasen's novel *Strip Tease*. Moore loses custody of her daughter to vengeful ex Robert Patrick, and turns to stripping. Made on location in Florida, mainly around **Fort Lauderdale**. Don Shula Hospital is **Broward General Hospital**. The Rojo sugar cane fields were filmed in **South Bay**. The interior of the sugar refinery is the **Pennsuco Cement Plant, NW 72nd Avenue** in Miami, near Lake Joanne. Garcia's cabin, on Lake Okeechobee was built at **Quiet Waters Park**. Filming also took place at **Miami Seaquarium**. The *Big Sugar* yacht is actually called the *Big Eagle*, and was shot at **Port Everglades**. The autopsy filmed in the real **Dade County Morgue**, while real autopsies were being conducted behind screens.

The Eager Beaver and Flesh Farm clubs used real strip joints in **Pompano**.

STROMBOLI
(1949, dir: Roberto Rossellini)
Ingrid Bergman, Mario Vitale, Renzo Cesana.
● **ITALY**

This melodrama, made at the height of Bergman's scandalous affair with Rossellini, was shot, naturally enough, around the volcano of **Stromboli**.

SUBWAY
(1985, dir: Luc Besson)
Christophe Lambert, Isabelle Adjani, Jean-Hugues Anglade.
● **PARIS**

Style, style, style is all in this designer thriller filmed almost entirely within the Paris Métro system, so it's play 'spot the station'. The station where Lambert, escaping the hitmen, first catches a train is **Dupleix** on Boulevard Grenelle just south of the Pont de Bir-Hakeim. The inspector meets up with flower-seller Bohringer at **Porte de Versailles**, south toward Mairie d'Issy. Lambert listens to the sax player at eastern terminus **Gallieni**. Roller-skater Anglade is followed onto the train at **Concorde**, before being handcuffed to the carriage pole at **La Motte-Picqet-Grenelle** – back toward Dupleix again. Most of the action centres around the vast interchange of the world's largest underground station, **Chatelet-Les Halles** beneath the Forum des Halles.

SUDDEN FEAR
(1952, dir: David Miller)
Joan Crawford, Jack Palance, Gloria Grahame.
● **SAN FRANCISCO**

Wealthy playwright Joan Crawford discovers that new

hubby Jack Palance is planning to bump her off in this neat suspenser made in San Francisco. Crawford's home is **2800 Scott Street**.

Crawford's house: Scott Street, San Francisco

SUDDEN IMPACT
(1983, dir: Clint Eastwood)
Clint Eastwood, Sondra Locke, Pat Hingle.
● **CALIFORNIA**

Fourth outing for Dirty Harry Callahan. Reputedly no longer welcome in cute, touristy and liberal San Francisco, most of the action takes place in the fictitious San Paula, which

'Go ahead, make my day...': Burger Island, Third Street, San Francisco

is, in fact, **Santa Cruz** just down the coast on Highway 1 (see *The Lost Boys* for details). The wedding party, where Harry provokes a suspect into a heart attack, filmed in the **Cocoanut Grove Ballroom** on the **Santa Cruz Boardwalk**. A pretty klutzy movie, but Eastwood's line as he deals with the robbery at a restaurant has passed into the language: "Go ahead, make my day." The restaurant, still there, is **Burger Island, 901 Third Street** at Townsend, San Francisco.

SUGARLAND EXPRESS, THE
(1974, dir: Steven Spielberg)
Goldie Hawn, William Atherton, Michael Sacks.
● **TEXAS**

Spielberg's first made-for-cinema movie (although *Duel* played cinemas in the UK, it was made for US TV) is a dazzlingly-directed comedy car chase which plunges into tragedy as Goldie Hawn springs husband William Atherton from Pre-release Center and sets off across Texas to reclaim her baby from care in Sugarland. The movie opens at **Rosenberg**, on I-59, 30 miles southwest of Houston and about 20 miles west of the real Sugarland. The fugitives stop for gas at **Humble**, I-59, just north of Houston. As the media circus surrounding their flight begins to grow, they call in at **San Antonio**; at **Pleasanton**, 30 miles south, where sheriff Ben Johnson has second thoughts about using snipers to pick the couple off, and at nearby **Floresville** ending up over in West Texas near the Mexico border, at **Del Rio**. Johnson finally resorts to the ultimate deterrent and the chase grinds to a halt in the Rio Grande.

SUMMER MADNESS (aka *Summertime*)
(1955, dir: David Lean)
Katharine Hepburn, Rossano Brazzi, Isa Miranda.
● **VENICE, ITALY**

Starchy 'spinster' Hepburn falls for married Rossano Brazzi

Hepburn's alfresco drink: Cafe Chioggia, Piazza San Marco

Rossano Brazzi's antique shop: 2808 Dorsoduro

Hepburn's hotel: Pensione Accademia, Fondamenta Bollani

on a European vacation. David Lean's lightweight travelogue-romance was made on location in Venice, in the days before mass tourism, though the film's release doubled the city's tourist trade overnight. Lean takes advantage of the audience's presumed unfamiliarity with the city by playing fast and loose with the geography.

Movie camera-toting Hepburn arrives by train at **Stazione Ferroviaria Santa Lucia**, the then-spanking new railway station, one of Venice's few unapologetically modern buildings, on **Fondamenta di Santa Lucia** at the northern end of Canal Grande. In order to conjure up an instant flavour of Venice, Lean has Hepburn's vaporetto trip to the hotel take a bizarrely circuitous route, taking in the church of **Santa Maria della Salute**, which stands at the canal's southern entrance. Likewise, the Pensioni Fiorini, where she stays, has windows which look out on totally different areas of the city. The actual hotel itself, a detached villa with canalside terrace, is **Pensione Accademia, Fondamenta Bollani 1058**, in the Dorsoduro district (© 5237846) just to the west of the Galleria dell'Accademia (*vaporetto: Accademia*).

Hepburn, inevitably for a Venice-set movie, enjoys a drink alfresco at **Cafe Chioggia**, opposite the Basilica San Marco in the **Piazzetta San Marco**, where she first meets Brazzi. Northwest of the Pensione Accademia is the site of the film's most famous scene, Hepburn falling into the canal. The canal is the Canal San Barnaba, at **Campo San Barnaba** in the Dorsoduro district. At the foot of the sweet

Hepburn falls into the canal: Campo San Barnaba

little Ponte San Barnaba on the campo is Brazzi's antique shop, **2808 Dorsoduro**. The church dominating the campo, by the way, is the major Venice location for *Indiana Jones and the Last Crusade*.

SUMMER OF '42
(1971, dir: Robert Mulligan)
Gary Grimes, Jennifer O'Neill, Jerry Houser.
● **CALIFORNIA**

Soft-focus, sentimental nostalgia, with schoolboy Grimes enjoying his first sexual experience with recently widowed O'Neill. Set in New England, the real location is over on the west coast, in the seaport of **Mendocino**, originally a Gold Rush town, then a mill town, now reinvented as an upmarket artists' colony, with filming at **Ten Mile Beach**.

SUMMER OF SAM
(1999, dir: Spike Lee)
John Leguizamo, Adrien Brody, Mira Sorvino.
● **NEW YORK CITY**

Spike Lee's evocation of the blistering summer of 1977 and the effect on the inhabitants of NY of serial killer the Son of Sam. The 'dead end street' neighbourhood is **Layton Avenue** in the **Country Club** district, on Eastchester Bay in the Bronx. John Leguizamo and Mira Sorvino chicken out of joining the, rather anachronistic, punk crowd at **CBGB's, 315 Bowery** between First and Second Streets (© 212.982.4052), and join the hopefuls lined up outside **Studio 54, 254 West 54th Street** between Broadway and Eighth Avenue, Manhattan. No longer the legendary nightclub of the seventies, it's now a performance space (see *54* for details).

SUMMER WITH MONIKA
(1952, dir: Ingmar Bergman)
Harriet Andersson, Lars Ekborg, John Harryson.
● **SWEDEN**

Early Bergman, a doomed summer romance, made on **Orno**, a large island in the south of the Stockholm archipelago.

SUNDAY, BLOODY SUNDAY
(1971, dir: John Schlesinger)
Peter Finch, Glenda Jackson, Murray Head.
● **LONDON**

Both Finch and Jackson are besotted with artist Head in this immaculately written, acted and directed slice of London life in the seventies. But the icing on the cake comes in the collection of priceless cameos and caricatures surrounding the central relationships. Jackson and Head take the precocious kids for a scamper around **Greenwich Park**, SE10, which is quite a walk from the family house. The passageway lined with gravestones, is alongside **St**

Dr Finch's surgery: Pembroke Square, Kensington

Home of the Hodson family: Spencer Park, Wandsworth

Daniel Day-Lewis' first screen appearance: St Alphege, Greenwich

Alphege, in Greenwich. One of the kids vandalising cars here is Daniel Day-Lewis, in his first screen appearance. Although the appalling Hodson family is quintessentially 'Hampstead', the house is actually in south London, about 12 miles from Greenwich, on the north side of Wandsworth Common, **5 Spencer Park**, SW18. Dr Finch's surgery, where he and Head raised a few eyebrows back in 1971 with a passionate screen kiss, is **37 Pembroke Square**, W8, just off Earls Court Road. The scene took the film crew by surprise, too. Until that point, they'd been led to believe the couple were uncle and nephew.

SUNSET BLVD.

(1950, dir: Billy Wilder)
Gloria Swanson, William Holden, Erich Von Stroheim.
● **LOS ANGELES**

The Paramount Gate, Hollywood

William Holden's digs: Alto Nido Apartments, North Ivar Street

Forget the musical, this is the real thing. Ageing silent movie star Swanson takes in flat-broke screenwriter Holden in Wilder's brilliant satire noir. The glorious old Renaissance-style mansion, which stood at 641 Irving on the corner of Wilshire and Crenshaw Boulevards, midtown LA, was demolished in 1957 to make way for the Getty headquarters, now the glumly nondescript Harbor Building. The mansion, seen also in *Rebel Without a Cause*, was built in the twenties for a former US Consul in Mexico, who abandoned the building, which stood vacant for over ten years until bought by J Paul Getty. At the time of filming *Sunset Blvd.*, the mansion had passed to Mrs J Paul Getty in a divorce settlement and she, in turn, rented the property out to Paramount on condition the film company built her a swimming pool. And if Mrs Getty didn't like the pool, she would have to remove it. Paramount built it, Mrs Getty liked it, and it stayed, which is just as well...

You can still, however, see the digs of scriptwriter Holden, the Mediterranean-style **Alto Nido Apartments, 1851 North Ivar Street**, Hollywood. Just down the road a bit, in the mock-Tudor Para Sed Apartments at 1817 North Ivar, lived real-life writer Nathanael West who began penning the classic Hollywood satire *Day of the Locust* here in 1935.

Gloria Swanson visits Cecil B DeMille on set at **Paramount Studios, 5555 Melrose Avenue** in Hollywood. The studio, built in 1917 as the Peralta Studios, became Brunton Studios in 1920, then United Studios in 1921, before being bought by Paramount in 1926. The studio has since expanded and swallowed up surrounding streets, which means that the main entrance is no longer the famous Paramount gate seen in the movie. The arch can now only be glimpsed from a distance across the lot, unless you can manage the under-publicised walking tour of the lot (three times a day, Monday to Friday, $15).

Disastrous previews (one in Evanston, Illinois, home to the Women's Christian Temperance Union – Wilder had earlier made *The Lost Weekend*) led to Wilder junking the original opening scene (the corpse of Holden and a bunch of other stiffs in the morgue discuss how they ended up dead) and trying something with the swimming pool. The rest is history.

SUNSHINE BOYS, THE

(1975, dir: Herbert Ross)
George Burns, Walter Matthau, Richard Benjamin.
● **NEW YORK CITY**

Burns and Matthau, two old vaudevillians who can't stand the sight of each other, are brought together for a TV reunion in this filming of Neil Simon's stage play. Matthau's New York apartment block is the **Ansonia Hotel, 2107-2109 Broadway** between West 73rd and West 74th Streets on the West Side. The Belle-Epoque block has never been a hotel, but private apartments whose thick, soundproofed walls have made it popular with musicians such as Caruso, Toscanini, Stravinsky and Lily Pons. The Ansonia basement, incidentally, was home to the Continental Baths, the gay bathhouse and cabaret where Bette Midler, accompanied by pianist Barry Manilow, began her career. Also featured is the **Friars Club, 57 East 55th Street**, the private actors' club famous for celebrity roasts, between Park and Madison Avenues, midtown New York.

SUPERMAN

(1978, dir: Richard Donner)
Christopher Reeve, Margot Kidder, Gene Hackman.
● **NEW YORK CITY; ALBERTA; CALIFORNIA; NEVADA; NEW MEXICO**

The wheatfields of Smallville, Clark Kent's childhood home, are around **Calgary** in Alberta, Canada, as is the beautiful lakeside setting where Lex Luthor and his cohorts commandeer missiles. The *Daily Planet* building is the splendid art-deco **News Building, 220 East 42nd Street** between Second and Third Avenues, New York, formerly the New York *Daily News* Building (the fifties TV series of *Superman* famously used Los Angeles City Hall, 200 North Spring Street, downtown). The

The *Daily Planet* building: News Building, East 42nd Street

roof, where Lois Lane is rescued from the 'copter crash, is the **US Post Office Building** on Lexington Avenue. Lois's apartment is **240 Central Park South,** from which she and Supes go for a night-time spin around the **Statue of Liberty.** Luthor's lair is supposedly beneath **Grand Central Station,** and that is the real course, where Otis is tailed to the rail lines beneath, though the hideout itself is an imaginative set built at Pinewood Studios in the UK. Superman's feats involve saving a school bus on San Francisco's **Golden Gate Bridge** and rescuing Jimmie Olsen from the collapsing **Boulder Dam,** Nevada. There was more filming at **Red Rock State Park** near Gallup, New Mexico (the area has been renamed Superman Canyon).

SUPERMAN II
(1980, dir: Richard Lester)
Christopher Reeve, Valerie Perrine, Terence Stamp.

Superman to the rescue: Niagara Falls

● **NEW YORK CITY; BUCKING-HAMSHIRE**

The three supervillains arrive on Earth at that old favourite location, **Black Park Lake, Black Park** behind Pinewood Studios at Iver Heath, Buckinghamshire. The small Western town was built at Chobham Common, Surrey. The Metropolis set was, at the time, the largest ever constructed at Pinewood. Superman rescues a little boy plummeting into **Niagara Falls.** The Honeymoon Haven Hotel is **Table Rock House,** alongside the Canadian side of Horseshoe Falls.

SUPERMAN III
(1983, dir: Richard Lester)
Christopher Reeve, Richard Pryor, Jackie Cooper.
● **ARIZONA; ALBERTA**

Superman is corrupted by synthetic Kryptonite, while villains Pryor and Robert Vaughn beaver away at a supercomputer. Filming took place at the **Glen Canyon Dam,** near Page, northern Arizona. The fallen chimney is **Turbo Resources Ltd Oil Refinery** in Alberta, Canada. There was more filming at **Calgary; Drumheller** and **High River** in Alberta.

SUPERMAN IV: THE QUEST FOR PEACE
(1987, dir: Sidney J Furie)
Christopher Reeve, Gene Hackman, Margot Kidder.
● **BUCKINGHAMSHIRE**

The saga trundles on… Metropolis, the bland, soulless city of the future is no longer New York, but **Milton Keynes,** the Buckinghamshire New Town. The United Nations Building is **Milton Keynes Central Railway Sta-**

tion. The *Daily Planet* building is nearby. Mariel Hemingway's hotel is the HQ of **Argos, Avebury Boulevard.** The studio work at Elstree ran into problems when the set for *Willow,* filming at the same time, began to impinge on the *Supman IV* set. It was all settled amicably, of course.

SUPERVIXENS
(1975, dir: Russ Meyer)
Shari Eubank, Charles Pitts, Charles Napier.
● **ARIZONA**

Another bizarre confection from breast-obsessed Meyer, though more bloody than usual, with Charles Pitts getting involved with a succession of Amazonian females after fleeing his job at Martin Bormann's gas station when he's accused of… well, you get the picture. It was shot in **Quartzsite,** Arizona.

SUSPECT
(1987, dir: Peter Yates)
Cher, Dennis Quaid, Liam Neeson.
● **WASHINGTON DC; ONTARIO, CANADA**

Cher defends deaf-mute Neeson, accused of murder, while getting involved with juror Quaid. Set in Washington DC, the movie's locations are split between the real DC and Toronto, Ontario. The opening shot is the **US Supreme Court, First Street NE,** between Maryland Avenue and East Capitol Street. The murder takes place at the parking lot on **K Street** beneath the Francis Scott Key Bridge, Georgetown. Cher lives in the Adams Morgan district of DC. Toronto locations include the **Ontario Hydro Substation, 451 Davenport Road;** the **Sutton Place Hotel, 955 Bay Street; Queen's Park; Liberty Street** and **Rosedale Road.**

SUSPICION
(1941, dir: Alfred Hitchcock)
Cary Grant, Joan Fontaine, Nigel Bruce.
● **CALIFORNIA**

Is playboy Cary Grant scheming to kill his poor, naïve, young wife Joan Fontaine? You bet. Until Hitch played safe to please the studio execs and refilmed a happy ending with Grant totally exonerated. Set in England, the coastscapes are the rugged seafront of northern California, between **Carmel** and **Big Sur.**

SWAMP THING
(1982, dir: Wes Craven)
Ray Wise, Adrienne Barbeau, Louis Jourdan.
● **SOUTH CAROLINA**

Ray Wise turns into lumbering green eco-warrior in this comicbook adaptation from a pre-*Nightmare* Craven. The fearful, impenetrable swamplands are the Cypress Gardens and the Magnolia Plantations of **Charleston,** down on the southeast coast of South Carolina.

SWAMP WATER
(1941, dir: Jean Renoir)
Walter Huston, Walter Brennan, Anne Baxter.
● **GEORGIA**

A fugitive hides out in the **Okeefenokee Swamp,** where

this was actually filmed, down in southwest Georgia.

SWAN, THE
(1956, dir: Charles Vidor)
Grace Kelly, Alec Guinness, Agnes Moorehead.
● NORTH CAROLINA

Why waste good publicity? If Grace Kelly is leaving the movies to marry a prince, why not quickly slip her into a romantic comedy about a woman about to marry a prince? Ferenc Molnar's play was duly exhumed. The house is Vanderbilt's French Renaissance-style chateau, **Biltmore House, Asheville**, North Carolina (see *Being There* for details).

SWEET AND LOWDOWN
(1999, dir: Woody Allen)
Sean Penn, Samantha Morton, Uma Thurman.
● NEW YORK STATE; NEW JERSEY

Although Allen's biopic of a fictitious jazz musician used the Teaneck Armory in New Jersey as a soundstage, plenty of thirties-style locations were found around the state, as well as in Upstate New York and new York City itself. The amateur talent contest won by Penn is at the **Eagles' Club, 7 Old Albany Post Road, Ossining**. The railroad yards are the **Sunnyside Railyards** in Queens, while the Chicago stockyards were found in **Patterson**, New Jersey.

The nightclub, where a drunken Sean Penn drags his companion off into the night to watch trains, is **Chumley's, 86 Bedford Street**, between Grove and Barrow Streets, Greenwich Village. This atmospheric little bar was once a speakeasy and still has no sign outside to indicate its presence. The unmodernised interior can also be seen in *Bright Lights, Big City*, Warren Beatty's epic *Reds* and Mike Wadleigh's eco-horror *Wolfen*. Another venue is the old **Gage and Tollner** restaurant in Brooklyn. The gas station is on Highway 9W, upstate New York, and the park is **Rockland Lake State Park**, Route 9W in **Congers**.

SWEET DREAMS
(1985, dir: Karel Reisz)
Jessica Lange, Ed Harris, Ann Wedgeworth.
● WEST VIRGINIA; TENNESSEE; CALIFORNIA

Biopic of country singer Patsy Cline, shot partly in Cline's hometown of **Martinsburg**, off I-81 way over in the northeastern corner of West Virginia. Locations here include the **Rainbow Road Club**, Route 340, and **Green Hill Cemetery, East Burke Street**. Filming also took place at the inevitable Grand Ol' Opry in the **Ryman Auditorium, 116 Opry Place, Nashville** and in LA.

SWEET HEREAFTER, THE
(1997, dir: Atom Egoyan)
Ian Holm, Sarah Polley, Bruce Greenwood.
● ONTARIO, CANADA

An adaptation of Russell Banks' novel. Filmed around Ontario: at **Barrie**, on the west shore of Lake Simcoe, I-400; **Caledon**, northwest of Toronto; **Stouffville**, twenty miles north of east Toronto; **Goodwood**, just to the northeast of Stouffville; **Whitevale** and **Lake Mussleman**.

SWEET SMELL OF SUCCESS
(1957, dir: Alexander Mackendrick)
Tony Curtis, Burt Lancaster, Marty Milner.
● NEW YORK CITY

Creepy journo Curtis carries out control-freak Lancaster's bidding in this brilliantly cynical melodrama. Lancaster's apartment is in the art deco **Brill Building, 1619 Broadway** between 49th and 50th Streets.

Burt Lancaster's place: Brill Building, Broadway

SWINGERS
(1996, dir: Doug Liman)
Jon Favreau, Vince Vaughn, Ron Livingston.
● LOS ANGELES; NEVADA

Liman's excruciatingly spot-on comedy of LA-scene manners is set against the retro-swing dance movement. The coffee shop, where the swingers meet up for their heart-to-hearts, is **Hills Coffee Shop**, within the **Best Western, 6145 Franklin Avenue**, east Hollywood – this is where much of the script was actually concoct-

"Vegas, Bob, Vegas.": The Stardust Hotel and Casino, Las Vegas Boulevard

Jon Favreau meets the Dresden waitress: Dresden Room, Los Feliz

ed. The Vegas trip takes Vaughn and Favreau to the **Fremont Hotel and Casino, 200 East Fremont Street** (℮ *702.385.3232*) in the old Downtown district, though the exterior is the **Stardust Hotel and Casino, 3000 Las Vegas Boulevard** (℮ *702.732.6111*) on the Strip.

Back in LA, Favreau plays a round at the **Los Feliz Golf Club**. The convoy of cars from the Hollywood Hills party passes a couple of familiar locations – **Canter's** on Fairfax, as seen in *Enemy of the State*, and the **Hollywood Star Lanes Bowling Alley** on Hollywood Boulevard, from *The Big Lebowski*. Their destination is the **Dresden Room Restaurant, 1760 North Vermont Avenue**, just north of Barnsdall Park in Los Feliz (℮ *323.665.4294*), one of the top swing venues, where Favreau meets the Starbucks waitress. The club where Liman parodies Scorsese's famous tracking shot from *Goodfellas* is **The Derby, 4500 Los Feliz Boulevard** (℮ *323.663.8979*). The old Brown Derby (though not the famed hat-shaped restaurant, which stood on Wilshire Boulevard) was reinvented in 1993 as a swing bar and restored to its Hollywood glory. And to top it all, the oval bar was used in the Joan Crawford noir *Mildred Pierce*. Check out the website at *www.the-derby.com*.

T

TAKING OF PELHAM ONE TWO THREE, THE
(1974, dir: Joseph Sargent)
Walter Matthau, Robert Shaw, Martin Balsam.
● **NEW YORK CITY**

The ransom delivery:
28th Street Station

This tense drama invented colour-coded villains, later picked up by Tarantino for *Reservoir Dogs*, while providing a rare serious role for Walter Matthau as the transport cop negotiating with the hijackers of a NY subway train. The subway scenes were shot on the **Pelham Bay Line** (and also in Filmways Studio, which is now the Foodways Supermarket on East 127th Street in East Harlem). Most of the interiors used the disused **Court Street Station** in Brooklyn, a forked section of track which looks different enough from various angles to provide multiple locations. The ransom is delivered to **28th Street Station**, at 28th Street and Park Avenue South.

TALENTED MR RIPLEY, THE
(1999 , dir: Anthony Minghella)
Matt Damon, Jude Law, Gwyneth Paltrow.
● **ITALY; NEW YORK CITY**

The second filming of Patricia Highsmith's novel (the first was *Plein Soleil*, which cast Alain Delon as the sexually ambiguous anti-hero) conjures up Italy of the 1960s from a patchwork of niftily chosen locations, not all of them what they seem.

The opening, though, is New York, where Tom Ripley works at the **Lyceum Theatre, 149 West 45th Street** between Sixth and Seventh Avenues (used in the 1947 George Cukor backstage melodrama *A Double Life*, starring Ronald Colman). The interior of Ripley's dismal basement apartment was actually the ground floor of a tene-

The theatre where Ripley works:
Lyceum, West 45th Street, New York

ment on Second Avenue at 26th Street in the Gramercy district, but you'll find the exterior, with the steep flight of iron steps, in the tiny passageway of **Franklin Place**, between White Street and Franklin Street in Tribeca.

Taking the job of tracking down spoiled rich kid Dickie Greenleaf,

Ripley's basement apartment: Franklin Place, Tribeca

Ripley arrives in Italy at the art deco terminal of **Palermo**, on the northwest coast of Sicily.

To represent the fictitious resort of Mongibello, where Dickie idles away his time with girlfriend Marge, the movie uses the island of **Ischia** in the Bay of Naples. The cobbled square where Ripley gets off the bus is **Ischia Ponte**, below the towering 12th century Castello Aragonese which dominates the island's northeast coast. The best way to reach Ischia Ponte is by catching a bus, about a mile east of the ferry landing at Ischia Porto. Between Ischia Ponte and Ischia Porte you'll find **Bagno Antonio**, the private beach where Ripley first discovers Dickie and Marge. Close by are Dickie's house and the small harbour where the body of Dickie's girlfriend Silvana turns up during the ceremony of the Madonna. The

Ripley meets Dickie Greenleaf: Bagno Antonio, Ischia

Marge has suspicions at the Venice café: Cafe Florian, Piazza San Marco, Venice

The Venetian church where Smith-Kingsley rehearses the choir: Chiesa Martorana, Piazza Bellini, Palermo

The Rome opera house: Teatro San Carlo, Naples

Freddie turns up at the cafe: Piazza Navona, Rome

main shopping street and town square of Mongibello, however, can be found on **Procida**, a neighbouring island, twenty minutes away by ferry.

The Vesuvio nightclub, supposedly in Naples, where Dickie and Ripley perform 'Tu Vuo' Fa L'Americano' is the **Caffè Latino, Via Monte Testaccio 96** (© 06.5728.8384) in Rome, whereas the Rome opera house, where Ripley poses as Dickie, is the **Teatro San Carlo,**

Tom Ripley arrives in Mongibello: Ischia Ponte, Ischia

Via San Carlo in Naples. And also in Naples is the imposing vaulted Galleria where Dickie draws his allowance. The San Remo jazz festival, where Ripley begins to realise that the idyll is coming to an end, is the seafront at **Anzio**, on the coast about 30 miles south of Rome (the real San Remo is up at the French border).

Ripley's Roman hotel, the sumptuous **Grand Hotel, Via Vittorio Emanuele Orlando 3** (*©* *06.47091*), off Piazza della Repubblica, really is in the Eternal City, as is the café where Dickie's obnoxious chum, Freddie Miles, turns up, on **Piazza Navona** opposite Bernini's Fountain of the Four Rivers. When he returns to Rome after Dickie's murder, surveying the ruins of the **Forum** from **Capitoline Hill** and viewing the monumental sculptures of the **Capitoline Museum**, Ripley stays in an apartment on the fictitious Piazza Gioia, which is actually near the old Jewish Ghetto, on **Piazza Mattei**. The interior of the apartment – which also functioned as the Grand Hotel suite – is the 14th century **Palazzo Taverna, Via di Monte Giordano 36**. The terrace café, where Ripley arranges for Meredith, Marge and Peter Smith-Kingsley to meet up, is **Cafe Dinelli, Piazza di Spagna**, at the foot of the Spanish Steps.

Moving on to Venice, Ripley stays in an apartment which is an amalgam of the abandoned **Ca' Sagredo** and the **Palazzo Mosto**. Marge, having arrived at the streamlined, fifties-style **Santa Lucia Railway Station**, at the northern end of Canal Grande, finally voices her suspicions about Dickie's disappearance at Venetian landmark **Cafe Florian, Piazza San Marco 56-59**. The hotel where Ripley meets Dickie's father is the **Europa e Regina, Calle Larga 22 Marzo, San Marco 2159**, (*©* *520.0477*) on the Canal Grande, facing the Chiesa della Salute.

The Venetian church, though, where Smith-Kingsley rehearses the 'Stabat Mater', is in fact the 14th century **Chiesa Martorana, Piazza Bellini** in Palermo, Sicily.

TARZAN AND HIS MATE
(1934, dir: Cedric Gibbons)
Johnny Weissmuller, Maureen O'Sullivan.
● **CALIFORNIA**

The jungle is **Sherwood Forest** and **Sherwood Lake**. The swamp is **Woodland Park**, near Pico-Rivera in Whittier. More CA locations include **Big Tujunga** and **China Flats** (now a restricted Naval Weapons Center, north of Ridgecrest in the Mojave Desert).

TARZAN AND THE AMAZONS
(1945, dir: Kurt Neumann)
Johnny Weissmuller, Brenda Joyce, Johnny Sheffield.
● **LOS ANGELES**

For the jungle scenes, the film-makers used the **Los Angeles State and County Arboretum, 301 North Baldwin Avenue**, Arcadia, east of Pasadena (*©* *818.821.3222*). This 127-acre tropical garden has supplied the lush backdrop to countless movies, including the other Tarzan adventures *Tarzan Escapes* and *Tarzan and the Leopard Woman*, as well as *Anaconda, Devil's Island, The Man in the Iron Mask* (1939), *Passage to Marseilles* and *Road to Singapore*.

TARZAN'S NEW YORK ADVENTURE
(1942, dir: Richard Thorpe)
Johnny Weissmuller, Maureen O'Sullivan, Johnny Sheffield.
● **NEW YORK CITY**

Tarzan leaves the jungle to reclaim his kidnapped son. The New York location filming famously includes Olympic swimmer Weissmuller's 200-foot dive from the **Brooklyn Bridge** into the East River.

TASTE OF HONEY, A
(1961, dir: Tony Richardson)
Rita Tushingham, Dora Bryan, Murray Melvin.
● **MANCHESTER; LANCASHIRE; LONDON**

A compendium of sixties hot potatoes – unmarried motherhood, race, homosexuality – baked in a cracking script from Shelagh Delaney's stage play. It was the first British feature film to be made entirely on location, around the streets and canals of Manchester and on **Blackpool**'s seafront and piers. Much of the terraced housing has gone, but you can still see the railway viaduct, where Rita Tushingham and Murray Melvin cut loose, at **Salford**. The strange, ricketty flat Rita finally moves into is the scenic workshop of the English Stage Company at the Royal Court Theatre in **Sloane Square**, London which also provided the yard outside for the fireworks scene.

TASTE THE BLOOD OF DRACULA
(1969, dir: Peter Sasdy)
Christopher Lee, Geoffrey Keen, Peter Sallis.
● **HERTFORDSHIRE**

One of Hammer's better sequels, with three jaded Victorian businessman conjuring up Dracula for kicks, and in turn being destroyed by their own children. Mostly setbound, with exteriors at **Tykes Water Lake**, **Aldenham Country Park**, off the A411 west of **Elstree, Hertfordshire**.

TAXI DRIVER
(1976, dir: Martin Scorsese)
Robert De Niro, Jodie Foster, Harvey Keitel.
● **NEW YORK CITY**

De Niro is so identified with the role of unhinged loner Travis Bickle, it's difficult to believe the first choice for the role was crooner Neil Diamond. Second up was Jeff Bridges, under the direction of Robert Mulligan. Thank-

The cab office: 57th Street at 11th Avenue

fully, the script finally passed to the dream team of Scorsese and De Niro, who produced arguably the greatest movie of the seventies.

Scorsese, naturally, uses real New York locations. The cab office De Niro works out of was at the western end of **57th Street**, at 11th Avenue. The building is still there, but the photogenic backdrop has been bulldozed to make way for the West Side Highway. Gone too is the café where De Niro meets with Peter Boyle and the other drivers. It was a real cabbies' hangout, the Belmore Cafeteria, which stood on Park Avenue South at 28th Street. The porno theatres, where De Niro spends his days, are along the 48th Street block of Eighth Avenue. The political rally is on Seventh Avenue at 38th Street. De Niro sports a mohican to shoot the senator at **Columbus Circle**. He's finally picked up by Cybill Shepherd outside the **St Regis-Sheraton Hotel, 2 East 55th Street** at Fifth Avenue.

The scuzzy hotel, where De Niro takes underage hooker Foster, and the site of the climactic bloodbath, is **226 13th Street**, between Second and Third Avenues in the East Village.

TEEN WOLF
(1985, dir: Rod Daniel)
Michael J Fox, James Hampton, Scott Paulin.
● CALIFORNIA

The hardware store: Mission Street, South Pasadena

Highschool basketball player Fox turns hairy in this amiable comedy. The family home is **1727 Bushnell Avenue, South Pasadena** (the same house Fox was taken into in *Back to the Future*). The hardware store, where Fox works, was Balk's, at **1518 Mission Street** in South Pasadena, which closed down in 2000. Tony's Liquor, where Fox uses his werewolf stare to buy beer, is in **Tujunga**, northwest of LA.

10
(1979, dir: Blake Edwards)
Dudley Moore, Julie Andrews, Bo Derek.
LOS ANGELES; HAWAII; MEXICO

Crude sex farce that briefly turned Moore into a diminutive sex symbol and Ravel's *Bolero* into the soundtrack for sex. Lustful Moore first spies buxom Derek in the **All Saints Episcopal Church, 504 Camden Drive** at Santa Monica Boulevard in Beverly Hills. Filming also took place at the **Pasadena Civic Auditorium, 300 East Green Street, Pasadena** (also seen as the concert venue for Bette

Moore's first glimpse of Bo Derek: All Saints Episcopal Church, Beverly Hills

Midler's *Divine Madness*). The Mexican scenes were filmed at the luxury resort of **Puerto Las Hadas**, on the Bay of Manzanillo, Mexico (© 52. 333.400.00). The beach scenes are the nearby cove of **Playa Audiencia**.

TEN COMMANDMENTS, THE
(1923, dir: Cecil B DeMille)
Theodore Roberts, Richard Dix, Charles de Roche.
● CALIFORNIA

DeMille's early silent version of the Biblical story of Moses and the Israelites bizarrely grafts on a modern morality fable. Plans to film in Egypt were rejected by producer Adolph Zukor as too expensive, so the epic sets were finally built on the **Nipomo Sand Dunes**, which extend from Point Sal to Pismo Beach, north of LA, around Guadalupe. The huge mountains of sand, up to 450 feet high, are held together by a network of ice plant, grasses, verbena and silver lupine. The city of Per Rameses, its grand boulevard lined with an avenue of sphinxes and pharaohs, was subsequently buried beneath the shifting sands, and is now being uncovered as a genuine archaeological relic.

The Israelites were chased by 250 Egyptian chariots across the famous **Muroc Dry Lake Bed** in the Mojave Desert. After the parting of the Red Sea, the Israelites journey across **Balboa Beach**, between Newport and Laguna Beaches, south of LA. Pharaoh's chariot host is stopped by the Pillar of Fire at **Anaheim Landing**.

The modern day sequences feature the **Cathedral of St Peter and St Paul, 666 Filbert Street** in San Francisco, which was still under construction (see *Dirty Harry* for details). Gutsy Leatrice Joy ascended 200 feet on the workmen's elevator, to cheers from an appreciative crowd below.

TEN COMMANDMENTS, THE
(1956, dir: Cecil B DeMille)
Charlton Heston, Anne Baxter, Yul Brynner.
● LOS ANGELES; EGYPT

Over 30 years later, DeMille returned to the subject, ditching the modern day moralities to produce the peak of Hollywood mega-kitsch, which lurches wildly from hysterical camp to heart-in-mouth drama. The epic was shot largely on the Paramount lot in Hollywood, though this time there was some genuine location filming in Egypt.

First off, where's Mount Sinai? Not on any map. There is, however, in the Sinai massif, a cluster of peaks among which **Jebel Musa** – the Mount of Moses – is the most popular candidate. And that's where CB and crew turned up in October 1954. The crew stayed at St Catherine's Monastery at the foot of the range. Footage was shot for the Burning Bush scene, though the bush itself, with risible cartoon flames, was obviously filmed in the studio. Pharaoh Cedric Hardwick's Treasure City was built at **Beni**

St Catharine's Monastery: base camp for the Egyptian location

Youssef, near Cairo, which is also where the moving Exodus scene was staged. 10,000 Arabs, playing the Children of Israel, were drafted in, along with 15,000 camels, water buffaloes, sheep, horses, oxen, goats, ducks, geese, pigeons, dogs, donkeys and, of course, many cattle.

Yul Brynner also shot some scenes on location, chasing the Children of Israel to the Red Sea. But clearly not the banishment of Moses into the wilderness, which crosscuts between Chuck Heston, very obviously alone and on location, and Yul Brynner, very obviously in a studio.

10 RILLINGTON PLACE
(1971, dir: Richard Fleischer)
Richard Attenborough, John Hurt, Pat Heywood.
● LONDON

Grim and sober account of mass-murderer John Christie, and the wrongful hanging of Timothy Evans, filmed in Rillington Place itself, before the notorious street was demolished and renamed. The cul-de-sac became Ruston Close, now Ruston Mews, W11. It's on the west side of St Mark's Road just before Lancaster Road, overshadowed by the Westway. Number ten was the last house on the left.

10 THINGS I HATE ABOUT YOU
(1999, dir: Gil Junger)
Heath Ledger, Julia Stiles, Joseph Gordon-Levitt.
● WASHINGTON STATE

Smart highschool reworking of Shakespeare's *The Taming of the Shrew*. Padua High is **Stadium High School, 111 North E Street, Tacoma** in Washington State. The striking building, on a bluff overlooking Commencement Bay, was built as a luxury hotel at the turn of the century. It is named for the school's huge athletic stadium, constructed in a ravine known as Old Woman's Gulch, after the widows of local fishermen who once squatted in little shacks here. The theatre is the **Paramount Theatre, 901 Pine Street** at Ninth Avenue, downtown, Seattle.

TENEBRAE (aka *Unsane*)
(1982, dir: Dario Argento)
Anthony Franciosa, Veronica Lario, John Saxon.
● ROME; NEW YORK CITY

Another of Argento's triumphs of style over content, with a superb shock effect cheekily lifted by Brian De Palma for the ending of *Raising Cain*. Apart from a brief opening sequence of author Franciosa cycling to **JFK Airport** in New York, the film was shot in Rome. Argento, unusually, chose to film in dazzling sunlight (the ironic title means 'darkness') around the near-deserted, antiseptic suburb of **EUR** (Esposizione Universale Romana), a grandiose project planned by Mussolini but not completed until the fifties, about four miles south of Rome on Via

Cristoforo Colombo. You can see more of the area's fascist architecture in *Titus*.

TEOREMA (aka *Theorem*)
(1968, dir: Pier Paolo Pasolini)
Terence Stamp, Silvana Mangano, Massimo Girotti.
● MILAN, ITALY

Allegorical fable, shot in Milan, with handsome stranger Stamp seducing all the members of a bourgeois family, and the maid. The family react in different ways: mother Silvana Mangano goes cruising the streets of Milan for men; father strips naked on the platform of **Milan Central Railroad Station**.

TERMINATOR, THE
(1984, dir: James Cameron)
Linda Hamilton, Michael Biehn, Arnold Schwarzenegger.
● LOS ANGELES

Schwarzenegger, the cyborg sent back from 2029AD to terminate future heroine Linda Hamilton, first materialises in a flurry of animated lightning at the **Griffith Park Ob-**

The Terminator materialises above LA: Griffith Observatory

servatory, Observatory Drive in Griffith Park, where he rips the hearts out of a couple of punks and takes their clothes (while thanking God he didn't land in a convent). The scene features some stunning nighttime views over the great flat expanse of LA.

The human resistance is not far behind, in the form of Michael Biehn, obviously travelling economy class, who lands in a backalley of LA's grubby downtown area. Hamilton works as a waitress in Big Buns café, which is actually **Carrows Restaurant, 815 South Fremont Avenue** at Mission Street, South Pasadena. The car chase is around downtown LA, on **Sixth** and **Seventh Streets** and **Broadway**, leading to a shootout in the huge indoor parking lot of the **Department of Power and Water, 111 North Hope Street**. The tunnel chase, with Arnie's bike dodging home-made bombs, was filmed in the **Second Street Tunnel**, which dives underground between Hill Street and

Big Buns, where Linda Hamilton works: Carrow's Restaurant, South Fremont Avenue, South Pasadena

Figueroa Street, also downtown. The final confrontation, with the Terminator reduced to a metal skeleton before being crushed in the jaws of a metal press, was filmed at **Kern's of California, 13010 East Temple Avenue**, down in City of Industry, southeast LA.

TERMINATOR 2: JUDGEMENT DAY

(1991, dir: James Cameron)
Arnold Schwarzenegger, Linda Hamilton, Robert Patrick.

● CALIFORNIA

The Pescadero State Hospital for the Criminally Insane: Phoenix Academy, Lake View

Some years on from *The Terminator*, and future resistance hero John Connor (Edward Furlong) is an eleven-year-old, farmed out to foster parents in the northern LA suburb of Reseda (don't go looking for South Almond Avenue – it's fictitious), while Mom Linda Hamilton is banged up in a maximum security asylum.

At $94 million, *T2* was the most expensive movie ever (the original *Terminator* came in at a neat $6 million). But that was before *Titanic*. Cameron took the opportunity to revisit ideas from the first *Terminator* movie on a grander scale. The opening 'future war' is reprised, using the ruins of a demolished steel plant at **Fontana**, on the outskirts of San Bernardino, Route 10 east of LA. With a sense of thrift that would gladden his old mentor (Cameron is a graduate of the Roger Corman school of moviemaking – at age 26 he handled the special effects on the Corman-produced *Battle Beyond the Stars*), the twisted bikes, burned-out cars and blackened cinders used as dressing are charred debris from the Universal Studio fire of 1989, when a disgruntled security guard torched the famous backlot.

The Pescadero State Hospital for the Criminally Insane, where Hamilton is incarcerated, has nothing to do with Pescadero, which is a small California fishing town between San Francisco and Santa Cruz. The institution of the movie is closer to LA. It's the **Phoenix Academy** (previously the Lake View Medical Center), **11600 Eldridge**

The truck dives into the flood-control channel: Bull Creek at Plummer and Hayvenhurst

350

The Cyberdyne HQ: Bayside Park, Fremont

at Kagel Canyon, off Foothill Boulevard to the north of Hansen Dam Park in the San Fernando Valley. Built as a medical facility in the early seventies, it was closed, either due to earthquake damage or lack of funding, according to which story you buy, and started a new career as a movie location, but now seems to be back on course.

Arnie, by another stroke of luck, finds himself naked in the San Fernando Valley at biker hangout, **The Corral Bar, 12002 Osborne Street, Lakeview Terrace** (*℃ 818.899.9944*), where he gets himself not only a leather jacket, but a cool bike and a large gun as well. Meanwhile, the T-1000 update Terminator, a liquid metal shapechanger, has tracked young Connor down to Reseda. The shopping mall chase and confrontation between the two Terminators wasn't filmed in Reseda, though. The exterior is nearby, the **Northridge Mall, 9301 Tampa Avenue, Northridge**, though the interior is on the coast at Santa Monica, in the 162-store **Santa Monica Place Shopping Center, Fourth Street** at Broadway. Escaping on his dirt bike, Connor tears into one of LA's concrete flood control channels, back in the San Fernando Valley. The spillway used is **Bull Creek**, which leads down to the Sepulveda Flood Control Area (in drier times, the Balboa and the Encino Golf Courses). The T-1000 gives chase in an eighteen-wheel truck, and, at the junction of **Plummer and Hayvenhurst**, makes the spectacular leap down into Bull Creek, tearing through the 40-foot wide spillway.

Having sprung Mom from Pescadero, Connor and the good Terminator head out to a desert compound on the western rim of the Mojave Desert, at **Lancaster** in Antelope Valley. Hamilton, spurred on by visions of LA engulfed in a nuclear firestorm, takes off to kill scientist Joe Morton, whose research is destined to lead to the Skynet System and hence the future war. Morton's house, where Arnie stomach-churningly demonstrates his non-human status, is a private home on **Pacific Coast Highway**, just west of South Malibu Canyon Road, west of Malibu (though it's not visible from the road).

The Cyberdyne HQ, high security home of the lethal cyborg chip, really is situated in California's Silicon Valley, the heart of the computer industry. The building is the **Renco Investment Company, 47131 Bayside Park**, at Gateway Boulevard, Fremont, a suburb of San Jose. A glass façade added a third storey to the building, and the (real glass) windows were wired to blow out simultaneously with a gasoline fireball. The commandeered SWAT truck crashes through a specially added lobby. Fremont is east of San Francisco Bay over the Dunbar Bridge where Route 17 intersects with Route 84.

The T-1000 oozes into the helicopter for the climactic chase sequence. LA's constantly packed freeways are vital arteries constantly teetering on the verge of terminal grid-lock. Closing a section down is risking fatal thrombosis, but LA is also movie city, and there's always a way. A four-lane section of freeway was discovered down toward San Pedro. In this scruffy industrial hinterland of the port is a three-mile north-south stretch of roadway linking Sepulveda Boulevard with the naval base on Terminal Island. The **Terminal Island Freeway** could be closed for the night without major disruption to the city's traffic flow. For most of the chase, the helicopter was suspended from a crane mounted on a flatbed truck which drove along the adjacent lane, but for one hair-raising stunt, a real heli-copter flew under the twenty-foot overpass of the **Pacific Coast Highway**.

The end of the chase brings the movie full circle. The steelworks, supposedly at the end of the freeway, is adja-cent to the ruins at Fontana used for the opening sequence. Here a steelmill, abandoned for seventeen years, was brought to life with a battery of trick effects. Molten metal gives insurance companies panic attacks – see *The Deer Hunter* – so the film uses rivers of white paint and illu-minated plastic panels amid showers of sparks.

TERMS OF ENDEARMENT
(1983, dir: James L Brooks)
Shirley MacLaine, Debra Winger, Jack Nicholson.
● **TEXAS; NEBRASKA**

Oscar-laden and well acted, but soapy, tearjerker, set in **Houston**, Texas (well, where else would you be living next door to an astronaut?).

In Houston, Jack Nicholson lives at **3068 Locke Lane**, in the smart **Avalon** district. Although the house has been completely renovated, you will recognise the home of Shirley MacLaine next door. The couple's lunch date is at **Brennan's Restaurant, 3300 Smith Street**, downtown Houston (✆ *713.522.9711*), originally a branch of the famous New Orleans eaterie, it's since severed connec-tions. Nicholson and MacLaine drive onto **East Beach, Galveston**. There was more filming at **River Oaks**, the posh area to the northwest of Houston.

MacLaine and Nicholson's lunch date: Brennan's, Smith Street, Houston

Shirley MacLaine's house: Locke Lane, Avalon, Houston

The town Debra Winger and Jeff Daniels move to is **Lincoln**, Nebraska, where their home is at **847 14th Street**. Winger meets John Lithgow at **Leon's Food Mart, North 32nd Street** at South Street, Lincoln, and confronts the errant Daniels at the **University of Nebraska, 14th Street** at R Street. Winger tearily expires at **Lincoln General Hospital, Van Dorn Street**, while MacLaine and Nicholson finally get to mumble "I lurve you" at **Lincoln Municipal Airport, 2400 West Adams**.

TERROR, THE
(1963, dir: Roger Corman)
Boris Karloff, Jack Nicholson, Sandra Knight.
● **CALIFORNIA**

'Mr Economy' Corman finished *The Raven* a couple of days ahead of schedule. He still had the sets and the cast, so he quickly cobbled together this little number, com-plete with vaguely generic title. The shots of the Baltic Coast are California's **Big Sur** coastline, between San Fran-cisco and Los Angeles, photographed by second unit direc-tor Francis Ford Coppola.

TESS
(1979, dir: Roman Polanski)
Nastassja Kinski, Leigh Lawson, Peter Firth.
● **FRANCE**

Thomas Hardy's *Tess of the D'Urbervilles* filmed, not in the West Country of England, but in Brittany, northern France, around the old town of **Morlaix**, towards the north-ern coast.

TESTAMENT D'ORPHEE, LE (aka *The Testament of Orpheus*)
(1960, dir: Jean Cocteau)
Jean Cocteau, Edouard Dermithe, Maria Casares.
● **FRANCE**

Cocteau's final film is a rambling, imaginative rumi-nation on the nature of his art, with contributions from Yul Brynner and Picasso. The strange under-ground street is **rue Obscure** in the old town of **Villefranche-sur-Mer**,

The underground street: rue Obscure, Villefranche-sur-Mer

the beautiful little fishing port just east of Nice on the French Riviera. It was in this subterranean warren that the French Resistance was able to evade the German army during WWII.

TEXAS CHAIN SAW MASSACRE, THE
(1974, dir: Tobe Hooper)
Marilyn Burns, Allen Danziger, Gunnar Hansen.
● **TEXAS**

Not as explicitly gory as its reputation, Hooper's slasher classic gets its nasty atmosphere across largely by sug-gestion. It was filmed in 16mm, with a mostly amateur cast recruited from the drama department of Austin's Uni-versity of Texas. The grisly farmhouse, since demolished, stood on **Quick Hill Road, Round Rock**, I-35, about ten miles north of Austin, Texas.

TEXASVILLE

(1990, dir: Peter
Bogdanovich)
Jeff Bridges,
Cybill Shepherd,
Timothy
Bottoms.

● **TEXAS**

The fictitious Anarene, Texas: Archer
City

19 years on, Peter
Bogdanovich returned to **Archer City**, Texas, for this disappointing sequel to *The Last Picture Show*.

THAT'LL BE THE DAY

(1973, dir: Claude Whatham)
David Essex, Ringo Starr, Rosemary Leach.
● **HAMPSHIRE**

Essex plays a 1950s working class drifter, then fairground worker, who finally makes it as a pop star. The title comes from the Buddy Holly song, which in turn came from John Wayne's line in *The Searchers*. It was made on the **Isle of Wight**. The sequel, following the rise and fall of Essex's character, is *Stardust*.

THAT TOUCH OF MINK

(1962, dir: Delbert Mann)
Cary Grant, Doris Day, Gig Young.
● **LOS ANGELES; NEW YORK CITY**

Sixties sex comedy, with exec Grant chasing secretary Day. The scenes set in Bermuda are actually LA, at the **Miramar Sheraton Hotel, 101 Wilshire Boulevard**, Santa Monica. Filming also took place at **Yankee Stadium** in the Bronx, NYC.

THEATRE OF BLOOD

(1973, dir: Douglas Hickox)
Vincent Price, Diana Rigg, Ian Hendry.
● **LONDON; BERKSHIRE**

Home of the the first victim: Digby Mansions,
Hammersmith

Price is the barnstorming Shakespearian actor, believed dead, who returns to kill off members of the despised Critics' Circle, using appropriately Shakespearian murders, in this gloriously tasteless black comedy, shot entirely on location around London.

Michael Hordern's flat is in **Digby Mansions, Hammersmith Bridge Road** at Lower Mall overlooking Hammersmith Bridge (just alongside the rowing club and pub seen in *Sliding Doors*). Jack Hawkins, who must be an *extremely* successful critic, strangles Diana Dors at his swanky Chelsea Embankment house, **8 Cheyne Walk**, SW3, overlooking Albert Bridge (another location for *Sliding Doors*). Blue Plaque spotters might notice that the house is sandwiched between the former homes of poet Dante Gabriel Rossetti and George Eliot. Coral Browne gets her ash highlights well and truly lit at (now gone) Robert Fielding,

Knightsbridge, SW7, opposite Harrods. Diana Rigg works on a movie filming at the **Long Walk** by Windsor Castle. Ian Hendry's apartment, and the meeting place of the Critics' Circle, from which Price plunges into the Thames, is **Alembic House** on the Albert Embankment between Lambeth and Vauxhall Bridges. The cemetery, where Dennis Price's body turns up, is **Kensal Green Cemetery**, Kensal Green.

Lionheart's suicide: The
Thames embankment

The theatre itself was Putney Hippodrome, on the corner of Putney High Street and Felsham Road, SW15, since demolished. Built in 1906 as a vaudeville variety house, it was converted into a cinema in the thirties but had been closed for fourteen years when it was chosen as Edward Lionheart's hideout. The proscenium was specially built for the film, a chandelier added and 500 seats (at 50p each) were bought from Croydon Odeon to fill the decrepit stalls.

THELMA & LOUISE

(1991, dir: Ridley Scott)
Susan Sarandon, Geena Davis, Brad Pitt.
● **CALIFORNIA; UTAH; COLORADO**

Feminist road movie or male fantasies in drag? You takes your choice. The movie's journey is from Arkansas through Oklahoma and Colorado to Arizona, but the master of deceptive locations, Scott, filmed only the last third of the movie in the desert, outside greater LA and Bakersfield. And that was in mainly in Utah.

The green, wet landscape of Arkansas is actually an area around **Gorman**, north of LA and the **Lockwood Valley**, dressed with appropriate cattle. The gradual descent into the central valley of California at **Bakersfield** is used for the transition from the crowded, narrow mountains of Arkansas to the open plains of Oklahoma. It's north to **Shafter** for the train sequence, then to the dust fields and oil rigs of **Taft** in the west central valley.

The mid-west C&W bar, where the attempted rape that turns the adventure sour takes place, is in southern LA. It's the (now closed, but instantly recognisable) **Silver Bullet, 3321 South Street**, between Obispo and Downey Avenues. The motel, where the pair meet up with studly

The mid-west motel: Vagabond Inn, South Figueroa Street, LA

The mid-west bar: The Silver Bullet, Long Beach

Brad Pitt, can also be found in LA. It's the **Vagabond Inn, 3101 South Figueroa Street** (℃ *213.746.1531*), south of downtown LA.

There's some filming in the real Colorado, at **Unaweep Canyon, Grand Junction** on I-70 in the west of the state. Sarandon phones the FBI agent from **Bedrock General Store, Bedrock**, Colorado. The desert scenes, while pretending to be the rather flat New Mexico, are the spectacular sandstone landscapes of the **La Sal Mountains**, Route 46, southeast of Moab in eastern Utah; **Arches National Park**, to the north of Moab and **Canyonlands** to the southwest. The police chase is at **Cisco**, Utah. Filming also took place at **Thompson Springs** and **Valley City**. And the Grand Canyon? Nope. The spectacular gorge of the final scene is not the Grand Canyon, but **Shafer Overlook**, at **Gooseneck State Park**, the snaking s-bends of the San Juan River near the bizarre rock formation of Mexican Hat, Route 163 down in the southeast corner of Utah.

THEM!
(1954, dir: Gordon Douglas)
Edmund Gwenn, James Whitmore, Joan Weldon.
● CALIFORNIA

Classic fifties sci-fi, with atomic tests giving rise to giant mutated ants. The ants appear initially in the New Mexico desert – actually the Mojave Desert around **Palmdale**, California – but soon they're headed for the concrete spillways of LA, popping out at the **Sixth Street Viaduct**, downtown.

THERE'S SOMETHING ABOUT MARY
(1998, dir: Bobby Farrelly, Peter Farrelly)
Cameron Diaz, Ben Stiller, Matt Dillon.
● MIAMI, FLORIDA; RHODE ISLAND

The high school, where nerdy Ben Stiller doesn't quite make it to the prom with Cameron Diaz, is **Plantation City Hall, Plantation**, Florida. The café where Matt Dillon meets Jeffrey Tambor is the **Big Pink Restaurant, 157 Collins Avenue**, south of South Beach's Art Deco district. Diaz takes faker Dillon to an architecture exhibition at the **Center for the Fine Arts**, in the **Miami Dade Cultural Center, 101 West Flagler Street**, downtown Miami.

Matt Dillon meets Jeffrey Tambor: Big Pink Restaurant, Collins Avenue, Miami Beach

Cameron Diaz's office, where Stiller meets up with her after thirteen years, is on the downtown Miami waterfront at **Brickell Park**, overlooking the Brickell Key Causeway. Stiller's

Cleaning the pipes: Cardozo Hotel, Ocean Drive, Miami Beach

Miami hotel, site of the movie's most infamous 'pipe cleaning' scene, is the **Cardozo Hotel, 1300 Ocean Drive** at 14th Street (℃ *305.535.6500; www.cardozohotel.com*). This art deco gem can also be seen in *A Hole in the Head*. The waterside bar, where Dillon reports back to Ben Stiller, is **The Hot Club, 575 South Water Street** off Bridge Street (℃ *401.861.9007*), **Providence**, Rhode Island.

The architecture exhibition: Dade Cultural Center, Miami

Cameron Diaz's office: Brickell Park, Miami

THEY DIED WITH THEIR BOOTS ON
(1941, dir: Raoul Walsh)
Errol Flynn, Olivia de Havilland, Arthur Kennedy.
● NEW YORK STATE

This highly fictionalised account of Custer's Last Stand was shot partly at **West Point Military Academy**, as a thinly disguised recruiting drive. Director Walsh was made a brother of the Sioux Nation in a publicity stunt toward the end of the shoot. Only the ninth white person to receive such an honour, he was named Thunder Hawk. The Academy is on the Hudson River, Route 9W, north of New York City.

THEY DRIVE BY NIGHT
(1940, dir: Raoul Walsh)
George Raft, Humphrey Bogart, Ann Sheridan.
● CALIFORNIA

Tough, pacy trucking drama, using locations around **Wharf No2, Monterey**, northern California.

THEY LIVE BY NIGHT
(1948, dir: Nicholas Ray)
Farley Granger, Cathy O'Donnell, Howard da Silva.
● LOS ANGELES

Ray's stylish melodrama, remade by Robert Altman in 1974 as *Thieves Like Us*, has Granger as a young con escaping with a couple of hardened criminals and enjoying a doomed romance with O'Donnell while on the run. Made in the RKO Studios and around LA. The opening helicopter shot is **Canoga Park**, northwest LA.

THEY SHOOT HORSES, DON'T THEY?

(1969, dir: Sydney Pollack)
Jane Fonda, Michael Sarrazin, Gig Young.
● **LOS ANGELES**

A clutch of great performances, as desperate couples struggle to survive a dance marathon during the thirties Depression, with Gig Young's cynical compere scooping Best Actor Oscar. The dance hall is on the **Santa Monica Pier, Colorado Avenue**, Santa Monica, LA. Additional filming took place at Myron's Ballroom, now dance club **Grand Avenue, 1024 South Grand Avenue**, downtown LA (seen in *New York, New York*).

THIEF OF BAGDAD, THE

(1940, dir: Ludwig Berger, Michael Powell, Tim Whelan)
Sabu, Conrad Veidt, John Justin.
● **CORNWALL; ARIZONA**

Alexander Korda's lavish Arabian Nights fantasy began filming in the UK, but ultimately shifted to the US as World War II threatened production. It had been intended to film in the Middle East but this obviously became impossible. The beach, where Sabu unleashes the Genie of the Bottle, is **Sennen Cove**, about mile north of Land's End on the western tip of Cornwall. The other spectacular locations were found in the US, at the **Grand Canyon** and in the **Painted Desert**, the multicoloured plateau of the Little Colorado River to the southeast.

THIEVES LIKE US

(1974, dir: Robert Altman)
Keith Carradine, Shelley Duvall, Louise Fletcher.
● **MISSISSIPPI**

Altman's remake of *They Live by Night* filmed in Mississippi at the towns of **Jackson** and **Canton**.

THIN RED LINE, THE

(1998, dir: Terrence Malick)
Sean Penn, Jim Caviezel, Ben Chaplin.
● **QUEENSLAND, AUSTRALIA; SOLOMON ISLANDS**

The eagerly-awaited return to film from reclusive director Malick (*Badlands* and *Days of Heaven*) is a war drama set during the crucial 1942-43 Guadalcanal campaign of WWII, and indeed part of the movie was shot near **Honiara**, the capital of Guadalcanal, largest of the Solomon Islands in the Pacific. For the most part, however, the lush jungle is the **Daintree Rainforest**, about 50 miles north of Cairns, Queensland, on the northeastern coast of Australia.

THING, THE (aka *The Thing From Another World*)

(1951, dir: Christian Nyby, and possibly Howard Hawks)
James Arness, Robert Cornthwaite, Kenneth Tobey.
● **LOS ANGELES; MONTANA**

The RKO original, with James Arness (Matt Dillon in TV's

Gunsmoke) as a human vegetable from space. The 'arctic' location, where the creature is discovered (a scene being shown on TV in John Carpenter's original *Halloween*) is Montana. The first choice had been Fairbanks or Nome in Alaska, but the presence of sensitive USAF bases saw the Pentagon stepping in to nix that idea. The final choice was **Cut Bank**, in Glacier National Park about 100 miles northwest of Great Falls on I-2, northern Montana, where the cast stayed at the Glacier Hotel. The fire and explosion were filmed out on the **Iverson Movie Ranch**, Chatsworth, 30 miles north of LA. Arctic scenes were also shot in the ice-house of a meat packing company on Mesquit Street, alongside the Los Angeles River, southeast of downtown, also used for filming snow scenes in Frank Capra's *Lost Horizon*.

THING, THE

(1982, dir: John Carpenter)
Kurt Russell, A Wilford Brimley, Richard Dysart.
● **BRITISH COLUMBIA, CANADA; ALASKA**

John Carpenter's FX-heavy remake bombed at the box-office but has since acquired a heavy reputation. The snow-bound locations were found in British Columbia. The opening icescapes are icefields above **Juneau**, Alaska.

THINGS TO DO IN DENVER WHEN YOU'RE DEAD

(1995, dir: Gary Fleder)
Andy Garcia, Christopher Lloyd, Treat Williams.
● **COLORADO**

Oddball crime drama, with small businessman Garcia putting together a bunch of misfits for a job that goes horribly wrong, and set, unsurprisingly, in Denver. The Silver Naked Lady is the **Casino Cabaret, 2637 Welton Street**. Andy Garcia meets up with Gabrielle Anwar in the **Denver Museum of Natural History, 2001 Colorado Boulevard**. Filming also took place at **Coors Field**.

THIRD MAN, THE

(1949, dir: Carol Reed)
Joseph Cotten, Orson Welles, Alida Valli.
● **AUSTRIA**

Graham Greene's story of black-marketeering in post-WWII Vienna is given heavy impressionist treatment with wildly tilting camera angles. After seeing the film, veteran director William Wyler sent Reed a spirit level. The movie was filmed on location in **Vienna**, though some of the sewers were reconstructed in the studio. Orson Welles makes his great entrance, glimpsed in a doorway, a kitten nibbling the laces of his shoes (the laces having been coated with pilchard). The doorway is still there, unchanged, at **8 Schreyvogelgasse**. The cemetery is Vienna's Central Cemetery, the **Zentral-Friedhof, Simmeringen Hauptstrasse** in District 11, though the establishing shot, making this clear by panning across the graves of Brahms and Beethoven, was cut.

The big wheel, where Welles and Cotten play their crucial scene, and Welles gives his (self-penned) cuckoo clock speech, is the **Riesenrad**, the Grand Ferris Wheel erected in 1896 and restored in 1948 after war damage. It still

Harry Lime's first appearance: Schreyvogelgasse, Vienna

Harry Lime's 'cuckoo clock' speech: Prater

stands in the **Prater**, Vienna's huge park in District 2, between the Danube and the Danube Canal (*subway: Praterstern*).

The **Casanova Club, Dorotheergasse 6**, still operates as a nightclub, and you can still attend performances at the **Theater in der Josefstadt Theatre, Josefstadterstrasse 26** (© *0222.4025127*). If you can afford it, you can, as Joseph Cotten did, stay at the venerable **Hotel Sacher, Philharmonikerstrasse 4** (© *0222.514560*), behind the Opera House. You can visit the famous Mozart Café, Albertinaplatz 2, but the scene for the movie was actually shot on **Tegetthofstrasse**. Welles' apartment is in **Palais Pallavicini, Josefsplatz 5**. Other locations included the **Stiftgasse Staircase** and **Vienna Railway Station**. You can take a guided *Third Man* walking tour of the city, *www.viennawalks.tix.at*.

39 STEPS, THE
(1935, dir: Alfred Hitchcock)
Robert Donat, Madeleine Carroll, Godfrey Tearle.
● LONDON; SCOTLAND

This Hitchcock classic was shot almost entirely in the studio, at the old Lime Grove Studios, Shepherds Bush, demolished in the nineties, apart from shots of the **Forth Bridge**, spanning the Firth of Forth, between Edinburgh and Dunfermline. The bland and boring 1959 remake (filmed virtually shot for shot) also features the bridge.

THIRTY-NINE STEPS, THE
(1978, dir: Don Sharp)
Robert Powell, Karen Dotrice, John Mills.
● LONDON; WORCESTERSHIRE; SCOTLAND

The third version wisely jettisons Hitchcock and returns to John Buchan's original story. Richard Hannay's flat is **Albert Court**, alongside the Albert Hall, Kensington, SW7. The killing of John

Richard Hannay's flat: Albert Court, SW7

Mills takes place at **Marylebone Station**. The railway scenes were filmed on the Severn Valley Railway, and instead of the Forth Bridge, we get the **Victoria Bridge** over the Severn. The Scottish locations include: **Castlemilk House**, near Lockerbie; **Morton Castle**, a ruin near Thornhill; the village of **Durisdeer**; the **Forest of Ae**; and the **Drumlanrig Estate**. For the movie's climax, Hannay famously dangles from a mock-up of Big Ben's clockface.

37°2 LE MATIN (aka *Betty Blue/37°2 in the Morning*)
(1986, dir: Jean-Jacques Beineix)
Jean-Hugues Anglade, Beatrice Dalle, Gerard Darmon.
● FRANCE

Anglade is the indolent under-achiever who realises his potential as a writer after an affair with irritatingly intolerable wacko Dalle. In the Director's Cut, there are an extra 60 minutes of stylishly photographed pouting and tantrums until the most welcome pillow job since *One Flew Over the Cuckoo's Nest*. The coastal village of the opening scenes, with its stilt houses, is **Gruissan**, ten miles southeast of Narbonne in the Languedoc-Rousillon area toward the Spanish border. The other French villages used are **Marvejois**, a tiny market town in the Colagne Valley about 100 miles north of Narbonne on E9/N9, and **Nogent-sur-Marne**, east of Paris.

THIS BOY'S LIFE
(1993, dir: Michael Caton-Jones)
Leonardo DiCaprio, Ellen Barkin, Robert De Niro.
● WASHINGTON STATE

DiCaprio's life is made hell when his mother marries the monstrously tyrannical De Niro. The small town they settle in is the evocatively-named **Concrete**, about 100 miles northwest of Seattle, Washington State.

THIS IS SPINAL TAP
(1984, dir: Rob Reiner)
Christopher Guest, Michael McKean, Harry Shearer.
● LOS ANGELES; TENNESSEE

Spot-on mockumentary, well-deserving its regular place in lists of the funniest movies of all time, following the rock group of the title. The Atlanta record of-

Tap's version of 'Heartbreak Hotel' at the King's grave: Graceland, Memphis

The concert scenes: Raymond Theatre, Pasadena

The Atlanta record office: Westin Bonaventure Hotel, LA

fice is the futuristic **Westin Bonaventure Hotel, 404 South Figueroa Street**, downtown LA. The group pays tribute to the King with a moving version of 'Heartbreak Hotel' at his tastefully restrained graveside in the grounds of **Graceland, 3717 Elvis Presley Boulevard, Memphis**, Tennessee (© *901.332.3322*). Spot how the necessarily reverential longshots, on location, are craftily spliced into wicked close-ups, which were filmed separately. Concert scenes used the **Raymond Theatre, 129 North Raymond Avenue**, Pasadena, seen also in *Pulp Fiction*.

THIS SPORTING LIFE
(1963, dir: Lindsay Anderson)
Richard Harris, Rachel Roberts, William Hartnell.
● YORKSHIRE

Grim tale of rugby playing in the dour monochrome north. The rugby club is **Wakefield Trinity Rugby League Club**.

THOMAS CROWN AFFAIR, THE
(1968, dir: Norman Jewison)
Steve McQueen, Faye Dunaway, Paul Burke.
● MASSACHUSETTS

The bank robbery: Congress Street, Boston

Unlikely insurance investigator Dunaway on the trail of bored tycoon McQueen, who's pulled off a bank heist, in Jewison's glossy, romantic thriller, set around the wealthier areas of **Boston**. The opening bank robbery used a real bank (even grabbing authentic reaction shots with a hidden camera), at **55 Congress Street** in the Financial district. The polo match, where Faye Dunaway first sees Steve McQueen, is at the **Myopia Hunt Club, Hamilton**, on Route 1A, twenty miles northeast of Boston.

THOMAS CROWN AFFAIR, THE
(1999, dir: John McTiernan)
Pierce Brosnan, Rene Russo, Denis Leary.
● NEW YORK CITY; NEW YORK STATE; MARTINIQUE

For McTiernan's witty and stylish update, Thomas Crown now robs an art gallery. The exterior of the gallery is, quite obviously, **New York's Metropolitan Museum of Art,**

The art gallery, exterior: Metropolitan Museum of Art, Fifth Avenue

The art gallery, interior: New York Library, Fifth Avenue

Fifth Avenue at 82nd Street (© *212.535.7710*; *www.metmuseum.org*), though it is never identified as such in the movie. The gallery had a problem admitting the possibility of such a robbery and refused cooperation. They couldn't, however, prevent filming of the exterior, which belongs to the city of New York, which is why the exhibition banners change from shot to shot. The interior galleries are impressive studio sets, but the entrance concourse is the **New York Public Library, Fifth Avenue** at 42nd Street (© *212.869.8089; www.nypl.org*) – the exterior of which was the haunted library in *Ghostbusters*.

The entrance to Crown Towers, Thomas Crown's luxury office building, was an unoccupied office near New York's Stock Exchange, but the terrific view over the east River is from the window of Lucent Technologies. The National Arts Club (you can see the real thing in Martin Scorsese's *The Age of Innocence* and Woody Allen's *Manhattan Murder Mystery*) is the **India Club, Hanover Square**, on the outside, while inside, it's **Manhattanville College, Purchase**, New York. The ballroom of the Pierre Hotel, where Catherine Banning comes on strong to Crown, is the old library of **Bronx College, University Avenue** at West 181st Street. Thomas Crown's exotic getaway is the island of **Martinique**.

THREE DAYS OF THE CONDOR
(1975, dir: Sydney Pollack)
Robert Redford, Max von Sydow, Faye Dunaway.
● NEW YORK CITY

NY-set conspiracy thriller, with Redford on the run from assassins after escaping a massacre in the office where he works. The office is the **Ansonia Hotel, 2107-2109 Broadway**, between West 73rd and West 74th Streets on the West Side. He's set up and narrowly escapes death in the alleyway behind the Ansonia. Villainous Cliff Robertson's office is in the **World Trade Center, Church Street**, between Vesey and Liberty Streets, Lower Manhattan. Dunaway lives in Brooklyn Heights, and Redford has a confrontation with villain Robertson on **Brooklyn Heights Promenade**, over the East River from Lower Manhattan.

THREE KINGS
(1999, dir: David O Russell)
George Clooney, Mark Wahlberg, Ice Cube.
● ARIZONA; MEXICO

Russell's intelligent, cinematically thrilling adventure, set in the aftermath of the Gulf War, needed a flat, blasted landscape to represent the featureless wastes of Iraq. The opening scene is a dry lake bed outside **Mexicali**, Mexico. Most of the film was shot at the abandoned **Sacaton Copper Mine** at **Casa Grande**, between Tucson and Phoenix, Arizona, where chemical poisoning had wiped out any vegetation. The 'Iraqi' villages were constructed on various plateaux left after the extraction of the mineral ore.

3 MEN AND A BABY
(1987, dir: Leonard Nimoy)
Ted Danson, Tom Selleck, Steve Guttenberg.
● **NEW YORK CITY; ONTARIO, CANADA**

This remake of the 1985 French film *Three Men and a Cradle* is set in New York, but is one of the increasing number of films shot, for financial reasons, largely in Toronto. Real NY locations include the bachelor apartment, **50 Central Park West** – next to Sigourney Weaver's haunted block from *Ghostbusters*.

The three men's apartment: 50 Central Park West

Much of the movie shot in Toronto: Royal Alex Theatre, King Street West

The Toronto locations include the **Royal Alex Theatre, 260 King Street West**; the **John Innes Community Centre**; **Scotia Plaza**; and **Duncan Street** at Pearl Street. As with many Toronto-based films, sets were built in the old **Gooderham and Worts Distillery Building**.

3 MEN AND A LITTLE LADY
(1990, dir: Emile Ardolino)
Ted Danson, Tom Selleck, Steve Guttenberg.
● **OXFORDSHIRE; BERKSHIRE**

The home of the man who is to marry the 'little lady's' mother is **Broughton Castle**, two miles west of Banbury, in Oxfordshire. See *The Madness of King George* for full details. Also featured is the Catholic theological school, **Douai Abbey School, Upper Woolhampton**, near Reading in Berkshire.

The English country home: Broughton Castle, Banbury

THREE MUSKETEERS: THE QUEEN'S DIAMONDS, THE
(1973, dir: Richard Lester)
Michael York, Oliver Reed, Richard Chamberlain.
● **SPAIN**

Quirkily off-centre version of the Dumas classic. Set, nat-

urally, in France, it was filmed back to back with the sequel, *The Four Musketeers: The Revenge of Milady*, around Spain. The decadent court of Versailles, where Geraldine Chaplin rides a human-powered roundabout, Jean-Pierre Cassel plays living chess and Michael York finally becomes a musketeer, is the **Palacio Real, Aranjuez**. The Royal Palace, dating from 1722, was built in the classical style after fire destroyed Charles V's extension to Philip II's original hunting lodge.

The Bastille, where Spike Milligan is questioned by Charlton Heston, is the **Alcazar, Segovia**, a mid-14th century building remodelled in the 15th century. A royal residence until 1570, it subsequently became a state prison. The Hotel de Ville, scene of the climactic ball, where the queen reveals her jewels, is **La Granja de San Ildefonso**, a mini-Versailles 30 miles northwest of Madrid, built in the 1720s as a summer lodge for Philip V. The firework display is by the **Gran Cascada** here. More 'French' locations were found at the palace of **Riofrío**, about 40 miles northwest of Madrid.

THREE MUSKETEERS, THE
(1993, dir: Stephen Herek)
Kiefer Sutherland, Charlie Sheen, Chris O'Donnell.
● **AUSTRIA; CORNWALL**

The bratpacky remake, from the director of the first *Bill and Ted* movie, was shot on location in Austria, where the town square was built next to the village church of **Perchtoldsdorf**, just southwest of Vienna. There was more filming in Cornwall (where Milady plummets to her death from the cliffs), at **Charlestown Harbour**, on the south coast by St Austell.

THRONE OF BLOOD (aka *Cobweb Castle*)
(1957, dir: Akira Kurosawa)
Toshiro Mifune, Isuzu Yamada, Takashi Shimura.
● **JAPAN**

Kurosawa's terrific adaptation of *Macbeth*. Macbeth's castle was constructed high up on **Mount Fuji**, though the courtyard (complete with sand brought in from Fuji) was recreated in the studio. The mansion is on Japan's **Izu Peninsula**.

THROUGH A GLASS, DARKLY
(1961, dir: Ingmar Bergman)
Harriet Andersson, Gunnar Bjornstrand, Max von Sydow.
● **SWEDEN**

One of Bergman's bleakest dramas of non-communication, with Harriet Andersson suffering a breakdown, culminating in a disturbing vision of God as a malign spider. The first of many of the director's movies to be filmed in the barren landscape of the private island of **Faro**.

THROW MOMMA FROM THE TRAIN
(1987, dir: Danny DeVito)
Billy Crystal, Danny DeVito, Anne Ramsey.
● **LOS ANGELES; HAWAII**

Blackish (though not quite as dark as it promises) comedy, with mother-ridden DeVito inspired by Hitchcock's

Strangers on a Train to swap murders with Billy Crystal. The college, where Billy Crystal teaches creative writing, is **Los Angeles Valley College, 5800 Fulton Avenue** at Burbank Boulevard, North Hollywood in the San Fernando Valley. DeVito sneaks off to Hawaii to bump off Crystal's wife, who stays at the **Sheraton Princeville Hotel**, at the end of **Ka Haku Road** overlooking Hanalei Bay on Kauai's spectacular north shore. It all ends (sort of) happily on nearby **Ke'e Beach**.

THUNDERBALL

(1965, dir: Terence Young)
Sean Connery, Claudine Auger, Adolfo Celi.
● **BAHAMAS; FRANCE; FLORIDA; NORTHAMPTONSHIRE**

The fourth Bond, eagerly awaited after *Goldfinger*, had the biggest budget of the series so far and was the first shot in full Panavision widescreen. It turned out to be phenomenally successful, despite a protracted underwater battle that just drags on forever. The opening teaser, with Bond beating the life out of the rather butch widow at the funeral and the jetpack escape, is at the **Chateau d'Anet**, a partly-destroyed palace built for Diane de Poitiers at Anet, about 50 miles west of Paris. Shrublands, the health farm where Bond roasts Count Lippe in the Sitz bath, was **Chalfont Park House, Chalfont Park**, a converted hotel near to the Pinewood studios. The incineration of Count Lippe, blown up in his car, uses **Silverstone** racetrack in Northamptonshire. The SPECTRE HQ is in Paris.

Most of the other locations are – surprise! – at Nassau, in the Bahamas. The swish nightspot, where Bond gambles with Largo and dances with Domino, is the **Cafe Martinique** on **Paradise Island**, a two-mile strip of sand and rock at the outer edge of Nassau harbour. The dressed-up-to-the-eyeballs extras are locals, tempted out in their poshest frocks, with the promise of free caviar and champers – very much director Terence Young's style. At the time, the island could be reached only by boat (there's now a bridge) and was called by its pre-tourism name of Hog Island.

Largo's Palmyra estate, with its shark-infested swimming pool, was the summer home of the Nicholas Sullivans of Philadelphia (no, I don't know who they are, either), **Rock Point, West Bay Street**, east of Compass Point on **New Providence Island**. The Junkanoo, Nassau's Boxing Day parade, used **Parade Street** in downtown Nassau.

The stolen Vulcan bomber crash-lands in the sea off **Rose Island**, on the northeastern coast of New Providence Island. It is hidden alongside **Clifton Wall**, part of Nassau Harbour, where the framework of the purpose-built prop (despite being blown up after filming) can still be seen, almost alongside the sunken freighter from the *Thunderball* remake, *Never Say Never Again*. The speargun sequence uses the Golden Grotto, now known as **Thunderball Reef**.

Clifton Pier in Nassau Harbour is the site of Bond and Domino's underwater tryst, though the beach where they come ashore is the aptly-named **Love Beach** (it's actually named for the Love family), west of Gambier Village

on the northwest shore of New Providence. The climactic, and tiresomely protracted, underwater battle is also alongside Clifton Pier. The underwater scenes were staged by Ricou Browning, the veteran diver inside the rubber suit as the original *Creature From the Black Lagoon*, and a few close-up shots were recreated at the all-purpose underwater location of **Silver Springs** in Florida, where much of the *Creature* movie was shot. Silver Springs is a tourist attraction just east of Ocala, Route 40, central Florida. Also in Florida are the skydiving frogmen – that's clearly the city of Miami in the background.

Bond's Aston Martin, which appears in both *Thunderball* and *Goldfinger*, can be seen in Carbo's Smoky Mountain Car Museum, Pigeon Forge, Route 66, southeast of Knoxville in eastern Tennessee.

THX 1138

(1970, dir: George Lucas)
Robert Duvall, Donald Pleasence, Maggie McOmie.
● **CALIFORNIA**

George Lucas' first feature film, before he went on to *American Graffiti* and the phenomenally successful *Star Wars*, is a self-consciously film-student art movie. Set in a clinically dystopian future, the film utilised a number of real Californian locations. The claustrophobic underground environment is the (uncompleted) tunnel system of the **San Francisco Bay Area Rapid Transit** system (BART). Other locations include the **Lawrence Hall of Science, 1 Centennial Drive**, in the hills above the main University of California campus at Berkeley, and Frank Lloyd Wright's magnificent fifties extravaganza, the **Marin County Civic Center, Civic Center Drive, San Rafael**, northern California (seen also in *Gattaca*).

The clinical future: Marin County Civic Center, San Rafael

TIGER BAY

(1959, dir: J Lee Thompson)
Hayley Mills, John Mills, Horst Buchholz.
● **WALES**

Hayley Mills is kidnapped by, but ends up protecting, Polish sailor Horst Buchholz, who is wanted by the police for the murder of his girlfriend. Made around **Cardiff**, and at sea in the Bristol Channel.

TIME AFTER TIME

(1980, dir: Nicholas Meyer)
Malcolm McDowell, David Warner, Mary Steenburgen.
● **CALIFORNIA**

Neat little conceit, with prim Victorian HG Wells using his time machine to follow Jack the Ripper to 1980s San Francisco. The museum, in which Wells materialises, is a conflation of the **California Academy of Sciences**, on Music Concourse in Golden Gate Park, and the **Oakland Museum**, 10th and Oak, in Oakland over the bridge from San Fran. Wells tracks Jack to his room at the **Hyatt**

HG Wells confronts Jack the Ripper: Palace of Fine Arts

Regency Hotel, 5 Embarcadero Center (its glass elevators were seen also in *The Towering Inferno* and *High Anxiety*), and gets to chase him in – yes – the glass lobby elevators.

The search for the Ripper continues at San Francisco General Hospital, 1001 Potrero Avenue near 22nd Street in the Mission District. The revolving restaurant, where Steenburgen takes Wells to lunch, is the Equinox, the rooftop restaurant back at the Hyatt Regency. There's the inevitable trip over the Golden Gate Bridge, to the Redwood forests of northern California. Steenburgen's place is 2340 Francisco Street in the Marina District, close to the Palace of Fine Arts. Bernard Maybeck's elaborate fantasy, set in a small park on the eastern border of Golden Gate National Recreation Area, is a major location for the rest of the movie. It was built initially as a temporary structure for the Panama-Pacific International Exposition of 1916, but proved so popular that it was retained after the exhibition closed. During the late sixties, the original wood and plaster structure was recreated in concrete. It's also featured in *Vertigo* and *The Rock*. The entrance is 3601 Lyon Street at Marina Boulevard.

TIME BANDITS
(1981, dir: Terry Gilliam)
Craig Warnock, David Rappaport, John Cleese.
● MOROCCO; WALES; BUCKINGHAMSHIRE

The home of young time-traveller Kevin is at Haywood, Birch Hill in Bracknell, Buckinghamshire. The ruined castle, where Napoleon enjoys watching little people hit each other, is Raglan Castle in Wales. Ancient Greece, where Kevin meets Agamemnon, is Aït Ben Haddou near Ouarzazate in southern Morocco (conveniently close to the Aloha Golf Course for Sean Connery), a familiar location from films like *The Jewel of the Nile* and *Gladiator*. The sinking of the Titanic is colourised footage from the British account of the disaster, *A Night to Remember*.

TIMECOP
(1994, dir: Peter Hyams)
Jean-Claude Van Damme, Mia Sara, Ron Silver.
● BRITISH COLUMBIA, CANADA; PENNSYLVANIA

Set in Pittsburgh, Pennsylvania, but partly made on Granville Island, Vancouver, British Columbia.

TIN MEN
(1987, dir: Barry Levinson)
Richard Dreyfuss, Danny DeVito, Barbara Hershey.
● MARYLAND

Dreyfuss and DeVito are feuding aluminium salesmen in sixties Baltimore. The house, where the *Life* magazine scam ("a monument to your good taste") is foisted on a gullible housewife, is director Berry Levinson's old home,

at 4211 Springdale Avenue, Forest Park, south of Liberty Heights Avenue. The Cadillac showroom, outside which Dreyfuss gets his new motor dented, is 242 West 29th Street, near Remington Avenue, south of Johns Hopkins University campus. DeVito lives, not on Pimlico Road, but at 3107 Cliffmount. The restaurant/piano lounge, where DeVito and pals hang out, is elegant dining room, the John Eager Howard Room of the Belvedere Hotel, 1 East Chase Street. The Belvedere, now a restaurant and residential condominiums, can be found in the Mount Vernon district. Outside, Dreyfuss kicks in headlights and zooms off down East Chase Street. The diner, where DeVito and Dreyfuss eat, is a nod to an earlier Levinson film. It's the Hollywood Diner, 400 East Saratoga Street, the main setting for *Diner*.

TIREZ SUR LE PIANISTE (aka *Shoot the Pianist*)
(1960, dir: François Truffaut)
Charles Aznavour, Marie Dubois, Nicole Berger.
● FRANCE

Truffaut's second full-length feature, from the novel *Down There* by David Goodis. Filmed at a café, A la Bonne Franquette, rue Mussard, Levallois near Paris, and at Le Sappey, fifteen miles from Grenoble.

TITANIC
(1997, dir: James Cameron)
Leonardo DiCaprio, Kate Winslet, Gloria Stuart.
● MEXICO; NORTH ATLANTIC; SAN FRANCISCO

Fourteen Academy Award nominations, eleven wins – tying with *Ben-Hur* for top Oscar winner of all time. The vast *Titanic* set was constructed, in 100 days, as a fully-functioning studio at Rosarito Beach, eighteen miles south of Tijuana on the Mexican coast, though not without a wave of protest from local residents. Footage of the real *Titanic* wreck on the floor of the North Atlantic is used in the opening scenes. Twelve dives were made down to the hulk of the ship, and on the last two the remotely operated camera, intended only as a prop, went deeper into the ship than any other previous dive.

The engine room is the Triple Expansion Engine of the SS Jeremiah O'Brien, the National Liberty Ship Memorial, which you can visit at Pier 45, Fisherman's Wharf, San Francisco (used also in sci-fi epic *Sphere*).

TITFIELD THUNDERBOLT, THE
(1952, dir: Charles Crichton)
Stanley Holloway, George Relph, Naunton Wayne.
● AVON; OXFORDSHIRE; LONDON

The scheming owner of a coach service attempts to close down an old steam train service. Just when all seems lost, the locals rally round to save the day, in this archetypal people-versus-business Ealing comedy. Filmed, in luscious colour, on the now-defunct railway line at Limpley Stoke, near Bath. The fictitious Titfield-Mallingford branch line is a seven mile stretch of track between Limpley Stoke and Camerton, just south of Bath. Junction Point is actually Bristol. The station was a derelict stop at Monckton Coombe, just a couple of miles south of Bath. The village, with its distinctive mill chimney, is still recognis-

The commuters off to work: Mill Lane

Site of the old station: Monckton Coombe

The farm: Mott Farm

able. The road down which the commuters march to catch the Thunderbolt is **Mill Lane**, which has changed only slightly over the years. The turning into the station entrance is now a sadly overgrown mess, and the site of Titfield Station is now buried under tennis courts, though you can still clearly make out the site, and the route of the old line along the valley of the River Misbourne. Across the valley, you can see **Mott Farm**, the farmhouse pillaged for pots and pans after the water tank is sabotaged. Stanley Holloway's house is in the village of **Freshford**.

There was one day's filming with loco *The Lion* at Bristol's **Temple Meads Station**, standing in for Mallingford. The derailed train, which takes to the road, isn't a train at all, but a shell built onto a lorry chassis. Its night-time journey filmed in the village of **Woodstock**, Oxfordshire. The railway museum, from which the locals steal a steam engine and manhandle it down a flight of steps, was the old Imperial Institute, since demolished, which stood on Exhibition Road, Kensington.

TITUS
(1999, dir: Julie Taymor)
Anthony Hopkins, Jessica Lange, Harry Lennix.
● **ITALY; CROATIA**

The underground catacombs: Villa Adriana

Thrilling, imaginative filming of Shakespeare's early bloodfest, which anticipated the Theatre of the Absurd by about 300 years. The colosseum – the world's sixth largest – is at **Pula**, on the southwest coast of the Istrian peninsula in Croatia. The underground catacombs are at **Villa Adriana**, Hadrian's villa on the outskirts of Rome, and the emperor's fascist palace is **EUR** (Esposizione Universale Romana), government buildings planned by Mussolini but not completed until the fifties, about four miles south of Rome on Via Cristoforo Colombo (the wide, near

deserted streets of the district were also used in Dario Argento's *Tenebrae*).

TO CATCH A THIEF
(1955, dir: Alfred Hitchcock)
Cary Grant, Grace Kelly, Jessie Royce Landis.
● **FRANCE; MONACO**

The flower market: cours Saleya, Nice

Minor Hitchcock, kept afloat by the sparkling interplay between Grant and Kelly, set against the glitzy background of the French Riviera, where Grant, suspected of being a cat burglar, sets out to unmask the real culprit. Grace Kelly stays at the **Carlton Hotel, 58 la Croisette, Cannes**. Monte Carlo has been drastically, and grossly, redeveloped, and the terrace restaurant on the bay is long gone. Cary Grant's villa is just below the huge rocky outcrop of **Baou de St Jeannet**. The flower market is on **cours Saleya**, in the old town of **Nice**. The bridge is at

Grace Kelly's hotel: Carlton Hotel, Cannes

Éze. The chase was shot on the **Grande Corniche**, above Monte Carlo.

TO DIE FOR
(1995, dir: Gus Van Sant)
Nicole Kidman, Joaquin Phoenix, Matt Dillon.
● **ONTARIO, CANADA; FLORIDA**

The observatory: McLaughlin Planetarium, Toronto

Black comedy from indie director Van Sant, shot around Toronto. The high school is **King City**, about 15 miles north of Toronto. The movie was shot at **Jackson's Point, Lake Simcoe**; **Brampton**, a western suburb of Toronto; **Georgetown**, just west of Toronto; **Hamilton**, a southern suburb on the south shore of Lake Ontario; **Mississauga**, to the southwest; **Oakville**, southwest Mississauga; **Schomberg**, north toward Lake Simcoe; **Whitby**, about 20 miles east of Toronto, and **Port Hope**, on the shore of Lake Ontario a further 60 miles east. The observatory is the **McLaughlin Planetarium**. Suzanne and Larry's honeymoon, however, did film in Florida.

TO KILL A MOCKINGBIRD
(1962, dir: Robert Mulligan)
Gregory Peck, Mary Badham, Philip Alford.
● **LOS ANGELES**

Peck takes home the Best Actor Oscar as the lawyer in the

Deep South who has his work cut out defending a black man accused of rape. Harper Lee, author of the original novel, based the fictitious setting of Maycomb on hometown Monroeville in Alabama, which seemed the obvious place to film. But the town had undergone too many changes and, in the end, the movie ended up being shot on the Universal backlot in Hollywood. Monroeville is on Route 21, between Mobile and Montgomery, Alabama.

TO THE DEVIL A DAUGHTER
(1975, dir: Peter Sykes)
Richard Widmark, Christopher Lee, Denholm Elliott.
● BUCKINGHAMSHIRE

When Satanists promise Natassja Kinski to the Devil, her father, Denholm Elliott, appeals to occult novelist Widmark for help, in this adaptation of a Dennis Wheatley novel. Filming took place at **West Wycombe Caves**, legendary haunt of the notorious Hellfire Club, off the A40 at West Wycombe, northwest of High Wycombe in Buckinghamshire. The caves, nondescript mining tunnels hewn out of the rock, are open to the public (*admission charge*), but they're a truly underwhelming experience.

Satanic goings-on at the home of the Hellfire club: West Wycombe Caves

TOM BROWN'S SCHOOLDAYS
(1951, dir: Gordon Parry)
John Howard Davies, Robert Newton, Diana Wynyard.
● WARWICKSHIRE; LONDON

The filming of the old classic does actually use the book's location of **Rugby School** in Warwickshire. The coaching tavern is the **George Inn, Borough**, one of London's last remaining galleried inns.

The old tavern: George Inn, Borough

TOM JONES
(1963, dir: Tony Richardson)
Albert Finney, Susannah York, Hugh Griffith.
● DORSET; SOMERSET; LONDON

Richardson pulls out all the cinematic stops for this picaresque sex adventure, made mainly in the West Country. One of the key locations is **Cranborne Manor**, on the B3078, about eighteen miles north of Bournemouth, Dorset. The 17th century gardens here are

Squire Allworthy's estate: Minterne, Dorset

open to the public March to September (*admission charge*). The famous eating scene, with Finney and Joyce Redman, uses the stables of **Nettlecombe Court**,

Tom contemplates marriage: Lincoln's Inn Fields

which in 1963 was a girls' boarding school, near **Williton** on the A39, eight miles east of Minehead, north Somerset. Newgate Jail is Nettlecombe's courtyard. Squire Allworthy's estate is **Minterne**, on the A352, two miles from Cerne Abbas and ten miles north of Dorchester in Dorset. The 18th century rhododendron and shrub garden is open April to October (*admission charge; © 01300.341370*). **Castle Street, Bridgwater**, in Somerset, provided more picturesque backdrops.

Lady Bellaston's house was Londonderry House, since demolished, which stood at Hyde Park Corner, while more period London street scenes used **Lincoln's Inn Fields** and the old warehouses along **Shad Thames, Southwark**.

TOMB OF LIGEIA, THE
(1964, dir: Roger Corman)
Vincent Price, Elizabeth Shepherd, John Westbrook
● NORFOLK

Price's dead wife becomes a cat, and thence the Lady Rowena, in this adaptation of an Edgar Allen Poe story by Robert Towne, the writer of *Chinatown*. Roger Corman left the AIP studios in LA, where he had filmed his series of atmospheric Poe/Price movies, to take advantage of the British studios' practice of reusing old sets for gratis. Unusually, Corman ventured out to a real location. The ruined abbey is **Castle Acre**, a 900-year-old priory four miles north of Swaffham in Norfolk. The graveyard is in **Swaffham** itself.

TOMBSTONE
(1993, dir: George P Cosmatos)
Kurt Russell, Val Kilmer, Michael Biehn.
● ARIZONA

Epic Western, filmed at the **Old Tucson** movie set-cum-tourist attraction, **201 South Kinney Road**, Tucson, Arizona. The real Tomb-

The Tombstone set at Old Tucson studios, Arizona.

stone, where you can see the OK Corral and Boot Hill Cemetery, is about 50 miles southeast of Tucson.

TOMMY
(1975, dir: Ken Russell)
Roger Daltrey, Ann-Margret, Oliver Reed.
● HAMPSHIRE; LAKE DISTRICT; LONDON; HERTFORDSHIRE

The film adaptation of The Who's rock opera has a great

Going up in flames: South Parade Pier, Southsea

The fifties holiday camp chalets: Eastney Esplanade

The 'Pinball Wizard' theatre: King's Theatre, Southsea

The Marilyn Monroe Church: Henderson Road, Eastney

The holiday camp pool: Hilsea Lido

Tommy's holiday camp: Fort Purbrook, Portsmouth

first half – virtually inventing the music video – as Russell gives full rein to his imagination, but then trips up on the obvious budgetary restrictions as the lumpen allegory takes over. The opening and closing countryside idylls are the Lake District.

Apart from Tommy's birth, a scene shot in **Harefield**, Hertfordshire the movie was shot around **Portsmouth** and nearby **Hayling Island**, Hampshire.

The opening Blitz scene was **Cumberland Road**, near Fratton Station, as the street was being demolished. It's now a smart new housing estate. The subterranean tunnel, through which Oliver Reed and Ann-Margret take the young Tommy to the funfair, is at **Southsea Castle**, south of Southsea Common. The fair itself is at the northwestern end of the common. You won't find Oliver Reed's campy fifties holiday camp. It's a composite of several different locations. The row of chalets, actually tiny sun huts, can be seen along **Eastney Esplanade** at St George's Road, east of Southsea. The swimming pool is **Hilsea Lido**, off London Road at the roundabout by Port Creek, Hilsea, north of Portsmouth.

The ballroom was the theatre on the old **South Parade Pier**, Southsea. The pier caught fire and burned down during filming. But waste not, want not – film of the pier burning is incorporated into the conflagration at the movie's climax. The replacement is a sad, bland reconstruction of the original. Elton John's 'Pinball Wizard' number uses the **King's Theatre**, Southsea. The Church of Marilyn Monroe, where Eric Clapton performs 'Eyesight to the Blind', was St Andrew's Church, now imaginatively converted to luxury housing, on **Henderson Road, Eastney**, east of Southsea.

Hang-gliding Tommy (and what seventies movie would be complete without its hang-gliding sequence?) perches atop the remaining tower of **Warblington Castle**, the rest of which was largely destroyed during the Civil War. It's on private land just east of the B2149 by the bridge to Hayling Island, south of Havant.

Tommy's Holiday Camp, where a manic Keith Moon flogs trinkets to the converts, is **Fort Purbrook**, one of five Victorian forts overlooking Portsmouth. Known collectively as Palmerston's Folly, after the Prime Minister who

oversaw their construction, they were meant to defend the south coast against a French invasion, which never materialised. Purbrook, most easterly of the five, is on **Portsdown Hill Road**, off London Road, northwest of Cosham. The entrance to Tommy's camp is the fort's westerly gate. The interior of the camp used piles of buoys, painted silver in an imaginative, if unsuccessful, attempt to resemble giant pinballs. The buoys were stacked at the now-gone Pound's Scrapyard, Twyford Avenue, by Alexandra Park.

TOMORROW NEVER DIES

(1997, dir: Roger Spottiswoode)
Pierce Brosnan, Jonathan Pryce, Michelle Yeoh.
● LONDON; SUFFOLK; OXFORDSHIRE; HERTFORDSHIRE; GERMANY; THAILAND; FRANCE; MEXICO

Brosnan's second outing as Bond. The opening terrorist arms bazaar 'on the Russian border' is **Peyresourde**, one of the world's few high-altitude airfields, in the central French Pyrenees.

The Oxford college, where Bond learns a new tongue, is **New College**. The MI6 HQ is **Somerset House** in the Strand, which served as St Petersburg in *Goldeneye*. Bond flies off to Germany, arriving at **Hamburg International Airport** (the real thing), where he meets Q. Elliot Carver's Hamburg HQ though, where Bond meets old flame Paris Carver at the party, is the **IBM Building** at **Bedfont Lakes** near Heathrow Airport. Carver's print works is an amalgamation of two London printers: **Harmsworth Quays Printers Ltd, Surrey Quays Road**, SE16 and **Westferry Printers, 235 Westferry Road**, E14, at Millwall Dock (printers of the London *Evening Standard* and the *Daily Telegraph*).

The hotel, where Bond finds Paris Carver dead, is the **Atlantic Hotel Kempinski, An der Alster 72-79** (© *49.40.288.80*) on the banks of the Aussenalster lake in central Hamburg. The carpark chase is in the fourth level of **Brent Cross Shopping Centre** in Golders Green, London, where the fire brigade were called out after the stunts produced a little more smoke than anticipated. The final leap into the fake Avis office, though, is the real Hamburg.

The US airbase at Okinawa in the South China Sea is really **RAF Lakenheath** in Suffolk, despite Joe Don Baker's floral shirt and shorts. The sea landing is **Rosarito** in Baja California, Mexico, where *Titanic* was filmed.

Bond pops up in **Phuket Bay**, Thailand, among the limestone towers familiar from *The Man With the Golden Gun*. The Saigon scenes are actually Bangkok, Thailand, where the skyscraper down which Bond and Wai Lin descend on a banner is the **Banyan Tree Hotel, 21/100 South Sathorn Road, Sathorn** (*© 66.2.679.1200; www.westin-bangkok.com*). The chase is through Bangkok, along **Tannery Row** and **Mahogany Wharf**, though climaxing on a set built at the **Eon Studios** in Frogmore, Hertfordshire.

TOOTSIE
(1982, dir: Sydney Pollack)
Dustin Hoffman, Jessica Lange, Teri Garr.
● **NEW YORK CITY; NEW YORK STATE; NEW JERSEY**

Hoffman, as a struggling actor, famously drags up to find work on a soap. Tootsie checks out 'her' new image by meeting up with agent Sydney Pollack in the **Russian Tea Room, 150 West 57th Street** – seen also in Woody Allen's *Manhattan*. Tootsie argues over a cab outside **Bloomingdale's, 1000 Third Avenue** at East 59th Street on the East Side.

Other NY locations include: **Central Park; East Riverside Drive; Fifth Avenue; Sixth Avenue;** the (now closed) Copacabana Nightclub, 10 East 60th Street at Madison Avenue (seen in *Goodfellas*). **Plaza West Shopping Center**; a loft in **SoHo**, and **Fort Lee**, over the Hudson in New Jersey. The farmhouse is in **Kingston**, New York State. The restaurant, where Hoffman sits after being outed as a man, is **Hurley Mountain Inn, Route 29A**, west of Route 209, between Esopus Creek and Brinks Lane, **Hurley**, New York State (*© 845.331.1780*).

TOP GUN
(1986, dir: Tony Scott)
Tom Cruise, Kelly McGillis, Val Kilmer.
● **CALIFORNIA; NEVADA**

Navy recruiting movie from a director grounded in advertising. The hardware looks good enough to eat and there's a choice of love interest – Kilmer or McGillis according to orientation. The movie is set in San Diego, home of the 11th Naval District HQ, one of the world's largest navy bases, Route 5, 120 miles south of LA. Also featured is the **US Naval Air Station** at **Fallon**. It's east of the town of Fallon, on I-50, Nevada. The flyers' hangout, where Anthony Edwards plays 'Great Balls of Fire', and Tom gets his big clinch with Kelly, is the **Kansas City Barbeque Restaurant, 610 West Market Street** at Kettner Boulevard, by the railroad tracks in downtown San Diego.

TOP SECRET!
(1984, dir: Jim Abrahams, David Zucker, Jerry Zucker)
Val Kilmer, Lucy Gutteridge, Omar Sharif.
● **NORTHAMPTONSHIRE; DEVON**

The *Airplane!* team takes on the Cold War spy movie.

Filming took place at **Rockingham Castle, Rockingham**, two miles north of Corby, Northamptonshire (*© 01536.770240, admission charge*). The California surfing opening is actually **Saunton Sands**, on the North Devon coast, west of Barnstaple (also seen in *A Matter of Life and Death* and *Pink Floyd – The Wall*).

TOPAZ
(1969, dir: Alfred Hitchcock)
Frederick Stafford, John Forsythe, Roscoe Lee Browne.
● **DENMARK; GERMANY; FRANCE; NEW YORK CITY; WASHINGTON DC; CALIFORNIA**

Far and away the worst Hitchcock ever, a confused, uninteresting, unfocused international spy thriller with a truncated ending that has to be seen to be believed. Hitch, feeling that his precise, storyboarded style was dated for the freewheeling sixties, unwisely attempted to wing it with an unfinished script and poor preparation. The movie shot all over, in **Copenhagen**, Denmark; **Wiesbaden**, Germany; **Paris**; New York; Washington DC; and **Salinas**, California (standing in for Cuba).

TOPKAPI
(1964, dir: Jules Dassin)
Melina Mercouri, Maximilian Schell, Peter Ustinov.
● **TURKEY**

Classic caper movie, with Schell stealing a dagger from the **Topkapi Palace Museum**, on Seraglio Point overlooking the Marmora and Bosphorus, Istanbul (*© 90.212.5120480; www.ee.bilkent.edu.tr/~history/topkapi*).

TOPPER
(1937, dir: Norman Z McLeod)
Cary Grant, Constance Bennett, Roland Young.
● **LOS ANGELES**

Cary Grant and Constance Bennett are the Kirbys, a smart – but dead – couple who haunt stuffy banker Roland Young. Young's's Connecticut estate is the Gothic mansion at **380 San Rafael Avenue, Pasadena** (a private home, not visible from the road). The entrance to the Sea Breeze Hotel, supposedly also in Connecticut, is the rear porte cochere of the striking Bullock's Department Store building. Long closed, the towering landmark has been restored as home to the **Southwestern Law School, 3050 Wilshire Boulevard**, midtown LA.

The Sea Breeze Inn: Southwestern Law School, Wilshire Boulevard, LA

TOPSY-TURVY
(1999, dir: Mike Leigh)
Jim Broadbent, Allan Corduner, Timothy Spall.
● SURREY; HERTFORDSHIRE

Mike Leigh springs a surprise with this genial, episodic analysis of the creative process, as Gilbert and Sullivan, stuck in a rut and about to go their separate ways,

The Savoy Theatre interiors: Richmond Theatre, Richmond

come up with *The Mikado*. The Savoy Theatre has changed beyond all recognition since the days of D'Oyly Carte, revamped in a twenties deco style. The theatre scenes filmed in **Richmond Theatre, The Green, Richmond** in Surrey (✆ *020.8940.0088*). Budgetary constraints meant that there are no exterior 'money shots'; in fact, most of the film was shot inside **Langleybury Mansion**, an abandoned Victorian school in King's Langley, Hertfordshire.

TORN CURTAIN
(1966, dir: Alfred Hitchcock)
Paul Newman, Julie Andrews, Lila Kedrova.
● CALIFORNIA; GERMANY

This second division Hitchcock is miscast, but has some great sequences. Paul Newman, whose methody style was anathema to Hitch, poses as a defector in order to get some macguffins from behind the Iron Curtain, but girlfriend Andrews almost scuppers the plan by doggedly tailing him. The story grew out of the Burgess-Maclean spying episode (a treatment of which Hitchcock was still working on at the time of his death), looking at political and sexual betrayal from the wife's point of view.

By the time Universal had junked the homosexual element of the story and lumbered Hitchcock with two unsuitable leads, the project was sinking fast. The film also marked the director's final rift with brilliant but temperamental composer Bernard Herrmann. In 1966, the studio felt him 'too old fashioned'. He went on to score *Obsession* for Brian De Palma, *Taxi Driver* for Martin Scorsese, and when *Cape Fear* and *Psycho* were remade, both films retained the original Herrmann scores.

The movie was made largely on the Universal backlot, and on the campus of the **University of Southern California**, in LA's Exposition Park area, south of downtown. The remote farm, where the gruesomely protracted killing of the East German agent takes place, was at **Camarillo**, on Route 101 between LA and Ventura. The airport is in San Fernando Valley. The port is **Long Beach**, southern LA. Surprisingly, there are a few shots of the real **East Berlin**, snatched surreptitiously by a second unit ostensibly filming a travelogue. When Newman leaves the hotel, looks up the street and sees the yellow bus, it really is in East Berlin. The bus he gets on board is a duplicate at Universal. The museum chase was tricked up with matte shots.

TOTAL RECALL
(1990, dir: Paul Verhoeven)
Arnold Schwarzenegger, Sharon Stone, Ronny Cox.
● MEXICO

Ingenious FX-packed sci-fi, with Schwarzenegger visiting Mars to discover why he's been implanted with a false memory, though it does feel like there's one last twist cut from the ending. Made almost entirely in Mexico City's Churubuscu Studios. Director Verhoeven wanted to film the futuristic cityscapes in Houston, but, ultimately, production costs determined that filming would be south of the border, and Arnie's neighbourhood on Earth is thus a military academy just outside Mexico City. Other scenes used the penthouse and the lobby of the 750-room **Hotel Nikko Mexico, Campos Eliseos 204**, Mexico City, north of Chapultepec Park.

TOTO LE HEROS (aka *Toto the Hero*)
(1991, dir: Jaco van Dormael)
Michel Bouquet, Jo De Backer, Thomas Godet.
● BRUSSELS, BELGIUM

Van Dormael's dazzling, off-centre black comedy has Bouquet, convinced that a mix-up at birth robbed him of his life, out to settle the score. The film is set in Brussels, mainly in the southeastern suburb of **Watermael-Boitsford**, in **rue Friquet**; **rue de la Hulotte**; **rue de Loriot** and **rue du Troglodyte**. Also seen are the suburbs of **Uccle**; **Ixelles**; **Saint-Josse-ten-Noode** and **Schaerbeek**.

TOUCH OF EVIL
(1958, dir: Orson Welles)
Charlton Heston, Janet Leigh, Orson Welles.
● LOS ANGELES

Welles tiptoed back to Hollywood to film Whit Masterson's novel *Badge of Evil*, and adapted the book himself. He wanted to film the corrupt and decaying labyrinth of a Mexican border town in Tijuana or Juarez, but the Mexican authorities objected to the sleaziness in the script. Universal wanted Welles to film in the studio. In the end, it was writer Aldous Huxley who came up with the inspired choice of **Venice**.

The once-elegant recreation of the Italian city, with canals and arched walkways, had degenerated into a decrepit backwater, the buildings crumbling, the stagnant canals stinking and oil derricks disfiguring the landscape. The ending of the screenplay was rewritten to accommo-

The Mexican border town: Windward Avenue, Venice

date the locale. The area has been spruced up no end since the fifties, and is now a lively, old-hippyish neighbourhood. The remaining arcades can be seen on **Windward Avenue**, between Pacific Avenue and Speedway; the canals are southeast of Pacific Avenue and Venice Boulevard.

TOWERING INFERNO, THE
(1974, dir: John Guillermin)
Paul Newman, Steve McQueen, William Holden.
● **CALIFORNIA**

The entrance to the glass tower: Bank of America World HQ, California Street

Fox and Warners both planned high-rise conflagration movies, based on books *The Tower* and *The Glass Inferno*. They decided to pool their resources and produce *The Towering Inferno*. Five storeys of the doomed building were built at Fox's Malibu Ranch. Set in San Francisco, the opening matte shot places the tower just about on the site of the Transamerica Pyramid. The entrance is actually the plaza entrance to the **Bank of America World Headquarters, California Street** at Kearney Street. The lobby, with its glass elevators, is the **Hyatt Regency Hotel, 5 Embarcadero**

The tower's lobby: Embarcadero Center

Center, a dizzying location seen also in Mel Brooks' *High Anxiety* and sci-fi adventure *Time After Time*. This being, in part, a Twentieth Century Fox movie, the computer controlled building surveillance centre was shot in the basement of a Century City office building.

TRADING PLACES
(1983, dir: John Landis)
Eddie Murphy, Dan Aykroyd, Ralph Bellamy.
● **PENNSYLVANIA; NEW YORK CITY; NEW YORK STATE; VIRGIN ISLANDS**

Rich old men Bellamy and Don Ameche get their comeuppance after swapping the lifestyles of beggar Murphy and stockbroker Aykroyd for a bet. Set mainly in Philadelphia, where 'legless' Murphy begs in a wintry **Rittenhouse Square**, at 18th and Walnut Streets, to the southwest of the city centre. In the classy district a little further southwest is Dan Aykroyd's house, taken over by Eddie Murphy, at **2014 Delancey Street** near 21st Street. Bellamy and Ameche's Duke and Duke bank is the **Fideli-**

'Legless' Murphy begs in Rittenhouse Square

ty Bank, 135 South Broad Street, just south of City Hall. After he's had his credit cards confiscated, the destitute Aykroyd is offered help by hooker Jamie Lee Curtis on **15th Street** in front of Claes Oldenburg's giant, 45-foot steel Clothespeg statue, Market Street west of City Hall. Murphy and Aykroyd set out for New York from the elegant deco concourse of **Thirtieth Street Station, 30th Street**, Philadelphia (seen also in *Blow Out, Marnie* and *Witness*). The Dukes' mansion isn't Pennsylvania at all, but **Mill Neck Manor for the Deaf, Mill Neck**, Nassau County, Long Island. The frantic climax, with Murphy and Aykroyd joining forces to bankrupt their tormentors, is in the **Comex Commodities Exchange Center**, of the **World Trade Center, Church Street** between Liberty and Vesey Streets in NYC. The good guys end up on the tropical beaches of **St Croix** in the Virgin Islands.

The Duke and Duke Bank: Fidelity Bank, South Broad Street, Philadelphia

Aykroyd is saved by Jamie Lee Curtis: the Clothespeg on 15th Street

Dan Aykroyd's house: Delancey Street

TRAINSPOTTING
(1996, dir: Danny Boyle)
Ewan McGregor, Ewen Bremner, Jonny Lee Miller.
● **SCOTLAND; LONDON**

Irvine Welsh's druggy novel, filmed by the *Shallow Grave* team with manic energy and a vow to keep the running time down to 90 minutes, deservedly turned out to be one of the UK's most profitable movies. Set in Edinburgh but, as with *Shallow Grave*, most of the filming took place in Glasgow.

The opening scene is the only real glimpse of Edinburgh, with Renton and co

Shoplifting: Princes Street, Edinburgh

Renton and the car: Calton Street Bridge

The football match: Firhill Complex, Hopehill Road, Glasgow

Gearing up for the job interview: Cafe d'Jaconelli, Maryhill Road, Glasgow

Begbie and the beermug: Crosslands, Queen Margaret Drive, Glasgow

Renton's London flat: Talgarth Road, West Kensington

Shooting the dog: Rouken Glen Park, Thornliebank, Glasgow

The drug deal: Craven Road, Bayswater

The drug deal hotel, exterior: Royal Eagle Hotel, Craven Road, Bayswater

The hotel interior: George Hotel, Buchanan Street, Glasgow

raiding **John Menzies Bookstore** and sprinting off down **Princes Street** to the **Calton Street Bridge**, where Renton is hit by the car. From here on it's Glasgow. The studio filming utilised a disused cigarette factory (it provides 30 of the film's 50 locations). The down-at-heel pub where the American tourist gets done over, and everyone gathers after the trial, is the old Social Club of the factory.

The football match filmed at the **Firhill Health Complex, Hopehill Road**, north from Maryhill Road, North Kelvin (*Underground: St Georges Cross*). The park where Renton and Sick Boy discuss the career of Sean Connery and shoot the dog's behind is **Rouken Glen Park, Rouken Glen Park Road, Thornliebank**, south of the city center on the line from Central Station. The park was also the site of the grave in *Shallow Grave*.

The disco: Volcano, Benalder Street

The café where Renton and Spud share a milkshake before speeding is **Cafe d'Jaconelli, 570 Maryhill Road**, in North Kelvin not far from the Firhill Health Complex. A little further up the road on the left is Queen Margaret Drive. A few minutes down the road you can find the galleried bar where Begbie entertains the crowd with his pool story and demonstrates how not to dispose of a beermug. It's **Crosslands, 182 Queen Margaret Drive**.

The nightclub where Renton meets the schoolgirl is **Volcano, 15 Benalder Street**, close to Kelvinhall Station. The rear of the club is the grey building facing Dumbarton Road. The railway station where Tommy tries vainly to whip up some enthusiasm for the Scottish countryside is **Rannoch Moor**, on the West Highland line up toward Fort William.

Renton's West London flat is on **Talgarth Road** in West Kensington. The London hotel, scene of the drug deal, is the **Royal Eagle Hotel, Craven Road**, Bayswater, though the interior is still in Glasgow. It's the **George Hotel, 235 Buchanan Street** not far from Central Station.

TRAMP, THE

(1915, dir: Charles Chaplin)
Charles Chaplin, Edna Purviance, Bud Jamison.
● CALIFORNIA

The tramp rescues Purviance from crooks. He's given a job on her parents' farm and gets looked after by her, until her lover turns up, and we get the original walk off into the sunset. The final shot filmed at **Niles**, California, which was the site of hundreds of old silent Westerns.

TRAPEZE

(1956, dir: Carol Reed)
Burt Lancaster, Tony Curtis, Gina Lollobrigida.
● PARIS

Lollobrigida comes between acrobats Burt and Tony in this sawdust melodrama. Much of the atmosphere comes from the location filming. Almost all of the movie was shot in, or around, the domed, 5,000 seat **Cirque d'Hiver, 110 rue Amelot**. Built as the Cirque Napoleon by Louis De-jean, one of the most acclaimed circus managers

The circus: Cirque d'Hiver, rue Amelot, Paris

of the 1850s, and opened in the presence of Napoleon III, it was here that the flying trapeze was invented by M. Leotard. A parade along the Grand Boulevard and the Champs Elysées filmed before a crowd of 9,000 Parisians.

TRAVELS WITH MY AUNT
(1972, dir: George Cukor)
Maggie Smith, Alec McCowen, Robert Stephens.
● LONDON; PARIS; ITALY; MOROCCO; SPAIN; TURKEY; YUGOSLAVIA

St James and Albany Hotel: George V Hotel, avenue George V, Paris

It all looked so promising. Then Katharine Hepburn dropped out of the cast and Maggie Smith came on board, with a performance so extravagantly OTT it's only safe to watch from behind a lead shield. She plays the 'liberating' aunt who opens up new horizons for dry old stick McCowen. In London, Smith's West End base is above The Salisbury pub in St Martin's Lane, at the time one of London's most famously theatrical gay bars. The money pick-up is not far away, at the Lamb and Flag pub in Rose Street, Covent Garden. The grandiose St James and Albany Hotel is Paris' lavish George V Hotel, 31 avenue George V, off the Champs Elysées. The fabulous fin-de-siècle restaurant, where Smith begins to get flashbacks to her youth, is Le Train Bleu, on the first floor of the Gare de Lyon, Paris (see it also in Luc Besson's stylish *Nikita*). The travels also filmed in Italy, Morocco, Spain, Turkey and Yugoslavia.

TREASURE ISLAND
(1934, dir: Victor Fleming)
Wallace Beery, Jackie Cooper, Lionel Barrymore.
● CALIFORNIA

The seafront location is Point Lobos State Reserve, northern California. This site is credited as being the inspira-

Treasure Island: Point Lobos State Reserve

tion for Robert Louis Stevenson's story.

TREASURE ISLAND
(1950, dir: Byron Haskin)
Robert Newton, Bobby Driscoll, Walter Fitzgerald.
● CORNWALL

Colourful Disney version of the classic yarn, filmed at Falmouth in Cornwall. Filming took place at Carrick Roads and River Fal. The *Hispaniola* is the Ryland Training Schooner, converted at Bideford. There was a little filming up the Helford River, but most of the shooting was at the entrance to the River Fal at Turnaware Bar, opposite Feock, and further upriver near to King Harry Ferry. For the Treasure Island itself, painted palm trees were matted in.

TREASURE OF THE SIERRA MADRE, THE
(1948, dir: John Huston)
Humphrey Bogart, Walter Huston, Tim Holt.
● MEXICO; LOS ANGELES

The somewhat obvious studio sets were at Warner Bros in Burbank, but there is real location filming in the mountains surrounding the village of Jungapeo, near San Jose Purua, Mexico, west from Mexico City, in the district of Michoacan; at Tampico and a few shots in Durango.

TREMORS
(1990, dir: Ron Underwood)
Kevin Bacon, Fred Ward, Finn Carter.
● CALIFORNIA

Horror comedy, with giant carnivorous worms popping up around the Alabama Hills of Lone Pine, Route 395 in central California, and at nearby Olancha.

TRIAL, THE
(1962, dir: Orson Welles)
Anthony Perkins, Orson Welles, Jeanne Moreau.
● YUGOSALVIA; PARIS; ROME; MILAN, ITALY

Gare d'Orsay, Paris

Part Kafka, part Welles, all brilliant. The grand, impressive locations, dotted all over Europe, are stitched together to form a nightmarish landscape. Joseph K's office, a huge exhibition hall outside Zagreb, in the former Yugoslavia, with 850 desks, typewriters and secretaries. Other locations include: Dubrovnik; Rome; Milan and Paris. A typical sequence has Perkins at the Gare d'Orsay, Paris, then walking down the steps of the Palazzo di Giustizia, Rome, to meet his cousin, strolling to a factory entrance in Milan, and returning to a council house in Zagreb.

TRIP, THE
(1967, dir: Roger Corman)
Peter Fonda, Susan Strasberg, Bruce Dern.
● CALIFORNIA

Jack Nicholson-scripted sixties acid movie, with Fonda

tripping out of his brain. The low dives are on the Strip, the stretch of **Sunset Boulevard** running through West Hollywood. The medieval flashbacks are the Californian coast at **Big Sur**, I-1; the deserts are at **Big Dune**, Yuma, Route 8 down in southeast California at the Arizona border.

TRIP TO BOUNTIFUL, THE
(1985, dir: Peter Masterson)
Geraldine Page, John Heard, Carlin Glynn.
● **TEXAS**

Near-senile Geraldine Page is obsessed with making one last trip, away from her ghastly family in Houston, to see the old family home, in this predictable tearjerker just about rescued from sentimentality-hell by the wonderful Page's Oscar-grabbing performance. It was shot in **Waxahachie**, that favourite Texas location, south of Dallas; and in **Venus**, some fifteen miles to the west, and **Five Points**. The Houston Bus Terminal is the old **Dallas Railroad Terminal**.

TRISTANA
(1970, dir: Luis Buñuel)
Catherine Deneuve, Fernando Rey, Franco Nero.
● **SPAIN**

Another surreal psychosexual puzzle from Buñuel, with Deneuve as a young woman given into the charge of ageing Spanish liberal Rey. The film is set in one of Spain's oldest cities, **Toledo**. The alabaster tomb, which so fascinates Deneuve, is modelled on the tomb of Cardinal Tavera, by Alonson Berruguete, in the Church of the Hospital Tavera, north of the Puerta de Bisagra, outside Toledo's city walls.

TROUBLE WITH HARRY, THE
(1955, dir: Alfred Hitchcock)
Edmund Gwenn, Mildred Natwick, Shirley MacLaine.
● **VERMONT**

One of Hitchcock's own favourites, this amiable, gently black comedy centres around the attempted disposal of a dead body. It's also Shirley MacLaine's screen début, and looks a treat thanks to Robert Burks' photography of the autumnal new England location of **East Craftsbury**, 30 miles north of Montpelier, northern Vermont. Much of the planned shooting had to be rearranged because of unexpected rainstorms. Interior sets were built inside a school gym in Morrisville, some fifteen miles away.

TRUE GRIT
(1969, dir: Henry Hathaway)
John Wayne, Glen Campbell, Kim Darby.
● **COLORADO; CALIFORNIA**

Wayne dons an eyepatch as crotchety marshall Rooster Cogburn in this likeable Western, made in the **Gunnison** area south of Montrose, in southwest Colorado. The opening shots are the **Wilson Peaks** in the San Juan national Forest. The frontier town is the main square of **Ridgway**, on I-550, about 30 miles to the south. Scenes were also shot at **Mammoth Lakes**, Route 395, east of Yosemite National Park in central California.

TRUE LIES
(1994, dir: James Cameron)
Arnold Schwarzenegger, Jamie Lee Curtis, Tia Carrere.
● **CALIFORNIA; WASHINGTON DC; FLORIDA; RHODE ISLAND**

Cameron's action thriller had a lot of location filming around Washington DC. Schwarzenegger chases terrorist Art Malik through the **George-town Park Mall**, out onto **M Street**, and borrows a policeman's horse in **Franklin Park**. However, the DC hotel, into which Arnie rides his horse, is actually the **Westin Bonaventure Hotel**,

The horse leap at the DC hotel: Westin Bonaventure Hotel, LA

The chase and shootout: Georgetown Mall, Washington DC

404 South Figueroa Street, in downtown LA. The most imaginative location, though, is the Swiss chateau on the lake. This is actually **Ochre Court** – now the Salve Regina University – **Ochre Point Avenue, Rhode Island**. A canal was dug alongside the mansion and the camera placed on the other side to give the impression of a lakeside setting. The interior is **Rosecliff, Bellevue Avenue** near Newport,

The Harrier jet climax: Colonial Bank Center, Brickell Avenue, Miami

another of the grand Rhode Island mansions (see *The Great Gatsby* for details of Rosecliff). Filming also took place in the High Sierra Mountains of Central California. The bridge that features in the epic helicopter/limo scene is the **Old Seven Mile Bridge** joining Key Vaca and Bahia Honda Key in the Florida Keys. Originally a railway bridge built in 1910, it once carried Overseas Highway, US1, but was replaced by a new bridge in 1982. The gleaming black highrise where the terrorists hole up, and which Arnie trashes with a Harrier jump jet, is the **Colonial Bank Centre, 1200 Brickell Avenue** at SE 13th Street, downtown Miami. The final tango is in the Crystal Ballroom of the **Biltmore Hotel**, in LA.

TRUE ROMANCE
(1993, dir: Tony Scott)
Christian Slater, Patricia Arquette, Gary Oldman.
● **LOS ANGELES; DETROIT, MICHIGAN**

Tony Scott's film of Tarantino's script shamelessly rips off the musical style and flat narrative voiceover of Terrence Malick's *Badlands*. But if you're going to borrow, borrow from the best. The movie opens in Detroit, and

The hideout: Safari Inn, Olive Boulevard, Burbank

indeed this is where you'll find Dennis Hopper's trailer park, on the Detroit River. He works at the **Packard Plant, East Grand Boulevard** at Mount Elliott. The cop station is at **1300 Beaubien**, and Slater and Arquette marry at the **Wayne County Building, 600 Randolph**. But the Sonny Chiba *Street Fighter* triple bill, where Slater and Arquette first meet, is in Hollywood, at the **Vista Theater, 4473 Sunset Drive** (used for the première of *Stab* in *Scream 2*). And the diner, where they eat pie afterwards, is the fifties-style **Rae's Restaurant, 2901 Pico Boulevard**, at the corner of 29th Street in **Santa Monica** (*© 310.828.7937*), seen also in the Eddie Murphy-Steve Martin satire *Bowfinger*.

Other locations include the mansions of **Pasadena**; **Hollywood** bungalows; downtown LA; the beach at **Malibu** and the desert at **Palmdale**. The construction site is alongside the landing strips of **Los Angeles International Airport**. The roller-coaster is the **Viper**, at **Six Flags Magic Mountain, Magic Mountain Parkway**, off I-5, Valencia, north of LA. Movie producer Lee Donowitz's lavish Beverly Ambassador suite filmed in the **Ambassador Hotel, 3400 Wilshire Boulevard**, midtown LA. The fabulously kitsch motel, where Slater and Arquette hide out, is the **Safari Inn, 1911 Olive Boulevard** (*© 818.845.8586*), near Buena Vista, just north of the Disney Studios in Burbank – though the leopardskin interior isn't for real.

Filming also took place at the **Athenaeum**, the dining club of the California Institute of Technology, at **551 South Hill Avenue** in Pasadena (see *Beverly Hills Cop* for details).

TRUMAN SHOW, THE

(1998, dir: Peter Weir)
Jim Carrey, Laura Linney, Ed Harris.
● FLORIDA

Weir's surprise sleeper, with Carrey as Truman Burbank – unwitting star of a 24-hour soap since his birth – needed a slightly stagey location. The town of Seahaven is in actuality one of those slightly creepy planned resorts. Called, generically, **Seaside**, this pastel newtown fantasy of a traditional resort can be found on the Gulf coast of Florida, on I-98 about 30 miles east of Panama City toward Fort Walton Beach.

TWELFTH NIGHT

(1996, dir: Trevor Nunn)
Imogen Stubbs, Helena Bonham Carter, Toby Stephens.
● CORNWALL

Shakespeare's romantic comedy, set in Illyria on Italy's sun-kissed Adriatic coast, is transposed to Cornwall. The two locations are **Lanhydrock**, a 17th century house two and a half miles southeast of Bodmin (*rail: Bodmin Park-*

way) on the B3268 Lostwithiel Road. The great house, containing 42 rooms open to the public, including the kitchen and servants' quarters, is set in extensive formal gardens with clipped yews and parterre. The house is open from the beginning of April to the end of October (except Mondays), the gardens and grounds all year (*© 01208.73320*).

The other location is **Prideaux Place**, an Elizabethan mansion set in extensive grounds above the little port of Padstow, about seven miles from Wadebridge (*rail: Wadebridge*). The house is open to the public for two weeks from Easter Saturday, and then from the Spring Bank Holiday to the end of September (*© 0841.532411 or 0841.532945*).

12 ANGRY MEN

(1957, dir: Sidney Lumet)
Henry Fonda, Lee J Cobb, EG Marshall.
● NEW YORK CITY

County Courthouse, Center Street

Claustrophobic jury room drama, filmed by Lumet at New York's **County Courthouse, 60 Center Street** on the northeast corner of Pearl Street and Foley Square, and inside the building's rotunda.

TWELVE MONKEYS

(1995, dir: Terry Gilliam)
Bruce Willis, Brad Pitt, Madeleine Stowe.
● PENNSYLVANIA; MARYLAND

Bruce Willis travels back to the 20th century: Philadelphia City Hall

Gilliam's best film to date is a dizzyingly time-shifting sci-fi, based on Chris Marker's experimental film, *La Jetée*. Sent back in time, Bruce Willis first appears outside a wintery **City Hall, Penn Square** between Broad and Market Streets, Philadelphia. The WWI battlefield is Baltimore. The asylum where he's subsequently incarcerated is Philadelphia's **Eastern State Penitentiary, 22nd Street** at Fairmount Avenue (*© 215.236.3300; www.easternstate.org*). When Charles Dickens visited the US, there were two things he wanted to see: Niagara Falls and the Eastern State Pen. This architectural wonder, a central hub with seven 'spokes' radiating outwards, was the brainchild of the Quaker movement, a humane alternative to the

The airport: Philadelphia Convention Center

The asylum: Eastern State Penitentiary, 22nd Street, Philadelphia

corrupt, disease-ridden dumping grounds that served as prisons in the 19th century. The guiding principal was solitary confinement. With only the Bible, a little daily work and no human contact whatsoever (even meals were served through holes in the wall so the prisoner could have no contact with the warder), the inmate, freed from temptation, would revert to a natural state of innocence. In fact, they mostly went mad. One who didn't was Al Capone, who resided here for eight months in 1929, in a tastefully decorated cell, with a desk, music and all the luxuries a crime boss could afford. You can see his restored cell on the prison tour. The Eastern State can also be seen in *Return to Paradise* (1998).

Madeleine Stowe gets the blond wig: Wanamaker's Store

The vagrants: Met Theatre, Broad Street

The homeless enclave where Willis battles with vicious vagrants is the old, abandoned **Met Theatre, Broad Street** at Poplar, in a poor area north of Philadelphia city centre. Also used is the once-majestic, now graffiti-covered Greek Revival **Ridgway Library, 901 South Broad Street** at Carpen-

ter Street, also Philadelphia. The library, which had been abandoned for 30 years when the film was made, has since won several awards for adaptive re-use since being renovated to house the Philadelphia High School for Creative and Performing Arts. The vast underground chamber is Philadelphia's abandoned **Delaware Power Station**, where the floodgates were opened for the first time in years.

The elegant home of Christopher Plummer, the scientist father of Brad Pitt, is the **Garrett-Jacobs Mansion, 11 West Vernon Place**, Baltimore (*© 410.539.6914*), home to the Engineers Club.

The future prison is Philadelphia's Richmond Power Station. The Engineering Room where Willis is interrogated, is the No.4 Turbine Basement of the **Westport Power Plant** on the shores of the Patapsco River in Baltimore. The University lecture hall is the **Memorial Hall, North Concourse Drive**, in West Fairmount Park, part of the Centennial Exhibition of 1876 on Benjamin Franklin Parkway towards the Schuylkill River, Philadelphia. The airport, seen in the recurring dream, is actually Philadelphia's spanking new **Convention Center** between 11th and 13th and at Market Street. There are daily tours. The vast department store where Moore buys wigs is **Wanamaker's Department Store, Market Street** at 13th Street (see *Mannequin* for details). The deco cinema where Willis and Moore sit through a 24-hour Hitchcock Fest is the **Senator Theater, 5904 York Road**, in Baltimore. You might recognise it from Barry Levinson's *Avalon*.

20,000 LEAGUES UNDER THE SEA

(1954, dir: Richard Fleischer)
Kirk Douglas, James Mason, Peter Lorre.
● **JAMAICA**

Jules Verne's fantasy about a group of Victorian scientists wrecked at sea and held captive by submariner Captain Nemo, with exotic location scenes filmed in Jamaica.

TWIN PEAKS: FIRE WALK WITH ME

(1992, dir: David Lynch)
Sheryl Lee, Kyle MacLachlan, David Bowie.
● **WASHINGTON STATE**

Disappointing prequel to the weird'n'wonderful TV series. The Double R Diner, home of the legendary cherry pie, is the **Mar T Cafe, 137 West North Bend Way** at North Bend Boulevard in, yes, **North Bend**, on I-90, about twenty miles east of Seattle, Washington State.

The Great Northern Hotel, sadly missing from the movie but heavily featured in the TV show, is the Salish Lodge, 37807 SE Snoqualmie Falls Road, Snoqualmie, Route 202 just north of North Bend. The Roadhouse bar is the **Colonial Inn, Fall City**, northwest of Snoqualmie.

TWISTER

(1996, dir: Jan De Bont)
Bill Paxton, Cary Elwes, Helen Hunt.
● **OKLAHOMA; TEXAS**

FX-laden but flimsy actioner as Paxton and Hunt chase computer generated tornados across the American midwest. Production was hampered by good weather. In order to make the skies look dark, the car interiors had to be compensatingly overlit, leading to temporary eye problems for Paxton. Shades of the industry's old Klieg Light problem from the early days of motion pictures. The stop-off is the **Hot Pit Bar-B-Q, 309 Avenue F**, Del Rio, Texas. A section of the town of **Wakita**, Oklahoma, scheduled for demolition, was 'blown down' for the movie. Warner Bros then spent $250,000 replacing the area with a park, the bricks of which are emblazoned with the legend 'Twister '95'.

TWO EVIL EYES
(1990, dir: George Romero, Dario Argento)
Adrienne Barbeau, EG Marshall, Harvey Keitel.
● PENNSYLVANIA

Portmanteau movie of two Edgar Allen Poe stories, both previously filmed – after a fashion – by Roger Corman: 'The Truth About the Valdemar Case' directed by Romero (previously seen as 'The Facts in the Case of M. Valdemar' section of Corman's *Tales of Terror)*, and 'The Black Cat' by Argento. Both were shot around **Pittsburgh**, Pennsylvania.

TWO MULES FOR SISTER SARA
(1969, dir: Don Siegel)
Clint Eastwood, Shirley MacLaine, Manolo Fabregas.
● MEXICO

Come on, did you really believe Shirley was a nun? Siegel's comedy Western was made on location out in **Cocoyoc**, a small town in the tiny state of Morelos, south of Mexico City. Clint and Shirl hide from the troops, and are threatened by a rattler, in the ruins of a sugarcane plantation, bombed by Zapata during the Revolution.

TWO RODE TOGETHER
(1961, dir: John Ford)
Jame Stewart, Richard Widmark, Shirley Jones.
● TEXAS

Stewart and Widmark attempt to rescue prisoners from the Comanches, in this minor Ford, shot in **Brackettville**, southern Texas, I-90, east of Del Rio and home of the giant set for *The Alamo*.

2001: A SPACE ODYSSEY
(1968, dir: Stanley Kubrick)
Keir Dullea, Gary Lockwood, Leonard Rossiter.
● HERTFORDSHIRE; SCOTLAND; ARIZONA

A giant step forward in the way space movies looked, made mostly in the studio at Borehamwood, Hertfordshire. The first scenes to be shot, the discovery of the giant monolith on the moon, had to be shot at Shepperton, where there was a soundstage large enough. 90 tons of dyed (that is, moon-coloured) sand had to be shipped in. The African landscapes, for the ape scenes, were achieved with a complex system of front projection. The alien landscapes, seen during the trippy ending through the Stargate, are optically distorted shots of the **Hebrides** and of **Monument Valley**, Arizona.

U

U.S. MARSHALS
(1998, dir: Stuart Baird)
Tommy Lee Jones, Wesley Snipes, Robert Downey Jr.
● **NEW YORK CITY; ILLINOIS; KENTUCKY; TENNESSEE**

Disappointing sequel to *The Fugitive*, with Marshall Tommy Lee Jones this time chasing wrongly-accused Wesley Snipes. Filming took place at the **United Nations**, New York, and in Chicago, at **O'Hare International Airport**; **Bohemian National Cemetery**; **Cook County Courthouse**; **St Ann's Hospital**; at **444 North Michigan Avenue**, and also in **West Vienna**, Illinois. Non-Illinois locations include **Benton**, Kentucky, and **Reelfoot Lake**, Tennessee (see *Raintree County* for details).

U TURN
(1997, dir: Oliver Stone)
Sean Penn, Jennifer Lopez, Nick Nolte.
● **ARIZONA**

When bigger projects fell through, Oliver Stone filmed this small, Western-noir. The location is the abandoned mining town of **Superior**, 60 miles from Phoenix, Arizona, which was dressed to look like a town decaying since the sixties. The Waldorf Café, where Penn meets a bizarre assortment of local characters, was a derelict café restored for the movie, though retaining its original name. The climax is at nearby **Apache Leap**, a rock bluff named for an incident in the 1800s when Apache tribesmen leapt to their deaths rather than face capture by the US Cavalry.

UNBELIEVABLE TRUTH, THE
(1990, dir: Hal Hartley)
Adrienne Shelly, Robert Burke, Christopher Cooke.
● **NEW YORK STATE**

Offbeat indie comedy from the master of the form, with Burke as a released murderer returning to his home community, made in **Suffolk County**, eastern Long Island.

UNDEAD, THE
(1957, dir: Roger Corman)
Richard Garland, Pamela Duncan, Allison Hayes.
● **LOS ANGELES**

Interesting early Corman pic, in which a woman is sent back to the Middle Ages when, in a previous life, she was burned as a witch. The medieval scenes make imaginative use of the famous 'Witch's House' in Beverly Hills. The gingerbread fairytale cottage is the **Spadena House, 516 Walden Drive**, off Santa Monica Boulevard. Built

The Middle Ages in Beverly Hills: Spadena House, Walden Drive

in 1921 as combined production offices and movie set for the Irving C Willat movie company, it stood originally at 6509 West Washington Boulevard, Culver City. It was moved to its present location in the thirties.

UNDER CAPRICORN
(1949, dir: Alfred Hitchcock)
Ingrid Bergman, Joseph Cotten, Michael Wilding.
● **CALIFORNIA**

Underrated Hitchcock costume melodrama, in lush colour. Set in Australia, the elaborate flyaway sets – Hitchcock was still experimenting with long unbroken takes after *Rope* – were constructed at MGM Studios in Elstree. The Australian village was on the backlot at the Warners' Ranch in LA. Government House, Sydney, is the pillared frontage of the old Canoga Park High School, since demolished. Filming also at **Los Angeles State and County Arboretum, 301 North Baldwin Avenue**, Arcadia, east of Pasadena (*©* *818.821.3222*). See *Tarzan and the Amazons* for details.

UNDER SIEGE
(1992, dir: Andrew Davis)
Steven Seagal, Tommy Lee Jones, Gary Busey.
● **ALABAMA**

Seagal is the ship's cook who saves the battleship from Jones and Busey in this actioner made aboard the **USS Alabama, Battleship Memorial Park, Mobile Bay, Mobile**, Alabama.

UNDER THE CLOCK (aka *The Clock*)
(1945, dir: Vincente Minnelli)
Judy Garland, Robert Walker, James Gleason.
● **NEW YORK CITY**

Judy Garland meets GI Robert Walker under the clock in the concourse of New York's **Grand Central Station**, and marries him during his 24-hour leave. With the help of a little back-projection, the couple walk in the Egyptian Gallery of the **Metropolitan Museum of Art, Fifth Avenue** at East 82nd Street.

UNFORGIVEN, THE
(1960, dir: John Huston)
Audrey Hepburn, Burt Lancaster, Audie Murphy.
● **MEXICO**

Audrey Hepburn might be an Indian! The Texas plains of 1850 are the flat, open land around **Durango**, central Mexico. 600 miles northwest of Mexico City, this is a favourite locale for Western movies, though generally regarded as 'bad territory'. As one local bigwig opined 'Why don't we get more tourists round here?' he was interrupted by the sound of gunfire. Nuff said.

UNFORGIVEN
(1992, dir: Clint Eastwood)
Clint Eastwood, Gene Hackman, Morgan Freeman.
● **ALBERTA, CANADA; CALIFORNIA**

After a series of forgettable lightweight knockabouts,

Eastwood's dark, introspective Western proved to be an unexpected box-office smash and an Oscar grabber. It was shot in various towns around Calgary, Alberta, Canada: **Brooks**; **Drumheller**; **Stettler**; and **Longview**.

Railroad scenes were shot on the dependable old **Sierra Railroad, Jamestown**, northern California (see the Marx Brothers' *Go West* for details)

UNION PACIFIC
(1939, dir: Cecil B DeMille)
Joel McCrea, Barbara Stanwyck, Akim Tamiroff.
● **OMAHA; NEBRASKA; IOWA; UTAH; CALIFORNIA**

Big-scale (well it is DeMille) account of the building of the railroad. Location filming included Omaha; Nebraska; and neighbouring **Council Bluffs**, just over the state line in Iowa, where the Union Pacific railroad began. A complete reproduction of the town of Cheyenne was built at the Frontier Movie Town in **Kanab**, Utah. The scene of the 'Golden Spike' – the last nail hammered home to complete the railway – was much closer to Hollywood, at **Canoga Park** in the San Fernando Valley, north LA. The actual spike, on loan from its vault at the Wells Fargo Bank in San Francisco, was used.

UNION STATION
(1950, dir: Rudolph Maté)
William Holden, Barry Fitzgerald, Nancy Olson.
● **CHICAGO; LOS ANGELES**

Kidnappers use Chicago's famous railway station as the ransom drop. Part of the fifties trend for getting out of the studio and into real locations. Well, almost. Although there is some filming at **Union Station, 210 South Canal Street, Chicago**, most of the time it's **Union Station, 800 North Alameda Street**, downtown Los Angeles.

UNIVERSAL SOLDIER
(1992, dir: Roland Emmerich)
Dolph Lundgren, Jean-Claude Van Damme, Ally Walker.
● **MEXICO; ARIZONA**

Sci-fi, with dead soldiers revived for more active service, made in Mexico; and in Arizona, at **Clarkdale**; **Verde Valley**; **Kingman** and **Prescott**.

UNTAMED HEART
(1993, dir: Tony Bill)
Christian Slater, Marisa Tomei, Rosie Perez.
● **MINNESOTA**

Christian Slater gets a baboon's heart in this offbeat drama, set in **Minneapolis**. Slater rescues Tomei from rapists in the park on **Main Street** along Minneapolis Riverplace. The coffee shop they work in is **Jim's Coffee Shop and Bakery, 328 Central Avenue East**, Minneapolis.

UNTOUCHABLES, THE
(1987, dir: Brian De Palma)
Kevin Costner, Sean Connery, Robert De Niro.
● **CHICAGO; MONTANA**

Terrific return to form for De Palma, and deserved Oscar

nominations for production design and costumes as the film recreates Prohibition era Chicago on location.

The café blown up by the protection racketeers' bomb at the opening was under the 'el' (elevated train) in Wrigleyville, north of town at the junction of **West Roscoe and North Clark Streets**. Just a couple of blocks south of Wrigley Field, the same location can be seen as John Candy's home in the John Hughes-Chris Columbus comedy *Only the Lonely*.

Blowing up the café: West Roscoe and North Clark Streets

Eliot Ness' police HQ is the **Rookery Building, 202 South La Salle Street**. Built in 1886, its lobby was remodelled in 1907 by Frank Lloyd Wright. It's recently been renovated. South La Salle Street, with its vista leading down to the Chicago Board of Trade Building, is prominently featured,

The Untouchables' HQ: Rookery Building, South La Salle Street

Ness meets Irish cop Malone: Michigan Avenue Bridge

The poster image: South La Salle Street

373

Capone's hotel: Chicago Theatre, North State Street

The lobby of Capone's hotel: Roosevelt University

Capone toasts Pagliacci: Preston Bradley Hall

The exterior of the much-used Chicago Theatre, North State Street

The bloody banquet: Blackstone Hotel, South Michigan Avenue

Capone's Lexington Hotel exterior: Roosevelt University

Ness wises up to Frank Nitti: The Grand Army of the Republic Rotunda

and is the image used on the movie poster. The liquor raid on the US Post Office is here, opposite the Rookery, at the **Continental Illinois Bank and Trust Company, 231 South La Salle Street**.

Ness meets up with incorruptible Irish cop Malone on the lower pedestrian deck of the **Michigan Avenue Bridge**, another familiar location you can also see in *Rent-a-Cop* and *The Package*. Malone's apartment is an in unchanged block of terraced houses, **1634 South Racine Avenue** at Harrison

The Lexington Hotel, where Al Capone kept a suite, is no longer in its original state. For the movie, the interior is a conflation of two different locations. The first view of the Lexington, with the newspaper being delivered to Capone in bed, is the upper foyer of the **Chicago Theater, 175 North State Street** at East Lake Street. The exterior of this movie house, with its convenient 'Chicago' sign, is the ubiquitous scene-setting shot for countless Windy City movies, but *The Untouchables* utilises its lavish Baroque interior. The Lexington's lower lobby is the foyer of **Roosevelt University, 430 South Michigan Avenue** – you can peek inside at the grand staircase, where Ness confronts Capone after the murder of his fellow Untouchables.

The station shoot-out: Union Station

The banquet scene, where Capone gives a pep talk on teamwork before braining a freelancer with a baseball bat, was filmed in the ballroom of the 1910 **Blackstone Hotel, 636 South Michigan Avenue** at East Balbo Drive (© *312.427.4300*) overlooking Grant Park.

The opera house lobby, where Capone pleads his innocence to the press, is the Grand Staircase of the **Chicago Public Library Cultural Center, 78 East Washington Street**. The staircase, of white Carrara marble inlaid with multi-coloured glass mosaic work, can be seen inside the main southern entrance on Washington Street (© *312.269.2900, free admission to the public daily except Sundays*). It leads up to the **Preston Bradley Hall** on the third floor, with its spectacular 38-foot glass dome – supposedly the largest Tiffany dome in the world, renovated in the 1970s and worth an estimated $35 million. This is the spot where Capone toasts Pagliacci after the murder of Malone.

The Center houses another grand glass dome, in the **Grand Army of the Republic Rotunda**, located on the second floor of the northern entrance on Randolph Street. The Rotunda walls are of Knoxville Pink Marble from Tennessee, the dome Renaissance-style stained glass. This is the courtroom lobby where Ness finds Malone's address in Frank Nitti's matchbook. The subsequent chase leads up to the Cultural Center's roof, from which Nitti is finally thrown.

The set-piece shootout, with De Palma paying homage to the Odessa Steps sequence from *Battleship Potemkin*, was staged in Chicago's imposing **Union Station, 210 South Canal Street**.

A non-Chicago location is the shootout with the rum-runners at the bridge, which uses **Hardy Bridge**, near **Great Falls** on the Missouri in Montana.

The real Eliot Ness operated out of Room 308 in the Transportation Building, 608 South Dearborn Street, still standing but now converted into stores and apartments.

URBAN COWBOY

(1980, dir: James Bridges)
John Travolta, Debra Winger, Scott Glenn.
● **TEXAS**

The C&W honky tonk with the famous mechanical bull, where John Travolta hangs out and finds Debra Winger, was Gilley's, 4500 Spencer Highway, Pasadena, southeast of Houston, East Texas. Don't bother to go looking though, as the bar has since burned down.

URBAN LEGEND

(1998, dir: Jamie Blanks)
Jared Leto, Alicia Witt, Rebecca Gayheart.
● **ONTARIO, CANADA**

College kids are offed in the style of various urban myths in this addition to the ironic-slasher genre. The New England college, Stanley Hall, Melbourne, New Hampshire, is the **University of Toronto** campus, smack in the middle of the city of Toronto, Ontario. The Frat house is **Lakeshore Psychiatric Hospital**.

Stanley Hall, New Hampshire: University of Toronto

USUAL SUSPECTS, THE

(1995, dir: Bryan Singer)
Gabriel Byrne, Chazz Palminteri, Kevin Spacey.
● **LOS ANGELES**

Bryan Singer's dazzling, convoluted who-dun-what was shot largely in the old **Herald Examiner Building, 1111 South Broadway**, downtown Los Angeles. The old newspaper offices supplied the interior of the police station, while the lobby became the New York restaurant for

Interior filming: Herald Examiner Building, South Broadway, downtown LA

Gabriel Byrne at the opening. The building was designed, in 1912, by Julia Morgan, the architect of William Randolph Hearst's San Simeon estate (see *Citizen Kane* for details of Hearst's

folly). It was inspired by the California Building from the 1893 Chicago World's Fair, and was home to the *Herald Examiner* newspaper. It has been empty, used only as an occasional movie location, since the paper closed. The huge bell, where the suspects meet up with Redfoot, is the **Korean Bell of Friendship, Angels Gate Park, South Gaffey Street** in San Pedro. The bell, presented by Korea during the US bicentennial celebrations in 1976, is on a breathtaking wild bluff overlooking the harbour of San Pedro to the east and the Palos Verdes Peninsula to the west.

The meeting with Redfoot: Korean Bell of Friendship, Angels Gate Park, San Pedro

V

VALENTINO

(1977, dir: Ken Russell)
Rudolf Nureyev, Leslie Caron, Michelle Phillips.
● SPAIN; BUCKINGHAMSHIRE; DORSET

Ken Russell's overlong biopic of the silent star does have its great moments, and the mix of luscious deco sets and imaginatively chosen locations makes it look a million dollars. Set, of course, in the US, the movie was shot in the UK and Spain.

The filming of *The Sheik* and *The Four Horsemen of the Apocalypse* takes place at **The Dunes**, a stretch of desert twenty miles inland from Almeria on the south coast of Spain. Many of the spaghetti Westerns were made at **Almeria**, and it's on one of these Western street sets that Valentino has a showdown with studio head Jesse Lasky, while a parallel showdown is played out in the background. The set for Lasky's office was built inside the gorilla house of **Barcelona Zoo, Parc de la Ciutadella**, in order to incorporate Snowflake, the unique albino gorilla.

The beach, where Natasha Rambova and the unemployed Valentino agree to an advertising deal, is at **S'Agaro**, on the Costa Brava. It leads to plugging 'Mineralava' beauty products at a tango demonstration, filmed in the gilt splendour of the **Blackpool Tower Ballroom**, Blackpool, on the Lancashire coast. And it's in the **Blackpool Tower Circus** that Valentino fights a boxing match with the editor of the *New York Evening News*.

Valentino's mansion is the turn-of-the-century **East Cliff Hall, the Russell-Cotes Art Gallery and Museum, East Cliff**, overlooking Poole Bay in Bournemouth (*© 01202.451800, www.russell-cotes.bournemouth.gov.uk*).

VALLEY OF THE DOLLS

(1967, dir: Mark Robson)
Barbara Parkins, Patty Duke, Susan Hayward.
● LOS ANGELES; NEW YORK CITY

Jacqueline Susann's soapy melodrama about an innocent actress heading down the path of drink and drugs is set in New York and LA. When smalltown girl Barbara Parkins leaves home to find work in the big city, she wisely stays at the Martha Washington Hotel for Women. This New York institution opened in 1903 to provide reputable accommodation for single women travellers in the city. It closed down, only to be reopened as the (mixed) **Thirty Thirty Hotel, 30 East 30th Street** between Madison and Fifth Avenues, Murray Hill.

The sweet little New England town Barbara Parkins hails from, and finally returns to, is **Mount Kisco**, about 30 miles north of New York City.

VALMONT

(1989, dir: Milos Forman)
Colin Firth, Annette Bening, Meg Tilly.
● FRANCE

One of those odd coincidences that sees two versions of the same story being filmed simultaneously. This version of de Laclos' *Les Liaisons Dangereuses*, with double the budget of Stephen Frears' enormously successful *Dangerous Liaisons*, went into production first and wrapped last, but ultimately disappeared in the wake of the smaller film. It was made in Paris, Caen and Bordeaux. Mme de Rosemonde's estate is **Chateau de la Motte-Tilly** (*© 03.25.39.99.67*), an 18th century chateau at Nogent-sur-Seine, about 50 miles east of Paris. The opera house, where Valmont first meets the innocent Cecile, is the **Opera Comique** in Paris. Interiors were shot in the **Musée Nissim de Camondo, 63 rue de Monceau**, a mansion on the edge of Parc Monceau in Paris (*© 45.63.26.32; metro: Villiers*) and the **Hotel des Ambassadeurs de Hollande, 47 rue Vieille-du-Temple** in the Marais district of Paris – where Beaumarchais wrote *The Marriage of Figaro*. Strangely, this splendid mansion has never been the Dutch embassy and, sadly, it's not open to the public.

The horse stables are **Musée Vivant du Cheval**, the Living Museum of the Horse, at the **Chateau of Chantilly** (see *A View to a Kill* for details). Filming also took place at **Chateau de Versailles**, and the **Abbaye aux Hommes** in Caen, built in 1064 for William, Duke of Normandy. The abbey is currently used as Caen's town hall (*guided tours; © 33.02.31.30.42.81*); **Meaux**, an old town about 35 miles east of Paris on the River Marne, and in **Bordeaux**.

VAMPIRE LOVERS, THE

(1970, dir: Roy Ward Baker)
Ingrid Pitt, Peter Cushing, Pippa Steele.
● HERTFORDSHIRE

Softcore vamping in a late-period Hammer filming of J Sheridan Le Fanu's lesbian vampire novella *Carmilla*. Peter Cushing's palatial home, where Marcilla first stays, is

George Cole's mansion: Wall Hall College, Aldenham

Moor Park Golf Club, Anson Walk, on the A404, northwest of Northwood (seen also in the colourful period romance *Jassy*). George Cole's rather more modest mansion is **Wall Hall College** (now the University of Hertfordshire), north of Aldenham, to the northeast of Watford – seen as the psychiatric clinic in Hammer's Bette Davis shocker *The Nanny*.

VAMPIRES (aka *John Carpenter's Vampires*)

(1998, dir: John Carpenter)
James Woods, Daniel Baldwin, Sheryl Lee.
● NEW MEXICO

John Carpenter's southwest vampires are closer to the bloodsucking family of Kathryn Bigelow's *Near Dark* than the mittel-European nobility of Hammer films. The movie is shot around the red deserts of **Santa Fe**, New Mexico. The Sun God Motel is a set built around the existing sign of a motel that burned down several years ago. Slayer Daniel Baldwin and on-the-change vamp victim Sheryl Lee hole up at the **Plaza Hotel, 230 Plaza, Las Vegas** (*℄ 505.425.3591*), east of Santa Fe. The hotel already has a footnote in film history. In 1913 it became the HQ of Romaine Fielding's Lubin Film Company, and later became home to silent Western star Tom Mix, who made many of his movies in the Las Vegas area, occasionally using the Plaza as a location. The fictitious town of Santiago is **Cerrillos**, a small desert town on I-14 between Santa Fe and Albuquerque, previously used in *Young Guns*.

VAMPIRES IN VENICE (aka *Nosferatu in Venice/Nosferatu A Venezia/Vampire in Venice*)
(1986, dir: Augusto Caminito)
Klaus Kinski, Christopher Plummer, Donald Pleasence.
● **VENICE, ITALY**

Nosferatu strikes: Chiesa di Santa Maria Valverde, Camppo dell'Abbazia

This slow, uneventful sequel to Werner Herzog's *Nosferatu* exploits the dank Gothic mistinesss of Venice so well that the city seems the natural home of the vampire movie. The home of the Princess, where vampire-hunter Christopher Plummer comes to stay, is **Palazzo Barbaro, Canal Grande** at Ponte dell'Accademia (seen also in Richard Attenborough's Hemingway pic *In Love and War*, and *Wings of the Dove*). Nosferatu prowls the misty **Piazza San Marco**, while one of his victims plummets dreamily from the **Campanile**. The funeral of the Princess heads for **San Michele in Isola** (which is also seen in *Wings of the Dove*), the cemetery island of the Venetian lagoon. Nosferatu sets up home at **Lazzaretto Vecchio**, once the hospital and graveyard for plague victims, now a dogs' home, scheduled for redevelopment. He bloodily feasts on a victim at **Chiesa di Santa Maria Valverde, Campo dell'Abbazia**.

VANISHING, THE
(1993, dir: George Sluizer)
Jeff Bridges, Kiefer Sutherland, Sandra Bullock.
● **WASHINGTON STATE; WYOMING; CALIFORNIA**

What's surprising is that this Hollywood remake of *Spoorloos*, which throws out the elements that made the original so great, was made by the same director. The locale is changed to *Twin Peaks* territory, around the Seattle area of the Pacific northwest. Kiefer Sutherland and Sandra Bullock drive through the blasted landscape of **Mount St Helens**, Washington State, but the tunnel, where they run out of gas, is on I-14/16/20, six miles west of **Cody**, leading to Yellowstone National Park, Wyoming. The gas station, where Bullock disappears, is the **Texaco Station, 742 SW Mount Si Boulevard, North Bend**, off I-90. Jeff Bridges' lakeside cabin is at **Camp Omache, 24225 Woods Creek Road, Snohomish**, on Lake Hughes near **Monroe** in the Cascade Mountains, Washington State. He

accosts women at Seattle's famous **Pike Place Market**. There was filming also in California, at **234 North Canyon Boulevard, Monrovia**, east of Pasadena.

VANISHING AMERICAN, THE
(1925, dir: George B Seitz)
Richard Dix, Lois Wilson, Noah Beery.
● **LOS ANGELES; ARIZONA**

History of the American Indian. Much of the movie was shot on **Catalina Island**, 20 miles off the coast of LA. The author of the original story, Western writer Zane Grey, came here with the crew and took up residence for 20 years in Avalon, the island's only town. The home he built is now the Zane Grey Pueblo Hotel, 199 Chimes Tower Road. Grey's contract stipulated that films of his stories must be shot at the specific locations he mentioned, thus the second unit filmed at **Monument Valley** (many years before it was discovered by John Ford) and at the **Betatakin Cliff Dwellings**, off I-160, west of Kayenta, northern Arizona.

VANISHING POINT
(1971, dir: Richard C Sarafian)
Barry Newman, Cleavon Little, Dean Jagger
● **UTAH; NEVADA; COLORADO**

If the studio suits sat down to assemble a post-*Easy Rider* cliché compendium, this is the market-led package they would have put together. Ex-cop, ex-racing driver, ex-surfer, turned drugs courier, Barry Newman races across the desert, establishing a psychic link with blind, soul DJ Cleavon Little, while flashbacks crop up with the regularity of ad breaks. Compensation comes in the form of the fabulous dusty wastes of the Nevada and Utah deserts. Newman's journey begins from Denver, Colorado, and crosses three central counties of Utah: Lander, Nye and Esmerelda. Blind DJ Super Soul broadcasts from the now-abandoned **Goldfield Hotel, Goldfield**, a near-ghost town in Utah. The small town where the cop car overturns is **Salina**, Utah. The towns Newman whizzes through are **Thompson Springs; Green River** and **Wendover**, Utah; **Glenwood Spring** and **Grand Junction**, Colorado; and **Tonopah; Elko** and **Austin**, Nevada. The climactic smash-up is at **Cisco**, on I-70, near Moab, Utah.

VELVET GOLDMINE
(1998, dir: Todd Haynes)
Jonathan Rhys Meyers, Ewan McGregor, Christian Bale.
● **LONDON**

Brave, but ultimately botched, fantasia on the seventies glam-rock phenomenon, structured as a pastiche of *Citizen Kane*, with Rhys Meyers a pouting Bowie-figure and McGregor an amalgam of Iggy Pop and Kurt Cobain. The bizarre opening, with aliens depositing baby Oscar Wilde on a Dublin doorstep in 1854, is **Elder Street, Spitalfields**, E1. Most of the rock concert scenes used the **Brixton Academy, 211 Stockwell Road, SW9**. Christian Bale's 1984 quest to New York to trace the disappeared rock star takes him no further than the sixties concrete canyons of **Croydon**. The orgy is at **Mentmore Towers**, the Gothic pile at the village of Mentmore in Buckinghamshire (the exterior of the Long Island mansion where Tom Cruise attends the bizarre orgy in Stanley Kubrick's *Eyes Wide Shut*; see Terry Gilliam's *Brazil* for details). The pop video is shot at the north end of Notting Hill's **Portobello Road**. Filming also took place at the **Bedford Arms, 409 Clapham Road**, SW9, Balham.

VERTIGO

(1958, dir: Alfred Hitchcock)

James Stewart, Kim Novak, Barbara Bel Geddes.

● CALIFORNIA

Starting out as as a conventional enough thriller, with ex-cop Scottie hired by worried husband Gavin Elster to keep an eye on the bizarre behaviour of his wife, Madeleine, acrophobia segues imperceptibly into the fear of sex and of death as Scottie becomes Hitchcock-by-proxy, recreating and controlling his unattainable object of desire.

Hitchcock signals the sudden flare-up of irrational passion by disrupting the pastel colour scheme and setting Scottie's first glimpse of Madeleine against the rich red silk interior of Ernie's Restaurant, near Washington Street in the Jackson Square Historic District. One of Hitch's own favourite San Francisco hangouts, Ernie's had been serving up *haute cuisine* to the well-heeled since 1934, but finally closed its doors only to reopen as the **Essex Supper Club, 537 Montgomery Street** (© *415.397.5969*). Although you'll recognise the bar area where James Stewart falls for Kim Novak, the scarlet Victorian decor was replaced in the 1980s by tastefully anodyne pink and no longer looks like an elegant Parisian bordello.

A few blocks southwest, on the summit of the appropriately named Nob Hill is Elster's imposing apartment block, from which the smitten Scottie tails Madeleine Elster. Its unmistakable entrance court guarded by elaborate lamps, the 277-room **Brocklebank Apartments, 1000 Mason Street** at Sacramento Street, is a major location for Gene Wilder's 1984 *The Woman in Red*, and also features in the TV adaptation of Armistead Maupin's *Tales of the City*.

There's nothing left to see on the northwest corner of Gough and Eddy Streets, where Scottie trails Mrs Elster to McKittrick's Hotel, the old house of long-dead Carlotta Valdes (the area, north of the Civic Center district, has been redeveloped, and the elaborate Gothic St Paulus Lutheran Church dating from 1872, which you can see behind James Stewart, was recently destroyed by fire). You can, though, visit the gleaming white-pillared palace in which Madeleine sits spellbound by Carlotta's portrait. Situated between China and Ocean Beaches on San Francisco's northwesterly tip, it's the **Palace of the Legion of Honor, Legion of Honor Drive** in Lincoln Park (*admission charge*; © *415.750.3659*). A twin of the Legion d'Honneur in Paris, the gallery houses a rather

The portrait of Carlotta: Palace of the Legion of Honor, Lincoln Park

more impressive collection of paintings than Carlotta Valdes' kitschy portrait, including works by Rembrandt, Titian, Monet, Renoir and Degas along with one of the world's finest collections of Rodin sculptures.

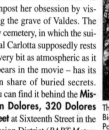
Scottie and Madeleine at the seashore: Seventeen Mile Drive

Madeleine continues to signpost her obsession by visiting the grave of Valdes. The tiny cemetery, in which the suicidal Carlotta supposedly rests – every bit as atmospheric as it appears in the movie – has its own share of buried secrets. You can find it behind the **Mission Dolores, 320 Dolores Street** at Sixteenth Street in the Mission District (*BART Metro: 16th Street-Mission*). Once you've seen the ornate exterior, you can forget the pompous basilica which was grafted on next door in 1913, the real interest here is the Misión San Francisco De Asis, completed in 1791. One of the 21 California missions established by the Spanish in the 18th century and the oldest intact survivor, its four-foot thick adobe walls having withstood the worst assaults of San Andreas, the mission of St Francis of Assisi is not only the oldest building in San Francisco but gives the city its name. Visit the cool, dark chapel interior with its unique Spanish-Mexican decoration and ceiling painting based on the designs of the Ramaytush people – dubbed Costanoans ("coast dwellers") by the 'kindly' Spanish Franciscans who occupied their land, resettled them and oversaw their complete extinction. By 1850 there was only one Ramaytush left alive. A small museum records sanitised highlights of the mission's history – for a while in the 1840s and 1850s under Mexican rule it became a hotel and a gambling den, and bullfights were held on the plaza where Dolores Street now stands. The museum exits into the cemetery itself. Don't be fooled by the size. Over 5,500 of the native people are buried here in a common grave, commemorated by a single stone shrine. The grander monuments record the founding Father Palou, the city's bigwigs and the, mainly Irish, immigrants who poured into the area after the Gold Rush.

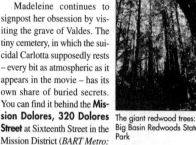
The giant redwood trees: Big Basin Redwoods State Park

Back northwest of the city is the granite sea wall beneath the southern anchoring of the Golden Gate Bridge at **Fort Point, Marine Drive** off Long Avenue, the spot where Madeleine takes a reckless plunge into the notoriously treacherous waters of the Bay. The site is named for the brick fort, built in the 1850s to defend the city from sea attack long before the bridge was conceived. It now houses a museum of militaria (© *415.556.1693*).

Falling for the possessed woman act, Scottie rescues Madeleine and takes her back to his apartment. Scottie's

The mission: San Juan Bautista

The interior of the mission: San Juan Bautista

The stables: San Juan Bautista

The inquest: Plaza Hall, San Juan Bautista

home stands, virtually unchanged, at **900 Lombard Street** on the corner of Jones Street, just at the foot of the series of famous hairpin bends on the 'Crookedest Street in the World'. Looking east along Lombard Street you can't miss Telegraph Hill, and crowning it, the **Coit Memorial Tower, Telegraph Hill Boulevard**, the l a n d m a r k Madeleine later uses to find her way back to Scottie's apartment. The tower was built 'to beautify San Francisco' with a bequest left to the city by Lillie Hitchcock Coit (no relation), a Bay City pioneer woman apparently fascinated by firemen (as a girl she was made an honorary member of the Knickerbocker No.5 Fire Company). It's claimed, presumably by people unfamiliar with the works of Freud, that the monument is intended to resemble a firehose nozzle. If your ambition is to visit the top of a reinforced concrete tower perched on the summit of a steep hill in a notorious earthquake zone, you can take the elevator to a 210-foot observation deck, which does actually give wonderful views of the Bay (*admission charge*).

Over the Golden Gate Bridge, about 15 miles north on Shoreline Drive, Mill Valley, off Route 1, are Muir Woods (*open 8am-sunset, © 415.388.2595*), the Giant Redwood grove, home to some of the largest and oldest living creatures on the earth, *Sequoia Sempervirens* – "Always green, ever living" – supposedly where Madeleine gets the heebie-jeebies contemplating the past. Although it's here, near the visitor centre, that you can find a section of tree trunk

on which significant dates in history are recorded, the actual filming location was **Big Basin Redwoods State Park, 21600 Big Basin Way** – Route 236 – at Boulder Creek (*© 408.338.6132*) off Pacific Coast Highway 1 south of San Francisco toward Santa Cruz. The seashore, where Scottie follows the apparently distraught Madeleine, is **Cypress Point** on **Seventeen-Mile Drive**, on the wild Monterey Peninsula.

When Madeleine finally succumbs to her suicidal impulse, Scottie suffers a nervous breakdown, recuperating in a sanitarium at **351 Buena Vista Avenue East**. Overwhelmed by his own obsession, he refashions lookalike actress Judy Barton into Madeleine's dead image. For the transformation of Judy back into Madeleine, Hitchcock pulls off one of his dazzling visual coups, filling the seedy hotel room with an unearthly green neon glow. Although the film's Hotel Empire has undergone a name change and a major facelift, you'll still recognise Judy's lodging. Not only is it now quite posh, it also houses one of the city's top cabaret spots, the Plush Room. You can see the **York Hotel** at **940 Sutter Street** (*© 415.885.6800*) between Hyde and Leavenworth Streets just west of the downtown area.

The movie's climax returns to the scene of Madeleine's suicide/murder. About 90 miles south of San Francisco, just east from Route 101, is the quiet little town of San Juan Bautista, home to a clutch of beautifully restored period buildings preserved as a State Historic Park. On the town's central plaza you'll find not only the mission, but the **Plaza Stables** Madeleine claims to remember from a previous existence, and **Plaza Hall**, the courtroom where the inquest is held (though, once again, the interior was recreated in the studio). The 19th century **Mission San Juan Bautista** is the largest of the Spanish missions and houses a small museum, open daily from 10am to 4pm. Don't expect to see the bell-tower, from which Judy finally plunges to her death. The church's tower had collapsed many years before and the movie's climax makes use of a superimposed painting.

VICTIM

(1961, dir: Basil Dearden)
Dirk Bogarde, Sylvia Syms, Peter McEnery.

● **LONDON**

Brave, for its time, attempt to encourage reform of the UK's anti-homosexual laws, with this melodrama about the blackmail of a bisexual barrister. Many of the locations are

The West End gay bar: The Salisbury, St Martin's Lane

around London's West End, including the gleaming glass-and-brass **Salisbury** pub, in St Martin's Lane (where Maggie Smith stayed in *Travels With My Aunt*), which at the time was one of the capital's most famous theatrical gay bars. Charles Lloyd Pack's gents hairdresser's was on **Cambridge Circus**.

VIDEODROME
(1982, dir: David Cronenberg)
James Woods, Deborah Harry, Sonja Smits.
● ONTARIO, CANADA

A TV signal induces the growth of a new organ within the brain in another of the director's explorations of the blurring borderline between the human body and new technology. If it's Cronenberg, chances are it's Toronto. It is. The 'Spectacular Optical' presentation, where James Woods rebels and blows away the Videodrome chief, is at the **Harbour Castle Westin 1 Harbour Square**, Toronto (℃ 416.869.1600).

VIEW TO A KILL, A
(1985, dir: John Glen)
Roger Moore, Christopher Walken, Grace Jones.
● CALIFORNIA; FRANCE; BERKSHIRE; SUSSEX; ICELAND; SWITZERLAND

Bond's leap onto the pleasure boat: Pont Alexandre III

Fourteenth in the mainstream Bond series uses much the same plot as the 1978 *Superman*, with electronics wiz Zorin attempting to trigger the San Andreas fault into action and flood California's Silicon Valley... or something.

The pre-credits Siberia teaser is actually **Glacier Lake**, on the

Bond meets CIA agent Jack Lee: Fisherman's Wharf, San Francisco

southeast tip of the huge **Vatnajökull Glacier** and the tiny hamlet of **Höfn** on the southeast coast of Iceland. You can visit the glacier on a trip from the Hotel Höfn, 781 Hornefjöur (℃ *478.1240*), though be warned, the Vatnajökull volcano erupted under the ice-sheet in 1996. The chase continues at a larger glacier, the **Vadretta di Scerscen Inferiore**

Zorin's Silicon Valley mine: Amberley Chalk Pits Museum

on the Swiss/Italian border.

M's London HQ is now in **Whitehall**. Bond first checks out Zorin at **Ascot Racecourse**, on the A330 five miles south of Windsor, Berkshire.

In Paris, Bond meets up with the unlikely French 'tec M. Aubergine, who's killed by a butterfly in the **Restaurant Jules Verne**, the pricey eaterie on the second floor of the Eiffel Tower (℃ *01.45.55.61.44*). After Zorin's henchwoman, May Day, makes a spectacular leap from the Tower, there's a car chase culminating in Bond's leap into the Seine pleasure boat from the **Pont Alexandre III**

Stacey's mansion: Dunsmuir House and Gardens

(a wonderfully over-the-top confection also used in *Anastasia* and Toulouse Lautrec biopic *Moulin Rouge*).

Zorin's estate is the 18th century (he says it's 16th century, but that's a Bond villain for you) **Chateau Chantilly**, twenty miles north of Paris on the N16 in the Picardy region. The dazzling chateau, open to the public (℃ *01.44.57.08.00, admission charge*), is set among gardens and lakes to the west of the town of Chantilly. It's a 30-minute walk from Chantilly-Gouvieux station, reached from the Gare du Nord. The racecourse here is the spectacular **Piste d'Avilly**. Bond pits himself against Zorin in a steeplechase in the Forest of Chantilly, while Sir Godfrey gets garotted in a carwash in the city of Chantilly itself.

Bond follows Zorin to San Francisco, where he meets CIA agent Jack Lee at bright but touristy **Fisherman's Wharf** on the bay. The State Office Building, where Zorin's corrupt official, Howe, has his Divisions of Oil and Mines office is **San Francisco City Hall, Van Ness Avenue** at McAllister Street. This 1915 domed building, modelled on St Peter's in Rome, is no stranger to movies – *Dirty Harry* seems to spend an inordinate amount of time being insubordinate to city officials here. The moviemakers were allowed plenty of licence to simulate Zorin's burning down of the building, including fitting out the balconies with gas jets. The fire-truck chase hares off down **Market Street** to the **Lefty O'Doul Drawbridge** on Third Street at China Basin (just past the Burger Island where Clint uttered the immortal line "Go ahead, make my day" in *Sudden Impact*). Lefty O'Doul, if you're wondering, was an old-time ball-player. The home of oil heiress Stacey Sutton is **Dunsmuir House and Gardens, 2960 Peralta Oaks Court, Oakland**, (℃ *510.615.5555, guided tours, April to September*) over the bay from San Fran. Zorin's Main Strike, the abandoned silver mine in Silicon Valley isn't in California at all, or even in the US. You can see the entrance to the mine at the 36-acre, open-air **Amberley Chalk Pits Museum** (℃ *01798.831370, admission charge, www.amberleymuseum.co.uk*) opposite Amberley Station in west Sussex.

VIKINGS, THE
(1958, dir: Richard Fleischer)
Kirk Douglas, Tony Curtis, Janet Leigh.
● NORWAY; FRANCE

Douglas and Curtis slug it out in this enjoyably butch Norse saga, shot on location in Norway, near to **Bergen**. Sea battles were filmed in the **Hardanger Fjord**. The castle is the 14th century **Fort Lalatte**, on the north Brittany coast between St Brieuc and St Malo.

VILLAGE OF THE DAMNED
(1960, dir: Wolf Rilla)
George Sanders, Barbara Shelley, Michael Gwynn.
● **HERTFORDSHIRE**

Creepy sci-fi horror, from John Wyndham's *The Midwich Cuckoo*s, with a clutch of unemotional, super-intelligent kids born simultaneously in a small English village. The damned village of Midwich is **Letchmore Heath**, just east of Watford and, conveniently, within four miles of MGM's Borehamwood Studios.

The 'village of the damned': Letchmore Heath, Hertfordshire

VILLAGE OF THE DAMNED
(1995, dir: John Carpenter)
Christopher Reeve, Kirstie Alley, Michael Paré.
● **CALIFORNIA**

The 'village of the damned': Point Reyes Station

John Carpenter's disappointing remake transposes the action to the same northern California locations he used for *The Fog*, which also happens to be the director's backyard. This time Midwich is the town of **Point Reyes Station**. More scenes filmed at nearby **Inverness**, and the picnic scene was shot at nearby **Nicasio**.

VILLAIN
(1971, dir: Michael Tuchner)
Richard Burton, Ian McShane, Joss Ackland.
● **LONDON**

Liz Taylor pulling pints: The Assembly House, Kentish Town Road

Horribly miscast Burton overacts as a mother-fixated gay East End gangster (not a million miles away from real life thug Ronnie Kray) in this violent thriller, filmed on location around London, largely in the **Nine Elms** area. The pub is the **Assembly House, Kentish Town Road** opposite Kentish Town tube station. A great publicity shot has Liz Taylor, visiting Burton on location, pulling pints behind the bar.

VIRGIN SPRING, THE
(1959, dir: Ingmar Bergman)
Max von Sydow, Gunnel Lindblom, Brigitta Valberg.
● **SWEDEN**

Von Sydow kills the three men who raped and murdered his daughter, at which point a spring bubbles up from the spot on which she died, in this odd medieval fable. It was loosely remade by Wes Craven, in 1972, as the notorious *Last House on the Left*. Bergman's original was shot in the forest around **Styggforsen**, in Dalarna, not far from Rattvik, central Sweden.

VIRIDIANA
(1961, dir: Luis Buñuel)
Silvia Pinal, Francisco Rabal, Fernando Rey.
● **SPAIN**

After years of exile in Mexico, Buñuel was accused of selling out when he returned to Spain to film this story of novice nun Pinal, whose noble intentions go wildly awry when she's sent to stay with her lecherous uncle. As it turned out, the film was immediately banned in Spain – after having won the Palme d'Or at Cannes, where it was mistakenly assumed to be the official Spanish entry.

The Catholic church declared it sacrilegious and blasphemous. Franco had egg all over his face. Fernando Rey's grand home, where the beggars, charitably installed by Pinal, stage their gloriously anarchic orgy, is a beautiful estate just outside Madrid. The 'Last Supper' scene was reproduced in Robert Altman's *M*A*S*H*.

VISITEURS DU SOIR, LES (aka *The Devil's Envoys*)
(1942, dir: Marcel Carné)
Arletty, Jules Berry, Marie Déa.
● **FRANCE**

A strange medieval fable, made in France under the German Occupation, with the Devil sending henchmen to Earth to corrupt two lovers. Intended as a political metaphor. The village is the beautiful **Tourette-Sur-Loup**, above Nice, in the south of France.

VIVA LAS VEGAS (aka *Love in Las Vegas*)
(1964, dir: George Sidney)
Elvis Presley, Ann-Margret, Cesare Danova.
● **LOS ANGELES; NEVADA**

Presley (apparently unknown in Vegas) enters a talent contest to pay for his racing car. The film was, as usual for Presley pictures, mostly shot in Hollywood, though there is some real Vegas. The 'Folies Bergere' number filmed at the **Hotel Tropicana, 3801 Las Vegas Boulevard South** at Tropicana Avenue. Last, fanciest and most expensive of the Strip hotels to be built in the fifties, the Tropicana houses the Strip's longest-running revue, *Les Folies Bergere*, which opened in 1959.

VIVEMENT DIMANCHE (aka *Confidentially Yours/Finally Sunday*)
(1982, dir: François Truffaut)
Fanny Ardant, Jean-Louis Trintignant, Philippe Laudenbach.
● **FRANCE**

Black and white Truffaut *film noir*, shot at the charming old town of **Hyeres**, lying beneath the ruins of a medieval fortress, about twelve miles east of Toulon on the Provence coast, France.

VOLCANO
(1997, dir: Mick Jackson)
Tommy Lee Jones, Anne Heche, Gaby Hoffman.
● **LOS ANGELES**

LA destroyed: Wilshire Boulevard at Fairfax Avenue

The eruption in LA: La Brea Tar Pits, Wilshire Boulevard

Wilshire Boulevard destroyed: May and Co building

Halting the lava flow: Beverly Center, Beverly Hills

You wait years for a volcano movie, then two come along at once. *Dante's Peak* spurted lava over a small town in Idaho, but *Volcano* staged the (geologically unlikely) eruption smack in the centre of LA. The first inkling of disaster comes when a burst of sulphurous flame kills underground workers in a storm drain in **MacArthur Park** at the junction of Seventh Street and Alvarado, downtown. This notoriously risky area has been cleaned up a lot of late. The park, once a centre for drug-related violence, is a bright, refreshing oasis in the downtown district, but it's still best to avoid after dark. Soon the park's lake is bubbling and there are strange disturbances at the **La Brea Tar Pits, 5801 Wilshire Boulevard**, where the volcano eventually erupts. Don't worry, it's still there. You can visit the **George C Page Museum of La Brea Discoveries** – that's the excellent museum (established in 1977) built at the site of the Pits, where the remains of thousands of Pleistocene Age animals were preserved as fossils. It's at **5801 Wilshire**

Boulevard, **Hancock Park** at Curson Avenue (a double ticket admits you to the LA County Museum of Art next door). The museum is also featured in Curtis Hanson's excellent *Bad Influence*, and the dark, satiric thriller *Miracle Mile*, while the pits were recreated down in Long Beach for the Schwarzenegger bomb *Last Action Hero*.

A section of Wilshire Boulevard, centering around the junction with Fairfax Avenue, with Johnie's Coffee Shop and the gold deco cylinder of the old May and Co building, was reconstructed at the studio for the destruction scenes. The lava flow is finally halted when it's just about to engulf the **Beverly Center, 8500 Beverly Boulevard** at La Cienega Boulevard.

W

WAGON MASTER
(1950, dir: John Ford)
Ben Johnson, Ward Bond, Joanne Dru.
● UTAH

Ben Johnson and Harry Carey help Ward Bond guide a Mormon wagon train to Utah, in the movie that gave rise to the TV series *Wagon Train*, which starred longtime Ford regular Bond. *Wagon Master* uses the landscapes around around **Moab**, Utah, at **Professor Valley**, the Colorado River and **Spanish Valley**. Ford wanted his beloved Monument Valley for the film's climax, but when he couldn't afford it, he faked the mountain using miniatures.

WAIT UNTIL DARK
(1967, dir: Terence Young)
Audrey Hepburn, Alan Arkin, Richard Crenna.
● NEW YORK CITY

A bunch of psychos are after a cache of drugs hidden in blind Audrey Hepburn's NY apartment. Marvellous little suspenser that contains one of the all-time great seat-

Audrey Hepburn is tormented: St Luke's Place, Greenwich Village

jumping moments. Hepburn's basement is the classic 1860s townhouse at **4 St Luke's Place**, off Hudson Street in a classy part of Greenwich Village. Incidentally, her neighbours include, at number 12, that nice family the Huxtables, from TV's *The Cosby Show*.

WAKING NED (aka *Waking Ned Devine*)
(1998, dir: Kirk Jones)
Ian Bannen, David Kelly, Fionnula Flanagan.
● ISLE OF MAN

A lottery win for a dead man in a tiny Irish village has oldsters Bannen and Kelly working a scam to get the money. The fictitious village of Tullymore is **Cregneish**, on the southern tip of the Isle of Man.

WALK IN THE CLOUDS, A
(1995, dir: Alfonso Arau)
Keanu Reeves, Aitana Sanchez-Gijon, Anthony Quinn.
● CALIFORNIA

Keanu Reeves, returning from WWII and stranded in the middle of nowhere, saves the accidentally-pregnant Aitana Sanchez-Gijon from the wrath of

The wine festival: Pasadena City hall, Pasadena

her family by passing himself off as her husband, in Arau's whimsical romance set in Northern California's Wine Country. The movie was shot around loads of the Napa Valley wineries, including **Mayacamus Vineyards, 1155 Lokoyo Road, Napa**; **Mount Veeder Winery, 1999 Mount Veeder Road, Napa**; the **Haywood Vineyards, Sonoma**; the **Beringer Vineyards, 1000 Pratt Avenue, Saint Helena**; the **Charles Krug Winery Redwood Cellar, 2800 Main Street (Hwy 29), Saint Helena**, and **Duckhorn Vineyards, 3027 Silverado Trail, Saint Helena**. Filming also took place in **San Pedro**, the harbour to the south of LA. The most intriguing location, though, must be the wine festival, which was actually staged in the Large Courtyard of **Pasadena City Hall, 100 North Garfield Avenue**, Pasadena, east of LA.

WALL STREET
(1987, dir: Oliver Stone)
Michael Douglas, Charlie Sheen, Daryl Hannah.
● NEW YORK CITY

The defining eighties movie, with Douglas' slimy Gordon Gekko providing a yuppie role model. The offices of both Sheen and Douglas were filmed at **222**

Exclusive NY hangout: 21 Club, West 52nd Street

Broadway, downtown Manhattan. Filming also took place at exclusive hangout, **The 21 Club, 21 West 52nd Street** between Fifth and Sixth Avenues, and at **PJ Moran's Pub and Restaurant, 3 East 48th Street**. The restaurant where Sheen wears a wire to entrap Douglas is the **Tavern on the Green, Central Park** at West 67th Street (see *Ghostbusters* for details).

WAR GAMES
(1983, dir: John Badham)
Matthew Broderick, Ally Sheedy, John Wood.
● WASHINGTON STATE; CALIFORNIA

Matthew Broderick (at 22) is a schoolkid hacker accessing the US defence system for a quick game of Global Nuclear War. The movie is set in the Pacific northwest, around

The Goose Island ferry: Steilacoom Ferry, Tacoma

Seattle and further northeast at Newhalen, Route 20, in the North Cascade Mountains, and Mount Vernon, north on I-5. Filming took place at **Lake Chelan**, in central Washington State. The Goose Island ferry Broderick catches is actually the **Steilacoom Ferry**, in a suburb of Tacoma. The university is **University of Washington**, Seattle, where the 'computer hacker department' is really the Psychology Building, on the west side of the campus.

Some of the locations are closer to Hollywood, though. John Wood's house, and the 7-11 Store are at **Big Bear**, the lakeside resort north of LA, while Broderick's house is smack in the centre of LA itself, in the exclusive neighbourhood of **Hancock Park**.

WAR OF THE ROSES, THE
(1989, dir: Danny DeVito)
Michael Douglas, Kathleen Turner, Danny DeVito.
● **LOS ANGELES; WASHINGTON STATE**

DeVito's gleefully pitch-black comedy sees high-flying professionals Michael Douglas and Kathleen Turner turning divorce into a fight to the death. Nantucket, where Douglas and Turner first meet up, is not the classy New England resort at all, but **Coupeville**, Route 20, on **Whidbey Island**, 40 miles north of Seattle, Washington State over on the Pacific Northwest coast. And the cutesy, snow-covered street, in Cambridge, Massachusetts, where Turner presents Douglas with a Morgan, is no more than the Universal backlot in LA.

The movie was shot largely, though, on stages at Twentieth Century-Fox in LA, where the huge, three-storey set was built, to match up with a real house on the exclusive **Fremont Place**, a private road in LA's posh Hancock Park district. The senate hearing is in LA's **City Hall, 200 North Spring Street**, downtown LA. There was filming also at the **California Institute of Technology (Cal Tech), 1201 East California Boulevard** between Hill and Wilson Avenues, Pasadena.

WAR OF THE WORLDS, THE
(1953, dir: Byron Haskin)
Gene Barry, Ann Robinson, Les Tremayne.
● **LOS ANGELES**

Byron Haskin's colourful adaptation transposes the HG Wells story from village England to California, and replaces the lumbering tripods of the book with sleek flying machines. **City Hall, 200 North Spring Street**, downtown LA, is destroyed by Martians. Filming also took place at the **United States Government District Court Building, 312 North Spring Street** at Aliso Street. The church, where Barry finally finds Ann Robinson, is **St Brendan's, Third Street** at Van Ness Avenue, Hollywood.

The troops are called out: US Government District Court Building, Spring Street, downtown LA

The ending: St Brendan's Church, Third Street

WARRIORS, THE
(1979, dir: Walter Hill)
Michael Beck, James Remar, Thomas Waites.
● **NEW YORK CITY**

Early, culty Walter Hill movie, with a NY street gang away from their territory trying to make it home to **Coney Island**. The opening scene, with thousands of extras, including real gang members and all the problems that entails, is in the **Riverside Park Playground, 96th Street** at Riverside Drive. Also filmed at **The Bathhouse**, Coney island.

WATERBOY, THE
(1998, dir: Frank Coraci)
Adam Sandler, Kathy Bates, Henry Winkler.
● **FLORIDA**

When waterboy Sandler gets riled he shows a ferocious talent for tackling, in this comedy, which the Harold Lloyd family felt bore a rather striking resemblance to *The Freshman*. The movie was shot in Florida. Sandler's Louisiana bayou home was built on the boat landing at **Deberry**. The Mud Dogs' training ground is the football field in **DeLand**, while more scenes were shot in **St Cloud**. The climactic Bourbon Bowl game is actually at the **Citrus Bowl**, the gamepark of **Central Florida University, Orlando**.

WATERLOO
(1970, dir: Sergei Bondarchuk)
Rod Steiger, Christopher Plummer, Orson Welles.
● **UKRAINE; ITALY**

A sumptuous Italian-Russian co-production, with Steiger as a wracked Napoleon and Plummer as an arrogant Duke of Wellington, about the events leading up to, and the battle of, Waterloo in 1815. The gigantic battle scenes were shot in the Ukraine. Louis XVIII's Paris court, the Tuileries, is the **Palazzo Reale, Caserta**, about fifteen miles from Naples, which you might recognise as Queen Amidala's palace (see *Star Wars Episode I: The Phantom Menace* for details).

Napoleon's triumphal return to Paris: the grand staircase, Palazzo Reale, Caserta

Louis XVIII flees the Tuileries: Palazzo Reale, Caserta

WATERLOO BRIDGE
(1931, dir: James Whale)
Mae Clarke, Kent Douglass, Bette Davis.
● **LOS ANGELES**

Mae Clarke is a chorus girl who descends into prostitution after her husband is declared missing in action in this tragic melodrama. Set in London, it was filmed in LA. A bridge over the Los Angeles River close to Universal Studios was dressed to resemble London's Waterloo Bridge. The English country estate, Wetherby House is in **Pasadena**.

WATERLOO BRIDGE
(1940, dir: Mervyn LeRoy)
Vivien Leigh, Robert Taylor, Lucile Watson.
● **CALIFORNIA**

Remake shot around **Chico**, central California, including **Bidwell Park**; **Pentz Road** and the **M and T Ranch**.

WATERLOO ROAD
(1944, dir: Sidney Gilliat)
John Mills, Stewart Granger, Alastair Sim.
● **LONDON**

A soldier goes AWOL to sort out his family life, in this London-set pre-kitchen sink piece of social realism, which includes a chase across the tracks at **Waterloo Station**.

WAY DOWN EAST
(1920, dir: DW Griffith)
Lillian Gish, Richard Barthelmess, Lowell Sherman.
● **NEW YORK STATE; VERMONT**

Old fashioned melodrama, saved by Griffith's bravura direction and Gish's performance as the naïve country girl seduced, abandoned, shamed and packed off to the icy wastes, where Barthelmess rescues her. Griffith's studio was at **Orienta Point, Mamaroneck**, New York State. The blizzard scenes were also filmed at Orienta Point, but outside on Long Island Sound, during a spell of genuine bad weather. Several crew members suffered exposure and were lost to pneumonia. For the rightly famous ice-floe climax, shot without stunt doubles at **White River Junction**, up in Vermont where the White River and the Connecticut River flow alongside each other, solid ice was dynamited to provide individual floes.

WAY WE WERE, THE
(1973, dir: Sydney Pollack)
Barbra Streisand, Robert Redford, James Woods.
● **LOS ANGELES; NEW YORK CITY; NEW YORK STATE**

Leftish firebrand Streisand endures a mismatched relationship with rich-kid writer Redford in Pollack's nostalgia-drenched star vehicle. The fictitious Wentworth College,

Streisand and Redford escape the red-baiters: Union Station, downtown LA

where the mismatched pair first meet up, is **Union College, Schenectady**, New York State. Streisand harangues the student activists in front of the domed, 16-sided **Nott Memorial**. Also featured is the **Chester Arthur statue**, and the prom scene is **Memorial Field House**. LA locations include the **Beverly Hills Hotel, 96641 Sunset Boulevard**, Beverly Hills. Streisand endures a demo of hysterical red-baiters at **Union Station, 800 North Alameda**

Street, downtown. The final meeting of Streisand and Redford takes place in NYC, outside the Fifth Avenue entrance of the **Plaza Hotel, 59th Street** .

WAYNE'S WORLD
(1992, dir: Penelope Spheeris)
Mike Myers, Dana Carvey, Rob Lowe.
● **LOS ANGELES; CHICAGO**

Saturday Night Live spinoff, getting the big screen treatment from one-time youth scene observer Spheeris. Set in Aurora, Illinois, 30 miles west of Chicago, the low-budget movie was shot mainly around LA, and often on the Paramount lot. The nightclub, where Garth seeks revenge on a bully, is the très chic **Arena, 6655 Santa Monica Boulevard**, West Hollywood.

WAYNE'S WORLD 2
(1993, dir: Stephen Surjik)
Mike Myers, Dana Carvey, Tia Carrere.
● **CALIFORNIA**

The sequel was also shot in California, in the LA suburb of Monrovia, east of Pasadena, on **Huntington Avenue** and **Lemon Avenue**.

WE FAW DOWN
(1928, dir: Leo McCarey)
Stan Laurel, Oliver Hardy, Bess Flowers.
● **LOS ANGELES**

On the town: Hotel Adams, Main Street, Culver City

Stan and Ollie fib to their wives when planning an evening out on the town. Filmed at the **Hotel Adams, 3896 Main Street**, Culver City, LA.

WEDDING, A
(1978, dir: Robert Altman)
Carol Burnett, Paul Dooley, Desi Arnaz.
● **CHICAGO**

Great ensemble cast of 48 (thus doubling *Nashville*'s cast of 24), and Altman in his best mode – overlapping dialogue, sharp cameos – at a smart society wedding. The setting is the posh Chicago suburb of **Lake Bluff**, where the palatial residence used for the reception is the **Armour Mansion**.

WEDDING SINGER, THE
(1998, dir: Frank Coraci)
Drew Barrymore, Adam Sandler, Steve Buscemi.
● **LOS ANGELES**

The wedding reception is held in one of the ballrooms of the **Ambassador Hotel, 3400 Wilshire Boulevard**, midtown LA.

WEEKEND AT BERNIE'S
(1989, dir: Ted Kotcheff)
Andrew McCarthy, Jonathan Silverman.
● **NORTH CAROLINA; NEW YORK CITY**

Broad, one-note black farce, along the lines of *The Trou-*

ble With Harry, with McCarthy and Silverman covering up the death of their boss while enjoying the highlife in his beach house. The insurance office where the two boys work is the **Metropolitan Life Insurance Building, 1 Madison Avenue**, between 23rd and 25th Streets, New York. Hampton Island was actually filmed in North Carolina, not far from the East Coast filming centre of Wilmington. Most of the movie was shot on **Bald Head Island**, about 30 miles south of Wilmington at the mouth of the Cape Fear River. The lighthouse, where Silverman gets temporarily blinded, is the **Old Baldy Light**. Bernie's ultramodern beach house was built specially for the movie (after shooting it was dismantled) on the **Fort Fisher Recreation Area**, between Bald Head Island and **Carolina Beach State Park**, which is where the corpse of Bernie ends up 'waterskiing'.

WEIRD SCIENCE
(1985, dir: John Hughes)
Anthony Michael Hall, Ilan Mitchell-Smith, Kelly LeBrock.
● **ILLINOIS**

Horny teen computer nerds create femme-fantasy Kelly LeBrock, but the premise goes nowhere in another Hughes teen-farce, shot – where else? – around Chicago. The boys' neighbourhood is **Highland Park**, north of the city. Featured is **Northbrook Court Mall, Northbrook**.

WELCOME TO THE DOLLHOUSE
(1995, dir: Todd Solondz)
Heather Matarazzo, Brendan Sexton Jr, Matthew Faber.
● **NEW JERSEY**

Family drama, with Matarazzo living through schoolday traumas, made in **West Caldwell**, New Jersey.

WENT THE DAY WELL (aka *Forty-eight Hours*)
(1942, dir: Alberto Cavalcanti)
Leslie Banks, Elizabeth Allan, Frank Lawton.
● **BUCKINGHAMSHIRE**

The village of Bramley End: Turville

The policeman's cottage, Bramley End: Turville

During WWII, a small English village is taken over by German fifth columnists in this excellent, low key propaganda piece, from a Graham Greene story, which still packs a punch. The fictitious village of Bramley End (though not the manor house, which filmed elsewhere) is **Turville**, off the B482 about five miles west of High Wycombe, Buckinghamshire. Pretty much unchanged to this day, the village is over-

Leslie Banks' cottage in Bramley End: Turville

looked by the windmill from *Chitty Chitty Bang Bang*, and was also the scene of the haunted wedding in the classic British chiller *Dead of Night*.

WEST SIDE STORY
(1961, dir: Robert Wise, Jerome Robbins)
Natalie Wood, Rita Moreno, Richard Beymer.
● **NEW YORK CITY**

Robert Wise's filming of the greatest Broadway musical of all time fizzes with the energy of Jerome Robbins' choreography, but suffers from some dreadful miscasting and a clumping staginess in the studio scenes. The opening twenty minutes, filmed by (the subsequently replaced) Robbins, show what might have been. They used the real about-to-be demolished slum tenements on the West Side, the area now occupied by the Lincoln Center for the Performing Arts. But after the exhilarating introduction it's off to the studio, with great music, cramped sets and naff filters.

WESTERNER, THE
(1940, dir: William Wyler)
Gary Cooper, Walter Brennan, Fred Stone.
● **ARIZONA**

Walter Brennan won an Oscar as Judge Roy Bean, and stole the show from a less-than-happy Cooper. The movie was shot in the town of **Goldwyn** (guess who it was named after) near Tucson, Arizona. Built as a replica of an early Texan town, movie mogul Sam Goldwyn promised to use it as a permanent set for all his Westerns.

WESTWORLD
(1973, dir: Michael Crichton)
Yul Brynner, Richard Benjamin, James Brolin.
● **LOS ANGELES**

Long before *Jurassic Park*, writer Crichton tackled the theme of technology running amok, and this time as director too. The 'Roman World' of the technically advanced theme park is **Greenacres**, the lavish Beverly Hills spread of ledge-dangling comic Harold Lloyd. The estate, which in 1928 covered twenty acres and included twelve themed gardens, had by the seventies been reduced to five acres. The 44-room house has 26 bathrooms and, for a while after the actor's death in 1971, was open to the public as a museum. No longer. It's at **1740 Greenacres Place, Beverly Hills**. The western landscapes are **Red Rock Canyon**, near Ridgecrest in central California (see *Jurassic Park* for details).

WHALES OF AUGUST, THE
(1987, dir: Lindsay Anderson)
Lillian Gish, Bette Davis, Vincent Price.
● **MAINE**

The incredible Lillian Gish, who first came to prominence

in DW Griffith's *Birth of a Nation*, is paired with Bette Davis – who proved just too much for her – in Lindsay Anderson's gentle drama set on **Cliff Island**, off the coast of Portland, Maine.

WHAT EVER HAPPENED TO BABY JANE?

(1962, dir: Robert Aldrich)
Bette Davis, Joan Crawford, Victor Buono.
● LOS ANGELES

Sold at the time as a psycho-horror, the movie has since turned out to be an all-time camp classic, as the two great screen queens of the thirties and forties were teamed for the first time in a low-budget schlocker. It was made by Warner Bros, but by the early sixties the two stars were seen as write-offs and the production was shunted off the lot to the ramshackle Producers Studio (now the independent Raleigh Studios), 650 North Bronson at Melrose Avenue, while the entire WB lot was given over to the big prestige production, *Gypsy*.

Momma's boy pianist Edwin Flagg was to have been played by Peter Lawford, but President Kennedy's bro-in-law got cold feet and was thankfully replaced by the wonderfully fey Victor Buono.

Set in a fast-decaying Hollywood, where Bette drives her battered old Merc along **Wilcox Avenue**, and at **Sunset** and **La Brea**. She calls in at the, now gone, Western Costume Co, which stood at 5339 Melrose Avenue. The beach, where Crawford finally croaks, is **Paradise Cove** on Zuma Beach, Malibu, north of LA. The old mansion, where the sisters live in a mutually-dependent hate-hate relationship, has had a bright facelift. It was 172, but has now been renumbered, **174 South McCadden Place** at Clinton Street, Hollywood.

The TV remake, *Whatever Happened to…*, with real-life sisters Lynn and Vanessa Redgrave, used a house a couple of blocks east at – coincidentally – 501 South Hudson Avenue.

The Hudson sisters' home: South McCadden Place, Hollywood

WHAT PRICE HOLLYWOOD?

(1932, dir: George Cukor)
Constance Bennett, Lowell Sherman, Neil Hamilton.
● LOS ANGELES

In Cukor's early version of *A Star Is Born*, Constance Bennett works in the original hat-shaped Brown Derby restaurant. Long closed, you can see the dome of the

Derby, now painted silver, on **Brown Derby Plaza, 3377 Wilshire Boulevard** at Alexandria, where it's now called **Café Mecca**. The original restaurant (there were other, more conventional, Derbys later) was built in 1926 as a coffeeshop by Gloria Swanson's hubby, Herbert Somborn. Bennett marries at **First United Methodist Church**, Highland Avenue at the northwest corner of Franklin Avenue, Hollywood. Still towering over Hollywood, you can see the church in *The Godfather*, behind Grauman's Chinese when Tom Hagen arrives in Hollywood. And it's to Grauman's Chinese Theater, **6925 Hollywood Boulevard** (now **Mann's Chinese Theater**) that the director takes Bennett to a première.

The old Brown Derby: Café Mecca, Brown Derby Plaza, Wilshire Boulevard

Constance Bennett gets married: First United Methodist Church, Highland Avenue

WHAT'S EATING GILBERT GRAPE?

(1993, dir: Lasse Hallström)
Johnny Depp, Leonardo DiCaprio, Juliette Lewis.
● TEXAS

Domestic drama has Depp dealing with disturbed younger brother DiCaprio and his grossly obese mother. Set in the fictitious Endora, Iowa, it was actually made in Texas, in the town of **Manor**, just east of state capital Austin. The town square is nearby **Lockhart**. The Grape house was on **Hodde Lane**, outside Pflugerville, but nothing remains from its conflagration at the climax of the movie.

WHAT'S LOVE GOT TO DO WITH IT?

(1993, dir: Brian Gibson)
Angela Bassett, Laurence Fishburne, Vanessa Bell Calloway.
● CALIFORNIA

The Tina Turner biopic, set all over the US, was made almost entirely around LA. Concert scenes were shot in the **State Theater, 703 South Broadway** and the **Embassy Auditorium, 851 South Grand Avenue**, both downtown. The Ritz Club, New York, which no longer exists, is the **Palace Theater, 1735 North Vine Street** – home to *This Is Your Life* in the fifties, when it was known as El Capitan (see *Against All Odds* for details).

Tina Turner performs: State Theater, South Broadway, downtown LA

Harlem's famous Apollo Theater is played by the **Warner Grand Theater, 478 West Sixth Street** in San Pedro, and the sixties dance show uses LA's **Star Search Theater**. The briefly-glimpsed theatre, where Turner is about to perform when she finally cracks and does a runner, is S Charles Lee's Streamline Moderne masterpiece, the **Academy Theater, 3100 Manchester Boulevard** at Crenshaw Boulevard (now used as a church), in Inglewood, just east of Los Angeles Airport. The Fairmont Hotel, San Francisco, where Tina makes her solo début, is the Ballroom of the **Park Plaza Hotel, 607 South Park View Street**, downtown LA. Ike and Tina have a massive bust-up at **Johnie's Broiler, 7447 Firestone Boulevard, Downey**.

It's the real Turner home seen in the movie. While researching the picture, it was discovered that the house had remained virtually untouched since the sixties, even down to the lamps, the wallpaper and a portrait of Ike Turner.

WHAT'S UP DOC?

(1972, dir: Peter Bogdanovich)
Barbra Streisand, Ryan O'Neal, Kenneth Mars.
● SAN FRANCISCO

The Hotel Bristol: Hilton Hotel, O'Farrell Street

The car chase: Alta Plaza Park

Bogdanovich's heavy-handed retread of thirties screwball comedies was shot around San Francisco. The Hotel Bristol, where wacky Barbra Streisand causes no end of trouble for meek geologist Ryan O'Neal, is the **Hilton Hotel, 333 O'Farrell Street** at Mason Street. The car chase is a joy but, much to the chagrin of the city, has left permanent cracks in the steps on the south side of **Alta Plaza Park**, on **Steiner Street** at Clay Street.

WHEN DINOSAURS RULED THE EARTH

(1970, dir: Val Guest)
Victoria Vetri, Patrick Allen, Robin Hawdon.
● CANARY ISLANDS

Cheapo sequel to Hammer's remake of *One Million Years BC*, with Vetri banished from her tribe for the crime of being blonde. The primaeval landscapes are the volcanic wastes around **Lanzarote** in the Canary Islands.

Prehistoric landscape: Lanzarote, Canary Islands

WHEN HARRY MET SALLY...

(1989, dir: Rob Reiner)
Billy Crystal, Meg Ryan, Carrie Fisher.
● NEW YORK CITY; CHICAGO

"I'll have what she's having...": Katz's Delicatessen, East Houston Street, East Village

It's oh-so-predictable that Crystal and Ryan are finally going to get it together, but the journey's plenty of fun. They actually meet up in the Main Quad of the **University of Chicago, University Avenue** at 58th Avenue. After driving from the University, Ryan drops Crystal off at **Washington Arch, Washington Square Park** in Greenwich Village, New York. Years later, the two meet up at **Shakespeare & Co Booksellers, 2259 Broadway** at 81st Street on the West Side, and they visit the **Metropolitan Museum of Art, Fifth Avenue** at 82nd Street. The café, where Ryan demonstrates how to fake it in the movie's most famous scene, is **Katz's Delicatessen, 205 East Houston Street** at Ludlow Street in the East Village. The restaurant has a sign: 'You are sitting at the table where Harry met Sally'.

Harry finally declares his love at the New Year party: Puck Building, Lafayette Street

Harry and Sally help make up a foursome at **Cafe Luxembourg, 200 West 70th Street** near Amsterdam Avenue, and singalong to the karaoke machine at the home of the executive toy, **The Sharper Image, 4 West 57th Street**. Filming also took place at **West 96th Street Station** on the Upper West Side. The New Year party, where Crystal finally declares his love, is in the **Puck Building, 295 Lafayette Street**.

WHERE EAGLES DARE

(1969, dir: Brian G Hutton)
Richard Burton, Clint Eastwood, Mary Ure.
● AUSTRIA

Bluff, double bluff and multiple bluff in this clever Alistair MacLean adventure, which has Burton and Eastwood posing as Nazis to rescue top military brass from the impregnable Schloss Adler in southern Germany. The village they arrive in is **Werfen**, about twenty miles south of Salzburg in the Salzach Valley, Austria (*rail: Wer-*

The fake Nazis arrive in Austria: Werfen

Schloss Adler: Schloss Hohenwerfen, Werfen, Austria

fen). The mountaintop fortress looming over the village is **Schloss Hohenwerfen**. But don't worry, you won't have to take a scary cable-car ride. In fact, there is no cable car. The castle, now a falconry centre and museum, is accessible by a short, if steep, road from the village.

WHISKY GALORE! (aka *Tight Little Island*)
(1948, dir: Alexander Mackendrick)
Basil Radford, Joan Greenwood, Gordon Jackson.
● SCOTLAND

Based on real events, when the *SS Politician*, carrying 50,000 cases of Scotch, was wrecked in 1941 on the Isle of Eriskay in the Outer Hebrides. In the movie, the island becomes Todday, and was filmed on the island of **Barra** in the Hebrides.

WHISTLE DOWN THE WIND
(1961, dir: Bryan Forbes)
Alan Bates, Hayley Mills, Bernard Lee.
● LANCASHIRE

"We three kings...": Pendle Hill

Before the Lloyd-Webber musical transposed the story to the Southern States, screenwriters Keith Waterhouse and Willis Hall already shifted the location for this story of a holed-up escapee being mistaken for Christ, from the pony-and-jodhpurs Home Counties to the gritty north of England. The film was shot on location in the village of **Downham**, off the A59,

The farmhouse: Worsaw End Farm

about ten miles northwest of Burnley, Lancashire. It's pretty much unchanged. You can still find the carpark, where the Salvation Army band played ("Do you want a kitten? It's not dead."). Bostock's farm itself is nearby on **Pendle Hill**. In reality **Worsaw End Farm**, it's still instantly recognisable, both the farmhouse (the kitchen interiors were the only studio shots in the film) and the barn – though a shelter has since been added to the door. The original tractor, driven by Bernard Lee, is still here, rusting away.

The farm's current owner, a child at the time of filming, was denied the opportunity of appearing as one of the 'disciples' by a sudden bout of appendicitis. Even the trees silhouetted on Pendle Hill (as the children sing "We three kings...") can still be seen.

The village: Downham

The barn: Worsaw End Farm

The village: Downham

The ending: Worsaw End Farm

WHITE HEAT
(1949, dir: Raoul Walsh)
James Cagney, Edmond O'Brien, Virginia Mayo.
● LOS ANGELES

Classic hardboiled gangster pic. The final chase leads through downtown LA, past City Hall. The climactic finale at the oil refinery ("Made it Ma, top of the world!") is **198th Street and Figueroa, Torrance**, southern LA.

WHITE HUNTER, BLACK HEART
(1990, dir: Clint Eastwood)
Clint Eastwood, Jeff Fahey, Charlotte Cornwell.
● AFRICA;
BUCKING-
HAMSHIRE

Eastwood as a thinly-disguised John Huston, on location in Africa to shoot both a film and an ele-

Eastwood's Irish estate: West Wycombe House, Buckinghamshire

phant, shot in Zimbabwe and Zambesi. Eastwood's Irish estate is **West Wycombe House**, two and a half miles west of High Wycombe, south of the A40, Buckinghamshire. See *The Music Lovers* for details.

WHITE MEN CAN'T JUMP
(1992, dir: Ron Shelton)
Wesley Snipes, Woody Harrelson, Rosie Perez.
● **LOS ANGELES**

Sport-movie specialist Shelton (*Bull Durham*) moves from baseball to basketball with this story of two scam artists in LA. The playground basketball courts are **La-**

The basketball courts: Lafayette Park, Wilshire Boulevard

fayette Park, Wilshire Boulevard between Hoover Street and Lafayette Park Place, where the swishy boulevard curves right into the scuzzy downtown district near MacArthur Park. Filming also took place at **Venice Beach Boardwalk** and a rundown motel in **Santa Monica**. The scam game filmed outside **Compton Church** near the Watts Towers.

WHITE PALACE
(1990, dir: Luis Mandoki)
James Spader, Susan Sarandon, Eileen Brennan.
● **MISSOURI**

Spader is a young yuppie falling for older waitress Sarandon in this low-key, well-acted class- and age-gap drama filmed in St Louis, Missouri. The White Palace burger house is the **White Knight Cafe, 1801 Olive Street**. The ad agency, where Spader works, is on **Laclede's Landing** on the St Louis Riverfront. The bachelor party was filmed in the **Lemp Mansion, 3322 DeMenil Place**. The New York restaurant, where the couple are finally reunited, is also St Louis. It's **Duff's Restaurant, 392 North Euclid Avenue**.

WHO FRAMED ROGER RABBIT
(1988, dir: Robert Zemeckis)
Bob Hoskins, Christopher Lloyd, Joanna Cassidy.
● **LONDON; CALIFORNIA**

Impressive blend of animation and live action, set around the Toontown ghetto of LA. The Acme factory on the Toontown border is an empty electrical testing station in **Shepherds Bush** in west London. The cinema, where Eddie and Roger watch a Goofy cartoon, is the now closed 2,000 seat **Gray's State Theatre, Grays** in Essex. The wonderful thirties movie palace was the largest single-screen auditorium still operating in

The movie house: Gray's State Theatre, Essex

Europe at the time, and has since been a nightclub but is currently closed.

The Ink and Paint Club, Eddie's office and the Terminal Bar are sets built at Elstree Studios.

LA locations include the **Dodger Stadium, 1000 Elysian Park Avenue** near Silverlake, and **Griffith Park**. Maroon Studios are the **Ren-Mar Studios, 846 North Cahuenga, Hollywood**. The LA street scenes are **Hope Street**, between 11th and 12th Streets, downtown LA, heavily disguised behind scads of period dressing. Filming also took place in **Oakland**, over the bay from San Francisco.

WHO'S AFRAID OF VIRGINIA WOOLF?
(1966, dir: Mike Nichols)
Elizabeth Taylor, Richard Burton, George Segal, Sandy Dennis.
● **MASSACHUSETTS**

Rivetting movie of Edward Albee's play. Burton and Taylor are, for once, perfect together. Interiors were shot on a closed set at Warner's Burbank Studio. The college is **Smith College, Northampton**, on I-91, north of Springfield, Massachusetts, where Burton-Taylor's home is the **Tyler Annex**.

WICKED LADY, THE
(1945, dir: Leslie Arliss)
Margaret Lockwood, James Mason, Griffith Jones.
● **NORFOLK**

Margaret Lockwood is the wicked Lady Skelton, stealing husbands, poisoning aged retainers and moonlighting as a highway robber in this Restoration romp. Scandalous in its time for the plunging necklines, scenes had to be reshot for the trembling innocents of the USA. Lady Skelton's stately pile, Maryiot Cells, supposedly at Maiden Worthy in Buckinghamshire, is **Blickling Hall**, northwest of Aylsham in Norfolk. The redbrick Jacobean mansion is open to the public on various days of the week between March and October (*admission charge;* ℂ *01263.733084*).

WICKED LADY, THE
(1983, dir: Michael Winner)
Faye Dunaway, Alan Bates, John Gielgud.
● **WARWICKSHIRE; HERTFORDSHIRE; YORKSHIRE; LONDON**

Sexed-up remake, with bare breasts and whip fights. Maryiot Cells is now a conflation of two houses: the turretted and gabled home of Lord Northampton, **Compton Wynyates** in Warwickshire, an ancient house rebuilt in the 16th century; and the Elizabethan mansion, **North Mymms Park**, in Hertfordshire. The Tyburn hanging scenes used the moors outside Sheffield.

The Duke's Theatre, where Lady Skelton meets Charles II,

The Duke's Theatre: Painted Hall, Royal Naval College, Greenwich

is the **Painted Hall** of the **Royal Naval College, Greenwich** (see *The Madness of King George* for details).

WICKER MAN, THE
(1973, dir: Robin Hardy)
Edward Woodward, Christopher Lee, Britt Ekland.
● SCOTLAND

Savagely cut down before release, and with some shaky performances, *The Wicker Man* has nevertheless achieved cult status since its initial release as a B-feature with *Don't Look Now*. Its success lies in the gameplaying of the clever plot and wicked script of Anthony Shaffer (*Sleuth*). Woodward is the puritanically Christian cop sent to investigate pagan rites on a remote Scottish isle. There is a real Summerisle, but it's way to the north of where this movie filmed. The near-tropical (warmed by the gulf stream) island estate of Lord Summerisle (so kindly thanked in the movie's credits – and as bogus as Eve Channing in *Sleuth*'s) is an amalgam of around 25 separate locations, all of them on the Scottish mainland.

The opening aerial shots were filmed en route to the Isle of Skye, though the harbour, where Woodward's seaplane touches down, is **Plockton**, a small town off the A890, at the mouth of Loch Carron, about 55 miles west of Inverness, on the west coast of Ross and Cromarty. The production was based at **Newton Stewart**, on the River Cree, north of Wigtown Bay in Galloway. Much of the filming was done here, including the schoolhouse and the inn. 20 miles southeast, at **Kirkcudbright** on the A711, you'll find the ruined church and the sweetshop. The Green Man Inn is a conflation of two locations: inside it's the **Ellan Gowan Hotel, Creetown**; the exterior is **Cally Estate office, Gatehouse of Fleet**. The schoolhouse and the old kirk are at **Anwoth**.

The exterior of Lord Summerisle's castle is **Culzean Castle**, a fine Adam house, just off the A719, twelve miles southwest of Ayr. It's open to the public from the end of March to the end of October (℗ *01655.760274, admission charge*). The interior, though, is **Lord Stair's Castle**, near **Wigtown** a few miles south of Newton Stewart. This was a tad too grand for the film – Lord Summerisle's palatial drawing room is Lord Stair's foyer. The tour of Summerisle's garden is in **Logan Botanic Garden, Port Logan**, 10 miles south of Stranraer.

The wicker man itself was built on the **Machars Peninsula**, the area of land between Luce and Wigtown Bays, south of Newton Stewart, around **St Ninian's Cave**, near the southern tip, off the A747.

WILD ANGELS, THE
(1966, dir: Roger Corman)
Peter Fonda, Nancy Sinatra, Bruce Dern.
● CALIFORNIA

Corman's biker movie, with real Hell's Angels in the cast, earned an inevitable cult reputation as a result of being banned in the UK for several years. It's set around LA, at **Venice Beach**; around the oil rigs of **San Pedro**; along the bike trails of **Palm Canyon** at Palm Springs, and at **Mecca**, in the desert south of I-10, near the Salton Sea.

The church, where the sacrilegious wake is held (the scene that was probably responsible for the ban) is the **Little Country Church, North Argyle Avenue**, Hollywood. The cemetery is the park at **Idyllwild**, off Route 74 in the San Bernardino National Forest, southwest of Palm Springs.

WILD AT HEART
(1990, dir: David Lynch)
Nicolas Cage, Laura Dern, Willem Dafoe.
● TEXAS; CALIFORNIA

Wilfully bizarre fantasy, a sick, violent road movie patterned on *The Wizard of Oz*, made around **El Paso**, Texas, and **Palmdale**, north of LA. The vast, vaulted lobby

The bloody murder: Park Plaza Hotel, downtown LA

(supposedly in Cape Fear) of the opening scenes, where Cage brains a guy on the staircase, is the lobby of the, now closed, **Park Plaza Hotel, 607 South Park View Street**, downtown LA.

WILD BUNCH, THE
(1969, dir: Sam Peckinpah)
William Holden, Robert Ryan, Ernest Borgnine.
● MEXICO

Peckinpah's masterpiece, conjuring poetry from dust and blood, was filmed in Mexico. The town of Starbuck is **Parras**, one of the oldest towns in north Mexico, some 600 miles north of Mexico City, midway between Saltillo and Torreon on Route 40. The ever-present dust of the Mexican desert required a camera mechanic to be permanently on duty dismantling and cleaning the cameras.

Pike puts the wounded Buck out of his misery at the **Duranzo Arroyo, Torreon**. And it's here, too, behind the Perote Winery, that the bounty hunters bed down for the night. Angel's village is **El Rincon del Motero**. Old man Sykes waits at **El Romeral** with horses for the bunch to return from Starbuck. The robbery of the munitions train involved the use of a period locomotive on a rail spur south of **La Goma**.

The blowing up of the bridge, and the river crossing, take place on the **Rio Nazas** just south of Torreon. The climactic massacre, supposedly in the town of Agua Verde, took eleven days to film, at the **Hacienda Cienga del Carmen**.

WILD ONE, THE
(1954, dir: Laslo Benedek)
Marlon Brando, Lee Marvin, Jay C Flippen.
● CALIFORNIA

Notorious for being banned, this is the original bad-boy biker movie. The big disappointment, if you want to slip on your leather jacket and get snapped mooching moodily about on Main Street, is that the movie was shot on the backlot at Columbia's San Fernando Valley ranch.

Second best is probably the town where the events that

inspired the movie actually happened, which is Hollister, east of Salinas, northern California. Hollister is on I-156, less than ten miles east of San Juan Bautista, site of the old mission from *Vertigo*.

WILD STRAWBERRIES

(1957, dir: Ingmar Bergman)
Victor Sjostrom, Ingrid Thulin, Gunnar Bjornstrand.
● SWEDEN

Archetypal fifties Bergman, with veteran movie director Sjostrom as an elderly professor travelling a physical and mental journey through a series of nightmares. Mostly studio-bound, but part of the 'phantom carriage' ride, when the carriage careers round a corner, was shot in a deserted Old Town. The professor recites a poem at a lunch overlooking **Lake Vattern**, and eventually arrives at the University in **Lund**, just north of Malmo at the southern tip of Sweden.

WILD WILD WEST

(1999, dir: Barry Sonnenfeld)
Will Smith, Kevin Kline, Kenneth Branagh.
● NEW MEXICO; ARIZONA; IDAHO

A real disappointment from Sonnenfeld after the hugely enjoyable *Men in Black*. The spectacular version of the gimmicky TV show is long on FX, but who lost the script? Wisely, George Clooney jumped ship early on, to be replaced by Kline. Most of the movie was shot on the **Cook Ranch**, near Galisteo, about 20 miles south of Santa Fe, New Mexico, a regular filming site used for the superior TV series *Lonesome Dove, Wyatt Earp* and Lawrence Kasdan's *Silverado* (a nice in-joke: the town in *WWW* is called Silverado, and the store, destroyed by Kenneth Branagh's giant mechanical spider, is 'Kasdan's'). Second unit rail scenes were shot at **Pierce**, Idaho. Spider Canyon is **Monument Valley**, Arizona, and there was more filming at the spectacular **Canyon de Chelly** (see *Mackenna's Gold* for details)

WILD WOMEN OF WONGO

(1958, dir: James L Wolcott)
Jean Hawkshaw, Johnny Walsh, Adrienne Bourbeau.
● FLORIDA

Just to prove that you don't always need the perverse genius of Ed Wood to produce one of the Worst Movies of All Time. The beautifully manicured island of Wongo is **Silver Springs** at Ocala, Florida.

WILDE

(1998, dir: Brian Gilbert)
Stephen Fry, Jude Law, Jennifer Ehle.

● LONDON; DORSET; OXFORDSHIRE; HAMPSHIRE; HERTFORDSHIRE; SPAIN

Stephen Fry in the role he was born to play, an explicitness missing from earlier versions and the use of striking period locations compensate for the familiarity of the flamboyant writer's fall from grace.

The startling Western opening, at Leadville, Colorado, is the desert at **Alicante** on the southeast coast of Spain, though the interior of the tin mine, where Wilde charms

the miners, was constructed at Grip House Studios near London.

The Cadogan Hotel: South Audley Street

The exterior of Wilde's West End apartment is the central courtyard of the recently renovated **Somerset House** in the Strand, a familiar location seen as New York in Tim Burton's *Sleepy Hollow* and as St Petersburg in *Goldeneye* among many other appearances. The imposing exterior of the St James Theatre, where *Lady Windermere's Fan* opens, is the **Palace Theatre, Cambridge Circus**, longtime home to *Les Miserables*.

Spoiled and petulant opportunist Bosie confides his fear of blackmail to Wilde alongside the River Cherwell in the grounds of **Magdalen College**, Oxford, which actually was Wilde's alma mater (see that other period gay romance, *Maurice*, for details of this location). Meanwhile, Wilde's wife, Constance, hints at marital problems to Lady Mount-Temple, on the beach overlooked by the spectacular natural arch of **Durdle Door**, west of West Lulworth between Weymouth and Swanage on the B3070 in Dorset (*rail: Wool*), a location also seen in John Schlesinger's *Far From the Madding Crowd*. And at **Swanage** is the pier where Wilde takes his kids fishing while suffering from a cold.

Period interiors: 25-26 Tredegar Square, Bow

The Queensberry country home, where Bosie gets a dire warning from his mother, is **Knebworth House** near Stevenage in Hertfordshire (see Tim Burton's *Batman* for details). Oscar relates the story of *The Selfish Giant* to his children at the country retreat where he can write in peace. The charming estate is **Houghton Lodge Gardens**, a cottage ornée just south of **Stockbridge**, about twelve miles east of Salisbury in Hampshire. The garden is open to the public from March to September (*admission charge; © 01264. 810177*).

The hotel where Wilde and Bosie make up after their blazing row is another familiar location, **Luton Hoo**, near Luton, Hertfordshire (see *Four Weddings and a Funeral* for details). The law court exteriors are **Middle Temple, Lincoln's Inn**, Lon-

Ross consoles Wilde's ex-lover: Jamaica Wine Lodge, Cornhill, E3

The prison: Oxford Gaol, New Road, Oxford

don. Reading Gaol, where Wilde is incarcerated, is **HM Prison Oxford, New Road**, alongside Castle Mound. Period interiors were filmed at London's **Athenaeum Club**; the **National Liberal Club** in Whitehall (seen also in *The Elephant Man*) and **25-26 Tredegar Square** in Bow, E3.

The pub, where Robbie Ross consoles Wilde's discarded love John Gray, is the **Jamaica Wine Lodge, St Michael's Alley, Cornhill**, E3, a historic pub tucked away in the heart of the City, which was England's first coffee house. The Cadogan Hotel, where Wilde is arrested, is the ornate red-brick private residence at **2 South Audley Street**, behind the Hilton Hotel. The Italian cemetery where Wilde visits his wife's grave, and the French sidewalk café, where he decides to meet Bosie again, can both be found in **Granada**, Spain.

WILLIAM SHAKESPEARE'S ROMEO & JULIET
(1996, dir: Baz Luhrmann)
Leonardo DiCaprio, Claire Danes, Pete Postlethwaite.
● **MEXICO**

Baz Luhrmann's brashly imaginative reinvention of the Shakespeare play sets the action in Verona Beach, using settings in Mexico. Sycamore Grove, the beachfront where the Montagues hang out and where Mercutio is killed, is the coastal village of **Veracruz**, on the Gulf of Mexico, about 200 miles east of Mexico City. Romeo's banishment sees him holed up in a trailer in the barren badlands of **Texcoco**.

The Capulet mansion is **Castillo de Chapultepec** in Chapultepec Park, Mexico City. Built from 1780 to 1840, this palace was the summer house of Mexican presidents until 1940, when it became a national museum of history. St Peter's, the Modern Gothic concrete church where Romeo and Juliet wed in secret, and where they die together at the movie's end, is the **Immaculate Heart of Mary Church, Colonia Guerrero** in Mexico City.

WILLY WONKA AND THE CHOCOLATE FACTORY
(1971, dir: Mel Stuart)
Gene Wilder, Jack Albertson, Peter Ostrum.
● **GERMANY**

Musical version of Roald Dahl's kiddie fantasy, shot in **Munich**. The ending (with the flying glass elevator) was filmed at **Nördlingen, Bavaria**.

WINCHESTER '73
(1950, dir: Anthony Mann)
James Stewart, Shelley Winters, Dan Duryea.
● **ARIZONA**

The classic Western filmed in **Tucson, Old Tucson** and **Nogales**, Arizona.

WIND, THE
(1928, dir: Victor Seastrom)
Lillian Gish, Lars Hanson, Montagu Love.
● **CALIFORNIA**

City girl Gish goes to live out on the prairie, and murders a potential rapist in this overwhelming (and recently-restored) silent classic, using the desert around the town of **Mojave**, Route 14 north of LA.

WIND AND THE LION, THE
(1975, dir: John Milius)
Sean Connery, Candice Bergen, Brian Keith.
● **SPAIN**

In turn-of-the-century Tangier, Bergen and kids are kidnapped by Scottish Berber bandit Connery in John Milius' talky epic, shot in Spain. The desert is at **Almeria**, southern Spain. The other locations are **Madrid; Seville** and **Granada**.

WIND IN THE WILLOWS, THE (aka *Mr Toad's Wild Ride*)
(1996, dir: Terry Jones)
Terry Jones, Eric Idle, Steve Coogan.
● **SUFFOLK**

Toad Hall is **Kentwell Hall**, Long Melford in Suffolk, seen also in *Witchfinder General*. The railway scenes were filmed on the Bluebell Railway.

WINGS
(1927, dir: William A Wellman)
Charles 'Buddy' Rogers, Richard Arlen, Clara Bow.
● **TEXAS**

The first ever Academy Award for Best Picture went to this WWI aerial melodrama. The flying sequences, filmed at **Carey Air Field** in **San Antonio**, Texas, are still breathtaking. A 100-foot tower was built to house the camera for some of the shots. There was help from the Air service Ground School at Brooks Field, and the Advanced Flying School at Kelly Field.

WINGS OF DESIRE (aka *Himmel Ueber Berlin*)
(1987, dir: Wim Wenders)
Bruno Ganz, Solveig Dommartin, Peter Falk.
● **BERLIN**

Wenders' romantic fantasy (remade in California as *City of Angels*) with Bruno Ganz, one of a pair of angels hovering above Berlin, yearning to exchange his wings for humanity. Beautifully shot around the then still-divided city, where Ganz perches alongside the giant golden angel atop the **Siegessäule, Strasse des 17 Juni**, the city's landmark victory column.

Angels' perch: The Siegessaul, Berlin

WINGS OF THE DOVE, THE
(1997, dir: Iain Softley)
Helena Bonham Carter, Linus Roache, Alison Elliott.
● **LONDON; HERTFORDSHIRE; SURREY; VENICE, ITALY**

Love takes second place to financial expediency in a beautifully photographed version of the Henry James tragedy.

Alison Elliott visits the Basilica San Marco

Elliott and Roache in the little piazza: Campo Dei SS Apostoli

Elliott's palazzo: Palazzo Barbaro, Canal Grande

Picnic on the church steps: Santa Maria della Salute

Helena Bonham Carter's London home is **10 Carlton House Terrace**, above the Mall in Westminster. The opening party, where she meets cynical aristo Alex Jennings, is the Great Hall of **Syon House, Brentford** (see *Accident* for details). Jennings' country castle, where he takes pot-shots at bunnies from the roof, is **Knebworth House**, Knebworth (see Tim Burton's *Batman* for details). Bonham Carter meets her lover Linus Roache and duped American heiress Alison Elliott at the **Serpentine Gallery** in Hyde Park, but the park which stands in for central London for most of the time is **Painshill Park, Portsmouth Road, Cobham** (*admission charge*), about twenty miles southwest of the capital in Surrey. The newspaper office, where Roache inveighs against social injustice, is the Library of the **Freemason's Hall, Great Queen Street , WC2** (*open daily, except Sunday, for guided tours*). Bonham Carter tends her mother's grave at **Brompton Cemetery, Old Brompton Road, Earls Court**, SW5, the last resting place of singer Richard Tauber and of suffragette Emmeline Pankhurst, which was also seen in the bizarre 1991 thriller *Afraid of the Dark*.

On a trip to Venice, Bonham Carter, Roache and Elliott picnic on the steps of **Santa Maria della Salute** at the mouth of Canal Grande, and sightsee in **Piazza San Marco** and the **Basilica San Marco**. Elliott's Venetian palazzo is **Palazzo Barbaro** (also known as Palazzo Leporelli), on the Canal Grande at Ponte dell'Accademia, where Henry James actually wrote *The Wings of the Dove*. Elliott and Linus Roach walk in the tiny piazza, **Campo Dei SS Apostoli**. The luxurious coffee house, where Roache spies Jennings and realises there's trouble afoot, is **Caffè Florian**, Piazza San Marco, where Gwyneth Paltrow also experiences dark forebodings in *The Talented Mr Ripley*.

WISE BLOOD
(1979, dir: John Huston)
Brad Dourif, Harry Dean Stanton, Ned Beatty.
● **GEORGIA**

Just when he was about to be dismissed as a has-been, Huston always seemed to storm back with a beaut. This story of religious heresy was shot around the town of **Macon**, Georgia.

WISH YOU WERE HERE
(1987, dir: David Leland)
Emily Lloyd, Tom Bell, Clare Clifford.
● **SUSSEX**

Loosely based on the early life of Cynthia Payne, this story of a feisty young girl growing up in the prudish fifties was made in **Worthing** and **Bognor** on the south coast of Sussex.

WITCHES OF EASTWICK, THE
(1987, dir: George Miller)
Susan Sarandon, Cher, Michelle Pfeiffer.
● **MASSACHUSETTS; CALIFORNIA**

Little Compton, Rhode Island, was the chosen location for George Miller's film of the John Updike novel, until the locals found out about the sacrilegious nature of the

Jack Nicholson's mansion: Castle Hill, Ipswich

script. The town council eventually voted in favour of the film, but by then Warner Bros had upped and found **Cohasset**, Massachusetts. The church is the **First Parish Unitarian Church, 23 North Main Street**. Jack Nicholson's mansion is **Castle Hill, 290 Argilla Road, Ipswich** (© 978.356.4351), about 30 miles north of Boston, though the interior is the familiar **Greystone Mansion, 905 Loma Vista Drive, Beverly Hills** (see *The Loved One* for full details).

WITCHFINDER GENERAL (aka *The Conqueror Worm*)
(1968, dir: Michael Reeves)
Vincent Price, Rupert Davies, Ian Ogilvy.
● **SUFFOLK; BUCKINGHAMSHIRE**

Director Reeves wanted Donald Pleasence for the role of Matthew Hopkins, who made a lucrative career in the 17th century searching out witches. The studio insisted on the more bankable Price, and after a running battle with the veteran star the 24-year-old director extracted a performance for once more sinister than camp, and produced a genuine English classic, violent, bleak and beautiful. This was the last of Reeves' three movies (the others are *The Sorcerers*, with Boris Karloff, and *Revenge of the Blood Beast*). The talented director died of a drug overdose in 1969.

Based on a true story, the film uses some of the real locations, including the church at **Brandeston**, ten miles northeast of Ipswich in Suffolk, where the priest John Lowes really was tried by water and executed for witchcraft.

The witch burning was filmed on the site of real witch burnings in the town square of **Lavenham**, on the A1141, fifteen miles west of Ipswich. The coastal scene, where Ian Ogilvy questions the fishermen, is **Dunwich**, on the coast north of Orford. The magistrate's house, site of John Lowes' trial by water, is the moat of **Kentwell, Long Melford**, on the A134, three miles north of Sudbury, Suffolk – also seen as Toad Hall in the 1996 *Wind in the Willows* (℗ *01787.310207, open certain days during summer, admission charge*).

The escape of the Witchfinder's henchmen is **Langley Park**, on the A412, north of Slough in Buckinghamshire; while the ambush of the soldiers is the oft-used **Black Park**, alongside Pinewood Studios, familiar from many Bond and Hammer movies.

The fortified tower, where vengeful Richard Marshall bloodily dispatches Hopkins, is **Orford Castle, Orford**, thirteen miles southeast on the B1084 on the River Alde. Built by Henry II around 1173, it was a pretty advanced design for its time, and was an important royal residence until being handed over to the Earl of Norfolk in 1280. It's open to the public (℗ *03944.50472*).

WITHNAIL & I

(1987, dir: Bruce Robinson)
Richard E Grant, Paul McGann, Richard Griffiths.
● **LONDON; CUMBRIA; BUCKINGHAMSHIRE**

Bruce Robinson's sixties-set comedy has acquired a vast cult following over the years. Set in Camden Town, most of the London scenes were actually filmed in Notting Hill, including the squalid flat, which has since been demolished. The film's Mother Black Cap pub (presumably a conflation of Camden's Black Cap and Mother Red Cap – now the World's End), where Withnail orders "Two large gins. Two pints of cider. Ice in the cider", is **Fudrucker's, Lancaster Road** at St Mark's Grove, W11. The wolf enclosure is in Camden, though the wolves have now gone. It's **Regents Park Zoo**, by the **Gloucester Gate** entrance from the Outer Circle. Crow Cragg, where they

Crow Cragg: Sleddale hall, Cumbria

Crow Cragg: Sleddale Hall, Cumbria

end up "on holiday by mistake", is **Sleddale Hall**, a derelict cottage alongside Wet Sleddale Reservoir just west from the A6, near Shap, about twelve miles south of Penrith, Cumbria (*rail: Penrith*). There's a limited bus service from Penrith to Shap. About a mile south of Shap, a narrow road runs west to Wet Sleddale, and from that, about two miles of footpath lead to Sleddale Hall. Although the cottage overlooks Wet Sleddale Reservoir, that's not the spectacular body of water seen in the movie. The King Henry pub is **The Crown, Stony Stratford**, near Milton Keynes, Buckinghamshire (*rail: Wolverton*).

The Mother Black Cap: Lancaster Road, Notting Hill

WITNESS
(1985, dir: Peter Weir)
Harrison Ford, Kelly McGillis, Lukas Haas.
● **PENNSYLVANIA**

When a small Amish boy witnesses a murder, a whole mess of police corruption is uncovered, and good cop Ford has to go into hiding with the austere religious community. In the original script, the opening murder took place at Philadelphia bus station, but the state film commission suggested the more photogenic **30th Street Railway Station**, where young Lukas Haas is entranced by the concourse's vast angel statue. The café where Harrison Ford neglects to say grace and where Haas enjoys a hot dog, is now **Xando Coffee Bar, 235 South 15th Street** at Locust Street, a designer-heavy orange, purple and lime coffee shop. The rest of the movie was actually shot in Amish country: in Lancaster County, Eastern Pennsylvania, with the cooperation of more liberal members of the community. The farm, where Ford hides out, is **Paul Krantz Farm**, near **Strasburg**, a few miles south of Lancaster, about 50 miles west of Philadelphia. The tourist-riddled

Lukas Haas is fascinated by the angelic statue: 30th Street Station

Kelly McGillis waits as Lukas Haas witnesses murder: 30th Street Station

Haas enjoys a hot dog: Xando, 15th Street at Locust

town that Ford visits is the racily-named **Intercourse**, ten miles east of Lancaster, where he makes a phonecall outside **WL Zimmerman & Sons** general store.

WIZARD OF OZ, THE
(1939, dir: Victor Fleming)
Judy Garland, Frank Morgan, Ray Bolger.
● **LOS ANGELES**

No, there are no locations for Oz, of course, but here are some studio details for completists. The classic fantasy was shot on stages at MGM's Culver City Studio, **10202 Washington Boulevard, Culver City** (the studio buildings are still there). The Tornado filmed on Stage 14; the cornfield and apple orchard on 15, 25 and 26; Munchkinland was Stage 27; and the Poppy field (the then new) Stage 29. The small people who played the Munchkins stayed just over the road at the Culver Hotel, though their legendary exploits seem to be largely based on Judy Garland's dubious recollection. 1997 saw a reunion of surviving Munchkins at the hotel – there's a photo in the lobby (see *We Faw Down* for more on the Culver Hotel).

Souvenir of the Munchkin reunion at the Culver Hotel

WOLF
(1994, dir: Mike Nichols)
Jack Nicholson, Michelle Pfeiffer, James Spader.
● **NEW YORK CITY; NEW YORK STATE; LOS ANGELES**

Considering the talent involved, this is a disappointing attempt to rework the werewolf myth in contemporary Manhattan. There are a couple of familiar locations: Christopher Plummer's estate is **Old Westbury Gardens, 71 Old Westbury Road, Old Westbury**, Long Island, which is probably more familiar as the Townsend house in Hitchcock's *North by Northwest*. And Nicholson's publishing company isn't in New York at all, but over on the West Coast in LA. It's the **Bradbury Building, 304 South Broadway** at Third Street, downtown LA, seen in plenty of movies, most famously *Blade Runner*. The upscale hotel Nicholson moves into can be found on New York's West Side. It's the **Mayflower Hotel, 15 Central Park West** at 61st Street.

Nicholson's hotel: The Mayflower, Central Park West

WOLFEN
(1981, dir: Michael Wadleigh)
Albert Finney, Diane Venora, Edward James Olmos.
● **NEW YORK CITY**

Stylish and bloody eco-horror, from the director of *Wood-*

stock, has strangely-accented cop Finney investigating a race of superwolves, descended from native American hunters, who live by scavenging on the Big Apple's down-and-outs. The Van de Veers and their chauffeur get chomped at **Battery Park**. Finney lives in a surprisingly elegant mansion block on **Staten Island**, from where he flies in by helicopter to investigate the deaths. The wolfen inhabit the blighted urban wastes of the **South Bronx**.

The Van de Veers' glitzy apartment is in the **Chase Manhattan Bank Building, 1 Chase Manhattan Plaza**, in Lower Manhattan. The strange black and white sculpture outside is Jean Dubuffet's *A Group of Four Trees*. After a scare in the South Bronx, Finney and Venora head for **Chumley's**, a former speakeasy (you need to look for it – there's still no sign), **86 Bedford Street**, between Grove and Barrow Streets in Greenwich Village (seen also in Woody Allen's *Sweet and Lowdown*).

Wolf-loving Dr Ferguson works out of **Central Park Zoo**, Fifth Avenue at East 64th Street. Finney questions Edward James Olmos in a dizzying scene atop the arch of the **Manhattan Bridge** high above the East River, after a queasy climb up the huge suspension wires. The climactic bloody wolf attack, with the Police Chief's head gaily bouncing off the car, is staged in front of the grandiose Parthenon-style **Federal Hall, 26 Wall Street** at Nassau Street.

WOMAN IN RED, THE
(1984, dir: Gene Wilder)
Gene Wilder, Charles Grodin, Kelly LeBrock.
● **SAN FRANCISCO**

The Seven Year Itch revisited, as middle-aged married man Wilder gets smitten by impossible sex object LeBrock. Set in San Francisco, where Wilder's house is one of the group of 'Painted Ladies', the Gingerbread houses on **Steiner Street** between Hayes Street and Fulton Street. The apartment block, where Wilder teeters on the ledge, is the **Brocklebank Apartments, 1000 Mason Street** (see *Vertigo*, where the Brocklebank features as Kim Novak's apartment, for details).

WOMEN IN LOVE
(1969, dir: Ken Russell)
Glenda Jackson, Alan Bates, Oliver Reed.
● **DERBYSHIRE; YORKSHIRE; SWITZERLAND**

The best filming of a Lawrence novel, with Glenda Jackson getting her first Oscar. The grand house of Alan Bates and Eleanor Bron is **Kedleston Hall**, four miles northwest of Derby on the Derby-Hulland Road, Derbyshire. This neo-classical masterpiece was built in 1759 for Sir Nathaniel Curzon by Robert Adam, who also designed the superb interior. The circular saloon, where Eleanor Bron's cultural performance gets sabotaged, is based on the design of a Roman temple (✆ *01332.842191, open April to November, admission charge*). Shortlands, the Crich house of Oliver Reed, where Christopher Gable drowns during the party, is **Elvaston Castle, Borrowash Road, Elvaston**, Derby. The park is open all year, the house, now a museum of traditional crafts, from April to November (✆ *01332.571342*). Other locations were found around Derbyshire and Sheffield. The snowy climax is **Zermatt**, at the foot of the Matterhorn, Switzerland.

WONDER BOYS
(2000, dir: Curtis Hanson)
Michael Douglas, Tobey Maguire, Frances McDormand.
● PITTSBURGH, PENNSYLVANIA

One-time wonderboy writer Douglas can't bring himself to complete his novel. Douglas' home is in Pittsburgh's Friendship district. His college is the **Carnegie-Mellon University**, with filming in **Baker Hall** and the **Fine Arts Building**. The Hi-Hat Club exterior is in Pittsburgh's historic African-American Hill District, but the interior is the **Modern Restaurant Cafe and Bar, 862 Western Avenue**, in the North Side neighbourhood. Filming also took place in **Pittsburgh International Airport** and in the **Beaver** district.

WONDERFUL LIFE
(1964, dir: Sidney J Furie)
Cliff Richard, The Shadows, Melvyn Hayes.
● CANARY ISLANDS; LONDON

Cliff and the Shads are sacked cruise line entertainers, who manage to get employed in the movies. Hey, just like real life! Made in the Canary Islands and at Elstree Studios, with the bonus of a musical number on a boat in the Thames.

WOODSTOCK
(1970, dir: Michael Wadleigh)
Jimi Hendrix, The Who, Richie Havens.
● NEW YORK STATE

The giant split-screen documentary record of the legendary four-day rock concert (edited by the young Martin Scorsese) wasn't filmed at Woodstock at all. The concert had grown too large for its original location, which is upstate New York on Route 212 near the Catskills. The final venue, Max Yasgur's 38-acre farm, was in **Bethel**, some 50 miles southwest on Route 17B.

WORKING GIRL
(1988, dir: Mike Nichols)
Melanie Griffith, Sigourney Weaver, Harrison Ford.
● NEW YORK CITY

Office worker Melanie Griffith finally betters bitch-boss Weaver to make it in the Big Apple in this Oscar-nominated comedy. The opening shot of Griffith and Joan Cusack (both Oscar nominees) was stolen during the morning rush hour as the **Staten Island Ferry** arrives at NY's **Battery Park**. A twenty-minute ride with fabulous views of the Lower Manhattan skyline, the ferry is now free.

Petty-Marsh, the broker house where they work, is a composite of four different locations: the huge secretarial pool is a set constructed on the 21st floor of **1 State Street Plaza** on Manhattan's southern tip overlooking Battery Park; the club room was filmed at the **Midday Club**; the company's lobby is that of **7 World Trade Center**; while the reading floor is that of **LF Rothschild Company**.

The offices of the Trask Company are the 1907 Beaux

Arts-style United States Custom House, now the **Museum of the Native American, Broadway** at Bowling Green, Lower Manhattan, seen also in *Batman Forever* and *Ghostbusters II*. Weaver's Manhattan town house is an early 19th century private home on **Irving Place**, south from Gramercy Park between Third and Park Avenues.

The fictitious Union Club, site of the Trask wedding reception, is also a composite. The exterior is the familiar **Carnegie Mansion**, home of the Cooper-Hewitt Museum, **2 East 91st Street** at Fifth Avenue on the East Side, while the interior was shot just across the street in the 1904 Burden Mansion, now the **Convent of the Sacred Heart, 1 East 91st Street** (see *The Anderson Tapes* for details).

WORLD ACCORDING TO GARP, THE
(1982, dir: George Roy Hill)
Robin Williams, Mary Beth Hurt, Glenn Close.
● NEW YORK STATE; NEW JERSEY; CONNECTICUT

Confused and tiresome film of John Irving's complex novel, with Robin Williams' Garp struggling to become a writer, Glenn Close as Jenny Fields, his bizarre proto-feminist mother, and John Lithgow as a sex-changed ex-footballer.

The beachfront home of Close's parents is a private estate on **Fishers Island**, New York State. Long fought over by New York and Connecticut, Fishers Island was eventually awarded to NY in 1879, despite being much closer to the New England state – the locals prefer to identify with Connecticut. The island is a remote summer getaway for the very, very rich. The Everett Steering School, where Garp grows up, is the expansive green 600-acre campus of **Millbrook School, School Road, Millbrook**, about 12 miles northeast of Poughkeepsie, Route 44, in the Hudson Valley, upstate New York (seen also in *Regarding Henry*).

The home Jenny Fields buys for Garp and his wife is **2 Brassie Road, Eastchester** on Route 22, north of New York City on the road to White Plains. A façade was constructed at the end of the runway of **Lincoln Park Airport**, off I-80, in northern New Jersey, for the scene where a plane crashes into the front of the house.

Also in Lincoln Park is the college where Garp's wife teaches, **Rutgers University Campus**. Fields is assassinated in front of the town hall of **Madison**, New Jersey, the **Hartley Dodge Memorial Building, Kings Road** at Green Avenue. Filming also took place at **Norwich**, Connecticut; **Roslyn**, Nassau County, Long Island and **Tuckahoe**, NY.

WORLD IS NOT ENOUGH, THE
(1999, dir: Michael Apted)
Pierce Brosnan, Robert Carlyle, Sophie Marceau.
● LONDON; SURREY; BUCKINGHAMSHIRE; HERTFORDSHIRE; WILTSHIRE; AZERBAIJAN; FRANCE; SPAIN; TURKEY; SCOTLAND; WALES

Third in the increasingly confident Brosnan Bonds, given a little more weight than usual by a top-drawer cast and the director of *Gorillas in the Mist*. The opening teaser is set against the backdrop of Frank O Gehry's stunning, titanium-plated **Guggenheim Museum**, on the Nerrión River in the centre of **Bilbao** (*www.guggenheim-bilbao/es*). But when test audiences felt a bit short-changed with a

The boat chase from the real MI6 HQ; Vauxhall

single stunt, the titles were shunted back to include the Thames boat chase as part of the pre-credits sequence. In a move which garnered plenty of publicity, the movie opens at the real MI6 headquarters on the Thames at **Vauxhall Bridge**. The subsequent boat chase (much cut down) was shot, not so much on the Thames, as on waterways and docks. The rollover is the **Royal Victoria Dock**, at Canning Town – actually over the Thames from the chase's climax. The opening bridge is **Glengall Bridge, Millwall Inner Dock** on the Isle of Dogs – the great loop of the Thames Bond appears to shortcut to reach the Dome. It's back toward Tower Bridge for the leap through the canoe clubhouse, at **Tobacco Dock** on the tiny **Ornamental Canal** at **Wapping Lane** near Shadwell, E1. A crafty cut has Bond's boat tearing ashore at **Chatham High Street**, in Kent, before emerging opposite the then uncompleted **Millennium Dome, Greenwich**.

The temporary MI6 HQ in Scotland is made up of two separate locations. The funeral scene uses the chapel at **Stowe School** in Buckinghamshire (see *Indiana Jones and the Last Crusade* for details), though Castle Thane itself really is north of the border. It's **Eilean Donan Castle**, at **Dornie** near the Kyle of Lochalsh, probably most familiar from *Highlander* (© *01599.555202, www.eileandonancastle.com*).

The vast, sprawling oilfields of Azerbaijan are the real thing, at **Baku** on the Caspian Sea, though closer shots are of the familiar old standby **Black Park**, near to the Pinewood Studios, and **Hankley Common, Tilford Road** south of Tilford in Surrey. The oil pipeline site itself is at **Cuenca**, central Spain (but don't go looking for the beautiful little chapel, which was only a set).

The skiing sequence, supposedly in the Caucasus Mountains, where the paragliders attack, is high on the slopes of Mont Blanc near **Chamonix** on the Italian-French border.

From here on Azerbaijan is largely fake. The exterior of Electra's Baku palace is a mansion on the Bosphorus in Istanbul, while its interior is **Luton Hoo**, Luton (see *Four Weddings and a Funeral* for details), a veteran location seen in *Eyes Wide Shut*, Pink Panther sequel *A Shot in the Dark* and *Wilde*, among many other films. And it provides more backdrops here too, as the casino bar. The casino itself is the RAF officers' mess at **Horton**, Buckinghamshire. The airport from which Bond makes his nighttime escape is **Northolt Airport**.

The Kazakhstan site, where Bond meets Christmas, is **Bardenas Reales** near Tudela in Spain, while the gleaming pipeline terminal is the **Motorola Building** at **Swindon** in Wiltshire. The pipeline itself is in the mountains of **Snowdonia** in Wales, but the explosion from which Bond and Christmas escape was faked in Black Park.

M is imprisoned in **Kiz Kulesi – Maiden's Tower** –

an 11th century lighthouse at the mouth of the Bosphorus at Istanbul, Turkey.

WRONG MAN, THE
(1957, dir: Alfred Hitchcock)
Henry Fonda, Vera Miles, Anthony Quayle.
● NEW YORK CITY; NEW YORK STATE

Hitchcock's untypically downbeat documentary-style drama, with jazz muso Fonda mistakenly arrested as an armed robber, is based on the true story of Manny Balastrero, and was shot, wherever possible, on the story's real locations.

The Stork Club, where Fonda plays jazz, stood at 3 East 53rd Street until it closed in 1965. Since 1967, Samuel Paley Plaza has stood on the site. Hitchcock uses the cells where Balastrero was held and the real court where he was tried. Other locations include the **Prudential Insurance Office** in the **Victor Moore Arcade, Queens**; the home of the real Christopher Balastrero on **74th Street, Queens**; the Balastreros' summer resort at the **Edelweiss Farm**, Cornwall, Route 9W by the Hudson just north of West Point Military Academy; the **Greenmont Sanatorium**, where Mrs Balastrero was treated after her breakdown, Ossining, Route 9 east of the Hudson River north of NYC.

Look out during the movie for the real culprit: outside the Stork Club, in the Victor Moore Arcade, and in one of the liquor stores where the cops take Manny.

WUTHERING HEIGHTS
(1939, dir: William Wyler)
Laurence Olivier, Merle Oberon, David Niven.
● LOS ANGELES; YORKSHIRE

The first sound adaptation of Emily Brontë's novel, with location shooting near **Chatsworth**, California. Kilos of heather were imported from northern England and replanted in California to match up with location shots of the Yorkshire moors. The ducks and geese look cute, and are remarkably quiet. That's because they had their vocal chords snipped to prevent extraneous noise on the soundtrack.

WUTHERING HEIGHTS
(1992, dir: Peter Kosminsky)
Juliette Binoche, Ralph Fiennes, Janet McTeer.
● YORKSHIRE

After Robert Fuest's stately but passionless version in 1970, shot in the West Riding of Yorkshire, comes this unsuccessful remake, with a miscast Binoche. Wuthering Heights is just north of **Grassington**, where the frontage of the house was erected. Thrushcross Grange, home of Edgar Linton, is **Broughton Hall, Skipton** (© *01756.792267, open during summer*). Heathcliff works in the barn and outhouses of the 17th century manor house **East Riddlesden Hall, Bradford Road, Keighley** (*admission charge; © 01535.607075, rail: Keighley*). Standing stones were erected at **Boss Moor**. Cathy and Heathcliff declare their love near **Aysgarth Falls**, seen in *Robin Hood: Prince of Thieves*. Also shot at **Malham Rocks** and **Malham Cove, Malham**, north Yorkshire.

X

X-FILES, THE
(1998, dir: Rob Bowman)
David Duchovny, Gillian Anderson, Martin Landau.
● CALIFORNIA; LONDON; WASHINGTON DC;
BRITISH COLUMBIA, CANADA

The old stamping ground of the smash TV series used to be Vancouver, where the first six series were shot (and you can find plenty of *X-Files* tours of the city), but the big screen version moved south to California. The Dallas Federal Building, blown up at the beginning of the movie, is the old **Unocal Building, Fifth Street** at Beaudry Street, downtown LA, now finding a new lease of life as a movie location (it also houses film location offices). The FBI lab was on the 26th floor. The 'bee domes'

Mulder meets Kurtzweil: Casey's Bar, South Grand Avenue, downtown LA

The meeting of elders, exterior: Queen Alexandra's House, Kensington Gore...

... though the interior is the Athenaeum, South Hill Avenue, Pasadena

in the cornfield are at **Bakersfield**, in the desert north of LA, as is the desert epilogue – supposedly in Tunisia at Foum Tatouine – a jokey reference to the *Star Wars* desert location.

Mulder meets Kurtzweil at **Casey's Bar, 613 South Grand Avenue**, downtown Los Angeles (seen also in Michelle Pfeiffer weepie *The Deep End of the Ocean*). Kurtzweil's apartment, where Mulder discovers the cops already searching, is the **Mira Monte Apartments** in LA.

The Well-Manicured Man attends the meeting of elders at **Queen Alexandra's House, Kensington Gore**, SW7, near the **Albert Hall** in Kensington, London, but the interior is the **Athenaeum**, the dining club of the California Institute of Technology, at **551 South Hill Avenue** in Pasadena (a frequently used location, seen in *Beverly Hills Cop* and *True Romance* among others). The railway crossing scene is at **Soledad Canyon** at Saugus, just north of LA, also the location for Steven Spielberg's classic road movie *Duel*. Mulder and the Well-Manicured Man drive by the **Department of Agriculture Building** in DC. While the Cigarette-Smoking Man watches, the unconscious Scully is loaded onto the plane at **LAX, Los Angeles International Airport**. The hospital is the **St Mary Medical Center, 1050 Linden Avenue** in Long Beach, California.

The Antarctic location is a glacier above the ski resort of **Whistler**, British Columbia.

X-MEN
(2000, dir: Bryan Singer)
Patrick Stewart, Ian McKellen, Hugh Jackman.
● ONTARIO, CANADA

Set mainly around New York, Singer's dark, intelligent comic-strip adaptation was made almost entirely in Ontario. The opening concentration camp scene, in 'Poland, 1944', used the old **Gooderham-Worts Distillery, Mill Street** toward the Toronto waterfront, an abandoned complex whose empty warehouses are frequently used as makeshift studios (*Blues Brothers 2000*, *The Long Kiss Goodnight*, *Mimic* and *Three Men and a Baby* are among many movies shot here). The lowlife bar in northern Alberta where Wolverine is first discovered is also the old distillery.

The concentration camp: Gooderham-Worts Distillery, Toronto

Also in central Toronto is the dazzling metal and glass centre of the senate hearings, the **Metro Hall Council Chamber, St John Street**, and the Ellis Island meeting place for the Conference of World Leaders, which is **Central Commerce Collegiate, 570 Shaw Street**, west of the city.

The interior of Dr Xavier's academy: Casa Loma, Toronto

The stretch of road where Wolverine's truck is attacked is east of Toronto in the nature conservation area, the **Rouge River Valley Park**. Further east still, in the city of **Oshawa** you'll find Mutant High, Dr Xavier's

The interior of Dr Xavier's academy, schoolroom: Casa Loma, Toronto

Cyclops' motorbike: The Stables, Casa Loma, Toronto

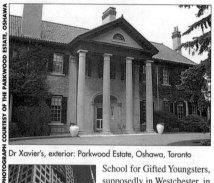

Dr Xavier's, exterior: Parkwood Estate, Oshawa, Toronto

The senate hearing: Metro Hall, St John Street, Toronto

School for Gifted Youngsters, supposedly in Westchester, in reality the **Parkwood Estate, 270 Simcoe Street North** (*admission charge;* © *905.433.4311*) which you might recognise from Adam Sandler comedy *Billy Madison* or Shirley MacLaine's *Mrs Winterbourne*. The interior of the school, though, is **Casa Loma, 1 Austin Terrace** at Spadina Road (*admission charge;* © *416.923.1171*), a turn-of-the-century mock-medieval folly overlooking northern Toronto. The building is a frequent film location (see it in David Cronenberg's *Dead Ringers* and in Jean-Claude van Damme actioner *Maximum Risk*), and here you'll find Xavier's study, the conservatory where mutant children learn to channel their skills, and the old Stables, where Cyclops' bike is stashed.

Magneto's lair was constructed in a forest clearing at the **Greenwood Conservation Area** in **Hamilton**, about 40 miles southwest of Toronto. Westchester Railway Station, where Cerebro traces Rogue, and Magneto uses his electromagnetic powers to levitate the police cars, is also Hamilton, the **Old Hamilton Train Station**, the location of the spectacular shoot-out in *The Long Kiss Goodnight*. Liberty Island is actually **Spencer Smith Park** in **Burlington**, east of Hamilton, while some of the interior shots of the statue are the **Bridgeman Transformer Station**.

X – THE MAN WITH X-RAY EYES (aka *The Man With X-Ray Eyes*)
(1963, dir: Roger Corman)
Ray Milland, John Hoyt, Diana Van Der Vlis.
● LOS ANGELES

Corman again makes the most of a microbudget in this story of a scientist who develops x-ray vision, only to be driven bonkers by what he sees. The Las Vegas scenes were shot on soundstages and around LA. The x-ray visions of transparent buildings were achieved by photographing construction sites from the same angle over a period of time, then reversing the shots so the buildings appear to dissolve.

Y

YANKS
(1979, dir: John Schlesinger)
Vanessa Redgrave, Richard Gere, William Devane.
● LANCASHIRE; YORKSHIRE

Schlesinger's tearjerker has GIs bringing a glimpse of romance, and not a little resentment, to a Lancashire town during WWII. The dance scene is in **Hyde Town Hall**, near Manchester, with more filming in **Stockport**. The army camp is in Yorkshire – **Steeton Ordinance Camp**, **Steeton**, an abandoned army facility a couple of miles northwest of Keighley – as is the railway station, **Keighley** itself.

YEAR MY VOICE BROKE, THE
(1987, dir: John Duigan)
Noah Taylor, Loene Carmen, Ben Mendelsohn.
● NEW SOUTH WALES, AUSTRALIA

Smalltown drama set in early sixties Australia. It was shot in the town of **Braidwood**, New South Wales.

YEAR OF LIVING DANGEROUSLY, THE
(1982, dir: Peter Weir)
Mel Gibson, Sigourney Weaver, Linda Hunt.
● PHILIPPINES; NEW SOUTH WALES, AUSTRALIA

The film's actual setting of Indonesia was obviously out from the start, and production began in the Philippines, but threats from Islamic fundamentalists soon closed the production down. The production relocated to the comparative safety of Australia, largely around Sydney. The café and wharf are **Metro Manila**, with more filming at **Chatsworth**, a northern suburb of Sydney.

YEAR OF THE DRAGON
(1985, dir: Michael Cimino)
Mickey Rourke, John Lone, Ariane.
● NORTH CAROLINA; NEW YORK CITY

Viet-vet Rourke fights corruption in New York's Chinatown in this thriller, written by Oliver Stone. Most of the Big Apple locations were recreated on the backlot of the de Laurentiis Studios in **Wilmington**, North Carolina.

YOU ONLY LIVE TWICE
(1967, dir: Lewis Gilbert)
Sean Connery, Tetsuro Tamba, Akiko Wakabayashi.
● JAPAN; GIBRALTAR; BAHAMAS; SCOTLAND; SPAIN

Bond gets killed off before the opening credits, but – surprise! – it's only a ruse. He's buried at sea in Hong Kong Harbour, but what happens to the buildings and the hills and the teeming boats after the initial establishing shot? The burial was actually shot aboard HMS *Tenby*, safely anchored in **Gibraltar Harbour**, while the undersea rescue was across the Atlantic in the Bahamas.

Bond's mission takes him to Japan, dispatched to Tokyo to see Mr Henderson – played by Blofeld-in-waiting Charles Gray. The headquarters of Osato Chemicals is Tokyo's **Hotel New Otani, 4-1 Kioi-cho, Chiyoda-Ku** (© *81.3.3265.1111, www.newotani.co.jp/tokyo/en*), a vast luxury block built in 1964 in time for the Olympic Games.

Bond dodges SPECTRE agents at the docks of **Kobe**, an industrial port near to Osaka (and, more recently, badly damaged in a disastrous earthquake). His crashlanding of Helga Brandt's plane, somewhere in Japan, is actually at **Finmere** in Scotland. Back in Japan, the helicopter flight was filmed above the village of **Ebino**, where aerial photographer Johnny Jordon lost a leg when the blades of another helicopter came too close. The sequence was later completed in the skies above **Torremolinos**, Spain.

The Ninja training school, where Bond limbers up and turns Japanese, is **Himeji Castle**, the White Heron Castle on a bluff overlooking the town of **Himeji**, 33 miles west of Kobe. It's about ten minutes from Himeji Station, from where you can see it clearly. There were a few problems with the press when it was claimed one of the steel darts became embedded in the venerable landmark's wooden wall. You can also see Himeji Castle in Kurosawa's epics *Kagemusha* and *Ran*. The extinct volcano, beneath which Blofeld establishes his hideout, can be found in **Kirishima National Park** near to Kagoshima, at the southern tip of Kyushu, the southern island of Japan. The interior is a vast $1 million set constructed under canvas on an outdoor site at Pinewood.

YOUNG FRANKENSTEIN
(1974, dir: Mel Brooks)
Gene Wilder, Peter Boyle, Marty Feldman.
● LOS ANGELES

Loving pastiche of the Universal horror movies of the thirties, which even utilises props and lab equipment from the 1931 *Frankenstein*. The lecture theatre, where Frankenstein teaches, is **Hoffman Hall, University of Southern California** in the Exposition Park area, south of downtown LA.

YOUNG GUNS
(1988, dir: Christopher Cain)
Emilio Estevez, Kiefer Sutherland, Lou Diamond Phillips.
● NEW MEXICO

Brat pack Western, filmed in New Mexico, mainly in and around **Cerrillos**, a small town on I-14 between Santa Fe and Albuquerque. Also at **Galisteo**; **Ojo Caliente** and at **Rancho de las Golondrinas**. Look out for a tiny uncredited cameo by Tom Cruise as a bewhiskered bad guy.

YOUNG GUNS II – BLAZE OF GLORY
(1990, dir: Geoff Murphy)
Emilio Estevez, Kiefer Sutherland, Lou Diamond Phillips.
● NEW MEXICO; ARIZONA

The sequel was shot around **White Sands National Mon-**

ument and **Santa Fe,** New Mexico; **Tumacacori Nation-al Monument; Willcox Playa** and **Old Tucson,** Arizona.

YOUNG SHERLOCK HOLMES (aka *Young Sherlock Holmes and the Pyramid of Fear*)
(1985, dir: Barry Levinson)
Nicholas Rowe, Alan Cox, Sophie Ward.
● **BERKSHIRE; OXFORDSHIRE; KENT; LEICESTERSHIRE; LONDON**

Disappointingly witless and FX-heavy story of Holmes and Watson's schooldays from producer Spielberg, director Barry Levinson – responsible for *Diner* and *Rain Man* – and written by Chris Columbus, the director of *Home Alone.* The fictional Brompton School is an elaborate composite. The exterior is **Brasenose College, Radcliffe Square** opposite the Radcliffe Camera in Oxford, with the tower of St Mary the Virgin in the background. Once through the gates, the school quad is the quad of **Eton College, Eton,** Berkshire (for details of Eton see *Chariots of Fire*). But when Holmes and Watson look up to see Waxflatter demonstrating his flying machine, the crenellated towers are those of **Belvoir Castle** near Grantham in Leicestershire.

Belvoir, the seat of the Dukes of Rutland, was built 1816 on the site of a Norman castle. It's seven miles west of Grantham between the A52 and the A607 and

Brompton School, gates: Brasenose College, Oxford

open to the public from the beginning of April to the end of September, except Mondays and Fridays (*admission charge,* ℗ *01476. 870262*).

Brompton School, quad: Eton College, Berkshire

The school gym, where Holmes fences with schoolmaster Rathe, is the **Barons Hall** of **Penshurst Place,** a Tudor mansion in Kent (see *Anne of the Thousand Days* for details) – "Are you alright, Penshurst?" asks Rathe of one of the schoolboys. The castellated home of Cragwitch is Belvoir Castle once again.

Brompton School, towers: Belvoir Castle, Lincolnshire

Brompton School, gym: Barons Hall, Penshurst Place, Kent

And once again **Shad Thames,** on the South Bank of the Thames in London SE1 and now redeveloped as shops and restaurants, stands in for Victorian London.

Z

Z
(1969, dir: Costa-Gavras)
Yves Montand, Irene Papas, Jean-Louis Trintignant.
● ALGERIA

Costa-Gavras' political thriller, though set in an unnamed country, was based on events in Greece under the rule of the Colonels, but was made in Algeria.

ZABRISKIE POINT
(1970, dir: Michelangelo Antonioni)
Rod Taylor, Mark Frechette, Daria Halprin.
● CALIFORNIA; ARIZONA; NEVADA

After his cool, stylish Italian dramas and his foray into Swinging London with *Blowup*, Antonioni was lured to Hollywood and the result was tears all around as the film ran wildly over budget, proved incomprehensible to the studio and the director's working methods flummoxed the Hollywood crew. Antonioni brought in an Italian crew, but US union rules meant that for every Italian, there had to be an American equivalent on the payroll, standing around doing nothing. The resulting film tells us that there are a lot of billboards in California, some of the scenery is very nice but businessmen are not. Harrison Ford was in the movie, but his part was cut. Glimpse him in the background of the jail scene.

Much of the movie was shot around LA. Rod Taylor's office is the **Mobil Oil Building**, at the corner of Wilshire Boulevard and Flower Street, downtown LA, where, at a cost of thousands of dollars, an extra storey was added to the roof. The fabulous black and gold deco tower seen through Taylor's window is the **Eastern Columbia Building** (see *Predator 2* for details). Taylor's business meeting is in Phoenix, Arizona, and the famous slo-mo exploding house – covered by seventeen cameras – is also near Phoenix. The city's air traffic was held up during the filming of this profound scene, which reminds us that rich Americans have homes full of consumer goods.

The wonderful desert locations, the only reason for sitting through this pretentious mishmash, are around **Blythe**, California, and **Overton**, Nevada. But greatest of all, of course, is the wondrous **Death Valley** and **Zabriskie Point** itself. The dizzying overlook, named for a Dutch businessman who mined borax in the area, is on the east-

The desert orgy: Zabriskie Point, Death Valley

ern fringe of Death Valley near the Nevada border, on Route 190 between the tiny town of Death Valley Junction (a location for David Lynch's *Lost Highway*) and the Death Valley Visitor Center. The breathtaking sea of yellow and grey canyons is the used for the movie's surreal orgy.

ZARDOZ
(1973, dir: John Boorman)
Sean Connery, Charlotte Rampling, John Alderton.
● IRELAND

Imaginative, muddled, pretentious, sometimes boring fantasy, filmed around County Wicklow, Ireland. The Brutals, of the fiercely divided futuristic society, live in **Glencree**, a former reformatory now the Glencree Centre for Reconciliation – an organisation dedicated to bringing peace to Ireland – at Glencree, Enniskerry. The immortal elite live in **Hollybrook**, now the Brennanstown Riding School, Kilmacanogue, near Bray.

ZAZIE DANS LE METRO
(1960, dir: Louis Malle)
Catherine Demongeot, Philippe Noiret, Vittorio Caprioli.
● PARIS

Little girl causes chaos in the Paris Métro, with filming at such Parisian landmarks as the **Gare de l'Est** and the **Eiffel Tower**.

ZELIG
(1983, dir: Woody Allen)
Woody Allen, Mia Farrow, Garrett Brown.
● NEW JERSEY; NEW YORK STATE

Fake documentary about Leonard Zelig, a fictitious media celeb with a chameleon-like ability to adapt his personality to his surroundings. Filmed around New Jersey, in **Englewood**; **Alpine**; **Paramus**; **Weehawken**; **Saddle River**; **Jersey City** and **Union City**. Filming also took place at the **Old Promenade, Long Beach**, Nassau County, Long Island.

ZORBA THE GREEK
(1964, dir: Michael Cacoyannis)
Anthony Quinn, Alan Bates, Lila Kedrova.
● CRETE, GREECE

Anthony Quinn teaches Alan Bates all about life, in this filming of Nikos Kazantzakis' novel, shot around **Chania**, on the northern coast of Crete. The beach is **Stavros Beach**, on the Akrotiri Peninsula, east of the town.

ZULU
(1964, dir: Cy Endfield)
Stanley Baker, Michael Caine, James Booth.
● SOUTH AFRICA

Star Stanley Baker himself produced this account of the last stand of the British garrison against 4,000 warriors

of the Zulu nation at Rorke's Drift in 1879. The movie
was shot in South Africa, with the cooperation of Chief
Buthelezi, who actually appears in the movie playing his
ancestor Cetewayo. The actual location of Rorke's Drift,
alongside the Buffalo River, had changed beyond recognition so the movie was shot 10,000 feet above Durban
against the backdrop of the country's longest mountain
range, the Drakensburg Mountains, in the **Royal Natal
National Park**, southeast South Africa.

GAZETTEER

● **ALGERIA:** Battaglia di Algeri, La; Sheltering Sky, The; Z

● **ANTARCTICA:** Scott of the Antarctic

● **ARGENTINA:** Evita; Mission, The

● **AUSTRALIA:** "Crocodile Dundee"; Muriel's Wedding

NEW SOUTH WALES: Adventures of Priscilla, Queen of the Desert, The; Babe; Babe, Pig in the City; Cars That Ate Paris, The; Chant of Jimmie Blacksmith, The; Mad Max 2; Mad Max Beyond Thunderdome; Matrix, The; Mission: Impossible 2; My Brilliant Career; Strictly Ballroom; Year My Voice Broke, The; Year of Living Dangerously, The

NORTHERN TERRITORY: Adventures of Priscilla, Queen of the Desert, The; "Crocodile" Dundee

QUEENSLAND: Dead Calm; Muriel's Wedding; Thin Red Line, The

SOUTH AUSTRALIA: Adventures of Priscilla, Queen of the Desert, The; Gallipoli; Mad Max Beyond Thunderdome; Picnic at Hanging Rock; Shine

VICTORIA: Mad Max; Picnic at Hanging Rock; Romper Stomper; Strictly Ballroom

● **AUSTRIA:** Bad Timing; Chitty Chitty Bang Bang; Day of the Jackal, The; Götterdammerung; Great Race, The; Help!; Living Daylights, The; Night Porter, The; Sound of Music, The; Third Man, The; Three Musketeers, The; Where Eagles Dare

● **AZERBAIJAN:** World Is Not Enough, The

● **BAHAMAS:** Cocoon; For Your Eyes Only; Help!; Jaws the Revenge; Never Say Never Again; Silence of the Lambs, The; Spy Who Loved Me, The; Thunderball; You Only Live Twice

● **BAVARIA:** Spy Who Came in from the Cold, The

● **BELGIAN CONGO:** King Solomon's Mines

● **BELGIUM:** C'est Arrivé pres de Chez Vous; Lust for Life; Toto le Heros

● **BELIZE:** Dogs of War, The; Mosquito Coast, The

● **BORA BORA:** Mutiny on the *Bounty* (1962)

● **BRAZIL:** Anaconda; Emerald Forest, The; Fitzcarraldo; Moonraker

● **CAMEROONS:** Greystoke: The Legend of Tarzan, Lord of the Apes

● **CANADA:** Atlantic City; Doctor Zhivago; Spy Who Loved Me, The

ALBERTA: Days of Heaven; Legends of the Fall; Little Big Man; River of No Return; Silver Streak; Superman; Superman III; Unforgiven

BRITISH COLUMBIA: Blade; Jumanji; Legends of the Fall; Little Women (1994); Look Who's Talking; McCabe and Mrs. Miller; Neverending Story, The; Rocky IV; Roxanne; Thing, The (1982); Timecop; X-Files, The. **Vancouver:** Carnal Knowledge

ONTARIO: American Psycho; Bride of Chucky; Cocktail; Crash; Dead Ringers; 54; Fly, The; Freshman, The; Good Will Hunting; Hurricane, The; In the Mouth of Madness; Johnny Mnemonic; Long Kiss Goodnight, The; Maximum Risk; Moonstruck; Murder at 1600; Naked Lunch, The; Network; Niagara; Nightbreed; Sea of Love; Silver Streak; Suspect; Sweet Hereafter, The; 3 Men and a Baby; To Die For; Urban Legend; Videodrome; X-Men

QUEBEC: Hotel New Hampshire, The; I Confess; Rabid; Jesus of Montreal; Scanners; Shivers; Snake Eyes

● **CANARY ISLANDS:** Land That Time Forgot, The; Moby Dick; When Dinosaurs Ruled the Earth; Wonderful Life

● **CAYMAN ISLANDS:** Firm, The

● **CHINA:** Armageddon; Empire of the Sun; Last Emperor, The; Raise the Red Lantern

● **COLOMBIA:** Mission, The

● **CORSICA:** Big Blue, The

● **COSTA RICA:** 1492: Conquest of Paradise

● **CROATIA:** Titus

● **CZECH REPUBLIC:** Mission: Impossible

● **CZECHOSLOVAKIA:** Amadeus; Closely Observed Trains; Nosferatu, Phantom der Nacht

● **DENMARK:** Anastasia; Babette's Feast; Breaking the Waves; Topaz

● **DOMINICAN REPUBLIC:** Godfather Part II, The

● **EGYPT:** Awakening, The; Death on the Nile; Gallipoli; Malcolm X; Spy Who Loved Me, The; Ten Commandments, The (1956)

● **ENGLAND:**

AVON: Agatha; Canterbury Tales, The; Music Lovers, The; Remains of the Day, The; Titfield Thunderbolt, The

BEDFORDSHIRE: Batman; Eyes Wide Shut; Four Weddings and a Funeral; Never Say Never Again

BERKSHIRE: Alien; Arabesque; Buster; Carry On Again Doctor; Carry On Behind; Carry On Dick; Carry On Loving; Carry On Regardless; Chariots of Fire; Die, Monster, Die; Dracula (1958); Eagle Has Landed, The; Elizabeth; Empire of the Sun; French Lieutenant's Woman, The; Genevieve; Land That Time Forgot, The; Madness of King George, The; Murder by Death; Music Lovers, The; Quatermass Xperiment, The; Rocky Horror Picture Show, The; Shakespeare in Love; Theatre of Blood; 3 Men and a Little Lady; View to a Kill, A; Young Sherlock Holmes

BUCKINGHAMSHIRE: Blithe Spirit; Brazil; Brief Encounter; Carry On at Your Convenience; Carry On Behind; Carry On Camping; Carry On Cowboy; Carry On Dick; Carry On—Don't Lose Your Head; Carry On Girls; Carry On Up the Khyber; Chitty Chitty Bang Bang; Clockwork Orange, A; Curse of Frankenstein, The; Dad's Army; Darling; Dead of Night; Devil Rides Out, The; Dracula (1958); Emma; First Knight; Four Weddings and a Funeral; Genevieve; Goldfinger; Help!; Isadora; Lolita (1961); Monty Python's The Meaning of Life; Mummy, The; Murder Ahoy; Murder at the Gallop; Murder She Said; Music Lovers, The; Never Say Never Again; Nightbreed; On Her Majesty's Secret Service; Plague of the Zombies, The; Robin Hood: Prince of Thieves; Ruling Class, The; Sleepy Hollow; Superman II; Superman IV: The Quest for Peace; To the Devil a Daughter; Time Bandits; Valentino; Went the Day Well; White Hunter, Black Heart; Witchfinder General; World Is Not Enough, The

CAMBRIDGESHIRE: Awakening, The; Full Metal Jacket; Maurice; Nightcomers, The; Revolution

CHESHIRE: Patton; Robin Hood

CORNWALL: Dracula (1979); Eagle Has Landed, The; Knights of the Round Table; Scott of the Antarctic; Straw Dogs; Thief of Bagdad, The; Three Musketeers, The; Treasure Island (1950); Twelfth Night

CUMBERLAND: Stars Look Down, The

CUMBRIA: Brazil; Julia; Mahler; Withnail & I. **Lake District:** Dam Busters, The; Paradine Case, The; Tommy

DERBYSHIRE: Elizabeth; Goodbye Mr. Chips (1939); Jane Eyre; Women in Love

DEVON: Catch Us If You Can; French Lieutenant's Woman, The; Howards End; I See a Dark Stranger; Isadora; Knights of the Round Table; Matter of Life and Death, A (1946); Remains of the Day, The; Revolution; Sense and Sensibility; Top Secret!

DORSET: Browning Version, The; Damned, The; Emma; Far from the Madding Crowd; French Lieutenant's Woman, The; Sleuth; Tom Jones; Valentino; Wilde

ESSEX: Canterbury Tales, The; Four Weddings and a Funeral; High Hopes; Quatermass II

GLOUCESTERSHIRE: Assam Garden, The; Barry Lyndon; Canterbury Tales, The; If . . . ; Maurice

HAMPSHIRE: Boyfriend, The; Emma; First Knight; Four Weddings and a Funeral; Inn of the Sixth Happiness, The; Lady Vanishes, The; Man for All Seasons, A; Mission: Impossible; Modesty Blaise; Music Lovers, The; Ruling Class, The; That'll Be the Day; Tommy; Wilde

HERTFORDSHIRE: Abominable Dr. Phibes, The; Anastasia; Batman; Clockwork Orange, A; Curse of the Crimson Altar; Devil Rides Out, The; Dirty Dozen, The; Dracula A.D. 1972; Four Weddings and a Funeral; Goldeneye; Greystoke: The Legend of Tarzan, Lord of the Apes; Henry VIII and His Six Wives; Here We Go Round the Mulberry Bush; Horror Hospital; In Which We Serve; Jassy; Kiss Before Dying, A; Lair of the White Worm, The; Mahler; Murder at the Gallop; Murder on the Orient Express; Nanny, The; Night of the Demon; Peter's Friends; Quatermass II; Satanic Rites of Dracula, The; Saving Private Ryan; School for Scoundrels; Shadowlands; Shakespeare in Love; Shot in the Dark, A; Sleepy Hollow; Taste the Blood of Dracula; Tommy; Tomorrow Never Dies; Topsy-Turvy; 2001: A Space Odyssey; Vampire Lovers, The; Village of the Damned (1960); Wicked Lady, The (1983); Wilde; Wings of the Dove, The; World Is Not Enough, The

ISLE OF MAN: I See a Dark Stranger; Waking Ned

ISLE OF WIGHT: Mrs. Brown

KENT: Anne of the Thousand Days; Brazil; Canterbury Tale, A; Collector, The; Draughtsman's Contract, The; Follow That Camel; Great Expectations (1946); Hamlet (1991); Henry VIII and His Six Wives; Kind Hearts and Coronets; Moonraker; Mummy, The; Room with a View, A; Saint, The; Young Sherlock Holmes

LANCASHIRE: Brief Encounter; Entertainer, The; Hear My Song; Kind of Loving, A; Richard III; Taste of Honey, A; Whistle Down the Wind; Yanks

LEICESTERSHIRE: Buster; Shadowlands; Young Sherlock Holmes

LINCOLNSHIRE: Dam Busters, The; Emerald Forest, The; Haunting, The (1999); Holiday Camp; Ruling Class, The

LONDON: Abominable Dr. Phibes, The; Absolute Beginners; Accident; African Queen, The; Agatha; Alfie; Aliens; American Werewolf in London, An; Angel at My Table, An; Anne of the Thousand Days; Arabesque; Around the World in Eighty Days; Awakening, The; Backbeat; Bad Timing; Batman; Billion Dollar Brain; Billy Liar; Blackmail; Blowup; Blue Lamp, The; Bounty, The; Brannigan; Brassed Off; Brazil; Brief Encounter; Britannia Hospital; Bunny Lake Is Missing; Buster; Carry On Regardless; Castaway; Catch Us If You Can; Chaplin; Charge of the Light Brigade, The (1968); Children of the Damned; Clockwork Orange, A; Collector, The; Crying Game, The; Dance with a Stranger; Darling; Day of the Jackal, The; Day of the Triffids, The; Day the Earth Caught Fire, The; Deep End; Doctor in the House; Dr. No; Dracula A.D. 1972; Duellists, The; 84 Charing Cross Road; Elephant Man, The; Empire of the Sun; Entertaining Mr. Sloane; Eyes Wide Shut; Fallen Idol, The; Fish Called Wanda, A; For Your Eyes Only; Four Weddings and a Funeral; French Lieutenant's Woman, The; Frenzy; Full Metal Jacket; Gandhi; Genevieve; Georgy Girl; Goldeneye; Great Expectations (1946); Greystoke: The Legend of Tarzan, Lord of the Apes; Hard Day's Night, A; Heat and Dust; Hellraiser; Help!; High Hopes; Howards End; Hudson Hawk; Hunger, The; Indiscreet; Ipcress File, The; Isadora; It Always Rains on Sunday; Italian Job, The; Jubilee; Kid for Two Farthings, A; Killing of Sister George, The; Kiss Before Dying, A; Knack . . . and How to Get It, The; Krays, The; L-Shaped Room, The; Lady Vanishes, The; Ladykillers, The; Lawrence of Arabia; Leather Boys, The; Life and Death of Colonel Blimp, The; Living Daylights, The; Loch Ness; Lock, Stock and Two Smoking Barrels; Long Good Friday, The; Look Back in Anger; Madness of King George, The; Man Who Knew Too Much, The (1934); Man Who Knew Too Much, The (1956); Maurice; Million Pound Note, The; Mission: Impossible; Modesty Blaise; Mona Lisa; Monty Python's The Meaning of Life; Murder on the Orient Express; Murder She Said; Music Lovers, The; My Beautiful Laundrette; Naked; Nanny, The; Night of the Demon; Nineteen Eighty-Four; Notting Hill; Paradine Case, The; Passenger, The; Passport to Pimlico; Patriot Games; Peeping Tom; Performance; Pink Floyd—The Wall; Prick Up Your Ears; Prince and the Showgirl, The; Private Life of Sherlock Holmes, The; Quadrophenia; Quatermass Xperiment, The; Red Shoes, The; Repulsion; Return of the Pink Panther, The; Richard III; Ring of Bright Water; Robin Hood: Prince of Thieves; Room with a View, A; Ruling Class, The; Sabotage; Saint, The; Satanic Rites of Dracula, The; Saturday Night and Sunday Morning; Scandal; Secret Ceremony; Secrets and Lies; Sense and Sensibility; Servant, The; Shadowlands; Shakespeare in Love; Shine; Shirley Valentine; Shooting Fish; Sid and Nancy; Sleepy Hollow; Sliding Doors; Smallest Show on Earth, The; Stage Fright; Sunday Bloody Sunday; 10 Rillington Place; Taste of Honey, A; Theatre of Blood; Titfield Thunderbolt, The; Tom Brown's Schooldays; Tom Jones; Tommy; Tomorrow Never Dies; Trainspotting; Travels with My Aunt; Velvet Goldmine; Victim; Villain; Waterloo Road; Who Framed Roger Rabbit?; Wicked Lady, The (1983); Wilde; Wings of the Dove, The; Withnail & I; Wonderful Life; World Is Not Enough, The; X-Files, The; Young Sherlock Holmes

MANCHESTER: Hobson's Choice; In the Name of the Father; A Kind of Loving; Raining Stones; Taste of Honey, A

MERSEYSIDE: Chariots of Fire; Scandal; Shirley Valentine. **Liverpool:** Backbeat; Hunt for Red October, The; In the Name of the Father

MIDDLESEX: Bounty, The; Clockwork Orange, A; Curse of the Crimson Altar; Elizabeth; Emma; Frankenstein Must Be Destroyed; Kiss Before Dying, A; Lavender Hill Mob, The; Madness of King George, The; Prime of Miss Jean Brodie, The; Richard III; Saint, The; Shirley Valentine; Thirty-Nine Steps, The

MIDLAND: Birmingham: Brassed Off

NORFOLK: Full Metal Jacket; Go-Between, The; Julia; Revolution; Shakespeare in Love; Tomb of Ligeia, The; Wicked Lady, The (1945)

NORTHAMPTONSHIRE: Another Country; Top Secret!; Thunderball

NORTHUMBERLAND: Alien 3; Cul-de-Sac; Devils, The; Elizabeth; Ivanhoe; Macbeth; Mary Queen of Scots (1971); Robin Hood: Prince of Thieves; Spaceman and King Arthur, The

NOTTINGHAMSHIRE: Saturday Night and Sunday Morning; Scandal; Sons and Lovers

OXFORDSHIRE: Accident; Another Country; Arabesque; Fish Called Wanda, A; Greystoke: The Legend of Tarzan, Lord of the Apes; Hamlet (1997); Heaven's Gate; Howards End; Julia; Madness of King George, The; Man for All Seasons, A; Saint, The; Saraband for Dead Lovers; Shadowlands; Shakespeare in Love; 3 Men and a Little Lady; Titfield Thunderbolt, The; Tomorrow Never Dies; Wilde; Young Sherlock Holmes

SHROPSHIRE: Gone to Earth; Howards End

SOMERSET: Remains of the Day, The; Sense and Sensibility; Tom Jones

SUFFOLK: Canterbury Tales, The; Tomorrow Never Dies; Wind in the Willows, The; Witchfinder General

SURREY: Accident; American Werewolf in London, An; Carry On Columbus; Carry On—Don't Lose Your Head; Carry On Sergeant; Darling; Dr. Strangelove or: How I Learned to Stop Worrying and Love the Bomb; Fish Called Wanda, A; Four Weddings and a Funeral; Gladiator; Goldeneye; Howards End; In the Bleak Midwinter; Lawrence of Arabia; Loneliness of the Long Distance Runner, The; Mummy, The; Pink Floyd—The Wall; Ruling Class, The; Topsy-Turvy; Wings of the Dove, The; World Is Not Enough, The

SUSSEX: Adventures of Quentin Durward, The; Barry Lyndon; Black Narcissus; Brighton Rock; Canterbury Tales, The; Carry On at Your Convenience; Carry On Girls; Chaplin; Henry V (1989); Innocents, The; Leather Boys, The; Loot; Madness of King George, The; Mary Queen of Scots (1971); Mona Lisa; Quadrophenia; Richard III; Robin Hood: Prince of Thieves; View to a Kill, A; Wish You Were Here

TYNESIDE: Get Carter; Mary Queen of Scots (1971)

WARWICKSHIRE: Death on the Nile; Haunting, The (1963); Tom Brown's Schooldays; Wicked Lady, The (1983)

WEST COUNTRY: Hard Day's Night, A

WILTSHIRE: Barry Lyndon; Bounty, The; Doctor Dolittle (1967); Far from the Madding Crowd; Help!; Madness of King George, The; Maurice; Mrs. Brown; Moon-Raker, The; Music Lovers, The; Night of the Demon; Nineteen Eighty-Four; Remains of the Day, The; Robin Hood: Prince of Thieves; Scandal; Sense and Sensibility; World Is Not Enough, The

WORCESTER: Howards End

WORCESTERSHIRE: Canterbury Tales, The; Thirty-Nine Steps, The

YORKSHIRE: Agatha; Barry Lyndon; Billy Liar; Brassed Off; Chariots of Fire; Elizabeth; Entertainer, The; Full Monty, The; Holiday Camp; It Shouldn't Happen to a Vet; Jane Eyre; Kes; Little Voice; Pink Floyd—The Wall; Private Function, A; Private Life of Sherlock Holmes, The; Railway Children, The; Robin Hood: Prince of Thieves; Room at the Top; This Sporting Life; Wicked Lady, The (1983); Women in Love; Wuthering Heights (1939); Wuthering Heights (1971); Wuthering Heights (1992); Yanks

● **FIJI:** Blue Lagoon, The; Contact

● **FINLAND:** Billion Dollar Brain; Doctor Zhivago; Eagle Has Landed, The

● **FORMER YUGOSLAVIA:** Cross of Iron; Fiddler on the Roof; Murder on the *Orient Express*

● **FRANCE:** Adventures of Quentin Durward, The; Amants, Les; Amants du Pont Neuf, Les; Amerikanische Freund, Der; Armageddon; L'Atalante; Belle et la Bête, La; Big Blue, The; Boucher, Le; Bride, The; Cage aux Folles, La; C'est Arrivé pres de Chez Vous; Cet Obscur Objet de Desir; Chitty Chitty Bang Bang; Cyrano de Bergerac; Dangerous Liaisons; Danton; Day of the Jackal, The; Dejeuner sur l'Herbe; Dirty Rotten Scoundrels; Double Life of Veronique, The; Duellists, The; Enfants du Paradis, Les; Et Dieu . . . Crea la Femme; Fahrenheit 451; French Connection, The; French Connection II; Germinal; Goldeneye; Grande Illusion, La; Homme et une Femme, Un; Isadora; Jewel of the Nile, The; Jour de Fête; Journal d'une Femme de Chambre, Le; Jules et Jim; Julia; Lacombe Lucien; Le Mans; Lion in Winter, The; Longest Day, The; Lust for Life; Ma Nuit Chez Maud; Man in the Iron Mask, The (1998); Manon des Sources; Maximum Risk; Mission: Impossible; Mon Oncle; Monsieur Hulot's Holiday; Monte Carlo or Bust; Moonraker; Never Say Never Again; Raiders of the Lost Ark; Red Shoes, The; Regle du Jeu, La; Return of the Pink Panther, The; Robin Hood: Prince of Thieves; Sabrina (1995); Tess; Testament d'Orphee, Le; 37°2 le Matin; Thunderball; Tirez sur le Pianiste; To Catch a Thief; Tomorrow Never Dies; Topaz; Valmont; View to a Kill, A; Vikings, The; Visiteurs du Soir, Les; Vivement Dimanche; World Is Not Enough, The. **Marseilles:** A Bout de Souffle. **Nice:** A Propos de Nice; Never Say Never Again. **Paris:** A Bout de Souffle; L'Age d'Or; Age of Innocence, The; Alphaville; Anastasia; Angel at My Table, An; Around the World in Eighty Days; Ascenseur pour l'Echafaud; Belle de Jour; Bête Humaine, La; Boudu Sauvé des Eaux; Brazil; Chant d'Amour, Un; Charade; Charme Discret de la Bourgeoisie, Le; Chien Andalou, Un; Conformista, Il; Dernier Metro, Le; Diva; Doors, The; Everyone Says I Love You; Femme Est une Femme, Une; Frantic; Gigi; Haine, La; Hotel du Nord; Interview with the Vampire: The Vampire Chronicles; Killing Zoe; Last Tango in Paris; Lavender Hill Mob, The; Léon; Love and Death; Marathon Man; Moulin Rouge; Murder on the *Orient Express*; Quatre Cents Coups, Les; Samourai, Le; Subway; Trapeze; Travels with My Aunt; Trial, The; Zazie dans le Metro

HAUTE-SAVOIE: Genou de Claire, Le

PAYS DE LA LOIRE: Au Revoir les Enfants

PROVENCE: Jean de Florette

● **FRENCH POLYNESIA:** Love Affair (1994)

● **GERMANY:** Amerikanische Freund, Der; Barry Lyndon; Cabaret; Chitty Chitty Bang Bang; Deep End; Diamonds Are Forever; Götterdammerung; Great

Escape, The; Kings of the Road; Name of the Rose, The; Nosferatu; Nosferatu, Phantom der Nacht; Passenger, The; Rollerball; Tomorrow Never Dies; Topaz; Torn Curtain; Vikings, The; Willy Wonka and the Chocolate Factory. **Berlin:** Man Between, The; Wings of Desire. **Hamburg:** Backbeat. **Munich:** L'Année Derniére à Marienbad; Fear Eats the Soul; Paths of Glory. **Wuppertal:** Alice in den Stadten

● **GIBRALTAR:** Living Daylights, The; You Only Live Twice

● **GREECE:** Big Blue, The; For Your Eyes Only; Guns of Navarone, The; Mediterraneo; Never on Sunday; Otello; Patton; Shirley Valentine; Zorba the Greek

● **GUATEMALA:** Moonraker; Star Wars

● **HOLLAND** see **NETHERLANDS**

● **HONG KONG:** Around the World in Eighty Days; Chungking Express; Enter the Dragon; Man with the Golden Gun, The; Rush Hour; Sand Pebbles, The

● **HUNGARY:** Cyrano de Bergerac; Evita; Hudson Hawk; Love and Death

● **ICELAND:** View to a Kill, A

● **INDIA:** Aparajito; Arabian Nights; Armageddon; Around the World in Eighty Days; Close Encounters of the Third Kind; Gandhi; Heat and Dust; Kim; Octopussy; Passage to India, A; Pather Panchali; Shakespeare Wallah

● **IRAN:** Arabian Nights

● **IRAQ:** Exorcist, The

● **IRELAND:** Angel; Angela's Ashes; Barry Lyndon; Braveheart; Butcher Boy, The; Commitments, The; Crying Game, The; Excalibur; Far and Away; Hear My Song; Italian Job, The; Henry V (1944); I See a Dark Stranger; Lion in Winter, The; Lock Up Your Daughters; Michael Collins; Moby Dick; My Left Foot; Quiet Man, The; Ryan's Daughter; Saving Private Ryan; Zardoz. **Dublin:** Awfully Big Adventure, An; Dead, The; Educating Rita; In the Name of the Father; Lonely Passion of Judith Hearne, The

● **ISRAEL:** Jesus Christ Superstar; Schindler's List

● **ITALY:** Adventures of Baron Munchausen, The; Agony and the Ecstasy, The; Amadeus; Amarcord; Avanti!; Barabbas; Beat the Devil; Ben Hur (1925); Ben Hur (1959); Big Blue, The; Cliffhanger; Day of the Jackal, The; Death in Venice; Deserto Rosso, Il; Edipo Re; English Patient, The; Fellini Satyricon; For Your Eyes Only; Giardino dei Finzi-Contini, Il; Godfather Part II, The; Gospel According to St. Matthew, The; Götterdammerung; Hannah and Her Sisters; Hudson Hawk; Isadora; Jason and the Argonauts; Mid-Summer Night's Dream, A (1999); Mighty Aphrodite; Modesty Blaise; Much Ado About Nothing; My Own Private Idaho; Novecento; Pink Panther, The; Plein Soleil; Prince of Foxes; Romeo and Juliet; Salo; Spider's Stratagem, The; Star Wars: Episode 1: The Phantom Menace; Strada, La; Stromboli; Talented Mr. Ripley, The; Titus; Travels with My Aunt; Waterloo. **Capri:** Mepris, Le. **Florence:** Darling; Room with a View, A. Milan: Teorema; Trial, The. **Naples:** Crimson Pirate, The. **Parma:** Prima Della Rivoluzione. **Rome:** Accattone; L'Avventura; Belly of an Architect, The; Conformista, Il; Dolce Vita, La; L'Eclisse; Fellini's Roma; Fistful of Dollars, A; Godfather Part III, The; Ladri di Biciclette; Mepris, Le; Night Porter, The; Roman Holiday; Stazione Termini; Tenebrae; Trial, The. **Turin:** Italian Job, The. **Venice:** Don't Look Now; Everyone Says I Love You; From Russia with Love; Indiana Jones and the Last Crusade; Moonraker; Senso; Summer Madness; Vampires in Venice; Wings of the Dove, The

● **SICILY:** L'Avventura; Canterbury Tales, The; Cinema Paradiso; Gattopardo, Il; Godfather, The; Godfather Part II, The; Godfather Part III, The; Maurice; Patton

● **JAMAICA:** Cocktail; Legends of the Fall; Live and Let Die; Papillon; 20,000 Leagues Under the Sea

● **JAPAN:** Around the World in Eighty Days; Black Rain; Godzilla, King of the Monsters (1955); Hidden Fortress, The; Kagemusha; Ran; Spy Who Loved Me, The; Throne of Blood; You Only Live Twice

● **JORDAN:** Indiana Jones and the Last Crusade; Lawrence of Arabia; Sinbad and the Eye of the Tiger

● **KENYA:** Born Free; King Solomon's Mines

● **LIBYA:** Ice Cold in Alex

● **MACAU:** Indiana Jones and the Temple of Doom; Man with the Golden Gun, The

● **MALAYSIA:** Anna and the King

● **MALTA:** Gladiator; Midnight Express; Sinbad and the Eye of the Tiger; Spy Who Loved Me, The

● **MARTINIQUE:** Thomas Crown Affair, The (1999)

● **MEXICO:** Against All Odds; Altered States; Born on the Fourth of July; Bring Me the Head of Alfredo Garcia; Buster; Butch Cassidy and the Sundance Kid; Catch 22; Desperado; Doña Herlinda y Su Hijo; Dune; El; Free Willy; Game, The; Hondo; In Cold Blood; Lady from Shanghai, The; Licence to Kill; Long Goodbye, The; Magnificent Seven, The; Major Dundee; Man Called Horse, A; Nazarin; Net, The; Night of the Iguana; Pat Garrett and Billy the Kid; Predator; Rambo: First Blood Part II; Romancing the Stone; Salvador; 10; Three Kings; Titanic; Tomorrow Never Dies; Total Recall; Treasure of the Sierra Madre, The; Two Mules for Sister Sara; Unforgiven, The; Universal Soldier; Wild Bunch, The; William Shakespeare's Romeo & Juliet

● **MONACO:** Goldeneye; Monte Carlo or Bust; Red Shoes, The; To Catch a Thief

● **MOROCCO:** Bad Timing; Edipo Re; Gladiator; Jewel of the Nile, The; Kundun; Last Days of Sodom and Gomorrah, The; Last Temptation of Christ, The; Lawrence of Arabia; Living Daylights, The; Man Who Knew Too Much, The (1956); Man Who Would Be King, The; Mummy, The; Othello; Patton; Prick Up Your Ears; Return of the Pink Panther, The; Time Bandits; Travels with My Aunt

● **NEPAL:** Arabian Nights

● **NETHERLANDS:** Alice in den Stadten; Amsterdammed; Bridge Too Far, A; Diamonds Are Forever; Lust for Life; Modesty Blaise; Nosferatu; Phantom der Nacht; Secret Ceremony

● **NEW ZEALAND:** Angel at My Table, An; Bad Taste; Bounty, The; Braindead; Midnight Run; Piano, The

● **NIGER:** Sheltering Sky, The

● **NORTH AFRICA:** Arabian Nights; Passenger, The

● **NORTH ATLANTIC:** Titanic

● **NORWAY:** Empire Strikes Back, The; Revolution; Scott of the Antarctic; Vikings, The

● **PERU:** Aguirre, The Wrath of God; Big Blue, The; Fitzcarraldo

● **PHILIPPINES:** Apocalypse Now; Born on the Fourth of July; Platoon; Year of Living Dangerously, The

● **POLAND:** Double Life of Veronique, The; Kanal; Popiol y Diament; Schindler's List

● **PORTUGAL:** On Her Majesty's Secret Service

● **PUERTO RICO:** Contact; Goldeneye; Lord of the Flies; Species

● **RUSSIA:** Air Force One; Alexander Nevsky; Andrei Roublev; Battleship Potemkin; Goldeneye; Saint, The

● **RWANDA:** Gorillas in the Mist

● **ST LUCIA:** Superman

● **SARDINIA:** Boom!; Spy Who Loved Me, The

● **SAUDI ARABIA:** Malcolm X

● **SCOTLAND:** Battle of the Sexes, The; Braveheart; Breaking the Waves; Carry On Regardless; Carry On Up the Khyber; Chariots of Fire; Duellists, The; From Russia with Love; Gregory's Girl; Greystoke: The Legend of Tarzan, Lord of the Apes; Hamlet (1991); Highlander; I Know Where I'm Going; Journey to the Centre of the Earth; Kidnapped; Local Hero; Loch Ness; Long Good Friday, The; Mary Queen of Scots (1971); Mission: Impossible; Mrs. Brown; Monty Python and the Holy Grail; Prime of Miss Jean Brodie, The; Private Life of Sherlock Holmes, The; Ring of Bright Water; Rob Roy; Shallow Grave; Spy Who Loved Me, The; 39 Steps, The; Thirty-Nine Steps, The; Trainspotting; 2001: A Space Odyssey; Whisky Galore!; Wicker Man, The; World Is Not Enough, The; You Only Live Twice

● **SEYCHELLES:** Castaway; Emmanuelle

● **SLOVAKIA:** Dragonheart

● **SOLOMON ISLANDS:** Thin Red Line, The

● **SOUTH AFRICA:** Malcolm X; Ryan's Daughter; Zulu

● **SOUTH PACIFIC:** Hell in the Pacific

● **SPAIN:** Accion Mutante; Adventures of Baron Munchausen, The; L'Age d'Or; Angel at My Table, An; Around the World in Eighty Days; Cet Obscur Objet de Desir; Chimes at Midnight; Conan the Barbarian; Day of the Triffids, The; Django; Doctor Zhivago; Duck, You Sucker; El Cid; Empire of the Sun; Fall of the Roman Empire, The; Fistful of Dollars, A; For a Few Dollars More; For Your Eyes Only; 1492: Conquest of Paradise; Good, the Bad and the Ugly, The; Indiana Jones and the Last Crusade; Jamon, Jamon; King of Kings (1961); Lawrence of Arabia; Man in the Wilderness; Never Say Never Again; Pandora and the Flying Dutchman; Passenger, The; Patton; Return of the Musketeers, The; Sinbad and the Eye of the Tiger; Spartacus; Three Musketeers: The Queen's Diamonds, The; Time Bandits; Travels with My Aunt; Tristana; Valentino; Viridiana; Wilde; Wind and the Lion, The; World Is Not Enough, The; You Only Live Twice

● **SRI LANKA:** Bridge on the River Kwai, The; Indiana Jones and the Temple of Doom

● **SUDAN:** Four Feathers

● **SWEDEN:** Cries and Whispers; Elvira Madigan; Face, The; Fanny and Alexander; Hour of the Wolf; Magic Flute, The; Monte Carlo or Bust; Persona; Scott of the Antarctic; Seventh Seal, The; Smiles of a Summer Night; Summer with Monika; Through a Glass, Darkly; Virgin Spring, The; Wild Strawberries

● **SWITZERLAND:** Chaplin; Goldeneye; Goldfinger; On Her Majesty's Secret Service; Phenomena; Return of the Pink Panther, The; Spy Who Loved Me, The; View to a Kill, A; Women in Love

● **TAHITI:** Bounty, The; Mutiny on the Bounty (1935); Mutiny on the Bounty (1962)

● **TAIWAN:** Sand Pebbles, The

● **TANGANYIKA:** King Solomon's Mines; Mogambo

● **TANZANIA:** Hatari!

● **THAILAND:** Beach, The; Deer Hunter, The; Good Morning, Vietnam; Heaven & Earth; Killing Fields, The; Man with the Golden Gun, The; Tomorrow Never Dies; Year of the Dragon

● **TUNISIA:** English Patient, The; Monty Python's Life of Brian; Raiders of the Lost Ark; Star Wars; Star Wars: Episode 1: The Phantom Menace

● **TURKEY:** Armageddon; Charge of the Light Brigade, The (1968); From Russia with Love; Midnight Express; Murder on the Orient Express; Topkapi; Travels with My Aunt; World Is Not Enough, The

● **UGANDA:** African Queen, The; King Solomon's Mines; Mogambo

● **UKRAINE:** Waterloo

● **UNITED STATES OF AMERICA:**

ALABAMA: Close Encounters of the Third Kind; Mississippi Burning; Under Siege

ALASKA: Star Trek VI: The Undiscovered Country; Thing, The (1982)

ARIZONA: Alice Doesn't Live Here Any More; Apache; Back to the Future, Part III; Ballad of Cable Hogue, The; Bill & Ted's Excellent Adventure; Billy the Kid; Broken Arrow; Bus Stop; Contact; Dead Man; Death Wish; Duel in the Sun; Easy Rider; El Dorado; Electra Glide in Blue; Exorcist II: The Heretic; Gunfight at the O.K. Corral; Jerry Maguire; Johnny Guitar; Junior Bonner; Karate Kid, The; Life and Times of Judge Roy Bean, The; Lost Patrol, The; Mackenna's Gold; Man Who Shot Liberty Valance, The; Mars Attacks!; Midnight Run; My Darling Clementine; Natural Born Killers; Nutty Professor, The (1963); Planet of the Apes; Raising Arizona; Red River; Return of the Jedi; Rio Bravo; Searchers, The; She Wore a Yellow Ribbon; Star Is Born, A (1976); Star Trek: First Contact; Stargate; Starman; Stir Crazy; Superman III; Supervixens; Thief of Bagdad, The; Three Kings; Tombstone; 2001: A Space Odyssey; U Turn; Unforgiven; Vanishing American, The; Westerner, The; Wild Wild West; Winchester '73; Young Guns II—Blaze of Glory; Zabriskie Point. **Phoenix:** Grifters, The; Psycho (1960); Psycho (1998)

ARKANSAS: Client, The; Firm, The

CALIFORNIA: Addams Family Values; Adventures of Robin Hood, The; Air Force One; Airport; All Quiet on the Western Front; All the King's Men; American Beauty; American Gigolo; American Graffiti; Anna Karenina; Apache; Apt Pupil; Arachnophobia; Army of Darkness; Around the World in Eighty Days; Assassin; Back to the Future Part II; Back to the Future Part III; Bad Day at Black Rock; Bagdad Cafe; Beverly Hills Cop III; Birdman of Alcatraz, The; Birds, The; Birdy; Black Rain; Bugsy; Cable Guy, The; Captain Courageous; Casino; Chaplin; Charge of the Light Brigade, The (1936); Chase, The; China Syndrome, The; Clash by Night; Close Encounters of the Third Kind; Cocoon; Color Purple, The; Con Air; Conquest; Coogan's Bluff; Cool Hand Luke; Dead, The; Defiant Ones, The; Demolition Man; Desiree; Devil in a Blue Dress; Diamonds Are Forever; Die Hard II: Die Harder; Doctor Dolittle (1967); Doctor Dolittle (1998); Dodge City; Doors, The; Duel; Duel in the Sun; East of

Eden; Empire of the Sun; Escape from the Planet of the Apes; Every Which Way but Loose; Explorers; Family Plot; Few Good Men, A; Final Analysis; Five Easy Pieces; Flintstones, The; Fog, The; Foolish Wives; For Whom the Bell Tolls; Forever Young; 48 Hours; Foul Play; Friendly Persuasion; From Dusk Till Dawn; From Here to Eternity; Game, The; Gattaca; Ghost and Mrs. Muir, The; Glenn Miller Story, The; Go West; Godfather Part II, The; Gold Rush, The; Gone with the Wind; Graduate, The; Grapes of Wrath, The; Great Dictator, The; Great Race, The; Greatest Story Ever Told, The; Greed; Grifters, The; Grosse Pointe Blank; Gunga Din; Halloween II; Halloween III: Season of the Witch; Heaven Can Wait; High Anxiety; High Noon; High Plains Drifter; High Sierra; Hitcher, The; Hot Shots!; House; Hunt for Red October, The; I Know What You Did Last Summer; I Want to Live; In the Heat of the Night; Independence Day; Indiana Jones and the Temple of Doom; Innerspace; Iron Mask, The; Island of Lost Souls; It's a Mad Mad Mad Mad World; Johnny Belinda; Jurassic Park; Kalifornia; Kid Millions; Killer Klowns from Outer Space; Killing Fields, The; Kim; King of the Khyber Rifles; King Solomon's Mines; Kings Go Forth; Kiss Me Deadly; Kiss Me, Stupid; Lady from Shanghai, The; Lassie Come Home; Lawrence of Arabia; Leaving Las Vegas; Life Less Ordinary, A; Little Big Man; Lives of a Bengal Lancer, The; Lolita (1997); Long Riders, The; Lost Boys, The; Lost Highway; Lost Horizon; Lost World: Jurassic Park, The; Love Bug, The; Magnificent Obsession; Magnolia; Maltese Falcon, The; Man on the Moon; M*A*S*H; Mrs. Doubtfire; Moonraker; Most Dangerous Game, The; Murder in the First; Mutiny on the *Bounty* (1935); National Velvet; Net, The; Nixon; North by Northwest; Nothing Sacred; Pacific Heights; Panther; Parent Trap, The; Patriot Games; Peggy Sue Got Married; Pete's Dragon; Phantasm; Place in the Sun, A; Plan 9 from Outer Space; Planet of the Apes; Play Misty for Me; Player, The; Point Blank; Pollyanna; Poseidon Adventure, The; Postman Always Rings Twice, The; Predator II; Pump Up the Volume; Raiders of the Lost Ark; Rain Man; Rainmaker, The; Raising Cain; Rebecca; Red Badge of Courage, The; Replacement Killers, The; Return of the Jedi; Ride the High Country; River's Edge; Road to Morocco; Rock, The; Saboteur; Sandpiper, The; Scarface; Scream; Scream 2; Scream 3; Searchers, The; Seconds; Shadow, The; Shadow of a Doubt; Sheltering Sky, The; Short Cuts; Sister Act; Sister Act II: Back in the Habit; Sleeper; Southerner, The; Spartacus; Spawn; Species; Speed; Stagecoach; Stand by Me; Star Is Born, A (1954); Star Trek: The Motion Picture; Star Trek IV: The Voyage Home; Star Trek V: The Final Frontier; Star Trek VI: The Undiscovered Country; Star Trek: Generations; Star Trek: First Contact; Star Trek: Insurrection; Star Wars; Stargate; Stolen Life, A; Sudden Impact; Summer of '42; Superman; Suspicion; Sweet Dreams; Tarzan and His Mate; Teen Wolf; Ten Commandments, The (1923); Terminator 2: Judgement Day; Terror, The; Thelma & Louise; Them!; They Drive by Night; THX 1138; Time After Time; Top Gun; Topaz; Torn Curtain; Towering Inferno, The; Tramp, The; Treasure Island (1934); Tremors; Trip, The; True Grit; True Lies; Under Capricorn; Union Pacific; Vanishing, The; Vertigo; View to a Kill, A; Village of the Damned (1995); Walk in the Clouds, The; War Games; Waterloo Bridge (1940); Wayne's World 2; What's Love Got to Do with It?; Who Framed Roger Rabbit?; Wild Angels, The; Wild at Heart; Wild One, The; Wind, The; Witches of Eastwick, The; X-Files, The; Zabriskie Point. **Los Angeles:** Absolute Power; Ace in the Hole; Adam's

Rib; Addams Family, The; Advise and Consent; African Queen, The; Against All Odds; Airplane; Alice Doesn't Live Here Any More; All the President's Men; Altered States; American Pie; Amistad; Anaconda; Anna and the King of Siam; Annie Hall; Apollo 13; Armageddon; As Good as It Gets; Asphalt Jungle, The; Assault on Precinct 13; Austin Powers: International Man of Mystery; Back to the Future; Barton Fink; Batman & Robin; Batman Forever; Beach Blanket Bingo; Beast from Twenty Thousand Fathoms, The; Being There; Beverly Hills Cop; Beverly Hills Cop II; Big Business; Big Lebowski, The; Big Sleep, The; Birth of a Nation, The; Blade; Blade Runner; Blazing Saddles; Blockheads; Body Double; Bodyguard, The; Bombshell; Bonfire of the Vanities, The; Boogie Nights; Bound; Boyz'n'the Hood; Brady Bunch Movie, The; Breathless; Bride of the Monster; Bucket of Blood, A; Buffy the Vampire Slayer; Busy Bodies; Caged Heat; Car Wash; Carrie; Casablanca; Chinatown; Citizen Kane; Clambake; Clueless; Collector, The; County Hospital; Creature from the Black Lagoon; Cruel Intentions; Day at the Races, A; Day of the Locust, The; Dead Men Don't Wear Plaid; Die Hard; Disorderly Orderly, The; D.O.A. (1950); Double Indemnity; Down and Out in Beverly Hills; Dracula (1931); Dragnet; Driver, The; Duck Soup; E.T. The Extra-Terrestrial; Earthquake; Easy Rider; Ed Wood; 8mm; Enemy of the State; Eraserhead; Escape from L.A.; Exorcist II: The Heretic; Fabulous Baker Boys, The; Face/Off; Falling Down; Fantastic Voyage, The; Farewell My Lovely (1944); Farewell My Lovely (1975); Fast Times at Ridgemont High; Father of the Bride; Feet First; Fight Club; Fisher King, The; Foreign Correspondent; Forrest Gump; Frankenstein; Get Shorty; Ghostbusters; Gigi; Go; Godfather, The; Gods and Monsters; Going My Way; Grease; Green Mile, The; Gremlins II: The New Batch; Halloween; Halloween H20: 20 Years Later; Heat; Heathers; Hello, Dolly!; Hook; House of Usher, The; House on Haunted Hill, The; How Green Was My Valley; Hunchback of Notre Dame, The; Hustler, The; Imitation of Life; In a Lonely Place; In the Line of Fire; Indecent Proposal; Internal Affairs; Intolerance; Invasion of the Body Snatchers (1956); It's a Wonderful Life; Jackie Brown; Jazz Singer, The; Jerk, The; Jerry Maguire; Kentucky Fried Movie; Key Largo; Killers, The; Killing Zoe; Kindergarten Cop; King Kong (1933); King of Kings (1927); L.A. Confidential; L.A. Story; Last Action Hero, The; Last Boy Scout, The; Lavender Hill Mob, The; Lethal Weapon; Lethal Weapon 2; Lethal Weapon 3; Lethal Weapon 4; Liar Liar; Little Shop of Horrors; Long Goodbye, The; Loved One, The; Madigan; Magnificent Ambersons, The; Man in the Iron Mask, The (1939); Man with Two Brains, The; Mask, The; Mean Streets; Men in Black; Mildred Pierce; Million Dollar Hotel; Mr. Blandings Builds His Dream House; Mr. Smith Goes to Washington; Mommie Dearest; Move Over Darling; Music Box, The; Naked Gun: From the Files of Police Squad!, The; Naked Gun 2½: The Smell of Fear, The; Naked Gun 33⅓: The Final Insult, The; Negotiator, The; New York, New York; Nightmare on Elm Street, A; Nightmare on Elm Street IV: The Dream Master, A; Now Voyager; Nutty Professor, The (1996); Paper Moon; Parallax View, The; Pee-Wee's Big Adventure; People vs. Larry Flynt, The; Phantom of the Paradise; Planes, Trains and Automobiles; Pleasant-Ville; Poltergeist; Pretty in Pink; Pretty Woman; Prizzi's Honor; Psycho (1960); Psycho (1998); Psycho II; Psycho III; Pulp Fiction; Raging Bull; Reality Bites; Rear Window; Rebel Without a Cause; Reservoir Dogs;

Robot Monster; Rocky; Rocky II; Rocky III; Rocky V; Rope; Rush Hour; Safety Last; Sand Pebbles, The; Sayonara; Scenes from a Mall; Se7en; Seven Year Itch, The; Shampoo; She's All That; Silver Streak; Society; Someone to Watch Over Me; Sophie's Choice; Sound of Music, The; Splash!; Star Is Born, A (1937); Star Is Born, A (1976); Starship Troopers; Sting, The; Strange Days; Strangers on a Train; Streetcar Named Desire, A; Sunset Boulevard; Swingers; Tarzan and the Amazons; 10; Ten Commandments, The (1956); Terminator, The; That Touch of Mink; They Live by Night; They Shoot Horses, Don't They?; Thing, The (1951); Things to Do in Denver When You're Dead; This Is Spinal Tap; Throw Momma from the Train; To Kill a Mockingbird; Topper; Touch of Evil; Treasure of the Sierra Madre, The; True Romance; Twins; Undead, The; Union Station; Usual Suspects, The; Valley of the Dolls; Vanishing American, The; Viva Las Vegas; Volcano; War of the Roses, The; War of the Worlds, The; Waterloo Bridge (1931); Way We Were, The; Wayne's World; We Faw Down; Wedding Singer, The; Westworld; What Ever Happened to Baby Jane? (1962); What Price Hollywood?; White Heat; White Men Can't Jump; Wizard of Oz, The; Wolf; Wuthering Heights (1939); X—The Man with X-Ray Eyes; Young Frankenstein. **San Diego:** Attack of the Killer Tomatoes!; Some Like It Hot. **San Francisco:** All About Eve; Basic Instinct; Bullitt; Chan Is Missing; Conversation, The; Dark Passage; Dim Sum; Dirty Harry; D.O.A. (1950); Escape from Alcatraz; Interview with the Vampire: The Vampire Chronicles; Invasion of the Body Snatchers (1978); Killer Elite, The; Pal Joey; Sudden Fear; Titanic; What's Up Doc?; Woman in Red, The

COLORADO: Around the World in Eighty Days; Badlands; Butch Cassidy and the Sundance Kid; Cat Ballou; Cheyenne Autumn; City Slickers; Die Hard II: Die Harder; Dumb and Dumber; Every Which Way but Loose; How the West Was Won; In Cold Blood; Indiana Jones and the Last Crusade; Searchers, The; Sleeper; Starman; Thelma & Louise; Things to Do in Denver When You're Dead; True Grit; Vanishing Point

CONNECTICUT: Amistad; Boomerang; Godfather Part II, The; Ice Storm, The; Last House on the Left, The; Scenes from a Mall; Seconds; Sleepers; Stepford Wives, The; Strangers on a Train; World According to Garp, The. **New Haven:** All About Eve

DELAWARE: Dead Poets Society

FLORIDA: Analyze This; Any Given Sunday; Apollo 13; Armageddon; Bad Boys; Birdcage, The; Body Heat; Bodyguard, The; Caddyshack; Cape Fear (1991); Clambake; Cocoon; Creature from the Black Lagoon; Day of the Dead; Devil's Advocate, The; Edward Scissorhands; Godfather Part II, The; Goldfinger; Great Expectations (1998); Greatest Show on Earth, The; Haunting, The (1999); Jaws 2; Jaws 3-D; Key Largo; Lethal Weapon 3; Licence to Kill; Matinee; Midnight Cowboy; Money Pit, The; Moonraker; My Girl; Scarface; Striptease; Thunderball; To Die For; True Lies; Truman Show, The; Waterboy, The; Wild Women of Wongo. **Miami:** Ace Ventura, Pet Detective; Bellboy, The; Goldfinger; Hole in the Head, A; There's Something About Mary

GEORGIA: Cape Fear (1962); Deliverance; Driving Miss Daisy; Forrest Gump; Fried Green Tomatoes at the Whistle Stop Cafe; Glory; Kalifornia; Long Riders, The; Manhunter; Robocop 3; Scream 2; Smokey and the Bandit; Swamp Water; Wise Blood

HAWAII: Blue Hawaii; Body Heat; Donovan's Reef; Feet First; From Here to Eternity; Godzilla (1998); Honeymoon in Vegas; Hook; Jurassic Park; King Kong (1976); Lost World: Jurassic Park, The; Mister Roberts; Mutiny on the Bounty (1962); Point Break; Raiders of the Lost Ark; South Pacific; 10; Throw Momma from the Train

IDAHO: Bus Stop; Dante's Peak; Heaven's Gate; Pale Rider; Wild Wild West

ILLINOIS: Blues Brothers, The; Color of Money, The; Five Easy Pieces; Fugitive, The; Groundhog Day; In the Heat of the Night; League of Their Own, A; Mission: Impossible; Natural Born Killers; North by Northwest; Risky Business; U.S. Marshals; Weird Science. **Chicago:** About Last Night . . . ; Backdraft; Breakfast Club, The; Candyman; Child's Play; Ferris Bueller's Day Off; Flatliners; Henry: Portrait of a Serial Killer; Home Alone; Home Alone 2: Lost in New York; Hudsucker Proxy, The; Midnight Run; Miracle on 34th Street (1994); My Best Friend's Wedding; Negotiator, The; Silver Streak; Sleepless in Seattle; Sting, The; Union Station; Untouchables, The; Wayne's World; Wedding, A; When Harry Met Sally . . .

INDIANA: Breaking Away; League of Their Own, A; Natural Born Killers; Rain Man; Some Came Running

IOWA: Bridges of Madison County, The; Field of Dreams; Starman; Straight Story, The; Twister; Union Pacific

KANSAS: Carnival of Souls; Dances with Wolves; In Cold Blood; Paper Moon; Picnic

KENTUCKY: Asphalt Jungle, The; Coal Miner's Daughter; Goldfinger; How the West Was Won; Lawn Dogs; League of Their Own, A; Rain Man; Raintree County; U.S. Marshals

LOUISIANA: Assassin; Beguiled, The; Client, The; Horse Soldiers, The; Hush . . . Hush, Sweet Charlotte; Interview with the Vampire: The Vampire Chronicles; JFK; Live and Let Die; Lolita (1997); Long, Hot Summer, The; Miller's Crossing; Passion Fish; Pelican Brief, The; Sex, Lies & Videotape; Southern Comfort; Steel Magnolias. **New Orleans:** Angel Heart; Big Easy, The; Cat People; Cincinnati Kid, The; Easy Rider; Hard Target; JFK; King Creole; Pretty Baby; Streetcar Named Desire, A

MAINE: Captain Courageous; Carousel; Forrest Gump; Jumanji; Man Without a Face; Peyton Place; Whales of August, The

MARYLAND: Absolute Power; Blair Witch Project, The; Cry-Baby; Die Hard with a Vengeance; Patriot Games; Pink Flamingos; Serial Mom; Sleepless in Seattle; Tin Men; Twelve Monkeys. **Baltimore:** Avalon; Cry-Baby; Diner; Female Trouble; Hairspray

MASSACHUSETTS: Altered States; Amistad; Carnal Knowledge; Field of Dreams; Firm, The; Glory; Jaws; Jaws 2; Jaws the Revenge; Last Detail, The; Little Women (1994); Love Story; Portrait of Jenny; River Wild, The; Sabrina (1995); Thomas Crown Affair, The (1968); Who's Afraid of Virginia Woolf?; Witches of Eastwick, The. **Boston:** Good Will Hunting

MICHIGAN: Anatomy of a Murder; Die Hard II: Die Harder; Evil Dead, The; Evil Dead II; Grosse Pointe Blank; Midnight Run. **Detroit:** Beverly Hills Cop; True Romance

MIDWAY ISLAND: Mister Roberts

MINNESOTA: Airport; Fargo; Simple Plan, A; Untamed Heart. **Minneapolis:** Mallrats

MISSISSIPPI: Baby Doll; Home from the Hill; Horse Soldiers, The; Mississippi Burning; Raintree County; Thieves Like Us

MISSOURI: In Cold Blood; Intruder, The; Manhunter; Paper Moon; Planes, Trains and Automobiles; White Palace. **St. Louis:** Escape from New York

MONTANA: Broken Arrow; Far and Away; Heaven's Gate; Little Big Man; River Runs Through It, A; River Wild, The; Thing, The (1951); Untouchables, The

NEBRASKA: Boys' Town; Election; Terms of Endearment; Union Pacific

NEVADA: Amazing Colossal Man, The; Ballad of Cable Hogue, The; Charley Varrick; Go; Godfather, The; Godfather Part II, The; Greatest Story Ever Told, The; High Plains Drifter; In Cold Blood; Independence Day; Iron Horse, The; Kill Me Again; Kiss Me, Stupid; Leaving Las Vegas; Lethal Weapon 4; Magnolia; Midnight Run; Misery; Misfits, The; Moonraker; Place in the Sun, A; Rain Man; Romancing the Stone; Saboteur; Shootist, The; Showgirls; Sister Act; Star Trek: Generations; Starman; Stir Crazy; Swingers; Top Gun; Vanishing Point; Viva Las Vegas; Zabriskie Point. **Las Vegas:** Austin Powers: International Man of Mystery; Casino; Con Air; Diamonds Are Forever; Godfather, The; Honeymoon in Vegas; Indecent Proposal; Mars Attacks!; Prizzi's Honor

NEW HAMPSHIRE: Jumanji; Last Detail, The; Little Women (1933)

NEW JERSEY: Amityville Horror, The; Analyze This; Big; Birdy; Broadway Danny Rose; Chasing Amy; Clerks; Color of Money, The; Cop Land; Creepshow; Desperately Seeking Susan; Dogma; Friday the 13TH; Godfather Part III, The; Goodfellas; Hurricane, The; In and Out; King of Marvin Gardens, The; Kiss of Death; Léon; Long Kiss Goodnight, The; Mallrats; Manhattan; Marnie; Meet Joe Black; Men in Black; Purple Rose of Cairo; The; Radio Days; Ransom; Reversal of Fortune; Rounders; Shaft (2000); Snake Eyes; Stardust Memories; Sweet and Lowdown; Tootsie; Welcome to the Dollhouse; World According to Garp, The; Zelig. **Atlantic City:** Atlantic City

NEW MEXICO: Ace in the Hole; All the Pretty Horses; Armageddon; City Slickers; Contact; Easy Rider; Every Which Way but Loose; Gas-S-S-S; Journey to the Center of the Earth; King Solomon's Mines; Lolita (1997); Lonely Are the Brave; Man from Laramie, The; Man Who Fell to Earth, The; Milagro Beanfield War, The; Natural Born Killers; Spider, The; Superman; Vampires; Wild Wild West; Young Guns; Young Guns II—Blaze of Glory

NEW YORK: Age of Innocence, The; Analyze This; Arthur; Basket Case; Batman Forever; Big; Boomerang; Cat on a Hot Tin Roof; Citizen Kane; Cruel Intentions; Fatal Attraction; Flesh Eaters, The; Fugitive Kind, The; Great Expectations (1998); Hannah and Her Sisters; Hello, Dolly!; Horse Whisperer, The; In and Out; King of Comedy, The; Kiss of Death; Last Seduction, The; League of Their Own, A; Long Day's Journey into Night; Malcolm X; Man on the Moon; Midsummer Night's Sex Comedy, A; Mighty Aphrodite; Money Pit, The; Natural, The; New Jack City; North by Northwest; Planes, Trains and Automobiles; Purple Rose of Cairo, The; Quiz Show; Raging Bull; Reversal of Fortune; Robocop; Sabrina (1954); Sabrina (1995); Scent of a Woman; Sleepers; Spanking the Monkey; Splendor in the Grass; Strangers on a Train; Sweet and Lowdown; They Died with Their Boots On; Thomas Crown Affair, The (1999); Tootsie; Trading Places; Unbelievable Truth,

The; Way Down East; Way We Were, The; Wolf; Woodstock; World According to Garp, The; Wrong Man, The; Zelig. **Long Island:** Bodyguard, The; Godfather, The; Goodfellas. **New York City:** Across 110th Street; Adam's Rib; After Hours; Alice; Alice in Den Stadten; All About Eve; All That Jazz; Altered States; Amateur; American Psycho; Amerikanische Freund, Der; Anderson Tapes, The; Angel Heart; Annie Hall; Another Woman; Apartment, The; Armageddon; Arthur; As Good as It Gets; Awakenings; Bad Lieutenant; Bad Timing; Barefoot in the Park; Beast from Twenty Thousand Fathoms, The; Bell, Book and Candle; Big; Big Blue, The; Black Rain; Bonfire of the Vanities, The; Breakfast at Tiffany's; Broadway Danny Rose; Bullets over Broadway; Carlito's Way; Carnal Knowledge; Chasing Amy; City Slickers; Clockers; Cocktail; Coogan's Bluff; Cotton Club, The; Crimes and Misdemeanors; Crocodile Dundee; Cruising; Death Wish; Deep Impact; Desperately Seeking Susan; Devil's Advocate, The; Die Hard with a Vengeance; Do the Right Thing; Dog Day Afternoon; Donnie Brasco; Doors, The; Dressed to Kill; 84 Charing Cross Road; Election; Escape from New York; Everyone Says I Love You; Exorcist, The; Fame; Fatal Attraction; 54; Fisher King, The; French Connection, The; Freshman, The; Ghost; Ghostbusters; Ghostbusters II; Godfather, The; Godfather Part II, The; Godfather Part III, The; (1998); Goodfellas; Great Gatsby, The; Gremlins II: The New Batch; Hackers; Hester Street; Highlander; Home Alone 2: Lost in New York; Honeymoon in Vegas; Hospital, The; House on 92nd St., The; How to Marry a Millionaire; Hudson Hawk; Hunger, The; Husbands and Wives; Hustler, The; Ice Storm, The; Independence Day; Jerry Maguire; Johnny Suede; Jungle Fever; King Kong (1933); King Kong (1976); King of New York; Kiss Before Dying, A; Kiss of Death; Klute; Kramer vs. Kramer; Last Action Hero, The; Last Detail, The; Last House on the Left, The; Léon; Light Sleeper; Live and Let Die; Lost Weekend, The; Love Affair (1939); Love Affair (1994); Love at First Bite; Love Story; Madigan; Malcolm X; Man Who Fell to Earth, The; Manchurian Candidate, The; Manhattan; Manhattan Murder Mystery; Marathon Man; Maximum Risk; Mean Streets; Meet Joe Black; Men in Black; Midnight Cowboy; Midnight Run; Miracle on 34th Street (1947); Miracle on 34th Street (1994); Mo' Better Blues; Money Pit, The; Moonstruck; My Dinner with Andre; Naked City, The; Network; New Jack City; New York Stories; Nine ½ Weeks; North by Northwest; Nothing Sacred; Pawnbroker, The; Pelican Brief, The; Phantom of Paradise; Portrait of Jenny; Prisoner of Second Avenue, The; Prizzi's Honor; Producers, The; Q—The Winged Serpent; Quiz Show; Radio Days; Raging Bull; Ransom; Reversal of Fortune; Romancing the Stone; Rosemary's Baby; Rounders; Saboteur; Saturday Night Fever; Scarface; Scenes from a Mall; Scent of a Woman; Sea of Love; Seconds; Serpico; Seven Year Itch, The; Shaft (1971); Shaft (2000); She's Gotta Have It; Sid and Nancy; Single White Female; Six Degrees of Separation; Sleepers; Sleepless in Seattle; Sliver; Someone to Watch Over Me; Splash!; Stir Crazy; Strangers on a Train; Summer of Sam; Sunshine Boys, The; Superman; Superman II; Sweet Smell of Success; Taking of Pelham One Two Three, The; Talented Mr. Ripley, The; Tarzan's New York Adventure; Taxi Driver; Teenage Mutant Ninja Turtles; Tenebrae; That Touch of Mink; Thomas Crown Affair, The; Three Days of the Condor; 3 Men and a Baby; Tootsie; Topaz; Trading Places; 12 Angry Men; Under the Clock; U.S. Marshals; Usual Suspects, The; Valley of the Dolls; Wait Until Dark; Wall Street; Warriors, The; Way We Were,

The; Weekend at Bernie's; West Side Story; When Harry Met Sally . . . ; Wolf; Wolfen; Working Girl; Wrong Man, The; Year of the Dragon

NORTH CAROLINA: Being There; Blue Velvet; Bull Durham; Color Purple, The; Crimes of the Heart; Crow, The; Dirty Dancing; Evil Dead II; Exorcist III, The; Fugitive, The; Hunt for Red October, The; I Know What You Did Last Summer; Last of the Mohicans, The; Lolita (1997); Manhunter; Starman; Swan, The; Teenage Mutant Ninja Turtles; Weekend at Bernie's; Year of the Dragon

NORTH DAKOTA: Fargo

OHIO: Air Force One; Deer Hunter, The; Rain Man; Shawshank Redemption, The

OKLAHOMA: Around the World in Eighty Days; Grapes of Wrath, The; Outsiders, The; Rain Man; Rumble Fish; Twister

OREGON: Dead Man; Drugstore Cowboy; Empire Strikes Back, The; Five Easy Pieces; Free Willy; General, The; Great Race, The; Kindergarten Cop; My Own Private Idaho; National Lampoon's Animal House; Northwest Passage; Paint Your Wagon; Point Break; River Wild, The; Shining, The; Short Circuit; Stand by Me

PENNSYLVANIA: Age of Innocence, The; Blob, The; Crazies, The; Creepshow; Dawn of the Dead; Day of the Dead; Deer Hunter, The; Dogma; Flashdance; Greatest Show on Earth, The; King of Marvin Gardens, The; Kiss Before Dying, A; Marnie; Maximum Risk; Robocop; Timecop; Trading Places; Twelve Monkeys; Two Evil Eyes; Witness. **Philadelphia:** Birdy; Blow Out; Dressed to Kill; Eraserhead; Philadelphia; Rocky; Rocky II; Rocky III; Sixth Sense, The. **Pittsburgh:** Night of the Living Dead; Silence of the Lambs, The; Wonder Boys

RHODE ISLAND: Amistad; Dumb and Dumber; Great Gatsby, The; High Society; Meet Joe Black; There's Something About Mary; True Lies

SOUTH CAROLINA: Abyss, The; Big Chill, The; Die Hard with a Vengeance; Forrest Gump; Swamp Thing

SOUTH DAKOTA: Armageddon; Dances with Wolves; How the West Was Won; North by Northwest; Starship Troopers

TENNESSEE: Client, The; Coal Miner's Daughter; Evil Dead, The; Green Mile, The; In the Heat of the Night; Nashville; Rainmaker, The; Raintree County; Starman; Sweet Dreams; This Is Spinal Tap; U.S. Marshals. **Memphis:** Firm, The; Mystery Train; People vs. Larry Flynt, The

TEXAS: Alamo, The; All the Pretty Horses; Any Given Sunday; Apollo 13; Armageddon; Baby, the Rain Must Fall; Blood Simple; Bonnie and Clyde; Born on the Fourth of July; Boys Don't Cry; Crow, The; Dazed and Confused; D.O.A. (1988); Faculty, The; Getaway, The; Giant; Home from the Hill; Hud; In Cold Blood; Last Picture Show, The; Local Hero; Lolita (1997); Long Riders, The; Midnight Cowboy; Paris, Texas; Pee-Wee's Big Adventure; Perfect World, A; Phantom of the Paradise; Problem Child; Reality Bites; Robocop 2; Slacker; Southern Comfort; Sugarland Express; Terms of Endearment; Texas Chain Saw Massacre, The; Texasville; Trip to Bountiful, The; Twister; Two Rode Together; Urban Cowboy; What's Eating Gilbert Grape?; Wild at Heart; Wings. **Dallas:** Gas-S-S-S; JFK; Robocop

UTAH: Butch Cassidy and the Sundance Kid; Carnival of Souls; Cheyenne Autumn; Con Air; Conqueror, The;

Dumb and Dumber; Electra Glide in Blue; Footloose; Forrest Gump; Fort Apache; Greatest Story Ever Told, The; Halloween 4: The Return of Michael Myers; How the West Was Won; Indiana Jones and the Last Crusade; Jeremiah Johnson; Jewel of the Nile, The; Life Less Ordinary, A; Mackenna's Gold; Mission: Impossible 2; Rio Grande; Romancing the Stone; Searchers, The; She Wore a Yellow Ribbon; Species; Stagecoach; Thelma & Louise; This Boy's Life; Union Pacific; Vanishing Point; Wagon Master

VERMONT: Beetlejuice; Trouble with Harry, The; Way Down East

VIRGINIA: Coal Miner's Daughter; Contact; Deep Impact; Dirty Dancing; Kiss Before Dying, A; Last Detail, The; Mission: Impossible; My Dinner with Andre; No Way Out; Patriot Games; Silence of the Lambs, The; Sommersby

WASHINGTON, D.C.: Absolute Power; Advise and Consent; Air Force One; All the President's Men; Armageddon; Assassin; Being There; Close Encounters of the Third Kind; Contact; Day the Earth Stood Still, The; Deep Impact; Die Hard II: Die Harder; Enemy of the State; Exorcist, The; Exorcist III, The; Few Good Men, A; Firm, The; Forrest Gump; French Connection, The; Greatest Show on Earth, The; In the Line of Fire; Independence Day; JFK; Last Detail, The; Manchurian Candidate, The; Manhunter; Mars Attacks!; Mr. Smith Goes to Washington; Net, The; Night of the Living Dead; Nixon; No Way Out; Pelican Brief, The; People vs. Larry Flynt, The; Strangers on a Train; Suspect; Topaz; True Lies; X-Files, The

WASHINGTON: Dante's Peak; Dead Man; Deer Hunter, The; Harry and the Hendersons; Hunt for Red October, The; I Love You to Death; Lassie Come Home; Long Kiss Goodnight, The; My Own Private Idaho; Parallax View, The; 10 Things I Hate About You; This Boy's Life; Twin Peaks: Fire Walk with Me; Vanishing, The; War Games; War of the Roses, The. **Seattle:** Fabulous Baker Boys, The; It Happened at the World's Fair; Singles; Sleepless in Seattle

WEST VIRGINIA: Deer Hunter, The; Sweet Dreams

WISCONSIN: Blues Brothers, The; Simple Plan, A; Straight Story, The

WYOMING: Cheyenne Autumn; Close Encounters of the Third Kind; Dances with Wolves; River Runs Through It, A; Rocky IV; Shane; Star Trek: The Motion Picture; Star Trek V: The Final Frontier; Starship Troopers; Vanishing, The

● **VENEZUELA:** Arachnophobia

● **VIRGIN ISLANDS:** Big Blue, The; Dinosaurus; Trading Places

● **WALES:** American Werewolf in London, An; Arabesque; Backbeat; Carry On Up the Khyber; Citadel, The; Dam Busters, The; Drum, The; First Knight; Inn of the Sixth Happiness; Jabberwocky; Lion in Winter, The; Macbeth (1971); Robin Hood; Tiger Bay; Time Bandits; World Is Not Enough, The

● **WEST INDIES:** Doctor Dolittle (1967); Dr. No

● **YUGOSLAVIA:** Isadora; Sophie's Choice; Travels with My Aunt; Trial, The

● **ZAIRE:** African Queen, The

● **ZAMBESE:** White Hunter, Black Heart

● **ZIMBABWE:** Cry Freedom; White Hunter, Black Heart

ALTERNATIVE TITLES INDEX

A

AMERICAN FRIEND, THE see **AMERIKANISCHE FREUND, DER**
AND GOD . . . CREATED WOMAN see **ET DIEU . . . CREA LA FEMME**
ANGST ESSEN SEELE AUF see **FEAR EATS THE SOUL**
ASHES AND DIAMONDS see **POPIOL Y DIAMENT**

B

BATTLE OF ALGIERS see **BATTAGLIA DI ALGERI, LA**
BEAUTY AND THE BEAST see **BELLE ET LA BÊTE, LA**
BEFORE THE REVOLUTION see **PRIMA DELLA RIVOLUZIONE**
BETTY BLUE see **37°2 LE MATIN**
BICYCLE THIEVES, THE see **LADRI DI BICICLETTE**
BIG CARNIVAL, THE see **ACE IN THE HOLE**
BIG HEART, THE see **MIRACLE ON 34TH STREET (1947)**
BIG TIME OPERATORS see **SMALLEST SHOW ON EARTH, THE**
BIGFOOT AND THE HENDERSONS see **HARRY AND THE HENDERSONS**
BIRDS OF A FEATHER see **CAGE AUX FOLLES, LA**
BLAZING SUN see **PLEIN SOLEIL**
BLONDE BOMBSHELL see **BOMBSHELL**
BOUDU SAVED FROM DROWNING see **BOUDU SAUVÉ DES EAUX**
BREATHLESS see **A BOUT DE SOUFFLE**
BUONO, IL BRUTO, IL CATTIVO, IL see **GOOD, THE BAD AND THE UGLY, THE**
BUTCHER, THE see **BOUCHER, LE**

C

CARRY ON–FOLLOW THAT CAMEL see **FOLLOW THAT CAMEL**
CHILDREN OF PARADISE see **ENFANTS DU PARADIS, LES**
CLAIRE'S KNEE see **GENOU DE CLAIRE, LE**
CLOCK, THE see **UNDER THE CLOCK**
CLOSELY WATCHED TRAINS see **CLOSELY OBSERVED TRAINS**
COBWEB CASTLE see **THRONE OF BLOOD**
CODE NAME: TRIXIE see **CRAZIES, THE**
COLOR OUT OF SPACE, THE see **DIE, MONSTER, DIE**
CONFIDENTIALLY YOURS see **VIVEMENT DIMANCHE**
CONFORMIST, THE see **CONFORMISTA**
CONQUEROR WORM, THE see **WITCHFINDER GENERAL**
CONTEMPT see **MEPRIS, LE**
COUNT DRACULA AND HIS VAMPIRE BRIDE see **SATANIC RITES OF DRACULA, THE**
CREEPERS see **PHENOMENA**
CREEPING UNKNOWN, THE see **QUATERMASS EXPERIMENT, THE**
CURSE OF THE DEMON see **NIGHT OF THE DEMON**

D

DAHONG DENGLONG GAOGAO GUA see **RAISE THE RED LANTERN**
DAMNED, THE see **GÖTTERDAMMERUNG**
DANNY BOY see **ANGEL**
DAY FOR NIGHT see **NUIT AMERICAINE, LA**
DESERT ATTACK see **ICE COLD IN ALEX**
DEVIL'S ENVOYS, THE see **VISITEURS DU SOIR, LES**
DIARY OF A CHAMBERMAID, THE see **JOURNAL D'UNE FEMME DE CHAMBRE**

DISCREET CHARM OF THE BOURGEOISIE, THE see **CHARME DISCRET DE LA BOURGEOISIE, LE**
DOÑA HERLINDA AND HER SONS see **DOÑA HERLINDA Y SU HIJO**
DRUMS see **DRUM, THE**

E

EARTH VERSUS THE SPIDER see **SPIDER, THE**
ECLIPSE, THE see **L'ECLISSE**
ENEMY FROM SPACE see **QUATERMASS II**

F

FALL OF THE HOUSE OF USHER, THE see **HOUSE OF USHER, THE**
FINALLY SUNDAY see **VIVEMENT DIMANCHE**
FISTFUL OF DYNAMITE, A see **DUCK, YOU SUCKER**
FORTY-EIGHT HOURS see **WENT THE DAY WELL**
FOUR HUNDRED BLOWS, THE see **QUATRE CENTS COUPS, LES**
FRANTIC see **ASCENSEUR POUR L'ECHAFAUD**

G

GARDEN OF THE FINZI-CONTINIS, THE see **GIARDINO DEI FINZI-CONTINI, IL**
GAS! OR IT BECAME NECESSARY TO DESTROY THE WORLD IN ORDER TO SAVE IT see **GAS-S-S-S**
GODSON, THE see **SAMOURAI, LE**
GRAND ILLUSION see **GRANDE ILLUSION, LA**

H

HANDLE WITH CARE see **CITIZEN'S BAND**
HATE see **HAINE, LA**
HAVING A WILD WEEKEND see **CATCH US IF YOU CAN**
HER MAJESTY, MRS. BROWN see **MRS. BROWN**
HIMMEL UEBER BERLIN see **WINGS OF DESIRE**
HORROR OF DRACULA see **DRACULA (1958)**
HOUNDS OF ZAROFF, THE see **MOST DANGEROUS GAME, THE**
HUMAN BEAST, THE see **BÊTE HUMAINE, LA**

I

IM LAUF DER ZEIT see **KINGS OF THE ROAD**
INDISCRETION OF AN AMERICAN WIFE see **STAZIONE TERMINI**

J

JOHN CARPENTER'S VAMPIRES see **VAMPIRES**
JUDAS WAS A WOMAN see **BÊTE HUMAINE, LA**

K

KAKUSHI TORIDE NO SAN AKUNIN see **HIDDEN FORTRESS, THE**

L

LAST METRO, THE see **DERNIER METRO, LE**
LAST YEAR IN MARIENBAD see **L'ANNÉE DERNIERE À MARIENBAD**
LEOPARD, THE see **GATTOPARDO, IL**
LIFT TO THE SCAFFOLD see **ASCENSEUR POUR L'ECHAFAUD**
LOST ILLUSION, THE see **FALLEN IDOL, THE**